CREATE YOUR ACCOUNT TODAY!

Access to eResources Selected by Your Instructor

Your instant access includes:

CengageNOW for College Accounting--2

To get started:

① **Go to www.cengage.com/login.**

② **Click on "Create My Account." Select user type "Student." Already have an account? Enter your email/password under "Sign In."**

③ **Enter account information and the access code below and click "Continue."**

ACCESS CODE

PPQS8WGP3KVBT6

www.cengage.com/login

④ **Record your e-mail address and password for future visits.**

TIPS AND TROUBLESHOOTING

- **Keep a record of your email address and password.** You will need them every time you sign in.
- **Your access code is NOT your password!** You will use this access code only once when your first access your eResources. Once your access code is successfully authenticated, you will not be asked for it again.
- **Problems with your access code?** For tech support, visit our website at www.cengage.com/support.

Access code may be used only one time.

Note: All media assets accessible through this program are available to college and university students in the United States and Canada. Some restrictions may apply in other markets or countries. Please contact Cengage Learning for details.

STOP! This is your personal PAID ACCESS CODE that is required to access your electronic materials for your CengageNOW course.

IMPORTANT: This code is for use by one student and cannot be copied.

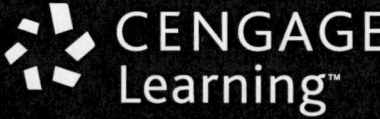

CENGAGE Learning™

College Accounting

Chapters 1-27
Included Inside: Two Semester CengageNOW Access

20th Edition

Heintz | Parry

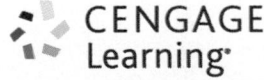

CENGAGE Learning®

Australia • Brazil • Japan • Korea • Mexico • Singapore • Spain • United Kingdom • United States

CENGAGE Learning

College Accounting: Chapters 1-27, Included Inside: Two Semester CengageNOW Access, 20th Edition

Senior Project Development Manager:
Linda deStefano

Market Development Manager:
Heather Kramer

Senior Production/Manufacturing Manager:
Donna M. Brown

Production Editorial Manager:
Kim Fry

Sr. Rights Acquisition Account Manager:
Todd Osborne

Printed in the United States of America

College Accounting, Chapters 1-27, 20th Edition
Heintz | Parry

ISBN-13: 978-1-285-89207-8

ISBN-10: 1-285-89207-0

Cengage Learning
5191 Natorp Boulevard
Mason, Ohio 45040
USA

Cengage Learning is a leading provider of customized learning solutions with office locations around the globe, including Singapore, the United Kingdom, Australia, Mexico, Brazil, and Japan. Locate your local office at: **international.cengage.com/region.**

Cengage Learning products are represented in Canada by Nelson Education, Ltd.
For your lifelong learning solutions, visit **www.cengage.com/custom.**
Visit our corporate website at **www.cengage.com.**

Where Accounting Education and the Real World Meet

Be your best in the classroom *and* in the workplace with the accounting skills and confidence you'll achieve with Heintz/Parry's ***College Accounting, 20e***!

The future belongs to those who possess the marketable skills learned from studying Heintz/Parry. With unmatched *clarity*, *accuracy*, and *technology*, our text provides you with the accounting knowledge you need to succeed. As you journey through this text, you will gain confidence as you learn accounting, which is the language of the business world.

Through 19 editions, we've fine-tuned the pedagogy in our text and supporting materials. Our proven step-by-step approach and inviting narrative style focus on the practical skills you'll need to transition from the classroom to the workplace. We've kept intact everything that has made *College Accounting* so successful and have added new features and ancillary materials to ensure that it remains **the best text** on the market.

We invite you to read the following preface, which serves as a guide to help you gain the most knowledge from this text and its supporting materials.

Best wishes to you for a successful college experience and business career!

Jim Heintz and Rob Parry

LEARNING OBJECTIVES CONNECT THE CHAPTER COVERAGE FROM BEGINNING TO END

By paying attention to the Learning Objectives, you can focus on what is important. The Learning Objectives appear in many places throughout the chapter. Here's where you will find the Learning Objectives (LOs):

CHAPTER OPENER PAGE

The first page of the chapter lists all of the Learning Objectives for the chapter.

LEARNING OBJECTIVES

Careful study of this chapter should enable you to:

LO1 **Prepare financial statements with the aid of a work sheet.**

LO2 **Journalize and post closing entries.**

LO3 **Prepare a post-closing trial balance.**

LO4 **List and describe the steps in the accounting cycle.**

MARGINS

When the chapter is presenting coverage for a certain Learning Objective, the LO is stated at the beginning of the section.

LO1 Prepare financial statements with the aid of a work sheet.

THE FINANCIAL STATEMENTS

The work sheet prepared in Chapter 5 supplies most of the information needed to prepare an income statement, a statement of owner's equity, and a balance sheet. The statements and work sheet columns from which they are derived for Jessie Jane's Campus Delivery Service are shown in Figures 6-1 and 6-2.

As you refer to the financial statements in Figures 6-1 and 6-2, notice the placement of dollar signs, single rulings, and double rulings. Dollar signs are placed at the top of each column and beneath rulings. Single rulings indicate addition or subtraction, and double rulings are placed under totals. Notice that each statement heading contains three lines: (1) company name, (2) statement title, and (3) period ended or date.

KEY POINTS TO REMEMBER

At the beginning of the Self-Study section, each Learning Objective is stated along with the most important information covered in the chapter.

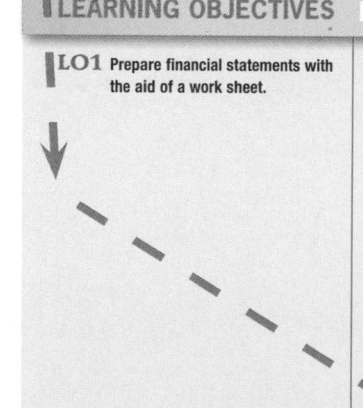

LEARNING OBJECTIVES	Key Points to Remember
LO1 **Prepare financial statements with the aid of a work sheet.**	The work sheet is used as an aid in preparing: 1. adjusting entries, 2. financial statements, and 3. closing entries. The following classifications are used for accounts reported on the balance sheet. • *Current assets* include cash and assets that will be converted into cash or consumed within either one year or the normal operating cycle of the business, whichever is longer. An *operating cycle* is the time required to purchase supplies and services and convert them back into cash. • *Property, plant, and equipment*, also called *plant assets* or *long-term assets*, represent assets that are expected to serve the business for many years. • *Current liabilities* are liabilities that are due within either one year or the normal operating cycle of the business, whichever is longer, and that are to be paid out of current assets. • *Long-term liabilities*, or *long-term debt*, are obligations that are not expected to be paid within a year and do not require the use of current assets.

U REVU BANNERS

Inside the banner, the Learning Objective number is indicated.

U REVU Complete U REVU-1 on **page 210** to test your basic understanding of LO1.

TRUE/FALSE AND MULTIPLE CHOICE QUESTIONS AND U REVU EXERCISES

Each of these Self-Study items indicates the related Learning Objective number(s). If you need to review the coverage in the chapter, use these LOs to guide you to the right place.

SELF-STUDY QUESTIONS AND EXERCISES

True/False Questions

1. LO1 Expenses are listed on the income statement as they appear in the chart of accounts or in descending order (by dollar amount).
2. LO1 Additional investments of capital during the month are not reported on the statement of owner's equity.
3. LO1 The income statement cannot be prepared using the work sheet alone.
4. LO1 A classified balance sheet groups similar items, such as current assets together.
5. LO2 Temporary accounts are closed at the end of each accounting period.

Multiple Choice Questions

1. LO2 Which of these types of accounts is considered a "permanent" account?
   (a) Revenue (c) Drawing
   (b) Asset (d) Expense
2. LO2 Which of these accounts is considered a "temporary" account?
   (a) Cash (c) J. Jones, Capital
   (b) Accounts Payable (d) J. Jones, Drawing
3. LO2 Which of these is the first step in the closing process?
   (a) Close revenue account(s). (c) Close the income summary account.
   (b) Close expense accounts. (d) Close the drawing account.
4. LO3 The _______ is prepared after closing entries are posted to prove the equality of debit and credit balances.
   (a) balance sheet (c) post-closing trial balance
   (b) income statement (d) statement of owner's equity
5. LO4 Steps that begin with analyzing source documents and conclude with the post-closing trial balance are called the
   (a) closing process. (c) adjusting entries.
   (b) accounting cycle. (d) posting process.

U REVU Exercises

1. LO1 Joe Fisher operates Fisher Consulting. A partial work sheet for August 20-- is provided below. Fisher made no additional investments during the month. Prepare an income statement, statement of owner's equity, and balance sheet.

Fisher Consulting
Work Sheet (Partial)
For Month Ended August 31, 20 - -

	ACCOUNT TITLE	INCOME STATEMENT DEBIT	INCOME STATEMENT CREDIT	BALANCE SHEET DEBIT	BALANCE SHEET CREDIT	
1	Cash			2,500 00		1
2	Accounts Receivable			800 00		2
3	Equipment			3,800 00		3
4	Accum. Depr.— Equipment				200 00	4
5	Accounts Payable				1,000 00	5
6	Joe Fisher, Capital				3,000 00	6
7	Joe Fisher, Drawing			300 00		7
8	Professional Fees		5,000 00			8
9	Wages Expense	1,000 00				9
10	Rent Expense	700 00				10
11	Depreciation Expense	100 00				11
12		1,800 00	5,000 00	7,400 00	4,200 00	12
13	Net Income	3,200 00			3,200 00	13
14		5,000 00	5,000 00	7,400 00	7,400 00	14
15						15
16						16

2. LO2 Using the work sheet provided in U REVU Exercise 1, prepare closing entries in general journal form.
3. LO3 Using the work sheet provided in U REVU Exercise 1 and financial statements prepared for that exercise, prepare a post-closing trial balance.

The answers to the Self-Study Questions and Exercises are at the end of the chapter (pages 213–215).

APPLYING YOUR KNOWLEDGE

REVIEW QUESTIONS

LO1 1. Identify the source of the information needed to prepare the income statement.
LO1 2. Describe two approaches to listing the expenses in the income statement.
LO1 3. Identify the sources of the information needed to prepare the statement of owner's equity.
LO1 4. If additional investments were made during the year, what information in addition to the work sheet would be needed to prepare the statement of owner's equity?
LO1 5. Identify the sources of the information needed to prepare the balance sheet.
LO2 6. What is a permanent account? On which financial statement are permanent accounts reported?

SERIES A EXERCISES

E 6-1A (LO1) ✓ Net income: $1,990
INCOME STATEMENT From the partial work sheet for Case Advising below, prepare an income statement.

E 6-2A (LO1) ✓ Capital 1/31: $5,190
STATEMENT OF OWNER'S EQUITY From the partial work sheet below, prepare a statement of owner's equity, assuming no additional investment was made by the owner.

SERIES A PROBLEMS

P 6-7A (LO1) ✓ Net income: $1,400; Capital 1/31: $7,400; Total assets: $8,650
FINANCIAL STATEMENTS Page 203 shows a work sheet for Monte's Repairs. No additional investments were made by the owner during the month.

REQUIRED

1. Prepare an income statement.
2. Prepare a statement of owner's equity.
3. Prepare a balance sheet.

REVIEW QUESTIONS, A & B EXERCISES, AND A & B PROBLEMS

Each of these assignments indicates the related Learning Objective number. If you need to review the coverage in the chapter, use these LOs to guide you to the right place.

COLOR CODING GUIDES YOU

Throughout the text, you will see special color coding used to help you quickly know how accounts are classified and help you follow the key transactions presented. A quick reference to these colors can be found on the second page of each part opener. For example, page 2 shows the following chart for the chapters in Part 1:

Add Some Color to Your Learning!

Throughout the text, you will be introduced to many important terms and types of accounts. To help you learn the different terms and types of accounts, we have coded many of them using the following color key in Part 1:

- Assets
- Contra-Assets
- Liabilities
- Capital
- Drawing
- Revenues
- Expenses
- Income Summary (Net Income/Net Loss)

As you move through the text, more color codes are added. So always check the Add Some Color To Your Learning! chart when you start a new part.

CHAPTER OPENERS PROVIDE CLUES

Don't miss the Learning Objectives! These tell you what you should know when you've completed studying the chapter.

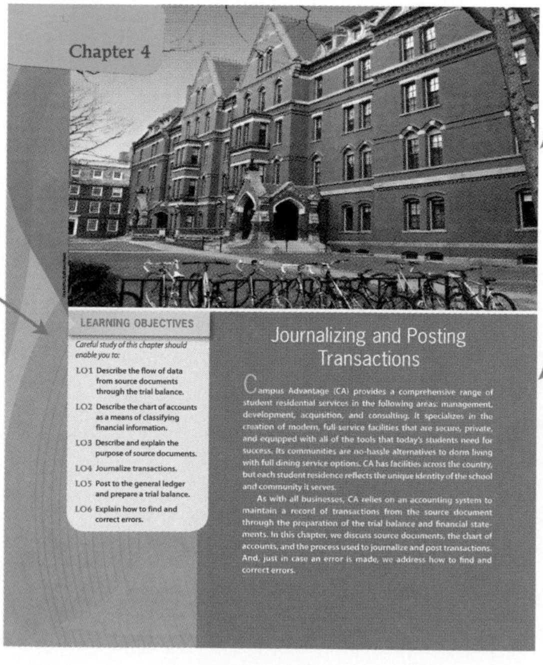

Chapter 4

LEARNING OBJECTIVES

Careful study of this chapter should enable you to:

LO1 Describe the flow of data from source documents through the trial balance.

LO2 Describe the chart of accounts as a means of classifying financial information.

LO3 Describe and explain the purpose of source documents.

LO4 Journalize transactions.

LO5 Post to the general ledger and prepare a trial balance.

LO6 Explain how to find and correct errors.

Journalizing and Posting Transactions

Campus Advantage (CA) provides a comprehensive range of student residential services in the following areas: management, development, acqusition, and consulting. It specializes in the creation of modern, full-service facilities that are secure, private, and equipped with all of the tools that today's students need for success. Its communities are no-hassle alternatives to dorm living with full dining service options. CA has facilities across the country, but each student residence reflects the unique identity of the school and community it serves.

As with all businesses, CA relies on an accounting system to maintain a record of transactions from the source document through the preparation of the trial balance and financial statements. In this chapter, we discuss source documents, the chart of accounts, and the process used to journalize and post transactions. And, just in case an error is made, we address how to find and correct errors.

Each chapter opens with a colorful image and a description of a real company. By reading the opening description, you will find out *why it's important* to master the information that is covered in the chapter. The openers can help you visualize how accounting is so used in the business world and, therefore, why it's known as the "language of business."

CALLOUTS AND ARROWS HELP YOU NAVIGATE

Along with color coding, callouts and arrows help you quickly find important elements in a figure and know how different parts of a figure are connected.

FIGURE 7-5 Checks and Check Stubs

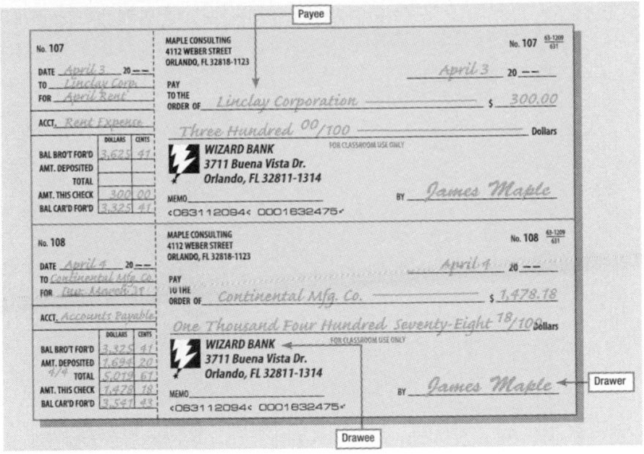

THE STEPS LEAD THE WAY

Where it's most helpful, we provide step-by-step instructions. Related figures guide you visually through the steps to reinforce the process. When you see these, take the time to "walk" through each step to strengthen your understanding.

FIGURE 4-10 Posting a Credit

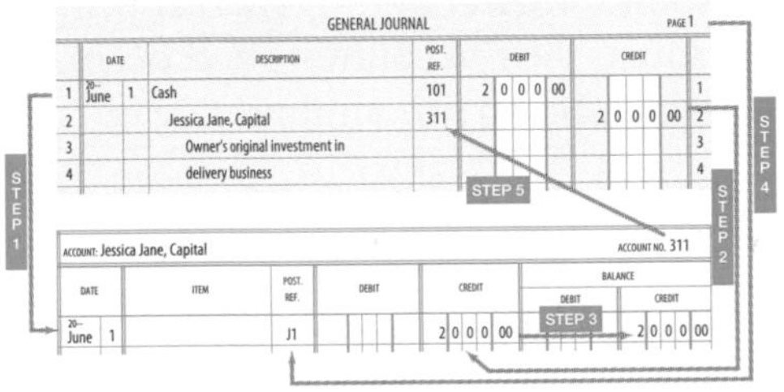

In the ledger account:

STEP 1 **Enter the date of the transaction in the Date column.** Enter the year, "20--," the month, "June," and the day, "1," in the Date column of the account Jessica Jane, Capital.

STEP 2 **Enter the credit.** Copy the $2,000 credit to Jessica Jane, Capital in the journal to the Credit column in the ledger.

STEP 3 **Enter the balance of the account.** Enter the $2,000 balance in the Balance columns under Credit. (If the balance of the account is zero, draw a line through the Debit and Credit columns.)

STEP 4 **Enter the journal page in the Posting Reference column.** Enter "J1" in the Posting Reference column since the posting came from page 1 of the journal.

LEARNING KEYS AND MARGIN NOTES REINFORCE AND EXPAND YOUR KNOWLEDGE

LEARNING KEY

1. Find the row for wages.
2. Find the column for withholding allowances.
3. Find the amount where they cross.

Watch for Learning Keys. Make sure you understand them. Learning Keys reinforce basic content as it's covered in the chapter.

When the Social Security program was established in 1937, the tax was 1% on earnings up to $3,000 per year!

Watch for the margin notes. They give you more information so that you will have a greater understanding of the topic.

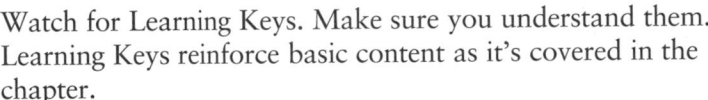

A BROADER VIEW WIDENS YOUR HORIZON

Each chapter expands your understanding by featuring a real situation or event. A Broader View puts accounting in perspective.

A BROADER VIEW

PHOTODISC/GETTY IMAGES

Payroll Fraud—Paying for Ghosts

A supervisor at Haas Transfer Warehouse embezzled $12,000 from the company by collecting paychecks for former employees. When an employee left the company, the supervisor continued to submit a department time report for the employee. This caused a paycheck to be generated for the "ghost" employee. The supervisor then simply kept this paycheck when others were distributed to actual employees.

This fraud shows the importance of two procedures that appear in this chapter: (1) a time card, plastic card, or badge should be used for each employee to keep an accurate record of time worked and (2) payment by direct deposit or electronic funds transfer to the employee's bank is a good internal control.

PROFILES IN ACCOUNTING LET YOU SEE WHAT OTHERS ARE DOING WITH THEIR ACCOUNTING EDUCATION

The individuals featured in Profiles in Accounting are real people who have learned the basics from the Heintz/Parry *College Accounting* text, continued their accounting and business education, and are now pursuing successful careers in the business world. As you will see, an accounting education can lead to many different careers.

Profiles in Accounting

Michael Burdish
Payroll Compliance Auditor

Michael Burdish graduated with an associate degree in accounting with honors from The College of Westchester. Michael excelled in his studies in accounting and knew this was the field for him. After graduation, Michael was hired as a payroll compliance auditor for an accounting firm. He is part of the team that audits companies and contractors that hire union members. The focus of the audits is to ensure that the correct amounts of benefits are paid. According to Michael he really enjoys his work. He especially likes meeting many new people and having new experiences. Michael intends to further his education and complete his baccalaureate degree in accounting.

SELF-STUDY QUESTIONS AND U REVU EXERCISES HELP YOU CHECK YOUR UNDERSTANDING

If you want to know how well you understand the chapter's information, watch for these banners and test yourself:

U REVU Complete U REVU-1 on **page 154** to test your basic understanding of LO1

Throughout each chapter, the U REVU banners let you know when to test your basic understanding of the section you have completed.

SELF-STUDY QUESTIONS AND EXERCISES

Find the true/false and multiple choice questions and U REVU exercises section by looking for this banner. Be sure to note the "LO" by each question/exercise. That will help you find the coverage in the chapter.

ANSWERS TO SELF-STUDY QUESTIONS AND EXERCISES

Once you have tested yourself using the Self-Study Questions and Exercises, you will find the answers under this banner at the end of the chapter.

KEY POINTS TO REMEMBER HELP YOU REVIEW QUICKLY

In the end-of-chapter section, at the beginning of the Self-Study section, each of the chapter's Learning Objectives is repeated along with the core information covered in the chapter. This information will help you when you are working on your assignments and when you are studying for a test.

COMPREHENSIVE PROBLEMS PULL CONTENT ALTOGETHER

Following Chapter 6, the first Comprehensive Problem gives you a chance to see how well you understand the coverage of Part 1. After Chapter 15, the second Comprehensive Problem checks your understanding of the content in Parts 1–3. Depending on whether or not you've studied special journals (Chapter 12), this second one gives you two different choices for solving the problem. The third Comprehensive Problem is presented after Chapter 19. This one involves a partnership and includes accounting for receivables, notes, interest, and long-term assets.

CENGAGENOW HELPS YOU WORK AND LEARN MORE EFFICIENTLY

Ask your instructor about getting access to this powerful Web site.

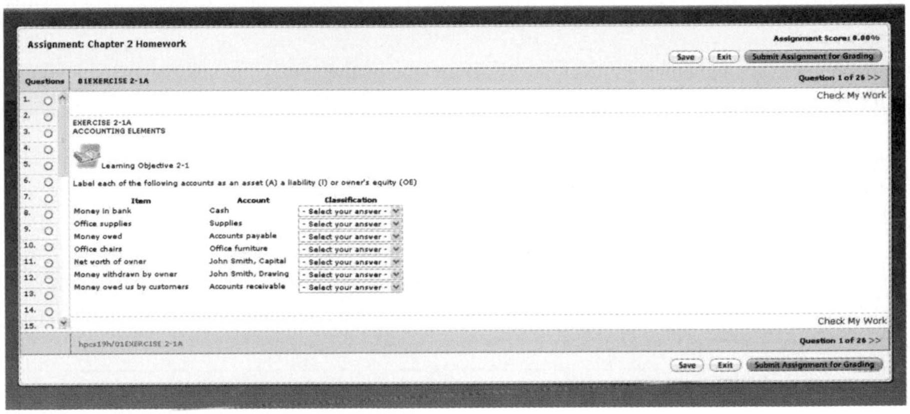

CengageNOW for Heintz/Parry's *College Accounting* online learning system helps you make the most of every minute of study and handle homework more efficiently. With CengageNOW's personalized study plans, you focus only on the areas of challenge to you with a variety of interactive learning tools to ensure you are prepared with the accounting skills most important for your future. Homework management tools help you efficiently complete homework assignments necessary to earn a successful grade in the course.

THE STUDY GUIDE PROVIDES MORE PRACTICE; WORKING PAPERS SHORTEN YOUR HOMEWORK TIME

The Heintz and Parry 20e Study Guide for Chapters 1–15 + Combination Journal Module (ISBN-10: 0538737042, ISBN-13: 9780538737043) and Chapters 16–27 (ISBN-10: 0538750707, ISBN-13: 9780538750707) offers you the opportunity to reinforce your learning experience with brief discussions of each chapter's key points and learning objectives. In addition, the Study Guide provides a third set of "C" assignments, which consists of review questions, exercises, and problems similar to those at the end of each chapter. (The solutions to the Study Guide assignments are available separately, at the discretion of your instructor.) Included with the Study Guide are the Working Papers for the text's end-of-chapter assignments. Journals, ledgers, work sheets, and other documents are provided to make completing the assignments less time consuming for you. Ask your instructor about this helpful resource.

OTHER SUPPLEMENTAL MATERIALS ENHANCE YOUR UNDERSTANDING

Student Supplements and Resources

Student Web Site

Now mastering accounting concepts is easier than ever with the rich array of learning resources at the Heintz/Parry *College Accounting*, 20e interactive companion Web site. Designed specifically to help you learn the most from your course and earn the grade you want, this Web site's interactive study center features chapter-by-chapter PowerPoint® lecture presentation slides, online quizzes, flashcards, outlines, key terms, and a final exam, as well as links to accounting resources, and more. These resources will help you develop the skills you need for progress now and success throughout the future!

Klooster & Allen General Ledger Software and Data Files CD-ROM

(ISBN-10: 0538750693/ISBN-13: 9780538750691)

Gain first-hand experience in working with full-functioning general ledger software. Use this proven software with selected problems in the main text that are clearly **identified by icons**. You'll learn to work with opening balances, to interpret a chart of accounts, and to set up functions to complete problems.

Peachtree and QuickBooks Data Files for Comprehensive Problems CD-ROM

(ISBN-10: 0538476168/ISBN-13: 9780538476164)

These data sets allow you to complete the requirements of the Comprehensive Problems using either Peachtree or QuickBooks software. (The software is **not** included on this CD-ROM.)

Online Excel Spreadsheet Templates

(ISBN-10: 0538753595/ISBN-13: 9780538753593)

These new templates are provided for selected end-of-chapter exercises and problems (**designated by an icon in the text**). They will assist you as you set up and work the assignment. To help you stay on track, certain cells are coded to display a red asterisk when an incorrect answer is entered.

Using Peachtree Complete for Accounting (w/ CD-ROM)
Glenn Owen, Allan Hancock College

(ISBN-10: 0324665512/ISBN-13: 9780324665512)

The textbook takes a user perspective by illustrating how accounting information is both used and created. In addition, the text uses proven and successful pedagogy to demonstrate the software's features and elicit student interaction. The text's foremost goal is to help you learn fundamental accounting concepts through the use of Peachtree and the analysis of business events. The content complements the first course in accounting.

Using QuickBooks Pro for Accounting (w/ CD-ROM)
Glenn Owen, Allan Hancock College

(ISBN-10: 0324664044/ISBN-13: 9780324664041)

Similar in description to the Peachtree text above, this book introduces QuickBooks Pro.

Using Excel and Access for Accounting
Glenn Owen, Allan Hancock College

(ISBN-10: 0324594399/ISBN-13: 9780324594393)

This textbook teaches how businesses use spreadsheets and databases in accounting. It serves as a primer explaining how to use these tools in solving real accounting problems.

Trey's Fast Cleaning Service Practice Set with Student CD
Toni R. Hartley, Laurel Business Institute

(ISBN-10: 0538753226/ISBN-13: 9780538753227)

This practice set features a sole proprietorship service business simulation. It reviews the accounting cycle and accounting for cash. The practice set can be solved manually, with Klooster & Allen General Ledger software, or with Peachtree software. The Student CD includes the installation files for both software packages as well as the relevant data files. (Appropriate for use after Chapter 7.)

Coolspring Furniture Practice Set with Student CD
Toni R. Hartley, Laurel Business Institute

(ISBN-10: 053875074X/ISBN-13: 9780538750745)

Practice your accounting success, including working with payroll taxes, within this sole proprietorship merchandising business. The accompanying CD contains both Klooster & Allen General Ledger software, Peachtree software, and the data files to complete the practice set using either software program. The practice set may also be completed manually. (Appropriate for use after Chapter 12.)

SPECIAL INFORMATION FOR INSTRUCTORS

In addition to the important pedagogical elements introduced to your students above, we have some new features and key changes that will enhance your course. Overall, these are:

- A greater use of portrait presentation of figures wherever possible

FIGURE 6-2 Linkages Between the Work Sheet, Statement of Owner's Equity, and Balance Sheet

Statement Heading
Name of company
Title of statement
Accounting period ended
Current assets: cash and items that will be converted to cash or consumed within a year.
Property, plant, and equipment: durable assets that will help produce revenues for several years.
Current liabilities: amounts owed that will be paid within a year (will require the use of current assets).

Note: The statement of owner's equity is prepared before the balance sheet. The S.O.E. is shown below the B.S. to enhance the illustration of the linkages between the work sheet and financial statements.

Jessie Jane's Campus Delivery Service
Work Sheet (Partial)
For Month Ended June 30, 20 - -

	ACCOUNT TITLE	BALANCE SHEET DEBIT	BALANCE SHEET CREDIT
1	Cash	370 00	
2	Accounts Receivable	650 00	
3	Supplies	20 00	
4	Prepaid Insurance	175 00	
5	Delivery Equipment	3600 00	
6	Accum. Depr.—Delivery Equip.		100 00
7	Accounts Payable		1800 00
8	Wages Payable		50 00
9	Jessica Jane, Capital		2000 00
10	Jessica Jane, Drawing	150 00	
11	Delivery Fees		
12	Wages Expense		
13	Rent Expense		
14	Supplies Expense		
15	Telephone Expense		
16	Insurance Expense		
17	Depr. Expense—Delivery Equip.		
18		4965 00	3950 00
19	Net Income		1015 00
20		4965 00	4965 00
21			

Prepare BS Third

Jessie Jane's Campus Delivery Service
Balance Sheet
June 30, 20 --

Assets		
Current assets:		
Cash	$ 370 00	
Accounts receivable	650 00	
Supplies	20 00	
Prepaid insurance	175 00	
Total current assets		$ 1215 00
Property, plant, and equipment:		
Delivery equipment	$3600 00	
Less accumulated depreciation	100 00	3500 00
Total assets		$ 4715 00
Liabilities		
Current liabilities:		
Accounts payable	$1800 00	
Wages payable	50 00	
Total current liabilities		$ 1850 00
Owner's Equity		
Jessica Jane, capital		2865 00
Total liabilities and owner's equity		$ 4715 00

Prepare SOE Second

Jessie Jane's Campus Delivery Service
Statement of Owner's Equity
For Month Ended June 30, 20 --

Jessica Jane, capital, June 1, 20--		$ —
Investments during June		2000 00
Total investment		$2000 00
Net income for June	$1015 00	
Less: withdrawals for June	150 00	
Increase in capital		865 00
Jessica Jane, capital, June 30, 20--		$2865 00

Ending capital is not taken from the work sheet. It is computed on the statement of owner's equity.
Dollar signs used at top of columns and under rulings.
Single rulings indicate addition or subtraction.
Double rulings indicate totals.

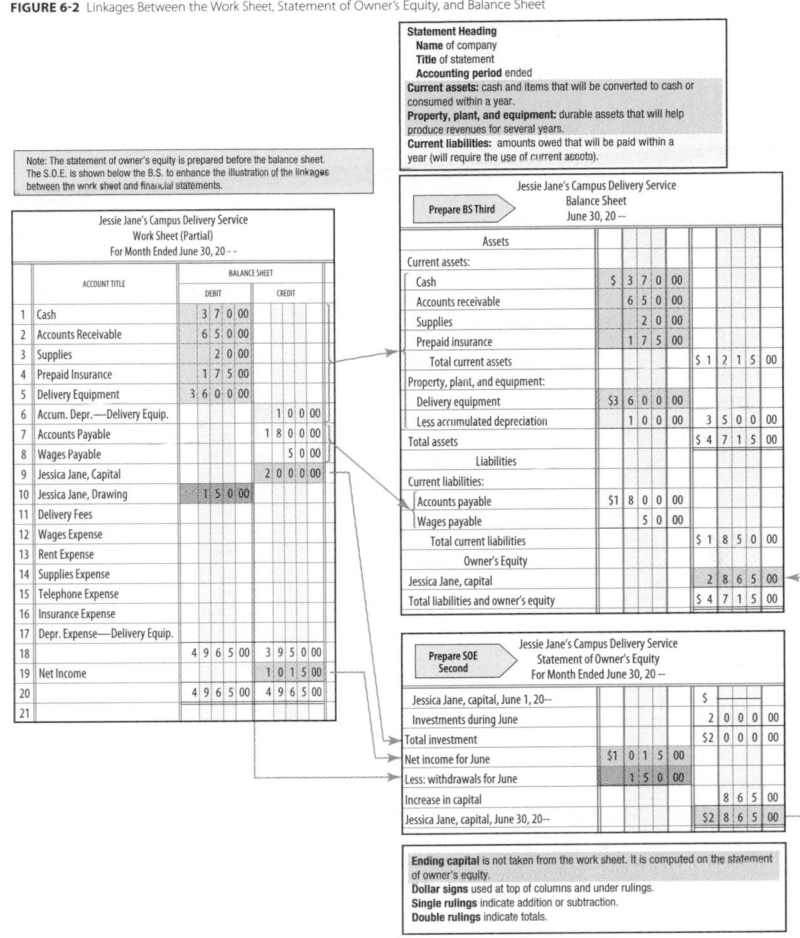

- Improved readability (shorter paragraphs, more listings/steps for easier understanding, etc.)

The adjustment for merchandise inventory is done in two steps.

1. Remove the beginning inventory from the merchandise inventory account by making the following entry:

Income Summary	old	
Merchandise Inventory		old

2. Enter the ending inventory in the merchandise inventory account by making the following entry:

Merchandise Inventory	new	
Income Summary		new

- The owner's initial investment is now shown as an investment during the period, instead of the beginning of the period.

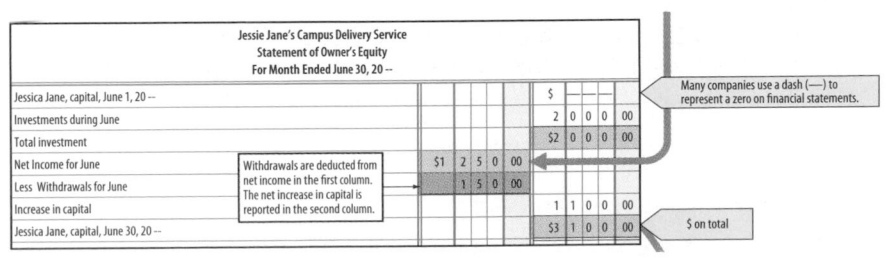

Jessie Jane's Campus Delivery Service
Statement of Owner's Equity
For Month Ended June 30, 20 --

Jessica Jane, capital, June 1, 20 --		$ —
Investments during June		2000 00
Total investment		$2000 00
Net Income for June	$1250 00	
Less Withdrawals for June	150 00	
Increase in capital		1100 00
Jessica Jane, capital, June 30, 20 --		$3100 00

Withdrawals are deducted from net income in the first column. The net increase in capital is reported in the second column.

Many companies use a dash (—) to represent a zero on financial statements.

$ on total

- New supplement—Excel templates (related exercises/problems are indicated by an icon in the text)

E 2-3A (LO3/4)
✓ Assets following (d): $22,000

EFFECTS OF TRANSACTIONS (BALANCE SHEET ACCOUNTS) Alice Stern started a business. During the first month (February 20--), the following transactions occurred. Show the effect of each transaction on the accounting equation: *Assets = Liabilities + Owner's Equity.* After each transaction, show the new totals.

(a) Invested cash in the business, $20,000.
(b) Bought office equipment on account, $3,500.
(c) Bought office equipment for cash, $1,200.
(d) Paid cash on account to supplier in transaction (b), $1,500.

By chapter:

Ch. 1—We have added brief coverage of International Financial Reporting Standards (IFRS) and forensic accounting.

Ch. 2—Redesigned accounting equation that clarifies the expanded owner's equity after students gain an understanding of the basic equation (A=L+OE); new color coding highlights key accounts by category.

	Assets (Items Owned)			=	Liabilities (Amounts Owed)	+	Owner's Equity (Owner's Investment)		+	(Earnings)		
	Cash +	Accounts Receivable +	Delivery Equipment	=	Accounts Payable	+	Jessica Jane, Capital –	Jessica Jane, Drawing	+	Revenues –	Expenses	Description
	$750		$2,100		$600		$2,000			$ 500	$250	
(h)		+ $600								+ 600		Deliv. Fees
	$750 +	$600 +	$2,100	=	$600	+	$2,000		+	$1,100 –	$250	
		$3,450		=				$3,450				

Ch. 3—Redesigned owner's equity umbrella featuring new color coding for greater clarity.

FIGURE 3-2 The Accounting Equation and the Owner's Equity Umbrella

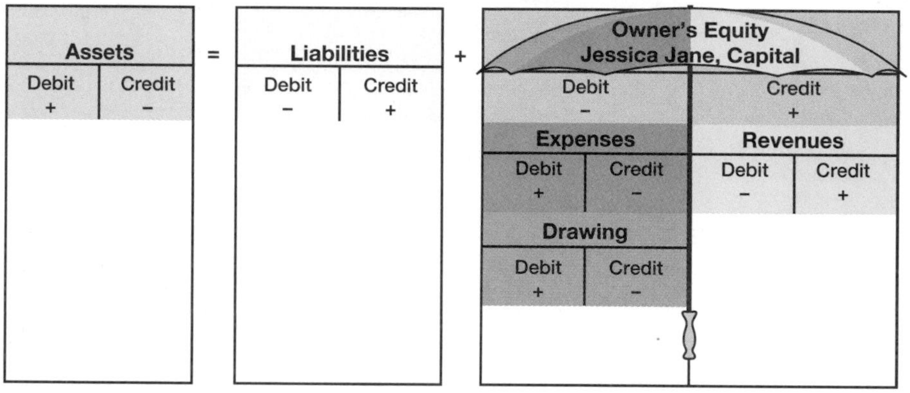

The color coding ties the narrative information with the T account presentation.

Analysis. This payment decreases the asset, Cash, and decreases the liability, Accounts Payable. Debit Accounts Payable and credit Cash for $300.

FIGURE 3-8 Transaction (d): Payment on Account

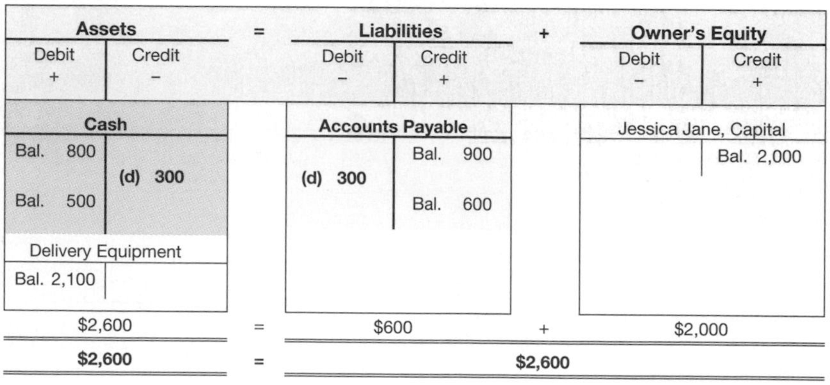

Assets
Debit +
Credit –
=
Liabilities
Debit –
Credit +
+
Owner's Equity
Debit –
Credit +
Cash
Bal. 800
(d) 300
Bal. 500
Delivery Equipment
Bal. 2,100
Accounts Payable
Bal. 900
(d) 300
Bal. 600
Jessica Jane, Capital
Bal. 2,000
$2,600 = $600 + $2,000
$2,600 = $2,600

Ch. 4—Financial statement illustration has been added to the demonstration problem. This helps students tie knowledge from earlier chapters together with information presented in the chapter.

Ch. 5—Journal entry for the adjusting entries now shown with T account presentations; chapter content presentation has been revised to cover posting of adjusting entries before work sheet coverage—this makes skipping work sheet coverage easier for those wanting to do so; for those using the work sheet, we enhanced the linkage between work sheet adjustments and adjusting entries. In the appendix, graphs have been added to the depreciation method examples to assist visual learners.

FIGURE 5-7 Adjustment for Unpaid Wages

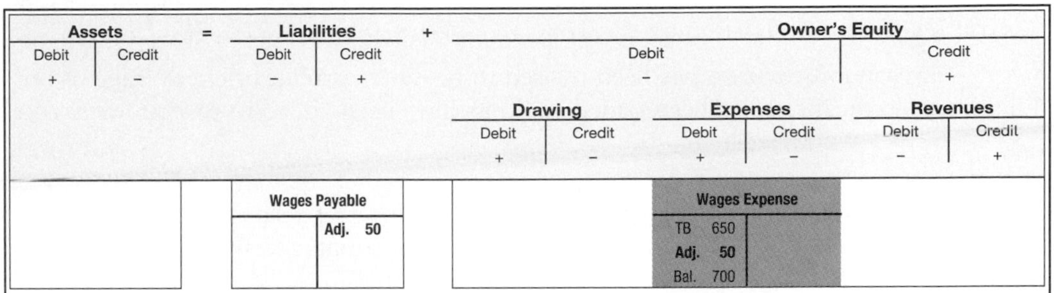

GENERAL JOURNAL PAGE 3

	DATE	DESCRIPTION	POST REF.	DEBIT	CREDIT	
1		Adjusting Entry				1
8		Wages Expense		50 00		8
9		Wages Payable			50 00	9
10						10

Ch. 6—Illustration of the closing process has been enhanced.

FIGURE 6-8 Closing Entries in Journal Form

Jessie Jane's Campus Delivery Service
Work Sheet (Partial)
For Month Ended June 30, 20 - -

	ACCOUNT TITLE	INCOME STATEMENT DEBIT	INCOME STATEMENT CREDIT	BALANCE SHEET DEBIT	BALANCE SHEET CREDIT
1	Cash			370 00	
2	Accounts Receivable			650 00	
3	Supplies			20 00	
4	Prepaid Insurance			175 00	
5	Delivery Equipment			3600 00	
6	Accum. Depr.—Delivery Equipment				100 00
7	Accounts Payable				1800 00
8	Wages Payable				50 00
9	Jessica Jane, Capital				2000 00
10	Jessica Jane, Drawing			150 00	
11	Delivery Fees		2150 00		
12	Wages Expense	700 00			
13	Rent Expense	200 00			
14	Supplies Expense	60 00			
15	Telephone Expense	50 00			
16	Insurance Expense	25 00			
17	Depr. Expense—Delivery Equipment	100 00			
18		1135 00	2150 00	4965 00	3950 00
19	Net Income	1015 00			1015 00
20		2150 00	2150 00	4965 00	4965 00

STEP 1: Close revenue accounts to Income Summary.

STEP 2: Close expense accounts to Income Summary.

STEP 3: Close Income Summary to the owner's capital account.

STEP 4: Close Drawing to the owner's capital account.

GENERAL JOURNAL PAGE 4

DATE		DESCRIPTION	POST. REF.	DEBIT	CREDIT	
		Closing Entries				1
20-- June	30	Delivery Fees	401	2150 00		2
		Income Summary	313		2150 00	3
						4
	30	Income Summary	313	1135 00		5
		Wages Expense	511		700 00	6
		Rent Expense	521		200 00	7
		Supplies Expense	523		60 00	8
		Telephone Expense	525		50 00	9
		Insurance Expense	535		25 00	10
		Depr. Expense—Delivery Equipment	541		100 00	11
						12
	30	Income Summary	313	1015 00		13
		Jessica Jane, Capital	311		1015 00	14
						15
	30	Jessica Jane, Capital	311	150 00		16
		Jessica Jane, Drawing	312		150 00	17
						18

LEARNING KEY

Each individual revenue, expense, and drawing account must be closed.

Comprehensive Problem—New data sets have been added so that students can complete the problem using either Peachtree or QuickBooks software or the Klooster & Allen General Ledger software.

Ch. 7—Coverage of lapping and kiting has been added to the cash internal control section.

Ch. 8—Payroll information has been revised to be more current; to assist in understanding the link between the payroll register and related journal entries, cross-reference coding has been added.

Ch. 9—Payroll information has been revised to be more current; brief coverage of Form I-9 (Employment Eligibility Verification) has been added; callouts have been added to several forms to enhance clarity.

Ch. 10—Expanded coverage of sales discounts, including a new figure illustrating the concept and accounting for sales when there are sales taxes and cash discounts.

Figure 10-11 shows how (1) a sale on account followed by (2) collection with a cash discount affects the accounts receivable, sales, and cash accounts.

FIGURE 10-11 Sales on Account → Collection with Cash Discount

	(1) Credit Sale	−	2% Cash Discount	=	(2) Cash Collection
Net Sales =	$100	−	$2	=	$98

		Debit	Credit
	ENTRY FOR CREDIT SALE		
(1)	Accounts Receivable	1 0 0 00	
	Sales		1 0 0 00

		Debit	Credit
	ENTRY FOR CASH COLLECTION		
(2)	Cash	9 8 00	
	Sales Discounts	2 00	
	Accounts Receivable		1 0 0 00

Ch. 11—Impact of sales discounts has been added to the gross profit coverage.

Ch. 14—Cost of goods sold illustration added to demo problem.

Ch. 15—Sales discounts added to demo problem; unearned revenue added to selected problems.

Comprehensive Problem 2—Significant reduction in number of transactions required in Part 1—thus decreasing redundancy.

Ch. 16—New illustrations of the percentage of sales and percentage of receivables provide a visualization of these two methods.

FIGURE 16-2 Percentage of Sales Method

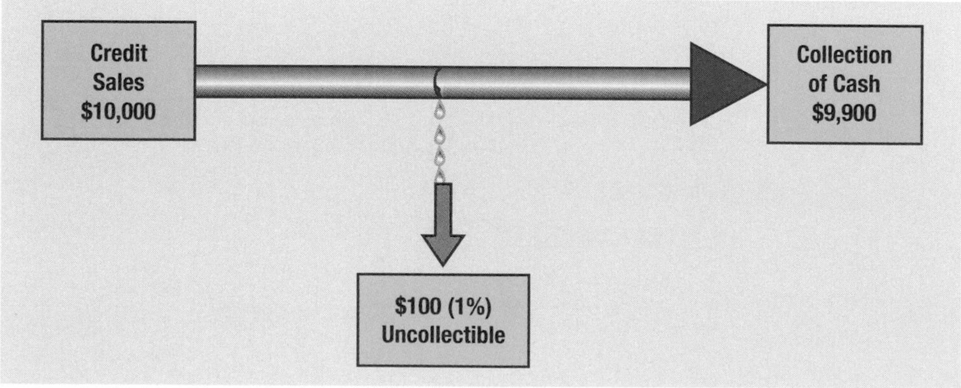

Ch. 18—Coverage of accounting for replacements has been expanded.

Ch. 19—A section on three types of partnerships and how they are formed has been added. This includes coverage of general, limited (LP), and limited liability (LLP) partnerships. In addition, the impact of periodic and perpetual inventory methods on partner drawings is explained.

Ch. 20—Capital stock coverage has been expanded to include new illustrations and coverage of convertible preferred stock.

FIGURE 20-4 Capital Stock

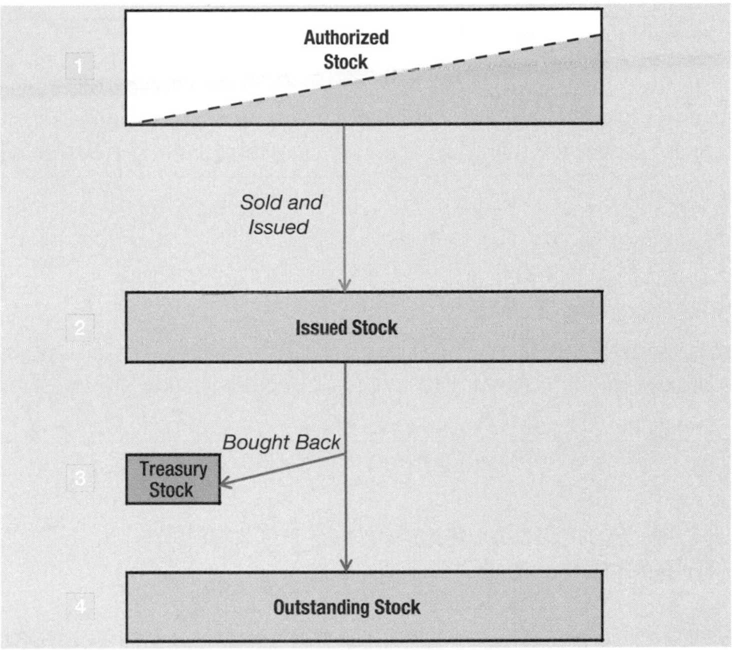

Ch. 21—New illustrations showing the effect of cash dividends and stock dividends have been added.

FIGURE 21-4 Effect of Cash Dividend

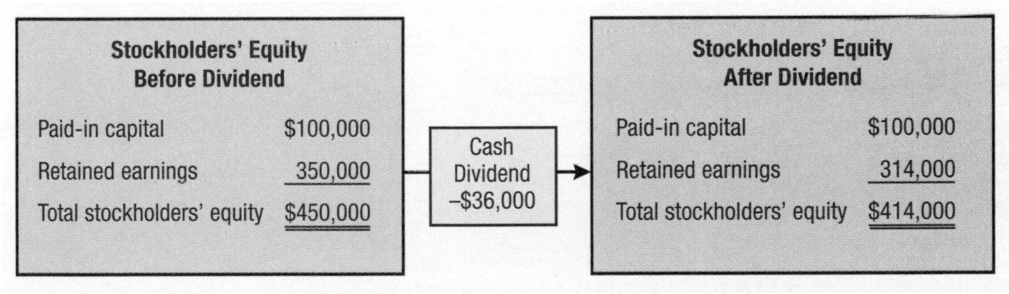

Ch. 22—New visuals have been added to the coverage of bonds issued at a premium and at a discount.

FIGURE 22-2 Bonds Issued at a Premium

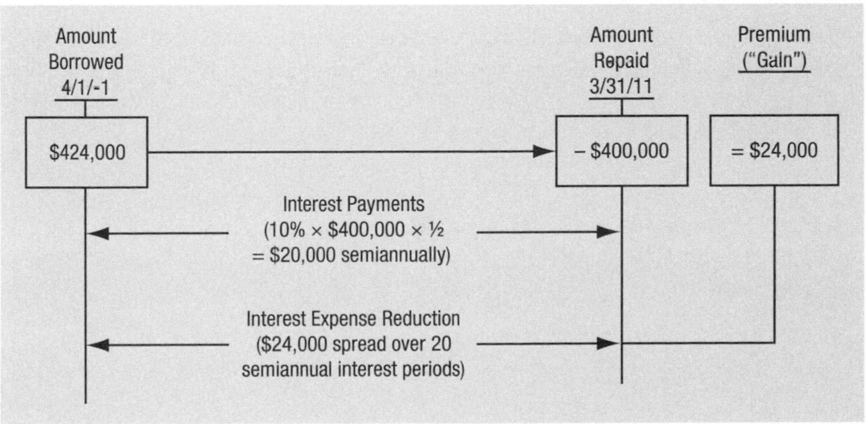

Ch. 24—The discussion of ratio analysis has been reorganized and expanded.

Ch. 26—The illustrated flow of manufacturing costs and the schedule of cost of goods manufactured have been revised. New illustrations have been added to the coverage of job order cost accounting.

Instructor Supplements and Resources

CengageNOW

NEW CengageNOW for Heintz/Parry's *College Accounting* online teaching and learning system provides the ultimate in flexibility and ease of use with the results you want NOW to ensure your students are building skills for the future. Save time as you efficiently plan your course, teach and reinforce content with interactive learning tools and personalized study plans, and grade results based on AACSB accreditation standards.

Solutions Manual
James Heintz and Robert Parry

Chapters 1-15 + Combination Journal Module (ISBN-10: 053875088X/ISBN-13: 9780538750882)
Chapters 16-27 (ISBN-10: 0538750898/ISBN-13: 9780538750899)

This printed version contains the complete, carefully verified solutions for all text assignments. Accounting rulings are used where appropriate. (*Note*: These are also the solutions to the working papers.) The solutions manual is also available on the Instructor's Resource CD-ROM and the Instructor's Web site, which are described below.

Study Guide Solutions
James Heintz and Robert Parry

Chapters 1-9 + Combination Journal Module (ISBN-10: 0538750715/ISBN-13: 9780538750714)
Chapters 10-15 (ISBN-10: 0538750723/ISBN-13: 9780538750721)
Chapters 16-27 (ISBN-10: 0538750731/ISBN-13: 9780538750738)

These solutions cover all set "C" assignments found in the Study Guide. **This may be packaged with the Study Guide at the instructor's discretion.**

Solutions Transparencies
James Heintz and Robert Parry

Chapters 1-15 + Combination Journal Module (ISBN-10: 0538752521/ISBN-13: 9780538752527)
Chapters 16-27 (ISBN-10: 053875253X/ISBN-13: 9780538752534)

Contains solutions for the Series A & B Exercises and Problems, Mastery Problems, Challenge Problems, and Comprehensive Problems in the text. Where appropriate, solutions appear on accounting rulings.

Test Bank

Alice Sineath, Forsyth Technical Community College
Bruce Gunning, Kent State University at East Liverpool

Chapters 1-15 + Combination Journal Module (ISBN-10: 0538752548/ISBN-13: 9780538752541)
Chapters 16-27 (ISBN-10: 0538752556/ISBN-13: 9780538752558)

Revised and verified to ensure accuracy, this printed version of the test bank includes questions clearly identified by Learning Objectives, level of difficulty, and AACSB standards to allow greater guidance in developing assessments and evaluating student progress. Question types include true/false, multiple choice, and problems. The complete test bank in both the Microsoft Word and ExamView® testing software versions is available on the Instructor's Resource CD-ROM, which is listed on the following page.

Instructor's Resource Guide

James M. Emig, Villanova University
Susan Jefferson, Reece, Campbell, Inc.

Chapters 1-15 + Combination Journal Module (ISBN-10: 0538754389/ISBN-13: 9780538754385)
Chapters 16-27 (ISBN-10: 0538754397/ISBN-13: 9780538754392)

This guide contains a wealth of resources to help instructors create an exciting and productive classroom experience. Included are enhanced chapter outlines and teaching tips; references to exhibits, PowerPoint® slides, and teaching transparencies; suggested enrichments and activities; check figures for text assignments; pretests tied to Learning Objectives; and Ten Questions Your Students Will Always Ask to help anticipate student learning needs. This guide is also available on the Instructor's Resource CD-ROM, which is listed below.

Instructor's Resource CD-ROM with ExamView®

(ISBN-10: 0538750650/ISBN-13: 9780538750653)

This all-in-one tool places the resources you need to plan and teach at your fingertips in one convenient CD-ROM. You'll find the Solutions Manual, Test Bank in Microsoft Word and Examview® testing software, PowerPoint® lecture presentation slides, Instructor's Resource Guide, Instructor's solutions, Excel template solutions, Teaching Transparencies, and Inspector software for checking solutions using the accompanying Klooster & Allen General Ledger software.

Instructor's Web Site

Ensure a higher level of understanding and success with this comprehensive, resource-rich text support site. An interactive student study center provides interactive quizzes and online tools that encourage learning. Password-protected teaching resources, including the Instructor's Manual, Teaching Transparencies, PowerPoint® lecture presentations, Test Bank, Instructor's solutions Excel templates, and Solutions Manual, are easy to download. You can link to Web Work assignments, ideal for Internet research, assign online quizzes with solutions, or assign other interactive assignments to help students test themselves during study. It's everything you need to deliver the skills your students need to enhance their future.

Trey's Fast Cleaning Service Practice Set Key + Inspector CD-ROM

Toni R. Hartley, Laurel Business Institute

(ISBN-10: 0538753234/ISBN-13: 9780538753234)

This Instructor's Key for the Trey's Fast Cleaning Service practice set includes the inspector CD, which contains the Klooster & Allen General Ledger solutions software for the practice set.

Coolspring Furniture Practice Set Key + Inspector CD-ROM

Toni R. Hartley, Laurel Business Institute

(ISBN-10: 0538752750/ISBN-13: 9780538752756)

This Instructor's Key for the Coolspring Furniture practice set includes the inspector CD, which contains the Klooster & Allen General Ledger solutions software for the practice set.

Additional Resources

Integrated Accounting for Windows (and software)

Dale Klooster and Warren Allen

(ISBN-10: 0538747978/ISBN-13: 9780538747974)

Quite possibly the easiest-to-understand learning program on the market, this textbook, with accompanying software, teaches students all the aspects of computerized accounting and the operating procedures for all Windows-based programs at the same time. The software was designed to be very similar to the commercial software packages used in business, which will help students hit the ground running when they get that first real job. With its updated design and improved directions, students won't become overwhelmed with the program.

DEDICATION

We are grateful to our wives, Celia Heintz and Jane Parry, and our children, Andrea Heintz, John Heintz, Jessica Jane Parry, and Mitch Parry, for their love, support, and assistance during the creation of this 20th edition. We especially appreciate Jessie Parry's willingness to let us use her name throughout the first six chapters.

ACKNOWLEDGMENTS

We thank the following individuals for their helpful contributions in assisting us in this revision of *College Accounting.*

Allan N. Aspelund, *Century College*
Lelia Austin, *Lake City Community College*
Anne Bikofsky, *The College of Westchester*
Juanita Garza Blankenship, *Del Mar College*
Jane Bloom, *Palm Beach Community College*
Anna Boulware, *St. Charles Community College*
Leonor Cabrera, *Cañada College*
Dan Carroll, *Miami University—Hamilton and Middletown*
Susan S. Davis, *Green River Community College*
Judith A. Dixon, *York Technical College*
Sharon Doherty, *Lincoln College of Technology*
Larry J. Dragosavac, *Edison Community College*
Richard Dugger, *Kilgore College*
Charles D. Edwards, *Miami University—Hamilton and Middletown*
Marina Grau, *Houston Community College*
Becky Hancock, *El Paso Community College*
Toni R. Hartley, *Laurel Business Institute*
Patricia H. Holmes, *Des Moines Area Community College*
James Hurst, *National College—Lexington*
Dieter M. Kiefer, *American River College*
Susan S. Lafferty, *National College of Business and Technology*
Sonja Lolland, *Sierra College*
Ted Lynch, *Hocking College*
Alfonso J. Maldonado, *Laredo Community College*
Michael S. Manis, *College of the Desert*
James Mann, *Huntington Junior College*
Josephine M. Mathias, *Mercer County Community College*
Marc Newman, *Hocking College*
Sonia M. Gipson Rankin, *IIA College*
Aaron Reeves, *Saint Louis Community College—Forest Park*
Carolyn M. Seefer, *Diablo Valley College*
Tom Shaffer, *Spencerian College—Louisville*
Judy Toland, *Bucks County Community College*

Special recognition and thanks go to Anne Bikofsky, The College of Westchester, who provided the all-new Profiles in Accounting, which feature five of her former students. In addition, we express our appreciation to the following consultants for their quality assistance in providing supporting materials: Alice Sineath of Forsyth Technical Community College, Leonor Cabrera of Canada College of Business, James Emig of Villanova University, Susan Jefferson, Patti Hudepohl, and Mark Sears. We would also like to thank Richard Dugger of Kilgore College, Sheila Viel of the University of Wisconsin—Milwaukee, Bruce Gunning of Kent State University East Liverpool, and Robert Osborne of Ohio Dominican University for their diligent verification of the supplements.

CONTENTS IN BRIEF

CONTENTS

PART 4 SPECIALIZED ACCOUNTING PROCEDURES FOR MERCHANDISING BUSINESSES AND PARTNERSHIPS 619

Accounting for a Service Business

PART 1

Add Some Color to Your Learning!

Throughout the text, you will be introduced to many important terms and types of accounts. To help you learn the different terms and types of accounts, we have coded many of them using the following color key in Part 1:

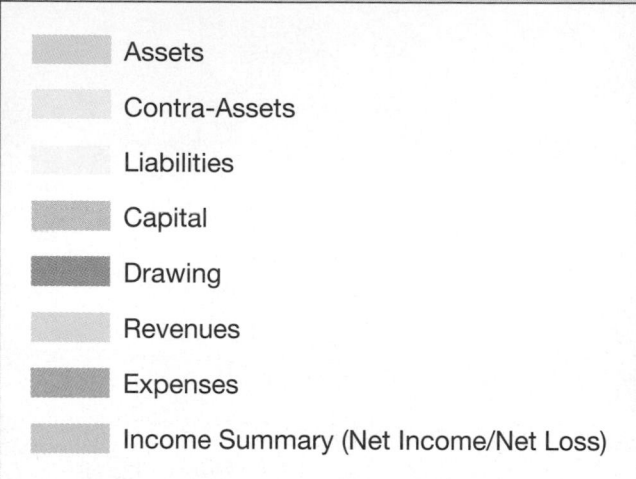

- Assets
- Contra-Assets
- Liabilities
- Capital
- Drawing
- Revenues
- Expenses
- Income Summary (Net Income/Net Loss)

Chapter 1

IAN BRACEGIRDLE PHOTOGRAPHY/ISTOCKPHOTO.COM

Introduction to Accounting

Need a private jet to get away for the weekend, attend a business meeting, or visit Mom? Call Jets.com. Established in 1999, Jets.com serves as a broker for private jet services. Call or go online, and its technology will automatically send your trip request/itinerary to a network of approved operators who will locate available aircraft. Operators will competitively bid for your business, resulting in significant savings and increased aircraft options for you.

In addition to a system that links customers with private jet service, Jets.com needs a system to account for its business transactions. Thus, it employs accounting professionals who understand the accounting process and generally accepted accounting principles.

Welcome to the world of accounting. We are delighted that you have decided to join us. A solid foundation in accounting concepts and techniques will serve you well. This is true whether you accept a professional position in accounting, work for or own a business, or simply seek a better understanding of your personal finances.

Oh, and what does it cost to take a private jet to the Super Bowl? Rates run from $2,000 to $7,000 per hour on the busiest weekend of the year.

LEARNING OBJECTIVES

Careful study of this chapter should enable you to:

LO1 Describe the purpose of accounting.

LO2 Describe the accounting process.

LO3 Define GAAP and describe the process used by FASB to develop these principles.

LO4 Define three types of business ownership structures.

LO5 Classify different types of businesses by activities.

LO6 Identify career opportunities in accounting.

Accounting is the language of business. You must learn this language to understand the impact of economic events on a specific company. Common, everyday terms have very precise meanings when used in accounting. For example, you have probably heard terms like asset, liability, revenue, expense, and net income. Take a moment to jot down how you would define each of these terms. After reading and studying Chapter 2, compare your definitions with those developed in this text. This comparison will show whether you can trust your current understanding of accounting terms. Whether you intend to pursue a career in accounting or simply wish to understand the impact of business transactions, you need a clear understanding of this language.

THE PURPOSE OF ACCOUNTING

LO1 Describe the purpose of accounting.

The purpose of accounting is to provide financial information about the current operations and financial condition of a business to individuals, agencies, and organizations. As shown in Figure 1-1, owners, managers, creditors, and government agencies all need accounting information. Other users of accounting information include customers, clients, labor unions, stock exchanges, and financial analysts.

FIGURE 1-1 Users of Accounting Information

USER	INFORMATION NEEDED	DECISIONS MADE BY USERS
Owners—Present and future	Company's profitability and current financial condition.	If business is good, owners may consider making additional investments for growth. If business is poor, they may want to talk to management to find out why and may consider closing the business.
Managers—May or may not own business	Detailed measures of business performance.	Managers need to make operating decisions. How much and what kinds of inventory should be carried? Is business strong enough to support higher wages for employees?
Creditors—Present and future	Company's profitability, debt outstanding, and assets that could be used to secure debt.	Should a loan be granted to this business? If so, what amount of debt can the business support, and what interest rate should be charged?
Government Agencies—National, state, and local	Company's profitability, cash flows, and overall financial condition.	The IRS will decide how much income tax the business must pay. Local governments may be willing to adjust property taxes paid by the business to encourage it to stay in town.

THE ACCOUNTING PROCESS

LO2 Describe the accounting process.

Accounting is a system of gathering financial information about a business and reporting this information to users. The six major steps of the accounting process are analyzing, recording, classifying, summarizing, reporting, and interpreting (Figure 1-2). Computers are often used in the recording, classifying, summarizing, and reporting steps. Whether or not computers are used, the accounting concepts and techniques are the same. Information entered into the computer system must reflect a proper application of these concepts. Otherwise, the output will be meaningless.

FIGURE 1-2 The Accounting Process

- **Analyzing** is looking at events that have taken place and thinking about how they affect the business.
- **Recording** is entering financial information about events into the accounting system. Although this can be done with paper and pencil, most businesses use computers to perform routine record-keeping operations.
- **Classifying** is sorting and grouping similar items together rather than merely keeping a simple, diary-like record of numerous events.
- **Summarizing** is the aggregation of many similar events to provide information that is easy to understand. For example, a firm may buy and sell baseballs during the year. Summarizing provides information on the total baseballs bought and sold and the change in the number of baseballs held from the beginning to the end of the period.
- **Reporting** is telling the results. In accounting, it is common to use tables of numbers to report results.
- **Interpreting** is deciding the meaning and importance of the information in various reports. This may include ratio analysis to help explain how pieces of information relate to one another.

GENERALLY ACCEPTED ACCOUNTING PRINCIPLES (GAAP)

LO3 Define GAAP and describe the process used by FASB to develop these principles.

Soon after the stock market crash of 1929, the federal government established the Securities and Exchange Commission (SEC). The purpose of this government agency is to help develop standards for reporting financial information to stockholders. The SEC currently has authority over 12,000 companies listed on the major stock exchanges (New York, American, and NASDAQ). It has the power to require these firms to follow certain rules when preparing their financial statements. These rules are referred to as **generally accepted accounting principles (GAAP)**.

Rather than developing GAAP on its own, the SEC encouraged the creation of a private standard-setting body. It did so because it believed the private sector had better access to the resources and talent necessary to develop these standards. Since 1973, the Financial Accounting Standards Board (FASB) has filled this role. In developing accounting standards, FASB follows a specific process and relies on the advice of many organizations. When an accounting issue is identified, the following steps are followed:

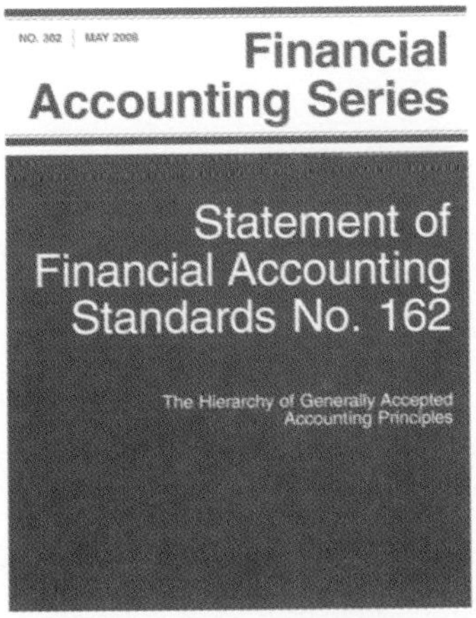

1. The issue is placed on FASB's agenda. This lets everyone know that the Board plans to develop a standard addressing this issue.
2. After researching an issue, FASB issues a **discussion memorandum.** This document identifies the pros and cons of various accounting treatments for an event.
3. To gather additional views on the issue, the Board will often hold **public hearings** around the country. Interested parties are invited to express their opinions at these hearings.

4. Following these hearings, the Board issues an **exposure draft**. This document explains the rules that FASB believes firms should follow in accounting for this event.
5. After considering feedback on the exposure draft, the Board issues a final **statement of financial accounting standards (SFAS)**.

Throughout this process, many parties participate by testifying at public hearings or by sending letters to the Board explaining why they agree or disagree with the proposed standard. These parties include the American Institute of Certified Public Accountants (AICPA), the American Accounting Association (AAA), the Institute of Management Accountants (IMA), the Financial Executives Institute (FEI), corporate executives and accountants, representatives from the investment community, analysts, bankers, industry associations, and the SEC and other government agencies. Clearly, FASB considers the views of a wide range of parties. By doing so, it maximizes the likelihood of developing and gaining acceptance of the most appropriate accounting and disclosure requirements.

The International Accounting Standards Board (IASB) issues accounting standards followed by many firms in countries outside the United States. These are called International Financial Reporting Standards (IFRS). In recent years, the IASB and FASB have worked together to try to minimize the differences in these standards. These standards may eventually converge into one set of standards used around the world.

THREE TYPES OF OWNERSHIP STRUCTURES

LO4 Define three types of business ownership structures.

One or more persons may own a business. Businesses are classified according to who owns them and the specific way they are organized. Three types of ownership structures are (1) sole proprietorship, (2) partnership, and (3) corporation (Figure 1-3). Accountants provide information to owners of all three types of ownership structures.

Most businesses in the United States operate as sole proprietorships or partnerships. However, corporations earn the highest amount of revenue.

FIGURE 1-3 Types of Ownership Structures—Advantages and Disadvantages

TYPES OF OWNERSHIP STRUCTURES

Sole Proprietorship	Partnership	Corporation
• One owner • Owner assumes all risk • Owner makes all decisions	• Two or more partners • Partners share risks • Partners may disagree on how to run business	• Stockholders • Stockholders have limited risk • Stockholders may have little influence on business decisions

The largest corporations in the United States are known as the "Fortune 500."

SOLE PROPRIETORSHIP

A **sole proprietorship** is owned by one person. The owner is usually called a proprietor. The proprietor often manages the business. The owner assumes all risks for the business, and personal assets can be taken to pay creditors. The advantage of a sole proprietorship is that the owner can make all decisions.

PARTNERSHIP

A **partnership** is owned by more than one person. One or more partners may manage the business. Like proprietors, partners assume the risks for the business, and their assets may be taken to pay creditors. An advantage of a partnership is that owners share risks and decision making. A disadvantage is that partners may disagree about the best way to run the business.

CORPORATION

A **corporation** is owned by stockholders (or shareholders). Corporations may have many owners, and they usually employ professional managers. The owners' risk is usually limited to their initial investment, and they often have very little influence on the business decisions.

TYPES OF BUSINESSES

LO5 Classify different types of businesses by activities.

Businesses are classified according to the type of service or product provided. Some businesses provide a service. Others sell a product. A business that provides a service is called a **service business**. A business that buys a product from another business to sell to customers is called a **merchandising business**. A business that makes a product to sell is called a **manufacturing business**. You will learn about all three types of businesses in this book. Figure 1-4 lists examples of types of businesses organized by activity.

FIGURE 1-4 Types and Examples of Businesses Organized by Activities

SERVICE	MERCHANDISING	MANUFACTURING
Travel Agency	Department Store	Automobile Manufacturer
Computer Consultant	Pharmacy	Furniture Maker
Physician	Grocery Store	Toy Factory

A BROADER VIEW

DESIGN PICS INC/PHOTOLIBRARY

All Kinds of Businesses Need Accounting Systems

Even small businesses like those that provide guided horse-back tours of the Rocky Mountains need good accounting systems. Proper records must be maintained for the cost of the horses, feed, food served, tour guides' salaries, and office expenses. Without this information, the company would not know how much to charge and whether a profit is made on these trips.

CAREER OPPORTUNITIES IN ACCOUNTING

LO6 Identify career opportunities in accounting.

Accounting offers many career opportunities. The positions described below require varying amounts of education, experience, and technological skill.

ACCOUNTING CLERK I
Performs accounting activities such as maintenance of the general ledger and preparation of various accounting statements and financial reports. Requires a high school diploma or its equivalent with 0–2 years of experience in the field or in a related area. $27,000–$34,000

ACCOUNTING CLERKS

Businesses with large quantities of accounting tasks to perform daily often employ **accounting clerks** to record, sort, and file accounting information. Often, accounting clerks will specialize in cash, payroll, accounts receivable, accounts payable, inventory, or purchases. As a result, they are involved with only a small portion of the total accounting responsibilities for the firm. Accounting clerks usually have at least one year of accounting education.

BOOKKEEPER
Maintains and records business transactions. Balances ledgers and prepares reports. May require an associate's degree or its equivalent with 2–4 years of experience in the field or in a related area. $32,000–$42,000

BOOKKEEPERS AND PARA-ACCOUNTANTS

Bookkeepers generally supervise the work of accounting clerks, help with daily accounting work, and summarize accounting information. In small-to-medium-sized businesses, the bookkeeper may also help managers and owners interpret the accounting information. Bookkeepers usually have one to two years of accounting education and experience as an accounting clerk.

Para-accountants provide many accounting, auditing, or tax services under the direct supervision of an accountant. A typical para-accountant has a two-year degree or significant accounting and bookkeeping experience.

BUDGET ANALYST I
Analyzes accounting records to determine financial resources required to implement programs and makes recommendations for budget allocations to ensure conformance to budgetary limits. Also responsible for reviewing operating budgets periodically in order to analyze trends affecting budget needs. Requires a bachelor's degree and 0–2 years of experience in the field or in a related area. $42,000–$54,000

ACCOUNTANTS

The difference between accountants and bookkeepers is not always clear, particularly in smaller companies where bookkeepers also help interpret the accounting information. In large companies, the distinction is clearer. Bookkeepers focus on the processing of accounting data. **Accountants** design the accounting information system and focus on analyzing and interpreting information. They also look for important trends in the data and study the impact of alternative decisions.

Most accountants enter the field with a college degree in accounting. In fact, since many states require 150 credit hours to sit for the CPA exam, many students are also earning a master's degree in accounting before entering the profession. Accountants are employed in public accounting, private (managerial) accounting, and governmental and not-for-profit accounting (Figure 1-5).

FIGURE 1-5 Accounting Careers

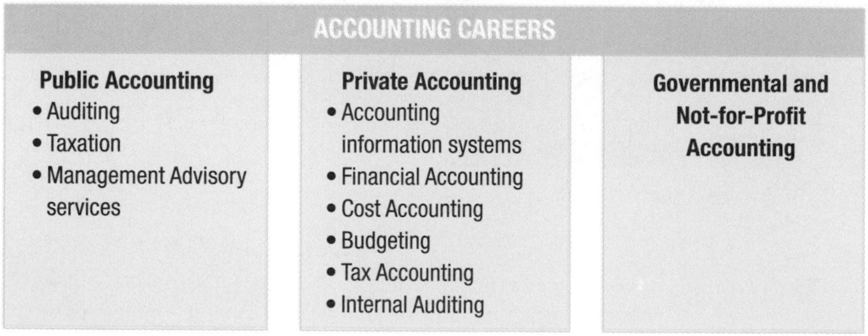

ACCOUNTING CAREERS
Public Accounting
• Auditing
• Taxation
• Management Advisory services
Private Accounting
• Accounting information systems
• Financial Accounting
• Cost Accounting
• Budgeting
• Tax Accounting
• Internal Auditing
Governmental and Not-for-Profit Accounting

ACCOUNTS PAYABLE MANAGER
Responsible for all activities in the accounts payable function. Ensures timely payments of vendor invoices and expense vouchers and maintains accurate records and control reports. Reviews applicable accounting reports and accounts payable register to ensure accuracy. May require a bachelor's degree in a related area and at least 7 years of experience in the field. Familiar with a variety of the field's concepts, practices, and procedures. Relies on experience and judgment to plan and accomplish goals. Manages a staff of administrators/clerks and typically reports to the controller. $59,000–$80,000

TOP AUDIT EXECUTIVE
Oversees all aspects of an organization's auditing function. Responsible for planning and directing all accounting and financial data. Requires a bachelor's degree with at least 15 years of experience in the field. Familiar with a variety of the field's concepts, practices, and procedures. Relies on extensive experience and judgment to plan and accomplish goals. Performs a variety of tasks. Leads and directs the work of others. A wide degree of creativity and latitude is expected. Typically reports to top management. $138,000–$200,000

Public Accounting

Public accountants offer services in much the same way as doctors and lawyers. The public accountant can achieve professional recognition as a **Certified Public Accountant** (CPA). This is done by meeting certain educational and experience requirements as determined by each state and passing a uniform examination prepared by the American Institute of Certified Public Accountants.

Many CPAs work alone, while others work for local, regional, or national accounting firms that vary in scope and size. The largest public accounting firms in the United States are known as the "Big Four." They are Deloitte, Ernst & Young, KPMG, and PricewaterhouseCoopers.

Services offered by public accountants are listed below.

- **Auditing.** Auditing involves the application of standard review and testing procedures to be certain that proper accounting policies and practices have been followed. The purpose of the audit is to provide an independent opinion that the financial information about a business is fairly presented in a manner consistent with generally accepted accounting principles.
- **Taxation.** Tax specialists advise on tax planning, prepare tax returns, and represent clients before governmental agencies such as the Internal Revenue Service.
- **Management Advisory Services.** Given the financial training and business experience of public accountants, many businesses seek their advice on a wide variety of managerial issues. Often, accounting firms are involved in designing computerized accounting systems.
- **Forensic Accounting.** Forensic accounting is a rapidly growing segment of accounting practice. It includes fraud detection, fraud prevention, litigation support, business valuations, expert witness services, and other investigative activities. Public accounting firms offer forensic accounting services, but forensic accountants also work for insurance companies, banks, law enforcement agencies, and other organizations. By meeting certain requirements, and passing the Certified Fraud Examiner exam, a forensic accountant may earn a **Certified Fraud Examiner** (CFE) designation.

In 2002, the **Sarbanes-Oxley Act** (**SOX**) was passed by Congress to help improve reporting practices of public companies. The act was in response to accounting scandals at firms like Enron, WorldCom, Cendant, Xerox, and others. Key provisions of SOX are listed below.

- The Public Company Accounting Oversight Board (PCAOB) was created to enforce SOX rules and regulations. The PCAOB also has authority to set auditing standards for public company audits and to perform inspections of auditing firms.
- External auditors are required to report on the effectiveness of a public company's accounting procedures.
- Auditing firms are prohibited from offering many nonaudit services to their public audit clients.
- Auditing firms must rotate audit partners off audit engagements every five years.
- The CEO and CFO must personally certify that the financial statements are accurate.

It is difficult to guarantee that information provided in financial statements is always complete and accurate. These measures are a step in the right direction. If our economy and financial markets are to function properly, information provided in financial statements must be reliable.

CONTROLLER
Responsible for directing an organization's accounting functions. These functions include establishing and maintaining the organization's accounting principles, practices, procedures, and initiatives. Prepares financial reports and presents findings and recommendations to top management. Requires a bachelor's degree and at least 15 years of direct experience in the field. Typically requires a CPA. Usually reports to top financial officer or CEO. $135,000–$201,000

Private (Managerial) Accounting

Many accountants are employees of private business firms. The **controller** oversees the entire accounting process and is the principal accounting officer of the company. Private or managerial accountants perform a wide variety of services for the business. These services are listed below.

- **Accounting Information Systems.** Accountants in this area design and implement manual and computerized accounting systems.
- **Financial Accounting.** Based on the accounting data prepared by the bookkeepers and accounting clerks, accountants prepare various reports and financial statements and help in analyzing operating, investing, and financing decisions.
- **Cost Accounting.** The cost of producing specific products or providing services must be measured. Further analysis is also done to determine whether the products and services are produced in the most cost-effective manner.
- **Budgeting.** In the budgeting process, accountants help managers develop a financial plan.
- **Tax Accounting.** Instead of hiring a public accountant, a company may have its own accountants. They focus on tax planning, preparation of tax returns, and dealing with the Internal Revenue Service and other governmental agencies.
- **Internal Auditing.** Internal auditors review the operating and accounting control procedures adopted by management to make sure the controls are adequate and are being followed. They also monitor the accuracy and timeliness of the reports provided to management and to external parties.

A managerial accountant can achieve professional status as a **Certified Management Accountant** (CMA). This is done by passing a uniform examination offered by the Institute of Management Accountants. An internal auditor can achieve professional recognition as a **Certified Internal Auditor** (CIA) by passing the uniform examination offered by the Institute of Internal Auditors.

Governmental and Not-for-Profit Accounting

Thousands of governmental and not-for-profit organizations (states, cities, schools, churches, and hospitals) gather and report financial information. These organizations employ a large number of accountants. Since these entities are not profit oriented, the rules are somewhat different for governmental and not-for-profit organizations. However, many accounting procedures are similar to those found in profit-seeking enterprises.

JOB OPPORTUNITIES

Job growth in some areas will be much greater than in others. Newspaper advertisements often indicate that accountants and accounting clerks are expected to have computer skills. Computer skills definitely increase the opportunities available to you in your career. Almost every business needs accountants, accounting clerks, and bookkeepers. Figure 1-6 shows the expected growth for different types of businesses. Notice that growth will be greatest in health care services. Chapters 2 through 9 introduce accounting skills that you will need to work in a service business, like health care. Chapter 10 begins the discussion of merchandising businesses. Accounting for manufacturing businesses is addressed in the last chapters of the book.

Figure 1-7 shows the expected demand for accounting skills. A 12.5% increase in demand is expected for bookkeeping, accounting, and auditing clerks. These types of

FIGURE 1-6 Expected Growth

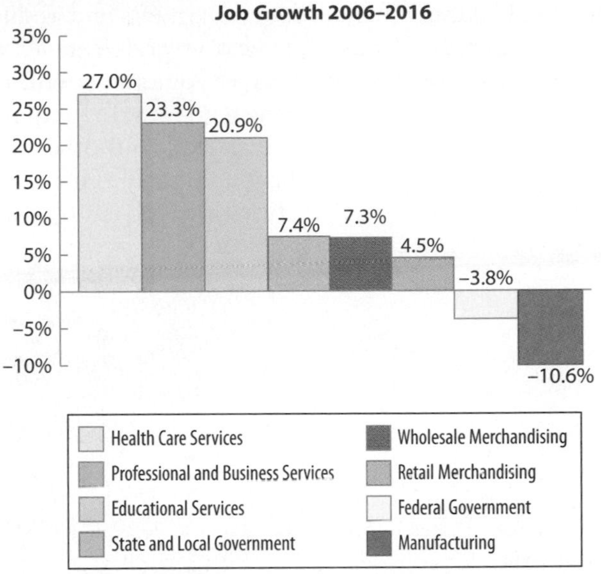

The growth in the number of new jobs from 2006 to 2016 will vary according to industry. The major area of growth will be in health care services. Businesses providing educational, health care, and professional/business services are expected to have the strongest employment growth. Moderate growth is expected in merchandising businesses and state and local governments. Employment in manufacturing and the federal government is expected to decline. Total employment for all industry sectors will increase 10.4%.

Source: U.S. Department of Labor—Bureau of Labor Statistics (http://www.bls.gov/news.release/ecopro.t01.htm) as of January 20, 2009.

FIGURE 1-7 Expected Demand

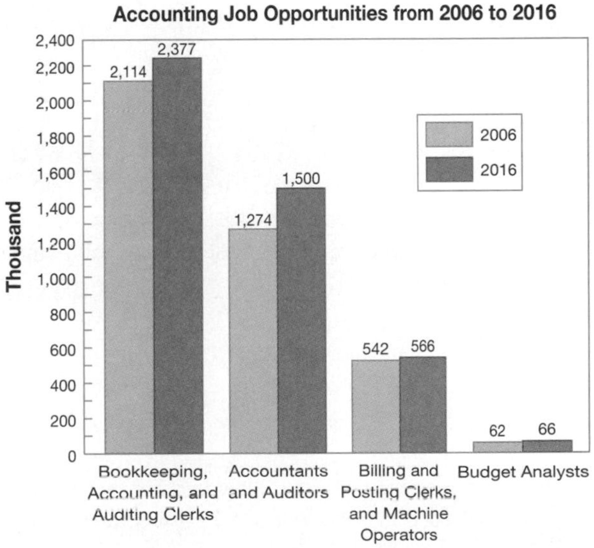

The highest number of jobs available will be for bookkeepers, accounting and auditing clerks, and accountants and auditors. The growth for each area shown from 2006 to 2016 will be as follows:

	Thousands	Percentage
Accountants and auditors	226	17.7%
Budget analysts	4	7.1%*
Bookkeeping, accounting, and auditing clerks	264*	12.5%*
Billing and posting clerks, and machine operators	24	4.4%

*Differences due to rounding.

Source: Arlene Dohm and Lynn Shniper, "Occupational Employment Projections to 2016," *Monthly Labor Review*, November 2007.

positions will offer the highest number of job opportunities over the next several years. The next highest demand is for accountants and auditors, and this demand is expected to increase by 17.7% over the next several years.

Regardless of the type of career you desire, writing skills are important in business and your personal life. Becoming a good writer requires practice and a strategy for the process used to prepare memos, letters, and other documents. On pages 12, 13, and 14, Ken Davis offers an excellent approach to managing your writing. Take a moment to read Ken's tips. Then, practice his approach by completing the writing assignments as you finish each chapter.

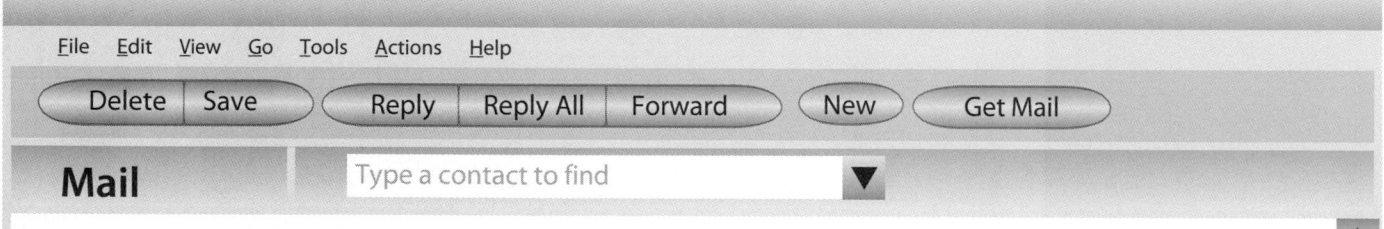

File Edit View Go Tools Actions Help

Delete | Save | Reply | Reply All | Forward | New | Get Mail

Mail Type a contact to find

From: Ken Davis
Subject: Managing Your Writing
To: Accounting Students

Here's a secret: the business writing that you and I do—the writing that gets the world's work done—requires no special gift. It can be managed, like any other business process.

Managing writing is largely a matter of managing time. Writing is a process, and like any process it can be done efficiently or inefficiently. Unfortunately, most of us are pretty inefficient writers. That's because we try to get each word, each sentence, right the first time. Given a letter to write, we begin with the first sentence. We think about that sentence, write it, revise it, even check its spelling, before going on to the second sentence. In an hour of writing, we might spend 45 or 50 minutes doing this kind of detailed drafting. We spend only a few minutes on overall planning at the beginning and only a few minutes on overall revising at the end.

That approach to writing is like building a house by starting with the front door: planning, building, finishing—even washing the windows—before doing anything with the rest of the house. No wonder most of us have so much trouble writing.

Efficient, effective writers take better charge of their writing time. They *manage* their writing. Like building contractors, they spend time planning before they start construction. Once construction has started, they don't try to do all of the finishing touches as they go.

As the following illustration shows, many good writers break their writing process into three main stages: planning, drafting, and revising. They spend more time at the first and third stages than at the second. They also build in some "management" time at the beginning and the end, and some break time in the middle. To manage *your* writing time, try the following steps.

To Do List

✓ At the MANAGING stage (perhaps two or three minutes for a one-hour writing job), remind yourself that writing *can* be managed and that it's largely a matter of managing time. Plan your next hour.

At the PLANNING stage (perhaps 20 minutes out of the hour):

1. **Find the "we."** Define the community to which you and your reader belong. Then ask, "How are my reader and I alike and different?"—in knowledge, attitudes, and circumstances.
2. **Define your purpose.** Remember the advice a consultant once gave Stanley Tool executives: "You're not in the business of making drills: you're in the business of making holes." Too many of us lose sight of the difference between making drills and making holes when we write letters and memos. We focus on the piece of writing—the tool itself—not its purpose. The result: our writing often misses the chance to be as effective as it could be. When you're still at the planning stage, focus on the outcome you want, not on the means you will use to achieve it.
3. **Get your stuff together.** Learn from those times when you've turned a one-hour home-improvement project into a three- or four-hour job by having to make repeated trips to the hardware store for tools or parts. Before you start the drafting stage of writing, collect the information you need.
4. **Get your ducks in a row.** Decide on the main points you want to make. Then, make a list or rough outline placing your points in the most logical order.

At the DRAFTING STAGE (perhaps 5 minutes out of the hour):

5. **Do it wrong the first time.** Do a "quick and dirty" draft, without editing. Think of your draft as a "prototype," written not for the end user but for your own testing and improvement. Stopping to edit while you draft breaks your train of thought and keeps you from being a good writer. (*Hint:* If you are writing at a computer, try turning off the monitor during the drafting stage.)

At the BREAK STAGE (perhaps 5 minutes):

6. **Take a break and change hats.** Get away from your draft, even if for only a few minutes. Come back with a fresh perspective—the reader's perspective.

At the REVISING STAGE (perhaps 25 minutes):

7. **Signal your turns.** Just as if you were driving a car, you're leading your reader through new territory. Use "turn signals"—*and, in addition, but, however, or, therefore, because, for example*—to guide your reader from sentence to sentence.
8. **Say what you mean.** Put the point of your sentences in the subjects and verbs. For example, revise "There are drawbacks to using this accounting method" to "This accounting method has some drawbacks." You'll be saying what you mean, and you'll be a more effective communicator.
9. **Pay by the word.** Reading your memo requires work. If your sentences are wordy and you are slow to get to the point, the reader may decide that it is not worth the effort. Pretend you are paying the reader by the word to read your memo. Then, revise your memo to make it as short and to the point as possible.
10. **Translate into English.** Keep your words simple. (Lee Iacocca put both these tips in one "commandment of good management": "Say it in English and keep it short.") Remember that you write to express, not impress.

11. **Finish the job.** Check your spelling, punctuation, and mechanics.

Finally, at the MANAGING STAGE again (2 to 3 minutes):

12. **Evaluate your writing process.** Figure out how to improve it next time.

By following these 12 steps, you can take charge of your writing time. Begin today to *manage your writing*. As a United Technologies Corporation advertisement in *The Wall Street Journal* admonished, "If you want to manage somebody, manage yourself. Do that well and you'll be ready to stop managing and start leading."

Dr. Kenneth W. Davis is Professor of English and Adjunct Professor of Communication Studies at Indiana University-Purdue University, Indianapolis. He is also president of Komei, Inc., a communication consulting and training company.

SELF-STUDY

LEARNING OBJECTIVES Key Points to Remember

LEARNING OBJECTIVES	Key Points to Remember
LO1 Describe the purpose of accounting.	The purpose of accounting is to provide financial information about a business to individuals and organizations.
LO2 Describe the accounting process.	The six major steps of the accounting process are analyzing, recording, classifying, summarizing, reporting, and interpreting.
LO3 Define GAAP and describe the process used by FASB to develop these principles.	Generally accepted accounting principles (GAAP) are the rules that businesses must follow when preparing financial statements. FASB takes the following steps to develop an accounting standard: 1. The issue is placed on the Board's agenda. 2. After researching the issue, a discussion memorandum is issued. 3. Public hearings are held. 4. An exposure draft is issued. 5. The statement of financial accounting standards is issued.
LO4 Define three types of business ownership structures.	Three types of business ownership structures are the sole proprietorship, the partnership, and the corporation.
LO5 Classify different types of businesses by activities.	Different types of businesses classified by activities are a service business, a merchandising business, and a manufacturing business.
LO6 Identify career opportunities in accounting.	Career opportunities in accounting include work in public accounting, private accounting, and governmental and not-for-profit accounting.

KEY TERMS

accountant (8) Designs the accounting information system and focuses on analyzing and interpreting information.

accounting (4) A system of gathering financial information about a business and reporting this information to users.

accounting clerk (8) Records, sorts, and files accounting information.

accounting information systems (10) Accountants in this area design and implement manual and computerized accounting systems.

analyzing (5) Looking at events that have taken place and thinking about how they affect the business.

auditing (9) Reviewing and testing to be certain that proper accounting policies and practices have been followed.

bookkeeper (8) Generally supervises the work of accounting clerks, helps with daily accounting work, and summarizes accounting information.

budgeting (10) The process in which accountants help managers develop a financial plan.

Certified Fraud Examiner (CFE) (9) A forensic accountant who has passed the exam offered by the Association of Certified Fraud Examiners.

Certified Internal Auditor (CIA) (10) An internal auditor who has achieved professional recognition by passing the uniform examination offered by the Institute of Internal Auditors.

Certified Management Accountant (CMA) (10) An accountant who has passed an examination offered by the Institute of Management Accountants.

Certified Public Accountant (CPA) (9) A public accountant who has met certain educational and experience requirements and has passed an examination prepared by the American Institute of Certified Public Accountants.

classifying (5) Sorting and grouping similar items together rather than merely keeping a simple, diary-like record of numerous events.

controller (10) The accountant who oversees the entire accounting process and is the principal accounting officer of a company.

corporation (7) A type of ownership structure in which stockholders own the business. The owners' risk is usually limited to their initial investment, and they usually have very little influence on the business decisions.

cost accounting (10) Determining the cost of producing specific products or providing services and analyzing for cost effectiveness.

discussion memorandum (5) The first document issued by FASB when developing an accounting standard. This document identifies the pros and cons of various accounting treatments for an event.

exposure draft (6) This document explains the rules that FASB believes firms should follow in accounting for a particular event. Based on the responses to the exposure draft, the Board will decide if any changes are necessary before issuing a final standard.

financial accounting (10) Includes preparing various reports and financial statements and analyzing operating, investing, and financing decisions.

forensic accounting (9) A specialized field that combines fraud detection, fraud prevention, litigation support, expert witnessing, business valuations, and other investigative activities.

generally accepted accounting principles (GAAP) (5) Procedures and guidelines developed by the Financial Accounting Standards Board to be followed in the accounting and reporting process.

internal auditing (10) Reviewing the operating and accounting control procedures adopted by management to make sure the controls are adequate and being followed; assuring that accurate and timely information is provided.

interpreting (5) Deciding the meaning and importance of the information in various reports.

management advisory services (9) Providing advice to businesses on a wide variety of managerial issues.

manufacturing business (7) A business that makes a product to sell.

merchandising business (7) A business that buys products to sell.

para-accountant (8) A paraprofessional who provides many accounting, auditing, or tax services under the direct supervision of an accountant.

partnership (6) A type of ownership structure in which more than one person owns the business.

public hearing (5) Following the issuance of a discussion memorandum, public meetings are often held by FASB to gather opinions on the accounting issue.

recording (5) Entering financial information about events affecting the company into the accounting system.

reporting (5) Telling the results of the financial information.

Sarbanes-Oxley Act (SOX) (9) An act passed by Congress to help improve reporting practices of public companies.

service business (7) A business that provides a service.

sole proprietorship (6) A type of ownership structure in which one person owns the business.

statement of financial accounting standards (SFAS) (6) A standard issued by the Financial Accounting Standards Board. These standards must be followed when preparing financial statements.

summarizing (5) Bringing the various items of information together to determine a result.

tax accounting (10) Services focused on tax planning, preparing tax returns, and dealing with the Internal Revenue Service and other governmental agencies.

taxation (9) See tax accounting.

APPLYING YOUR KNOWLEDGE

REVIEW QUESTIONS

LO1 1. What is the purpose of accounting?

LO1 2. Identify four user groups normally interested in financial information about a business.

LO2 3. Identify the six major steps of the accounting process and explain each step.

LO3 4. What are generally accepted accounting principles (GAAP)?

LO3 5. Describe the steps followed by the Financial Accounting Standards Board when developing an accounting standard.

LO3 6. What is the name of the organization that issues accounting standards followed by many firms in countries outside the United States?

LO4 7. Identify the three types of ownership structures and discuss the advantages and disadvantages of each.

LO5 8. Identify three types of businesses according to activities.

LO6 9. What are the main functions of an accounting clerk?

LO6 10. Name and describe three areas of specialization for a public accountant.

LO6 11. What is the purpose of the Sarbanes-Oxley Act?

LO6 12. Name and describe six areas of specialization for a managerial accountant.

SERIES A EXERCISES

E 1-1A (LO1)

PURPOSE OF ACCOUNTING Match the following users with the information needed.

1. Owners	a. Whether the firm can pay its bills on time
2. Managers	b. Detailed, up-to-date information to measure business performance (and plan for future operations)
3. Creditors	c. To determine taxes to be paid and whether other regulations are met
4. Government agencies	d. The firm's current financial condition

E 1-2A (LO2)

ACCOUNTING PROCESS List the six major steps of the accounting process in order (1–6) and define each.

_______ Recording
_______ Summarizing
_______ Reporting
_______ Analyzing
_______ Interpreting
_______ Classifying

SERIES B EXERCISES

E 1-1B (LO1)

PURPOSE OF ACCOUNTING Describe the kind of information needed by the users listed.

Owners (present and future)
Managers
Creditors (present and future)
Government agencies

E 1-2B (LO2)

ACCOUNTING PROCESS Match the following steps of the accounting process with their definitions.

Analyzing	a. Telling the results
Recording	b. Looking at events that have taken place and thinking about how they affect the business
Classifying	c. Deciding the importance of the various reports
Summarizing	d. Aggregating many similar events to provide information that is easy to understand
Reporting	e. Sorting and grouping like items together
Interpreting	f. Entering financial information into the accounting system

MANAGING YOUR WRITING

Take a moment to think about what it would be like to run your own business. If you started a business, what would it be? Prepare a one-page memo that describes the type of business you would enjoy the most. Would it be a service, merchandising, or manufacturing business? Explain what form of ownership you would prefer and why.

Chapter 2

RICH ABRAHAMSON/FORT COLLINS COLORADOAN

Analyzing Transactions: The Accounting Equation

At Rob's Bike Courier Service in Fort Collins, Colorado, Rob believes "less is more." His small company doesn't "have a fleet of vehicles, just some pretty cool bicycles." His mission is providing successful bike delivery service, perfect for both traditional business delivery services and residential errands. Since January of 2005, Rob's Bike Courier Service has been the alternative to gas-powered vehicle delivery. Thus, besides great rates and friendly, reliable service, Rob offers earth-friendly service.

Currently, he delivers wholesale bagels from a mid-town baker to several downtown coffee shops. He does the same for another pastry chef. Rob also picks up recycling materials and will go to a customer's home to fix flat bike tires and make repairs.

Though his company is small, Rob still needs an accounting system to maintain records of his business transactions and to prepare financial statements. Currently, he uses Quickbooks®, an accounting program used by many small companies. In Chapters 2 through 6, we learn how to account for a service business like Rob's by using an example of a similar company: Jessie Jane's Campus Delivery Service.

LEARNING OBJECTIVES

Careful study of this chapter should enable you to:

LO1 Define the accounting elements.

LO2 Construct the accounting equation.

LO3 Analyze business transactions.

LO4 Show the effects of business transactions on the accounting equation.

LO5 Prepare and describe the purposes of a simple income statement, statement of owner's equity, and balance sheet.

LO6 Define the three basic phases of the accounting process.

The entire accounting process is based on one simple equation, called the accounting equation. In this chapter, you will learn how to use this equation to analyze business transactions. You also will learn how to prepare financial statements that report the effect of these transactions on the financial condition of a business.

THE ACCOUNTING ELEMENTS

LO1 Define the accounting elements.

Before the accounting process can begin, the entity to be accounted for must be defined. A **business entity** is an individual, association, or organization that engages in economic activities and controls specific economic resources. This definition allows the personal and business finances of an owner to be accounted for separately.

Three basic accounting elements exist for every business entity: assets, liabilities, and owner's equity. These elements are defined below.

LEARNING KEY

Pay close attention to the definitions for the basic accounting elements. A clear understanding of these definitions will help you analyze even the most complex business transactions.

ASSETS

Assets are items that are owned by a business and will provide future benefits. Examples of assets include cash, merchandise, furniture, fixtures, machinery, buildings, and land. Businesses may also have an asset called **accounts receivable.** This asset represents the amount of money owed to the business by its customers as a result of making sales "on account," or "on credit." Making sales on account simply means that the customers have promised to pay sometime in the future.

LIABILITIES

Liabilities represent something owed to another business entity. The amount owed represents a probable future outflow of assets as a result of a past event or transaction. Liabilities are debts or obligations of the business that can be paid with cash, goods, or services.

The most common liabilities are accounts payable and notes payable. An **account payable** is an unwritten promise to pay a supplier for assets purchased or services received. Acquiring assets or services by promising to make payments in the future is referred to as making a purchase "on account," or "on credit." Formal written promises to pay suppliers or lenders specified sums of money at definite future times are known as **notes payable.**

OWNER'S EQUITY

Owner's equity is the amount by which the business assets exceed the business liabilities. Other terms used for owner's equity include **net worth** and **capital.** If there are no business liabilities, the owner's equity is equal to the total assets.

LEARNING KEY

The business entity's assets and liabilities are separate from the owner's nonbusiness assets and liabilities.

The owner of a business may have business assets and liabilities as well as nonbusiness assets and liabilities. For example, the business owner probably owns a home, clothing, and a car, and perhaps owes the dentist for dental service. These are personal, nonbusiness assets and liabilities. According to the **business entity concept,** nonbusiness assets and liabilities are not included in the business entity's accounting records.

If the owner invests money or other assets in the business, the item invested is reclassified from a nonbusiness asset to a business asset. If the owner withdraws money or other assets from the business for personal use, the item withdrawn is reclassified from a business asset to a nonbusiness asset. These distinctions are important and allow the owner to make decisions based on the financial condition and results of the business apart from nonbusiness activities.

A BROADER VIEW

IMAGE COPYRIGHT MARK YUILL 2009. USED UNDER LICENSE FROM SHUTTERSTOCK.COM

Assets and the Cost of Products We Buy

Next time you buy something, think of all the assets a company needs to produce that product. If the product comes from a capital-intensive industry, one that requires heavy investments in assets, the company must price the product high enough to cover the cost of using the assets and replacing them when they wear out. For example, Procter & Gamble recently reported that the cost of property, plant, and equipment used for operating purposes came to over $38 billion.

U REVU Complete U REVU-1 on **page 41** to test your basic understanding of LO1.

THE ACCOUNTING EQUATION

LO2 Construct the accounting equation.

The relationship between the three basic accounting elements—assets, liabilities, and owner's equity—can be expressed in the form of a simple equation known as the **accounting equation.**

Assets	=	Liabilities	+	Owner's Equity

This equation reflects the fact that both outsiders and insiders have an interest in the assets of a business.

- Liabilities represent the outside interests of creditors.
- Owner's equity represents the inside interests of owners.

Or, viewed another way,

The left side of the equation shows the assets.

The right side of the equation shows where the money came from to buy the assets.

When two elements are known, the third can always be calculated. For example, assume that assets on December 31 total $60,400. On that same day, the business liabilities consist of $5,400 owed for equipment. Owner's equity is calculated by subtracting total liabilities from total assets, $60,400 – $5,400 = $55,000.

LEARNING KEY

If you know two accounting elements, you can calculate the third element.

Total assets	$60,400
Total liabilities	–5,400
Owner's equity	$55,000

Assets	=	Liabilities	+	Owner's Equity
$60,400	=	$5,400	+	$55,000
$60,400	=		**$60,400**	

If during the next accounting period, assets increased by $10,000 and liabilities increased by $3,000, owner's equity must have increased by $7,000 ($10,000 – $3,000) as shown below.

	Assets	=	Liabilities	+	Owner's Equity
BB	$60,400		$5,400		$55,000
	+10,000	=	+3,000	+	+7,000
EB	$70,400	=	$8,400	+	$62,000
	$70,400	=		**$70,400**	

BB: Beginning balance

EB: Ending balance

Note also that after computing the ending balances for assets, liabilities, and owner's equity, the accounting equation remains in balance.

U REVU Complete U REVU-2 on page 41 to test your basic understanding of LO2.

ANALYZING BUSINESS TRANSACTIONS

LO3 Analyze business transactions.

A **business transaction** is an economic event that has a direct impact on the business. A business transaction almost always requires an exchange between the business and another outside entity. We must be able to measure this exchange in dollars. Examples of business transactions include buying goods and services, selling goods and services, buying and selling assets, making loans, and borrowing money.

All business transactions affect the accounting equation through specific accounts. An **account** is a separate record used to summarize changes in each asset, liability, and owner's equity of a business. **Account titles** provide a description of the particular type of asset, liability, or owner's equity affected by a transaction.

Three basic questions must be answered when analyzing the effects of a business transaction on the accounting equation. These questions help address the steps in the accounting process discussed in Chapter 1.

1. **What happened?**
    - Make certain you understand the event that has taken place.
2. **Which accounts are affected?**
    - Identify the accounts that are affected.
    - Classify these accounts as assets, liabilities, or owner's equity.
3. **How is the accounting equation affected?**
    - Determine which accounts have increased or decreased.
    - Make certain that the accounting equation remains in balance after the transaction has been entered.

EFFECT OF TRANSACTIONS ON THE ACCOUNTING EQUATION

LO4 Show the effects of business transactions on the accounting equation.

In Chapters 2 through 6, we will focus on learning how to account for a business similar to Rob's Bike Courier Service, discussed in the chapter opener. In these chapters, we will focus on Jessie Jane's Campus Delivery Service. By studying Jessie's business transactions and accounting techniques, you will learn about business and accounting. A major advantage of studying accounting is that it helps you learn a great deal about business.

As explained above, we must first understand the economic substance of events. Then, we must determine how that information is entered into the accounting system. If Jessie does not understand the economic events affecting her delivery business and their impact on the accounting equation, the events will not be correctly entered into the accounting system.

Each transaction affects at least two accounts and one or more of the three basic accounting elements. A transaction increases or decreases specific asset, liability, or owner's equity accounts. Assume that the following transactions occurred during June 20--, the first month of operations for Jessie Jane's Campus Delivery Service.

Remember, capital does not mean cash. The cash is shown in the cash account.

Transaction (a): Investment by owner

An Increase in an Asset Offset by an Increase in Owner's Equity. Jessica Jane opened a bank account with a deposit of $2,000 for her business. The new business now has $2,000 of the asset Cash. Since Jessie contributed the asset, the owner's equity element, Jessica Jane, Capital, increases by the same amount.

	Assets (Items owned)	**=**	**Liabilities** (Amounts owed)	**+**	**Owner's Equity** (Owner's Investment)
	Cash	=			Jessica Jane, Capital
(a)	**$2,000**	=			**$2,000**

Transaction (b): Purchase of an asset for cash

An Increase in an Asset Offset by a Decrease in Another Asset. Jessie decided that the fastest and easiest way to get around campus and find parking is on a motor scooter. Thus, she bought a motor scooter (delivery equipment) for $1,200 cash. Jessie exchanged one asset, cash, for another, delivery equipment. This transaction reduces Cash and creates a new asset, Delivery Equipment.

	Assets (Items owned)			**=**	**Liabilities** (Amounts owed)	**+**	**Owner's Equity** (Owner's Investment)
	Cash	+	Delivery Equipment	=			Jessica Jane, Capital
	$2,000						$2,000
(b)	**−1,200**		**+ $1,200**				
	$ 800	+	$1,200	=			$2,000
	$2,000			=			**$2,000**

LEARNING KEY

If transactions are entered correctly, the accounting equation always remains in balance.

Transaction (c): Purchase of an asset on account

An Increase in an Asset Offset by an Increase in a Liability. Jessie hired a friend to work for her, which meant that a second scooter would be needed. Given Jessie's limited cash, she bought the dealer's demonstration model for $900. The seller agreed to allow Jessie to spread the payments over the next three months. This transaction increased an asset, Delivery Equipment, by $900 and increased the liability, Accounts Payable, by an equal amount.

	Assets (Items owned)			=	Liabilities (Amounts owed)	+	Owner's Equity (Owner's Investment)
	Cash	+	Delivery Equipment	=	Accounts Payable	+	Jessica Jane, Capital
	$800		$1,200				$2,000
(c)			**+ 900**		**+ $900**		
	$800	+	$2,100	=	$900	+	$2,000
	$2,900			=	**$2,900**		

Transaction (d): Payment on a loan

A Decrease in an Asset Offset by a Decrease in a Liability. Jessie paid the first installment on the scooter of $300 [see transaction (c)]. This payment decreased the asset, Cash, and the liability, Accounts Payable, by $300.

	Assets (Items owned)			=	Liabilities (Amounts owed)	+	Owner's Equity (Owner's Investment)
	Cash	+	Delivery Equipment	=	Accounts Payable	+	Jessica Jane, Capital
	$800		$2,100		$900		$2,000
(d)	**– 300**				**– 300**		
	$500	+	$2,100	=	$600	+	$2,000
	$2,600			=	**$2,600**		

EXPANDING THE ACCOUNTING EQUATION: REVENUES, EXPENSES, AND WITHDRAWALS

In the preceding sections, three key accounting elements of every business entity were defined and explained: assets, liabilities, and owner's equity. To complete the explanation of the accounting process, three additional elements must be added to the discussion: revenues, expenses, and withdrawals.

Revenues

Revenues represent the amount a business charges customers for products sold or services performed. Customers generally pay with cash or a credit card, or they promise to pay at a later date. Most businesses recognize revenues when earned, even if cash has not yet been received. Separate accounts are used to recognize different types of revenue. Examples include Delivery Fees; Consulting Fees; Rent Revenue, if the business rents space to others; Interest Revenue, for interest earned on bank deposits; and Sales, for sales of merchandise. *Revenues increase both assets and owner's equity.*

Expenses

Expenses represent the *decrease* in assets (or *increase* in liabilities) as a result of a company's efforts to produce revenues. Common examples of expenses are rent, salaries, supplies consumed, and taxes. As with revenues, separate accounts are used to keep the accounting records for each different type of expense. Expenses are "incurred" as

- assets are consumed (such as supplies), or
- services are provided (by employees, for example) to the business.

LEARNING KEY

It is important to remember that expenses do not always reduce cash and revenues do not always increase cash right away.

The two main purposes of recognizing an expense are (a) to keep track of the amount and types of expenses incurred and (b) to show the reduction in owner's equity. Again, an expense can cause a reduction in assets or an increase in liabilities. Wages earned by employees is a good example.

- If paid, the expense reduces owner's equity and an asset, Cash.
- If not paid, the expense reduces owner's equity and increases a liability, Wages Payable.

Either way, owner's equity is reduced. If total revenues are greater than total expenses for the period, the excess is the **net income,** or net profit, for the period. On the other hand, if total expenses are greater than total revenues for the period, the excess is a **net loss** for the period.

Revenues	$900	Revenues	$ 300
Expenses	500	Expenses	500
Net income	$400	Net loss	$(200)

The owner can determine the time period used in the measurement of net income or net loss. It may be a month, a quarter (three months), a year, or some other time period. The concept that income determination can be made on a periodic basis is known as the **accounting period concept.** Any accounting period of 12 months is called a **fiscal year.** The fiscal year frequently coincides with the calendar year.

Withdrawals

LEARNING KEY

Owner's Equity	
Decrease	Increase
Expenses	Revenues
Drawing	Investments

Withdrawals, or **drawing,** reduce owner's equity as a result of the owner taking cash or other assets out of the business for personal use. Since earnings are expected to offset withdrawals, this reduction is viewed as temporary.

The accounting equation is expanded to include revenues, expenses, and withdrawals. Note that revenues increase owner's equity, while expenses and drawing reduce owner's equity.

	Assets (Items Owned)			=	Liabilities (Amounts Owed)	+	Owner's Equity (Owner's Investment)			+	(Earnings)		
	Cash	+	Delivery Equipment	=	Accounts Payable	+	Jessica Jane, Capital	–	Jessica Jane, Drawing	+	Revenues	–	Expenses
Balance	$500	+	$2,100	=	$600	+	$2,000						
	$2,600			=	**$2,600**								

EFFECT OF REVENUE, EXPENSE, AND WITHDRAWAL TRANSACTIONS ON THE ACCOUNTING EQUATION

To show the effects of revenue, expense, and withdrawal transactions, the example of Jessie Jane's Campus Delivery Service will be continued. Assume that the following transactions took place in Jessie's business during June 20--.

Transaction (e): Delivery revenues earned in cash

An Increase in an Asset Offset by an Increase in Owner's Equity Resulting from Revenue. Jessie received $500 cash from clients for delivery services. This transaction increased the asset, Cash, and increased owner's equity by $500. The increase in owner's equity is shown by increasing the revenue account, Delivery Fees, by $500.

	Assets (Items Owned)			=	Liabilities (Amounts Owed)	+	Owner's Equity (Owner's Investment)			+	(Earnings)			
	Cash	+	Delivery Equipment	=	Accounts Payable	+	Jessica Jane, Capital	−	Jessica Jane, Drawing	+	Revenues	−	Expenses	Description
	$ 500		$2,100		$600		$2,000							
(e)	+ 500										+ $500			Deliv. Fees
	$1,000	+	$2,100	=	$600	+	$2,000			+	$500			
	$3,100			=	$3,100									

Transaction (f): Paid rent for month

A Decrease in an Asset Offset by a Decrease in Owner's Equity Resulting from an Expense. Jessie rents a small office on campus. She paid $200 for office rent for June. This transaction decreased both Cash and owner's equity by $200. The decrease in owner's equity is shown by increasing an expense called Rent Expense by $200. An increase in an expense decreases owner's equity.

	Assets (Items Owned)			=	Liabilities (Amounts Owed)	+	Owner's Equity (Owner's Investment)			+	(Earnings)			
	Cash	+	Delivery Equipment	=	Accounts Payable	+	Jessica Jane, Capital	−	Jessica Jane, Drawing	+	Revenues	−	Expenses	Description
	$1,000	+	$2,100		$600		$2,000				$500			
(f)	− 200												+ $200	Rent Exp.
	$ 800	+	$2,100	=	$600	+	$2,000			+	$500	−	$200	
	$2,900			=	$2,900									

Transaction (g): Paid telephone bill

A Decrease in an Asset Offset by a Decrease in Owner's Equity Resulting from an Expense. Jessie paid $50 in cash for telephone service. This transaction, like the previous one, decreased both Cash and owner's equity. This decrease in owner's equity is shown by increasing an expense called Telephone Expense by $50.

	Assets (Items Owned)			=	Liabilities (Amounts Owed)	+	Owner's Equity (Owner's Investment)			+	(Earnings)			
	Cash	+	Delivery Equipment	=	Accounts Payable	+	Jessica Jane, Capital	−	Jessica Jane, Drawing	+	Revenues	−	Expenses	Description
	$800		$2,100		$600		$2,000				$500		$200	
(g)	− 50												+ 50	Tele. Expense
	$750	+	$2,100	=	$600	+	$2,000			+	$500	−	$250	
	$2,850			=			$2,850							

LEARNING KEY

Revenue is recognized when it is earned even though cash is not received.

Transaction (h): Delivery revenues earned on account

An Increase in an Asset Offset by an Increase in Owner's Equity Resulting from Revenue. Jessie extends credit to regular customers. Often, delivery services are performed for which payment will be received later. Since revenues are recognized when earned, an increase in owner's equity must be reported by increasing the revenue account. Since no cash is received at this time, Cash cannot be increased. Instead, an increase is reported for another asset, Accounts Receivable. *The total of Accounts Receivable at any point in time reflects the amount owed to Jessie by her customers.* Deliveries made on account amounted to $600. Accounts Receivable and Delivery Fees are increased.

	Assets (Items Owned)					=	Liabilities (Amounts Owed)	+	Owner's Equity (Owner's Investment)			+	(Earnings)			
	Cash	+	Accounts Receivable	+	Delivery Equipment	=	Accounts Payable	+	Jessica Jane, Capital	−	Jessica Jane, Drawing	+	Revenues	−	Expenses	Description
	$750				$2,100		$600		$2,000				$ 500		$250	
(h)			+ $600										+ 600			Deliv. Fees
	$750	+	$600	+	$2,100	=	$600	+	$2,000			+	$1,100	−	$250	
			$3,450			=			$3,450							

Transaction (i): Purchase of supplies

An Increase in an Asset Offset by a Decrease in an Asset. Jessie bought pens, paper, delivery envelopes, and other supplies for $80 cash. These supplies should last for several months. Since they will generate future benefits, the supplies should be recorded as an asset. The accounting equation will show an increase in an asset, Supplies, and a decrease in Cash.

	Assets (Items Owned)							=	Liabilities (Amounts Owed)	+	Owner's Equity (Owner's Investment)			+	(Earnings)			
	Cash	+	Accounts Receivable	+	Supplies	+	Delivery Equipment	=	Accounts Payable	+	Jessica Jane, Capital	−	Jessica Jane, Drawing	+	Revenues	−	Expenses	Description
	$750		$600				$2,100		$600		$2,000				$1,100		$250	
(i)	− 80				+ $80													
	$670	+	$600	+	$80	+	$2,100	=	$600	+	$2,000			+	$1,100	−	$250	
					$3,450			=			$3,450							

LEARNING KEY

Both supplies and insurance are recorded as assets because they will provide benefits for several months.

Transaction (j): Payment of insurance premium

An Increase in an Asset Offset by a Decrease in an Asset. Since Jessie plans to graduate and sell the business next January, she paid $200 for an eight-month liability insurance policy. Insurance is paid in advance and will provide future benefits. Thus, it is treated as an asset. We must expand the equation to include another asset, Prepaid Insurance, and show that Cash has been reduced.

	Assets (Items Owned)					=	Liabilities (Amounts Owed)	+	Owner's Equity (Owner's Investment)		+	Owner's Equity (Earnings)		
	Cash +	Accounts Receivable +	Supplies +	Prepaid Insurance +	Delivery Equipment	=	Accounts Payable	+	Jessica Jane, Capital −	Jessica Jane, Drawing	+	Revenues −	Expenses	Description
	$670	$600	$80		$2,100		$600		$2,000			$1,100	$250	
(j)	− 200			+ $200										
	$470 +	$600 +	$80 +	$200 +	$2,100	=	$600	+	$2,000		+	$1,100 −	$250	
			$3,450			=				$3,450				

As shown in transactions (i), (j), and (k), transactions do not always affect both sides of the accounting equation.

Transaction (k): Cash receipts from prior sales on account

An Increase in an Asset Offset by a Decrease in an Asset. Jessie received $570 in cash for delivery services performed for customers earlier in the month [see transaction (h)]. Receipt of this cash increases the cash account and reduces the amount due from customers reported in the accounts receivable account. *Notice that owner's equity is not affected in this transaction. Owner's equity increased in transaction (h) when revenue was recognized as it was earned, rather than now when cash is received.*

	Assets (Items Owned)					=	Liabilities (Amounts Owed)	+	Owner's Equity (Owner's Investment)		+	Owner's Equity (Earnings)		
	Cash +	Accounts Receivable +	Supplies +	Prepaid Insurance +	Delivery Equipment	=	Accounts Payable	+	Jessica Jane, Capital −	Jessica Jane, Drawing	+	Revenues −	Expenses	Description
	$ 470	$600	$80	$200	$2,100		$600		$2,000			$1,100	$250	
(k)	+ 570	− 570												
	$1,040 +	$ 30 +	$80 +	$200 +	$2,100	=	$600	+	$2,000		+	$1,100 −	$250	
			$3,450			=				$3,450				

Transaction (l): Purchase of an asset on account making a partial payment

An Increase in an Asset Offset by a Decrease in an Asset and an Increase in a Liability. With business increasing, Jessie hired a second employee and bought a third motor scooter. The scooter cost $1,500. Jessie paid $300 in cash and will spread the remaining payments over the next four months. The asset Delivery Equipment increases by $1,500, Cash decreases by $300, and the liability Accounts Payable increases by $1,200. *Note that this transaction changes three accounts. Even so, the accounting equation remains in balance.*

	Assets (Items Owned)					=	Liabilities (Amounts Owed)	+ Owner's Equity (Owner's Investment) +		(Earnings)		
	Cash +	Accounts Receivable +	Supplies +	Prepaid Insurance +	Delivery Equipment	=	Accounts Payable +	Jessica Jane, Capital −	Jessica Jane, Drawing +	Revenues −	Expenses	Description
	$1,040	$30	$80	$200	$2,100		$ 600	$2,000		$1,100	$250	
(l)	− 300				+ 1,500		+ 1,200					
	$ 740 +	$30 +	$80 +	$200 +	$3,600	=	$1,800 +	$2,000 +		$1,100 −	$250	
	$4,650					=	$4,650					

Transaction (m): Payment of wages

A Decrease in an Asset Offset by a Decrease in Owner's Equity Resulting from an Expense. Jessie paid her part-time employees $650 in wages. This represents an additional business expense. As with other expenses, Cash is reduced and owner's equity is reduced by increasing an expense.

	Assets (Items Owned)					=	Liabilities (Amounts Owed)	+ Owner's Equity (Owner's Investment) +		(Earnings)		
	Cash +	Accounts Receivable +	Supplies +	Prepaid Insurance +	Delivery Equipment	=	Accounts Payable +	Jessica Jane, Capital −	Jessica Jane, Drawing +	Revenues −	Expenses	Description
	$740	$30	$80	$200	$3,600		$1,800	$2,000		$1,100	$250	
(m)	− 650										+ 650	**Wages Exp.**
	$ 90 +	$30 +	$80 +	$200 +	$3,600	=	$1,800 +	$2,000 +		$1,100 −	$900	
	$4,000					=	$4,000					

Transaction (n): Deliveries made for cash and on account

An Increase in Two Assets Offset by an Increase in Owner's Equity. Total delivery fees for the remainder of the month amounted to $1,050: $430 in cash and $620 on account. Since all of these delivery fees have been earned, the revenue account increases by $1,050. Also, Cash increases by $430 and Accounts Receivable increases by $620. Thus, revenues increase assets and owner's equity. Note, once again, that one event impacts three accounts while the equation remains in balance.

	Assets (Items Owned)					=	Liabilities (Amounts Owed)	+ Owner's Equity (Owner's Investment) +		(Earnings)		
	Cash +	Accounts Receivable +	Supplies +	Prepaid Insurance +	Delivery Equipment	=	Accounts Payable +	Jessica Jane, Capital −	Jessica Jane, Drawing +	Revenues −	Expenses	Description
	$ 90	$ 30	$80	$200	$3,600		$1,800	$2,000		$1,100	$900	
(n)	+ 430	+ 620								+ 1,050		**Deliv. Fees**
	$ 520 +	$ 650 +	$80 +	$200 +	$3,600	=	$1,800 +	$2,000 +		$2,150 −	$900	
	$5,050					=	$5,050					

LEARNING KEY

Withdrawals by the owner are reported in the drawing account. Withdrawals are the opposite of investments by the owner.

Transaction (o): Withdrawal of cash from business

A Decrease in an Asset Offset by a Decrease in Owner's Equity Resulting from a Withdrawal by the Owner. At the end of the month, Jessie took $150 in cash from the business to purchase books for her classes. Since the books are not business related, this is a withdrawal. Withdrawals can be viewed as the opposite of investments by the owner. Both owner's equity and Cash decrease.

	Assets (Items Owned)					=	Liabilities (Amounts Owed)	+	Owner's Equity (Owner's Investment)		+	(Earnings)		
	Cash +	Accounts Receivable +	Supplies +	Prepaid Insurance +	Delivery Equipment	=	Accounts Payable	+	Jessica Jane, Capital −	Jessica Jane, Drawing	+	Revenues −	Expenses	Description
	$520	$650	$80	$200	$3,600		$1,800		$2,000			$2,150	$900	
(o)	− 150									+ $150				
	$370 +	$650 +	$80 +	$200 +	$3,600	=	$1,800	+	$2,000 −	$150	+	$2,150 −	$900	
			$4,900			=				$4,900				

Figure 2-1 shows a summary of the transactions. Use this summary to test your understanding of transaction analysis by describing the economic event represented by each transaction. At the bottom of Figure 2-1, the asset accounts and their totals are compared with the liability and owner's equity accounts and their totals.

U REVU Complete U REVU-3 on **page 41** to test your basic understanding of LO3/4.

FINANCIAL STATEMENTS

LO5 Prepare and describe the purposes of a simple income statement, statement of owner's equity, and balance sheet.

Three financial statements commonly prepared by a business entity are the income statement, statement of owner's equity, and balance sheet. The transaction information gathered and summarized in the accounting equation may be used to prepare these financial statements. Figure 2-2 shows the following:

1. A summary of the specific revenue and expense transactions and the ending totals for the asset, liability, capital, and drawing accounts from the accounting equation.
2. The financial statements and their linkages with the accounting equation and each other.

Note that each of the financial statements in Figure 2-2 has a heading consisting of:

HEADING FOR FINANCIAL STATEMENTS	
1. The name of the company	Jessie Jane's Campus Delivery Service
2. The title of the statement	Income Statement, Statement of Owner's Equity, or Balance Sheet
3. The time period covered or the date of the statement	For Month Ended June 30, 20--, or June 30, 20--

FIGURE 2-1 Summary of Transactions Illustrated

	Assets (Items Owned)					= Liabilities (Amounts Owed)	+ Owner's Equity (Owner's Investment) +		(Earnings)		
Transaction	Cash	+ Accounts Receivable	+ Supplies	+ Prepaid Insurance	+ Delivery Equipment	= Accounts Payable	+ Jessica Jane, Capital	− Jessica Jane, Drawing	+ Revenues	− Expenses	Description
Balance											
(a)	2,000						2,000				
Balance	2,000						2,000				
(b)	(1,200)				1,200						
Balance	800				1,200		2,000				
(c)					900	900					
Balance	800				2,100	900	2,000				
(d)	(300)					(300)					
Balance	500				2,100	600	2,000				
(e)	500								500		Deliv. Fees
Balance	1,000				2,100	600	2,000		500		
(f)	(200)									200	Rent Exp.
Balance	800				2,100	600	2,000		500	200	
(g)	(50)									50	Tele. Exp.
Balance	750				2,100	600	2,000		500	250	
(h)		600							600		Deliv. Fees
Balance	750	600			2,100	600	2,000		1,100	250	
(i)	(80)		80								
Balance	670	600	80		2,100	600	2,000		1,100	250	
(j)	(200)			200							
Balance	470	600	80	200	2,100	600	2,000		1,100	250	
(k)	570	(570)									
Balance	1,040	30	80	200	2,100	600	2,000		1,100	250	
(l)	(300)				1,500	1,200					
Balance	740	30	80	200	3,600	1,800	2,000		1,100	250	
(m)	(650)									650	Wages Exp.
Balance	90	30	80	200	3,600	1,800	2,000		1,100	900	
(n)	430	620							1,050		Deliv. Fees
Balance	520	650	80	200	3,600	1,800	2,000		2,150	900	
(o)	(150)							150			
Balance	**370**	**+ 650**	**+ 80**	**+ 200**	**+ 3,600**	**= 1,800**	**+ 2,000**	**− 150**	**+ 2,150**	**− 900**	

Cash	$ 370
Accounts Receivable	650
Supplies	80
Prepaid Insurance	200
Delivery Equipment	3,600
Total Assets	$ 4,900

Accounts Payable	$ 1,800
Jessica Jane, Capital	2,000
Jessica Jane, Drawing	(150)
Delivery Fees	2,150
Rent Expense	(200)
Telephone Expense	(50)
Wages Expense	(650)
Total Liabilities and Owner's Equity	$ 4,900

Amounts in ( ) are subtracted

As with the running totals in the table, the listing immediately below the table provides proof that the accounting equation is in balance.

The income statement and statement of owner's equity provide information concerning events covering a period of time, in this case, *the month ended* June 30, 20--. The balance sheet, on the other hand, offers a picture of the business on *a specific date*, June 30, 20--.

FIGURE 2-2 Summary and Financial Statements

	Assets (Items Owned)									=	Liabilities (Amounts Owed)	+	Owner's Equity (Owner's Investment)			+	(Earnings)			
Trans-action	Cash	+	Accounts Receivable	+	Supplies	+	Prepaid Insurance	+	Delivery Equipment	=	Accounts Payable	+	Jessica Jane, Capital	−	Jessica Jane, Drawing	+	Revenues	−	Expenses	Description
(e)																	500			Deliv. Fees
(f)																			200	Rent Exp.
(g)																			50	Tele. Exp.
(h)																	600			Deliv. Fees
(m)																			650	Wages Exp.
(n)																	1,050			Deliv. Fees
Balance	370	+	650	+	80	+	200	+	3,600	=	1,800	+	2,000	−	150	+	2,150	−	900	

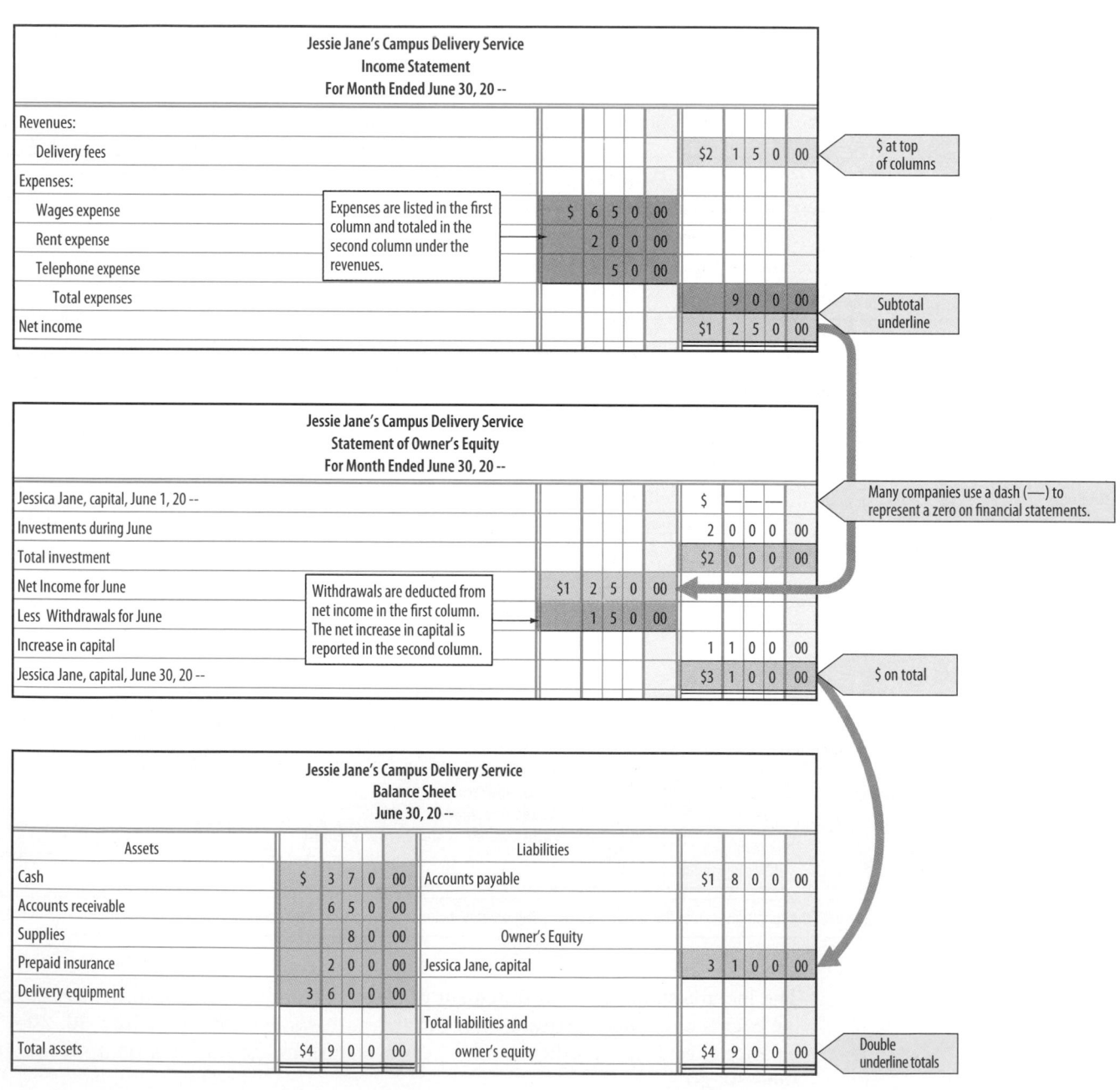

Jessie Jane's Campus Delivery Service
Income Statement
For Month Ended June 30, 20 --

Revenues:			
Delivery fees		$2 1 5 0 00	$ at top of columns
Expenses:			
Wages expense	$ 6 5 0 00		
Rent expense	2 0 0 00		
Telephone expense	5 0 00		
Total expenses		9 0 0 00	Subtotal underline
Net income		$1 2 5 0 00	

Expenses are listed in the first column and totaled in the second column under the revenues.

Jessie Jane's Campus Delivery Service
Statement of Owner's Equity
For Month Ended June 30, 20 --

Jessica Jane, capital, June 1, 20 --		$ — — —	Many companies use a dash (—) to represent a zero on financial statements.
Investments during June		2 0 0 0 00	
Total investment		$2 0 0 0 00	
Net Income for June	$1 2 5 0 00		
Less Withdrawals for June	1 5 0 00		
Increase in capital		1 1 0 0 00	
Jessica Jane, capital, June 30, 20 --		$3 1 0 0 00	$ on total

Withdrawals are deducted from net income in the first column. The net increase in capital is reported in the second column.

Jessie Jane's Campus Delivery Service
Balance Sheet
June 30, 20 --

Assets		Liabilities		
Cash	$ 3 7 0 00	Accounts payable	$1 8 0 0 00	
Accounts receivable	6 5 0 00			
Supplies	8 0 00	Owner's Equity		
Prepaid insurance	2 0 0 00	Jessica Jane, capital	3 1 0 0 00	
Delivery equipment	3 6 0 0 00			
		Total liabilities and		
Total assets	$4 9 0 0 00	owner's equity	$4 9 0 0 00	Double underline totals

LEARNING KEY

Income Statement

Revenues	$500
Expenses	400
Net income	$100

Income Statement

Revenues	$ 500
Expenses	700
Net loss	$(200)

THE INCOME STATEMENT

The **income statement**, sometimes called the **profit and loss statement or operating statement**, reports the profitability of business operations for a specific period of time. Jessie's income statement shows the revenues earned for the month of June. Next, the expenses incurred as a result of the efforts made to earn these revenues are deducted. If the revenues are greater than the expenses, net income is reported. If the expenses are greater than the revenue, a net loss is reported.

By carefully studying the income statement, it is clear that Jessie earns revenues in only one way: by making deliveries. If other types of services were offered, these revenues would also be identified on the statement. Further, the reader can see the kinds of expenses that were incurred. The reader can make a judgment as to whether these seem reasonable given the amount of revenue earned. Finally, the most important number on the statement is the net income. This is known as the "bottom line."

THE STATEMENT OF OWNER'S EQUITY

The **statement of owner's equity** illustrated in Figure 2-2 reports on these activities for the month of June. Jessie started her business with an investment of $2,000. During the month of June, she earned $1,250 in net income and withdrew $150 for personal expenses. Jessie's $2,000 original investment, plus the net increase of $1,100, results in her ending capital of $3,100.

Note that Jessie's original investment and later withdrawal are taken from the accounting equation. *The net income figure could have been computed from information in the accounting equation. However, it is easier to simply transfer net income as reported on the income statement to the statement of owner's equity.* This is an important linkage between the income statement and statement of owner's equity.

If Jessie had a net loss of $500 for the month, the statement of owner's equity would be prepared as shown in Figure 2-3.

FIGURE 2-3 Statement of Owner's Equity with Net Loss

Jessie Jane's Campus Delivery Service Statement of Owner's Equity For Month Ended June 30, 20 --		
Jessica Jane, capital, June 1, 20 --		$ —
Investments during June		2,000.00
Total investment		$2,000.00
Less: Net loss for June	$ 500.00	
Withdrawals for June	150.00	
Decrease in capital		650.00
Jessica Jane, capital, June 30, 20 --		$1,350.00

THE BALANCE SHEET

The **balance sheet** reports a firm's assets, liabilities, and owner's equity on a specific date. It is called a balance sheet because it confirms that the accounting equation has remained in balance. It is also referred to as a **statement of financial position** or **statement of financial condition.**

As illustrated in Figure 2-2, the asset and liability accounts are taken from the accounting equation and reported on the balance sheet. *The total of Jessie's capital account on June 30 could have been computed from the owner's equity accounts in the accounting equation ($2,000 – $150 + $2,150 – $900). However, it is simpler to take the June 30, 20--, capital as computed on the statement of owner's equity and transfer it to the balance sheet.* This is an important linkage between these two statements.

Most firms also prepare a statement of cash flows. Given the complexity of this statement, we will postpone its discussion until later in this text.

GUIDELINES FOR PREPARING FINANCIAL STATEMENTS

1. Financial statements are prepared primarily for users not associated with the company. To make a good impression and enhance understanding, financial statements must follow a standard form with careful attention to placement, spacing, and indentations.
2. All statements have a heading with the name of the company, name of the statement, and accounting period or date.
3. Single rules (lines) indicate that the numbers above the line have been added or subtracted. Double rules (double underlines) indicate a total.
4. Dollar signs are used at the top of columns and for the first amount entered in a column beneath a ruling.
5. On the income statement, some companies list expenses from highest to lowest dollar amount, with miscellaneous expense listed last.
6. On the balance sheet, assets are listed from most liquid to least liquid. **Liquidity** measures the ease with which the asset will be converted to cash. Liabilities are listed from most current to least current.

U REVU

Complete U REVU-4 on **page 41** to test your basic understanding of LO5.

OVERVIEW OF THE ACCOUNTING PROCESS

LO6 Define the three basic phases of the accounting process.

Figure 2-4 shows the three basic phases of the accounting process in terms of input, processing, and output.

- **Input.** Business transactions provide the necessary *input.*
- **Processing.** Recognizing the effect of these transactions on the assets, liabilities, owner's equity, revenues, and expenses of a business is the *processing* function.
- **Output.** The financial statements are the *output.*

FIGURE 2-4 Input, Processing, and Output

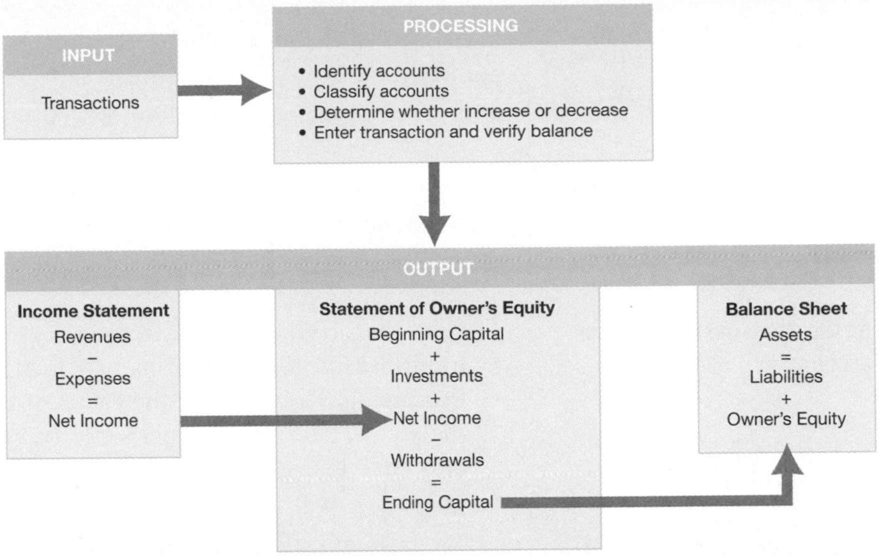

SELF-STUDY

LEARNING OBJECTIVES Key Points to Remember

LO1 Define the accounting elements.	The three key accounting elements are assets, liabilities, and owner's equity. Owner's equity is expanded in L04 to include revenues, expenses, and drawing.
LO2 Construct the accounting equation.	The accounting equation is: Assets = Liabilities + Owner's Equity
LO3 Analyze business transactions.	Three questions must be answered in analyzing business transactions: 1. What happened? 2. Which accounts are affected? 3. How is the accounting equation affected?
LO4 Show the effects of business transactions on the accounting equation.	Each transaction affects at least two accounts and one or more of the three basic accounting elements. The transactions described in this chapter can be classified into five groups: 1. Increase in an asset offset by an increase in owner's equity. 2. Increase in an asset offset by a decrease in another asset. 3. Increase in an asset offset by an increase in a liability. 4. Decrease in an asset offset by a decrease in a liability. 5. Decrease in an asset offset by a decrease in owner's equity.
LO5 Prepare and describe the purposes of a simple income statement, statement of owner's equity, and balance sheet.	The purposes of the income statement, statement of owner's equity, and balance sheet can be summarized as follows: **STATEMENT** — **PURPOSE** Income statement — Reports net income or loss Revenues − Expenses = Net Income or Loss *(continued)*

LEARNING OBJECTIVES Key Points to Remember

LO5 (concluded)	Statement of owner's equity	Shows changes in the owner's capital account Beginning Capital + Investments + Net Income – Withdrawals = Ending Capital
	Balance sheet	Verifies balance of accounting equation Assets = Liabilities + Owner's Equity
LO6 Define the three basic phases of the accounting process.	The three basic phases of the accounting process are shown below. • **Input.** Business transactions provide the necessary input. • **Processing.** Recognizing the effect of these transactions on the assets, liabilities, owner's equity, revenues, and expenses of a business is the processing function. • **Output.** The financial statements are the output.	

DEMONSTRATION PROBLEM

Damon Young has started his own business, Home and Away Inspections. He inspects property for buyers and sellers of real estate. Young rents office space and has a part-time assistant to answer the phone and help with inspections. The transactions for the month of September are as follows:

(a) On the first day of the month, Young invested cash by making a deposit in a bank account for the business, $15,000.

(b) Paid rent for September, $300.

(c) Bought a used truck for cash, $8,000.

(d) Purchased tools on account from Crafty Tools, $3,000.

(e) Paid electricity bill, $50.

(f) Paid two-year premium for liability insurance on truck, $600.

(g) Received cash from clients for services performed, $2,000.

(h) Paid part-time assistant (wages) for first half of month, $200.

(i) Performed inspection services for clients on account, $1,000.

(j) Paid telephone bill, $35.

(k) Bought office supplies costing $300. Paid $100 cash and will pay the balance next month, $200.

(l) Received cash from clients for inspections performed on account in (i), $300.

(m) Paid part-time assistant (wages) for last half of month, $250.

(n) Made partial payment on tools bought in (d), $1,000.

(o) Earned additional revenues amounting to $2,000: $1,400 in cash and $600 on account.

(p) Young withdrew cash at the end of the month for personal expenses, $500.

REQUIRED

1. Enter the transactions in an accounting equation similar to the one illustrated on the following page.

Assets (Items Owned)						= Liabilities (Amounts Owed)	+ Owner's Equity (Owner's Investment) +		(Earnings)		
Cash	+ Accounts Receivable	+ Supplies	+ Prepaid Insurance	+ Tools	+ Truck =	Accounts Payable	+ Damon Young, Capital	− Damon Young, Drawing	+ Revenues	− Expenses	Description

2. Compute the ending balances for all accounts.
3. Prepare an income statement for Home and Away Inspections for the month of September 20--.
4. Prepare a statement of owner's equity for Home and Away Inspections for the month of September 20--.
5. Prepare a balance sheet for Home and Away Inspections as of September 30, 20--.

Solution 1, 2.

	Assets (Items Owned)						= Liabilities (Amounts Owed)	+ Owner's Equity (Owner's Investment) +		(Earnings)		
	Cash	+ Accounts Receivable	+ Supplies	+ Prepaid Insurance	+ Tools	+ Truck =	Accounts Payable	+ Damon Young, Capital	− Damon Young, Drawing	+ Revenues	− Expenses	Description
(a)	15,000							15,000				
(b)	(300)										300	Rent Exp.
(c)	(8,000)					8,000						
(d)					3,000		3,000					
(e)	(50)										50	Utilities Exp.
(f)	(600)			600								
(g)	2,000									2,000		Inspect. Fees
(h)	(200)										200	Wages Exp.
(i)		1,000								1,000		Inspect. Fees
(j)	(35)										35	Tele. Exp.
(k)	(100)		300				200					
(l)	300	(300)										
(m)	(250)										250	Wages Exp.
(n)	(1,000)						(1,000)					
(o)	1,400	600								2,000		Inspect. Fees
(p)	(500)								500			
Bal.	**7,665**	**+ 1,300**	**+ 300**	**+ 600**	**+ 3,000**	**+ 8,000 =**	**2,200**	**+ 15,000**	**− 500**	**+ 5,000**	**− 835**	

(continued)

3.

Home and Away Inspections Income Statement For Month Ended September 30, 20 --		
Revenues:		
Inspection fees		$5 000 00
Expenses:		
Wages expense	$ 450 00	
Rent expense	300 00	
Utilities expense	50 00	
Telephone expense	35 00	
Total expenses		835 00
Net income		$4 165 00

4.

Home and Away Inspections Statement of Owner's Equity For Month Ended September 30, 20 - -		
Damon Young, capital, September 1, 20 - -		$ —
Investment during September		15 000 00
Total investment		$15 000 00
Net income for September	$ 4 165 00	
Less withdrawals for September	500 00	
Increase in capital		3 665 00
Damon Young, capital, September 30, 20 - -		$18 665 00

5.

Home and Away Inspections Balance Sheet September 30, 20 --			
Assets		Liabilities	
Cash	$ 7 665 00	Accounts payable	$ 2 200 00
Accounts receivable	1 300 00		
Supplies	300 00	Owner's Equity	
Prepaid insurance	600 00	Damon Young, capital	18 665 00
Tools	3 000 00		
Truck	8 000 00		
		Total liabilities and	
Total assets	$20 865 00	owner's equity	$20 865 00

KEY TERMS

account (22) A separate record used to summarize changes in each asset, liability, and owner's equity of a business.

account title (22) Provides a description of the particular type of asset, liability, owner's equity, revenue, or expense.

accounting equation (21) The accounting equation consists of the three basic accounting elements: Assets = Liabilities + Owner's Equity.

accounting period concept (25) The concept that income determination can be made on a periodic basis.

accounts payable (20) An unwritten promise to pay a supplier for assets purchased or services received.

accounts receivable (20) An amount owed to a business by its customers as a result of the sale of goods or services.

asset (20) An item that is owned by a business and will provide future benefits.

balance sheet (34) Reports assets, liabilities, and owner's equity on a specific date. It is called a balance sheet because it confirms that the accounting equation is in balance.

business entity (20) An individual, association, or organization that engages in economic activities and controls specific economic resources.

business entity concept (20) The concept that nonbusiness assets and liabilities are not included in the business entity's accounting records.

business transaction (22) An economic event that has a direct impact on the business.

capital (20) Another term for owner's equity, the amount by which the business assets exceed the business liabilities.

drawing (25) Withdrawals that reduce owner's equity as a result of the owner taking cash or other assets out of the business for personal use.

expenses (25) The decrease in assets (or increase in liabilities) as a result of efforts to produce revenues.

fiscal year (25) Any accounting period of 12 months' duration.

income statement (33) Reports the profitability of business operations for a specific period of time.

input (34) Business transactions provide the necessary input for the accounting information system.

liability (20) Something owed to another business entity.

liquidity (34) A measure of the ease with which an asset will be converted to cash.

net income (25) The excess of total revenues over total expenses for the period.

net loss (25) The excess of total expenses over total revenues for the period.

net worth (20) Another term for owner's equity, the amount by which the business assets exceed the business liabilities.

notes payable (20) A formal written promise to pay a supplier or lender a specified sum of money at a definite future time.

operating statement (33) Another name for the income statement, which reports the profitability of business operations for a specific period of time.

output (34) The financial statements are the output of the accounting information system.

owner's equity (20) The amount by which the business assets exceed the business liabilities.

processing (34) Recognizing the effect of transactions on the assets, liabilities, owner's equity, revenues, and expenses of a business.

profit and loss statement (33) Another name for the income statement, which reports the profitability of business operations for a specific period of time.

revenues (24) The amount a business charges customers for products sold or services performed.

statement of financial condition (34) Another name for the balance sheet, which reports assets, liabilities, and owner's equity on a specific date.

statement of financial position (34) Another name for the balance sheet, which reports assets, liabilities, and owner's equity on a specific date.

statement of owner's equity (33) Reports beginning capital plus net income less withdrawals to compute ending capital.

withdrawals (25) Reduce owner's equity as a result of the owner taking cash or other assets out of the business for personal use.

SELF-STUDY QUESTIONS AND EXERCISES

True/False Questions

1. LO1 Assets are items that are owned by the business and are expected to provide future benefits.
2. LO1 Accounts Payable is an example of an asset account.
3. LO1 According to the business entity concept, nonbusiness assets and liabilities are not included in the business's accounting records.
4. LO2 The accounting equation (Assets = Liabilities + Owner's Equity) must always be in balance.
5. LO2 When an asset increases, a liability must also increase.
6. LO3 Expenses represent outflows of assets or increases in liabilities as a result of efforts to produce revenues.
7. LO5 When total revenues exceed total expenses, the difference is called net loss.

Multiple Choice Questions

1. LO4 An increase to which of these accounts will increase owner's equity?
   (a) Accounts Payable
   (b) Drawing
   (c) Client Fees
   (d) Rent Expense
2. LO4 When delivery revenue is earned in cash, which accounts increase or decrease?
   (a) Cash increases; Revenue increases.
   (b) Cash decreases; Revenue increases.
   (c) Cash decreases; Revenue decreases.
   (d) Cash does not change; owner's equity increases.

3. LO4 When delivery revenue is earned on account, which accounts increase or decrease?

(a) Cash increases; Revenue increases.
(b) Accounts Receivable increases; Revenue increases.
(c) Accounts Receivable increases; Revenue decreases.
(d) Accounts Receivable decreases; Revenue decreases.

4. LO4 When payment is made on an existing debt, which accounts increase or decrease?

(a) Cash increases; Accounts Receivable increases.
(b) Cash decreases; Accounts Payable increases.
(c) Cash increases; Accounts Payable increases.
(d) Cash decreases; Accounts Payable decreases.

5. LO5 Which of the following accounts does not appear on the income statement?

(a) Delivery Fees
(b) Wages Expense
(c) Drawing
(d) Rent Expense

U REVU Exercises

1. LO1 Label each of the following accounts as an asset (A), a liability (L), or owner's equity (OE), using the following format:

Account	Classification
Accounts Receivable	________
Accounts Payable	________
Judy Smith, Capital	________

2. LO2 What is missing from the accounting equation below?

___?___ = Liabilities + Owner's Equity

3. LO3/4 What are the effects of the following transactions on the accounting equation? Indicate an increase (+) or decrease (–) under the appropriate asset, liability, and owner's equity headings.

Transaction	Assets	Liabilities	Owner's Equity
a. Purchase of an asset on account.	________	________	________
b. Made payment on account for transaction (a).	________	________	________

4. LO5 Classify the following accounts as assets (A), liabilities (L), owner's equity (OE), revenue (R), or expense (E). Indicate the financial statement on which the account belongs—income statement (IS), statement of owner's equity (SOE), or balance sheet (BS).

Account	Classification	Financial Statement
Accounts Payable	________	________
Peggy Welsch, Drawing	________	________
Rent Expense	________	________
Sales	________	________
Equipment	________	________

The answers to the Self-Study Questions and Exercises are at the end of the chapter (page 49).

APPLYING YOUR KNOWLEDGE

REVIEW QUESTIONS

LO1 1. Why is it necessary to distinguish between business assets and liabilities and nonbusiness assets and liabilities of a single proprietor?

LO1/4 2. Name and define the six major elements of the accounting equation.

LO3 3. List the three basic questions that must be answered when analyzing the effects of a business transaction on the accounting equation.

LO5 4. What is the function of an income statement?

LO5 5. What is the function of a statement of owner's equity?

LO5 6. What is the function of a balance sheet?

LO6 7. What are the three basic phases of the accounting process?

SERIES A EXERCISES

E 2-1A (LO1)

ACCOUNTING ELEMENTS Label each of the following accounts as an asset (A), a liability (L), or owner's equity (OE), using the following format:

Item	Account	Classification
Money in bank	Cash	
Office supplies	Supplies	
Money owed	Accounts Payable	
Office chairs	Office Furniture	
Net worth of owner	John Smith, Capital	
Money withdrawn by owner	John Smith, Drawing	
Money owed by customers	Accounts Receivable	

E 2-2A (LO2)

THE ACCOUNTING EQUATION Using the accounting equation, compute the missing elements.

Assets	=	Liabilities	+	Owner's Equity
______	=	\$24,000	+	\$10,000
\$25,000	=	\$18,000	+	______
\$40,000	=	______	+	\$15,000

E 2-3A (LO3/4)

✓ Assets following (d): \$22,000

EFFECTS OF TRANSACTIONS (BALANCE SHEET ACCOUNTS) Alice Stern started a business. During the first month (February 20--), the following transactions occurred. Show the effect of each transaction on the accounting equation: *Assets = Liabilities + Owner's Equity.* After each transaction, show the new totals.

(a) Invested cash in the business, \$20,000.
(b) Bought office equipment on account, \$3,500.
(c) Bought office equipment for cash, \$1,200.
(d) Paid cash on account to supplier in transaction (b), \$1,500.

E 2-4A (LO3/4)

✓ Assets following (k): \$23,427

EFFECTS OF TRANSACTIONS (REVENUE, EXPENSE, WITHDRAWALS) This exercise is an extension of Exercise 2-3A. Assume Alice Stern completed the following additional transactions during February. Show the effect of each transaction on the basic elements of the expanded accounting equation: *Assets = Liabilities + Owner's Equity (Capital – Drawing + Revenues – Expenses)*. After transaction (k), report the totals for each element. Demonstrate that the accounting equation has remained in balance.

(e) Received cash from a client for professional services, $2,500.
(f) Paid office rent for February, $900.
(g) Paid February telephone bill, $73.
(h) Withdrew cash for personal use, $500.
(i) Performed services for clients on account, $1,000.
(j) Paid wages to part-time employee, $600.
(k) Received cash for services performed on account in transaction (i), $600.

E 2-5A **(LO1/4/5)**

FINANCIAL STATEMENT ACCOUNTS Label each of the following accounts as an asset (A), liability (L), owner's equity (OE), revenue (R), or expense (E). Indicate the financial statement on which the account belongs—income statement (IS), statement of owner's equity (SOE), or balance sheet (BS)—in a format similar to the following.

Account	Classification	Financial Statement
Cash		
Rent Expense		
Accounts Payable		
Service Fees		
Supplies		
Wages Expense		
Ramon Martinez, Drawing		
Ramon Martinez, Capital		
Prepaid Insurance		
Accounts Receivable		

E 2-6A **(LO5)**
✓ Capital, 6/30: $22,000

STATEMENT OF OWNER'S EQUITY REPORTING NET INCOME Betsy Ray started an accounting service on June 1, 20--, by investing $20,000. Her net income for the month was $10,000, and she withdrew $8,000. Prepare a statement of owner's equity for the month of June.

E 2-7A **(LO5)**
✓ Capital, 6/30: $9,000

STATEMENT OF OWNER'S EQUITY REPORTING NET LOSS Based on the information provided in Exercise 2-6A, prepare a statement of owner's equity assuming Ray had a net loss of $3,000.

SERIES A PROBLEMS

P 2-8A **(LO1/2)**
✓ 3: $34,920 = $12,570 + $22,350

THE ACCOUNTING EQUATION Dr. John Schleper is a chiropractor. As of December 31, he owned the following property that related to his professional practice.

Cash	$ 4,750
Office Equipment	6,200
X-ray Equipment	11,680
Laboratory Equipment	7,920

He also owes the following business suppliers:

Chateau Gas Company	$ 2,420
Aloe Medical Supply Company	3,740

(continued)

REQUIRED

1. From the preceding information, compute the accounting elements and enter them in the accounting equation shown as follows.

Assets	=	Liabilities	+	Owner's Equity
________	=	________	+	________

2. During January, the assets increase by $7,290, and the liabilities increase by $4,210. Compute the resulting accounting equation.
3. During February, the assets decrease by $2,920, and the liabilities increase by $2,200. Compute the resulting accounting equation.

P 2-9A (LO3/4)
✓ Total cash following (g): $12,950

EFFECT OF TRANSACTIONS ON ACCOUNTING EQUATION Jay Pembroke started a business. During the first month (April 20--), the following transactions occurred.

(a) Invested cash in business, $18,000.
(b) Bought office supplies for $4,600: $2,000 in cash and $2,600 on account.
(c) Paid one-year insurance premium, $1,200.
(d) Earned revenues totaling $3,300: $1,300 in cash and $2,000 on account.
(e) Paid cash on account to the company that supplied the office supplies in transaction (b), $2,300.
(f) Paid office rent for the month, $750.
(g) Withdrew cash for personal use, $100.

REQUIRED

Show the effect of each transaction on the individual accounts of the expanded accounting equation: *Assets = Liabilities + Owner's Equity (Capital – Drawing + Revenues – Expenses)*. After transaction (g), report the totals for each element. Demonstrate that the accounting equation has remained in balance.

P 2-10A (LO5)
✓ Net income: $2,550

INCOME STATEMENT Based on Problem 2-9A, prepare an income statement for Jay Pembroke for the month of April 20--.

P 2-11A (LO5)
✓ Capital, 4/30: $20,450

STATEMENT OF OWNER'S EQUITY Based on Problem 2-9A, prepare a statement of owner's equity for Jay Pembroke for the month of April 20--.

P 2-12A (LO5)
✓ Total assets, 4/30: $20,750

BALANCE SHEET Based on Problem 2-9A, prepare a balance sheet for Jay Pembroke as of April 30, 20--.

SERIES B EXERCISES

E 2-1B **(LO1)**

ACCOUNTING ELEMENTS Label each of the following accounts as an asset (A), liability (L), or owner's equity (OE) using the following format.

Account	Classification
Cash	
Accounts Payable	
Supplies	
Bill Jones, Drawing	
Prepaid Insurance	
Accounts Receivable	
Bill Jones, Capital	

E 2-2B **(LO2)**

THE ACCOUNTING EQUATION Using the accounting equation, compute the missing elements.

Assets	=	Liabilities	+	Owner's Equity
________	=	$20,000	+	$5,000
$30,000	=	$15,000	+	________
$20,000	=	________	+	$10,000

E 2-3B **(LO3/4)**
✓ Assets following (d): $32,500

EFFECTS OF TRANSACTIONS (BALANCE SHEET ACCOUNTS) Jon Wallace started a business. During the first month (March 20--), the following transactions occurred. Show the effect of each transaction on the accounting equation: *Assets = Liabilities + Owner's Equity*. After each transaction, show the new account totals.

(a) Invested cash in the business, $30,000.
(b) Bought office equipment on account, $4,500.
(c) Bought office equipment for cash, $1,600.
(d) Paid cash on account to supplier in transaction (b), $2,000.

E 2-4B **(LO3/4)**
✓ Assets following (k): $34,032

EFFECTS OF TRANSACTIONS (REVENUE, EXPENSE, WITHDRAWALS) This exercise is an extension of Exercise 2-3B. Assume Jon Wallace completed the following additional transactions during March. Show the effect of each transaction on the basic elements of the expanded accounting equation: *Assets = Liabilities + Owner's Equity (Capital − Drawing + Revenues − Expenses)*. After transaction (k), report the totals for each element. Demonstrate that the accounting equation has remained in balance.

(e) Performed services and received cash, $3,000.
(f) Paid rent for March, $1,000.
(g) Paid March telephone bill, $68.
(h) Jon Wallace withdrew cash for personal use, $800.
(i) Performed services for clients on account, $900.
(j) Paid wages to part-time employee, $500.
(k) Received cash for services performed on account in transaction (i), $500.

E 2-5B **(LO1/4/5)**

FINANCIAL STATEMENT ACCOUNTS Label each of the following accounts as an asset (A), liability (L), owner's equity (OE), revenue (R), or expense (E). Indicate the financial statement on which the account belongs—income statement (IS), statement of owner's equity (SOE), or balance sheet (BS)—in a format similar to the following.

(continued)

Account	Classification	Financial Statement
Cash		
Rent Expense		
Accounts Payable		
Service Fees		
Supplies		
Wages Expense		
Amanda Wong, Drawing		
Amanda Wong, Capital		
Prepaid Insurance		
Accounts Receivable		

E 2-6B (LO5)
✓ Capital, 6/30: $14,000

STATEMENT OF OWNER'S EQUITY REPORTING NET INCOME Efran Lopez started a financial consulting service on June 1, 20--, by investing $15,000. His net income for the month was $6,000, and he withdrew $7,000 for personal use. Prepare a statement of owner's equity for the month of June.

E 2-7B (LO5)

STATEMENT OF OWNER'S EQUITY REPORTING NET LOSS Based on the information provided in Exercise 2-6B, prepare a statement of owner's equity assuming Lopez had a net loss of $2,000.

SERIES B PROBLEMS

P 2-8B (LO1/2)
✓ 3: $25,235 = $10,165 + $15,070

THE ACCOUNTING EQUATION Dr. Patricia Parsons is a dentist. As of January 31, Parsons owned the following property that related to her professional practice:

Cash	$3,560
Office Equipment	4,600
X-ray Equipment	8,760
Laboratory Equipment	5,940

She also owes the following business suppliers:

Cupples Gas Company	$1,815
Swan Dental Lab	2,790

REQUIRED

1. From the preceding information, compute the accounting elements and enter them in the accounting equation as shown below.

Assets	=	Liabilities	+	Owner's Equity
________	=	________	+	________

2. During February, the assets increase by $4,565, and the liabilities increase by $3,910. Compute the resulting accounting equation.
3. During March, the assets decrease by $2,190, and the liabilities increase by $1,650. Compute the resulting accounting equation.

P 2-9B (LO3/4)

✓ Total cash following (g): $11,300

EFFECT OF TRANSACTIONS ON ACCOUNTING EQUATION David Segal started a business. During the first month (October 20--), the following transactions occurred.

(a) Invested cash in the business, $15,000.
(b) Bought office supplies for $3,800: $1,800 in cash and $2,000 on account.
(c) Paid one-year insurance premium, $1,000.
(d) Earned revenues amounting to $2,700: $1,700 in cash and $1,000 on account.
(e) Paid cash on account to the company that supplied the office supplies in transaction (b), $1,800.
(f) Paid office rent for the month, $650.
(g) Withdrew cash for personal use, $150.

REQUIRED

Show the effect of each transaction on the individual accounts of the expanded accounting equation: *Assets = Liabilities + Owner's Equity (Capital − Drawing + Revenues − Expenses)*. After transaction (g), report the totals for each element. Demonstrate that the accounting equation has remained in balance.

P 2-10B (LO5)

✓ Net income: $2,050

INCOME STATEMENT Based on Problem 2-9B, prepare an income statement for David Segal for the month of October 20--.

P 2-11B (LO5)

✓ Capital, 10/31: $16,900

STATEMENT OF OWNER'S EQUITY Based on Problem 2-9B, prepare a statement of owner's equity for David Segal for the month of October 20--.

P 2-12B (LO5)

✓ Total assets, 10/31: $17,100

BALANCE SHEET Based on Problem 2-9B, prepare a balance sheet for David Segal as of October 31, 20--.

MANAGING YOUR WRITING

Write a brief memo that explains the differences and similarities between expenses and withdrawals.

MASTERY PROBLEM

✓ Cash following (p): $3,105; Revenue following (p): $2,100

Lisa Vozniak started her own business, We Do Windows. She offers interior and exterior window cleaning for local area residents. Lisa rents a garage to store her tools and cleaning supplies and has a part-time assistant to answer the phone and handle third-story work. (Lisa is afraid of heights.) The transactions for the month of July are as follows:

(a) On the first day of the month, Vozniak invested cash by making a deposit in a bank account for the business, $8,000.

(continued)

(b) Paid rent for July, $150.
(c) Purchased a used van for cash, $5,000.
(d) Purchased tools on account from Clean Tools, $600.
(e) Purchased cleaning supplies that cost $300. Paid $200 cash and will pay the balance next month, $100.
(f) Paid part-time assistant (wages) for first half of month, $100.
(g) Paid for advertising, $75.
(h) Paid two-year premium for liability insurance on van, $480.
(i) Received cash from clients for services performed, $800.
(j) Performed cleaning services for clients on account, $500.
(k) Paid telephone bill, $40.
(l) Received cash from clients for window cleaning performed on account in transaction (j), $200.
(m) Paid part-time assistant (wages) for last half of month, $150.
(n) Made partial payment on tools purchased in transaction (d), $200.
(o) Earned additional revenues amounting to $800: $600 in cash and $200 on account.
(p) Vozniak withdrew cash at the end of the month for personal expenses, $100.

REQUIRED

1. Enter the above transactions in an accounting equation similar to the one illustrated below.

Assets (Items Owned)						=	**Liabilities** + (Amounts Owed)	**Owner's Equity** (Owner's Investment) +		(Earnings)		
Cash +	Accounts Receivable +	Supplies +	Prepaid Insurance +	Tools +	Van	=	Accounts Payable	+ Lisa Vozniak, Capital –	Lisa Vozniak, Drawing	+ Revenues –	Expenses	Description

2. After transaction (p), compute the balance of each account.
3. Prepare an income statement for We Do Windows for the month of July 20--.
4. Prepare a statement of owner's equity for We Do Windows for the month of July 20--.
5. Prepare a balance sheet for We Do Windows as of July 31, 20--.

CHALLENGE PROBLEM

This problem challenges you to apply your cumulative accounting knowledge to move a step beyond the material in the chapter.

✓ Cash difference: $2,165

In this chapter, you learned about three important financial statements: the income statement, statement of owner's equity, and balance sheet. As mentioned in the margin note on page 34, most firms also prepare a statement of cash flows. Part of this statement reports the **cash received** from customers and **cash paid** for goods and services.

REQUIRED

Take another look at the Demonstration Problem for Damon Young's "Home and Away Inspections." Note that when revenues are measured based on the amount earned, and expenses are measured based on the amount incurred, net income for the period was $4,165. Now, compute the difference between cash received from customers and cash paid to suppliers of goods and services by completing the form provided below. Are these measures different? Which provides a better measure of profitability?

Cash from customers		______
Cash paid for wages	______	
Cash paid for rent	______	
Cash paid for utilities	______	
Cash paid for insurance	______	
Cash paid for supplies	______	
Cash paid for telephone	______	
Total cash paid for operating items		______
Difference between cash received from customers and cash paid for goods and services		______

ANSWERS TO SELF-STUDY QUESTIONS AND EXERCISES

True/False Questions

1. T
2. F (Accounts Payable is a liability.)
3. T
4. T
5. F (Other changes could occur: capital could increase, revenue could increase, etc.)
6. T
7. F (net income)

Multiple Choice Questions

1. c 2. a 3. b 4. d 5. c

U REVU Exercises

1.

Account	Classification
Accounts Receivable	A
Accounts Payable	L
Judy Smith, Capital	OE

2. Assets = Liabilities + Owner's Equity

3.

Transaction	Assets	Liabilities	Owner's Equity
a. Purchase of an asset on account.	+	+	
b. Made payment on account for transaction (a).	–	–	

4.

Account	Classification	Financial Statement
Accounts Payable	L	BS
Peggy Welsch, Drawing	OE	SOE
Rent Expense	E	IS
Sales	R	IS
Equipment	A	BS

Chapter 3

LEARNING OBJECTIVES

Careful study of this chapter should enable you to:

LO1 Define the parts of a T account.

LO2 Foot and balance a T account.

LO3 Describe the effects of debits and credits on specific types of accounts.

LO4 Use T accounts to analyze transactions.

LO5 Prepare a trial balance and explain its purposes and linkages with the financial statements.

The Double-Entry Framework

Tired of receiving spam e-mail messages? Or, are you worried about your computer picking up a virus? Businesses have the same concerns. Computer viruses can cause serious financial damage to a business. In response to demand for e-mail security, AppRiver was founded in April of 2002 to provide simple, yet powerful e-mail security solutions to businesses of any size. The company is based in Gulf Breeze, Florida, and maintains multiple data centers at secure locations in the United States and Europe. AppRiver's 100 employees protect more than 35,000 customers around the world from spam, viruses, and Internet pollution.

Just as e-mail security is important to you in your personal life and to businesses, the same can be said about accounting. A solid understanding of financial accounting will help you manage your personal finances and help you understand business transactions in your professional life. In this chapter, you will learn about the double-entry framework used by businesses to enter transactions into an accounting system. You could use the same concepts for your personal transactions or for a business you might start.

The terms asset, liability, owner's equity, revenue, and expense were explained in Chapter 2. Examples showed how individual business transactions change one or more of these basic accounting elements. Each transaction had a dual effect. An increase or decrease in any asset, liability, owner's equity, revenue, or expense was *always* accompanied by an offsetting change within the basic accounting elements. The fact that each transaction has a dual effect upon the accounting elements provides the basis for what is called **double-entry accounting**. To understand double-entry accounting, it is important to learn how T accounts work and the role of debits and credits in accounting.

THE T ACCOUNT

LO1 Define the parts of a T account.

The assets of a business may consist of a number of items, such as cash, accounts receivable, equipment, buildings, and land. The liabilities may consist of one or more items, such as accounts payable and notes payable. Similarly, owner's equity may consist of the owner's investments and various revenue and expense items. A separate account is used to record the increases and decreases in each type of asset, liability, owner's equity, revenue, and expense.

The T account gets its name from the fact that it resembles the letter T. The three major parts of an account are as follows:

1. the title,
2. the debit, or left side, and
3. the credit, or right side.

Title	
Debit = Left	Credit = Right

LEARNING KEY

Debit means left and credit means right.

The debit side is always on the left, and the credit side is always on the right. This is true for all types of asset, liability, owner's equity, revenue, and expense accounts.

BALANCING A T ACCOUNT

LO2 Foot and balance a T account

To determine the balance of a T account at any time, simply total the dollar amounts on the debit and credit sides. These totals are known as **footings**. The difference between the footings is called the **balance** of the account. This amount is then written on the side with the larger footing.

In Chapter 2, the accounting equation was used to analyze business transactions. This required columns in which to record the increases and decreases in various accounts. Let's compare this approach with the use of a T account for the transactions affecting cash. When a T account is used, increases in cash are recorded on the debit side and decreases are recorded on the credit side. Transactions for Jessie Jane's Campus Delivery Service are shown in Figure 3-1.

FIGURE 3-1 Cash T Account

COLUMNAR SUMMARY (From Chapter 2, page 31)

Transaction	Cash
(a)	2,000
(b)	(1,200)
(d)	(300)
(e)	500
(f)	(200)
(g)	(50)
(i)	(80)
(j)	(200)
(k)	570
(l)	(300)
(m)	(650)
(n)	430
(o)	(150)
Balance	370

T ACCOUNT FORM

	Cash			
	(a)	2,000	(b)	1,200
	(e)	500	(d)	300
	(k)	570	(f)	200
	(n)	430	(g)	50
footing →		**3,500**	(i)	80
			(j)	200
			(l)	300
			(m)	650
			(o)	150
Balance →		370		**3,130** ← footing

U REVU

Complete U REVU-1 on **page 74** to test your basic understanding of LO2.

DEBITS AND CREDITS

LO3 Describe the effects of debits and credits on specific types of accounts.

To **debit** an account means to enter an amount on the left or debit side of the account. To **credit** an account means to enter an amount on the right or credit side of the account. *Debits may increase or decrease the balances of specific accounts. This is also true for credits. To learn how to use debits and credits, it is best to focus on the accounting equation.*

Abbreviations:
Often debit and credit are abbreviated as: Dr. = Debit, Cr. = Credit (based on the Latin terms "debere" and "credere")

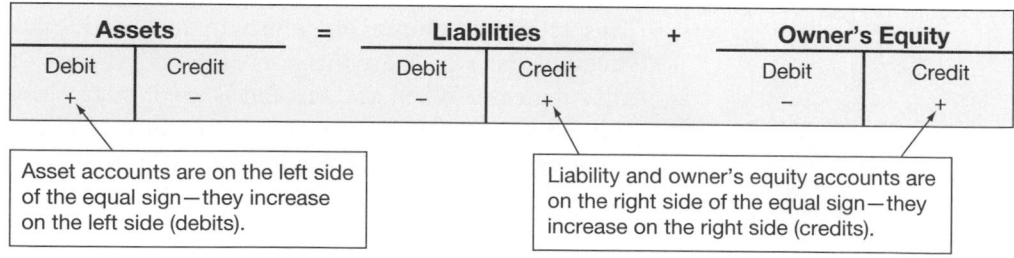

Assets		=	Liabilities		+	Owner's Equity	
Debit	Credit		Debit	Credit		Debit	Credit
+	−		−	+		−	+

Asset accounts are on the left side of the equal sign—they increase on the left side (debits).

Liability and owner's equity accounts are on the right side of the equal sign—they increase on the right side (credits).

ASSETS

Assets are on the left side of the accounting equation. Therefore, increases are entered on the left (debit) side of an asset account, and decreases are entered on the right (credit) side.

LIABILITIES AND OWNER'S EQUITY

Liabilities and owner's equity are on the right side of the equation. Therefore, increases are entered on the right (credit) side, and decreases are entered on the left (debit) side.

THE OWNER'S EQUITY UMBRELLA

Owner's equity includes four types of accounts: Owner's Capital, Revenues, Expenses, and Drawing. Expanding the accounting equation helps illustrate the use of debits and credits. Since these accounts affect owner's equity, they are shown under the "umbrella" of owner's equity in the accounting equation in Figure 3-2.

FIGURE 3-2 The Accounting Equation and the Owner's Equity Umbrella

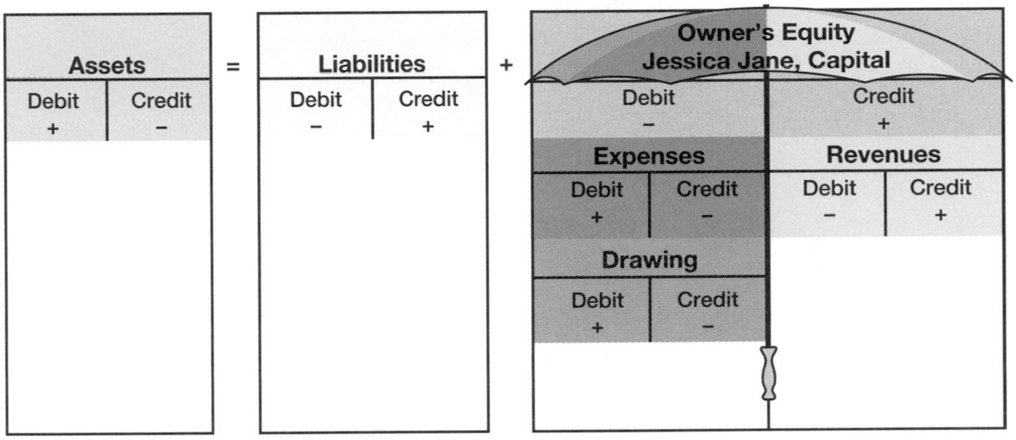

OWNER'S CAPITAL

The owner's capital account, Jessica Jane, Capital, in Figure 3-2 reports the amount the owner has invested in the business. These investments increase the owner's equity and are credited to the owner's capital account.

DRAWING

Withdrawals of cash and other assets by the owner for personal reasons decrease owner's equity. Withdrawals could be debited directly to the owner's capital account. However, readers of financial statements want to know the amount of withdrawals for the accounting period. Thus, as shown in Figure 3-2, withdrawals are debited to a separate account, Drawing.

LEARNING KEY

You could credit the owner's capital account for revenues and debit the capital account for expenses and withdrawals. However, this is not a good idea. Using specific accounts provides additional information. Remember: An increase in an expense decreases owner's equity.

REVENUES

Revenues increase owner's equity. Revenues could be recorded directly on the credit side of the owner's capital account. However, readers of financial statements are interested in the specific types of revenues earned. Therefore, specific revenue accounts, like Delivery Fees, Sales, and Service Fees, are used. These specific accounts are credited when revenue is earned.

EXPENSES

Expenses decrease owner's equity. Expenses could be recorded on the debit side of the owner's capital account. However, readers of financial statements want to see the types of expenses incurred during the accounting period. Thus, specific expense accounts are maintained for items like rent, wages, advertising, and utilities. These specific accounts are debited as expenses are incurred.

NORMAL BALANCES

A **normal balance** is the side of an account that is used to increase the account. Thus, the normal balances for the accounts illustrated in Figure 3-2 are shown with a "+" sign. Since assets are debited for increases, these accounts normally have **debit balances**. Liability and owner's capital accounts are credited for increases; thus, these accounts normally have **credit balances**. Since expense and drawing accounts are debited for increases (reducing owner's equity), these accounts normally have debit balances. Finally, revenue accounts are credited for increases (increasing owner's equity); thus, these accounts normally have credit balances. A summary of normal balances is provided in Figure 3-3.

FIGURE 3-3 Normal Balances

ACCOUNT	INCREASE	DECREASE	NORMAL BALANCE
Assets	Debit	Credit	Debit
Liabilities	Credit	Debit	Credit
Owner's Capital	Credit	Debit	Credit
Revenues	Credit	Debit	Credit
Expenses	Debit	Credit	Debit
Drawing	Debit	Credit	Debit

U REVU

Complete U REVU-2 on **page 74** to test your basic understanding of LO3.

TRANSACTION ANALYSIS

LO4 Use T accounts to analyze transactions.

LEARNING KEY

If you have a debit, you must always have at least one credit. If you have a credit, you must always have at least one debit.

In Chapter 2, you learned how to analyze transactions by using the accounting equation. Here, we continue to use the accounting equation, but add debits and credits by using T accounts. As shown in Figure 3-4, the three basic questions that must be answered when analyzing a transaction are essentially the same but are expanded slightly to address the use of the owner's equity umbrella and T accounts. You must determine the location of the account within the accounting equation and/or the owner's equity umbrella. You must also determine whether the accounts should be debited or credited.

FIGURE 3-4 Steps in Transaction Analysis

1. **What happened?**
   Be sure you understand the event that has taken place.
2. **Which accounts are affected?**
   Once you understand what happened, you must:
   - Identify the accounts that are affected.
   - Classify these accounts as assets, liabilities, owner's equity, revenues, or expenses.
   - Identify the location of the accounts in the accounting equation and/or the owner's equity umbrella—left or right.
3. **How is the accounting equation affected?**
   - Determine whether the accounts have increased or decreased.
   - Determine whether the accounts should be debited or credited.
   - Make certain the accounting equation remains in balance after the transaction has been entered.
     (1) Assets = Liabilities + Owner's Equity.
     (2) Debits = Credits for every transaction.

DEBITS AND CREDITS: ASSET, LIABILITY, AND OWNER'S EQUITY ACCOUNTS

Transactions (a) through (d) from Jessie Jane's Campus Delivery Service (Chapter 2) demonstrate the double-entry process for transactions affecting asset, liability, and owner's equity accounts.

As you study each transaction, answer the three questions: (1) What happened? (2) Which accounts are affected? and (3) How is the accounting equation affected? The transaction statement tells you what happened. The analysis tells which accounts are affected. The illustration shows you how the accounting equation is affected.

Transaction (a): Investment by owner

Jessica Jane opened a bank account with a deposit of $2,000 for her business (Figure 3-5).

Analysis. As a result of this transaction, the business acquired an asset, Cash. In exchange for the asset, the business gave Jessica Jane owner's equity. The owner's equity account is called Jessica Jane, Capital. The transaction is entered as an increase in an asset and an increase in owner's equity. Debit Cash and credit Jessica Jane, Capital for $2,000.

FIGURE 3-5 Transaction (a): Investment by Owner

Assets		=	Liabilities		+	Owner's Equity	
Debit +	Credit −		Debit −	Credit +		Debit −	Credit +
Cash						Jessica Jane, Capital	
(a) 2,000							(a) 2,000
$2,000		=	$0		+	$2,000	
$2,000		=			**$2,000**		

Transaction (b): Purchase of an asset for cash

Jessie bought a motor scooter (delivery equipment) for $1,200 cash (Figure 3-6).

Analysis. Jessie exchanged one asset, Cash, for another, Delivery Equipment. Debit Delivery Equipment and credit Cash for $1,200. Notice that the total assets are still $2,000 as they were following transaction (a). Transaction (b) shifted assets from cash to delivery equipment, but total assets remained the same.

FIGURE 3-6 Transaction (b): Purchase of an Asset for Cash

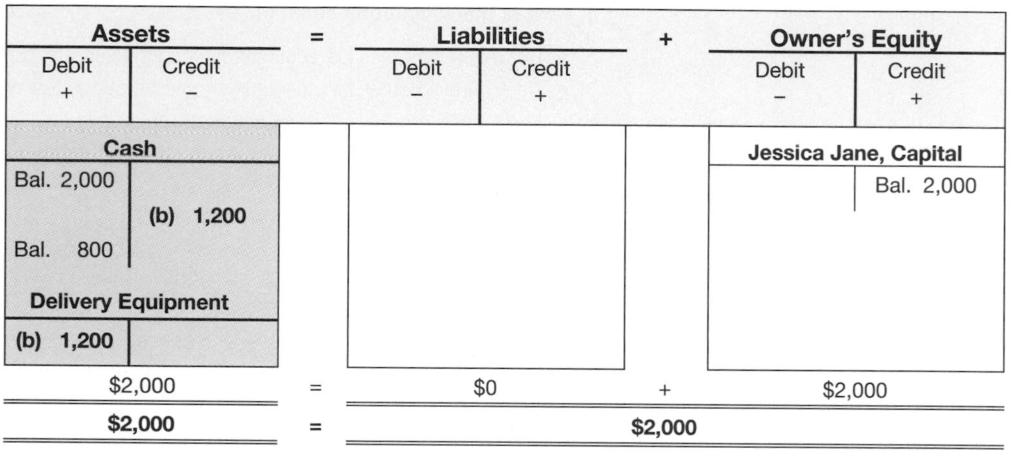

Transaction (c): Purchase of an asset on account

Jessie bought a second motor scooter on account for $900 (Figure 3-7). Recall from chapter 2 that "on account" means Jessie will pay for the asset later.

Analysis. The asset, Delivery Equipment, increases by $900 and the liability, Accounts Payable, increases by the same amount. Thus, debit Delivery Equipment and credit Accounts Payable for $900.

FIGURE 3-7 Transaction (c): Purchase of an Asset on Account

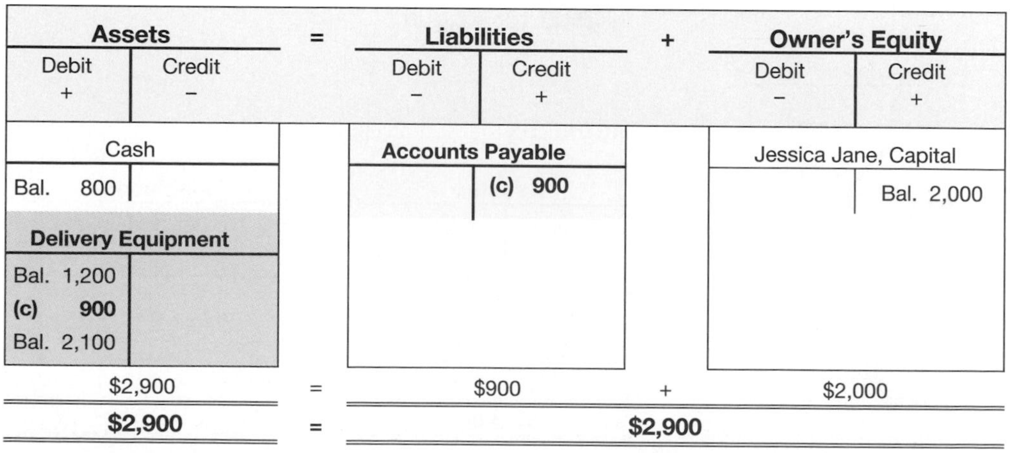

Transaction (d): Payment on account

Jessie made the first $300 payment on the scooter purchased in transaction (c) (Figure 3-8).

Analysis. This payment decreases the asset, Cash, and decreases the liability, Accounts Payable. Debit Accounts Payable and credit Cash for $300.

FIGURE 3-8 Transaction (d): Payment on Account

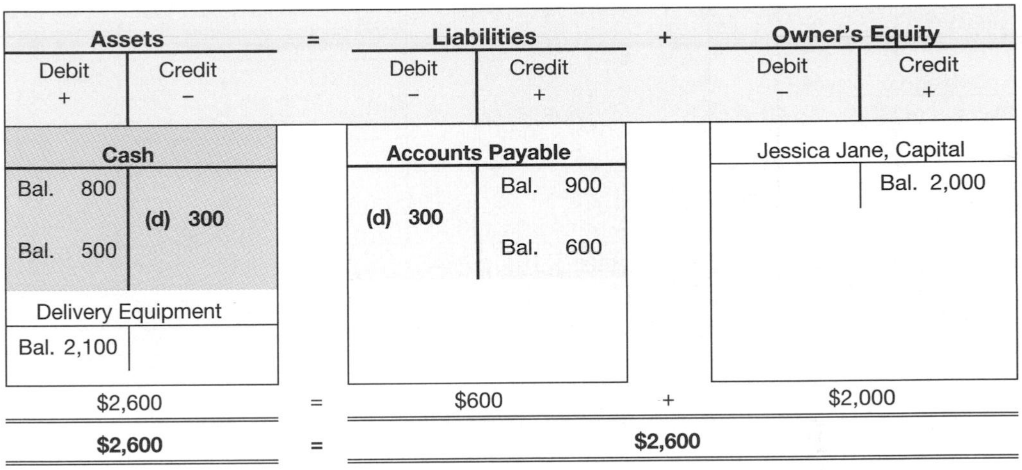

Notice that for transactions (a) through (d), the debits equal credits and the accounting equation is in balance. Review transactions (a) through (d). Again, identify the accounts that were affected and how they were classified (assets, liabilities, or owner's equity). Finally, note each account's location within the accounting equation.

LEARNING KEY

Credits increase the capital account. Revenues increase capital. Thus, revenues are shown under the credit side of the capital account. Debits decrease the capital account. Expenses and drawing reduce owner's equity. Thus, they are shown under the debit side of the capital account.

DEBITS AND CREDITS: INCLUDING REVENUES, EXPENSES, AND DRAWING

Transactions (a) through (d) involved only assets, liabilities, and the owner's capital account. To complete the illustration of Jessie Jane's Campus Delivery Service, the equation is expanded to include revenues, expenses, and drawing. Remember, revenues increase owner's equity and are shown under the credit side of the capital account. Expenses and drawing decrease owner's equity and are shown under the debit side of the capital account. The expanded equation is shown in Figure 3-9.

FIGURE 3-9 The Expanded Accounting Equation

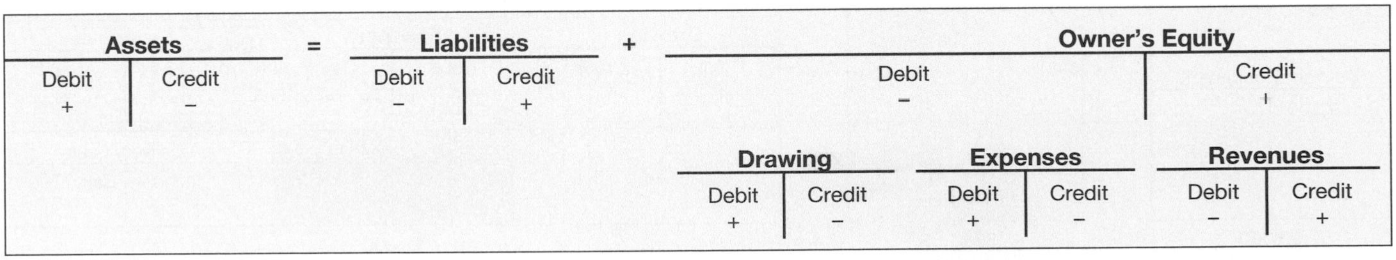

Transaction (e): Delivery revenues earned in cash

Jessie made deliveries and received $500 cash from clients (Figure 3-10).

Analysis. The asset, Cash, and the revenue, Delivery Fees, increase. Debit Cash and credit Delivery Fees for $500.

FIGURE 3-10 Transaction (e): Delivery Revenues Earned in Cash

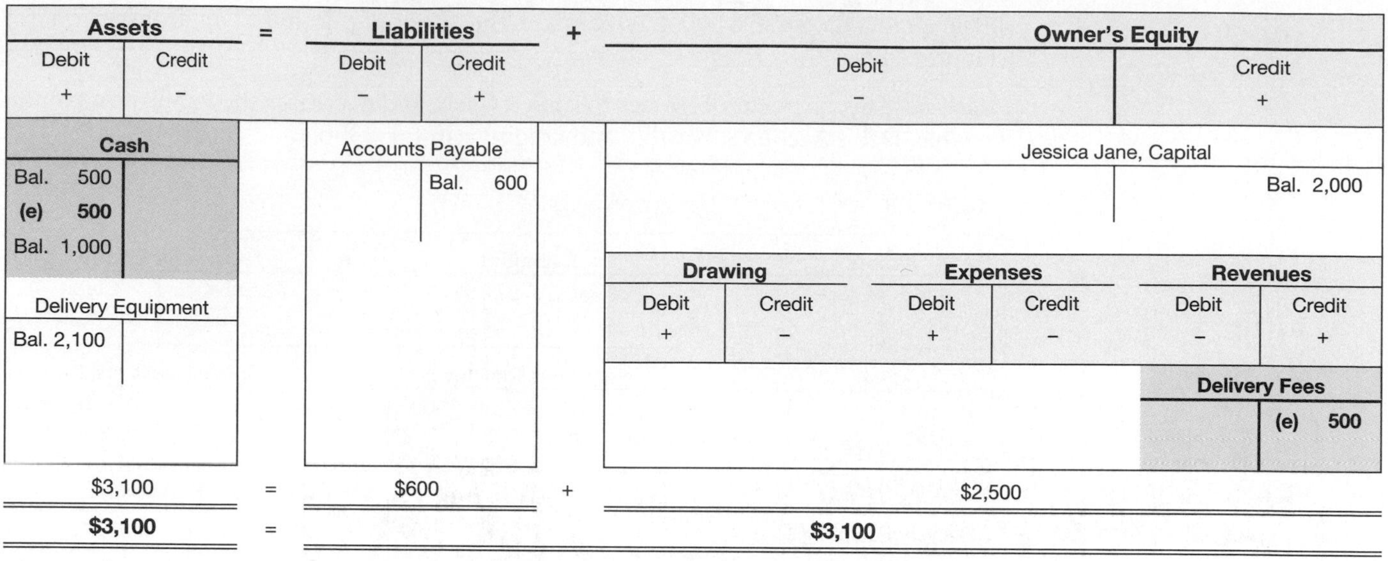

Assets
Debit +
Credit −
=
Liabilities
Debit −
Credit +
+
Owner's Equity
Debit −
Credit +
Cash
Bal. 500
(e) 500
Bal. 1,000
Delivery Equipment
Bal. 2,100
Accounts Payable
Bal. 600
Jessica Jane, Capital
Bal. 2,000
Drawing
Debit +
Credit −
Expenses
Debit +
Credit −
Revenues
Debit −
Credit +
Delivery Fees
(e) 500
$3,100 = $600 + $2,500
$3,100 = $3,100

Transaction (f): Paid rent for month

Jessie paid $200 for office rent for June (Figure 3-11).

Analysis. Rent Expense increases and Cash decreases. Debit Rent Expense and credit Cash for $200.

A debit to an expense account *increases* that expense and *decreases* owner's equity. Notice that the placement of the plus and minus signs for expenses is opposite the placement of the signs for owner's equity. Note also that expenses are located on the left (debit) side of the owner's equity umbrella.

FIGURE 3-11 Transaction (f): Paid Rent for Month

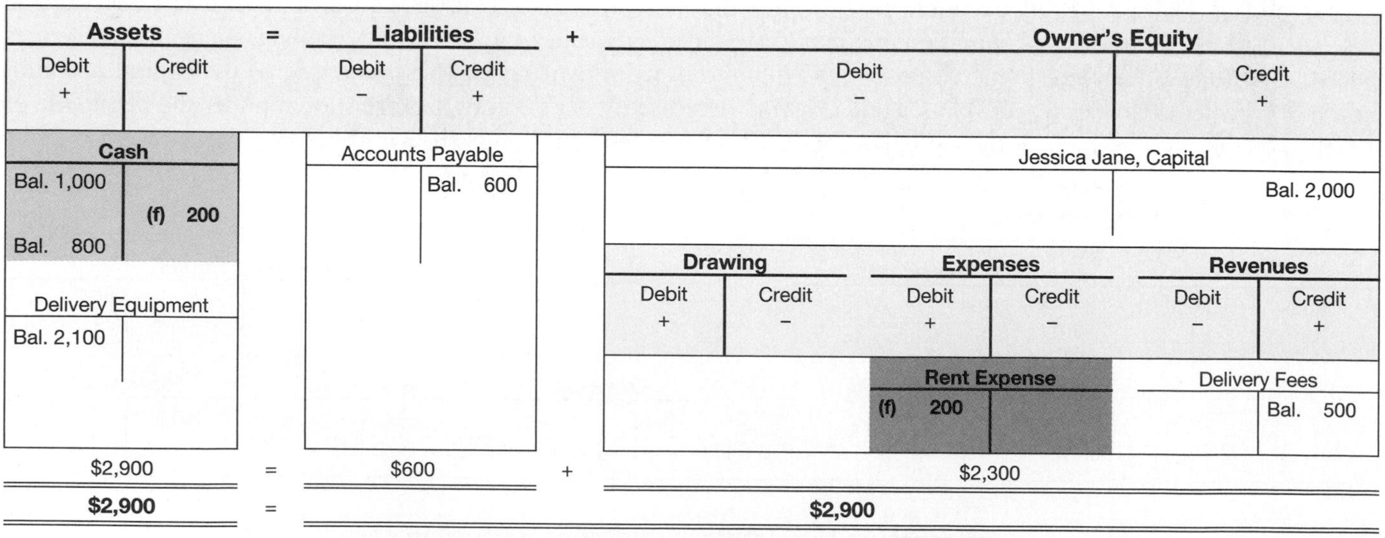

Transaction (g): Paid telephone bill

Jessie paid for telephone service, $50 (Figure 3-12).

Analysis. This transaction, like the previous one, increases an expense and decreases an asset. Debit Telephone Expense and credit Cash for $50.

FIGURE 3-12 Transaction (g): Paid Telephone Bill

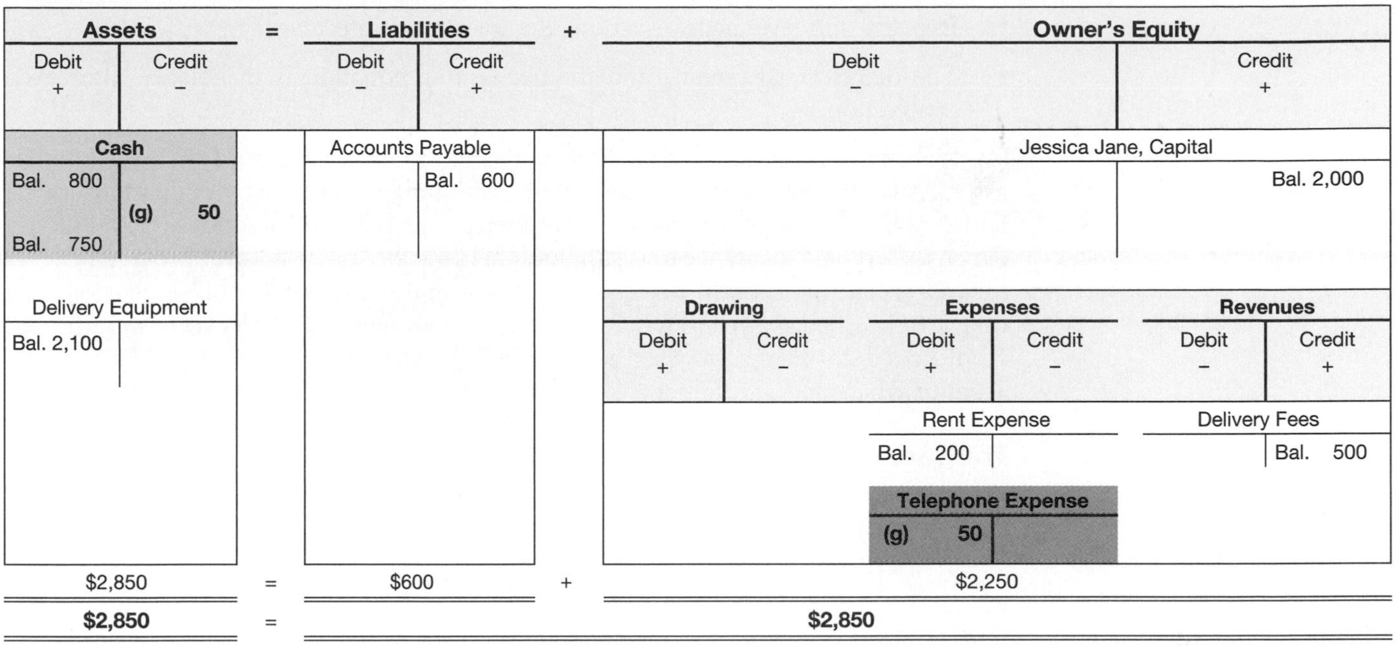

Transaction (h): Delivery revenues earned on account

Jessie made deliveries on account for $600 (Figure 3-13).

Analysis. As discussed in Chapter 2, delivery services are performed for which payment will be received later. This is called offering services "on account" or "on credit." Instead of receiving cash, Jessie receives a promise that her customers will pay cash in the future. Therefore, the asset, Accounts Receivable, increases. Since revenues are recognized when earned, the revenue account, Delivery Fees, also increases. Debit Accounts Receivable and credit Delivery Fees for $600.

FIGURE 3-13 Transaction (h): Delivery Revenues Earned on Account

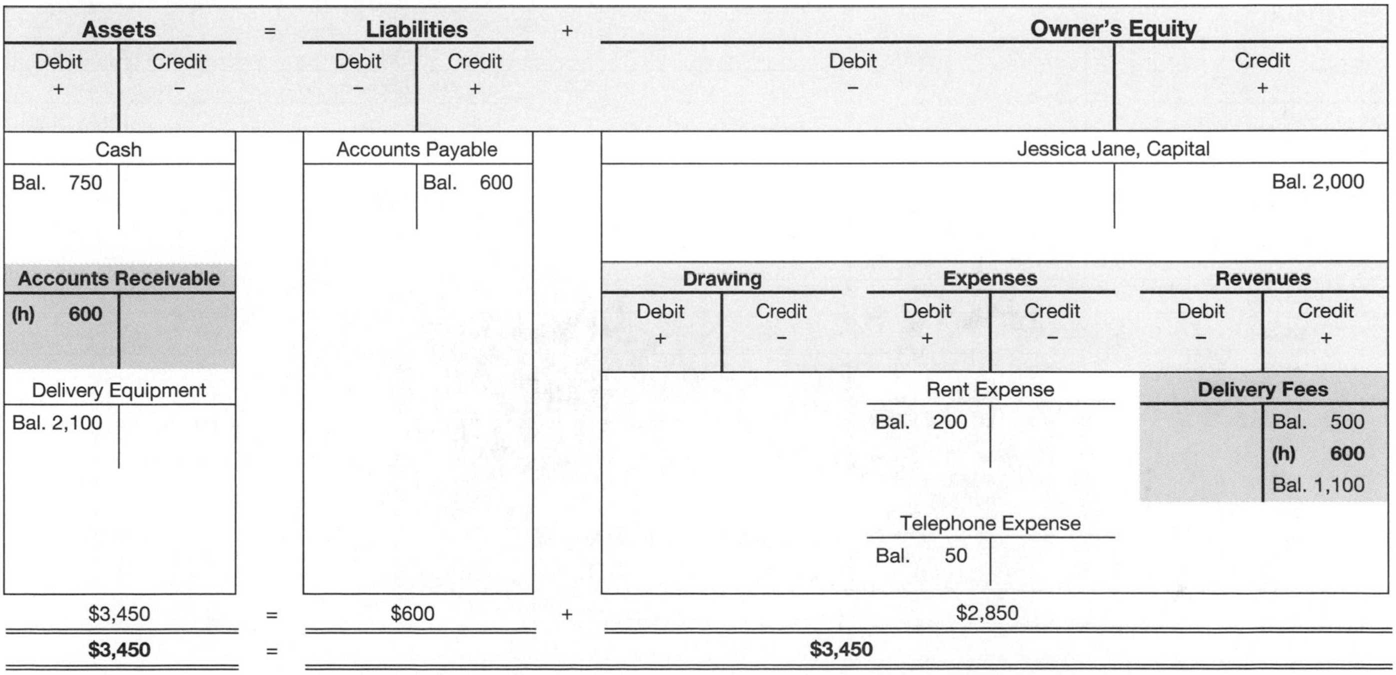

Review transactions (e) through (h). Note the following:

- Expense and revenue transactions do not always affect cash.
- The debits equal credits, and the accounting equation is in balance after each transaction.

Upcoming transactions (i) and (j) both involve an exchange of cash for another asset. As you analyze these two transactions, you may wonder why prepaid insurance and supplies are assets while the rent and telephone bill in transactions (f) and (g) are expenses. Prepaid insurance and supplies are assets because they will provide benefits for more than one month. Jessie pays her rent and her telephone bill each month so they are classified as expenses. If Jessie paid her rent only once every three months, she would need to set up an asset account called Prepaid Rent. She would debit this account when she paid the rent.

Transaction (i): Purchase of supplies

Jessie bought pens, paper, delivery envelopes, and other supplies for $80 cash (Figure 3-14).

Analysis. These supplies will last for several months. Since they will generate future benefits, the supplies should be recorded as an asset. An asset, Supplies, increases, and an asset, Cash, decreases. Debit Supplies and credit Cash for $80.

FIGURE 3-14 Transaction (i): Purchase of Supplies

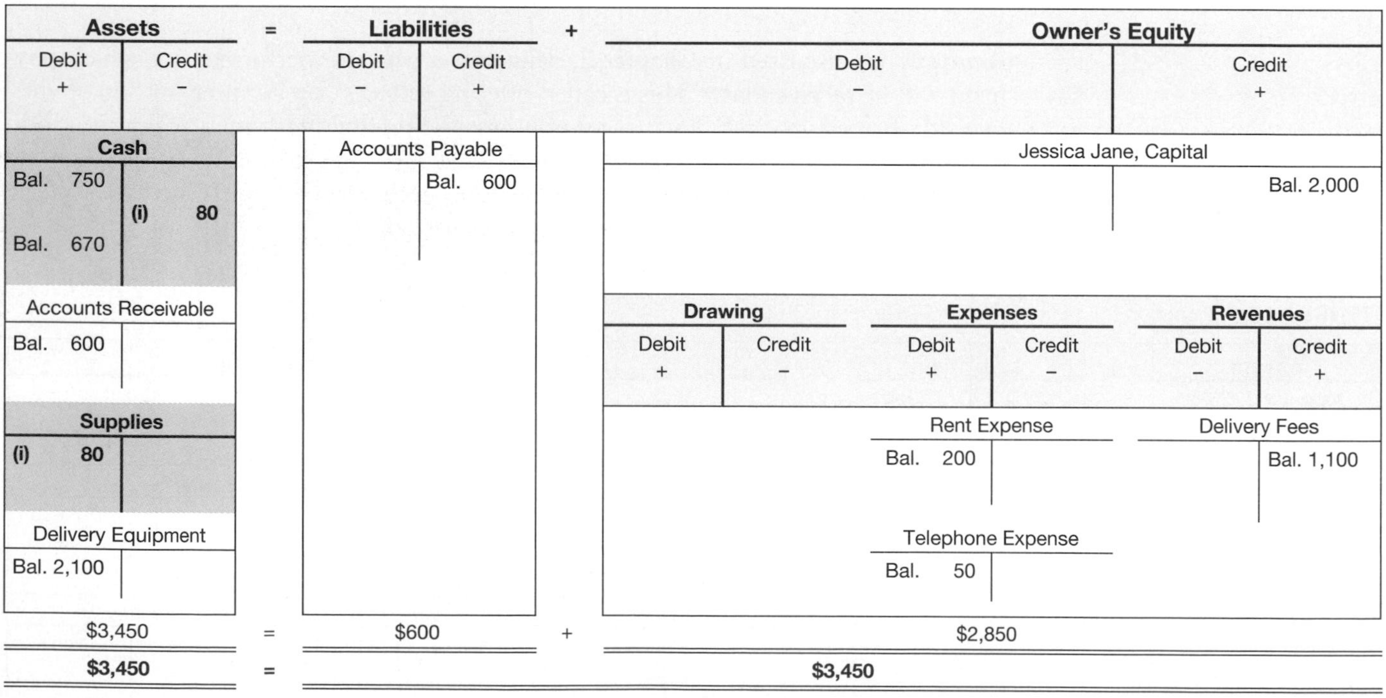

A BROADER VIEW

MELANIE KINTZ / ISTOCKPHOTO.COM

Supplies—Asset or Expense?

When businesses buy office supplies from Staples or other suppliers, the supplies are initially recorded as assets. This is done because the supplies will provide future benefits. Those still remaining in inventory at the end of the accounting period are reported on the balance sheet as assets. Supplies actually used during the period are recognized as an expense on the income statement. We will discuss how to account for the expense in Chapter 5.

Transaction (j): Payment of insurance premium

Jessie paid $200 for an eight-month liability insurance policy (Figure 3-15).

Analysis. Since insurance is paid in advance and will provide future benefits, it is treated as an asset. Therefore, one asset, Prepaid Insurance, increases and another, Cash, decreases. Debit Prepaid Insurance and credit Cash for $200.

FIGURE 3-15 Transaction (j): Payment of Insurance Premium

Assets		=	Liabilities		+	Owner's Equity	
Debit +	Credit −		Debit −	Credit +		Debit −	Credit +

Assets

Cash	
Bal. 670	(j) 200
Bal. 470	

Accounts Receivable	
Bal. 600	

Supplies	
Bal. 80	

Prepaid Insurance	
(j) 200	

Delivery Equipment	
Bal. 2,100	

Liabilities

Accounts Payable	
	Bal. 600

Owner's Equity

Jessica Jane, Capital	
	Bal. 2,000

Drawing		Expenses		Revenues	
Debit +	Credit −	Debit +	Credit −	Debit −	Credit +

Rent Expense	
Bal. 200	

Telephone Expense	
Bal. 50	

Delivery Fees	
	Bal. 1,100

Assets		Liabilities		Owner's Equity
$3,450	=	$600	+	$2,850
$3,450	=	**$3,450**		

Transaction (k): Cash receipts from prior sales on account

Jessie received $570 in cash for delivery services performed for customers earlier in the month [see transaction (h)] (Figure 3-16).

Analysis. This transaction increases Cash and reduces the amount due from customers reported in Accounts Receivable. Debit Cash and credit Accounts Receivable $570.

As you analyze transaction (k), notice which accounts are affected and the location of these accounts in the accounting equation. Jessie received cash, but this transaction did not affect revenue. The revenue was recorded in transaction (h). Transaction (k) is an exchange of one asset (Accounts Receivable) for another asset (Cash).

FIGURE 3-16 Transaction (k): Cash Receipts from Prior Sales on Account

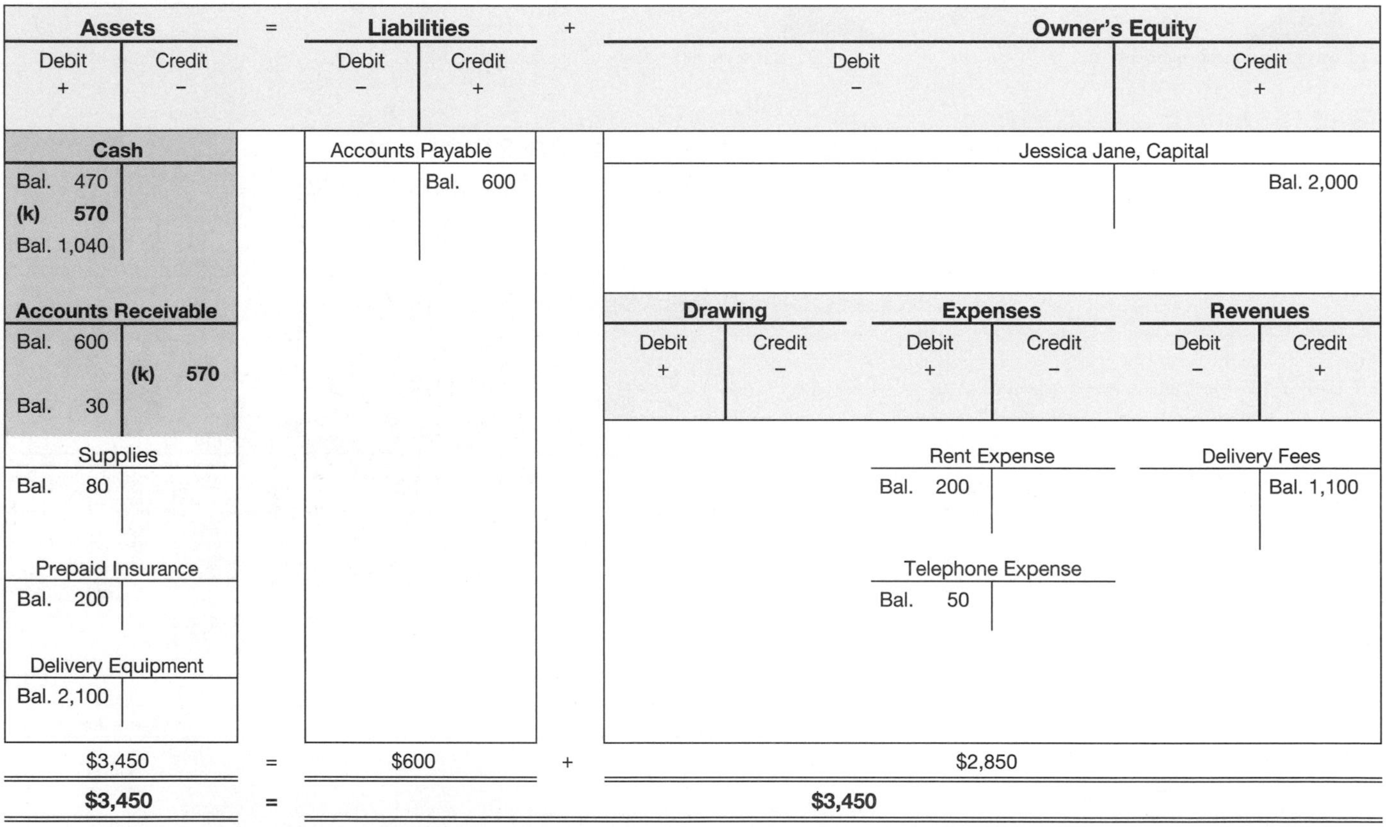

As you analyze transactions (l) through (o), make certain that you understand what has happened in each transaction. Identify the accounts that are affected and the locations of these accounts within the accounting equation. Notice that the accounting equation remains in balance after every transaction and debits equal credits for each transaction.

Profiles in Accounting

Maria Giorgio, Assistant Manager

Maria Giorgio graduated with an associate degree in accounting with honors from The College of Westchester. After working as an intern at Rosenberg, Chesnov & Co., LLP, she became the assistant manager of the company's New York Office on 5th Ave. Maria has found that working in a CPA firm exposes her to every aspect of accounting from tax to audit. Because she enjoys accounting so much, she is in the process of furthering her education. In addition, she thrives on the interpersonal daily experiences at the office and has found that you can be a people person and an aspiring CPA too.

Transaction (l): Purchase of an asset on credit making a partial payment

Jessie bought a third motor scooter for $1,500. Jessie made a down payment of $300 and spread the remaining payments over the next four months (Figure 3-17).

Analysis. The asset, Delivery Equipment, increases by $1,500, Cash decreases by $300, and the liability, Accounts Payable, increases by $1,200. Thus, debit Delivery Equipment for $1,500, credit Cash for $300, and credit Accounts Payable for $1,200. This transaction requires one debit and two credits. Even so, total debits ($1,500) equal the total credits ($1,200 + $300) and the accounting equation remains in balance.

FIGURE 3-17 Transaction (l): Purchase of an Asset on Credit Making a Partial Payment

Assets		=	Liabilities		+	Owner's Equity	
Debit +	Credit −		Debit −	Credit +		Debit −	Credit +

Assets

Cash	
Bal. 1,040	
	(l) 300
Bal. 740	

Accounts Receivable	
Bal. 30	

Supplies	
Bal. 80	

Prepaid Insurance	
Bal. 200	

Delivery Equipment	
Bal. 2,100	
(l) 1,500	
Bal. 3,600	

Liabilities

Accounts Payable	
	Bal. 600
	(l) 1,200
	Bal. 1,800

Owner's Equity

Jessica Jane, Capital	
	Bal. 2,000

Drawing		Expenses		Revenues	
Debit +	Credit −	Debit +	Credit −	Debit −	Credit +

Rent Expense	
Bal. 200	

Telephone Expense	
Bal. 50	

Delivery Fees	
	Bal. 1,100

$4,650	=	$1,800	+	$2,850
$4,650	=	**$4,650**		

Transaction (m): Payment of wages

Jessie paid her part-time employees $650 in wages (Figure 3-18).

Analysis. This is an additional business expense. Wages Expense increases and Cash decreases. Debit Wages Expense and credit Cash for $650.

FIGURE 3-18 Transaction (m): Payment of Wages

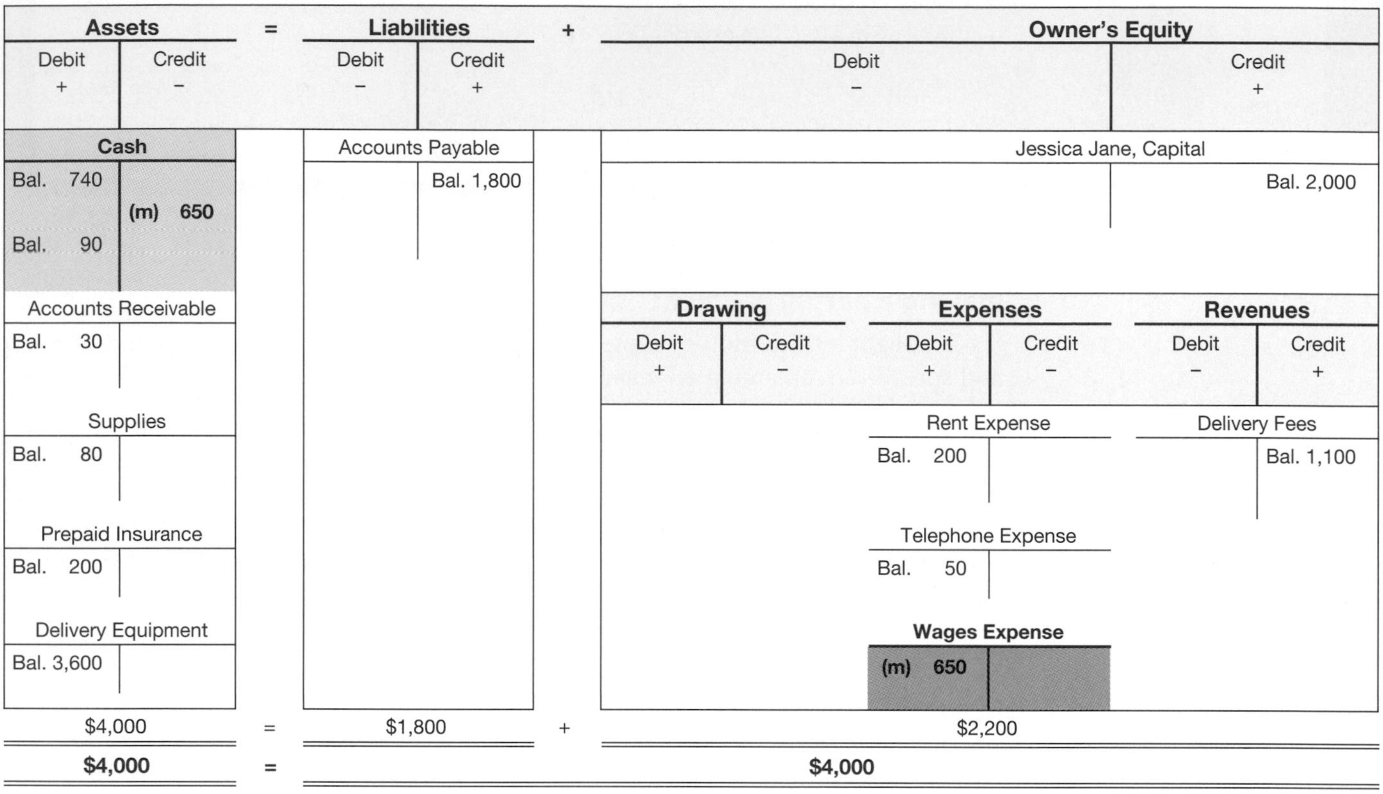

Transaction (n): Deliveries made for cash and credit

Total delivery fees for the remainder of the month amounted to $1,050: $430 in cash and $620 on account (Figure 3-19 on the next page).

Analysis. Since the delivery fees have been earned, the revenue account increases by $1,050. Also, Cash increases by $430 and Accounts Receivable increases by $620. Note once again that one event impacts three accounts. This time we have debits of $430 to Cash and $620 to Accounts Receivable, and a credit of $1,050 to Delivery Fees. As before, the total debits ($430 + $620) equal the total credits ($1,050) and the accounting equation remains in balance.

Transaction (o): Withdrawal of cash from business

At the end of the month, Jessie withdrew $150 in cash from the business to purchase books for her classes (Figure 3-20 on the next page).

Analysis. Cash withdrawals decrease owner's equity and decrease cash. Debit Jessica Jane, Drawing and credit Cash for $150.

Withdrawals are reported in the drawing account. Withdrawals by an owner are the opposite of an investment. You could debit the owner's capital account for withdrawals. However, using a specific account tells the user of the accounting information how much was withdrawn for the period.

FIGURE 3-19 Transaction (n): Deliveries Made for Cash and Credit

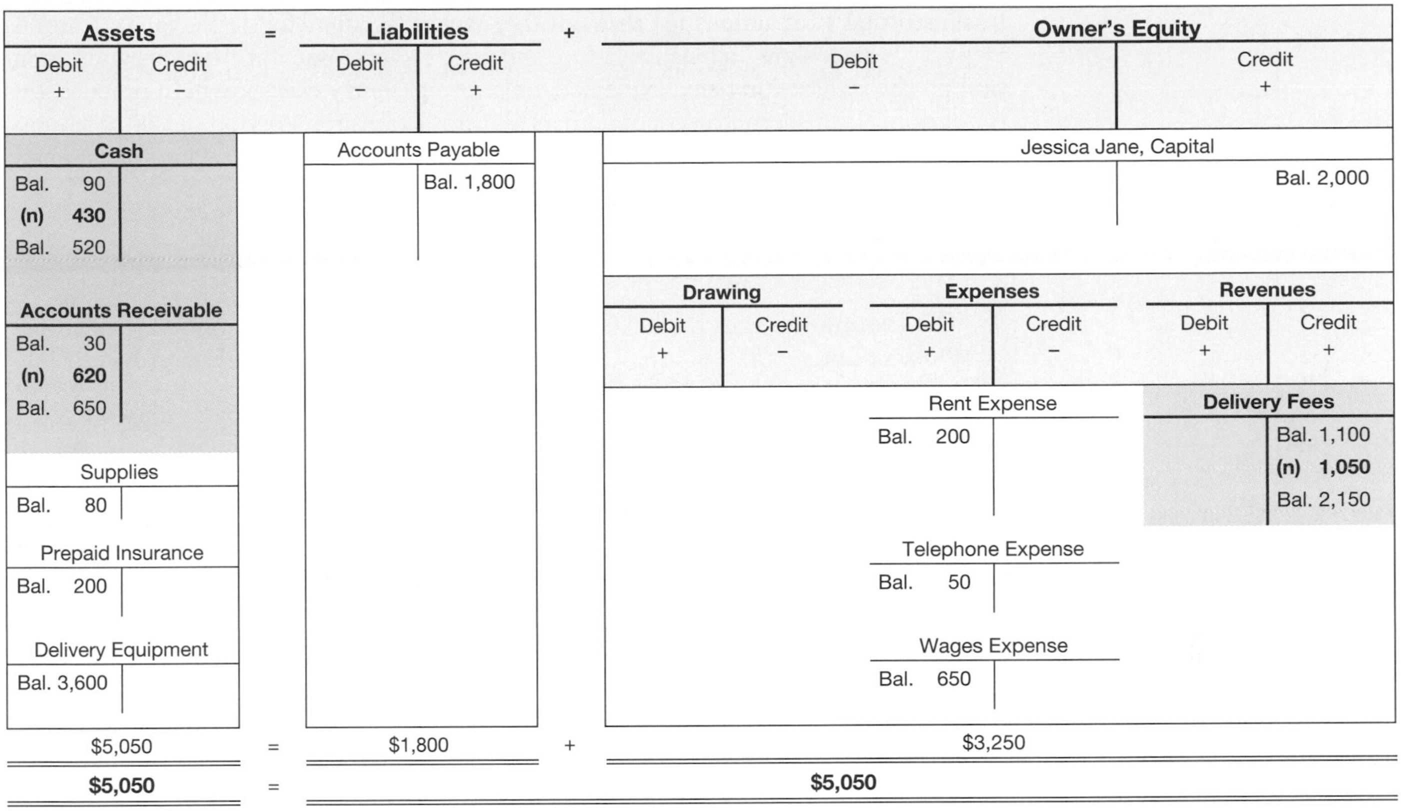

FIGURE 3-20 Transaction (o): Withdrawal of Cash from Business

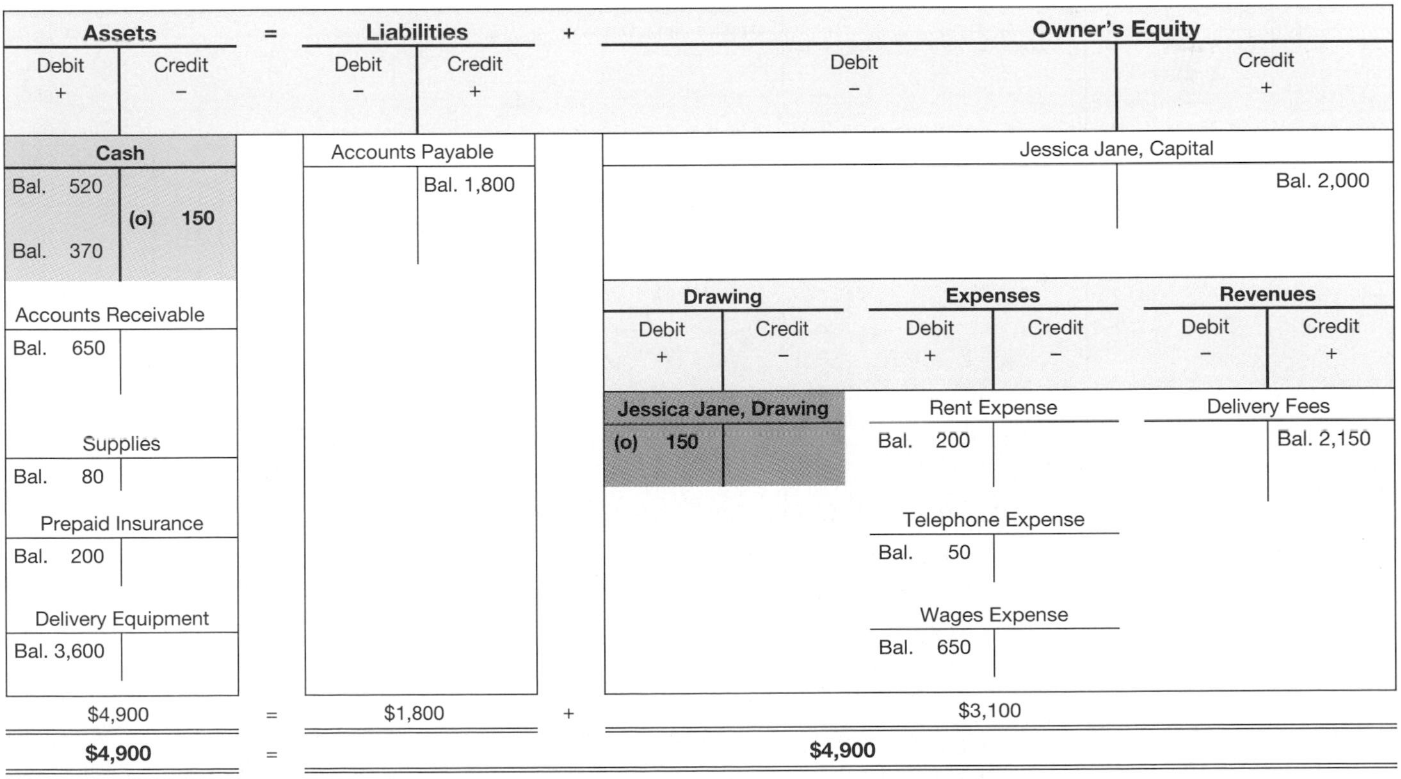

SUMMARY OF TRANSACTIONS

In illustrating transactions (a) through (o), each T account for Jessie Jane's Campus Delivery Service shows a balance before and after each transaction. To focus your attention on the transaction being explained, only a single entry was shown. In practice, this is not done. Instead, each account gathers all transactions for a period. Jessie's accounts, with all transactions listed, are shown in Figure 3-21. Note the following four items:

1. The footings are directly under the debit (left) and credit (right) sides of the T account for those accounts with more than one debit or credit.
2. The balance is shown on the side with the larger footing.
3. The footing serves as the balance for accounts with entries on only one side of the account.
4. If an account has only a single entry, it is not necessary to enter a footing or balance.

FIGURE 3-21 Summary of Transactions (a) Through (o)

Assets		=	Liabilities		+	Owner's Equity	
Debit +	Credit −		Debit −	Credit +		Debit −	Credit +

Assets

Cash	
(a) 2,000	(b) 1,200
(e) 500	(d) 300
(k) 570	(f) 200
(n) 430	(g) 50
3,500	(i) 80
	(j) 200
	(l) 300
	(m) 650
	(o) 150
	3,130
Bal. 370	

Accounts Receivable	
(h) 600	(k) 570
(n) 620	
1,220	
Bal. 650	

Supplies	
(i) 80	

Prepaid Insurance	
(j) 200	

Delivery Equipment	
(b) 1,200	
(c) 900	
(l) 1,500	
Bal. 3,600	

Liabilities

Accounts Payable	
(d) 300	(c) 900
	(l) 1,200
	2,100
	Bal. 1,800

Owner's Equity

Jessica Jane, Capital	
	(a) 2,000

Drawing		Expenses		Revenues	
Debit +	Credit −	Debit +	Credit −	Debit −	Credit +

Jessica Jane, Drawing	
(o) 150	

Rent Expense	
(f) 200	

Telephone Expense	
(g) 50	

Wages Expense	
(m) 650	

Delivery Fees	
	(e) 500
	(h) 600
	(n) 1,050
	Bal. 2,150

Assets	=	Liabilities	+	Owner's Equity
$4,900	=	$1,800	+	$3,100
$4,900	=	**$4,900**		

U REVU

Complete U REVU-3 on **page 74** to test your basic understanding of LO4.

THE TRIAL BALANCE

LO5 Prepare a trial balance and explain its purposes and linkages with the financial statements.

Recall the following two very important rules in double-entry accounting:

1. The sum of the debits must equal the sum of the credits.

   At least two accounts are affected by each transaction. This rule is so important that many computer accounting programs will not permit a transaction to be entered into the accounting system unless the debits equal the credits.

2. The accounting equation must remain in balance.

In illustrating the transactions for Jessie Jane's Campus Delivery Service, the equality of the accounting equation was verified after each transaction. Because of the large number of transactions entered each day, this is not done in practice. Instead, a trial balance is prepared periodically to determine the equality of the debits and credits. A **trial balance** is a list of all accounts showing the title and balance of each account. By totaling the debits and credits, their equality can be tested.

LEARNING KEY

A trial balance provides proof that total debits equal total credits and shows that the accounting equation is in balance.

A trial balance of Jessie's accounts, taken on June 30, 20--, is shown in Figure 3-22. This date is shown on the third line of the heading. The trial balance shows that the debit and credit totals are equal in amount. This is proof that (1) in entering transactions (a) through (o), the total of the debits was equal to the total of the credits, and (2) the accounting equation has remained in balance.

A trial balance is not a formal statement or report. Normally, only the accountant sees it. As shown in Figure 3-23, a trial balance can be used as an aid in preparing the financial statements.

Since a trial balance is not a formal statement, dollar signs are not used.

FIGURE 3-22 Trial Balance

Jessie Jane's Campus Delivery Service
Trial Balance
June 30, 20 --

ACCOUNT TITLE	DEBIT BALANCE	CREDIT BALANCE
Cash	370 00	
Accounts Receivable	650 00	
Supplies	80 00	
Prepaid Insurance	200 00	
Delivery Equipment	3600 00	
Accounts Payable		1800 00
Jessica Jane, Capital		2000 00
Jessica Jane, Drawing	150 00	
Delivery Fees		2150 00
Rent Expense	200 00	
Telephone Expense	50 00	
Wages Expense	650 00	
	5950 00	5950 00

FIGURE 3-23 Linkages Between the Trial Balance and Financial Statements

Jessie Jane's Campus Delivery Service
Trial Balance
June 30, 20 --

ACCOUNT TITLE	DEBIT BALANCE	CREDIT BALANCE
Cash	370 00	
Accounts Receivable	650 00	
Supplies	80 00	
Prepaid Insurance	200 00	
Delivery Equipment	3600 00	
Accounts Payable		1800 00
Jessica Jane, Capital		2000 00
Jessica Jane, Drawing	150 00	
Delivery Fees		2150 00
Rent Expense	200 00	
Telephone Expense	50 00	
Wages Expense	650 00	
	5950 00	5950 00

Jessie Jane's Campus Delivery Service
Income Statement
For Month Ended June 30, 20 --

Revenue:		
Delivery fees		$2150 00
Expenses:		
Wages expense	$ 650 00	
Rent expense	200 00	
Telephone expense	50 00	
Total expenses		900 00
Net income		$1250 00

Jessie Jane's Campus Delivery Service
Statement of Owner's Equity
For Month Ended June 30, 20 --

Jessica Jane, capital, June 1, 20 --		$ —
Investments during June		2000 00
Total investment		$2000 00
Net income for June	$1250 00	
Less withdrawals for June	150 00	
Increase in capital		1100 00
Jessica Jane, capital, June 30, 20 --		$3100 00

Jessie Jane's Campus Delivery Service
Balance Sheet
June 30, 20 --

Assets		Liabilities	
Cash	$ 370 00	Accounts payable	$1800 00
Accounts receivable	650 00		
Supplies	80 00	Owner's Equity	
Prepaid insurance	200 00	Jessica Jane, capital	3100 00
Delivery equipment	3600 00		
Total assets	$4900 00	Total liabilities and owner's equity	$4900 00

If the beginning capital balance was $2,000 and Jessie made no additional investments, the statement would be prepared as follows:

Jessie Jane's Campus Delivery Service
Statement of Owner's Equity
For Month Ended June 30, 20 --

Jessica Jane, capital, June 1, 20 --		$2000 00
Net income for June	$1250 00	
Less withdrawals for June	150 00	
Increase in capital		1100 00
Jessica Jane, Capital, June 30, 20 --		$3100 00

U REVU Complete U REVU-4 on **page 74** to test your basic understanding of LO5.

LEARNING OBJECTIVES — Key Points to Remember

LO1 Define the parts of a T account.

The parts of a T account are:
1. the title,
2. the debit or left side, and
3. the credit or right side.

Title	
Debit = Left	Credit = Right

LO2 Foot and balance a T account.

Rules for footing and balancing T accounts are:
1. The footings are directly under the debit (left) and credit (right) sides of the T account for those accounts with more than one debit or credit.
2. The balance is shown on the side with the larger footing.
3. The footing serves as the balance for accounts with entries on only one side of the account.
4. If an account has only a single entry, it is not necessary to enter a footing or balance.

LO3 Describe the effects of debits and credits on specific types of accounts.

Rules for debits and credits. (See illustration below.)
1. Assets are on the left side of the accounting equation. There fore, increases are entered on the left (debit) side of an asset account and decreases are entered on the right (credit) side.
2. Liabilities and owner's equity are on the right side of the accounting equation. Therefore, increases are entered on the right (credit) side and decreases are entered on the left (debit) side.
3. Revenues increase owner's equity. Therefore, increases are entered on the right (credit) side and decreases are entered on the left (debit) side.
4. Expenses and drawing decrease owner's equity. Therefore, increases are entered on the left (debit) side and decreases are entered on the right (credit) side.

Accounting Equation with Owner's Equity Umbrella

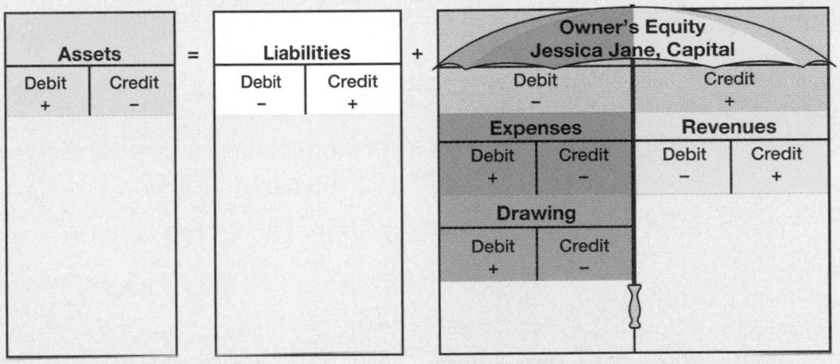

LO4 Use T accounts to analyze transactions.

Picture the accounting equation in your mind as you analyze transactions. When entering transactions in T accounts:
1. The sum of the debits must equal the sum of the credits.
2. At least two accounts are affected by each transaction.
3. When finished, the accounting equation must remain in balance.

LO5 Prepare a trial balance and explain its purposes and linkages with the financial statements.

A trial balance shows that the debit and credit totals are equal. A trial balance also can be used in preparing the financial statements.

DEMONSTRATION PROBLEM

Celia Pints opened We-Buy, You-Pay Shopping Services. For a fee that is based on the amount of research and shopping time required, Pints and her associates will shop for almost anything from groceries to home furnishings. Business is particularly heavy around Christmas and in early summer. The business operates from a rented store front. The associates receive a commission based on the revenues they produce and a mileage reimbursement for the use of their personal automobiles for shopping trips. Pints decided to use the following accounts to record transactions.

Assets
- Cash
- Accounts Receivable
- Office Equipment
- Computer Equipment

Liabilities
- Accounts Payable
- Notes Payable

Owner's Equity
- Celia Pints, Capital
- Celia Pints, Drawing

Revenue
- Shopping Fees

Expenses
- Rent Expense
- Telephone Expense
- Commissions Expense
- Utilities Expense
- Travel Expense

The following transactions are for the month of December 20--.

(a) Pints invested cash in the business, $30,000.

(b) Bought office equipment for $10,000. Paid $2,000 in cash and promised to pay the balance over the next four months.

(c) Paid rent for December, $500.

(d) Provided shopping services for customers on account, $5,200.

(e) Paid telephone bill, $90.

(f) Borrowed cash from the bank by signing a note payable, $5,000.

(g) Bought a computer and printer, $4,800.

(h) Collected cash from customers for services performed on account, $4,000.

(i) Paid commissions to associates for revenues generated during the first half of the month, $3,500.

(j) Paid utility bill, $600.

(k) Paid cash on account for the office equipment purchased in transaction (b), $2,000.

(l) Earned shopping fees of $13,200: $6,000 in cash and $7,200 on account.

(m) Paid commissions to associates for last half of month, $7,000.

(n) Paid mileage reimbursements for the month, $1,500.

(o) Paid cash on note payable to bank, $1,000.

(p) Pints withdrew cash for personal use, $2,000.

REQUIRED

1. Enter the transactions for December in T accounts. Use the accounting equation as a guide for setting up the T accounts.
2. Foot the T accounts and determine their balances as necessary.
3. Prepare a trial balance of the accounts as of December 31 of the current year.
4. Prepare an income statement for the month ended December 31 of the current year.
5. Prepare a statement of owner's equity for the month ended December 31 of the current year.
6. Prepare a balance sheet as of December 31 of the current year.

Solution 1, 2.

Assets		=	Liabilities		+	Owner's Equity	
Debit +	Credit −		Debit −	Credit +		Debit −	Credit +

Assets

Cash

Debit	Credit
(a) 30,000	(b) 2,000
(f) 5,000	(c) 500
(h) 4,000	(e) 90
(l) 6,000	(g) 4,800
45,000	(i) 3,500
	(j) 600
	(k) 2,000
	(m) 7,000
	(n) 1,500
	(o) 1,000
	(p) 2,000
	24,990
Bal. 20,010	

Accounts Receivable

Debit	Credit
(d) 5,200	(h) 4,000
(l) 7,200	
12,400	
Bal. 8,400	

Office Equipment

Debit	Credit
(b) 10,000	

Computer Equipment

Debit	Credit
(g) 4,800	

Liabilities

Accounts Payable

Debit	Credit
(k) 2,000	(b) 8,000
	Bal. 6,000

Notes Payable

Debit	Credit
(o) 1,000	(f) 5,000
	Bal. 4,000

Owner's Equity

Celia Pints, Capital

Debit	Credit
	(a) 30,000

Drawing		Expenses		Revenues	
Debit +	Credit −	Debit +	Credit −	Debit −	Credit +

Celia Pints, Drawing

Debit	Credit
(p) 2,000	

Rent Expense

Debit	Credit
(c) 500	

Telephone Expense

Debit	Credit
(e) 90	

Commissions Expense

Debit	Credit
(i) 3,500	
(m) 7,000	
Bal. 10,500	

Utilities Expense

Debit	Credit
(j) 600	

Travel Expense

Debit	Credit
(n) 1,500	

Shopping Fees

Debit	Credit
	(d) 5,200
	(l) 13,200
	Bal. 18,400

Assets		Liabilities		Owner's Equity
$43,210	=	$10,000	+	$33,210
$43,210	=	**$43,210**		

(continued)

3.

We-Buy, You-Pay Shopping Services
Trial Balance
December 31, 20 --

ACCOUNT TITLE	DEBIT BALANCE	CREDIT BALANCE
Cash	20,010.00	
Accounts Receivable	8,400.00	
Office Equipment	10,000.00	
Computer Equipment	4,800.00	
Accounts Payable		6,000.00
Notes Payable		4,000.00
Celia Pints, Capital		30,000.00
Celia Pints, Drawing	2,000.00	
Shopping Fees		18,400.00
Rent Expense	500.00	
Telephone Expense	90.00	
Commissions Expense	10,500.00	
Utilities Expense	600.00	
Travel Expense	1,500.00	
	58,400.00	58,400.00

4.

We-Buy, You-Pay Shopping Services
Income Statement
For Month Ended December 31, 20 --

Revenue:		
Shopping fees		$18,400.00
Expenses:		
Commissions expense	$10,500.00	
Travel expense	1,500.00	
Utilities expense	600.00	
Rent expense	500.00	
Telephone expense	90.00	
Total expenses		13,190.00
Net income		$ 5,210.00

5.

We-Buy, You-Pay Shopping Services
Statement of Owner's Equity
For Month Ended December 31, 20 - -

Celia Pints, capital, December 1, 20 --		$ —
Investments during December		30,000.00
Total investment		$30,000.00
Net income for December	$5,210.00	
Less withdrawals for December	2,000.00	
Increase in capital		3,210.00
Celia Pints, capital, December 31, 20 --		$33,210.00

6.

We-Buy, You-Pay Shopping Services
Balance Sheet
December 31, 20 - -

Assets		Liabilities	
Cash	$20 0 1 0 00	Accounts payable	$ 6 0 0 0 00
Accounts receivable	8 4 0 0 00	Notes payable	4 0 0 0 00
Office equipment	10 0 0 0 00	Total liabilities	$10 0 0 0 00
Computer equipment	4 8 0 0 00		
		Owner's Equity	
		Celia Pints, capital	33 2 1 0 00
Total assets	$43 2 1 0 00	Total liabilities and owner's equity	$43 2 1 0 00

KEY TERMS

balance (51) The difference between the footings of an account.

credit (52) To enter an amount on the right side of an account.

credit balance (54) The normal balance of liability, owner's equity, and revenue accounts.

debit (52) To enter an amount on the left side of an account.

debit balance (54) The normal balance of asset, expense, and drawing accounts.

double-entry accounting (51) A system in which each transaction has a dual effect on the accounting elements.

footings (51) The total dollar amounts on the debit and credit sides of an account.

normal balance (54) The side of an account that is increased.

trial balance (67) A list of all accounts, showing the title and balance of each account, used to prove that the sum of the debits equals the sum of the credits.

SELF-STUDY QUESTIONS AND EXERCISES

True/False Questions

1. LO3 To debit an account is to enter an amount on the left side of the account.
2. LO3 Liability accounts normally have debit balances.
3. LO3 Increases in owner's equity are entered as credits.
4. LO3 Revenue accounts normally have debit balances.
5. LO3 To credit an account is to enter an amount on the right side of the account.
6. LO3 A debit to an asset account will decrease it.

Multiple Choice Questions

1. LO3 A common example of an asset is

   (a) Professional Fees.
   (b) Rent Expense.
   (c) Accounts Receivable.
   (d) Accounts Payable.

2. LO3 The accounting equation may be expressed as

(a) Assets = Liabilities − Owner's Equity.
(b) Assets = Liabilities + Owner's Equity.
(c) Liabilities = Owner's Equity − Assets.
(d) all of the above.

3. LO3 Liability, owner's equity, and revenue accounts normally have

(a) debit balances.
(b) large balances.
(c) negative balances.
(d) credit balances.

4. LO4 To record the payment of rent expense, an accountant would

(a) debit Cash; credit Rent Expense.
(b) debit Rent Expense; debit Cash.
(c) debit Rent Expense; credit Cash.
(d) credit Rent Expense; credit Cash.

5. LO4 An investment of cash by the owner will

(a) increase assets and owner's equity.
(b) increase assets and liabilities.
(c) increase liabilities and owner's equity.
(d) increase owner's equity and decrease liabilities.

U REVU Exercises

1. LO2 Foot and balance the accounts receivable T account shown below.

Accounts Receivable

100	50
200	30

2. LO3 Complete the following questions using either "debit" or "credit":

(a) The asset account Supplies is increased with a __________.
(b) The owner's capital account is increased with a __________.
(c) The rent expense account is increased with a __________.

3. LO4 Analyze the following transaction using the T accounts provided below. Robb Todd purchased equipment for $300 cash.

Cash

Equipment

4. LO5 The following accounts have normal balances. Prepare a trial balance. Accounts Payable, $20; Accounts Receivable, $90; Capital, $40; Sales, $200; Cash, $100; Rent Expense, $70.

The answers to the Self-Study Questions and Exercises are at the end of the chapter (page 85).

REVIEW QUESTIONS

LO1 1. What are the three major parts of a T account?

LO1 2. What is the left side of the T account called? the right side?

LO2 3. What is a footing?

LO3 4. What is the relationship between the revenue and expense accounts and the owner's equity account?

LO5 5. What is the function of the trial balance?

SERIES A EXERCISES

E 3-1A (LO2)
✓ Cash bal.: $1,200 (Dr.)

FOOT AND BALANCE A T ACCOUNT Foot and balance the cash T account shown below.

Cash	
500	100
400	200
600	

E 3-2A (LO3)

DEBIT AND CREDIT ANALYSIS Complete the following statements using either "debit" or "credit":

(a) The cash account is increased with a ________.
(b) The owner's capital account is increased with a ________.
(c) The delivery equipment account is increased with a ________.
(d) The cash account is decreased with a ________.
(e) The liability account Accounts Payable is increased with a ________.
(f) The revenue account Delivery Fees is increased with a ________.
(g) The asset account Accounts Receivable is increased with a ________.
(h) The rent expense account is increased with a ________.
(i) The owner's drawing account is increased with a ________.

E 3-3A (LO2/3/4)
✓ Cash bal. after (c): $2,700 (Dr.)

ANALYSIS OF T ACCOUNTS Jim Arnold began a business called Arnold's Shoe Repair.

1. Create T accounts for Cash; Supplies; Jim Arnold, Capital; and Utilities Expense. Identify the following transactions by letter and place them on the proper side of the T accounts:

   (a) Invested cash in the business, $5,000.
   (b) Purchased supplies for cash, $800.
   (c) Paid utility bill, $1,500.

2. Foot the T account for cash and enter the ending balance.

E 3-4A (LO3)

NORMAL BALANCE OF ACCOUNT Indicate the normal balance (debit or credit) for each of the following accounts:

1. Cash
2. Wages Expense
3. Accounts Payable
4. Owner's Drawing
5. Supplies
6. Owner's Capital
7. Equipment

E 3-5A (LO4)

TRANSACTION ANALYSIS Sheryl Hansen started a business on May 1, 20--. Analyze the following transactions for the first month of business using T accounts. Label each T account with the title of the account affected and then place the transaction letter and the dollar amount on the debit or credit side.

(a) Invested cash in the business, $4,000.
(b) Bought equipment for cash, $500.
(c) Bought equipment on account, $800.
(d) Paid cash on account for equipment purchased in transaction (c), $300.
(e) Withdrew cash for personal use, $700.

E 3-6A (LO2)
✓ Cash bal. after (e): $2,500 (Dr.)

FOOT AND BALANCE T ACCOUNTS Foot and balance the T accounts prepared in Exercise 3-5A if necessary.

E 3-7A (LO2/4)
✓ Cash bal. after (k): $24,400 (Dr.)

ANALYSIS OF TRANSACTIONS Charles Chadwick opened a business called Charlie's Detective Service in January 20--. Set up T accounts for the following accounts: Cash; Accounts Receivable; Office Supplies; Computer Equipment; Office Furniture; Accounts Payable; Charles Chadwick, Capital; Charles Chadwick, Drawing; Professional Fees; Rent Expense; and Utilities Expense.

The following transactions occurred during the first month of business. Record these transactions in T accounts. After all transactions are recorded, foot and balance the accounts if necessary.

(a) Invested cash in the business, $30,000.
(b) Bought office supplies for cash, $300.
(c) Bought office furniture for cash, $5,000.
(d) Purchased computer and printer on account, $8,000.
(e) Received cash from clients for services, $3,000.
(f) Paid cash on account for computer and printer purchased in transaction (d), $4,000.
(g) Earned professional fees on account during the month, $9,000.
(h) Paid cash for office rent for January, $1,500.
(i) Paid utility bills for the month, $800.
(j) Received cash from clients billed in transaction (g), $6,000.
(k) Withdrew cash for personal use, $3,000.

E 3-8A (LO5)
✓ Trial bal. total debits: $46,000

TRIAL BALANCE Based on the transactions recorded in Exercise 3-7A, prepare a trial balance for Charlie's Detective Service as of January 31, 20--.

E 3-9A (LO5)
✓ Trial bal. total debits: $42,800

TRIAL BALANCE The following accounts have normal balances. Prepare a trial balance for Damon's Lawn Service as of September 30, 20--.

Cash	$ 10,000
Accounts Receivable	6,000
Supplies	1,600
Prepaid Insurance	1,200
Delivery Equipment	16,000
Accounts Payable	4,000
Damon Young, Capital	20,000
Damon Young, Drawing	2,000
Delivery Fees	18,800
Wages Expense	4,200
Rent Expense	1,800

Provided below is a trial balance for Juanita's Delivery Service. **Use this trial balance for Exercises 3-10A, 3-11A, and 3-12A.**

Juanita's Delivery Service Trial Balance September 30, 20 --		
ACCOUNT TITLE	DEBIT BALANCE	CREDIT BALANCE
Cash	5 0 0 0 00	
Accounts Receivable	3 0 0 0 00	
Supplies	8 0 0 00	
Prepaid Insurance	6 0 0 00	
Delivery Equipment	8 0 0 0 00	
Accounts Payable		2 0 0 0 00
Juanita Raye, Capital		10 0 0 0 00
Juanita Raye, Drawing	1 0 0 0 00	
Delivery Fees		9 4 0 0 00
Wage Expense	2 1 0 0 00	
Rent Expense	9 0 0 00	
	21 4 0 0 00	21 4 0 0 00

E 3-10A (LO5)
✓ Net income: $6,400

INCOME STATEMENT From the information in the trial balance presented above, prepare an income statement for Juanita's Delivery Service for the month ended September 30, 20--.

E 3-11A (LO5)
✓ Capital, 9/30: $15,400

STATEMENT OF OWNER'S EQUITY From the information in the trial balance presented above, prepare a statement of owner's equity for Juanita's Delivery Service for the month ended September 30, 20--.

E 3-12A (LO5)
✓ Total assets, 9/30: $17,400

BALANCE SHEET From the information in the trial balance presented above, prepare a balance sheet for Juanita's Delivery Service as of September 30, 20--.

SERIES A PROBLEMS

P 3-13A (LO2/4/5)
✓ Cash bal. after (p): $14,820 (Dr.); Trial bal. total debits: $38,200

T ACCOUNTS AND TRIAL BALANCE Harold Long started a business in May 20-- called Harold's Home Repair. Long hired a part-time college student as an assistant. Long has decided to use the following accounts for recording transactions:

Assets
- Cash
- Accounts Receivable
- Office Supplies
- Prepaid Insurance
- Equipment
- Van

Liabilities
- Accounts Payable

Owner's Equity
- Harold Long, Capital
- Harold Long, Drawing

Revenue
- Service Fees

Expenses
- Rent Expense
- Wages Expense
- Telephone Expense
- Gas and Oil Expense

(continued)

The following transactions occurred during May:

(a) Invested cash in the business, $20,000.
(b) Purchased a used van for cash, $7,000.
(c) Purchased equipment on account, $5,000.
(d) Received cash for services rendered, $6,000.
(e) Paid cash on account owed from transaction (c), $2,000.
(f) Paid rent for the month, $900.
(g) Paid telephone bill, $200.
(h) Earned revenue on account, $4,000.
(i) Purchased office supplies for cash, $120.
(j) Paid wages to student, $600.
(k) Purchased a one-year insurance policy, $1,200.
(l) Received cash from services performed in transaction (h), $3,000.
(m) Paid cash for gas and oil expense on the van, $160.
(n) Purchased additional equipment for $3,000, paying $1,000 cash and spreading the remaining payments over the next 10 months.
(o) Earned service fees for the remainder of the month of $3,200: $1,800 in cash and $1,400 on account.
(p) Withdrew cash at the end of the month, $2,800.

REQUIRED

1. Enter the transactions in T accounts, identifying each transaction with its corresponding letter.
2. Foot and balance the accounts where necessary.
3. Prepare a trial balance as of May 31, 20--.

P 3-14A (LO5)
✓ Net income: $11,340
✓ Owner's equity, 5/31: $28,540
✓ Total assets, 5/31: $33,540

NET INCOME AND CHANGE IN OWNER'S EQUITY Refer to the trial balance of Harold's Home Repair in Problem 3-13A to determine the following information. Use the format provided below.

1. a. Total revenue for the month ________
   b. Total expenses for the month ________
   c. Net income for the month ________
2. a. Harold Long's original investment in the business ________
   + Net income for the month ________
   − Owner's drawing ________
   Increase (decrease) in capital ________
   = Ending owner's equity ________
   b. End of month accounting equation:

Assets	=	Liabilities	+	Owner's Equity
________	=	________	+	________

P 3-15A (LO5)
✓ NI: $11,340; Capital, 5/31/20--: $28,540; Total assets: $33,540

FINANCIAL STATEMENTS Refer to the trial balance in Problem 3-13A and to the analysis of the change in owner's equity in Problem 3-14A.

REQUIRED

1. Prepare an income statement for Harold's Home Repair for the month ended May 31, 20--.
2. Prepare a statement of owner's equity for Harold's Home Repair for the month ended May 31, 20--.
3. Prepare a balance sheet for Harold's Home Repair as of May 31, 20--.

SERIES B EXERCISES

E 3-1B (LO2)
✓ Accts. Pay: $400 (Cr.)

FOOT AND BALANCE A T ACCOUNT Foot and balance the accounts payable T account shown below.

Accounts Payable	
300	450
250	350
	150

E 3-2B (LO3)

DEBIT AND CREDIT ANALYSIS Complete the following statements using either "debit" or "credit":

(a) The asset account Prepaid Insurance is increased with a ________.
(b) The owner's drawing account is increased with a ________.
(c) The asset account Accounts Receivable is decreased with a ________.
(d) The liability account Accounts Payable is decreased with a ________.
(e) The owner's capital account is increased with a ________.
(f) The revenue account Professional Fees is increased with a ________.
(g) The expense account Repair Expense is increased with a ________.
(h) The asset account Cash is decreased with a ________.
(i) The asset account Delivery Equipment is decreased with a ________.

E 3-3B (LO2/3/4)
✓ Cash bal. after (c): $3,900 (Dr.)

ANALYSIS OF T ACCOUNTS Roberto Alvarez began a business called Roberto's Fix-It Shop.

1. Create T accounts for Cash; Supplies; Roberto Alvarez, Capital; and Utilities Expense. Identify the following transactions by letter and place them on the proper side of the T accounts:

   (a) Invested cash in the business, $6,000.
   (b) Purchased supplies for cash, $1,200.
   (c) Paid utility bill, $900.

2. Foot the T account for cash and enter the ending balance.

E 3-4B (LO3)

NORMAL BALANCE OF ACCOUNT Indicate the normal balance (debit or credit) for each of the following accounts:

1. Cash
2. Rent Expense
3. Notes Payable
4. Owner's Drawing
5. Accounts Receivable
6. Owner's Capital
7. Tools

E 3-5B (LO4)

TRANSACTION ANALYSIS George Atlas started a business on June 1, 20--. Analyze the following transactions for the first month of business using T accounts. Label each T account with the title of the account affected and then place the transaction letter and the dollar amount on the debit or credit side.

(a) Invested cash in the business, $7,000.
(b) Purchased equipment for cash, $900.
(c) Purchased equipment on account, $1,500.
(d) Paid cash on account for equipment purchased in transaction (c), $800.
(e) Withdrew cash for personal use, $1,100.

E 3-6B (LO2)
✓ Cash bal. after (e): $4,200 (Dr.)

FOOT AND BALANCE T ACCOUNTS Foot and balance the T accounts prepared in Exercise 3-5B if necessary.

E 3-7B (LO2/4)
✓ Cash bal. after (k): $9,000 (Dr.)

ANALYSIS OF TRANSACTIONS Nicole Lawrence opened a business called Nickie's Neat Ideas in January 20--. Set up T accounts for the following accounts: Cash; Accounts Receivable; Office Supplies; Computer Equipment; Office Furniture; Accounts Payable; Nicole Lawrence, Capital; Nicole Lawrence, Drawing; Professional Fees; Rent Expense; and Utilities Expense.

The following transactions occurred during the first month of business. Record these transactions in T accounts. After all transactions have been recorded, foot and balance the accounts if necessary.

(a) Invested cash in the business, $18,000.
(b) Purchased office supplies for cash, $500.
(c) Purchased office furniture for cash, $8,000.
(d) Purchased computer and printer on account, $5,000.
(e) Received cash from clients for services, $4,000.
(f) Paid cash on account for computer and printer purchased in transaction (d), $2,000.
(g) Earned professional fees on account during the month, $7,000.
(h) Paid office rent for January, $900.
(i) Paid utility bills for the month, $600.
(j) Received cash from clients that were billed previously in transaction (g), $3,000.
(k) Withdrew cash for personal use, $4,000.

E 3-8B (LO5)
✓ Trial bal. total debits: $32,000

TRIAL BALANCE Based on the transactions recorded in Exercise 3-7B, prepare a trial balance for Nickie's Neat Ideas as of January 31, 20--.

E 3-9B (LO5)
✓ Trial bal. total debits: $55,000

TRIAL BALANCE The following accounts have normal balances. Prepare a trial balance for Betty's Cleaning Service as of September 30, 20--.

Cash	$14,000	Betty Par, Capital	$24,000
Accounts Receivable	8,000	Betty Par, Drawing	4,000
Supplies	1,200	Delivery Fees	25,000
Prepaid Insurance	1,800	Wages Expense	6,000
Delivery Equipment	18,000	Rent Expense	2,000
Accounts Payable	6,000		

Provided below is a trial balance for Bill's Delivery Service. **Use this trial balance for Exercises 3-10B, 3-11B, and 3-12B.**

Bill's Delivery Service
Trial Balance
September 30, 20 --

ACCOUNT TITLE	DEBIT BALANCE	CREDIT BALANCE
Cash	7,000.00	
Accounts Receivable	4,000.00	
Supplies	600.00	
Prepaid Insurance	900.00	
Delivery Equipment	9,000.00	
Accounts Payable		3,000.00
Bill Swift, Capital		12,000.00
Bill Swift, Drawing	2,000.00	
Delivery Fees		12,500.00
Wage Expense	3,000.00	
Rent Expense	1,000.00	
	27,500.00	27,500.00

E 3-10B (LO5)
✓ Net income: $8,500

INCOME STATEMENT From the information in the trial balance presented above, prepare an income statement for Bill's Delivery Service for the month ended September 30, 20--.

E 3-11B (LO5)
✓ Capital, 9/30: $18,500

STATEMENT OF OWNER'S EQUITY From the information in the trial balance presented above, prepare a statement of owner's equity for Bill's Delivery Service for the month ended September 30, 20--.

E 3-12B (LO5)
✓ Total assets, 9/30: $21,500

BALANCE SHEET From the information in the trial balance presented above, prepare a balance sheet for Bill's Delivery Service as of September 30, 20--.

SERIES B PROBLEMS

P 3-13B (LO2/4/5)
✓ Cash bal. after (p): $20,200 (Dr.); Trial bal. total debits: $44,300

KA KLOOSTER & ALLEN

T ACCOUNTS AND TRIAL BALANCE Sue Jantz started a business in August 20-- called Jantz Plumbing Service. Jantz hired a part-time college student as an administrative assistant. Jantz has decided to use the following accounts:

Assets
- Cash
- Accounts Receivable
- Office Supplies
- Prepaid Insurance
- Plumbing Equipment
- Van

Liabilities
- Accounts Payable

Owner's Equity
- Sue Jantz, Capital
- Sue Jantz, Drawing

Revenue
- Service Fees

Expenses
- Rent Expense
- Wages Expense
- Telephone Expense
- Advertising Expense

(continued)

The following transactions occurred during August:

(a) Invested cash in the business, $30,000.
(b) Purchased a used van for cash, $8,000.
(c) Purchased plumbing equipment on account, $4,000.
(d) Received cash for services rendered, $3,000.
(e) Paid cash on account owed from transaction (c), $1,000.
(f) Paid rent for the month, $700.
(g) Paid telephone bill, $100.
(h) Earned revenue on account, $4,000.
(i) Purchased office supplies for cash, $300.
(j) Paid wages to student, $500.
(k) Purchased a one-year insurance policy, $800.
(l) Received cash from services performed in transaction (h), $3,000.
(m) Paid cash for advertising expense, $2,000.
(n) Purchased additional plumbing equipment for $2,000, paying $500 cash and spreading the remaining payments over the next six months.
(o) Earned revenue from services for the remainder of the month of $2,800: $1,100 in cash and $1,700 on account.
(p) Withdrew cash at the end of the month, $3,000.

REQUIRED

1. Enter the transactions in T accounts, identifying each transaction with its corresponding letter.
2. Foot and balance the accounts where necessary.
3. Prepare a trial balance as of August 31, 20--.

P 3-14B (LO5)
✓ Net income: $6,500
✓ Owner's equity, 8/31: $33,500
✓ Total assets, 8/31: $38,000

NET INCOME AND CHANGE IN OWNER'S EQUITY Refer to the trial balance of Jantz Plumbing Service in Problem 3-13B to determine the following information. Use the format provided below.

1.	a.	Total revenue for the month		________
	b.	Total expenses for the month		________
	c.	Net income for the month		________
2.	a.	Sue Jantz's original investment in the business		
		+ Net income for the month	________	
		– Owner's drawing	________	________
		Increase (decrease) in capital		________
		= Ending owner's equity		________
	b.	End of month accounting equation:		

Assets	=	Liabilities	+	Owner's Equity
________	=	________	+	________

P 3-15B (LO5)

✓ NI: $6,500
✓ Capital, 8/31/20--: $33,500
✓ Total assets: $38,000

FINANCIAL STATEMENTS Refer to the trial balance in Problem 3-13B and to the analysis of the change in owner's equity in Problem 3-14B.

REQUIRED

1. Prepare an income statement for Jantz Plumbing Service for the month ended August 31, 20--.
2. Prepare a statement of owner's equity for Jantz Plumbing Service for the month ended August 31, 20--.
3. Prepare a balance sheet for Jantz Plumbing Service as of August 31, 20--.

MANAGING YOUR WRITING

Write a one-page memo to your instructor explaining how you could use the double-entry system to maintain records of your personal finances. What types of accounts would you use for the accounting elements?

MASTERY PROBLEM

✓ Cash bal. after (p): $1,980 (Dr.); Trial bal. debit total: $5,840; Net income: $500; Total assets: $4,300

Craig Fisher started a lawn service called Craig's Quick Cut to earn money over the summer months. Fisher has decided to use the following accounts for recording transactions:

Assets
- Cash
- Accounts Receivable
- Mowing Equipment
- Lawn Tools

Liabilities
- Accounts Payable
- Notes Payable

Owner's Equity
- Craig Fisher, Capital
- Craig Fisher, Drawing

Revenue
- Lawn Fees

Expenses
- Rent Expense
- Wages Expense
- Telephone Expense
- Gas and Oil Expense
- Transportation Expense

Transactions for the month of June are listed below.

(a) Invested cash in the business, $3,000.
(b) Bought mowing equipment for $1,000: paid $200 in cash and promised to pay the balance over the next four months.
(c) Paid garage rent for June, $50.
(d) Provided lawn services for customers on account, $520.
(e) Paid telephone bill, $30.
(f) Borrowed cash from the bank by signing a note payable, $500.
(g) Bought lawn tools, $480.
(h) Collected cash from customers for services performed on account in transaction (d), $400.
(i) Paid associates for lawn work done during the first half of the month, $350.
(j) Paid for gas and oil for the equipment, $60.
(k) Paid cash on account for the mowing equipment purchased in transaction (b), $200.
(l) Earned lawn fees of $1,320: $600 in cash and $720 on account.
(m) Paid associates for last half of month, $700.

(continued)

(n) Reimbursed associates for costs incurred using their own vehicles for transportation, $150.
(o) Paid on note payable to bank, $100.
(p) Withdrew cash for personal use, $200.

REQUIRED

1. Enter the transactions for June in T accounts. Use the accounting equation as a guide for setting up the T accounts.
2. Foot and balance the T accounts where necessary.
3. Prepare a trial balance of the accounts as of June 30, 20--.
4. Prepare an income statement for the month ended June 30, 20--.
5. Prepare a statement of owner's equity for the month ended June 30, 20--.
6. Prepare a balance sheet as of June 30, 20--.

This problem challenges you to apply your cumulative accounting knowledge to move a step beyond the material in the chapter.

✓ Capital, 8/31/20--: $600

CHALLENGE PROBLEM

Your friend Chris Stevick started a part-time business in June and has been keeping her own accounting records. She has been preparing monthly financial statements. At the end of August, she stopped by to show you her performance for the most recent month. She prepared the following income statement and balance sheet:

Income Statement		Balance Sheet	End of Month	Beginning of Month
Revenues	$500	Cash	$600	$400
Expenses	200	Capital	600	400
Net income	$300			

Chris has also heard that there is a statement of owner's equity, but she is not familiar with that statement. She asks if you can help her prepare one. After confirming that she has no assets other than cash, no liabilities, and made no additional investments in the business in August, you agree.

REQUIRED

1. Prepare the statement of owner's equity for your friend's most recent month.
2. What suggestions might you give to Chris that would make her income statement more useful?

ANSWERS TO SELF-STUDY QUESTIONS AND EXERCISES

True/False Questions

1. T 2. F (Liability accounts normally have credit balances.) 3. T 4. F (credit balances) 5. T 6. F (increase)

Multiple Choice Questions

1. c 2. b 3. d 4. c 5. a

U REVU Exercises

1.

Accounts Receivable	
100	50
200	30
300	80
220	

2. (a) The asset account Supplies is increased with a debit.
   (b) The owner's capital account is increased with a credit.
   (c) The rent expense account is increased with a debit.

3.

Cash	
	300

Equipment	
300	

4.

Trial Balance		
Cash	100	
Accounts Receivable	90	
Accounts Payable		20
Capital		40
Sales		200
Rent Expense	70	
	260	260

Chapter 4

COLEONG/DREAMSTIME

LEARNING OBJECTIVES

Careful study of this chapter should enable you to:

LO1 Describe the flow of data from source documents through the trial balance.

LO2 Describe the chart of accounts as a means of classifying financial information.

LO3 Describe and explain the purpose of source documents.

LO4 Journalize transactions.

LO5 Post to the general ledger and prepare a trial balance.

LO6 Explain how to find and correct errors.

Journalizing and Posting Transactions

Campus Advantage (CA) provides a comprehensive range of student residential services in the following areas: management, development, acquisition, and consulting. It specializes in the creation of modern, full-service facilities that are secure, private, and equipped with all of the tools that today's students need for success. Its communities are no-hassle alternatives to dorm living with full dining service options. CA has facilities across the country, but each student residence reflects the unique identity of the school and community it serves.

As with all businesses, CA relies on an accounting system to maintain a record of transactions from the source document through the preparation of the trial balance and financial statements. In this chapter, we discuss source documents, the chart of accounts, and the process used to journalize and post transactions. And, just in case an error is made, we address how to find and correct errors.

The double-entry framework of accounting was explained and illustrated in Chapter 3. To demonstrate the use of debits and credits, business transactions were entered directly into T accounts. Now we will take a more detailed look at the procedures used to account for business transactions.

FLOW OF DATA

LO1 Describe the flow of data from source documents through the trial balance.

This chapter traces the flow of financial data from the source documents through the accounting information system. This process includes the following steps:

1. Analyze what happened by using information from source documents and the firm's chart of accounts.
2. Enter business transactions in the general journal in the form of journal entries.
3. Post these journal entries to the accounts in the general ledger.
4. Prepare a trial balance.

The flow of data from the source documents through the preparation of a trial balance is shown in Figure 4-1.

FIGURE 4-1 Flow of Data from Source Documents through Trial Balance

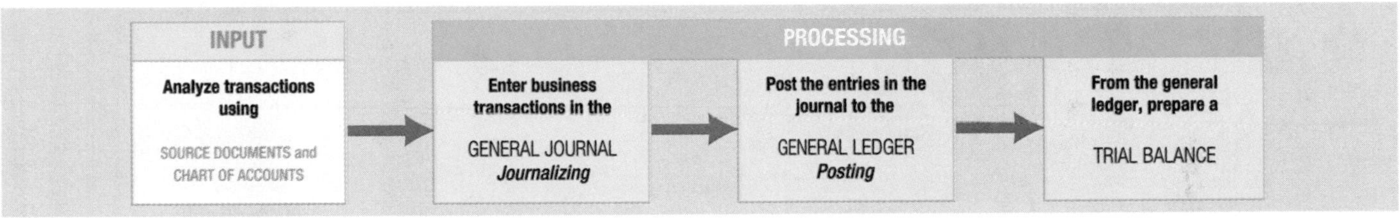

THE CHART OF ACCOUNTS

LO2 Describe the chart of accounts as a means of classifying financial information.

You learned in Chapters 2 and 3 that there are three basic questions that must be answered when analyzing transactions.

1. What happened?
2. Which accounts are affected?
3. How is the accounting equation affected?

To determine which accounts are affected (step 2), the accountant must know the accounts being used by the business. A list of all accounts used by a business is called a **chart of accounts**.

The chart of accounts includes the account titles in numeric order for all assets, liabilities, owner's equity, revenues, and expenses. The numbering should follow a consistent pattern. In Jessie Jane's Campus Delivery Service, asset accounts begin with "1," liability accounts begin with "2," owner's equity accounts begin with "3," revenue accounts begin with "4," and expense accounts begin with "5." Jessie uses three-digit numbers for all accounts.

A chart of accounts for Jessie Jane's Campus Delivery Service is shown in Figure 4-2. Jessie would not need many accounts initially because the business is new. Additional accounts can easily be added as needed. Note that the accounts are arranged according to the accounting equation.

FIGURE 4-2 Chart of Accounts

JESSIE JANE'S CAMPUS DELIVERY SERVICE CHART OF ACCOUNTS			
Assets	**(100–199)**	**Revenues**	**(400–499)**
101	Cash	401	Delivery Fees
122	Accounts Receivable		
141	Supplies	**Expenses**	**(500–599)**
145	Prepaid Insurance	511	Wages Expense
185	Delivery Equipment	521	Rent Expense
		525	Telephone Expense
Liabilities	**(200–299)**		
202	Accounts Payable		
Owner's Equity	**(300–399)**		
311	Jessica Jane, Capital		
312	Jessica Jane, Drawing		

Assets begin with 1

Liabilities begin with 2

Owner's Equity begin with 3

Revenues begin with 4

Expenses begin with 5

SOURCE DOCUMENTS

LO3 Describe and explain the purpose of source documents.

Almost any document that provides information about a business transaction can be called a **source document**. A source document triggers the analysis of what happened. It begins the process of entering transactions in the accounting system. Examples of source documents are shown in Figure 4-3. These source documents provide information that is useful in determining the effect of business transactions on specific accounts.

In addition to serving as input for transaction analysis, source documents serve as objective evidence of business transactions. If anyone questions the accounting records, these documents may be used as objective, verifiable evidence of the accuracy of the accounting records. For this reason, source documents are filed for possible future reference. *Having objective, verifiable evidence that a transaction occurred is an important accounting concept.*

FIGURE 4-3 Source Documents

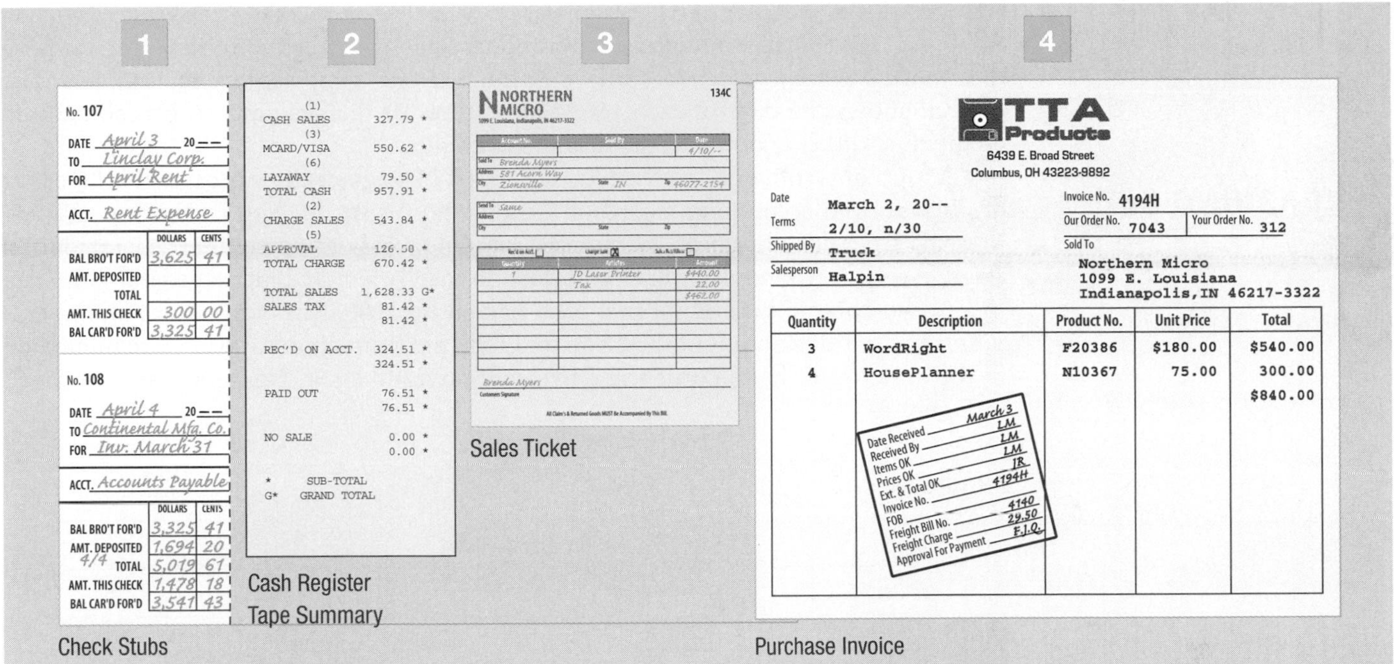

SOURCE DOCUMENTS	
Example	**Provides Information About**
1. Check stubs or copies of checks	Cash payments
2. Receipt stubs, copies of receipts, cash register tapes, or memos of cash register totals	Cash receipts
3. Copies of sales tickets or sales invoices issued to customers or clients	Sales of goods or services
4. Purchase invoices received from suppliers	Purchase of goods or services

A Broader View

Electronic Source Documents

With the ability to go shopping in cyberspace, more transactions are being initiated electronically. Even Best Buy, known for its low prices and excellent in-store service, has "online" shopping at http://www.bestbuy.com. Customers can place orders and these orders can be filled, all based on electronic communications. This means that more and more "source documents" will be in an electronic form.

U REVU

Complete U REVU-1 on **page 114** to test your basic understanding of LO3.

THE GENERAL JOURNAL

LO4 Journalize transactions.

LEARNING KEY

A journal provides a day-by-day listing of all transactions completed by the business.

A day-by-day listing of the transactions of a business is called a **journal.** The purpose of a journal is to provide a record of all transactions completed by the business. The journal shows the date of each transaction, titles of the accounts to be debited and credited, and the amounts of the debits and credits.

A journal is commonly referred to as a **book of original entry** because it is here that the first formal accounting record of a transaction is made. Although many types of journals are used in business, the simplest journal form is a two-column general journal (Figure 4-4). Any kind of business transaction may be entered into a general journal.

A **two-column general journal** is so-named because it has only two amount columns, one for debit amounts and one for credit amounts. Journal pages are numbered in the upper right-hand corner. The five column numbers in Figure 4-4 are explained in Figure 4-5.

FIGURE 4-4 Two-Column General Journal

GENERAL JOURNAL PAGE 1

	DATE		DESCRIPTION	POST. REF.	DEBIT	CREDIT	
1	20--	1	2	3	4	5	1
2							2
3							3

FIGURE 4-5 The Columns in a Two-Column General Journal

Column 1 Date	The year is entered in small figures at the top of the column immediately below the column heading. The year is repeated only at the top of each new page. The month is entered for the first entry on the page and for the first transaction of the month. The day of the month is recorded for every transaction, even if it is the same as the prior entry.
Column 2 Description	The *Description* or *Explanation* column is used to enter the titles of the accounts affected by each transaction and to provide a very brief description of the transaction. Each transaction affects two or more accounts. The account(s) to be debited are entered first at the extreme left of the column. The account(s) to be credited are listed after the debits and indented. The description should be entered immediately following the last credit entry with an additional indentation.
Column 3 Posting Reference	No entries are made in the *Posting Reference* column during journalizing. Entries are made in this column when the debits and credits are copied to the proper accounts in the ledger. This process will be explained in detail later in this chapter.
Column 4 Debit Amount	The *Debit amount column* is used to enter the amount to be debited to an account. The amount should be entered on the same line as the title of that account.
Column 5 Credit Amount	The *Credit amount column* is used to enter the amount to be credited to an account. The amount should be entered on the same line as the title of that account.

JOURNALIZING

LEARNING KEY

When journalizing, the exact account titles shown in the chart of accounts must be used. Refer to the chart of accounts in Figure 4-2 as you review the entries for Jessie Jane's Campus Delivery Service.

Entering the transactions in a journal is called **journalizing.** For every transaction, the entry should include the date, the title of each account affected, the amounts, and a brief description.

To illustrate the journalizing process, transactions for the first month of operations of Jessie Jane's Campus Delivery Service will be journalized. The transactions are listed in Figure 4-6. Since you analyzed these transactions in Chapters 2 and 3, the journalizing process should be easier to understand. Let's start with a close look at the steps followed when journalizing the first transaction, Jessie's initial investment of $2,000.

FIGURE 4-6 Summary of Transactions

SUMMARY OF TRANSACTIONS JESSIE JANE'S CAMPUS DELIVERY SERVICE		
Transaction		
(a)	June 1	Jessica Jane invested cash in her business, $2,000.
(b)	3	Bought delivery equipment for cash, $1,200.
(c)	5	Bought delivery equipment on account from Big Red Scooters, $900.
(d)	6	Paid first installment from transaction (c) to Big Red Scooters, $300.
(e)	6	Received cash for delivery services rendered, $500.
(f)	7	Paid cash for June office rent, $200.
(g)	15	Paid telephone bill, $50.
(h)	15	Made deliveries on account for a total of $600: Accounting Department ($400) and the School of Music ($200).
(i)	16	Bought supplies for cash, $80.
(j)	18	Paid cash for an eight-month liability insurance policy, $200. Coverage began on June 1.
(k)	20	Received $570 in cash for services performed in transaction (h): $400 from the Accounting Department and $170 from the School of Music.
(l)	25	Bought a third scooter from Big Red Scooters, $1,500. Paid $300 cash, with the remaining payments expected over the next four months.
(m)	27	Paid wages of part-time employees, $650.
(n)	30	Earned delivery fees for the remainder of the month amounting to $1,050: $430 in cash and $620 on account. Deliveries on account: Accounting Department ($250) and Athletic Ticket Office ($370).
(o)	30	Jessie withdrew cash for personal use, $150.

Transaction (a)

June 1 Jessica Jane opened a bank account with a deposit of $2,000 for her business.

STEP 1 **Enter the date.** Since this is the first entry on the journal page, the year is entered on the first line of the Date column (in small print at the top of the line). The month and day are entered on the same line, below the year, in the Date column.

GENERAL JOURNAL PAGE 1

	DATE		DESCRIPTION	POST. REF.	DEBIT	CREDIT	
1	20-- June	1					1
2							2

STEP 2 **Enter the debit.** Cash is entered on the first line at the extreme left of the Description column. The amount of the debit, $2,000, is entered on the same line in the Debit column. Since this is not a formal financial statement, dollar signs are not used.

In Chapter 3, we simply debited the T account.

Cash	
(a) 2,000	

GENERAL JOURNAL PAGE 1

	DATE		DESCRIPTION	POST. REF.	DEBIT	CREDIT	
1	20-- June	1	Cash		2 0 0 0 00		1
2							2

STEP 3 **Enter the credit.** The title of the account to be credited, Jessica Jane, Capital, is entered on the second line, **indented one-half inch from the left side of the Description column.** The amount of the credit, $2,000, is entered on the same line in the Credit column.

In Chapter 3, we simply credited the T account.

Jessica Jane, Capital	
	(a) 2,000

GENERAL JOURNAL PAGE 1

	DATE		DESCRIPTION	POST. REF.	DEBIT	CREDIT	
1	20-- June	1	Cash		2 0 0 0 00		1
2			Jessica Jane, Capital			2 0 0 0 00	2

STEP 4 **Enter the explanation.** The explanation of the entry is entered on the next line, **indented an additional one-half inch.** The second line of the explanation, if needed, is also indented the same distance as the first.

GENERAL JOURNAL PAGE 1

	DATE		DESCRIPTION	POST. REF.	DEBIT	CREDIT	
1	20-- June	1	Cash		2 0 0 0 00		1
2			Jessica Jane, Capital			2 0 0 0 00	2
3			Owner's original investment in				3
4			delivery business				4

Enter the next transaction. To enter transaction (b), the purchase of a motor scooter for $1,200 cash, we skip a line and follow the same four steps. Note that the month and year do not need to be repeated. The day of the month must, however, be entered.

GENERAL JOURNAL PAGE 1

	DATE		DESCRIPTION	POST. REF.	DEBIT	CREDIT	
1	20-- June	1	Cash		2 0 0 0 00		1
2			Jessica Jane, Capital			2 0 0 0 00	2
3			Owner's original investment in				3
4			delivery business				4
5 (Skip a line)							5
6		3	Delivery Equipment		1 2 0 0 00		6
7			Cash			1 2 0 0 00	7
8			Purchased delivery equipment for cash				8

The journal entries for the month of June are shown in Figure 4-7. Note that the entries on June 25 and June 30 affect more than two accounts. Entries requiring more than one debit and/or one credit are called **compound entries**. The entry on June 25 has two credits. The credits are listed after the debit, indented and listed one under the other. The entry on June 30 has two debits. They are aligned with the left margin of the Description column and listed one under the other. In both cases, the debits equal the credits.

FIGURE 4-7 General Journal Entries

GENERAL JOURNAL PAGE 1

	DATE		DESCRIPTION	POST. REF.	DEBIT	CREDIT	
1	20-- June	1	Cash		2000 00		1
2			Jessica Jane, Capital			2000 00	2
3			Owner's original investment in				3
4			delivery business				4
5							5
6			Delivery Equipment		1200 00		6
7			Cash			1200 00	7
8			Purchased delivery equipment for cash				8
9							9
10		5	Delivery Equipment		900 00		10
11			Accounts Payable			900 00	11
12			Purchased delivery equipment on account				12
13			from Big Red Scooters				13
14							14
15		6	Accounts Payable		300 00		15
16			Cash			300 00	16
17			Made partial payment to Big Red Scooters				17
18							18
19		6	Cash		500 00		19
20			Delivery Fees			500 00	20
21			Received cash for delivery services				21
22							22
23		7	Rent Expense		200 00		23
24			Cash			200 00	24
25			Paid office rent for June				25
26							26
27		15	Telephone Expense		50 00		27
28			Cash			50 00	28
29			Paid telephone bill for June				29
30							30
31		15	Accounts Receivable		600 00		31
32			Delivery Fees			600 00	32
33			Deliveries made on account for Accounting				33
34			Department ($400) and School of Music ($200)				34
35							35

List debits first.

List credits second and indented.

Explanation is third and indented.

Space to make entries easier to read. To prevent improper changes to entries, the extra spacing might not be used in practice.

(continued)

FIGURE 4-7 General Journal Entries (*concluded*)

GENERAL JOURNAL PAGE 2

DATE		DESCRIPTION	POST. REF.	DEBIT	CREDIT
20-- June	16	Supplies		80 00	
		Cash			80 00
		Purchased supplies for cash			
	18	Prepaid Insurance		200 00	
		Cash			200 00
		Paid premium for eight-month			
		insurance policy			
	20	Cash		570 00	
		Accounts Receivable			570 00
		Received cash on account from Accounting			
		Department ($400) and School of Music ($170)			
	25	Delivery Equipment		1 500 00	
		Accounts Payable			1 200 00
		Cash			300 00
		Purchased scooter with down payment;			
		balance on account with Big Red Scooters			
	27	Wages Expense		650 00	
		Cash			650 00
		Paid employees			
	30	Cash		430 00	
		Accounts Receivable		620 00	
		Delivery Fees			1 050 00
		Deliveries made for cash and on account to			
		Accounting Department ($250) and			
		Athletic Ticket Office ($370)			
	30	Jessica Jane, Drawing		150 00	
		Cash			150 00
		Owner's withdrawal			

Line up credits

Compound entry

Debits = Credits

Line up debits

Compound entry

Debits = Credits

U REVU

Complete U REVU-2 on **page 114** to test your basic understanding of LO4.

THE GENERAL LEDGER

LO5 Post to the general ledger and prepare a trial balance.

The journal provides a day-by-day record of business transactions. To determine the current balance of specific accounts, however, the information in the journal must be transferred to accounts similar to the T accounts illustrated in Chapter 3. This process is called posting.

LEARNING KEY

While the journal provides a day-by-day record of business transactions, the ledger provides a record of the transactions entered in each account.

A complete set of all the accounts used by a business is known as the **general ledger.** The general ledger accumulates a complete record of the debits and credits made to each account as a result of entries made in the journal. The accounts are numbered and arranged in the same order as the chart of accounts. That is, accounts are numbered and grouped by classification: assets, liabilities, owner's equity, revenues, and expenses.

GENERAL LEDGER ACCOUNT

For purposes of illustration, the T account was introduced in Chapter 3. In practice, businesses are more likely to use a version of the account called the **general ledger account.** Figure 4-8 compares the cash T account from Chapter 3 for Jessie Jane's Campus Delivery Service and a general ledger account summarizing the same cash transactions.

A three-column account with just one column for the normal balance also may be used for some purposes.

A four-column general ledger account contains columns for the debit or credit transaction and columns for the debit or credit running balance. In addition, there are columns for the date, description of the item, and posting reference.

The Item column is used to provide descriptions of special entries. For example, "Balance" is written in this column when the balance of an account is transferred to a new page. In addition, "Correcting," "Adjusting," "Closing," or "Reversing" may be written in this column when these types of entries are made. Correcting entries are described later in the chapter. Adjusting, closing, and reversing entries are illustrated in Chapters 5, 6, and 15, respectively.

The Posting Reference (Post. Ref.) column is used to indicate the journal page from which an entry was posted, or a check mark (✓) is inserted to indicate that no posting was required.

As shown in Figure 4-8, the primary advantage of the T account is that the debit and credit sides of the account are easier to identify. Thus, for demonstration purposes

FIGURE 4-8 Comparison of T Account and General Ledger Account

Cash

(a) 2,000	(b) 1,200
(e) 500	(d) 300
(k) 570	(f) 200
(n) 430	(g) 50
3,500	(i) 80
	(j) 200
	(l) 300
	(m) 650
	(o) 150
Bal. 370	*3,130*

GENERAL LEDGER

ACCOUNT: Cash ACCOUNT NO. 101

DATE		ITEM	POST. REF.	DEBIT	CREDIT	BALANCE DEBIT	BALANCE CREDIT
20-- June	1			2 0 0 0 00		2 0 0 0 00	
	3				1 2 0 0 00	8 0 0 00	
	6				3 0 0 00	5 0 0 00	
	6			5 0 0 00		1 0 0 0 00	
	7				2 0 0 00	8 0 0 00	
	15				5 0 00	7 5 0 00	
	16				8 0 00	6 7 0 00	
	18				2 0 0 00	4 7 0 00	
	20			5 7 0 00		1 0 4 0 00	
	25				3 0 0 00	7 4 0 00	
	27				6 5 0 00	9 0 00	
	30			4 3 0 00		5 2 0 00	
	30				1 5 0 00	3 7 0 00	

Transaction Amount (Debit and Credit columns) — Running Balance (Balance columns)

LEARNING KEY

The general ledger account is similar to the T account, but makes it easier to maintain a running balance.

and analyzing what happened, T accounts are very helpful. However, computing the balance of a T account is cumbersome. The primary advantage of the general ledger account is that it maintains a running balance.

Note that the heading for the general ledger account has the account title and an account number. The account number is taken from the chart of accounts and is used in the posting process.

POSTING TO THE GENERAL LEDGER

LEARNING KEY

Posting is simply the process of copying the exact dates and dollar amounts from the journal to the ledger.

The process of copying the debits and credits from the journal to the ledger accounts is known as **posting.** All amounts entered in the journal must be posted to the general ledger accounts. Posting from the journal to the ledger is done daily or at frequent intervals.

To illustrate the posting process, the first journal entry for Jessie Jane's Campus Delivery Service will be posted step by step. There are five steps in the process of posting each debit and credit. First, let's post the debit to Cash (Figure 4-9).

FIGURE 4-9 Posting a Debit

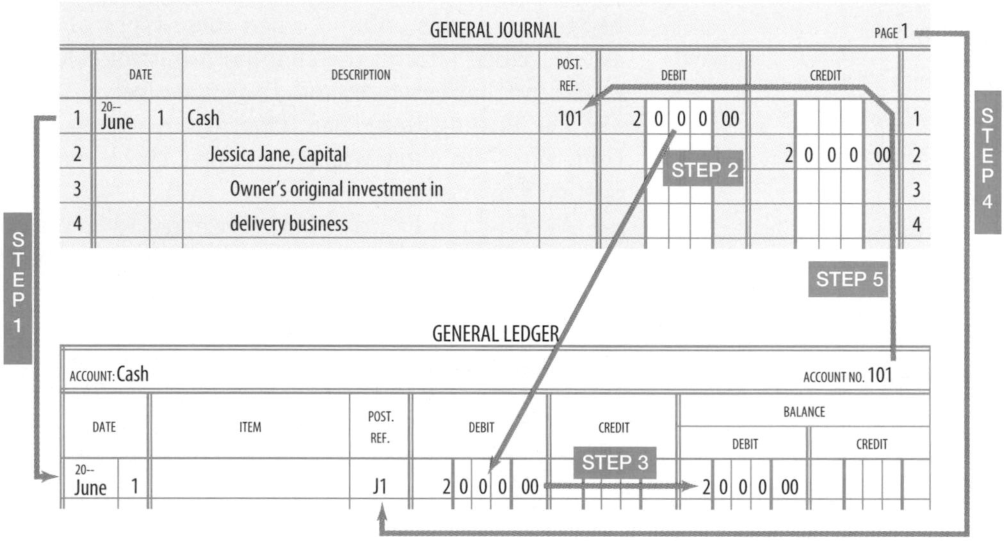

In the ledger account:

STEP 1 **Enter the date of the transaction in the Date column.** Enter the year, "20--," the month, "June," and the day, "1," in the Date column of the cash account.

STEP 2 **Enter the debit.** Copy the $2,000 debit to Cash in the journal to the Debit column of the ledger. Since this is not a formal financial statement, dollar signs are not used.

STEP 3 **Enter the balance of the account.** Enter the $2,000 balance in the Balance columns under Debit. (If the balance of the account is zero, draw a line through the Debit and Credit columns.)

STEP 4 **Enter the journal page in the Posting Reference column.** Enter "J1" in the Posting Reference column since the posting came from page 1 of the journal.

The Item column is left blank, except for special reasons such as indicating the beginning balance, adjusting, correcting, closing, or reversing entries.

LEARNING KEY

Posting references indicate that a journal entry has been posted to the general ledger.

In the journal:

STEP 5 **Enter the ledger account number in the Posting Reference column.** Enter the account number for Cash, 101 (see chart of accounts in Figure 4-2 on page 88), in the Posting Reference column of the journal on the same line as the debit to Cash for $2,000.

Step 5 is the last step in the posting process. After this step is completed, the posting references will indicate which journal entries have been posted to the ledger accounts. This is very helpful, particularly if you are interrupted during the posting process. The information in the Posting Reference columns of the journal and ledger provides a link between the journal and ledger known as a **cross-reference.**

Now let's post the credit portion of the first entry (Figure 4-10).

FIGURE 4-10 Posting a Credit

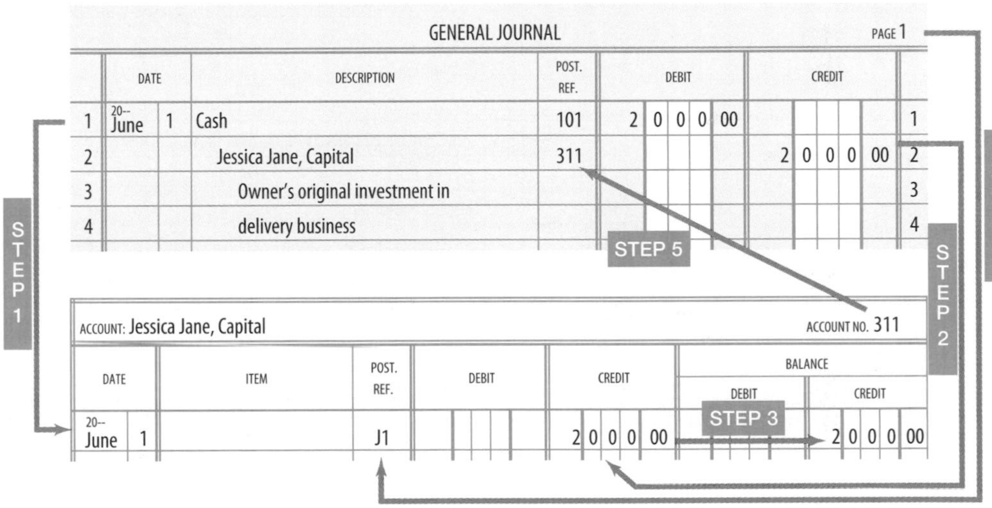

In the ledger account:

STEP 1 **Enter the date of the transaction in the Date column.** Enter the year, "20--," the month, "June," and the day, "1," in the Date column of the account Jessica Jane, Capital.

STEP 2 **Enter the credit.** Copy the $2,000 credit to Jessica Jane, Capital in the journal to the Credit column in the ledger.

STEP 3 **Enter the balance of the account.** Enter the $2,000 balance in the Balance columns under Credit. (If the balance of the account is zero, draw a line through the Debit and Credit columns.)

STEP 4 **Enter the journal page in the Posting Reference column.** Enter "J1" in the Posting Reference column since the posting came from page 1 of the journal.

In the journal:

STEP 5 **Enter the ledger account number in the Posting Reference column.** Enter the account number for Jessica Jane, Capital, 311, in the Posting Reference column. Again, this last step indicates that the credit has been posted to the general ledger.

After posting the journal entries for Jessie Jane's Campus Delivery Service for the month of June, the general journal and general ledger should appear as illustrated in Figures 4-11 and 4-12 on pages 98–101. *Note that the Posting Reference column of the journal has been filled in because the entries have been posted.*

FIGURE 4-11 General Journal After Posting

GENERAL JOURNAL PAGE 1

	DATE		DESCRIPTION	POST. REF.	DEBIT	CREDIT	
1	20-- June	1	Cash	101	2000 00		1
2			Jessica Jane, Capital	311		2000 00	2
3			Owner's original investment in				3
4			delivery business				4
5							5
6		3	Delivery Equipment	185	1200 00		6
7			Cash	101		1200 00	7
8			Purchased delivery equipment for cash				8
9							9
10		5	Delivery Equipment	185	900 00		10
11			Accounts Payable	202		900 00	11
12			Purchased delivery equipment on account				12
13			from Big Red Scooters				13
14							14
15		6	Accounts Payable	202	300 00		15
16			Cash	101		300 00	16
17			Made partial payment to Big Red Scooters				17
18							18
19		6	Cash	101	500 00		19
20			Delivery Fees	401		500 00	20
21			Received cash for delivery services				21
22							22
23		7	Rent Expense	521	200 00		23
24			Cash	101		200 00	24
25			Paid office rent for June				25
26							26
27		15	Telephone Expense	525	50 00		27
28			Cash	101		50 00	28
29			Paid telephone bill for June				29
30							30
31		15	Accounts Receivable	122	600 00		31
32			Delivery Fees	401		600 00	32
33			Deliveries made on account for Accounting				33
34			Department ($400) and School of Music ($200)				34
35							35

FIGURE 4-11 General Journal After Posting *(concluded)*

GENERAL JOURNAL PAGE 2

DATE		DESCRIPTION	POST. REF.	DEBIT	CREDIT
20-- June	16	Supplies	141	80 00	
		Cash	101		80 00
		Purchased supplies for cash			
	18	Prepaid Insurance	145	200 00	
		Cash	101		200 00
		Paid premium for eight-month			
		insurance policy			
	20	Cash	101	570 00	
		Accounts Receivable	122		570 00
		Received cash on account from Accounting			
		Department ($400) and School of Music ($170)			
	25	Delivery Equipment	185	1,500 00	
		Accounts Payable	202		1,200 00
		Cash	101		300 00
		Purchased scooter with down payment;			
		balance on account with Big Red Scooters			
	27	Wages Expense	511	650 00	
		Cash	101		650 00
		Paid employees			
	30	Cash	101	430 00	
		Accounts Receivable	122	620 00	
		Delivery Fees	401		1,050 00
		Deliveries made for cash and on account to			
		Accounting Department ($250) and			
		Athletic Ticket Office ($370)			
	30	Jessica Jane, Drawing	312	150 00	
		Cash	101		150 00
		Owner's withdrawal			

FIGURE 4-12 General Ledger After Posting

GENERAL LEDGER

ACCOUNT: Cash — ACCOUNT NO. 101

DATE		ITEM	POST. REF.	DEBIT	CREDIT	BALANCE DEBIT	BALANCE CREDIT
20-- June	1		J1	2,000.00		2,000.00	
	3		J1		1,200.00	800.00	
	6		J1		300.00	500.00	
	6		J1	500.00		1,000.00	
	7		J1		200.00	800.00	
	15		J1		50.00	750.00	
	16		J2		80.00	670.00	
	18		J2		200.00	470.00	
	20		J2	570.00		1,040.00	
	25		J2		300.00	740.00	
	27		J2		650.00	90.00	
	30		J2	430.00		520.00	
	30		J2		150.00	370.00	

ACCOUNT: Accounts Receivable — ACCOUNT NO. 122

DATE		ITEM	POST. REF.	DEBIT	CREDIT	BALANCE DEBIT	BALANCE CREDIT
20-- June	15		J1	600.00		600.00	
	20		J2		570.00	30.00	
	30		J2	620.00		650.00	

ACCOUNT: Supplies — ACCOUNT NO. 141

DATE		ITEM	POST. REF.	DEBIT	CREDIT	BALANCE DEBIT	BALANCE CREDIT
20-- June	16		J2	80.00		80.00	

ACCOUNT: Prepaid Insurance — ACCOUNT NO. 145

DATE		ITEM	POST. REF.	DEBIT	CREDIT	BALANCE DEBIT	BALANCE CREDIT
20-- June	18		J2	200.00		200.00	

ACCOUNT: Delivery Equipment — ACCOUNT NO. 185

DATE		ITEM	POST. REF.	DEBIT	CREDIT	BALANCE DEBIT	BALANCE CREDIT
20-- June	3		J1	1,200.00		1,200.00	
	5		J1	900.00		2,100.00	
	25		J2	1,500.00		3,600.00	

For asset, expense, and drawing accounts, a running balance is maintained by adding the debit or subtracting the credit from the balance shown on the line above.

FIGURE 4-12 General Ledger After Posting *(concluded)*

For liability, revenue, and capital accounts, a running balance is maintained by adding the credit or subtracting the debit from the balance shown on the line above.

ACCOUNT: Accounts Payable — ACCOUNT NO. 202

DATE		ITEM	POST. REF.	DEBIT	CREDIT	BALANCE DEBIT	BALANCE CREDIT
20-- June	5		J1		900 00		900 00
	6		J1	300 00			600 00
	25		J2		1200 00		1800 00

ACCOUNT: Jessica Jane, Capital — ACCOUNT NO. 311

DATE		ITEM	POST. REF.	DEBIT	CREDIT	BALANCE DEBIT	BALANCE CREDIT
20-- June	1		J1		2000 00		2000 00

ACCOUNT: Jessica Jane, Drawing — ACCOUNT NO. 312

DATE		ITEM	POST. REF.	DEBIT	CREDIT	BALANCE DEBIT	BALANCE CREDIT
20-- June	30		J2	150 00		150 00	

ACCOUNT: Delivery Fees — ACCOUNT NO. 401

DATE		ITEM	POST. REF.	DEBIT	CREDIT	BALANCE DEBIT	BALANCE CREDIT
20-- June	6		J1		500 00		500 00
	15		J1		600 00		1100 00
	30		J2		1050 00		2150 00

ACCOUNT: Wages Expense — ACCOUNT NO. 511

DATE		ITEM	POST. REF.	DEBIT	CREDIT	BALANCE DEBIT	BALANCE CREDIT
20-- June	27		J2	650 00		650 00	

ACCOUNT: Rent Expense — ACCOUNT NO. 521

DATE		ITEM	POST. REF.	DEBIT	CREDIT	BALANCE DEBIT	BALANCE CREDIT
20-- June	7		J1	200 00		200 00	

ACCOUNT: Telephone Expense — ACCOUNT NO. 525

DATE		ITEM	POST. REF.	DEBIT	CREDIT	BALANCE DEBIT	BALANCE CREDIT
20-- June	15		J1	50 00		50 00	

THE TRIAL BALANCE

In Chapter 3, a **trial balance** was used to prove that the totals of the debit and credit balances in the T accounts were equal. In this chapter, a trial balance is used to prove the equality of the debits and credits in the ledger accounts. A trial balance can be prepared daily, weekly, monthly, or whenever desired. Before preparing a trial balance, all transactions should be journalized and posted so that the effect of all transactions will be reflected in the ledger accounts.

The trial balance for Jessie Jane's Campus Delivery Service shown in Figure 4-13 was prepared from the balances in the general ledger in Figure 4-12. The accounts are listed in the order used in the chart of accounts. This order is also often used when preparing financial statements. In Chapter 2, we pointed out that many firms list expenses from highest to lowest amounts. Some firms list expenses according to the chart of accounts, which is the method we will follow.

LEARNING KEY

The chart of accounts determines the order for listing accounts in the general ledger and trial balance. This order may also be used when preparing financial statements.

FIGURE 4-13 Trial Balance

Jessie Jane's Campus Delivery Service
Trial Balance
June 30, 20 - -

ACCOUNT TITLE	ACCOUNT NO.	DEBIT BALANCE	CREDIT BALANCE
Cash	101	370 00	
Accounts Receivable	122	650 00	
Supplies	141	80 00	
Prepaid Insurance	145	200 00	
Delivery Equipment	185	3600 00	
Accounts Payable	202		1800 00
Jessica Jane, Capital	311		2000 00
Jessica Jane, Drawing	312	150 00	
Delivery Fees	401		2150 00
Wages Expense	511	650 00	
Rent Expense	521	200 00	
Telephone Expense	525	50 00	
		5950 00	5950 00

Even though the trial balance indicates that the ledger is in balance, the ledger can still contain errors. For example, if a journal entry was made debiting or crediting the wrong accounts, or if an item was posted to the wrong account, the ledger will still be in balance. It is important, therefore, to be very careful in preparing the journal entries and in posting them to the ledger accounts.

U REVU

Complete U REVU-3 on **page 114** to test your basic understanding of LO5.

FINDING AND CORRECTING ERRORS IN THE TRIAL BALANCE

LO6 Explain how to find and correct errors.

Tips are available to help if your trial balance has an error. Figure 4-14 offers hints for finding the error when your trial balance does not balance.

FIGURE 4-14 Tips for Finding Errors in the Trial Balance

1. Double check your addition. Review balances to see if they are too large or small, relative to other accounts, or entered in the wrong column.
2. Find the difference between the debits and the credits.
   a. If the difference is equal to the amount of a specific transaction, perhaps you forgot to post the debit or credit portion of this transaction.
   b. Divide the difference by 2. If the difference is evenly divisible by 2, you may have posted two debits or two credits for a transaction. If a debit was posted as a credit, it would mean that one transaction had two credits and no debits. The difference between the total debits and credits would be twice the amount of the debit that was posted as a credit.
   c. Divide the difference by 9. If the difference is evenly divisible by 9, you may have committed a **slide error** or a **transposition error**. A slide occurs when debit or credit amounts "slide" a digit or two to the left or right when entered. For example, if *$250* was entered as *$25*:

$250	−	$25	=	$225
$225	÷	9	=	$25

The difference is evenly divisible by 9.

A transposition occurs when two digits are reversed. For example, if *$250* was entered as *$520*:

$520	−	$250	=	$270
$270	÷	9	=	$30

Again, the difference is evenly divisible by 9.

If the tips in Figure 4-14 don't work, you must retrace your steps through the accounting process. Double check your addition for the ledger accounts. Also trace all postings. Be patient as you search for your error. Use this process as an opportunity to reinforce your understanding of the flow of information through the accounting system. Much can be learned while looking for an error.

Once you have found an error, there are two methods of making the correction. Although you may want to erase when correcting your homework, this is not acceptable in practice. An erasure may suggest that you are trying to hide something. You should use the ruling method or make a correcting entry instead.

RULING METHOD

The **ruling method** should be used to correct two types of errors.

1. When an incorrect journal entry has been made, but not yet posted.
2. When a proper entry has been made but posted to the wrong account or for the wrong amount.

When using the ruling method, draw a single line through the incorrect account title or amount and write the correct information directly above the line. Corrections should be initialed by someone authorized to make such changes. This is done so the source and reason for the correction can be traced. This type of correction may be made in the journal or ledger accounts, as shown in Figure 4-15.

FIGURE 4-15 Ruling Method of Making a Correction

GENERAL JOURNAL PAGE 2

	DATE		DESCRIPTION	POST. REF.	DEBIT	CREDIT	
	20--						
1	Sept.	17	~~Entertainment Expense~~ Wages Expense MP		650 00		1
2			Cash			650 00	2
3			Paid employees				3
4							4
5		18	Prepaid Insurance		~~20 00~~ MP 200 00		5
6			Cash			~~20 00~~ MP 200 00	6
7			Paid premium for eight-month				7
8			insurance policy				8
9							9

Slide

GENERAL LEDGER

ACCOUNT: Accounts Payable ACCOUNT NO. 202

DATE		ITEM	POST. REF.	DEBIT	CREDIT	BALANCE DEBIT	BALANCE CREDIT
20--							
Sept.	8		J1		700 00		700 00
	15		J1	200 00			500 00
	25		J2		~~2,100 00~~ 1,200 00 MP		~~2,600 00~~ MP 1,700 00

Transposition

CORRECTING ENTRY METHOD

If an incorrect entry has been journalized and posted to the wrong account, a **correcting entry** should be made. For example, assume that a $400 payment for Rent Expense was incorrectly debited to Repair Expense and correctly credited to Cash. This requires a correcting entry and explanation as shown in Figure 4-16. Figure 4-17 shows the effects of the correcting entry on the ledger accounts. Generally, "Correcting" is written in the Item column of the general ledger account.

FIGURE 4-16 Correcting Entry Method

GENERAL JOURNAL PAGE 6

	DATE		DESCRIPTION	POST. REF.	DEBIT	CREDIT	
	20--						
1	Sept.	25	Rent Expense	521	400 00		1
2			Repair Expense	537		400 00	2
3			To correct error in which payment for rent				3
4			was debited to Repair Expense				4
5							5

FIGURE 4-17 Effects of Correcting Entry on Ledger Accounts

GENERAL LEDGER

ACCOUNT: Rent Expense — ACCOUNT NO. 521

DATE		ITEM	POST. REF.	DEBIT	CREDIT	BALANCE DEBIT	BALANCE CREDIT
20-- Sept.	25	Correcting	J6	400 00		400 00	

ACCOUNT: Repair Expense — ACCOUNT NO. 537

DATE		ITEM	POST. REF.	DEBIT	CREDIT	BALANCE DEBIT	BALANCE CREDIT
20-- Sept.	10		J5	50 00		50 00	
	15		J5	400 00		450 00	
	25	Correcting	J6		400 00	50 00	

U REVU Complete U REVU-4 on **page 114** to test your basic understanding of LO6

SELF-STUDY

LEARNING OBJECTIVES Key Points to Remember

LO1 Describe the flow of data from source documents through the trial balance.

The flow of data from the source documents through the trial balance is as follows:

1. Analyze business transactions.
2. Journalize transactions in the general journal.
3. Post journal entries to the general ledger.
4. Prepare a trial balance.

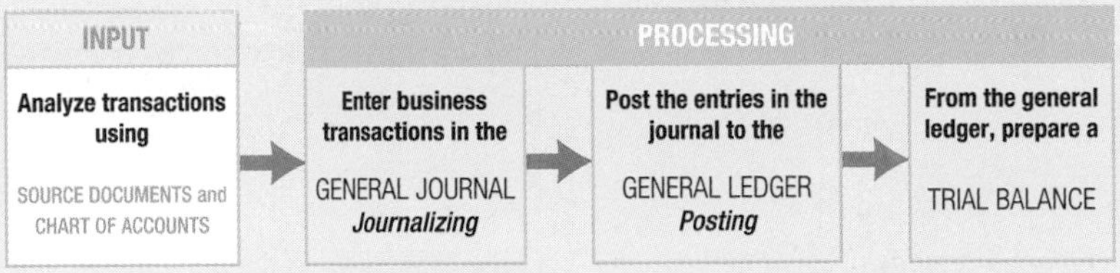

LEARNING OBJECTIVES Key Points to Remember

LO2 Describe the chart of accounts as a means of classifying financial information.	The chart of accounts includes the account titles in numerical order for all assets, liabilities, owner's equity, revenues, and expenses. The chart of accounts is used in classifying information about transactions.
LO3 Describe and explain the purpose of source documents.	Source documents trigger the analysis of business transactions and the entries into the accounting system.
LO4 Journalize transactions.	A journal provides a day-by-day listing of transactions. The journal shows the date, titles of the accounts to be debited or credited, and the amounts of the debits and credits. The steps in the journalizing process are as follows: 1. Enter the date. 2. Enter the debit. Accounts to be debited are entered first. 3. Enter the credit. Accounts to be credited are entered after the debits and are indented one-half inch. 4. Enter the explanation. A brief explanation of the transaction should be entered in the description column on the line following the last credit. The explanation should be indented an additional one-half inch.
LO5 Post to the general ledger and prepare a trial balance.	The general ledger is a complete set of all accounts used by the business. The steps in posting from the general journal to the general ledger are as follows: In the general ledger: 1. Enter the date of each transaction. 2. Enter the amount of each debit or credit in the Debit or Credit column. 3. Enter the new balance. 4. Enter the journal page number from which each transaction is posted in the Posting Reference column. In the journal: 5. Enter the account number to which each transaction is posted in the Posting Reference column. The trial balance provides a check to make sure the total of all debit balances in the ledger accounts equals the total of all credit balances in the ledger accounts.
LO6 Explain how to find and correct errors.	Errors may be found by verifying your addition, by dividing the difference between the debits and credits by 2 or 9, and by retracing your steps through the accounting process. Use the ruling method or the correcting entry method to correct the error.

DEMONSTRATION PROBLEM

George Fielding is a financial planning consultant. He provides budgeting, estate planning, tax planning, and investing advice for professional golfers. He developed the following chart of accounts for his business:

Assets	**Revenues**
101 Cash	401 Professional Fees
142 Office Supplies	
	Expenses
Liabilities	511 Wages Expense
202 Accounts Payable	521 Rent Expense
	525 Telephone Expense
Owner's Equity	533 Utilities Expense
311 George Fielding, Capital	534 Charitable Contributions Expense
312 George Fielding, Drawing	538 Automobile Expense

The following transactions took place during the month of December of the current year:

Dec. 1	Fielding invested cash to start the business, $20,000.
3	Paid Bollhorst Real Estate for December office rent, $1,000.
4	Received cash from Aaron Patton, a client, for services, $2,500.
6	Paid T. Z. Anderson Electric for December heating and light, $75.
7	Received cash from Andrew Conder, a client, for services, $2,000.
12	Paid Fichter's Super Service for gasoline and oil purchases for the company car, $60.
14	Paid Hillenburg Staffing for temporary secretarial services during the past two weeks, $600.
17	Bought office supplies from Bowers Office Supply on account, $280.
20	Paid Mitchell Telephone Co. for business calls during the past month, $100.
21	Fielding withdrew cash for personal use, $1,100.
24	Made donation to the National Multiple Sclerosis Society, $100.
27	Received cash from Billy Walters, a client, for services, $2,000.
28	Paid Hillenburg Staffing for temporary secretarial services during the past two weeks, $600.
29	Made payment on account to Bowers Office Supply, $100.

REQUIRED

1. Record the preceding transactions in a general journal.
2. Post the entries to the general ledger.
3. Prepare a trial balance.
4. Prepare an income statement, statement of owner's equity, and balance sheet for the month of December.

(continued)

Solution 1, 2.

GENERAL JOURNAL PAGE 1

DATE		DESCRIPTION	POST. REF.	DEBIT	CREDIT
20-- Dec.	1	Cash	101	20,000.00	
		George Fielding, Capital	311		20,000.00
		Owner's original investment in			
		consulting business			
	3	Rent Expense	521	1,000.00	
		Cash	101		1,000.00
		Paid rent for December			
	4	Cash	101	2,500.00	
		Professional Fees	401		2,500.00
		Received cash for services rendered			
	6	Utilities Expense	533	75.00	
		Cash	101		75.00
		Paid utilities			
	7	Cash	101	2,000.00	
		Professional Fees	401		2,000.00
		Received cash for services rendered			
	12	Automobile Expense	538	60.00	
		Cash	101		60.00
		Paid for gas and oil			
	14	Wages Expense	511	600.00	
		Cash	101		600.00
		Paid temporary secretaries			
	17	Office Supplies	142	280.00	
		Accounts Payable	202		280.00
		Purchased office supplies on account from			
		Bowers Office Supply			

GENERAL JOURNAL PAGE 2

DATE		DESCRIPTION	POST. REF.	DEBIT	CREDIT
20-- Dec.	20	Telephone Expense	525	100 00	
		Cash	101		100 00
		Paid telephone bill			
	21	George Fielding, Drawing	312	1100 00	
		Cash	101		1100 00
		Owner's withdrawal			
	24	Charitable Contributions Expense	534	100 00	
		Cash	101		100 00
		Contribution to National Multiple			
		Sclerosis Society			
	27	Cash	101	2000 00	
		Professional Fees	401		2000 00
		Received cash for services rendered			
	28	Wages Expense	511	600 00	
		Cash	101		600 00
		Paid temporary secretaries			
	29	Accounts Payable	202	100 00	
		Cash	101		100 00
		Payment on account to Bowers Office Supply			

2.

GENERAL LEDGER

ACCOUNT: Cash ACCOUNT NO. 101

DATE		ITEM	POST. REF.	DEBIT	CREDIT	BALANCE DEBIT	BALANCE CREDIT
20-- Dec.	1		J1	20000 00		20000 00	
	3		J1		1000 00	19000 00	
	4		J1	2500 00		21500 00	
	6		J1		75 00	21425 00	
	7		J1	2000 00		23425 00	
	12		J1		60 00	23365 00	
	14		J1		600 00	22765 00	
	20		J2		100 00	22665 00	
	21		J2		1100 00	21565 00	
	24		J2		100 00	21465 00	
	27		J2	2000 00		23465 00	
	28		J2		600 00	22865 00	
	29		J2		100 00	22765 00	

(continued)

ACCOUNT: Office Supplies ACCOUNT NO. 142

DATE		ITEM	POST. REF.	DEBIT	CREDIT	BALANCE DEBIT	BALANCE CREDIT
20-- Dec.	17		J1	280 00		280 00	

ACCOUNT: Accounts Payable ACCOUNT NO. 202

DATE		ITEM	POST. REF.	DEBIT	CREDIT	BALANCE DEBIT	BALANCE CREDIT
20-- Dec.	17		J1		280 00		280 00
	29		J2	100 00			180 00

ACCOUNT: George Fielding, Capital ACCOUNT NO. 311

DATE		ITEM	POST. REF.	DEBIT	CREDIT	BALANCE DEBIT	BALANCE CREDIT
20-- Dec.	1		J1		20 000 00		20 000 00

ACCOUNT: George Fielding, Drawing ACCOUNT NO. 312

DATE		ITEM	POST. REF.	DEBIT	CREDIT	BALANCE DEBIT	BALANCE CREDIT
20-- Dec.	21		J2	1 100 00		1 100 00	

ACCOUNT: Professional Fees ACCOUNT NO. 401

DATE		ITEM	POST. REF.	DEBIT	CREDIT	BALANCE DEBIT	BALANCE CREDIT
20-- Dec.	4		J1		2 500 00		2 500 00
	7		J1		2 000 00		4 500 00
	27		J2		2 000 00		6 500 00

ACCOUNT: Wages Expense ACCOUNT NO. 511

DATE		ITEM	POST. REF.	DEBIT	CREDIT	BALANCE DEBIT	BALANCE CREDIT
20-- Dec.	14		J1	600 00		600 00	
	28		J2	600 00		1 200 00	

ACCOUNT: Rent Expense ACCOUNT NO. 521

DATE		ITEM	POST. REF.	DEBIT	CREDIT	BALANCE DEBIT	BALANCE CREDIT
20-- Dec.	3		J1	1 000 00		1 000 00	

ACCOUNT: Telephone Expense ACCOUNT NO. 525

DATE		ITEM	POST. REF.	DEBIT	CREDIT	BALANCE DEBIT	BALANCE CREDIT
20-- Dec.	20		J2	100.00		100.00	

ACCOUNT: Utilities Expense ACCOUNT NO. 533

DATE		ITEM	POST. REF.	DEBIT	CREDIT	BALANCE DEBIT	BALANCE CREDIT
20-- Dec.	6		J1	75.00		75.00	

ACCOUNT: Charitable Contributions Expense ACCOUNT NO. 534

DATE		ITEM	POST. REF.	DEBIT	CREDIT	BALANCE DEBIT	BALANCE CREDIT
20-- Dec.	24		J2	100.00		100.00	

ACCOUNT: Automobile Expense ACCOUNT NO. 538

DATE		ITEM	POST. REF.	DEBIT	CREDIT	BALANCE DEBIT	BALANCE CREDIT
20-- Dec.	12		J1	60.00		60.00	

3.

George Fielding, Financial Planning Consultant
Trial Balance
December 31, 20 --

ACCOUNT TITLE	ACCOUNT NO.	DEBIT BALANCE	CREDIT BALANCE
Cash	101	22,765.00	
Office Supplies	142	280.00	
Accounts Payable	202		180.00
George Fielding, Capital	311		20,000.00
George Fielding, Drawing	312	1,100.00	
Professional Fees	401		6,500.00
Wages Expense	511	1,200.00	
Rent Expense	521	1,000.00	
Telephone Expense	525	100.00	
Utilities Expense	533	75.00	
Charitable Contributions Expense	534	100.00	
Automobile Expense	538	60.00	
		26,680.00	26,680.00

(continued)

4.

George Fielding, Financial Planning Consultant
Income Statement
For Month Ended December 31, 20 --

Revenue:		
Proffessional fees		$6,500.00
Expenses:		
Wages expense	$1,200.00	
Rent expense	1,000.00	
Telephone expense	100.00	
Utilities expense	75.00	
Charitable contributions expense	100.00	
Automobile expense	60.00	
Total expenses		2,535.00
Net income		$3,965.00

George Fielding, Financial Planning Consultant
Statement of Owner's Equity
For Month Ended December 31, 20 --

George Fielding, capital, December 1, 20 --		$ —
Investments during December		20,000.00
Total investment		$20,000.00
Net income for December	$3,965.00	
Less withdrawals for December	1,100.00	
Increase in capital		2,865.00
George Fielding, Capital, December 1, 20 --		$22,865.00

George Fielding, Financial Planning Consultant
Balance Sheet
December 31, 20 --

Assets		Liabilities	
Cash	$22,765.00	Accounts payable	$ 180.00
Office Supplies	280.00	Owner's equity	
		George Fielding, capital	22,865.00
Total assets	$23,045.00	Total liabilities and owner's equity	$23,045.00

KEY TERMS

book of original entry (90) The journal or the first formal accounting record of a transaction.

chart of accounts (87) A list of all accounts used by a business.

compound entry (93) A general journal entry that affects more than two accounts.

correcting entry (104) An entry to correct an incorrect entry that has been journalized and posted to the wrong account.

cross-reference (97) The information in the Posting Reference columns of the journal and ledger that provides a link between the journal and ledger.

general ledger (95) A complete set of all the accounts used by a business. The general ledger accumulates a complete record of the debits and credits made to each account as a result of entries made in the journal.

general ledger account (95) An account with columns for the debit or credit transaction and columns for the debit or credit running balance.

journal (90) A day-by-day listing of the transactions of a business.

journalizing (90) Entering the transactions in a journal.

posting (96) Copying the debits and credits from the journal to the ledger accounts.

ruling method (103) A method of correcting an entry in which a line is drawn through the error and the correct information is placed above it.

slide error (103) An error that occurs when debit or credit amounts "slide" a digit or two to the left or right.

source document (88) Any document that provides information about a business transaction.

transposition error (103) An error that occurs when two digits are reversed.

trial balance (102) A list used to prove that the totals of the debit and credit balances in the ledger accounts are equal.

two-column general journal (90) A journal with only two amount columns, one for debit amounts and one for credit amounts.

SELF-STUDY QUESTIONS AND EXERCISES

True/False Questions

1. LO2 The chart of accounts lists capital accounts first, followed by liabilities, assets, expenses, and revenue.
2. LO3 Source documents serve as historical evidence of business transactions.
3. LO4 No entries are made in the Posting Reference column at the time of journalizing.
4. LO4 When entering the credit item in a general journal, it should be listed after all debits and indented.
5. LO6 When an incorrect entry has been journalized and posted to the wrong account, a correcting entry should be made.

Multiple Choice Questions

1. LO2 A revenue account will begin with the number ________ in the chart of accounts.

   (a) 1 (c) 3
   (b) 2 (d) 4

(continued)

2. LO3 Which of the following is not a source document?
   (a) Check stub
   (b) Cash register tape
   (c) Journal entry
   (d) Purchase invoice

3. LO4 To purchase an asset such as office equipment on account, you would credit which account?
   (a) Cash
   (b) Accounts Receivable
   (c) Accounts Payable
   (d) Capital

4. LO4 When fees are earned and the customer promises to pay later, which account is debited?
   (a) Cash
   (b) Accounts Receivable
   (c) Accounts Payable
   (d) Capital

5. LO6 When the correct numbers are used but are in the wrong order, the error is called a
   (a) transposition.
   (b) slide.
   (c) ruling.
   (d) correcting entry.

U REVU Exercises

1. LO3 A check stub serves as a source document for what kind of transaction?
2. LO4 Indicate the information that would be entered for each of the lettered items in the general journal provided below.

GENERAL JOURNAL — PAGE

	DATE		DESCRIPTION	POST. REF.	DEBIT	CREDIT	
1	A B	C	D	G	H		1
2			E	J		I	2
3			F				3
4							4
5							5

3. LO5 Indicate the information that would be entered for each of the lettered items in the general ledger account provided below.

GENERAL LEDGER

ACCOUNT: A — ACCOUNT NO. B

DATE		ITEM	POST. REF.	DEBIT	CREDIT	BALANCE DEBIT	BALANCE CREDIT
C D	E	F	G	H	I	J	K

4. LO6 Dunkin Company made the following entry for the payment of $500 cash for rent expense:

Rent Expense	500	
Rent Payable		500

   Prepare a correcting entry.

The answers to the Self-Study Questions and Exercises are at the end of the chapter (pages 128–129).

REVIEW QUESTIONS

LO1 1. Trace the flow of accounting information through the accounting system.

LO2 2. Explain the purpose of a chart of accounts.

LO2 3. Name the five types of financial statement classifications for which it is ordinarily desirable to keep separate accounts.

LO3 4. Name a source document that provides information about each of the following types of business transactions:
   a. Cash payment
   b. Cash receipt
   c. Sale of goods or services
   d. Purchase of goods or services

LO4 5. Where is the first formal accounting record of a business transaction usually made?

LO4 6. Describe the four steps required to journalize a business transaction in a general journal.

LO5 7. In what order are the accounts customarily placed in the ledger?

LO5 8. Explain the primary advantage of a general ledger account.

LO5 9. Explain the five steps required when posting the journal to the ledger.

LO5 10. What information is entered in the Posting Reference column of the journal as an amount is posted to the proper account in the ledger?

LO6 11. Explain why the ledger can still contain errors even though the trial balance is in balance. Give examples of two such types of errors.

LO6 12. What is a slide error?

LO6 13. What is a transposition error?

LO6 14. What is the ruling method of correcting an error?

LO6 15. What is the correcting entry method?

SERIES A EXERCISES

E 4-1A **(LO3)**

SOURCE DOCUMENTS Source documents trigger the analysis of events requiring an accounting entry. Match the following source documents with the type of information they provide.

1. Check stubs or check register
2. Purchase invoice from suppliers (vendors)
3. Sales tickets or invoices to customers
4. Receipts or cash register tapes

a. A good or service has been sold.
b. Cash has been received by the business.
c. Cash has been paid by the business.
d. Goods or services have been purchased by the business.

E 4-2A **(LO4)**

GENERAL JOURNAL ENTRIES For each of the following transactions, list the account to be debited and the account to be credited in the general journal.

(continued)

1. Invested cash in the business, $5,000.
2. Paid office rent, $500.
3. Purchased office supplies on account, $300.
4. Received cash for services rendered (fees), $400.
5. Paid cash on account, $50.
6. Rendered services on account, $300.
7. Received cash for an amount owed by a customer, $100.

E 4-3A **(LO5)**
✓ Final Cash bal.: $4,950

GENERAL LEDGER ACCOUNTS Set up T accounts for each of the general ledger accounts needed for Exercise 4-2A and post debits and credits to the accounts. Foot the accounts and enter the balances. Prove that total debits equal total credits.

E 4-4A **(LO4)**

GENERAL JOURNAL ENTRIES Jean Jones has opened Jones Consulting. Journalize the following transactions that occurred during January of the current year. Use the following journal pages: January 1–10, page 1, and January 11–29, page 2. Use the following chart of accounts:

Chart of Accounts

Assets
101 Cash
142 Office Supplies
181 Office Equipment

Liabilities
202 Accounts Payable

Owner's Equity
311 Jean Jones, Capital
312 Jean Jones, Drawing

Revenues
401 Consulting Fees

Expenses
511 Wages Expense
521 Rent Expense
525 Telephone Expense
533 Utilities Expense
549 Miscellaneous Expense

Jan. 1 Jones invested cash in the business, $10,000.
2 Paid office rent, $500.
3 Purchased office equipment on account, $1,500.
5 Received cash for services rendered, $750.
8 Paid telephone bill, $65.
10 Paid for a magazine subscription (miscellaneous expense), $15.
11 Purchased office supplies on account, $300.
15 Made a payment on account (see Jan. 3 transaction), $150.
18 Paid part-time employee, $500.
21 Received cash for services rendered, $350.
25 Paid utilities bill, $85.
27 Jones withdrew cash for personal use, $100.
29 Paid part-time employee, $500.

E 4-5A **(LO5)**
✓ Final Cash bal.: $9,185;
Trial bal. total debits: $12,750

GENERAL LEDGER ACCOUNTS; TRIAL BALANCE Set up general ledger accounts using the chart of accounts provided in Exercise 4-4A. Post the transactions from Exercise 4-4A to the general ledger accounts and prepare a trial balance.

E 4-6A **(LO5)**

✓ Total assets, Jan. 31: $10,985

FINANCIAL STATEMENTS From the information in Exercises 4-4A and 4-5A, prepare an income statement, a statement of owner's equity, and a balance sheet.

E 4-7A **(LO5)**

✓ Total assets, July 31: $7,100

FINANCIAL STATEMENTS From the following trial balance taken after one month of operation, prepare an income statement, a statement of owner's equity, and a balance sheet.

TJ's Paint Service
Trial Balance
July 31, 20 - -

ACCOUNT TITLE	ACCOUNT NO.	DEBIT BALANCE	CREDIT BALANCE
Cash	101	4 3 0 0 00	
Accounts Receivable	122	1 1 0 0 00	
Supplies	141	8 0 0 00	
Paint Equipment	183	9 0 0 00	
Accounts Payable	202		2 1 5 0 00
TJ Ulza, Capital	311		3 2 0 5 00
TJ Ulza, Drawing	312	5 0 0 00	
Painting Fees	401		3 6 0 0 00
Wages Expense	511	9 0 0 00	
Rent Expense	521	2 5 0 00	
Telephone Expense	525	5 0 00	
Transportation Expense	526	6 0 00	
Utilities Expense	533	7 0 00	
Miscellaneous Expense	549	2 5 00	
		8 9 5 5 00	8 9 5 5 00

E 4-8A **(LO6)**

FINDING AND CORRECTING ERRORS Joe Adams bought $500 worth of office supplies on account. The following entry was recorded on May 17. Find the error(s) and correct it (them) using the ruling method.

	Date		Description	Post. Ref.	Debit	Credit	
14							14
15	20-- May	17	Office Equipment		4 0 0 00		15
16			Cash			4 0 0 00	16
17			Purchased copy paper				17

On May 25, after the transactions had been posted, Adams discovered that the following entry contains an error. The cash received represents a collection on account, rather than new service fees. Correct the error in the general journal using the correcting entry method.

	Date		Description	Post. Ref.	Debit	Credit	
22							22
23	20-- May	23	Cash	101	1 0 0 0 00		23
24			Service Fees	401		1 0 0 0 00	24
25			Received cash for services previously earned				25

SERIES A PROBLEMS

P 4-9A (LO4/5)

✓ Cash bal., Jan. 31: $10,021; Trial bal. total debits: $13,460

JOURNALIZING AND POSTING TRANSACTIONS Annette Creighton opened Creighton Consulting. She rented a small office and paid a part-time worker to answer the telephone and make deliveries. Her chart of accounts is as follows:

Chart of Accounts

Assets		Revenues	
101	Cash	401	Consulting Fees
142	Office Supplies		
181	Office Equipment	Expenses	
		511	Wages Expense
Liabilities		512	Advertising Expense
202	Accounts Payable	521	Rent Expense
		525	Telephone Expense
Owner's Equity		526	Transportation Expense
311	Annette Creighton, Capital	533	Utilities Expense
312	Annette Creighton, Drawing	549	Miscellaneous Expense

Creighton's transactions for the first month of business are as follows:

Jan. 1 Creighton invested cash in the business, $10,000.
1 Paid rent, $500.
2 Purchased office supplies on account, $300.
4 Purchased office equipment on account, $1,500.
6 Received cash for services rendered, $580.
7 Paid telephone bill, $42.
8 Paid utilities bill, $38.
10 Received cash for services rendered, $360.
12 Made payment on account, $50.
13 Paid for car rental while visiting an out-of-town client (transportation expense), $150.
15 Paid part-time worker, $360.
17 Received cash for services rendered, $420.
18 Creighton withdrew cash for personal use, $100.
20 Paid for a newspaper ad, $26.
22 Reimbursed part-time employee for cab fare incurred delivering materials to clients (transportation expense), $35.
24 Paid for books on consulting practices (miscellaneous expense), $28.
25 Received cash for services rendered, $320.
27 Made payment on account for office equipment purchased, $150.
29 Paid part-time worker, $360.
30 Received cash for services rendered, $180.

REQUIRED

1. Set up general ledger accounts from the chart of accounts.
2. Journalize the transactions for January in a two-column general journal. Use the following journal page numbers: January 1–10, page 1; January 12–24, page 2; January 25–30, page 3.

3. Post the transactions to the general ledger.
4. Prepare a trial balance.
5. Prepare an income statement and a statement of owner's equity for the month of January and a balance sheet as of January 31, 20--.

P 4-10A **(LO4/5)**
✓ Cash bal., June 30: $3,958;
Trial bal. total debits: $22,358

JOURNALIZING AND POSTING TRANSACTIONS Jim Andrews opened a delivery business in March. He rented a small office and has a part-time assistant. His trial balance shows accounts for the first three months of business.

Jim's Quick Delivery
Trial Balance
May 31, 20 - -

ACCOUNT TITLE	ACCOUNT NO.	DEBIT BALANCE	CREDIT BALANCE
Cash	101	3,826.00	
Accounts Receivable	122	1,212.00	
Office Supplies	142	648.00	
Office Equipment	181	2,100.00	
Delivery Truck	185	8,000.00	
Accounts Payable	202		6,000.00
Jim Andrews, Capital	311		4,478.00
Jim Andrews, Drawing	312	1,800.00	
Delivery Fees	401		9,880.00
Wages Expense	511	1,200.00	
Advertising Expense	512	90.00	
Rent Expense	521	900.00	
Telephone Expense	525	126.00	
Electricity Expense	533	98.00	
Charitable Contributions Expense	534	60.00	
Gas and Oil Expense	538	186.00	
Miscellaneous Expense	549	112.00	
		20,358.00	20,358.00

Andrews' transactions for the month of June are as follows:

June 1 Paid rent, $300.
2 Performed delivery services for $300: $100 in cash and $200 on account.
4 Paid for newspaper advertising, $15.
6 Purchased office supplies on account, $180.
7 Received cash for delivery services rendered, $260.
9 Paid cash on account (truck payment), $200.
10 Purchased a copier (office equipment) for $700: paid $100 in cash and put $600 on account.
11 Made a contribution to the Red Cross (charitable contributions), $20.
12 Received cash for delivery services rendered, $380.
13 Received cash on account for services previously rendered, $100.
15 Paid a part-time worker, $200.
16 Paid electric bill, $36.
18 Paid telephone bill, $46.
19 Received cash on account for services previously rendered, $100.

(continued)

June 20	Andrews withdrew cash for personal use, $200.
21	Paid for gas and oil, $32.
22	Made payment on account (for office supplies), $40.
24	Received cash for services rendered, $340.
26	Paid for a magazine subscription (miscellaneous expense), $15.
27	Received cash for services rendered, $180.
27	Received cash on account for services previously rendered, $100.
29	Paid for gasoline, $24.
30	Paid a part-time worker, $200.

REQUIRED

1. Set up general ledger accounts by entering the balances as of June 1.
2. Journalize the transactions for June in a two-column general journal. Usc thc following journal pages: June 1–10, page 7; June 11–20, page 8; June 21–30, page 9.
3. Post the entries to the general ledger.
4. Prepare a trial balance.

P 4-11A **(LO6)**

CORRECTING ERRORS Assuming that all entries have been posted, prepare correcting entries for each of the following errors.

1. The following entry was made to record the purchase of $500 in supplies on account:

Supplies	142	500	
Cash	101		500

2. The following entry was made to record the payment of $300 in wages:

Rent Expense	521	300	
Cash	101		300

3. The following entry was made to record a $200 payment to a supplier on account:

Supplies	142	100	
Cash	101		100

SERIES B EXERCISES

E 4-1B **(LO3)**

SOURCE DOCUMENTS What type of information is found on each of the following source documents?

1. Cash register tape
2. Sales ticket (issued to customer)
3. Purchase invoice (received from supplier or vendor)
4. Check stub

E 4-2B **(LO4)**

GENERAL JOURNAL ENTRIES For each of the following transactions, list the account to be debited and the account to be credited in the general journal.

1. Invested cash in the business, $1,000.
2. Performed services on account, $200.

3. Purchased office equipment on account, $500.
4. Received cash on account for services previously rendered, $200.
5. Made a payment on account, $100.

E 4-3B **(LO5)**
✓ Final Cash bal.: $1,100

GENERAL LEDGER ACCOUNTS Set up T accounts for each of the general ledger accounts needed for Exercise 4-2B and post debits and credits to the accounts. Foot the accounts and enter the balances. Prove that total debits equal total credits.

E 4-4B **(LO4)**

GENERAL JOURNAL ENTRIES Sengel Moon opened The Bike Doctor. Journalize the following transactions that occurred during the month of October of the current year. Use the following journal pages: October 1–12, page 1, and October 14–29, page 2. Use the following chart of accounts:

Chart of Accounts

Assets
101 Cash
141 Bicycle Parts
142 Office Supplies

Liabilities
202 Accounts Payable

Owner's Equity
311 Sengel Moon, Capital
312 Sengel Moon, Drawing

Revenues
401 Repair Fees

Expenses
511 Wages Expense
521 Rent Expense
525 Telephone Expense
533 Utilities Expense
549 Miscellaneous Expense

Oct. 1	Moon invested cash in the business, $15,000.
2	Paid shop rental for the month, $300.
3	Purchased bicycle parts on account, $2,000.
5	Purchased office supplies on account, $250.
8	Paid telephone bill, $38.
9	Received cash for services, $140.
11	Paid a sports magazine subscription (miscellaneous expense), $15.
12	Made payment on account (see Oct. 3 transaction), $100.
14	Paid part-time employee, $300.
15	Received cash for services, $350.
16	Paid utilities bill, $48.
19	Received cash for services, $250.
23	Moon withdrew cash for personal use, $50.
25	Made payment on account (see Oct. 5 transaction), $50.
29	Paid part-time employee, $300.

E 4-5B **(LO5)**
✓ Final Cash bal.: $14,539; Trial bal. total debits: $17,840

GENERAL LEDGER ACCOUNTS; TRIAL BALANCE Set up general ledger accounts using the chart of accounts provided in Exercise 4-4B. Post the transactions from Exercise 4-4B to the general ledger accounts and prepare a trial balance.

E 4-6B **(LO5)**
✓ Total assets, Oct. 31: $16,789

FINANCIAL STATEMENTS From the information in Exercises 4-4B and 4-5B, prepare an income statement, a statement of owner's equity, and a balance sheet.

E 4-7B (LO5)

✓ Total assets, Mar. 31: $11,900

FINANCIAL STATEMENTS From the following trial balance taken after one month of operation, prepare an income statement, a statement of owner's equity, and a balance sheet.

AT Speaker's Bureau Trial Balance March 31, 20 - -			
ACCOUNT TITLE	ACCOUNT NO.	DEBIT BALANCE	CREDIT BALANCE
Cash	101	6600 00	
Accounts Receivable	122	2800 00	
Office Supplies	142	1000 00	
Office Equipment	181	1500 00	
Accounts Payable	202		3000 00
AT Speaker, Capital	311		6098 00
AT Speaker, Drawing	312	800 00	
Speaking Fees	401		4800 00
Wages Expense	511	400 00	
Rent Expense	521	200 00	
Telephone Expense	525	35 00	
Travel Expense	526	450 00	
Utilities Expense	533	88 00	
Miscellaneous Expense	549	25 00	
		13898 00	13898 00

E 4-8B (LO6)

FINDING AND CORRECTING ERRORS Mary Smith purchased $350 worth of office equipment on account. The following entry was recorded on April 6. Find the error(s) and correct it (them) using the ruling method.

7							7
8	20-- Apr.	6	Office Supplies		530 00		8
9			Cash			530 00	9
10			Purchased office equipment				10

On April 25, after the transactions had been posted, Smith discovered the following entry contains an error. When her customer received services, Cash was debited, but no cash was received. Correct the error in the journal using the correcting entry method.

27							27
28	20-- Apr.	21	Cash	101	300 00		28
29			Service Fees	401		300 00	29
30			Revenue earned from services				30
31			previously rendered				31

SERIES B PROBLEMS

P 4-9B **(LO4/5)**

✓ Cash bal., May 31: $4,500; Trial bal. total debits: $8,790

JOURNALIZING AND POSTING TRANSACTIONS Benito Mendez opened Mendez Appraisals. He rented office space and has a part-time secretary to answer the telephone and make appraisal appointments. His chart of accounts is as follows:

Chart of Accounts

Assets		Revenues	
101	Cash	401	Appraisal Fees
122	Accounts Receivable		
142	Office Supplies	Expenses	
181	Office Equipment	511	Wages Expense
		512	Advertising Expense
Liabilities		521	Rent Expense
202	Accounts Payable	525	Telephone Expense
		526	Transportation Expense
Owner's Equity		533	Electricity Expense
311	Benito Mendez, Capital	549	Miscellaneous Expense
312	Benito Mendez, Drawing		

Mendez's transactions for the first month of business are as follows:

May 1	Mendez invested cash in the business, $5,000.
2	Paid rent, $500.
3	Purchased office supplies, $100.
4	Purchased office equipment on account, $2,000.
5	Received cash for services rendered, $280.
8	Paid telephone bill, $38.
9	Paid electric bill, $42.
10	Received cash for services rendered, $310.
13	Paid part-time employee, $500.
14	Paid car rental for out-of-town trip, $200.
15	Paid for newspaper ad, $30.
18	Received cash for services rendered, $620.
19	Paid mileage reimbursement for part-time employee's use of personal car for business deliveries (transportation expense), $22.
21	Mendez withdrew cash for personal use, $50.
23	Made payment on account for office equipment purchased earlier, $200.
24	Earned appraisal fee, which will be paid in a week, $500.
26	Paid for newspaper ad, $30.
27	Paid for local softball team sponsorship (miscellaneous expense), $15.
28	Paid part-time employee, $500.
29	Received cash on account, $250.
30	Received cash for services rendered, $280.
31	Paid cab fare (transportation expense), $13.

(continued)

REQUIRED

1. Set up general ledger accounts from the chart of accounts.
2. Journalize the transactions for May in a two-column general journal. Use the following journal page numbers: May 1–10, page 1; May 13–24, page 2; May 26–31, page 3.
3. Post the transactions to the general ledger.
4. Prepare a trial balance.
5. Prepare an income statement and a statement of owner's equity for the month of May, and a balance sheet as of May 31, 20--.

P 4-10B **(LO4/5)**

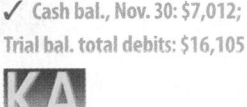

✓ Cash bal., Nov. 30: $7,012; Trial bal. total debits: $16,105

JOURNALIZING AND POSTING TRANSACTIONS Ann Taylor owns a suit tailoring shop. She opened business in September. She rented a small work space and has an assistant to receive job orders and process claim tickets. Her trial balance shows her account balances for the first two months of business.

Taylor Tailoring
Trial Balance
October 31, 20 --

ACCOUNT TITLE	ACCOUNT NO.	DEBIT BALANCE	CREDIT BALANCE
Cash	101	6 211 00	
Accounts Receivable	122	484 00	
Tailoring Supplies	141	1 000 00	
Tailoring Equipment	183	3 800 00	
Accounts Payable	202		4 125 00
Ann Taylor, Capital	311		6 130 00
Ann Taylor, Drawing	312	800 00	
Tailoring Fees	401		3 600 00
Wages Expense	511	800 00	
Advertising Expense	512	34 00	
Rent Expense	521	600 00	
Telephone Expense	525	60 00	
Electricity Expense	533	44 00	
Miscellaneous Expense	549	22 00	
		13 855 00	13 855 00

Taylor's transactions for November are as follows:

Nov. 1 Paid rent, $300.
2 Purchased tailoring supplies on account, $150.
3 Purchased a new button hole machine on account, $300.
5 Earned first week's revenue, $400: $100 in cash and $300 on account.
8 Paid for newspaper advertising, $13.
9 Paid telephone bill, $28.
10 Paid electric bill, $21.
11 Received cash on account from customers, $200.
12 Earned second week's revenue, $450: $200 in cash and $250 on account.
15 Paid assistant, $400.
16 Made payment on account, $100.
17 Paid for magazine subscription (miscellaneous expense), $12.

Nov. 19	Earned third week's revenue, $450: $300 in cash, $150 on account.
23	Received cash on account from customers, $300.
24	Paid for newspaper advertising, $13.
26	Paid for postage (miscellaneous expense), $12.
27	Earned fourth week's revenue, $600: $200 in cash and $400 on account.
30	Received cash on account from customers, $400.

REQUIRED

1. Set up general ledger accounts by entering the balances as of November 1, 20--.
2. Journalize the transactions for November in a two-column general journal. Use the following journal page numbers: November 1–11, page 7; November 12–24, page 8; November 26–30, page 9.
3. Post the entries to the general ledger.
4. Prepare a trial balance.

P 4-11B **(LO6)**

CORRECTING ERRORS Assuming that all entries have been posted, prepare correcting entries for each of the following errors.

1. The following entry was made to record the purchase of $400 in equipment on account:

Supplies	142	400	
Cash	101		400

2. The following entry was made to record the payment of $200 for advertising:

Repair Expense	537	200	
Cash	101		200

3. The following entry was made to record a $600 payment to a supplier on account:

Prepaid Insurance	145	400	
Cash	101		400

MANAGING YOUR WRITING

You are a public accountant with many small business clients. During a recent visit to a client's business, the bookkeeper approached you with a problem. The columns of the trial balance were not equal. You helped the bookkeeper find and correct the error, but believe you should go one step further. Write a memo to all of your clients that explains the purpose of the double-entry framework, the importance of maintaining the equality of the accounting equation, the errors that might cause an inequality, and suggestions for finding the errors.

MASTERY PROBLEM

✓ Cash bal., June 30: $45,495; Trial bal. total debits: $96,200

KA KLOOSTER & ALLEN

Barry Bird opened the Barry Bird Basketball Camp for children ages 10 through 18. Campers typically register for one week in June or July, arriving on Sunday and returning home the following Saturday. College players serve as cabin counselors and assist the local college and high school coaches who run the practice sessions. The registration fee includes a room, meals at a nearby restaurant, and basketball instruction.

(continued)

In the off-season, the facilities are used for weekend retreats and coaching clinics. Bird developed the following chart of accounts for his service business:

Chart of Accounts

Assets		Revenues	
101	Cash	401	Registration Fees
142	Office Supplies		
183	Athletic Equipment	Expenses	
184	Basketball Facilities	511	Wages Expense
		512	Advertising Expense
Liabilities		524	Food Expense
202	Accounts Payable	525	Telephone Expense
		533	Utilities Expense
Owner's Equity		536	Postage Expense
311	Barry Bird, Capital		
312	Barry Bird, Drawing		

The following transactions took place during the month of June:

June 1	Bird invested cash in the business, $10,000.
1	Purchased basketballs and other athletic equipment, $3,000.
2	Paid Hite Advertising for flyers that had been mailed to prospective campers, $5,000.
2	Collected registration fees, $15,000.
2	Rogers Construction completed work on a new basketball court that cost $12,000. Arrangements were made to pay the bill in July.
5	Purchased office supplies on account from Gordon Office Supplies, $300.
6	Received bill from Magic's Restaurant for meals served to campers on account, $5,800.
7	Collected registration fees, $16,200.
10	Paid wages to camp counselors, $500.
14	Collected registration fees, $13,500.
14	Received bill from Magic's Restaurant for meals served to campers on account, $6,200.
17	Paid wages to camp counselors, $500.
18	Paid postage, $85.
21	Collected registration fees, $15,200.
22	Received bill from Magic's Restaurant for meals served to campers on account, $6,500.
24	Paid wages to camp counselors, $500.
28	Collected registration fees, $14,000.
30	Received bill from Magic's Restaurant for meals served to campers on account, $7,200.
30	Paid wages to camp counselors, $500.
30	Paid Magic's Restaurant on account, $25,700.
30	Paid utility bill, $500.
30	Paid telephone bill, $120.
30	Bird withdrew cash for personal use, $2,000.

REQUIRED

1. Enter the transactions in a general journal. Use the following journal pages: June 1–6, page 1; June 7–22, page 2; June 24–30, page 3.
2. Post the entries to the general ledger.
3. Prepare a trial balance.

This problem challenges you to apply your cumulative accounting knowledge to move a step beyond the material in the chapter.

✓ **Total debits: $19,150**

CHALLENGE PROBLEM

Journal entries and a trial balance for Fred Phaler Consulting follow. As you will note, the trial balance does not balance, suggesting that there are errors. Recall that the chapter offers tips on identifying individual posting errors. These techniques are not as effective when there are two or more errors. Thus, you will need to first carefully inspect the trial balance to see if you can identify any obvious errors due to amounts that either look out of proportion or are simply reported in the wrong place. Then, you will need to carefully evaluate the other amounts by using the techniques offered in the text, or tracing the journal entries to the amounts reported on the trial balance. (*Hint*: Four errors were made in the posting process and preparation of the trial balance.)

GENERAL JOURNAL PAGE 1

	DATE		DESCRIPTION	POST. REF.	DEBIT	CREDIT	
1	20-- June	1	Cash	101	10,000.00		1
2			Fred Phaler, Capital	311		10,000.00	2
3							3
4		2	Rent Expense	521	500.00		4
5			Cash	101		500.00	5
6							6
7		3	Cash	101	4,000.00		7
8			Professional Fees	401		4,000.00	8
9							9
10		4	Utilities Expense	533	100.00		10
11			Cash	101		100.00	11
12							12
13		7	Cash	101	3,000.00		13
14			Professional Fees	401		3,000.00	14
15							15
16		12	Automobile Expense	526	50.00		16
17			Cash	101		50.00	17
18							18
19		14	Wages Expense	511	500.00		19
20			Cash	101		500.00	20
21							21
22		14	Office Supplies	142	250.00		22
23			Accounts Payable	202		250.00	23
24							24
25		20	Telephone Expense	525	100.00		25
26			Cash	101		100.00	26
27							27
28		21	Fred Phaler, Drawing	312	1,200.00		28
29			Cash	101		1,200.00	29
30							30
31		24	Accounts Receivable	122	2,000.00		31
32			Professional Fees	401		2,000.00	32
33							33
34		25	Accounts Payable	202	100.00		34
35			Cash	101		100.00	35
36							36
37		30	Wages Expense	511	300.00		37
38			Cash	101		300.00	38

(continued)

Fred Phaler Consulting
Trial Balance
June 30, 20 - -

ACCOUNT TITLE	ACCOUNT NO.	DEBIT BALANCE	CREDIT BALANCE
Cash	101		13,900.00
Accounts Receivable	122	2,000.00	
Office Supplies	142	250.00	
Accounts Payable	202	100.00	
Fred Phaler, Capital	311		10,000.00
Fred Phaler, Drawing	312	2,100.00	
Professional Fees	401		9,000.00
Wages Expense	511	800.00	
Rent Expense	521	500.00	
Telephone Expense	525	100.00	
Automobile Expense	526	50,000.00	
Utilities Expense	533	100.00	
		55,950.00	32,900.00

REQUIRED

1. Find the errors.
2. Explain what caused the errors.
3. Prepare a corrected trial balance.

ANSWERS TO SELF-STUDY QUESTIONS AND EXERCISE

True/False Questions

1. F (A, L, OE, R, E)
2. T
3. T
4. T
5. T

Multiple Choice Questions

1. d
2. c
3. c
4. b
5. a

U REVU Exercises

1. A cash payment.

2. A Year in which entry was made. (Needed for first transaction on this page.)
   B Month in which entry was made. (Needed for first transaction on this page.)
   C Day of the month entry was made. (Needed for every transaction.)
   D Account debited.
   E Account credited.
   F Description of transaction.
   G Account number for account debited to indicate the debit has been posted.
   H Amount for account debited.
   I Amount for account credited.
   J Account number for account credited to indicate the credit has been posted.

3. A Account title.
   B Account number.
   C Year of transaction. (Needed for first transaction on this page.)
   D Month of transaction. (Needed for first transaction on this page.)
   E Day of month transaction was made. (Needed for every transaction.)
   F Generally left blank, except for special reasons such as indicating the beginning balance, adjusting, correcting, closing, or reversing entries.
   G Journal page from which entry was posted.
   H Dollar amount of debit.
   I Dollar amount of credit.
   J Balance if account has a debit balance.
   K Balance if account has a credit balance.

4.

GENERAL JOURNAL PAGE 1

	DATE		DESCRIPTION	POST. REF.	DEBIT	CREDIT	
1			Rent Payable		500 00		1
2			Cash			500 00	2
3			To correct error in which payment for rent				3
4			was credited to Rent Payable rather than Cash.				4
5							5

Chapter 5

COURTESY OF FLOYD'S 99 BARBERSHOPS

LEARNING OBJECTIVES

Careful study of this chapter should enable you to:

LO1 Prepare end-of-period adjustments.

LO2 Post adjusting entries to the general ledger.

LO3 Prepare a work sheet.

LO4 Describe methods for finding errors on the work sheet.

LO5 Journalize adjusting entries from the work sheet.

LO6 Explain the cash, modified cash, and accrual bases of accounting.

Adjusting Entries and the Work Sheet

Floyd's 99 Barbershops was founded in 2001 and currently has 350 employees. The company generates over $15 million in revenues annually. Floyd's 99 is a contemporary full-service barbershop/hair-care concept offering haircuts, coloring, styling, and shaves. In a setting where *Hard Rock* meets haircuts, customers listen to custom designed Floyd's 99 Radio, watch TV, surf the internet, and get a signature shoulder massage and hot lather neck shave all as a part of their overall haircut experience. About 80% of Floyd's 99 customers are male. The company has an aggressive expansion program and requires that franchisees be able to immediately fund and open three to five branches. Headquartered in Greenwood Village, Colorado, Floyd's 99 has shops in nine states, primarily Colorado, California, and Texas. Over half of the current 40 locations are corporately owned, and the rest are franchise owned.

As a rapidly growing company, Floyd's 99 uses the accrual basis of accounting, which requires making end-of-period adjusting entries. In this chapter, you will learn why adjusting entries are important, how they are made, and how they affect the financial statements. In addition, you will learn how to use a work sheet to help in the preparation of adjusting entries and the financial statements.

Up to this point, you have learned how to journalize business transactions, post to the ledger, and prepare a trial balance. Now it is time to learn how to make end-of-period adjustments to the accounts listed in the trial balance. This chapter explains the need for adjustments and illustrates how they are made with or without the use of a work sheet.

END-OF-PERIOD ADJUSTMENTS

LO1 Prepare end-of-period adjustments.

Transactions are entered as they occur throughout the year. Adjustments are made at the end of the accounting period for items that do not involve exchanges with an outside party.

Throughout the accounting period, business transactions are entered in the accounting system. These transactions are based on exchanges between the business and other companies and individuals. During the accounting period, other changes occur that affect the business's financial condition. For example, equipment is wearing out, prepaid insurance and supplies are being used up, and employees are earning wages that have not yet been paid. Since these events have not been entered into the accounting system, **adjusting entries** must be made prior to the preparation of financial statements.

The **matching principle** in accounting requires the matching of revenues earned during an accounting period with the expenses incurred to produce the revenues. This approach offers the best measure of net income. The income statement reports earnings for a specific period of time, and the balance sheet reports the assets, liabilities, and owner's equity on a specific date. Thus, to follow the matching principle, the accounts must be brought up to date before financial statements are prepared. This requires adjusting some of the accounts listed in the trial balance. Figure 5-1 lists reasons to adjust the trial balance.

LEARNING KEY

Matching revenues earned with expenses incurred to produce those revenues offers the best measure of net income.

FIGURE 5-1 Reasons to Adjust the Trial Balance

1. To report all revenues earned during the accounting period.
2. To report all expenses incurred to produce the revenues earned in the accounting period.
3. To accurately report the assets on the balance sheet date. Some assets may have been used up during the accounting period.
4. To accurately report the liabilities on the balance sheet date. Expenses may have been incurred but not yet paid.

Generally, adjustments are made and financial statements prepared at the end of a 12-month period called a **fiscal year**. This period does not need to be the same as a calendar year. In fact, many businesses schedule their fiscal year-end for a time when business is slow. In this chapter, we continue the illustration of Jessie Jane's Campus Delivery Service and will prepare adjustments at the end of the first month of operations. We will focus on the following accounts: Supplies, Prepaid Insurance, Wages Expense, and Delivery Equipment.

A BROADER VIEW

TRISH LEASE/GETTY IMAGES

Adjusting Entries

Are adjusting entries important? The Walt Disney Company and Mattel, Inc., probably think so. The Walt Disney Company granted Mattel, Inc., the right to make and sell toys based on Disney characters. In return, Mattel agreed to make payments to Disney as the toys were sold. One of the issues in a court case was whether Mattel should have made an adjusting entry when it fell behind on these payments. The entry would have been:

Royalty Expense	17,000,000	
Accounts Payable (Disney)		17,000,000

This adjusting entry would have reduced Mattel's fourth-quarter earnings for that year by more than 15%. Following an investigation by the Securities and Exchange Commission, Mattel eventually agreed to make an adjustment to later financial statements.

SUPPLIES

During June, Jessie purchased supplies consisting of paper, pens, and delivery envelopes for $80. *Since these supplies were expected to provide future benefits, Supplies, an asset, was debited at the time of the purchase.* No other entries were made to the supplies account during June. As reported on the trial balance in Figure 5-2, the $80 balance remains in the supplies account at the end of the month.

FIGURE 5-2 Trial Balance

Jessie Jane's Campus Delivery Service
Trial Balance
June 30, 20 - -

ACCOUNT TITLE	ACCOUNT NO.	DEBIT BALANCE	CREDIT BALANCE
Cash	101	370 00	
Accounts Receivable	122	650 00	
Supplies	141	80 00	
Prepaid Insurance	145	200 00	
Delivery Equipment	185	3600 00	
Accounts Payable	202		1800 00
Jessica Jane, Capital	311		2000 00
Jessica Jane, Drawing	312	150 00	
Delivery Fees	401		2150 00
Wages Expense	511	650 00	
Rent Expense	521	200 00	
Telephone Expense	525	50 00	
		5950 00	5950 00

As supplies are used, an expense is incurred. However, it is not practical to make a journal entry to recognize this expense and the reduction in the supplies account every time someone uses an envelope. It is more efficient to wait until the end of the accounting period to make one adjusting entry to reflect the expense incurred for the use of supplies for the entire month.

LEARNING KEY

Since it is not practical to make a journal entry for supplies expense each time supplies are used, one adjusting entry is made at the end of the accounting period.

At the end of the month, an inventory, or physical count, of the remaining supplies is taken. The inventory shows that supplies costing $20 were still unused at the end of June. Since Jessie bought supplies costing $80, and only $20 worth remain, supplies costing $60 must have been used ($80 – $20 = $60). Thus, supplies expense for the month is $60.

Since $60 worth of supplies have been used, Supplies Expense is debited and Supplies (asset) is credited for $60. This entry is illustrated in Figure 5-3 in T account and general journal form. Thus, as shown in Figure 5-4, supplies with a cost of $20 will be reported as an asset on the balance sheet and a supplies expense of $60 will be reported on the income statement. The adjusting entry affected an income statement account (Supplies Expense) and a balance sheet account (Supplies).

FIGURE 5-3 Adjustment for Supplies

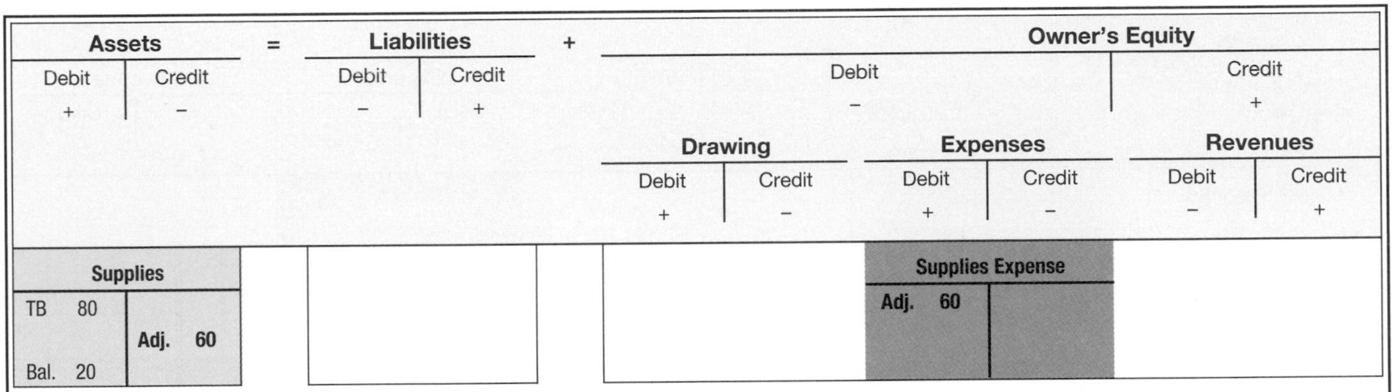

TB: Trial Balance

GENERAL JOURNAL — PAGE 3

	DATE	DESCRIPTION	POST REF.	DEBIT	CREDIT	
1		Adjusting Entry				1
2		Supplies Expense		6 0 00		2
3		Supplies			6 0 00	3
4						4

LEARNING KEY

By making an adjusting entry that debits Supplies Expense and credits Supplies, you are taking the amount of supplies used out of Supplies and putting it in Supplies Expense.

FIGURE 5-4 Effect of Adjusting Entry for Supplies on Financial Statements

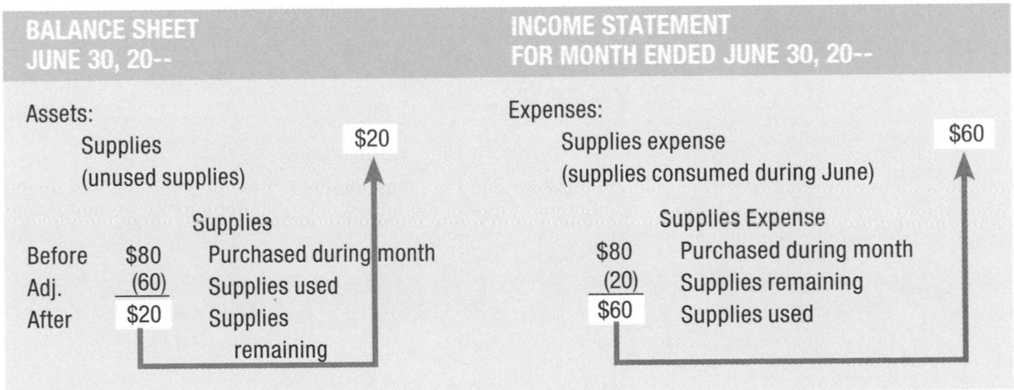

PREPAID INSURANCE

On June 18, Jessie paid $200 for an eight-month liability insurance policy with coverage beginning on June 1. *Prepaid Insurance, an asset, was debited because the insurance policy is expected to provide future benefits.* The $200 balance is reported on the trial balance. As the insurance policy expires with the passage of time, the asset should be reduced and an expense recognized.

Since the $200 premium covers eight months, the cost of the expired coverage for June is $25 ($200 ÷ 8 months). As shown in Figure 5-5, the adjusting entry is to debit Insurance Expense for $25 and credit Prepaid Insurance for $25. Figure 5-6 shows that the unexpired portion of the insurance premium will be reported on the balance sheet as Prepaid Insurance of $175. The expired portion will be reported on the income statement as Insurance Expense of $25.

FIGURE 5-5 Adjustment for Expired Insurance

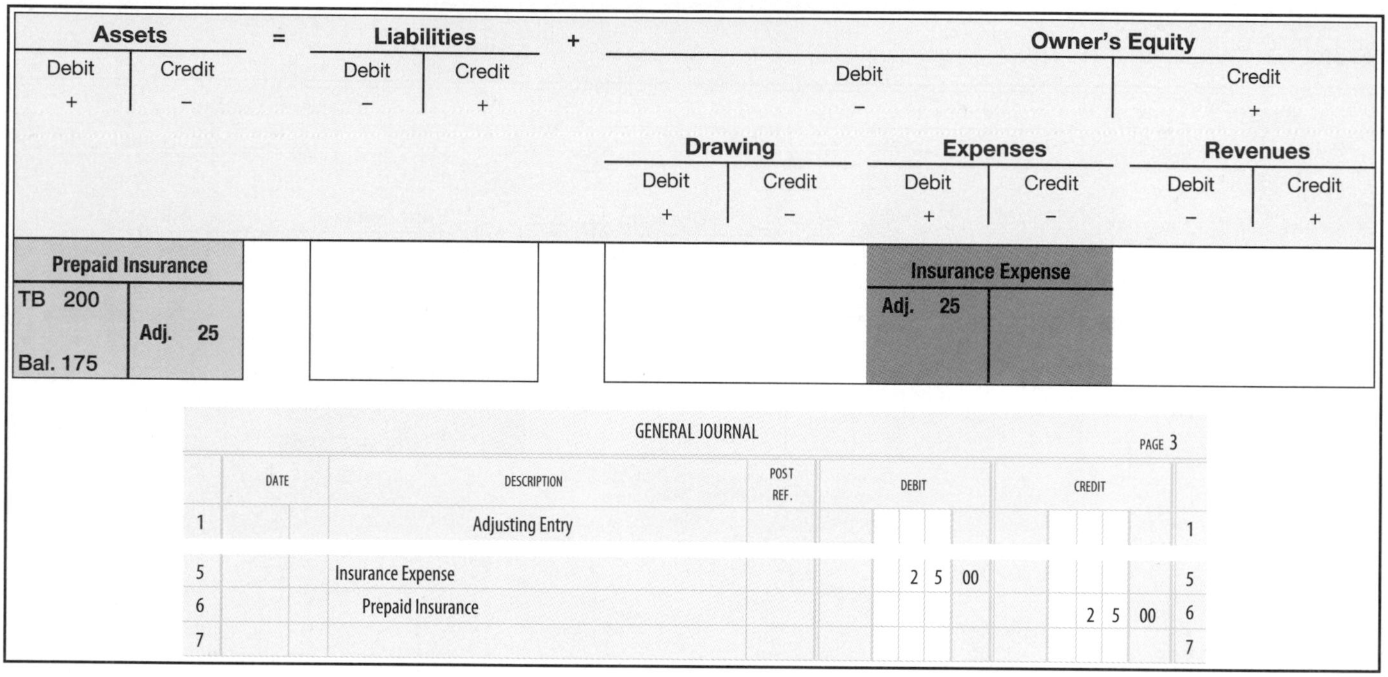

FIGURE 5-6 Effect of Adjusting Entry for Prepaid Insurance on Financial Statements

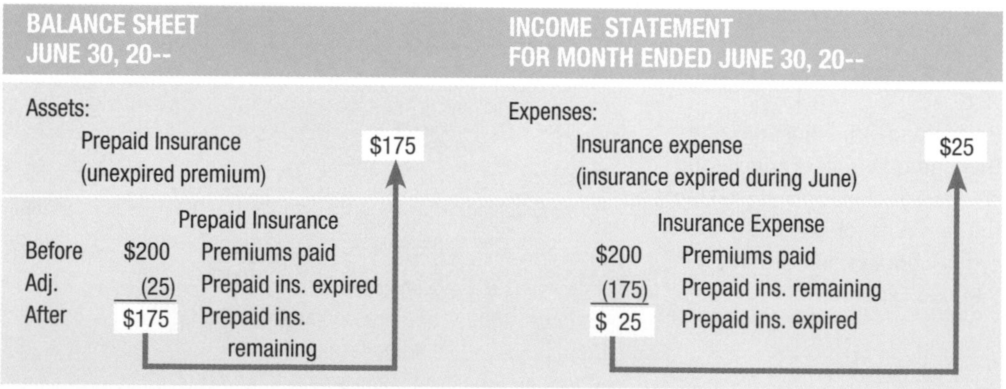

WAGES EXPENSE

Jessie paid her part-time employees $650 on June 27. Since then, they have earned an additional $50, but have not yet been paid. The additional wages expense must be recognized.

Since the employees have not been paid, Wages Payable, a liability, should be established. Thus, Wages Expense is debited and Wages Payable is credited for $50 in

Figure 5-7. Note in Figure 5-8 that Wages Expense of $700 is reported on the income statement and Wages Payable of $50 is reported on the balance sheet.

FIGURE 5-7 Adjustment for Unpaid Wages

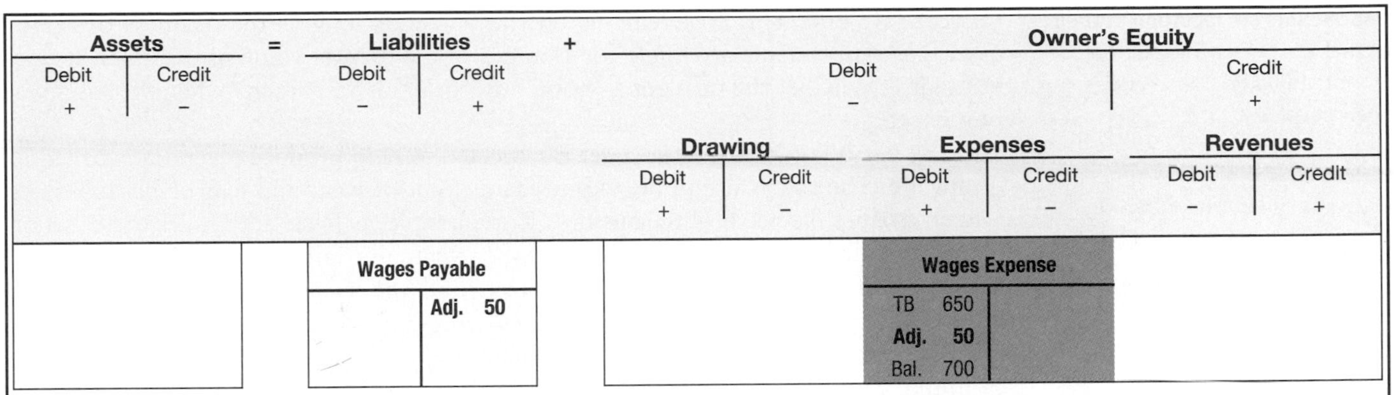

GENERAL JOURNAL PAGE 3

	DATE		DESCRIPTION	POST REF.	DEBIT	CREDIT	
1			Adjusting Entry				1
8			Wages Expense		50 00		8
9			Wages Payable			50 00	9
10							10

FIGURE 5-8 Effect of Adjusting Entry for Wages on Financial Statements

BALANCE SHEET JUNE 30, 20--		INCOME STATEMENT FOR MONTH ENDED JUNE 30, 20--	
Liabilities:		Expenses:	
Wages Payable (owed to employees)	$50	Wages expense (incurred for June)	$700

Wages Payable	
$700	Total wages expense incurred
(650)	Paid to employees
$ 50	Owed to employees

Wages Expense		
Before	$650	Wages paid
Adj.	50	Wages owed
After	$700	Total wages expense

Profiles in Accounting

Mezaun Akeera Ramjohn, Accounts Payable Coordinator

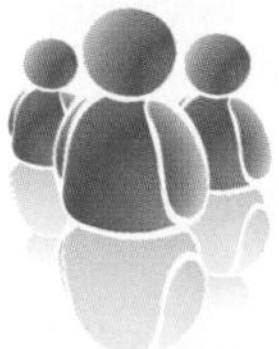

Mezaun Akeera Ramjohn has an AAS degree in accounting and is currently completing her baccalaureate degree at The College of Westchester at night. She is a member of Sigma Beta Delta and is on the President's List. Mezaun is employed full time as accounts payable coordinator at an international importing/exporting company located in Westchester, NY. According to Mezaun, she loves her job and is learning a lot. Working full time and going to school at night is a challenge, which she enjoys. Mezaun's educational goal is to acquire her master's degree in accounting and sit for the CPA exam.

DEPRECIATION EXPENSE

During the month of June, Jessie purchased three motor scooters. Since the scooters will provide future benefits, they were recorded as assets in the delivery equipment account. Under the **historical cost principle**, assets are recorded at their actual cost, in this case $3,600. This cost remains on the books as long as the business owns the asset. No adjustments are made for changes in the market value of the asset. It does not matter whether the firm got a "good buy" or paid "too much" when the asset was purchased.

LEARNING KEY

The historical cost principle is an important accounting concept. Assets are recorded at their actual cost. This historical cost is not adjusted for changes in market values.

To learn about other depreciation methods, see the appendix to this chapter.

The period of time that an asset is expected to help produce revenues is called its **useful life.** The asset's useful life expires as a result of wear and tear or because it no longer satisfies the needs of the business. For example, as Jessie adds miles to her scooters, they will become less reliable and will eventually fail to run. As this happens, depreciation expense should be recognized and the value of the asset should be reduced. **Depreciation** is a method of *matching* an asset's original cost against the revenues produced over its useful life. There are many depreciation methods. In our example, we will use the **straight-line method**.

Let's assume that Jessie's motor scooters have estimated useful lives of three years and will have no salvage value at the end of that time period. **Salvage value** (also called scrap value, or residual value) is the expected **market value** or selling price of the asset at the end of its useful life. The **depreciable cost** of these scooters is the original cost, less salvage value, or $3,600. It is this amount that is subject to depreciation. Let's also assume that a full month's depreciation is recognized in the month in which an asset is purchased.

Depreciation expense is based on estimates of useful lives and salvage values.

The depreciable cost is spread over 36 months (3 years × 12 months). Thus, the straight-line depreciation expense for the month of June is $100 ($3,600 ÷ 36 months).

STRAIGHT-LINE DEPRECIATION

$$\text{Original Cost} - \text{Salvage Value} = \text{Depreciable Cost}$$

$$\frac{\text{Depreciable Cost}}{\text{Estimated Useful Life}} = \frac{\$3,600}{36 \text{ months}} = \$100 \text{ per month}$$

LEARNING KEY

Depreciable assets provide benefits over more than one year. Therefore, the historical cost of the asset remains in the asset account. To show that it has been depreciated, a *contra-asset* account is used.

When we made adjustments for supplies and prepaid insurance, the asset accounts were credited to show that they had been consumed. Assets of a durable nature that are expected to provide benefits over several years or more, called **plant assets**, require a different approach. The business maintains a record of the original cost and the amount of depreciation taken since the asset was acquired. By comparing these two amounts, the reader can estimate the relative age of the assets. Thus, instead of crediting Delivery Equipment for the amount of depreciation, a contra-asset account, Accumulated Depreciation—Delivery Equipment, is credited. "Contra" means opposite or against. Thus, a **contra-asset** has a credit balance (the opposite of an asset) and is deducted from the related asset account on the balance sheet.

As shown in Figure 5-9, the appropriate adjusting entry consists of a debit to Depreciation Expense—Delivery Equipment and a credit to Accumulated Depreciation—Delivery Equipment. Note the position of the accumulated depreciation account in the accounting equation. It is shown in the assets section, directly beneath Delivery Equipment. Contra-asset accounts should always be shown along with the related asset account. Therefore, Delivery Equipment and Accumulated Depreciation—Delivery Equipment are shown together.

FIGURE 5-9 Adjustment for Depreciation of Delivery Equipment

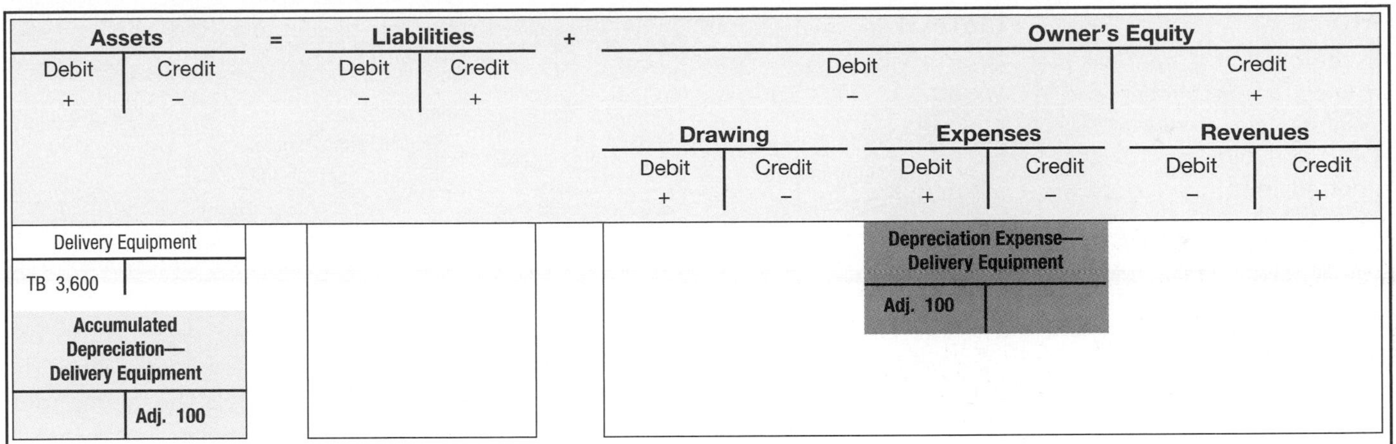

GENERAL JOURNAL — PAGE 3

	DATE	DESCRIPTION	POST REF.	DEBIT	CREDIT	
1		Adjusting Entry				1
11		Depreciation Expense—Delivery Equipment		1 0 0 00		11
12		Accumulated Depreciation—Delivery Equipment			1 0 0 00	12
13						13

LEARNING KEY

There is no individual account that reports book value. It must be computed.

Cost of Plant Assets
− Accumulated Depreciation
= Book Value

The same concept is used on the balance sheet. Note in Figure 5-10 that Accumulated Depreciation is reported immediately beneath Delivery Equipment as a deduction. The difference between these accounts is known as the **book value**, or **undepreciated cost**, of the delivery equipment. Book value simply means the value carried on the books or in the accounting records. It does *not* represent the market value, or selling price, of the asset.

FIGURE 5-10 Effect of Adjusting Entry for Depreciation on Financial Statements for June

BALANCE SHEET JUNE 30, 20--			INCOME STATEMENT FOR MONTH ENDED JUNE 30, 20--	
Assets:			Expenses:	
Delivery equipment	$3,600		Depreciation expense (Expired cost for June)	$100
Less: Accumulated depreciation	100	$3,500 (Book value)		

If no delivery equipment is bought or sold during the next month, the same adjusting entry would be made at the end of July. If an income statement for the month of July and a balance sheet as of July 31 were prepared, the amounts shown in Figure 5-11 would be reported for the delivery equipment.

FIGURE 5-11 Effect of Adjusting Entry for Depreciation on Financial Statements for July

BALANCE SHEET JULY 31, 20--			INCOME STATEMENT FOR MONTH ENDED JULY 31, 20--	
Assets:			Expenses:	
Delivery equipment	$3,600		Depreciation expense	$100
Less: Accumulated depreciation	200	$3,400 (Book value)	(Expired cost for July)	

The cost ($3,600) remains unchanged, but the accumulated depreciation has increased to $200. This represents *the depreciation that has accumulated* since the delivery equipment was purchased ($100 in June and $100 in July). The depreciation expense for July is $100, the same as reported for June. Depreciation expense is reported for a specific time period. It does not accumulate across reporting periods.

If financial statements are prepared at the end of the year, December 31, 20--, the results for the seven months of operations would be presented as shown in Figure 5-12. Depreciation expense for the year is $700 ($100 × 7 months), and the accumulated depreciation would be the same because this is the first year of operation.

Cost	$3,600	= $100
Useful life	36 months	
Dep./month	$100	
Months in service	× 7	
Dep. June–Dec.	$700	

FIGURE 5-12 Straight-Line Depreciation for Seven Months

BALANCE SHEET DECEMBER 31, 20--			INCOME STATEMENT FOR YEAR ENDED DECEMBER 31, 20--	
Assets:			Expenses:	
Delivery equipment	$3,600		Depreciation expense	$700
Less: Accumulated depreciation	700	$2,900 (Book value)	(Expired cost from June through December)	

EXPANDED CHART OF ACCOUNTS

Several new accounts were needed to make the adjusting entries. New accounts are easily added to the chart of accounts, as shown in Figure 5-13. Note the close relationship between assets and contra-assets in the numbering of the accounts. Contra-accounts carry the same number as the related asset account with a ".1" suffix. For example, Delivery Equipment is account number 185 and the contra-asset account, Accumulated Depreciation—Delivery Equipment, is account number 185.1.

U REVU Complete U REVU-1 on **page 154** to test your basic understanding of LO1

POSTING ADJUSTING ENTRIES

LO2 Post adjusting entries to the general ledger.

Adjusting entries are posted to the general ledger in the same manner as all other entries, except that "*Adjusting*" is written in the Item column of the general ledger. Figure 5-14 shows the posting of the adjusting entries. The posting reference numbers are inserted as each entry is posted.

FIGURE 5-13 Expanded Chart of Accounts

JESSIE JANE'S CAMPUS DELIVERY SERVICE
CHART OF ACCOUNTS

Assets		**Revenues**	
101	Cash	401	**Delivery Fees**
122	Accounts Receivable		
141	Supplies	**Expenses**	
145	Prepaid Insurance	511	Wages Expense
185	Delivery Equipment	521	Rent Expense
185.1	Accumulated Depr.—	523	Supplies Expense
	Delivery Equipment	525	Telephone Expense
		535	Insurance Expense
Liabilities		541	Depr. Expense —
202	Accounts Payable		Delivery Equipment
219	Wages Payable		
Owner's Equity			
311	Jessica Jane, Capital		
312	Jessica Jane, Drawing		

FIGURE 5-14 Posting the Adjusting Entries

GENERAL JOURNAL PAGE 3

	DATE		DESCRIPTION	POST. REF.	DEBIT	CREDIT	
1			Adjusting Entries				1
2	20-- June	30	Supplies Expense	523	60 00		2
3			Supplies	141		60 00	3
4							4

(a) (entries on lines 2–3)

	DATE		DESCRIPTION	POST. REF.	DEBIT	CREDIT	
5		30	Insurance Expense	535	25 00		5
6			Prepaid Insurance	145		25 00	6
7							7

(b) (entries on lines 5–6)

GENERAL LEDGER

(a)

ACCOUNT: Supplies ACCOUNT NO. 141

DATE		ITEM	POST. REF.	DEBIT	CREDIT	BALANCE DEBIT	BALANCE CREDIT
20-- June	16		J1	80 00		80 00	
	30	Adjusting	J3		60 00	20 00	

ACCOUNT: Supplies Expense ACCOUNT NO. 523

DATE		ITEM	POST. REF.	DEBIT	CREDIT	BALANCE DEBIT	BALANCE CREDIT
20-- June	30	Adjusting	J3	60 00		60 00	

(b)

ACCOUNT: Prepaid Insurance ACCOUNT NO. 145

DATE		ITEM	POST. REF.	DEBIT	CREDIT	BALANCE DEBIT	BALANCE CREDIT
20-- June	18		J1	200 00		200 00	
	30	Adjusting	J3		25 00	175 00	

ACCOUNT: Insurance Expense ACCOUNT NO. 535

DATE		ITEM	POST. REF.	DEBIT	CREDIT	BALANCE DEBIT	BALANCE CREDIT
20-- June	30	Adjusting	J3	25 00		25 00	

(continued)

FIGURE 5-14 Posting the Adjusting Entries (*concluded*)

(c)

8	30	Wages Expense	511	50 00		8
9		Wages Payable	219		50 00	9
10						10

(c)

ACCOUNT: Wages Payable ACCOUNT NO. 219

DATE		ITEM	POST. REF.	DEBIT	CREDIT	BALANCE DEBIT	BALANCE CREDIT
20-- June	30	Adjusting	J3		50 00		50 00

ACCOUNT: Wages Expense ACCOUNT NO. 511

DATE		ITEM	POST. REF.	DEBIT	CREDIT	BALANCE DEBIT	BALANCE CREDIT
20-- June	27		J1	650 00		650 00	
	30	Adjusting	J3	50 00		700 00	

(d)

11	30	Depr. Expense — Delivery Equipment	541	100 00		11
12		Accum. Depr. — Delivery Equipment	185.1		100 00	12

(d)

ACCOUNT: Accumulated Depreciation—Delivery Equipment ACCOUNT NO. 185.1

DATE		ITEM	POST. REF.	DEBIT	CREDIT	BALANCE DEBIT	BALANCE CREDIT
20-- June	30	Adjusting	J3		100 00		100 00

ACCOUNT: Depreciation Expense—Delivery Equipment ACCOUNT NO. 541

DATE		ITEM	POST. REF.	DEBIT	CREDIT	BALANCE DEBIT	BALANCE CREDIT
20-- June	30	Adjusting	J3	100 00		100 00	

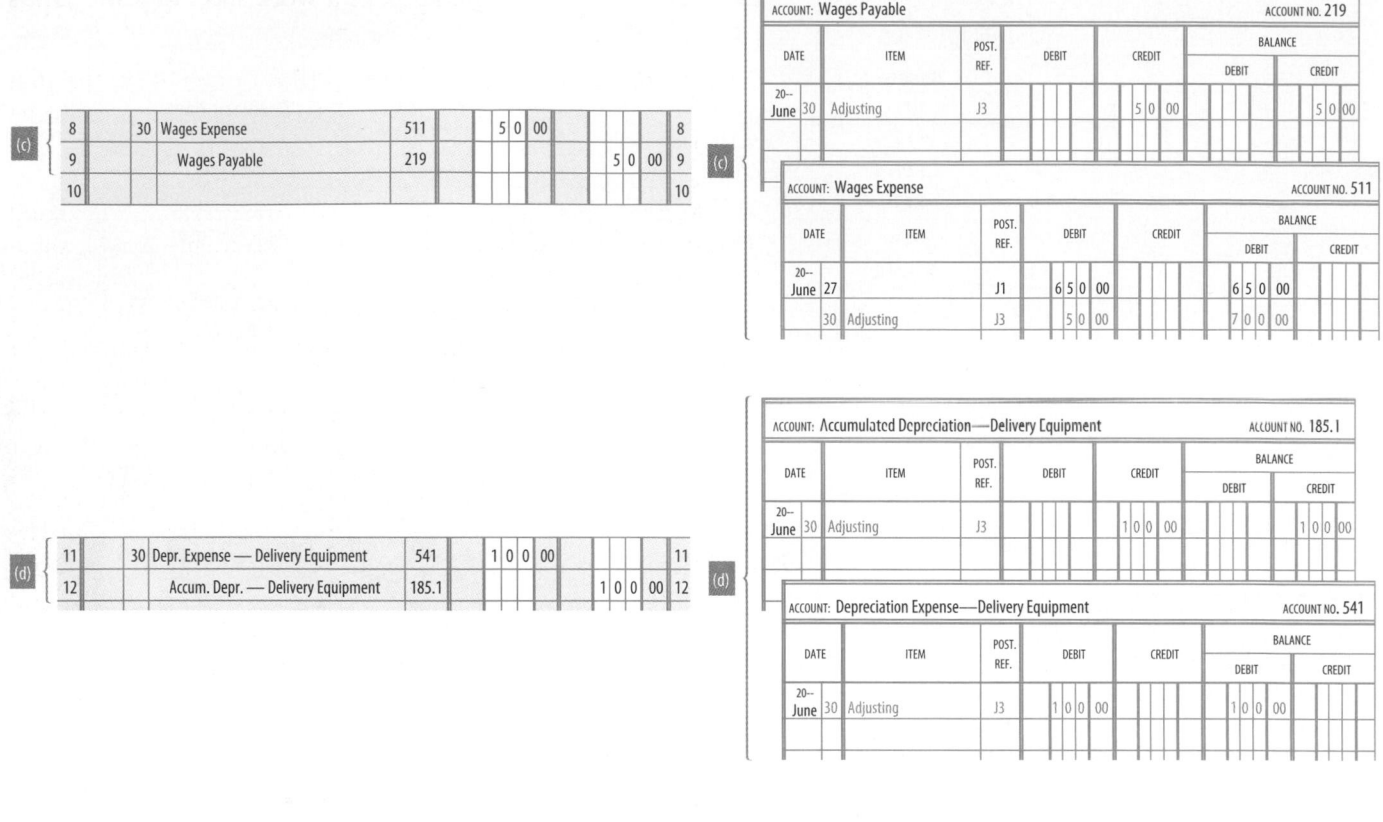

U REVU Complete U REVU-2 on **page 154** to test your basic understanding of LO2

THE WORK SHEET

LO3 Prepare a work sheet.

A **work sheet** pulls together all of the information needed to enter adjusting entries and prepare the financial statements. Work sheets are not financial statements, are not a formal part of the accounting system, and are not a required part of the accounting process. However, many accountants prepare them because they are very helpful in planning the adjustments and preparing the financial statements. Ordinarily, only the accountant uses a work sheet. For this reason, a work sheet is usually prepared in pencil or as a computer spreadsheet. As computer use has become more common, the term "spreadsheet" is often used in place of "work sheet."

THE 10-COLUMN WORK SHEET

Although a work sheet can take several forms, a common format has a column for account titles and 10 amount columns grouped into five pairs. The work sheet format and the five steps in preparing the work sheet are illustrated in Figure 5-15 on page 142A. As with financial statements, the work sheet has a heading consisting of the name of the company, name of the working paper, and the date of the accounting period just ended. The five major column headings for the work sheet are Trial Balance, Adjustments, Adjusted Trial Balance, Income Statement, and Balance Sheet.

PREPARING THE WORK SHEET

Let's apply the five steps required for the preparation of a work sheet to Jessie Jane's Campus Delivery Service.

STEP 1 **Prepare the Trial Balance.** As shown in Figure 5-16 on page 142B, the first pair of amount columns is for the trial balance. The trial balance assures the equality of the debits and credits before the adjustment process begins. The columns should be double ruled to show that they are equal.

Note that all accounts listed in the expanded chart of accounts are included in the Trial Balance columns of the work sheet. This is done even though some accounts have zero balances. The accounts with zero balances could be added to the bottom of the list as they are needed for adjusting entries. However, it is easier to include them now, especially if preparing the work sheet on an electronic spreadsheet. Listing the accounts within their proper classifications (assets, liabilities, etc.) also makes it easier to extend the amounts to the proper columns.

STEP 2 **Prepare the Adjustments.** As shown in Figure 5-17 on page 142C, the second pair of amount columns is used to prepare the adjusting entries. Enter the adjustments directly in these columns. When an account is debited or credited, the amount is entered on the same line as the name of the account and in the appropriate Adjustments Debit or Credit column. A small letter in parentheses identifies each adjusting entry made on the work sheet.

LEARNING KEY

For adjustments (a), (b), and (d), we are simply recognizing that assets have been used. When this happens, the asset must be decreased and an expense recognized. Note that the reported amount for delivery equipment is reduced by crediting a contra-asset.

ADJUSTMENT (a):

Supplies costing $60 were used during June.

	Debit	Credit
Supplies Expense	60	
Supplies		60

ADJUSTMENT (b):

One month's insurance premium has expired.

	Debit	Credit
Insurance Expense	25	
Prepaid Insurance		25

LEARNING KEY

Adjustment (c) recognizes an economic event that has not required an actual transaction yet. Employees earned wages, but have not been paid. The adjustment recognizes an expense and a liability.

ADJUSTMENT (c):

Employees earned $50 that has not yet been paid.

	Debit	Credit
Wages Expense	50	
Wages Payable		50

ADJUSTMENT (d):

Depreciation on the motor scooters is recognized.

	Debit	Credit
Depreciation Expense—Delivery Equipment	100	
Accumulated Depreciation—Delivery Equipment		100

When all adjustments have been entered on the work sheet, each column should be totaled to assure that the debits equal the credits for all entries. After balancing the columns, they should be double ruled.

STEP 3 **Prepare the Adjusted Trial Balance.** As shown in Figure 5-18 on page 142D, the third pair of amount columns on the work sheet is the **Adjusted Trial Balance columns.**

- When an account balance is not affected by entries in the Adjustments columns, the amount in the Trial Balance columns is extended directly to the Adjusted Trial Balance columns.
- *When affected by an entry in the Adjustments columns, the account balance to be entered in the Adjusted Trial Balance columns increases or decreases by the amount of the adjusting entry.*

For example, in Jessica Jane's business, Supplies is listed in the Trial Balance Debit column as $80. Since the entry of $60 is in the Adjustments Credit column, the amount extended to the Adjusted Trial Balance Debit column is $20 ($80 – $60).

Wages Expense is listed in the Trial Balance Debit column as $650. Since $50 is in the Adjustments Debit column, the amount extended to the Adjusted Trial Balance Debit column is $700 ($650 + $50).

After all extensions have been made, the Adjusted Trial Balance columns are totaled to prove the equality of the debits and the credits. Once balanced, the columns are double ruled.

STEP 4 **Extend Adjusted Balances to the Income Statement and Balance Sheet Columns.** As shown in Figure 5-19 on page 142E, each account listed in the Adjusted Trial Balance must be extended to either the Income Statement or Balance Sheet columns. The **Income Statement columns** show the amounts that will be reported in the income statement. All revenue accounts are extended to the Income Statement Credit column and expense accounts are extended to the Income Statement Debit column.

The asset, liability, drawing, and capital accounts are extended to the **Balance Sheet columns.** Although called the Balance Sheet columns, these columns of the work sheet show the amounts that will be reported in the balance sheet and the statement of owner's equity. The asset and drawing accounts are extended to the Balance Sheet Debit column. The liability and owner's capital accounts are extended to the Balance Sheet Credit column.

LEARNING KEY

The Balance Sheet columns show the amounts for both the balance sheet and the statement of owner's equity.

STEP 5 **Complete the Work Sheet.** To complete the work sheet, first total the Income Statement columns. If the total of the credits (revenues) exceeds the total of the debits (expenses), the difference represents net income. If the total of the debits exceeds the total of the credits, the difference represents a net loss.

The Income Statement columns of Jessie's work sheet in Figure 5-20 on page 142F show total credits of $2,150 and total debits of $1,135. The difference, $1,015, is the net income for the month of June. This amount should be added to the Debit column to balance the Income Statement columns. "Net Income" should be written on the same line in the Account Title column. If the business had a net loss, the amount of the loss would be added to the Income Statement Credit column and the words "Net Loss" would be written in the Account Title column. Once balanced, the columns should be double ruled.

Finally, the Balance Sheet columns are totaled. The difference between the totals of these columns also is the amount of net income or net loss for the accounting period. If the total debits exceed the total credits, the difference is net income. If the total credits exceed the total debits, the difference is a net loss. This difference should be the same as the difference we found for the Income Statement columns.

LEARNING KEY

In the Balance Sheet columns of the work sheet, total debits minus total credits equals net *income* if greater than zero and equals net *loss* if less than zero.

FIGURE 5-15 Steps In Preparing The Work Sheet

Name of Company
Work Sheet
For Month Ended June 30, 20 --

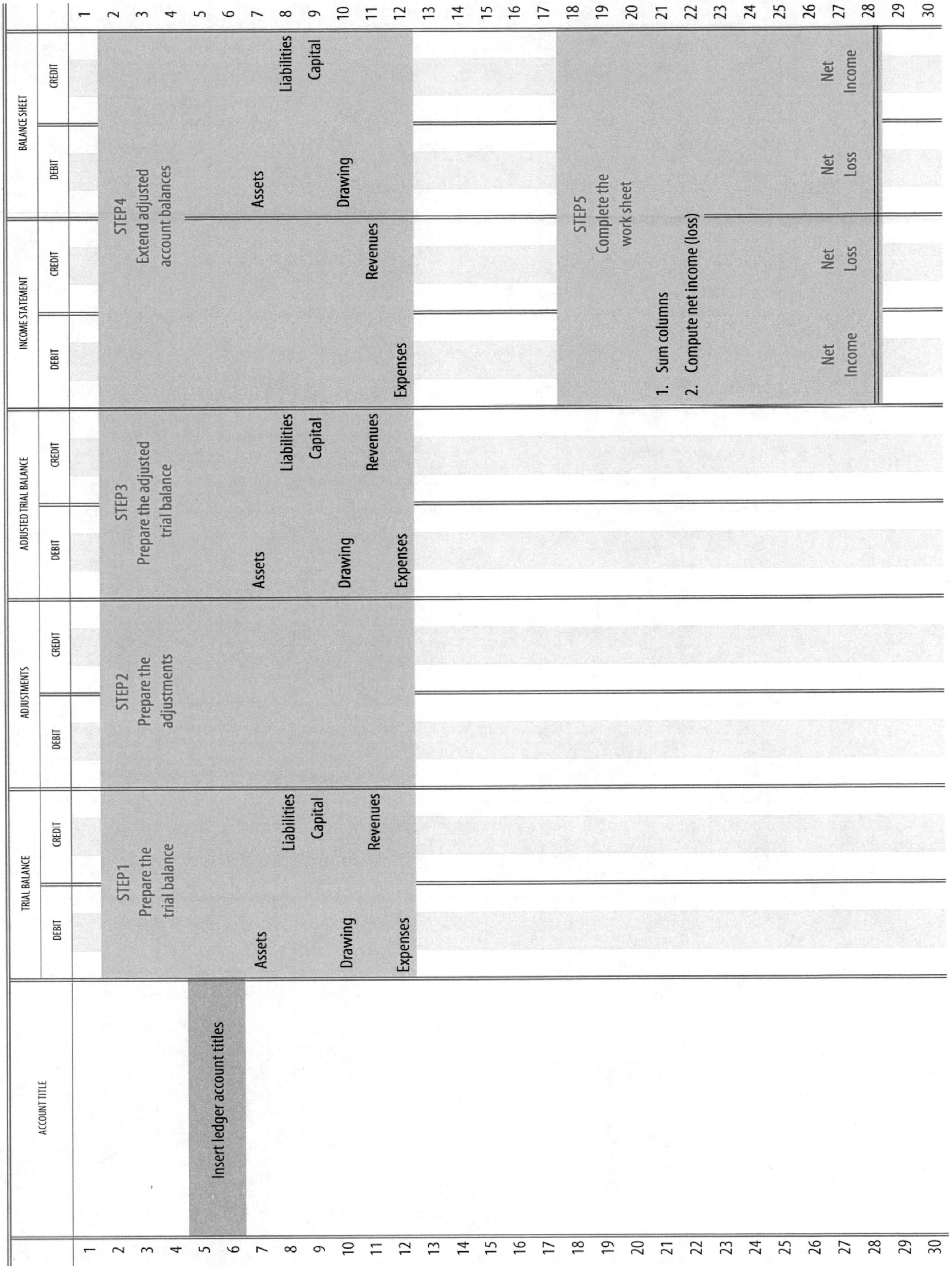

FIGURE 5-16 Step 1—Prepare the Trial Balance

Jessica Jane's Campus Delivery Service
Work Sheet
For Month Ended June 30, 20 - -

	ACCOUNT TITLE	TRIAL BALANCE		ADJUSTMENTS		ADJUSTED TRIAL BALANCE		INCOME STATEMENT		BALANCE SHEET		
		DEBIT	CREDIT	DEBIT	CREDIT	DEBIT	CREDIT	DEBIT	CREDIT	DEBIT	CREDIT	
1	Cash	370 00										1
2	Accounts Receivable	650 00										2
3	Supplies	80 00										3
4	Prepaid Insurance	200 00										4
5	Delivery Equipment	3600 00										5
6	Accum. Depr.—Delivery Equipment											6
7	Accounts Payable		1800 00									7
8	Wages Payable											8
9	Jessica Jane, Capital		2000 00									9
10	Jessica Jane, Drawing	150 00										10
11	Delivery Fees		2150 00									11
12	Wages Expense	650 00										12
13	Rent Expense	200 00										13
14	Supplies Expense											14
15	Telephone Expense	50 00										15
16	Insurance Expense											16
17	Depr. Expense—Delivery Equipment											17
18		5950 00	5950 00									18
19												19
20												20
21												21
22												22
23												23
24												24
25												25
26												26
27												27
28												28
29												29
30												30

STEP 1

Preparing the Work Sheet

STEP 1 Prepare the Trial Balance.

- Write the heading, account titles, and the debit and credit amounts from the general ledger.
- Place a single rule across the Trial Balance columns and total the debit and credit amounts.
- Place a double rule under the totals for each column.
- Total debits must equal total credits.

STEP 2 Prepare the Adjustments.

- Record the adjustments.
  Hint: Make certain that each adjustment is on the same line as the account name and in the appropriate column.
  Hint: Identify each adjusting entry by a letter in parentheses.
- Rule the Adjustments columns.
- Total the Debit and Credit columns and double rule the columns.
- Total debits must equal total credits.

STEP 3 Prepare the Adjusted Trial Balance.

- Extend those debits and credits that are not adjusted directly to the appropriate Adjusted Trial Balance column.
- Enter the adjusted balances in the appropriate Adjusted Trial Balance column.
  Hint: If an account has a debit and a credit, subtract the adjustment. If an account has two debits or two credits, add the adjustment.
- Single rule the Adjusted Trial Balance columns. Total and double rule the Debit and Credit columns.
- Total debits must equal total credits.

STEP 4 Extend Adjusted Balances to the Income Statement and Balance Sheet Columns.

- Extend all revenue accounts to the Income Statement Credit column.
- Extend all expense accounts to the Income Statement Debit column.
- Extend the asset and drawing accounts to the Balance Sheet Debit column.
- Extend the liability and owner's capital accounts to the Balance Sheet Credit column.

STEP 5 Complete the Work Sheet.

- Rule and total the Income Statement and Balance Sheet columns.
- Calculate the difference between the Income Statement Debit and Credit columns.
- Calculate the difference between the Balance Sheet Debit and Credit columns.
  Hint: If the Income Statement credits exceed debits, net income has occurred; otherwise, a net loss has occurred. If the Balance Sheet debits exceed the credits, the difference is net income; otherwise, a net loss has occurred.
  Hint: The difference between the Balance Sheet columns should be the same as the difference between the Income Statement columns.
- Add the net income to the Income Statement Debit column or add the net loss to the Income Statement Credit column. Add the net income to the Balance Sheet Credit column or the net loss to the Balance Sheet Debit column. Write "Net Income" or "Net Loss" in the Account Title column.
- Total and double rule the columns.

The Balance Sheet columns of Jessie's work sheet show total debits of $4,965 and total credits of $3,950. The difference of $1,015 represents the amount of net income for the month. This amount is added to the Credit column to balance the Balance Sheet columns. If the business had a net loss, this amount would be added to the Balance Sheet Debit column. Once balanced, the columns should be double ruled.

A trick for remembering the appropriate placement of the net income and net loss is the following: Net Income *apart*; Net Loss *together*. Figure 5-21 illustrates this learning aid.

FIGURE 5-21 Net Income Apart, Net Loss Together

	INCOME STATEMENT		BALANCE SHEET	
	DEBIT	CREDIT	DEBIT	CREDIT
Net Income	1 1 3 5 00	2 0 0 0 00	4 8 1 5 00	3 9 5 0 00
	8 6 5 00			8 6 5 00
	2 0 0 0 00	2 0 0 0 00	4 8 1 5 00	4 8 1 5 00

Apart

	INCOME STATEMENT		BALANCE SHEET	
	DEBIT	CREDIT	DEBIT	CREDIT
Net Loss	2 5 0 0 00	2 0 0 0 00	5 0 1 5 00	5 5 1 5 00
		5 0 0 00	5 0 0 00	
	2 5 0 0 00	2 5 0 0 00	5 5 1 5 00	5 5 1 5 00

Together

U REVU Complete U REVU-3 on **page 154** to test your basic understanding of LO3.

FINDING ERRORS ON THE WORK SHEET

LO4 Describe methods for finding errors on the work sheet.

If any of the columns on the work sheet do not balance, you must find the error before you continue. Once you are confident that the work sheet is accurate, you are ready to journalize the adjusting entries and prepare financial statements. Figure 5-22 offers tips for finding errors on the work sheet.

FIGURE 5-22 Finding Errors on the Work Sheet

TIPS FOR FINDING ERRORS ON THE WORK SHEET
1. Check the addition of all columns.
2. Check the addition and subtraction required when extending to the Adjusted Trial Balance columns.
3. Make sure the adjusted account balances have been extended to the appropriate columns.
4. Make sure that the net income or net loss has been added to the appropriate columns.

U REVU Complete U REVU-4 on **page 154** to test your basic understanding of LO4.

JOURNALIZING ADJUSTING ENTRIES FROM THE WORK SHEET

LO5 Journalize adjusting entries from the work sheet.

Keep in mind that the work sheet simply helps the accountant organize the end-of-period work. *Writing the adjustments on the work sheet has no effect on the ledger accounts in the accounting system. The only way to change the balance of a ledger account is to make a journal entry.* Once the work sheet has been completed, simply copy the adjustments from the work sheet to the journal, as shown in Figure 5-23.

FIGURE 5-23 Journalizing Adjusting Entries from the Work Sheet

Jessica Jane's Campus Delivery Service
Work Sheet (Partial)
For Month Ended June 30, 20--

	ACCOUNT TITLE	TRIAL BALANCE		ADJUSTMENTS	
		DEBIT	CREDIT	DEBIT	CREDIT
1	Cash	370 00			
2	Accounts Receivable	650 00			
3	Supplies	80 00			(a) 60 00
4	Prepaid Insurance	200 00			(b) 25 00
5	Delivery Equipment	3600 00			
6	Accum. Depr.—Delivery Equipment				(d) 100 00
7	Accounts Payable		1800 00		
8	Wages Payable				(c) 50 00
9	Jessica Jane, Capital		2000 00		
10	Jessica Jane, Drawing	150 00			
11	Delivery Fees		2150 00		
12	Wages Expense	650 00		(c) 50 00	
13	Rent Expense	200 00			
14	Supplies Expense			(a) 60 00	
15	Telephone Expense	50 00			
16	Insurance Expense			(b) 25 00	
17	Depr. Expense—Delivery Equipment			(d) 100 00	
18		5950 00	5950 00	235 00	235 00

GENERAL JOURNAL PAGE 3

		DATE		DESCRIPTION	POST. REF.	DEBIT	CREDIT	
	1			Adjusting Entries				1
(a)	2	20-- June	30	Supplies Expense	523	60 00		2
	3			Supplies	141		60 00	3
	4							4
(b)	5		30	Insurance Expense	535	25 00		5
	6			Prepaid Insurance	145		25 00	6
	7							7
(c)	8		30	Wages Expense	511	50 00		8
	9			Wages Payable	219		50 00	9
	10							10
(d)	11		30	Depr. Expense—Delivery Equipment	541	100 00		11
	12			Accum. Depr.—Delivery Equipment	185.1		100 00	12

Jessie's adjusting entries are illustrated in Figure 5-23 as they would appear in a general journal. Note that the last day of the accounting period, June 30, has been entered in the date column and "*Adjusting Entries*" is written in the Description column prior to the first adjusting entry. No explanation is required in the Description column for individual adjusting entries. We simply label them as adjusting entries.

U REVU

Complete U REVU-5 on **page 155** to test your basic understanding of LO5.

METHODS OF ACCOUNTING: CASH, MODIFIED CASH, AND ACCRUAL

LO6 Explain the cash, modified cash, and accrual bases of accounting.

The accrual basis of accounting offers the best matching of revenues and expenses and is required under generally accepted accounting principles. GAAP financial statements prepared using the accrual method are particularly important when major businesses want to raise large amounts of money. Investors and creditors expect GAAP financial statements and generally will not invest or make loans without them.

However, many small professional service organizations are not concerned with raising large amounts of money from investors and creditors. These organizations include CPAs, doctors, dentists, lawyers, engineers, and architects. Since these organizations do not need to prepare GAAP financial statements, they often use the cash or modified cash basis. If one of these organizations needs to borrow money from a bank that requires GAAP financial statements, an accountant can convert the financial statements to the accrual basis.

Under the **accrual basis of accounting**, revenues are recorded when earned. Revenues are considered earned when a service is provided or a product sold, regardless of whether cash is received. If cash is not received, a receivable is set up.

The accrual basis also assumes that expenses are recorded when incurred. Expenses are incurred when a service is received or an asset consumed, regardless of when cash is paid. If cash is not paid when a service is received, a payable is set up. When assets are consumed, prepaid assets are decreased or long-term assets are depreciated. Since the accrual basis accounts for long-term assets, prepaid assets, receivables, and payables, it is the most comprehensive system and best method of measuring income for the vast majority of businesses.

LEARNING KEY

Accrual Basis

Accounting for:		
Revenues and Expenses	**Assets and Liabilities**	
Record revenue when earned.	Accounts receivable:	Yes
Record expenses when incurred.	Accounts payable:	Yes
	Prepaid assets:	Yes
	Long-term assets:	Yes

Under the **cash basis of accounting**, revenues are recorded when cash is received and expenses are recorded when cash is paid. This method will provide results that are similar to the accrual basis if there are few receivables, payables, and assets. However, as shown in Figure 5-24, the cash and accrual bases can result in very different measures of net income if a business has significant amounts of receivables, payables, and assets.

LEARNING KEY

Cash Basis

Accounting for:		**Assets and Liabilities**	
Revenues and Expenses		Accounts receivable:	No
	Record revenue when cash is received.	Accounts payable:	No
	Record expenses when cash is paid.	Prepaid assets:	No
		Long-term assets:	No

FIGURE 5-24 Cash versus Accrual Accounting

RECOGNITION OF REVENUES AND EXPENSES: ACCRUAL BASIS VS. CASH BASIS

	Method of Accounting			
	Accrual Basis		Cash Basis	
Transaction	Expense	Revenue	Expense	Revenue
(a) Provided services on account, $600.		$600		
(b) Paid wages earned this period, $300	$300		$300	
(c) Received cash for services performed on account last month, $200				$ 200
(d) Received cleaning bill for month, $250	250			
(e) Paid on account for last month's advertising, $100			100	
(f) Purchase of supplies, $50			50	
(g) Supplies used during month, $40	40			
	$590	$600	$450	$ 200
Revenue		$600		$ 200
Expense		590		450
Net Income (Loss)		$ 10		$(250)
Revenues are recognized when:		earned		cash is received
Expenses are recognized when:		incurred		cash is paid

The modified cash basis is the same as the accrual basis, except receivables and payables are not recognized for revenues and operating expenses.

A third method of accounting combines aspects of the cash and accrual methods. With the **modified cash basis**, a business uses the cash basis for recording revenues and most expenses. Exceptions are made when cash is paid for assets with useful lives greater than one accounting period. For example, under a strict cash basis, if cash is paid for equipment, buildings, supplies, or insurance, the amount is immediately recorded as an expense. This approach could cause major distortions when measuring net income. Under the modified cash basis, cash payments like these are recorded as assets, and adjustments are made each period as under the accrual basis. Liabilities associated with the acquisition of these assets are also recognized.

Although similar to the accrual basis, the modified cash basis does not account for receivables or for payables for services received. Thus, the modified cash basis is a combination of the cash and accrual methods of accounting. The differences and similarities among the cash, modified cash, and accrual methods of accounting are demonstrated in Figure 5-25.

LEARNING KEY

Modified Cash Basis

Accounting for:
Revenues and Expenses

Record revenue when cash is received.
Record expenses when cash is paid, except for assets with useful lives greater than one accounting period. Accrual accounting is used for prepaid assets (insurance and supplies) and long-term assets.

Assets and Liabilities	
Accounts receivable:	No
Accounts payable	
for purchase of assets:	Yes
for services received:	No
Prepaid assets:	Yes
Long-term assets:	Yes

If all businesses were the same, only one method of accounting would be needed. However, businesses vary in their need for major assets like buildings and equipment, the amount of customer receivables, and payables to suppliers. For example, if a business were rather small with no major assets, receivables, or payables, it would be simpler to use the cash basis of accounting. In addition, under these circumstances, the difference in net income under the accrual and cash bases of accounting would be small. Most individuals fit this description and use the cash basis on their tax returns.

Businesses with buildings and equipment, but few receivables and payables, might use the modified cash basis. Again, the accounting would be a little simpler and differences between net income computed under the modified cash and accrual bases would be small. Finally, businesses with buildings and equipment, and receivables and payables, should use the accrual basis of accounting to achieve the best matching of revenues and expenses.

LEARNING KEY

The shaded areas in Figure 5-25 show that sometimes the modified cash basis is the same as the cash basis and sometimes it is the same as the accrual basis. For some transactions, all methods are the same.

FIGURE 5-25 Comparison of Cash, Modified Cash, and Accrual Methods

ENTRIES MADE UNDER EACH ACCOUNTING METHOD			
Event	**Cash**	**Modified Cash**	**Accrual**
Revenues: Perform services for cash	Cash Professional Fees	Cash Professional Fees	Cash Professional Fees
Perform services on account	No entry	No entry	Accounts Receivable Professional Fees
Expenses: Pay cash for operating expenses: wages, advertising, rent, telephone, etc.	Expense Cash	Expense Cash	Expense Cash
Pay cash for prepaid items: insurance, supplies, etc.	Expense Cash	Prepaid Asset Cash	Prepaid Asset Cash
Pay cash for property, plant, and equipment (PP&E)	Expense Cash	PP&E Asset Cash	PP&E Asset Cash
Receive bill for services received	No entry	No entry	Expense Accounts Payable
End-of-period adjustments: Wages earned by employees but not paid	No entry	No entry	Wages Expense Wages Payable
Prepaid items used	No entry	Expense Prepaid Asset	Expense Prepaid Asset
Depreciation on property, plant, and equipment	No entry	Depreciation Expense Accumulated Depreciation	Depreciation Expense Accumulated Depreciation
Other: Purchase of assets on account	No entry	Asset Accounts Payable	Asset Accounts Payable
Payments for assets purchased on account	Expense Cash	Accounts Payable Cash	Accounts Payable Cash

U REVU Complete U REVU-6 on **page 155** to test your basic understanding of LO6.

LEARNING OBJECTIVES Key Points to Remember

LEARNING OBJECTIVES	Key Points to Remember
LO1 Prepare end-of-period adjustments.	End-of-period adjustments are necessary to bring the general ledger accounts up to date prior to preparing financial statements. Reasons to adjust the trial balance are as follows: 1. To report all revenues earned during the accounting period. 2. To report all expenses incurred to produce the revenues during the accounting period. 3. To accurately report the assets on the balance sheet. Some assets may have expired, depreciated, or been used up during the accounting period. 4. To accurately report the liabilities on the balance sheet date. Expenses may have been incurred, but not yet paid.
LO2 Post adjusting entries to the general ledger.	Adjusting entries are posted to the general ledger in the same manner as all other entries, except that "Adjusting" is written in the Item column of the general ledger.
LO3 Prepare a work sheet.	Steps in preparing the work sheet are as follows: 1. Prepare the trial balance. 2. Prepare the adjustments. 3. Prepare the adjusted trial balance. 4. Extend the adjusted account balances to the Income Statement and Balance Sheet columns. 5. Total the Income Statement and Balance Sheet columns to compute the net income or net loss.
LO4 Describe methods for finding errors on the work sheet.	Tips for finding errors on the work sheet include the following: 1. Check the addition of all columns. 2. Check the addition and subtraction required when extending to the Adjusted Trial Balance columns. 3. Make sure the adjusted account balances have been extended to the appropriate columns. 4. Make sure that the net income or net loss has been added to the appropriate columns.
LO5 Journalize adjusting entries from the work sheet.	The adjustments are copied from the work sheet to the journal. The last day of the accounting period is entered in the Date column and "Adjusting Entries" is written in the Description column.
LO6 Explain the cash, modified cash, and accrual bases of accounting.	Cash Basis—Record revenues when cash is received and expenses when cash is paid. Accrual Basis—Record revenues when earned and expenses as incurred. Modified Cash Basis—Same as accrual, except no accounts receivable and no accounts payable for operating expenses.

DEMONSTRATION PROBLEM

Justin Park is a lawyer specializing in corporate tax law. He began his practice on January 1. A chart of accounts and trial balance taken on December 31, 20--, are provided below.

Information for year-end adjustments is as follows:

(a) Office supplies on hand at year-end amounted to $300.

(b) On January 1, 20--, Park purchased office equipment costing $15,000 with an expected life of five years and no salvage value.

(c) Computer equipment costing $6,000 with an expected life of three years and no salvage value was purchased on July 1, 20--. Assume that Park computes depreciation to the nearest full month.

(d) A premium of $1,200 for a one-year insurance policy was paid on December 1, 20--.

(e) Wages earned by Park's part-time secretary, which have not yet been paid, amount to $300.

REQUIRED

1. Prepare the work sheet for the year ended December 31, 20--.
2. Prepare adjusting entries in a general journal.

JUSTIN PARK LEGAL SERVICES
CHART OF ACCOUNTS

Assets		**Revenue**	
101	Cash	401	Client Fees
142	Office Supplies		
145	Prepaid Insurance	**Expenses**	
181	Office Equipment	511	Wages Expense
181.1	Accumulated Depr.—	521	Rent Expense
	Office Equipment	523	Office Supplies Expense
187	Computer Equipment	525	Telephone Expense
187.1	Accumulated Depr.—	533	Utilities Expense
	Computer Equipment	535	Insurance Expense
Liabilities		541	Depr. Expense—
201	Notes Payable		Office Equipment
202	Accounts Payable	542	Depr. Expense—
219	Wages Payable		Computer Equipment
Owner's Equity			
311	Justin Park, Capital		
312	Justin Park, Drawing		

(continued)

Justin Park Legal Services
Trial Balance
December 31, 20 --

ACCOUNT TITLE	ACCOUNT NO.	DEBIT BALANCE	CREDIT BALANCE
Cash	101	7,000.00	
Office Supplies	142	800.00	
Prepaid Insurance	145	1,200.00	
Office Equipment	181	15,000.00	
Computer Equipment	187	6,000.00	
Notes Payable	201		5,000.00
Accounts Payable	202		500.00
Justin Park, Capital	311		11,400.00
Justin Park, Drawing	312	5,000.00	
Client Fees	401		40,000.00
Wages Expense	511	12,000.00	
Rent Expense	521	5,000.00	
Telephone Expense	525	1,000.00	
Utilities Expense	533	3,900.00	
		56,900.00	56,900.00

The solution to part (1) is found on page 151.

2.

GENERAL JOURNAL PAGE 11

	DATE		DESCRIPTION	POST. REF.	DEBIT	CREDIT	
1			Adjusting Entries				1
2	20-- Dec.	31	Office Supplies Expense		500.00		2
3			Office Supplies			500.00	3
4							4
5		31	Depr. Expense—Office Equipment		3,000.00		5
6			Accum. Depr.—Office Equipment			3,000.00	6
7							7
8		31	Depr. Expense—Computer Equipment		1,000.00		8
9			Accum. Depr.—Computer Equipment			1,000.00	9
10							10
11		31	Insurance Expense		100.00		11
12			Prepaid Insurance			100.00	12
13							13
14		31	Wages Expense		300.00		14
15			Wages Payable			300.00	15

SOLUTION 1.

Justin Park Legal Services
Work Sheet
For Year Ended December 31, 20--

	ACCOUNT TITLE	TRIAL BALANCE DEBIT	TRIAL BALANCE CREDIT	ADJUSTMENTS DEBIT	ADJUSTMENTS CREDIT	ADJUSTED TRIAL BALANCE DEBIT	ADJUSTED TRIAL BALANCE CREDIT	INCOME STATEMENT DEBIT	INCOME STATEMENT CREDIT	BALANCE SHEET DEBIT	BALANCE SHEET CREDIT	
1	Cash	7,000.00				7,000.00				7,000.00		1
2	Office Supplies	800.00			(a) 500.00	300.00				300.00		2
3	Prepaid Insurance	1,200.00			(d) 100.00	1,100.00				1,100.00		3
4	Office Equipment	15,000.00				15,000.00				15,000.00		4
5	Accum. Depr.—Office Equip.				(b) 3,000.00		3,000.00				3,000.00	5
6	Computer Equipment	6,000.00				6,000.00				6,000.00		6
7	Accum. Depr.—Computer Equip.				(c) 1,000.00		1,000.00				1,000.00	7
8	Notes Payable		5,000.00				5,000.00				5,000.00	8
9	Accounts Payable		500.00				500.00				500.00	9
10	Wages Payable				(e) 300.00		300.00				300.00	10
11	Justin Park, Capital		11,400.00				11,400.00				11,400.00	11
12	Justin Park, Drawing	5,000.00				5,000.00				5,000.00		12
13	Client Fees		40,000.00				40,000.00		40,000.00			13
14	Wages Expense	12,000.00		(e) 300.00		12,300.00		12,300.00				14
15	Rent Expense	5,000.00				5,000.00		5,000.00				15
16	Office Supplies Expense			(a) 500.00		500.00		500.00				16
17	Telephone Expense	1,000.00				1,000.00		1,000.00				17
18	Utilities Expense	3,900.00				3,900.00		3,900.00				18
19	Insurance Expense			(d) 100.00		100.00		100.00				19
20	Depr. Expense—Office Equip.			(b) 3,000.00		3,000.00		3,000.00				20
21	Depr. Expense—Computer Equip.			(c) 1,000.00		1,000.00		1,000.00				21
22		56,900.00	56,900.00	4,900.00	4,900.00	61,200.00	61,200.00	26,800.00	40,000.00	34,400.00	21,200.00	22
23	Net Income							13,200.00			13,200.00	23
24								40,000.00	40,000.00	34,400.00	34,400.00	24
25												25
26												26
27												27
28												28
29												29
30												30

KEY TERMS

accrual basis of accounting (144) A method of accounting under which revenues are recorded when earned and expenses are recorded when incurred.

Adjusted Trial Balance columns (142) The third pair of amount columns on the work sheet. They are used to prove the equality of the debits and credits in the general ledger accounts after making all end-of-period adjustments.

adjusting entries (131) Journal entries made at the end of an accounting period to reflect changes in account balances that are not the direct result of an exchange with an outside party.

Balance Sheet columns (142) The work sheet columns that show the amounts that will be reported in the balance sheet and the statement of owner's equity.

book value (137) The difference between the asset account and its related accumulated depreciation account. The value reflected by the accounting records.

cash basis of accounting (145) A method of accounting under which revenues are recorded when cash is received and expenses are recorded when cash is paid.

contra-asset (136) An account with a credit balance that is deducted from the related asset account on the balance sheet.

depreciable cost (136) The cost of an asset that is subject to depreciation.

depreciation (136) A method of matching an asset's original cost against the revenues produced over its useful life.

fiscal year (131) A 12-month period for which financial reports are prepared.

historical cost principle (136) A principle that requires assets to be recorded at their actual cost.

Income Statement columns (142) The work sheet columns that show the amounts that will be reported in the income statement.

market value (136) The amount an item can be sold for under normal economic conditions.

matching principle (131) A principle that requires the matching of revenues earned during an accounting period with the expenses incurred to produce the revenues.

modified cash basis (145) A method of accounting that combines aspects of the cash and accrual methods. It uses the cash basis for recording revenues and most expenses. Exceptions are made when cash is paid for assets with useful lives greater than one accounting period.

plant assets (136) Assets of a durable nature that will be used for operations over several years. Examples include buildings and equipment.

salvage value (136) The expected market value of an asset at the end of its useful life.

straight-line method (136) A depreciation method in which the depreciable cost is divided by the estimated useful life.

undepreciated cost (137) The difference between the asset account and its related accumulated depreciation account. Also known as book value.

useful life (136) The period of time that an asset is expected to help produce revenues.

work sheet (140) A form used to pull together all of the information needed to enter adjusting entries and prepare the financial statements.

SELF-STUDY QUESTIONS AND EXERCISES

True/False Questions

1. LO1 The matching principle in accounting requires the matching of debits and credits.
2. LO1 Adjusting entries are required at the end of the accounting period because of mistakes in the journal and ledger.
3. LO1 As part of the adjustment of supplies, an expense account is debited and Supplies is credited for the amount of supplies used during the accounting period.
4. LO1 Depreciable cost is the difference between the original cost of the asset and its accumulated depreciation.
5. LO1 The purpose of depreciation is to record the asset's market value in the accounting records.

Multiple Choice Questions

1. LO1 The purpose of depreciation is to
   (a) spread the cost of an asset over its useful life.
   (b) show the current market value of an asset.
   (c) set up a reserve fund to purchase a new asset.
   (d) expense the asset in the year it was purchased.
2. LO1 Depreciable cost is the
   (a) difference between original cost and accumulated depreciation.
   (b) difference in actual cost and true market value.
   (c) difference between original cost and estimated salvage value.
   (d) difference between estimated salvage value and the actual salvage value.
3. LO1 Book value is the
   (a) difference between market value and estimated value.
   (b) difference between market value and historical cost.
   (c) difference between original cost and salvage value.
   (d) difference between original cost and accumulated depreciation.
4. LO1 The adjustment for wages earned by employees but not yet paid is
   (a) debit Wages Payable and credit Wages Expense.
   (b) debit Wages Expense and credit Cash.
   (c) debit Wages Expense and credit Wages Payable.
   (d) debit Wages Expense and credit Accounts Receivable.
5. LO3 The first step in preparing a work sheet is to
   (a) prepare the trial balance.
   (b) prepare the adjustments.
   (c) prepare the adjusted trial balance.
   (d) extend the amounts from the Adjusted Trial Balance to the Income Statement and Balance Sheet columns.

U REVU Exercises

1. LO1 On December 31, the trial balance indicates that the supplies account has a balance, prior to the adjusting entry, of $100. A physical count of the supplies inventory shows that $70 of supplies remain. What adjustment should be made to the supplies account?
2. LO2 When posting adjusting entries to the general ledger, what is written in the Item column?
3. LO3 Indicate the heading for the columns of the work sheet A through F below.

	A	B		C		D		E		F		
		DEBIT	CREDIT	DEBIT	CREDIT	DEBIT	CREDIT	DEBIT	CREDIT	DEBIT	CREDIT	
1												1
2												2

4. LO4 Find the error(s) in the work sheet below.

	ACCOUNT TITLE	TRIAL BALANCE		ADJUSTMENTS		ADJUSTED TRIAL BALANCE		INCOME STATEMENT		BALANCE SHEET		
		DEBIT	CREDIT	DEBIT	CREDIT	DEBIT	CREDIT	DEBIT	CREDIT	DEBIT	CREDIT	
1	Cash	370 00				370 00				370 00		1
2	Accounts Receivable	650 00				650 00				650 00		2
3	Supplies	80 00			(a) 60 00	140 00				140 00		3
4	Prepaid Insurance	200 00			(b) 25 00	175 00				175 00		4
5	Delivery Equipment	3600 00				3600 00				3600 00		5
6	Accum. Depr.—Delivery Equipment				(d) 100 00		100 00				100 00	6
7	Accounts Payable		1800 00				1800 00				1800 00	7
8	Wages Payable				(c) 50 00		50 00				50 00	8
9	Jessica Jane, Capital		2000 00				2000 00				2000 00	9
10	Jessica Jane, Drawing	150 00				150 00				150 00		10
11	Delivery Fees		2150 00				2150 00		2150 00			11
12	Wages Expense	650 00		(c) 50 00		700 00		700 00				12
13	Rent Expense	200 00				200 00		200 00				13
14	Supplies Expense			(a) 60 00		60 00		60 00				14
15	Telephone Expense	50 00				50 00		50 00				15
16	Insurance Expense			(b) 25 00		25 00		25 00				16
17	Depr. Expense—Delivery Equipment			(d) 100 00		100 00		100 00				17
18		5950 00	5950 00	235 00	235 00	6220 00	6100 00	1135 00	2150 00	5085 00	3950 00	18
19								1015 00			1135 00	19
20								2150 00	2150 00	5085 00	5085 00	20
21												21
22												22
23												23
24												24

5. LO5 Using the following partial work sheet prepared on December 31, 20--, journalize the adjusting entry.

	ACCOUNT TITLE	TRIAL BALANCE		ADJUSTMENTS	
		DEBIT	CREDIT	DEBIT	CREDIT
1	Cash	370 00			
2	Accounts Receivable	650 00			
3	Supplies	80 00			
4	Prepaid Insurance	200 00			(b) 50 00
5	Delivery Equipment	3600 00			
6	Accum. Depr.—Delivery Equipment				
7	Accounts Payable		1800 00		
8	Wages Payable				
9	Jessica Jane, Capital		2000 00		
10	Jessica Jane, Drawing	150 00			
11	Delivery Fees		2150 00		
12	Wages Expense	650 00			
13	Rent Expense	200 00			
14	Supplies Expense				
15	Telephone Expense	50 00			
16	Insurance Expense			(b) 50 00	
17	Depr. Expense—Delivery Equipment				
18		5950 00	5950 00	50 00	50 00
19					

6. LO6 Bill Roberts provided legal advice to a client for $500 on account. Roberts paid a legal assistant $50 for research on this engagement and used office supplies costing $10. If these are the only transactions for the period, compute net income under the cash, accrual, and modified cash bases.

The answers to the Self-Study Questions and Exercises are at the end of the chapter (pages 173–174).

APPLYING YOUR KNOWLEDGE

REVIEW QUESTIONS

LO1 1. Explain the matching principle.

LO1 2. Explain the historical cost principle.

LO1 3. Describe a plant asset.

LO1 4. What is a contra-asset?

LO1 5. What is the useful life of an asset?

LO1 6. What is the purpose of depreciation?

LO1 7. What is an asset's depreciable cost?

LO1 8. What is the book value of an asset?

LO3 9. Explain the purpose of the work sheet.

LO3 10. Identify the five major column headings on a work sheet.

LO3 11. List the five steps taken in preparing a work sheet.

LO4 12. Describe four tips for finding errors on the work sheet.

LO6 13. Explain when revenues are recorded under the cash basis, modified cash basis, and accrual basis of accounting.

LO6 14. Explain when expenses are recorded under the cash basis, modified cash basis, and accrual basis of accounting.

SERIES A EXERCISES

E 5-1A (LO1)

ADJUSTMENT FOR SUPPLIES On December 31, the trial balance indicates that the supplies account has a balance, prior to the adjusting entry, of $320. A physical count of the supplies inventory shows that $90 of supplies remain. Analyze this adjustment for supplies using T accounts, and then formally enter this adjustment in the general journal.

E 5-2A (LO1)

ADJUSTMENT FOR INSURANCE On December 1, a six-month liability insurance policy was purchased for $900. Analyze the required adjustment as of December 31 using T accounts, and then formally enter this adjustment in the general journal.

E 5-3A (LO1)

ADJUSTMENT FOR WAGES On December 31, the trial balance shows wages expense of $600. An additional $200 of wages was earned by the employees, but has not yet been paid. Analyze this adjustment for wages using T accounts, and then formally enter this adjustment in the general journal.

E 5-4A (LO1)

ADJUSTMENT FOR DEPRECIATION OF ASSET On December 1, delivery equipment was purchased for $7,200. The delivery equipment has an estimated useful life of four years (48 months) and no salvage value. Using the straight-line depreciation method, analyze the necessary adjusting entry as of December 31 (one month) using T accounts, and then formally enter this adjustment in the general journal.

E 5-5A (LO1)

CALCULATION OF BOOK VALUE On June 1, 20--, a depreciable asset was acquired for $5,400. The asset has an estimated useful life of five years (60 months) and no salvage value. Using the straight-line depreciation method, calculate the book value as of December 31, 20--.

E 5-6A (LO1)

ANALYSIS OF ADJUSTING ENTRY FOR SUPPLIES Analyze each situation and indicate the correct dollar amount for the adjusting entry. (Trial balance is abbreviated as TB.)

1. Ending inventory of supplies is $130.

(Balance Sheet) Supplies

TB 460	
	Adj. ______
Bal. ______	

(Income Statement) Supplies Expense

Adj. ______	

2. Amount of supplies used is $320.

(Balance Sheet) Supplies

TB 545	
	Adj. ______
Bal. ______	

(Income Statement) Supplies Expense

Adj. ______	

E 5-7A (LO1)

ANALYSIS OF ADJUSTING ENTRY FOR INSURANCE Analyze each situation and indicate the correct dollar amount for the adjusting entry.

1. Amount of insurance expired is $900.

(Balance Sheet) Prepaid Insurance

TB 1,300	
	Adj. ______
Bal. ______	

(Income Statement) Insurance Expense

Adj. ______	

2. Amount of unexpired insurance is $185.

(Balance Sheet) Prepaid Insurance

TB 860	
	Adj. ______
Bal. ______	

(Income Statement) Insurance Expense

Adj. ______	

E 5-8A (LO2)

POSTING ADJUSTING ENTRIES Two adjusting entries are in the following general journal. Post these adjusting entries to the four general ledger accounts. The following account numbers were taken from the chart of accounts: 141, Supplies; 219, Wages Payable; 511, Wages Expense; and 523, Supplies Expense. If you are not using the working papers that accompany this text, enter the following balances before posting the entries: Supplies, $200 Dr.; Wages Expense, $1,200 Dr.

(continued)

	GENERAL JOURNAL					PAGE 9	
	DATE		DESCRIPTION	POST. REF.	DEBIT	CREDIT	
1			Adjusting Entries				1
2	20-- Dec.	31	Supplies Expense		85 00		2
3			Supplies			85 00	3
4							4
5		31	Wages Expense		220 00		5
6			Wages Payable			220 00	6

E 5-9A (LO3)

✓ Adjustments col. total: $1,550

WORK SHEET AND ADJUSTING ENTRIES A partial work sheet for Jim Jacobs' Furniture Repair is shown as follows. Indicate by letters (a) through (d) the four adjustments in the Adjustments columns of the work sheet, properly matching each debit and credit. Complete the Adjustments columns.

Jim Jacobs' Furniture Repair
Work Sheet (Partial)
For Year Ended December 31, 20 - -

	ACCOUNT TITLE	TRIAL BALANCE		ADJUSTMENTS		ADJUSTED TRIAL BALANCE		
		DEBIT	CREDIT	DEBIT	CREDIT	DEBIT	CREDIT	
1	Cash	100 00				100 00		1
2	Supplies	850 00				200 00		2
3	Prepaid Insurance	900 00				300 00		3
4	Delivery Equipment	3,600 00				3,600 00		4
5	Accum. Depr.—Delivery Equipment		600 00				800 00	5
6	Wages Payable						100 00	6
7	Jim Jacobs, Capital		4,000 00				4,000 00	7
8	Repair Fees		1,650 00				1,650 00	8
9	Wages Expense	600 00				700 00		9
10	Advertising Expense	200 00				200 00		10
11	Supplies Expense					650 00		11
12	Insurance Expense					600 00		12
13	Depr. Expense—Delivery Equipment					200 00		13
14		6,250 00	6,250 00			6,550 00	6,550 00	14

E 5-10A (LO5)

JOURNALIZING ADJUSTING ENTRIES From the adjustments columns in Exercise 5-9A, journalize the four adjusting entries, as of December 31, in proper general journal format.

E 5-11A (LO3)

EXTENDING ADJUSTED BALANCES TO THE INCOME STATEMENT AND BALANCE SHEET COLUMNS Indicate with an "X" whether each account total should be extended to the Income Statement Debit or Credit or to the Balance Sheet Debit or Credit columns on the work sheet.

	Income Statement		Balance Sheet	
	Debit	Credit	Debit	Credit
Cash	______	______	______	______
Accounts Receivable	______	______	______	______
Supplies	______	______	______	______
Prepaid Insurance	______	______	______	______
Delivery Equipment	______	______	______	______
Accum. Depr.—Delivery Equipment	______	______	______	______
Accounts Payable	______	______	______	______
Wages Payable	______	______	______	______
Owner, Capital	______	______	______	______
Owner, Drawing	______	______	______	______
Delivery Fees	______	______	______	______
Wages Expense	______	______	______	______
Rent Expense	______	______	______	______
Supplies Expense	______	______	______	______
Insurance Expense	______	______	______	______
Depr. Exp.—Delivery Equipment	______	______	______	______

E 5-12A (LO3)

ANALYSIS OF NET INCOME OR NET LOSS ON THE WORK SHEET Indicate with an "X" in which columns, Income Statement Debit or Credit or Balance Sheet Debit or Credit, a net income or a net loss would appear on a work sheet.

	Income Statement		Balance Sheet	
	Debit	Credit	Debit	Credit
Net Income	______	______	______	______
Net Loss	______	______	______	______

E 5-13A (LO6)

✓ See Figure 5-25 in text

CASH, MODIFIED CASH, AND ACCRUAL BASES OF ACCOUNTING Prepare the entry for each of the following transactions, using the (a) cash basis, (b) modified cash basis, and (c) accrual basis of accounting.

1. Purchase supplies on account.
2. Make payment on asset previously purchased.
3. Purchase supplies for cash.
4. Purchase insurance for cash.
5. Pay cash for wages.
6. Pay cash for telephone expense.
7. Pay cash for new equipment.

End-of-Period Adjusting Entries:

8. Wages earned but not paid.
9. Prepaid item purchased, partly used.
10. Depreciation on long-term assets.

SERIES A PROBLEMS

P 5-14A (LO1/3)

✓ Adjustments col. total: $1,895; Net income: $1,060

ADJUSTMENTS AND WORK SHEET SHOWING NET INCOME The trial balance after one month of operation for Mason's Delivery Service as of September 30, 20--, is shown below. Data to complete the adjustments are as follows:

(a) Supplies inventory as of September 30, $165.
(b) Insurance expired (used), $800.
(c) Depreciation on delivery equipment, $400.
(d) Wages earned by employees but not paid as of September 30, $225.

REQUIRED

1. Enter the adjustments in the Adjustments columns of the work sheet.
2. Complete the work sheet.

Mason's Delivery Service
Work Sheet (Partial)
For Month Ended September 30, 20 - -

	ACCOUNT TITLE	TRIAL BALANCE		ADJUSTMENTS		
		DEBIT	CREDIT	DEBIT	CREDIT	
1	Cash	1600 00				1
2	Accounts Receivable	940 00				2
3	Supplies	635 00				3
4	Prepaid Insurance	1200 00				4
5	Delivery Equipment	6400 00				5
6	Accum. Depr.—Delivery Equipment					6
7	Accounts Payable		1220 00			7
8	Wages Payable					8
9	Jill Mason, Capital		8000 00			9
10	Jill Mason, Drawing	1400 00				10
11	Delivery Fees		6200 00			11
12	Wages Expense	1500 00				12
13	Advertising Expense	460 00				13
14	Rent Expense	800 00				14
15	Supplies Expense					15
16	Telephone Expense	165 00				16
17	Insurance Expense					17
18	Repair Expense	230 00				18
19	Oil and Gas Expense	90 00				19
20	Depr. Expense—Delivery Equipment					20
21		15420 00	15420 00			21

P 5-15A (LO1/3)

✓ Adjustments col. total: $1,380; Net loss: $2,495

ADJUSTMENTS AND WORK SHEET SHOWING A NET LOSS Jason Armstrong started a business called Campus Delivery Service. After the first month of operations, the trial balance as of November 30, 20--, is as shown on the next page.

REQUIRED

1. Analyze the following adjustments and enter them on the work sheet.
   (a) Ending inventory of supplies on November 30, $185.
   (b) Unexpired (remaining) insurance as of November 30, $800.
   (c) Depreciation expense on van, $300.
   (d) Wages earned but not paid as of November 30, $190.
2. Complete the work sheet.

Campus Delivery Service
Work Sheet (Partial)
For Month Ended November 30, 20 - -

	ACCOUNT TITLE	TRIAL BALANCE DEBIT	TRIAL BALANCE CREDIT	ADJUSTMENTS DEBIT	ADJUSTMENTS CREDIT	
1	Cash	980 00				1
2	Accounts Receivable	590 00				2
3	Supplies	575 00				3
4	Prepaid Insurance	1300 00				4
5	Van	5800 00				5
6	Accum. Depr.—Van					6
7	Accounts Payable		960 00			7
8	Wages Payable					8
9	Jason Armstrong, Capital		10000 00			9
10	Jason Armstrong, Drawing	600 00				10
11	Delivery Fees		2600 00			11
12	Wages Expense	1800 00				12
13	Advertising Expense	380 00				13
14	Rent Expense	900 00				14
15	Supplies Expense					15
16	Telephone Expense	220 00				16
17	Insurance Expense					17
18	Repair Expense	315 00				18
19	Oil and Gas Expense	100 00				19
20	Depr. Expense—Van					20
21		13560 00	13560 00			21

P 5-16A (LO2/5)

KA KLOOSTER & ALLEN

JOURNALIZE AND POST ADJUSTING ENTRIES FROM THE WORK SHEET

Refer to Problem 5-15A and the following additional information:

Account Name	Account Number	Balance in Account Before Adjusting Entry
Supplies	141	$ 575
Prepaid Insurance	145	1,300
Accum. Depr.—Van	185.1	0
Wages Payable	219	0
Wages Expense	511	1,800
Supplies Expense	523	0
Insurance Expense	535	0
Depr. Expense—Van	541	0

(continued)

REQUIRED

1. Journalize the adjusting entries on page 5 of the general journal.
2. Post the adjusting entries to the general ledger. (If you are not using the working papers that accompany this text, enter the balances provided in this problem before posting the adjusting entries.)

P 5-17A (LO4)

✓ Adjustments col. total: $1,160; Net income: $1,575

CORRECTING WORK SHEET WITH ERRORS A beginning accounting student tried to complete a work sheet for Joyce Lee's Tax Service. The following adjusting entries were to have been analyzed and entered onto the work sheet. The work sheet is shown on page 163.

(a) Ending inventory of supplies as of March 31, $160.
(b) Unexpired insurance as of March 31, $520.
(c) Depreciation of office equipment, $275.
(d) Wages earned, but not paid as of March 31, $110.

REQUIRED

The accounting student made a number of errors. Review the work sheet for addition mistakes, transpositions, and other errors and make all necessary corrections.

SERIES B EXERCISES

E 5-1B (LO1)

ADJUSTMENT FOR SUPPLIES On July 31, the trial balance indicates that the supplies account has a balance, prior to the adjusting entry, of $430. A physical count of the supplies inventory shows that $120 of supplies remain. Analyze the adjustment for supplies using T accounts, and then formally enter this adjustment in the general journal.

E 5-2B (LO1)

ADJUSTMENT FOR INSURANCE On July 1, a six-month liability insurance policy was purchased for $750. Analyze the required adjustment as of July 31 using T accounts, and then formally enter this adjustment in the general journal.

E 5-3B (LO1)

ADJUSTMENT FOR WAGES On July 31, the trial balance shows wages expense of $800. An additional $150 of wages was earned by the employees but has not yet been paid. Analyze the required adjustment using T accounts, and then formally enter this adjustment in the general journal.

E 5-4B (LO1)

ADJUSTMENT FOR DEPRECIATION OF ASSET On July 1, delivery equipment was purchased for $4,320. The delivery equipment has an estimated useful life of three years (36 months) and no salvage value. Using the straight-line depreciation method, analyze the necessary adjusting entry as of July 31 (one month) using T accounts, and then formally enter this adjustment in the general journal.

E 5-5B (LO1)

CALCULATION OF BOOK VALUE On January 1, 20--, a depreciable asset was acquired for $5,760. The asset has an estimated useful life of four years (48 months) and no salvage value. Use the straight-line depreciation method to calculate the book value as of July 1, 20--.

PROBLEM 5-17A

Joyce Lee's Tax Service
Work Sheet
For Month Ended March 31, 20--

	ACCOUNT TITLE	TRIAL BALANCE		ADJUSTMENTS		ADJUSTED TRIAL BALANCE		INCOME STATEMENT		BALANCE SHEET		
		DEBIT	CREDIT	DEBIT	CREDIT	DEBIT	CREDIT	DEBIT	CREDIT	DEBIT	CREDIT	
1	Cash	1725 00				1725 00				1752 00		1
2	Accounts Receivable	960 00				960 00				96 00		2
3	Supplies	525 00			(a) 160 00	365 00				365 00		3
4	Prepaid Insurance	930 00			(b) 410 00	540 00				540 00		4
5	Office Equipment	5450 00			(c) 275 00	5175 00				5175 00		5
6	Accum. Depr.– Office Equipment											6
7	Accounts Payable		480 00				480 00				480 00	7
8	Wages Payable				(d) 110 00		110 00		110 00			8
9	Joyce Lee, Capital		7500 00				7500 00				7500 00	9
10	Joyce Lee, Drawing	1125 00				1125 00		1125 00				10
11	Professional Fees		5700 00				5700 00		5700 00			11
12	Wages Expense	1420 00		(d) 110 00		1420 00		1420 00			1580 00	12
13	Advertising Expense	350 00				350 00		350 00				13
14	Rent Expense	700 00				700 00		700 00				14
15	Supplies Expense			(a) 160 00		160 00		160 00				15
16	Telephone Expense	130 00				130 00		130 00				16
17	Utilities Expense	190 00				190 00		190 00				17
18	Insurance Expense			(b) 410 00		410 00		41 00				18
19	Depr. Expense–Office Equipment			(c) 275 00		275 00		275 00				19
20	Miscellaneous Expense	175 00				175 00		175 00				20
21												21
22		13680 00	13680 00	955 00	955 00	13160 00	13790 00	4566 00	5810 00	9508 00	7980 00	22
23								1244 00			1528 00	23
24								5810 00	5810 00	9508 00	9508 00	24
25												25
26												26
27												27
28												28
29												29
30												30

Contains Errors

This work sheet contains errors.

E 5-6B (LO1)

ANALYSIS OF ADJUSTING ENTRY FOR SUPPLIES Analyze each situation and indicate the correct dollar amount for the adjusting entry.

1. Ending inventory of supplies is $95.

(Balance Sheet)
Supplies

TB 540	
	Adj. ______
Bal. ______	

(Income Statement)
Supplies Expense

Adj. ______	

2. Amount of supplies used is $280.

(Balance Sheet)
Supplies

TB 330	
	Adj. ______
Bal. ______	

(Income Statement)
Supplies Expense

Adj. ______	

E 5-7B (LO1)

ANALYSIS OF ADJUSTING ENTRY FOR INSURANCE Analyze each situation and indicate the correct dollar amount for the adjusting entry.

1. Amount of insurance expired (used) is $830.

(Balance Sheet)
Prepaid Insurance

TB 960	
	Adj. ______
Bal. ______	

(Income Statement)
Insurance Expense

Adj. ______	

2. Amount of unexpired (remaining) insurance is $340.

(Balance Sheet)
Prepaid Insurance

TB 1,135	
	Adj. ______
Bal. ______	

(Income Statement)
Insurance Expense

Adj. ______	

E 5-8B (LO2)

POSTING ADJUSTING ENTRIES Two adjusting entries are shown in the following general journal. Post these adjusting entries to the four general ledger accounts. The following account numbers were taken from the chart of accounts: 145, Prepaid Insurance; 183.1, Accumulated Depreciation—Cleaning Equipment; 541, Depreciation Expense—Cleaning Equipment; and 535, Insurance Expense. If you are not using the working papers that accompany this text, enter the following balances before posting the entries: Prepaid Insurance, $960 Dr.; Accumulated Depreciation—Cleaning Equipment, $870 Cr.

GENERAL JOURNAL PAGE 7

	DATE		DESCRIPTION	POST. REF.	DEBIT	CREDIT	
1			Adjusting Entries				1
2	20-- July	31	Insurance Expense		320 00		2
3			Prepaid Insurance			320 00	3
4							4
5		31	Depr. Expense—Cleaning Equipment		145 00		5
6			Accum. Depr.—Cleaning Equipment			145 00	6

E 5-9B (LO3)

✓ Adjustments col. total: $1,530

WORK SHEET AND ADJUSTING ENTRIES A partial work sheet for Jasmine Kah's Auto Detailing is shown below. Indicate by letters (a) through (d) the four adjustments in the Adjustments columns of the work sheet, properly matching each debit and credit. Complete the Adjustments columns.

Jasmine Kah's Auto Detailing
Work Sheet (Partial)
For Month Ended June 30, 20 - -

	ACCOUNT TITLE	TRIAL BALANCE		ADJUSTMENTS		ADJUSTED TRIAL BALANCE		
		DEBIT	CREDIT	DEBIT	CREDIT	DEBIT	CREDIT	
1	Cash	150 00				150 00		1
2	Supplies	520 00				90 00		2
3	Prepaid Insurance	750 00				200 00		3
4	Cleaning Equipment	5400 00				5400 00		4
5	Accum. Depr.— Cleaning Equipment		850 00				1150 00	5
6	Wages Payable						250 00	6
7	Jasmine Kah, Capital		4600 00				4600 00	7
8	Detailing Fees		2220 00				2220 00	8
9	Wages Expense	700 00				950 00		9
10	Advertising Expense	150 00				150 00		10
11	Supplies Expense					430 00		11
12	Insurance Expense					550 00		12
13	Depr. Expense—Cleaning Equipment					300 00		13
14		7670 00	7670 00			8220 00	8220 00	14

E 5-10B (LO5)

JOURNALIZING ADJUSTING ENTRIES From the Adjustments columns in Exercise 5-9B, journalize the four adjusting entries as of June 30, in proper general journal format.

E 5-11B (LO3)

EXTENDING ADJUSTED BALANCES TO THE INCOME STATEMENT AND BALANCE SHEET COLUMNS Indicate with an "X" whether each account total should be extended to the Income Statement Debit or Credit or to the Balance Sheet Debit or Credit columns on the work sheet.

(continued)

	Income Statement		Balance Sheet	
	Debit	Credit	Debit	Credit
Cash	______	______	______	______
Accounts Receivable	______	______	______	______
Supplies	______	______	______	______
Prepaid Insurance	______	______	______	______
Automobile	______	______	______	______
Accum. Depr.—Automobile	______	______	______	______
Accounts Payable	______	______	______	______
Wages Payable	______	______	______	______
Owner, Capital	______	______	______	______
Owner, Drawing	______	______	______	______
Service Fees	______	______	______	______
Wages Expense	______	______	______	______
Supplies Expense	______	______	______	______
Utilities Expense	______	______	______	______
Insurance Expense	______	______	______	______
Depr. Exp.—Automobile	______	______	______	______

E 5-12B (LO3)

ANALYSIS OF NET INCOME OR NET LOSS ON THE WORK SHEET Insert the dollar amounts where the net income or net loss would appear on the work sheet.

	Income Statement		Balance Sheet	
	Debit	Credit	Debit	Credit
Net Income: $2,500	______	______	______	______
Net Loss: $1,900	______	______	______	______

E 5-13B (LO6)

✓ See Figure 5-25 in text

CASH, MODIFIED CASH, AND ACCRUAL BASES OF ACCOUNTING For each journal entry shown below, indicate the accounting method(s) for which the entry would be appropriate. If the journal entry is not appropriate for a particular accounting method, explain the proper accounting treatment for that method.

1. Office Equipment
   Cash
   Purchased equipment for cash
2. Office Equipment
   Accounts Payable
   Purchased equipment on account
3. Cash
   Revenue
   Cash receipts for week
4. Accounts Receivable
   Revenue
   Services performed on account
5. Prepaid Insurance
   Cash
   Purchased prepaid asset
6. Supplies
   Accounts Payable
   Purchased prepaid asset

7. Telephone Expense
   Cash
      Paid telephone bill

8. Wages Expense
   Cash
      Paid wages for month

9. Accounts Payable
   Cash
      Made payment on account

Adjusting Entries:

10. Supplies Expense
    Supplies

11. Wages Expense
    Wages Payable

12. Depreciation Expense—Office Equipment
    Accumulated Depreciation—Office Equipment

SERIES B PROBLEMS

P 5-14B (LO1/3)

✓ Adjustments col. total: $805; Net income: $2,410

ADJUSTMENTS AND WORK SHEET SHOWING NET INCOME Louie Long started a business called Louie's Lawn Service. The trial balance as of March 31, after the first month of operation, is as follows:

Louie's Lawn Service
Work Sheet
For Month Ended March 31, 20 --

	ACCOUNT TITLE	TRIAL BALANCE		ADJUSTMENTS		
		DEBIT	CREDIT	DEBIT	CREDIT	
1	Cash	1375 00				1
2	Accounts Receivable	880 00				2
3	Supplies	490 00				3
4	Prepaid Insurance	800 00				4
5	Lawn Equipment	5700 00				5
6	Accum. Depr.—Lawn Equipment					6
7	Accounts Payable		780 00			7
8	Wages Payable					8
9	Louie Long, Capital		6500 00			9
10	Louie Long, Drawing	1250 00				10
11	Lawn Service Fees		6100 00			11
12	Wages Expense	1145 00				12
13	Advertising Expense	540 00				13
14	Rent Expense	725 00				14
15	Supplies Expense					15
16	Telephone Expense	160 00				16
17	Insurance Expense					17
18	Repair Expense	250 00				18
19	Depr. Expense—Lawn Equipment					19
20	Miscellaneous Expense	65 00				20
21		13380 00	13380 00			21

(continued)

REQUIRED

1. Analyze the following adjustments and enter them on a work sheet.
   (a) Ending supplies inventory as of March 31, $165.
   (b) Insurance expired (used), $100.
   (c) Depreciation of lawn equipment, $200.
   (d) Wages earned but not paid as of March 31, $180.
2. Complete the work sheet.

P 5-15B (LO1/3)

✓ Adjustments col. total: $990; Net loss: $1,625

ADJUSTMENTS AND WORK SHEET SHOWING A NET LOSS Val Nolan started a business called Nolan's Home Appraisals. The trial balance as of October 31, after the first month of operations, is as follows:

Nolan's Home Appraisals
Work Sheet
For Month Ended October 31, 20 - -

	ACCOUNT TITLE	TRIAL BALANCE DEBIT	TRIAL BALANCE CREDIT	ADJUSTMENTS DEBIT	ADJUSTMENTS CREDIT	
1	Cash	830 00				1
2	Accounts Receivable	760 00				2
3	Supplies	625 00				3
4	Prepaid Insurance	950 00				4
5	Automobile	6 500 00				5
6	Accum. Depr.—Automobile					6
7	Accounts Payable		1 500 00			7
8	Wages Payable					8
9	Val Nolan, Capital		9 900 00			9
10	Val Nolan, Drawing	1 100 00				10
11	Appraisal Fees		3 000 00			11
12	Wages Expense	1 560 00				12
13	Advertising Expense	420 00				13
14	Rent Expense	1 050 00				14
15	Supplies Expense					15
16	Telephone Expense	255 00				16
17	Insurance Expense					17
18	Repair Expense	270 00				18
19	Oil and Gas Expense	80 00				19
20	Depr. Expense—Automobile					20
21		14 400 00	14 400 00			21

REQUIRED

1. Analyze the following adjustments and enter them on the work sheet.
   (a) Supplies inventory as of October 31, $210.
   (b) Unexpired (remaining) insurance as of October 31, $800.
   (c) Depreciation of automobile, $250.
   (d) Wages earned but not paid as of October 31, $175.
2. Complete the work sheet.

P 5-16B (LO2/5)

JOURNALIZE AND POST ADJUSTING ENTRIES FROM THE WORK SHEET
Refer to Problem 5-15B and the following additional information:

Account Name	Account Number	Balance in Account Before Adjusting Entry
Supplies	141	$ 625
Prepaid Insurance	145	950
Accum. Depr.—Automobile	185.1	0
Wages Payable	219	0
Wages Expense	511	1,560
Supplies Expense	523	0
Insurance Expense	535	0
Depr. Expense—Automobile	541	0

REQUIRED

1. Journalize the adjusting entries on page 3 of the general journal.
2. Post the adjusting entries to the general ledger. (If you are not using the working papers that accompany this text, enter the balances provided in this problem before posting the adjusting entries.)

P 5-17B (LO4)

✓ Adjustments col. total: $1,640; Net income: $1,405

CORRECTING WORK SHEET WITH ERRORS A beginning accounting student tried to complete a work sheet for Dick Ady's Bookkeeping Service. The following adjusting entries were to have been analyzed and entered in the work sheet:

(a) Ending inventory of supplies on July 31, $130.
(b) Unexpired insurance on July 31, $420.
(c) Depreciation of office equipment, $325.
(d) Wages earned, but not paid as of July 31, $95.

REQUIRED

Review the work sheet shown on page 170 for addition mistakes, transpositions, and other errors and make all necessary corrections.

MANAGING YOUR WRITING

Delia Alvarez, owner of Delia's Lawn Service, wants to borrow money to buy new lawn equipment. A local bank has asked for financial statements. Alvarez has asked you to prepare financial statements for the year ended December 31, 20--. You have been given the unadjusted trial balance on page 171 and suspect that Alvarez expects you to base your statements on this information. You are concerned, however, that some of the account balances may need to be adjusted. Write a memo to Alvarez explaining what additional information you need before you can prepare the financial statements. Alvarez is not familiar with accounting issues. Therefore, explain in your memo why you need this information, the potential impact of this information on the financial statements, and the importance of making these adjustments before approaching the bank for a loan.

(continued)

PROBLEM 5-17B

Dick Ady's Bookkeeping Service
Work Sheet
For Month Ended July 31, 20--

	ACCOUNT TITLE	TRIAL BALANCE		ADJUSTMENTS		ADJUSTED TRIAL BALANCE		INCOME STATEMENT		BALANCE SHEET	
		DEBIT	CREDIT	DEBIT	CREDIT	DEBIT	CREDIT	DEBIT	CREDIT	DEBIT	CREDIT
1	Cash	1365 00				1365 00				1356 00	
2	Accounts Receivable	845 00				845 00			845 00		
3	Supplies	620 00			(a) 490 00	130 00				130 00	
4	Prepaid Insurance	1150 00			(b) 420 00	730 00				730 00	
5	Office Equipment	6400 00			(c) 325 00	6725 00				6725 00	
6	Accum. Depr.—Office Equipment										
7	Accounts Payable		735 00				735 00				735 00
8	Wages Payable				(d) 95 00		95 00				59 00
9	Dick Ady, Capital		7800 00				7800 00				7800 00
10	Dick Ady, Drawing	1200 00				1200 00				1200 00	
11	Professional Fees		6350 00				6350 00		6350 00		
12	Wages Expense	1495 00		(d) 95 00		1590 00		1590 00			
13	Advertising Expense	380 00				380 00		380 00			
14	Rent Expense	850 00				850 00		850 00			
15	Supplies Expense			(a) 490 00		490 00		490 00			
16	Telephone Expense	205 00				205 00		250 00			
17	Utilities Expense	285 00				285 00		285 00			
18	Insurance Expense			(b) 420 00		420 00		420 00			
19	Depr. Expense—Office Equipment			(c) 325 00		325 00		325 00			
20	Miscellaneous Expense	90 00				90 00		90 00			
21	Net Income	14885 00	14885 00	1330 00	1330 00	15630 00	14980 00	4880 00	7195 00	10141 00	8594 00
22								2315 00			1547 00
23								7195 00	7195 00	10141 00	10141 00
24											
25											
26											
27											
28											
29											
30											

Contains Errors

This work sheet contains errors.

Delia's Lawn Service
Trial Balance
December 31, 20 - -

ACCOUNT TITLE	ACCOUNT NO.	DEBIT BALANCE		CREDIT BALANCE	
Cash	101	770	00		
Accounts Receivable	122	1700	00		
Supplies	142	280	00		
Prepaid Insurance	145	400	00		
Lawn Equipment	183	13800	00		
Accounts Payable	202			2200	00
Delia Alvarez, Capital	311			3000	00
Delia Alvarez, Drawing	312	350	00		
Lawn Cutting Fees	401			52400	00
Wages Expense	511	35850	00		
Rent Expense	521	1200	00		
Gas and Oil Expense	538	3250	00		
		57600	00	57600	00

MASTERY PROBLEM

✓ Adjusted Trial Bal. total: $58,500; Net income: $13,630

Kristi Williams offers family counseling services specializing in financial and marital problems. A chart of accounts and a trial balance taken on December 31, 20--, follow.

KRISTI WILLIAMS FAMILY COUNSELING SERVICES
CHART OF ACCOUNTS

Assets		**Revenue**	
101	Cash	401	Client Fees
142	Office Supplies		
145	Prepaid Insurance	**Expenses**	
181	Office Equipment	511	Wages Expense
181.1	Accumulated Depr.—	521	Rent Expense
	Office Equipment	523	Office Supplies Expense
187	Computer Equipment	533	Utilities Expense
187.1	Accumulated Depr.—	535	Insurance Expense
	Computer Equipment	541	Depr. Expense—
Liabilities			Office Equipment
201	Notes Payable	542	Depr. Expense—
202	Accounts Payable		Computer Equipment
		549	Miscellaneous Expense
Owner's Equity			
311	Kristi Williams, Capital		
312	Kristi Williams, Drawing		

(continued)

Kristi Williams Family Counseling Services
Trial Balance
December 31, 20 - -

ACCOUNT TITLE	ACCOUNT NO.	DEBIT BALANCE	CREDIT BALANCE
Cash	101	8,730 00	
Office Supplies	142	700 00	
Prepaid Insurance	145	600 00	
Office Equipment	181	18,000 00	
Computer Equipment	187	6,000 00	
Notes Payable	201		8,000 00
Accounts Payable	202		500 00
Kristi Williams, Capital	311		11,400 00
Kristi Williams, Drawing	312	3,000 00	
Client Fees	401		35,800 00
Wages Expense	511	9,500 00	
Rent Expense	521	6,000 00	
Utilities Expense	533	2,170 00	
Miscelleneous Expense	549	1,000 00	
		55,700 00	55,700 00

Information for year-end adjustments is as follows:

(a) Office supplies on hand at year-end amounted to $100.
(b) On January 1, 20--, Williams purchased office equipment that cost $18,000. It has an expected useful life of 10 years and no salvage value.
(c) On July 1, 20--, Williams purchased computer equipment costing $6,000. It has an expected useful life of three years and no salvage value. Assume that Williams computes depreciation to the nearest full month.
(d) On December 1, 20--, Williams paid a premium of $600 for a six-month insurance policy.

REQUIRED

1. Prepare the work sheet for the year ended December 31, 20--.
2. Prepare adjusting entries in a general journal.

CHALLENGE PROBLEM

This problem challenges you to apply your cumulative accounting knowledge to move a step beyond the material in the chapter.

Your friend, Diane Kiefner, teaches elementary school and operates her own wilderness kayaking tours in the summers. She thinks she has been doing fine financially, but has never really measured her profits. Until this year, her business has always had more money at the end of the summer than at the beginning. She enjoys kayaking and as long as she came out a little ahead, that was fine. Unfortunately, Diane had to dip into her savings to make up for "losses" on her kayaking tours this past summer. Hearing that you have been studying accounting, she brought a list of cash receipts and expenditures and would like you to try to figure out what happened.

Cash balance beginning of summer		$15,000
Cash receipts from kayakers over the summer	$10,000	
Cash expenditures over the summer	13,500	
Amount taken from savings		(3,500)
Cash balance end of summer		$11,500

When asked for more details on the expenditures and the kayaking gear that you saw in her garage, Diane provided the following information:

Expenditures were made on the following items:	
Brochures used to advertise her services (Diane only used about 1/4 of them and plans to use the remainder over the next three summers.)	$1,000
Food for trips (nothing left)	2,000
Rent on equipment used by kayakers on trips	3,000
Travel expenses	4,000
A new kayak and paddles (At the beginning of the summer, Diane bought a new kayak and paddles. Up to this time, she had always borrowed her father's. Diane expects to use the equipment for about five years. At that time, she expects it to have no value.)	3,500

A trial balance based on this information follows. As you will note, Diane's trial balance is not consistent with some of the concepts discussed in this chapter.

Diane Kiefner's Wilderness Kayaking Tours
Work Sheet
For Summer Ended 20 - -

	ACCOUNT TITLE	TRIAL BALANCE		ADJUSTMENTS		ADJUSTED TRIAL BALANCE		INCOME STATEMENT		BALANCE SHEET		
		DEBIT	CREDIT	DEBIT	CREDIT	DEBIT	CREDIT	DEBIT	CREDIT	DEBIT	CREDIT	
1	Cash	11 500 00										1
2	Diane Kiefner, Capital		15 000 00									2
3	Tour Revenue		10 000 00									3
4	Advertising Supplies Expense	1 000 00										4
5	Food Expense	2 000 00										5
6	Equipment Rental Expense	3 000 00										6
7	Travel Expense	4 000 00										7
8	Kayak Expense	3 500 00										8
9		25 000 00	25 000 00									9

REQUIRED

1. Complete Diane's work sheet by making appropriate adjustments and extensions. *Note*: (a) You may need to add new accounts. (b) Some of the adjustments you need to make are actually "corrections of errors" Diane has made in classifying certain items.
2. What is your best measure of Diane's net income for the summer of 20--?

ANSWERS TO SELF-STUDY QUESTIONS AND EXERCISES

True/False Questions

1. F (match revenues and expenses) **2.** F (to bring accounts up to date) **3.** T
4. F (depreciable cost = cost – salvage value) **5.** F (to match cost of asset against revenues it will help generate)

Multiple Choice Questions

1. a **2.** c **3.** d **4.** c **5.** a

U REVU Exercises

1. Supplies should be reduced (credited) for $30.
2. Adjusting.
3. A. Account Title
   B. Trial Balance
   C. Adjustments
   D. Adjusted Trial Balance
   E. Income Statement
   F. Balance Sheet
4. Errors are highlighted in yellow.

	ACCOUNT TITLE	TRIAL BALANCE		ADJUSTMENTS		ADJUSTED TRIAL BALANCE		INCOME STATEMENT		BALANCE SHEET		
		DEBIT	CREDIT	DEBIT	CREDIT	DEBIT	CREDIT	DEBIT	CREDIT	DEBIT	CREDIT	
1	Cash	370 00				370 00				370 00		1
2	Accounts Receivable	650 00				650 00				650 00		2
3	Supplies	80 00			(a) 60 00	140 00				140 00		3
4	Prepaid Insurance	200 00			(b) 25 00	175 00				175 00		4
5	Delivery Equipment	3600 00				3600 00				3600 00		5
6	Accum. Depr.—Delivery Equipment				(d) 100 00		100 00				100 00	6
7	Accounts Payable		1800 00				1800 00				1800 00	7
8	Wages Payable				(c) 50 00		50 00				50 00	8
9	Jessica Jane, Capital		2000 00				2000 00				2000 00	9
10	Jessica Jane, Drawing	150 00				150 00				150 00		10
11	Delivery Fees		2150 00				2150 00		2150 00			11
12	Wages Expense	650 00		(c) 50 00		700 00		700 00				12
13	Rent Expense	200 00				200 00		200 00				13
14	Supplies Expense			(a) 60 00		60 00		60 00				14
15	Telephone Expense	50 00				50 00		50 00				15
16	Insurance Expense			(b) 25 00		25 00		25 00				16
17	Depr. Expense—Delivery Equipment			(d) 100 00		100 00		100 00				17
18		5950 00	5950 00	235 00	235 00	6220 00	6100 00	1135 00	2150 00	5085 00	3950 00	18
19	Net Income							1015 00			1135 00	19
20								2150 00	2150 00	5085 00	5085 00	20
21												21

5.

	Adjusting Entry		
Dec. 31	Insurance Expense	50.00	
	Prepaid Insurance		50.00

6.

Transaction	Cash Basis	Accrual Basis	Modified Cash Basis
Services on account,	$ —	$500.00	$ —
Payment for legal research assistance	(50.00)	(50.00)	(50.00)
Office supplies used		(10.00)	(10.00)
Net Income (Net Loss)	$(50.00)	$440.00	$(60.00)

Chapter 5 Appendix

Depreciation Methods

LEARNING OBJECTIVES

Careful study of this appendix should enable you to:

LO1 **Prepare a depreciation schedule using the straight-line method.**

LO2 **Prepare a depreciation schedule using the sum-of-the-years'-digits method.**

LO3 **Prepare a depreciation schedule using the double-declining-balance method.**

LO4 **Prepare a depreciation schedule for tax purposes using the Modified Accelerated Cost Recovery System.**

In Chapter 5, we introduced the straight-line method of depreciation. Here, we will review this method and illustrate three others: sum-of-the-years'-digits; double-declining-balance; and, for tax purposes, the Modified Accelerated Cost Recovery System. For all illustrations, we will assume that a delivery van was purchased for $40,000. It has a five-year useful life and salvage value of $4,000.

STRAIGHT-LINE METHOD

LO1 Prepare a depreciation schedule using the straight-line method.

Under the **straight-line depreciation method**, an equal amount of depreciation will be taken each period. First, compute the depreciable cost by subtracting the salvage value from the cost of the asset. This is done because we expect to sell the asset for $4,000 at the end of its useful life. Thus, the total cost to be recognized as an expense over the five years is $36,000, not $40,000.

Cost	−	Salvage Value	=	Depreciable Cost
$40,000	−	$4,000	=	$36,000

Next, we divide the depreciable cost by the expected life of the asset, five years.

Depreciation Expense per Year	=	Depreciable Cost / Years of Life
$7,200 per year	=	$36,000 / 5 years

When preparing a depreciation schedule, it is often convenient to use a depreciation rate per year. In this case, it would be 20% (100% ÷ 5 years of life). Figure 5A-1 shows the depreciation expense, accumulated depreciation, and book value for each of the five years.

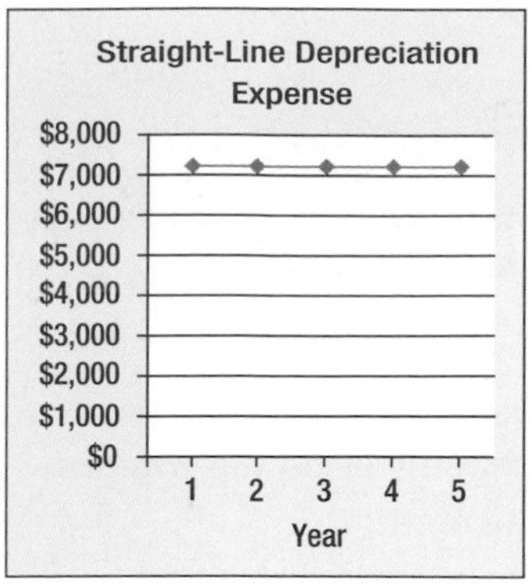

FIGURE 5A-1 Depreciation Schedule Using Straight-Line Method

STRAIGHT-LINE DEPRECIATION

Year	Depreciable Cost	×	Rate	=	Depreciation Expense	Accumulated Depreciation (End of Year)	Book Value (End of Year)
1	$36,000		20%		$7,200	$ 7,200	$32,800
2	36,000		20%		7,200	14,400	25,600
3	36,000		20%		7,200	21,600	18,400
4	36,000		20%		7,200	28,800	11,200
5	36,000		20%		7,200	36,000	4,000

Depreciable Cost	Rate	Depreciation Expense	Accumulated Depreciation	Book Value
Cost $40,000 – Salvage Value 4,000 Depreciable Cost $36,000	100% / 5 Years = 20%	Same amount each year	Accum. Depr. increases by the same amount each year, $7,200.	Cost – Accum. Depr. = Book Value

SUM-OF-THE-YEARS'-DIGITS

LO2 Prepare a depreciation schedule using the sum-of-the-years'-digits method.

Under the **sum-of-the-years'-digits depreciation method,** depreciation is determined by multiplying the depreciable cost by a schedule of fractions. The numerator of the fraction for a specific year is the number of years of remaining useful life for the asset, measured from the beginning of the year. The denominator for all fractions is determined by adding the digits that represent the years of the estimated life of the asset. The calculation of the **sum-of-the-years'-digits** for our delivery van with a five-year useful life is shown below.

Sum-of-the-Years'-Digits = 5 + 4 + 3 + 2 + 1 = 15

A depreciation schedule using these fractions is shown in Figure 5A-2.

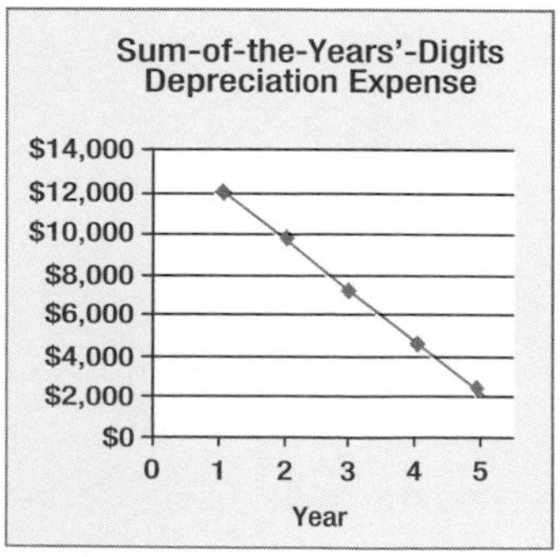

FIGURE 5A-2 Depreciation Schedule Using Sum-of-the-Years'-Digits Method

SUM-OF-THE-YEARS'-DIGITS

Year	Depreciable Cost	×	Rate	=	Depreciation Expense	Accumulated Depreciation (End of Year)	Book Value (End of Year)
1	$36,000		5/15		$12,000	$12,000	$28,000
2	36,000		4/15		9,600	21,600	18,400
3	36,000		3/15		7,200	28,800	11,200
4	36,000		2/15		4,800	33,600	6,400
5	36,000		1/15		2,400	36,000	4,000

Depreciable Cost	Rate	Depreciation Expense	Accumulated Depreciation	Book Value
Cost $40,000 – Salvage Value 4,000 Depreciable Cost $36,000	Remaining life from beginning of period / SYD	Expense gets smaller each year	Accum. Depr. increases by amount of current year's depreciation expense.	Cost – Accum. Depr. = Book Value

DOUBLE-DECLINING-BALANCE METHOD

LO3 Prepare a depreciation schedule using the double-declining-balance method.

Under the **double-declining-balance depreciation method**, the book value is multiplied by a fixed rate, often double the straight-line rate. The van has a five-year life, so the straight-line rate is 1 ÷ 5, or 20%. Double the straight-line rate is 2 × 20%, or 40%. The double-declining-balance depreciation schedule is shown in Figure 5A-3. Note that the rate is applied to the book value of the asset. Once the book value is reduced to the expected salvage value, $4,000, no more depreciation may be recognized.

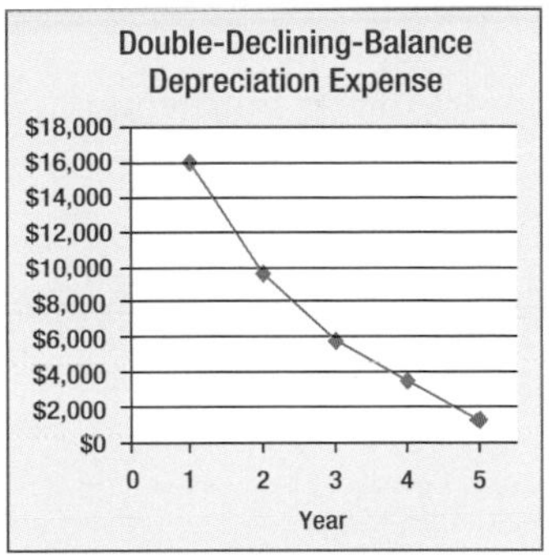

FIGURE 5A-3 Depreciation Schedule Using Double-Declining-Balance Method

DOUBLE-DECLINING-BALANCE METHOD

Year	Book Value (Beginning of Year)	×	Rate	=	Depreciation Expense	Accumulated Depreciation (End of Year)	Book Value (End of Year)
1	$40,000		40%		$16,000	$16,000	$24,000
2	24,000		40%		9,600	25,600	14,400
3	14,400		40%		5,760	31,360	8,640
4	8,640		40%		3,456	34,816	5,184
5	5,184				1,184	36,000	4,000

Cost
– Accum.Depr.
Book Value

Double the Straight Line Rate 1/5 x 2 = 2/5 = 40%

LEARNING KEY

Double means double the straight-line rate. Declining-balance means that the rate is multiplied by the *book value* (not depreciable cost) at the beginning of each year. This amount is *declining* each year.

MODIFIED ACCELERATED COST RECOVERY SYSTEM

LO4 Prepare a depreciation schedule for tax purposes using the Modified Accelerated Cost Recovery System.

For assets purchased since 1986, many firms use the **Modified Accelerated Cost Recovery System (MACRS)** for tax purposes. Under this method, the Internal Revenue Service (IRS) classifies various assets according to useful life and sets depreciation rates for each year of the asset's life. These rates are then multiplied by the cost of the asset. Even though the van is expected to have a useful life of five years, and a salvage value of $4,000, the IRS schedule, shown in Figure 5A-4, spreads the depreciation over a six-year period and assumes no salvage value.

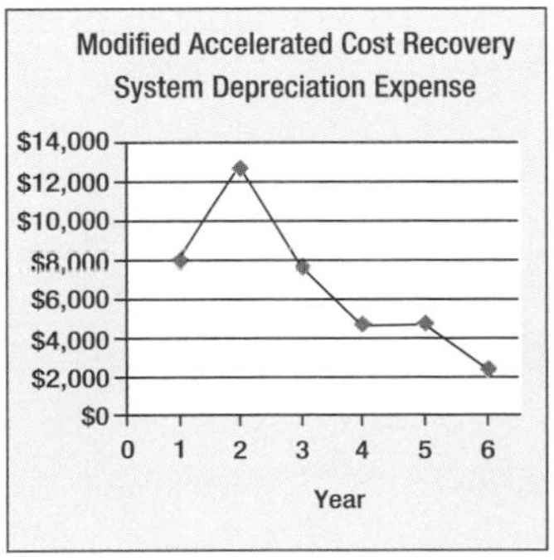

FIGURE 5A-4 Depreciation Schedule Using Modified Accelerated Cost Recovery System

MODIFIED ACCELERATED COST RECOVERY SYSTEM

Year	Cost	×	Rate	=	Depreciation Expense	Accumulated Depreciation (End of Year)	Book Value (End of Year)
1	$40,000		20.00%		$ 8,000	$ 8,000	$32,000
2	40,000		32.00%		12,800	20,800	19,200
3	40,000		19.20%		7,680	28,480	11,520
4	40,000		11.52%		4,608	33,088	6,912
5	40,000		11.52%		4,608	37,696	2,304
6	40,000		5.76%		2,304	40,000	0

Rate set by IRS

Cost
–Accum. Depr.
Book Value

LEARNING OBJECTIVES Key Points to Remember

LO1 Prepare a depreciation schedule using the straight-line method.	Under straight-line depreciation, an equal amount of depreciation is taken each period. Depreciation expense for each year is computed as follows: Cost – Salvage Value = Depreciable Cost/Expected Years of Life = Depreciation Expense per Year
LO2 Prepare a depreciation schedule using the sum-of-the-years'-digits method.	Under the sum-of-the-years'-digits method, the depreciable cost is multiplied by a fraction. The fraction consists of the following: Remaining Years of Life Measured from the Beginning of the Current Year / Sum-of-the-Years'-Digits If an asset has a life of three years, the sum-of-the-years'-digits is equal to: 3 + 2 + 1 = 6 Depreciation would be computed as follows: Year 1: 3/6 × Depreciable Cost Year 2: 2/6 × Depreciable Cost Year 3: 1/6 × Depreciable Cost
LO3 Prepare a depreciation schedule using the double-declining-balance method.	Under this method, the book value (the declining balance) is multiplied by a fixed rate, often double the straight-line rate.
LO4 Prepare a depreciation schedule for tax purposes using the Modified Accelerated Cost Recovery System.	Under this method, the IRS provides the depreciation rates to be applied to the cost of the asset. Simply multiply the rate provided by the IRS by the cost of the asset.

KEY TERMS

double-declining-balance depreciation method (177) A depreciation method that recognizes depreciation each year by multiplying a rate (typically double the straight-line rate) by the book value of the asset.

Modified Accelerated Cost Recovery System (MACRS) (177) A depreciation method in which rates determined by the IRS are multiplied by the cost of the asset to determine depreciation expense for the year.

straight-line depreciation method (175) A depreciation method that recognizes an equal amount of depreciation each year.

sum-of-the-years'-digits (176) If an asset has a five-year life, the sum-of-the-years'-digits is computed as follows: 5 + 4 + 3 + 2 + 1 = 15.

sum-of-the-years'-digits depreciation method (176) A depreciation method that recognizes depreciation each year by multiplying a fraction by the depreciable cost. The numerator of the fraction is the remaining life of the asset, measured from the beginning of the year. The denominator is the sum-of-the-years'-digits.

REVIEW QUESTIONS

1. List three depreciation methods used for financial reporting.
2. Which depreciation method is used for tax purposes?

SERIES A EXERCISES

E 5Apx-1A (LO1)
✓ Accum. depr. end of Yr. 2: $10,000

STRAIGHT-LINE DEPRECIATION A small delivery truck was purchased on January 1 at a cost of $25,000. It has an estimated useful life of four years and an estimated salvage value of $5,000. Prepare a depreciation schedule showing the depreciation expense, accumulated depreciation, and book value for each year under the straight-line method.

E 5Apx-2A (LO2)
✓ Accum. depr. end of Yr. 2: $14,000

SUM-OF-THE-YEARS'-DIGITS DEPRECIATION Using the information given in Exercise 5Apx-1A, prepare a depreciation schedule showing the depreciation expense, accumulated depreciation, and book value for each year under the sum-of-the-years'-digits method.

E 5Apx-3A (LO3)
✓ Accum. depr. end of Yr. 2: $18,750

DOUBLE-DECLINING-BALANCE DEPRECIATION Using the information given in Exercise 5Apx-1A, prepare a depreciation schedule showing the depreciation expense, accumulated depreciation, and book value for each year under the double-declining-balance method.

E 5Apx-4A (LO4)
✓ Accum. depr. end of Yr. 2: $13,000

MODIFIED ACCELERATED COST RECOVERY SYSTEM Using the information given in Exercise 5Apx-1A and the rates shown in Figure 5A-4, prepare a depreciation schedule showing the depreciation expense, accumulated depreciation, and book value for each year under the Modified Accelerated Cost Recovery System. For tax purposes, assume that the truck has a useful life of five years. (The IRS schedule will spread depreciation over six years.)

SERIES B EXERCISES

E 5Apx-1B (LO1)
✓ Accum. depr. end of Yr. 2: $1,800

STRAIGHT-LINE DEPRECIATION A computer was purchased on January 1 at a cost of $5,000. It has an estimated useful life of five years and an estimated salvage value of $500. Prepare a depreciation schedule showing the depreciation expense, accumulated depreciation, and book value for each year under the straight-line method.

E 5Apx-2B (LO2)
✓ Accum. depr. end of Yr. 2: $2,700

SUM-OF-THE-YEARS'-DIGITS DEPRECIATION Using the information given in Exercise 5Apx-1B, prepare a depreciation schedule showing the depreciation expense, accumulated depreciation, and book value for each year under the sum-of-the-years'-digits method.

E 5Apx-3B (LO3)
✓ Accum. depr. end of Yr. 2: $3,200

DOUBLE-DECLINING-BALANCE DEPRECIATION Using the information given in Exercise 5Apx-1B, prepare a depreciation schedule showing the depreciation expense, accumulated depreciation, and book value for each year under the double-declining-balance method.

E 5Apx-4B (LO4)
✓ Accum. depr. end of Yr. 2: $2,600

MODIFIED ACCELERATED COST RECOVERY SYSTEM Using the information given in Exercise 5Apx-1B and the rates shown in Figure 5A-4, prepare a depreciation schedule showing the depreciation expense, accumulated depreciation, and book value for each year under the Modified Accelerated Cost Recovery System. For tax purposes, assume that the computer has a useful life of five years. (The IRS schedule will spread depreciation over six years.)

Chapter 6

COURTESY OF THE INDY EXPRESS BAND

LEARNING OBJECTIVES

Careful study of this chapter should enable you to:

LO1 Prepare financial statements with the aid of a work sheet.

LO2 Journalize and post closing entries.

LO3 Prepare a post-closing trial balance.

LO4 List and describe the steps in the accounting cycle.

Financial Statements and the Closing Process

Indy Express Band is central Indiana's premier variety band. It offers a popular mix of musical styles from Top 40 to Big Band. The eight-piece band is led by Greg Imboden, fronted by Cozette Myers, driven by a three-piece horn section, and backed by a tight rhythm section. The **Indy Express Band is** perfect for a wedding reception, corporate function, conference event, dinner dance, or charity ball. Members of Indy Express Band have provided music for entertainers such as Jay Leno, Rod Stewart, Natalie Cole, Dionne Warwick, and Al Jarreau.

In addition to playing at Jessie Jane's wedding and other events, the band generally performs on New Year's Eve, the same day many businesses prepare closing entries. In this chapter, we complete the accounting cycle by demonstrating how to make closing entries and prepare the Post-Closing Trial Balance.

The work sheet, introduced in Chapter 5, is used for three major end-of-period activities:

1. journalizing adjusting entries,
2. preparing financial statements, and
3. journalizing closing entries.

This chapter illustrates the use of the work sheet for preparing financial statements and closing entries. In addition, the post-closing trial balance is explained and illustrated. All of these activities take place at the end of the firm's fiscal year. However, to continue our illustration of Jessie Jane's Campus Delivery Service, we demonstrate these activities at the end of the first month of operations.

THE FINANCIAL STATEMENTS

LO1 Prepare financial statements with the aid of a work sheet.

The work sheet prepared in Chapter 5 supplies most of the information needed to prepare an income statement, a statement of owner's equity, and a balance sheet. The statements and work sheet columns from which they are derived for Jessie Jane's Campus Delivery Service are shown in Figures 6-1 and 6-2.

As you refer to the financial statements in Figures 6-1 and 6-2, notice the placement of dollar signs, single rulings, and double rulings. Dollar signs are placed at the top of each column and beneath rulings. Single rulings indicate addition or subtraction, and double rulings are placed under totals. Notice that each statement heading contains three lines: (1) company name, (2) statement title, and (3) period ended or date.

THE INCOME STATEMENT

Figure 6-1 shows how the Income Statement columns of the work sheet provide the information needed to prepare an income statement. Revenue is shown first, followed by an itemized and totaled list of expenses. Then, net income is calculated to double check the accuracy of the work sheet. It is presented with a double ruling as the last item in the statement.

Multiple columns are used on the financial statements to make them easier to read. There are no debit or credit columns on the financial statements.

The expenses could be listed in the same order that they appear in the chart of accounts or in descending order by dollar amount. The second approach helps the reader identify the most important expenses.

THE STATEMENT OF OWNER'S EQUITY

The Balance Sheet columns of the work sheet provide most of the information needed to prepare a statement of owner's equity. Figure 6-2 shows that Jessie's capital account balance and the drawing account balance are in the Balance Sheet columns. Be careful, however, when using the capital account balance reported on the work sheet. This account balance is the beginning balance *plus any investments made during the period*. Recall that Jessie's beginning capital balance was zero. During June, she made an investment of $2,000. Thus, as reported previously, the beginning balance on the statement of owner's equity must be zero with the $2,000 reported as an investment during June. The net income for the month can be found either on the work sheet at the bottom of the Income Statement (see Figure 6-1) and Balance Sheet columns or on the income statement itself. With these items of information, the statement of owner's equity can be prepared.

LEARNING KEY

The owner's capital account in the general ledger must be reviewed to determine if additional investments were made during the accounting period.

FIGURE 6-1 Linkages Between the Work Sheet and Income Statement

Jessie Jane's Campus Delivery Service
Work Sheet (Partial)
For Month Ended June 30, 20 - -

	ACCOUNT TITLE	INCOME STATEMENT DEBIT	INCOME STATEMENT CREDIT
1	Cash		
2	Accounts Receivable		
3	Supplies		
4	Prepaid Insurance		
5	Delivery Equipment		
6	Accum. Depr.—Delivery Equipment		
7	Accounts Payable		
8	Wages Payable		
9	Jessica Jane, Capital		
10	Jessica Jane, Drawing		
11	Delivery Fees		2 150 00
12	Wages Expense	700 00	
13	Rent Expense	200 00	
14	Supplies Expense	60 00	
15	Telephone Expense	50 00	
16	Insurance Expense	25 00	
17	Depr. Expense—Delivery Equipment	100 00	
18		1 135 00	2 150 00
19	Net Income	1 015 00	
20		2 150 00	2 150 00
21			
22			
23			

Formatting Reminders:
Statement Heading
Name of company
Title of statement
Accounting period ended
Revenues listed first
Expenses listed second by amount (largest to smallest), or in chart of accounts order. Amounts are itemized in left column, subtotaled in right column.

Prepare Income Statement First

Jessie Jane's Campus Delivery Service
Income Statement
For Month Ended June 30, 20 --

Revenue:		
Delivery fees		$ 2 150 00
Expenses:		
Wages expense	$ 700 00	
Rent expense	200 00	
Supplies expense	60 00	
Telephone expense	50 00	
Insurance expense	25 00	
Depr. expense—delivery equip.	100 00	
Total expenses		1 135 00
Net income		$ 1 015 00

Dollar signs used at top of columns and under rulings.
Single rulings indicate addition or subtraction.
Double rulings indicate totals.

THE BALANCE SHEET

As shown in Figure 6-2, the work sheet and the statement of owner's equity are used to prepare Jessie's balance sheet. The asset and liability amounts can be found in the Balance Sheet columns of the work sheet. The ending balance in Jessica Jane, Capital has been computed on the statement of owner's equity. This amount should be copied from the statement of owner's equity to the balance sheet.

Two important features of the balance sheet in Figure 6-2 should be noted. First, it is a **report form of balance sheet,** which means that the liabilities and owner's equity sections are shown below the assets section. It differs from an **account form of balance sheet** in which the assets are on the left and the liabilities and owner's equity sections are on the right. (See Jessie's balance sheet illustrated in Figure 2-2 on page 32 in Chapter 2.)

Second, it is a **classified balance sheet,** which means that similar items are grouped together on the balance sheet. Assets are classified as current assets and property, plant, and equipment. Similarly, liabilities are broken down into current and long-term sections. The following major balance sheet classifications are generally used.

FIGURE 6-2 Linkages Between the Work Sheet, Statement of Owner's Equity, and Balance Sheet

Statement Heading
Name of company
Title of statement
Accounting period ended
Current assets: cash and items that will be converted to cash or consumed within a year.
Property, plant, and equipment: durable assets that will help produce revenues for several years.
Current liabilities: amounts owed that will be paid within a year (will require the use of current assets).

Note: The statement of owner's equity is prepared before the balance sheet. The S.O.E. is shown below the B.S. to enhance the illustration of the linkages between the work sheet and financial statements.

Jessie Jane's Campus Delivery Service
Work Sheet (Partial)
For Month Ended June 30, 20 - -

	ACCOUNT TITLE	BALANCE SHEET DEBIT	BALANCE SHEET CREDIT
1	Cash	370 00	
2	Accounts Receivable	650 00	
3	Supplies	20 00	
4	Prepaid Insurance	175 00	
5	Delivery Equipment	3600 00	
6	Accum. Depr.—Delivery Equip.		100 00
7	Accounts Payable		1800 00
8	Wages Payable		50 00
9	Jessica Jane, Capital		2000 00
10	Jessica Jane, Drawing	150 00	
11	Delivery Fees		
12	Wages Expense		
13	Rent Expense		
14	Supplies Expense		
15	Telephone Expense		
16	Insurance Expense		
17	Depr. Expense—Delivery Equip.		
18		4965 00	3950 00
19	Net Income		1015 00
20		4965 00	4965 00
21			

Prepare BS Third

Jessie Jane's Campus Delivery Service
Balance Sheet
June 30, 20 --

Assets		
Current assets:		
Cash	$ 370 00	
Accounts receivable	650 00	
Supplies	20 00	
Prepaid insurance	175 00	
Total current assets		$ 1215 00
Property, plant, and equipment:		
Delivery equipment	$3600 00	
Less accumulated depreciation	100 00	3500 00
Total assets		$ 4715 00
Liabilities		
Current liabilities:		
Accounts payable	$1800 00	
Wages payable	50 00	
Total current liabilities		$ 1850 00
Owner's Equity		
Jessica Jane, capital		2865 00
Total liabilities and owner's equity		$ 4715 00

Prepare SOE Second

Jessie Jane's Campus Delivery Service
Statement of Owner's Equity
For Month Ended June 30, 20 --

Jessica Jane, capital, June 1, 20--		$ —
Investments during June		2000 00
Total investment		$2000 00
Net income for June	$1015 00	
Less: withdrawals for June	150 00	
Increase in capital		865 00
Jessica Jane, capital, June 30, 20--		$2865 00

Ending capital is not taken from the work sheet. It is computed on the statement of owner's equity.
Dollar signs used at top of columns and under rulings.
Single rulings indicate addition or subtraction.
Double rulings indicate totals.

Current Assets

Current assets include cash and assets that will be converted into cash or consumed within either one year or the normal operating cycle of the business, whichever is longer. Examples include cash, accounts receivable, supplies, and prepaid insurance. As shown in Figure 6-3, an **operating cycle** is the period of time required to purchase supplies and services and convert them back into cash.

FIGURE 6-3 Operating Cycle

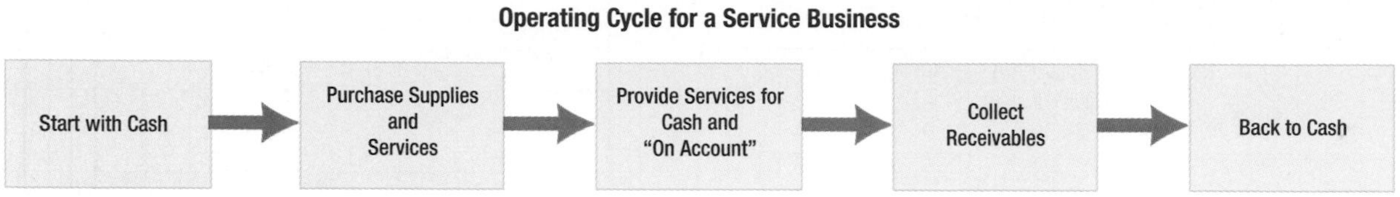

Property, Plant, and Equipment

Property, plant, and equipment, also called **plant assets** or **long-term assets**, represent assets that are expected to serve the business for many years. Examples include land, buildings, and equipment.

Current Liabilities

Current liabilities are due within either one year or the normal operating cycle of the business, whichever is longer. They will be paid out of current assets. Accounts payable and wages payable are classified as current liabilities.

Long-Term Liabilities

Long-term liabilities, or **long-term debt**, are obligations that are not expected to be paid within a year and do not require the use of current assets. A mortgage on an office building is an example of a long-term liability. Jessie has no long-term debts. If she did, they would be listed on the balance sheet in the long-term liabilities section immediately following the current liabilities.

ADDITIONAL INVESTMENTS BY THE OWNER (REVISITED)

If the owner of a business made additional investments during the accounting period, the owner's capital reported in the Balance Sheet columns of the work sheet represents the beginning balance plus any additional investments made during the accounting period. If this amount were used as the beginning balance on the statement of owner's equity, it would not equal the ending balance from last period and would create confusion for those comparing the two statements. In addition, the statement would not reflect all of the activities affecting the owner's capital account during the period.

Thus, we must also review the owner's capital account in the general ledger to get the information needed to prepare the statement of owner's equity. Figure 6-4 illustrates this situation for another business, Ramon's Shopping Service. The $5,000 balance of July 1, 20--, in Ramon Balboa's general ledger capital account is used as the beginning balance on the statement of owner's equity. Note that this is also the ending balance on June 30, 20--. The additional investment of $3,000 made on July 5 and posted to Balboa's general ledger capital account is reported by writing "Investments during period" on the line immediately after the beginning balance. The beginning

FIGURE 6-4 Statement of Owner's Equity with Additional Investment

GENERAL LEDGER

ACCOUNT: Ramon Balboa, Capital ACCOUNT NO. 311

DATE		ITEM	POST. REF.	DEBIT	CREDIT	BALANCE DEBIT	BALANCE CREDIT
20-- July	1	Balance	J5		5 0 0 0 00		5 0 0 0 00
	5		J5		3 0 0 0 00		8 0 0 0 00

Additional investment

Amount reported on work sheet

Ramon's Shopping Service
Statement of Owner's Equity
For Months Ended June 30 and July 31, 20 - -

	June		July	
Ramon Balboa, beginning capital		$ 4 0 0 0 00		$ 5 0 0 0 00
Investments during period				3 0 0 0 00
Total investment				$ 8 0 0 0 00
Net income for the month	$ 1 5 0 0 00		$ 2 1 0 0 00	
Less withdrawals for the month	5 0 0 00		2 5 0 00	
Increase in capital		1 0 0 0 00		1 8 5 0 00
Ramon Balboa, ending capital		$ 5 0 0 0 00		$ 9 8 5 0 00

From general ledger

From work sheet

balance plus investments during the period equals the total investment by the owner in the business and is the amount reported in the Balance Sheet columns of the work sheet. From this point, the preparation of the statement is the same as for businesses without additional investments.

U REVU Complete U REVU-1 on **page 199** to test your basic understanding of LO1.

THE CLOSING PROCESS

LO2 Journalize and post closing entries.

Assets, liabilities, and the owner's capital account accumulate information across accounting periods. For example, the cash balance at the end of one accounting period must be the same as the cash balance at the beginning of the next period. Thus, the balance reported for Cash is a result of all cash transactions since the business first opened. This is true for all accounts reported on the balance sheet. For this reason, they are called **permanent accounts**.

Revenue, expense, and drawing accounts accumulate information *for only a specific accounting period*. When preparing the financial statements, only revenues, expenses, and withdrawals for *this year* should be reported. Revenues, expenses, and withdrawals from prior years should not be included in *this year's* financial statements. Similarly, *this year's* revenues, expenses, and withdrawals should not be included in next year's financial statements. Thus, at the end of the fiscal year, these accounts must be *closed*. The **closing process** gives these accounts zero balances so they are prepared to accumulate new information for the next accounting period. Since these accounts are closed at the end of each period, they are called **temporary accounts**.

LEARNING KEY

Permanent accounts contain the results of all transactions since the business started. Their balances are carried forward to each new accounting period.

LEARNING KEY

Temporary accounts contain information for one accounting period. These accounts are closed at the end of each accounting period.

The income summary account is not really needed for the closing process. Revenue and expense accounts can be closed to the owner's capital account. One benefit of using the income summary account is that its balance before closing to the capital account equals the net income or net loss for the period. Thus, it can serve as a check of the accuracy of the closing entries for revenues and expenses.

The accounting records are closed "as of" December 31, or another fiscal year-end chosen by the business. The actual adjusting entries, closing entries, and financial statements are generally prepared several weeks after the official closing date. However, it is important to include all transactions occurring prior to year-end in the *current* year's financial statements. Similarly, transactions taking place after year-end must be included in the *next* year's financial statements. Improper timing of the recognition of transactions taking place around the end of the year can have major effects on the reported profits. For example, some businesses have been found to "leave the books open" for a few days to include a major sale, or other profitable transactions, that actually took place after the end of the fiscal year. Thus, proper treatment of transactions taking place around the end of the year is carefully monitored by auditors.

The closing process is most clearly demonstrated by returning to the accounting equation and T accounts. As shown in Figure 6-5, revenue, expense, and drawing accounts impact owner's equity and should be considered "under the umbrella" of the capital account. The effect of these accounts on owner's equity is formalized at the end of the accounting period when the balances of the temporary accounts are transferred to the owner's capital account (a permanent account) during the closing process.

The four basic steps in the closing process are illustrated in Figure 6-5. As you can see, a new account, **Income Summary**, is used in the closing process. This account may also be called *Expense and Revenue Summary*. This temporary account is used to close the revenue and expense accounts. After closing the revenues and expenses to Income Summary, the balance of this account is equal to the net income. This is why it is called Income Summary. Income Summary is opened during the closing process. Then it is closed to the owner's capital account. It does not appear on any financial statement. The four steps in the closing process are explained on page 197.

FIGURE 6-5 The Closing Process

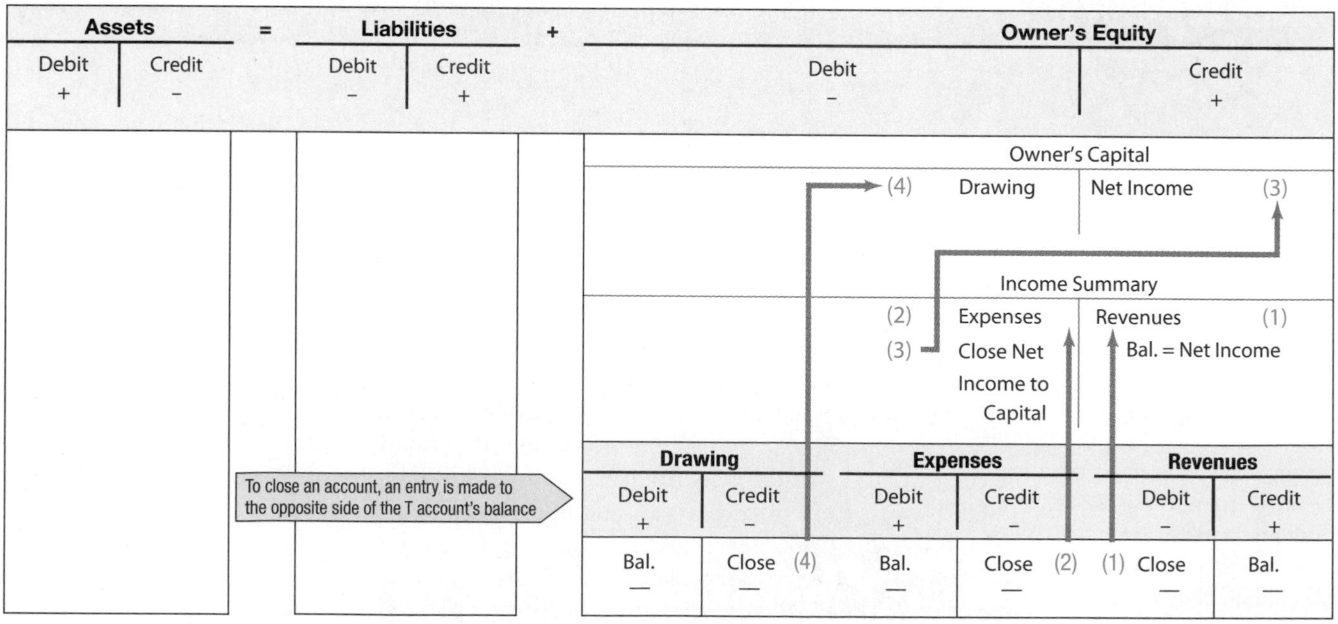

Dashes are entered on the debit and credit sides of the T accounts to indicate a zero balance.

STEPS IN THE CLOSING PROCESS

STEP 1 **Close Revenue Accounts to Income Summary.** Revenues have credit balances and increase owner's equity. Therefore, the revenue account is debited to create a zero balance. Income Summary is credited for the same amount.

STEP 2 **Close Expense Accounts to Income Summary.** Expenses have debit balances and reduce owner's equity. Therefore, the expense accounts are credited to create a zero balance. Income Summary must be debited for the total of the expenses.

STEP 3 **Close Income Summary to the Owner's Capital Account.** The balance in Income Summary represents the net income (credit balance) or net loss (debit balance). If net income has been earned, Income Summary is debited to create a zero balance, and the owner's capital account is credited. If a net loss has been incurred, the owner's capital account is debited and Income Summary is credited to create a zero balance. Figure 6-6 shows examples for closing net income and net loss.

FIGURE 6-6 Step 3: Closing Net Income and Closing Net Loss

NET INCOME

Capital

		1,000	STEP 3 (Net Income)

Income Summary

(Expenses)	4,000	5,000	(Revenues)
STEP 3 to close	1,000	1,000	(Bal. before closing)
	—	—	

NET LOSS

Capital

STEP 3 (Net Loss)	2,000		

Income Summary

(Expenses)	6,000	4,000	(Revenues)
(Bal. before closing)	2,000	2,000	STEP 3 to close
	—	—	

LEARNING KEY

The owner can make withdrawals from the business at any time, as long as the assets are available. These withdrawals have nothing to do with measuring the profitability of the firm. Thus, they are closed directly to the owner's capital account.

STEP 4 **Close Drawing to the Owner's Capital Account.** Drawing has a debit balance and reduces owner's equity. Therefore, it is credited to create a zero balance. The owner's capital account is debited.

Upon completion of these four steps, all temporary accounts have zero balances. The earnings and withdrawals for the period have been transferred to the owner's capital account. Closing entries for Jessie Jane's Campus Delivery Service, in T account form, are illustrated in Figure 6-7.

JOURNALIZE CLOSING ENTRIES

Of course, to actually change the ledger accounts, the closing entries must be journalized and posted to the general ledger. As shown in Figure 6-8, the balances of the accounts to be closed are readily available from the Income Statement and Balance Sheet columns of the work sheet. These balances are used to illustrate the closing entries for Jessie Jane's Campus Delivery Service, in general journal form. Remember: Closing entries are made at the end of the *fiscal year*. Closing entries made at the end of June are illustrated here so you can see the completion of the accounting cycle for Jessie Jane's Campus Delivery Service. Like adjusting entries, the closing entries are made on the last day of the accounting period. "Closing Entries" is written in the Description column before the first entry and no explanations are required. Note that it is best to make one compound entry to close the expense accounts.

FIGURE 6-7 Closing Entries in T Account Form

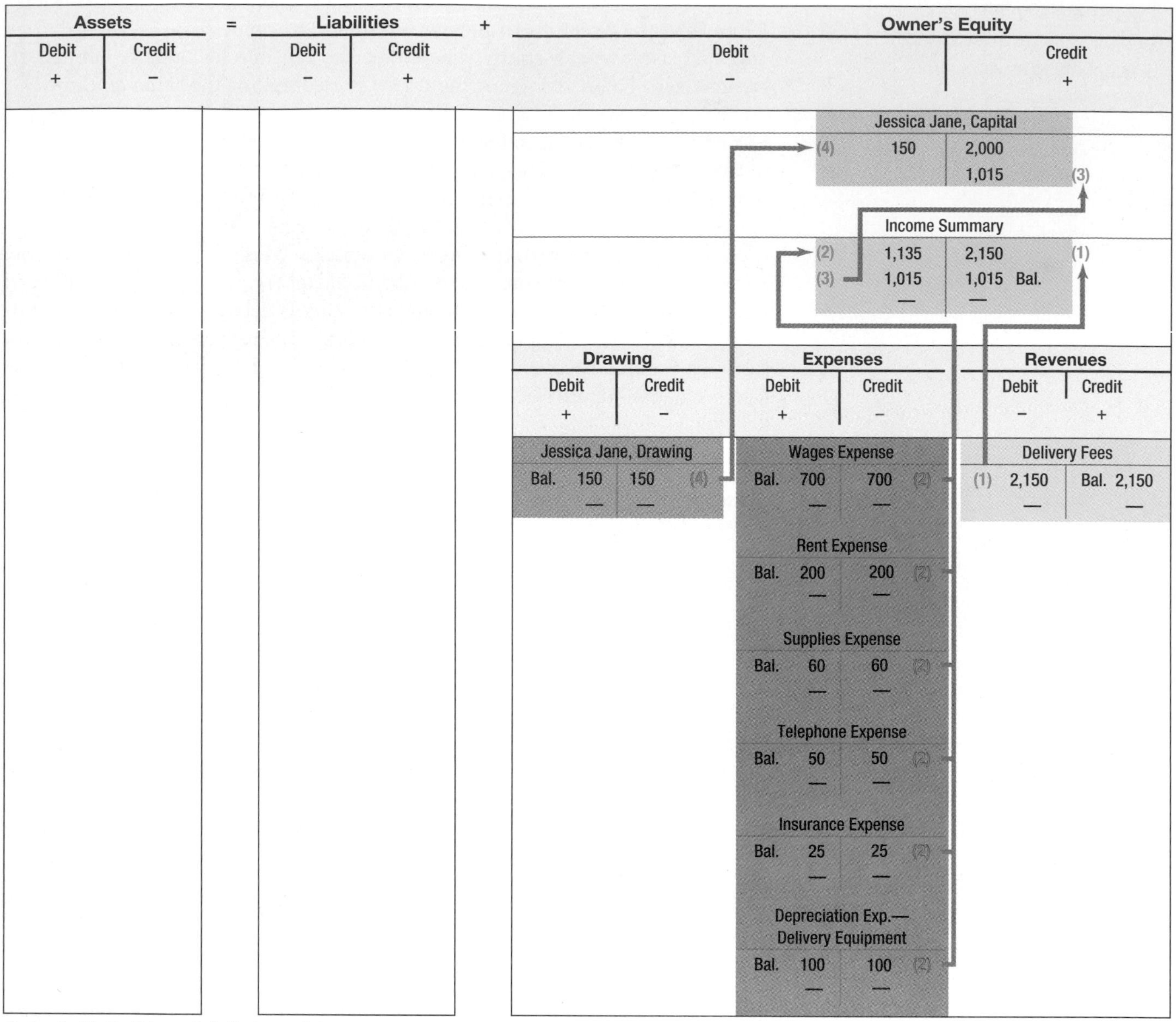

Dashes (—) in the T Accounts indicate zero balances

POST THE CLOSING ENTRIES

Computer programs post the closing entries to the owner's capital account automatically.

The account numbers have been entered in the Posting Reference column of the journal to show that the entries have been posted to the ledger accounts illustrated in Figure 6-9. Note that "Closing" has been written in the Item column of each account to identify the closing entries. Zero account balances are recorded by entering dashes in both the Balance Debit and Credit columns.

FIGURE 6-8 Closing Entries in Journal Form

Jessie Jane's Campus Delivery Service
Work Sheet (Partial)
For Month Ended June 30, 20 - -

	ACCOUNT TITLE	INCOME STATEMENT DEBIT	INCOME STATEMENT CREDIT	BALANCE SHEET DEBIT	BALANCE SHEET CREDIT
1	Cash			370 00	
2	Accounts Receivable			650 00	
3	Supplies			20 00	
4	Prepaid Insurance			175 00	
5	Delivery Equipment			3600 00	
6	Accum. Depr.—Delivery Equipment				100 00
7	Accounts Payable				1800 00
8	Wages Payable				50 00
9	Jessica Jane, Capital				2000 00
10	Jessica Jane, Drawing			150 00	
11	Delivery Fees		2150 00		
12	Wages Expense	700 00			
13	Rent Expense	200 00			
14	Supplies Expense	60 00			
15	Telephone Expense	50 00			
16	Insurance Expense	25 00			
17	Depr. Expense—Delivery Equipment	100 00			
18		1135 00	2150 00	4965 00	3950 00
19	Net Income	1015 00			1015 00
20		2150 00	2150 00	4965 00	4965 00

STEP 1: Close revenue accounts to Income Summary.

STEP 2: Close expense accounts to Income Summary.

STEP 3: Close Income Summary to the owner's capital account.

STEP 4: Close Drawing to the owner's capital account.

GENERAL JOURNAL PAGE 4

DATE		DESCRIPTION	POST. REF.	DEBIT	CREDIT	
		Closing Entries				1
20-- June	30	Delivery Fees	401	2150 00		2
		Income Summary	313		2150 00	3
						4
	30	Income Summary	313	1135 00		5
		Wages Expense	511		700 00	6
		Rent Expense	521		200 00	7
		Supplies Expense	523		60 00	8
		Telephone Expense	525		50 00	9
		Insurance Expense	535		25 00	10
		Depr. Expense—Delivery Equipment	541		100 00	11
						12
	30	Income Summary	313	1015 00		13
		Jessica Jane, Capital	311		1015 00	14
						15
	30	Jessica Jane, Capital	311	150 00		16
		Jessica Jane, Drawing	312		150 00	17
						18

STEP 1 STEP 2 STEP 3 STEP 4

LEARNING KEY

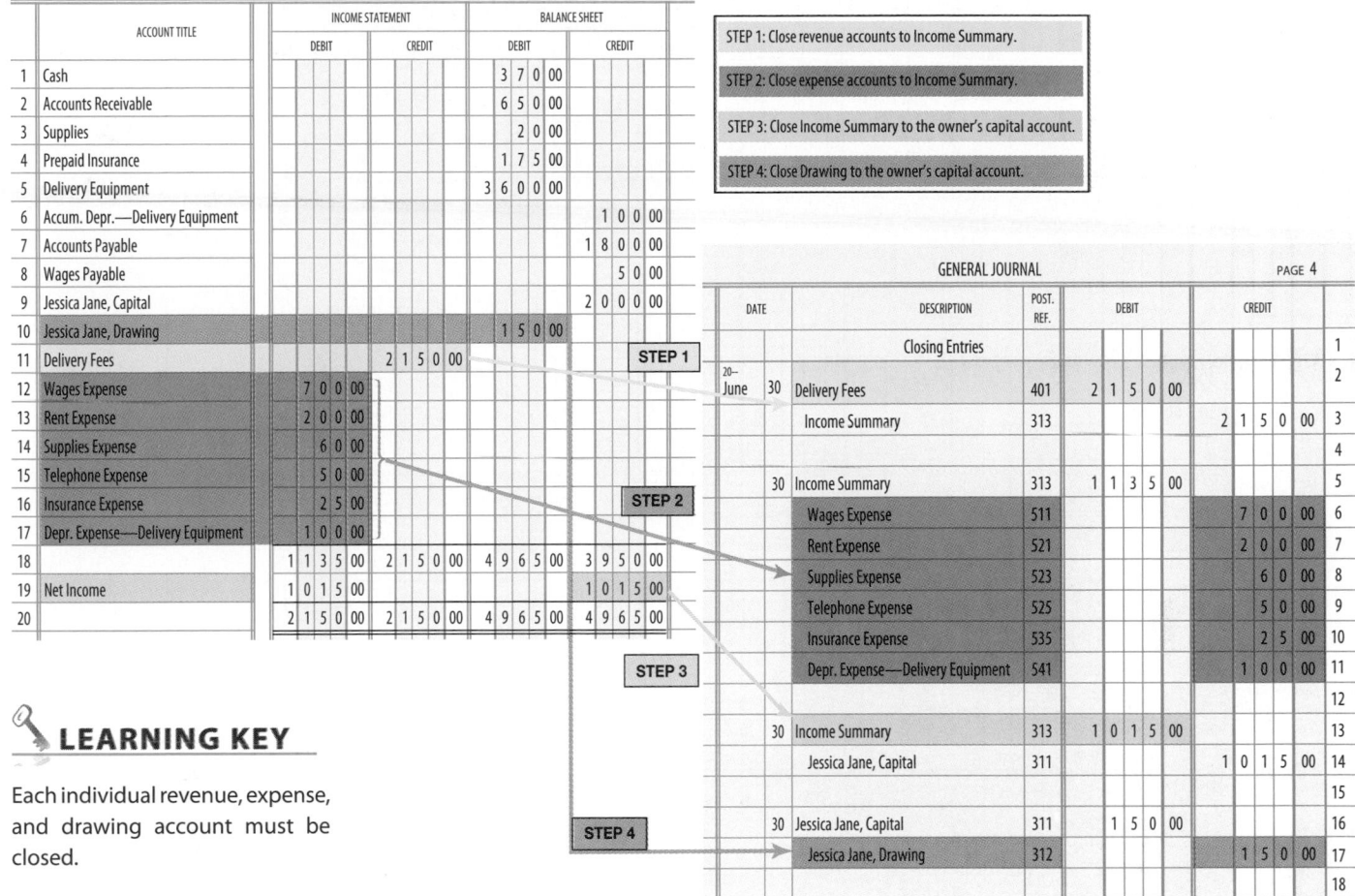

Each individual revenue, expense, and drawing account must be closed.

FIGURE 6-9 Closing Entries Posted to the General Ledger

GENERAL LEDGER

ACCOUNT: Jessica Jane, Capital ACCOUNT NO. 311

DATE		ITEM	POST. REF.	DEBIT	CREDIT	BALANCE DEBIT	BALANCE CREDIT
20-- June	1		J1		2000 00		2000 00
	30	Closing	J4		1015 00		3015 00
	30	Closing	J4	150 00			2865 00

ACCOUNT: Jessica Jane, Drawing ACCOUNT NO. 312

DATE		ITEM	POST. REF.	DEBIT	CREDIT	BALANCE DEBIT	BALANCE CREDIT
20-- June	30		J2	150 00		150 00	
	30	Closing	J4		150 00	—	—

(continued)

FIGURE 6-9 Closing Entries Posted to the General Ledger *(continued)*

ACCOUNT: Income Summary — ACCOUNT NO. 313

DATE		ITEM	POST. REF.	DEBIT	CREDIT	BALANCE DEBIT	BALANCE CREDIT
20-- June	30	Closing	J4		2,150.00		2,150.00
	30	Closing	J4	1,135.00			1,015.00
	30	Closing	J4	1,015.00		—	—

ACCOUNT: Delivery Fees — ACCOUNT NO. 401

DATE		ITEM	POST. REF.	DEBIT	CREDIT	BALANCE DEBIT	BALANCE CREDIT
20-- June	6		J1		500.00		500.00
	15		J1		600.00		1,100.00
	30		J2		1,050.00		2,150.00
	30	Closing	J4	2,150.00		—	—

ACCOUNT: Wages Expense — ACCOUNT NO. 511

DATE		ITEM	POST. REF.	DEBIT	CREDIT	BALANCE DEBIT	BALANCE CREDIT
20-- June	27		J2	650.00		650.00	
	30	Adjusting	J3	50.00		700.00	
	30	Closing	J4		700.00	—	—

ACCOUNT: Rent Expense — ACCOUNT NO. 521

DATE		ITEM	POST REF.	DEBIT	CREDIT	BALANCE DEBIT	BALANCE CREDIT
20-- June	7		J1	200.00		200.00	
	30	Closing	J4		200.00	—	—

ACCOUNT: Supplies Expense — ACCOUNT NO. 523

DATE		ITEM	POST. REF.	DEBIT	CREDIT	BALANCE DEBIT	BALANCE CREDIT
20-- June	30	Adjusting	J3	60.00		60.00	
	30	Closing	J4		60.00	—	—

ACCOUNT: Telephone Expense — ACCOUNT NO. 525

DATE		ITEM	POST. REF.	DEBIT	CREDIT	BALANCE DEBIT	BALANCE CREDIT
20-- June	15		J1	50.00		50.00	
	30	Closing	J4		50.00	—	—

ACCOUNT: Insurance Expense — ACCOUNT NO. 535

DATE		ITEM	POST. REF.	DEBIT	CREDIT	BALANCE DEBIT	BALANCE CREDIT
20-- June	30	Adjusting	J3	25.00		25.00	
	30	Closing	J4		25.00	—	—

FIGURE 6-9 Closing Entries Posted to the General Ledger *(concluded)*

ACCOUNT: Depreciation Expense—Delivery Equipment ACCOUNT NO. 541

DATE		ITEM	POST. REF.	DEBIT	CREDIT	BALANCE DEBIT	BALANCE CREDIT
20-- June	30	Adjusting	J3	100 00		100 00	
	30	Closing	J4		100 00	—	—

U REVU Complete U REVU-2 on **page 199** to test your basic understanding of LO2.

POST-CLOSING TRIAL BALANCE

LO3 Prepare a post-closing trial balance.

After posting the closing entries, a **post-closing trial balance** should be prepared to prove the equality of the debit and credit balances in the general ledger accounts. The ending balance of each general ledger account that remains open at the end of the year is listed. Remember: Only the permanent accounts remain open after the closing process is completed. Figure 6-10 shows the post-closing trial balance for Jessie's ledger.

Note that all amounts reflected on the post-closing trial balance are the same as reported in the Balance Sheet columns of the work sheet except Drawing and Owner's Capital. Drawing was closed. Owner's Capital was updated to reflect revenues, expenses, and drawing for the accounting period.

LEARNING KEY

Once the closing entries are posted, the general ledger capital account balance will agree with the amount reported on the balance sheet.

FIGURE 6-10 Post-Closing Trial Balance

Jessie Jane's Campus Delivery Service
Post-Closing Trial Balance
June 30, 20 - -

ACCOUNT TITLE	ACCOUNT NO.	DEBIT BALANCE	CREDIT BALANCE
Cash	101	370 00	
Accounts Receivable	122	650 00	
Supplies	141	20 00	
Prepaid Insurance	145	175 00	
Delivery Equipment	185	3,600 00	
Accumulated Depreciation—Delivery Equipment	185.1		100 00
Accounts Payable	202		1,800 00
Wages Payable	219		50 00
Jessica Jane, Capital	311		2,865 00
		4,815 00	4,815 00

U REVU Complete U REVU-3 on **page 199** to test your basic understanding of LO3.

A BROADER VIEW

FLUXFOTO/ISTOCKPHOTO.COM

Importance of Earnings to the Stock Market

Investors in the stock market pay close attention to earnings reported on the income statement. This information is so important that corporate officials often announce expected earnings before the financial statements are actually distributed to the public. If the announcement is different from what investors are expecting, the price of the stock may go up or down. For example, when Aetna, a leader in the managed health care industry, warned that earnings would be about 27% lower than expected by stock analysts, its stock price fell more than 10%.

THE ACCOUNTING CYCLE

LO4 List and describe the steps in the accounting cycle.

The steps involved in accounting for all of the business activities during an accounting period are called the **accounting cycle**. The cycle begins with the analysis of source documents and ends with a post-closing trial balance. A brief summary of the steps in the cycle follows.

STEPS IN THE ACCOUNTING CYCLE

During Accounting Period

STEP 1 Analyze source documents.

STEP 2 Journalize the transactions.

STEP 3 Post to the general ledger accounts.

End of Accounting Period

STEP 4 Prepare a trial balance.

STEP 5 Determine and prepare the needed adjustments on the work sheet.

STEP 6 Complete an end-of-period work sheet.

STEP 7 Journalize and post the adjusting entries.

STEP 8 Prepare an income statement, a statement of owner's equity, and a balance sheet.

STEP 9 Journalize and post the closing entries.

STEP 10 Prepare a post-closing trial balance.

LEARNING KEY

Properly analyzing and journalizing transactions is very important. A mistake made in step 1 is carried through the entire accounting cycle.

Steps 4 through 10 in the preceding list are performed *as of* the last day of the accounting period. This does not mean that they are actually done on the last day. The accountant may not be able to do any of these things until the first few days (sometimes weeks) of the next period. Nevertheless, the work sheet, statements, and entries are prepared as of the closing date.

LEARNING OBJECTIVES Key Points to Remember

LO1 Prepare financial statements with the aid of a work sheet.

The work sheet is used as an aid in preparing:

1. adjusting entries,
2. financial statements, and
3. closing entries.

The following classifications are used for accounts reported on the balance sheet.

- *Current assets* include cash and assets that will be converted into cash or consumed within either one year or the normal operating cycle of the business, whichever is longer. An *operating cycle* is the time required to purchase supplies and services and convert them back into cash.
- *Property, plant, and equipment*, also called *plant assets* or *long-term assets*, represent assets that are expected to serve the business for many years.
- *Current liabilities* are liabilities that are due within either one year or the normal operating cycle of the business, whichever is longer, and that are to be paid out of current assets.
- *Long-term liabilities,* or *long-term debt*, are obligations that are not expected to be paid within a year and do not require the use of current assets.

LO2 Journalize and post closing entries.

Steps in the closing process are:

1. Close revenue accounts to Income Summary.
2. Close expense accounts to Income Summary.
3. Close Income Summary to the owner's capital account.
4. Close Drawing to the owner's capital account.

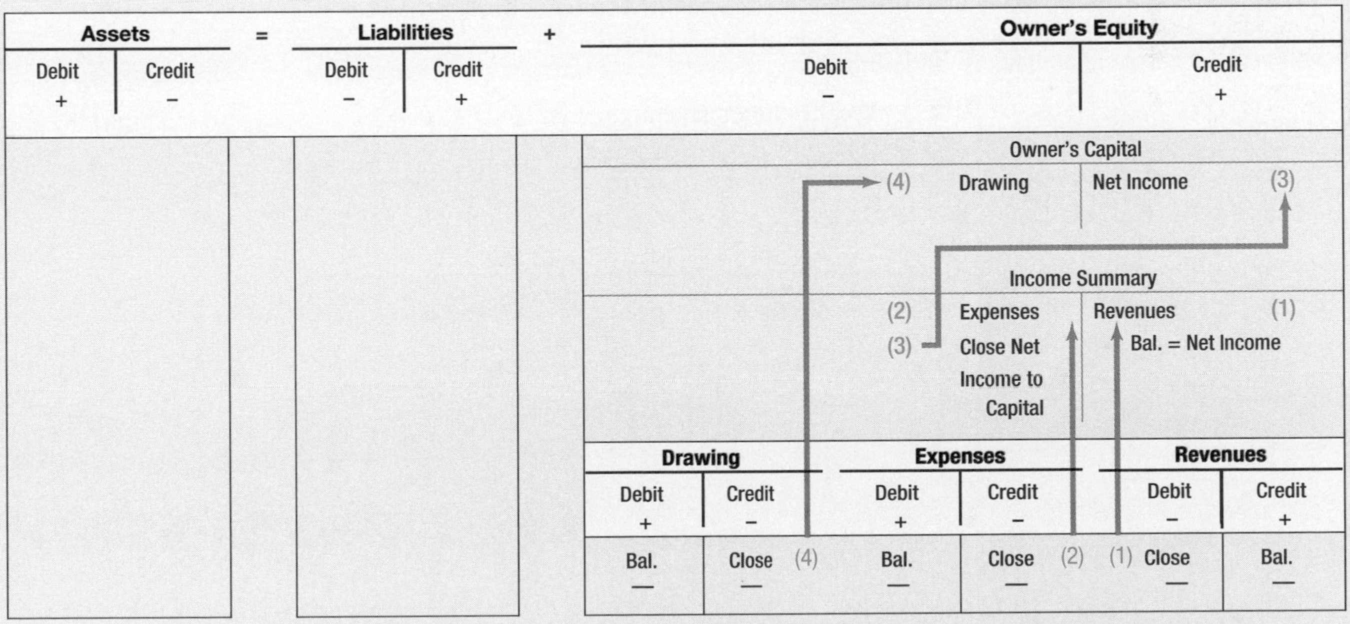

LEARNING OBJECTIVES Key Points to Remember

LO3 Prepare a post-closing trial balance.	After posting the closing entries, a post-closing trial balance should be prepared to prove the equality of the debit and credit balances in the general ledger accounts. The accounts shown in the post-closing trial balance are the permanent accounts.
LO4 List and describe the steps in the accounting cycle.	Steps in the accounting cycle are: *During Accounting Period* 1. Analyze source documents. 2. Journalize the transactions. 3. Post to the general ledger accounts. *End of Accounting Period* 4. Prepare a trial balance. 5. Determine and prepare the needed adjustments on the work sheet. 6. Complete an end-of-period work sheet. 7. Journalize and post the adjusting entries. 8. Prepare an income statement, a statement of owner's equity, and a balance sheet. 9. Journalize and post the closing entries. 10. Prepare a post-closing trial balance.

DEMONSTRATION PROBLEM

Timothy Chang owns and operates Hard Copy Printers. A work sheet for the year ended December 31, 20--, is provided on the next page. Chang made no additional investments during the year.

REQUIRED

1. Prepare financial statements.
2. Prepare closing entries.

Hard Copy Printers
Work Sheet
For Year Ended December 31, 20--

	ACCOUNT TITLE	TRIAL BALANCE DEBIT	TRIAL BALANCE CREDIT	ADJUSTMENTS DEBIT	ADJUSTMENTS CREDIT	ADJUSTED TRIAL BALANCE DEBIT	ADJUSTED TRIAL BALANCE CREDIT	INCOME STATEMENT DEBIT	INCOME STATEMENT CREDIT	BALANCE SHEET DEBIT	BALANCE SHEET CREDIT	
1	Cash	1,180 00				1,180 00				1,180 00		1
2	Paper Supplies	3,600 00			(a) 3,550 00	50 00				50 00		2
3	Prepaid Insurance	1,000 00			(b) 505 00	495 00				495 00		3
4	Printing Equipment	5,800 00				5,800 00				5,800 00		4
5	Accum. Depr.—Printing Equipment				(d) 1,200 00		1,200 00				1,200 00	5
6	Accounts Payable		500 00				500 00				500 00	6
7	Wages Payable				(c) 30 00		30 00				30 00	7
8	Timothy Chang, Capital		10,000 00				10,000 00				10,000 00	8
9	Timothy Chang, Drawing	13,000 00				13,000 00				13,000 00		9
10	Printing Fees		35,100 00				35,100 00		35,100 00			10
11	Wages Expense	11,970 00		(c) 30 00		12,000 00		12,000 00				11
12	Rent Expense	7,500 00				7,500 00		7,500 00				12
13	Paper Supplies Expense			(a) 3,550 00		3,550 00		3,550 00				13
14	Telephone Expense	550 00				550 00		550 00				14
15	Utilities Expense	1,000 00				1,000 00		1,000 00				15
16	Insurance Expense			(b) 505 00		505 00		505 00				16
17	Depr. Expense—Printing Equipment			(d) 1,200 00		1,200 00		1,200 00				17
18		45,600 00	45,600 00	5,285 00	5,285 00	46,830 00	46,830 00	26,305 00	35,100 00	20,525 00	11,730 00	18
19	Net Income							8,795 00			8,795 00	19
20								35,100 00	35,100 00	20,525 00	20,525 00	20
21												21
22												22
23												23
24												24
25												25
26												26
27												27
28												28
29												29
30												30

(continued)

Solution 1.

Hard Copy Printers
Income Statement
For Year Ended December 31, 20 --

Revenue:		
Printing fees		$35,100.00
Expenses:		
Wages expense	$12,000.00	
Rent expense	7,500.00	
Paper supplies expense	3,550.00	
Telephone expense	550.00	
Utilities expense	1,000.00	
Insurance expense	505.00	
Depreciation expense—printing equipment	1,200.00	
Total expenses		26,305.00
Net income		$ 8,795.00

Hard Copy Printers
Statement of Owner's Equity
For Year Ended December 31, 20 --

Timothy Chang, capital, January 1, 20 - -		$10,000.00
Net income for 20 - -	$ 8,795.00	
Less withdrawals for 20 - -	13,000.00	
Decrease in capital		(4,205.00)
Timothy Chang, capital, December 31, 20 - -		$ 5,795.00

Hard Copy Printers
Balance Sheet
December 31, 20 - -

Assets		
Current assets:		
Cash	$ 1,180.00	
Paper supplies	50.00	
Prepaid insurance	495.00	
Total current assets		$ 1,725.00
Property, plant, and equipment:		
Printing equipment	$ 5,800.00	
Less accumulated depreciation	1,200.00	4,600.00
Total assets		$ 6,325.00
Liabilities		
Current liabilities:		
Accounts payable	$ 500.00	
Wages payable	30.00	
Total current liabilities		$ 530.00
Owner's Equity		
Timothy Chang, capital		5,795.00
Total liabilities and owner's equity		$ 6,325.00

2.

GENERAL JOURNAL PAGE 4

	DATE		DESCRIPTION	POST. REF.	DEBIT	CREDIT	
1			Closing Entries				1
2	20-- Dec.	31	Printing Fees		35,100.00		2
3			Income Summary			35,100.00	3
4							4
5		31	Income Summary		26,305.00		5
6			Wages Expense			12,000.00	6
7			Rent Expense			7,500.00	7
8			Paper Supplies Expense			3,550.00	8
9			Telephone Expense			550.00	9
10			Utilities Expense			1,000.00	10
11			Insurance Expense			505.00	11
12			Depr. Expense—Printing Equipment			1,200.00	12
13							13
14		31	Income Summary		8,795.00		14
15			Timothy Chang, Capital			8,795.00	15
16							16
17		31	Timothy Chang, Capital		13,000.00		17
18			Timothy Chang, Drawing			13,000.00	18
19							19

KEY TERMS

account form of balance sheet (182) A balance sheet in which the assets are on the left and the liabilities and the owner's equity sections are on the right.

accounting cycle (192) The steps involved in accounting for all of the business activities during an accounting period.

classified balance sheet (182) A balance sheet with separate categories for current assets; property, plant, and equipment; current liabilities; and long-term liabilities.

closing process (185) The process of giving zero balances to the temporary accounts so that they can accumulate information for the next accounting period.

current assets (184) Cash and assets that will be converted into cash or consumed within either one year or the normal operating cycle of the business, whichever is longer.

current liabilities (184) Liabilities that are due within either one year or the normal operating cycle of the business, whichever is longer, and that are to be paid out of current assets.

Income Summary (186) A temporary account used in the closing process to summarize the effects of all revenue and expense accounts.

long-term assets (184) See property, plant, and equipment.

long-term debt (184) See long-term liabilities.

long-term liabilities (184) Obligations that are not expected to be paid within a year and do not require the use of current assets. Also called long-term debt.

operating cycle (184) The period of time required to purchase supplies and services and convert them back into cash.

permanent accounts (185) Accounts that accumulate information across accounting periods; all accounts reported on the balance sheet.

plant assets (184) See property, plant, and equipment.

post-closing trial balance (191) Prepared after posting the closing entries to prove the equality of the debit and credit balances in the general ledger accounts.

property, plant, and equipment (184) Assets that are expected to serve the business for many years. Also called plant assets or long-term assets.

report form of balance sheet (182) A balance sheet in which the liabilities and the owner's equity sections are shown below the assets section.

temporary accounts (185) Accounts that do not accumulate information across accounting periods but are closed, such as the drawing account and all income statement accounts.

SELF-STUDY QUESTIONS AND EXERCISES

True/False Questions

1. LO1 Expenses are listed on the income statement as they appear in the chart of accounts or in descending order (by dollar amount).
2. LO1 Additional investments of capital during the month are not reported on the statement of owner's equity.
3. LO1 The income statement cannot be prepared using the work sheet alone.
4. LO1 A classified balance sheet groups similar items, such as current assets together.
5. LO2 Temporary accounts are closed at the end of each accounting period.

Multiple Choice Questions

1. LO2 Which of these types of accounts is considered a "permanent" account?
   (a) Revenue
   (b) Asset
   (c) Drawing
   (d) Expense
2. LO2 Which of these accounts is considered a "temporary" account?
   (a) Cash
   (b) Accounts Payable
   (c) J. Jones, Capital
   (d) J. Jones, Drawing
3. LO2 Which of these is the first step in the closing process?
   (a) Close revenue account(s).
   (b) Close expense accounts.
   (c) Close the income summary account.
   (d) Close the drawing account.
4. LO3 The _______ is prepared after closing entries are posted to prove the equality of debit and credit balances.
   (a) balance sheet
   (b) income statement
   (c) post-closing trial balance
   (d) statement of owner's equity
5. LO4 Steps that begin with analyzing source documents and conclude with the post-closing trial balance are called the
   (a) closing process.
   (b) accounting cycle.
   (c) adjusting entries.
   (d) posting process.

U REVU Exercises

1. LO1 Joe Fisher operates Fisher Consulting. A partial work sheet for August 20-- is provided below. Fisher made no additional investments during the month. Prepare an income statement, statement of owner's equity, and balance sheet.

Fisher Consulting
Work Sheet (Partial)
For Month Ended August 31, 20 - -

	ACCOUNT TITLE	INCOME STATEMENT DEBIT	INCOME STATEMENT CREDIT	BALANCE SHEET DEBIT	BALANCE SHEET CREDIT	
1	Cash			2 500 00		1
2	Accounts Receivable			800 00		2
3	Equipment			3 800 00		3
4	Accum. Depr.— Equipment				200 00	4
5	Accounts Payable				1 000 00	5
6	Joe Fisher, Capital				3 000 00	6
7	Joe Fisher, Drawing			300 00		7
8	Professional Fees		5 000 00			8
9	Wages Expense	1 000 00				9
10	Rent Expense	700 00				10
11	Depreciation Expense	100 00				11
12	Net Income	1 800 00	5 000 00	7 400 00	4 200 00	12
13		3 200 00			3 200 00	13
14		5 000 00	5 000 00	7 400 00	7 400 00	14
15						15
16						16

2. LO2 Using the work sheet provided in U REVU Exercise 1, prepare closing entries in general journal form.
3. LO3 Using the work sheet provided in U REVU Exercise 1 and financial statements prepared for that exercise, prepare a post-closing trial balance.

The answers to the Self-Study Questions and Exercises are at the end of the chapter (pages 213–215).

APPLYING YOUR KNOWLEDGE

REVIEW QUESTIONS

LO1 1. Identify the source of the information needed to prepare the income statement.

LO1 2. Describe two approaches to listing the expenses in the income statement.

LO1 3. Identify the sources of the information needed to prepare the statement of owner's equity.

LO1 4. If additional investments were made during the year, what information in addition to the work sheet would be needed to prepare the statement of owner's equity?

LO1 5. Identify the sources of the information needed to prepare the balance sheet.

LO2 6. What is a permanent account? On which financial statement are permanent accounts reported?

LO2 7. Name three types of temporary accounts.

LO2 8. List the four steps for closing the temporary accounts.

LO2 9. Describe the net effect of the four closing entries on the balance of the owner's capital account. Where else is this same amount calculated?

LO3 10. What is the purpose of the post-closing trial balance?

LO4 11. List the 10 steps in the accounting cycle.

SERIES A EXERCISES

E 6-1A (LO1)
✓ Net income: $1,990

INCOME STATEMENT From the partial work sheet for Case Advising below, prepare an income statement.

E 6-2A (LO1)
✓ Capital 1/31: $5,190

STATEMENT OF OWNER'S EQUITY From the partial work sheet below, prepare a statement of owner's equity, assuming no additional investment was made by the owner.

E 6-3A (LO1)
✓ Total assets: $6,390

BALANCE SHEET From the partial work sheet below, prepare a balance sheet.

(FOR EXERCISES 6-1A, 6-2A, AND 6-3A)

Case Advising
Work Sheet (Partial)
For Month Ended January 31, 20 - -

	ACCOUNT TITLE	INCOME STATEMENT DEBIT	INCOME STATEMENT CREDIT	BALANCE SHEET DEBIT	BALANCE SHEET CREDIT	
1	Cash			1212 00		1
2	Accounts Receivable			896 00		2
3	Supplies			482 00		3
4	Prepaid Insurance			900 00		4
5	Office Equipment			3000 00		5
6	Accum. Depr.—Office Equipment				100 00	6
7	Accounts Payable				1000 00	7
8	Wages Payable				200 00	8
9	Bill Case, Capital				4000 00	9
10	Bill Case, Drawing			800 00		10
11	Advising Fees		3793 00			11
12	Wages Expense	800 00				12
13	Advertising Expense	80 00				13
14	Rent Expense	500 00				14
15	Supplies Expense	120 00				15
16	Telephone Expense	58 00				16
17	Electricity Expense	44 00				17
18	Insurance Expense	30 00				18
19	Gas and Oil Expense	38 00				19
20	Depr. Expense—Office Equipment	100 00				20
21	Miscellaneous Expense	33 00				21
22		1803 00	3793 00	7290 00	5300 00	22
23	Net Income	1990 00			1990 00	23
24		3793 00	3793 00	7290 00	7290 00	24

E 6-4A (LO2)

✓ Capital 1/31: $5,190

CLOSING ENTRIES (NET INCOME) Set up T accounts for Case Advising based on the work sheet in Exercise 6-1A and the chart of accounts provided below. Enter the existing balance for each account. Prepare closing entries in general journal form. Then post the closing entries to the T accounts.

Chart of Accounts

No.	Account	No.	Account
Assets		**Revenues**	
101	Cash	401	Advising Fees
122	Accounts Receivable		
141	Supplies	**Expenses**	
145	Prepaid Insurance	511	Wages Expense
181	Office Equipment	512	Advertising Expense
181.1	Accum. Depr.—Office Equip.	521	Rent Expense
		524	Supplies Expense
Liabilities		525	Telephone Expense
202	Accounts Payable	533	Electricity Expense
219	Wages Payable	535	Insurance Expense
		538	Gas and Oil Expense
		541	Depr. Exp.—Office Equip.
Owner's Equity		549	Miscellaneous Expense
311	Bill Case, Capital		
312	Bill Case, Drawing		
313	Income Summary		

E 6-5A (LO2)

CLOSING ENTRIES (NET INCOME) Using the following partial listing of T accounts, prepare closing entries in general journal form dated April 30, 20--. Then post the closing entries to the T accounts.

Account	No.	Debit	Credit
Cash	101	Bal. 500	
Income Summary	313		
Supplies Expense	524	Bal. 500	
Accounts Receivable	122	Bal. 1,500	
Golf Instruction Fees	401		Bal. 4,000
Insurance Expense	535	Bal 100	
Wages Payable	219		Bal. 400
Wages Expense	511	Bal. 800	
Postage Expense	536	Bal. 50	
Chris Williams, Capital	311		Bal. 9,000
Advertising Expense	512	Bal. 200	
Gas and Oil Expense	538	Bal. 150	
Chris Williams, Drawing	312	Bal. 1,000	
Travel Expense	515	Bal. 600	
Miscellaneous Expense	549	Bal. 80	

E 6-6A (LO2)

✓ Capital 1/31: $2,597

CLOSING ENTRIES (NET LOSS) Using the following partial listing of T accounts, prepare closing entries in general journal form dated January 31, 20--. Then post the closing entries to the T accounts.

Accum. Depr.—Del. Equip. 185.1	
	Bal. 100

Wages Payable 219	
	Bal. 200

Saburo Goto, Capital 311	
	Bal. 4,000

Saburo Goto, Drawing 312	
Bal. 800	

Income Summary 313	

Delivery Fees 401	
	Bal. 2,200

Wages Expense 511	
Bal. 1,800	

Advertising Expense 512	
Bal. 80	

Rent Expense 521	
Bal. 500	

Supplies Expense 523	
Bal. 120	

Telephone Expense 525	
Bal. 58	

Electricity Expense 533	
Bal. 44	

Insurance Expense 535	
Bal 30	

Gas and Oil Expense 538	
Bal. 38	

Depr. Exp.—Del. Equip. 541	
Bal. 100	

Miscellaneous Expense 549	
Bal. 33	

SERIES A PROBLEMS

P 6-7A (LO1)

✓ Net income: $1,400; Capital 1/31: $7,400; Total assets: $8,650

FINANCIAL STATEMENTS Page 203 shows a work sheet for Monte's Repairs. No additional investments were made by the owner during the month.

REQUIRED

1. Prepare an income statement.
2. Prepare a statement of owner's equity.
3. Prepare a balance sheet.

PROBLEM 6-7A

Monte's Repairs
Work Sheet
For Month Ended January 31, 20--

	ACCOUNT TITLE	TRIAL BALANCE		ADJUSTMENTS		ADJUSTED TRIAL BALANCE		INCOME STATEMENT		BALANCE SHEET		
		DEBIT	CREDIT	DEBIT	CREDIT	DEBIT	CREDIT	DEBIT	CREDIT	DEBIT	CREDIT	
1	Cash	3080.00				3080.00				3080.00		1
2	Accounts Receivable	1200.00				1200.00				1200.00		2
3	Supplies	800.00			(a) 200.00	600.00				600.00		3
4	Prepaid Insurance	900.00			(b) 100.00	800.00				800.00		4
5	Delivery Equipment	3000.00				3000.00				3000.00		5
6	Accum. Depr.—Delivery Equipment				(d) 30.00		30.00				30.00	6
7	Accounts Payable		1100.00				1100.00				1100.00	7
8	Wages Payable				(c) 150.00		150.00				150.00	8
9	Monte Eli, Capital		7000.00				7000.00				7000.00	9
10	Monte Eli, Drawing	1000.00				1000.00				1000.00		10
11	Repair Fees		4230.00				4230.00		4230.00			11
12	Wages Expense	1650.00		(c) 150.00		1800.00		1800.00				12
13	Advertising Expense	170.00				170.00		170.00				13
14	Rent Expense	420.00				420.00		420.00				14
15	Supplies Expense			(a) 200.00		200.00		200.00				15
16	Telephone Expense	49.00				49.00		49.00				16
17	Insurance Expense			(b) 100.00		100.00		100.00				17
18	Gas and Oil Expense	33.00				33.00		33.00				18
19	Depr. Expense—Delivery Equipment			(d) 30.00		30.00		30.00				19
20	Miscellaneous Expense	28.00				28.00		28.00				20
21		12330.00	12330.00	480.00	480.00	12510.00	12510.00	2830.00	4230.00	9680.00	8280.00	21
22	Net Income							1400.00			1400.00	22
23								4230.00	4230.00	9680.00	9680.00	23
24												24
25												25
26												26
27												27
28												28
29												29
30												30

P 6-8A (LO1)

✓ Capital 1/31: $6,820

STATEMENT OF OWNER'S EQUITY The capital account for Autumn Chou, including an additional investment, and a partial work sheet are shown below.

REQUIRED

Prepare a statement of owner's equity.

GENERAL LEDGER

ACCOUNT: Autumn Chou, Capital — ACCOUNT NO. 311

DATE		ITEM	POST. REF.	DEBIT	CREDIT	BALANCE DEBIT	BALANCE CREDIT
20-- Jan.	1	Balance	✔				4,800.00
	18		J1		1,200.00		6,000.00

Autumn's Home Designs
Work Sheet (Partial)
For Month Ended January 31, 20 --

	ACCOUNT TITLE	INCOME STATEMENT DEBIT	INCOME STATEMENT CREDIT	BALANCE SHEET DEBIT	BALANCE SHEET CREDIT	
1	Cash			3,200.00		1
2	Accounts Receivable			1,600.00		2
3	Supplies			800.00		3
4	Prepaid Insurance			900.00		4
5	Office Equipment			2,500.00		5
6	Accum. Depr.—Office Equipment				50.00	6
7	Accounts Payable				1,950.00	7
8	Wages Payable				180.00	8
9	Autumn Chou, Capital				6,000.00	9
10	Autumn Chou, Drawing			1,000.00		10
11	Design Fees		4,866.00			11
12	Wages Expense	1,900.00				12
13	Advertising Expense	21.00				13
14	Rent Expense	600.00				14
15	Supplies Expense	200.00				15
16	Telephone Expense	85.00				16
17	Electricity Expense	48.00				17
18	Insurance Expense	60.00				18
19	Gas and Oil Expense	32.00				19
20	Depr. Expense—Office Equipment	50.00				20
21	Miscellaneous Expense	50.00				21
22		3,046.00	4,866.00	10,000.00	8,180.00	22
23	Net Income	1,820.00			1,820.00	23
24		4,866.00	4,866.00	10,000.00	10,000.00	24

P 6-9A (LO2/3)

✓ Capital 1/31:$7,400; Post-closing trial bal. total debits: $8,680

KA KLOOSTER & ALLEN

CLOSING ENTRIES AND POST-CLOSING TRIAL BALANCE Refer to the work sheet in Problem 6-7A for Monte's Repairs. The trial balance amounts (before adjustments) have been entered in the ledger accounts provided in the working papers. If you are not using the working papers that accompany this book, set up ledger accounts and enter these balances as of January 31, 20--. A chart of accounts is provided below.

Monte's Repairs
Chart of Accounts

Assets		Revenues	
101	Cash	401	Repair Fees
122	Accounts Receivable		
141	Supplies	Expenses	
145	Prepaid Insurance	511	Wages Expense
185	Delivery Equipment	512	Advertising Expense
185.1	Accum. Depr.—Delivery Equip.	521	Rent Expense
		523	Supplies Expense
Liabilities		525	Telephone Expense
202	Accounts Payable	535	Insurancc Expense
219	Wages Payable	538	Gas and Oil Expense
		541	Depr. Exp.--Delivery Equip.
Owner's Equity		549	Miscellaneous Expense
311	Monte Eli, Capital		
312	Monte Eli, Drawing		
313	Income Summary		

REQUIRED

1. Journalize (page 10) and post the adjusting entries.
2. Journalize (page 11) and post the closing entries.
3. Prepare a post-closing trial balance.

SERIES B EXERCISES

E 6-1B (LO1)
✓ Net income: $1,826

INCOME STATEMENT From the partial work sheet for Adams' Shoe Shine below, prepare an income statement.

E 6-2B (LO1)
✓ Capital 6/30: $5,826

STATEMENT OF OWNER'S EQUITY From the partial work sheet below, prepare a statement of owner's equity, assuming no additional investment was made by the owner.

E 6-3B (LO1)
✓ Total assets: $7,936

BALANCE SHEET From the partial work sheet below, prepare a balance sheet for Adams' Shoe Shine.

(FOR EXERCISES 6-1B, 6-2B, AND 6-3B)

Adams' Shoe Shine
Work Sheet (Partial)
For Month Ended June 30, 20 - -

	ACCOUNT TITLE	INCOME STATEMENT DEBIT	INCOME STATEMENT CREDIT	BALANCE SHEET DEBIT	BALANCE SHEET CREDIT	
1	Cash			3,262 00		1
2	Accounts Receivable			1,244 00		2
3	Supplies			800 00		3
4	Prepaid Insurance			640 00		4
5	Office Equipment			2,100 00		5
6	Accum. Depr.—Office Equipment				110 00	6
7	Accounts Payable				1,850 00	7
8	Wages Payable				260 00	8
9	Mary Adams, Capital				6,000 00	9
10	Mary Adams, Drawing			2,000 00		10
11	Service Fees		4,813 00			11
12	Wages Expense	1,080 00				12
13	Advertising Expense	34 00				13
14	Rent Expense	900 00				14
15	Supplies Expense	322 00				15
16	Telephone Expense	133 00				16
17	Utilities Expense	102 00				17
18	Insurance Expense	120 00				18
19	Gas and Oil Expense	88 00				19
20	Depr. Expense—Office Equipment	110 00				20
21	Miscellaneous Expense	98 00				21
22		2,987 00	4,813 00	10,046 00	8,220 00	22
23	Net Income	1,826 00			1,826 00	23
24		4,813 00	4,813 00	10,046 00	10,046 00	24

E 6-4B (LO2)
✓ Capital 6/30: $5,826

CLOSING ENTRIES (NET INCOME) Set up T accounts for Adams' Shoe Shine based on the work sheet above and the chart of accounts provided on the next page. Enter the existing balance for each account. Prepare closing entries in general journal form. Then post the closing entries to the T accounts.

Chart of Accounts

Assets		Revenues	
101	Cash	401	Service Fees
122	Accounts Receivable		
141	Supplies	**Expenses**	
145	Prepaid Insurance	511	Wages Expense
181	Office Equipment	512	Advertising Expense
181.1	Accum. Depr.—Office Equip.	521	Rent Expense
		523	Supplies Expense
Liabilities		525	Telephone Expense
202	Accounts Payable	533	Utilities Expense
219	Wages Payable	535	Insurance Expense
		538	Gas and Oil Expense
Owner's Equity		542	Depr. Exp.—Office Equip.
311	Mary Adams, Capital	549	Miscellaneous Expense
312	Mary Adams, Drawing		
313	Income Summary		

E 6-5B **(LO2)**

CLOSING ENTRIES (NET INCOME) Using the following partial listing of T accounts, prepare closing entries in general journal form dated May 31, 20--. Then post the closing entries to the T accounts.

Cash 101

Bal. 600	

Income Summary 313

Supplies Expense 524

Bal. 900	

Accounts Receivable 122

Bal. 1,800	

Lawn Service Fees 401

	Bal. 5,000

Insurance Expense 535

Bal. 300	

Wages Payable 219

	Bal. 500

Wages Expense 511

Bal. 400	

Postage Expense 536

Bal. 40	

Mark Thrasher, Capital 311

	Bal. 8,000

Advertising Expense 512

Bal. 600	

Gas and Oil Expense 538

Bal. 700	

Mark Thrasher, Drawing 312

Bal. 800	

Travel Expense 515

Bal. 100	

Miscellaneous Expense 549

Bal. 200	

E 6-6B (LO2)
✓ Capital 6/30: $3,826

CLOSING ENTRIES (NET LOSS) Using the following partial listing of T accounts, prepare closing entries in general journal form dated June 30, 20--. Then post the closing entries to the T accounts.

Accum. Depr.—Office Equip. 181.1	
	Bal. 110

Wages Payable 219	
	Bal. 260

Raquel Zapata, Capital 311	
	Bal. 6,000

Raquel Zapata, Drawing 312	
Bal. 2,000	

Income Summary 313	

Referral Fees 401	
	Bal. 2,813

Wages Expense 511	
Bal. 1,080	

Advertising Expense 512	
Bal. 34	

Rent Expense 521	
Bal. 900	

Supplies Expense 523	
Bal. 322	

Telephone Expense 525	
Bal. 133	

Utilities Expense 533	
Bal. 102	

Insurance Expense 535	
Bal. 120	

Gas and Oil Expense 538	
Bal. 88	

Depr. Exp.—Office Equip. 541	
Bal. 110	

Miscellaneous Expense 549	
Bal. 98	

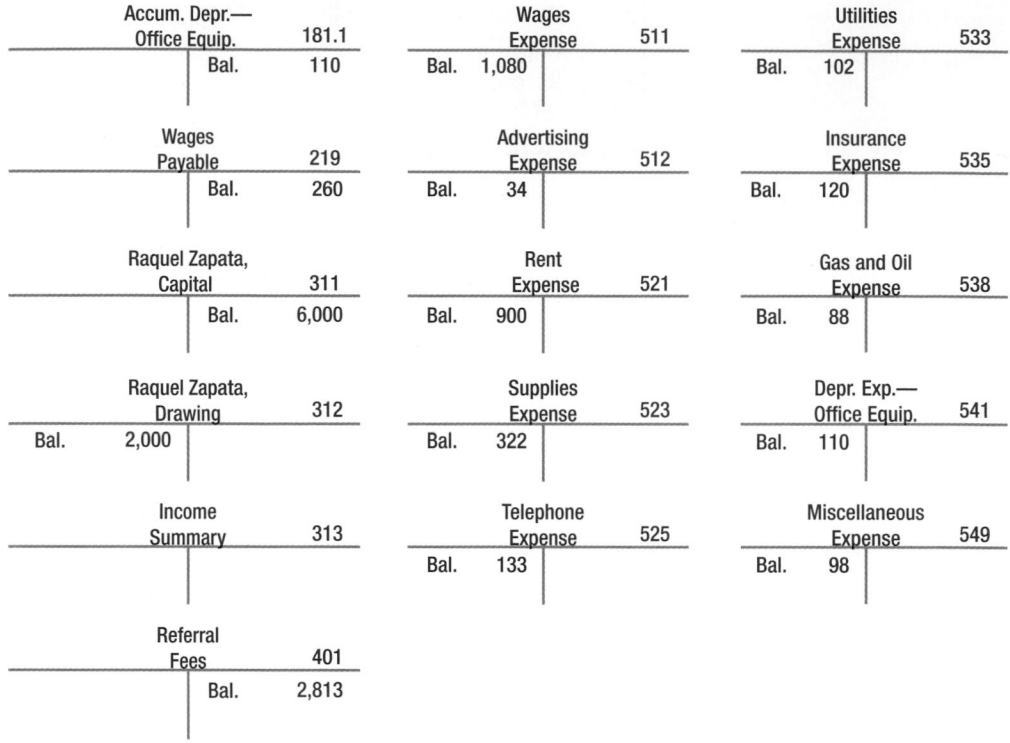

SERIES B PROBLEMS

P 6-7B (LO1)
✓ Net income: $1,450;
Capital 6/30: $7,650;
Total assets: $9,350

FINANCIAL STATEMENTS A work sheet for Juanita's Consulting is shown on the following page. There were no additional investments made by the owner during the month.

REQUIRED

1. Prepare an income statement.
2. Prepare a statement of owner's equity.
3. Prepare a balance sheet.

PROBLEM 6-7B

Juanita's Consulting
Work Sheet
For Month Ended June 30, 20--

	ACCOUNT TITLE	TRIAL BALANCE		ADJUSTMENTS		ADJUSTED TRIAL BALANCE		INCOME STATEMENT		BALANCE SHEET		
		DEBIT	CREDIT	DEBIT	CREDIT	DEBIT	CREDIT	DEBIT	CREDIT	DEBIT	CREDIT	
1	Cash	5285 00				5285 00				5285 00		1
2	Accounts Receivable	1075 00				1075 00				1075 00		2
3	Supplies	750 00			(a) 250 00	500 00				500 00		3
4	Prepaid Insurance	500 00			(b) 100 00	400 00				400 00		4
5	Office Equipment	2200 00				2200 00				2200 00		5
6	Accum. Depr.—Office Equipment				(d) 110 00		110 00				110 00	6
7	Accounts Payable		1500 C0				1500 00				1500 00	7
8	Wages Payable				(c) 200 00		200 00				200 00	8
9	Juanita Alvarez, Capital		7000 00				7000 00				7000 00	9
10	Juanita Alvarez, Drawing	800 00				800 00				800 00		10
11	Consulting Fees		4204 00				4204 00		4204 00			11
12	Wages Expense	1400 00		(c) 200 00		1600 00		1600 00				12
13	Advertising Expense	60 00				60 00		60 00				13
14	Rent Expense	500 00				500 00		500 00				14
15	Supplies Expense			(a) 250 00		250 00		250 00				15
16	Telephone Expense	46 00				46 00		46 00				16
17	Electricity Expense	39 00				39 00		39 00				17
18	Insurance Expense			(b) 100 00		100 00		100 00				18
19	Gas and Oil Expense	28 00				28 00		28 00				19
20	Depr. Expense—Office Equipment			(d) 110 00		110 00		110 00				20
21	Miscellaneous Expense	21 00				21 00		21 00				21
22		12704 00	12704 00	660 00	660 00	13014 00	13014 00	2754 00	4204 00	10260 00	8810 00	22
23	Net Income							1450 00			1450 00	23
24								4204 00	4204 00	10260 00	10260 00	24
25												25
26												26
27												27
28												28
29												29
30												30

P 6-8B (LO1)
✓ Capital 1/31: $9,975

STATEMENT OF OWNER'S EQUITY The capital account for Minta's Editorial Services, including an additional investment, and a partial work sheet are shown below.

GENERAL LEDGER

ACCOUNT: Minta Berry, Capital — ACCOUNT NO. 311

DATE		ITEM	POST. REF.	DEBIT	CREDIT	BALANCE DEBIT	BALANCE CREDIT
20-- Jan.	1	Balance	✔				3,600 00
	22		J1		2,900 00		6,500 00

Minta's Editorial Services
Work Sheet (Partial)
For Month Ended January 31, 20 --

	ACCOUNT TITLE	INCOME STATEMENT DEBIT	INCOME STATEMENT CREDIT	BALANCE SHEET DEBIT	BALANCE SHEET CREDIT	
1	Cash			3,800 00		1
2	Accounts Receivable			2,200 00		2
3	Supplies			1,000 00		3
4	Prepaid Insurance			950 00		4
5	Computer Equipment			4,500 00		5
6	Accum. Depr.—Computer Equipment				225 00	6
7	Accounts Payable				2,100 00	7
8	Wages Payable				150 00	8
9	Minta Berry, Capital				6,500 00	9
10	Minta Berry, Drawing			1,700 00		10
11	Editing Fees		7,012 00			11
12	Wages Expense	600 00				12
13	Advertising Expense	49 00				13
14	Rent Expense	450 00				14
15	Supplies Expense	288 00				15
16	Telephone Expense	44 00				16
17	Utilities Expense	38 00				17
18	Insurance Expense	125 00				18
19	Depr. Expense—Computer Equipment	225 00				19
20	Miscellaneous Expense	18 00				20
21		1,837 00	7,012 00	14,150 00	8,975 00	21
22	Net Income	5,175 00			5,175 00	22
23		7,012 00	7,012 00	14,150 00	14,150 00	23

REQUIRED

Prepare a statement of owner's equity.

P 6-9B (LO2/3)

✓ Capital 6/30: $7,650;
Post-closing trial bal.
total debits: $9,460

CLOSING ENTRIES AND POST-CLOSING TRIAL BALANCE Refer to the work sheet for Juanita's Consulting in Problem 6-7B. The trial balance amounts (before adjustments) have been entered in the ledger accounts provided in the working papers. If you are not using the working papers that accompany this book, set up ledger accounts and enter these balances as of June 30, 20--. A chart of accounts is provided below.

Juanita's Consulting
Chart of Accounts

Assets		Revenues	
101	Cash	401	Consulting Fees
122	Accounts Receivable		
141	Supplies	Expenses	
145	Prepaid Insurance	511	Wages Expense
181	Office Equipment	512	Advertising Expense
181.1	Accum. Depr.—Office Equip.	521	Rent Expense
		523	Supplies Expense
Liabilities		525	Telephone Expense
202	Accounts Payable	533	Electricity Expense
219	Wages Payable	535	Insurance Expense
		538	Gas and Oil Expense
Owner's Equity		541	Depr. Exp.—Office Equip.
311	Juanita Alvarez, Capital	549	Miscellaneous Expense
312	Juanita Alvarez, Drawing		
313	Income Summary		

REQUIRED

1. Journalize (page 10) and post the adjusting entries.
2. Journalize (page 11) and post the closing entries.
3. Prepare a post-closing trial balance.

MANAGING YOUR WRITING

At lunch, two bookkeepers got into a heated discussion about whether closing entries should be made before or after preparing the financial statements. They have come to you to resolve this issue and have agreed to accept your position. Write a memo explaining the purpose of closing entries and whether they should be made before or after preparing the financial statements.

MASTERY PROBLEM

✓ Total assets: $4,740;
E. Soltis, capital, Dec. 31: $4,475

Elizabeth Soltis owns and operates Aunt Ibby's Styling Salon. A year-end work sheet is provided on the next page. Using this information, prepare adjusting entries, financial statements, and closing entries. Soltis made no additional investments during the year.

(continued)

MASTERY PROBLEM

Aunt Ibby's Styling Salon
Work Sheet
For Year Ended December 31, 20--

	ACCOUNT TITLE	TRIAL BALANCE		ADJUSTMENTS		ADJUSTED TRIAL BALANCE		INCOME STATEMENT		BALANCE SHEET	
		DEBIT	CREDIT	DEBIT	CREDIT	DEBIT	CREDIT	DEBIT	CREDIT	DEBIT	CREDIT
1	Cash	940 00				940 00				940 00	
2	Styling Supplies	1500 00			(a) 1450 00	50 00				50 00	
3	Prepaid Insurance	800 00			(b) 650 00	150 00				150 00	
4	Salon Equipment	4500 00				4500 00				4500 00	
5	Accum. Depr.—Salon Equipment				(d) 900 00		900 00				900 00
6	Accounts Payable		225 00				225 00				225 00
7	Wages Payable				(c) 40 00		40 00				40 00
8	Elizabeth Soltis, Capital		2765 00				2765 00				2765 00
9	Elizabeth Soltis, Drawing	12000 00				12000 00				12000 00	
10	Styling Fees		32000 00				32000 00		32000 00		
11	Wages Expense	8000 00		(c) 40 00		8040 00		8040 00			
12	Rent Expense	6000 00				6000 00		6000 00			
13	Styling Supplies Expense			(a) 1450 00		1450 00		1450 00			
14	Telephone Expense	450 00				450 00		450 00			
15	Utilities Expense	800 00				800 00		800 00			
16	Insurance Expense			(b) 650 00		650 00		650 00			
17	Depr. Expense—Salon Equipment			(d) 900 00		900 00		900 00			
18		34990 00	34990 00	3040 00	3040 00	35930 00	35930 00	18290 00	32000 00	17640 00	3930 00
19	Net Income							13710 00			13710 00
20								32000 00	32000 00	17640 00	17640 00
21											
22											
23											
24											
25											
26											
27											
28											
29											
30											

CHALLENGE PROBLEM

This problem challenges you to apply your cumulative accounting knowledge to move a step beyond the material in the chapter.

✓ **Net loss: $2,100; Capital, 1/31/20--: ($700)**

Provided below is a partial work sheet for Ardery Advising.

Ardery Advising
Work Sheet (Partial)
For Month Ended January 31, 20 - -

	ACCOUNT TITLE	INCOME STATEMENT		BALANCE SHEET		
		DEBIT	CREDIT	DEBIT	CREDIT	
1	Cash			2,412.00		1
2	Accounts Receivable			896.00		2
3	Supplies			482.00		3
4	Prepaid Insurance			900.00		4
5	Office Equipment			3,000.00		5
6	Accum. Depr.—Office Equipment				2,000.00	6
7	Accounts Payable				2,190.00	7
8	Wages Payable				1,200.00	8
9	Notes Payable				3,000.00	9
10	Sam Ardery, Capital				2,200.00	10
11	Sam Ardery, Drawing			800.00		11
12	Advising Fees		3,802.00			12
13	Wages Expense	1,800.00				13
14	Advertising Expense	400.00				14
15	Rent Expense	1,500.00				15
16	Supplies Expense	120.00				16
17	Telephone Expense	300.00				17
18	Electricity Expense	44.00				18
19	Insurance Expense	200.00				19
20	Gas and Oil Expense	38.00				20
21	Depr. Expense—Office Equipment	1,000.00				21
22	Miscellaneous Expense	500.00				22
23		5,902.00	3,802.00	8,490.00	10,590.00	23
24	Net Loss		2,100.00	2,100.00		24
25		5,902.00	5,902.00	10,590.00	10,590.00	25

REQUIRED

During January, Ardery made an additional investment of $1,200. Prepare an income statement, statement of owner's equity, and balance sheet for Ardery Advising.

ANSWERS TO SELF-STUDY QUESTIONS AND EXERCISES

True/False Questions

1. T
2. F (additional investments are shown as an addition to the beginning balance)
3. F 4. T 5. T

Multiple Choice Questions

1. b 2. d 3. a 4. c 5. b

U REVU

Exercises

1.

Fisher Consulting Income Statement For Month Ended August 31, 20 --		
Revenue:		
Professional fees		$5,000.00
Expenses:		
Wages expense	$1,000.00	
Rent expense	700.00	
Depreciation expense	100.00	
Total expenses		1,800.00
Net income		$3,200.00

Fisher Consulting Statement of Owner's Equity For Month Ended August 31, 20 --		
Joe Fisher, capital, August 1, 20 - -		$3,000.00
Net income for August	$3,200.00	
Less withdrawals for August	300.00	
Increase in capital		2,900.00
Joe Fisher, capital, August 31, 20 - -		$5,900.00

Fisher Consulting Balance Sheet August 31, 20 --		
Assets		
Current assets:		
Cash	$2,500.00	
Accounts receivable	800.00	
Total current assets		$3,300.00
Property, plant, and equipment:		
Equipment	$3,800.00	
Less accumulated depreciation	200.00	3,600.00
Total assets		$6,900.00
Liabilities		
Current liabilities:		
Accounts payable		$1,000.00
Owner's Equity		
Joe Fisher, capital, August 31, 20--		5,900.00
Total liabilities and owner's equity		$6,900.00

2.

DATE		DESCRIPTION	POST. REF.	DEBIT	CREDIT
		Closing Entries			
20-- Aug.	31	Professional Fees		5 0 0 0 00	
		Income Summary			5 0 0 0 00
	31	Income Summary		1 8 0 0 00	
		Wages Expense			1 0 0 0 00
		Rent Expense			7 0 0 00
		Depreciation Expense			1 0 0 00
	31	Income Summary		3 2 0 0 00	
		Joe Fisher, capital			3 2 0 0 00
	31	Joe Fisher, Capital		3 0 0 00	
		Joe Fisher, Drawing			3 0 0 00

3

Joe Fisher, Consulting
Post-Closing Trial Balance
August 31, 20 - -

ACCOUNT TITLE	ACCOUNT NO	DEBIT BALANCE	CREDIT BALANCE
Cash		2 5 0 0 00	
Accounts Receivable		8 0 0 00	
Equipment		3 8 0 0 00	
Accumulated Depr.—Equipment			2 0 0 00
Accounts Payable			1 0 0 0 00
Joe Fisher, Capital			5 9 0 0 00
		7 1 0 0 00	7 1 0 0 00

Chapter 6 Appendix

Statement of Cash Flows

LEARNING OBJECTIVES

Careful study of this appendix should enable you to:

LO1 **Classify business transactions as operating, investing, or financing.**

LO2 **Prepare a statement of cash flows by analyzing and categorizing a series of business transactions.**

Thus far, we have discussed three financial statements: the income statement, the statement of owner's equity, and the balance sheet. A fourth statement, the statement of cash flows, is also very important. It explains what the business did to generate cash and how the cash was used. This is done by categorizing all cash transactions into three types of activities: operating, investing, and financing.

TYPES OF BUSINESS ACTIVITIES

LO1 Classify business transactions as operating, investing, or financing.

Cash flows from **operating activities** are related to the revenues and expenses reported on the income statement. Examples include cash received for services performed and the payment of cash for expenses.

Investing activities are those transactions involving the purchase and sale of long-term assets, lending money, and collecting the principal on the related loans.

Financing activities are those transactions dealing with the exchange of cash between the business and its owners and creditors. Examples include cash received from the owner to finance the operations and cash paid to the owner as withdrawals. Financing activities also include borrowing cash and repaying the loan principal.

Figure 6A-1 provides a review of the transactions for Jessie Jane's Campus Delivery Service for the month of June. The transactions are classified as operating, investing, or financing, and an explanation for the classification is provided.

LEARNING KEY

There are three types of business activities: operating, investing, and financing.

LEARNING KEY

Lending money to another entity is an outflow of cash from investing activities. The collection of the principal when the loan is due is an inflow of cash from investing activities. Borrowing cash is an inflow from financing activities. Repayment of the loan principal is an outflow from financing activities.

FIGURE 6A-1 Summary of Transactions for Jessie Jane's Campus Delivery Service

SUMMARY OF TRANSACTIONS FOR JESSIE JANE'S CAMPUS DELIVERY SERVICE	TYPE OF TRANSACTION	EXPLANATION
(a) Jessica Jane invested cash in her business, $2,000.	Financing	Cash received from the owner is an inflow from financing activities. Don't be fooled by the word "invested." From the company's point of view, this is a way to *finance* the business.
(b) Purchased delivery equipment for cash, $1,200.	Investing	Purchases of long-term assets are investments.
(c) Purchased delivery equipment on account from Big Red Scooters, $900. (*Note*: Big Red has loaned Jane $900.)	No cash involved	This transaction will not affect the main sections of the statement of cash flows. (This is a noncash investing and financing activity.)
(d) Paid first installment to Big Red Scooters, $300. [See transaction (c).]	Financing	Repayments of loans are financing activities.
(e) Received cash for delivery services rendered, $500.	Operating	Cash received as a result of providing services is classified as an operating activity.
(f) Paid cash for June office rent, $200.	Operating	Cash payments for expenses are classified as operating activities.
(g) Paid telephone bill, $50.	Operating	Cash payments for expenses are classified as operating activities.
(h) Made deliveries on account for a total of $600: $400 for the Accounting Department and $200 for the School of Music.	No cash involved	This transaction will not affect the statement of cash flows.
(i) Purchased supplies for cash, $80.	Operating	Cash payments for expenses are classified as operating activities. Most of these supplies were used up. Those that remain will be used in the near future. These are not long-term assets and, thus, do not qualify as investments.
(j) Paid cash for an eight-month liability insurance policy, $200. Coverage began on June 1.	Operating	Cash payments for expenses are classified as operating activities. Prepaid Insurance is not considered a long-term asset and, thus, does not qualify as an investment.
(k) Received $570 in cash for services performed in transaction (h): $400 from the Accounting Department and $170 from the School of Music.	Operating	Cash received as a result of providing services is classified as an operating activity.
(l) Purchased a third scooter from Big Red Scooters, $1,500. A down payment of $300 was made with the remaining payments expected over the next four months.	Investing	Purchases of long-term assets are investments. Only the $300 cash paid will be reported on the statement of cash flows.
(m) Paid wages of part-time employees, $650.	Operating	Cash payments for expenses are classified as operating activities.
(n) Earned delivery fees for the remainder of the month amounting to $1,050: $430 in cash and $620 on account. Deliveries on account: $250 for the Accounting Department and $370 for the Athletic Ticket Office.	Operating	Cash received ($430) as a result of providing services is classified as an operating activity.
(o) Jane withdrew cash for personal use, $150.	Financing	Cash payments to owners are classified as a financing activity.

PREPARING THE STATEMENT OF CASH FLOWS

LO2 Prepare a statement of cash flows by analyzing and categorizing a series of business transactions.

The classifications of the cash transactions for Jessie Jane's Campus Delivery Service are summarized in the expanded cash T account shown in Figure 6A-2. Using this information, we can prepare a statement of cash flows. As shown in Figure 6A-3, the heading is similar to that used for the income statement. Since the statement of cash flows reports on the flow of cash for a period of time, the statement is dated for the month ended June 30, 20--.

FIGURE 6A-2 Cash T Account for Jessie Jane's Campus Delivery Service with Classifications of Cash Transactions

CASH						
Event	**Classification**	**Amount**	**Amount**	**Classification**	**Event**	
(a) Investment by Jessie.	Financing	2,000	1,200	Investing	Purchased delivery equipment.	(b)
(e) Cash received for services.	Operating	500	300	Financing	Made payment on loan.	(d)
(k) Cash received for services.	Operating	570	200	Operating	Paid office rent.	(f)`
(n) Cash received for services.	Operating	430	50	Operating	Paid telephone bill.	(g)
		3,500	80	Operating	Purchased supplies.	(i)
			200	Operating	Paid for insurance.	(j)
			300	Investing	Purchased delivery equipment.	(l)
			650	Operating	Paid wages.	(m)
			150	Financing	Withdrawal by owner.	(o)
			3,130			
	Bal.	370				

FIGURE 6A-3 Statement of Cash Flows for Jessie Jane's Campus Delivery Service

Jessie Jane's Campus Delivery Service Statement of Cash Flows For Month Ended June 30, 20 - -		
Cash flows from operating activities:		
Cash received from customers for delivery services		$ 1,500 00
Cash paid for wages	$ (650 00)	
Cash paid for rent	(200 00)	
Cash paid for supplies	(80 00)	
Cash paid for telephone	(50 00)	
Cash paid for insurance	(200 00)	
Total cash paid for operations		(1,180 00)
Net cash provided by operating activities		$ 320 00
Cash flows from investing activities:		
Cash paid for delivery equipment	$(1,500 00)	
Net cash used for investing activities		(1,500 00)
Cash flows from financing activities:		
Cash investment by owner	$ 2,000 00	
Cash withdrawal by owner	(150 00)	
Payment made on loan	(300 00)	
Net cash provided by financing activities		1,550 00
Net increase in cash		$ 370 00

The main body of the statement is arranged in three sections: operating, investing, and financing activities. First, cash received from customers is listed under operating activities. Then, cash payments for operating activities are listed and totaled. The net amount is reported as net cash provided by operating activities. Since this is the main purpose of the business, it is important to be able to generate positive cash flows from operating activities.

The next two sections list the inflows and outflows from investing and financing activities. Debits to the cash account are inflows and credits are outflows. Note that there was an outflow, or net use of cash, from investing activities resulting from the purchase of the motor scooters. In addition, cash was provided from financing activities because Jessie's initial investment more than covered her withdrawal and the payment on the loan. These investing and financing activities are typical for a new business.

LEARNING KEY

To prove the accuracy of the statement of cash flows, compare the net increase or decrease reported on the statement with the change in the balance of the cash account.

The sum of the inflows and outflows from operating, investing, and financing activities equals the net increase (or decrease) in the cash account during the period. Since this is a new business, the cash account had a beginning balance of zero. The ending balance is $370. This agrees with the net increase in cash of $370 reported on the statement of cash flows.

This appendix introduces you to the purpose and format of the statement of cash flows. Here, we classified entries made to the cash account as operating, investing, or financing. These classifications were then used to prepare the statement. Businesses have thousands of entries to the cash account. Thus, this approach to preparing the statement is not really practical. Other approaches to preparing the statement will be discussed in Chapter 23. However, the purpose and format of the statements are the same.

LEARNING OBJECTIVES Key Points to Remember

LO1 Classify business transactions as operating, investing, or financing.

The purpose of the statement of cash flows is to report what the firm did to generate cash and how the cash was used. Business transactions are classified as operating, investing, and financing activities.

Operating activities are those transactions related to the revenues and expenses reported on the income statement.

Investing activities are those transactions involving the purchase and sale of long-term assets, lending money, and collecting the principal on the related loans.

Financing activities are those transactions dealing with the exchange of cash between the business and its owners and creditors.

LO2 Prepare a statement of cash flows by analyzing and categorizing a series of business transactions.

The main body of the statement of cash flows consists of three sections: operating, investing, and financing activities.

Name of Business
Statement of Cash Flows
For Period Ended Date

Cash flows from operating activities:		
Cash received from customers		$x x x x xx
List cash paid for various expenses	$ (x x x xx)	
Total cash paid for operations		(x x x x xx)
Net cash provided by (used for) operating activities		$ x x x xx
Cash flows from investing activities:		
List cash received from the sale of long-term assets and other investing activities	$x x x x xx	
List cash paid for the purchase of long-term assets and other investing activities	(x x x x xx)	
Net cash provided by (used for) investing activities		x x x x xx
Cash flows from financing activities:		
List cash received from owners and creditors	$x x x x xx	
List cash paid to owners and creditors	(x x x xx)	
Net cash provided by (used for) financing activities		x x x x xx
Net increase (decrease) in cash		$ x x x xx

KEY TERMS

financing activities (216) Those transactions dealing with the exchange of cash between the business and its owners and creditors.

investing activities (216) Those transactions involving the purchase and sale of long-term assets, lending money, and collecting the principal on the related loans.

operating activities (216) Those transactions related to the revenues and expenses reported on the income statement.

REVIEW QUESTIONS

LO1 1. Explain the purpose of the statement of cash flows.

LO1 2. Define and provide examples of the three types of business activities.

SERIES A EXERCISE

E 6Apx-1A (LO1)

CLASSIFYING BUSINESS TRANSACTIONS Dolores Lopez opened a new consulting business. The following transactions occurred during January of the current year. Classify each transaction as an operating, an investing, or a financing activity.

(a) Invested cash in the business, $10,000.
(b) Paid office rent, $500.
(c) Purchased office equipment. Paid $1,500 cash and agreed to pay the balance of $2,000 in four monthly installments.
(d) Received cash for services rendered, $900.
(e) Paid telephone bill, $65.
(f) Made payment on loan in transaction (c), $500.
(g) Paid wages to part-timse employee, $500.
(h) Received cash for services rendered, $800.
(i) Paid electricity bill, $85.
(j) Withdrew cash for personal use, $100.
(k) Paid wages to part-time employee, $500.

SERIES A PROBLEM

P 6Apx-2A (LO2)
✓ Operating activities: $50;
Investing activities: ($1,500);
Financing activities: $9,400

PREPARING A STATEMENT OF CASH FLOWS Prepare a statement of cash flows based on the transactions reported in Exercise 6Apx-1A.

SERIES B EXERCISE

E 6Apx-1B **(LO1)**

CLASSIFYING BUSINESS TRANSACTIONS Bob Jacobs opened an advertising agency. The following transactions occurred during January of the current year. Classify each transaction as an operating, an investing, or a financing activity.

(a) Invested cash in the business, $5,000.
(b) Purchased office equipment. Paid $2,500 cash and agreed to pay the balance of $2,000 in four monthly installments.
(c) Paid office rent, $400.
(d) Received cash for services rendered, $700.
(e) Paid telephone bill, $95.
(f) Received cash for services rendered, $600.
(g) Made payment on loan in transaction (b), $500.
(h) Paid wages to part-time employee, $800.
(i) Paid electricity bill, $100.
(j) Withdrew cash for personal use, $500.
(k) Paid wages to part-time employee, $600.

SERIES B PROBLEM

P 6Apx-2B **(LO2)**

✓Operating activities: ($695);
Investing activities: ($2,500);
Financing activities: $4,000

PREPARING A STATEMENT OF CASH FLOWS Prepare a statement of cash flows based on the transactions reported in Exercise 6Apx-1B.

COMPREHENSIVE PROBLEM 1: THE ACCOUNTING CYCLE

Bob Night opened "The General's Favorite Fishing Hole." The fishing camp is open from April through September and attracts many famous college basketball coaches during the off-season. Guests typically register for one week, arriving on Sunday afternoon and returning home the following Saturday afternoon. The registration fee includes room and board, the use of fishing boats, and professional instruction in fishing techniques. The chart of accounts for the camping operations is provided below.

This comprehensive problem is intended to serve as a mini-practice set without the source documents. As such, students should plan on about three to four hours to complete this problem.

The General's Favorite Fishing Hole
Chart of Accounts

Assets		**Revenues**	
101	Cash	401	Registration Fees
142	Office Supplies		
144	Food Supplies	**Expenses**	
145	Prepaid Insurance	511	Wages Expense
181	Fishing Boats	521	Rent Expense
181.1	Accum. Depr.—Fishing Boats	523	Office Supplies Expense
		524	Food Supplies Expense
Liabilities		525	Telephone Expense
202	Accounts Payable	533	Utilities Expense
219	Wages Payable	535	Insurance Expense
		536	Postage Expense
Owner's Equity		542	Depr. Exp.—Fishing Boats
311	Bob Night, Capital		
312	Bob Night, Drawing		
313	Income Summary		

The following transactions took place during April 20--.

Apr. 1	Night invested cash in business, $90,000.
1	Paid insurance premium for six-month camping season, $9,000.
2	Paid rent for lodge and campgrounds for the month of April, $40,000.
2	Deposited registration fees, $35,000.
2	Purchased 10 fishing boats on account for $60,000. The boats have estimated useful lives of five years, at which time they will be donated to a local day camp. Arrangements were made to pay for the boats in July.
3	Purchased food supplies from Acme Super Market on account, $7,000.
5	Purchased office supplies from Gordon Office Supplies on account, $500.
7	Deposited registration fees, $38,600.
10	Purchased food supplies from Acme Super Market on account, $8,200.
10	Paid wages to fishing guides, $10,000.
14	Deposited registration fees, $30,500.
16	Purchased food supplies from Acme Super Market on account, $9,000.
17	Paid wages to fishing guides, $10,000.
18	Paid postage, $150.

Apr. 21 Deposited registration fees, $35,600.

24 Purchased food supplies from Acme Super Market on account, $8,500.

24 Paid wages to fishing guides, $10,000.

28 Deposited registration fees, $32,000.

29 Paid wages to fishing guides, $10,000.

30 Purchased food supplies from Acme Super Market on account, $6,000.

30 Paid Acme Super Market on account, $32,700.

30 Paid utilities bill, $2,000.

30 Paid telephone bill, $1,200.

30 Bob Night withdrew cash for personal use, $6,000.

Adjustment information for the end of April is provided below.

(a) Office supplies remaining on hand, $100.
(b) Food supplies remaining on hand, $8,000.
(c) Insurance expired during the month of April, $1,500.
(d) Depreciation on the fishing boats for the month of April, $1,000.
(e) Wages earned, but not yet paid, at the end of April, $500.

REQUIRED

1. Enter the transactions in a general journal. Enter transactions from April 1–5 on page 1, April 7–18 on page 2, April 21–29 and the first two entries for April 30 on page 3, and the remaining entries for April 30 on page 4.
2. Post the entries to the general ledger. (If you are not using the working papers that accompany this text, you will need to enter the account titles and account numbers in the general ledger accounts.)
3. Prepare a trial balance on a work sheet.
4. Complete the work sheet.
5. Journalize the adjusting entries (page 5).
6. Post the adjusting entries to the general ledger.
7. Prepare the income statement.
8. Prepare the statement of owner's equity.
9. Prepare the balance sheet.
10. Journalize the closing entries (pages 5 and 6).
11. Post the closing entries to the general ledger.
12. Prepare a post-closing trial balance.

COMPREHENSIVE PROBLEM 1, PERIOD 2: THE ACCOUNTING CYCLE

During the month of May 20--, The General's Favorite Fishing Hole engaged in the following transactions. These transactions required an expansion of the chart of accounts as shown below.

> This comprehensive problem is intended to serve as a mini-practice set without the source documents. As such, students should plan on about three to four hours to complete this problem.

Assets

101	Cash
122	Accounts Receivable
142	Office Supplies
144	Food Supplies
145	Prepaid Insurance
146	Prepaid Subscriptions
161	Land
171	Buildings
171.1	Accum. Depr.—Buildings
181	Fishing Boats
181.1	Accum. Depr.—Fishing Boats
182	Surround Sound System
182.1	Accum. Depr.—Surround Sound Sys.
183	Big Screen TV
183.1	Accum. Depr.—Big Screen TV

Liabilities

202	Accounts Payable
219	Wages Payable

Owner's Equity

311	Bob Night, Capital
312	Bob Night, Drawing
313	Income Summary

Revenues

401	Registration Fees
404	Vending Commission Revenue

Expenses

511	Wages Expense
512	Advertising Expense
521	Rent Expense
523	Office Supplies Expense
524	Food Supplies Expense
525	Telephone Expense
533	Utilities Expense
535	Insurance Expense
536	Postage Expense
537	Repair Expense
540	Depr. Exp.—Buildings
541	Depr. Exp.—Surround Sound Sys.
542	Depr. Exp.—Fishing Boats
543	Depr. Exp.—Big Screen TV
546	Satellite Programming Exp.
548	Subscriptions Expense

May 1 In order to provide snacks for guests on a 24-hour basis, Night signed a contract with Snack Attack. Snack Attack will install vending machines with food and drinks and pay a 10% commission on all sales. Estimated payments are made at the beginning of each month. Night received a check for $200, the estimated commission on sales for May.

2 Night purchased a surround sound system and big screen TV with a digital satellite system for the guest lounge. The surround sound system cost $3,600 and has an estimated useful life of five years and no salvage value. The TV cost $8,000, has an estimated useful life of eight years, and has a salvage value of $800. Night paid cash for both items.

2 Paid for May's programming on the new digital satellite system, $125.

3 Night's office manager returned $100 worth of office supplies to Gordon Office Supply. Night received a $100 reduction on the account.

3 Deposited registration fees, $52,700.

3 Paid rent for lodge and campgrounds for the month of May, $40,000.

3 In preparation for the purchase of a nearby campground, Night invested an additional $600,000.

May 4 Paid Gordon Office Supply on account, $400.

4 Purchased the assets of a competing business and paid cash for the following: land, $100,000; lodge, $530,000; and fishing boats, $9,000. The lodge has a remaining useful life of 50 years and a $50,000 salvage value. The boats have remaining lives of five years and no salvage value.

5 Paid May's insurance premium for the new camp, $1,000. (See above transaction.)

5 Purchased food supplies from Acme Super Market on account, $22,950.

5 Purchased office supplies from Gordon Office Supplies on account, $1,200.

7 Night paid $40 each for one-year subscriptions to *Fishing Illustrated, Fishing Unlimited*, and *Fish Master*. The magazines are published monthly.

10 Deposited registration fees, $62,750.

13 Paid wages to fishing guides, $30,000. (Don't forget wages payable.)

14 A guest became ill and was unable to stay for the entire week. A refund was issued in the amount of $1,000.

17 Deposited registration fees, $63,000.

19 Purchased food supplies from Acme Super Market on account, $18,400.

21 Deposited registration fees, $63,400.

23 Paid $2,500 for advertising spots on National Sports Talk Radio.

25 Paid repair fee for damaged boat, $850.

27 Paid wages to fishing guides, $30,000.

28 Paid $1,800 for advertising spots on billboards.

29 Purchased food supplies from Acme Super Market on account, $14,325.

30 Paid utilities bill, $3,300.

30 Paid telephone bill, $1,800.

30 Paid Acme Super Market on account, $47,350.

31 Bob Night withdrew cash for personal use, $7,500.

Adjustment information at the end of May is provided below.

(a) Total vending machine sales were $2,300 for the month of May.
(b) Straight-line depreciation is used for the 10 boats purchased on April 2 for $60,000. The useful life for these assets is five years and there is no salvage value. A full month's depreciation was taken in April on these boats. Straight-line depreciation is also used for the two boats purchased in May. Make one adjusting entry for all depreciation on the boats.
(c) Straight-line depreciation is used to depreciate the surround sound system.
(d) Straight-line depreciation is used to depreciate the big screen TV.
(e) Straight-line depreciation is used for the building purchased in May.
(f) On April 2, Night paid $9,000 for insurance during the six-month camping season. May's portion of this premium was used up during this month.

(continued)

(g) Night received his May issues of *Fishing Illustrated, Fishing Unlimited*, and *Fish Master*.
(h) Office supplies remaining on hand, $150.
(i) Food supplies remaining on hand, $5,925.
(j) Wages earned, but not yet paid, at the end of May, $6,000.

REQUIRED

1. Enter the transactions in a general journal. Enter transactions from May 1–4 on page 5, May 5–28 on page 6, and the remaining entries on page 7. To save time and space, don't enter descriptions for the journal entries.
2. Post the entries to the general ledger. (If you are not using the working papers that accompany this text, you will need to enter the account titles, account numbers, and balances from April 30 in the general ledger accounts.)
3. Prepare a trial balance on a work sheet.
4. Complete the work sheet.
5. Journalize the adjusting entries on page 8 of the general journal.
6. Post the adjusting entries to the general ledger.
7. Prepare the income statement.
8. Prepare the statement of owner's equity.
9. Prepare the balance sheet.
10. Journalize the closing entries on page 9 of the general journal.
11. Post the closing entries to the general ledger.
12. Prepare a post-closing trial balance.

Accounting for Cash and Payroll

PART 2

Add Some Color to Your Learning!

Throughout the text, you will be introduced to many important terms and types of accounts. To help you learn the different terms and types of accounts, we have coded many of them using the following color key in Part 2:

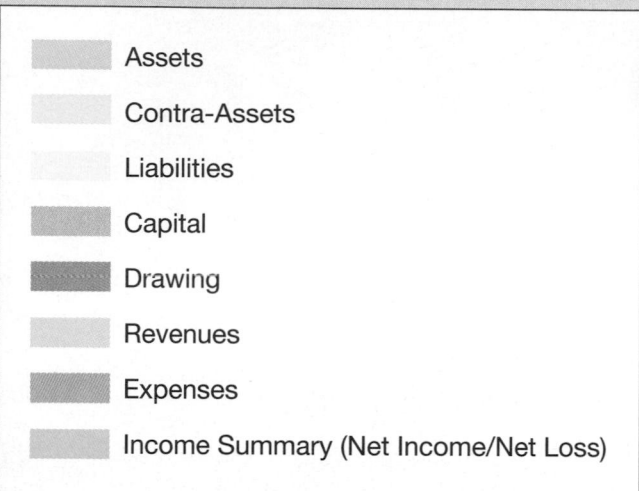

- Assets
- Contra-Assets
- Liabilities
- Capital
- Drawing
- Revenues
- Expenses
- Income Summary (Net Income/Net Loss)

Chapter 7

COURTESY OF H_2O AUDIO

Accounting for Cash

H2O Audio was founded in 2003 and has its home office in San Diego, California. Its key products are waterproof headphones, armbands and cases, and headsets designed to enable swimmers, surfers, and divers to use their iPods underwater. H2O sells its merchandise online, in major electronics stores such as Best Buy, and in many outdoor and sports shops throughout the United States. The company started quite small, but its revenues increased from $440,000 in 2004 to $4 million in 2008, for a growth of over 800% in just four years.

Two of the challenges for a company growing as fast as H2O Audio are managing and protecting its cash. H2O has multiple checking accounts, receives cash receipts from multiple sources, and makes cash payments for many different bills. The company must have clear procedures and complete and accurate records in order to properly control cash and to plan for future needs. In this chapter, you will learn some of the ways to manage this critical business asset.

LEARNING OBJECTIVES

Careful study of this chapter should enable you to:

LO1 Describe how to open and use a checking account.

LO2 Prepare a bank reconciliation and related journal entries.

LO3 Establish and use a petty cash fund.

LO4 Establish a change fund and use the cash short and over account.

Cash is an asset that is quite familiar and important to all of us. We generally think of **cash** as the currency and coins in our pockets and the money we have in our checking accounts. To a business, cash also includes checks received from customers, money orders, and bank cashier's checks.

Because it plays such a central role in operating a business, cash must be carefully managed and controlled. A business should have a system of **internal control**—a set of policies and procedures designed to ensure proper accounting for transactions. For good internal control of cash transactions, all cash received should be deposited daily in a bank. All disbursements, except for payments from petty cash, should be made by check.

CHECKING ACCOUNT

LO1 Describe how to open and use a checking account.

The key documents and forms required in opening and using a checking account are the signature card, deposit tickets, checks, and bank statements.

OPENING A CHECKING ACCOUNT

To open a checking account, each person authorized to sign checks must complete and sign a **signature card** (Figure 7-1). The bank uses this card to verify the depositor's

FIGURE 7-1 Signature Card

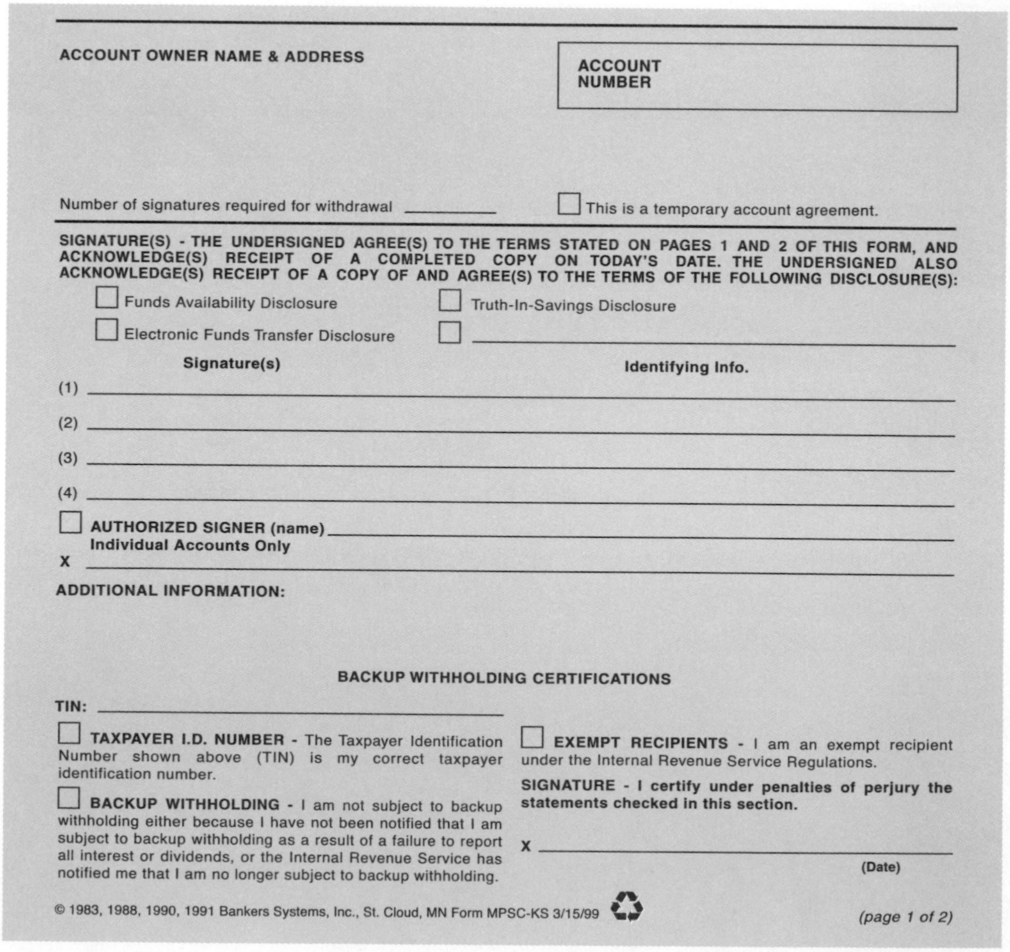
ACCOUNT OWNER NAME & ADDRESS

ACCOUNT NUMBER

Number of signatures required for withdrawal ______

☐ This is a temporary account agreement.

SIGNATURE(S) - THE UNDERSIGNED AGREE(S) TO THE TERMS STATED ON PAGES 1 AND 2 OF THIS FORM, AND ACKNOWLEDGE(S) RECEIPT OF A COMPLETED COPY ON TODAY'S DATE. THE UNDERSIGNED ALSO ACKNOWLEDGE(S) RECEIPT OF A COPY OF AND AGREE(S) TO THE TERMS OF THE FOLLOWING DISCLOSURE(S):

☐ Funds Availability Disclosure ☐ Truth-In-Savings Disclosure

☐ Electronic Funds Transfer Disclosure ☐ ______

Signature(s) Identifying Info.

(1) ______

(2) ______

(3) ______

(4) ______

☐ AUTHORIZED SIGNER (name) ______
Individual Accounts Only
X ______

ADDITIONAL INFORMATION:

BACKUP WITHHOLDING CERTIFICATIONS

TIN: ______

☐ TAXPAYER I.D. NUMBER - The Taxpayer Identification Number shown above (TIN) is my correct taxpayer identification number.

☐ BACKUP WITHHOLDING - I am not subject to backup withholding either because I have not been notified that I am subject to backup withholding as a result of a failure to report all interest or dividends, or the Internal Revenue Service has notified me that I am no longer subject to backup withholding.

☐ EXEMPT RECIPIENTS - I am an exempt recipient under the Internal Revenue Service Regulations.

SIGNATURE - I certify under penalties of perjury the statements checked in this section.

X ______ (Date)

© 1983, 1988, 1990, 1991 Bankers Systems, Inc., St. Cloud, MN Form MPSC-KS 3/15/99

(page 1 of 2)

signature on any banking transactions. The taxpayer identification number (TIN) is the depositor's social security number or employer identification number (EIN). This number is shown on the card to identify the depositor for income tax purposes. An EIN can be obtained from the Internal Revenue Service.

MAKING DEPOSITS

A **deposit ticket** (Figure 7-2) is a form showing a detailed listing of items being deposited. Currency, coins, and checks are listed separately. Each check should be identified by its **ABA (American Bankers Association) Number**. This number is the small fraction printed in the upper right-hand corner of each check (see Figure 7-5 on page 233). Part of this number also appears in **magnetic ink character recognition (MICR) code** on the lower left side of the front of each check. The code is used to sort and route checks throughout the U.S. banking system. Normally, only the numerator of the fraction is used in identifying checks on the deposit ticket.

FIGURE 7-2 Deposit Ticket

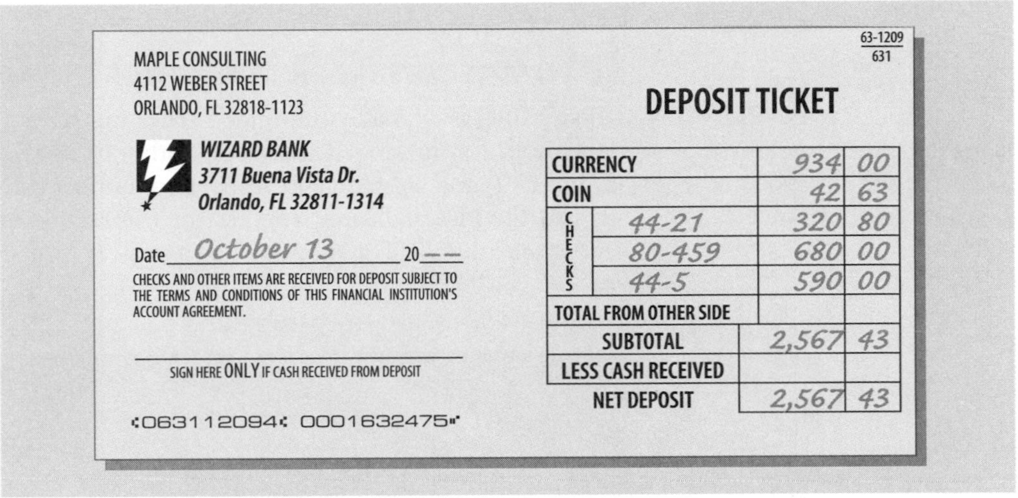
MAPLE CONSULTING
4112 WEBER STREET
ORLANDO, FL 32818-1123

63-1209
631

DEPOSIT TICKET

WIZARD BANK
3711 Buena Vista Dr.
Orlando, FL 32811-1314

Date October 13 20 — —

CHECKS AND OTHER ITEMS ARE RECEIVED FOR DEPOSIT SUBJECT TO THE TERMS AND CONDITIONS OF THIS FINANCIAL INSTITUTION'S ACCOUNT AGREEMENT.

SIGN HERE ONLY IF CASH RECEIVED FROM DEPOSIT

CURRENCY		934	00
COIN		42	63
CHECKS	44-21	320	80
	80-459	680	00
	44-5	590	00
TOTAL FROM OTHER SIDE			
SUBTOTAL		2,567	43
LESS CASH RECEIVED			
NET DEPOSIT		2,567	43

⑆063112094⑆ 0001632475⑈

The depositor delivers or mails the deposit ticket and all items being deposited to the bank. The bank then gives or mails a receipt to the depositor. The deposit also can be made after business hours by using the night depository provided by most banks. The deposit is put in a locked bag, which is placed in a secure drawer or chute at the bank, for processing the following morning.

ENDORSEMENTS

Each check being deposited must be endorsed by the depositor. The **endorsement** consists of stamping or writing the depositor's name and sometimes other information on the back of the check, in the space provided near the left end. There are two basic types of endorsements.

1. **Blank endorsement**—the depositor simply signs the back of the check. This makes the check payable to any bearer.
2. **Restrictive endorsement**—the depositor adds words such as "For deposit," "Pay to any bank," or "Pay to Daryl Beck only" to restrict the payment of the check.

Businesses commonly use a rubber stamp to endorse checks for deposit. The check shown in Figure 7-3 has been stamped with a restrictive endorsement.

FIGURE 7-3 Restrictive Endorsement

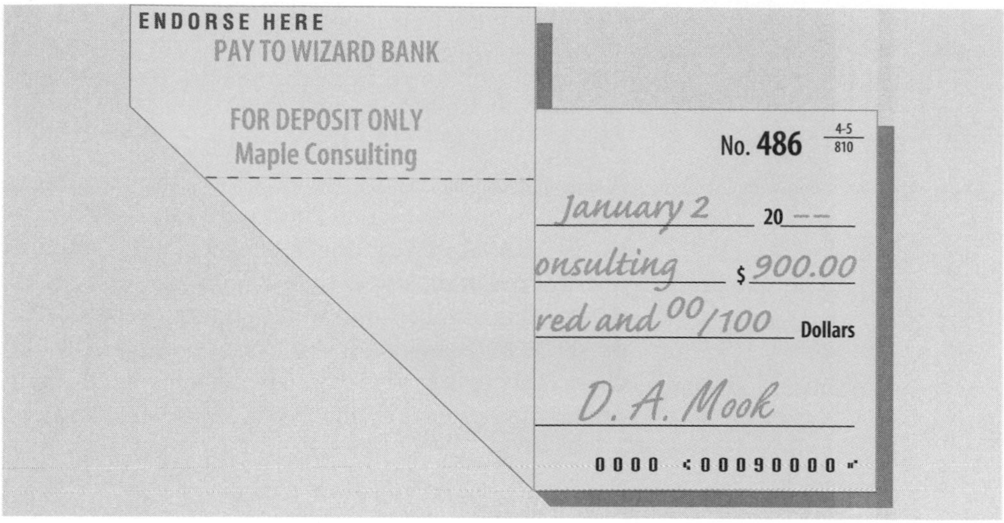

Postage stamps can be purchased at some ATMs. For deposits, some ATMs can provide an image of any checks being deposited.

AUTOMATED TELLER MACHINES

Most banks now make **automated teller machines (ATMs)** available at all times to depositors for making deposits or withdrawals. Each depositor has a plastic card (Figure 7-4) and a personal identification number (PIN). The depositor inserts the card, keys in the PIN, indicates whether the transaction is a withdrawal or a deposit, and enters the amount. The machine has a drawer or door for the withdrawal or deposit.

FIGURE 7-4 Automated Teller Machine Card

Most ATMs are now on a system such as Cirrus that allows noncustomers to use other ATMs in both the United States and foreign countries. There are also "cash machines" that supply only cash and do not take deposits. These are often found at airports and convenience stores.

It is important for the depositor to keep an accounting record of ATM withdrawals and deposits. This is done on the check stub or register described in the following section, and with an appropriate journal entry.

WRITING CHECKS

A **check** is a document ordering a bank to pay cash from a depositor's account. There are three parties to every check.

1. **Drawer**—the depositor who orders the bank to pay the cash.
2. **Drawee**—the bank on which the check is drawn.
3. **Payee**—the person being paid the cash.

Checks used by businesses are usually bound in the form of a book. In some checkbooks, each check is attached to a **check stub** (Figure 7-5) that contains space to record all relevant information about the check. Other checkbooks are accompanied by a small register book in which the relevant information is noted. If a financial computer software package is used, both the check and the register can be prepared electronically.

It is sometimes necessary to void a check. Proper procedures for doing so are to tear off or deface the signature box and to file the voided check numerically with the canceled checks.

Note that the check stubs in Figure 7-5 contain space to record amounts deposited. It generally is a good idea also to indicate the date of the deposit, as shown on check stub No. 108.

Use the following three steps in preparing a check:

STEP 1 Complete the check stub or register.

STEP 2 Enter the date, payee name, and amount on the check.

STEP 3 Sign the check.

FIGURE 7-5 Checks and Check Stubs

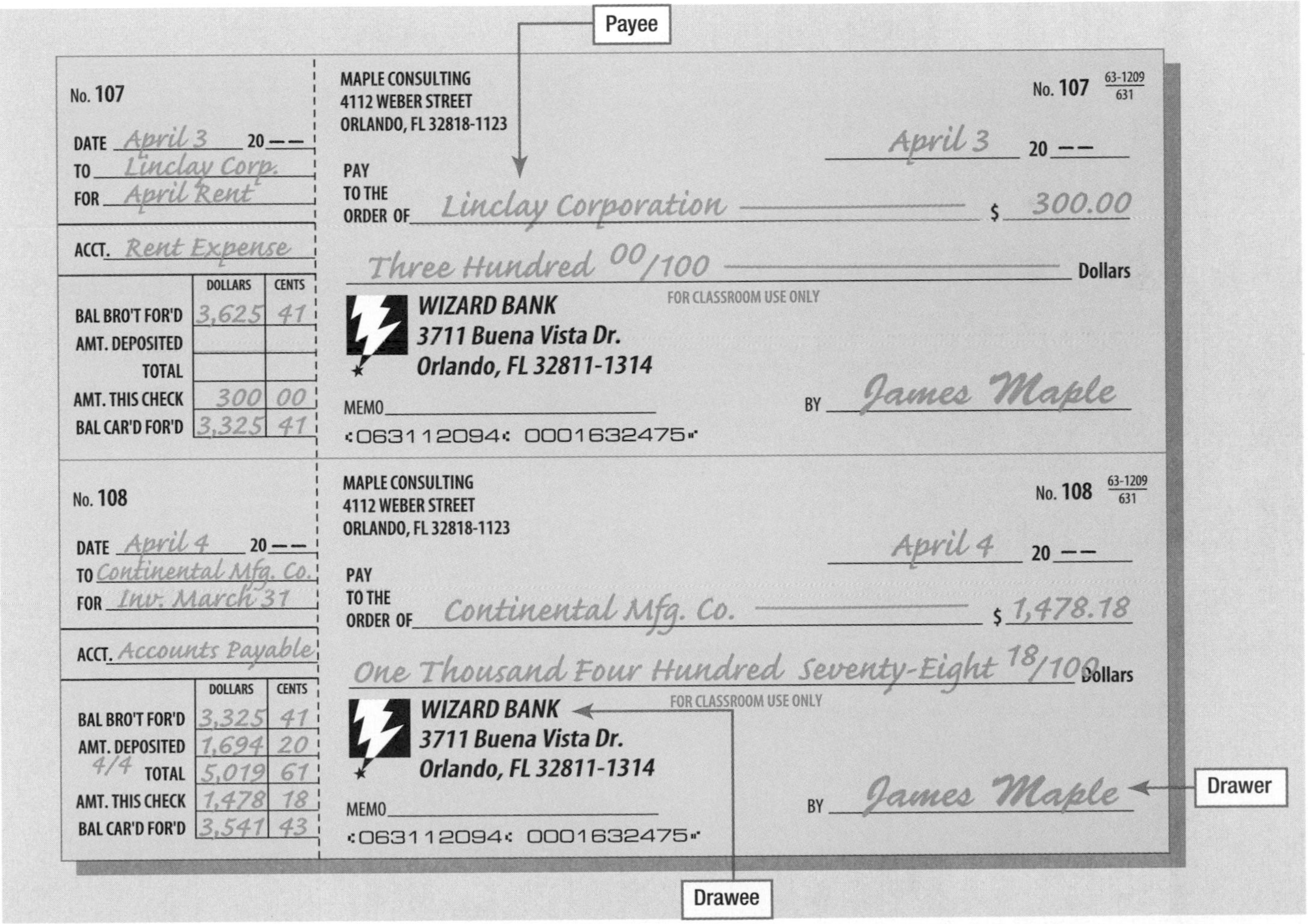

The payee and amount written in words should be followed by something, such as a line, to make it difficult to alter the payee or the amount.

LEARNING KEY

The check should not be signed until the check signer has verified that all aspects of the check are correct.

The check stub is completed first so that the drawer retains a record of each check issued. This information is needed to determine the proper journal entry for the transaction.

The payee name is entered on the first long line on the check, followed by the amount in figures. The amount in words is then entered on the second long line. If the amount in figures does not agree with the amount in words, the bank usually contacts the drawer for the correct amount or returns the check unpaid.

The most critical point in preparing a check is signing it, and this should be done last. The signature authorizes the bank to pay cash from the drawer's account. The check signer should make sure that all other aspects of the check are correct before signing it.

BANK STATEMENT

A statement of account issued by a bank to each depositor once a month is called a **bank statement**. Figure 7-6 is a bank statement for a checking account. The statement shows the following:

1. The balance at the beginning of the period.
2. Deposits and other amounts added during the period.
3. Checks and other amounts subtracted during the period.
4. The balance at the end of the period.

FIGURE 7-6 Bank Statement

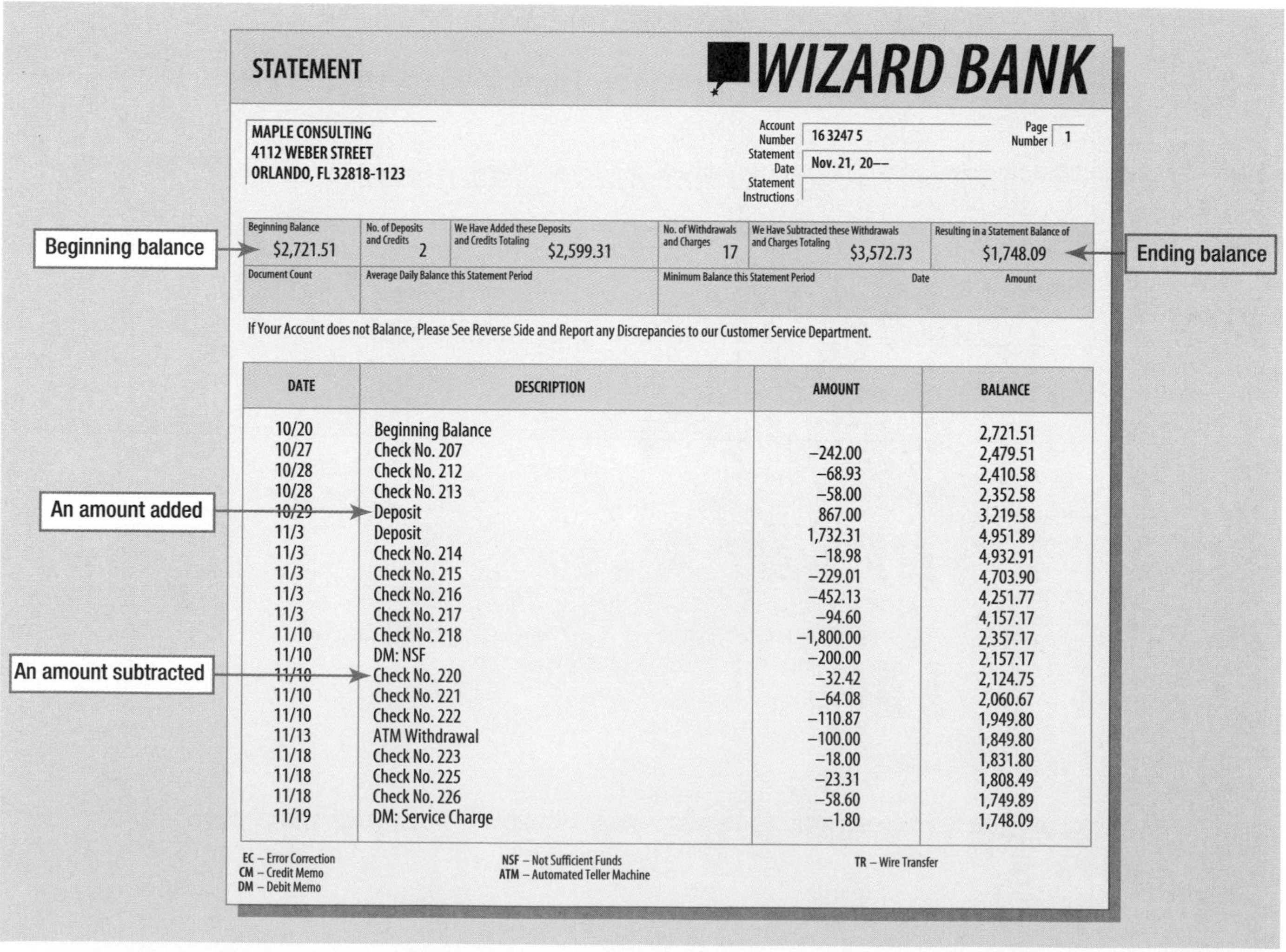

STATEMENT — WIZARD BANK

MAPLE CONSULTING
4112 WEBER STREET
ORLANDO, FL 32818-1123

Account Number: 16 3247 5
Statement Date: Nov. 21, 20––
Statement Instructions:
Page Number: 1

Beginning Balance	No. of Deposits and Credits	We Have Added these Deposits and Credits Totaling	No. of Withdrawals and Charges	We Have Subtracted these Withdrawals and Charges Totaling	Resulting in a Statement Balance of
$2,721.51	2	$2,599.31	17	$3,572.73	$1,748.09

Document Count	Average Daily Balance this Statement Period	Minimum Balance this Statement Period	Date	Amount

If Your Account does not Balance, Please See Reverse Side and Report any Discrepancies to our Customer Service Department.

DATE	DESCRIPTION	AMOUNT	BALANCE
10/20	Beginning Balance		2,721.51
10/27	Check No. 207	−242.00	2,479.51
10/28	Check No. 212	−68.93	2,410.58
10/28	Check No. 213	−58.00	2,352.58
10/29	Deposit	867.00	3,219.58
11/3	Deposit	1,732.31	4,951.89
11/3	Check No. 214	−18.98	4,932.91
11/3	Check No. 215	−229.01	4,703.90
11/3	Check No. 216	−452.13	4,251.77
11/3	Check No. 217	−94.60	4,157.17
11/10	Check No. 218	−1,800.00	2,357.17
11/10	DM: NSF	−200.00	2,157.17
11/10	Check No. 220	−32.42	2,124.75
11/10	Check No. 221	−64.08	2,060.67
11/10	Check No. 222	−110.87	1,949.80
11/13	ATM Withdrawal	−100.00	1,849.80
11/18	Check No. 223	−18.00	1,831.80
11/18	Check No. 225	−23.31	1,808.49
11/18	Check No. 226	−58.60	1,749.89
11/19	DM: Service Charge	−1.80	1,748.09

EC – Error Correction
CM – Credit Memo
DM – Debit Memo
NSF – Not Sufficient Funds
ATM – Automated Teller Machine
TR – Wire Transfer

It is increasingly common for banks to return only a listing of checks with the bank statement. A check "image" can be obtained by making a special request to the bank.

With the bank statement, the bank normally sends the following to the depositor:

1. **Canceled checks**—the depositor's checks paid by the bank during the period. The bank may send the checks themselves, "imaged" sheets showing only the faces of the checks, or simply a listing of the checks on the bank statement.
2. Any other forms representing items added to or subtracted from the account.

U REVU Complete U REVU-1 on **page 252** to test your basic understanding of LO1.

RECONCILING THE BANK STATEMENT

LO2 Prepare a bank reconciliation and related journal entries.

On any given day, the balance in the cash account on the depositor's books (the book balance) is unlikely to be the same as that on the bank's books (the bank balance). This difference can be due to errors, but it usually is caused by timing. Transactions generally are recorded by the business at a time that is different from when the bank records them.

DEPOSITS

Suppose there are cash receipts of $600 on April 30. These cash receipts would be recorded on the depositor's books on April 30, and a deposit of $600 would be sent to the bank. The deposit would not reach the bank, however, until at least the following day, May 1. This timing difference in recording the $600 of cash receipts is illustrated in Figure 7-7. Notice that on April 30, the balances in the depositor's books and in the bank's books would be different.

FIGURE 7-7 Depositor and Bank Records—Deposits

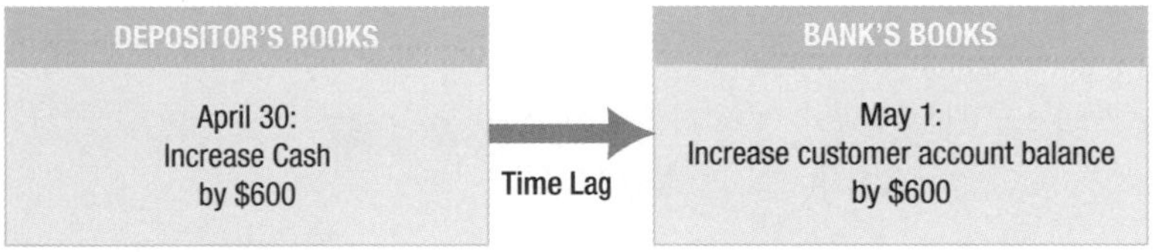

CASH PAYMENTS

Similar timing differences occur with cash payments. Suppose a check for $350 is written on April 30. This cash payment would be recorded on the depositor's books on April 30 and the check mailed to the payee. The check probably would not be received by the payee until May 3. If the payee deposited the check promptly, it still would not clear the bank until May 4. This timing difference in recording the $350 cash payment is illustrated in Figure 7-8. Notice once again that on April 30, the balances in the depositor's books and in the bank's books would be different.

FIGURE 7-8 Depositor and Bank Records—Cash Payments

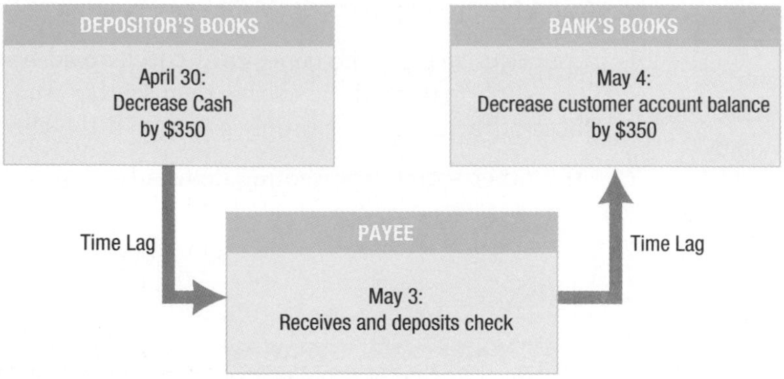

REASONS FOR DIFFERENCES BETWEEN BANK AND BOOK BALANCES

When the bank statement is received, the depositor examines the records to identify the items that explain the difference between the book and bank balances. This process of bringing the book and bank balances into agreement is called preparing a **bank reconciliation.**

The most common reasons for differences between the book and bank balances are the following:

1. **Deposits in transit.** Deposits that have not reached or been recorded by the bank before the statement is prepared.
2. **Outstanding checks.** Checks issued that have not been presented to the bank for payment before the statement is prepared.
3. **Service charges.** Bank charges for services such as check printing and processing.
4. **Collections.** Collections of promissory notes or charge accounts made by the bank on behalf of the depositor.
5. **Not sufficient funds** (**NSF**) **checks.** Checks deposited by the depositor that are not paid because the drawer did not have sufficient funds.
6. **Errors.** Errors made by the bank or the depositor in recording cash transactions.

STEPS IN PREPARING THE BANK RECONCILIATION

Use the following three steps in preparing the bank reconciliation:

STEP 1 Identify deposits in transit and any related errors.

STEP 2 Identify outstanding checks and any related errors.

STEP 3 Identify additional reconciling items.

Deposits in Transit and Related Errors

Follow these steps:

STEP 1 Compare deposits listed on the bank statement with deposits in transit on last month's bank reconciliation. All of last month's deposits in transit should appear on the current month's bank statement.

STEP 2 Compare the remaining deposits on the bank statement with deposits listed in the accounting records. Any deposits listed in the accounting records but not on the bank statement are deposits in transit on the current bank reconciliation.

STEP 3 Compare the individual deposit amounts on the bank statement and in the accounting records. If they differ, the error needs to be corrected.

Outstanding Checks and Related Errors

Follow these steps:

STEP 1 Compare canceled checks with the bank statement and the accounting records. If the amounts differ, the error needs to be corrected.

STEP 2 As each canceled check is compared with the accounting records, place a check mark on the check stub or other accounting record to indicate that the check has cleared.

STEP 3 Any checks written that have not been checked off represent outstanding checks on the bank reconciliation. This includes outstanding checks from last month's bank reconciliation that have not yet cleared.

Additional Reconciling Items

Some banks pay interest on checking account balances. This reconciling item would be handled in the same manner as a bank credit memo.

Compare any additions and deductions on the bank statement that are not deposits or checks with the accounting records. Items that the bank adds to the account are called **credit memos.** Items that the bank deducts from the account are called **debit memos.** Remember that a depositor's account is a liability to the bank. Thus, a credit memo increases this liability; a debit memo reduces the liability. Any of these items not appearing in the accounting records represent additional items on the bank reconciliation.

ILLUSTRATION OF A BANK RECONCILIATION

A general format for the bank reconciliation is shown in Figure 7-9. Not every item shown in this illustration would be in every bank reconciliation, but this format is helpful in determining where to put items. A bank reconciliation form also can be found on the back of most bank statements. Some banks also include a reconciliation form on their Web site.

FIGURE 7-9 Bank Reconciliation Format

BANK RECONCILIATION		
Bank statement balance		$xxxx
Add: Deposits in transit	$xxxx	
Bank errors (that understate balance)	xxxx	xxxx
		$xxxx
Deduct: Outstanding checks	$xxxx	
Bank errors (that overstate balance)	xxxx	xxxx
Adjusted bank balance		$xxxx
Book balance		$xxxx
Add: Bank credit memos	$xxxx	
Book errors (that understate balance)	xxxx	xxxx
		$xxxx
Deduct: Bank debit memos	$xxxx	
Book errors (that overstate balance)	xxxx	xxxx
Adjusted book balance		$xxxx

To illustrate the preparation of a bank reconciliation, we will use the Maple Consulting bank statement shown in Figure 7-6. That statement shows a balance of $1,748.09 as of November 21. The balance in Maple's check stubs and general ledger cash account is $2,393.23. The three steps described on page 236 were used to identify the following items, and the reconciliation in Figure 7-10 was prepared.

1. A deposit of $637.02 recorded on November 21 had not been received by the bank. Maple has received the funds but the amount has not yet been counted by the bank. This deposit in transit is added to the bank statement balance.
2. Check numbers 219, 224, and 227 are outstanding. The funds have been disbursed by Maple but have not yet been paid out by the bank. The amount of these outstanding checks is subtracted from the bank statement balance.
3. Check number 214 was written for $18.98 but was entered on the check stub and on the books as $19.88. This $0.90 error is added to the book balance because $0.90 too much had been deducted from the book balance.
4. Maple made an ATM withdrawal of $100.00 on November 13 for personal use but did not record the withdrawal on the books. The bank has reduced Maple's balance by this amount. Thus, this amount is deducted from the book balance.
5. The bank returned an NSF check of $200.00. This was a check received by Maple from a customer. The bank has reduced Maple's balance by $200.00, but Maple has not yet recorded it. This amount is deducted from the book balance.
6. The bank service charge was $1.80. The bank has reduced Maple's balance by this amount, but Maple has not yet recorded it. This amount is deducted from the book balance.

FIGURE 7-10 Bank Reconciliation

Maple Consulting
Bank Reconciliation
November 21, 20 - -

Bank statement balance, November 21			$1748	09
Add deposit in transit			637	02
			$2385	11
Deduct outstanding checks:				
No. 219	$200	00		
No. 224	25	00		
No. 227	67	78	292	78
Adjusted bank balance			$2092	33
Book balance, November 21			$2393	23
Add error on Check No. 214			0	90
			$2394	13
Deduct:				
Unrecorded ATM withdrawal	$100	00		
NSF check	200	00		
Bank service charge	1	80	301	80
Adjusted book balance			$2092	33

Requires journal entry (1)

Require journal entries (2), (3), and (4)

Reconciled balances

JOURNAL ENTRIES

Only two kinds of items appearing on a bank reconciliation require journal entries.

1. Errors in the depositor's books.
2. Bank additions and deductions that do not already appear in the books.

LEARNING KEY

Journal entries are needed to correct errors in the books and to record bank additions and deductions that are not in the books.

Note the four items in the lower portion of the bank reconciliation in Figure 7-10. A journal entry always is required for each item in this book balance portion of the bank reconciliation. The four journal entries for Maple Consulting are shown below, using entry numbers matching those noted in Figure 7-10.

The $0.90 item is an error in the accounting records that occurred when the check amount was incorrectly entered. Assume the $18.98 was in payment of an account payable which had been incorrectly debited for $19.88. The entry to correct this error is as follows:

					Debit	Credit	
4		(1)	Cash		0 90		4
5			Accounts Payable			0 90	5
6			Error in recording check				6

The $100.00 ATM withdrawal has been deducted from Maple's account by the bank. Maple has not yet recorded the withdrawal. Maple withdrew the funds for personal use, so the following journal entry is required:

					Debit	Credit	
8		(2)	James Maple, Drawing		1 0 0 00		8
9			Cash			1 0 0 00	9
10			Unrecorded ATM withdrawal				10

The $200.00 NSF check is a deduction by the bank for a check deposited by Maple that proved to be worthless. This amount must be deducted from the book balance. Assuming the $200.00 was received from a customer on account, the following journal entry is required:

					Debit	Credit	
12		(3)	Accounts Receivable		2 0 0 00		12
13			Cash			2 0 0 00	13
14			Unrecorded NSF check				14

The $1.80 bank service charge is a fee for bank services received by Maple. The bank has deducted this amount from Maple's account. Bank service charges are usually small and are charged to Miscellaneous Expense.

					Debit	Credit	
16		(4)	Miscellaneous Expense		1 80		16
17			Cash			1 80	17
18			Bank service charge				18

Figure 7-11 contains a detailed list of items that require journal entries.

FIGURE 7-11 Bank Reconciliation Items that Require Journal Entries

ADDITIONS TO CASH BALANCE	DEDUCTIONS FROM CASH BALANCE
* Unrecorded deposits (including ATM) * Note collected by bank * Interest earned * Errors: 1. Added too little as a deposit 2. Deducted too much as a check	* Unrecorded ATM withdrawals * NSF checks * Bank service charges * Deposits recorded twice * Unrecorded checks * Loan payments * Interest payments * Errors: 1. Added too much as a deposit 2. Deducted too little as a check

ELECTRONIC FUNDS TRANSFER

Electronic funds transfer (EFT) uses a computer rather than paper checks to complete transactions with the bank. This technique is being used increasingly today. Applications of EFT include payrolls, social security payments, retail purchases, mortgage payments, and the ATM transactions described earlier in the chapter.

Heavy use of EFT can present a challenge in preparing bank reconciliations. Many of the documents handled in a purely manual environment disappear when EFT is used. Bank accounts are just one of many areas where computers require accountants to think in new ways. Regardless of what system is used, the key point to remember is that the accounting records must be correctly updated.

U REVU

Complete U REVU-2 on **page 252** to test your basic understanding of LO2.

A BROADER VIEW

DON FARRALL/PHOTODISC/GETTY IMAGES

Fraud—A Real Threat to Small Business

Every two years, the Association of Certified Fraud Examiners (ACFE) surveys its members on the occupational fraud they have investigated during the preceding two years. The most recent survey showed that 40% of the frauds occurred in private companies. In addition, the median loss suffered by small businesses was $200,000. The most commonly cited factor that allowed the fraud to occur was a lack of adequate internal control. And 85% of the asset misappropriation cases involved theft or misuse of cash.

These survey findings show the importance of the kinds of internal controls over cash described in this chapter and the appendix.

THE PETTY CASH FUND

LO3 Establish and use a petty cash fund.

For good control over cash, payments generally should be made by check. Unfortunately, payments of very small amounts by check can be both inconvenient and inefficient. For example, the time and cost required to write a check for $0.70 to mail a letter might be greater than the cost of the postage. Therefore, businesses customarily establish a **petty cash fund** to pay for small items with cash. "Petty" means small, and both the amount of the fund and the maximum amount of any bill that can be paid from the fund are small.

ESTABLISHING A PETTY CASH FUND

To establish a petty cash fund, a check is written to the petty cash custodian for the amount to be set aside in the fund. The amount may be $50.00, $100.00, $200.00, or any amount considered necessary. The journal entry to establish a petty cash fund of $100.00 would be as follows:

4			Petty Cash		1 0 0 00		4
5			Cash			1 0 0 00	5
6			Establish petty cash fund				6

Petty Cash is an asset that is listed immediately below Cash on the balance sheet.

The custodian cashes the check and places the money in a petty cash box. For good control, the custodian should be the only person authorized to make payments from the fund. The custodian should be able to account for the full amount of the fund at any time.

MAKING PAYMENTS FROM A PETTY CASH FUND

A receipt called a **petty cash voucher** (Figure 7-12) should be prepared for every payment from the fund. The voucher shows the name of the payee, the purpose of the payment, and the account to be charged for the payment. Each voucher should be signed by the custodian and by the person receiving the cash. The vouchers should be numbered consecutively so that all vouchers can be accounted for.

FIGURE 7-12 Petty Cash Voucher

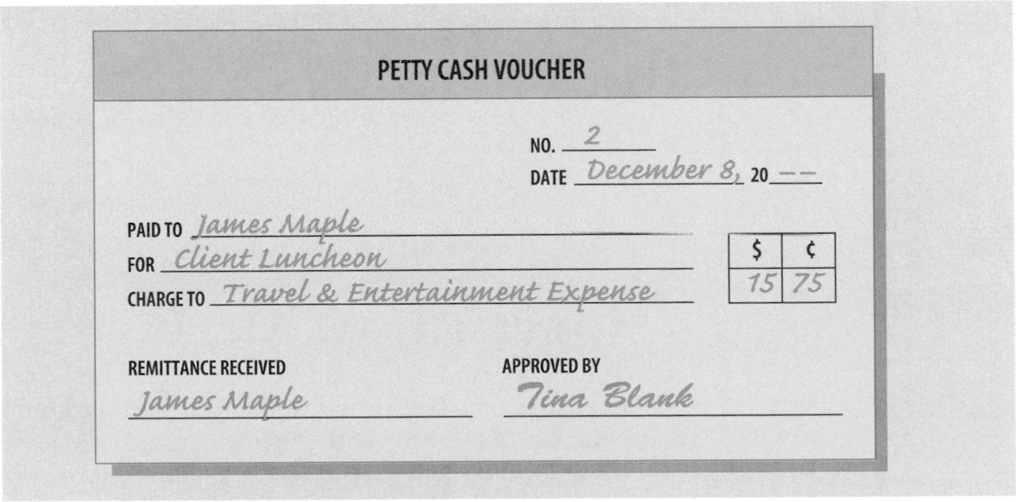

PETTY CASH PAYMENTS RECORD

When a petty cash fund is maintained, a formal record is often kept of all payments from the fund. The **petty cash payments record** (Figure 7-13) is a special multi-column record that supplements the regular accounting records. It is not a journal. The headings of the Distribution of Payments columns may vary, depending upon the types of expenditures.

The petty cash payments record of Maple Consulting is shown in Figure 7-13. A narrative of the petty cash transactions shown in Figure 7-13 is as follows:

Dec. 1 Maple issued a check for $200.00 payable to Tina Blank, Petty Cash Custodian. Blank cashed the check and placed the money in a secure cash box.

A notation of the amount received is made in the Description column of the petty cash payments record. In addition, this transaction is entered in the journal as follows:

8	Dec. 1	Petty Cash		200 00		8
9		Cash			200 00	9
10		Establish petty cash fund				10

During the month of December, the following payments were made from the petty cash fund:

Dec. 5 Paid $32.80 to Jerry's Auto for servicing the company automobile. Voucher No. 1.

8 Reimbursed Maple $15.75 for the amount spent for lunch with a client. Voucher No. 2.

9 Gave Maple $30.00 for personal use. Voucher No. 3.

There is no special Distribution column for entering amounts withdrawn by the owner for personal use. Therefore, this payment is entered by writing the account name in the Account column and $30.00 in the Amount column at the extreme right of the petty cash payments record.

15 Paid $38.25 for printer repairs. Voucher No. 4.

17 Reimbursed Maple $14.50 for travel expenses. Voucher No. 5.

19 Paid $8.00 to Big Red Car Care for washing the company automobile. Voucher No. 6.

22 Paid $9.50 for mailing a package. Voucher No. 7.

29 Paid $30.00 for postage stamps. Voucher No. 8.

REPLENISHING THE PETTY CASH FUND

The petty cash fund should be replenished whenever the fund runs low and at the end of each accounting period, so that the accounts are brought up to date. The amount columns of the petty cash payments record are totaled to verify that the total of the Total Amount column equals the total of the Distribution columns. The amount columns are then ruled as shown in Figure 7-13.

FIGURE 7-13 Maple Consulting's Petty Cash Payments Record

PETTY CASH PAYMENTS FOR THE MONTH OF December 20--

PAGE 1

DAY	DESCRIPTION		VOU. NO.	TOTAL AMOUNT	DISTRIBUTION OF PAYMENTS					
					AUTO EXP.	POST. EXP.	TRAVEL/ ENTERT. EXP.	MISC. EXP.	ACCOUNT	AMOUNT
1	Received in fund	200.00								
5	Automobile repairs		1	32 80	32 80					
8	Client luncheon		2	15 75			15 75			
9	James Maple, personal use		3	30 00					James Maple, Drawing	30 00
15	Printer repairs		4	38 25				38 25		
17	Traveling expenses		5	14 50			14 50			
19	Washing automobile		6	8 00	8 00					
22	Postage expense		7	9 50		9 50				
29	Postage stamps		8	30 00		30 00				
				178 80	40 80	39 50	30 25	38 25		30 00
31	Balance	21.20								
31	Replenished fund	178.80								
	Total	200.00								

Credit to replenish petty cash fund and reduce Cash.

Debits to replenish petty cash fund and recognize expenses paid out of petty cash.

The information in the petty cash payments record is then used to replenish the petty cash fund. On December 31, a check for $178.80 is issued to the petty cash custodian. The journal entry to record the replenishment of the fund is as follows:

18	Dec.	31	Automobile Expense		40 80		18
19			Postage Expense		39 50		19
20			Travel and Entertainment Expense		30 25		20
21			Miscellaneous Expense		38 25		21
22			James Maple, Drawing		30 00		22
23			Cash			178 80	23
24			Replenishment of petty cash fund				24

LEARNING KEY

Once the petty cash fund is established, an entry is made to Petty Cash only if the amount of the fund is being changed.

Note two important aspects of the functioning of a petty cash fund.

1. Once the fund is established by debiting Petty Cash and crediting Cash, no further entries are made to Petty Cash. Notice in the journal entry to replenish the fund that the debits are to appropriate expense accounts and the credit is to Cash. Only if the amount of the fund itself is being changed would there be a debit or credit to Petty Cash.
2. The petty cash payments record is strictly a supplement to the regular accounting records. Because it is not a journal, no posting is done from this record. A separate entry must be made in the journal to replenish the fund and update the expense accounts.

U REVU Complete U REVU-3 on **page 252** to test your basic understanding of LO3.

THE CHANGE FUND AND CASH SHORT AND OVER

LO4 Establish a change fund and use the cash short and over account.

Businesses generally must be able to make change when customers use cash to pay for goods or services received. To do so, generally it is a good idea to establish a **change fund**. A change fund is a supply of currency and coins kept in a cash register or cash drawer for use in handling cash sales.

ESTABLISHING AND OPERATING THE CHANGE FUND

The journal entries for establishing and maintaining a change fund are very similar to the ones just used for petty cash. To establish a change fund of $200.00 on June 1, the following entry would be made:

8	June 1	Change Fund		200 00		8
9		Cash			200 00	9
10		Establish change fund				10

At the end of the day, cash received during the day is deposited, but the change fund is held back for use the following business day. For example, if cash of $1,250.00 was received on June 3 for services provided, the cash drawer would contain $1,450.00, as follows:

Change fund	$ 200.00
Cash sales	1,250.00
Total cash on hand	$1,450.00

The $1,250 would be deposited in the bank, and the following journal entry would be made:

12	June 3	Cash		1,250 00		12
13		Service Fees			1,250 00	13
14		Cash received for services				14

LEARNING KEY

Once the change fund is established, an entry is made to Change Fund only if the amount of the fund is being changed.

Notice the additional similarity between the change fund and the petty cash fund. Once the change fund is established by a debit to Change Fund and a credit to Cash, no further entries are made to the change fund. Only if the amount of the change fund itself is being changed would there be a debit or credit to Change Fund.

CASH SHORT AND OVER

An unavoidable part of the change-making process is that errors can occur. It is important to know whether such errors have occurred and how to account for them.

Businesses commonly use cash registers with tapes that accumulate a record of the day's receipts. The amount of cash according to the tapes plus the amount of the change fund can be compared with the amount of cash in the register to determine any error. For example, assume a cash shortage is identified for June 19.

Change fund	$ 200.00
Receipts per register tapes	963.00
Total	$1,163.00
Cash count	1,161.00
Cash shortage	$ 2.00

Similarly, assume a cash overage is identified for June 20.

Change fund	$ 200.00
Receipts per register tapes	814.00
Total	$1,014.00
Cash count	1,015.00
Cash overage	$ 1.00

We account for such errors by using an account called Cash Short and Over. In T account form, Cash Short and Over appears as follows:

Cash Short and Over	
Shortage (Expense)	Overage (Revenue)

The register tapes on June 19 showed receipts of $963.00 and the change fund was $200.00, but only $1,161.00 in cash was counted. The journal entry on June 19 to record the revenues and cash shortage (remember that we hold back the change fund) would be as follows:

18	June	19	Cash		961 00		18
19			Cash Short and Over		2 00		19
20			Service Fees			963 00	20
21			Record service fees and cash shortage				21

The entry on June 20 to record the revenues and cash overage (holding back the change fund) would be as follows:

23	June	20	Cash		815 00		23
24			Service Fees			814 00	24
25			Cash Short and Over			1 00	25
26			Record service fees and cash overage				26

The cash short and over account is used to accumulate cash shortages and overages throughout the accounting period. At the end of the period, a debit balance in the account (a net shortage) is treated as an expense. A credit balance in the account (a net overage) is treated as revenue.

U REVU Complete U REVU-4 on **page 252** to test your basic understanding of LO4.

SELF-STUDY

LEARNING OBJECTIVES	Key Points to Remember
LO1 Describe how to open and use a checking account.	Three steps to follow in preparing a check are as follows: 1. Complete the check stub or register. 2. Enter the date, payee name, and amount on the check. 3. Sign the check.

LEARNING OBJECTIVES	Key Points to Remember
LO2 Prepare a bank reconciliation and related journal entries.	The most common reasons for differences between the book and bank cash balances are as follows: 1. Deposits in transit 2. Outstanding checks 3. Bank service charges 4. Bank collections for the depositor 5. NSF checks 6. Errors by the bank or the depositor Three steps to follow in preparing a bank reconciliation are as follows: 1. Identify deposits in transit and any related errors. 2. Identify outstanding checks and any related errors. 3. Identify additional reconciling items. Only two kinds of items on a bank reconciliation require journal entries. 1. Errors in the depositor's books. 2. Bank additions and deductions that do not already appear in the books.
LO3 Establish and use a petty cash fund.	Two important aspects of the functioning of a petty cash fund are as follows: 1. Once the fund is established, subsequent entries do not affect the petty cash account balance, unless the size of the fund itself is being changed. 2. The petty cash payments record is supplemental to the regular accounting records. No posting is done from this record.
LO4 Establish a change fund and use the cash short and over account.	A change fund is established by debiting Change Fund and crediting Cash. Cash shortages and overages are accounted for using the cash short and over account. A debit balance in this account represents expense; a credit balance represents revenue.

DEMONSTRATION PROBLEM

Jason Kuhn's check stubs indicated a balance of $4,565.12 for Kuhn's Wilderness Outfitters on March 31. This included a record of a deposit of $926.10 mailed to the bank on March 30, but not credited to Kuhn's account until April 1. In addition, the following checks were outstanding on March 31:

No. 462	$524.26
No. 465	$213.41
No. 473	$543.58
No. 476	$351.38
No. 477	$197.45

(continued)

The bank statement showed a balance of $5,419.00 as of March 31. The bank statement included a service charge of $4.10 with the date of March 29. In matching the canceled checks and record of deposits with the stubs, it was discovered that Check No. 456, a payment on account to Office Suppliers, Inc., for $39.00 was erroneously recorded on the stub as $93.00. This caused the bank balance on that stub and those following to be $54.00 too small. It was also discovered that an ATM withdrawal of $100.00 for personal use was not recorded on the books.

Kuhn maintains a $200.00 petty cash fund. His petty cash payments record showed the following totals at the end of March of the current year:

Automobile expense	$ 32.40
Postage expense	27.50
Charitable contributions expense	35.00
Telephone expense	6.20
Travel and entertainment expense	38.60
Miscellancous expense	17.75
Jason Kuhn, drawing	40.00
Total	$197.45

This left a balance of $2.55 in the petty cash fund, and the fund was replenished.

REQUIRED

1. Prepare a bank reconciliation for Jason Kuhn as of March 31, 20--.
2. Journalize the entries that should be made by Kuhn on his books as of March 31, 20--, (a) as a result of the bank reconciliation and (b) to replenish the petty cash fund.
3. Show proof that, after these entries, the total of the cash and petty cash account balances equals $4,715.02.

Solution

1.

Kuhn's Wilderness Outfitters
Bank Reconciliation
March 31, 20 --

Bank statement balance, March 31		$5,419.00
Add deposit in transit		926.10
		$6,345.10
Deduct outstanding checks:		
No. 462	$524.26	
No. 465	213.41	
No. 473	543.58	
No. 476	351.38	
No. 477	197.45	1,830.08
Adjusted bank balance		$4,515.02
Book balance, March 31		$4,565.12
Add error on Check No. 456		54.00
		$4,619.12
Deduct: Bank service charge	$4.10	
Unrecorded ATM withdrawal	100.00	104.10
Adjusted book balance		$4,515.02

2a.

	Date		Description	Post. Ref.	Debit	Credit	
3							3
4	Mar.	31	Miscellaneous Expense		4 10		4
5			Cash			4 10	5
6			Bank service charge				6
7							7
8			Cash		5 4 00		8
9			Accounts Payable—Office Suppliers, Inc.			5 4 00	9
10			Error on Check No. 456				10
11							11
12			Jason Kuhn, Drawing		1 0 0 00		12
13			Cash			1 0 0 00	13
14			Unrecorded ATM withdrawal				14
15							15

b.

	Date		Description	Post. Ref.	Debit	Credit	
16		31	Automobile Expense		3 2 40		16
17			Postage Expense		2 7 50		17
18			Charitable Contributions Expense		3 5 00		18
19			Telephone Expense		6 20		19
20			Travel and Entertainment Expense		3 8 60		20
21			Miscellaneous Expense		1 7 75		21
22			Jason Kuhn, Drawing		4 0 00		22
23			Cash			1 9 7 45	23
24			Replenishment of petty cash fund				24
25							25

3.

Cash in bank:		
Check stub balance, March 31	$4,565.12	
Plus error on Ck. No. 456	54.00	
Less bank charges	(104.10)	
Adjusted cash in bank		$4,515.02
Cash on hand:		
Petty cash fund	$ 2.55	
Add replenishment	197.45	
Adjusted cash on hand		200.00
Total cash in bank and petty cash on hand		$4,715.02

KEY TERMS

ABA (American Bankers Association) Number (231) The small fraction printed in the upper right-hand corner of each check.

automated teller machine (ATM) (232) A machine used by depositors to make withdrawals or deposits at any time.

bank reconciliation (236) A report used to bring the book and bank balances into agreement.

bank statement (234) A statement of account issued by a bank to each depositor once a month.

blank endorsement (231) An endorsement where the depositor simply signs the back of the check, making the check payable to any bearer.

canceled check (235) A depositor's check paid by the bank during the bank statement period.

cash (230) To a business, cash includes currency, coins, checks received from customers, money orders, and bank cashier's checks.

change fund (244) A supply of currency and coins kept in a cash register or cash drawer for use in handling cash sales.

check (233) A document ordering a bank to pay cash from a depositor's account.

check stub (233) In some checkbooks, a document attached to a check that contains space for relevant information about the check.

credit memo (237) An item that the bank adds to the account.

debit memo (237) An item that the bank deducts from the account.

deposit ticket (231) A form showing a detailed listing of items being deposited.

deposits in transit (236) Deposits that have not reached or been recorded by the bank before the bank statement is prepared.

drawee (233) The bank on which the check is drawn.

drawer (233) The depositor who orders the bank to pay the cash.

electronic funds transfer (EFT) (240) A process using a computer rather than paper checks to complete transactions with the bank.

endorsement (231) Stamping or writing the depositor's name and sometimes other information on the back of the check.

internal control (230) A set of procedures designed to ensure proper accounting for transactions.

magnetic ink character recognition (MICR) code (231) The character code used to print identifying information on the lower left front side of each check.

not sufficient funds (NSF) check (236) A check deposited by the depositor that is not paid because the drawer did not have sufficient funds.

outstanding check (236) A check issued that has not been presented to the bank for payment before the statement is prepared.

payee (233) The person being paid the cash.

petty cash fund (241) A fund established to pay for small items with cash.

petty cash payments record (242) A special multi-column record that supplements the regular accounting records.

petty cash voucher (241) A receipt that is prepared for every payment from the petty cash fund.

restrictive endorsement (231) An endorsement where the depositor adds words such as "For deposit" to restrict the payment of the check.

service charge (236) A bank charge for services such as check printing and processing.

signature card (230) A card that is completed and signed by each person authorized to sign checks.

SELF-STUDY QUESTIONS AND EXERCISES

True/False Questions

1. LO2 The primary purpose of a bank reconciliation is to detect and correct errors made by the bank in its records.
2. LO2 NSF checks are subtracted from the bank's ending balance on the bank reconciliation.
3. LO2 The bank service charge requires a journal entry to record its effects on the cash account.
4. LO2 Unrecorded ATM withdrawals are added to the checkbook balance on the bank reconciliation.
5. LO3 The petty cash record is a journal of original entry (entries are posted from it to the general ledger accounts).

Multiple Choice Questions

1. LO2 Which of these could be *added* to the ending checkbook balance?

(a) service charges
(b) NSF check
(c) checkbook errors
(d) outstanding checks

2 LO2 Which of these is *subtracted* from the ending checkbook balance?

(a) deposits in transit
(b) service charges
(c) note collection
(d) bank errors

3. LO2 Which of these is *added* to the ending bank statement balance?

(a) outstanding checks
(b) service charges
(c) checkbook errors
(d) deposits in transit

4. LO3 To establish a petty cash fund, which account is debited?

(a) Cash
(b) Petty Cash
(c) Miscellaneous Expense
(d) Revenue

5. LO4 When the cash short and over account has a debit balance at the end of the month, it is considered

(a) an expense.
(b) an asset.
(c) revenue.
(d) a liability.

U REVU Exercises

1. LO1 Match the following words with their definitions by entering the correct number in the spaces below.
   1. deposit ticket
   2. ATM
   3. check
   4. bank statement
   5. blank endorsement

   ____ a. A document ordering a bank to pay cash from a depositor's account.

   ____ b. An endorsement where the depositor simply signs the back of the check, making the check payable to any bearer.

   ____ c. Automated teller machine—a machine used by depositors to make withdrawals or deposits at any time.

   ____ d. A statement of account issued by a bank to each depositor once a month.

   ____ e. A form showing a detailed listing of items being deposited.

2. LO2 Indicate how each of the following items should be treated in a bank reconciliation by entering the correct letter in the spaces provided.

   a. Add to bank statement balance
   b. Subtract from bank statement balance
   c. Add to book balance
   d. Subtract from book balance

   ____ 1. Interest earned on checking account balance
   ____ 2. Error in checkbook whereby a check for $82 was entered in the checkbook as $28
   ____ 3. Deposit in transit
   ____ 4. Outstanding checks

3. LO3 A petty cash fund established for $200 had the following cash payments during the month:

Telephone expense	$23.50
Automobile expense	49.10
H. Appy, drawing	50.00

   Prepare the journal entry to replenish the petty cash fund at the end of the month.

4. LO4 The cash register tape for June 30 showed cash receipts of $876, and the cash in the register drawer was $1,070. A change fund of $200 is maintained.

   Prepare the journal entry for service fees and cash short and over at June 30.

The answers to the Self-Study Questions and Exercises are at the end of the chapter (page 265).

REVIEW QUESTIONS

LO1 1. Why must a signature card be filled out and signed to open a checking account?

LO1 2. Explain the difference between a blank endorsement and a restrictive endorsement.

LO1 3. Who are the three parties to every check?

LO1 4. What are the three steps to follow in preparing a check?

LO2 5. What are the most common reasons for differences between the book and bank cash balances?

LO2 6. What are the three steps to follow in preparing a bank reconciliation?

LO2 7. What two kinds of items on a bank reconciliation require journal entries?

LO2 8. Name five applications of electronic funds transfer in current use.

LO3 9. What is the purpose of a petty cash fund?

LO3 10. What should be prepared every time a petty cash payment is made?

LO3 11. At what two times should the petty cash fund be replenished?

LO3 12. From what source is the information obtained for issuing a check to replenish the petty cash fund?

LO4 13. At what two times would an entry be made affecting the change fund?

LO4 14. What does a debit balance in the cash short and over account represent? What does a credit balance in this account represent?

SERIES A EXERCISES

E 7-1A (LO1)

CHECKING ACCOUNT TERMS Match the following words with their definitions:

1. An endorsement where the depositor simply signs on the back of the check
2. An endorsement that contains words like "For Deposit Only" together with the signature
3. A card filled out and signed by each person authorized to sign checks on an account
4. The depositor who orders the bank to pay cash from the depositor's account
5. The bank on which the check is drawn
6. The person being paid the cash
7. A check that has been paid by the bank and is being returned to the depositor

a. signature card
b. canceled check
c. blank endorsement
d. drawer
e. restrictive endorsement
f. drawee
g. payee

E 7-2A (LO1)
✓ Total deposit: $817.00

PREPARE DEPOSIT TICKET Based on the following information, prepare a deposit ticket:

Date:		January 15, 20--
Currency:		$334.00
Coin:		26.00
Checks:	No. 4-11	311.00
	No. 80-322	108.00
	No. 3-9	38.00

E 7-3A (LO1)

PREPARE CHECK AND STUB Based on the following information, prepare a check and stub:

Date:	January 15, 20--
Balance brought forward:	$2,841.50
Deposit:	(from Exercise 7-2A)
Check to:	J. M. Suppliers
Amount:	$150.00
For:	Office Supplies
Signature:	Sign your name

E 7-4A (LO2)

BANK RECONCILIATION PROCEDURES In a format similar to the following, indicate whether the action at the left will result in an addition to (+) or subtraction from (–) the ending bank balance or the ending checkbook balance.

	Ending Bank Balance	Ending Checkbook Balance
1. Deposits in transit to the bank	______	______
2. Error in checkbook: check recorded as $32.00 but was actually for $23.00	______	______
3. Service fee charged by bank	______	______
4. Outstanding checks	______	______
5. NSF check deposited earlier	______	______
6. Error in checkbook: check recorded as $22.00 but was actually for $220.00	______	______
7. Bank credit memo advising a note was collected for us	______	______

E 7-5A (LO2)

✓ NSF check: Dr. Accounts Receivable, $390.00

PREPARE JOURNAL ENTRIES FOR BANK RECONCILIATION Based on the following bank reconciliation, prepare the journal entries:

Lisa Chai Associates
Bank Reconciliation
July 31, 20 - -

Bank statement balance, July 31		$2764.40
Add deposits in transit	$250.00	
	98.00	348.00
		$3112.40
Deduct outstanding checks:		
No. 387	$353.50	
No. 393	17.80	
No. 398	33.20	404.50
Adjusted bank balance		$2707.90
Book balance, July 31		$3084.90
Add error on Check No. 394*		23.00
		$3107.90
Deduct: NSF check	$390.00	
Bank service charge	10.00	400.00
Adjusted book balance		$2707.90
*Accounts Payable was debited in original entry.		

E 7-6A (LO3)

✓ Replenishment: Cr. Cash, $197.00

PETTY CASH JOURNAL ENTRIES Based on the following petty cash information, prepare (a) the journal entry to establish a petty cash fund, and (b) the journal entry to replenish the petty cash fund.

On January 1, 20--, a check was written in the amount of $200.00 to establish a petty cash fund. During January, the following vouchers were written for cash removed from the petty cash drawer:

Voucher No.	Account Debited	Amount
1	Telephone Expense	$17.50
2	Automobile Expense	33.00
3	Joseph Levine, Drawing	70.00
4	Postage Expense	12.50
5	Charitable Contributions Expense	15.00
6	Miscellaneous Expense	49.00

E 7-7A (LO4)

✓ Apr. 16: Cr. Cash Short and Over, $1.75

CASH SHORT AND OVER ENTRIES Based on the following information, prepare the weekly entries for cash receipts from service fees and cash short and over. A change fund of $100.00 is maintained.

Date	Change Fund	Cash Register Receipt Amount	Actual Cash Counted
Apr. 2	$100.00	$268.50	$366.50
9	100.00	237.75	333.50
16	100.00	309.25	411.00
23	100.00	226.50	324.00
30	100.00	318.00	422.00

SERIES A PROBLEMS

P 7-8A (LO2)
✓ Adjusted book balance: $4,182.00

BANK RECONCILIATION AND RELATED JOURNAL ENTRIES The book balance in the checking account of Volman Enterprises as of October 31 is $4,765.00. The bank statement shows an ending balance of $4,348.00. The following information is discovered by (1) comparing last month's deposits in transit and outstanding checks with this month's bank statement, (2) comparing deposits and checks written per books and per bank in the current month, and (3) noting service charges and other debit and credit memos shown on the bank statement.

Deposits in transit:	10/29	$175.00
	10/30	334.00
Outstanding checks:	No. 1764	47.00
	No. 1767	146.00
	No. 1772	113.00
	No. 1781	369.00
Unrecorded ATM withdrawal:*		180.00
Bank service charge:		43.00
NSF check:		370.00

Error on Check No. 1754 — Checkbook shows it was for $72.00, but it was actually written for $62.00. Accounts Payable was debited.

*Funds were withdrawn by Gary Volman for personal use.

REQUIRED

1. Prepare a bank reconciliation as of October 31, 20--.
2. Prepare the required journal entries.

P 7-9A (LO2)
✓ Adjusted bank balance: $3,069.95

BANK RECONCILIATION AND RELATED JOURNAL ENTRIES The book balance in the checking account of Lyle's Salon as of November 30 is $3,282.95. The bank statement shows an ending balance of $2,127.00. By examining last month's bank reconciliation, comparing the deposits and checks written per books and per bank in November, and noting the service charges and other debit and credit memos shown on the bank statement, the following were found:

(a) An ATM withdrawal of $150.00 on November 18 by Lyle for personal use was not recorded on the books.
(b) A bank debit memo issued for an NSF check from a customer of $19.50.
(c) A bank credit memo issued for interest of $19.00 earned during the month.
(d) On November 30, a deposit of $1,177.00 was made, which is not shown on the bank statement.
(e) A bank debit memo issued for $17.50 for bank service charges.
(f) Checks No. 549, 561, and 562 for the amounts of $185.00, $21.00, and $9.40, respectively, were written during November but have not yet been received by the bank.
(g) The reconciliation from the previous month showed outstanding checks totaling $271.95. One of those checks, No. 471 for $18.65, has not yet been received by the bank.
(h) Check No. 523 written to a creditor in the amount of $372.90 was recorded in the books as $327.90.

REQUIRED

1. Prepare a bank reconciliation as of November 30.
2. Prepare the required journal entries.

P 7-10A (LO3)

✓ Replenishment: Cr. Cash, $149.00

PETTY CASH RECORD AND JOURNAL ENTRIES On May 1, a petty cash fund was established for $150.00. The following vouchers were issued during May:

Date	Voucher No.	Purpose	Amount
May 1	1	postage due	$ 3.50
3	2	office supplies	11.00
5	3	auto repair (miscellaneous)	43.00
7	4	drawing (Joy Adams)	25.00
11	5	donation (Red Cross)	10.00
15	6	travel expenses	28.00
22	7	postage stamps	3.50
26	8	telephone call	5.00
30	9	donation (Boy Scouts)	20.00

REQUIRED

1. Prepare the journal entry to establish the petty cash fund.
2. Record the vouchers in the petty cash record. Total and rule the petty cash record.
3. Prepare the journal entry to replenish the petty cash fund. Make the appropriate entry in the petty cash record.

P 7-11A (LO4)

✓ July 23: Dr. Cash Short and Over, $2.50

CASH SHORT AND OVER ENTRIES Listed below are the weekly cash register tape amounts for service fees and the related cash counts during the month of July. A change fund of $100.00 is maintained.

Date	Change Fund	Cash Register Receipt Amount	Actual Cash Counted
July 2	$100.00	$289.50	$387.00
9	100.00	311.50	411.50
16	100.00	306.00	408.50
23	100.00	317.50	415.00
30	100.00	296.00	399.50

REQUIRED

1. Prepare the journal entries to record the cash service fees and cash short and over for each of the five weeks.
2. Post to the cash short and over account (use Account No. 516).
3. Determine the ending balance of the cash short and over account. Does it represent an expense or revenue?

SERIES B EXERCISES

E 7-1B (LO1)

CHECKING ACCOUNT TERMS Match the following words with their definitions:

1. Banking number used to identify checks for deposit tickets
2. A card filled out to open a checking account
3. A machine from which withdrawals can be taken or deposits made to accounts
4. A place where relevant information is recorded about a check
5. A set of procedures designed to ensure proper accounting for transactions
6. A statement of account issued to each depositor once a month
7. A detailed listing of items being deposited to an account

a. bank statement
b. deposit ticket
c. signature card
d. internal control
e. check stub
f. ATM
g. ABA number

E 7-2B (LO1)

✓ Total deposit: $645.00

PREPARE DEPOSIT TICKET Based on the following information, prepare a deposit ticket:

Date:	November 15, 20--	
Currency:		$283.00
Coin:		19.00
Checks:	No. 3-22	201.00
	No. 19-366	114.00
	No. 3-2	28.00

E 7-3B (LO1)

PREPARE CHECK AND STUB Based on the following information, prepare a check and stub:

Date:	November 15, 20--
Balance brought forward:	$3,181.00
Deposit:	(from Exercise 7-2B)
Check to:	R. J. Smith Co.
Amount:	$120.00
For:	Payment on account
Signature:	Sign your name

E 7-4B (LO2)

BANK RECONCILIATION PROCEDURES In a format similar to the following, indicate whether the action at the left will result in an addition to (+) or subtraction from (–) the ending bank balance or the ending checkbook balance.

		Ending Bank Balance	Ending Checkbook Balance
1.	Service fee of $12 charged by bank	______	______
2.	Outstanding checks______	______	
3.	Error in checkbook: check recorded as $36.00 was actually for $28.00	______	______
4.	NSF check deposited earlier	______	______
5.	Bank credit memo advising a note was collected for us	______	______
6.	Deposits in transit to the bank	______	______
7.	Error in checkbook: check recorded as $182.00 was actually for $218.00	______	______

E 7-5B (LO2)

✓ NSF check: Dr. Accounts Receivable, $66.00

PREPARE JOURNAL ENTRIES FOR BANK RECONCILIATION Based on the following bank reconciliation, prepare the journal entries:

Ruggero Celini Associates
Bank Reconciliation
July 31, 20 --

Bank statement balance, July 31		$1 7 8 4 00
Add deposits in transit	$ 4 1 8 50	
	1 0 0 50	5 1 9 00
		$2 3 0 3 00
Deduct outstanding checks:		
No. 185	$ 2 0 6 50	
No. 203	3 1 7 40	
No. 210	5 6 10	5 8 0 00
Adjusted bank balance		$1 7 2 3 00
Book balance, July 31		$1 7 9 2 00
Add: Error on Check No. 191*	1 0 00	
Interest earned	2 00	1 2 00
		$1 8 0 4 00
Deduct: NSF check	$ 6 6 00	
Bank service charge	1 5 00	8 1 00
Adjusted book balance		$1 7 2 3 00
*Accounts Payable was debited in original entry.		

E 7-6B (LO3)

✓ Replenishment: Cr. Cash, $190.00

PETTY CASH JOURNAL ENTRIES Based on the following petty cash information, prepare (a) the journal entry to establish a petty cash fund, and (b) the journal entry to replenish the petty cash fund.

On October 1, 20--, a check was written in the amount of $200.00 to establish a petty cash fund. During October, the following vouchers were written for cash taken from the petty cash drawer:

(continued)

Voucher No.	Account Debited	Amount
1	Postage Expense	$13.00
2	Miscellaneous Expense	17.00
3	John Flanagan, Drawing	45.00
4	Telephone Expense	36.00
5	Charitable Contributions Expense	50.00
6	Automobile Expense	29.00

E 7-7B (LO4)

✓ June 15: Dr. Cash Short and Over, $2.00

CASH SHORT AND OVER ENTRIES Based on the following information, prepare the weekly entries for cash receipts from service fees and cash short and over. A change fund of $100.00 is maintained.

Date	Change Fund	Cash Register Receipt Amount	Actual Cash Counted
June 1	$100.00	$330.00	$433.00
8	100.00	297.00	400.00
15	100.00	233.00	331.00
22	100.00	302.00	396.50
29	100.00	316.00	412.00

SERIES B PROBLEMS

P 7-8B (LO2)

✓ Adjusted book balance: $2,674.00

BANK RECONCILIATION AND RELATED JOURNAL ENTRIES The book balance in the checking account of Kyri Enterprises as of November 30 is $2,964.00. The bank statement shows an ending balance of $2,525.00. The following information is discovered by (1) comparing last month's deposits in transit and outstanding checks with this month's bank statement, (2) comparing deposits and checks written per books and per bank in the current month, and (3) noting service charges and other debit and credit memos shown on the bank statement.

Deposits in transit:	11/29	$125.00
	11/30	200.00
Outstanding checks:	No. 322	17.00
	No. 324	105.00
	No. 327	54.00
Unrecorded ATM withdrawal:*		100.00
Bank service charge:		25.00
NSF check:		185.00

Error on Check No. 321 Checkbook shows it was for $64.00, but it was actually written for $44.00. Accounts Payable was debited.

*Funds were withdrawn by Susan Kyri for personal use.

REQUIRED

1. Prepare a bank reconciliation as of November 30, 20--.
2. Prepare the required journal entries.

P 7-9B (LO2)

✓ Adjusted bank balance: $4,518.70

BANK RECONCILIATION AND RELATED JOURNAL ENTRIES The book balance in the checking account of Tori's Health Center as of April 30 is $4,690.30. The bank statement shows an ending balance of $3,275.60. By examining last month's bank reconciliation, comparing the deposits and checks written per books and per bank in April, and noting the service charges and other debit and credit memos shown on the bank statement, the following were found:

(a) An ATM withdrawal of $200.00 on April 20 by Tori for personal use was not recorded on the books.
(b) A bank debit memo issued for an NSF check from a customer of $29.10.
(c) A bank credit memo issued for interest of $28.00 earned during the month.
(d) On April 30, a deposit of $1,592.00 was made, which is not shown on the bank statement.
(e) A bank debit memo issued for $24.50 for bank service charges.
(f) Checks No. 481, 493, and 494 for the amounts of $215.00, $71.00, and $24.30, respectively, were written during April but have not yet been received by the bank.
(g) The reconciliation from the previous month showed outstanding checks totaling $418.25. One of these checks, No. 397 for $38.60, has not yet been received by the bank.
(h) Check No. 422 written to a creditor in the amount of $217.90 was recorded in the books as $271.90.

REQUIRED

1. Prepare a bank reconciliation as of April 30.
2. Prepare the required journal entries.

P 7-10B (LO3)

✓ Replenishment: Cr. Cash, $87.00

PETTY CASH RECORD AND JOURNAL ENTRIES On July 1, a petty cash fund was established for $100.00. The following vouchers were issued during July:

Date	Voucher No.	Purpose	Amount
July 1	1	office supplies	$ 3.00
3	2	donation (Goodwill)	15.00
5	3	travel expenses	5.00
7	4	postage due	2.00
8	5	office supplies	4.00
11	6	postage due	3.50
15	7	telephone call	5.00
21	8	travel expenses	11.00
25	9	withdrawal by owner (L. Ortiz)	20.00
26	10	copier repair (miscellaneous)	18.50

REQUIRED

1. Prepare the journal entry to establish the petty cash fund.
2. Record the vouchers in the petty cash record. Total and rule the petty cash record.
3. Prepare the journal entry to replenish the petty cash fund. Make the appropriate entry in the petty cash record.

P 7-11B (LO4)

✓ Aug. 8: Dr. Cash Short and Over, $3.50

CASH SHORT AND OVER ENTRIES Listed below are the weekly cash register tape amounts for service fees and the related cash counts during the month of July. A change fund of $200.00 is maintained.

Date	Change Fund	Cash Register Receipt Amount	Actual Cash Counted
Aug. 1	$200.00	$292.50	$495.00
8	200.00	305.00	501.50
15	200.00	286.00	486.00
22	200.00	330.25	532.75
29	200.00	299.20	495.00

REQUIRED

1. Prepare the journal entries to record the cash service fees and cash short and over for each of the five weeks.
2. Post to the cash short and over account (use Account No. 516).
3. Determine the ending balance of the cash short and over account. Does it represent an expense or revenue?

MANAGING YOUR WRITING

The current month's bank statement for your account arrives in the mail. In reviewing the statement, you notice a deposit listed for $400.00 that you did not make. It has been credited in error to your account.

Discuss whether you have an ethical or legal obligation to inform the bank of the error. What action should you take?

ETHICS CASE

Ben Thomas works as a teller for First National Bank. When he arrived at work on Friday, the branch manager, Frank Mills, asked him to get his cash drawer out early because the head teller, Naomi Ray, was conducting a surprise cash count for all the tellers. Surprise cash counts are usually done four or five times a year by the branch manager or the head teller and once or twice a year by internal auditors. Ben's drawer was $100.00 short and his reconciliation tape showed that he was in balance on Thursday night. Naomi asked Ben for an explanation, and Ben immediately took $100.00 out of his pocket and handed it to her. He went on to explain he needed the cash to buy prescriptions for his son and pay for groceries and intended to put the $100.00 back in his cash drawer on Monday, which was pay day. He also told Naomi that this was the first time he had ever "borrowed" money from his cash drawer and that he would never do it again.

1. What are the ethical considerations in this case from both Ben's and Naomi's perspectives?
2. What options does Naomi have to address this problem?
3. Assume Naomi chooses to inform the branch manager. Write a short incident report describing the findings.

4. In small groups, come up with as many ideas as possible on how to safeguard cash on hand in a bank (petty cash, teller drawer cash, and vault cash) from employee theft and mismanagement.

MASTERY PROBLEM

✓ Adjusted bank balance: $4,324.05

Turner Excavation maintains a checking account and has decided to open a petty cash fund. The following petty cash fund transactions occurred during July:

July 2	Established a petty cash fund by issuing Check No. 301 for $100.00.
5	Paid $25.00 from the petty cash fund for postage. Voucher No. 1.
7	Paid $30.00 from the petty cash fund for delivery of flowers (Miscellaneous Expense). Voucher No. 2.
8	Paid $20.00 from the petty cash fund to repair a tire on the company truck. Voucher No. 3.
12	Paid $22.00 from the petty cash fund for a newspaper advertisement. Voucher No. 4.
13	Issued Check No. 303 to replenish the petty cash fund. (Total and rule the petty cash payments record. Record the balance and the amount needed to replenish the fund in the Description column of the petty cash payments record.)
20	Paid $26.00 from the petty cash fund to reimburse an employee for expenses incurred to repair the company truck. Voucher No. 5.
24	Paid $12.50 from the petty cash fund for telephone calls made from a phone booth. Voucher No. 6.
28	Paid $25.00 from the petty cash fund as a contribution to the YMCA. Voucher No. 7.
31	Issued Check No. 308 to replenish the petty cash fund. (Total and rule the petty cash payments record. Record the balance and the amount needed to replenish the fund in the Description column of the petty cash payments record.)

The following additional transactions occurred during July:

July 5	Issued Check No. 302 to pay office rent, $650.00.
15	Issued Check No. 304 for office equipment, $525.00.
17	Issued Check No. 305 for the purchase of supplies, $133.00.
18	Issued Check No. 306 to pay attorney fees, $1,000.00.
30	Issued Check No. 307 to pay newspaper for an advertisement, $200.20.

REQUIRED

1. Record the petty cash transactions in a petty cash payments record.
2. Make all required general journal entries for the cash transactions. (*Note*: The petty cash fund was established and replenished twice during July.)
3. The bank statement on page 264 was received in the mail. Deposits were made on July 6 for $3,500.00 and on July 29 for $2,350.00. The checkbook balance on July 31 is $4,331.55. Notice the discrepancy in Check No. 302 that cleared the bank for $655.00. This check was written on July 5 for rent expense, but was incorrectly entered on the check stub and in the journal as $650.00. Prepare a bank reconciliation and make any necessary journal entries as of July 31.

(continued)

STATEMENT **Merchant's National Bank**

TURNER EXCAVATION
220 MAIN STREET
OAKHURST, NJ 07755-1461

Account Number 16 32475
Statement Date July 31, 20––
Statement Instructions
Page Number

Beginning Balance	No. of Deposits and Credits	We have added these deposits and credits totaling	No. of withdrawals and charges	We have subtracted these withdrawals and charges totaling	Resulting in a statement balance of
$1,250.25	1	$3,500.00	6	$1,512.50	$3,237.75
Document Count	Average Daily Balance this Statement Period		Minimum Balance this Statement Period	Date	Amount

If Your Account does not Balance, Please See Reverse Side and Report any Discrepancies to our Customer Service Department.

7/1	Beginning Balance		1,250.25
7/5	Check No. 301	−100.00	1,150.25
7/8	Check No. 302	−655.00	495.25
7/9	Deposit	3,500.00	3,995.25
7/15	Check No. 303	−97.00	3,898.25
7/20	Check No. 304	−525.00	3,373.25
7/28	Check No. 305	−133.00	3,240.25
7/31	Service Charge	−2.50	3,237.75

EC – Error Correction
ATM – Automated Teller Machine
OD – Overdrawn
TR – Wire Transfer
RC – Return Check Charge
D/N – Day/Night

Depositor Agrees and Bank Accepts Business Upon the Terms and Conditions of Bank's Rules and Regulations Now in Effect or as May be Hereafter Adopted.

CHALLENGE PROBLEM

This problem challenges you to apply your cumulative accounting knowledge to move a step beyond the material in the chapter.

✓ 2. Item 4: Dr. Depositor Accounts, $350.00

Susan Panera is preparing the June 30 bank reconciliation for Panera Bakery. She discovers the following items that explain the difference between the cash balance on her books and the balance as reported by Lawrence Bank:

1. An ATM withdrawal of $200.00 for personal use was not recorded by Susan.
2. A deposit of $850.00 was recorded by Susan but has not been received by Lawrence Bank as of June 30.
3. A check written in payment on account to Jayhawk Supply for $340.00 was recorded by Susan as $430.00 and by Lawrence Bank as $530.00.
4. An ATM deposit of $350.00 was recorded twice by Lawrence Bank.
5. An electronic funds transfer of $260.00 to Sunflower Mills as a payment on account was not recorded by Susan.
6. Checks No. 103 for $235.00 and No. 110 for $127.00 had not cleared Lawrence Bank as of June 30.

REQUIRED

1. Prepare the journal entries required to correct Panera Bakery's books as of June 30.
2. Prepare the journal entries required to correct Lawrence Bank's books as of June 30.

ANSWERS TO SELF-STUDY QUESTIONS AND EXERCISES

True/False Questions

1. F (primary purpose is to reconcile book balance with bank balance)
2. F (deducted from book balance)
3. T
4. F (deducted from book balance)
5. F (entries are not posted from petty cash record to general ledger)

Multiple Choice Questions

1. c 2. b 3. d 4. b 5. a

U REVU Exercises

1. __3__ a. A document ordering a bank to pay cash from a depositor's account.
   __5__ b. An endorsement where the depositor simply signs the back of the check, making the check payable to any bearer.
   __2__ c. Automated teller machine—a machine used by depositors to make withdrawals or deposits at any time.
   __4__ d. A statement of account issued by a bank to each depositor once a month.
   __1__ e. A form showing a detailed listing of items being deposited.

2. __c__ 1. Interest earned on checking account balance
   __d__ 2. Error in checkbook whereby a check for $82 was entered in the checkbook as $28
   __a__ 3. Deposit in transit
   __b__ 4. Outstanding checks

3.

Telephone Expense	23.50	
Automobile Expense	49.10	
H. Appy, Drawing	50.00	
Cash		122.60
Replenished petty cash fund		

4.

Cash	870.00	
Cash Short and Over	6.00	
Service Fees		876.00
Recorded service fees and cash shortage		

Chapter 7 Appendix

Internal Controls

LEARNING OBJECTIVES

Careful study of this appendix should enable you to:

LO1 **Explain the importance of internal control.**

LO2 **Define internal control and describe its key components.**

LO3 **Describe selected internal controls over cash receipts.**

LO4 **Describe selected internal controls over cash payments and the use of a voucher system.**

In Chapter 7, we introduced the concept of internal control and provided some examples of good internal control over cash transactions. Here, we examine internal control in greater depth.

We do the following:

1. Explain why internal control has achieved greater importance today.
2. Identify the key components of internal control.
3. Give examples of internal control over cash receipts.
4. Describe internal control of cash payments using a voucher system.

IMPORTANCE OF INTERNAL CONTROL

LO1 Explain the importance of internal control.

To be successful, management must have adequate control of the operations of the business. For example, the records of business activities must be reliable and timely, so that management has the information it needs to take necessary actions. The assets of the business must be known and protected. Employees must follow the rules and procedures defined by management. Accurate information must be available to report to owners, lenders, and regulatory bodies, such as the IRS. Without good internal control, it simply would not be possible to effectively and efficiently run a business.

The importance of strong internal control for managing a business has been known for years. But in 2002, the importance of internal control was raised to a whole new level. In July 2002, Congress passed the Sarbanes-Oxley Act (SOX). SOX applies to all **publicly held companies**—companies whose stock is traded on the major stock exchanges. Section 404 of SOX requires these companies to report annually on the effectiveness of internal control over financial reporting. For decades, these corporations have been required to provide audited financial statements. Now, they must also report on the quality of their internal control system. Figure 7A-1 provides an example of management's Section 404 report for Microsoft.

One of the interesting effects of SOX is how widely its rules are being felt. Officially, SOX applies to all publicly held companies and their external auditors. But SOX is causing many other companies and managements to look closely at the quality of their internal controls. The logic is simple: if internal controls are so important for publicly held companies, they probably deserve attention in other companies as well. Clearly, internal controls are a hot topic today.

FIGURE 7A-1 Section 404 Internal Control Report

REPORT OF MANAGEMENT ON INTERNAL CONTROL OVER FINANCIAL REPORTING

Our management [of Microsoft] is responsible for establishing and maintaining adequate internal control over financial reporting for the company. Internal control over financial reporting is a process to provide reasonable assurance regarding the reliability of our financial reporting for external purposes in accordance with accounting principles generally accepted in the United States of America. Internal control over financial reporting includes maintaining records that in reasonable detail accurately and fairly reflect our transactions; providing reasonable assurance that transactions are recorded as necessary for preparation of our financial statements; providing reasonable assurance that receipts and expenditures of company assets are made in accordance with management authorization; and providing reasonable assurance that unauthorized acquisition, use, or disposition of company assets that could have a material effect on our financial statements would be prevented or detected on a timely basis. Because of its inherent limitations, internal control over financial reporting is not intended to provide absolute assurance that a misstatement of our financial statements would be prevented or detected.

Management conducted an evaluation of the effectiveness of our internal control over financial reporting based on the framework in Internal Control—Integrated Framework issued by the Committee of Sponsoring Organizations of the Treadway Commission. Based on this evaluation, management concluded that the company's internal control over financial reporting was effective as of June 30, 2008. There were no changes in our internal control over financial reporting during the quarter ended June 30, 2008 that have materially affected, or are reasonably likely to materially affect, our internal control over financial reporting. Deloitte & Touche LLP has audited our internal control over financial reporting as of June 30, 2008; their report follows.

KEY COMPONENTS OF INTERNAL CONTROL

LO2 Define internal control and describe its key components.

Internal control is really important. So what exactly do we mean by internal control? Both the concept and attempts to define it have existed for many years. For our purposes, the following is a good definition:

> Internal control is a system developed by a company to provide reasonable assurance of achieving (1) effective and efficient operations, (2) reliable financial reporting, and (3) compliance with laws and regulations.

Several internal control frameworks have been developed that are consistent with this definition. The most widely accepted framework in the United States contains the following five components:

- Control environment
- Risk assessment
- Control activities
- Information and communication system
- Monitoring processes

CONTROL ENVIRONMENT

The control environment is the policies, procedures, and attitudes of the top management and owners of the business. It is often referred to as the "tone at the top." It includes the organization structure, management's philosophy and operating style, integrity and ethical values, and commitment to competent, trustworthy employees. The control environment provides the foundation for all other components of internal control.

RISK ASSESSMENT

Risk assessment is management's process for identifying, analyzing, and responding to its business risks. All businesses face various and changing risks from both external and internal sources. These risks include error and fraud. As part of the risk assessment component of internal control, management must deal with these risks. For example, if a business sells products like computers that are affected by rapid technology changes, its marketing and inventory plans should carefully guard against obsolete inventory. If a business has high employee turnover, its employee screening and training programs should be very thorough and up to date. If a business is growing rapidly, it should regularly review its internal controls to see that they fit the size and activities of the business.

CONTROL ACTIVITIES

Control activities are the policies and procedures established to help management meet its control objectives. Control activities can be classified in various ways. Four types of control activities are particularly important for our purposes.

1. Segregation of duties
2. Authorization procedures and related responsibilities
3. Adequate documents and records
4. Protection of assets and records

Segregation of duties means that:

1. Different employees should be responsible for different parts of a transaction; and
2. Employees who account for transactions should not also have custody of the assets.

For example, one employee should be responsible for ordering goods and another employee should be responsible for issuing the check to pay for them. One employee should be responsible for recording the purchase of goods and another employee should be responsible for receiving and placing the goods in inventory. This segregation of duties provides a built-in check by one employee on another. One employee cannot obtain goods for personal use without being caught by another employee.

Authorization procedures and related responsibilities means that every business activity should be properly authorized. In addition, it should be possible to identify who is responsible for every activity that has occurred. For example, to acquire new equipment, a signed document should authorize the purchase. After the purchase is made, this signed document shows who is responsible for the action.

Adequate documents and records means that accounting documents and records should be used so that all business transactions are recorded. For example, every purchase that occurs should be supported by a document. These documents should be:

- prenumbered,
- used in sequence, and
- subsequently accounted for.

In this way, the business can be sure that it has made a record of each transaction.

Protection of assets and records means that assets and records should be physically and logically protected. For assets, this generally means physical protection. Some examples are vaults for cash, securities and precious gems, or secure storage rooms for inventory. For records, this can mean storing journals, ledgers, and key documents in physically secure locations. In computerized systems, both physical and logical protection are needed. Passwords are a common form of logical protection of data files and processing programs.

INFORMATION AND COMMUNICATION SYSTEM

The information and communication system is the set of procedures, processes, and records used to initiate, process, record, and report the business's transactions. In addition, the system accounts for the related assets and liabilities. Typically, the system has several subcomponents for different business processes, such as:

- sales,
- cash receipts,
- purchases, and
- cash payments.

The journals and ledgers we learned to use in the previous chapters would be part of an information and communication system.

MONITORING PROCESSES

Monitoring processes are the methods used by management to determine that controls are operating properly, and that the controls are modified in response to changes in assessed risks. Figure 7A-2 provides some examples of such processes. Monitoring can be part of the ongoing activities of the business or a separate process. One ongoing activity could be comparisons of financial reports with expectations. If financial reports differ from expectations, it could indicate internal control failures. Follow-up on customer complaints regarding account balances might also uncover internal control weaknesses. The most common form of separate process is the work of the internal audit department. Internal auditors evaluate the design of the internal control system in light of the business risks. They also perform specific tests to determine whether internal controls are operating properly. If a business is not large enough to have an internal audit department, these responsibilities must be assumed by top management.

FIGURE 7A-2 Sample Monitoring Processes

- Comparison of results with expectations
- Review of customer correspondence
- Internal audit

INTERNAL CONTROLS OVER CASH RECEIPTS

LO3 Describe selected internal controls over cash receipts.

The main purposes of internal controls over cash receipts are to make sure that

- all cash received by the business is recorded in the accounts, and
- the cash is promptly deposited in the business bank account.

The exact form of some of these controls will vary depending on whether the cash is received directly from customers for sales, or is received by mail as a collection on account. Some of the key internal controls are shown in Figure 7A-3 and described in the following paragraphs.

FIGURE 7A-3 Sample Controls over Cash Receipts

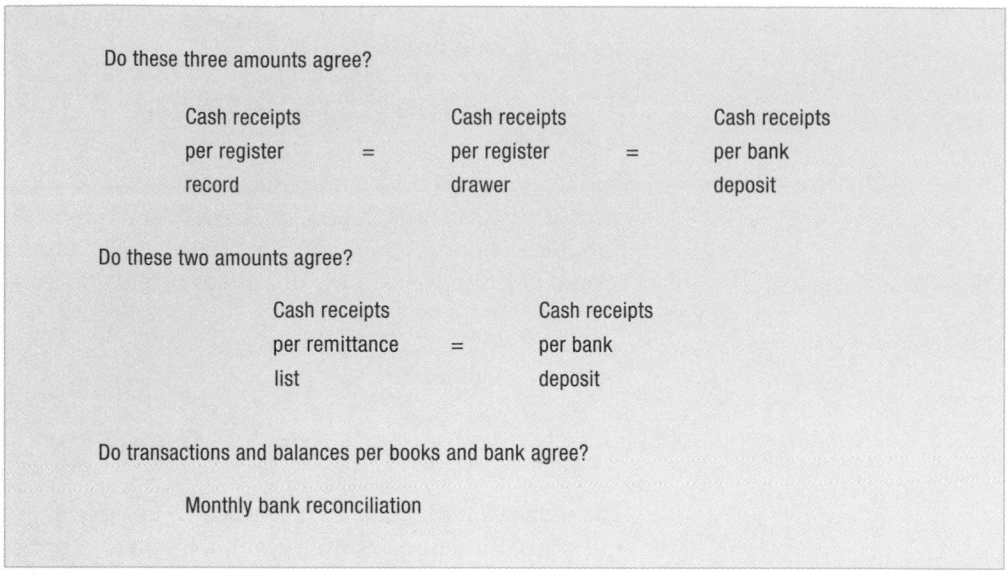

Do these three amounts agree?

Cash receipts per register record	=	Cash receipts per register drawer	=	Cash receipts per bank deposit

Do these two amounts agree?

Cash receipts per remittance list	=	Cash receipts per bank deposit

Do transactions and balances per books and bank agree?

Monthly bank reconciliation

If cash is received directly from customers, the use of a cash register or terminal with a printed receipt is essential. Only authorized employees should be allowed to operate the register. The register should generate an internal record of all transactions entered, including a total of cash receipts. This amount should be reconciled with the actual cash (and checks) in the register drawer. Any differences greater than a small amount to allow for errors in making change should be investigated. All cash receipts should be deposited daily in the business bank account. The total deposited and the total cash receipts according to the register should be reconciled and any differences investigated.

If cash is received as collections on account, the mail room should be supervised and employees who handle the cash (checks) should have no access to the accounting records. One reason for separating the handling of cash from the accounting records is to prevent lapping. **Lapping** means stealing cash received on account from one customer and hiding the theft by applying the cash received on account from another customer to the first customer's account. For example, assume customer A sends a check for $500 as a payment on account and that the employee keeps the $500 for him/herself. This causes customer A's account to be in error by $500. So when customer B makes a $500 payment on account, the employee applies this cash receipt to customer A's account. The dishonest employee must continue lapping the accounts receivable in this manner to continue to conceal the theft.

When the mail is opened, a remittance list should be prepared showing all amounts received and from whom they are received. Checks should be immediately endorsed "For deposit" to the business bank account.

The remittance list is sent to the accounting department for use in recording the collections in the journal and ledgers. The cash is sent to the cash receipts department to deposit in the business bank account. The total of the remittance list and the amount of the bank deposit should be independently verified and any differences investigated.

An additional internal control common to both systems described above is the independent monthly preparation of a bank reconciliation. Procedures for preparing the bank reconciliation are described in Chapter 7. The cash receipts, cash payments, and beginning and ending balances per bank and per books must be reconciled. The reconciliation should be prepared by employees who have no access to cash. Any differences should be investigated.

Many businesses have multiple bank accounts and transfer cash among them. When there are multiple bank accounts, it is possible to overstate the cash balance by engaging in kiting. **Kiting** consists of recording a transfer of cash *into* one bank account in the current period, but not recording the transfer *out of* another bank account until the following period. For example, assume a $1,000 check is written on bank account A on June 30, but not recorded as a cash payment until July 1. This check is deposited in bank account B and recorded as a cash receipt on June 30. By recording the transaction in this manner, the cash balance in both bank accounts includes the $1,000 at June 30. The total cash balance is thus overstated by $1,000 on June 30.

One of the reasons internal controls over cash are so important is that they help businesses manage their cash resources. Naturally, it is important to plan to have sufficient cash to meet current obligations. But it is also important not to allow too much cash to lie idle. Management should carefully monitor and plan for its cash needs. Strong internal controls help with this process.

INTERNAL CONTROLS OVER CASH PAYMENTS

LO4 Describe selected internal controls over cash payments and the use of a voucher system.

The main purpose of internal controls over cash payments is to make sure cash is paid only for goods and services received by the business, consistent with its best interests. To achieve this objective, controls are needed from the beginning of the process of acquiring goods and services through the payment of cash for those goods and services. An effective way to do so is with a voucher system.

VOUCHER SYSTEM

The three control activities described above can be combined to control cash payments by using a **voucher system**. A voucher system is a control technique that requires every acquisition and subsequent payment to be supported by an approved voucher. A **voucher** is a document which shows that an acquisition is proper and that payment is authorized.

THE PURCHASING PROCESS

Figure 7A-4 is a simplified illustration of how the purchasing portion of a voucher system operates. An authorized person or department prepares a purchase requisition to indicate the need for goods. The purchasing department reviews and approves the purchase requisition and prepares a purchase order to send to the supplier. When the goods are received, a receiving report is prepared. A copy of each of these documents is sent to the vouchers payable section in the accounting department.

When the purchase invoice arrives, it is compared with the purchase requisition, purchase order, and receiving report. If the purchase invoice is

- for the goods ordered (purchase requisition and purchase order),
- at the correct price (purchase order),
- and for the correct quantity (receiving report),

then a voucher like the one in Figure 7A-5 on page 273 is prepared. This is the first key control provided by the voucher system. If any aspect of the purchase is improper, it will be caught when the voucher is prepared.

FIGURE 7A-4 Voucher System—Purchasing Process

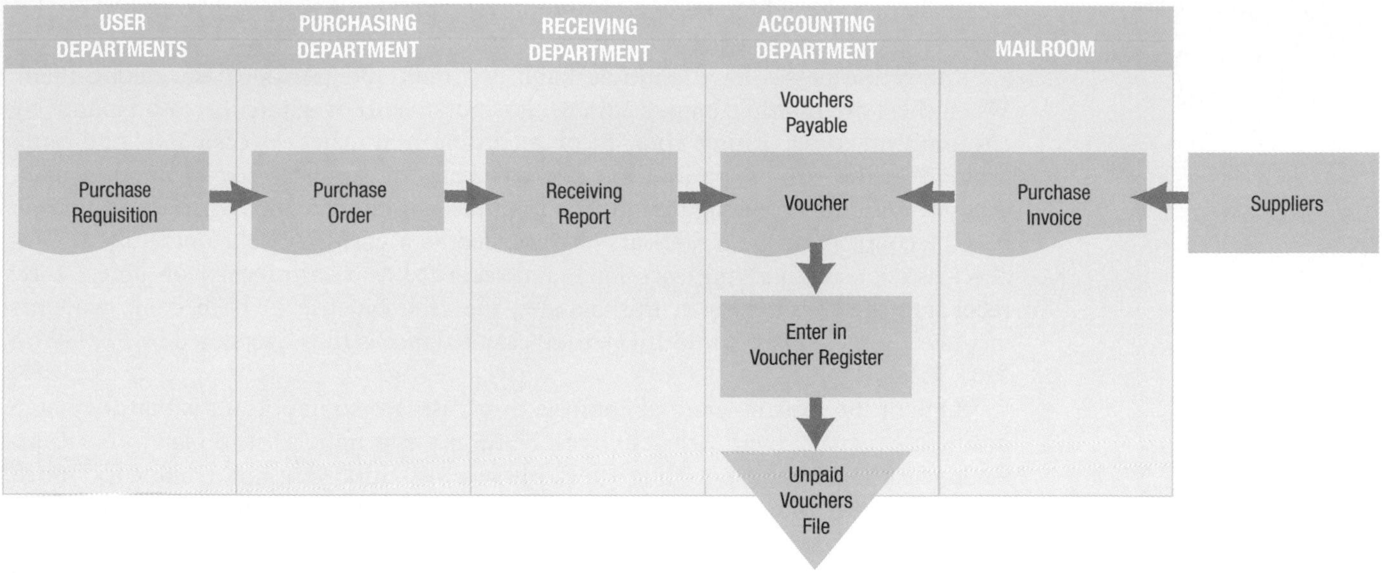

The front of the voucher usually shows the voucher number, date, supplier, and what was purchased. The back indicates the accounts to be debited and the payment date, check number, and amount.

After the voucher is prepared and approved, it is entered in a special journal called a **voucher register**. A voucher register is used to record purchases of all types of assets and services.

After the voucher is entered in the voucher register, the voucher and supporting documents (purchase requisition, purchase order, receiving report, and purchase invoice) are stapled together. This "voucher packet" is then filed in an **unpaid vouchers file**, normally by due date. Alternatively, vouchers can be filed by supplier name. Filing by due date is preferred because this helps management plan for cash needs. It also helps ensure that vouchers are paid on the due date and cash discounts are taken.

The completed voucher provides the basis for paying the supplier's invoice on the due date. This is the second key control provided by the voucher system. No payment may be made without an approved voucher.

Notice how three of the four control activities that are part of an internal control system can be seen in this system.

- *Duties are segregated* because different employees order, receive, and record the purchases.
- *Authorization* is required to order the goods and to prepare the voucher.
- The *documents and records* include purchase requisitions, purchase orders, receiving reports, and vouchers that are prenumbered and accounted for. This means that every recorded purchase is supported by the following five documents:

  1. Voucher
  2. Purchase invoice
  3. Receiving report
  4. Purchase order
  5. Purchase requisition

This provides management with strong assurance that purchasing activities are properly controlled.

LEARNING KEY

The voucher system contains elements of internal control such as segregation of duties, authorization to order the goods and prepare the voucher, and accounting procedures that require prenumbering and accounting for the supporting documents.

FIGURE 7A-5 Voucher

NORTHERN MICRO
1099 E. Louisiana, Indianapolis, IN 46217-3322

Voucher No. **111**

Date 4/11/-- Terms: 1/15, n/30 Due: 4/24/--

To: EZX Corp.
2928 Rhodes Ave.
Chicago, IL 60658

Invoice Date	Invoice No.	Description	Amount
4/9/--	4973	P75 Computers-3	$5,700.00
		Q19 Laser Printers-3	3,000.00
			$8,700.00

Authorization J. Jensen (Supervisor) Prepared By B. Zimmer (Clerk)

Front

Voucher No. **111**

Account Debited	Account No.	Amount	Summary	
Purchases	501	$8,700.00	Invoice	$8,700.00
			Discount	87.00
			Net	$8,613.00

Payment Date 4/24/-- Check No. 437 Amount $8,613.00

Approved Distribution J. G. Payment

Back

THE PAYMENT PROCESS

Figure 7A-6 on page 274 is a simplified illustration of the payment process when a voucher system is used. On the due date, the voucher is pulled from the unpaid vouchers file. The voucher is given to the person responsible for preparing and signing checks (the cashier in this illustration). The cashier reviews each voucher and supporting documents to see that the expenditure is proper. The cashier then prepares and signs the check and sends it to the supplier. It is important for internal control that no check be prepared without a supporting voucher and that the check be mailed as soon as it is signed.

LEARNING KEY

For good internal control of cash payments, it is important for the check to be mailed as soon as it is signed.

Ordinary checks may be used to make payments, but under the voucher system, voucher checks often are used. A **voucher check** is a check with space for entering data about the voucher being paid. Figure 7A-7 on page 274 shows a voucher check used to pay Voucher No. 111 (Figure 7A-5).

The voucher check has two parts:

1. The check itself, which is similar to an ordinary check, and
2. An attached statement, which indicates the invoice being paid and any deductions.

In addition, the voucher check stub identifies the voucher number being paid.

FIGURE 7A-6 Voucher System—Payment Process

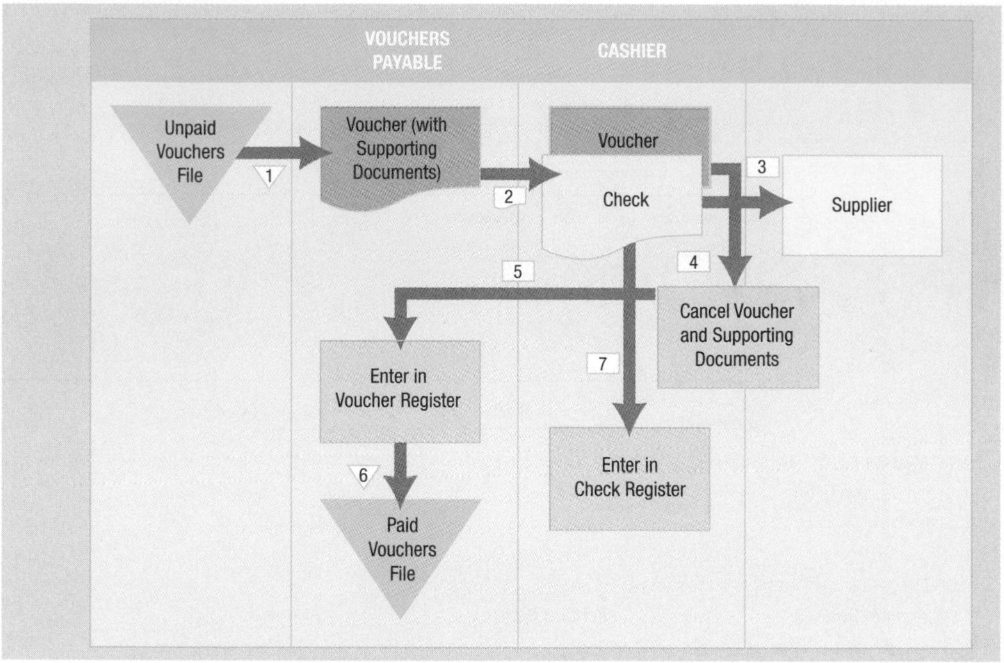

1. Pull Voucher and Supporting Documents; Send to Cashier.
2. Review Voucher and Documents; Prepare and Sign Check.
3. Send Check to Supplier.
4. Cancel Voucher and Documents.
5. Return Voucher and Documents to Vouchers Payable; Record Payment in Voucher Register.
6. File Voucher and Documents in Paid Vouchers File.
7. Record Payment in Check Register.

FIGURE 7A-7 Voucher Check

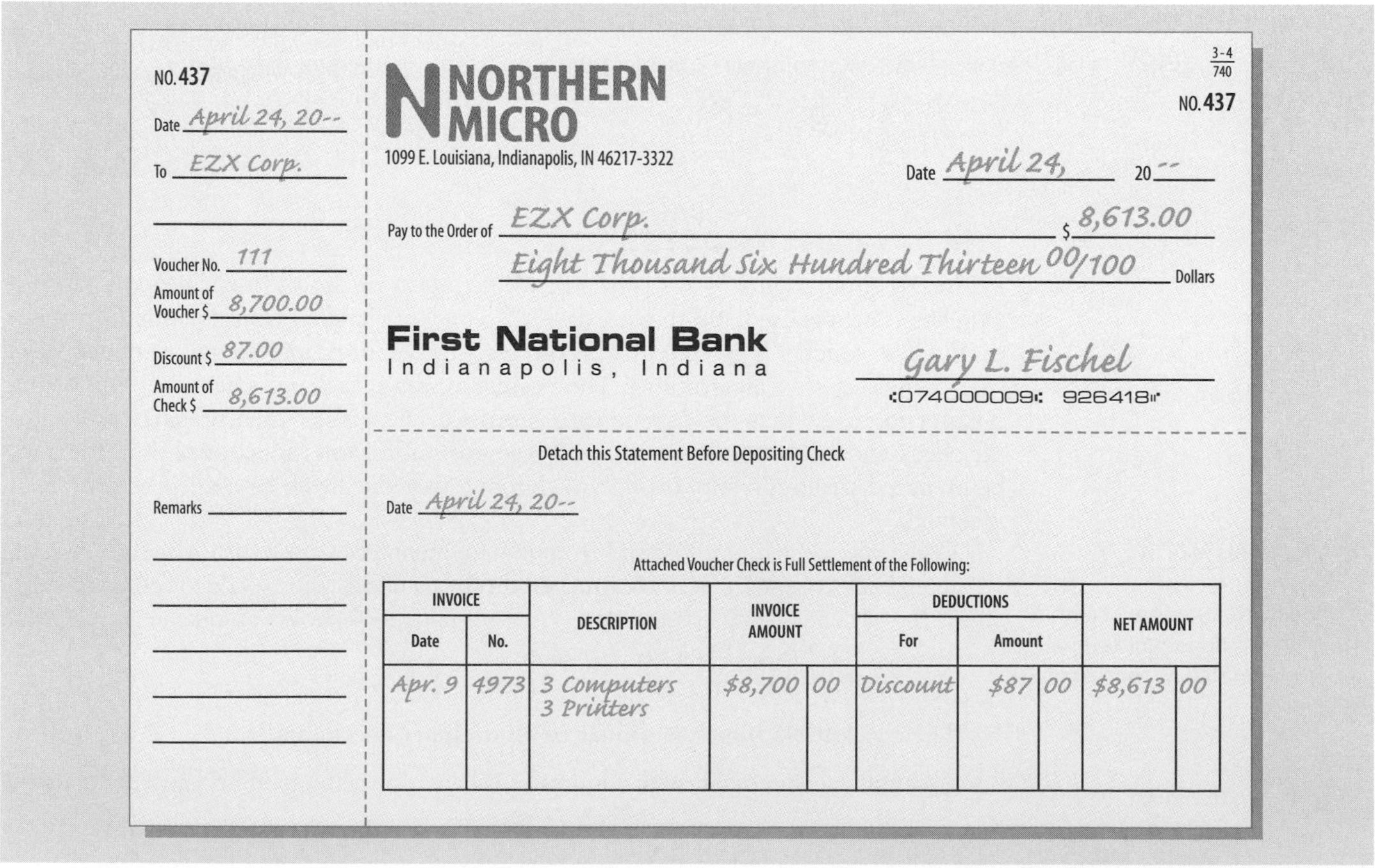

NO. 437
Date *April 24, 20--*
To *EZX Corp.*
Voucher No. *111*
Amount of Voucher $ *8,700.00*
Discount $ *87.00*
Amount of Check $ *8,613.00*
Remarks

NORTHERN MICRO
1099 E. Louisiana, Indianapolis, IN 46217-3322

3-4/740
NO. 437

Date *April 24,* 20*--*

Pay to the Order of *EZX Corp.* $ *8,613.00*
Eight Thousand Six Hundred Thirteen 00/100 Dollars

First National Bank
Indianapolis, Indiana

Gary L. Fischel

⑆074000009⑆ 926418⑈

Detach this Statement Before Depositing Check

Date *April 24, 20--*

Attached Voucher Check is Full Settlement of the Following:

INVOICE		DESCRIPTION	INVOICE AMOUNT		DEDUCTIONS			NET AMOUNT	
Date	No.				For	Amount			
Apr. 9	*4973*	*3 Computers 3 Printers*	*$8,700*	*00*	*Discount*	*$87*	*00*	*$8,613*	*00*

After the voucher has been paid, the cashier completes the "Payment" information and approval on the back of the voucher. The voucher and supporting documents are then canceled to indicate payment. The canceling can be done with a rubber stamp, by perforating, or by simply writing "paid" on all relevant documents. This prevents a voucher from being processed again to create a duplicate payment. The canceled voucher and supporting documents are then returned to the vouchers payable section. The canceled voucher is used to record the payment of the voucher in the voucher register. The voucher and supporting documents are then filed either numerically or by supplier in a **paid vouchers file.** In either case, the numerical sequence should be accounted for to identify possible missing or duplicate vouchers.

A copy of the check is used to enter the payment in a check register. A **check register** is a special journal used to record all checks written in a voucher system. This completes the payment process using the voucher system.

This appendix provides an introduction to internal control concepts and procedures. We have focused on cash here, but internal controls are important in every area of the business. Internal controls can be a very complicated subject, particularly in dealing with computerized operations. More thorough analysis of internal controls is a subject for a more advanced text.

LEARNING OBJECTIVES Key Points to Remember

LO1 Explain the importance of internal control.	Internal controls help assure management that it has reliable records to run the business and prepare needed reports. In addition, SOX requires publicly held companies to report annually on the quality of their internal control system.
LO2 Define internal control and describe its key components.	Internal control is a system developed by a company to provide reasonable assurance of achieving (1) effective and efficient operations, (2) reliable financial reporting, and (3) compliance with laws and regulations. The key components are as follows: • Control environment • Risk assessment • Control activities • Information and communication system • Monitoring processes
LO3 Describe selected internal controls over cash receipts.	If cash is received directly from customers, a cash register should be used. The record of cash receipts per the register should be reconciled with the actual cash in the drawer. If cash is received by mail, a remittance list should be prepared and sent to accounting. The checks should be endorsed immediately "For deposit" and sent to the cash receipts department for deposit in the bank. The remittance list and bank deposit should be independently reconciled.
LO4 Describe selected internal controls over cash payments and the use of a voucher system.	Every acquisition and subsequent payment should be supported by an approved voucher. The voucher should be supported by a purchase requisition, purchase order, receiving report, and purchase invoice. On the due date, checks are written only for approved vouchers, and vouchers and supporting documents are canceled to prevent reuse.

KEY TERMS

check register (275) A special journal used to record all checks written in a voucher system.

kiting (271) Recording a transfer of cash *into* one bank account in the current period, but not recording the transfer *out of* another bank account until the following period.

lapping (270) Stealing cash received on account from one customer and hiding the theft by applying the cash received on account from another customer to the first customer's account.

paid vouchers file (275) A file in which paid vouchers and supporting documents are placed, organized either numerically or by supplier.

publicly held companies (266) Companies whose stock is traded on the major stock exchanges.

unpaid vouchers file (272) A file in which unpaid voucher packets are placed, normally organized by due date.

voucher (271) A document that shows that an acquisition is proper and that payment is authorized.

voucher check (273) A check with space for entering data about the voucher being paid.

voucher register (272) A special journal used to record purchases of all types of assets and services.

voucher system (271) A control technique that requires that every acquisition and subsequent payment be supported by an approved voucher.

REVIEW QUESTIONS

LO1 1. What does Section 404 of the Sarbanes-Oxley Act require?

LO2 2. What is the meaning of internal control?

LO2 3. What are the five components of internal control?

LO2 4. What are the four types of control activities?

LO3 5. What are the main purposes of internal controls over cash receipts?

LO4 6. What is the main purpose of internal controls over cash payments?

LO4 7. What is a voucher system?

LO4 8. In a voucher system, each recorded purchase is supported by what five documents?

LO4 9. What is the purpose of canceling the voucher and supporting documents when a payment is made?

SERIES A EXERCISES

E 7Apx-1A (LO2)

INTERNAL CONTROL COMPONENTS The most widely accepted internal control framework in the United States contains the following five components. Describe each of them.

1. Control environment
2. Risk assessment
3. Control activities
4. Information and communication system
5. Monitoring processes

E 7Apx-2A (LO2)

INTERNAL CONTROL PROCEDURES AND PROCESSES In the left column below, five different internal control procedures and processes are described. In the right column, the five components of internal control are listed. Match the procedures and processes with the components by placing the letter of the appropriate component on the blank provided.

1. ____ A company publishes and uses a code of ethical conduct.
2. ____ The accounting system automatically generates monthly sales reports for each product line.
3. ____ A company has established an internal audit department.
4. ____ All purchases above $5,000 must be approved in writing by the head of the purchasing department.
5. ____ A company invests heavily in employee training programs because of the technical nature of its products.

a. Control environment
b. Risk assessment
c. Control activities
d. Information and communication system
e. Monitoring processes

E 7Apx-3A (LO4)

PURCHASING PROCESS USING A VOUCHER SYSTEM In the following flowchart, identify the documents, records, and procedures that illustrate the purchasing process in a voucher system.

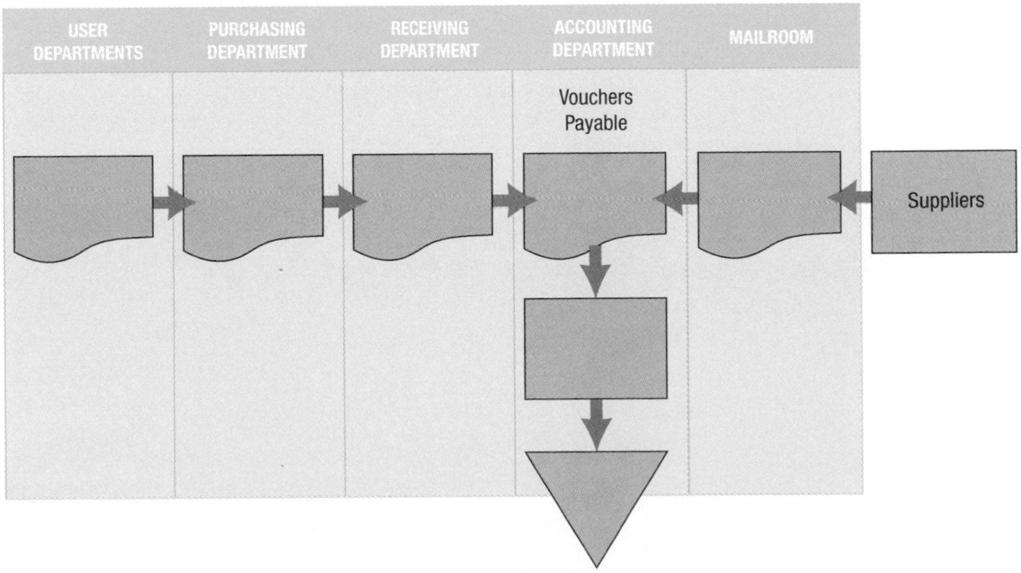

SERIES A PROBLEM

P 7Apx-4A (LO2/3/4)

USING INTERNAL CONTROLS TO PREVENT ERRORS. The following misstatements occurred in the records of ICW Company. For each misstatement, suggest a control to prevent it from happening.

1. A bill from a supplier was paid even though the shipment was not received.
2. A supplier's bill was paid twice for the same purchase.
3. A plant employee increased his pay rate by entering the computer system using a plant terminal and altering the payroll records.
4. The cash receipts clerk kept a portion of the regular bank deposits for personal use and concealed the theft by manipulating the monthly bank reconciliation she prepared.

SERIES B EXERCISES

E 7Apx-1B (LO2)

INTERNAL CONTROL COMPONENTS Four types of internal control activities are listed below. Describe each of them.

1. Segregation of duties
2. Authorization procedures and related responsibilities
3. Adequate documents and records
4. Protection of assets and records

E 7Apx-2B (LO2)

INTERNAL CONTROL PROCEDURES AND PROCESSES In the left column below, four different internal control procedures are described. In the right column, the four basic types of internal control activities are listed. Match the procedures with the activities by placing the letter of the appropriate activity on the blank provided.

1. ____ All passwords for access to sales and inventory databases must be changed monthly.
2. ____ All new hires must be approved by the department of human resources.
3. ____ All sales invoices are prenumbered and accounted for.
4. ____ Bank reconciliations are prepared by an employee with no other cash responsibilities.

a. Segregation of duties
b. Authorization procedures and related responsibilities
c. Adequate documents and records
d. Protection of assets and records

E 7Apx-3B **(LO4)**

PAYMENT PROCESS USING A VOUCHER SYSTEM In the following flowchart, identify the documents, records, and procedures that illustrate the payment process using a voucher system.

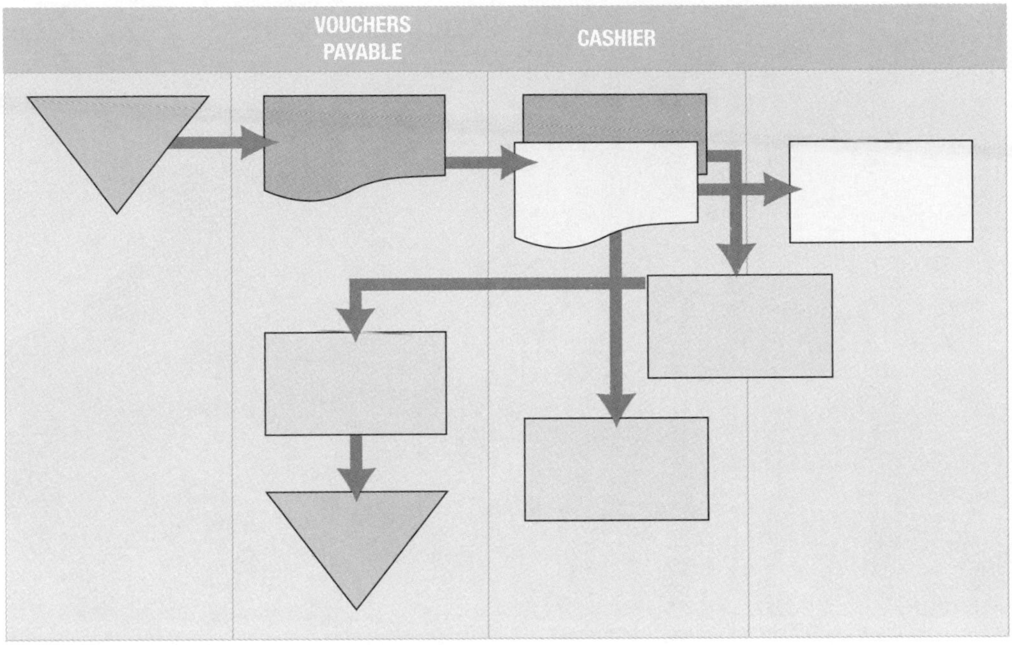

SERIES B PROBLEM

P 7Apx-4B **(LO2/3/4)**

USING INTERNAL CONTROLS TO PREVENT ERRORS The following misstatements occurred in the records of MW Company. For each misstatement, suggest a control to prevent it from happening.

1. A bill from a supplier was paid for goods that had not been ordered.
2. A supplier's bill for 50 boxes of materials was paid even though only 40 boxes were received.
3. Expensive product components were stolen by an employee from a loading dock area after hours.
4. No bill was sent to a customer for a shipment because the shipping document was lost after the shipment was made.

Chapter 8

EJLA/DREAMSTIME

LEARNING OBJECTIVES

Careful study of this chapter should enable you to:

LO1 Distinguish between employees and independent contractors.

LO2 Calculate employee earnings and deductions.

LO3 Describe and prepare payroll records.

LO4 Account for employee earnings and deductions.

LO5 Describe various payroll record-keeping methods.

Payroll Accounting: Employee Earnings and Deductions

Intechra provides computer hardware, software, and database disposal and recycling services. The company has grown rapidly in response to environmental and privacy concerns about the use of IT assets. Founded in 2004, Intechra has already become the largest electronics life cycle management company in the United States. The company currently recycles more than 200,000 units per month. With more than 600 employees, it offers both on-site services and secure transport of assets to its locations. The recycling function provides companies with value recovery for used IT products. And this enables other users to acquire name-brand computer equipment at greatly reduced prices. Consistent with environmental concerns, the entire recycling operation is performed under a zero-landfill policy for e-waste.

A company such as Intechra requires a variety of employees—from highly technical to basic materials handling staff—with very different rates of pay. For legal and operating efficiency reasons, a company must accurately track and control its payroll costs. It needs to know not only what to pay its people, but also what taxes to withhold from their wages. In this chapter, you will learn how to identify and account for payroll expenses for multiple employees.

The only contact most of us have with payroll is receiving a paycheck. Few of us have seen the large amount of record keeping needed to produce that paycheck.

Employers maintain complete payroll accounting records for two reasons. First, payroll costs are major expenditures for most companies. Payroll accounting records provide data useful in analyzing and controlling these expenditures. Second, federal, state, and local laws require employers to keep payroll records. Companies must accumulate payroll data both for the business as a whole and for each employee.

There are two major types of payroll taxes: those paid by the employee and those paid by the employer. In this chapter, we discuss employee taxes. In Chapter 9, we address payroll taxes paid by the employer.

EMPLOYEES AND INDEPENDENT CONTRACTORS

LO1 Distinguish between employees and independent contractors.

Not every person who performs services for a business is considered an employee. An **employee** works under the control and direction of an employer. Examples include secretaries, maintenance workers, salesclerks, and plant supervisors. In contrast, an **independent contractor** performs a service for a fee and does not work under the control and direction of the company paying for the service. Examples of independent contractors include public accountants, real estate agents, and lawyers.

The distinction between an employee and an independent contractor is important for payroll purposes. Government laws and regulations regarding payroll are much more complex for employees than for independent contractors. Employers must deduct certain taxes, maintain payroll records, and file numerous reports for all employees. Only one form (Form 1099) must be filed for independent contractors. The payroll accounting procedures described in this chapter apply only to employer/employee relationships.

EMPLOYEE EARNINGS AND DEDUCTIONS

LO2 Calculate employee earnings and deductions.

Three steps are required to determine how much to pay an employee for a pay period:

1. Calculate total earnings.
2. Determine the amounts of deductions.
3. Subtract deductions from total earnings to compute net pay.

SALARIES AND WAGES

Compensation for managerial or administrative services usually is called **salary**. A salary normally is expressed in biweekly (every two weeks), monthly, or annual terms. Compensation for skilled or unskilled labor usually is referred to as **wages**. Wages ordinarily are expressed in terms of hours, weeks, or units produced. The terms "salaries" and "wages" often are used interchangeably in practice.

The **Fair Labor Standards Act (FLSA)** requires employers to pay overtime at 1½ times the regular rate to any hourly employee who works over 40 hours in a week. Some companies pay a higher rate for hours worked on Saturday or Sunday, but this is not required by the FLSA. Some salaried employees are exempt from the FLSA rules and are not paid overtime.

COMPUTING TOTAL EARNINGS

Compensation usually is based on the time worked during the payroll period. Sometimes it is based on sales or units of output during the period. When compensation is based on time, a record must be kept of the time worked by each employee. Time cards (Figure 8-1) are helpful for this purpose. In large businesses with computer-based timekeeping systems, plastic cards or badges with special magnetic strips or bar codes (Figure 8-2) can be used. Employees use the cards to clock in and out at terminals with card readers. For increased security, these terminals also are available with fingerprint readers.

FIGURE 8-1 Time Card

Westly, Inc.
Time Card — Hourly Payroll

Emp. Name: Kuzmik, Helen   Base Dept.: Sales
Emp. ID: 359-47-1138   Pay Per. End: 12/19/20--

					HOURS			
Date	Time In	Time Out	Time In	Time Out	Reg	OT	DT	Total
12/13	8:00	12:30	13:00	17:30	8	1		9
12/14	8:00	12:30	13:00	17:30	8	1		9
12/15	8:00	12:30	13:00	17:30	8	1		9
12/16	8:00	12:30	13:00	17:30	8	1		9
12/17	8:00	12:30	13:00	17:30	8	1		9
12/18	10:00	16:00				6		6
12/19	13:00	17:00					4	4
TOTAL					40	11	4	55

Remarks

Approval: TM
Dept. Head

To illustrate the computation of total earnings, look at the time card of Helen Kuzmik in Figure 8-1. The card shows that Kuzmik worked 55 hours for the week.

Regular hours	40 hours
Overtime	11
Double time	4
Total hours worked	55 hours

Kuzmik's regular rate of pay is $12 per hour. She is paid 1½ times the regular rate for hours in excess of 8 on Monday through Friday and any hours worked on

FIGURE 8-2 Time Cards and Clock Terminal

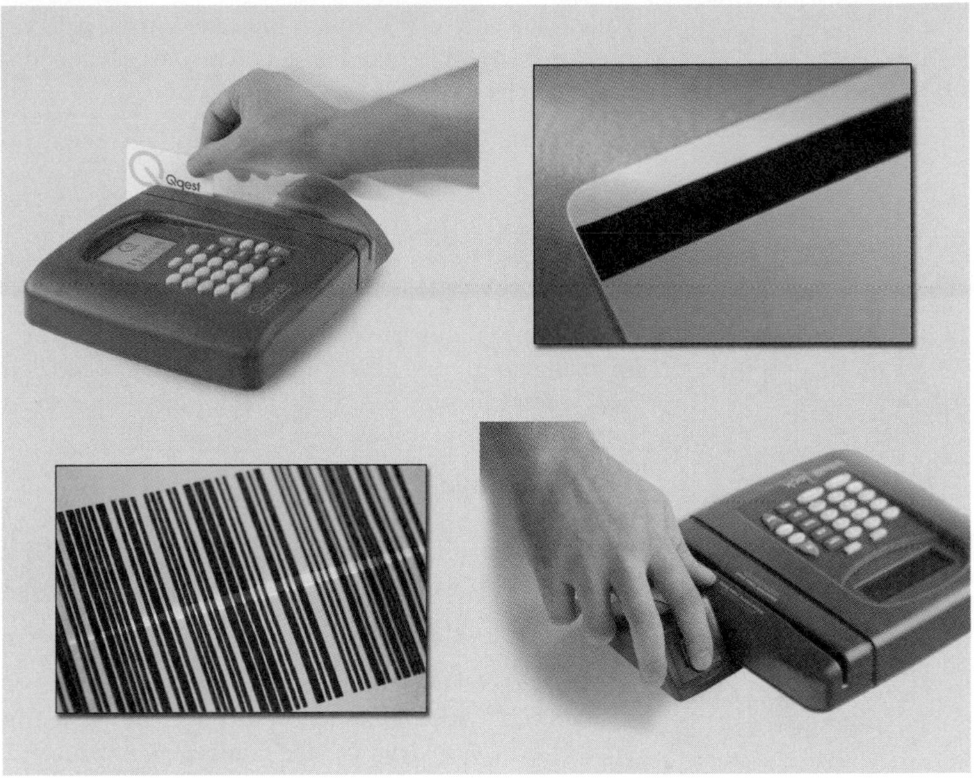

GETTY IMAGES/PHOTODISC, TIMECLOCK PHOTOS – COURTESY OF Qqest Software; www.qqesttime.com

Saturday, and twice the regular rate for hours on Sunday. Kuzmik's total earnings for the week ended December 19 are computed as follows:

40 hours × \$12	\$480
11 hours × \$18 (1½ × \$12 = \$18)	198
4 hours (on Sunday) × \$24 (2 × \$12 = \$24)	96
Total earnings for the week	\$774

Salaried employees who are not exempt from the FSLA rules may also be entitled to premium pay for overtime. If this is the case, it is necessary to compute the regular hourly rate of pay before computing the overtime rate. To illustrate, assume that Linda Swaney has a salary of \$2,288 a month plus 1½ times the regular hourly rate for hours in excess of 40 per week. Swaney's overtime rate of pay is computed as follows:

There are 52 weeks in each year but not 4 weeks in each month. That is why monthly salaries must be annualized in order to determine the hourly rate.

\$2,288 × 12 months	\$27,456 annual pay
\$27,456 ÷ 52 weeks	\$528.00 pay per week
\$528.00 ÷ 40 hours	\$13.20 pay per regular hour
\$13.20 × 1½	\$19.80 overtime pay per hour

If Swaney worked 50 hours during the week ended December 19, her total earnings for the week would be computed as follows:

40 hours × \$13.20	\$528.00
10 hours × \$19.80	198.00
Total earnings for the week	\$726.00

DEDUCTIONS FROM TOTAL EARNINGS

An employee's total earnings are called **gross pay**. Various deductions are made from gross pay to yield take-home or **net pay**. Deductions from gross pay fall into three major categories:

1. Federal (and possibly state and city) income tax withholding
2. Employee FICA tax withholding
3. Voluntary deductions

Income Tax Withholding

Federal law requires employers to withhold certain amounts from the total earnings of each employee. These withholdings are applied toward the payment of the employee's federal income tax. Four factors determine the amount to be withheld from an employee's gross pay each pay period:

1. Total earnings
2. Marital status
3. Number of withholding allowances claimed
4. Length of the pay period

Withholding Allowances. Each employee is required to furnish the employer an Employee's Withholding Allowance Certificate, Form W-4 (Figure 8-3). The marital status of the employee and the number of allowances claimed on Form W-4 determine the dollar amount of earnings subject to withholding. A **withholding allowance** exempts a specific dollar amount of an employee's gross pay from federal income tax withholding. In general, each employee is permitted one personal withholding allowance, one for a spouse who does not also claim an allowance, and one for each dependent.

FIGURE 8-3 Employee's Withholding Allowance Certificate (Form W-4)

Form **W-4**
Department of the Treasury
Internal Revenue Service

Employee's Withholding Allowance Certificate

► **Whether you are entitled to claim a certain number of allowances or exemption from withholding is subject to review by the IRS. Your employer may be required to send a copy of this form to the IRS.**

OMB No. 1545-0074
20--

1 Type or print your first name and middle initial. Ken M. | Last name Istone | 2 Your social security number 393 58 8194

Home address (number and street or rural route) 1546 Swallow Drive | 3 ☐ Single ☒ Married ☐ Married, but withhold at higher Single rate.
Note. *If married, but legally separated, or spouse is a nonresident alien, check the "Single" box.*

City or town, state, and ZIP code St. Louis, MO 63144-4752 | 4 **If your last name differs from that shown on your social security card, check here. You must call 1-800-772-1213 for a replacement card.** ► ☐

5 Total number of allowances you are claiming (from line **H** above **or** from the applicable worksheet on page 2) . . . 5 | 4
6 Additional amount, if any, you want withheld from each paycheck . . . . 6 | $
7 I claim exemption from withholding for 20--, and I certify that I meet **both** of the following conditions for exemption.
- Last year I had a right to a refund of **all** federal income tax withheld because I had **no** tax liability **and**
- This year I expect a refund of **all** federal income tax withheld because I expect to have **no** tax liability.

If you meet both conditions, write "Exempt" here . . . . ► 7

Under penalties of perjury, I declare that I have examined this certificate and to the best of my knowledge and belief, it is true, correct, and complete.

Employee's signature
(Form is not valid unless you sign it.) ► Ken M. Istone   **Date** ► January 3, 20--

8 Employer's name and address (Employer: Complete lines 8 and 10 only if sending to the IRS.) | 9 Office code (optional) | 10 Employer identification number (EIN)

For Privacy Act and Paperwork Reduction Act Notice, see page 2.   Cat. No. 10220Q   Form **W-4** (20--)

A withholding certificate completed by Ken Istone is shown in Figure 8-3. Istone is married, has a spouse who does not claim an allowance, and has two dependent children. On line 5 of the W-4 form, Istone claims four allowances, calculated as follows:

Personal allowance	1
Spouse allowance	1
Allowances for dependents	2
Total withholding allowances	4

A large number of IRS publications and forms can be found at the IRS Web site: http://www.irs.gov

Wage-Bracket Method. Employers generally use the **wage-bracket method** to determine the amount of tax to be withheld from an employee's pay. The employee's gross pay for a specific time period is traced into the appropriate wage-bracket table provided by the Internal Revenue Service (IRS). These tables cover various time periods, and there are separate tables for single and married taxpayers. Copies are provided in *Circular E—Employer's Tax Guide*, which may be obtained from any local IRS office or at the IRS Internet site.

Portions of weekly income tax wage-bracket withholding tables for single and married persons are illustrated in Figure 8-4. Assume that Ken Istone (who claims 4 allowances) had gross earnings of $545 for the week ending December 19, 20--. The amount to withhold for Istone is determined by using the following steps, as shown in Figure 8-4 for married persons (on page 287):

LEARNING KEY

1. Find the row for wages.
2. Find the column for withholding allowances.
3. Find the amount where they cross.

1. Find the row for wages of "at least $540, but less than $550."
2. Find the column headed "4 withholding allowances."
3. Where the row and column cross, $11.00 is given as the amount to be withheld.

For state or city income taxes, withholding generally is handled in one of two ways: (1) forms and tables similar to those provided by the IRS are used or (2) an amount equal to a percentage of the federal withholding amount is withheld.

Employee FICA Tax Withholding

When the Social Security program was established in 1937, the tax was 1% on earnings up to $3,000 per year!

The Federal Insurance Contributions Act requires employers to withhold **FICA taxes** from employees' earnings. FICA taxes include amounts for both Social Security and Medicare programs. Social Security provides pensions and disability benefits. Medicare provides health insurance.

Congress has frequently changed the tax rates and the maximum amounts of earnings subject to FICA taxes. For this text, we assume the Social Security rate is 6.2% on maximum earnings of $106,800. The Medicare rate is 1.45% on all earnings; there is no maximum.

To illustrate the calculation of FICA taxes, assume the following earnings for Sarah Cadrain:

	Earnings	
Pay Period	Week	Year-to-Date
Dec. 6–12	$2,000	$106,140
Dec. 13–19	$1,660	$107,800

For the week of December 6–12, FICA taxes on Cadrain's earnings would be:

Gross Pay	×	Tax Rate		=	Tax
$2,000		Social Security	6.2%		$124.00
		Medicare	1.45%		29.00
					$153.00

FIGURE 8-4 Federal Withholding Tax Table: Single Persons

SINGLE Persons—WEEKLY Payroll Period

(For Wages Paid in 2009)

If the wages are–		And the number of withholding allowances claimed is–										
At least	But less than	0	1	2	3	4	5	6	7	8	9	10
		The amount of income tax to be withheld is–										
$200	$210	$16	$8	$1	$0	$0	$0	$0	$0	$0	$0	$0
210	220	17	9	2	0	0	0	0	0	0	0	0
220	230	19	10	3	0	0	0	0	0	0	0	0
230	240	20	11	4	0	0	0	0	0	0	0	0
240	250	22	12	5	0	0	0	0	0	0	0	0
250	260	23	13	6	0	0	0	0	0	0	0	0
260	270	25	14	7	0	0	0	0	0	0	0	0
270	280	26	16	8	1	0	0	0	0	0	0	0
280	290	28	17	9	2	0	0	0	0	0	0	0
290	300	29	19	10	3	0	0	0	0	0	0	0
300	310	31	20	11	4	0	0	0	0	0	0	0
310	320	32	22	12	5	0	0	0	0	0	0	0
320	330	34	23	13	6	0	0	0	0	0	0	0
330	340	35	25	14	7	0	0	0	0	0	0	0
340	350	37	26	16	8	1	0	0	0	0	0	0
350	360	38	28	17	9	2	0	0	0	0	0	0
360	370	40	29	19	10	3	0	0	0	0	0	0
370	380	41	31	20	11	4	0	0	0	0	0	0
380	390	43	32	22	12	5	0	0	0	0	0	0
390	400	44	34	23	13	6	0	0	0	0	0	0
400	410	46	35	25	14	7	0	0	0	0	0	0
410	420	47	37	26	16	8	1	0	0	0	0	0
420	430	49	38	28	17	9	2	0	0	0	0	0
430	440	50	40	29	19	10	3	0	0	0	0	0
440	450	52	41	31	20	11	4	0	0	0	0	0
450	460	53	43	32	22	12	5	0	0	0	0	0
460	470	55	44	34	23	13	6	0	0	0	0	0
470	480	56	46	35	25	14	7	0	0	0	0	0
480	490	58	47	37	26	16	8	1	0	0	0	0
490	500	59	49	48	28	17	9	2	0	0	0	0
500	510	61	50	40	29	19	10	3	0	0	0	0
510	520	62	52	41	31	20	11	4	0	0	0	0
520	530	64	53	43	32	22	12	5	0	0	0	0
530	540	65	55	44	34	23	13	6	0	0	0	0
540	550	67	56	46	35	25	14	7	0	0	0	0
550	560	68	58	47	37	26	16	8	1	0	0	0
560	570	70	59	49	38	28	17	9	2	0	0	0
570	580	71	61	50	40	29	19	10	3	0	0	0
580	590	73	62	52	41	31	20	11	4	0	0	0
590	600	74	64	53	43	32	22	12	5	0	0	0
600	610	76	65	55	44	34	23	13	6	0	0	0
610	620	77	67	56	46	35	25	14	7	0	0	0
620	630	79	68	58	47	37	26	15	8	1	0	0
630	640	80	70	59	49	38	28	17	9	2	0	0
640	650	82	71	61	50	40	29	18	10	3	0	0
650	660	83	73	62	52	41	31	20	11	4	0	0
660	670	85	74	64	53	43	32	21	12	5	0	0
670	680	86	76	65	55	44	34	23	13	6	0	0
680	690	88	77	67	56	46	35	24	14	7	0	0
690	700	91	79	68	58	47	37	26	15	8	1	0
700	710	93	80	70	59	49	38	27	17	9	2	0
710	720	96	82	71	61	50	40	29	18	10	3	0
720	730	98	83	73	62	52	41	30	20	11	4	0
730	740	101	85	74	64	53	43	32	21	12	5	0
740	750	103	86	76	65	55	44	33	23	13	6	0
750	760	106	88	77	67	56	46	35	24	14	7	0
760	770	108	91	79	68	58	47	36	26	15	8	1
770	780	111	93	80	70	59	49	38	27	17	9	2
780	790	113	96	82	71	61	50	39	29	18	10	3
790	800	116	98	83	73	62	52	41	30	20	11	4

FIGURE 8-4 Federal Withholding Tax Table: (*concluded*) Married Persons

MARRIED Persons—WEEKLY Payroll Period

(For Wages Paid in 2009)

If the wages are–		And the number of withholding allowances claimed is–										
At least	But less than	0	1	2	3	(2) 4	5	6	7	8	9	10
		The amount of income tax to be withheld is–										
$200	$210	$5	$0	$0	$0	$0	$0	$0	$0	$0	$0	$0
210	220	6	0	0	0	0	0	0	0	0	0	0
220	230	7	0	0	0	0	0	0	0	0	0	0
230	240	8	1	0	0	0	0	0	0	0	0	0
240	250	9	2	0	0	0	0	0	0	0	0	0
250	260	10	3	0	0	0	0	0	0	0	0	0
260	270	11	4	0	0	0	0	0	0	0	0	0
270	280	12	5	0	0	0	0	0	0	0	0	0
280	290	13	6	0	0	0	0	0	0	0	0	0
290	300	14	7	0	0	0	0	0	0	0	0	0
300	310	15	8	1	0	0	0	0	0	0	0	0
310	320	16	9	2	0	0	0	0	0	0	0	0
320	330	17	10	3	0	0	0	0	0	0	0	0
330	340	18	11	4	0	0	0	0	0	0	0	0
340	350	19	12	5	0	0	0	0	0	0	0	0
350	360	20	13	6	0	0	0	0	0	0	0	0
360	370	21	14	7	0	0	0	0	0	0	0	0
370	380	22	15	8	1	0	0	0	0	0	0	0
380	390	23	16	9	2	0	0	0	0	0	0	0
390	400	24	17	10	3	0	0	0	0	0	0	0
400	410	25	18	11	4	0	0	0	0	0	0	0
410	420	26	19	12	5	0	0	0	0	0	0	0
420	430	27	20	13	6	0	0	0	0	0	0	0
430	440	28	21	14	7	0	0	0	0	0	0	0
440	450	29	22	15	8	1	0	0	0	0	0	0
450	460	30	23	16	9	2	0	0	0	0	0	0
460	470	31	24	17	10	3	0	0	0	0	0	0
470	480	33	25	18	11	4	0	0	0	0	0	0
480	490	34	26	19	12	5	0	0	0	0	0	0
490	500	35	27	20	13	6	0	0	0	0	0	0
500	510	37	28	21	14	7	0	0	0	0	0	0
510	520	39	29	22	15	8	1	0	0	0	0	0
520	530	40	30	23	16	9	2	0	0	0	0	0
530	540	42	31	24	17	10	3	0	0	0	0	0
(1) 540	550	43	33	25	18	(3) 11	4	0	0	0	0	0
550	560	45	34	26	19	12	5	0	0	0	0	0
560	570	46	36	27	20	13	6	0	0	0	0	0
570	580	48	37	28	21	14	7	0	0	0	0	0
580	590	49	39	29	22	15	8	1	0	0	0	0
590	600	51	40	30	23	16	9	2	0	0	0	0
600	610	52	42	31	24	17	10	3	0	0	0	0
610	620	54	43	33	25	18	11	4	0	0	0	0
620	630	55	45	34	26	19	12	5	0	0	0	0
630	640	57	46	36	27	20	13	6	0	0	0	0
640	650	58	48	37	28	21	14	7	0	0	0	0
650	660	60	49	39	29	22	15	8	1	0	0	0
660	670	61	51	40	30	23	16	9	2	0	0	0
670	680	63	52	42	31	24	17	10	3	0	0	0
680	690	64	54	43	33	25	18	11	4	0	0	0
690	700	66	55	45	34	26	19	12	5	0	0	0
1,300	1,310	157	147	136	126	115	105	94	84	73	63	52
1,310	1,320	159	148	138	127	117	106	96	85	75	64	54
1,320	1,330	160	150	139	129	118	108	97	87	76	66	55
1,330	1,340	162	151	141	130	120	109	99	88	78	67	57
1,340	1,350	163	153	142	132	121	111	100	90	79	69	58
1,350	1,360	165	154	144	133	123	112	102	91	81	70	60
1,360	1,370	166	156	145	135	124	114	103	93	82	72	61
1,370	1,380	168	157	147	136	126	115	105	94	84	73	63
1,380	1,390	169	159	148	138	127	117	106	96	85	75	64
1,390	1,400	171	160	150	139	129	118	108	97	87	76	66

During the week of December 13–19, Cadrain's earnings for the calendar year went over the $106,800 Social Security maximum by $1,000 ($107,800 – $106,800). Therefore, $1,000 of her $1,660 earnings for the week would not be subject to the Social Security tax.

Year-to-date earnings	$107,800
Social Security maximum	106,800
Amount not subject to Social Security tax	$ 1,000

The Social Security tax on Cadrain's December 13–19 earnings would be:

Gross pay	$1,660.00
Amount not subject to Social Security tax	1,000.00
Amount subject to Social Security tax	$ 660.00
Tax rate	6.2%
Social Security tax	$ 40.92

Since there is no Medicare maximum, all of Cadrain's December 13–19 earnings would be subject to the Medicare tax.

Gross pay	$1,660.00
Tax rate	1.45%
Medicare tax	$ 24.07

The total FICA tax would be:

Social Security tax	$40.92
Medicare tax	24.07
Total FICA tax	$64.99

For the rest of the calendar year through December 31, Cadrain's earnings would be subject only to Medicare taxes.

Voluntary Deductions

In addition to the mandatory deductions from employee earnings for income and FICA taxes, many other deductions are possible. These deductions are usually voluntary and depend on specific agreements between the employee and employer. Examples of voluntary deductions are:

1. U.S. savings bond purchases
2. Health insurance premiums
3. Credit union deposits
4. Pension plan payments
5. Charitable contributions

> If you use computer software, such as Microsoft® Excel, to create a payroll register, you may notice a column or row that is off by a penny or two. Usually, this occurs in the Social Security and Medicare tax calculations. These are not errors. They are simply differences caused when rounding numbers to the nearest penny.

COMPUTING NET PAY

To compute an employee's net pay for the period, subtract all tax withholdings and voluntary deductions from the gross pay. Ken Istone's net pay for the week ended December 19 would be calculated as follows:

Gross pay		$545.00
Deductions:		
Federal income tax withholding	$11.00	
Social Security tax withholding	33.79	
Medicare tax withholding	7.90	
Health insurance premiums	10.00	
Total deductions		62.69
Net pay		$482.31

U REVU

Complete U REVU-1 on **page 303** to test your basic understanding of LO2.

PAYROLL RECORDS

LO3 Describe and prepare payroll records.

Payroll records should provide the following information for each employee:

1. Name, address, occupation, social security number, marital status, and number of withholding allowances
2. Gross amount of earnings, date of payment, and period covered by each payroll
3. Gross amount of earnings accumulated for the year
4. Amounts of taxes and other items withheld

Three types of payroll records are used to accumulate this information:

1. The payroll register
2. The payroll check with earnings statement attached
3. The employee earnings record

These records can be prepared by either manual or automated methods. The illustrations in this chapter are based on a manual system. The forms and procedures illustrated are equally applicable to both manual and automated systems.

PAYROLL REGISTER

A **payroll register** is a form used to assemble the data required at the end of each payroll period. Figure 8-5 on pages 290 and 291 illustrates Westly, Inc.'s payroll register for the payroll period ended December 19, 20--. Detailed information on earnings, taxable earnings, deductions, and net pay is provided for each employee. Column headings for deductions may vary, depending on which deductions are commonly used by a particular business. The sources of key information in the register are indicated in Figure 8-5.

A good example of a deduction column that could be added is State Income Tax. In the payroll register in Figure 8-5, the column could be inserted immediately after Federal Income Tax.

Note four important things about Westly's payroll register:

1. The first $106,800 of earnings of each employee is subject to Social Security tax. The Cumulative Total column, under the Earnings category, shows that Sarah Cadrain has exceeded this limit during the period. Thus, only $660 of her earnings for this pay period is subject to Social Security tax, as shown in the Taxable Earnings columns.
2. There are two Taxable Earnings columns: Unemployment Compensation and Social Security. Only one of these columns (Social Security) is needed to determine employee taxes. Both columns are shown here because they are a standard part of a payroll register. The Unemployment Compensation column is needed to determine this payroll tax on employers. The Social Security column is needed to determine both employee and employer Social Security taxes. The two employer taxes (Unemployment Compensation and Social Security) are discussed in Chapter 9.
3. Regular deductions are made from employee earnings for federal income tax and Social Security and Medicare taxes.

FIGURE 8-5 Payroll Register (left side)

PAYROLL

	NAME	ALLOWANCES	MARITAL STATUS	EARNINGS: REGULAR	EARNINGS: OVERTIME	EARNINGS: TOTAL	EARNINGS: CUMULATIVE TOTAL	TAXABLE EARNINGS: UNEMPLOYMENT COMPENSATION	TAXABLE EARNINGS: SOCIAL SECURITY	
1	Cadrain, Sarah	4	M	1,600.00	60.00	1,660.00	107,800.00	0.00	660.00	1
2	Gruder, James	1	S	760.00	140.00	900.00	43,400.00	0.00	900.00	2
3	Istone, Ken	4	M	545.00		545.00	27,025.00	0.00	545.00	3
4	Kuzmik, Helen	2	M	480.00	294.00	774.00	31,000.00	0.00	774.00	4
5	Lee, Hoseoup	3	M	440.00		440.00	22,340.00	0.00	440.00	5
6	Swaney, Linda	2	S	528.00	198.00	726.00	27,500.00	0.00	726.00	6
7	Tucci, Paul	3	M	490.00		490.00	25,050.00	0.00	490.00	7
8	Wiles, Harry	1	S	300.00		300.00	6,300.00	300.00	300.00	8
9				5,143.00	692.00	5,835.00	290,415.00	300.00	4,835.00	9
10										10

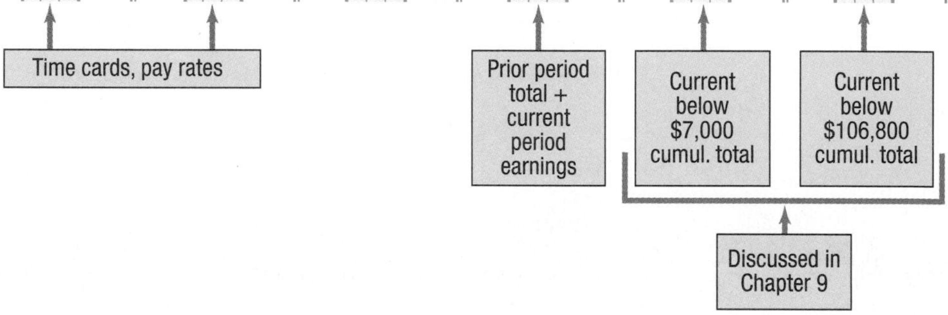

4. Voluntary deductions are made for health insurance and United Way contributions, based on agreements with individual employees.

After the data for each employee have been entered, the amount columns in the payroll register should be totaled and the totals verified as follows:

Regular earnings		$5,143.00
Overtime earnings		692.00
Gross earnings		$5,835.00
Deductions:		
Federal income tax	$476.00	
Social Security tax	299.77	
Medicare tax	84.61	
Health insurance premiums	46.00	
United Way	40.00	946.38
Net amount of payroll		$4,888.62

In a computerized accounting system, the payroll software performs this proof. An error in the payroll register could cause the payment of an incorrect amount to an employee. It also could result in sending an incorrect amount to the government or other agencies for whom funds are withheld.

PAYROLL CHECK

Employees may be paid in cash or by check. Data needed to prepare a paycheck for each employee are contained in the payroll register. In a computer-based system, the paychecks and payroll register normally are prepared at the same time. The employer furnishes an earnings statement to each employee along with each paycheck. Paychecks with detachable earnings statements, like the one for Ken Istone illustrated in Figure 8-6, are widely used for this purpose. Before the check is deposited or cashed, the employee should detach the stub and keep it.

FIGURE 8-5 Payroll Register (right side)

REGISTER—WEEK ENDED 12/19/--

	DEDUCTIONS									
	FEDERAL INCOME TAX	SOCIAL SECURITY TAX	MEDICARE TAX	HEALTH INSURANCE	UNITED WAY	OTHER	TOTAL	NET PAY	CHECK NO.	
1	168.00	40.92	24.07				232.99	1,427.01	409	1
2	126.00	55.80	13.05		20.00		214.85	685.15	410	2
3	11.00	33.79	7.90	10.00			62.69	482.31	411	3
4	57.00	47.99	11.22	13.00	20.00		149.21	624.79	412	4
5	8.00	27.28	6.38	13.00			54.66	385.34	413	5
6	73.00	45.01	10.53				128.54	597.46	414	6
7	13.00	30.38	7.11	10.00			60.49	429.51	415	7
8	20.00	18.60	4.35				42.95	257.05	416	8
9	476.00	299.77	84.61	46.00	40.00		946.38	4,888.62		9
10										10

Withholding Tax Table (Federal Income Tax)

6.2% × Social Security taxable earnings (Social Security Tax)

1.45% × total earnings (Medicare Tax)

Specific employer–employee agreements (Health Insurance, United Way)

Total earnings – total deductions (Net Pay)

FIGURE 8-6 Paycheck and Earnings Statement

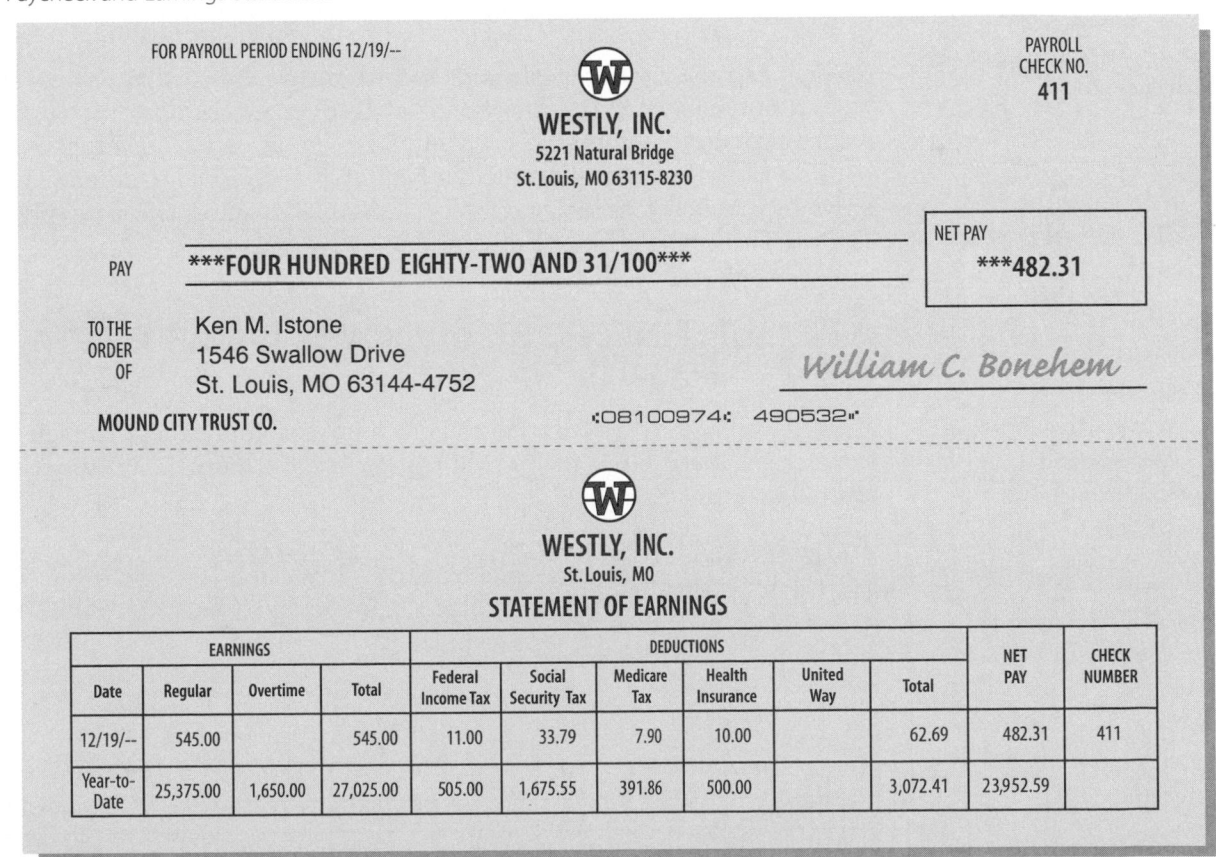

FOR PAYROLL PERIOD ENDING 12/19/--

PAYROLL CHECK NO. 411

WESTLY, INC.
5221 Natural Bridge
St. Louis, MO 63115-8230

NET PAY ***482.31

PAY ***FOUR HUNDRED EIGHTY-TWO AND 31/100***

TO THE ORDER OF
Ken M. Istone
1546 Swallow Drive
St. Louis, MO 63144-4752

William C. Bonehem

MOUND CITY TRUST CO.

⑆08100974⑆ 490532⑈

WESTLY, INC.
St. Louis, MO

STATEMENT OF EARNINGS

EARNINGS				DEDUCTIONS						NET PAY	CHECK NUMBER
Date	Regular	Overtime	Total	Federal Income Tax	Social Security Tax	Medicare Tax	Health Insurance	United Way	Total		
12/19/--	545.00		545.00	11.00	33.79	7.90	10.00		62.69	482.31	411
Year-to-Date	25,375.00	1,650.00	27,025.00	505.00	1,675.55	391.86	500.00		3,072.41	23,952.59	

FIGURE 8-7 Employee Earnings Record (left side)

EMPLOYEE EARNINGS RECORD

PERIOD ENDED	EARNINGS				TAXABLE EARNINGS	
	REGULAR	OVERTIME	TOTAL	CUMULATIVE TOTAL	UNEMPLOYMENT COMPENSATION	SOCIAL SECURITY
11/28	545.00	75.00	620.00	25,240.00		620.00
12/5	545.00	75.00	620.00	25,860.00		620.00
12/12	545.00	75.00	620.00	26,480.00		620.00
12/19	545.00		545.00	27,025.00		545.00

GENDER M	GENDER F	DEPARTMENT	OCCUPATION	SOCIAL SECURITY NUMBER	MARITAL STATUS	ALLOWANCES
✓		Maintenance	Service	393-58-8194	M	4

In many cases, the employee does not even handle the paycheck. Rather, payment is made by **direct deposit** or electronic funds transfer (EFT) by the employer to the employee's bank. The employee receives only the earnings statement from the check indicating the deposit has been made. Payment by check or direct deposit provides better internal accounting control than payment by cash.

EMPLOYEE EARNINGS RECORD

LEARNING KEY

The payroll register and employee earnings record are linked. The payroll register shows the earnings of all employees for a single pay period. The employee earnings record summarizes the earnings of an individual employee for all pay periods.

A separate record of each employee's earnings is called an **employee earnings record.** An employee earnings record for Ken M. Istone for a portion of the last quarter of the calendar year is illustrated in Figure 8-7 above.

The information in this record is obtained from the payroll register. In a computer-based system, the employee earnings record can be updated at the same time the payroll register is prepared.

Istone's earnings for four weeks of the last quarter of the year are shown on this form. Note that the entry for the pay period ended December 19 is the same as that in the payroll register illustrated in Figure 8-5. This linkage between the payroll register and the employee earnings record always exists. The payroll register provides a summary of the earnings of all employees for each pay period. The earnings record provides a summary of the annual earnings of an individual employee.

The earnings record illustrated in Figure 8-7 is designed to accumulate both quarterly and annual totals. The employer needs this information to prepare several reports. These reports will be discussed in Chapter 9.

ACCOUNTING FOR EMPLOYEE EARNINGS AND DEDUCTIONS

LO4 Account for employee earnings and deductions.

The payroll register described in the previous section provides complete payroll data for each pay period. But the payroll register is not a journal. We still need to make a journal entry for payroll.

JOURNALIZING PAYROLL TRANSACTIONS

The totals at the bottom of the columns of the payroll register in Figure 8-5 are reproduced here.

PAYROLL REGISTER (LEFT SIDE)

EARNINGS				TAXABLE EARNINGS	
REGULAR	OVERTIME	TOTAL	CUMULATIVE TOTAL	UNEMPLOYMENT COMPENSATION	SOCIAL SECURITY
5,143.00	692.00	5,835.00	290,415.00	300.00	4,835.00

(1)

FIGURE 8-7 Employee Earnings Record (right side)

FOR PERIOD ENDED 20--

DEDUCTIONS								
FEDERAL INCOME TAX	SOCIAL SECURITY TAX	MEDICARE TAX	HEALTH INSURANCE	UNITED WAY	OTHER	TOTAL	CHECK NO.	AMOUNT
19 00	38 44	8 99	10 00			76 43	387	543 57
19 00	38 44	8 99	10 00			76 43	395	543 57
19 00	38 44	8 99	10 00			76 43	403	543 57
11 00	33 79	7 90	10 00			62 69	411	482 31

PAY RATE	DATE OF BIRTH	DATE HIRED	NAME/ADDRESS	EMPLOYEE NUMBER
$545/wk	8/17/64	1/3/87	Ken M. Istone 1546 Swallow Drive St. Louis, MO 63144-4752	3

A BROADER VIEW

PHOTODISC/GETTY IMAGES

Payroll Fraud—Paying for Ghosts

A supervisor at Haas Transfer Warehouse embezzled $12,000 from the company by collecting paychecks for former employees. When an employee left the company, the supervisor continued to submit a department time report for the employee. This caused a paycheck to be generated for the "ghost" employee. The supervisor then simply kept this paycheck when others were distributed to actual employees.

This fraud shows the importance of two procedures that appear in this chapter: (1) a time card, plastic card, or badge should be used for each employee to keep an accurate record of time worked and (2) payment by direct deposit or electronic funds transfer to the employee's bank is a good internal control.

The numbered amounts in the payroll register column totals thus provide the basis for recording the payroll. If the employee paychecks are written from the regular bank account, the following journal entry is made:

PAYROLL REGISTER (RIGHT SIDE) 20--

DEDUCTIONS								
FEDERAL INCOME TAX	SOCIAL SECURITY TAX	MEDICARE TAX	HEALTH INSURANCE	UNITED WAY	OTHER	TOTAL		NET PAY
476 00	299 77	84 61	46 00	40 00	0 00 0 00	946 38		4 888 62
(2)	(3)	(4)	(5)	(6)				(7)

		DATE		DESCRIPTION	POST REF.	DEBIT		CREDIT		
(1)	5	Dec.	19	Wages and Salaries Expense		5835	00			5
(2)	6			Employee Income Tax Payable				476	00	6
(3)	7			Social Security Tax Payable				299	77	7
(4)	8			Medicare Tax Payable				84	61	8
(5)	9			Health Insurance Premiums Payable				46	00	9
(6)	10			United Way Contributions Payable				40	00	10
(7)	11			Cash				4888	62	11
	12			Payroll for week ended Dec. 19						12

Employee paychecks also can be written from a special payroll bank account. Large businesses with many employees commonly use a payroll bank account. If Westly used a payroll bank account, it first would have made the following entry on December 19 to transfer funds from the regular bank account to the payroll bank account:

	DATE		DESCRIPTION	POST REF.	DEBIT		CREDIT		
1	Dec.	19	Payroll Cash		4888	62			1
2			Cash				4888	62	2
3			Cash for Dec. 19 payroll						3

Then, the payroll entry shown above would be made, except that the credit of $4,888.62 would be to Payroll Cash rather than Cash.

If a payroll bank account is used, individual checks totaling $4,888.62 are written to the employees from that account. Otherwise, individual checks totaling that amount are written to the employees from the regular bank account.

Notice two important facts about the payroll entry. First, Wages and Salaries Expense is debited for the gross pay of the employees. The expense to the employer is the gross pay, not the employees' net pay after deductions. Second, a separate account is kept for each deduction.

LEARNING KEY

Wages and Salaries Expense is debited for the gross pay. A separate account is kept for each earnings deduction. Cash is credited for the net pay.

The accounts needed in entering deductions depend upon the deductions involved. To understand the accounting for these deductions, consider what the employer is doing. By deducting amounts from employees' earnings, the employer is simply serving as an agent for the government and other groups. Amounts that are deducted from an employee's gross earnings must be paid by the employer to these groups. Therefore, a separate account should be kept for the liability for each type of deduction.

To help us understand the journal entry for payroll, let's use the accounting equation to examine the accounts involved. The seven accounts affected by the payroll entry above are shown in the accounting equation in Figure 8-8.

FIGURE 8-8 Accounting for Payroll

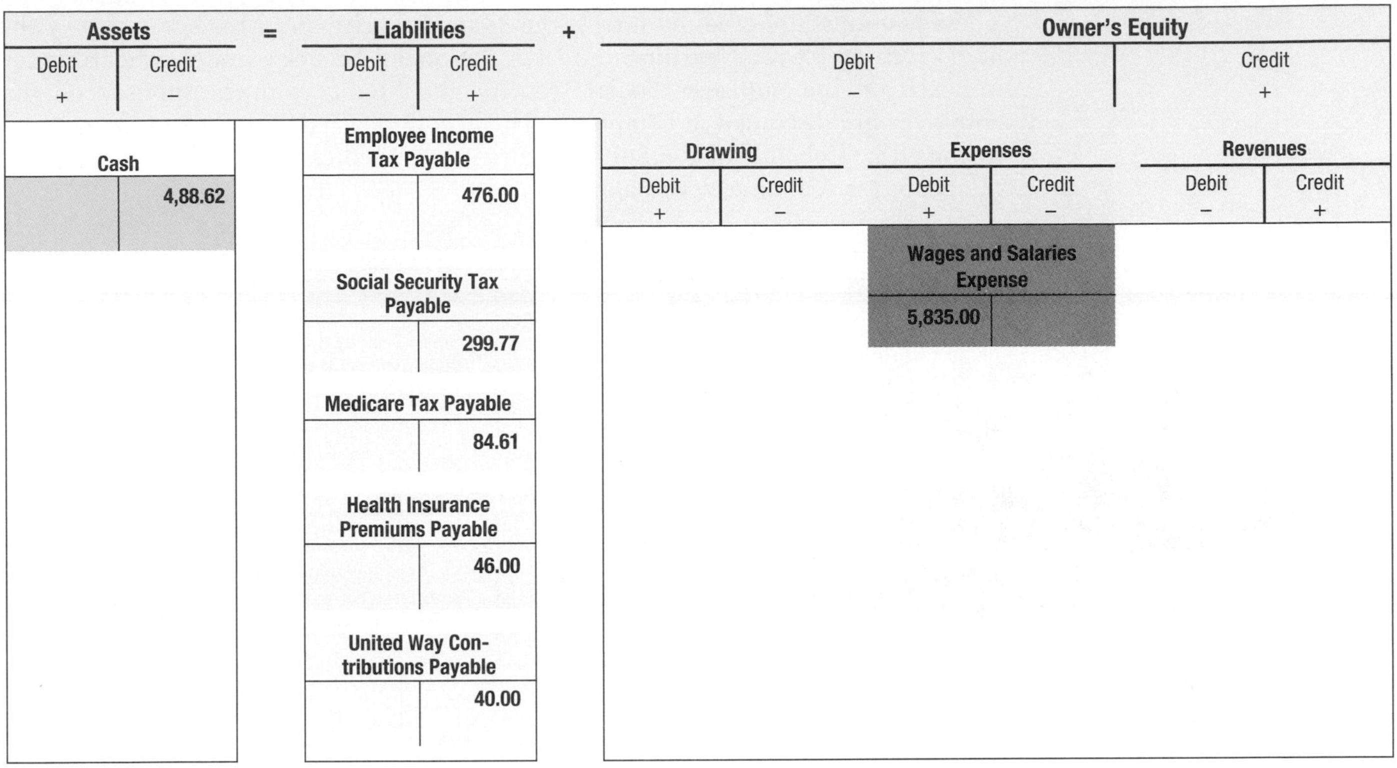

WAGES AND SALARIES EXPENSE

This account is debited for the gross pay of all employees for each pay period. Sometimes separate expense accounts are kept for the employees of different departments. Thus, separate accounts may be kept for Office Salaries Expense, Sales Salaries Expense, and Factory Wages Expense.

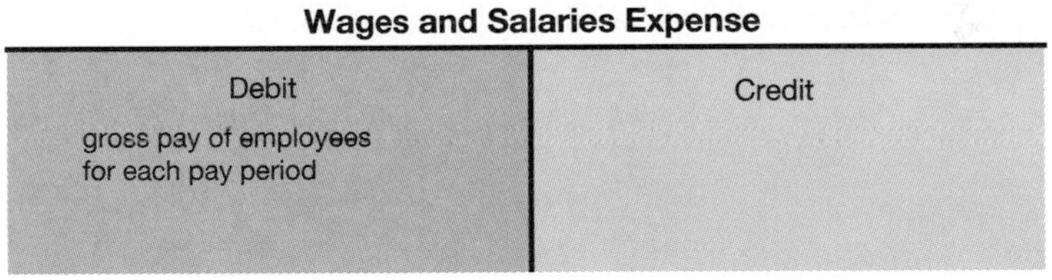

Wages and Salaries Expense
Debit
gross pay of employees
for each pay period
Credit

EMPLOYEE INCOME TAX PAYABLE

This account is credited for the total federal income tax withheld from employees' earnings. The account is debited for amounts paid to the IRS. When all of the income taxes withheld have been paid, the account will have a zero balance. A state or city income tax payable account is used in a similar manner.

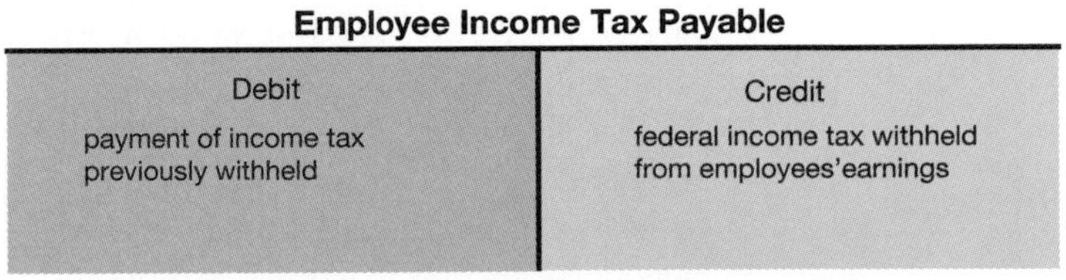

SOCIAL SECURITY AND MEDICARE TAXES PAYABLE

These accounts are credited for (1) the Social Security and Medicare taxes withheld from employees' earnings and (2) the Social Security and Medicare taxes imposed on the employer. Social Security and Medicare taxes imposed on the employer are discussed in Chapter 9. The accounts are debited for amounts paid to the IRS. When all of the Social Security and Medicare taxes have been paid, the accounts will have zero balances.

Social Security Tax Payable

Debit	Credit
payment of Social Security tax previously withheld or imposed	Social Security taxes (1) withheld from employees'earnings and (2) imposed on the employer

Medicare Tax Payable

Debit	Credit
payment of Medicare tax previously withheld or imposed	Medicare taxes (1) withheld from employees'earnings and (2) imposed on the employer

OTHER DEDUCTIONS

Health Insurance Premiums Payable is credited for health insurance contributions deducted from an employee's pay. The account is debited for the subsequent payment of these amounts to the health insurer. United Way Contributions Payable is handled in a similar manner.

U REVU Complete U REVU-2 on **page 303** to test your basic understanding of LO4.

PAYROLL RECORD-KEEPING METHODS

LO5 Describe various payroll record-keeping methods.

Payroll typically is one of the first functions to be computerized by businesses.

You probably noticed that the same information appears in several places in the payroll records—in the payroll register, paycheck and stub, and employee earnings records. If all records are prepared by hand (a **manual system**), the same information would be recorded several times. Unless an employer has only a few employees, this can be very inefficient. Various approaches are available to make payroll accounting more efficient and accurate.

Both medium- and large-size businesses commonly use two approaches for payroll record keeping: payroll processing centers and electronic systems. A **payroll processing center** is a business that sells payroll record-keeping services. The employer provides the center with all basic employee data and each period's report of hours worked. The processing center maintains all payroll records and prepares each period's payroll checks. Payroll processing center fees tend to be much less than the cost to an employer of handling payroll internally.

An **electronic system** is a computer system based on a software package that performs all payroll record keeping and prepares payroll checks. In this system, only the employee number and hours worked need to be entered into a computer each pay period, as shown in Figure 8-9. All other payroll data needed to prepare the payroll records can be stored in the computer. The computer uses the employee number and hours worked to determine the gross pay, deductions, and net pay. The payroll register, checks, and employee earnings records are provided as outputs.

FIGURE 8-9 Electronic Payroll System

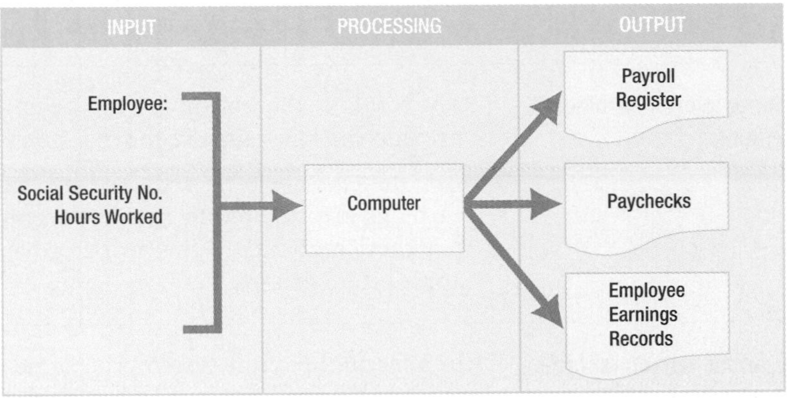

The same inputs and outputs are required in all payroll systems. Even with a computer, the data required for payroll processing have to be entered into the system at some point. The outputs—the payroll register, paychecks, and employee earnings records—are basically the same under each system.

SELF-STUDY

LEARNING OBJECTIVES Key Points to Remember

LO1 Distinguish between employees and independent contractors.

Employees work under the control and direction of an employer. Independent contractors perform a service for a fee and do not work under the control and direction of the company paying for the service. Payroll accounting procedures apply only to employees, not to independent contractors.

LO2 Calculate employee earnings and deductions.

Three steps are required to determine how much to pay an employee for a pay period:

1. Calculate total earnings.
2. Determine the amounts of deductions.
3. Subtract deductions from total earnings to compute net pay.

Deductions from gross pay fall into three categories:

1. Income tax withholding
2. Employee Social Security and Medicare taxes withholding
3. Voluntary deductions

Four factors determine the amount to be withheld from an employee's gross pay each pay period:

1. Total earnings
2. Marital status
3. Number of withholding allowances claimed
4. Length of the pay period

LEARNING OBJECTIVES Key Points to Remember

LO3 Describe and prepare payroll records.	The payroll register and the employee earnings record are linked. The payroll register provides a summary of earnings of all employees for each pay period. The earnings record provides a summary of the annual earnings of an individual employee.
LO4 Account for employee earnings and deductions.	The totals at the bottom of the columns of the payroll register provide the basis for the journal entry for payroll. Amounts withheld or deducted by the employer from employee earnings are credited to liability accounts. The employer must pay these amounts to the proper government groups and other appropriate groups.
LO5 Describe various payroll record-keeping methods.	In a manual payroll system, the same information needs to be recorded several times. An electronic payroll system is much more efficient.

DEMONSTRATION PROBLEM

Carole Vohsen operates a pet grooming salon called Canine Coiffures. She has five employees, all of whom are paid on a weekly basis. Canine Coiffures uses a payroll register, individual employee earnings records, a journal, and a general ledger.

The payroll data for each employee for the week ended January 21, 20--, are given below. Employees are paid 1½ times the regular rate for work over 40 hours a week and double time for work on Sunday.

Name	Employee No.	No. of Allowances	Marital Status	Total Hours Worked Jan. 15–21	Rate	Total Earnings Jan. 1–14
DeNourie, Katie	1	2	S	44	$11.50	$1,058.00
Garriott, Pete	2	1	M	40	12.00	1,032.00
Martinez, Sheila	3	3	M	39	12.50	987.50
Parker, Nancy	4	4	M	42	11.00	957.00
Shapiro, John	5	2	S	40	11.50	931.50

Sheila Martinez is the manager of the Shampooing Department. Her social security number is 500-88-4189, and she was born April 12, 1969. She lives at 46 Darling Crossing, Norwich, CT 06360. Martinez was hired September 1 of last year.

Canine Coiffures uses a federal income tax withholding table. A portion of this weekly table is provided in Figure 8-4 on pages 286 and 287. Social Security tax is withheld at the rate of 6.2% of the first $106,800 earned. Medicare tax is withheld at the rate of 1.45%, and city earnings tax at the rate of 1%, both applied to gross pay. Garriott and Parker each have $14.00 and DeNourie and Martinez each have $4.00 withheld for health insurance. DeNourie, Martinez, and Shapiro each have $15.00 withheld to be invested in the groomers' credit union. Garriott and Shapiro each have $18.75 withheld under a savings bond purchase plan.

Canine Coiffures' payroll is met by drawing checks on its regular bank account. This week, the checks were issued in sequence, beginning with No. 811.

REQUIRED

1. Prepare a payroll register for Canine Coiffures for the week ended January 21, 20--. (In the Taxable Earnings/Unemployment Compensation column, enter the same amounts as in the Social Security column.) Total the amount columns, verify the totals, and rule with single and double lines.
2. Prepare an employee earnings record for Sheila Martinez for the week ended January 21, 20--.
3. Assuming that the wages for the week ended January 21 were paid on January 23, prepare the journal entry for the payment of this payroll.
4. Post the entry in requirement (3) to the affected accounts in the ledger of Canine Coiffures. Do not enter any amounts in the Balance columns. Use account numbers as follows: Cash—101; Employee Income Tax Payable—211; Social Security Tax Payable—212; Medicare Tax Payable—213; City Earnings Tax Payable—215; Health Insurance Premiums Payable—216; Credit Union Payable—217; Savings Bond Deductions Payable—218; Wages and Salaries Expense—511.

Solution 1.

PAYROLL REGISTER—WEEK ENDED January 21, 20--

	NAME	EMPLOYEE NO.	ALLOWANCES	MARITAL STATUS	EARNINGS: REGULAR	EARNINGS: OVERTIME	EARNINGS: TOTAL	EARNINGS: CUMULATIVE TOTAL	TAXABLE EARNINGS: UNEMPLOYMENT COMPENSATION	TAXABLE EARNINGS: SOCIAL SECURITY	
1	DeNourie, Katie	1	2	S	460 00	69 00	529 00	1587 00	529 00	529 00	1
2	Garriott, Pete	2	1	M	480 00		480 00	1512 00	480 00	480 00	2
3	Martinez, Sheila	3	3	M	487 50		487 50	1475 00	487 50	487 50	3
4	Parker, Nancy	4	4	M	440 00	33 00	473 00	1430 00	473 00	473 00	4
5	Shapiro, John	5	2	S	460 00		460 00	1391 50	460 00	460 00	5
6					2327 50	102 00	2429 50	7395 50	2429 50	2429 50	6
7											7

	DEDUCTIONS: FEDERAL INCOME TAX	DEDUCTIONS: SOCIAL SECURITY TAX	DEDUCTIONS: MEDICARE TAX	DEDUCTIONS: CITY TAX	DEDUCTIONS: HEALTH INSURANCE	DEDUCTIONS: CREDIT UNION	DEDUCTIONS: OTHER	DEDUCTIONS: TOTAL	NET PAY	CHECK NO.	
1	43 00	32 80	7 67	5 29	4 00	15 00		107 76	421 24	811	1
2	26 00	29 76	6 96	4 80	14 00		18 75	100 27	379 73	812	2
3	12 00	30 23	7 07	4 88	4 00	15 00		73 18	414 32	813	3
4	4 00	29 33	6 86	4 73	14 00			58 92	414 08	814	4
5	34 00	28 52	6 67	4 60		15 00	18 75	107 54	352 46	815	5
6	119 00	150 64	35 23	24 30	36 00	45 00	37 50	447 67	1981 83		6
7											7

(continued)

2.

EMPLOYEE EARNINGS RECORD

20-- PERIOD ENDED	EARNINGS: REGULAR	EARNINGS: OVERTIME	EARNINGS: TOTAL	EARNINGS: CUMULATIVE TOTAL	TAXABLE EARNINGS: UNEMPLOYMENT COMPENSATION	TAXABLE EARNINGS: SOCIAL SECURITY
1/7						
1/14						
1/21	487 50		487 50	1475 00	487 50	487 50
1/28						

GENDER M	GENDER F	DEPARTMENT	OCCUPATION	SOCIAL SECURITY NUMBER	MARITAL STATUS	ALLOWANCES
	✔	Shampooing	Manager	500-88-4189	M	3

FOR PERIOD ENDED 20--

DEDUCTIONS: FEDERAL INCOME TAX	SOCIAL SECURITY TAX	MEDICARE TAX	CITY TAX	HEALTH INSURANCE	CREDIT UNION	OTHER	TOTAL	CHECK NO.	AMOUNT
12 00	30 23	7 07	4 88	4 00	15 00		73 18	813	414 32

PAY RATE	DATE OF BIRTH	DATE HIRED	NAME/ADDRESS	EMPLOYEE NUMBER
$12.50	4/12/69	9/1/--	Sheila Martinez 46 Darling Crossing Norwich, CT 06360	3

3.

GENERAL JOURNAL PAGE 1

	DATE		DESCRIPTION	POST. REF.	DEBIT	CREDIT	
1	20-- Jan.	23	Wages and Salaries Expense	511	2,429 50		1
2			Employee Income Tax Payable	211		119 00	2
3			Social Security Tax Payable	212		150 64	3
4			Medicare Tax Payable	213		35 23	4
5			City Earnings Tax Payable	215		24 30	5
6			Health Insurance Premiums Payable	216		36 00	6
7			Credit Union Payable	217		45 00	7
8			Savings Bond Deductions Payable	218		37 50	8
9			Cash	101		1,981 83	9
10			Payroll for week ended Jan. 21				10

4.

GENERAL LEDGER

ACCOUNT: Cash ACCOUNT NO. 101

DATE		ITEM	POST. REF.	DEBIT	CREDIT	BALANCE DEBIT	BALANCE CREDIT
20-- Jan.	23		J1		1,981.83		

ACCOUNT: Employee Income Tax Payable ACCOUNT NO. 211

DATE		ITEM	POST. REF.	DEBIT	CREDIT	BALANCE DEBIT	BALANCE CREDIT
20-- Jan.	23		J1		119.00		

ACCOUNT: Social Security Tax Payable ACCOUNT NO. 212

DATE		ITEM	POST. REF.	DEBIT	CREDIT	BALANCE DEBIT	BALANCE CREDIT
20-- Jan.	23		J1		150.64		

ACCOUNT: Medicare Tax Payable ACCOUNT NO. 213

DATE		ITEM	POST. REF.	DEBIT	CREDIT	BALANCE DEBIT	BALANCE CREDIT
20-- Jan.	23		J1		35.23		

ACCOUNT: City Earnings Tax Payable ACCOUNT NO. 215

DATE		ITEM	POST. REF.	DEBIT	CREDIT	BALANCE DEBIT	BALANCE CREDIT
20-- Jan.	23		J1		24.30		

ACCOUNT: Health Insurance Premiums Payable ACCOUNT NO. 216

DATE		ITEM	POST. REF.	DEBIT	CREDIT	BALANCE DEBIT	BALANCE CREDIT
20-- Jan.	23		J1		36.00		

ACCOUNT: Credit Union Payable ACCOUNT NO. 217

DATE		ITEM	POST. REF.	DEBIT	CREDIT	BALANCE DEBIT	BALANCE CREDIT
20-- Jan.	23		J1		45.00		

ACCOUNT: Savings Bond Deductions Payable ACCOUNT NO. 218

DATE		ITEM	POST. REF.	DEBIT	CREDIT	BALANCE DEBIT	BALANCE CREDIT
20-- Jan.	23		J1		37.50		

ACCOUNT: Wages and Salaries Expense ACCOUNT NO. 511

DATE		ITEM	POST. REF.	DEBIT	CREDIT	BALANCE DEBIT	BALANCE CREDIT
20-- Jan.	23		J1	2,429.50			

KEY TERMS

direct deposit (292) A payroll method in which the employee does not handle the paycheck; payment is made by the employer directly to the employee's bank.

electronic system (296) A computer system based on a software package that performs all payroll record keeping and prepares payroll checks.

employee (281) Someone who works under the control and direction of an employer.

employee earnings record (292) A separate record of each employee's earnings.

Fair Labor Standards Act (FLSA) (281) A law that requires employers to pay overtime at 1½ times the regular rate to any hourly employee who works over 40 hours in a week.

FICA taxes (285) Payroll taxes withheld to provide Social Security and Medicare benefits.

gross pay (284) An employee's total earnings.

independent contractor (281) Someone who performs a service for a fee and does not work under the control and direction of the company paying for the service.

manual system (296) Payroll system in which all records are prepared by hand.

net pay (284) Gross pay less mandatory and voluntary deductions.

payroll processing center (296) A business that sells payroll record-keeping services.

payroll register (289) A form used to assemble the data required at the end of each payroll period.

salary (281) Compensation for managerial or administrative services.

wage-bracket method (285) A method of determining the amount to withhold from an employee's gross pay for a specific time period. Wage-bracket tables are provided by the Internal Revenue Service.

wages (281) Compensation for skilled or unskilled labor.

withholding allowance (284) A specific dollar amount of an employee's gross pay that is exempt from federal income tax withholding.

SELF-STUDY QUESTIONS AND EXERCISES

True/False Questions

1. LO1 An independent contractor is one who works under the control and direction of an employer.
2. LO1 Government laws and regulations regarding payroll are more complex for employees than for independent contractors.
3. LO2 Compensation for skilled or unskilled labor expressed in terms of hours, weeks, or units is called salary.
4. LO2 An employee's total earnings is called gross pay.
5. LO3 A payroll register is a multi-column form used to assemble the data required at the end of each payroll period.

Multiple Choice Questions

1. LO2 Jack Smith is married, has a spouse who is not employed and has five dependent children. How many withholding allowances is Smith entitled to?

   (a) 5 (c) 7
   (b) 6 (d) 8

2. LO2 Nancy Summers worked 44 hours during the past week. She is entitled to 1½ times her regular pay for all hours worked in excess of 40 during the week. Her regular rate of pay is $12.00. Social Security tax is withheld at the rate of 6.2% and Medicare tax is withheld at the rate of 1.45%; federal income tax withheld is $68; and $5 of union dues are withheld. Her net pay for the week is

   (a) $440.89. (c) $552.00.
   (b) $472.00. (d) $436.78.

3. LO2 Which of the following is *not* a factor that determines the amount of federal income tax to be withheld from an employee's gross pay?

   (a) marital status (c) total earnings
   (b) number of withholding allowances claimed (d) age of employee

4. LO3 A separate record of each employee's earnings is called a(n)

   (a) payroll register. (c) W-4.
   (b) employee earnings record. (d) earnings statement.

5. LO4 Social Security Tax Payable and Medicare Tax Payable are classified as

   (a) liabilities. (c) owner's equity.
   (b) assets. (d) expenses.

U REVU Exercises

1. LO2 Qian Wang is paid a regular rate of $14 per hour and 1½ times the regular rate for hours worked over 40 in a week. During the past week, Qian worked 45 hours.

   (a) Compute Qian's gross pay for the week.
   (b) Assume Qian is married and claims two withholding allowances. Compute the amount of federal income tax her employer should withhold for the week.

2. LO4 The column totals from the payroll register of Jawhawk Supplies for the week ended February 9 were as follows:

Total earnings	$4,600.00
Federal income tax	417.00
Social Security tax	285.20
Medicare tax	66.70
State income tax	46.00
Health insurance	181.00

   Prepare the journal entry to record the payroll, crediting Cash for the net pay.

The answers to the Self-Study Questions and Exercises are at the end of the chapter (page 314).

REVIEW QUESTIONS

LO1 1. Why is it important for payroll accounting purposes to distinguish between an employee and an independent contractor?

LO2 2. Name three major categories of deductions from an employee's gross pay.

LO2 3. Identify the four factors that determine the amount of federal income tax that is withheld from an employee's pay each pay period.

LO2 4. In general, an employee is entitled to withholding allowances for what purposes?

LO3 5. Identify the three payroll records usually needed by an employer.

LO3 6. Describe the information contained in the payroll register.

LO3 7. Why is it important to total and verify the totals of the payroll register after the data for each employee have been entered?

LO3 8. Distinguish between the payroll register and the employee earnings record.

LO4 9. Explain what an employer does with the amounts withheld from an employee's pay.

LO5 10. Explain why payroll processing centers and electronic systems are commonly used in payroll accounting.

SERIES A EXERCISES

E 8-1A (LO2)

✓ Net pay: $446.51

COMPUTING NET PAY Mary Sue Guild works for a company that pays its employees 1½ times the regular rate for all hours worked in excess of 40 per week. Guild's pay rate is $10.00 per hour. Her wages are subject to deductions for federal income tax, Social Security tax, and Medicare tax. She is married and claims four withholding allowances. Guild has a ½-hour lunch break during an 8½-hour day. Her time card is shown below.

Name	Mary Sue Guild					
Week Ending	March 30, 20--					
Day	In	Out	In	Out	Hours Worked: Regular	Hours Worked: Overtime
M	7:57	12:05	12:35	4:33	8	
T	7:52	12:09	12:39	5:05	8	½
W	7:59	12:15	12:45	5:30	8	1
T	8:00	12:01	12:30	6:31	8	2
F	7:56	12:05	12:34	4:30	8	
S	8:00	10:31				2½

Complete the following:

(a) __________ regular hours × $10.00 per hour $__________

(b) __________ overtime hours × $15.00 per hour $__________

(c) Total gross wages $________

(d) Federal income tax withholding (from tax tables in Figure 8-4, pages 286 and 287) $________

(e) Social Security withholding at 6.2% $________

(f) Medicare withholding at 1.45% $________

(g) Total withholding $________

(h) Net pay $________

E 8-2A (LO2)
✓ Gross pay: $795.00

COMPUTING WEEKLY GROSS PAY Ryan Lawrence's regular hourly rate is $15.00. He receives 1½ times the regular rate for any hours worked over 40 a week and double the rate for work on Sunday. During the past week, Lawrence worked 8 hours each day Monday through Thursday, 10 hours on Friday, and 5 hours on Sunday. Compute Lawrence's gross pay for the past week.

E 8-3A (LO2)
✓ b: $712.50

COMPUTING OVERTIME RATE OF PAY AND GROSS WEEKLY PAY Rebecca Huang receives a regular salary of $2,600 a month and is paid 1½ times the regular hourly rate for hours worked in excess of 40 per week.

(a) Calculate Huang's overtime rate of pay.
(b) Calculate Huang's total gross weekly pay if she works 45 hours during the week.

E 8-4A (LO2)
✓ e: $10.00

COMPUTING FEDERAL INCOME TAX Using the table in Figure 8-4 on pages 286 and 287, determine the amount of federal income tax an employer should withhold weekly for employees with the following marital status, earnings, and withholding allowances:

	Marital Status	Total Weekly Earnings	Number of Allowances	Amount of Withholding
(a)	S	$327.90	2	________
(b)	S	410.00	1	________
(c)	M	438.16	3	________
(d)	S	518.25	0	________
(e)	M	603.98	5	________

E 8-5A (LO2)
✓ 3d row, Soc. Sec. tax: $161.20

CALCULATING SOCIAL SECURITY AND MEDICARE TAXES Assume a Social Security tax rate of 6.2% is applied to maximum earnings of $106,800 and a Medicare tax rate of 1.45% is applied to all earnings. Calculate the Social Security and Medicare taxes for the following situations:

Cumul. Pay Before Current Weekly Payroll	Current Gross Pay	Year-to-Date Earnings	Soc. Sec. Maximum	Amount Over Max. Soc. Sec.	Amount Subject to Soc. Sec.	Soc. Sec. Tax Withheld	Medicare Tax Withheld
$ 22,000	$1,200	________	$106,800	________	________	________	________
54,000	4,200	________	106,800	________	________	________	________
104,200	3,925	________	106,800	________	________	________	________
106,200	4,600	________	106,800	________	________	________	________

E 8-6A (LO4)
✓ Med. tax: $126.15

JOURNALIZING PAYROLL TRANSACTIONS On December 31, the payroll register of Hamstreet Associates indicated the following information:

Wages and Salaries Expense	$8,700.00
Employee Income Tax Payable	920.00
United Way Contributions Payable	200.00
Earnings subject to Social Security tax	8,000.00

Determine the amount of Social Security and Medicare taxes to be withheld and record the journal entry for the payroll, crediting Cash for the net pay.

E 8-7A (LO4)
✓ Cr. Cash: $4,756.49

PAYROLL JOURNAL ENTRY Journalize the following data taken from the payroll register of University Printing as of April 15, 20—:

Regular earnings	$5,418.00
Overtime earnings	824.00
Deductions:	
Federal income tax	593.00
Social Security tax	387.00
Medicare tax	90.51
Pension plan	90.00
Health insurance premiums	225.00
United Way contributions	100.00

SERIES A PROBLEMS

P 8-8A (LO2/4)
✓ Net pay: $180.19

GROSS PAY, DEDUCTIONS, AND NET PAY Donald Chin works for Northwest Supplies. His rate of pay is $8.50 per hour, and he is paid 1½ times the regular rate for all hours worked in excess of 40 per week. During the last week of January of the current year, he worked 48 hours. Chin is married and claims three withholding allowances on his W-4 form. His weekly wages are subject to the following deductions:

(a) Employee income tax (use Figure 8-4 on pages 286 and 287)
(b) Social Security tax at 6.2%
(c) Medicare tax at 1.45%
(d) Health insurance premium, $85.00
(e) Credit union, $125.00
(f) United Way contribution, $10.00

REQUIRED

1. Compute Chin's regular pay, overtime pay, gross pay, and net pay.
2. Journalize the payment of his wages for the week ended January 31, crediting Cash for the net amount.

P 8-9A (LO2/3/4)
✓ Cr. Cash: $1,827.03

PAYROLL REGISTER AND PAYROLL JOURNAL ENTRY Don McCullum operates a travel agency called Don's Luxury Travel. He has five employees, all of whom are paid on a weekly basis. The travel agency uses a payroll register, individual employee earnings records, and a general journal.

Don's Luxury Travel uses a weekly federal income tax withholding table. The payroll data for each employee for the week ended March 22, 20—, are given on the following page. Employees are paid 1½ times the regular rate for working over 40 hours a week.

Name	No. of Allowances	Marital Status	Total Hours Worked Mar. 16–22	Rate	Total Earnings Jan. 1–Mar. 15
Ali, Loren	4	M	45	$11.00	$5,280.00
Carson, Judy	1	S	40	12.00	5,760.00
Hernandez, Maria	3	M	43	9.50	4,560.00
Knox, Wayne	1	S	39	11.00	5,125.50
Paglione, Jim	2	M	40	10.50	4,720.50

Social Security tax is withheld from the first $106,800 of earnings at the rate of 6.2%. Medicare tax is withheld at the rate of 1.45%, and city earnings tax at the rate of 1%, both applied to gross pay. Ali and Knox have $15.00 withheld and Carson and Hernandez have $5.00 withheld for health insurance. Ali and Knox have $20.00 withheld to be invested in the travel agency's credit union. Carson has $38.75 withheld and Hernandez has $18.75 withheld under a savings bond purchase plan.

Don's Luxury Travel's payroll is met by drawing checks on its regular bank account. The checks were issued in sequence, beginning with Check No. 423.

REQUIRED

1. Prepare a payroll register for Don's Luxury Travel for the week ended March 22, 20--. (In the Taxable Earnings/Unemployment Compensation column, enter the same amounts as in the Social Security column.) Total the amount columns, verify the totals, and rule with single and double lines.
2. Assuming that the wages for the week ended March 22 were paid on March 24, prepare the journal entry for the payment of the payroll.

P 8-10A (LO3)
✓ Soc. Sec. tax: $29.76

EMPLOYEE EARNINGS RECORD Don's Luxury Travel in Problem 8-9A keeps employee earnings records. Judy Carson, employee number 62, is employed as a manager in the ticket sales department. She was born on May 8, 1959, and was hired on June 1 of last year. Her social security number is 544-67-1283. She lives at 28 Quarry Drive, Vernon, CT 06066.

REQUIRED

For the week ended March 22, complete an employee earnings record for Judy Carson. (Insert earnings data only for the week of March 22.)

SERIES B EXERCISES

E 8-1B (LO2)
✓ Net pay: $527.70

COMPUTING NET PAY Tom Hallinan works for a company that pays its employees 1½ times the regular rate for all hours worked in excess of 40 per week. Hallinan's pay rate is $12.00 per hour. His wages are subject to deductions for federal income tax, Social Security tax, and Medicare tax. He is married and claims five withholding allowances. Hallinan has a ½-hour lunch break during an 8½-hour day. His time card is shown on page 308.

(continued)

Name Tom Hallinan

Week Ending March 30, 20--

Day	In	Out	In	Out	Hours Worked	
					Regular	Overtime
M	7:55	12:02	12:32	5:33	8	1
T	7:59	12:04	12:34	6:05	8	1½
W	7:59	12:05	12:35	4:30	8	
T	8:00	12:01	12:30	5:01	8	½
F	7:58	12:02	12:31	5:33	8	1
S	7:59	9:33				1½

Complete the following:

(a) _________ regular hours × \$12.00 per hour \$_________

(b) _________ overtime hours × \$18.00 per hour \$_________

(c) Total gross wages \$_________

(d) Federal income tax withholding (from tax tables in Figure 8-4, pages 286 and 287) \$_________

(e) Social Security withholding at 6.2% \$_________

(f) Medicare withholding at 1.45% \$_________

(g) Total withholding \$_________

(h) Net pay \$_________

E 8-2B (LO2)
✓ Gross pay: \$678.00

COMPUTING WEEKLY GROSS PAY Manuel Soto's regular hourly rate is \$12.00. He receives 1½ times the regular rate for hours worked in excess of 40 a week and double the rate for work on Sunday. During the past week, Soto worked 8 hours each day Monday through Thursday, 11 hours on Friday, and 6 hours on Sunday. Compute Soto's gross pay for the past week.

E 8-3B (LO2)
✓ b: \$918.75

COMPUTING OVERTIME RATE OF PAY AND GROSS WEEKLY PAY Mike Fritz receives a regular salary of \$3,250 a month and is paid 1½ times the regular hourly rate for hours worked in excess of 40 per week.

(a) Calculate Fritz's overtime rate of pay. (Compute to the nearest half cent.)
(b) Calculate Fritz's total gross weekly pay if he works 46 hours during the week.

E 8-4B (LO2)
✓ e: \$77.00

COMPUTING FEDERAL INCOME TAX Using the table in Figure 8-4 on pages 286 and 287, determine the amount of federal income tax an employer should withhold weekly for employees with the following marital status, earnings, and withholding allowances:

	Marital Status	Total Weekly Earnings	Number of Allowances	Amount of Withholding
(a)	M	\$546.00	4	_________
(b)	M	390.00	3	_________
(c)	S	461.39	2	_________
(d)	M	522.88	2	_________
(e)	S	612.00	0	_________

E 8-5B (LO2)

✓ 3rd row, Soc. Sec. tax: $179.80

CALCULATING SOCIAL SECURITY AND MEDICARE TAXES Assume a Social Security tax rate of 6.2% is applied to maximum earnings of $106,800 and a Medicare tax rate of 1.45% is applied to all earnings. Calculate the Social Security and Medicare taxes for the following situations:

Cumul. Pay Before Current Weekly Payroll	Current Gross Pay	Year-to-Date Earnings	Soc. Sec. Maximum	Amount Over Max. Soc. Sec.	Amount Subject to Soc. Sec.	Soc. Sec. Tax Withheld	Medicare Tax Withheld
$ 31,000	$1,500		$106,800				
53,000	2,860		106,800				
103,900	3,140		106,800				
106,200	2,920		106,800				

E 8-6B (LO4)

✓ Med. tax: $136.30

JOURNALIZING PAYROLL TRANSACTIONS On November 30, the payroll register of Webster & Smith indicated the following information:

Wages and Salaries Expense	$9,400.00
Employee Income Tax Payable	985.00
United Way Contributions Payable	200.00
Earnings subject to Social Security tax	9,400.00

Determine the amount of Social Security and Medicare taxes to be withheld and record the journal entry for the payroll, crediting Cash for the net pay.

E 8-7B (LO4)

✓ Cr. Cash: $5,696.54

PAYROLL JOURNAL ENTRY Journalize the following data taken from the payroll register of Himes Bakery as of June 12, 20--:

Regular earnings	$6,520.00
Overtime earnings	950.00
Deductions:	
Federal income tax	782.00
Social Security tax	463.14
Medicare tax	108.32
Pension plan	80.00
Health insurance premiums	190.00
United Way contributions	150.00

SERIES B PROBLEMS

P 8-8B (LO2/4)

✓ Net pay: $185.27

GROSS PAY, DEDUCTIONS, AND NET PAY Elyse Lin works for Columbia Industries. Her rate of pay is $9.00 per hour, and she is paid 1½ times the regular rate for all hours worked in excess of 40 per week. During the last week of January of the current year, she worked 46 hours. Lin is married and claims two withholding allowances on her W-4 form. Her weekly wages are subject to the following deductions:

(a) Employee income tax (use Figure 8-4 on pages 286 and 287)
(b) Social Security tax at 6.2%
(c) Medicare tax at 1.45%
(d) Health insurance premium, $92.00
(e) Credit union, $110.00
(f) United Way contribution, $5.00

(continued)

REQUIRED

1. Compute Lin's regular pay, overtime pay, gross pay, and net pay.
2. Journalize the payment of her wages for the week ended January 31, crediting Cash for the net amount.

P 8-9B (LO2/3/4)
✓ Cr. Cash: $1,777.42

PAYROLL REGISTER AND PAYROLL JOURNAL ENTRY Karen Jolly operates a bakery called Karen's Cupcakes. She has five employees, all of whom are paid on a weekly basis. Karen's Cupcakes uses a payroll register, individual employee earnings records, and a general journal.

Karen's Cupcakes uses a weekly federal income tax withholding table. The payroll data for each employee for the week ended February 15, 20--, are given below. Employees are paid 1½ times the regular rate for working over 40 hours a week.

Name	No. of Allowances	Marital Status	Total Hours Worked Feb. 9–15	Rate	Total Earnings Jan. 1–Feb. 8
Barone, William	1	S	40	$10.00	$2,400.00
Hastings, Gene	4	M	45	12.00	3,360.00
Nitobe, Isako	3	M	46	8.75	2,935.00
Smith, Judy	4	M	42	11.00	2,745.00
Tarshis, Dolores	1	S	39	10.50	2,650.75

Social Security tax is withheld from the first $106,800 of earnings at the rate of 6.2%. Medicare tax is withheld at the rate of 1.45%, and city earnings tax at the rate of 1%, both applied to gross pay. Hastings and Smith have $35.00 withheld and Nitobe and Tarshis have $15.00 withheld for health insurance. Nitobe and Tarshis have $25.00 withheld to be invested in the bakers' credit union. Hastings has $18.75 withheld and Smith has $43.75 withheld under a savings bond purchase plan.

Karen's Cupcakes' payroll is met by drawing checks on its regular bank account. The checks were issued in sequence, beginning with No. 365.

REQUIRED

1. Prepare a payroll register for Karen's Cupcakes for the week ended February 15, 20--. (In the Taxable Earnings/Unemployment Compensation column, enter the same amounts as in the Social Security column.) Total the amount columns, verify the totals, and rule with single and double lines.
2. Assuming that the wages for the week ended February 15 were paid on February 17, prepare the journal entry for the payment of this payroll.

P 8-10B (LO3)
✓ Soc. Sec. tax: $24.80

EMPLOYEE EARNINGS RECORD Karen's Cupcakes in Problem 8-9B keeps employee earnings records. William Barone, employee number 19, is employed as a baker in the desserts department. He was born on August 26, 1959, and was hired on October 1 of last year. His social security number is 342-73-4681. He lives at 30 Timber Lane, Willington, CT 06279.

REQUIRED

For the week ended February 15, complete an employee earnings record for William Barone. (Insert earnings data only for the week of February 15.)

MANAGING YOUR WRITING

The minimum wage originally was only 25 cents an hour. Today it is $7.25 an hour. Assume that Congress is considering raising the minimum wage again and your U.S. representative is asking for public opinion on this issue. Write a letter to your representative with arguments for and against a higher minimum wage.

ETHICS CASE

Maura Lowe is a payroll accountant for N & L Company. She prepares and processes the company's payroll on a weekly basis and has been at N & L for only three months. All employees are paid on Friday. On Wednesday afternoon, Simon Lentz, one of the company's top sales associates, asks Maura to not take out any payroll deductions from his pay this week. He explains that he is short of cash and needs the full amount of his gross salary just to put food on the table and make his past-due car payment. He promises Maura that she can catch up on the deductions over the next month. The deductions include employee income tax, Social Security tax, Medicare tax, and health insurance premiums.

1. Is Simon's request of Maura ethical? Why or why not?
2. If this were the first pay period of the year and Maura agreed not to take out deductions from Simon's pay, what effect would this have on the liabilities section of the balance sheet?
3. Write a short paragraph from Maura to Simon explaining how omitting deductions from a pay period will cause errors in the company's financial statements.
4. In small groups, discuss what action Maura should take regarding Simon's request.

MASTERY PROBLEM

✓ Cr. Cash: $4,253.54

KA KLOOSTER & ALLEN

Abigail Trenkamp owns and operates the Trenkamp Collection Agency. Listed on the following page are the name, number of allowances claimed, marital status, information from time cards on hours worked each day, and the hourly rate of each employee. All hours worked in excess of 40 hours for Monday through Friday are paid at 1½ times the regular rate. All weekend hours are paid at double the regular rate.

Trenkamp uses a weekly federal income tax withholding table (see Figure 8-4 on pages 286 and 287). Social Security tax is withheld at the rate of 6.2% for the first $106,800 earned. Medicare tax is withheld at 1.45% and state income tax at 3.5%. Each employee has $5.00 withheld for health insurance. All employees use payroll deduction to the credit union for varying amounts as listed.

(continued)

Trenkamp Collection Agency
Payroll Information for the Week Ended November 18, 20--

Name	Employee No.	No of Allow.	Marital Status	S	S	M	T	W	T	F	Hourly Rate	Credit Union Deposit	Total Earnings 1/1–11/11
				Regular Hours Worked									
Berling, James	1	3	M	2	2	9	8	8	9	10	$12.00	$149.60	$24,525.00
Merz, Linda	2	4	M	4	3	8	8	8	8	11	10.00	117.00	20,480.00
Goetz, Ken	3	2	M	0	0	6	7	8	9	10	11.00	91.30	21,500.00
Menick, Judd	4	2	S	8	8	0	0	8	8	9	11.00	126.50	22,625.00
Morales, Eva	5	3	M	0	0	8	8	8	6	8	13.00	117.05	24,730.00
Heimbrock, Jacob	6	5	M	0	0	8	8	8	8	8	34.00	154.25	105,840.00
Townsley, Sarah	7	2	M	4	0	6	6	6	6	4	9.00	83.05	21,425.00
Salzman, Ben	8	4	M	6	2	8	8	6	6	6	11.00	130.00	6,635.00
Layton, Esther	9	3	M	0	0	8	8	8	8	8	11.00	88.00	5,635.00
Thompson, David	10	5	M	0	2	10	9	7	7	10	11.00	128.90	21,635.00
Vadillo, Carmen	11	2	S	8	0	4	8	8	8	9	13.00	139.11	24,115.00

The Trenkamp Collection Agency follows the practice of drawing a single check for the net amount of the payroll and depositing the check in a special payroll account at the bank. Individual checks issued were numbered consecutively, beginning with No. 331.

REQUIRED

1. Prepare a payroll register for Trenkamp Collection Agency for the week ended November 18, 20--. (In the Taxable Earnings/Unemployment Compensation column, enter $365 for Salzman and $440 for Layton. Leave this column blank for all other employees.) Total the amount columns, verify the totals, and rule with single and double lines.
2. Assuming that the wages for the week ended November 18 were paid on November 21, prepare the journal entry for the payment of this payroll.
3. The current employee earnings record for Ben Salzman is provided in the working papers. Update Salzman's earnings record to reflect the November 18 payroll. Although this information should have been entered earlier, complete the required information on the earnings record. The necessary information is as follows:

Name	Ben F. Salzman
Address	12 Windmill Lane Trumbull, CT 06611
Employee No.	8
Gender	Male
Department	Administration
Occupation	Office Manager
Social Security No.	446-46-6321
Marital Status	Married
Allowances	4
Pay Rate	$11.00 per hour
Date of Birth	4/5/64
Date Hired	7/22/--

CHALLENGE PROBLEM

This problem challenges you to apply your cumulative accounting knowledge to move a step beyond the material in the chapter.

✓ **Dr. Wages and Salaries Expense: $1,596**

Irina Company pays its employees weekly. The last pay period for 20-1 was on December 28. From December 28 through December 31, the employees earned $1,754.00, so the following adjusting entry was made:

	20-1					
5	Dec.	31	Wages and Salaries Expense	1 7 5 4 00		5
6			Wages and Salaries Payable		1 7 5 4 00	6
7			To record accrued wages and salaries			7

The first pay period in 20-2 was on January 4. The totals line from Irina Company's payroll register for the week ended January 4, 20-2, was as follows:

PAYROLL

			EARNINGS				TAXABLE EARNINGS		
			REGULAR	OVERTIME	TOTAL	CUMULATIVE TOTAL	UNEMPLOYMENT COMPENSATION	SOCIAL SECURITY	
1	Totals		3 3 5 0 00		3 3 5 0 00	3 3 5 0 00	3 3 5 0 00	3 3 5 0 00	1

REGISTER—WEEK ENDED January 4, 20-2

	DEDUCTIONS								
	FEDERAL INCOME TAX	SOCIAL SECURITY TAX	MEDICARE TAX	HEALTH INSURANCE	UNITED WAY	OTHER	TOTAL	NET PAY	
1	3 4 2 00	2 0 7 70	4 8 58	5 0 00	8 0 00		7 2 8 28	2 6 2 1 72	1

REQUIRED

1. Prepare the journal entry for the payment of the payroll on January 4, 20-2.
2. Prepare T accounts for Wages and Salaries Expense and Wages and Salaries Payable showing the beginning balance, January 4, 20-2, entry, and ending balance as of January 4, 20-2.

ANSWERS TO SELF-STUDY QUESTIONS AND EXERCISES

True/False Questions

1. F (does *not* work under control and direction)
2. T
3. F (is called wages)
4. T
5. T

Multiple Choice Questions

1. c **2.** d **3.** d **4.** b **5.** a

U REVU Exercises

1.

(a)

40 × $14 =	$560
5 × $14 × 1.5 =	105
Gross pay	$665

(b) $40

2.

Wages and Salaries Expense	4,600.00	
Employee Income Tax Payable		417.00
Social Security Tax Payable		285.20
Medicare Tax Payable		66.70
State Income Tax Payable		46.00
Health Insurance Premiums Payable		181.00
Cash		3,604.10

Chapter 9

LISEGAGNE/ISTOCKPHOTO.COM

Payroll Accounting: Employer Taxes and Reports

LEARNING OBJECTIVES

Careful study of this chapter should enable you to:

LO1 **Describe and calculate employer payroll taxes.**

LO2 **Account for employer payroll taxes expense.**

LO3 **Describe employer reporting and payment responsibilities.**

LO4 **Describe and account for workers' compensation insurance.**

As competition has become more global, many challenges to businesses have developed. Learning how to function in many different languages and cultures is one of these challenges. Lingualinx is a full-service translation company that offers help with language issues. Founded in 2002, Lingualinx has offices in the United States, the United Kingdom, France, and China. It hires qualified professional linguists with skills tailored to provide services in more than 100 languages. Some examples of its capabilities include simple text translation, simultaneous interpretation, sign language, copywriting, and even Braille production. It can also provide on-site language instruction classes.

Lingualinx faces the same kinds of payroll issues as Intechra, the company described in the introduction to Chapter 8. But Lingualinx would face the added challenge of employees in multiple countries, so it would need to know the regulations in each location. In addition, you will learn in this chapter that employers must account for not just *employee* wages and taxes but also *employer* taxes. The complexity of payroll accounting is a major reason why many businesses hire an outside company to manage their payroll. You will also learn about two of these payroll service companies in this chapter's "A Broader View."

The taxes we discussed in Chapter 8 had one thing in common—they all were levied on the employee. The employer withheld them from employees' earnings and paid them to the government. They did not add anything to the employer's payroll expenses.

In this chapter, we will examine several taxes that are imposed directly on the employer. All of these taxes represent additional payroll expenses. You will see that the total cost of employees includes not only wages but also payroll taxes and benefits such as vacation and sick pay.

EMPLOYER PAYROLL TAXES

LO1 Describe and calculate employer payroll taxes.

Most employers must pay FICA, FUTA (Federal Unemployment Tax Act), and SUTA (state unemployment tax) taxes.

EMPLOYER FICA TAXES

Employer FICA taxes are levied on employers at the same rates and on the same earnings bases as the employee FICA taxes. As explained in Chapter 8, we are assuming the Social Security component is 6.2% on maximum earnings of $106,800 for each employee. Since there is no maximum on the Medicare component, this tax is 1.45% on all earnings.

The payroll register we saw in Chapter 8 is a key source of information for computing employer payroll taxes. That payroll register is reproduced in Figure 9-1. The Taxable Earnings Social Security column shows that $4,835 of employee earnings were subject to Social Security tax for the pay period. The employer's Social Security tax on these earnings is computed as follows:

FIGURE 9-1 Payroll Register (left side)

PAYROLL

	NAME	ALLOWANCES	MARITAL STATUS	EARNINGS REGULAR	EARNINGS OVERTIME	EARNINGS TOTAL	EARNINGS CUMULATIVE TOTAL	TAXABLE EARNINGS UNEMPLOYMENT COMPENSATION	TAXABLE EARNINGS SOCIAL SECURITY	
1	Cadrain, Sarah	4	M	1600 00	60 00	1660 00	107800 00	0 00	660 00	1
2	Gruder, James	1	S	760 00	140 00	900 00	43400 00	0 00	900 00	2
3	Istone, Ken	4	M	545 00		545 00	27025 00	0 00	545 00	3
4	Kuzmik, Helen	2	M	480 00	294 00	774 00	31000 00	0 00	774 00	4
5	Lee, Hoseoup	3	M	440 00		440 00	22340 00	0 00	440 00	5
6	Swaney, Linda	2	S	528 00	198 00	726 00	27500 00	0 00	726 00	6
7	Tucci, Paul	3	M	490 00		490 00	25050 00	0 00	490 00	7
8	Wiles, Harry	1	S	300 00		300 00	6300 00	300 00	300 00	8
9				5143 00	692 00	5835 00	290415 00	300 00	4835 00	9
10										10

Time cards, pay rates (Regular, Overtime)

Prior period total + current period earnings (Cumulative Total)

Current below $7,000 cumul. total (Unemployment Compensation)

Current below $106,800 cumul. total (Social Security)

Social Security Taxable Earnings	×	Tax Rate	=	Tax
$4,835		0.062		$299.77

LEARNING KEY

Use the information in the payroll register to compute employer payroll taxes.

The Medicare tax applies to the total earnings of $5,835. The employer's Medicare tax on these earnings is computed as follows:

Total Earnings	×	Tax Rate	=	Tax
$5,835		0.0145		$84.61

These amounts plus the employees' Social Security and Medicare taxes withheld must be paid by the employer to the Internal Revenue Service (IRS).

SELF-EMPLOYMENT TAX

The self-employment tax rate is double the employee and employer Social Security and Medicare rates because the self-employed person is considered both the employer and employee.

Individuals who own and run their own business are considered self-employed. These individuals can be viewed as both employer and employee. They do not receive salary or wages from the business, but they do have earnings in the form of the business net income. **Self-employment income** is the net income of a trade or business run by an individual. Currently, persons earning net self-employment income of $400 or more must pay a **self-employment tax**. Self-employment tax is a contribution to the FICA program. The tax rates are double the Social Security and Medicare rates (12.4% + 2.9% = 15.3% total). They are applied to the same income bases as those used for the Social Security and Medicare taxes. *Publication 334, Tax Guide for Small Business,* contains helpful information for self-employed persons.

EMPLOYER FUTA TAX

The **FUTA (Federal Unemployment Tax Act) tax** is levied only on employers. It is not deducted from employees' earnings. The purpose of this tax is to raise funds to administer the combined federal/state unemployment compensation program. The maximum

FIGURE 9-1 Payroll Register (right side)

REGISTER—WEEK ENDED 12/19/--

	DEDUCTIONS							NET PAY	CHECK NO.	
	FEDERAL INCOME TAX	SOCIAL SECURITY TAX	MEDICARE TAX	HEALTH INSURANCE	UNITED WAY	OTHER	TOTAL			
1	168.00	40.92	24.07				232.99	1,427.01	409	1
2	126.00	55.80	13.05		20.00		214.85	685.15	410	2
3	11.00	33.79	7.90	10.00			62.69	482.31	411	3
4	57.00	47.99	11.22	13.00	20.00		149.21	624.79	412	4
5	8.00	27.28	6.38	13.00			54.66	385.34	413	5
6	73.00	45.01	10.53				128.54	597.46	414	6
7	13.00	30.38	7.11	10.00			60.49	429.51	415	7
8	20.00	18.60	4.35				42.95	257.05	416	8
9	476.00	299.77	84.61	46.00	40.00		946.38	4,888.62		9
10										10

Withholding Tax Table

6.2% × Social Security taxable earnings

1.45% × total earnings

Specific employer–employee agreements

Total earnings – total deductions

amount of earnings subject to the FUTA tax and the tax rate can be changed by Congress. The current rate is 6.2% applied to maximum earnings of $7,000 for each employee, but employers are allowed a credit of up to 5.4% for participation in state unemployment programs. Thus, the effective federal rate is commonly 0.8%.

Gross FUTA rate	6.2%
Credit for state unemployment taxes	5.4%
Net FUTA rate	0.8%

To illustrate the computation of the FUTA tax, refer to Figure 9-1. The Taxable Earnings Unemployment Compensation column shows that only $300 of employee earnings were subject to the FUTA tax. This amount is low because the payroll period is late in the calendar year (December 19, 20--). It is common for most employees to exceed the $7,000 earnings limit by this time. The FUTA tax is computed as shown in Figure 9-2.

FIGURE 9-2 Computation of FUTA Tax

	UNEMPLOYMENT COMPENSATION
5	
6	
7	
8	300 00
9	300 00

FUTA Taxable Earnings	×	Tax Rate	=	Tax
$300		0.008		$2.40

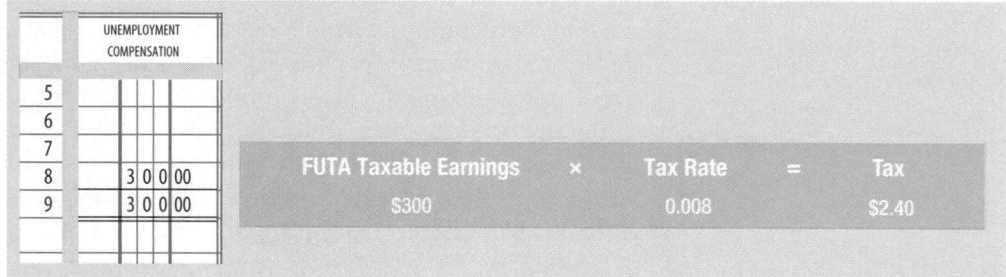

EMPLOYER SUTA TAX

State unemployment tax rates and maximum earnings amounts vary greatly. Current rates range from 5.4% to 11%. Maximum earnings amounts are $7,000 to $35,700.

The **SUTA (state unemployment tax) tax** is also levied only on employers in most states. The purpose of this tax is to raise funds to pay unemployment benefits. Tax rates and unemployment benefits vary among the states. A common rate is 5.4% applied to maximum earnings of $7,000 for each employee. Most states have an **experience-rating system** to encourage employers to provide regular employment to workers. If an employer has very few former employees receiving unemployment compensation, the employer qualifies for a lower state unemployment tax rate. If an employer qualifies for a lower state rate, the full credit of 5.4% would still be allowed in computing the federal unemployment tax due.

Refer to the payroll register in Figure 9-1. As we saw with the FUTA tax, only $300 of employee earnings for this pay period are subject to the state unemployment tax. The tax is computed as shown in Figure 9-3.

FIGURE 9-3 Computation of SUTA Tax

	UNEMPLOYMENT COMPENSATION
5	
6	
7	
8	300 00
9	300 00

State Unemployment Taxable Earnings	×	Tax Rate	=	Tax
$300		0.054		$16.20

U REVU Complete U REVU-1 on **page 339** to test your basic understanding of LO1.

ACCOUNTING FOR EMPLOYER PAYROLL TAXES

LO2 Account for employer payroll taxes expense.

Now that we have computed the employer payroll taxes, we need to journalize them. It is common to debit all employer payroll taxes to a single account—Payroll Taxes Expense. However, we usually credit separate liability accounts for Social Security, Medicare, FUTA, and SUTA taxes payable.

JOURNALIZING EMPLOYER PAYROLL TAXES

The employer payroll taxes computed in the previous section can be summarized as follows:

Employer's Social Security tax	$299.77
Employer's Medicare tax	84.61
FUTA tax	2.40
SUTA tax	16.20
Total employer payroll taxes	$402.98

These amounts provide the basis for the following journal entry:

					Debit	Credit	
5	Dec.	19	Payroll Taxes Expense		402.98		5
6			Social Security Tax Payable			299.77	6
7			Medicare Tax Payable			84.61	7
8			FUTA Tax Payable			2.40	8
9			SUTA Tax Payable			16.20	9
10			Employer payroll taxes for week ended Dec. 19				10

The steps needed to prepare this journal entry for employer payroll taxes are:

STEP 1 Obtain the total earnings and taxable earnings amounts from the Earnings—Total and Taxable Earnings columns of the payroll register. In this case, total earnings were $5,835; Social Security taxable earnings were $4,835; and Unemployment Compensation taxable earnings were $300.

STEP 2 Compute the amount of employer Social Security tax by multiplying the Social Security taxable earnings by 6.2%.

STEP 3 Compute the amount of employer Medicare tax by multiplying total earnings by 1.45%.

STEP 4 Compute the amount of FUTA tax by multiplying the Unemployment Taxable earnings by 0.8%.

STEP 5 Compute the amount of SUTA tax by multiplying the Unemployment Taxable earnings by 5.4%.

STEP 6 Prepare the appropriate journal entry using the amounts computed in steps 2–5.

To understand the journal entry for employer payroll taxes, let's use the accounting equation to examine the accounts involved. The five accounts affected by the payroll taxes entry above are shown in the accounting equation in Figure 9-4.

FIGURE 9-4 Accounting for Payroll Taxes

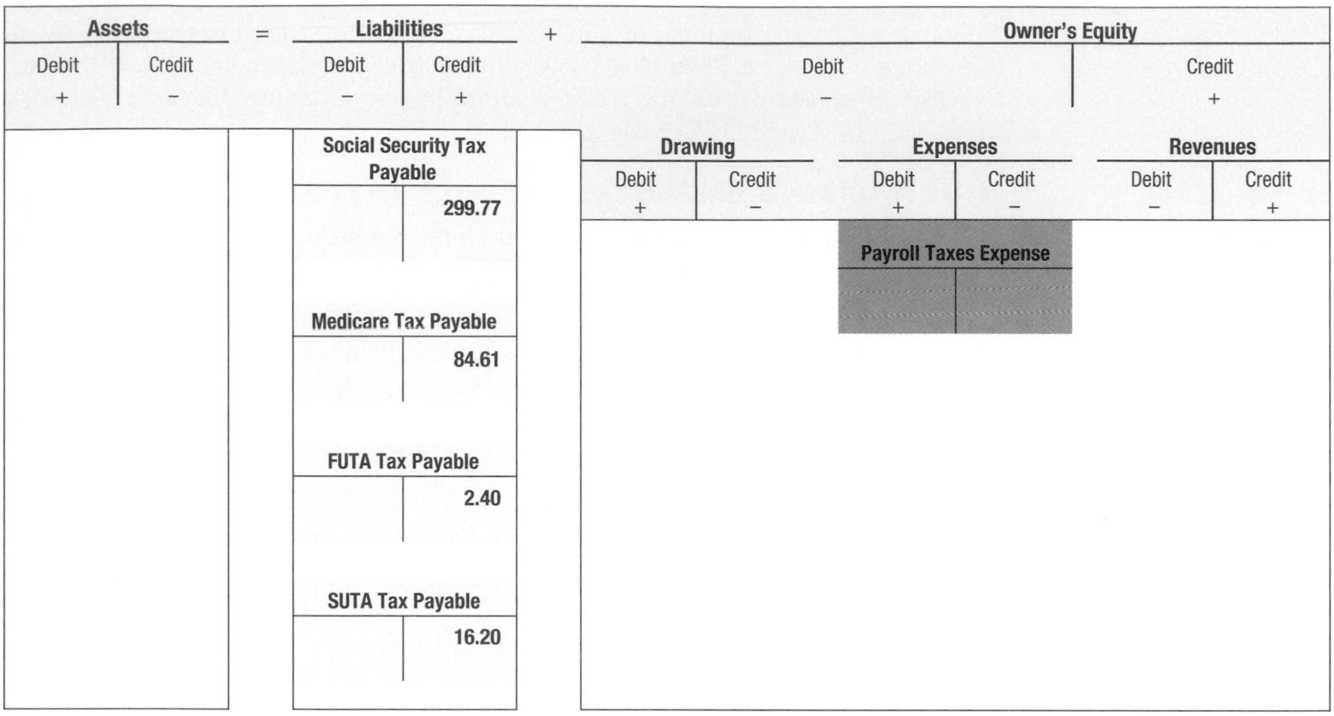

PAYROLL TAXES EXPENSE

The Social Security, Medicare, FUTA, and SUTA taxes imposed on the employer are expenses of doing business. Each of the employer taxes is debited to Payroll Taxes Expense.

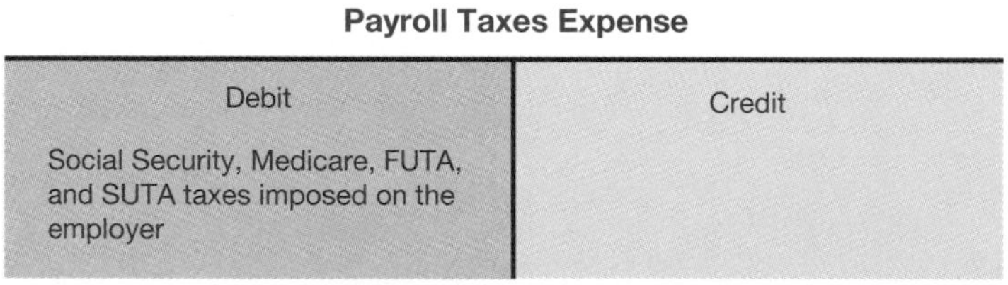

SOCIAL SECURITY AND MEDICARE TAXES PAYABLE

These are the same liability accounts used in Chapter 8 to record the Social Security and Medicare taxes withheld from employees' earnings. The accounts are credited to enter the Social Security and Medicare taxes imposed on the employer. They are debited when the taxes are paid to the IRS. When all of the Social Security and Medicare taxes have been paid, the accounts will have zero balances.

LEARNING KEY

Employer and employee Social Security and Medicare taxes are credited to the same liability accounts because both of these taxes are due and will be paid to the IRS.

Social Security Tax Payable

Debit	Credit
Payment of Social Security tax	Social Security taxes (1) withheld from employees' earnings and (2) imposed on the employer

Medicare Tax Payable

Debit	Credit
Payment of Medicare tax	Medicare taxes (1) withheld from employees' earnings and (2) imposed on the employer

FUTA TAX PAYABLE

A separate liability account entitled FUTA Tax Payable is kept for the employer's FUTA tax. This account is credited for the tax imposed on employers under the Federal Unemployment Tax Act. The account is debited when this tax is paid. When all of the FUTA taxes have been paid, the account will have a zero balance.

FUTA Tax Payable

Debit	Credit
Payment of FUTA tax	FUTA tax imposed on the employer

SUTA TAX PAYABLE

A separate liability account entitled SUTA Tax Payable is kept for the state unemployment tax. This account is credited for the tax imposed on employers under the state unemployment compensation laws. The account is debited when this tax is paid. When all of the state unemployment taxes have been paid, the account will have a zero balance.

SUTA Tax Payable

Debit	Credit
Payment of SUTA tax	SUTA tax imposed on the employer

TOTAL PAYROLL COST OF AN EMPLOYEE

It is interesting to note what it really costs to employ a person. The employer must, of course, pay the gross wages of an employee. In addition, the employer must pay payroll taxes on employee earnings up to certain dollar limits.

To illustrate, assume that an employee earns $26,000 a year. The total cost of this employee to the employer is calculated as follows:

Gross wages	$26,000
Employer Social Security tax, 6.2% of $26,000	1,612
Employer Medicare tax, 1.45% of $26,000	377
State unemployment tax, 5.4% of $7,000	378
FUTA tax, 0.8% of $7,000	56
	$28,423

Thus, the total payroll cost of employing a person whose stated compensation is $26,000 is $28,423. Employer payroll taxes clearly are a significant cost of doing business. Employer-paid medical insurance and pension plans can further increase total payroll costs.

U REVU

Complete U REVU-2 on **page 339** to test your basic understanding of LO2.

REPORTING AND PAYMENT RESPONSIBILITIES

LO3 Describe employer reporting and payment responsibilities.

Employer payroll reporting and payment responsibilities fall into six areas:

1. Federal income tax withholding and Social Security and Medicare taxes
2. FUTA taxes
3. SUTA taxes
4. Employee Wage and Tax Statement (Form W-2)
5. Summary of employee wages and taxes (Form W-3)
6. Employment eligibility verification (Form I-9)

FEDERAL INCOME TAX WITHHOLDING AND SOCIAL SECURITY AND MEDICARE TAXES

Three important aspects of employer reporting and payment responsibilities for federal income tax withholding and Social Security and Medicare taxes are:

1. Determining when payments are due
2. Use of Form 8109, Federal Tax Deposit Coupon
3. Use of Form 941, Employer's Quarterly Federal Tax Return

When Payments Are Due

The date by which federal income tax withholding and Social Security and Medicare taxes must be paid depends on the amount of these taxes. Figure 9-5 summarizes the deposit rules stated in *Circular E—Employer's Tax Guide*. In general, the larger the amount that needs to be deposited, the more frequently payments must be made. For simplicity, we will assume that deposits must be made 15 days after the end of each month.

FIGURE 9-5 Summary of Deposit Rules

ACCUMULATED TAX LIABILITY	DEPOSIT DUE
1. Less than $2,500 at the end of the current quarter	1. Pay with Form 941 at end of the month following end of the quarter
2. $2,500 or more at the end of the current quarter and $50,000 or less in total during the lookback period*	2. Deposit 15 days after end of the month
3. $2,500 or more at the end of the current quarter and more than $50,000 in total during the lookback period*	3. Deposit every other Wednesday or Friday, depending on day of the week payroll payments are made
4. $100,000 or more on any day during the current quarter	4. Deposit by the end of the next banking day

*Lookback period is the four quarters beginning July 1, two years ago, and ending June 30, one year ago.

Form 8109

Taxpayers who are not required to make electronic deposits may voluntarily participate in EFTPS.

Deposits may be made using either the **Electronic Federal Tax Payment System (EFTPS)** or Form 8109. The EFTPS is an electronic funds transfer system for making federal tax deposits. Any taxpayer whose deposits in the prior year exceeded $200,000 is required to use this system. Deposits other than EFTPS are made at an authorized commercial bank using Form 8109, Federal Tax Deposit Coupon (Figure 9-6). The **Employer Identification Number (EIN)** shown on this form is obtained by the employer from the IRS. This number identifies the employer and must be shown on all payroll forms and reports filed with the IRS.

FIGURE 9-6 Federal Tax Deposit Coupon (Form 8109)

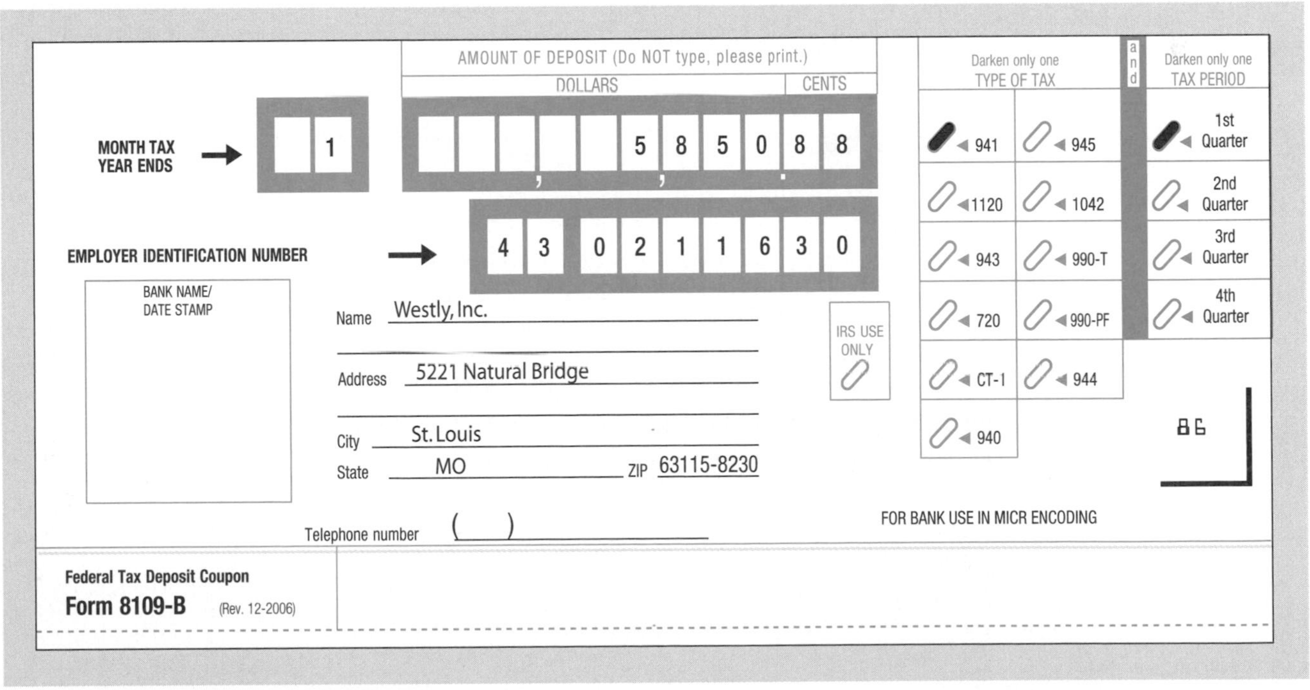

The $5,850.88 deposit shown in Figure 9-6 for Westly, Inc., was for the following taxes on wages paid in January:

Employees' income tax withheld from wages		$2,526.80
Social Security tax:		
Withheld from employees' wages	$1,346.24	
Imposed on employer	1,346.24	2,692.48
Medicare tax:		
Withheld from employees' wages	$ 315.80	
Imposed on employer	315.80	631.60
Amount of check		$5,850.88

The journal entry for this deposit would be as follows:

5	Feb.	15	Employee Income Tax Payable		2,526.80		5
6			Social Security Tax Payable		2,692.48		6
7			Medicare Tax Payable		631.60		7
8			Cash			5,850.88	8
9			Deposit of employee federal income tax and				9
10			Social Security and Medicare taxes				10

Form 941

Form 941, Employer's Quarterly Federal Tax Return, must be filed with the IRS at the end of the month following each calendar quarter. This form reports the following taxes for the quarter:

1. Employee federal income tax withheld
2. Employee Social Security and Medicare taxes withheld
3. Employer Social Security and Medicare taxes

A completed form for Westly, Inc., for the first quarter of the calendar year is shown in Figure 9-7. Instructions for completing the form are provided with the form and in *Circular E.*

FUTA TAXES

Federal unemployment taxes must be calculated on a quarterly basis. If the accumulated liability exceeds $500, the total must be paid to an authorized commercial bank. The total is due by the end of the month following the close of the quarter. If the liability is $500 or less, no deposit is necessary. The amount is simply added to the amount to be deposited for the next quarter. FUTA taxes are deposited using either EFTPS or Form 8109 (Figure 9-6).

Assume that an employer's accumulated FUTA tax liability for the first quarter of the calendar year is $508. The employer would use Form 8109 to deposit this amount on April 30. The journal entry for this transaction would be as follows:

15	Apr.	30	FUTA Tax Payable		508.00		15
16			Cash			508.00	16
17			Deposit of federal unemployment tax				17

FIGURE 9-7 Employer's Quarterly Federal Tax Return (Form 941)

Form **941 for 20--: Employer's QUARTERLY Federal Tax Return** 950109

(Rev. January 20--) Department of the Treasury — Internal Revenue Service OMB No. 1545-0029

(EIN) Employer identification number: 4 3 – 0 2 1 1 6 3 0

Name (*not your trade name*):

Trade name (*if any*): Westly, Inc.

Address: 5221 Natural Bridge
Number Street Suite or room number

St. Louis | MO | 63115-8230
City State ZIP code

Report for this Quarter of 20--
(Check one.)

- [X] 1: January, February, March
- [ ] 2: April, May, June
- [ ] 3: July, August, September
- [ ] 4: October, November, December

Read the separate instructions before you complete Form 941. Type or print within the boxes.

Part 1: Answer these questions for this quarter.

Line	Description			Line	Amount
1	**Number of employees who received wages, tips, or other compensation for the pay period including:** ***Mar. 12*** **(Quarter 1),** ***June 12*** **(Quarter 2),** ***Sept. 12*** **(Quarter 3),** ***Dec. 12*** **(Quarter 4)**			1	8
2	**Wages, tips, and other compensation**			2	65,160.00
3	**Income tax withheld from wages, tips, and other compensation**			3	7,595.80 ← Employee federal income tax withheld
4	**If no wages, tips, and other compensation are subject to social security or Medicare tax**				[ ] Check and go to line 6.
5	**Taxable social security and Medicare wages and tips:**	*Column 1*	*Column 2*		
5a	**Taxable social security wages**	65,160.00 × .124 =	8,079.84 ← Employee and employer Social Security taxes		
5b	**Taxable social security tips**	. × .124 =	.		
5c	**Taxable Medicare wages & tips**	65,160.00 × .029 =	1,889.64 ← Employee and employer Medicare taxes		
5d	**Total social security and Medicare taxes** (*Column 2,* lines 5a + 5b + 5c = line 5d)			5d	9,969.48
6	**Total taxes before adjustments** (lines 3 + 5d = line 6)			6	17,565.28
7	**CURRENT QUARTER'S ADJUSTMENTS,** for example, a fractions of cents adjustment. **See the instructions.**				
7a	**Current quarter's fractions of cents**		.		
7b	**Current quarter's sick pay**		.		
7c	**Current quarter's adjustments for tips and group-term life insurance**		.		
7d	**TOTAL ADJUSTMENTS.** Combine all amounts on lines 7a through 7c			7d	.0
8	**Total taxes after adjustments.** Combine lines 6 and 7d			8	17,565.28
9	**Advance earned income credit (EIC) payments made to employees**			9	.0
10	**Total taxes after adjustment for advance EIC** (line 8 – line 9 = line 10)			10	17,565.28
11	**Total deposits for this quarter, including overpayment applied from a prior quarter and overpayment applied from Form 941-X or Form 944-X**		17,565.28		
12a	**COBRA premium assistance payments** (see instructions)		.		
12b	**Number of individuals provided COBRA premium assistance reported on line 12a**				
13	**Add lines 11 and 12a**			13	17,565.28
14	**Balance due.** If line 10 is more than line 13, write the difference here. For information on how to pay, see the instructions.			14	.0
15	**Overpayment.** If line 13 is more than line 10, write the difference here		.		Check one [ ] Apply to next return. [ ] Send a refund.

▶ You **MUST** complete both pages of Form 941 and **SIGN** it. **Next →**

For Privacy Act and Paperwork Reduction Act Notice, see the back of the Payment Voucher. Cat. No. 17001Z Form **941** (Rev. 1-20--)

FIGURE 9-7 Employer's Quarterly Federal Tax Return (Form 941) (*concluded*)

950209

Name *(not your trade name)* | **Employer identification number (EIN)**

Part 2: Tell us about your deposit schedule and tax liability for this quarter.

If you are unsure about whether you are a monthly schedule depositor or a semiweekly schedule depositor, see *Pub. 15 (Circular E)*, section 11.

16 [M][O] **Write the state abbreviation for the state where you made your deposits OR write "MU" if you made your deposits in multiple states.**

17 **Check one:** ☐ **Line 10 is less than $2,500.** Go to Part 3.

☒ **You were a monthly schedule depositor for the entire quarter. Enter your tax liability for each month.** Then go to Part 3.

Tax liability:	**Month 1**	5,850.88
	Month 2	5,690.77
	Month 3	6,023.63
Total liability for quarter		17,565.28 **Total must equal line 10.**

☐ **You were a semiweekly schedule depositor for any part of this quarter.** Complete *Schedule B (Form 941): Report of Tax Liability for Semiweekly Schedule Depositors,* and attach it to Form 941.

Part 3: Tell us about your business. If a question does NOT apply to your business, leave it blank.

18 **If your business has closed or you stopped paying wages** . . . . ☐ Check here, and

enter the final date you paid wages ___ / ___ / ___ .

19 **If you are a seasonal employer and you do not have to file a return for every quarter of the year** . ☐ Check here.

Part 4: May we speak with your third-party designee?

Do you want to allow an employee, a paid tax preparer, or another person to discuss this return with the IRS? See the instructions for details.

☐ Yes. Designee's name and phone number ______ ( ) –

Select a 5-digit Personal Identification Number (PIN) to use when talking to the IRS. ☐☐☐☐☐

☒ No.

Part 5: Sign here. You MUST complete both pages of Form 941 and SIGN it.

Under penalties of perjury, I declare that I have examined this return, including accompanying schedules and statements, and to the best of my knowledge and belief, it is true, correct, and complete. Declaration of preparer (other than taxpayer) is based on all information of which preparer has any knowledge.

X Sign your name here *William P. Jones*

Print your name here: William P Jones

Print your title here: Treasurer

Date 4/30/--

Best daytime phone ( ) –

Paid preparer's use only

Check if you are self-employed . . . ☐

Preparer's name		Preparer's SSN/PTIN	
Preparer's signature		Date	/ /
Firm's name (or yours if self-employed)		EIN	
Address		Phone	( ) –
City	State	ZIP code	

Form 940

In addition to making quarterly deposits, employers are required to file an annual report of federal unemployment tax using Form 940 (Figure 9-8). This form must be

FIGURE 9-8 Employer's Annual Federal Unemployment (FUTA) Tax Return (Form 940)

Form **940 for 20--: Employer's Annual Federal Unemployment (FUTA) Tax Return** 850108

Department of the Treasury — Internal Revenue Service OMB No. 1545-0028

(EIN) Employer identification number: 4 3 - 0 2 1 1 6 3 0

Name (*not your trade name*):

Trade name (*if any*): Westly, Inc.

Address: 5221 Natural Bridge (Number, Street, Suite or room number)

St. Louis (City) MO (State) 63115-8230 (ZIP code)

Type of Return (Check all that apply.)

- ☐ a. Amended
- ☐ b. Successor employer
- ☐ c. No payments to employees in 20--
- ☐ d. Final: Business closed or stopped paying wages

Read the separate instructions before you fill out this form. Please type or print within the boxes.

Part 1: Tell us about your return. If any line does NOT apply, leave it blank.

1 **If you were required to pay your state unemployment tax in ...**

1a **One state only,** write the state abbreviation . . . 1a M O

- OR -

1b **More than one state** (You are a multi-state employer) . . . . 1b ☐ Check here. Fill out Schedule A.

Skip line 2 for 20-- and go to line 3.

2 If you paid wages in a state that is subject to CREDIT REDUCTION . . . . 2 ☐ Check here. Fill out Schedule A (Form 940), Part 2.

Part 2: Determine your FUTA tax before adjustments for 20--. If any line does NOT apply, leave it blank.

3	**Total payments to all employees**	3	258,954.00
4	**Payments exempt from FUTA tax**	4	.
	Check all that apply: 4a ☐ Fringe benefits; 4b ☐ Group-term life insurance; 4c ☐ Retirement/Pension; 4d ☐ Dependent care; 4e ☐ Other		
5	**Total of payments made to each employee in excess of $7,000**	5	203,254.00
6	**Subtotal** (line 4 + line 5 = line 6)	6	203,254.00
7	**Total taxable FUTA wages** (line 3 – line 6 = line 7)	7	55,700.00 ← FUTA taxable wages
8	**FUTA tax before adjustments** (line 7 × .008 = line 8)	8	445.60

Part 3: Determine your adjustments. If any line does NOT apply, leave it blank.

9	**If ALL of the taxable FUTA wages you paid were excluded from state unemployment tax, multiply line 7 by .054** (line 7 × .054 = line 9). Then go to line 12	9	.
10	**If SOME of the taxable FUTA wages you paid were excluded from state unemployment tax, OR you paid ANY state unemployment tax late** (after the due date for filing Form 940), fill out the worksheet in the instructions. Enter the amount from line 7 of the worksheet onto line 10	10	.
	Skip line 11 for 20-- and go to line 12.		
11	If credit reduction applies, enter the amount from line 3 of Schedule A (Form 940)	11	.

Part 4: Determine your FUTA tax and balance due or overpayment for 20--. If any line does NOT apply, leave it blank.

12	**Total FUTA tax after adjustments** (lines 8 + 9 + 10 + 11 = line 12)	12	445.60 ← FUTA tax
13	**FUTA tax deposited for the year, including any payment applied from a prior year**	13	427.60 ← FUTA tax paid
14	**Balance due** (If line 12 is more than line 13, enter the difference on line 14.) • If line 14 is more than $500, you must deposit your tax. • If line 14 is $500 or less, you may pay with this return. For more information on how to pay, see the separate instructions	14	18.00 ← FUTA tax due
15	**Overpayment** (If line 13 is more than line 12, enter the difference on line 15 and check a box below.)	15	.

Check one: ☐ Apply to next return. ☐ Send a refund.

▶ You **MUST** fill out both pages of this form and **SIGN** it.

Next ➔

For Privacy Act and Paperwork Reduction Act Notice, see the back of Form 940-V, Payment Voucher. Cat. No. 11234O Form **940** (20--)

FIGURE 9-8 Employer's Annual Federal Unemployment (FUTA) Tax Return (Form 940) (*concluded*)

850208

Name *(not your trade name)*	**Employer identification number (EIN)**

Part 5: Report your FUTA tax liability by quarter only if line 12 is more than $500. If not, go to Part 6.

16 **Report the amount of your FUTA tax liability for each quarter; do NOT enter the amount you deposited. If you had no liability for a quarter, leave the line blank.**

16a **1st quarter** (January 1 – March 31)	16a	.
16b **2nd quarter** (April 1 – June 30)	16b	.
16c **3rd quarter** (July 1 – September 30)	16c	.
16d **4th quarter** (October 1 – December 31)	16d	.
17 **Total tax liability for the year** (lines 16a + 16b + 16c + 16d = line 17)	17	. **Total must equal line 12.**

Part 6: May we speak with your third-party designee?

Do you want to allow an employee, a paid tax preparer, or another person to discuss this return with the IRS? See the instructions for details.

☐ **Yes.** Designee's name and phone number [ ] ( ) –

Select a 5-digit Personal Identification Number (PIN) to use when talking to IRS [ ][ ][ ][ ][ ]

☒ **No.**

Part 7: Sign here. You MUST fill out both pages of this form and SIGN it.

Under penalties of perjury, I declare that I have examined this return, including accompanying schedules and statements, and to the best of my knowledge and belief, it is true, correct, and complete, and that no part of any payment made to a state unemployment fund claimed as a credit was, or is to be, deducted from the payments made to employees. Declaration of preparer (other than taxpayer) is based on all information of which preparer has any knowledge.

✗ Sign your name here	*William P. Jones*	Print your name here	WILLIAM P. JONES
		Print your title here	TREASURER
Date	1/ 31 /--	Best daytime phone	( ) –

Paid preparer's use only Check if you are self-employed . . ☐

Preparer's name		Preparer's SSN/PTIN	
Preparer's signature		Date	/ /
Firm's name (or yours if self-employed)		EIN	
Address		Phone	( ) –
City	State:	ZIP code	

filed with the IRS by the beginning of the second week of February. Figure 9-8 shows a completed Form 940 for Westly, Inc. If a balance is due, it may be paid using EFTPS or Form 940-V. Figure 9-9 shows a completed Form 940-V for Westly.

FIGURE 9-9 Payment Voucher (Form 940-V)

Form **940-V**
Department of the Treasury
Internal Revenue Service

Payment Voucher
▶ **Do not staple or attach this voucher to your payment.**

OMB No. 1545-0028
20--

1 Enter your employer identification number (EIN).
43-0211630

2 **Enter the amount of your payment.** ▶ Dollars 18 Cents 00

3 Enter your business name (individual name if sole proprietor).
Westly, Inc.
Enter your address.
5221 Natural Bridge
Enter your city, state, and ZIP code.
St. Louis, MO 63115-8230

SUTA TAXES

Deposit rules and forms for state unemployment taxes vary among the states. Deposits usually are required on a quarterly basis. Assume that Westly's accumulated state unemployment liability for the first quarter of the calendar year is $2,754. The journal entry for the deposit of this amount with the state on April 30 would be as follows:

19	Apr.	30	SUTA Tax Payable		2 7 5 4 00		19
20			Cash			2 7 5 4 00	20
21			Deposit of state unemployment tax				21

EMPLOYEE WAGE AND TAX STATEMENT

By January 31 of each year, employers must furnish each employee with a Wage and Tax Statement, Form W-2 (Figure 9-10). This form shows the total amount of wages paid to the employee and the amounts of taxes withheld during the preceding taxable year. The employee earnings record contains the information needed to complete this form.

Multiple copies of Form W-2 are needed for the following purposes:

- Copy A—Employer sends to Social Security Administration
- Copy B—Employee attaches to federal income tax return
- Copy C—Employee retains for his or her own records
- Copy D—Employer retains for business records
- Copy 1—Employer sends to state or local tax department
- Copy 2—Employee attaches to state, city, or local income tax return

FIGURE 9-10 Wage and Tax Statement (Form W-2)

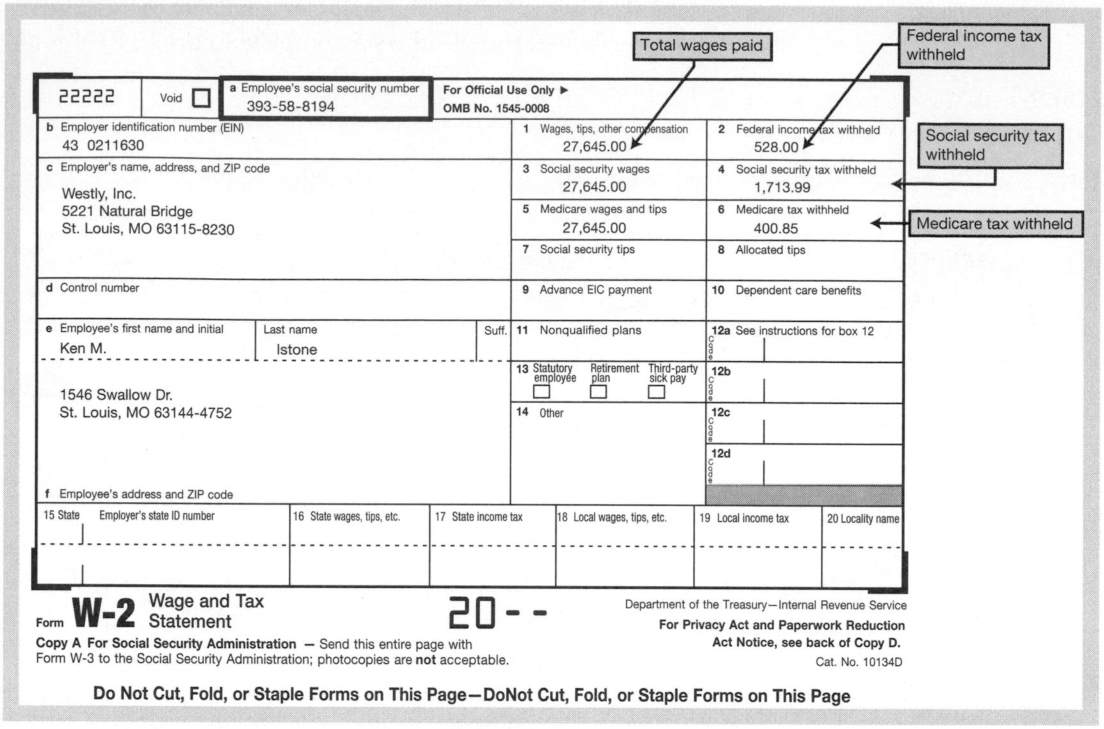

22222 Void ☐ a Employee's social security number 393-58-8194 For Official Use Only ▶ OMB No. 1545-0008

b Employer identification number (EIN) 43 0211630	1 Wages, tips, other compensation 27,645.00 / 2 Federal income tax withheld 528.00
c Employer's name, address, and ZIP code: Westly, Inc. 5221 Natural Bridge St. Louis, MO 63115-8230	3 Social security wages 27,645.00 / 4 Social security tax withheld 1,713.99
	5 Medicare wages and tips 27,645.00 / 6 Medicare tax withheld 400.85
	7 Social security tips / 8 Allocated tips
d Control number	9 Advance EIC payment / 10 Dependent care benefits
e Employee's first name and initial: Ken M. Last name: Istone Suff.	11 Nonqualified plans / 12a See instructions for box 12
1546 Swallow Dr. St. Louis, MO 63144-4752	13 Statutory employee ☐ Retirement plan ☐ Third-party sick pay ☐ / 12b
f Employee's address and ZIP code	14 Other / 12c / 12d

15 State	Employer's state ID number	16 State wages, tips, etc.	17 State income tax	18 Local wages, tips, etc.	19 Local income tax	20 Locality name

Form **W-2** Wage and Tax Statement 20- -

Department of the Treasury—Internal Revenue Service
For Privacy Act and Paperwork Reduction Act Notice, see back of Copy D.
Cat. No. 10134D

Copy A For Social Security Administration — Send this entire page with Form W-3 to the Social Security Administration; photocopies are **not** acceptable.

Do Not Cut, Fold, or Staple Forms on This Page—DoNot Cut, Fold, or Staple Forms on This Page

SUMMARY OF EMPLOYEE WAGES AND TAXES

Employers send Form W-3, Transmittal of Wage and Tax Statements (Figure 9-11), with Copy A of Forms W-2 to the Social Security Administration. Form W-3 must be filed by February 28 following the end of each taxable year. This form summarizes the employee earnings and tax information presented on Forms W-2 for the year. Information needed to complete Form W-3 is contained in the employee earnings records.

EMPLOYMENT ELIGIBILITY VERIFICATION

Every employee hired after November 6, 1986, must complete Form I-9, Employment Eligibility Verification. The purpose of this form is to document that each employee is authorized to work in the United States. The employee completes Section 1 of the form and provides the employer with evidence of the employee's identity and authorization to work. The employer completes Section 2 of the form indicating what evidence the employer examined.

Form I-9 is not filed with any government agency. Instead, it must be retained by the employer and made available for inspection if requested by the Department of Homeland Security or the Department of Labor.

SUMMARY OF TAXES, REPORTS, AND PAYMENTS

Keeping track of the many payroll taxes can be a challenge for an employer. Figure 9-12 summarizes the various employee and employer taxes we have discussed in Chapters 8 and 9. Figure 9-13 shows a calendar that highlights the due dates for the various reports and deposits. The calendar assumes the following for an employer:

1. Undeposited FIT (federal income tax) and Social Security and Medicare taxes of $2,500 at the end of each quarter and less than $50,000 during the lookback period.
2. Undeposited FUTA taxes of more than $500 at the end of each quarter.
3. SUTA taxes deposited quarterly.

The combination of payroll taxes, reports, deposit rules, and due dates can make payroll accounting rather complex. In fact, this is a major reason why small businesses often hire an accountant or an outside company to handle payroll.

FIGURE 9-11 Transmittal of Wage and Tax Statements (Form W-3)

DO NOT STAPLE

33333	a Control number	**For Official Use Only ▶** **OMB No. 1545-0008**	
b **Kind of Payer** ▶ 941 ☐ Military ☐ 943 ☐ 944 ☐ CT-1 ☐ Hshld. emp. ☐ Medicare govt. emp. ☐ **Third-party sick pay** ☐		1 Wages, tips, other compensation 276,917.00	2 Federal income tax withheld 30,370.00
		3 Social security wages 274,217.00	4 Social security tax withheld 17,001.45
c Total number of Forms W-2 8	d Establishment number	5 Medicare wages and tips 276,917.00	6 Medicare tax withheld 4,015.30
e Employer identification number (EIN) 43-0211630		7 Social security tips	8 Allocated tips
f Employer's name Westly, Inc.		9 Advance EIC payments	10 Dependent care benefits
5221 Natural Bridge St. Louis, MO 63115-8230		11 Nonqualified plans	12 Deferred compensation
		13 For third-party sick pay use only	
g Employer's address and ZIP code		14 Income tax withheld by payer of third-party sick pay	
h Other EIN used this year			
15 State MO	Employer's state ID number 21686001	16 State wages, tips, etc. 276,917.00	17 State income tax
		18 Local wages, tips, etc.	19 Local income tax
Contact person		Telephone number ( )	For Official Use Only
Email address		Fax number ( )	

Under penalties of perjury, I declare that I have examined this return and accompanying documents, and, to the best of my knowledge and belief, they are true, correct, and complete.

Signature ▶ Title ▶ Date ▶

Form **W-3 Transmittal of Wage and Tax Statements** 20- -   Department of the Treasury Internal Revenue Service

FIGURE 9-12 Summary of Employee and Employer Taxes

TAX	TAX APPLIES TO EMPLOYEE	TAX APPLIES TO EMPLOYER
Federal income tax	X	
State income tax	X	
Social Security	X	X
Medicare	X	X
FUTA		X
SUTA		X*

*Also applies to employees in some states.

FIGURE 9-13 Payroll Calendar

File Forms 940, 941, state unemployment tax report, and send W-2 to employees.	File Form 940	File form W-3 with CopyA ofW-2s.	File Form 941 and make FUTA and SUTA tax deposits.	Deposit FIT and Social Security and Medicare taxes from previous month.

January

S	M	T	W	T	F	S
			1	2	3	4
5	6	7	8	9	10	11
12	13	14	**15**	16	17	18
19	20	21	22	23	24	25
26	27	28	29	30	**31**	

February

S	M	T	W	T	F	S
						1
2	3	4	5	6	7	8
9	**10**	11	12	13	14	15
16	**17**	18	19	20	21	22
23	24	25	26	27	**28**	29

March

S	M	T	W	T	F	S
1	2	3	4	5	6	7
8	9	10	11	12	13	14
15	**16**	17	18	19	20	21
22	23	24	25	26	27	28
29	30	31				

April

S	M	T	W	T	F	S
			1	2	3	4
5	6	7	8	9	10	11
12	13	14	**15**	16	17	18
19	20	21	22	23	24	25
26	27	28	29	**30**		

May

S	M	T	W	T	F	S
					1	2
3	4	5	6	7	8	9
10	11	12	13	14	**15**	16
17	18	19	20	21	22	23
24	25	26	27	28	29	30
31						

June

S	M	T	W	T	F	S
	1	2	3	4	5	6
7	8	9	10	11	12	13
14	**15**	16	17	18	19	20
21	22	23	24	25	26	27
28	29	30				

July

S	M	T	W	T	F	S
			1	2	3	4
5	6	7	8	9	10	11
12	13	14	**15**	16	17	18
19	20	21	22	23	24	25
26	27	28	29	30	**31**	

August

S	M	T	W	T	F	S
						1
2	3	4	5	6	7	8
9	10	11	12	13	14	15
16	**17**	18	19	20	21	22
23	24	25	26	27	28	29
30	31					

September

S	M	T	W	T	F	S
		1	2	3	4	5
6	7	8	9	10	11	12
13	14	**15**	16	17	18	19
20	21	22	23	24	25	26
27	28	29	30			

October

S	M	T	W	T	F	S
				1	2	3
4	5	6	7	8	9	10
11	12	13	14	**15**	16	17
18	19	20	21	22	23	24
25	26	27	28	29	30	31

November

S	M	T	W	T	F	S
1	**2**	3	4	5	6	7
8	9	10	11	12	13	14
15	**16**	17	18	19	20	21
22	23	24	25	26	27	28
29	30					

December

S	M	T	W	T	F	S
		1	2	3	4	5
6	7	8	9	10	11	12
13	14	**15**	16	17	18	19
20	21	22	23	24	25	26
27	28	29	30	31		

A BROADER VIEW

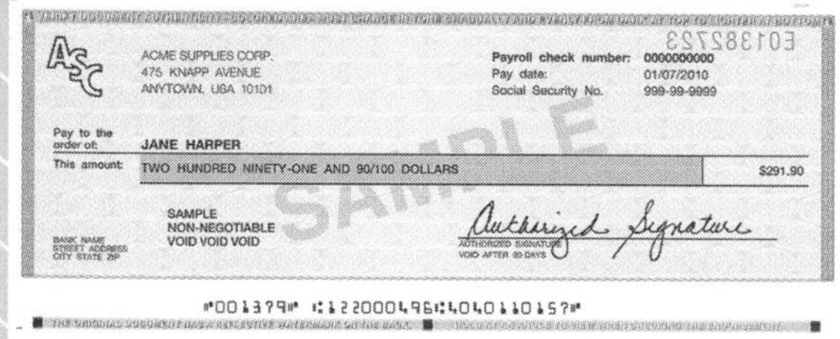

ADP, INC.

Dealing with Payroll Complexity—Let Someone Else Do It

A common way for both small and large businesses to deal with the complexity of payroll reports, deposit rules, and due dates is to hire an outside company to handle the payroll. Payroll processing companies have combined payroll expertise with the power of computers to create a major business enterprise based on the efficient and effective provision of payroll services.

The extent to which businesses use outside companies to handle payroll can be seen in the two largest payroll processing companies: Automatic Data Processing, Inc. (ADP) and Paychex, Inc. ADP has operations in 26 countries, provides payroll services to 585,000 clients (500,000 in the United States), and has revenues of $9 billion. Paychex has 100 locations nationwide, provides services to 572,000 clients, and has revenues of $2 billion. These companies prepare employee paychecks, journals, and summary reports; collect and remit funds for federal, state, and local payroll taxes; and file all required forms with government taxing authorities.

U REVU Complete U REVU-3 on **page 339** to test your basic understanding of LO3.

WORKERS' COMPENSATION INSURANCE

LO4 Describe and account for workers' compensation insurance.

Most states require employers to carry workers' compensation insurance. **Workers' compensation insurance** provides insurance for employees who suffer a job-related illness or injury.

The employer usually pays the entire cost of workers' compensation insurance. The cost of the insurance depends on the number of employees, riskiness of the job, and the company's accident history. For example, the insurance premium for workers in a chemical plant could be higher than for office workers. Employers generally obtain the insurance either from the state in which they operate or from a private insurance company.

The employer usually pays the premium at the beginning of the year, based on the estimated payroll for the year. At the end of the year, after the actual amount of payroll is known, an adjustment is made. If the employer has overpaid, a credit is received from the state or insurance company. If the employer has underpaid, an additional premium is paid.

To illustrate the accounting for workers' compensation insurance, assume that Lockwood Co. expects its payroll for the year to be $210,000. If Lockwood's insurance premium rate is 0.2%, its payment for workers' compensation insurance at the beginning of the year would be $420.

Estimated Payroll	×	Rate	=	Estimated Insurance Premium
$210,000		0.002		$420.00

The journal entry for the payment of this $420 premium would be as follows:

7	Jan.	2	Workers' Compensation Insurance Expense		420 00		7
8			Cash			420 00	8
9			Paid insurance premium				9

If Lockwood's actual payroll for the year is $220,000, Lockwood would owe an additional premium of $20 at year-end.

Actual Payroll	×	Rate	=	Insurance Premium
$220,000		0.002		$440.00
Less premium paid				420.00
Additional premium due				$ 20.00

The adjusting entry at year-end for this additional expense would be as follows:

11	Dec.	31	Workers' Compensation Insurance Expense		20 00		11
12			Workers' Compensation Insurance Payable			20 00	12
13			Adjustment for insurance premium				13

In T account form, the total Workers' Compensation Insurance Expense of $440.00 would look like this.

Workers' Compensation Insurance Expense

Debit	Credit
420.00	
20.00	
440.00	

If Lockwood's actual payroll for the year is only $205,000, Lockwood would be due a refund of $10:

Payroll	×	Rate	=	Insurance Premium
$205,000		0.002		$410.00
Less premium paid				420.00
Refund due				$(10.00)

The adjusting entry at year-end for this refund due would be as follows:

16	Dec.	31	Insurance Refund Receivable		10 00		16
17			Workers' Compensation Insurance Expense			10 00	17
18			Adjustment for insurance premium				18

In T account form, the total Workers' Compensation Insurance Expense of $410 would look like this.

Workers' Compensation Insurance Expense

Debit	Credit
420.00	10.00
410.00	

U REVU

Complete U REVU-4 on **page 339** to test your basic understanding of LO4.

Profiles in Accounting

Michael Burdish
Payroll Compliance Auditor

Michael Burdish graduated with an associate degree in accounting with honors from The College of Westchester. Michael excelled in his studies in accounting and knew this was the field for him. After graduation, Michael was hired as a payroll compliance auditor for an accounting firm. He is part of the team that audits companies and contractors that hire union members. The focus of the audits is to ensure that the correct amounts of benefits are paid. According to Michael he really enjoys his work. He especially likes meeting many new people and having new experiences. Michael intends to further his education and complete his baccalaureate degree in accounting.

LEARNING OBJECTIVES Key Points to Remember

LO1 Describe and calculate employer payroll taxes.

LO2 Account for employer payroll taxes expense.

Employer payroll taxes include FICA, FUTA, and SUTA taxes. These taxes represent additional payroll expenses of the employer. The journal entry for payroll taxes is as follows:

8		Payroll Taxes Expense	x x x xx		8
9		Social Security Tax Payable		x x x xx	9
10		Medicare Tax Payable		x x x xx	10
11		FUTA Tax Payable		x x x xx	11
12		SUTA Tax Payable		x x x xx	12

The steps to be followed in preparing this journal entry are as follows:

1. Obtain the total earnings and taxable earnings amounts from the Earnings—Total and Taxable Earnings columns of the payroll register.
2. Compute the amount of employer Social Security tax by multiplying the Social Security taxable earnings by 6.2%.
3. Compute the amount of employer Medicare tax by multiplying total earnings by 1.45%.
4. Compute the amount of FUTA tax by multiplying the Unemployment Taxable earnings by 0.8%.
5. Compute the amount of SUTA tax by multiplying the Unemployment Taxable earnings by 5.4%.
6. Prepare the appropriate journal entry using the amounts computed in steps 2–5.

LO3 Describe employer reporting and payment responsibilities.

Employer payroll reporting and payment responsibilities fall into six areas.

1. Federal income tax withholding and Social Security and Medicare taxes
2. FUTA taxes
3. SUTA taxes
4. Employee Wage and Tax Statement (Form W-2)
5. Summary of employee wages and taxes (Form W-3)
6. Employment eligibility verification (Form I-9)

Key forms needed in reporting and paying employer payroll taxes are as follows:

1. Form 8109, Federal Tax Deposit Coupon
2. Form 941, Employer's Quarterly Federal Tax Return
3. Form 940, Employer's Annual Federal Unemployment Tax Return

By January 31 of each year, employers must provide each employee with a Wage and Tax Statement, Form W-2.

By February 28 of each year, employers must file Form W-3 and Copy A of Form W-2 with the Social Security Administration.

LEARNING OBJECTIVES Key Points to Remember

LO4 Describe and account for workers' compensation insurance.	Workers' compensation insurance provides insurance for employees who suffer a job-related illness or injury. Employers generally are required to carry and pay the entire cost of this insurance.

DEMONSTRATION PROBLEM

The Totals line from Hart Company's payroll register for the week ended December 31, 20--, is as follows:

(left side) PAYROLL

	NAME	EMPLOYEE NUMBER	ALLOWANCES	MARITAL STATUS	EARNINGS				TAXABLE EARNINGS		
					REGULAR	OVERTIME	TOTAL	CUMULATIVE TOTAL	UNEMPLOYMENT COMPENSATION	SOCIAL SECURITY	
21	Totals				3 500 00	300 00	3 800 00	197 600 00	400 00	3 800 00	21

REGISTER—PERIOD ENDED December 31, 20-- (right side)

	DEDUCTIONS							NET PAY	CHECK NO.	
	FEDERAL INCOME TAX	SOCIAL SECURITY TAX	MEDICARE TAX	HEALTH INSURANCE	UNITED WAY	OTHER	TOTAL			
21	380 00	235 60	55 10	50 00	100 00		820 70	2 979 30		21

Payroll taxes are imposed as follows: Social Security, 6.2%; Medicare, 1.45%; FUTA, 0.8%; and SUTA, 5.4%.

REQUIRED

1. a. Prepare the journal entry for payment of this payroll on December 31, 20--.

   b. Prepare the journal entry for the employer's payroll taxes for the period ended December 31, 20--.

2. Hart Company had the following balances in its general ledger *after* the entries for requirement (1) were made:

Employee Income Tax Payable	$1,620.00
Social Security Tax Payable	1,847.00
Medicare Tax Payable	433.00
FUTA Tax Payable	27.20
SUTA Tax Payable	183.60

   a. Prepare the journal entry for payment of the liabilities for employee federal income taxes and Social Security and Medicare taxes on January 15, 20--.

   b. Prepare the journal entry for payment of the liability for FUTA tax on January 31, 20--.

c. Prepare the journal entry for payment of the liability for SUTA tax on January 31, 20--.

3. Hart Company paid a premium of $280 for workers' compensation insurance based on estimated payroll as of the beginning of the year. Based on actual payroll as of the end of the year, the premium is $298. Prepare the adjusting entry to reflect the underpayment of the insurance premium.

Solution 1.

GENERAL JOURNAL — PAGE 1

	DATE		DESCRIPTION	POST. REF.	DEBIT	CREDIT	
	20--						
1	Dec.	31	Wages and Salaries Expense		3800 00		1
2			Employee Income Tax Payable			380 00	2
3			Social Security Tax Payable			235 60	3
4			Medicare Tax Payable			55 10	4
5			Health Insurance Premiums Payable			50 00	5
6			United Way Contributions Payable			100 00	6
7			Cash			2979 30	7
8			To record Dec. 31 payroll				8
9							9
10		31	Payroll Taxes Expense		315 50		10
11			Social Security Tax Payable			235 60	11
12			Medicare Tax Payable			55 10	12
13			FUTA Tax Payable			3 20	13
14			SUTA Tax Payable			21 60	14
15			Employer payroll taxes for week ended Dec. 31				15

2. and 3.

18	Jan.	15	Employee Income Tax Payable		1620 00		18
19			Social Security Tax Payable		1847 00		19
20			Medicare Tax Payable		433 00		20
21			Cash			3900 00	21
22			Deposit of employee federal income tax and				22
23			Social Security and Medicare taxes				23
24							24
25		31	FUTA Tax Payable		27 20		25
26			Cash			27 20	26
27			Paid FUTA tax				27
28							28
29		31	SUTA Tax Payable		183 60		29
30			Cash			183 60	30
31			Paid SUTA tax				31
32							32
33	Dec.	31	Workers' Compensation Insurance Expense		18 00		33
34			Workers' Compensation Insurance Payable			18 00	34
35			Adjustment for insurance premium				35

KEY TERMS

Electronic Federal Tax Payment System (EFTPS) (323) An electronic funds transfer system for making federal tax deposits.

employer FICA taxes (316) Taxes levied on employers at the same rates and on the same earnings bases as the employee FICA taxes.

Employer Identification Number (EIN) (323) A number that identifies the employer on all payroll forms and reports filed with the IRS.

experience-rating system (318) A system to encourage employers to provide regular employment to workers.

FUTA (Federal Unemployment Tax Act) tax (317) A tax levied on employers to raise funds to administer the federal/state unemployment compensation program.

self-employment income (317) The net income of a trade or business run by an individual.

self-employment tax (317) A tax on the earnings of a self-employed person at double the Social Security and Medicare rates.

SUTA (state unemployment tax) tax (318) A tax levied on employers to raise funds to pay unemployment benefits.

workers' compensation insurance (333) Insurance carried by employers for employees who suffer a job-related illness or injury.

SELF-STUDY QUESTIONS AND EXERCISES

True/False Questions

1. LO1 Employer payroll taxes are deducted from the employee's pay.
2. LO1 The payroll register is a key source of information for computing employer payroll taxes.
3. LO1 Self-employment income is the net income of a trade or business owned and run by an individual.
4. LO1 The FUTA tax is levied only on the employees.
5. LO3 The W-4, which shows total annual earnings and deductions for federal and state income taxes, must be completed by the employer and given to the employee by January 31.

Multiple Choice Questions

1. LO2 The general ledger accounts commonly used to record the employer's Social Security, Medicare, FUTA, and SUTA taxes are classified as

   (a) assets.
   (b) liabilities.
   (c) expenses.
   (d) owner's equity.

2. LO2 Joyce Lee earns $30,000 a year. Her employer pays a matching Social Security tax of 6.2% on the first $106,800 in earnings, a Medicare tax of 1.45% on gross earnings, and a FUTA tax of 0.8% and a SUTA tax of 5.4%, both on the first $7,000 in earnings. What is the total cost of Joyce Lee to her employer?

   (a) $32,250
   (b) $30,000
   (c) $30,434
   (d) $32,729

3. LO3 The Form 941 tax deposit includes which of the following types of taxes withheld from the employee and paid by the employer?
   (a) Federal income tax and FUTA tax
   (b) Federal income tax and Social Security and Medicare taxes
   (c) Social Security and Medicare taxes and SUTA tax
   (d) FUTA tax and SUTA tax
4. LO4 Workers' compensation provides insurance for employees who
   (a) are unemployed due to a layoff.
   (b) are unemployed due to a plant closing.
   (c) are underemployed and need additional compensation.
   (d) suffer a job-related illness or injury.
5. LO4 The journal entry at the end of the year that recognizes an additional premium owed under workers' compensation insurance will include a
   (a) debit to Workers' Compensation Insurance Expense.
   (b) debit to Cash.
   (c) debit to Workers' Compensation Insurance Payable.
   (d) credit to Workers' Compensation Insurance Expense.

U REVU Exercises

1. LO1 Total earnings for the employees of Gary's Grill for the week ended January 14, 20--, were $6,400. The following payroll taxes were levied on these earnings:

Social Security	6.2%
Medicare	1.45%
FUTA	0.8%
SUTA	5.4%

   Calculate Gary's payroll taxes expense for the week ended January 14, 20--.
2. LO2 Liu's Lounge had the following payroll taxes expense for the week ended February 10, 20--:

Social Security	$595.20
Medicare	139.20
FUTA	76.80
SUTA	518.40

   Prepare the journal entry for these payroll taxes.
3. LO3 ARC Co. owes the following amounts for payroll taxes and employees' withholding of Social Security, Medicare, and federal income tax as of April 15:

Social Security Tax Payable	$6,750.00
Medicare Tax Payable	1,575.00
FUTA Tax Payable	360.00
SUTA Tax Payable	2,646.00
Employee Income Tax Payable	4,095.00

   Prepare the journal entries for:
   (a) Deposit of the employees' federal income taxes and the Social Security and Medicare taxes on April 15.
   (b) Deposits of the FUTA and SUTA taxes on April 30.
4. LO4 LC Co. estimates that its total payroll for the year will be $260,000. LC's workers' compensation insurance premium rate is 0.22%. Calculate LC's estimated workers' compensation insurance premium and prepare the journal entry for the payment of this amount.

The answers to the Self-Study Questions and Exercises are at the end of the chapter (page 350).

REVIEW QUESTIONS

LO1 1. Why do employer payroll taxes represent an additional expense to the employer, whereas the various employee payroll taxes do not?

LO1 2. At what rate and on what earnings base is the employer's Social Security tax levied?

LO1 3. What is the purpose of the FUTA tax, and who must pay it?

LO1 4. What is the purpose of the state unemployment tax, and who must pay it?

LO2 5. What accounts are affected when employer payroll tax expenses are properly recorded?

LO2 6. Identify all items that are debited or credited to Social Security Tax Payable and to Medicare Tax Payable.

LO2 7. Explain why an employee whose gross salary is $20,000 costs an employer more than $20,000 to employ.

LO3 8. What is the purpose of Form 8109, Federal Tax Deposit Coupon?

LO3 9. What is the purpose of Form 941, Employer's Quarterly Federal Tax Return?

LO3 10. What is the purpose of Form 940, Employer's Annual Federal Unemployment Tax Return?

LO3 11. What information appears on Form W-2, the employee's Wage and Tax Statement?

LO3 12. What is the purpose of Form I-9, Employment Eligibility Verification?

LO4 13. What is the purpose of workers' compensation insurance, and who must pay for it?

SERIES A EXERCISES

E 9-1A (LO1/2)

✓ Payroll taxes expense: $1,584.30

CALCULATION AND JOURNAL ENTRY FOR EMPLOYER PAYROLL TAXES

Portions of the payroll register for Barney's Bagels for the week ended July 15 are shown below. The SUTA tax rate is 5.4%, and the FUTA tax rate is 0.8%, both of which are levied on the first $7,000 of earnings. The Social Security tax rate is 6.2% on the first $106,800 of earnings. The Medicare rate is 1.45% on gross earnings.

Barney's Bagels
Payroll Register

	Total Taxable Earnings of All Employees	
Total Earnings	**Unemployment Compensation**	**Social Security**
$12,200	$10,500	$12,200

Calculate the employer's payroll taxes expense and prepare the journal entry to record the employer's payroll taxes expense for the week ended July 15 of the current year.

E 9-2A (LO1/2)
✓ Payroll taxes expense: $350.02

CALCULATION AND JOURNAL ENTRY FOR EMPLOYER PAYROLL TAXES Earnings for several employees for the week ended March 12, 20--, are as follows:

		Taxable Earnings	
Employee Name	Current Earnings	Unemployment Compensation	Social Security
Aus, Glenn E.	$ 700	$200	$ 700
Diaz, Charles K.	350	350	350
Knapp, Carol S.	1,200	—	1,200
Mueller, Deborah F.	830	125	830
Yeager, Jackie R.	920	35	920

Calculate the employer's payroll taxes expense and prepare the journal entry as of March 12, 20--, assuming that FUTA tax is 0.8%, SUTA tax is 5.4%, Social Security tax is 6.2%, and Medicare tax is 1.45%.

E 9-3A (LO1/2)
✓ Payroll taxes expense: $886.86

CALCULATION OF TAXABLE EARNINGS AND EMPLOYER PAYROLL TAXES AND PREPARATION OF JOURNAL ENTRY Selected information from the payroll register of Raynette's Boutique for the week ended September 14, 20--, is as follows. Social Security tax is 6.2% on the first $106,800 of earnings for each employee. Medicare tax is 1.45% of gross earnings. FUTA tax is 0.8% and SUTA tax is 5.4% on the first $7,000 of earnings.

			Taxable Earnings	
Employee Name	Cumulative Pay Before Current Earnings	Current Gross Pay	Unemployment Compensation	Social Security
Burgos, Juan	$ 6,800	$1,250		
Ellis, Judy A.	6,300	1,100		
Lewis, Arlene S.	54,200	2,320		
Mason, Jason W.	53,900	2,270		
Yates, Ruby L.	27,650	1,900		
Zielke, Ronald M.	104,930	2,680		

Calculate the amount of taxable earnings for unemployment, Social Security, and Medicare taxes, and prepare the journal entry to record the employer's payroll taxes as of September 14, 20--.

E 9-4A (LO1/2)
✓ Total cost: $34,882.00

TOTAL COST OF EMPLOYEE J. B. Kenton employs Sharla Knox at a salary of $32,000 a year. Kenton is subject to employer Social Security taxes at a rate of 6.2% and Medicare taxes at a rate of 1.45% on Knox's salary. In addition, Kenton must pay SUTA tax at a rate of 5.4% and FUTA tax at a rate of 0.8% on the first $7,000 of Knox's salary.

Compute the total cost to Kenton of employing Knox for the year.

E 9-5A (LO3)
✓ 941 deposit: $20,700

JOURNAL ENTRIES FOR PAYMENT OF EMPLOYER PAYROLL TAXES Angel Ruiz owns a business called Ruiz Construction Co. He does his banking at Citizens National Bank in Portland, Oregon. The amounts in his general ledger for payroll taxes and the employees' withholding of Social Security, Medicare, and federal income tax payable as of April 15 of the current year are as follows:

Social Security tax payable (includes both employer and employee)	$11,250
Medicare tax payable (includes both employer and employee)	2,625
FUTA tax payable	600
SUTA tax payable	4,050
Employee income tax payable	6,825

(continued)

Journalize the payment of the employee federal income taxes and Social Security and Medicare taxes on April 15, 20--, and the payments of the FUTA and SUTA taxes on April 30, 20--.

E 9-6A (LO4)

✓ 2. Additional premium due: $14.00

WORKERS' COMPENSATION INSURANCE AND ADJUSTMENT General Manufacturing estimated that its total payroll for the coming year would be $425,000. The workers' compensation insurance premium rate is 0.2%.

REQUIRED

1. Calculate the estimated workers' compensation insurance premium and prepare the journal entry for the payment as of January 2, 20--.
2. Assume that General Manufacturing's actual payroll for the year is $432,000. Calculate the total insurance premium owed and prepare a journal entry as of December 31, 20--, to record the adjustment for the underpayment. The actual payment of the additional premium will take place in January of the next year.

SERIES A PROBLEMS

P 9-7A (LO1/2)

✓ Payroll taxes expense: $662.06

CALCULATING PAYROLL TAXES EXPENSE AND PREPARING JOURNAL ENTRY Selected information from the payroll register of Anderson's Dairy for the week ended July 7, 20--, is shown below. The SUTA tax rate is 5.4%, and the FUTA tax rate is 0.8%, both on the first $7,000 of earnings. Social Security tax on the employer is 6.2% on the first $106,800 of earnings, and Medicare tax is 1.45% on gross earnings.

			Taxable Earnings	
Employee Name	Cumulative Pay Before Current Earnings	Current Weekly Earnings	Unemployment Compensation	Social Security
Barnum, Alex	$ 6,750	$ 820		
Duel, Richard	6,340	725		
Hunt, J. B.	23,460	1,235		
Larson, Susan	6,950	910		
Mercado, Denise	105,450	3,520		
Swan, Judy	25,470	1,125		
Yates, Keith	28,675	1,300		

REQUIRED

1. Calculate the total employer payroll taxes for these employees.
2. Prepare the journal entry to record the employer payroll taxes as of July 7, 20--.

P 9-8A (LO2/3)

✓ Payroll taxes expense: $3,864.00

KA KLOOSTER & ALLEN

JOURNALIZING AND POSTING PAYROLL ENTRIES Cascade Company has four employees. All are paid on a monthly basis. The fiscal year of the business is June 1 to May 31.

The accounts kept by Cascade include the following:

Account Number	Title	Balance on June 1
101	Cash	$70,200
211	Employee Income Tax Payable	3,553
212	Social Security Tax Payable	5,103
213	Medicare Tax Payable	1,197
218	Savings Bond Deductions Payable	1,225
221	FUTA Tax Payable	574
222	SUTA Tax Payable	2,835
511	Wages and Salaries Expense	0
530	Payroll Taxes Expense	0

The following transactions relating to payrolls and payroll taxes occurred during June and July:

June 15	Paid $9,853 covering the following May taxes:		
	Social Security tax		$ 5,103
	Medicare tax		1,197
	Employee income tax withheld		3,553
	Total		$ 9,853
30	June payroll:		
	Total wages and salaries expense		$42,000
	Less amounts withheld:		
	Social Security tax	$2,604	
	Medicare tax	609	
	Employee income tax	3,570	
	Savings bond deductions	1,225	8,008
	Net amount paid		$33,992
30	Purchased savings bonds for employees, $2,450		
30	Employer payroll taxes expenses for June were:		
	Social Security		$2,604
	Medicare		609
	FUTA		84
	SUTA		567
	Total		$3,864
July 15	Paid $9,996 covering the following June taxes:		
	Social Security tax		$ 5,208
	Medicare tax		1,218
	Employee income tax withheld		3,570
	Total		$ 9,996
31	Paid SUTA tax for the quarter, $3,402		
31	Paid FUTA tax, $658		

REQUIRED

1. Journalize the preceding transactions using a general journal.
2. Open T accounts for the payroll expenses and liabilities. Enter the beginning balances and post the transactions recorded in the journal.

P 9-9A (LO4)
✓ 3. Refund due: $48.00

WORKERS' COMPENSATION INSURANCE AND ADJUSTMENT Willamette Manufacturing estimated that its total payroll for the coming year would be $650,000. The workers' compensation insurance premium rate is 0.3%.

REQUIRED

1. Calculate the estimated workers' compensation insurance premium and prepare the journal entry for the payment as of January 2, 20--.
2. Assume that Willamette Manufacturing's actual payroll for the year was $672,000. Calculate the total insurance premium owed and prepare a journal entry as of December 31, 20--, to record the adjustment for the underpayment. The actual payment of the additional premium will take place in January of the next year.
3. Assume instead that Willamette Manufacturing's actual payroll for the year was $634,000. Prepare a journal entry as of December 31, 20--, for the total amount that should be refunded. The refund will not be received until the next year.

SERIES B EXERCISES

E 9-1B (LO1/2)
✓ Payroll taxes expense: $1,962.74

CALCULATION AND JOURNAL ENTRY FOR EMPLOYER PAYROLL TAXES Portions of the payroll register for Kathy's Cupcakes for the week ended June 21 are shown below. The SUTA tax rate is 5.4%, and the FUTA tax rate is 0.8%, both on the first $7,000 of earnings. The Social Security tax rate is 6.2% on the first $106,800 of earnings. The Medicare rate is 1.45% on gross earnings.

Kathy's Cupcakes
Payroll Register

	Total Taxable Earnings of All Employees	
Total Earnings	**Unemployment Compensation**	**Social Security**
$15,680	$12,310	$15,680

Calculate the employer's payroll taxes expense and prepare the journal entry to record the employer's payroll taxes expense for the week ended June 21 of the current year.

E 9-2B (LO1/2)
✓ Payroll taxes expense: $503.63

CALCULATION AND JOURNAL ENTRY FOR EMPLOYER PAYROLL TAXES Earnings for several employees for the week ended April 7, 20--, are as follows:

		Taxable Earnings	
Employee Name	Current Earnings	Unemployment Compensation	Social Security
Boyd, Glenda L.	$ 850	$300	$ 850
Evans, Sheryl N.	970	225	970
Fox, Howard J.	830	830	830
Jacobs, Phyllis J.	1,825	—	1,825
Roh, William R.	990	25	990

Calculate the employer's payroll taxes expense and prepare the journal entry as of April 7, 20--, assuming that FUTA tax is 0.8%, SUTA tax is 5.4%, Social Security tax is 6.2%, and Medicare tax is 1.45%.

E 9-3B (LO1/2)
✓ Payroll taxes expense: $788.04

CALCULATION OF TAXABLE EARNINGS AND EMPLOYER PAYROLL TAXES, AND PREPARATION OF JOURNAL ENTRY Selected information from the payroll register of Howard's Cutlery for the week ended October 7, 20--, is presented below. Social Security tax is 6.2% on the first $106,800 of earnings for each employee. Medicare tax is 1.45% on gross earnings. FUTA tax is 0.8% and SUTA tax is 5.4% on the first $7,000 of earnings.

			Taxable Earnings	
Employee Name	Cumulative Pay Before Current Earnings	Current Gross Pay	Unemployment Compensation	Social Security
Carlson, David J.	$ 6,635	$ 950		
Delgado, Luisa	6,150	1,215		
Lewis, Arlene S.	54,375	2,415		
Nixon, Robert R.	53,870	1,750		
Shippe, Lance W.	24,830	1,450		
Watts, Brandon Q.	105,400	2,120		

Calculate the amount of taxable earnings for unemployment, Social Security, and Medicare taxes, and prepare the journal entry to record the employer's payroll taxes as of October 7, 20--.

E 9-4B (LO1/2)
✓ Total cost: $49,953.00

TOTAL COST OF EMPLOYEE B. F. Goodson employs Eduardo Gonzales at a salary of $46,000 a year. Goodson is subject to employer Social Security taxes at a rate of 6.2% and Medicare taxes at a rate of 1.45% on Gonzales's salary. In addition, Goodson must pay SUTA tax at a rate of 5.4% and FUTA tax at a rate of 0.8% on the first $7,000 of Gonzales's salary.

Compute the total cost to Goodson of employing Gonzales for the year.

E 9-5B (LO3)
✓ 941 deposit: $19,058.00

JOURNAL ENTRIES FOR PAYMENT OF EMPLOYER PAYROLL TAXES Francis Baker owns a business called Baker Construction Co. She does her banking at the American National Bank in Seattle, Washington. The amounts in her general ledger for payroll taxes and employees' withholding of Social Security, Medicare, and federal income tax payable as of July 15 of the current year are as follows:

Social Security tax payable (includes both employer and employee)	$9,563
Medicare tax payable (includes both employer and employee)	2,250
FUTA tax payable	504
SUTA tax payable	3,402
Employee federal income tax payable	7,245

Journalize the payment of the employee federal income taxes and Social Security and Medicare taxes on July 15, 20--, and the payments of the FUTA and state unemployment taxes on July 31, 20--.

E 9-6B (LO4)
✓ 2. Additional premium due: $22.00

WORKERS' COMPENSATION INSURANCE AND ADJUSTMENT Columbia Industries estimated that its total payroll for the coming year would be $385,000. The workers' compensation insurance premium rate is 0.2%.

REQUIRED

1. Calculate the estimated workers' compensation insurance premium and prepare the journal entry for the payment as of January 2, 20--.

(continued)

2. Assume that Columbia Industries' actual payroll for the year is $396,000. Calculate the total insurance premium owed and prepare a journal entry as of December 31, 20--, to record the adjustment for the underpayment. The actual payment of the additional premium will take place in January of the next year.

SERIES B PROBLEMS

P 9-7B (LO1/2)

✓ Payroll taxes expense: $738.34

CALCULATING PAYROLL TAXES EXPENSE AND PREPARING JOURNAL ENTRY Selected information from the payroll register of Wray's Drug Store for the week ended July 14, 20--, is shown below. The SUTA tax rate is 5.4%, and the FUTA tax rate is 0.8%, both on the first $7,000 of earnings. Social Security tax on the employer is 6.2% on the first $106,800 of earnings, and Medicare tax is 1.45% on gross earnings.

			Taxable Earnings	
Employee Name	Cumulative Pay Before Current Earnings	Current Weekly Earnings	Unemployment Compensation	Social Security
Ackers, Alice	$ 6,460	$ 645		
Conley, Dorothy	27,560	1,025		
Davis, James	6,850	565		
Lawrence, Kevin	52,850	2,875		
Rawlings, Judy	16,350	985		
Tanaka, Sumio	22,320	835		
Vadillo, Raynette	104,960	3,540		

REQUIRED

1. Calculate the total employer payroll taxes for these employees.
2. Prepare the journal entry to record the employer payroll taxes as of July 14, 20--.

P 9-8B (LO2/3)

✓ Payroll taxes expense: $2,105.33

JOURNALIZING AND POSTING PAYROLL ENTRIES Oxford Company has five employees. All are paid on a monthly basis. The fiscal year of the business is June 1 to May 31.

The accounts kept by Oxford Company include the following:

Account Number	Title	Balance on June 1
101	Cash	$69,500.00
211	Employee Income Tax Payable	2,018.00
212	Social Security Tax Payable	2,735.00
213	Medicare Tax Payable	641.00
218	Savings Bond Deductions Payable	787.50
221	FUTA Tax Payable	540.00
222	SUTA Tax Payable	1,380.00
511	Wages and Salaries Expense	0.00
530	Payroll Taxes Expense	0.00

The following transactions relating to payrolls and payroll taxes occurred during June and July:

June 15	Paid $5,394.00 covering the following May taxes:		
	Social Security tax		$2,735.00
	Medicare tax		641.00
	Employee income tax withheld		2,018.00
	Total		$5,394.00
30	June payroll:		
	Total wages and salaries expense		$22,050.00
	Less amounts withheld:		
	Social Security tax	$1,367.10	
	Medicare tax	319.73	
	Employee income tax	1,920.00	
	Savings bond deductions	787.50	4,394.33
	Net amount paid		$17,655.67
30	Purchased savings bonds for employees, $1,575.00		
30	Employer payroll taxes expenses for June were:		
	Social Security		$1,367.10
	Medicare		319.73
	FUTA		54.00
	SUTA		364.50
	Total		$2,105.33
July 15	Paid $5,293.66 covering the following June taxes:		
	Social Security tax		$ 2,734.20
	Medicare tax		639.46
	Employee income tax withheld		1,920.00
	Total		$ 5,293.66
31	Paid SUTA tax for the quarter, $1,744.50		
31	Paid FUTA tax, $594.00		

REQUIRED

1. Journalize the preceding transactions using a general journal.
2. Open T accounts for the payroll expenses and liabilities. Enter the beginning balances and post the transactions recorded in the journal.

P 9-9B (LO4)

✓ 3. Refund due: $16.00

WORKERS' COMPENSATION INSURANCE AND ADJUSTMENT Multnomah Manufacturing estimated that its total payroll for the coming year would be $540,000. The workers' compensation insurance premium rate is 0.2%.

REQUIRED

1. Calculate the estimated workers' compensation insurance premium and prepare the journal entry for the payment as of January 2, 20--.
2. Assume that Multnomah Manufacturing's actual payroll for the year was $562,000. Calculate the total insurance premium owed and prepare a journal entry as of December 31, 20--, to record the adjustment for the underpayment. The actual payment of the additional premium will take place in January of the next year.

(continued)

3. Assume instead that Multnomah Manufacturing's actual payroll for the year was \$532,000. Prepare a journal entry as of December 31, 20--, for the total amount that should be refunded. The refund will not be received until the next year.

MANAGING YOUR WRITING

The director of the art department at an advertising company, Wilson Watson, wants to hire new office staff. His boss tells him that to do so he must find in his budget not only the base salary for this position but an additional 30% for "fringe benefits." Wilson explodes: "How in the world can there be 30% in fringe benefits?" Write a memo to Wilson Watson explaining the costs that probably make up these fringe benefits.

ETHICS CASE

Bob Estes works at Cliffrock Company in the central receiving department. He unpacks incoming shipments and verifies quantities of goods received. Over the weekend, Bob pulled a muscle in his back while playing basketball. When he came to work on Monday and started unpacking shipments, his back started to hurt again. Bob called the human resources department and told them he hurt his back lifting a package at work. He was told to fill out an accident report and sent to an orthopedic clinic with a workers' compensation form. The doctor at the clinic told Bob not to lift anything heavy for two weeks and to stay home from work for at least one week.

1. Is Bob entitled to workers' compensation? Why or why not?
2. What effect will Bob's claim have on Cliffrock Company's workers' compensation insurance premium?
3. Write a short memo from the human resources department to Cliffrock Company's employees explaining the purpose of workers' compensation.
4. In small groups, discuss the job-related illness or injury risks of a computer input operator and measures an employer might take to minimize these risks.

MASTERY PROBLEM

✓ Payroll taxes expense: \$730.75

The totals line from Nix Company's payroll register for the week ended March 31, 20--, is as follows:

(left side)

PAYROLL

	NAME	EMPLOYEE NUMBER	ALLOWANCES	MARITAL STATUS	EARNINGS: REGULAR	EARNINGS: OVERTIME	EARNINGS: TOTAL	CUMULATIVE TOTAL	TAXABLE EARNINGS: UNEMPLOYMENT COMPENSATION	TAXABLE EARNINGS: SOCIAL SECURITY	
21	Totals				5400 00	100 00	5500 00	71500 00	5000 00	5500 00	21

REGISTER—PERIOD ENDED March 31, 20--

(right side)

	DEDUCTIONS: FEDERAL INCOME TAX	SOCIAL SECURITY TAX	MEDICARE TAX	HEALTH INSURANCE	LIFE INSURANCE	OTHER	TOTAL	NET PAY	CHECK NO.	
21	500 00	341 00	79 75	165 00	200 00		1285 75	4214 25		21

KLOOSTER & ALLEN

Payroll taxes are imposed as follows: Social Security tax, 6.2%; Medicare tax, 1.45%; FUTA tax, 0.8%; and SUTA tax, 5.4%.

REQUIRED

1. a. Prepare the journal entry for payment of this payroll on March 31, 20--.
   b. Prepare the journal entry for the employer's payroll taxes for the period ended March 31, 20--.
2. Nix Company had the following balances in its general ledger before the entries for requirement (1) were made:

Employee income tax payable	$2,500
Social Security tax payable	2,008
Medicare tax payable	470
FUTA tax payable	520
SUTA tax payable	3,510

   a. Prepare the journal entry for payment of the liabilities for federal income taxes and Social Security and Medicare taxes on April 15, 20--.
   b. Prepare the journal entry for payment of the liability for FUTA tax on April 30, 20--.
   c. Prepare the journal entry for payment of the liability for SUTA tax on April 30, 20--.
3. Nix Company paid a premium of $420 for workers' compensation insurance based on the estimated payroll as of the beginning of the year. Based on actual payroll as of the end of the year, the premium is only $400. Prepare the adjusting entry to reflect the overpayment of the insurance premium at the end of the year (December 31, 20--).

CHALLENGE PROBLEM

This problem challenges you to apply your cumulative accounting knowledge to move a step beyond the material in the chapter.

✓ Payroll taxes expense: $1,306.25

Payrex Co. has six employees. All are paid on a weekly basis. For the payroll period ending January 7, total employee earnings were $12,500, all of which were subject to SUTA, FUTA, Social Security, and Medicare taxes. The SUTA tax rate in Payrex's state is 5.4%, but Payrex qualifies for a rate of 2.0% because of its good record of providing regular employment to its employees. Other employer payroll taxes are at the rates described in the chapter.

REQUIRED

1. Calculate Payrex's FUTA, SUTA, Social Security, and Medicare taxes for the week ended January 7.
2. Prepare the journal entry for Payrex's payroll taxes for the week ended January 7.
3. What amount of payroll taxes did Payrex save because of its good employment record?

ANSWERS TO SELF-STUDY QUESTIONS AND EXERCISE

True/False Questions

1. F (these taxes are paid by the employer)
2. T
3. T
4. F (FUTA tax is levied on employers)
5. F (this Form is W-2)

Multiple Choice Questions

1. b **2.** d **3.** b **4.** d **5.** a

U REVU Exercises

1.

Social Security	$396.80
Medicare	92.80
FUTA	51.20
SUTA	345.60
Total	$886.40

2.

Payroll Taxes Expense	1,329.60	
Social Security Tax Payable		595.20
Medicare Tax Payable		139.20
FUTA Tax Payable		76.80
SUTA Tax Payable		518.40
Employer payroll taxes for week ended Feb. 10		

3. (a)

Social Security Tax Payable	6,750.00	
Medicare Tax Payable	1,575.00	
Employee Income Tax Payable	4,095.00	
Cash		12,420.00
Deposit of employee federal income tax and Social Security and Medicare taxes		

(b)

FUTA Tax Payable		
Cash	360.00	
Paid FUTA tax		360.00
SUTA Tax Payable		
Cash	2,646.00	
Paid SUTA tax		2,646.00

4.

Workers' Compensation Insurance Expense		
Cash	572.00	
Paid insurance premium		572.00

PART 3

Accounting for a Merchandising Business

BOB KRIST/DOCUMENTARY VALUE/CORBIS

Add Some Color to Your Learning!

Throughout the text, you will be introduced to many important terms and types of accounts. To help you learn the different terms and types of accounts, we have coded many of them using the following color key in Part 3:

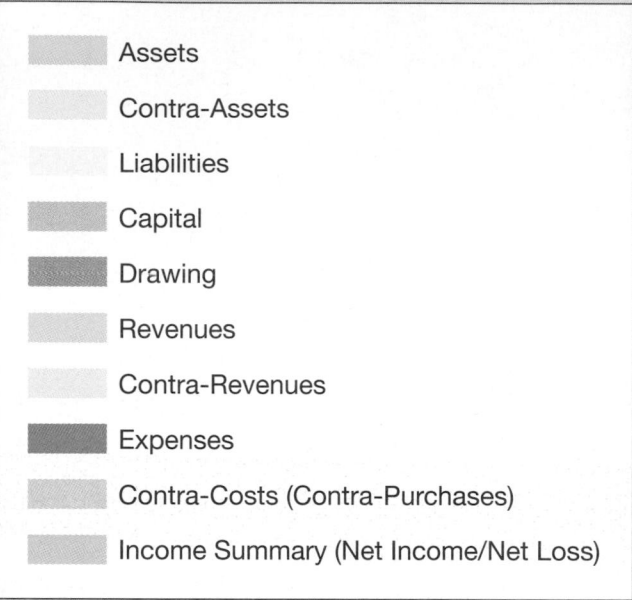

- Assets
- Contra-Assets
- Liabilities
- Capital
- Drawing
- Revenues
- Contra-Revenues
- Expenses
- Contra-Costs (Contra-Purchases)
- Income Summary (Net Income/Net Loss)

IMAGE COPYRIGHT GALINA BARSKAYA, 2009/USED UNDER LICENSE FROM SHUTTERSTOCK.COM

Chapter 10

Accounting for Sales and Cash Receipts

In recent years, we have seen increasing concern about how our actions affect the environment. Planet Shoes is an example of a young company whose business reflects this concern. Planet Shoes is an online shoe retailer specializing in eco-friendly shoes. It markets vegan shoes, shoes made from recycled chemicals, and a number of name brands such as Birkenstock, Clarks, Geox, and New Balance. At checkout, it even offers the option of carbon-free shipping and shoe recycling. And it donates 1% of its sales to environmental organizations.

Operating from Waltham, Massachusetts, Planet's revenues have grown from $541 thousand to $5.9 million in only 10 years. Planet must have a good system to manage and account for its high volume of sales. In addition, since all of its sales are via the Internet, it must know how to handle credit card sales. In this chapter, you will learn how to account for sales transactions, including credit card sales.

LEARNING OBJECTIVES

Careful study of this chapter should enable you to:

LO1 Describe merchandise sales transactions.

LO2 Describe and use merchandise sales accounts.

LO3 Describe and use the accounts receivable ledger.

LO4 Prepare a schedule of accounts receivable.

Over the last nine chapters, we have learned how to account for a service business. We are now ready to consider accounting for a different kind of business—merchandising. A **merchandising business** purchases merchandise such as clothing, furniture, or computers, and sells that merchandise to customers. For example, Planet Shoes buys shoes from vendors and manufacturers and sells them to its customers online.

This chapter examines how to account for the sale of merchandise using the accrual basis of accounting. We will learn how to use four new accounts and a subsidiary ledger.

MERCHANDISE SALES TRANSACTIONS

LO1 Describe merchandise sales transactions.

A **sale** is a transfer of merchandise from one business or individual to another in exchange for cash or a promise to pay cash. Sales procedures and documents vary greatly, depending on the nature and size of the business.

RETAILER

A retailer such as Planet Shoes makes all sales online. For Web-based transactions, companies use electronic forms that are similar to the paper documents described in this chapter.

Retail businesses generally sell to customers who enter the store, select the merchandise they want, and bring it to a salesclerk. The salesclerk enters the sale in some type of electronic cash register that generates a receipt for the customer. A copy of the receipt is retained in the register. Most registers can print a summary of the day's sales activity, like the one in Figure 10-1. This summary can be used to journalize sales in the accounting records.

FIGURE 10-1 Cash Register Tape Summary

(1)		
CASH SALES	327.79	*
(3)		
MCARD/VISA	550.62	*
(6)		
LAYAWAY	79.50	*
TOTAL CASH	957.91	*
(2)		
CHARGE SALES	543.84	*
(5)		
APPROVAL	126.58	*
TOTAL CHARGE	670.42	*
TOTAL SALES	1,628.33	G*
SALES TAX	81.42	*
	81.42	*
REC'D ON ACCT.	324.51	*
	324.51	*
PAID OUT	76.51	*
	76.51	*
NO SALE	0.00	*
	0.00	*
* SUB-TOTAL		
G* GRAND TOTAL		

An additional document often created as evidence of a sale in a retail business is a **sales ticket** (Figure 10-2). One copy of the sales ticket is given to the customer, and the other copy is sent to accounting.

FIGURE 10-2 Sales Ticket

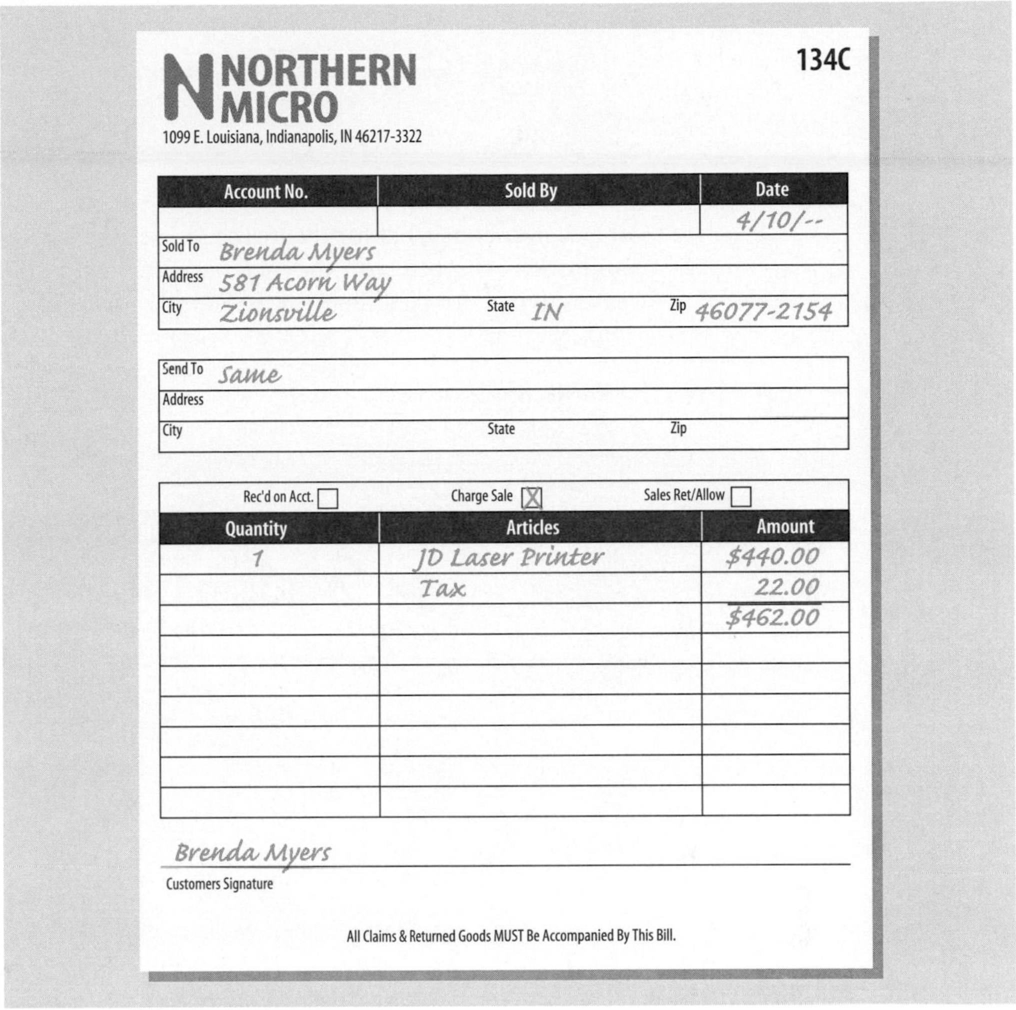
NORTHERN MICRO 134C

1099 E. Louisiana, Indianapolis, IN 46217-3322

Account No.	Sold By	Date
		4/10/--

Sold To: Brenda Myers
Address: 581 Acorn Way
City: Zionsville State: IN Zip: 46077-2154

Send To: Same
Address:
City: State: Zip:

Rec'd on Acct. ☐ Charge Sale ☒ Sales Ret/Allow ☐

Quantity	Articles	Amount
1	JD Laser Printer	$440.00
	Tax	22.00
		$462.00

Brenda Myers
Customers Signature

All Claims & Returned Goods MUST Be Accompanied By This Bill.

WHOLESALER

Figure 10-3 shows how the wholesaler plays a different role than the retailer in the marketing chain. Retailers usually sell to final consumers, whereas wholesalers tend to sell to retailers. This causes the wholesale sales transaction process to differ, as shown in Figure 10-4.

FIGURE 10-3 Marketing Chain

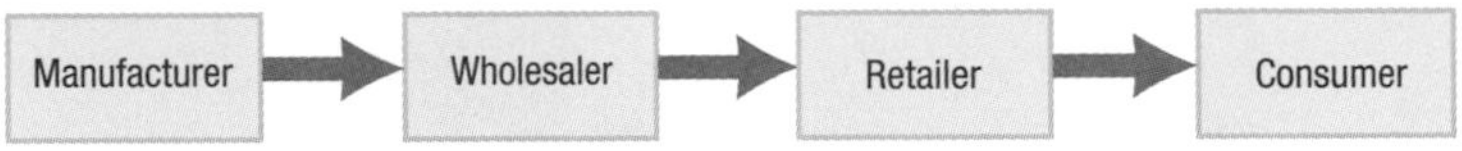

In a computerized system, customer orders can be submitted electronically. Even the credit approval process can be handled by the computer.

Customers commonly mail or fax written orders to buy merchandise from wholesalers. When the customer purchase order arrives, the customer name and items being ordered are determined. Since wholesalers typically make sales on account, credit approval is needed. Three copies of a **sales invoice** are then generated. One is sent to

FIGURE 10-4 Wholesale Sales Transaction Process

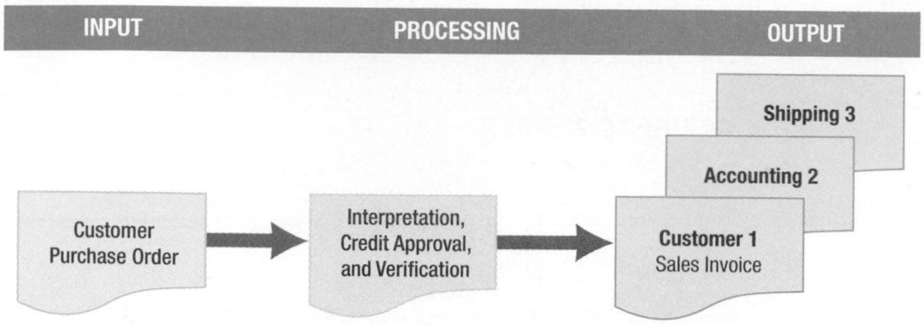

the customer as a bill for the merchandise, one is sent to accounting to record the sale, and one is shipped with the merchandise. Figure 10-5 shows the customer copy of a sales invoice for Aladdin Electric Supply.

FIGURE 10-5 Sales Invoice

Sales Invoice No. 513

Aladdin Electric Supply
204 Main St., Hartford, CT 06103

CUSTOMER: Crafters Builders
P.O. Box 502
Storrs, CT 06268

DATE: May 5, 20--
TERMS: 2/10, n/30

QUANTITY	DESCRIPTION	UNIT PRICE	AMOUNT
6	#DC-26-AB Fixtures	$25	$150.00
5	#HPS-50-P Fixtures	$50	250.00
TOTAL			$400.00

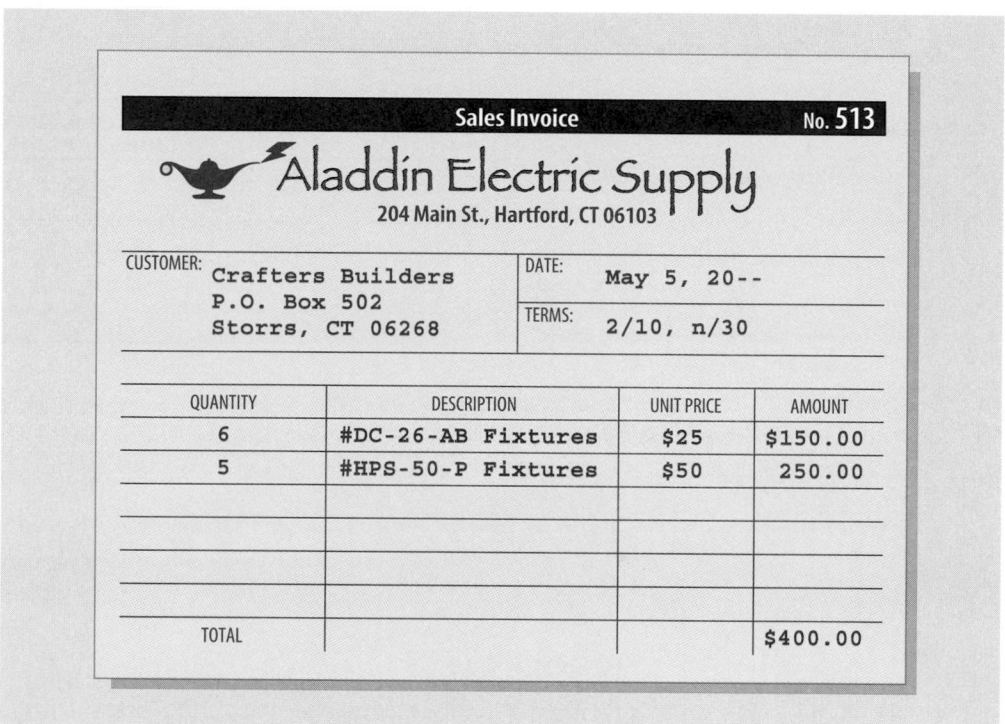

CREDIT MEMORANDUM

Both retailers and wholesalers sometimes have customers return goods or seek price reductions for damaged goods. Merchandise returned by a customer for a refund is called a **sales return**. Price reductions granted by the seller because of defects or other problems with the merchandise are called **sales allowances**. When credit is given for merchandise returned or for an allowance, a **credit memo** is issued for the amount involved. This document gets its name from the same debit and credit concepts you learned in Chapter 3. It is called a credit memo because the customer's account receivable is *credited* to reduce the amount the customer owes. One copy of the credit memo is given to the customer and one copy is sent to accounting. Figure 10-6 shows a credit memo issued by Northern Micro for merchandise returned by a customer.

FIGURE 10-6 Credit Memo

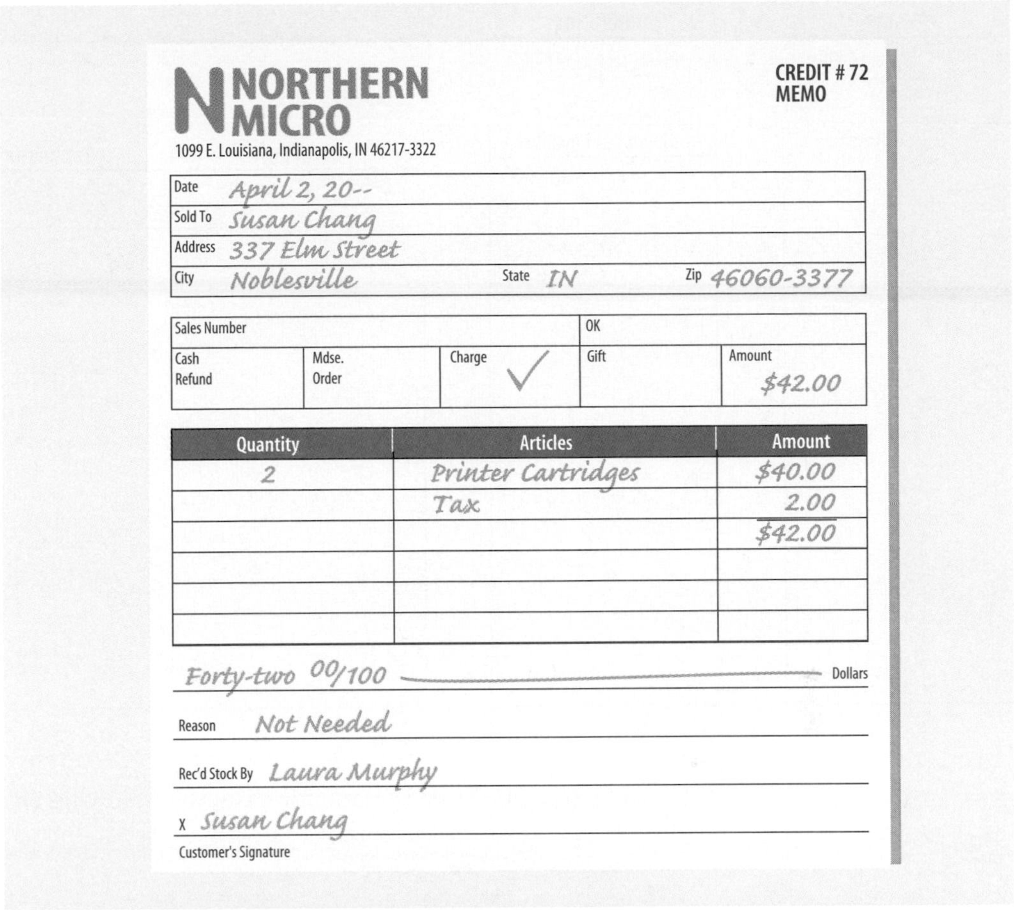
NORTHERN MICRO
1099 E. Louisiana, Indianapolis, IN 46217-3322

CREDIT MEMO # 72

Date: April 2, 20--
Sold To: Susan Chang
Address: 337 Elm Street
City: Noblesville State: IN Zip: 46060-3377

Sales Number			OK	
Cash Refund	Mdse. Order	Charge ✓	Gift	Amount $42.00

Quantity	Articles	Amount
2	Printer Cartridges	$40.00
	Tax	2.00
		$42.00

Forty-two 00/100 Dollars

Reason: Not Needed

Rec'd Stock By: Laura Murphy

X Susan Chang
Customer's Signature

U REVU Complete U REVU-1 on **page 381** to test your basic understanding of LO1.

MERCHANDISE SALES ACCOUNTS

LO2 Describe and use merchandise sales accounts.

To account for merchandise sales transactions, we will use four new accounts:

1. Sales
2. Sales Tax Payable
3. Sales Returns and Allowances
4. Sales Discounts

The position of these accounts in the accounting equation and their normal balances are shown in Figure 10-7.

SALES ACCOUNT

The sales account is a revenue account used to record sales of merchandise. The account is credited for the selling price of merchandise sold during the period.

Sales

Debit	Credit
	to enter the selling price of merchandise sold

FIGURE 10-7 Accounting for Merchandise Sales Transactions

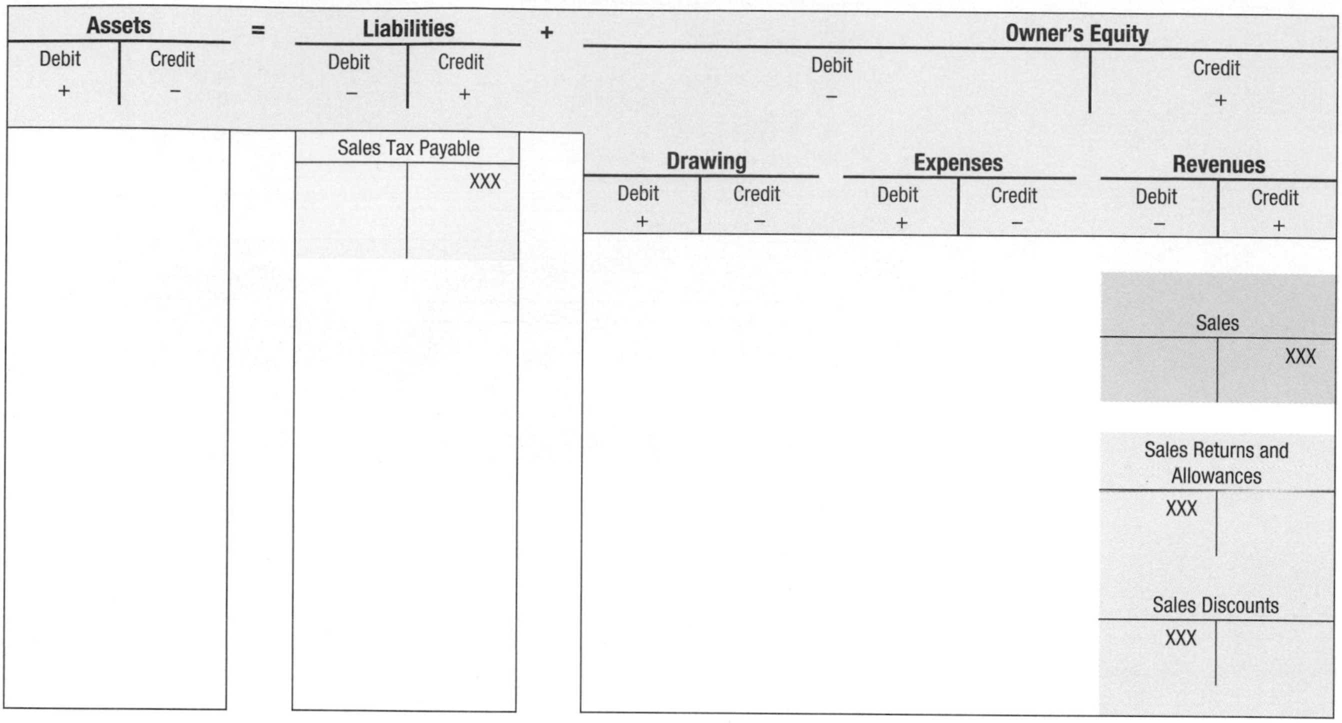

If a $100 sale is made for cash, the following entry is made:

5		Cash		100 00		5
6		Sales			100 00	6
7		Made cash sale				7

If the same sale is made on account, the entry is as follows:

The customer's name is placed after Accounts Receivable

5		Accounts Receivable/Customer		100 00		5
6		Sales			100 00	6
7		Made credit sale				7

Accounts Receivable is followed by a slash (/) and the name of the specific customer who owes the money. Accounts Receivable is the same account we first saw in Chapter 2. It is a general ledger account. The "Customer" name is for the customer's account in the accounts receivable ledger. This ledger is explained later in this chapter.

SALES TAX PAYABLE ACCOUNT

Most states require retailers to collect sales tax on sales to final consumers. When sales tax is imposed on merchandise sold, a separate account for Sales Tax Payable is kept. This is a liability account that is credited for the taxes imposed on sales. The account is debited for sales taxes paid to the proper taxing authority or for sales taxes on merchandise returned by customers. A credit balance in the account indicates the amount owed to the taxing authority for taxes collected.

Sales Tax Payable

Debit	Credit
to enter payment of tax to taxing authority or adjustment of tax on merchandise returned by customers	to enter tax imposed on sales

If a cash sale for $100 plus 5% sales tax (5% × $100 = $5) occurs, the following entry is made:

10		Cash		1 0 5 00		10
11		Sales			1 0 0 00	11
12		Sales Tax Payable			5 00	12
13		Made cash sale				13

If the same sale is made on account, the entry is as follows:

10		Accounts Receivable/Customer		1 0 5 00		10
11		Sales			1 0 0 00	11
12		Sales Tax Payable			5 00	12
13		Made credit sale				13

The debit to Accounts Receivable indicates that the amount owed by customers to the business has increased. Since the buyer has accepted the merchandise and promised to pay for it, revenue is recognized by crediting Sales. Sales Tax Payable is credited because the amount of sales tax owed to the taxing authority has increased.

SALES RETURNS AND ALLOWANCES ACCOUNT

Sales Returns and Allowances is a **contra-revenue account,** which has a debit balance and is deducted from the related revenue account. Sales returns and sales allowances are debited to this account. As shown in Figure 10-8, this account is reported as a deduction from Sales on the income statement. Returns and allowances are debited to a separate account rather than directly to Sales so that the business can more readily keep track of this activity.

Sales Returns and Allowances

Debit	Credit
to enter returns and allowances	

Look at the credit memo in Figure 10-6 on page 357. The entry for the return of these printer cartridges by Susan Chang would be as follows:

19		Sales Returns and Allowances		4 0 00		19
20		Sales Tax Payable		2 00		20
21		Accounts Receivable/Susan Chang			4 2 00	21
22		Returned merchandise — Credit Memo #72				22

FIGURE 10-8 Sales Returns and Allowances on the Income Statement

Sales	$38 5 0 0 00	
Less sales returns and allowances	2 0 0 00	
Net sales		$38 3 0 0 00

LEARNING KEY

To record returns and allowances, debit Sales Returns and Allowances for the amount of the sale excluding the sales tax.

Note carefully the parts of this entry. Sales Returns and Allowances is debited for the amount of the sale, *excluding* the sales tax. Sales Tax Payable is debited separately for the sales tax on the original sale amount. Accounts Receivable is credited for the total amount originally billed to Chang.

SALES DISCOUNTS ACCOUNT

Another type of discount sometimes offered between businesses is a trade discount. This discount is explained in Chapter 11.

Some businesses offer **cash discounts** to encourage prompt payment by customers who buy merchandise on account. When credit is tight and businesses are short of cash, it is particularly important to convert accounts receivable into cash as soon as possible. Prompt collection of accounts receivable also reduces the risk that those receivables will become uncollectible. Some possible credit terms are shown in Figure 10-9.

FIGURE 10-9 Credit Terms

TERMS	MEANING
2/10, n/30*	2% discount off sales price if paid within 10 days Total amount due within 30 days
1/10, n/30	Same as 2/10, n/30, except 1% discount instead of 2%
2/eom, n/60	2% discount if paid before end of month Total amount due within 60 days
3/10 eom, n/60	3% discount if paid within 10 days after end of month Total amount due within 60 days

*See Figure 10-5. A discount of $8 (2% × $400) is allowed if this invoice is paid by May 15 (invoice date of May 5 + 10 days).

To the seller, cash discounts are considered **sales discounts**. Sales Discounts is a contra-revenue account to which cash discounts allowed are debited. Like Sales Returns and Allowances, this account is reported as a deduction from Sales on the income statement, as shown in Figure 10-10.

Sales

Debit	Credit
to enter cash discounts	

FIGURE 10-10 Sales Discounts on the Income Statement

Sales		$38 500 00	
Less: Sales returns and allowances	$ 200 00		
Sales discounts	140 00	340 00	
Net sales			$38 160 00

If merchandise is sold for $100 with credit terms of 2/10, n/30, and cash is received within the discount period, two entries are made.

At time of sale:

26	Accounts Receivable/Customer	100 00		26
27	Sales		100 00	27
28	Made sale on account			28

At time of collection:

30	Cash	98 00		30
31	Sales Discounts	2 00		31
32	Accounts Receivable/Customer		100 00	32
33	Received cash on account			33

Figure 10-11 shows how (1) a sale on account followed by (2) collection with a cash discount affects the accounts receivable, sales, and cash accounts.

FIGURE 10-11 Sales on Account → Collection with Cash Discount

	(1) Credit Sale		2% Cash Discount		(2) Cash Collection
Net Sales =	$100	−	$2	=	$98

	ENTRY FOR CREDIT SALE		
(1)	Accounts Receivable	100 00	
	Sales		100 00

	ENTRY FOR CASH COLLECTION		
(2)	Cash	98 00	
	Sales Discounts	2 00	
	Accounts Receivable		100 00

If any merchandise has been returned, the sales discount is calculated on the sale amount after deducting the return. For the above sale for $100, if $30 of merchandise had been returned, the discount on the remaining $70 collection would be 2% × $70 = $1.40. The journal entry for the collection is:

1	Cash	68 60		1
2	Sales Discount	1 40		2
3	Accounts Receivable		70 00	3
4	Received cash on account			4

If there is a sales tax, the discount is calculated on the sale amount excluding the sales tax. Assume merchandise is sold for $100 plus 5% sales tax (5% × $100 = $5), with credit terms of 2/10, n/30. At the time of the sale, the following entry is made:

1		Accounts Receivable		1 0 5 00		1
2		Sales			1 0 0 00	2
3		Sales Tax Payable			5 00	3
4		Made sale on account				4

If cash is received within the discount period, the discount is 2% × $100 = $2, and the entry is:

1		Cash		1 0 3 00		1
2		Sales Discounts		2 00		2
3		Accounts Receivable			1 0 5 00	3
4		Received cash on account				4

Note that this entry does not affect Sales Tax Payable. The sales tax is based on the amount of the sale, which is not affected by the timing of the collection on account.

U REVU

Complete U REVU-2 on **page 381** to test your basic understanding of LO2.

JOURNALIZING AND POSTING SALES AND CASH RECEIPTS TRANSACTIONS

LO3 Describe and use the accounts receivable ledger.

To illustrate the journalizing and posting of sales and cash receipts transactions, we use Northern Micro, a retail computer business.

SALES

Assume the following sales transactions occurred during April 20--:

Apr.	4	Made Sale No. 133C on account to Enrico Lorenzo, $1,520 plus $76 sales tax.
	10	Made Sale No. 134C on account to Brenda Myers, $440 plus $22 sales tax.
	18	Made Sale No. 105D on account to Edith Walton, $980 plus $49 sales tax.
	21	Made Sale No. 202B on account to Susan Chang, $620 plus $31 sales tax.
	24	Made Sale No. 162A on account to Heidi Schwitzer, $1,600 plus $80 sales tax.

These transactions are entered in a general journal, as shown in Figure 10-12.

POSTING SALES TO THE GENERAL LEDGER

Sales transactions are posted from the general journal to the general ledger in the same manner as was illustrated in Chapter 4. Several steps are used, as indicated in Figure 10-13, for Northern Micro's April 4 and 10 sales transactions.

In the general ledger account:

STEP 1 Enter the date of the transaction in the Date column.

STEP 2 Enter the amount of the debit or credit in the Debit or Credit column.

STEP 3 Enter the new balance in the Balance columns under Debit or Credit.

STEP 4 Enter the journal page number from which each transaction is posted in the Posting Reference column.

FIGURE 10-12 Sales Entered in General Journal

Date		Description	Post. Ref.	Debit	Credit
Apr.	4	Accounts Receivable/E. Lorenzo		1596 00	
		Sales			1520 00
		Sales Tax Payable			76 00
		Sale No. 133C			
	10	Accounts Receivable/B. Myers		462 00	
		Sales			440 00
		Sales Tax Payable			22 00
		Sale No. 134C			
	18	Accounts Receivable/E. Walton		1029 00	
		Sales			980 00
		Sales Tax Payable			49 00
		Sale No. 105D			
	21	Accounts Receivable/S. Chang		651 00	
		Sales			620 00
		Sales Tax Payable			31 00
		Sale No. 202B			
	24	Accounts Receivable/H. Schwitzer		1680 00	
		Sales			1600 00
		Sales Tax Payable			80 00
		Sale No. 162A			

In the journal:

STEP 5 Enter the ledger account number in the Posting Reference column of the journal for each transaction that is posted.

Other sales transactions would be posted in the same manner.

POSTING SALES TO THE ACCOUNTS RECEIVABLE LEDGER

After all posting to the general ledger is completed, the accounts receivable, sales tax payable, and sales accounts in the general ledger are up to date. But at this point, Northern Micro has no complete record of the account receivable from *individual customers*. To run the business properly, Northern Micro needs this information.

A common approach to keeping a record of each customer's account receivable is to use an **accounts receivable ledger**. This is a separate ledger containing an individual account receivable for each customer. It is called a **subsidiary ledger**. A summary accounts receivable account called a **controlling account** is still maintained in the general ledger. The accounts receivable ledger is "subsidiary" to this account. If there are many customer accounts, it is good practice to assign each customer an account number. The subsidiary ledger accounts are kept in either alphabetical or numerical order, depending on whether customer accounts are identified by number. Figure 10-14 shows part of the accounts receivable ledger for Northern Micro.

Figure 10-14 illustrates the use of the accounts receivable ledger for Northern Micro's April 4 and 10 sales transactions. The accounts receivable ledger is posted

FIGURE 10-13 Posting Sales to the General Ledger

GENERAL JOURNAL (Partial) — Page 8

Date		Description	Post. Ref.	Debit	Credit
20--					
Apr.	4	Accounts Receivable/E. Lorenzo	122/	1,596.00	
		Sales	401		1,520.00
		Sales Tax Payable	231		76.00
		Sale No.133C			
	10	Accounts Receivable/B. Myers	122/	462.00	
		Sales	401		440.00
		Sales Tax Payable	231		22.00
		Sale No.134C			

GENERAL LEDGER (Partial)

ACCOUNT Accounts Receivable — ACCOUNT NO.122

Date		Item	Post. Ref.	Debit	Credit	Balance Debit	Balance Credit
20--							
Apr.	1	Bal.	✓			12,000.00	
	4		J8	1,596.00		13,596.00	
	10		J8	462.00		14,058.00	

ACCOUNT Sales Tax Payable — ACCOUNT NO.231

Date		Item	Post. Ref.	Debit	Credit	Balance Debit	Balance Credit
20--							
Apr.	4		J8		76.00		76.00
	10		J8		22.00		98.00

ACCOUNT Sales — ACCOUNT NO. 401

Date		Item	Post. Ref.	Debit	Credit	Balance Debit	Balance Credit
20--							
Apr.	1	Bal.	✓				27,000.00
	4		J8		1,520.00		28,520.00
	10		J8		440.00		28,960.00

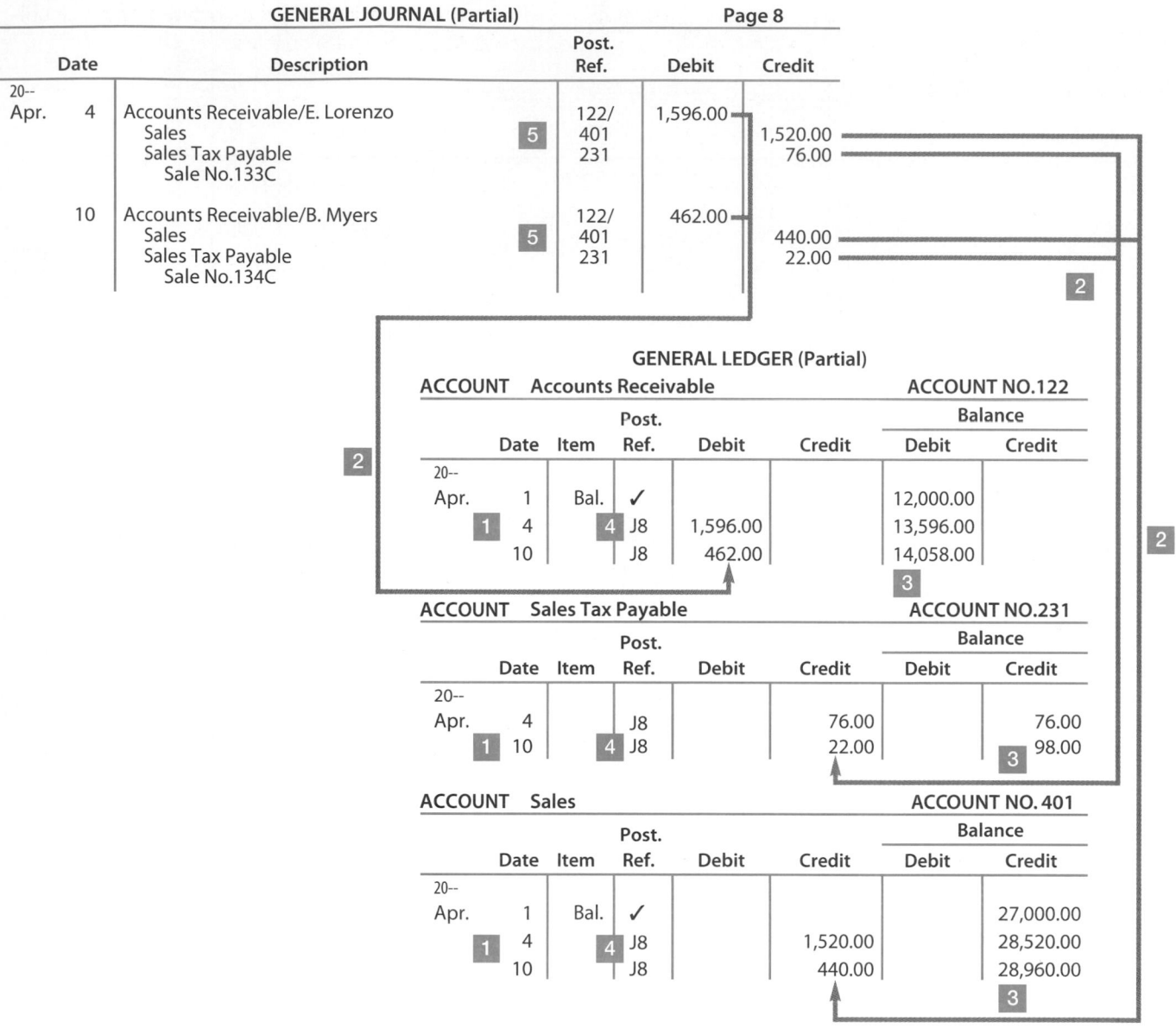

from the journal *daily* so that current information is available for each customer at all times. Note that including the individual customer name after Accounts Receivable in each journal entry helps in the posting process. Several steps are used to post from the general journal to the accounts receivable ledger, as shown in Figure 10-14.

In the accounts receivable ledger account:

STEP 1 Enter the date of the transaction in the Date column.

STEP 2 Enter the amount of the debit or credit in the Debit or Credit column.

STEP 3 Enter the new balance in the Balance column.

STEP 4 Enter the journal page number from which each transaction is posted in the Posting Reference column.

In the journal:

STEP 5 Enter a slash (/) followed by a check mark (✓) in the Posting Reference column of the journal for each transaction that is posted.

FIGURE 10-14 Posting Sales to the Accounts Receivable Ledger

GENERAL JOURNAL (Partial) **Page 8**

Date		Description	Post. Ref.	Debit	Credit
20--					
Apr.	4	Accounts Receivable/E. Lorenzo	5 122/✓	1,596.00	
		Sales	401		1,520.00
		Sales Tax Payable	231		76.00
		Sale No.133C			
	10	Accounts Receivable/B. Myers	5 122/✓	462.00	
		Sales	401		440.00
		Sales Tax Payable	231		22.00
		Sale No.134C			

2

ACCOUNTS RECEIVABLE LEDGER (Partial)

NAME Enrico Lorenzo
ADDRESS 5240 Tousley Court, Indianapolis, IN 46224-5678

Date		Item	Post. Ref.	Debit	Credit	Balance
20--						
Apr.	1 4		4 J8	1,596.00		1,596.00 3

NAME Brenda Myers
ADDRESS 581 Acorn Way, Zionsville, IN 46077-2154

Date		Item	Post. Ref.	Debit	Credit	Balance
20--						
Apr.	1 10		4 J8	462.00		462.00 3

GENERAL LEDGER (Partial)

ACCOUNT Accounts Receivable ACCOUNT NO. 122

Date		Item	Post. Ref.	Debit	Credit	Balance Debit	Balance Credit
20--							
Apr.	1	Bal.	✓			12,000.00	
	4		J8	1,596.00		13,596.00	
	10		J8	462.00		14,058.00	

ACCOUNT Sales Tax Payable ACCOUNT NO. 231

Date		Item	Post. Ref.	Debit	Credit	Balance Debit	Balance Credit
20--							
Apr.	4		J8		76.00		76.00
	10		J8		22.00		98.00

ACCOUNT Sales ACCOUNT NO. 401

Date		Item	Post. Ref.	Debit	Credit	Balance Debit	Balance Credit
20--							
Apr.	1	Bal.	✓				27,000.00
	4		J8		1,520.00		28,520.00
	10		J8		440.00		28,960.00

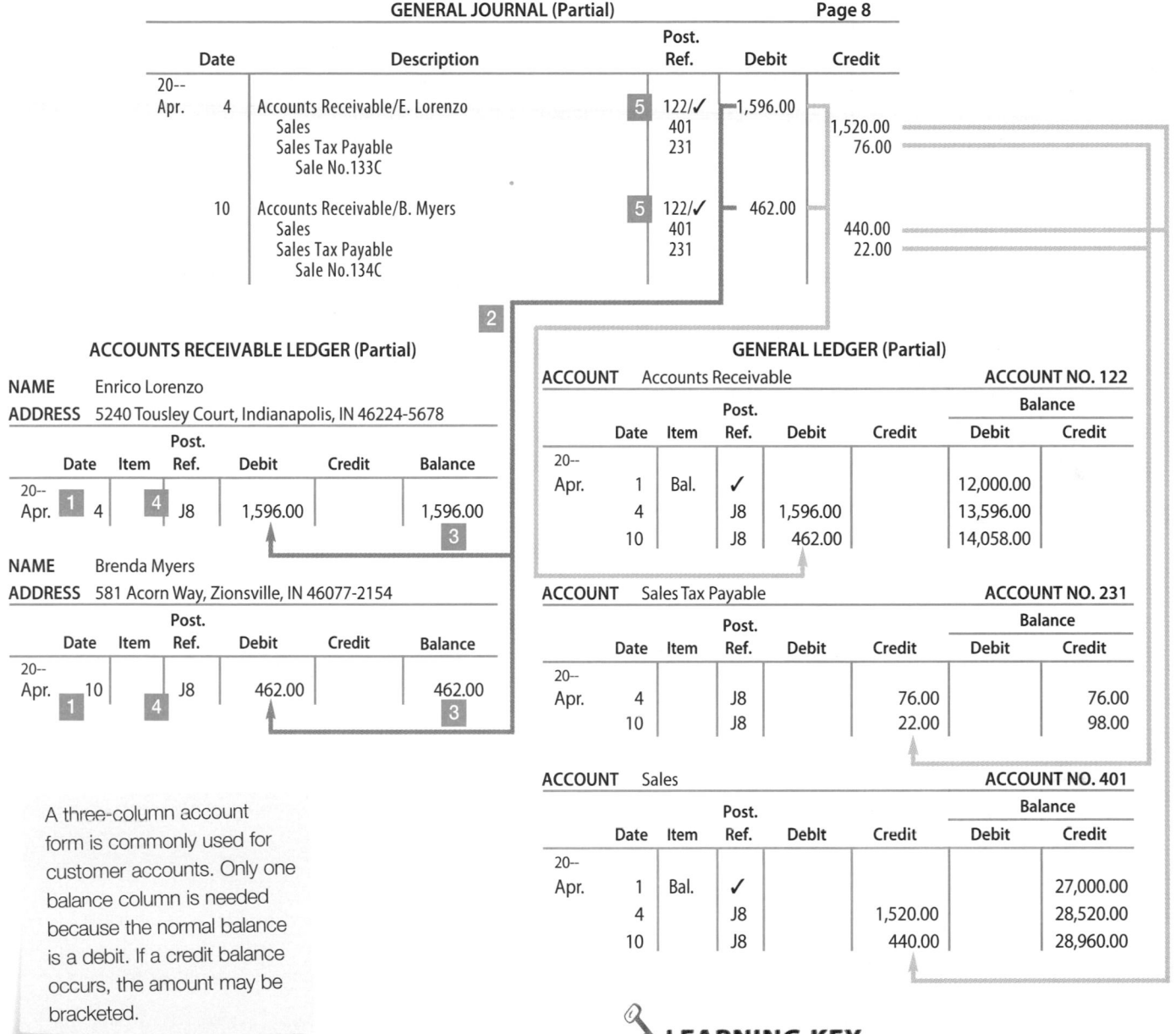

A three-column account form is commonly used for customer accounts. Only one balance column is needed because the normal balance is a debit. If a credit balance occurs, the amount may be bracketed.

LEARNING KEY

When an accounts receivable ledger is used, the Posting Reference column in the general journal can serve two purposes. (1) The account number is inserted to indicate the general ledger account has been posted. (2) A slash (/) and a check mark (✓) can be inserted to indicate the accounts receivable ledger account has been posted.

The accounts receivable ledger also can be posted from the source document used to make the general journal entry. For example, Sales Ticket No. 134C (see Figure 10-2) could be used to post that sale to Brenda Myers' account in the accounts receivable ledger. In this case, 134C would be inserted in the Posting Reference column of her account.

LEARNING KEY

The total of the accounts receivable ledger balances must equal the Accounts Receivable balance in the general ledger.

Note the relationship between the general journal, accounts receivable ledger, and general ledger. Entries in the general journal are posted to the general ledger and accounts receivable ledger. After the posting of the accounts receivable ledger and the general ledger is completed, the total of the accounts receivable ledger balances should equal the Accounts Receivable balance in the general ledger. Remember, the accounts receivable ledger is simply a detailed listing of the same information that is summarized in Accounts Receivable in the general ledger.

SALES RETURNS AND ALLOWANCES

If a customer returns merchandise or is given an allowance for damaged merchandise, a general journal entry is required. On May 5, Susan Chang returned two printer cartridges costing $40 plus $2 sales tax (Figure 10-6, page 357). Figure 10-15 shows the general journal entry, general ledger posting, and accounts receivable ledger posting for this transaction.

The general journal entry is made in the usual manner. The general ledger is posted using the same five steps as were illustrated for sales transactions in Figure 10-13. The accounts receivable ledger is posted using the five steps below, as illustrated in Figure 10-15.

In the accounts receivable ledger account:

STEP 1 Enter the date of the transaction in the Date column.

STEP 2 Enter the amount of the debit or credit in the Debit or Credit column.

STEP 3 Enter the new balance in the Balance column.

STEP 4 Enter the journal page number from which each transaction is posted in the Posting Reference column.

In the journal:

STEP 5 Enter a slash (/) followed by a check mark (✓) in the Posting Reference column of the journal for each transaction that is posted.

CASH RECEIPTS

Like sales transactions, cash receipt transactions occur frequently in most businesses. Three common types of cash receipts from sales are collections on account, cash sales, and bank credit card sales.

Collections on Account

Sales on account lead to cash receipts, which are entered in the general journal. For example, assume that Northern Micro receives cash from Enrico Lorenzo for Sale No. 133C on April 14. The transaction is recorded in the general journal as follows:

25	Apr.	14	Cash		1,596.00		25
26			Accounts Receivable/E. Lorenzo			1,596.00	26
27			Received cash on account				27

Cash Sales

Most businesses also regularly make cash sales. The following entry shows cash sales of $500 recorded in the general journal on May 5:

3	May	5	Cash		500.00		3
4			Sales			500.00	4
5			Made cash sales				5

FIGURE 10-15 Accounting for Sales Returns and Allowances

GENERAL JOURNAL (Partial) Page 9

Date		Description	Post. Ref.	Debit	Credit
20--					
May	5	Sales Returns and Allowances	401.1	40.00	
		Sales Tax Payable	231	2.00	
		Accounts Receivable/S.Chang	122 / ✓		42.00
		Returned merchandise—Credit Memo #72	5		

ACCOUNTS RECEIVABLE LEDGER (Partial)

NAME Susan Chang
ADDRESS 337 Elm Street, Noblesville, IN 46060-3377

Date		Item	Post. Ref.	Debit	Credit	Balance
20--						
May	1	Bal.	✓			651.00
1	5	4	J9		42.00	609.00 3

2

GENERAL LEDGER (Partial)

ACCOUNT Accounts Receivable ACCOUNT NO. 122

Date		Item	Post. Ref.	Debit	Credit	Balance Debit	Balance Credit
20--							
May	1	Bal.	✓			14,331.00	
	5		J9		42.00	14,289.00	

ACCOUNT Sales Tax Payable ACCOUNT NO. 231

Date		Item	Post. Ref.	Debit	Credit	Balance Debit	Balance Credit
20--							
May	1	Bal.	✓				563.00
	5		J9	2.00			561.00

ACCOUNT Sales Returns and Allowances ACCOUNT NO. 401.1

Date		Item	Post. Ref.	Debit	Credit	Balance Debit	Balance Credit
20--							
May	1	Bal.	✓			274.00	
	5		J9	40.00		314.00	

Bank Credit Card Sales

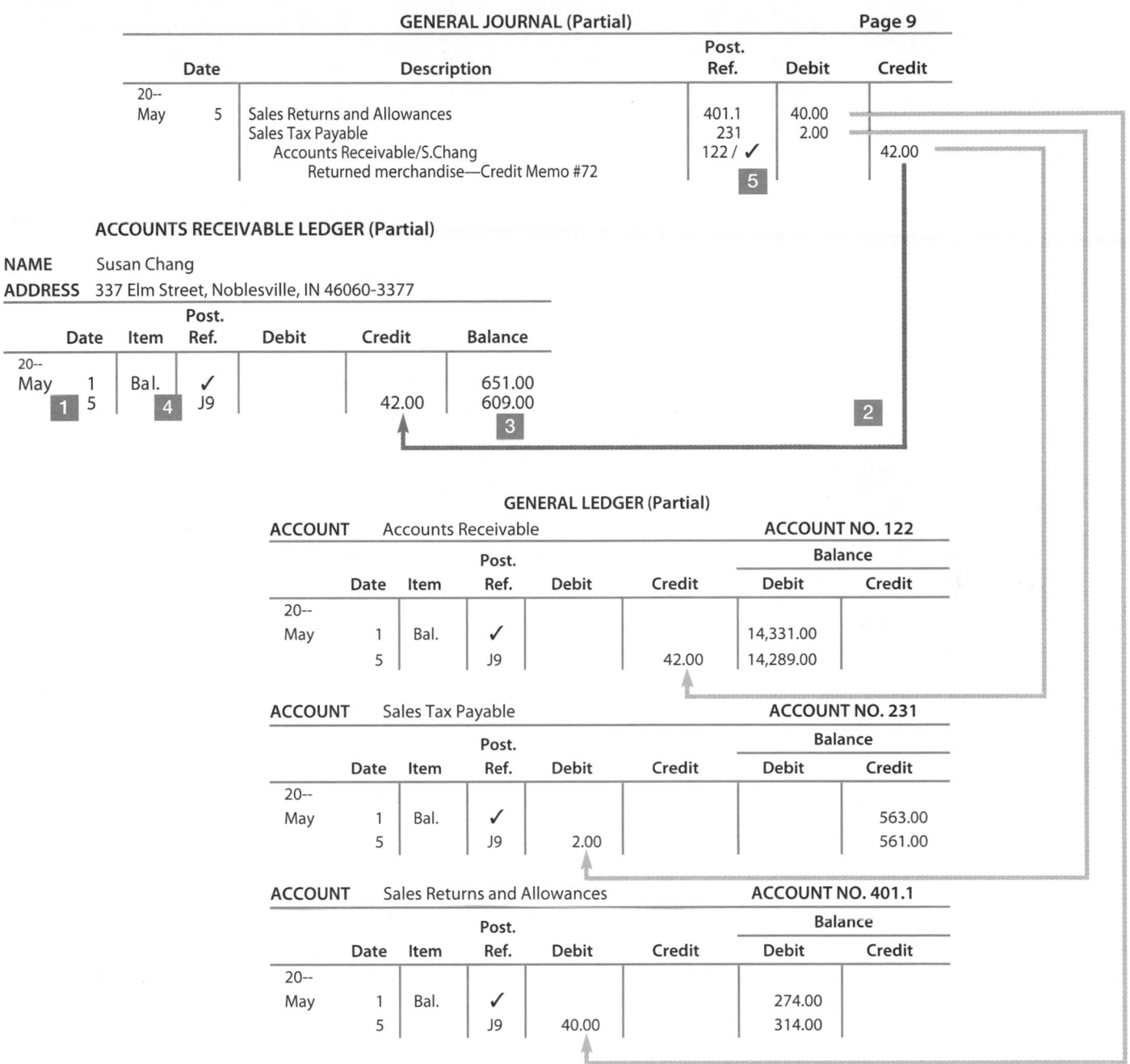

An increasing amount of sales today are made using bank credit cards. In fact, consider Planet Shoes, the company in the chapter introduction. Planet operates totally online, so virtually all of its sales would be by bank credit card. Bank credit card sales are similar to cash sales because the cash is available to the business as soon as an electronic deposit is made at the end of the day. The credit card company makes the electronic deposit to the merchandiser's bank account for the gross amount of credit card sales less a processing fee. The fee is based on the gross amount of the sale, including the sales tax. Thus, on a sale of $100 plus sales tax of $5, the credit card fee at 4%

would be $4.20 (4% × $105). The following entry shows this credit card sale recorded on May 6:

8	May	6	Cash		100	80			8
9			Bank Credit Card Expense		4	20			9
10			Sales				100	00	10
11			Sales Tax Payable				5	00	11
12			Made credit card sale						12

A BROADER VIEW

IMAGE COPYRIGHT MORGAN LANE PHOTOGRAPHY, 2009/USED UNDER LICENSE FROM SHUTTERSTOCK .COM

Is This Sale for Real?

U.S. businesses lose billions of dollars annually because of credit card fraud and bad checks. To reduce credit card fraud, cashiers should do two things: (1) Watch the customer sign the credit card slip and match it to the signature on the card. (2) Obtain an approval code on all credit card transactions. To reduce bad check losses, cashiers should accept only a driver's license as identification. They should compare the picture with the customer, watch the check being signed, and match the check signature with that on the driver's license.

JOURNALIZING CASH RECEIPTS

To illustrate the journalizing and posting of cash receipts transactions, we continue to use Northern Micro. Assume the following cash receipts transactions related to sales occurred during April 20--. (To simplify the illustration, cash sales and bank credit card sales for the month are summarized as single transactions at the end of the month.)

Apr. 14 Received cash on account from Enrico Lorenzo for Sale No. 133C, $1,596.

20 Received cash on account from Brenda Myers for Sale No. 134C, $462.

28 Received cash on account from Edith Walton for Sale No. 105D, $1,029.

30 Cash sales for the month are $3,600 plus tax of $180.

30 Bank credit card sales for the month are $2,500 plus tax of $125. Bank credit card expenses on these sales are $100.

These transactions are entered in a general journal as shown in Figure 10-16.

FIGURE 10-16 Cash Receipts Entered in General Journal

4	Apr.	14	Cash		1596 00		4
5			Accounts Receivable/E. Lorenzo			1596 00	5
6			Received cash on account				6
7							7
8		20	Cash		462 00		8
9			Accounts Receivable/B. Myers			462 00	9
10			Received cash on account				10
11							11
12		28	Cash		1029 00		12
13			Accounts Receivable/E. Walton			1029 00	13
14			Received cash on account				14
15							15
16		30	Cash		3780 00		16
17			Sales			3600 00	17
18			Sales Tax Payable			180 00	18
19			Made cash sales				19
20							20
21		30	Cash		2525 00		21
22			Bank Credit Card Expense		100 00		22
23			Sales			2500 00	23
24			Sales Tax Payable			125 00	24
25			Made credit card sales				25

POSTING CASH RECEIPTS TO THE GENERAL LEDGER AND ACCOUNTS RECEIVABLE LEDGER

Cash receipts transactions are posted to the general ledger in the same manner as was illustrated for sales transactions in Figure 10-13. To post cash receipts to the accounts receivable ledger, the steps below are used, as illustrated in Figure 10-17 for Northern Micro's April 14 and 20 cash receipts transactions.

In the accounts receivable ledger account:

STEP 1 Enter the date of the transaction in the Date column.

STEP 2 Enter the amount of the debit or credit in the Debit or Credit column.

STEP 3 Enter the new balance in the Balance column.

STEP 4 Enter the journal page number from which each transaction is posted in the Posting Reference column.

In the journal:

STEP 5 Enter a slash (/) followed by a check mark (✓) in the Posting Reference column of the journal for each transaction that is posted.

LEARNING OBJECTIVES Key Points to Remember

LO1 Describe merchandise sales transactions.	A merchandising business buys and sells merchandise. Retailers generally make sales in the store. Important accounting documents are cash register tapes and sales tickets. Wholesalers generally ship merchandise to retailers. A key accounting document is the sales invoice. When customers return merchandise or obtain price adjustments, a credit memo is issued.
LO2 Describe and use merchandise sales accounts.	Four accounts are used in accounting for merchandise sales transactions. 1. Sales 2. Sales Tax Payable 3. Sales Returns and Allowances 4. Sales Discounts
LO3 Describe and use the accounts receivable ledger.	To post sales transactions to the general ledger, use these five steps. **In the general ledger account:** STEP 1 Enter the date of the transaction in the Date column. STEP 2 Enter the amount of the debit or credit in the Debit or Credit column. STEP 3 Enter the new balance in the Balance columns under Debit or Credit. STEP 4 Enter the journal page number from which each transaction is posted in the Posting Reference column. **In the journal:** STEP 5 Enter the ledger account number in the Posting Reference column of the journal for each transaction that is posted. An accounts receivable ledger is a separate ledger containing an individual account receivable for each customer. To post sales transactions to the accounts receivable ledger, use these five steps. **In the accounts receivable ledger account:** STEP 1 Enter the date of the transaction in the Date column. STEP 2 Enter the amount of the debit or credit in the Debit or Credit column. STEP 3 Enter the new balance in the Balance column. STEP 4 Enter the journal page number from which each transaction is posted in the Posting Reference column. **In the journal:** STEP 5 Enter a slash (/) followed by a check mark (✓) in the Posting Reference column of the journal for each transaction that is posted. To post cash receipts transactions to the general ledger, use these five steps. **In the general ledger account:** STEP 1 Enter the date of the transaction in the Date column. STEP 2 Enter the amount of the debit or credit in the Debit or Credit column. STEP 3 Enter the new balance in the Balance columns under Debit or Credit.

(continued)

LEARNING OBJECTIVES Key Points to Remember

LO3 (concluded)	STEP 4 Enter the journal page number from which each transaction is posted in the Posting Reference column. **In the journal:** STEP 5 Enter the ledger account number in the Posting Reference column of the journal for each transaction that is posted. To post cash receipts transactions to the accounts receivable ledger, use these five steps. **In the accounts receivable ledger account:** STEP 1 Enter the date of the transaction in the Date column. STEP 2 Enter the amount of the debit or credit in the Debit or Credit column. STEP 3 Enter the new balance in the Balance column. STEP 4 Enter the journal page number from which each transaction is posted in the Posting Reference column. **In the journal:** STEP 5 Enter a slash (/) followed by a check mark (✓) in the Posting Reference column of the journal for each transaction that is posted.
LO4 Prepare a schedule of accounts receivable.	The schedule of accounts receivable is used to verify that the sum of the accounts receivable ledger balances equals the Accounts Receivable balance.

DEMONSTRATION PROBLEM

Karen Hunt operates Hunt's Audio-Video Store. The books include a general journal, general ledger, and accounts receivable ledger. The following transactions related to sales on account and cash receipts occurred during April 20--:

Apr. 3	Sold merchandise on account to Susan Haberman, \$159.50 plus tax of \$11.17. Sale No. 41.
4	Sold merchandise on account to Goro Kimura, \$299.95 plus tax of \$21.00. Sale No. 42.
6	Received payment from Tera Scherrer on account, \$69.50.
7	Issued Credit Memo No. 48 to Kenneth Watt for merchandise returned that had been sold on account, \$42.75 including tax of \$2.80.
10	Received payment from Kellie Cokley on account, \$99.95.
11	Sold merchandise on account to Victor Cardona, \$499.95 plus tax of \$35.00. Sale No. 43.
14	Received payment from Kenneth Watt in full settlement of account, \$157.00.
17	Sold merchandise on account to Susan Haberman, \$379.95 plus tax of \$26.60. Sale No. 44.

(continued)

Apr. 19 Sold merchandise on account to Tera Scherrer, $59.95 plus tax of $4.20. Sale No. 45.

21 Issued Credit Memo No. 49 to Goro Kimura for merchandise returned that had been sold on account, $53.45 including tax of $3.50.

24 Received payment from Victor Cardona on account, $299.95.

25 Sold merchandise on account to Kellie Cokley, $179.50 plus tax of $12.57. Sale No. 46.

26 Received payment from Susan Haberman on account, $250.65.

28 Sold merchandise on account to Kenneth Watt, $49.95 plus tax of $3.50. Sale No. 47.

30 Bank credit card sales for the month were $1,220.00 plus tax of $85.40. Bank credit card expense on these sales was $65.27.

30 Cash sales for the month were $2,000.00 plus tax of $140.00.

Hunt had the following general ledger account balances as of April 1:

Account Title	Account No.	General Ledger Balance on April 1
Cash	101	$5,000.00
Accounts Receivable	122	1,208.63
Sales Tax Payable	231	72.52
Sales	401	8,421.49
Sales Returns and Allowances	401.1	168.43
Bank Credit Card Expense	513	215.00

Hunt also had the following accounts receivable ledger account balances as of April 1:

Customer	Accounts Receivable Balance
Victor Cardona 6300 Washington Blvd. St. Louis, MO 63130-9523	$299.95
Kellie Cokley 4220 Kingsbury Blvd. St. Louis, MO 63130-1645	$99.95
Susan Haberman 9421 Garden Ct. Kirkwood, MO 63122-1878	$79.98
Goro Kimura 6612 Arundel Pl. Clayton, MO 63150-9266	$379.50
Tera Scherrer 315 W. Linden St. Webster Groves, MO 63119-9881	$149.50
Kenneth Watt 11742 Fawnridge Dr. St. Louis, MO 63131-1726	$199.75

REQUIRED

1. Open general ledger accounts and three-column accounts receivable ledger accounts for Hunt's Audio-Video Store as of April 1, 20--. Enter the April 1 balance in each of the accounts.
2. Enter each transaction in a general journal (page 7).
3. Post directly from the journal to the proper customers' accounts in the accounts receivable ledger. Each subsidiary ledger account should show the initial "J," followed by the appropriate journal page number as a posting reference for each transaction.
4. Post from the journal to the proper general ledger accounts. Each general ledger account should show the initial "J," followed by the appropriate journal page number as a posting reference for each transaction.
5. Prove the balance of the summary accounts receivable account by preparing a schedule of accounts receivable as of April 30, based on the accounts receivable ledger.

Solution 1. and 3.

ACCOUNTS RECEIVABLE LEDGER

NAME: Victor Cardona

DATE		ITEM	POST. REF.	DEBIT	CREDIT	BALANCE
20-- Apr.	1	Balance	✓			299 95
	11		J7	534 95		834 90
	24		J8		299 95	534 95

NAME: Kellie Cokley

DATE		ITEM	POST. REF.	DEBIT	CREDIT	BALANCE
20-- Apr.	1	Balance	✓			99 95
	10		J7		99 95	—
	25		J8	192 07		192 07

NAME: Susan Haberman

DATE		ITEM	POST. REF.	DEBIT	CREDIT	BALANCE
20-- Apr.	1	Balance	✓			79 98
	3		J7	170 67		250 65
	17		J7	406 55		657 20
	26		J8		250 65	406 55

NAME: Goro Kimura

DATE		ITEM	POST REF.	DEBIT	CREDIT	BALANCE
20-- Apr.	1	Balance	✓			379 50
	4		J7	320 95		700 45
	21		J8		53 45	647 00

(continued)

NAME: Tera Scherrer

DATE		ITEM	POST. REF.	DEBIT	CREDIT	BALANCE
20-- Apr.	1	Balance	✓			149 50
	6		J7		69 50	80 00
	19		J8	64 15		144 15

NAME: Kenneth Watt

DATE		ITEM	POST REF.	DEBIT	CREDIT	BALANCE
20-- Apr.	1	Balance	✓			199 75
	7		J7		42 75	157 00
	14		J7		157 00	—
	28		J8	53 45		53 45

2., 3., and 4.

GENERAL JOURNAL PAGE 7

	DATE		DESCRIPTION	POST. REF.	DEBIT	CREDIT	
1	20-- Apr.	3	Accounts Receivable/Susan Haberman	122/✓	170 67		1
2			Sales	401		159 50	2
3			Sales Tax Payable	231		11 17	3
4			Sale No. 41				4
5							5
6		4	Accounts Receivable/Goro Kimura	122/✓	320 95		6
7			Sales	401		299 95	7
8			Sales Tax Payable	231		21 00	8
9			Sale No. 42				9
10							10
11		6	Cash	101	69 50		11
12			Accounts Receivable/Tera Scherrer	122/✓		69 50	12
13			Received cash on account				13
14							14
15		7	Sales Returns and Allowances	401.1	39 95		15
16			Sales Tax Payable	231	2 80		16
17			Accounts Receivable/Kenneth Watt	122/✓		42 75	17
18			Returned merchandise				18
19							19
20		10	Cash	101	99 95		20
21			Accounts Receivable/Kellie Cokley	122/✓		99 95	21
22			Received cash on account				22
23							23
24		11	Accounts Receivable/Victor Cardona	122/✓	534 95		24
25			Sales	401		499 95	25
26			Sales Tax Payable	231		35 00	26
27			Sale No. 43				27
28							28
29		14	Cash	101	157 00		29
30			Accounts Receivable/Kenneth Watt	122/✓		157 00	30
31			Received cash on account				31
32							32
33		17	Accounts Receivable/Susan Haberman	122/✓	406 55		33
34			Sales	401		379 95	34
35			Sales Tax Payable	231		26 60	35
36			Sale No. 44				36

2., 3., and 4.

GENERAL JOURNAL PAGE 8

	DATE		DESCRIPTION	POST. REF.	DEBIT	CREDIT	
1	20-- Apr.	19	Accounts Receivable/Tera Scherrer	122/✓	64 15		1
2			Sales	401		59 95	2
3			Sales Tax Payable	231		4 20	3
4			Sale No. 45				4
5							5
6		21	Sales Returns and Allowances	401.1	49 95		6
7			Sales Tax Payable	231	3 50		7
8			Accounts Receivable/Goro Kimura	122/✓		53 45	8
9			Returned merchandise—Credit Memo #49				9
10							10
11		24	Cash	101	299 95		11
12			Accounts Receivable/Victor Cardona	122/✓		299 95	12
13			Received cash on account				13
14							14
15		25	Accounts Receivable/Kellie Cokley	122/✓	192 07		15
16			Sales	401		179 50	16
17			Sales Tax Payable	231		12 57	17
18			Sale No. 46				18
19							19
20		26	Cash	101	250 65		20
21			Accounts Receivable/Susan Haberman	122/✓		250 65	21
22			Received cash on account				22
23							23
24		28	Accounts Receivable/Kenneth Watt	122/✓	53 45		24
25			Sales	401		49 95	25
26			Sales Tax Payable	231		3 50	26
27			Sale No. 47				27
28							28
29		30	Cash	101	1,240 13		29
30			Bank Credit Card Expense	513	65 27		30
31			Sales	401		1,220 00	31
32			Sales Tax Payable	231		85 40	32
33			Credit card sales				33
34							34
35		30	Cash	101	2,140 00		35
36			Sales	401		2,000 00	36
37			Sales Tax Payable	231		140 00	37
38			Made cash sales				38

1. and 4.

GENERAL LEDGER (PARTIAL)

ACCOUNT: Cash ACCOUNT NO. 101

DATE		ITEM	POST. REF.	DEBIT	CREDIT	BALANCE DEBIT	BALANCE CREDIT
20-- Apr.	1	Balance	✓			5,000 00	
	6		J7	69 50		5,069 50	
	10		J7	99 95		5,169 45	
	14		J7	157 00		5,326 45	
	24		J8	299 95		5,626 40	
	26		J8	250 65		5,877 05	
	30		J8	1,240 13		7,117 18	
	30		J8	2,140 00		9,257 18	

(continued)

1. and 4.

ACCOUNT: Accounts Receivable — ACCOUNT NO. 122

DATE		ITEM	POST. REF.	DEBIT	CREDIT	BALANCE DEBIT	BALANCE CREDIT
20-- Apr.	1	Balance	✓			1208.63	
	3		J7	170.67		1379.30	
	4		J7	320.95		1700.25	
	6		J7		69.50	1630.75	
	7		J7		42.75	1588.00	
	10		J7		99.95	1488.05	
	11		J7	534.95		2023.00	
	14		J7		157.00	1866.00	
	17		J7	406.55		2272.55	
	19		J8	64.15		2336.70	
	21		J8		53.45	2283.25	
	24		J8		299.95	1983.30	
	25		J8	192.07		2175.37	
	26		J8		250.65	1924.72	
	28		J8	53.45		1978.17	

ACCOUNT: Sales Tax Payable — ACCOUNT NO. 231

DATE		ITEM	POST. REF.	DEBIT	CREDIT	BALANCE DEBIT	BALANCE CREDIT
20-- Apr.	1	Balance	✓				72.52
	3		J7		11.17		83.69
	4		J7		21.00		104.69
	7		J7	2.80			101.89
	11		J7		35.00		136.89
	17		J7		26.60		163.49
	19		J8		4.20		167.69
	21		J8	3.50			164.19
	25		J8		12.57		176.76
	28		J8		3.50		180.26
	30		J8		85.40		265.66
	30		J8		140.00		405.66

ACCOUNT: Sales — ACCOUNT NO. 401

DATE		ITEM	POST. REF.	DEBIT	CREDIT	BALANCE DEBIT	BALANCE CREDIT
20-- Apr.	1	Balance	✓				8421.49
	3		J7		159.50		8580.99
	4		J7		299.95		8880.94
	11		J7		499.95		9380.89
	17		J7		379.95		9760.84
	19		J8		59.95		9820.79
	25		J8		179.50		10000.29
	28		J8		49.95		10050.24
	30		J8		1220.00		11270.24
	30		J8		2000.00		13270.24

1. and 4.

ACCOUNT: Sales Returns and Allowances — ACCOUNT NO. 401.1

DATE		ITEM	POST. REF.	DEBIT	CREDIT	BALANCE DEBIT	BALANCE CREDIT
20-- Apr.	1	Balance	✓			168.43	
	7		J7	39.95		208.38	
	21		J8	49.95		258.33	

ACCOUNT: Bank Credit Card Expense — ACCOUNT NO. 513

DATE		ITEM	POST. REF.	DEBIT	CREDIT	BALANCE DEBIT	BALANCE CREDIT
20-- Apr.	1	Balance	✓			215.00	
	30		J8	65.27		280.27	

5.

Hunt's Audio-Video Store
Schedule of Accounts Receivable
April 30, 20--

Victor Cardona		534.95
Kellie Cokley		192.07
Susan Haberman		406.55
Goro Kimura		647.00
Tera Scherrer		144.15
Kenneth Watt		53.45
Total		1,978.17

KEY TERMS

accounts receivable ledger (363) A separate ledger containing an individual account receivable for each customer, kept in either alphabetical or numerical order.

cash discounts (360) Discounts to encourage prompt payment by customers who buy merchandise on account.

contra-revenue account (359) An account with a debit balance that is deducted from the related revenue account.

controlling account (363) A summary account maintained in the general ledger with a subsidiary ledger (for example, the accounts receivable ledger).

credit memo (356) A document issued when credit is given for merchandise returned or for an allowance.

merchandising business (354) A business that purchases merchandise such as clothing, furniture, or computers, and sells that merchandise to its customers.

sale (354) A transfer of merchandise from one business or individual to another in exchange for cash or a promise to pay cash.

sales allowances (356) Reductions in the price of merchandise granted by the seller because of defects or other problems with the merchandise.

sales discounts (360) To the seller, cash discounts are considered sales discounts.

sales invoice (355) A document that is generated to bill the customer to whom the sale was made.

sales return (356) Merchandise returned by a customer for a refund.

sales ticket (355) A document created as evidence of a sale in a retail business.

schedule of accounts receivable (370) An alphabetical or numerical listing of customer accounts and balances, usually prepared at the end of the month.

subsidiary ledger (363) A separate ledger made up of individual accounts that contain the detail for a controlling account.

SELF-STUDY QUESTIONS AND EXERCISES

True/False Questions

1. LO1 Reductions in the price of merchandise granted by the seller because of defects or other problems with the merchandise are called sales allowances.
2. LO2 All sales, for cash or on credit, can be recorded in the general journal.
3. LO2 Sales Tax Payable is a liability account that is credited for the amount of tax imposed on sales.
4. LO2 Sales Returns and Allowances is debited for the amount of the sale, including the sales tax on that amount.
5. LO2 Cash discounts are offered to encourage prompt payment by customers who buy on account.

Multiple Choice Questions

1. LO2 A credit sale of $250 plus a 6% sales tax would require a debit to Accounts Receivable of
   (a) $15.
   (b) $280.
   (c) $30.
   (d) $265.
2. LO2 When $25 of merchandise is returned for a credit on account, what is the amount of the credit to Accounts Receivable, assuming a 6% sales tax rate?
   (a) $1.50
   (b) $25.00
   (c) $26.50
   (d) $31.00
3. LO3 When $300, plus sales tax of 6%, is received for an amount previously owed, Cash is debited for what amount?
   (a) $18
   (b) $318
   (c) $300
   (d) $282
4. LO3 When credit sales are $325 plus sales tax of 5%, and there is a bank credit card fee of 3%, what is the debit to Bank Credit Card Expense?
   (a) $16.25
   (b) $10.24
   (c) $341.25
   (d) $331.01
5. LO3 Cash receipts should
   (a) be posted to customer accounts daily.
   (b) be posted to customer accounts weekly.
   (c) be posted to customer accounts at the end of the month.
   (d) not be posted.

U REVU Exercises

1. LO1 The sales transaction process for a wholesale business is shown below.

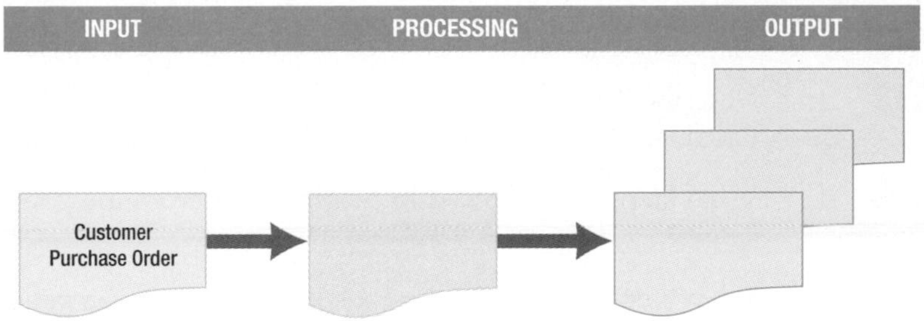

Complete the illustration by providing the missing information in the blank symbols.

2. LO2 Prepare journal entries for the following sales and cash receipts transactions.
   (a) Merchandise is sold on account for $300 plus 3% sales tax, with 2/10, n/30 cash discount terms.
   (b) Part of the merchandise sold in transaction (a) for $70 plus sales tax is returned for credit.
   (c) The balance on account for the merchandise sold in transaction (a) is paid in cash within the discount period.

3. LO3 The following journal entries are for current sales and cash receipts transactions. Using T accounts, post these transactions to Cash, Accounts Receivable, Sales, Sales Returns and Allowances, and Sales Tax Payable in the general ledger, and to the customer account in the accounts receivable ledger.

(a)		Accounts Receivable/M. Schapiro		288 40	
		Sales			280 00
		Sales Tax Payable			8 40
		Made sale on account			
(b)		Sales Returns and Allowances		60 00	
		Sales Tax Payable		1 80	
		Accounts Receivable/M. Shapiro			61 80
		Returned merchandise			
(c)		Cash		226 60	
		Accounts Receivable/M. Shapiro			226 60
		Received on account			

4. LO4 On March 24, MS Company's Accounts Receivable consisted of the following customer balances:

S. Burton	$310
A. Tangier	240
J. Holmes	504
F. Fullman	110
P. Molty	90

During the following week, MS made a sale of $104 to Molty and collected cash on account of $207 from Burton and $360 from Holmes. Prepare a schedule of accounts receivable for MS at March 31, 20--.

The answers to the Self-Study Questions and Exercises are at the end of the chapter (pages 395–396).

REVIEW QUESTIONS

LO1 1. Identify the sales documents commonly used in retail and wholesale businesses.

LO1 2. What is the purpose of a credit memo?

LO2 3. Describe how each of the following accounts is used: (1) Sales, (2) Sales Tax Payable, (3) Sales Returns and Allowances, and (4) Sales Discounts.

LO3 4. What steps are followed in posting sales from the general journal to the general ledger?

LO3 5. What steps are followed in posting sales from the general journal to the accounts receivable ledger?

LO3 6. What steps are followed in posting sales returns and allowances from the general journal to the general ledger and accounts receivable ledger?

LO3 7. What steps are followed in posting cash receipts from the general journal to the general ledger?

LO3 8. What steps are followed in posting cash receipts from the general journal to the accounts receivable ledger?

LO4 9. If the total of the schedule of accounts receivable does not agree with the Accounts Receivable balance, what procedures should be used to search for the error?

SERIES A EXERCISES

E 10-1A (LO1)

SALES DOCUMENTS For each document or procedure listed below, indicate whether it would be used for a retail business or a wholesale business, as described in the chapter.

1. sales ticket
2. sales invoice
3. credit approval
4. cash register tape summary
5. credit memo
6. customer purchase order

E 10-2A (LO2)

✓ 3(d):
Sales Ret. & Allow. 35
Accts. Rec. 35

SALES TRANSACTIONS AND T ACCOUNTS Using T accounts for Cash, Accounts Receivable, Sales Tax Payable, Sales, Sales Returns and Allowances, and Sales Discounts, enter the following sales transactions. Use a new set of accounts for each part, 1–5.

1. No sales tax.
   (a) Merchandise is sold for $300 cash.
   (b) Merchandise is sold on account for $285.
   (c) Payment is received for merchandise sold on account.
2. 5% sales tax.
   (a) Merchandise is sold for $300 cash plus sales tax.
   (b) Merchandise is sold on account for $285 plus sales tax.
   (c) Payment is received for merchandise sold on account.

3. Cash and credit sales, with returned merchandise.
   (a) Merchandise is sold for $325 cash.
   (b) $25 of merchandise sold for $325 is returned for refund.
   (c) Merchandise is sold on account for $350.
   (d) $35 of merchandise sold for $350 is returned for a credit.
   (e) Payment is received for balance owed on merchandise sold on account.

4. 5% sales tax, with returned merchandise.
   (a) Merchandise is sold on account for $400 plus sales tax.
   (b) Merchandise sold on account for $40 plus sales tax is returned for a credit.
   (c) Balance on account is paid in cash.
   (d) Merchandise is sold for $280 cash plus sales tax.
   (e) $20 of merchandise sold for $280 cash plus sales tax is returned for a refund.

5. Sales on account, with 2/10, n/30 cash discount terms.
   (a) Merchandise is sold on account for $350.
   (b) The balance is paid within the discount period.
   (c) Merchandise is sold on account for $290.
   (d) The balance is paid after the discount period.

E 10-3A (LO2)

✓ Net sales: $3,079

COMPUTING NET SALES Based on the following information, compute net sales.

Gross sales	$3,580
Sales returns and allowances	428
Sales discounts	73

E 10-4A (LO2)

✓ Aug 20:
Cash 135.20
Accts Rec/B.Feikert 135.20

JOURNALIZING SALES, SALES RETURNS AND ALLOWANCES, AND CASH RECEIPTS Prepare journal entries for the following transactions.

Aug. 4 Sold merchandise on account to F. Graves for $340 plus sales tax of 4%, with 2/10, n/30 cash discount terms.

6 Sold merchandise on account to B. Feikert for $180 plus sales tax of 4%.

10 F. Graves returned merchandise purchased on August 4 for $30 plus sales tax for credit.

13 F. Graves paid the balance due on her account.

15 B. Feikert returned merchandise purchased on August 6 for $50 plus sales tax for credit.

20 B. Feikert paid the balance due on his account.

E 10-5A (LO3)

✓ May 1:
A/R–J. Adams 2,120
Sales 2,000
Sales Tax Payable 120

JOURNALIZING SALES TRANSACTIONS Enter the following transactions in a general journal. Use a 6% sales tax rate.

May 1 Sold merchandise on account to J. Adams, $2,000 plus sales tax. Sale No. 488.

4 Sold merchandise on account to B. Clark, $1,800 plus sales tax. Sale No. 489.

8 Sold merchandise on account to A. Duck, $1,500 plus sales tax. Sale No. 490.

11 Sold merchandise on account to E. Hill, $1,950 plus sales tax. Sale No. 491.

E 10-6A (LO3)

✓ Ending Accts. Rec. balance: $4,059

JOURNALIZING SALES RETURNS AND ALLOWANCES Enter the following transactions in a general journal and post them to the appropriate general ledger and accounts receivable ledger accounts. Use account numbers as shown in the chapter. Beginning balance in Accounts Receivable is $4,200. Beginning balances in selected customer accounts are Abramowitz, $850; Gruder, $428; and Perez, $1,018.

June 1 John B. Abramowitz returned merchandise previously purchased on account (Sale No. 329), $73.

6 Marie L. Perez returned merchandise previously purchased on account (Sale No. 321), $44.

8 L. B. Gruder returned merchandise previously purchased on account (Sale No. 299), $24.

E 10-7A (LO3)

✓ July 6:
Cash 643
A/R–J. Adler 643

JOURNALIZING CASH RECEIPTS Enter the following transactions in a general journal:

July 6 James Adler made payment on account, $643.

10 Cash sales for the week were $2,320.

14 Betty Havel made payment on account, $430.

15 J. L. Borg made payment on account, $117.

17 Cash sales for the week were $2,237.

E 10-8A (LO4)

✓ Accts. Rec. balance: $4,586

SCHEDULE OF ACCOUNTS RECEIVABLE From the accounts receivable ledger shown, prepare a schedule of accounts receivable for Pheng Co. as of August 31, 20--.

ACCOUNTS RECEIVABLE LEDGER

NAME B & G Distributors
ADDRESS 2628 Burlington Avenue, Chicago, IL 60604-1329

DATE		ITEM	POST. REF.	DEBIT	CREDIT	BALANCE
20--						
Aug.	3		J1	1,380.00		1,380.00
	8		J1		140.00	1,240.00

NAME M. Chang
ADDRESS 1422 SW Pacific, Chicago, IL 60603-8596

DATE		ITEM	POST. REF.	DEBIT	CREDIT	BALANCE
20--						
Aug.	5		J1	2,136.00		2,136.00
	11		J2		2,136.00	—

NAME B. J. Hinschliff & Co.
ADDRESS 133 College Blvd., Des Plaines, IL 60611-4431

DATE		ITEM	POST. REF.	DEBIT	CREDIT	BALANCE
20--						
Aug.	15		J2	1,106.00		1,106.00
	21		J3	384.00		1,490.00

NAME Sally M. Pitts

ADDRESS 213 East 29th Place, Chicago, IL 60601-6287

DATE		ITEM	POST. REF.	DEBIT	CREDIT	BALANCE
20-- Aug.	21		J3	8 3 8 00		8 3 8 00

NAME Trendsetters, Inc.

ADDRESS 29 Industrial Way, Chicago, IL 60600-5918

DATE		ITEM	POST. REF.	DEBIT	CREDIT	BALANCE
20-- Aug.	28		J4	1 0 1 8 00		1 0 1 8 00

SERIES A PROBLEMS

P 10-9A (LO3)

✓ Accts. Rec. balance: $16,345.20

SALES TRANSACTIONS J. K. Bijan owns a retail business and made the following sales on account during the month of August 20--. There is a 6% sales tax on all sales.

Aug. 1 Sale No. 213 to Jung Manufacturing Co., $1,200 plus sales tax.

3 Sale No. 214 to Hassad Co., $3,600 plus sales tax.

7 Sale No. 215 to Helsinki, Inc., $1,400 plus sales tax. (Open a new account for this customer. Address is 125 Fishers Dr., Noblesville, IN 47870-8867.)

11 Sale No. 216 to Ardis Myler, $1,280 plus sales tax.

18 Sale No. 217 to Hassad Co., $4,330 plus sales tax.

22 Sale No. 218 to Jung Manufacturing Co., $2,000 plus sales tax.

30 Sale No. 219 to Ardis Myler, $1,610 plus sales tax.

REQUIRED

1. Record the transactions in a general journal.
2. Post from the journal to the general ledger and accounts receivable ledger accounts. Use account numbers as shown in the chapter.

P 10-10A (LO3)

✓ Accts. Rec. balance: $3,533.08

CASH RECEIPTS TRANSACTIONS Zebra Imaginarium, a retail business, had the following cash receipts during December 20--. The sales tax is 6%.

Dec. 1 Received payment on account from Michael Anderson, $1,360.

2 Received payment on account from Ansel Manufacturing, $382.

7 Cash sales for the week were $3,160 plus tax. Bank credit card sales for the week were $1,000 plus tax. Bank credit card fee is 3%.

8 Received payment on account from J. Gorbea, $880.

11 Michael Anderson returned merchandise for a credit, $60 plus tax.

14 Cash sales for the week were $2,800 plus tax. Bank credit card sales for the week were $800 plus tax. Bank credit card fee is 3%.

(continued)

Dec. 20 Received payment on account from Tom Wilson, $1,110.

21 Ansel Manufacturing returned merchandise for a credit, $22 plus tax.

21 Cash sales for the week were $3,200 plus tax.

24 Received payment on account from Rachel Carson, $2,000.

Beginning general ledger account balances were:

Cash	$9,862
Accounts Receivable	9,352

Beginning customer account balances were:

M. Anderson	$2,480
Ansel Manufacturing	982
J. Gorbea	880
R. Carson	3,200
T. Wilson	1,810

REQUIRED

1. Record the transactions in a general journal.
2. Post from the journal to the general ledger and accounts receivable ledger accounts. Use account numbers as shown in the chapter.

P 10-11A (LO3)

✓ Accts. Rec. balance: $8,133.33

SALES AND CASH RECEIPTS TRANSACTIONS Owens Distributors is a retail business. The following sales, returns, and cash receipts occurred during March 20--. There is an 8% sales tax. Beginning general ledger account balances were Cash, $9,741.00; and Accounts Receivable, $1,058.25. Beginning customer account balances included Thompson Group, $1,058.25.

Mar. 1 Sale on account No. 33C to Able & Co., $1,800 plus sales tax.

3 Sale on account No. 33D to R. J. Kalas, Inc., $2,240 plus sales tax.

5 Able & Co. returned merchandise from Sale No. 33C for a credit (Credit Memo No. 66), $30 plus sales tax.

7 Cash sales for the week were $3,160 plus sales tax.

10 Received payment from Able & Co. for Sale No. 33C less Credit Memo No. 66.

11 Sale on account No. 33E to Blevins Bakery, $1,210 plus sales tax.

13 Received payment from R. J. Kalas for Sale No. 33D.

14 Cash sales for the week were $4,200 plus sales tax.

16 Blevins Bakery returned merchandise from Sale No. 33E for a credit (Credit Memo No. 67), $44 plus sales tax.

18 Sale on account No. 33F to R. J. Kalas, Inc., $2,620 plus sales tax.

20 Received payment from Blevins Bakery for Sale No. 33E less Credit Memo No. 67.

21 Cash sales for the week were $2,400 plus sales tax.

25 Sale on account No. 33G to Blevins Bakery, $1,915 plus sales tax.

27 Sale on account No. 33H to Thompson Group, $2,016 plus sales tax.

28 Cash sales for the week were $3,500 plus sales tax.

REQUIRED

1. Record the transactions in a general journal.
2. Post from the journal to the general ledger and accounts receivable ledger accounts. Use account numbers as shown in the chapter.

P 10-12A (LO4)
✓ Accts. Rec. balance, Thompson Group: $3,235.53

SCHEDULE OF ACCOUNTS RECEIVABLE Based on the information provided in Problem 10-11A, prepare a schedule of accounts receivable for Owens Distributors as of March 31, 20--. Verify that the accounts receivable account balance in the general ledger agrees with the schedule of accounts receivable total.

SERIES B EXERCISES

E 10-1B (LO1)

SALES DOCUMENTS Indicate whether each of the following documents or procedures is for a retail business or for a wholesale business, as described in the chapter.

1. A cash register receipt is given to the customer.
2. Credit approval is required since sales are almost always "on account."
3. Three copies of the sales invoice are prepared: one for shipping, one for the customer (as a bill), and one for accounting.
4. A sales ticket is given to a customer and another copy is sent to accounting.
5. The sales process begins with a customer purchase order.
6. The sales invoice itemizes what is sold, its cost, and the total amount owed.

E 10-2B (LO2)
✓ 3(d):

Sales Ret. & Allow.	24	
Accts. Rec.		24

SALES TRANSACTIONS AND T ACCOUNTS Using T accounts for Cash, Accounts Receivable, Sales Tax Payable, Sales, Sales Returns and Allowances, and Sales Discounts, enter the following sales transactions. Use a new set of accounts for each part, 1–5.

1. No sales tax.
   (a) Merchandise is sold for $250 cash.
   (b) Merchandise is sold on account for $225.
   (c) Payment is received for merchandise sold on account.
2. 6% sales tax.
   (a) Merchandise is sold for $250 cash plus sales tax.
   (b) Merchandise is sold on account for $225 plus sales tax.
   (c) Payment is received for merchandise sold on account.
3. Cash and credit sales, with returned merchandise.
   (a) Merchandise is sold for $481 cash.
   (b) $18 of merchandise sold for $481 is returned for a refund.
   (c) Merchandise is sold on account for $388.
   (d) $24 of merchandise sold for $388 is returned for a credit.
   (e) Payment is received for balance owed on merchandise sold on account.

(continued)

4. 6% sales tax, with returned merchandise.
   (a) Merchandise is sold on account for $480 plus sales tax.
   (b) Merchandise sold on account for $30 plus sales tax is returned.
   (c) The balance on the account is paid in cash.
   (d) Merchandise is sold for $300 cash plus sales tax.
   (e) $30 of merchandise sold for $300 cash plus sales tax is returned for a refund.
5. Sales on account, with 2/10, n/30 cash discount terms.
   (a) Merchandise is sold on account for $280.
   (b) The balance is paid within the discount period.
   (c) Merchandise is sold on account for $203.
   (d) The balance is paid after the discount period.

E 10-3B (LO2)

✓ Net sales: $2,502

COMPUTING NET SALES Based on the following information, compute net sales:

Gross sales	$2,880
Sales returns and allowances	322
Sales discounts	56

E 10-4B (LO2)

✓ Oct. 20:
Cash 228.80
Accts Rec/B. Farnsby 228.80

JOURNALIZING SALES, SALES RETURNS AND ALLOWANCES, AND CASH RECEIPTS Prepare journal entries for the following transactions.

Oct. 5 Sold merchandise on account to B. Farnsby for $280 plus sales tax of 4%.

8 Sold merchandise on account to F. Preetee for $240 plus sales tax of 4%, with 2/10, n/30 cash discount terms.

11 F. Preetee returned merchandise purchased on October 8 for $50 plus sales tax for credit.

17 F. Preetee paid the balance due on her account.

18 B. Farnsby returned merchandise purchased on October 5 for $60 plus sales tax for credit.

20 B. Farnsby paid the balance due on his account.

E 10-5B (LO3)

✓ Sept. 1:
A/R–K. Smith 1,890
Sales 1800
Sales Tax Payable 90

JOURNALIZING SALES TRANSACTIONS Enter the following transactions in a general journal. Use a 5% sales tax rate.

Sept. 1 Sold merchandise on account to K. Smith, $1,800 plus sales tax. Sale No. 228.

3 Sold merchandise on account to J. Arnes, $3,100 plus sales tax. Sale No. 229.

5 Sold merchandise on account to M. Denison, $2,800 plus sales tax. Sale No. 230.

7 Sold merchandise on account to B. Marshall, $1,900 plus sales tax. Sale No. 231.

E 10-6B (LO3)

✓ Ending Accts. Rec. balance: $3,777

JOURNALIZING SALES RETURNS AND ALLOWANCES Enter the following transactions in a general journal and post them to the appropriate general ledger and accounts receivable ledger accounts. Use account numbers as shown in the chapter. Beginning balance in Accounts Receivable is $3,900. Beginning balances in selected customer accounts are Adams, $850; Greene, $428; and Phillips, $1,018.

June 1 Marie L. Phillips returned merchandise previously purchased on account (Sale No. 33), $43.

11 John B. Adams returned merchandise previously purchased on account (Sale No. 34), $59.

15 L. B. Greene returned merchandise previously purchased on account (Sale No. 35), $21.

E 10-7B (LO3)
✓ Nov. 1:
Cash 750
A/R–J. Haghighat 750

JOURNALIZING CASH RECEIPTS Enter the following transactions in a general journal:

Nov. 1	Jean Haghighat made payment on account, $750.
12	Marc Antonoff made payment on account, $464.
15	Cash sales were $3,763.
18	Will Mossein made payment on account, $241.
25	Cash sales were $2,648.

E 10-8B (LO4)
✓ Accts. Rec. balance: $6,402

SCHEDULE OF ACCOUNTS RECEIVABLE From the accounts receivable ledger shown, prepare a schedule of accounts receivable for Gelph Co. as of November 30, 20--.

ACCOUNTS RECEIVABLE LEDGER

NAME James L. Adams Co.
ADDRESS 24481 McAdams Road, Dallas, TX 77001-3465

DATE		ITEM	POST. REF.	DEBIT	CREDIT	BALANCE
20-- Nov.	1		J1	3180 00		3180 00
	5		J1		180 00	3000 00
	7		J2	200 00		3200 00

NAME Trish Berens
ADDRESS 34 West 55th Avenue, Fort Worth, TX 76310-8182

DATE		ITEM	POST. REF.	DEBIT	CREDIT	BALANCE
20-- Nov.	3		J1	1360 00		1360 00

NAME M and T Jenkins, Inc.
ADDRESS 100 NW Richfield, Austin, TX 78481-3791

DATE		ITEM	POST. REF.	DEBIT	CREDIT	BALANCE
20-- Nov.	5		J1	2628 00		2628 00
	12		J2		2628 00	—

NAME R & J Travis
ADDRESS 288 Beacon Street, Dallas, TX 79301-6642

DATE		ITEM	POST. REF.	DEBIT	CREDIT	BALANCE
20-- Nov.	22		J3	1842 00		1842 00

SERIES B PROBLEMS

P 10-9B (LO3)

✓ Accts. Rec. balance: $13,072.50

SALES TRANSACTIONS T. M. Maxwell owns a retail business and made the following sales on account during the month of July 20--. There is a 5% sales tax on all sales.

July 1	Sale No. 101 to Saga, Inc., $1,200 plus sales tax.
8	Sale No. 102 to Vinnie Ward, $2,100 plus sales tax.
15	Sale No. 103 to Dvorak Manufacturing, $4,300 plus sales tax.
21	Sale No. 104 to Vinnie Ward, $1,800 plus sales tax.
24	Sale No. 105 to Zapata Co., $1,600 plus sales tax. (Open a new account for this customer. Address is 789 N. Stafford Dr., Bloomington, IN 47401-6201.)
29	Sale No. 106 to Saga, Inc., $1,450 plus sales tax.

REQUIRED

1. Record the transactions in a general journal.
2. Post from the journal to the general ledger and accounts receivable ledger accounts. Use account numbers as shown in the chapter.

P 10-10B (LO3)

✓ Accts. Rec. balance: $2,744.45

CASH RECEIPTS TRANSACTIONS Color Florists, a retail business, had the following cash receipts during January 20--. The sales tax is 5%.

Jan. 1	Received payment on account from Ray Boyd, $880.
3	Received payment on account from Clint Hassell, $271.
5	Cash sales for the week were $2,800 plus tax. Bank credit card sales for the week were $1,200 plus tax. Bank credit card fee is 3%.
8	Received payment on account from Jan Sowada, $912.
11	Ray Boyd returned merchandise for a credit, $40 plus tax.
12	Cash sales for the week were $3,100 plus tax. Bank credit card sales for the week were $1,900 plus tax. Bank credit card fee is 3%.
15	Received payment on account from Robert Zehnle, $1,100.
18	Robert Zehnle returned merchandise for a credit, $31 plus tax.
19	Cash sales for the week were $2,230 plus tax.
25	Received payment on account from Dazai Manufacturing, $318.

Beginning general ledger account balances were:

Cash	$2,890.75
Accounts Receivable	6,300.00

Beginning customer account balances were:

R. Boyd	$1,400
Dazai Manufacturing	318
C. Hassell	815
J. Sowada	1,481
R. Zehnle	2,286

REQUIRED

1. Record the transactions in a general journal.
2. Post from the journal to the general ledger and accounts receivable ledger accounts. Use account numbers as shown in the chapter.

P 10-11B (LO3)
✓ Accts. Rec. balance: $6,104.25

SALES AND CASH RECEIPTS TRANSACTIONS Paul Jackson owns a retail business. The following sales, returns, and cash receipts are for April 20--. There is a 7% sales tax.

Apr. 1	Sale on account No. 111 to O. L. Meyers, $2,100 plus sales tax.
3	Sale on account No. 112 to Andrew Plaa, $1,000 plus sales tax.
6	O. L. Meyers returned merchandise from Sale No. 111 for a credit (Credit Memo No. 42), $50 plus sales tax.
7	Cash sales for the week were $3,240 plus sales tax.
9	Received payment from O. L. Meyers for Sale No. 111 less Credit Memo No. 42.
12	Sale on account No. 113 to Melissa Richfield, $980 plus sales tax.
14	Cash sales for the week were $2,180 plus sales tax.
17	Melissa Richfield returned merchandise from Sale No. 113 for a credit (Credit Memo No. 43), $40 plus sales tax.
19	Sale on account No. 114 to Kelsay Munkres, $1,020 plus sales tax.
21	Cash sales for the week were $2,600 plus sales tax.
24	Sale on account No. 115 to O. L. Meyers, $920 plus sales tax.
27	Sale on account No. 116 to Andrew Plaa, $1,320 plus sales tax.
28	Cash sales for the week were $2,800 plus sales tax.
29	Received payment from Melissa Richfield for $2,186.

Beginning general ledger account balances were:

Cash	$2,864.54
Accounts Receivable	2,726.25

Beginning customer account balances were:

K. Munkres	$ 482.00
M. Richfield	2,244.25

REQUIRED

1. Record the transactions in a general journal.
2. Post from the journal to the general ledger and accounts receivable ledger accounts. Use account numbers as shown in the chapter.

P 10-12B (LO4)
✓ Accts. Rec. balance, Melissa Richfield: $1,064.05

SCHEDULE OF ACCOUNTS RECEIVABLE Based on the information provided in Problem 10-11B, prepare a schedule of accounts receivable for Paul Jackson as of April 30, 20--. Verify that the accounts receivable account balance in the general ledger agrees with the schedule of accounts receivable total.

MANAGING YOUR WRITING

You and your spouse have separate charge accounts at a local department store. When you tried to use your card last week, you were told that you were over your credit limit. This puzzled you because you had paid the entire account balance several weeks ago. When the monthly statements arrived yesterday, the error was clear. The store had credited your payment to your spouse's account.

(continued)

Your account was treated as over the limit, and the store charged you interest on the unpaid balance. You suspect that part of the problem is that you and your spouse use the same last name (Morales) and have similar first names (Carmen and Carmelo).

Write a letter to the store requesting correction of your accounts and suggesting a way to identify your accounts so that this error does not happen again.

ETHICS CASE

Wholesale Health Supply sells a variety of medical equipment and supplies to retailers. When a new retailer is approved for credit, one of the criteria is that the retailer must have been in business for at least six months. Good Earth Foods placed a large order with Wholesale Health Supply and requested credit terms. Wholesale Health Supply faxed a credit request form to Good Earth Foods, and the buyer at Good Earth Foods faxed the completed form back to Wholesale Health Supply. Robin Sylvester, the sales manager at Wholesale Health Supply, saw the credit application and noticed Good Earth Foods had only been in business for two months. Thinking she might lose the order if Good Earth Foods wasn't extended credit, Robin authorized the shipment. She figured by the time the credit department rejected the application, Good Earth Foods would have received the order and the vice president would override the rejection to keep a new customer. Robin was sure that everything would turn out alright.

1. Do you think Robin's decision to ship the order was unethical? Why or why not?
2. What would you have done if you were in Robin's position?
3. Write a memo from the credit department manager to Robin Sylvester explaining the reasoning behind requiring a new credit customer to be in business for at least six months.
4. In small groups, discuss ways to prevent a situation like this from happening.

MASTERY PROBLEM

✓ Accts. Rec. balance: $1,900.54

Geoff and Sandy Harland own and operate Wayward Kennel and Pet Supply. Their motto is, "If your pet is not becoming to you, he should be coming to us." The Harlands maintain a sales tax payable account throughout the month to account for the 6% sales tax. They use a general journal, general ledger, and accounts receivable ledger. The following sales and cash collections took place during the month of September:

Sept. 2 Sold a fish aquarium on account to Ken Shank, $125.00 plus tax of $7.50, terms n/30. Sale No. 101.

3 Sold dog food on account to Nancy Truelove, $68.25 plus tax of $4.10, terms n/30. Sale No. 102.

5 Sold a bird cage on account to Jean Warkentin, $43.95 plus tax of $2.64, terms n/30. Sale No. 103.

8 Cash sales for the week were $2,332.45 plus tax of $139.95.

10 Received cash for boarding and grooming services, $625.00 plus tax of $37.50.

11 Jean Warkentin stopped by the store to point out a minor defect in the bird cage purchased in Sale No. 103. The Harlands offered a sales allowance of $10.00 plus tax on the price of the cage which satisfied Warkentin.

Sept. 12	Sold a cockatoo on account to Tully Shaw, $1,200.00 plus tax of $72.00, terms n/30. Sale No. 104.
14	Received cash on account from Rosa Alanso, $256.00.
15	Rosa Alanso returned merchandise, $93.28 including tax of $5.28.
15	Cash sales for the week were $2,656.85 plus tax of $159.41.
16	Received cash on account from Nancy Truelove, $58.25.
18	Received cash for boarding and grooming services, $535.00 plus tax of $32.10.
19	Received cash on account from Ed Cochran, $63.25.
20	Sold pet supplies on account to Susan Hays, $83.33 plus tax of $5.00, terms n/30. Sale No. 105.
21	Sold three Labrador Retriever puppies to All American Day Camp, $375.00 plus tax of $22.50, terms n/30. Sale No. 106.
22	Cash sales for the week were $3,122.45 plus tax of $187.35.
23	Received cash for boarding and grooming services, $515.00 plus tax of $30.90.
25	Received cash on account from Ken Shank, $132.50.
26	Received cash on account from Nancy Truelove, $72.35.
27	Received cash on account from Joe Gloy, $273.25.
28	Borrowed cash to purchase a pet limousine, $11,000.00.
29	Cash sales for the week were $2,835.45 plus tax of $170.13.
30	Received cash for boarding and grooming services, $488.00 plus tax of $29.28.

Wayward had the following general ledger account balances as of September 1:

Account Title	Account No.	General Ledger Balance on Sept. 1
Cash	101	$23,500.25
Accounts Receivable	122	850.75
Notes Payable	201	2,500.00
Sales Tax Payable	231	909.90
Sales	401	13,050.48
Sales Returns and Allowances	401.1	86.00
Boarding and Grooming Revenue	402	2,115.00

Wayward also had the following accounts receivable ledger balances as of September 1:

Customer	Accounts Receivable Balance
Rosa Alanso 2541 East 2nd Street Bloomington, IN 47401-5356	$456.00
Ed Cochran 2669 Windcrest Drive Bloomington, IN 47401-5446	$63.25
Joe Gloy 1458 Parnell Avenue Muncie, IN 47304-2682	$273.25
Nancy Truelove 2300 E. National Road Cumberland, IN 46229-4824	$58.25

(continued)

New customers opening accounts during September were as follows:

All American Day Camp
3025 Old Mill Run
Bloomington, IN 47408-1080

Susan Hays
1424 Jackson Creek Road
Nashville, IN 47448-2245

Ken Shank
6422 E. Bender Road
Bloomington, IN 47401-7756

Tully Shaw
3315 Longview Avenue
Bloomington, IN 47401-7223

Jean Warkentin
1813 Deep Well Court
Bloomington, IN 47401-5124

REQUIRED

1. Enter the transactions for the month of September in a general journal. (Begin with page 7.)
2. Post the entries to the general and subsidiary ledgers. Open new accounts for any customers who did not have a balance as of September 1.
3. Prepare a schedule of accounts receivable.
4. Compute the net sales for the month of September.

This problem challenges you to apply your cumulative accounting knowledge to move a step beyond the material in the chapter.

✓ June 14: Dr. Sales Discount, $12

KA KLOOSTER & ALLEN

CHALLENGE PROBLEM

Enter the following transactions in a general journal:

June 4	Sold merchandise on account to T. Allen, $1,500.00 plus 6% sales tax, with 1/10, n/30 cash discount terms.
7	Sold merchandise on account to K. Bryant, $1,800.00 plus 6% sales tax, with 1/10, n/30 cash discount terms.
11	T. Allen returned merchandise totaling $300.00 from the June 4 sale, for credit.
14	T. Allen paid the balance due from the June 4 sale, less discount.
17	K. Bryant paid the balance due from the June 7 sale, less discount.

ANSWERS TO SELF-STUDY QUESTIONS AND EXERCISES

True/False Questions

1. T
2. T
3. T
4. F (the debit *excludes* the sales tax)
5. T

Multiple Choice Questions

1. d **2.** c **3.** b **4.** b **5.** a

U REVU Exercises

1.

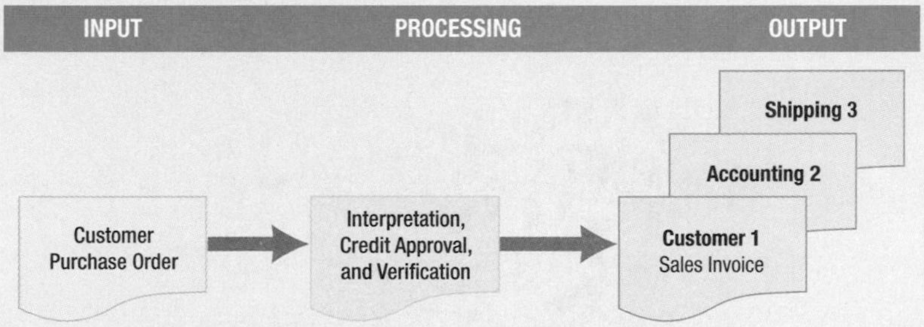

2.

		Description	PR	Debit	Credit
(a)		Accounts Receivable		309 00	
		Sales			300 00
		Sales Tax Payable			9 00
		Made credit sale			

		Description	PR	Debit	Credit
(b)		Sales Returns and Allowances		70 00	
		Sales Tax Payable		2 10	
		Accounts Receivable			72 10
		Returned merchandise			

		Description	PR	Debit	Credit
(c)		Cash		232 30	
		Sales Discounts		4 60	
		Accounts Receivable			236 90
		Received cash on account			

3. GENERAL LEDGER

Cash

(c)	226.60		

Accounts Receivable

(a)	288.40	(b)	61.80
		(c)	226.60

Sales Tax Payable

(b)	1.80	(a)	8.40

Sales Returns and Allowances

(b)	60.00		

Sales

		(a)	280.00

Accounts Receivable Ledger

M. Schapiro

(a)	288.40	(b)	61.80
		(c)	226.60

4. Schedule of Accounts Receivable
March 31, 20--

S. Burton	$103
A. Tangier	240
J. Holmes	144
F. Fullman	110
P. Molty	194
Total	$791

Chapter 11

THINK GREEN
operates under the Countryside
Environmental Policy.
Tree
Protection
Policy

Accounting for Purchases and Cash Payments

In Chapter 10, we heard about Planet Shoes, the company whose eco-friendly shoes reflect a concern about the environment. Innovar Environmental is a different kind of company that addresses environmental issues in a totally different way. Innovar provides services to enable government and businesses to become green through construction and renovation. Its projects include lead paint, asbestos, and mold abatement; facilities demolition; site enhancements; green construction; natural disaster recovery; storage tank removal, and more.

Innovar was founded in 2000 and is based in Littleton, Colorado. It has benefited from the nationwide interest in going green, increasing its revenues in a recent four-year period by 400%, to $6.1 million. You might recall that one of Planet Shoes' biggest challenges was accounting for its high volume of sales activity. In contrast, Innovar has far fewer but larger sales transactions. Its challenge is accounting for the many purchases of items used in its major construction and renovation projects. In this chapter, you will learn how to account for purchases transactions, including various discounts, freight charges, and the return of items to the manufacturer.

LEARNING OBJECTIVES

Careful study of this chapter should enable you to:

LO1 **Define merchandise purchases transactions.**

LO2 **Describe and use merchandise purchases accounts and compute gross profit.**

LO3 **Describe and use the accounts payable ledger.**

LO4 **Prepare a schedule of accounts payable.**

Chapter 10 demonstrated how to account for sales in a merchandising business. This chapter continues the study of the merchandising business by examining how to account for merchandise purchases. We will learn how to use four new accounts and another subsidiary ledger.

MERCHANDISE PURCHASES TRANSACTIONS

LO1 Define merchandise purchases transactions.

In everyday language, purchases can refer to almost anything we have bought. For a merchandising business, however, **purchases** refers to merchandise acquired for resale. These are the goods a business buys for the sole purpose of selling them to its customers.

Purchasing procedures and documents vary, depending on the nature and size of a business. For example, in a small business, the owner or an employee might do the buying on a part-time basis. In a large business, there might be a separate purchasing department with a full-time manager and staff. In addition, the procedures and documents used can be affected by whether purchases are made on account or for cash.

The flowchart in Figure 11-1 shows some of the major documents used in the purchasing process of a merchandising business. In discussing the purchasing process, we will assume that the business makes purchases on account and has a purchasing department.

FIGURE 11-1 Purchasing Process Documents

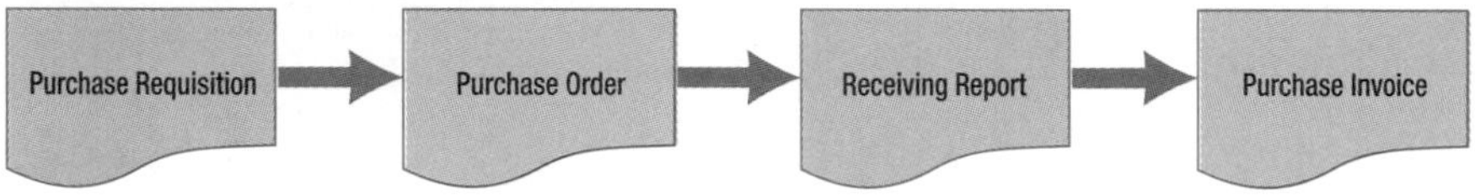

In a computerized system, companies use electronic forms that are similar to the paper documents described in this chapter.

PURCHASE REQUISITION

A **purchase requisition** is a form used to request the purchase of merchandise or other property. Any authorized person or department can prepare this form and submit it to the purchasing department. Figure 11-2 shows a purchase requisition used by Northern Micro. One copy of this form is sent to the purchasing department, one goes to the accounting department, and one is kept by the department that prepared the requisition.

When purchase orders are submitted electronically, signals are sent to the vendor and the accounting and purchasing departments at the same time.

PURCHASE ORDER

The purchasing department reviews and approves the purchase requisition and prepares a purchase order. A **purchase order** is a written order to buy goods from a specific vendor (supplier). Figure 11-3 shows a purchase order prepared by Northern Micro based on the purchase requisition in Figure 11-2. One copy of the purchase order is sent to the vendor to order the goods, one goes to the accounting department, and one copy is kept in the purchasing department. Other copies may be sent to the department that prepared the purchase requisition and to the receiving area.

FIGURE 11-2 Purchase Requisition

NORTHERN MICRO
1099 E. Louisiana, Indianapolis, IN 46217-3322

PURCHASE REQUISITION NO. **A-106**

Date Issued February 24, 20--	Order From TTA Products 6439 E. Broad St. Columbus, OH 43223-9892
Date Required March 12, 20--	
Required For Department Computer Software	
Deliver To Gary L. Fischel	

Quantity	Description
3	WordRight, No. F20386
2	TaxPro, No. N10367

Purchasing Department Memorandum

Placed By *Emily Green*	Date February 26, 20--
Approved By *Chris Lynders*	Issued To TTA Products 6439 E. Broad St. Columbus, OH 43223-9892
Purchase Order No. 312	

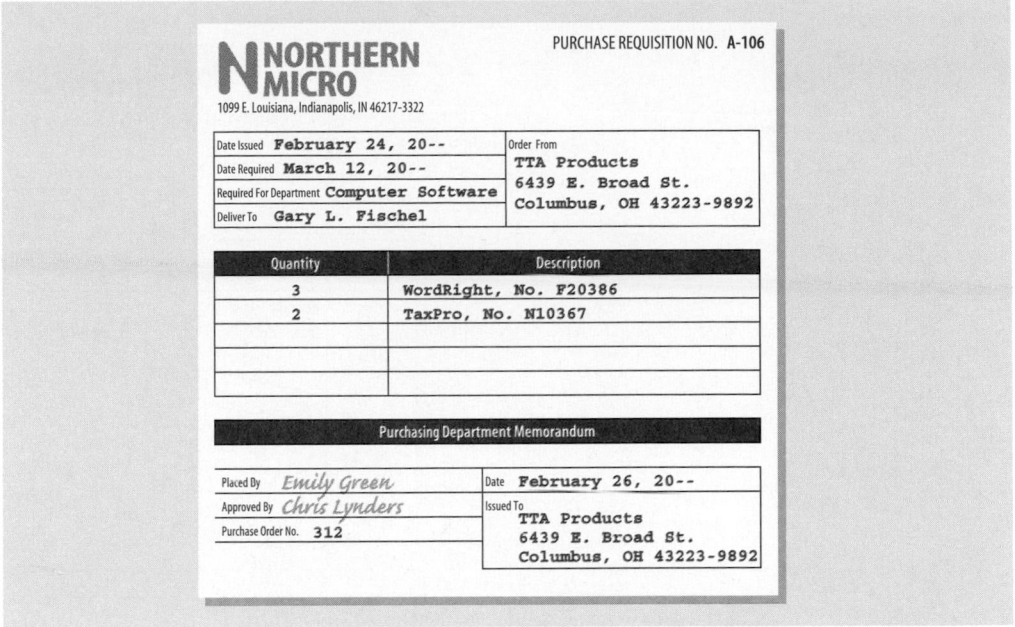

FIGURE 11-3 Purchase Order

NORTHERN MICRO
1099 E. Louisiana, Indianapolis, IN 46217-3322

PURCHASE ORDER NO. **312**

Date February 26, 20--	Order From TTA Products 6439 E. Broad St. Columbus, OH 43223-9892
Deliver By March 12, 20--	
Ship By Ajax Transfer Co.	
FOB Columbus	

Quantity	Description	Unit Price	Total
3	WordRight, No. F20386	$180.00	$540.00
2	TaxPro, No. N10367	150.00	300.00
	Total		$840.00

Chris Lynders

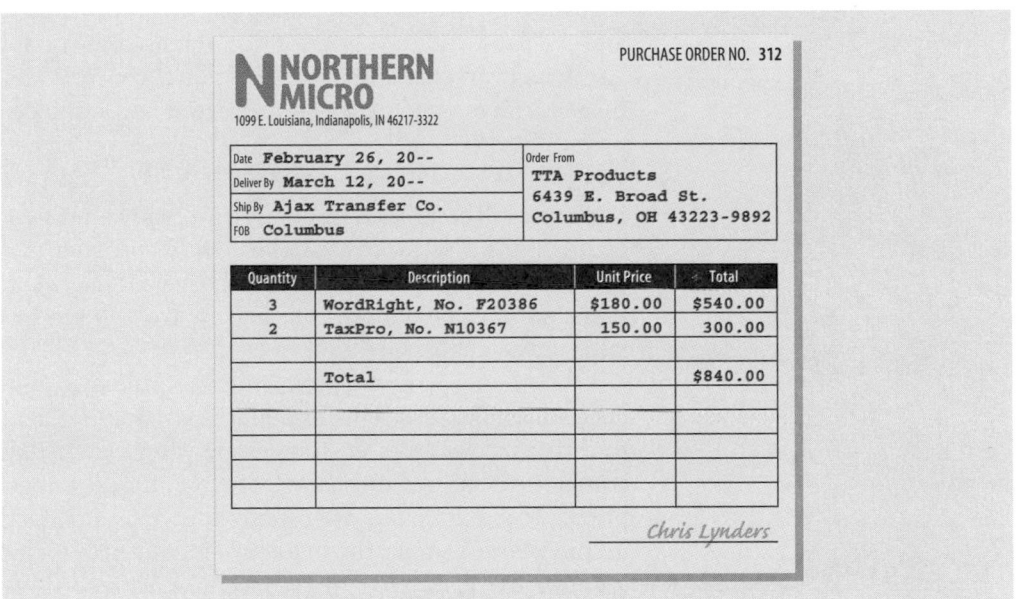

RECEIVING REPORT AND PURCHASE INVOICE

When the merchandise is received, a **receiving report** indicating what has been received is prepared. The receiving report can be a separate form, or one can be created from the vendor's purchase invoice. Figure 11-4 shows a vendor invoice on which a rubber stamp has been used to imprint a type of receiving report. The receiving clerk has indicated on the form the date and condition of the goods received.

An **invoice** is a document prepared by the seller as a bill for the merchandise shipped. To the seller, this is a sales invoice, as explained in Chapter 10. To the buyer, this is a **purchase invoice.** Figure 11-4 shows an invoice sent by TTA Products to Northern Micro for the goods ordered with the purchase order in Figure 11-3.

FIGURE 11-4 Purchase Invoice

TTA Products
6439 E. Broad Street
Columbus, OH 43223-9892

Date: March 2, 20--
Terms: 2/10, n/30
Shipped By: Truck
Salesperson: Halpin

Invoice No. 4194H
Our Order No. 7043 | Your Order No. 312
Sold To:
Northern Micro
1099 E. Louisiana
Indianapolis, IN 46217-3322

Quantity	Description	Product No.	Unit Price	Total
3	WordRight	F20386	$180.00	$540.00
2	TaxPro	N10367	150.00	300.00
				$840.00

Date Received: March 3
Received By: LM
Items OK: LM
Prices OK: LM
Ext. & Total OK: JK
Invoice No.: 4194H
FOB: Columbus
Freight Bill No.: 4140
Freight Charge: 29.50
Approval For Payment: F.I.O.

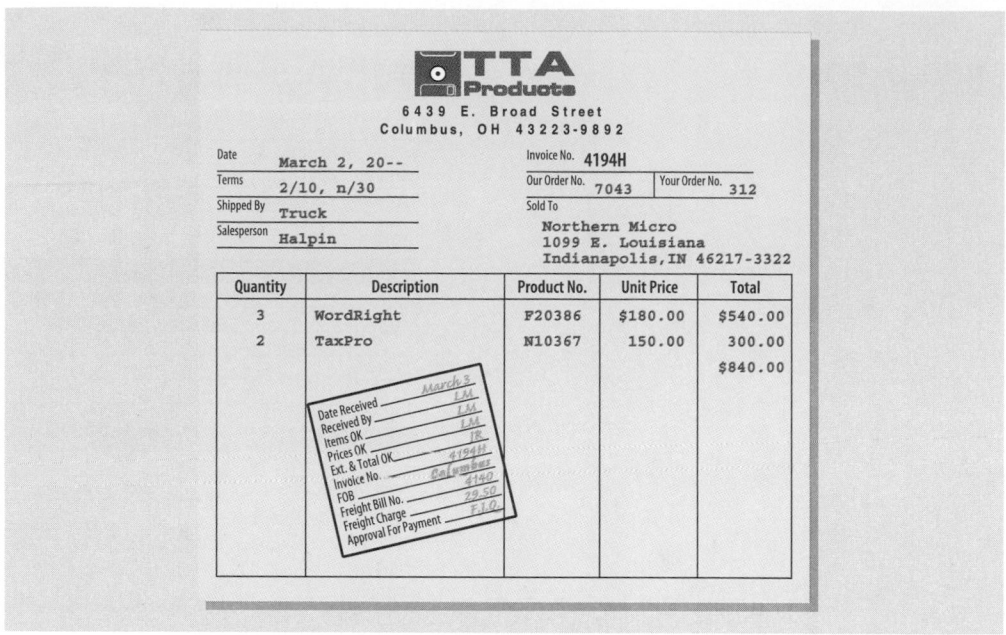

The accounting department compares the purchase invoice with the purchase requisition, purchase order, and receiving report. If the invoice is for the goods ordered and received and the correct price, the invoice is paid by the due date.

This is an example of good internal control. The procedure helps ensure that the business pays only for goods it ordered and received, and at the correct price.

CASH AND TRADE DISCOUNTS

Notice that the invoice in Figure 11-4 shows terms of 2/10, n/30. These are the same credit terms discussed in Chapter 10. A discount is available if the bill is paid within the discount period. The only difference is that we are now looking from the buyer's point of view rather than the seller's. We will see how to account for these discounts later in the chapter.

Another type of discount, called a **trade discount**, is often offered by manufacturers and wholesalers. This discount is a reduction from the list or catalog price offered to different classes of customers. By simply adjusting the trade discount percentages, companies can avoid the cost of reprinting catalogs every time there is a change in prices. Trade discounts are usually shown as a deduction from the total amount of the invoice. For example, the invoice in Figure 11-5 includes a trade discount of 10%. The amount to be entered in the accounting records for this invoice is $756, the net amount after deducting the trade discount of $84. Trade discounts represent a reduction in the price of the merchandise and should not be entered in the accounts of either the seller or the buyer.

LEARNING KEY

Purchases and sales subject to trade discounts should be recorded in the accounting records at the *net amount* after deducting the trade discounts.

We need to be careful in computing the cash discount when an invoice has both cash and trade discounts. The cash discount applies to the *net amount* after deducting the trade discount. For example, the cash discount and amount to be paid on the invoice in Figure 11-5 would be calculated as follows:

Gross amount	$840.00
Less 10% trade discount	84.00
Net amount	$756.00
Less 2% cash discount	15.12
Amount to be paid	$740.88

FIGURE 11-5 Purchase Invoice with Trade Discount

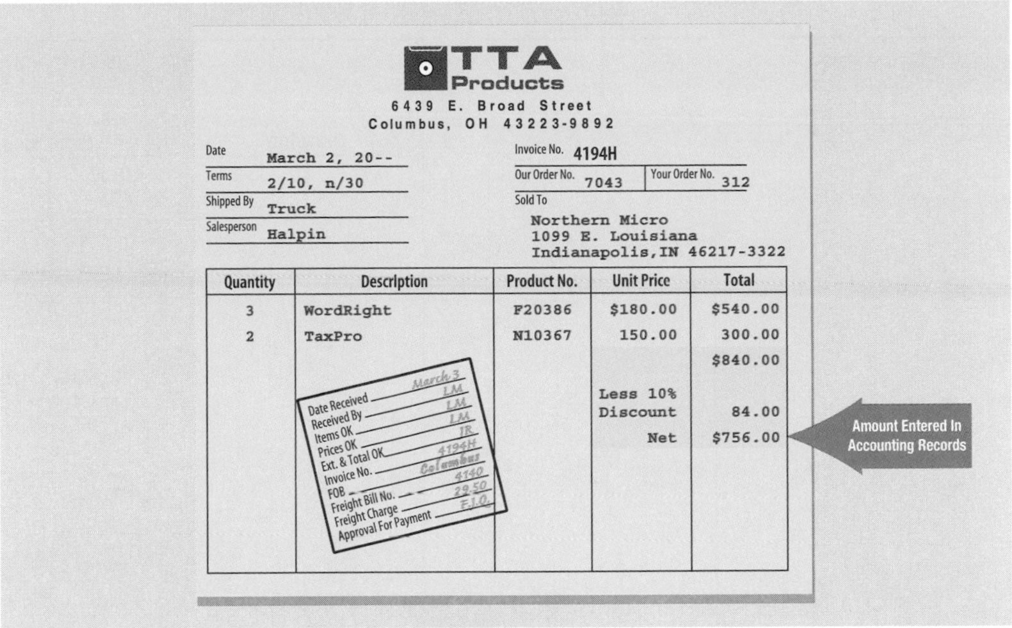
TTA Products
6439 E. Broad Street
Columbus, OH 43223-9892

Date March 2, 20--
Terms 2/10, n/30
Shipped By Truck
Salesperson Halpin

Invoice No. 4194H
Our Order No. 7043 Your Order No. 312
Sold To
Northern Micro
1099 E. Louisiana
Indianapolis, IN 46217-3322

Quantity	Description	Product No.	Unit Price	Total
3	WordRight	F20386	$180.00	$540.00
2	TaxPro	N10367	150.00	300.00
				$840.00
			Less 10% Discount	84.00
			Net	$756.00

Date Received March 3
Received By LM
Items OK LM
Prices OK LM
Ext. & Total OK JR
Invoice No. 4194H
FOB Columbus
Freight Bill No. 4140
Freight Charge 29.50
Approval For Payment F.L.O.

U REVU

Complete U REVU-1 on **page 421** to test your basic understanding of LO1.

MERCHANDISE PURCHASES ACCOUNTS

LO2 Describe and use merchandise purchases accounts and compute gross profit.

To account for merchandise purchases transactions, we will use four new accounts.

1. Purchases
2. Purchases Returns and Allowances
3. Purchases Discounts
4. Freight-In

The position of these accounts in the accounting equation and their normal balances are shown in Figure 11-6.

PURCHASES ACCOUNT

The purchases account is used to record the cost of merchandise purchased.

The approach to accounting for merchandise purchases shown in this chapter is known as the periodic method. Both the periodic and perpetual methods are covered in Chapter 13.

Purchases

Debit	Credit
to enter the cost of merchandise purchased	

FIGURE 11-6 Accounting for Merchandise Purchases Transactions

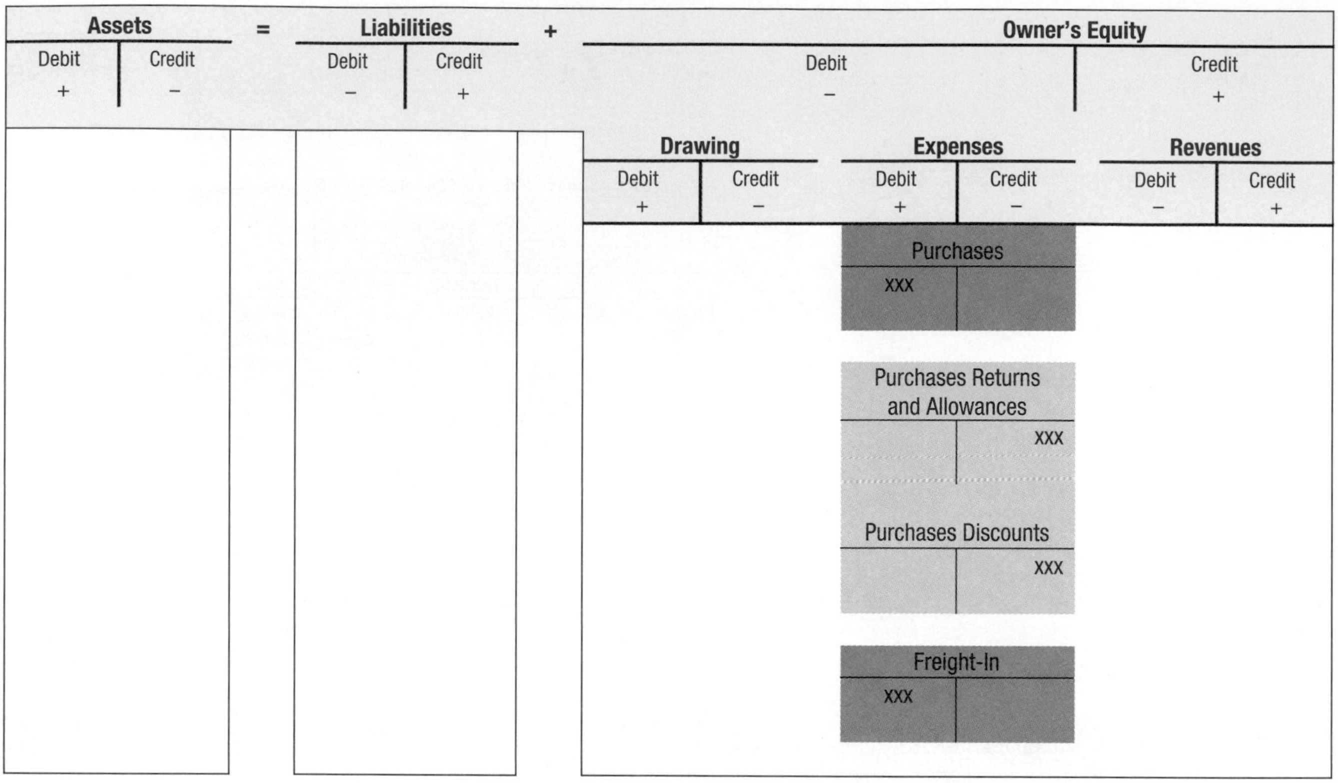

If a $100 purchase is made for cash, the following entry is made:

5		Purchases	100 00		5
6		Cash		100 00	6
7		Made cash purchase			7

If the same purchase is made on account, the entry is as follows:

The vendor's name is placed after Accounts Payable.

5		Purchases	100 00		5
6		Accounts Payable/Vendor		100 00	6
7		Made purchase on account			7

Accounts Payable is followed by a slash (/) and the name of the specific vendor to whom the purchaser owes money. The vendor name is for the vendor's account in the accounts payable ledger. This ledger is explained later in this chapter.

PURCHASES RETURNS AND ALLOWANCES ACCOUNT

Purchases	XXX	
Less: Purch. ret. & all.	XX	
Net purchases		XXX

Purchases Returns and Allowances is a **contra-cost** (or **contra-purchases**) **account,** which has a credit balance and is deducted from the related cost account. Purchases returns and purchases allowances are credited to this account. It is reported as a deduction from Purchases on the income statement to compute net purchases (see Figure 11-7 on page 407).

Purchases returns and allowances are similar to the sales returns and allowances we discussed in Chapter 10. We are simply looking at returns and allowances from the buyer's point of view. If merchandise is returned to a supplier, or the supplier grants a price reduction because of defects or other problems with merchandise purchased, Purchases Returns and Allowances is credited.

Purchases Returns and Allowances

Debit	Credit
	to enter returns and allowances

If merchandise that was purchased on account for $200 is defective and is returned to the supplier, the following entry is made:

9		Accounts Payable/Vendor	200.00		9
10		Purchases Returns and Allowances		200.00	10
11		Returned merchandise			11

If the same merchandise is retained but the supplier grants a price reduction of $45 because of the defects, the entry is as follows:

9		Accounts Payable/Vendor	45.00		9
10		Purchases Returns and Allowances		45.00	10
11		Allowance for defective merchandise			11

PURCHASES DISCOUNTS ACCOUNT

Purchases Discounts is a contra-purchases account used to record cash discounts allowed on purchases. Like Purchases Returns and Allowances, it is reported as a deduction from Purchases on the income statement to compute net purchases (see Figure 11-7).

Purchases	XXX	
Less: Purchases discounts	XX	
Net purchases		XXX

Purchases Discounts

Debit	Credit
	to enter cash discounts taken

If merchandise is purchased for $100 on account, with credit terms of 2/10, n/30, the following entry is made:

14		Purchases	100.00		14
15		Accounts Payable/Vendor		100.00	15
16		Made purchase on account			16

If payment for the merchandise is then made within the discount period, the entry is as follows:

18		Accounts Payable/Vendor	1 0 0 00		18
19		Cash		9 8 00	19
20		Purchases Discounts		2 00	20
21		Made payment on account			21

This approach to accounting for purchases discounts is known as the "gross-price method." The "net-price method" is described in the appendix.

Note the parts of this entry. Accounts Payable is debited for $100, the full amount of the invoice, because the entire debt has been satisfied. Cash is credited for only $98 because that is all that was required to pay the debt. The difference of $2 ($100 – $98) is credited to Purchases Discounts, which represents a reduction in the purchase price of the merchandise. That is why Purchases Discounts is deducted from Purchases on the income statement.

A Broader View

PHOTOLINK/PHOTODISC/GETTY IMAGES

Cash Management—Those Discounts Matter

If a business makes a $2,000 purchase on account, with terms of 2/10, n/30, the available discount is only $40 ($2,000 × 0.02). On the surface, this seems unimportant, like "small change." But take a closer look. If the business does not pay $1,960 ($2,000 – $40) within 10 days, it must pay $2,000 within 30 days. This means that the business would pay $40 for the use of $1,960 for 20 more days. If we assume a 360-day year, the approximate annual interest rate for using the $1,960 for 20 days is 36%.

The innocent looking 2% cash discount represents a very high rate of interest. If a business regularly misses cash discount opportunities, the annual dollar cost can be substantial. For sound cash management, take advantage of discounts.

In Chapter 17, we discuss how to compute interest. There you will learn to compute the exact interest rate.

FREIGHT-IN ACCOUNT

Freight-In is an adjunct-purchases account used to record transportation charges on merchandise purchases. It is added to net purchases on the income statement to compute cost of goods purchased (see Figure 11-7).

Freight-In

Debit	Credit
to enter transportation charges on merchandise purchases	

Net purchases	XXX	
Add freight–in	XX	
Cost of goods purchased		XXX

Transportation charges are expressed in FOB (free on board) terms that indicate who is responsible for paying the freight costs. **FOB shipping point** means that transportation charges are paid by the buyer. **FOB destination** means that transportation charges are paid by the seller. FOB terms also tell us who owns the inventory and who should count it in their inventory account. Under FOB shipping point, the buyer owns the inventory as soon as it is shipped and should count it in inventory. Under FOB destination, the seller owns the inventory until it is delivered to the buyer and should count it in inventory.

When the terms are FOB shipping point, either the freight charges will be listed separately on the purchase invoice or a separate freight bill will be sent. Assume Northern Micro receives an invoice for $400 plus freight charges of $38. The entry for this purchase is as follows:

25		Purchases		400 00		25
26		Freight-In		38 00		26
27		Accounts Payable/Vendor			438 00	27
28		Made purchase on account				28

Assume instead that Northern Micro receives an invoice for $400 for the same merchandise, shipped FOB shipping point. Northern Micro then receives a separate bill from the transportation company for $38. These two transactions are entered as follows:

30		Purchases		400 00		30
31		Accounts Payable/Vendor			400 00	31
32		Made purchase on account				32
33						33
34		Freight-In		38 00		34
35		Accounts Payable/Vendor			38 00	35
36		Freight charges on merchandise purchase				36

When the terms are FOB destination, generally no freight charges appear on the purchase invoice. The buyer simply records the purchase at the amount of the invoice. The freight-in account is not used in recording this purchase.

COMPUTATION OF GROSS PROFIT

An important step in determining net income for a merchandising business is the calculation of its gross profit. **Gross profit** (also called **gross margin**) is the difference between net sales and cost of goods sold. **Cost of goods sold** (also called **cost of merchandise sold**) is the difference between the goods available for sale and the ending inventory. It indicates the cost of the goods sold during the period. Gross profit provides very important information. It tells management the amount of sales dollars available to cover expenses, after covering the cost of the goods sold.

As a simple example, gross profit is computed as follows:

Net sales	\$8,400
Cost of goods sold	5,300
Gross profit	\$3,100

In a more realistic situation, we must compute net sales and cost of goods sold, in order to compute gross profit. Multiple steps are involved. To illustrate, we use three of the four new accounts described in Chapter 10, the four new accounts described in this chapter, and the merchandise inventory balances. Assume that Northern Micro has the following sales, purchases, and merchandise inventory balances for the year ended December 31, 20--:

From Chapter 10	Sales	\$201,500
	Sales returns and allowances	1,200
	Sales discounts	1,000
From Chapter 11	Purchases	105,000
	Purchases returns and allowances	800
	Purchases discounts	1,000
	Freight-in	300
	Merchandise inventory, January 1, 20--	26,000
	Merchandise inventory, December 31, 20--	18,000

Figure 11-7 uses these balances to compute net sales, net purchases, cost of goods sold, and gross profit. The following four steps in computing gross profit are labeled in the figure:

STEP 1 Compute net sales.

(Sales – Sales Returns and Allowances – Sales Discounts)

STEP 2 Compute goods available for sale.

(Beginning Inventory + Cost of Goods Purchased)

STEP 3 Compute cost of goods sold.

(Goods Available for Sale – Ending Inventory)

STEP 4 Compute gross profit.

(Net Sales – Cost of Goods Sold)

LEARNING KEY

Cost of Goods Sold = Beginning Inventory + Net Purchases + Freight-In – Ending Inventory

Gross Profit = Net Sales – Cost of Goods Sold

FIGURE 11-7 Computation of Gross Profit on a Partial Income Statement

Income Statement (partial)

	Revenue from sales:				
	Sales			$201,500.00	
	Less: Sales returns and allowances		$ 1,200.00		
	Sales discounts		1,000.00	2,200.00	
Step 1	**Net sales**				$199,300.00
	Cost of goods sold:				
	Merchandise inventory, Jan. 1			$ 26,000.00	
	Purchases		$105,000.00		
	Less: Purchases returns and allowances	$ 800.00			
	Purchases discounts	1,000.00	1,800.00		
	Net purchases		$103,200.00		
	Add freight-in		300.00		
	Cost of goods purchased			103,500.00	
Step 2	**Goods available for sale**			$129,500.00	
	Less merchandise inventory, Dec. 31			18,000.00	
Step 3	**Cost of goods sold**				111,500.00
Step 4	**Gross profit**				$ 87,800.00

U REVU

Complete U REVU-2 on **page 422** to test your basic understanding of LO2.

JOURNALIZING AND POSTING PURCHASES AND CASH PAYMENTS TRANSACTIONS

LO3 Describe and use the accounts payable ledger.

To illustrate the journalizing and posting of purchases transactions, we will continue with the transactions of Northern Micro.

PURCHASES

Assume the following purchases on account occurred during the month of April:

Apr. 4 Purchased merchandise from Compucraft, Inc., $3,300.
Invoice No. 631, dated April 2, terms, n/30.

8 Purchased merchandise from Datasoft, $2,500.
Invoice No. 927D, dated April 6, terms, n/30.

11 Purchased merchandise from EZX Corp., $8,700.
Invoice No. 804, dated April 9, terms, 1/15, n/30.

17 Purchased merchandise from Printpro Corp., $800.
Invoice No. 611, dated April 16, terms, n/30.

23 Purchased merchandise from Televax, Inc., $5,300.
Invoice No. 1465, dated April 22, terms, 1/10, n/30.

These transactions are entered in a general journal as shown in Figure 11-8.

FIGURE 11-8 Purchases Entered in General Journal

GENERAL JOURNAL PAGE 6

	DATE		DESCRIPTION	POST. REF.	DEBIT	CREDIT	
	20--						
1	Apr.	4	Purchases		3 3 0 0 00		1
2			Accounts Payable/Compucraft, Inc.			3 3 0 0 00	2
3			Invoice No. 631				3
4							4
5		8	Purchases		2 5 0 0 00		5
6			Accounts Payable/Datasoft			2 5 0 0 00	6
7			Invoice No. 927D				7
8							8
9		11	Purchases		8 7 0 0 00		9
10			Accounts Payable/EZX Corp.			8 7 0 0 00	10
11			Invoice No. 804				11
12							12
13		17	Purchases		8 0 0 00		13
14			Accounts Payable/Printpro Corp.			8 0 0 00	14
15			Invoice No. 611				15
16							16
17		23	Purchases		5 3 0 0 00		17
18			Accounts Payable/Televax, Inc.			5 3 0 0 00	18
19			Invoice No. 1465				19

POSTING PURCHASES TO THE GENERAL LEDGER

Purchases transactions are posted from the general journal to the general ledger in the same manner as was illustrated for sales in Chapter 10. The following steps are used, as indicated in Figure 11-9 for Northern Micro's April 4 and 8 purchases transactions:

In the general ledger account:

STEP 1 Enter the date of the transaction in the Date column.

STEP 2 Enter the amount of the debit or credit in the Debit or Credit column.

STEP 3 Enter the new balance in the Balance columns under Debit or Credit.

STEP 4 Enter the journal page number from which each transaction is posted in the Posting Reference column.

In the journal:

STEP 5 Enter the ledger account number in the Posting Reference column of the journal for each transaction that is posted.

Other purchases transactions would be posted in the same manner.

POSTING PURCHASES TO THE ACCOUNTS PAYABLE LEDGER

The Purchases and Accounts Payable resulting from merchandise purchases on account are now up to date in the general ledger. A record can be kept of the amount owed to each supplier by using an **accounts payable ledger**. This is a separate ledger containing an individual account payable for each supplier. It is similar to the accounts receivable ledger we saw in Chapter 10. A summary accounts payable account called

FIGURE 11-9 Posting Purchases to the General Ledger

GENERAL JOURNAL (Partial) **Page 6**

Date		Description		Post. Ref.	Debit	Credit
20--						
Apr.	4	Purchases		501	3,300.00	
		Accounts Payable/Compucraft, Inc.	5	202		3,300.00
		Invoice No. 631				
	8	Purchases		501	2,500.00	
		Accounts Payable/Datasoft	5	202		2,500.00
		Invoice No. 927D				

GENERAL LEDGER (Partial)

ACCOUNT Accounts Payable **ACCOUNT NO.** 202

Date		Item	Post. Ref.	Debit	Credit	Balance Debit	Balance Credit
20--							
Apr.	1	Bal.	✓				4,800.00
	1 4		4 J6		3,300.00		8,100.00
	8		J6		2,500.00		10,600.00

ACCOUNT Purchases **ACCOUNT NO.** 501

Date		Item	Post. Ref.	Debit	Credit	Balance Debit	Balance Credit
20--							
Apr.	1	Bal.	✓			17,400.00	
	1 4		4 J6	3,300.00		20,700.00	
	8		J6	2,500.00		23,200.00	

A three-column account form is commonly used for supplier accounts. Only one balance column is needed because the normal balance is a credit. If a debit balance occurs, the amount may be bracketed.

a controlling account is maintained in the general ledger. The accounts payable ledger is "subsidiary" to this account. If there are many supplier accounts, it is a good practice to assign each supplier an account number. The subsidiary ledger accounts are kept in either alphabetical or numerical order, depending on whether the supplier accounts are identified by number.

Figure 11-10 illustrates the use of the accounts payable ledger for Northern Micro's April 4 and 8 purchases transactions. Note that the individual vendor name follows accounts payable in each journal entry affecting Accounts Payable. The following steps are used to post from the general journal to the accounts payable ledger, as shown in Figure 11-10:

In the accounts payable ledger account:

STEP 1 Enter the date of the transaction in the Date column.

STEP 2 Enter the amount of the debit or credit in the Debit or Credit column.

STEP 3 Enter the new balance in the Balance column.

STEP 4 Enter the journal page number from which each transaction is posted in the Posting Reference column.

In the journal:

STEP 5 Enter a slash (/) followed by a check mark (✓) in the Posting Reference column of the journal for each transaction that is posted.

LEARNING KEY

When an accounts payable ledger is used, the Posting Reference column in the general journal serves two purposes. (1) The account number is inserted to indicate the general ledger account has been posted. (2) A slash (/) and a check mark (✓) are inserted to indicate the accounts payable ledger account has been posted.

FIGURE 11-10 Posting Purchases to the Accounts Payable Ledger

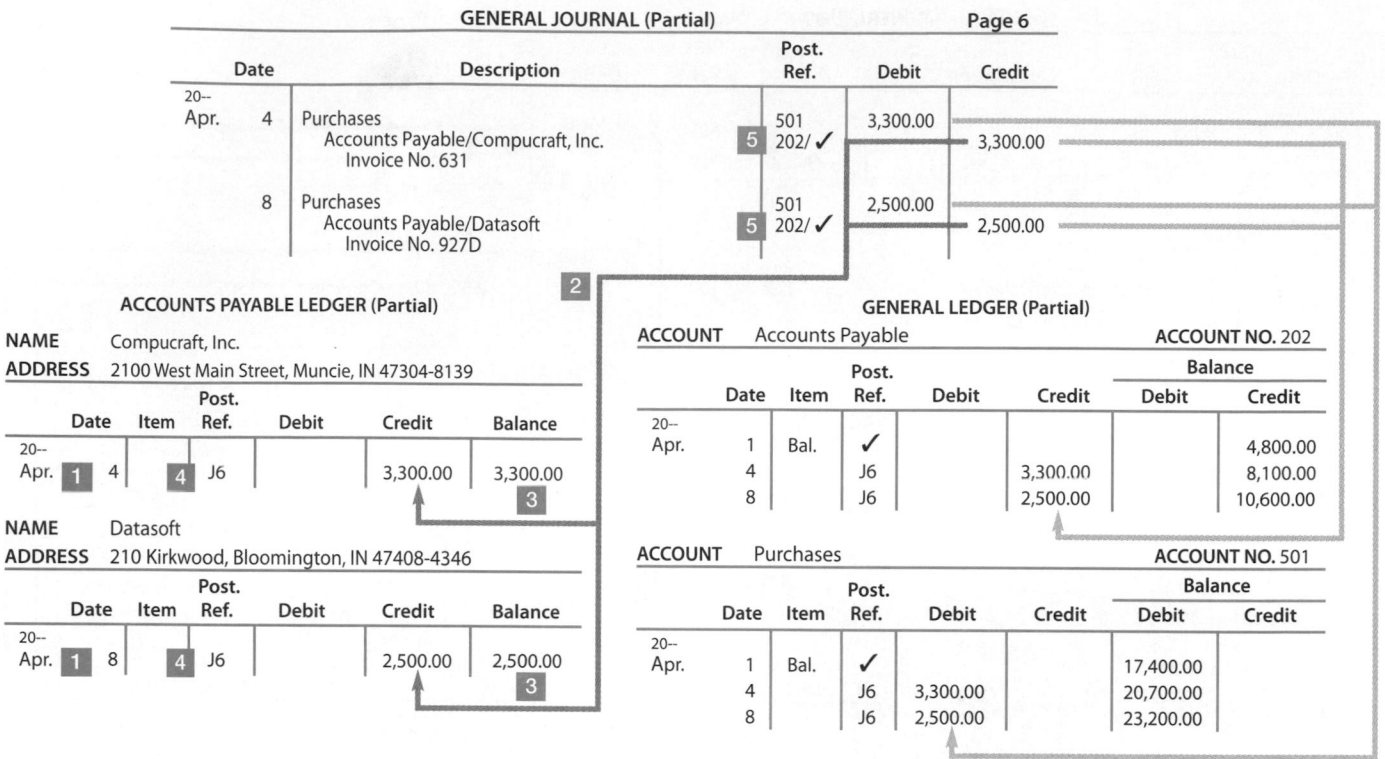

GENERAL JOURNAL (Partial) Page 6

Date		Description	Post. Ref.	Debit	Credit
20--					
Apr.	4	Purchases	501	3,300.00	
		Accounts Payable/Compucraft, Inc.	5 202/ ✓		3,300.00
		Invoice No. 631			
	8	Purchases	501	2,500.00	
		Accounts Payable/Datasoft	5 202/ ✓		2,500.00
		Invoice No. 927D			

2

ACCOUNTS PAYABLE LEDGER (Partial)

NAME Compucraft, Inc.
ADDRESS 2100 West Main Street, Muncie, IN 47304-8139

Date		Item	Post. Ref.	Debit	Credit	Balance
20--						
Apr. 1	4		4 J6		3,300.00	3,300.00 3

NAME Datasoft
ADDRESS 210 Kirkwood, Bloomington, IN 47408-4346

Date		Item	Post. Ref.	Debit	Credit	Balance
20--						
Apr. 1	8		4 J6		2,500.00	2,500.00 3

GENERAL LEDGER (Partial)

ACCOUNT Accounts Payable ACCOUNT NO. 202

Date		Item	Post. Ref.	Debit	Credit	Balance Debit	Balance Credit
20--							
Apr.	1	Bal.	✓				4,800.00
	4		J6		3,300.00		8,100.00
	8		J6		2,500.00		10,600.00

ACCOUNT Purchases ACCOUNT NO. 501

Date		Item	Post. Ref.	Debit	Credit	Balance Debit	Balance Credit
20--							
Apr.	1	Bal.	✓			17,400.00	
	4		J6	3,300.00		20,700.00	
	8		J6	2,500.00		23,200.00	

LEARNING KEY

The total of the accounts payable ledger balances must equal the Accounts Payable balance in the general ledger.

Note the relationship between the general journal, accounts payable ledger, and general ledger. All general journal entries are posted to both the general ledger and the accounts payable ledger. After the posting of the accounts payable ledger and general ledger is completed, the total of the accounts payable ledger balances should equal the Accounts Payable balance in the general ledger.

PURCHASES RETURNS AND ALLOWANCES

If a buyer returns merchandise or is given an allowance for damaged merchandise, a general journal entry is required. Assume that on May 4, Northern Micro returns $200 of merchandise to Televax, Inc. These goods were part of a purchase made on April 23. Figure 11-11 shows the general journal entry, general ledger posting, and accounts payable ledger posting for this transaction.

The general journal entry is made in the usual manner. The general ledger is posted using the same five steps as were illustrated for purchases transactions in Figure 11-9. The accounts payable ledger is posted using the following five steps, as illustrated in Figure 11-11:

In the accounts payable ledger account:

STEP 1 Enter the date of the transaction in the Date column.

STEP 2 Enter the amount of the debit or credit in the Debit or Credit column.

STEP 3 Enter the new balance in the Balance column.

STEP 4 Enter the journal page number from which each transaction is posted in the Posting Reference column.

In the journal:

STEP 5 Enter a slash (/) followed by a check mark (✓) in the Posting Reference column of the journal for each transaction that is posted.

FIGURE 11-11 Accounting for Purchases Returns and Allowances

GENERAL JOURNAL (Partial) **Page 8**

Date		Description	Post. Ref.	Debit	Credit
20-- May	4	Accounts Payable/Televax, Inc.	5 202/✓	200.00	
		Purchases Returns and Allowances	501.1		200.00
		Returned merchandise			

ACCOUNTS PAYABLE LEDGER (Partial) 2

NAME Televax, Inc.
ADDRESS 1500 North Walnut Street, Addison, IL 60101-2417

Date		Item	Post. Ref.	Debit	Credit	Balance
20-- May	1	Bal.				5,300.00
1	4	4	J8	200.00		5,100.00

3

GENERAL LEDGER (Partial)

ACCOUNT Accounts Payable ACCOUNT NO. 202

Date		Item	Post. Ref.	Debit	Credit	Balance Debit	Balance Credit
20-- May	1	Bal.	✓				11,900.00
	4		J8	200.00			11,700.00

ACCOUNT Purchases Returns and Allowances ACCOUNT NO. 501.1

Date		Item	Post. Ref.	Debit	Credit	Balance Debit	Balance Credit
20-- May	1	Bal.	✓				370.00
	4		J8		200.00		570.00

CASH PAYMENTS

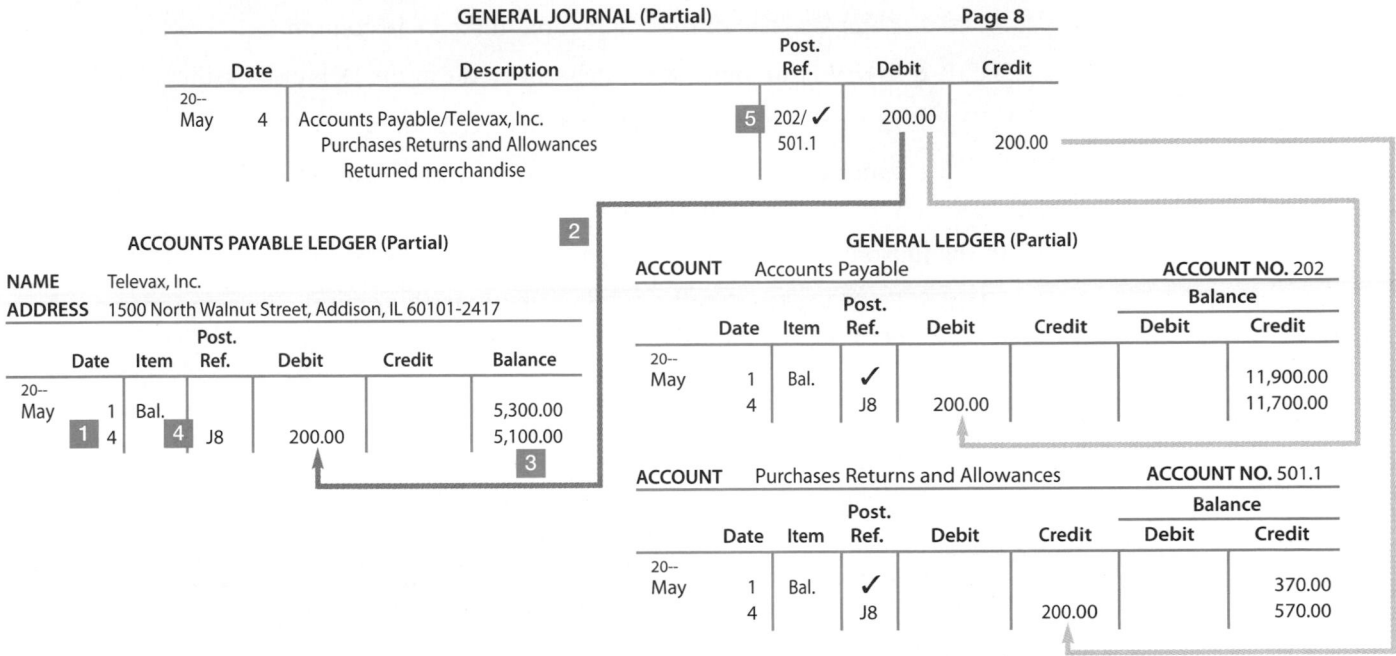

To illustrate the journalizing and posting of cash payments, we will use Northern Micro's cash payment transactions. Assume Northern Micro made the following two payments on account during the month of April:

Apr. 10 Paid B. B. Small $4,800 for purchases made on account.

24 Paid EZX Corp. $8,700 less discount of 1% for purchases made on account.

These transactions are entered in a general journal as shown in Figure 11-12.

FIGURE 11-12 Cash Payments Entered in a General Journal

30	Apr.	10	Accounts Payable/B. B. Small		4,800.00		30
31			Cash			4,800.00	31
32			Made payment on account				32
33							33
34		24	Accounts Payable/EZX Corp.		8,700.00		34
35			Cash			8,613.00	35
36			Purchases Discounts			87.00	36
37			Made payment less discount on account				37

POSTING CASH PAYMENTS TO THE GENERAL LEDGER AND ACCOUNTS PAYABLE LEDGER

Cash payment transactions are posted to the general ledger in the same manner as was illustrated for purchases transactions in Figure 11-9. To post cash payments to the accounts payable ledger, the following steps are used, as indicated in Figure 11-13 for Northern Micro's April 10 and 24 cash payment transactions:

In the accounts payable ledger account:

STEP 1 Enter the date of the transaction in the Date column.

STEP 2 Enter the amount of the debit or credit in the Debit or Credit column.

STEP 3 Enter the new balance in the Balance column.

STEP 4 Enter the journal page number from which each transaction is posted in the Posting Reference column.

In the journal:

STEP 5 Enter a slash (/) followed by a check mark (✓) in the Posting Reference column of the journal for each transaction that is posted.

FIGURE 11-13 Posting Cash Payments to the General Ledger and Accounts Payable Ledger

GENERAL JOURNAL (Partial) — Page 6

Date		Description	Post. Ref.	Debit	Credit
20--					
Apr.	10	Accounts Payable/B. B. Small	5 202/ ✓	4,800.00	
		Cash	101		4,800.00
		Made payment on account			
	24	Accounts Payable/EZX Corp.	5 202/ ✓	8,700.00	
		Cash	101		8,613.00
		Purchases Discounts	501.2		87.00
		Made payment less discount on account			

2

ACCOUNTS PAYABLE LEDGER (Partial)

NAME B. B. Small
ADDRESS 2323 High Street, Gurnee, IL 60031-5524

Date		Item	Post. Ref.	Debit	Credit	Balance
20--						
Apr.	1	Bal.	✓			4,800.00
	1 10		4 J6	4,800.00		3 —

NAME EZX Corp.
ADDRESS 2928 Rhodes Ave., Chicago, IL 60658-5036

Date		Item	Post. Ref.	Debit	Credit	Balance
20--						
Apr.	11		J6		8,700.00	8,700.00
	1 24		4 J6	8,700.00		3 —

GENERAL LEDGER (Partial)

ACCOUNT Cash — ACCOUNT NO. 101

Date		Item	Post. Ref.	Debit	Credit	Balance Debit	Balance Credit
20--							
Apr.	1	Bal.	✓			20,000.00	
	10		J6		4,800.00	15,200.00	
	24		J6		8,613.00	6,587.00	

ACCOUNT Accounts Payable — ACCOUNT NO. 202

Date		Item	Post. Ref.	Debit	Credit	Balance Debit	Balance Credit
20--							
Apr.	1	Bal.	✓				4,800.00
	4		J6		3,300.00		8,100.00
	8		J6		2,500.00		10,600.00
	10		J6	4,800.00			5,800.00
	11		J6		8,700.00		14,500.00
	17		J6		800.00		15,300.00
	23		J6		5,300.00		20,600.00
	24		J6	8,700.00			11,900.00

ACCOUNT Purchases Discounts — ACCOUNT NO. 501.2

Date		Item	Post. Ref.	Debit	Credit	Balance Debit	Balance Credit
20--							
Apr.	1	Bal.	✓				330.00
	24		J6		87.00		417.00

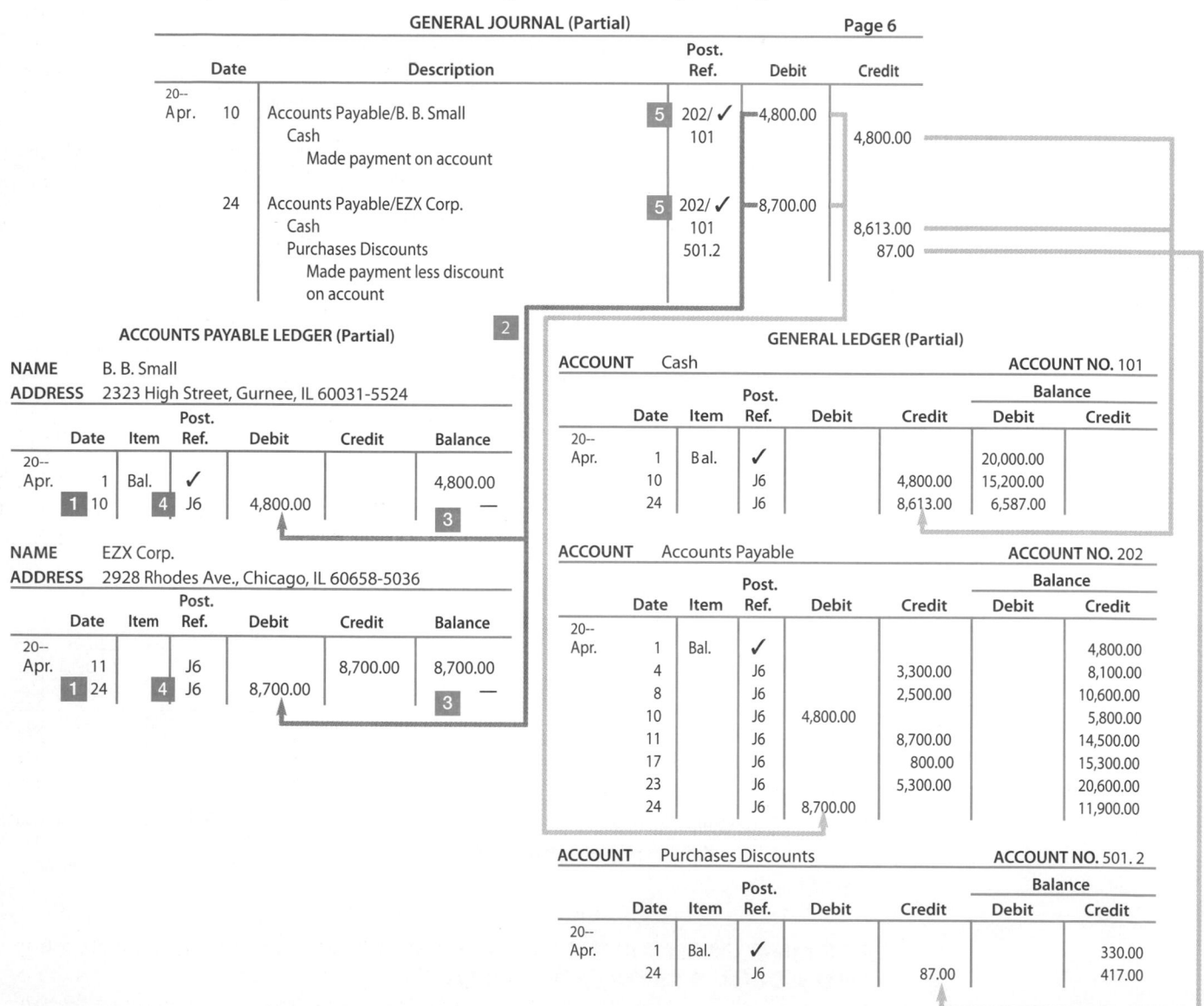

U REVU Complete U REVU-3 on **page 422** to test your basic understanding of LO3.

SCHEDULE OF ACCOUNTS PAYABLE

LO4 Prepare a schedule of accounts payable.

At the end of the month, all postings to Accounts Payable in the general ledger and to the accounts payable ledger should be complete, as shown in Figure 11-14. At this point, the Accounts Payable balance in the general ledger should equal the sum of the supplier balances in the accounts payable ledger.

FIGURE 11-14 General Ledger and Accounts Payable Ledger after Posting

ACCOUNTS PAYABLE LEDGER

NAME B. B. Small
ADDRESS 2323 High Street,Gurnee, IL 60031-5524

Date		Item	Post. Ref.	Debit	Credit	Balance
20--						
Apr.	1	Bal.	✓			4,800.00
	10		J6	4,800.00		—

NAME Compucraft, Inc.
ADDRESS 2100 West Main Street, Muncie, IN 47304-8139

Date		Item	Post. Ref.	Debit	Credit	Balance
20--						
Apr.	4		J6		3,300.00	3,300.00

NAME Datasoft
ADDRESS 210 Kirkwood, Bloomington, IN 47408-4346

Date		Item	Post. Ref.	Debit	Credit	Balance
20--						
Apr.	8		J6		2,500.00	2,500.00

NAME EZX Corp.
ADDRESS 2928 Rhodes Ave., Chicago, IL 60658-5036

Date		Item	Post. Ref.	Debit	Credit	Balance
20--						
Apr.	11		J6		8,700.00	8,700.00
	24		J6	8,700.00		—

NAME Printpro Corp.
ADDRESS 1200 Chambers Pike, Lincolnwood, IL 60648-2417

Date		Item	Post. Ref.	Debit	Credit	Balance
20--						
Apr.	17		J6		800.00	800.00

NAME Televax,Inc.
ADDRESS 1500 North Walnut Street, Addison, IL 60101-2417

Date		Item	Post. Ref.	Debit	Credit	Balance
20--						
Apr.	23		J6		5,300.00	5,300.00

GENERAL LEDGER (Partial)

ACCOUNT Accounts Payable **ACCOUNT NO.** 202

Date		Item	Post. Ref.	Debit	Credit	Balance Debit	Balance Credit
20--							
Apr.	1	Bal.	✓				4,800.00
	4		J6		3,300.00		8,100.00
	8		J6		2,500.00		10,600.00
	10		J6	4,800.00			5,800.00
	11		J6		8,700.00		14,500.00
	17		J6		800.00		15,300.00
	23		J6		5,300.00		20,600.00
	24		J6	8,700.00			11,900.00

To verify that the sum of the accounts payable ledger balances equals the Accounts Payable balance, a **schedule of accounts payable** is prepared. This is an alphabetical or numerical listing of supplier accounts and balances, usually prepared at the end of the month. Figure 11-15 shows the schedule of accounts payable for Northern Micro as of April 30. Note that suppliers whose account balance is zero are not included.

This schedule is prepared from the list of supplier accounts in the accounts payable ledger. The total calculated in the schedule is compared with the balance in Accounts Payable in the general ledger. Note that the $11,900 total listed in the schedule equals

FIGURE 11-15 Schedule of Accounts Payable

Northern Micro
Schedule of Accounts Payable
April 30, 20--

Compucraft, Inc.	$ 3 3 0 0 00
Datasoft	2 5 0 0 00
Printpro Corp.	8 0 0 00
Televax, Inc.	5 3 0 0 00
	$11 9 0 0 00

the Accounts Payable balance shown in Figure 11-14. If the schedule total and the Accounts Payable balance do not agree, the error must be located and corrected. To find the error, use the following procedures:

STEP 1 Verify the total of the schedule.

STEP 2 Verify the postings to the accounts payable ledger.

STEP 3 Verify the postings to Accounts Payable in the general ledger.

U REVU Complete U REVU-4 on **page 422** to test your basic understanding of LO4.

SELF-STUDY

LEARNING OBJECTIVES	Key Points to Remember
LO1 Define merchandise purchases transactions.	For a merchandising business, purchases refers to merchandise acquired for resale. Major documents used in the purchasing process are the purchase requisition, purchase order, receiving report, and purchase invoice.
LO2 Describe and use merchandise purchases accounts and compute gross profit.	Four accounts are used in accounting for merchandise purchases transactions. 1. Purchases 2. Purchases Returns and Allowances 3. Purchases Discounts 4. Freight-In Cost of Goods Sold = Beginning Inventory + Net Purchases + Freight-In – Ending Inventory Gross Profit = Net Sales – Cost of Goods Sold
LO3 Describe and use the accounts payable ledger.	To post purchases transactions to the general ledger: **In the general ledger account:** STEP 1 Enter the date of the transaction in the Date column. STEP 2 Enter the amount of the debit or credit in the Debit or Credit column. STEP 3 Enter the new balance in the Balance columns under Debit or Credit. STEP 4 Enter the journal page number from which each transaction is posted in the Posting Reference column. *(continued)*

LEARNING OBJECTIVES	Key Points to Remember
LO3 **(concluded)**	**In the journal:** STEP 5 Enter the ledger account number in the Posting Reference column of the journal for each transaction that is posted. An accounts payable ledger is a separate ledger containing an individual account payable for each supplier. To post from the general journal to the accounts payable ledger: **In the accounts payable ledger account:** STEP 1 Enter the date of the transaction in the Date column. STEP 2 Enter the amount of the debit or credit in the Debit or Credit column. STEP 3 Enter the new balance in the Balance column. STEP 4 Enter the journal page number from which each transaction is posted in the Posting Reference column. **In the journal:** STEP 5 Enter a slash (/) followed by a check mark (✓) in the Posting Reference column of the journal for each transaction that is posted. To post cash payments transactions to the general ledger: **In the general ledger account:** STEP 1 Enter the date of the transaction in the Date column. STEP 2 Enter the amount of the debit or credit in the Debit or Credit column. STEP 3 Enter the new balance in the Balance columns under Debit or Credit. STEP 4 Enter the journal page number from which each transaction is posted in the Posting Reference column. **In the journal:** STEP 5 Enter the ledger account number in the Posting Reference column of the journal for each transaction that is posted. To post cash payments transactions to the accounts payable ledger: **In the accounts payable ledger account:** STEP 1 Enter the date of the transaction in the Date column. STEP 2 Enter the amount of the debit or credit in the Debit or Credit column. STEP 3 Enter the new balance in the Balance column. STEP 4 Enter the journal page number from which each transaction is posted in the Posting Reference column. **In the journal:** STEP 5 Enter a slash (/) followed by a check mark (✓) in the Posting Reference column of the journal for each transaction that is posted.
LO4 **Prepare a schedule of accounts payable.**	The schedule of accounts payable is used to verify that the sum of the accounts payable ledger balances equals the Accounts Payable balance.

DEMONSTRATION PROBLEM

Jodi Rutman operates a retail pharmacy called Rutman Pharmacy. The books include a general journal, a general ledger, and an accounts payable ledger. The following transactions are related to purchases and cash payments for the month of June 20--:

June 1	Purchased merchandise from Sullivan Co. on account, $234.20. Invoice No. 71 dated June 1, terms 2/10, n/30.
2	Issued Check No. 536 for payment of June rent (Rent Expense), $1,000.00.
5	Purchased merchandise from Amfac Drug Supply on account, $562.40. Invoice No. 196 dated June 2, terms 1/15, n/30.
7	Purchased merchandise from University Drug Co. on account, $367.35. Invoice No. 914A dated June 5, terms 3/10 eom, n/30.
9	Issued Check No. 537 to Sullivan Co. in payment of Invoice No. 71 less 2% discount.
12	Received a credit memo from Amfac Drug Supply for merchandise returned that was purchased on June 5, $46.20.
14	Purchased merchandise from Mutual Drug Co. on account, $479.40. Invoice No. 745 dated June 14, terms 2/10, n/30.
15	Received a credit memo from University Drug Co. for merchandise returned that was purchased on June 7, $53.70.
16	Issued Check No. 538 to Amfac Drug Supply in payment of Invoice No. 196 less the credit memo of June 12 and less 1% discount.
23	Issued Check No. 539 to Mutual Drug Co. in payment of Invoice No. 745 less 2% discount.
27	Purchased merchandise from Flites Pharmaceuticals on account, $638.47. Invoice No. 675 dated June 27, terms 2/10 eom, n/30.
29	Issued Check No. 540 to Dolgin Candy Co. for a cash purchase of merchandise, $270.20.
30	Issued Check No. 541 to Vashon Medical Supply in payment of Invoice No. 416, $1,217.69. No discount allowed.

REQUIRED

1. Enter the transactions in a general journal (start with page 7).
2. Post from the journal to the general ledger accounts and the accounts payable ledger. Account numbers and June 1 balances are as indicated in the accounts presented below. Then, update the account balances.
3. Prepare a schedule of accounts payable from the accounts payable ledger in the problem. Verify that the total of accounts payable in the schedule equals the June 30 balance of Accounts Payable in the general ledger.

Solution 1.

GENERAL JOURNAL Page 7

DATE		DESCRIPTION	POST. REF.	DEBIT	CREDIT
20-- June	1	Purchases	501	234.20	
		Accounts Payable/Sullivan Co.	202/✓		234.20
		Invoice No. 71			
	2	Rent Expense	521	1000.00	
		Cash	101		1000.00
		Check No. 536			
	5	Purchases	501	562.40	
		Accounts Payable/Amfac Drug Supply	202/✓		562.40
		Invoice No. 196			
	7	Purchases	501	367.35	
		Accounts Payable/University Drug Co.	202/✓		367.35
		Invoice No. 914A			
	9	Accounts Payable/Sullivan Co.	202/✓	234.20	
		Cash	101		229.52
		Purchases Discounts	501.2		4.68
		Check No. 537			
	12	Accounts Payable/Amfac Drug Supply	202/✓	46.20	
		Purchases Returns and Allowances	501.1		46.20
		Returned merchandise			
	14	Purchases	501	479.40	
		Accounts Payable/Mutual Drug Co.	202/✓		479.40
		Invoice No. 745			

GENERAL JOURNAL Page 8

DATE		DESCRIPTION	POST. REF.	DEBIT	CREDIT
20-- June	15	Accounts Payable/University Drug Co.	202/✓	53.70	
		Purchases Returns and Allowances	501.1		53.70
		Returned merchandise			
	16	Accounts Payable/Amfac Drug Supply	202/✓	516.20	
		Cash	101		511.04
		Purchases Discounts	501.2		5.16
		Check No. 538			
	23	Accounts Payable/Mutual Drug Co.	202/✓	479.40	
		Cash	101		469.81
		Purchases Discounts	501.2		9.59
		Check No. 539			
	27	Purchases	501	638.47	
		Accounts Payable/Flites Pharmaceuticals	202/✓		638.47
		Invoice No. 675			
	29	Purchases	501	270.20	
		Cash	101		270.20
		Check No. 540			
	30	Accounts Payable/Vashon Medical Supply	202/✓	1217.69	
		Cash	101		1217.69
		Check No. 541			

(continued)

2.

ACCOUNT: Cash — ACCOUNT NO. 101

DATE		ITEM	POST. REF.	DEBIT	CREDIT	BALANCE DEBIT	BALANCE CREDIT
20-- June	1	Balance	✓			9,180.00	
	2		J7		1,000.00	8,180.00	
	9		J7		229.52	7,950.48	
	16		J8		511.04	7,439.44	
	23		J8		469.81	6,969.63	
	29		J8		270.20	6,699.43	
	30		J8		1,217.69	5,481.74	

ACCOUNT: Accounts Payable — ACCOUNT NO. 202

DATE		ITEM	POST. REF.	DEBIT	CREDIT	BALANCE DEBIT	BALANCE CREDIT
20-- June	1	Balance	✓				1,217.69
	1		J7		234.20		1,451.89
	5		J7		562.40		2,014.29
	7		J7		367.35		2,381.64
	9		J7	234.20			2,147.44
	12		J7	46.20			2,101.24
	14		J7		479.40		2,580.64
	15		J8	53.70			2,526.94
	16		J8	516.20			2,010.74
	23		J8	479.40			1,531.34
	27		J8		638.47		2,169.81
	30		J8	1,217.69			952.12

ACCOUNT: Purchases — ACCOUNT NO. 501

DATE		ITEM	POST. REF.	DEBIT	CREDIT	BALANCE DEBIT	BALANCE CREDIT
20-- June	1	Balance	✓			13,826.25	
	1		J7	234.20		14,060.45	
	5		J7	562.40		14,622.85	
	7		J7	367.35		14,990.20	
	14		J7	479.40		15,469.60	
	27		J8	638.47		16,108.07	
	29		J8	270.20		16,378.27	

ACCOUNT: Purchases Returns and Allowances — ACCOUNT NO. 501.1

DATE		ITEM	POST. REF.	DEBIT	CREDIT	BALANCE DEBIT	BALANCE CREDIT
20-- June	1	Balance	✓				312.63
	12		J7		46.20		358.83
	15		J8		53.70		412.53

ACCOUNT: Purchases Discounts — ACCOUNT NO. 501.2

DATE		ITEM	POST. REF.	DEBIT	CREDIT	BALANCE DEBIT	BALANCE CREDIT
20-- June	1	Balance	✓				2,1 1 45
	9		J7		4 68		2,1 6 13
	16		J8		5 16		2,2 1 29
	23		J8		9 59		2,3 0 88

ACCOUNT: Rent Expense — ACCOUNT NO. 521

DATE		ITEM	POST. REF.	DEBIT	CREDIT	BALANCE DEBIT	BALANCE CREDIT
20-- June	1	Balance	✓			5,0 0 0 00	
	2		J7	1,0 0 0 00		6,0 0 0 00	

ACCOUNTS PAYABLE LEDGER

NAME: Amfac Drug Supply

DATE		ITEM	POST. REF.	DEBIT	CREDIT	BALANCE
20-- June	5		J7		5 6 2 40	5 6 2 40
	12		J7	4 6 20		5 1 6 20
	16		J8	5 1 6 20		—

NAME: Flites Pharmaceuticals

DATE		ITEM	POST. REF.	DEBIT	CREDIT	BALANCE
20-- June	27		J8		6 3 8 47	6 3 8 47

NAME: Mutual Drug Co.

DATE		ITEM	POST. REF.	DEBIT	CREDIT	BALANCE
20-- June	14		J7		4 7 9 40	4 7 9 40
	23		J8	4 7 9 40		—

NAME: Sullivan Co.

DATE		ITEM	POST. REF.	DEBIT	CREDIT	BALANCE
20-- June	1		J7		2 3 4 20	2 3 4 20
	9		J7	2 3 4 20		—

NAME: University Drug Co.

DATE		ITEM	POST. REF.	DEBIT	CREDIT	BALANCE
20-- June	7		J7		3 6 7 35	3 6 7 35
	15		J8	5 3 70		3 1 3 65

NAME: Vashon Medical Supply

DATE		ITEM	POST. REF.	DEBIT	CREDIT	BALANCE
20-- June	1	Balance	✓			1,2 1 7 69
	30		J8	1,2 1 7 69		—

(continued)

3.

Rutman Pharmacy Schedule of Accounts Payable June 30, 20--	
Flites Pharmaceuticals	$ 6 3 8 47
University Drug Co.	3 1 3 65
	$ 9 5 2 12
Proof	
Balance of Accounts Payable, June 30	$ 9 5 2 12

KEY TERMS

accounts payable ledger (408) A separate ledger containing an individual account payable for each supplier.

contra-cost account (402) An account with a credit balance that is deducted from the related cost account.

contra-purchases account (402) see contra-cost account.

cost of goods sold (405) The difference between the goods available for sale and the ending inventory.

cost of merchandise sold (405) See cost of goods sold.

FOB destination (405) Shipping terms indicating that transportation charges are paid by the seller.

FOB shipping point (405) Shipping terms indicating that transportation charges are paid by the buyer.

gross margin (405) See gross profit.

gross profit (405) The difference between net sales and cost of goods sold.

invoice (399) A document prepared by the seller as a bill for the merchandise shipped. To the seller, this is a sales invoice. To the buyer, this is a purchase invoice.

purchase invoice (399) A document prepared by the seller as a bill for the merchandise shipped. To the buyer, this is a purchase invoice.

purchase order (398) A written order to buy goods from a specific vendor (supplier).

purchase requisition (398) A form used to request the purchase of merchandise or other property.

purchases (398) Merchandise acquired for resale to customers.

receiving report (399) A report indicating what has been received.

schedule of accounts payable (413) An alphabetical or numerical listing of supplier accounts and balances, usually prepared at the end of the month.

trade discount (400) A reduction from the list or catalog price offered to different classes of customers.

SELF-STUDY QUESTIONS AND EXERCISES

True/False Questions

1. LO1 In the purchasing process, the purchase invoice is the first document prepared.
2. LO1 A sales invoice prepared by the seller is called a purchase invoice by the buyer.
3. LO1 A trade discount is a reduction from the list or catalog price offered to different classes of customers.
4. LO2 Purchases Returns and Allowances is debited when merchandise is returned for credit.
5. LO2 FOB shipping point means that transportation charges are paid by the seller.

Multiple Choice Questions

1. LO1 A purchase of merchandise for $300 with a trade discount of 10% would require a debit to Purchases of

   (a) $330.
   (b) $300.
   (c) $297.
   (d) $270.

2. LO2 In the income statement, Freight-In is

   (a) added to purchases.
   (b) subtracted from purchases.
   (c) added to sales.
   (d) subtracted from cost of goods sold.

3. LO2 The difference between net sales and cost of goods sold is called

   (a) gross profit.
   (b) net purchases.
   (c) goods available for sale.
   (d) the bottom line.

4. LO2 The difference between merchandise available for sale and the end-of-period merchandise inventory is called

   (a) gross profit.
   (b) net purchases.
   (c) net sales.
   (d) cost of goods sold.

5. LO2 A purchase invoice for $1,200 with credit terms 2/10, n/30, and a return of $300 received by the seller prior to payment, is paid within the discount period. A check should be sent for

   (a) $1,200.
   (b) $882.
   (c) $900.
   (d) $810.

U REVU Exercises

1. LO1 Deering Housewares purchased merchandise for $1,200 less a 10% trade discount with credit terms of 1/10, n/30.

   a. Compute the trade discount.
   b. Compute the amount at which to record this purchase.
   c. Compute the cash discount if the payment for the merchandise is made within the discount period.

2. LO2 Based on the following data for Dave's Supply House, determine the gross profit.

Net sales	$92,000
Merchandise inventory, January 1, 20--	27,000
Purchases during the year	60,800
Purchases returns and allowances during the year	3,100
Purchases discounts during the year	1,300
Merchandise inventory, December 31, 20--	24,000

3. LO3 The following journal entries are for current purchases and cash payments transactions. Using T accounts, post these transactions to Cash, Accounts Payable, Purchases, Purchases Returns and Allowances, and Purchases Discounts in the general ledger, and the vendor account in the accounts payable ledger.

a. Purchases	350.00	
Accounts Payable/J. Bedas		350.00
b. Accounts Payable/J. Bedas	70.00	
Purchases Returns and Allowances		70.00
c. Accounts Payable/J. Bedas	280.00	
Cash		274.40
Purchases Discounts		5.60

4. LO4 On June 23, Felini Plumbing's accounts payable consisted of the following vendor balances:

B. Sutton	$245
A. Gagne	703
L. Mohler	410
P. Luffman	190
Z. Quary	263

During the following week, Felini Plumbing made a purchase of $180 from Mohler and made cash payments on account of $375 to Gagne and $110 to Quary. Prepare a schedule of accounts payable for Felini Plumbing at June 30, 20--.

The answers to the Self-Study Questions and Exercises are at the end of the chapter (pages 434–435).

APPLYING YOUR KNOWLEDGE

REVIEW QUESTIONS

LO1 1. Identify the major documents commonly used in the purchasing process.

LO1 2. Distinguish between a cash discount and a trade discount.

LO2 3. Describe how each of the following accounts is used: (1) Purchases, (2) Purchases Returns and Allowances, (3) Purchases Discounts, and (4) Freight-In.

LO2 4. How are cost of goods sold and gross profit computed?

LO3 5. What steps are followed in posting purchases from the general journal to the general ledger?

LO3 6. What steps are followed in posting purchases from the general journal to the accounts payable ledger?

LO3 7. What steps are followed in posting purchases returns and allowances from the general journal to the general ledger and accounts payable ledger?

LO3 8. What steps are followed in posting cash payments from the general journal to the general ledger?

LO3 9. What steps are followed in posting cash payments from the general journal to the accounts payable ledger?

LO4 10. If the total of the schedule of accounts payable does not agree with the Accounts Payable balance, what procedures should be used to search for the error?

SERIES A EXERCISES

E 11-1A **(LO1)**

PURCHASING DOCUMENTS AND FLOWCHART LABELING A partially completed flowchart showing some of the major documents commonly used in the purchasing function of a merchandise business is presented below. Identify documents 1, 3, and 4.

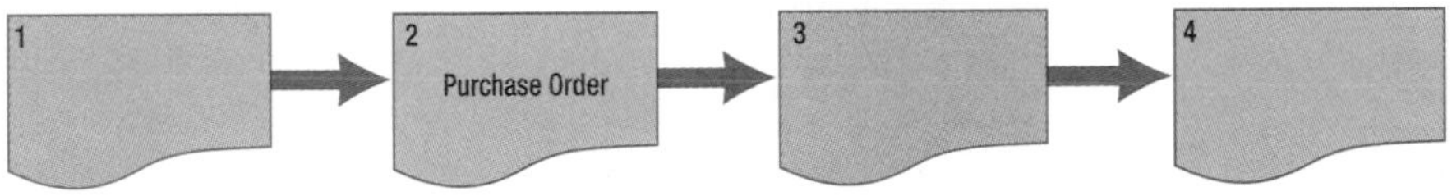

E 11-2A **(LO1/2)**
✓ 2: $1,764

TRADE DISCOUNT AND CASH DISCOUNTS Merchandise was purchased on account from Jacob's Distributors on May 17. The purchase price was $2,000, less a 10% trade discount and credit terms of 2/10, n/30.

1. Calculate the net amount to record the invoice, less the 10% trade discount.
2. Calculate the amount to be paid on this invoice within the discount period.
3. Journalize the purchase of the merchandise on May 17 in a general journal. Journalize the payment on May 27 (within the discount period).

E 11-3A **(LO2)**
✓ 3(c): Purchases Discounts: $70

PURCHASE TRANSACTIONS AND T ACCOUNTS Using T accounts for Cash, Accounts Payable, Purchases, Purchases Returns and Allowances, Purchases Discounts, and Freight-In, enter the following purchase transactions. Identify each transaction with its corresponding letter. Use a new set of T accounts for each set of transactions, 1–4.

1. Purchase of merchandise with cash.
   (a) Merchandise is purchased for cash, $1,500.
   (b) Merchandise listed at $3,500, less a trade discount of 15%, is purchased for cash.

(continued)

2. Purchase of merchandise on account with credit terms.
   (a) Merchandise is purchased on account, credit terms 2/10, n/30, $2,000.
   (b) Merchandise is purchased on account, credit terms 3/10, n/30, $1,200.
   (c) Payment is made on invoice (a) within the discount period.
   (d) Payment is made on invoice (b) too late to receive the cash discount.
3. Purchase of merchandise on account with return of merchandise.
   (a) Merchandise is purchased on account, credit terms 2/10, n/30, $4,000.
   (b) Merchandise is returned for credit before payment is made, $500.
   (c) Payment is made within the discount period.
4. Purchase of merchandise with freight-in.
   (a) Merchandise is purchased on account, $2,500 plus freight charges of $100. Terms of the sale were FOB shipping point.
   (b) Payment is made for the cost of merchandise and the freight charge.

E 11-4A (LO2)
✓ Cost of goods sold: $74,500

COMPUTING GROSS PROFIT The following data were taken from the accounts of Delhi Hardware, a small retail business. Determine the gross profit.

Sales	$113,500
Sales returns and allowances	800
Sales discounts	500
Merchandise inventory, January 1	34,000
Purchases during the period	76,000
Purchases returns and allowances during the period	4,000
Purchases discounts taken during the period	3,000
Freight-in on merchandise purchased during the period	1,500
Merchandise inventory, December 31	30,000

E 11-5A (LO3)
✓ May 9: Dr. Purchases, $2,300

JOURNALIZING PURCHASES TRANSACTIONS Journalize the following transactions in a general journal:

May 3 Purchased merchandise from Cintron, $6,500. Invoice No. 321, dated May 1, terms n/30.

9 Purchased merchandise from Mitsui, $2,300. Invoice No. 614, dated May 8, terms 2/10, n/30.

18 Purchased merchandise from Aloha Distributors, $4,200. Invoice No. 180, dated May 15, terms 1/15, n/30.

23 Purchased merchandise from Soto, $6,300. Invoice No. 913, dated May 22, terms 1/10, n/30.

E 11-6A (LO3)
✓ Ending Accounts Payable balance: $8,600

JOURNALIZING PURCHASES RETURNS AND ALLOWANCES AND POSTING TO GENERAL LEDGER AND ACCOUNTS PAYABLE LEDGER Using page 3 of a general journal and the following general ledger and accounts payable ledger accounts, journalize and post the following transactions:

July 7 Returned merchandise to Starcraft Industries, $700.

15 Returned merchandise to XYZ, Inc., $450.

27 Returned merchandise to Datamagic, $900.

General Ledger

Account No.	Account	Balance July 1, 20--
202	Accounts Payable	$10,650
501.1	Purchases Returns and Allowances	---

Accounts Payable Ledger

Name	Balance July 1, 20--
Datamagic	$2,600
Starcraft Industries	4,300
XYZ, Inc.	3,750

E 11-7A (LO3)
✓ Sept. 12: Cr. Cash, $6,930

JOURNALIZING CASH PAYMENTS TRANSACTIONS Enter the following cash payments transactions in a general journal:

Sept. 5 Issued Check No. 318 to Clinton Corp. for merchandise purchased August 28, $6,000, terms 2/10, n/30. Payment is made within the discount period.

12 Issued Check No. 319 to Mitchell Company for merchandise purchased September 2, $7,500, terms 1/10, n/30. A credit memo had been received on September 8 from Mitchell Company for merchandise returned, $500. Payment is made within the discount period after deduction for the return dated September 8.

19 Issued Check No. 320 to Expert Systems for merchandise purchased August 20, $4,100, terms n/30.

27 Issued Check No. 321 to Graphic Data for merchandise purchased September 17, $9,000, terms 2/10, n/30. Payment is made within the discount period.

E 11-8A (LO4)
✓ Total Accounts Payable: $14,370

SCHEDULE OF ACCOUNTS PAYABLE Ryan's Express, a retail business, had the following beginning balances and purchases and payments activity in its accounts payable ledger during October. Prepare a schedule of accounts payable for Ryan's Express as of October 31, 20--.

Accounts Payable Ledger

Name	Balance Oct. 1, 20--	Purchases	Payments
Columbia Products	$4,350	$3,060	$2,060
Favorite Fashions	4,910	1,970	2,600
Rustic Legends	5,130	2,625	3,015

SERIES A PROBLEMS

P 11-9A (LO3)
✓ Purchases balance: $20,790

PURCHASES TRANSACTIONS J. B. Speck, owner of Speck's Galleria, made the following purchases of merchandise on account during the month of September:

Sept. 3 Purchase Invoice No. 415, $2,650, from Smith Distributors.

8 Purchase Invoice No. 132, $3,830, from Michaels Wholesaler.

11 Purchase Invoice No. 614, $3,140, from J. B. Sanders & Co.

18 Purchase Invoice No. 329, $2,250, from Bateman & Jones, Inc.

(continued)

Sept. 23 Purchase Invoice No. 767, $4,160, from Smith Distributors.

27 Purchase Invoice No. 744, $1,980, from Anderson Company.

30 Purchase Invoice No. 652, $2,780, from Michaels Wholesaler.

REQUIRED

1. Record the transactions in a general journal.
2. Post from the general journal to the general ledger accounts and to the accounts payable ledger accounts. Use general ledger account numbers as shown in the chapter.

P 11-10A (LO3)
✓ Accounts Payable balance: $1,900

CASH PAYMENTS TRANSACTIONS Sam Santiago operates a retail variety store. The books include a general journal and an accounts payable ledger.

Selected account balances on May 1 are as follows:

General Ledger	
Cash	$40,000
Accounts Payable	20,000
Accounts Payable Ledger	
Fantastic Toys	$5,200
Goya Outlet	3,800
Mueller's Distributors	3,600
Van Kooning	7,400

The following are the transactions related to cash payments for the month of May:

May 1 Issued Check No. 426 in payment of May rent (Rent Expense), $2,400.

3 Issued Check No. 427 to Mueller's Distributors in payment of merchandise purchased on account, $3,600, less a 3% discount. Check was written for $3,492.

7 Issued Check No. 428 to Van Kooning in partial payment of merchandise purchased on account, $5,500. A cash discount was not allowed.

12 Issued Check No. 429 to Fantastic Toys for merchandise purchased on account, $5,200, less a 1% discount. Check was written for $5,148.

15 Issued Check No. 430 to City Power and Light (Utilities Expense), $1,720.

18 Issued Check No. 431 to A-1 Warehouse for a cash purchase of merchandise, $4,800.

26 Issued Check No. 432 to Goya Outlet for merchandise purchased on account, $3,800, less a 2% discount. Check was written for $3,724.

30 Issued Check No. 433 to Mercury Transit Company for freight charges on merchandise purchased (Freight-In), $1,200.

31 Issued Check No. 434 to Town Merchants for a cash purchase of merchandise, $3,000.

REQUIRED

1. Enter the transactions in a general journal.
2. Post from the general journal to the general ledger and the accounts payable ledger. Use general ledger account numbers as shown in the chapter.

P 11-11A (LO3)
✓ Cash balance: $11,805

PURCHASES AND CASH PAYMENTS TRANSACTIONS Freddy Flint owns a small retail business called Flint's Fantasy. The cash account has a balance of $20,000 on July 1. The following transactions occurred during July:

July 1	Issued Check No. 414 in payment of July rent, $1,500.
1	Purchased merchandise on account from Tang's Toys, Invoice No. 311, $2,700, terms 2/10, n/30.
3	Purchased merchandise on account from Sillas & Company, Invoice No. 812, $3,100, terms 1/10, n/30.
5	Returned merchandise purchased from Tang's Toys, receiving a credit memo on the amount owed, $500.
8	Purchased merchandise on account from Daisy's Dolls, Invoice No. 139, $1,900, terms 2/10, n/30.
11	Issued Check No. 415 to Tang's Toys for merchandise purchased on account, less return of July 5 and less 2% discount.
13	Issued Check No. 416 to Sillas & Company for merchandise purchased on account, less 1% discount.
15	Returned merchandise purchased from Daisy's Dolls, receiving a credit memo on the amount owed, $400.
18	Issued Check No. 417 to Daisy's Dolls for merchandise purchased on account, less return of July 15 and less 2% discount.
25	Purchased merchandise on account from Allied Business, Invoice No. 489, $2,450, terms n/30.
26	Purchased merchandise on account from Tang's Toys, Invoice No. 375, $1,980, terms 2/10, n/30.
29	Purchased merchandise on account from Sillas & Company, Invoice No. 883, $3,460, terms 1/10, n/30.

REQUIRED

1. Enter the transactions in a general journal.
2. Post from the journal to the general ledger and accounts payable ledger accounts. Use general ledger account numbers as shown in the chapter.

P 11-12A (LO4)
✓ Accounts Payable balance, Tang's Toys: $1,980

SCHEDULE OF ACCOUNTS PAYABLE Based on the information provided in Problem 11-11A, prepare a schedule of accounts payable for Flint's Fantasy as of July 31, 20--. Verify that the accounts payable account balance in the general ledger agrees with the schedule of accounts payable total.

SERIES B EXERCISES

E 11-1B (LO1)

PURCHASING DOCUMENTS AND FLOWCHART LABELING A flowchart showing some of the major documents commonly used in the purchasing function of a merchandise business is presented below. Briefly describe each document.

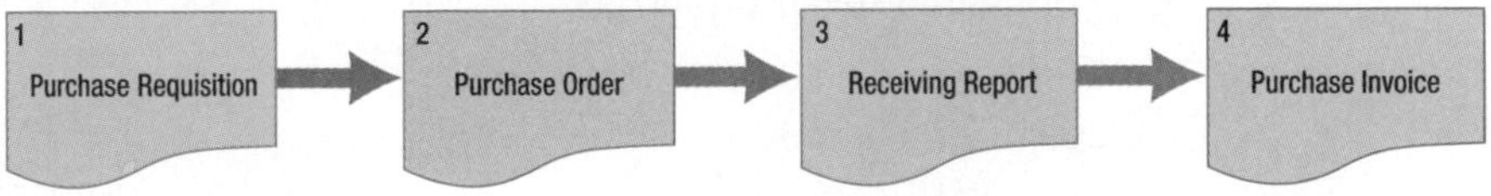

E 11-2B (LO1)
✓ 2: $4,365

TRADE DISCOUNT AND CASH DISCOUNTS Merchandise was purchased on account from Grant's Distributors on June 12. The purchase price was $5,000, less a 10% trade discount and credit terms of 3/10, n/30.

1. Calculate the net amount to record the invoice, less the 10% trade discount.
2. Calculate the amount to be paid on this invoice within the discount period.
3. Journalize the purchase of the merchandise on June 12 and the payment on June 22 (within the discount period) in a general journal.

E 11-3B (LO2)
✓ 3(c): Purchases Discounts, $100

PURCHASE TRANSACTIONS AND T ACCOUNTS Using T accounts for Cash, Accounts Payable, Purchases, Purchases Returns and Allowances, Purchases Discounts, and Freight-In, enter the following purchase transactions. Identify each transaction with its corresponding letter. Use a new set of T accounts for each set of transactions, 1–4.

1. Purchase of merchandise with cash.
   (a) Merchandise is purchased for cash, $2,300.
   (b) Merchandise listed at $4,000, less a trade discount of 10%, is purchased for cash.
2. Purchase of merchandise on account with credit terms.
   (a) Merchandise is purchased on account, credit terms 2/10, n/30, $4,000.
   (b) Merchandise is purchased on account, credit terms 3/10, n/30, $2,800.
   (c) Payment is made on invoice (a) within the discount period.
   (d) Payment is made on invoice (b) too late to receive the cash discount.
3. Purchase of merchandise on account with return of merchandise.
   (a) Merchandise is purchased on account, credit terms 2/10, n/30, $5,600.
   (b) Merchandise is returned for credit before payment is made, $600.
   (c) Payment is made within the discount period.
4. Purchase of merchandise with freight-in.
   (a) Merchandise is purchased on account, $3,800 plus freight charges of $200. Terms of the sale were FOB shipping point.
   (b) Payment is made for the cost of merchandise and the freight charge.

E 11-4B (LO2)
✓ Cost of goods sold: $76,700

COMPUTING GROSS PROFIT The following data were taken from the accounts of Burnside Bedknobs, a retail business. Determine the gross profit.

Sales	$116,900
Sales returns and allowances	1,100
Sales discounts	400
Merchandise inventory, January 1	30,000
Purchases during the period	100,000
Purchases returns and allowances during the period	2,000
Purchases discounts taken during the period	2,800
Freight-in on merchandise purchased during the period	1,500
Merchandise inventory, December 31	50,000

E 11-5B (LO3)
✓ Jan. 12: Dr. Purchases, $9,000

JOURNALIZING PURCHASES TRANSACTIONS Journalize the following transactions in a general journal:

Jan. 3 Purchased merchandise from Feng, $6,000. Invoice No. 416, dated January 1, terms 2/10, n/30.

12 Purchased merchandise from Miranda, $9,000. Invoice No. 624, dated January 10, terms n/30.

Jan. 19 Purchased merchandise from J. B. Barba, $6,400. Invoice No. 190, dated January 18, terms 1/10, n/30.

26 Purchased merchandise from Ramirez, $3,700. Invoice No. 923, dated January 25, terms 1/15, n/30.

E 11-6B (LO3)
✓ Ending Accounts Payable balance: $6,950

JOURNALIZING PURCHASES RETURNS AND ALLOWANCES AND POSTING TO GENERAL LEDGER AND ACCOUNTS PAYABLE LEDGER Using page 3 of a general journal and the following general ledger accounts and accounts payable ledger accounts, journalize and post the following transactions:

Mar. 5 Returned merchandise to Tower Industries, $500.

11 Returned merchandise to A & D Arms, $625.

23 Returned merchandise to Mighty Mansion, $275.

General Ledger

Account No.	Account	Balance Mar 1, 20--
202	Accounts Payable	$8,350
501.1	Purchases Returns and Allowances	---

Accounts Payable Ledger

Name	Balance Mar 1, 20--
A & D Arms	$2,300
Mighty Mansion	1,450
Tower Industries	4,600

E 11-7B (LO3)
✓ Apr. 19: Cr. Cash, $4,950

JOURNALIZING CASH PAYMENTS TRANSACTIONS Enter the following cash payments transactions in a general journal:

Apr. 5 Issued Check No. 429 to Standard Industries for merchandise purchased March 27, $8,000, terms 2/10, n/30. Payment is made within the discount period.

19 Issued Check No. 430 to Finest Company for merchandise purchased April 10, $5,300, terms 1/10, n/30. A credit memo had been received on April 12 from Finest Company for merchandise returned, $300. Payment is made within the discount period after deduction for the return dated April 12.

21 Issued Check No. 431 to Funny Follies for merchandise purchased March 22, $3,250, terms n/30.

29 Issued Check No. 432 to Classic Data for merchandise purchased April 20, $7,000, terms 2/10, n/30. Payment is made within the discount period.

E 11-8B (LO4)
✓ Total accounts payable: $10,565

SCHEDULE OF ACCOUNTS PAYABLE Crystal's Candles, a retail business, had the following balances and purchases and payments activity in its accounts payable ledger during November. Prepare a schedule of accounts payable for Crystal's Candles as of November 30, 20--.

Accounts Payable Ledger

Name	Balance Nov. 1, 20--	Purchases	Payments
Carl's Candle Wax	$4,135	$ 955	$1,610
Handy Supplies	3,490	1,320	1,850
Wishy Wicks	3,300	1,905	1,080

SERIES B PROBLEMS

P 11-9B (LO3)
✓ Purchases balance: $18,515

PURCHASES TRANSACTIONS Ann Benton, owner of Benton's Galleria, made the following purchases of merchandise on account during the month of October:

Oct. 2 Purchase Invoice No. 321, $1,950, from Boggs Distributors.
7 Purchase Invoice No. 152, $2,915, from Wolfs Wholesaler.
10 Purchase Invoice No. 634, $3,565, from Komuro & Co.
16 Purchase Invoice No. 349, $2,845, from Fritz & McCord, Inc.
24 Purchase Invoice No. 587, $3,370, from Boggs Distributors.
26 Purchase Invoice No. 764, $2,240, from Sanderson Company.
31 Purchase Invoice No. 672, $1,630, from Wolfs Wholesaler.

REQUIRED

1. Record the transactions in a general journal.
2. Post from the general journal to the general ledger accounts and to the accounts payable ledger accounts. Use general ledger account numbers as shown in the chapter.

P 11-10B (LO3)
✓ Accounts Payable balance: $600

CASH PAYMENTS TRANSACTIONS Kay Zembrowski operates a retail variety store. The books include a general journal and an accounts payable ledger. Selected account balances on May 1 are as follows:

General Ledger	
Cash	$40,000
Accounts Payable	20,000
Accounts Payable Ledger	
Cortez Distributors	$4,200
Indra & Velga	6,800
Toy Corner	4,600
Troutman Outlet	4,400

The following transactions are related to cash payments for the month of May:

May 1 Issued Check No. 326 in payment of May rent (Rent Expense), $2,600.
4 Issued Check No. 327 to Cortez Distributors in payment of merchandise purchased on account, $4,200, less a 3% discount. Check was written for $4,074.
7 Issued Check No. 328 to Indra & Velga in partial payment of merchandise purchased on account, $6,200. A cash discount was not allowed.
11 Issued Check No. 329 to Toy Corner for merchandise purchased on account, $4,600, less a 1% discount. Check was written for $4,554.
15 Issued Check No. 330 to County Power and Light (Utilities Expense), $1,500.
19 Issued Check No. 331 to Builders Warehouse for a cash purchase of merchandise, $3,500.
25 Issued Check No. 332 to Troutman Outlet for merchandise purchased on account, $4,400, less a 2% discount. Check was written for $4,312.

May 30 Issued Check No. 333 to Rapid Transit Company for freight charges on merchandise purchased (Freight-In), $800.

31 Issued Check No. 334 to City Merchants for a cash purchase of merchandise, $2,350.

REQUIRED

1. Enter the transactions in a general journal.
2. Post from the general journal to the general ledger and the accounts payable ledger. Use general ledger account numbers as shown in the chapter.

P 11-11B (LO3)

✓ Cash balance: $12,790

PURCHASES AND CASH PAYMENTS TRANSACTIONS Debbie Mueller owns a small retail business called Debbie's Doll House. The cash account has a balance of $20,000 on July 1. The following transactions occurred during July:

July 1 Issued Check No. 314 for July rent, $1,400.

1 Purchased merchandise on account from Topper's Toys, Invoice No. 211, $2,500, terms 2/10, n/30.

3 Purchased merchandise on account from Jones & Company, Invoice No. 812, $2,800, terms 1/10, n/30.

5 Returned merchandise purchased from Topper's Toys receiving a credit memo on the amount owed, $400.

8 Purchased merchandise on account from Downtown Merchants, Invoice No. 159, $1,600, terms 2/10, n/30.

11 Issued Check No. 315 to Topper's Toys for merchandise purchased on account, less return of July 5 and less 2% discount.

13 Issued Check No. 316 to Jones & Company for merchandise purchased on account, less 1% discount.

15 Returned merchandise purchased from Downtown Merchants receiving a credit memo on the amount owed, $600.

18 Issued Check No. 317 to Downtown Merchants for merchandise purchased on account, less return of July 15 and less 2% discount.

25 Purchased merchandise on account from Columbia Products, Invoice No. 468, $3,200, terms n/30.

26 Purchased merchandise on account from Topper's Toys, Invoice No. 395, $1,430, terms 2/10, n/30.

29 Purchased merchandise on account from Jones & Company, Invoice No. 853, $2,970, terms 1/10, n/30.

REQUIRED

1. Enter the transactions in a general journal.
2. Post from the journal to the general ledger and accounts payable ledger accounts. Use general ledger account numbers as shown in the chapter.

P 11-12B (LO4)

✓ Accounts Payable balance, Topper's Toys: $1,430

SCHEDULE OF ACCOUNTS PAYABLE Based on the information provided in Problem 11-11B, prepare a schedule of accounts payable for Debbie's Doll House as of July 31, 20--. Verify that the accounts payable account balance in the general ledger agrees with the schedule of accounts payable total.

MANAGING YOUR WRITING

You are working as a summer intern at a rapidly growing organic food distributor. Part of your responsibility is to assist in the accounts payable department. You notice that most bills from suppliers are not paid within the discount period. The manager of accounts payable says the bills are organized by vendor, like the accounts payable ledger, and she is too busy to keep track of the discount periods. Besides, the owner has told her that the 1% and 2% discounts available are not worth worrying about.

Write a memo to the owner explaining why it is expensive not to take advantage of cash discounts on credit purchases. In addition, suggest a way to file (organize) supplier invoices so that they are paid within the discount period.

ETHICS CASE

Bob's Discount Auto Parts receives a cash discount of 2% from Auto Warehouse if it pays an invoice within 10 days. Bob, the owner, consistently sends payments 15 to 20 days after receiving the invoice and still deducts the amount of the discount. Last week, Bob received a call from Auto Warehouse reminding him that in order to get the discount, an invoice must be paid within 10 days. When Bob received the next invoice, he dated the check exactly 10 days from the date of the invoice but didn't mail the check for another week. The receivables manager from Auto Warehouse called Bob and again reminded him that the check should be mailed by the 10th day in order to receive the 2% discount. When Bob received the next invoice, he mailed it on time but post-dated the check for the following week.

1. Are Bob's attempts to extend the discount period unethical?
2. What alternatives can Auto Warehouse take to prevent Bob's Discount Auto Parts from stretching the discount period?
3. Write a short note from Auto Warehouse to Bob's Discount Auto Parts explaining cash discounts and credit terms.
4. In small groups, make a list of the advantages and disadvantages of offering cash discounts.

MASTERY PROBLEM

✓ Accounts Payable balance: $10,000

KA KLOOSTER & ALLEN

Michelle French owns and operates Books and More, a retail book store. Selected account balances on June 1 are as follows:

General Ledger	
Cash	$32,200.00
Accounts Payable	2,000.00
M. French, Drawing	18,000.00
Purchases	67,021.66
Purchases Returns and Allowances	2,315.23
Purchases Discounts	905.00
Freight-In	522.60
Rent Expense	3,125.00
Utilities Expense	1,522.87
Accounts Payable Ledger	
Northeastern Publishing Co.	$ 2,000.00

The following purchases and cash payments transactions took place during the month of June:

June 1 Purchased books on account from Irving Publishing Company, \$2,100. Invoice No. 101, terms 2/10, n/30, FOB destination.

2 Issued Check No. 300 to Northeastern Publishing Co. for goods purchased on May 23, terms 2/10, n/30, \$1,960 (the \$2,000 invoice amount less the 2% discount).

3 Purchased books on account from Broadway Publishing, Inc., \$2,880. Invoice No. 711, less a 20% trade discount, and invoice terms of 3/10, n/30, FOB shipping point.

3 Issued Check No. 301 to Mayday Shipping for delivery from Broadway Publishing, Inc., \$250.

4 Issued Check No. 302 for June rent, \$625.

8 Purchased books on account from Northeastern Publishing Co., \$5,825. Invoice No. 268, terms 2/eom, n/60, FOB destination.

10 Received a credit memo from Irving Publishing Company, \$550. Books had been returned because the covers were on upside down.

13 Issued Check No. 304 to Broadway Publishing, Inc., for the purchase made on June 3. (Check No. 303 was voided because an error was made in preparing it.)

28 Made the following purchases:

Invoice No.	Company	Amount	Terms
579	Broadway Publishing, Inc.	\$2,350	2/10, n/30, FOB destination
406	Northeastern Publishing Co.	4,200	2/eom, n/60, FOB destination
964	Riley Publishing Co.	3,450	3/10, n/30, FOB destination

30 Issued Check No. 305 to Taylor County Utility Co. for June utilities, \$325.

30 French withdrew cash for personal use, \$4,500. Issued check no. 306.

30 Issued Check No. 307 to Irving Publishing Company for purchase made on June 1 less returns made on June 10.

30 Issued Check No. 308 to Northeastern Publishing Co. for purchase made on June 8.

30 Issued Check No. 309 for books purchased at an auction, \$1,328.

REQUIRED

1. Enter the transactions in a general journal (start with page 16).
2. Post from the journal to the general ledger accounts and the accounts payable ledger. Use general ledger account numbers as indicated in the chapter.
3. Prepare a schedule of accounts payable.
4. If merchandise inventory was \$35,523 on January 1 and \$42,100 as of June 30, prepare the cost of goods sold section of the income statement for the six months ended June 30, 20--.

CHALLENGE PROBLEM

This problem challenges you to apply your cumulative accounting knowledge to move a step beyond the material in the chapter.

✓ May 14: Cr. Purchases Discounts, $9

KLOOSTER & ALLEN

Record the following transactions in a general journal:

May 4	Merchandise listed at $2,900, less a trade discount of 10%, is purchased on account, credit terms of 1/10, n/30, shipping terms FOB destination.
8	Merchandise purchased on May 4, listed at $520, is returned for credit.
14	Partial payment is made for the merchandise purchased on May 4, listed at $1,000, less 1% discount.
June 3	Payment is made of the balance due on the May 4 purchase.

ANSWERS TO SELF-STUDY QUESTIONS AND EXERCISES

True/False Questions

1. F (purchase requisition)
2. T
3. T
4. F (credited)
5. F (buyer)

Multiple Choice Questions

1. d **2.** a **3.** a **4.** d **5.** b

U REVU Exercises

1. a. $1,200 × 10% = $120
b. $1,200 – $120 = $1,080
c. $1,200 – $120 = $1,080 × 1% = $10.80

2.

Net sales				$92,000
Cost of goods sold:				
Merchandise inventory, Jan. 1			$27,000	
Purchases		$60,800		
Less: Purchases returns and allowances	$3,100			
Purchases discounts	1,300	4,400		
Cost of goods purchased			56,400	
Goods available for sale			$83,400	
Less merchandise inventory, Dec. 31			24,000	
Cost of goods sold				59,400
Gross profit				$32,600

3.

GENERAL LEDGER

Cash

		(c)	274.40

Accounts Payable

(b)	70.00	(a)	350.00
(c)	280.00		

Purchases

(a)	350.00		

Purchases Returns and Allowances

		(b)	70.00

Purchases Discounts

		(c)	5.60

Accounts Payable Ledger

J. Bedas

(b)	70.00	(a)	350.00
(c)	280.00		

4.

Felini Plumbing
Schedule of Accounts Payable
June 30, 20--

B. Sutton	$ 245
A. Gagne	328
L. Mohler	590
P. Luffman	190
Z. Quary	153
Total	$1,506

Chapter 11 Appendix

The Net-Price Method of Recording Purchases

LEARNING OBJECTIVES

Careful study of this appendix should enable you to:

LO1 **Describe the net-price method of recording purchases.**

LO2 **Record purchases and cash payments using the net-price method.**

NET-PRICE METHOD

LO1 Describe the net-price method of recording purchases.

In this chapter, purchases were recorded using the **gross-price method.** Under this method, purchases are recorded at the gross amount, regardless of available cash discounts. An alternative approach to accounting for purchases is the **net-price method.** Under this method, purchases are recorded at the net amount, assuming that all available cash discounts will be taken.

RECORDING WITH THE NET-PRICE METHOD

LO2 Record purchases and cash payments using the net-price method.

To compare the gross-price and net-price methods, reconsider the purchase for $100 on account, with credit terms of 2/10, n/30, on page 403. At the time of the purchase, the following entries are made under the two methods:

Gross-Price			Net-Price		
Purchases	100.00		Purchases	98.00*	
Accounts Payable		100.00	Accounts Payable		98.00

*$100—$2 (2% cash discount)

If the payment for the merchandise is made within the discount period, the entries are as follows:

Gross-Price			Net-Price		
Accounts Payable	100.00		Accounts Payable	98.00	
Cash		98.00	Cash		98.00
Purchases Discounts		2.00			

If payment for the merchandise is not made until after the discount period, the entries are as follows:

Gross-Price			Net-Price		
Accounts Payable	100.00		Accounts Payable	98.00	
Cash		100.00	Purchases Discounts Lost	2.00	
			Cash		100.00

Note that under the net-price method a new account, Purchases Discounts Lost, is used. Purchases Discounts Lost is a temporary owner's equity account used to record cash discounts lost on purchases. It is reported as an expense on the income statement.

Purchases Discounts Lost

Debit	Credit
to enter discounts lost because of late payment of invoices	

Purchases Discounts Lost represents a finance charge for postponing the payment for merchandise. If the balance in this account is large relative to the amount of gross purchases, management should review its cash payment procedures.

LEARNING OBJECTIVES Key Points to Remember

LO1 Describe the net-price method of recording purchases.	Under the net-price method, purchases are recorded at the net amount, assuming all available cash discounts will be taken.

LO2 Record purchases and cash payments using the net-price method.	Assume a purchase is made for $100 on account, with credit terms of 2/10, n/30. Under the net-price method, the entry at the time of purchase is as follows:
	Purchases 98.00
	  Accounts Payable 98.00
	If payment is made within the discount period, the entry is as follows:
	Accounts Payable 98.00
	  Cash 98.00
	If payment is not made until after the discount period, the entry is as follows:
	Accounts Payable 98.00
	Purchases Discounts Lost 2.00
	  Cash 100.00

KEY TERMS

gross-price method (436) Under this method, purchases are recorded at the gross amount.

net-price method (436) Under this method, purchases are recorded at the net amount, assuming all available cash discounts are taken.

REVIEW QUESTIONS

LO1 1. At what amount are purchases recorded under the net-price method?

LO2 2. Under the net-price method, if payment for merchandise is not made within the discount period, what accounts are debited when the payment is made?

LO2 3. (a) What kind of an account is Purchases Discounts Lost?
(b) How is this item reported on the income statement?

SERIES A EXERCISE

E 11Apx-1A (LO2)
✓ 1. Apr. 11: Cr. Purchases Discounts, $20

PURCHASES TRANSACTIONS—GROSS-PRICE AND NET-PRICE METHODS Romero's Heating and Cooling had the following transactions during April:

Apr. 2 Purchased merchandise on account from Alanon Valve for $1,000, terms 2/10, n/30.

5 Purchased merchandise on account from Leon's Garage for $1,400, terms 1/10, n/30.

11 Paid the amount due to Alanon Valve for the purchase on April 2.

25 Paid the amount due to Leon's Garage for the purchase on April 5.

1. Prepare general journal entries for these transactions using the gross-price method.
2. Prepare general journal entries for these transactions using the net-price method.

SERIES B EXERCISE

E 11Apx-1B (LO2)
✓ 2. May 27: Dr. Purchases Discounts Lost, $12

PURCHASES TRANSACTIONS—GROSS-PRICE AND NET-PRICE METHODS Gloria's Repair Shop had the following transactions during May:

May 2 Purchased merchandise on account from Delgado's Supply for $900, terms 2/10, n/30.

6 Purchased merchandise on account from Goro's Auto Care for $1,200, terms 1/10, n/30.

11 Paid the amount due to Delgado's Supply for the purchase on May 2.

27 Paid the amount due to Goro's Auto Care for the purchase on May 6.

1. Prepare general journal entries for these transactions using the gross-price method.
2. Prepare general journal entries for these transactions using the net-price method.

Chapter 12

Special Journals

If you are an active health and fitness enthusiast, you might already know of NewHealth Nutrition, perhaps through its nutraplanet.com Web site. NewHealth Nutrition was founded in 2001 in Fayetteville, Georgia. In 2004, after a slow start operating from a traditional storefront, the company began selling on the Internet and the business took off. In the last four years, sales have quadrupled to more than $4 million.

NewHealth Nutrition sells a wide array of sports nutrition and health supplements. Many are targeted at bodybuilding, but its product categories include amino acids, carbohydrates, cardiovascular support, fat burners, herbs, joint support, and many others. Its products tend to be priced in the $13–$70 range. Most of the sales for a company like this probably would be for relatively small dollar amounts. This means the volume of transactions to generate annual sales of $4 million would be huge. NewHealth Nutrition would need a way to record all of this activity that is more efficient than the methods we have seen in Chapters 10 and 11. In Chapter 12, you will learn about a more efficient way to record transactions. In the "A Broader View Feature," you will see how computer software can add even greater efficiency.

LEARNING OBJECTIVES

Careful study of this chapter should enable you to:

LO1 **Describe, explain the purpose of, and identify transactions recorded in special journals.**

LO2 **Describe and use the sales journal.**

LO3 **Describe and use the cash receipts journal.**

LO4 **Describe and use the purchases journal.**

LO5 **Describe and use the cash payments journal.**

Chapters 10 and 11 demonstrated how to account for sales, cash receipts, purchases, and cash payments in a merchandising business. We also saw how to use accounts receivable and accounts payable ledgers to keep track of individual customer and supplier accounts. In this chapter, we continue to study how to account for sales, cash receipts, purchases, and cash payments, but our objective is to find a way to be more efficient. We will learn how to use four special journals that enable us to achieve this objective.

SPECIAL JOURNALS

LO1 Describe, explain the purpose of, and identify transactions recorded in special journals.

A **special journal** is a journal designed for recording only certain kinds of transactions. A special journal can be created for almost any kind of transaction. The types of special journals a business uses should depend on the types of transactions that occur most frequently for a business. The more transactions of a specific type that occur, the more likely a special journal of that type would be useful for the business.

The primary purpose of using special journals is to save time journalizing and posting transactions. In a general journal, we recorded transactions by writing the account names, debit and credit amounts, and an explanation for each transaction on several lines in the journal. In contrast, most transactions are entered in a special journal on a single line, with the debit and credit amounts indicated in special columns provided for each account. This enables substantial time saving. The posting process also is more efficient. Using the general journal, each transaction is posted separately to the appropriate general ledger accounts. With a special journal, summary postings of column totals are made to appropriate accounts on a periodic basis.

Of course, even if a business uses special journals, there still is a need for a general journal. For example, transactions that occur infrequently, and adjusting and closing entries, usually are recorded in the general journal.

Four special journals commonly used by businesses are as follows:

- Sales journal
- Cash receipts journal
- Purchases journal
- Cash payments journal

LEARNING KEY

The special journals and general journal are books of original entry. Each transaction is recorded in only <u>one</u> of these journals.

Figure 12-1 identifies the types of transactions recorded in each of the four special journals and the general journal. You might find it helpful to refer back to Figure 12-1 as the four special journals are introduced in this chapter.

FIGURE 12-1 Types of Journals and Transactions

TYPE OF JOURNAL	TYPE OF TRANSACTIONS RECORDED
Sales journal	All sales of merchandise on account
Cash receipts journal	All cash receipts
Purchases journal	All purchases of merchandise on account
Cash payments journal	All cash payments
General journal	All other transactions

In the following sections, we will examine the journalizing and posting process using each of the four special journals.

SALES JOURNAL

LO2 Describe and use the sales journal.

A **sales journal** is a special journal used to record only sales of merchandise on account. To illustrate the journalizing and posting of sales transactions in the sales journal, we use the following five sales transactions for Northern Micro from Chapter 10.

Apr. 4 Made Sale No. 133C on account to Enrico Lorenzo, $1,520, plus $76 sales tax.

10 Made Sale No. 134C on account to Brenda Myers, $440, plus $22 sales tax.

18 Made Sale No. 105D on account to Edith Walton, $980, plus $49 sales tax.

21 Made Sale No. 202B on account to Susan Chang, $620, plus $31 sales tax.

24 Made Sale No. 162A on account to Heidi Schwitzer, $1,600, plus $80 sales tax.

The general journal entries for these five transactions are shown in Figure 12-2.

FIGURE 12-2 Sales Entered in General Journal

4	Apr.	4	Accounts Receivable/E. Lorenzo		1 5 9 6 00		4
5			Sales			1 5 2 0 00	5
6			Sales Tax Payable			7 6 00	6
7			Sale No. 133C				7
8							8
9		10	Accounts Receivable/B. Myers		4 6 2 00		9
10			Sales			4 4 0 00	10
11			Sales Tax Payable			2 2 00	11
12			Sale No. 134C				12
13							13
14		18	Accounts Receivable/E. Walton		1 0 2 9 00		14
15			Sales			9 8 0 00	15
16			Sales Tax Payable			4 9 00	16
17			Sale No. 105D				17
18							18
19		21	Accounts Receivable/S. Chang		6 5 1 00		19
20			Sales			6 2 0 00	20
21			Sales Tax Payable			3 1 00	21
22			Sale No. 202B				22
23							23
24		24	Accounts Receivable/H. Schwitzer		1 6 8 0 00		24
25			Sales			1 6 0 0 00	25
26			Sales Tax Payable			8 0 00	26
27			Sale No. 162A				27

LEARNING KEY

Use a sales journal only for recording sales of merchandise on account.

Notice that each of these five entries involved the same three accounts. The same account titles were recorded five times. Similarly, to post these entries to the general ledger, five separate postings would be made to each of the three accounts, a total of 15 postings.

These transactions can be recorded more efficiently by using a sales journal. To illustrate, reconsider the five sales made on account by Northern Micro. They are entered in the sales journal in Figure 12-3. The sales journal provides separate columns for Accounts Receivable Debit, Sales Credit, and Sales Tax Payable Credit, the three

Remember that sales returns and allowances are recorded in the general journal, as illustrated in Chapter 10, not in the sales journal.

accounts used repeatedly in the general journal in Figure 12-2. A sale is recorded in the sales journal by entering the following information:

1. Date
2. Sale number
3. Customer (to whom sold)
4. Dollar amounts

There is no need to enter any general ledger account titles, since they appear in the column headings.

FIGURE 12-3 Northern Micro Sales Journal

SALES JOURNAL PAGE 6

	DATE		SALE NO.	TO WHOM SOLD	POST. REF.	ACCOUNTS RECEIVABLE DEBIT		SALES CREDIT		SALES TAX PAYABLE CREDIT		
	20--											
1	Apr.	4	133C	Enrico Lorenzo		1596	00	1520	00	76	00	1
2		10	134C	Brenda Myers		462	00	440	00	22	00	2
3		18	105D	Edith Walton		1029	00	980	00	49	00	3
4		21	202B	Susan Chang		651	00	620	00	31	00	4
5		24	162A	Heidi Schwitzer		1680	00	1600	00	80	00	5

This chapter illustrates a manual accounting system. With a computerized system, journals/ledgers can be updated simultaneously when a transaction is entered. (see A Broader View on p, 450).

The sales journal in Figure 12-3 is designed for a company, like Northern Micro, that charges sales tax. For a wholesaler or any other company that does not charge sales tax, a sales journal like that in Figure 12-4 would be sufficient. In this case, there is only a single amount column headed Accounts Receivable Debit/Sales Credit. With no sales tax, the Accounts Receivable Debit and Sales Credit amounts are identical for each sale. Thus, only a single column is needed.

FIGURE 12-4 Sales Journal Without Sales Tax

SALES JOURNAL PAGE 1

DATE		SALE NO.	TO WHOM SOLD	POST. REF.	ACCOUNTS RECEIVABLE DEBIT/ SALES CREDIT

POSTING FROM THE SALES JOURNAL

Posting from the sales journal also is very efficient. Each general ledger account used in the sales journal requires only one posting each period. Figure 12-5 illustrates the general ledger posting process for Northern Micro's sales journal for the month of April.

The following steps are used to post from the sales journal to the general ledger at the end of each month, as indicated in Figure 12-5:

Step 1 is the main difference in posting the sales journal to the general ledger. The remaining steps 2–6 are essentially the same as steps 1–5 used to post from the general journal.

In the sales journal:

STEP 1 Total the amount columns, verify that the total of the debit column equals the total of the credit columns, and rule the columns.

In the ledger account:

STEP 2 Enter the date of the transaction in the Date column.

STEP 3 Enter the amount of the debit or credit in the Debit or Credit column.

STEP 4 Enter the new balance in the Balance columns under Debit or Credit.

STEP 5 Enter the initial "S" and the journal page number in the Posting Reference column.

In the sales journal:

STEP 6 Enter the ledger account number immediately below the column totals for each account that is posted.

FIGURE 12-5 Posting the Sales Journal to the General Ledger

SALES JOURNAL — **Page 6**

Date		Sale No.	To Whom Sold	Post. Ref.	Accounts Receivable Debit	Sales Credit	Sales Tax Payable Credit	
20--								
Apr.	4	133C	Enrico Lorenzo		1,596.00	1,520.00	76.00	
	10	134C	Brenda Myers		462.00	440.00	22.00	
	18	105D	Edith Walton		1,029.00	980.00	49.00	
	21	202B	Susan Chang		651.00	620.00	31.00	
	24	162A	Heidi Schwitzer		1,680.00	1,600.00	80.00	
					5,418.00	5,160.00	258.00	1
					(122)	(401)	(231)	6

3

GENERAL LEDGER (Partial)

ACCOUNT Accounts Receivable — ACCOUNT NO. 122

	Date		Item	Post. Ref.	Debit	Credit	Balance Debit	Balance Credit
	20--							
	Apr.	1	Bal.	✔			12,000.00	
2		30	5	S6	5,418.00		17,418.00 (4)	

ACCOUNT Sales Tax Payable — ACCOUNT NO. 231

	Date		Item	Post. Ref.	Debit	Credit	Balance Debit	Balance Credit
	20--							
2	Apr.	30	5	S6		258.00		258.00 (4)

ACCOUNT Sales — ACCOUNT NO. 401

	Date		Item	Post. Ref.	Debit	Credit	Balance Debit	Balance Credit
	20--							
	Apr.	1	Bal.	✔				27,000.00
2		30	5	S6		5,160.00		32,160.00 (4)

1 Debit total: $5,418

Credit total: $5,160
258
$5,418

LEARNING KEY

All special journal entries are posted to the general and subsidiary ledger accounts, *not* to the general journal.

As we saw in Chapter 10, Northern Micro also needs a record of the accounts receivable from *individual customers*. Figure 12-6 illustrates the use of the accounts receivable ledger. The accounts receivable ledger is posted *daily* so that current information is available for each customer at all times. The following steps are used to post the sales journal to the accounts receivable ledger, as shown in Figure 12-6:

FIGURE 12-6 Posting from the Sales Journal to the Accounts Receivable Ledger

SALES JOURNAL — Page 6

Date		Sale No.	To Whom Sold	Post. Ref.	Accounts Receivable Debit	Sales Credit	Sales Tax Payable Credit
20--							
Apr.	4	133C	Enrico Lorenzo	✔	1,596.00	1,520.00	76.00
	10	134C	Brenda Myers	✔	462.00	440.00	22.00
	18	105D	Edith Walton	✔	1,029.00	980.00	49.00
	21	202B	Susan Chang	✔	651.00	620.00	31.00
	24	162A	Heidi Schwitzer	✔	1,680.00	1,600.00	80.00
				5	5,418.00	5,160.00	258.00
					(122)	(401)	(231)

2

ACCOUNTS RECEIVABLE LEDGER

NAME Helen Avery
ADDRESS 1739 Woodsage Trace, Indianapolis, IN 46237-1199

Date		Item	Post. Ref.	Debit	Credit	Balance
20--						
Apr.	1	Bal.	✔			2,302.00

NAME Susan Chang
ADDRESS 337 Elm Street, Noblesville, IN 46060-3377

Date		Item	Post. Ref.	Debit	Credit	Balance
20--						
1 Apr.	21	4	S6	651.00		651.00 3

NAME Enrico Lorenzo
ADDRESS 5240 Tousley Court, Indianapolis, IN 46224-5678

Date		Item	Post. Ref.	Debit	Credit	Balance
20--						
1 Apr.	4	4	S6	1,596.00		1,596.00 3

NAME Brenda Myers
ADDRESS 581 Acorn Way, Zionsville, IN 46077-2154

Date		Item	Post. Ref.	Debit	Credit	Balance
20--						
1 Apr.	10	4	S6	462.00		462.00 3

NAME Heidi Schwitzer
ADDRESS 5858 Wildflower Cir., Bloomington, IN 47401-6209

Date		Item	Post. Ref.	Debit	Credit	Balance
20--						
Apr.	1	Bal.	✔			1,883.00
1	24	4	S6	1,680.00		3,563.00 3

NAME Ken Ulmet
ADDRESS 5260 Eagle Creek, Indianapolis, IN 46254-8275

Date		Item	Post. Ref.	Debit	Credit	Balance
20--						
Apr.	1	Bal.	✔			3,315.00

NAME Edith Walton
ADDRESS 1113 Stones Crossing, Zionsville, IN 46077-6601

Date		Item	Post. Ref.	Debit	Credit	Balance
20--						
1 Apr.	18	4	S6	1,029.00		1,029.00 3

NAME Vivian Winston
ADDRESS 124 Main St., Zionsville, IN 46077-1358

Date		Item	Post. Ref.	Debit	Credit	Balance
20--						
Apr.	1	Bal.	✔			4,500.00

GENERAL LEDGER (Partial)

ACCOUNT Accounts Receivable — ACCOUNT NO. 122

Date		Item	Post. Ref.	Debit	Credit	Balance Debit	Balance Credit
20--							
Apr.	1	Bal.	✔			12,000.00	
	30		S6	5,418.00		17,418.00	

ACCOUNT Sales Tax Payable — ACCOUNT NO. 231

Date		Item	Post. Ref.	Debit	Credit	Balance Debit	Balance Credit
20--							
Apr.	30		S6		258.00		258.00

ACCOUNT Sales — ACCOUNT NO. 401

Date		Item	Post. Ref.	Debit	Credit	Balance Debit	Balance Credit
20--							
Apr.	1	Bal.	✔				27,000.00
	30		S6		5,160.00		32,160.00

If the accounts receivable ledger is posted daily and the general ledger is posted at the end of the month, the accounts receivable ledger total will equal the general ledger Accounts Receivable total only at the end of the month.

In the accounts receivable ledger account:

STEP 1 Enter the date of the transaction in the Date column.

STEP 2 Enter the amount of the debit or credit in the Debit or Credit column.

STEP 3 Enter the new balance in the Balance column.

STEP 4 Enter the initial "S" and the journal page number in the Posting Reference column.

In the sales journal:

STEP 5 Enter a check mark (✓) in the Posting Reference column of the journal for each transaction that is posted.

The accounts receivable ledger also can be posted from the source document used to make the sales journal entry. For example, sales ticket #134C (see Figure 10-2) could be used to post that sale to Brenda Myers' account in the accounts receivable ledger. In this case, 134C would be inserted in the Posting Reference column of her account.

LEARNING KEY

The total of the accounts receivable ledger balances must equal the Accounts Receivable balance in the general ledger.

Note the relationship between the sales journal, accounts receivable ledger, and general ledger. All individual entries in the sales journal are posted to the accounts receivable ledger. The totals of all entries in the sales journal are posted to the general ledger accounts. After the posting of the accounts receivable ledger and the general ledger is completed, the total of the accounts receivable ledger balances should equal the Accounts Receivable balance in the general ledger.

U REVU Complete U REVU-1 on **page 468** to test your basic understanding of LO2.

CASH RECEIPTS JOURNAL

LO3 Describe and use the cash receipts journal.

A **cash receipts journal** is a special journal used to record only cash receipts transactions. To illustrate its use, we continue with the transactions of Northern Micro. Northern Micro's cash receipts journal for the month of April is shown in Figure 12-7, with the following transactions:

Apr. 14	Received cash on account from Enrico Lorenzo for Sale No. 133C, $1,596.
20	Received cash on account from Brenda Myers for Sale No. 134C, $462.
28	Received cash on account from Edith Walton for Sale No. 105D, $1,029.
30	Made cash sales for the month of $3,600 plus tax of $180.
30	Made bank credit card sales for the month of $2,500 plus tax of $125. Bank credit card expenses on these sales are $100.
30	Received cash for rent revenue, $600.
30	Borrowed cash from the bank by signing a note, $3,000.

Northern Micro's cash receipts journal provides separate columns for Accounts Receivable Credit, Sales Credit, Sales Tax Payable Credit, Bank Credit Card Expense Debit, and Cash Debit. These are the accounts most frequently affected by Northern

FIGURE 12-7 Northern Micro Cash Receipts Journal

CASH RECEIPTS JOURNAL PAGE 7

	DATE		ACCOUNT CREDITED	POST. REF.	GENERAL CREDIT	ACCOUNTS RECEIVABLE CREDIT	SALES CREDIT	SALES TAX PAYABLE CREDIT	BANK CREDIT CARD EXPENSE DEBIT	CASH DEBIT	
	20--										
1	Apr.	14	Enrico Lorenzo			1,596 00				1,596 00	1
2		20	Brenda Myers			462 00				462 00	2
3		28	Edith Walton			1,029 00				1,029 00	3
4		30					3,600 00	180 00		3,780 00	4
5		30					2,500 00	125 00	100 00	2,525 00	5
6		30	Rent Revenue		600 00					600 00	6
7		30	Notes Payable		3,000 00					3,000 00	7
8											8

LEARNING KEY

Use a cash receipts journal to streamline journalizing and posting of cash receipts.

Micro's cash receipts transactions. In addition, a General Credit column is provided for credits to any other accounts affected by cash receipts transactions.

A cash receipt is recorded in the cash receipts journal by entering the following information:

1. Date
2. Account credited (if applicable)
3. Dollar amounts

The Account Credited column is used for two purposes.

1. To identify the customer name for any collection on account. This column is used whenever the Accounts Receivable Credit column is used.
2. To enter the appropriate account name whenever the General Credit column is used.

The Account Credited column is left blank whenever the entry is for cash sales or bank credit card sales.

The cash receipts journal in Figure 12-7 is designed for a company like Northern Micro, which charges sales tax, makes bank credit card sales, and offers no cash discounts. For a wholesaler that does not charge sales tax, makes no bank credit card sales, and offers cash discounts, a cash receipts journal like the one in Figure 12-8 would be used. Recall that a special journal should be designed with column headings for frequently used accounts. Thus, the cash receipts journal in Figure 12-8 has no Sales Tax Payable Credit or Bank Credit Card Expense Debit column. Instead, a Sales Discounts Debit column is provided. In this way, the common cash receipts transactions of the wholesaler can be easily and efficiently recorded.

FIGURE 12-8 Cash Receipts Journal Without Sales Tax

CASH RECEIPTS JOURNAL PAGE 1

	DATE		ACCOUNT CREDITED	POST. REF.	GENERAL CREDIT	ACCOUNTS RECEIVABLE CREDIT	SALES CREDIT	SALES DISCOUNTS DEBIT	CASH DEBIT	
1										1

POSTING FROM THE CASH RECEIPTS JOURNAL

The cash receipts journal is posted to the general ledger in two stages, as illustrated in Figure 12-9. First, on a daily basis, the individual amounts in the General Credit column are posted. Second, at the end of the month, the totals of each of the other amount columns are posted.

FIGURE 12-9 Posting from the Cash Receipts Journal to the General Ledger

CASH RECEIPTS JOURNAL — Page 7

Date		Account Credited	Post. Ref.	General Credit	Accounts Receivable Credit	Sales Credit	Sales Tax Payable Credit	Bank Credit Card Expense Debit	Cash Debit
20--									
Apr.	14	Enrico Lorenzo			1,596.00				1,596.00
	20	Brenda Myers			462.00				462.00
	28	Edith Walton			1,029.00				1,029.00
	30		✔			3,600.00	180.00		3,780.00
	30		✔			2,500.00	125.00	100.00	2,525.00
	30	Rent Revenue	412	600.00					600.00
	30	Notes Payable	201	3,000.00					3,000.00
				3,600.00	3,087.00	6,100.00	305.00	100.00	12,992.00
				(✔)	(122)	(401)	(231)	(513)	(101)

Debit total:	
	$ 100
	12,992
	$13,092
Credit total:	$ 3,600
	3,087
	6,100
	305
	$13,092

GENERAL LEDGER (Partial)

ACCOUNT Cash — ACCOUNT NO. 101

Date		Item	Post. Ref.	Debit	Credit	Balance Debit	Balance Credit
20--							
Apr.	1	Bal.	✔			20,000.00	
	30		CR7	12,992.00		32,992.00	

ACCOUNT Accounts Receivable — ACCOUNT NO. 122

Date		Item	Post. Ref.	Debit	Credit	Balance Debit	Balance Credit
20--							
Apr.	1	Bal.	✔			12,000.00	
	30		S6	5,418.00		17,418.00	
	30		CR7		3,087.00	14,331.00	

ACCOUNT Notes Payable — ACCOUNT NO. 201

Date		Item	Post. Ref.	Debit	Credit	Balance Debit	Balance Credit
20--							
Apr.	1	Bal.	✔				6,000.00
	30		CR7		3,000.00		9,000.00

ACCOUNT Sales Tax Payable — ACCOUNT NO. 231

Date		Item	Post. Ref.	Debit	Credit	Balance Debit	Balance Credit
20--							
Apr.	30		S6		258.00		258.00
	30		CR7		305.00		563.00

ACCOUNT Sales — ACCOUNT NO. 401

Date		Item	Post. Ref.	Debit	Credit	Balance Debit	Balance Credit
20--							
Apr.	1	Bal.	✔				27,000.00
	30		S6		5,160.00		32,160.00
	30		CR7		6,100.00		38,260.00

ACCOUNT Rent Revenue — ACCOUNT NO. 412

Date		Item	Post. Ref.	Debit	Credit	Balance Debit	Balance Credit
20--							
Apr.	1	Bal.	✔				1,800.00
	30		CR7		600.00		2,400.00

ACCOUNT Bank Credit Card Expense — ACCOUNT NO. 513

Date		Item	Post. Ref.	Debit	Credit	Balance Debit	Balance Credit
20--							
Apr.	1	Bal.	✔			430.00	
	30		CR7	100.00		530.00	

To post the General Credit column, on a daily basis, use the following steps:

In the general ledger account:

STEP 1 Enter the date of the transaction in the Date column.

STEP 2 Enter the amount of the debit or credit in the Debit or Credit column.

STEP 3 Enter the new balance in the Balance columns under Debit or Credit.

STEP 4 Enter the initials "CR" and the journal page number in the Posting Reference column.

In the cash receipts journal:

STEP 5 Enter the ledger account number in the Posting Reference column for each account that is posted.

To post the other amount columns, at the end of the month, use the following steps:

In the cash receipts journal:

STEP 6 Total the amount columns, verify that the total of the debit columns equals the total of the credit columns, and rule the columns.

In the general ledger account:

STEP 7 Enter the date in the Date column.

STEP 8 Enter the amount of the debit or credit in the Debit or Credit column.

STEP 9 Enter the new balance in the Balance columns under Debit or Credit.

STEP 10 Enter the initials "CR" and the journal page number in the Posting Reference column.

In the cash receipts journal:

STEP 11 Enter the ledger account number immediately below the column totals for each account that is posted.

STEP 12 Enter a check mark (✓) in the Posting Reference column for the cash sales and bank credit card sales, and immediately below the General Credit column.

The general ledger accounts affected by the cash receipts transactions are now up to date. Postings to the accounts receivable ledger also must be made. These postings are made daily. Figure 12-10 illustrates the posting procedures, as follows:

In the accounts receivable ledger account:

STEP 1 Enter the date of the transaction in the Date column.

STEP 2 Enter the amount of the debit or credit in the Debit or Credit column.

STEP 3 Enter the new balance in the Balance column.

STEP 4 Enter the initials "CR" and the journal page number in the Posting Reference column.

In the cash receipts journal:

STEP 5 Enter a check mark (✓) in the Posting Reference column of the journal for each transaction that is posted.

FIGURE 12-10 Posting from the Cash Receipts Journal to the Accounts Receivable Ledger

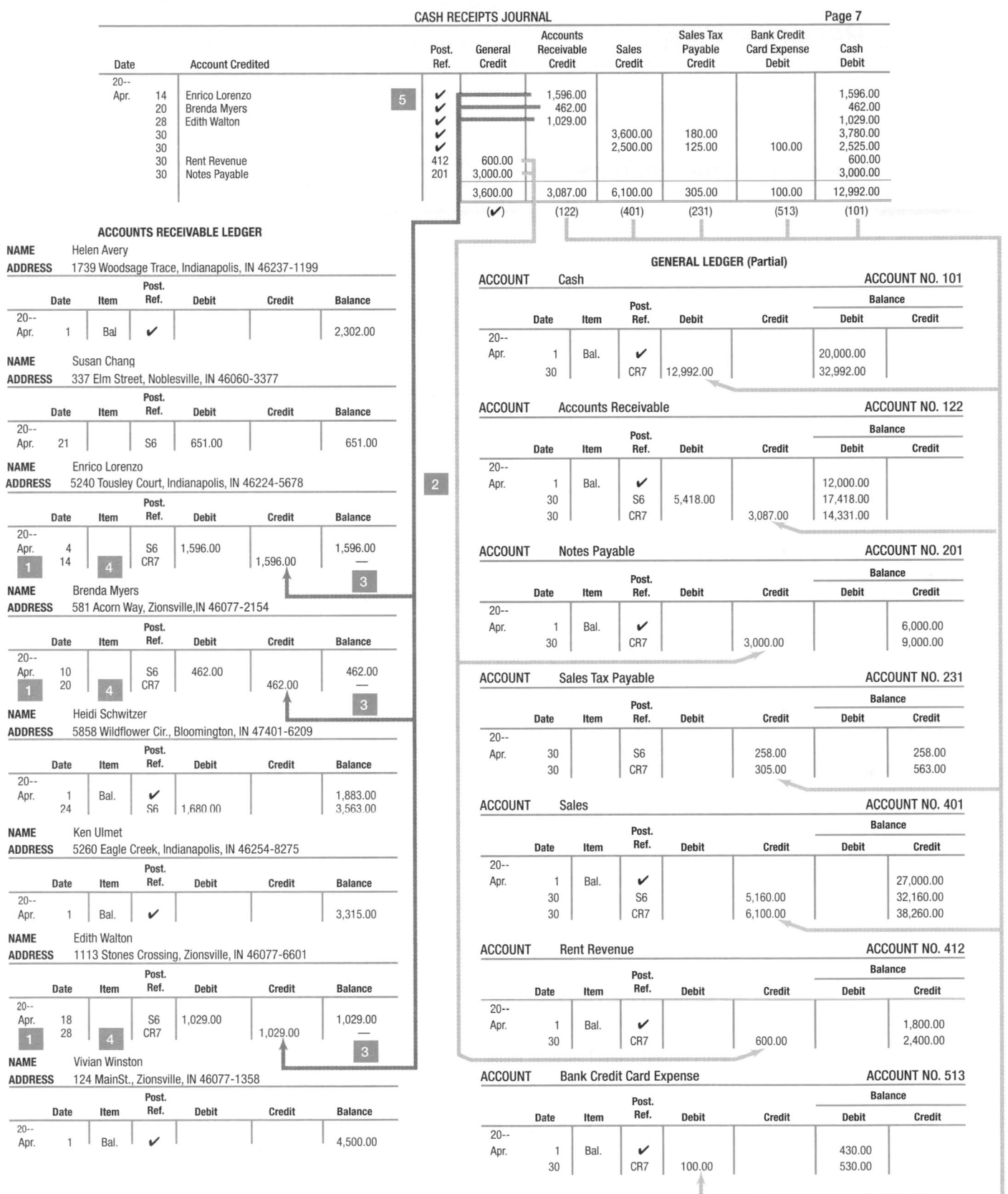

CASH RECEIPTS JOURNAL — Page 7

Date		Account Credited	Post. Ref.	General Credit	Accounts Receivable Credit	Sales Credit	Sales Tax Payable Credit	Bank Credit Card Expense Debit	Cash Debit
20--									
Apr.	14	Enrico Lorenzo	✔		1,596.00				1,596.00
	20	Brenda Myers	✔		462.00				462.00
	28	Edith Walton	✔		1,029.00				1,029.00
	30		✔			3,600.00	180.00		3,780.00
	30		✔			2,500.00	125.00	100.00	2,525.00
	30	Rent Revenue	412	600.00					600.00
	30	Notes Payable	201	3,000.00					3,000.00
				3,600.00	3,087.00	6,100.00	305.00	100.00	12,992.00
				(✔)	(122)	(401)	(231)	(513)	(101)

ACCOUNTS RECEIVABLE LEDGER

NAME Helen Avery
ADDRESS 1739 Woodsage Trace, Indianapolis, IN 46237-1199

Date		Item	Post. Ref.	Debit	Credit	Balance
20--						
Apr.	1	Bal	✔			2,302.00

NAME Susan Chang
ADDRESS 337 Elm Street, Noblesville, IN 46060-3377

Date		Item	Post. Ref.	Debit	Credit	Balance
20--						
Apr.	21		S6	651.00		651.00

NAME Enrico Lorenzo
ADDRESS 5240 Tousley Court, Indianapolis, IN 46224-5678

Date		Item	Post. Ref.	Debit	Credit	Balance
20--						
Apr.	4		S6	1,596.00		1,596.00
	14		CR7		1,596.00	—

NAME Brenda Myers
ADDRESS 581 Acorn Way, Zionsville,IN 46077-2154

Date		Item	Post. Ref.	Debit	Credit	Balance
20--						
Apr.	10		S6	462.00		462.00
	20		CR7		462.00	—

NAME Heidi Schwitzer
ADDRESS 5858 Wildflower Cir., Bloomington, IN 47401-6209

Date		Item	Post. Ref.	Debit	Credit	Balance
20--						
Apr.	1	Bal.	✔			1,883.00
	24		S6	1,680.00		3,563.00

NAME Ken Ulmet
ADDRESS 5260 Eagle Creek, Indianapolis, IN 46254-8275

Date		Item	Post. Ref.	Debit	Credit	Balance
20--						
Apr.	1	Bal.	✔			3,315.00

NAME Edith Walton
ADDRESS 1113 Stones Crossing, Zionsville, IN 46077-6601

Date		Item	Post. Ref.	Debit	Credit	Balance
20--						
Apr.	18		S6	1,029.00		1,029.00
	28		CR7		1,029.00	—

NAME Vivian Winston
ADDRESS 124 MainSt., Zionsville, IN 46077-1358

Date		Item	Post. Ref.	Debit	Credit	Balance
20--						
Apr.	1	Bal.	✔			4,500.00

GENERAL LEDGER (Partial)

ACCOUNT Cash — ACCOUNT NO. 101

Date		Item	Post. Ref.	Debit	Credit	Balance Debit	Balance Credit
20--							
Apr.	1	Bal.	✔			20,000.00	
	30		CR7	12,992.00		32,992.00	

ACCOUNT Accounts Receivable — ACCOUNT NO. 122

Date		Item	Post. Ref.	Debit	Credit	Balance Debit	Balance Credit
20--							
Apr.	1	Bal.	✔			12,000.00	
	30		S6	5,418.00		17,418.00	
	30		CR7		3,087.00	14,331.00	

ACCOUNT Notes Payable — ACCOUNT NO. 201

Date		Item	Post. Ref.	Debit	Credit	Balance Debit	Balance Credit
20--							
Apr.	1	Bal.	✔				6,000.00
	30		CR7		3,000.00		9,000.00

ACCOUNT Sales Tax Payable — ACCOUNT NO. 231

Date		Item	Post. Ref.	Debit	Credit	Balance Debit	Balance Credit
20--							
Apr.	30		S6		258.00		258.00
	30		CR7		305.00		563.00

ACCOUNT Sales — ACCOUNT NO. 401

Date		Item	Post. Ref.	Debit	Credit	Balance Debit	Balance Credit
20--							
Apr.	1	Bal.	✔				27,000.00
	30		S6		5,160.00		32,160.00
	30		CR7		6,100.00		38,260.00

ACCOUNT Rent Revenue — ACCOUNT NO. 412

Date		Item	Post. Ref.	Debit	Credit	Balance Debit	Balance Credit
20--							
Apr.	1	Bal.	✔				1,800.00
	30		CR7		600.00		2,400.00

ACCOUNT Bank Credit Card Expense — ACCOUNT NO. 513

Date		Item	Post. Ref.	Debit	Credit	Balance Debit	Balance Credit
20--							
Apr.	1	Bal.	✔			430.00	
	30		CR7	100.00		530.00	

FIGURE 12-13 Posting from the Purchases Journal to the General Ledger

PURCHASES JOURNAL — Page 8

Date		Invoice No.	From Whom Purchased	Post. Ref.	Purchases Debit/ Accounts Payable Credit	
20--						
Apr.	4	631	Compucraft, Inc.		3,300.00	
	8	927D	Datasoft		2,500.00	
	11	804	EZX Corp.		8,700.00	
	17	611	Printpro Corp.		800.00	
	23	1465	Televax, Inc.		5,300.00	
					20,600.00	1
					(501) (202)	6

3

GENERAL LEDGER (Partial)

ACCOUNT Accounts Payable — ACCOUNT NO. 202

	Date	Item	Post. Ref.	Debit	Credit	Balance Debit	Balance Credit
20--							
Apr.	1	Bal	✔				4,800.00
2	30	5	P8		20,600.00		25,400.00
							4

ACCOUNT Purchases — ACCOUNT NO.501

	Date	Item	Post. Ref.	Debit	Credit	Balance Debit	Balance Credit
20--							
Apr.	1	Bal	✔			17,400.00	
2	30	5	P8	20,600.00		38,000.00	
						4	

In the purchases journal:

STEP 6 Enter the Purchases and Accounts Payable account numbers immediately below the column total.

> If the accounts payable ledger is posted daily and the general ledger is posted at the end of the month, the accounts payable ledger total will equal the general ledger Accounts Payable total only at the end of the month.

To maintain a record of the amount owed to each supplier, an accounts payable ledger is used. Figure 12-14 illustrates the use of the accounts payable ledger. The following steps are used to post from the purchases journal to the accounts payable ledger daily, as shown in Figure 12-14:

In the accounts payable ledger account:

STEP 1 Enter the date of the transaction in the Date column.

STEP 2 Enter the amount of the debit or credit in the Debit or Credit column.

STEP 3 Enter the new balance in the Balance column.

STEP 4 Enter the initial "P" and the journal page number in the Posting Reference column.

In the purchases journal:

STEP 5 Enter a check mark (✓) in the Posting Reference column of the journal for each transaction that is posted.

After the posting of the accounts payable ledger and general ledger is completed, the total of the accounts payable ledger balances should equal the Accounts Payable balance in the general ledger.

FIGURE 12-14 Posting from the Purchases Journal to the Accounts Payable Ledger

PURCHASES JOURNAL Page 8

Date		Invoice No.	From Whom Purchased	Post. Ref.	Purchases Debit/ Accounts Payable Credit
20--					
Apr.	4	631	Compucraft, Inc.	✔	3,300.00
	8	927D	Datasoft	✔	2,500.00
	11	804	EZX Corp.	✔	8,700.00
	17	611	Printpro Corp.	✔	800.00
	23	1465	Televax, Inc.	✔	5,300.00
				5	20,600.00
					(501) (202)

2

ACCOUNTS PAYABLE LEDGER (Partial)

NAME B.B.Small
ADDRESS 2323 High Street, Gurnee, IL 60031-5524

Date		Item	Post. Ref.	Debit	Credit	Balance
20--						
Apr.	1	Bal.	✔			4,800.00

NAME Compucraft, Inc.
ADDRESS 2100 West Main Street, Muncie, IN 47304-8139

	Date		Item	Post. Ref.	Debit	Credit	Balance
	20--						
1	Apr.	4	4	P8		3,300.00	3,300.00
							3

NAME Datasoft
ADDRESS 210 Kirkwood, Bloomington, IN 47408-4346

	Date		Item	Post. Ref.	Debit	Credit	Balance
	20--						
1	Apr.	8	4	P8		2,500.00	2,500.00
							3

NAME EZX Corp.
ADDRESS 2928 Rhodes Ave., Chicago, IL 60658-5036

	Date		Item	Post. Ref.	Debit	Credit	Balance
	20--						
1	Apr.	11	4	P8		8,700.00	8,700.00
							3

NAME Printpro Corp.
ADDRESS 1200 Chambers Pike, Lincolnwood, IL 60648-2417

	Date		Item	Post. Ref.	Debit	Credit	Balance
	20--						
1	Apr.	17	4	P8		800.00	800.00
							3

NAME Televax, Inc.
ADDRESS 1500 North Walnut Street, Addison, IL 60101-7328

	Date		Item	Post. Ref.	Debit	Credit	Balance
	20--						
1	Apr.	23	4	P8		5,300.00	5,300.00
							3

GENERAL LEDGER (Partial)

ACCOUNT Accounts Payable — ACCOUNT NO. 202

Date		Item	Post. Ref.	Debit	Credit	Balance Debit	Balance Credit
20--							
Apr.	1	Bal.	✔				4,800.00
	30		P8		20,600.00		25,400.00

ACCOUNT Purchases — ACCOUNT NO. 501

Date		Item	Post. Ref.	Debit	Credit	Balance Debit	Balance Credit
20--							
Apr.	1	Bal.	✔			17,400.00	
	30		P8	20,600.00		38,000.00	

U REVU Complete U REVU-3 on **page 468** to test your basic understanding of LO4.

CASH PAYMENTS JOURNAL

LO5 **Describe and use the cash payments journal.**

A **cash payments journal** is a special journal used to record only cash payments transactions. To illustrate its use, we will record the cash payments transactions of Northern Micro. Northern Micro's cash payments journal for the month of April is shown in Figure 12-15. Five types of cash payments transactions are shown as follows:

1. Payment of an expense (April 2)
2. Cash purchase (April 4)
3. Payment of an account payable (April 10 and 24)
4. Payment of a note payable (April 14)
5. Withdrawal by the owner (April 22)

FIGURE 12-15 Northern Micro Cash Payments Journal

CASH PAYMENTS JOURNAL

	DATE		CK. NO.	ACCOUNT DEBITED	POST. REF.	GENERAL DEBIT	ACCOUNTS PAYABLE DEBIT	PURCHASES DEBIT	PURCHASES DISCOUNTS CREDIT	CASH CREDIT	
1	Apr.	2	307	Rent Expense		2400 00				2400 00	1
2		4	308					1400 00		1400 00	2
3		10	309	B. B. Small			4800 00			4800 00	3
4		14	310	Notes Payable		2000 00				2000 00	4
5		22	311	Gary L. Fishel, Drawing		1600 00				1600 00	5
6		24	312	EZX Corp.			8700 00		87 00	8613 00	6
7						6000 00	13500 00	1400 00	87 00	20813 00	7

LEARNING KEY

Use a cash payments journal to streamline journalizing and posting of cash payments.

Northern Micro's cash payments journal provides separate columns for Accounts Payable Debit, Purchases Debit, Purchases Discounts Credit, and Cash Credit. These are the accounts most frequently affected by Northern Micro's cash payments transactions. In addition, a General Debit column is provided for debits to any other accounts affected by cash payments transactions. For good internal control over cash payments, all payments (except out of petty cash) should be made by check. Therefore, the cash payments journal also includes a Check No. column.

A cash payment is recorded in the cash payments journal by entering the following information:

1. Date
2. Check number
3. Account debited (if applicable)
4. Dollar amounts

The Account Debited column is used for two purposes:

1. To identify the supplier name for any payment on account. This column is used whenever the Accounts Payable Debit column is used.
2. To enter the appropriate account name whenever the General Debit column is used.

   Note that the column is left blank if the entry is for cash purchases.

Posting from the Cash Payments Journal

The cash payments journal is posted to the general ledger in two stages, as illustrated in Figure 12-16. First, on a daily basis, the individual amounts in the General Debit column are posted. Second, at the end of the month, the totals of each of the other amount columns are posted.

To post the General Debit column, on a daily basis, the following steps are used:

In the general ledger account:

STEP 1 Enter the date of the transaction in the Date column.

STEP 2 Enter the amount of the debit or credit in the Debit or Credit column.

STEP 3 Enter the new balance in the Balance columns under Debit or Credit.

STEP 4 Enter the initials "CP" and the journal page number in the Posting Reference column.

In the cash payments journal:

STEP 5 Enter the ledger account number in the Posting Reference column for each account that is posted.

To post the other amount columns, at the end of the month, the following steps are used:

In the cash payments journal:

STEP 6 Total the amount columns, verify that the total of the debit columns equals the total of the credit columns, and rule the columns.

In the general ledger account:

STEP 7 Enter the date in the Date column.

STEP 8 Enter the amount of the debit or credit in the Debit or Credit column.

STEP 9 Enter the new balance in the Balance columns under Debit or Credit.

STEP 10 Enter the initials "CP" and the journal page number in the Posting Reference column.

In the cash payments journal:

STEP 11 Enter the ledger account number immediately below the column totals for each account that is posted.

STEP 12 Enter a check mark (✓) in the Posting Reference column for the cash purchases, and immediately below the General Debit column.

Postings from the cash payments journal to the accounts payable ledger also must be made. These postings are made daily. Posting procedures are as follows, as shown in Figure 12-17:

In the accounts payable ledger account:

STEP 1 Enter the date of the transaction in the Date column.

STEP 2 Enter the amount of the debit or credit in the Debit or Credit column.

STEP 3 Enter the new balance in the Balance column.

STEP 4 Enter the initials "CP" and the journal page number in the Posting Reference column.

In the cash payments journal:

STEP 5 Enter a check mark (✓) in the Posting Reference column of the journal for each transaction that is posted.

FIGURE 12-16 Posting from the Cash Payments Journal to the General Ledger

CASH PAYMENTS JOURNAL Page 12

Date	Check No.	Account Debited		Post. Ref.	General Debit	Accounts Payable Debit	Purchases Debit	Purchases Discounts Credit	Cash Credit	
20--										
Apr. 2	307	Rent Expense	5	521	2,400.00				2,400.00	
4	308		12	✔			1,400.00		1,400.00	
10	309	B. B. Small				4,800.00			4,800.00	
14	310	Notes Payable	5	201	2,000.00				2,000.00	
22	311	Gary L. Fishel, Drawing	5	312	1,600.00				1,600.00	
24	312	EZX Corp.				8,700.00		87.00	8,613.00	
					6,000.00	13,500.00	1,400.00	87.00	20,813.00	6
					(✔)	(202)	(501)	(501.2)	(101)	11

12 8 2

6 Debit total:

	$ 6,000
	13,500
	1,400
Debit total	$ 20,900
	$ 87
	20,813
Credit total	$ 20,900

GENERAL LEDGER (Partial)

ACCOUNT Cash — ACCOUNT NO. 101

Date		Item	Post. Ref.	Debit	Credit	Balance Debit	Balance Credit
20-- Apr.	1	Bal.	✔			20,000.00	
	30		CR7	12,992.00		32,992.00	
7	30	10	CP12		20,813.00	12,179.00	9

ACCOUNT Notes Payable — ACCOUNT NO. 201

Date		Item	Post. Ref.	Debit	Credit	Balance Debit	Balance Credit
20-- Apr.	1	Bal.	✔				6,000.00
1	14	4	CP12	2,000.00			4,000.00 3

ACCOUNT Accounts Payable — ACCOUNT NO. 202

Date		Item	Post. Ref.	Debit	Credit	Balance Debit	Balance Credit
20-- Apr.	1	Bal.	✔				4,800.00
	30		P8		20,600.00		25,400.00
7	30	10	CP12	13,500.00			11,900.00 9

ACCOUNT Gary L. Fishel, Drawing — ACCOUNT NO. 312

Date		Item	Post. Ref.	Debit	Credit	Balance Debit	Balance Credit
20-- Apr.	1	Bal.	✔			4,500.00	
1	22	4	CP12	1,600.00		6,100.00	3

ACCOUNT Purchases — ACCOUNT NO. 501

Date		Item	Post. Ref.	Debit	Credit	Balance Debit	Balance Credit
20-- Apr.	1	Bal.	✔			17,400.00	
	30		P8	20,600.00		38,000.00	
7	30	10	CP12	1,400.00		39,400.00	9

ACCOUNT Purchases Discounts — ACCOUNT NO. 501.2

Date		Item	Post. Ref.	Debit	Credit	Balance Debit	Balance Credit
20-- Apr.	1	Bal.	✔				330.00
7	30	10	CP12		87.00		417.00 9

ACCOUNT Rent Expense — ACCOUNT NO. 521

Date		Item	Post. Ref.	Debit	Credit	Balance Debit	Balance Credit
20-- Apr.	1	Bal.	✔			6,600.00	
1	2	4	CP12	2,400.00		9,000.00	3

FIGURE 12-17 Posting from the Cash Payments Journal to the Accounts Payable Ledger

CASH PAYMENTS JOURNAL Page 12

Date		Check No.	Account Debited	Post. Ref.	General Debit	Accounts Payable Debit	Purchases Debit	Purchases Discounts Credit	Cash Credit
20--									
Apr.	2	307	Rent Expense	521	2,400.00				2,400.00
	4	308		✔			1,400.00		1,400.00
	10	309	B. B. Small	✔		4,800.00			4,800.00
	14	310	Notes Payable	201	2,000.00				2,000.00
	22	311	Gary L.Fishel, Drawing	312	1,600.00				1,600.00
	24	312	EZX Corp.	✔		8,700.00		87.00	8,613.00
					6,000.00	13,500.00	1,400.00	87.00	20,813.00
					(✔)	(202)	(501)	(501.2)	(101)

ACCOUNTS PAYABLE LEDGER (Partial)

NAME B. B. Small
ADDRESS 2323 High Street, Gurnee, IL 60031-5524

Date		Item	Post. Ref.	Debit	Credit	Balance
20--						
Apr.	1	Bal.	✔			4,800.00
	10		CP12	4,800.00		—

NAME Compucraft, Inc.
ADDRESS 2100 West Main Street, Muncie, IN 47304-8139

Date		Item	Post. Ref.	Debit	Credit	Balance
20--						
Apr.	4		P8		3,300.00	3,300.00

NAME Datasoft
ADDRESS 210 Kirkwood, Bloomington, IN 47408-4346

Date		Item	Post. Ref.	Debit	Credit	Balance
20--						
Apr.	8		P8		2,500.00	2,500.00

NAME EZX Corp.
ADDRESS 2928 Rhodes Ave., Chicago, IL 60658-5036

Date		Item	Post. Ref.	Debit	Credit	Balance
20--						
Apr.	11		P8		8,700.00	8,700.00
	24		CP12	8,700.00		—

NAME Printpro Corp.
ADDRESS 1200 Chambers Pike, Lincolnwood, IL 60648-2417

Date		Item	Post. Ref.	Debit	Credit	Balance
20--						
Apr.	17		P8		800.00	800.00

NAME Televax, Inc.
ADDRESS 1500 North Walnut Street, Addison, IL 60101-7328

Date		Item	Post. Ref.	Debit	Credit	Balance
20--						
Apr.	23		P8		5,300.00	5,300.00

GENERAL LEDGER (Partial)

ACCOUNT Cash ACCOUNT NO. 101

Date		Item	Post. Ref.	Debit	Credit	Balance Debit	Balance Credit
20--							
Apr.	1	Bal.	✔			20,000.00	
	30		CR7	12,992.00		32,992.00	
	30		CP12		20,813.00	12,179.00	

ACCOUNT Notes Payable ACCOUNT NO. 201

Date		Item	Post. Ref.	Debit	Credit	Balance Debit	Balance Credit
20--							
Apr.	1	Bal.	✔				6,000.00
	14		CP12	2,000.00			4,000.00

ACCOUNT Accounts Payable ACCOUNT NO. 202

Date		Item	Post. Ref.	Debit	Credit	Balance Debit	Balance Credit
20--							
Apr.	1	Bal.	✔				4,800.00
	30		P8		20,600.00		25,400.00
	30		CP12	13,500.00			11,900.00

ACCOUNT Gary L. Fishel, Drawing ACCOUNT NO. 312

Date		Item	Post. Ref.	Debit	Credit	Balance Debit	Balance Credit
20--							
Apr.	1	Bal.	✔			4,500.00	
	22		CP12	1,600.00		6,100.00	

ACCOUNT Purchases ACCOUNT NO. 501

Date		Item	Post. Ref.	Debit	Credit	Balance Debit	Balance Credit
20--							
Apr.	1	Bal.	✔			17,400.00	
	30		P8	20,600.00		38,000.00	
	30		CP12	1,400.00		39,400.00	

ACCOUNT Purchases Discounts ACCOUNT NO. 501.2

Date		Item	Post. Ref.	Debit	Credit	Balance Debit	Balance Credit
20--							
Apr.	1	Bal.	✔				330.00
	30		CP12		87.00		417.00

ACCOUNT Rent Expense ACCOUNT NO. 521

Date		Item	Post. Ref.	Debit	Credit	Balance Debit	Balance Credit
20--							
Apr.	1	Bal.	✔			6,600.00	
	2		CP12	2,400.00		9,000.00	

U REVU Complete U REVU-4 on **page 468** to test your basic understanding of LO5.

LEARNING OBJECTIVES Key Points to Remember

LEARNING OBJECTIVES	Key Points to Remember
LO1 Describe, explain the purpose of, and identify transactions recorded in special journals.	A special journal is a journal designed for recording only certain kinds of transactions. The primary purpose of using special journals is to save time journalizing and posting transactions.
LO2 Describe and use the sales journal.	A sales journal is a special journal for recording sales of merchandise on account. A sale is recorded by entering the following: 1. Date 2. Sale number 3. Customer (to whom sold) 4. Dollar amounts To post from the sales journal to the general ledger, use the following steps: **In the sales journal:** STEP 1 Total the amount columns, verify that the total of the debit column equals the total of the credit columns, and rule the columns. **In the general ledger account:** STEP 2 Enter the date of the transaction in the Date column. STEP 3 Enter the amount of the debit or credit in the Debit or Credit column. STEP 4 Enter the new balance in the Balance columns under Debit or Credit. STEP 5 Enter the initial "S" and the journal page number in the Posting Reference column. **In the sales journal:** STEP 6 Enter the ledger account number immediately below the column totals for each account that is posted. To post from the sales journal to the accounts receivable ledger: **In the accounts receivable ledger account:** STEP 1 Enter the date of the transaction in the Date column. STEP 2 Enter the amount of the debit or credit in the Debit or Credit column. STEP 3 Enter the new balance in the Balance column. STEP 4 Enter the initial "S" and the journal page number in the Posting Reference column. **In the sales journal:** STEP 5 Enter a check mark (✓) in the Posting Reference column of the journal for each transaction that is posted.
LO3 Describe and use the cash receipts journal.	A cash receipts journal is a special journal for recording cash receipts. A cash receipt is recorded by entering the following: 1. Date 2. Account credited (if applicable) 3. Dollar amounts

(continued)

LEARNING OBJECTIVES Key Points to Remember

LO3 (continued)

To post from the cash receipts journal to the general ledger:

To post the General Credit column, on a daily basis, use the following steps:

In the general ledger account:

STEP 1 Enter the date of the transaction in the Date column.

STEP 2 Enter the amount of the debit or credit in the Debit or Credit column.

STEP 3 Enter the new balance in the Balance columns under Debit or Credit.

STEP 4 Enter the initials "CR" and the journal page number in the Posting Reference column.

In the cash receipts journal:

STEP 5 Enter the ledger account number in the Posting Reference column for each account that is posted.

To post the other amount columns, at the end of the month, use the following steps:

In the cash receipts journal:

STEP 6 Total the amount columns, verify that the total of the debit columns equals the total of the credit columns, and rule the columns.

In the general ledger account:

STEP 7 Enter the date in the Date column.

STEP 8 Enter the amount of the debit or credit in the Debit or Credit column.

STEP 9 Enter the new balance in the Balance columns under Debit or Credit.

STEP 10 Enter the initials "CR" and the journal page number in the Posting Reference column.

In the cash receipts journal:

STEP 11 Enter the ledger account number immediately below the column totals for each account that is posted.

STEP 12 Enter a check mark (✓) in the Posting Reference column for the cash sales and bank credit card sales, and immediately below the General Credit column.

To post from the cash receipts journal to the accounts receivable ledger, use the following steps:

In the accounts receivable ledger account:

STEP 1 Enter the date of the transaction in the Date column.

STEP 2 Enter the amount of the debit or credit in the Debit or Credit column.

STEP 3 Enter the new balance in the Balance column.

STEP 4 Enter the initials "CR" and the journal page number in the Posting Reference column.

(continued)

LEARNING OBJECTIVES	Key Points to Remember
LO3 (concluded)	**In the cash receipts journal:** STEP 5 Enter a check mark (✓) in the Posting Reference column of the journal for each transaction that is posted.
LO4 Describe and use the purchases journal.	A purchases journal is a special journal for recording purchases of merchandise on account. A purchase is recorded by entering the following: 1. Date 2. Invoice number 3. Supplier (from whom purchased) 4. Dollar amount To post from the purchases journal to the general ledger, use the following steps: **In the purchases journal:** STEP 1 Total and rule the amount column. **In the general ledger account:** STEP 2 Enter the date in the Date column. STEP 3 Enter the amount of the debit or credit in the Debit or Credit column. STEP 4 Enter the new balance in the Balance columns under Debit or Credit. STEP 5 Enter the initial "P" and the journal page number in the Posting Reference column. **In the purchases journal:** STEP 6 Enter the Purchases and Accounts Payable account numbers immediately below the column total. To post from the purchases journal to the accounts payable ledger, use the following steps: **In the accounts payable ledger account:** STEP 1 Enter the date of the transaction in the Date column. STEP 2 Enter the amount of the debit or credit in the Debit or Credit column. STEP 3 Enter the new balance in the Balance column. STEP 4 Enter the initial "P" and the journal page number in the Posting Reference column. **In the purchases journal:** STEP 5 Enter a check mark (✓) in the Posting Reference column of the journal for each transaction that is posted.
LO5 Describe and use the cash payments journal.	A cash payments journal is a special journal for recording cash payments. A cash payment is recorded by entering the following: 1. Date 2. Check number 3. Account debited (if applicable) 4. Dollar amounts

(continued)

LEARNING OBJECTIVES Key Points to Remember

LO5 (concluded)

To post from the cash payments journal to the general ledger:

To post the General Debit column, on a daily basis, use the following steps:

In the general ledger account:

STEP 1 Enter the date of the transaction in the Date column.

STEP 2 Enter the amount of the debit or credit in the Debit or Credit column.

STEP 3 Enter the new balance in the Balance columns under Debit or Credit.

STEP 4 Enter the initials "CP" and the journal page number in the Posting Reference column.

In the cash payments journal:

STEP 5 Enter the ledger account number in the Posting Reference column for each account that is posted.

To post the other amount columns, at the end of the month, use the following steps:

In the cash payments journal:

STEP 6 Total the amount columns, verify that the total of the debit columns equals the total of the credit columns, and rule the columns.

In the general ledger account:

STEP 7 Enter the date in the Date column.

STEP 8 Enter the amount of the debit or credit in the Debit or Credit column.

STEP 9 Enter the new balance in the Balance columns under Debit or Credit.

STEP 10 Enter the initials "CP" and the journal page number in the Posting Reference column.

In the cash payments journal:

STEP 11 Enter the ledger account number immediately below the column totals for each account that is posted.

STEP 12 Enter a check mark (✓) in the Posting Reference column for the cash purchases, and immediately below the General Debit column.

To post from the cash payments journal to the accounts payable ledger, use the following steps:

In the accounts payable ledger account:

STEP 1 Enter the date of the transaction in the Date column.

STEP 2 Enter the amount of the debit or credit in the Debit or Credit column.

STEP 3 Enter the new balance in the Balance column.

STEP 4 Enter the initials "CP" and the journal page number in the Posting Reference column.

In the cash payments journal:

STEP 5 Enter a check mark (✓) in the Posting Reference column of the journal for each transaction that is posted.

DEMONSTRATION PROBLEM

During the month of May 20--, David's Specialty Shop engaged in the following transactions:

May	1	Sold merchandise on account to Molly Mac, $2,000, plus tax of $100. Sale No. 533.
	2	Issued Check No. 750 to Kari Co. in partial payment of May 1 balance, $800, less 2% discount.
	3	Purchased merchandise on account from Scanlan Wholesalers, $2,000. Invoice No. 621, dated May 3, terms 2/10, n/30.
	4	Purchased merchandise on account from Simpson Enterprises, $1,500. Invoice No. 767, dated May 4, terms 2/15, n/30.
	4	Issued Check No. 751 in payment of telephone expense for the month of April, $200.
	8	Sold merchandise for cash, $3,600, plus tax of $180.
	9	Received payment from Cody Slaton in full settlement of account, $2,500.
	10	Issued Check No. 752 to Scanlan Wholesalers in payment of May 1 balance of $1,200.
	12	Sold merchandise on account to Cody Slaton, $3,000, plus tax of $150. Sale No. 534.
	12	Received payment from Kori Reynolds on account, $2,100.
	13	Issued Check No. 753 to Simpson Enterprises in payment of May 4 purchase. Invoice No. 767, less 2% discount.
	13	Cody Slaton returned merchandise for a credit, $1,000, plus sales tax of $50.
	17	Returned merchandise to Johnson Essentials for credit, $500.
	22	Received payment from Natalie Gabbert on account, $1,555.
	27	Sold merchandise on account to Natalie Gabbert, $2,000, plus tax of $100. Sale No. 535.
	29	Issued Check No. 754 in payment of wages (Wages Expense) for the four-week period ending May 30, $1,100.

Selected account balances as of May 1 were as follows:

Account	Account No.	Debit	Credit
Cash	101	$10,050.00	
Accounts Receivable	122	6,900.00	
Accounts Payable	202		$4,550.00

David's also had the following subsidiary ledger balances as of May 1:

Accounts Receivable:

Customer	Accounts Receivable Balance
Natalie Gabbert 12 Jude Lane Hartford, CT 06117	$1,821.00
Molly Mac 52 Juniper Road Hartford, CT 06118	279.00

Kori Reynolds
700 Hobbes Dr.
Avon, CT 06108 $2,300.00

Cody Slaton
5200 Hamilton Ave.
Hartford, CT 06111 2,500.00

Accounts Payable:

Vendor	**Accounts Payable Balance**
Johnson Essentials 34 Harry Ave. East Hartford, CT 05234	$2,350.00
Kari Co. 1009 Drake Rd. Farmington, CT 06082	1,000.00
Scanlan Wholesalers 43 Lucky Lane Bristol, CT 06007	1,200.00
Simpson Enterprises 888 Anders Street Newington, CT 06789	—

REQUIRED

1. Record the transactions in the sales journal, cash receipts journal, purchases journal, cash payments journal, and general journal. Total, verify, and rule the columns where appropriate at the end of the month.
2. Post from the journals to the general ledger, accounts receivable ledger, and accounts payable ledger accounts. Use account numbers as shown in the chapter.

Solution 1.

SALES JOURNAL PAGE 7

	DATE		SALE NO.	TO WHOM SOLD	POST. REF.	ACCOUNTS RECEIVABLE DEBIT	SALES CREDIT	SALES TAX PAYABLE CREDIT	
1	20-- May	1	533	Molly Mac	✔	2,100.00	2,000.00	100.00	1
2		12	534	Cody Slaton	✔	3,150.00	3,000.00	150.00	2
3		27	535	Natalie Gabbert	✔	2,100.00	2,000.00	100.00	3
4						7,350.00	7,000.00	350.00	4
5						(122)	(401)	(231)	5

PURCHASES JOURNAL PAGE 6

	DATE		INVOICE NO.	FROM WHOM PURCHASED	POST. REF.	PURCHASES DEBIT/ACCOUNTS PAYABLE CREDIT	
1	20-- May	3	621	Scanlan Wholesalers	✔	2,000.00	1
2		4	767	Simpson Enterprises	✔	1,500.00	2
3						3,500.00	3
4						(501) (202)	4

(continued)

GENERAL JOURNAL PAGE 5

	DATE		DESCRIPTION	POST. REF.	DEBIT	CREDIT	
1	20-- May	13	Sales Returns and Allowances	401.1	1 0 0 0 00		1
2			Sales Tax Payable	231	5 0 00		2
3			Accounts Receivable/Cody Slaton	122/✔		1 0 5 0 00	3
4			Accepted returned merchandise				4
5							5
6		17	Accounts Payable/Johnson Essentials	202/✔	5 0 0 00		6
7			Purchases Returns and Allowances	501.1		5 0 0 00	7
8			Returned merchandise				8
9							9

CASH PAYMENTS JOURNAL PAGE 11

	DATE		CK. NO.	ACCOUNT DEBITED	POST. REF.	GENERAL DEBIT	ACCOUNTS PAYABLE DEBIT	PURCHASES DEBIT	PURCHASES DISCOUNTS CREDIT	CASH CREDIT	
1	20-- May	2	750	Kari Co.	✔		8 0 0 00		1 6 00	7 8 4 00	1
2		4	751	Telephone Expense	525	2 0 0 00				2 0 0 00	2
3		10	752	Scanlan Wholesalers	✔		1 2 0 0 00			1 2 0 0 00	3
4		13	753	Simpson Enterprises	✔		1 5 0 0 00		3 0 00	1 4 7 0 00	4
5		29	754	Wages Expense	511	1 1 0 0 00				1 1 0 0 00	5
6						1 3 0 0 00	3 5 0 0 00		4 6 00	4 7 5 4 00	6
7						(✓)	(2 0 2)		(5 0 1 .2)	(1 0 1)	7

CASH RECEIPTS JOURNAL PAGE 10

	DATE		ACCOUNT CREDITED	POST. REF.	GENERAL CREDIT	ACCOUNTS RECEIVABLE CREDIT	SALES CREDIT	SALES TAX PAYABLE CREDIT	CASH DEBIT	
1	20-- May	8					3 6 0 0 00	1 8 0 00	3 7 8 0 00	1
2		9	C. Slaton	✔		2 5 0 0 00			2 5 0 0 00	2
3		12	K. Reynolds	✔		2 1 0 0 00			2 1 0 0 00	3
4		22	N. Gabbert	✔		1 5 5 5 00			1 5 5 5 00	4
5						6 1 5 5 00	3 6 0 0 00	1 8 0 00	9 9 3 5 00	5
6						(1 2 2)	(4 0 1)	(2 3 1)	(1 0 1)	6

2. GENERAL LEDGER

ACCOUNT: Cash ACCOUNT NO. 101

DATE		ITEM	POST. REF.	DEBIT	CREDIT	BALANCE DEBIT	BALANCE CREDIT
20-- May	1	Balance	✔			10 0 5 0 00	
	31		CR10	9 9 3 5 00		19 9 8 5 00	
	31		CP11		4 7 5 4 00	15 2 3 1 00	

ACCOUNT: Accounts Receivable — ACCOUNT NO. 122

DATE		ITEM	POST. REF.	DEBIT	CREDIT	BALANCE DEBIT	BALANCE CREDIT
20-- May	1	Balance	✔			6,900.00	
	13		J5		1,050.00	5,850.00	
	31		S7	7,350.00		13,200.00	
	31		CR10		6,155.00	7,045.00	

ACCOUNT: Accounts Payable — ACCOUNT NO. 202

DATE		ITEM	POST. REF.	DEBIT	CREDIT	BALANCE DEBIT	BALANCE CREDIT
20-- May	1	Balance	✔				4,550.00
	17		J5	500.00			4,050.00
	31		P6		3,500.00		7,550.00
	31		CP11	3,500.00			4,050.00

ACCOUNT: Sales Tax Payable — ACCOUNT NO. 231

DATE		ITEM	POST. REF.	DEBIT	CREDIT	BALANCE DEBIT	BALANCE CREDIT
20-- May	13		J5	50.00		50.00	
	31		S7		350.00		300.00
	31		CR10		180.00		480.00

ACCOUNT: Sales — ACCOUNT NO. 401

DATE		ITEM	POST. REF.	DEBIT	CREDIT	BALANCE DEBIT	BALANCE CREDIT
20-- May	31		S7		7,000.00		7,000.00
	31		CR10		3,600.00		10,600.00

ACCOUNT: Sales Returns and Allowances — ACCOUNT NO. 401.1

DATE		ITEM	POST. REF.	DEBIT	CREDIT	BALANCE DEBIT	BALANCE CREDIT
20-- May	13		J5	1,000.00		1,000.00	

ACCOUNT: Purchases — ACCOUNT NO. 501

DATE		ITEM	POST. REF.	DEBIT	CREDIT	BALANCE DEBIT	BALANCE CREDIT
20-- May	31		P6	3,500.00		3,500.00	

ACCOUNT: Purchases Returns and Allowances — ACCOUNT NO. 501.1

DATE		ITEM	POST. REF.	DEBIT	CREDIT	BALANCE DEBIT	BALANCE CREDIT
20-- May	17		J5		500.00		500.00

ACCOUNT: Purchases Discounts — ACCOUNT NO. 501.2

DATE		ITEM	POST. REF.	DEBIT	CREDIT	BALANCE DEBIT	BALANCE CREDIT
20-- May	31		CP11		46.00		46.00

(continued)

ACCOUNT: Wages Expense **ACCOUNT NO.** 511

DATE		ITEM	POST. REF.	DEBIT	CREDIT	BALANCE DEBIT	BALANCE CREDIT
20-- May	29		CP11	1100.00		1100.00	

ACCOUNT: Telephone Expense **ACCOUNT NO.** 525

DATE		ITEM	POST. REF.	DEBIT	CREDIT	BALANCE DEBIT	BALANCE CREDIT
20-- May	4		CP11	200.00		200.00	

ACCOUNTS RECEIVABLE LEDGER

NAME: Natalie Gabbert
ADDRESS: 12 Jude Lane, Hartford, CT 06117

DATE		ITEM	POST. REF.	DEBIT	CREDIT	BALANCE
20-- May	1	Balance	✔			1821.00
	22		CR10		1555.00	266.00
	27		S7	2100.00		2366.00

NAME: Molly Mac
ADDRESS: 52 Juniper Road, Hartford, CT 06118

DATE		ITEM	POST. REF.	DEBIT	CREDIT	BALANCE
20-- May	1	Balance	✔			279.00
	1		S7	2100.00		2379.00

NAME: Kori Reynolds
ADDRESS: 700 Hobbes Dr., Avon, CT 06108

DATE		ITEM	POST. REF.	DEBIT	CREDIT	BALANCE
20-- May	1	Balance	✔			2300.00
	12		CR10		2100.00	200.00

NAME: Cody Slaton
ADDRESS: 5200 Hamilton Ave., Hartford, CT 06111

DATE		ITEM	POST. REF.	DEBIT	CREDIT	BALANCE
20-- May	1	Balance	✔			2500.00
	9		CR10		2500.00	—
	12		S7	3150.00		3150.00
	13		J5		1050.00	2100.00

ACCOUNTS PAYABLE LEDGER

NAME: Johnson Essentials
ADDRESS: 34 Harry Ave., East Hartford, CT 05234

DATE		ITEM	POST. REF.	DEBIT	CREDIT	BALANCE
20-- May	1	Balance	✔			2350 00
	17		J5	500 00		1850 00

NAME: Kari Co.
ADDRESS: 1009 Drake Rd., Farmington, CT 06082

DATE		ITEM	POST. REF.	DEBIT	CREDIT	BALANCE
20-- May	1	Balance	✔			1000 00
	2		CP11	800 00		200 00

NAME: Scanlan Wholesalers
ADDRESS: 43 Lucky Lane, Bristol, CT 06007

DATE		ITEM	POST. REF.	DEBIT	CREDIT	BALANCE
20-- May	1	Balance	✔			1200 00
	3		P6		2000 00	3200 00
	10		CP11	1200 00		2000 00

NAME: Simpson Enterprises
ADDRESS: 888 Anders Street, Newington, CT 06789

DATE		ITEM	POST. REF.	DEBIT	CREDIT	BALANCE
20-- May	1	Balance	✔			—
	4		P6		1500 00	1500 00
	13		CP11	1500 00		—

KEY TERMS

cash payments journal (454) A special journal used to record only cash payments transactions.

cash receipts journal (445) A special journal used to record only cash receipts transactions.

purchases journal (450) A special journal used to record only purchases of merchandise on account.

sales journal (441) A special journal used to record only sales of merchandise on account.

special journal (440) A journal designed for recording only certain kinds of transactions.

SELF-STUDY QUESTIONS AND EXERCISES

True/False Questions

1. LO1 The types of special journals a business uses should depend on the types of transactions it has most frequently.
2. LO1 If a business uses special journals, it generally will not need a general journal.
3. LO2 All sales, for cash or on credit, are recorded in the sales journal.
4. LO3 A cash receipts journal is used to record all cash receipts transactions.
5. LO4 Purchases returns and allowances are recorded in the general journal.

Multiple Choice Questions

1. LO2 The first step in posting the sales journal to the general ledger is to
   (a) total and verify the equality of the amount columns.
   (b) enter the date in the Date column of the ledger account.
   (c) enter the new balance in the Balance columns of the ledger account.
   (d) enter the ledger account number below the column totals in the journal.
2. LO3 In the cash receipts journal, each amount in the General Credit column is posted
   (a) daily.
   (b) weekly.
   (c) at the end of the month.
   (d) at the end of the year.
3. LO4 The journal that should be used to record the return of merchandise for credit is the
   (a) purchases journal.
   (b) cash payments journal.
   (c) general journal.
   (d) accounts payable journal.
4. LO4 A purchases journal is used to record all
   (a) purchases.
   (b) cash purchases.
   (c) purchases of merchandise on account.
   (d) purchases returns and allowances.
5. LO5 In the cash payments journal, each amount in the General Debit column is posted
   (a) daily.
   (b) weekly.
   (c) at the end of the month.
   (d) at the end of the year.

U REVU Exercises

1. LO2 Enter the following transaction in a sales journal like the one illustrated in the chapter:

   June 1 Made Sale No. 214 on account to Erin Lucas, $840, plus $42 sales tax.
2. LO3 Enter the following transactions in a cash receipts journal like the one illustrated in the chapter:

   June 7 Received cash on account from Erin Lucas, $882.
   30 Made cash sales for the month of $2,150, plus sales tax of $107.50.
   30 Received cash for rent revenue, $750.
3. LO4 Enter the following transaction in a purchases journal like the one illustrated in the chapter:

   Apr. 6 Purchased merchandise from Clever, $1,680. Invoice No. 131, dated April 6, terms n/30.
4. LO5 Enter the following transactions in a cash payments journal like the one illustrated in the chapter:

   Aug. 2 Issued Check No. 193 in payment of August rent (Rent Expense), $2,200.

6 Issued Check No. 194 to Mason Hardware in payment of merchandise purchased on account, \$1,700, less 2% discount. The check was written for \$1,666.
10 Issued Check No. 195 to Augie's Wholesale for cash purchase of merchandise, \$2,730.

The answers to the Self-Study Questions and Exercises are at the end of the chapter (page 485).

APPLYING YOUR KNOWLEDGE

REVIEW QUESTIONS

LO1 1. What is the primary purpose of using special journals?

LO2 2. List four items of information about each sale entered in the sales journal.

LO2 3. What steps are followed in posting from the sales journal to the general ledger?

LO2 4. What steps are followed in posting from the sales journal to the accounts receivable ledger?

LO3 5. List three items of information about each cash receipt entered in the cash receipts journal.

LO3 6. What steps are followed in posting from the cash receipts journal to the general ledger?

LO3 7. What steps are followed in posting from the cash receipts journal to the accounts receivable ledger?

LO4 8. List four items of information about each purchase entered in the purchases journal.

LO4 9. What steps are followed in posting from the purchases journal to the general ledger?

LO4 10. What steps are followed in posting from the purchases journal to the accounts payable ledger?

LO5 11. List four items of information about each cash payment entered in the cash payments journal.

LO5 12. What steps are followed in posting from the cash payments journal to the general ledger?

LO5 13. What steps are followed in posting from the cash payments journal to the accounts payable ledger?

SERIES A EXERCISES

E 12-1A (LO1)

RECORDING TRANSACTIONS IN THE PROPER JOURNAL Identify the journal (sales, cash receipts, purchases, cash payments, or general) in which each of the following transactions should be recorded:

(a) Sold merchandise on account.
(b) Purchased delivery truck on account for use in the business.

(continued)

(c) Received payment from customer on account.
(d) Purchased merchandise on account.
(e) Issued check in payment of electric bill.
(f) Recorded depreciation on factory building.

E 12-2A (LO2)

✓ May 1:Dr. Accounts Receivable/ J. Adams, $2,120

JOURNALIZING SALES TRANSACTIONS Enter the following transactions in a sales journal. Use a 6% sales tax rate.

May 1 Sold merchandise on account to J. Adams, $2,000, plus sales tax. Sale No 488.

4 Sold merchandise on account to B. Clark, $1,800, plus sales tax. Sale No. 489.

8 Sold merchandise on account to A. Duck, $1,500, plus sales tax. Sale No. 490.

11 Sold merchandise on account to E. Hill, $1,950, plus sales tax. Sale No. 491.

E 12-3A (LO3)

✓ July 6: Cr. Accounts Receivable/ J. Adler, $643

JOURNALIZING CASH RECEIPTS Enter the following transactions in a cash receipts journal:

July 6 James Adler made payment on account, $643.

10 Made cash sales for the week, $2,320.

14 Betty Havel made payment on account, $430.

15 J. L. Borg made payment on account, $117.

17 Made cash sales for the week, $2,237.

E 12-4A (LO4)

✓ May 9: Purchases Dr./Accounts Payable Cr., $2,300

JOURNALIZING PURCHASES TRANSACTIONS Enter the following transactions in a purchases journal like the one below.

May 3 Purchased merchandise from Cintron, $6,500. Invoice No. 321, dated May 1, terms n/30.

9 Purchased merchandise from Mitsui, $2,300. Invoice No. 614, dated May 8, terms 2/10, n/30.

18 Purchased merchandise from Aloha Distributors, $4,200. Invoice No. 180, dated May 15, terms 1/15, n/30.

23 Purchased merchandise from Soto, $6,300. Invoice No. 913, dated May 22, terms 1/10, n/30.

PURCHASES JOURNAL PAGE

DATE	INVOICE NO.	FROM WHOM PURCHASED	POST. REF.	PURCHASES DEBIT/ACCOUNTS PAYABLE CREDIT

E 12-5A (LO5)

✓ Sept. 12: Cash Cr., $6,930

JOURNALIZING CASH PAYMENTS Landmark Industries uses a cash payments journal. Prepare a cash payments journal using the same format and account titles as illustrated in the chapter. Record the following payments for merchandise purchased:

Sept. 5 Issued Check No. 318 to Clinton Corp. for merchandise purchased August 28, $6,000, terms 2/10, n/30. Payment is made within the discount period.

12 Issued Check No. 319 to Mitchell Co. for merchandise purchased September 2, $7,500, terms 1/10, n/30. A credit memo had previously been received from Mitchell Co. for merchandise returned, $500. Payment is made within the discount period after deduction for the return dated September 8.

Sept. 19 Issued Check No. 320 to Expert Systems for merchandise purchased August 19, $4,100, terms n/30.

27 Issued Check No. 321 to Graphic Data for merchandise purchased September 17, $9,000, terms 2/10, n/30. Payment is made within the discount period.

SERIES A PROBLEMS

P 12-6A (LO2)

✓ Total Accounts Receivable Dr.: $16,345.20

SALES JOURNAL J. K. Bijan owns a retail business and made the following sales during the month of August 20--. There is a 6% sales tax on all sales.

Aug. 1 Sale No. 213 to Jung Manufacturing Co., $1,200, plus sales tax.

3 Sale No. 214 to Hassad Co., $3,600, plus sales tax.

7 Sale No. 215 to Helsinki, Inc., $1,400, plus sales tax. (Open a new account for this customer. Address is 125 Fishers Dr., Noblesville, IN 47870–8867.)

11 Sale No. 216 to Ardis Myler, $1,280, plus sales tax.

18 Sale No. 217 to Hassad Co., $4,330, plus sales tax.

22 Sale No. 218 to Jung Manufacturing Co., $2,000, plus sales tax.

30 Sale No. 219 to Ardis Myler, $1,610, plus sales tax.

REQUIRED

1. Record the transactions in the sales journal. Total and verify the column totals and rule the columns.
2. Post from the sales journal to the general ledger and accounts receivable ledger accounts. Use account numbers as shown in the chapter.

P 12-7A (LO3)

✓ Total Accounts Receivable Cr.: $5,732

CASH RECEIPTS JOURNAL Zebra Imaginarium, a retail business, had the following cash receipts during December 20--. The sales tax is 6%.

Dec. 1 Received payment on account from Michael Anderson, $1,360.

2 Received payment on account from Ansel Manufacturing, $382.

7 Made cash sales for the week, $3,160, plus tax. Bank credit card sales for the week, $1,000, plus tax. Bank credit card fee is 3%.

8 Received payment on account from J. Gorbea, $880.

11 Michael Anderson returned merchandise for a credit, $60, plus tax.

14 Made cash sales for the week, $2,800, plus tax. Bank credit card sales for the week, $800, plus tax. Bank credit card fee is 3%.

20 Received payment on account from Tom Wilson, $1,110.

21 Ansel Manufacturing returned merchandise for a credit, $22, plus tax.

21 Made cash sales for the week, $3,200, plus tax.

24 Received payment on account from Rachel Carson, $2,000.

(continued)

Beginning general ledger account balances were as follows:

Cash	$9,862
Accounts Receivable	9,352

Beginning customer account balances were as follows:

M. Anderson	$2,480
Ansel Manufacturing	982
J. Gorbea	880
R. Carson	3,200
T. Wilson	1,810

REQUIRED

1. Record the transactions in the cash receipts journal. Total and verify column totals and rule the columns. Use the general journal to record sales returns and allowances.
2. Post from the journals to the general ledger and accounts receivable ledger accounts. Use account numbers as shown in the chapter.

P 12-8A (LO2/3)

✓ Total Accounts Receivable Dr.: $12,745.08

KA KLOOSTER & ALLEN

SALES JOURNAL, CASH RECEIPTS JOURNAL, AND GENERAL JOURNAL Owens Distributors is a retail business. The following sales, returns, and cash receipts occurred during March 20--. There is an 8% sales tax. Beginning general ledger account balances were Cash, $9,741.00; and Accounts Receivable, $1,058.25. Beginning customer account balances were Thompson Group, $1,058.25.

Mar. 1	Sold merchandise to Able & Co., $1,800, plus sales tax. Sale No. 33C.
3	Sold merchandise to R. J. Kalas, Inc., $2,240, plus sales tax. Sale No. 33D.
5	Able & Co. returned merchandise from Sale No. 33C for a credit (Credit Memo No. 66), $30, plus sales tax.
7	Made cash sales for the week, $3,160, plus sales tax.
10	Received payment from Able & Co. for Sale No. 33C less Credit Memo No. 66.
11	Sold merchandise to Blevins Bakery, $1,210, plus sales tax. Sale No. 33E.
13	Received payment from R. J. Kalas for Sale No. 33D.
14	Made cash sales for the week, $4,200, plus sales tax.
16	Blevins Bakery returned merchandise from Sale No. 33E for a credit (Credit Memo No. 67), $44, plus sales tax.
18	Sold merchandise to R. J. Kalas, Inc., $2,620, plus sales tax. Sale No. 33F.
20	Received payment from Blevins Bakery for Sale No. 33E less Credit Memo No. 67.
21	Made cash sales for the week, $2,400, plus sales tax.
25	Sold merchandise to Blevins Bakery, $1,915, plus sales tax. Sale No. 33G.
27	Sold merchandise to Thompson Group, $2,016, plus sales tax. Sale No. 33H.
28	Made cash sales for the week, $3,500, plus sales tax.

REQUIRED

1. Record the transactions in the sales journal, cash receipts journal, and general journal. Total, verify, and rule the columns where appropriate at the end of the month.
2. Post from the journals to the general ledger and accounts receivable ledger accounts. Use account numbers as shown in the chapter.

P 12-9A (LO4)

✓ Total Purchases Dr.: $20,790

PURCHASES JOURNAL J. B. Speck, owner of Speck's Galleria, made the following purchases of merchandise on account during the month of September:

Sept. 3 Purchase Invoice No. 415, $2,650, from Smith Distributors.

8 Purchase Invoice No. 132, $3,830, from Michaels Wholesaler.

11 Purchase Invoice No. 614, $3,140, from J. B. Sanders & Co.

18 Purchase Invoice No. 329, $2,250, from Bateman & Jones, Inc.

23 Purchase Invoice No. 867, $4,160, from Smith Distributors.

27 Purchase Invoice No. 744, $1,980, from Anderson Company.

30 Purchase Invoice No. 652, $2,780, from Michaels Wholesaler.

REQUIRED

1. Record the transactions in the purchases journal. Total and rule the journal.
2. Post from the purchases journal to the general ledger and accounts payable ledger accounts. Use account numbers as shown in the chapter.

P 12-10A (LO4)

✓ Helmut's Hair Supply account balance: $4,240

PURCHASES JOURNAL, GENERAL LEDGER, AND ACCOUNTS PAYABLE LEDGER The purchases journal of Kevin's Kettle, a small retail business, is as follows:

PURCHASES JOURNAL PAGE 1

	DATE		INVOICE NO.	FROM WHOM PURCHASED	POST. REF.	PURCHASES DEBIT/ACCOUNTS PAYABLE CREDIT	
	20--						
1	Jan.	2	101	Ruiz Imports		3,000.00	1
2		3	621	Helmut's Hair Supply		2,480.00	2
3		7	195	Viola's Boutique		4,360.00	3
4		12	267	Royal Flush		1,950.00	4
5		18	903	Maria's Melodies		4,700.00	5
6		25	680	Helmut's Hair Supply		1,760.00	6
7						18,250.00	7

REQUIRED

1. Post the total of the purchases journal to the appropriate general ledger accounts. Use account numbers as shown in the chapter.
2. Post the individual purchase amounts to the accounts payable ledger.

P 12-11A (LO5)
✓ Total Cash Cr.: $30,984

CASH PAYMENTS JOURNAL Sam Santiago operates a retail variety store. The books include a cash payments journal and an accounts payable ledger. All cash payments (except petty cash) are entered in the cash payments journal.

Selected account balances on May 1 are as follows:

General Ledger	
Cash	$40,000
Accounts Payable	20,000

Accounts Payable Ledger	
Fantastic Toys	$5,200
Goya Outlet	3,800
Mueller's Distributors	3,600
Van Kooning	7,400

The following are the transactions related to cash payments for the month of May:

May 1 Issued Check No. 426 in payment of May rent (Rent Expense), $2,400.

3 Issued Check No. 427 to Mueller's Distributors in payment of merchandise purchased on account, $3,600, less a 3% discount. Check was written for $3,492.

7 Issued Check No. 428 to Van Kooning in partial payment of merchandise purchased on account, $5,500. A cash discount was not allowed.

12 Issued Check No. 429 to Fantastic Toys for merchandise purchased on account, $5,200, less a 1% discount. Check was written for $5,148.

15 Issued Check No. 430 to City Power and Light (Utilities Expense), $1,720.

18 Issued Check No. 431 to A-1 Warehouse for a cash purchase of merchandise, $4,800.

26 Issued Check No. 432 to Goya Outlet for merchandise purchased on account, $3,800, less a 2% discount. Check was written for $3,724.

30 Issued Check No. 433 to Mercury Transit Company for freight charges on merchandise purchased (Freight-In), $1,200.

31 Issued Check No. 434 to Town Merchants for a cash purchase of merchandise, $3,000.

REQUIRED

1. Enter the transactions in a cash payments journal. Total, rule, and prove the cash payments journal.
2. Post from the cash payments journal to the general ledger and accounts payable ledger. Use general ledger account numbers as shown in the chapter.

P 12-12A (LO4/5)
✓ Total Cash Cr.: $11,170

KA KLOOSTER & ALLEN

PURCHASES JOURNAL, CASH PAYMENTS JOURNAL, AND GENERAL JOURNAL Freddy Flint owns a small retail business called Flint's Fantasy. The cash account has a balance of $20,000 on July 1. The following transactions occurred during July:

July 1 Issued Check No. 414 in payment of July rent, $1,500.

1 Purchased merchandise on account from Tang's Toys, Invoice No. 311, $2,700, terms 2/10, n/30.

July 3 Purchased merchandise on account from Sillas & Company, Invoice No. 812, $3,100, terms 1/10, n/30.

5 Returned merchandise purchased from Tang's Toys, receiving a credit memo on the amount owed, $500.

8 Purchased merchandise on account from Daisy's Dolls, Invoice No. 139, $1,900, terms 2/10, n/30.

11 Issued Check No. 415 to Tang's Toys for merchandise purchased on account, less return of July 5 and less 2% discount.

13 Issued Check No. 416 to Sillas & Company for merchandise purchased on account, less 1% discount.

15 Returned merchandise purchased from Daisy's Dolls, receiving a credit memo on the amount owed, $400.

18 Issued Check No. 417 to Daisy's Dolls for merchandise purchased on account, less return of July 15 and less 2% discount.

25 Purchased merchandise on account from Allied Business, Invoice No. 489, $2,450, terms n/30.

26 Purchased merchandise on account from Tang's Toys, Invoice No. 375, $1,980, terms 2/10, n/30.

29 Purchased merchandise on account from Sillas & Company, Invoice No. 883, $3,460, terms 1/10, n/30.

31 Freddy Flint withdrew cash for personal use, $2,000. Issued Check No. 418.

31 Issued Check No. 419 to Glisan Distributors for a cash purchase of merchandise, $975.

REQUIRED

1. Record the transactions in the purchases journal, cash payments journal, and general journal. Total and rule the purchases and cash payments journals. Prove the cash payments journal.
2. Post from the journals to the general ledger and accounts payable ledger accounts. Use general ledger account numbers as shown in the chapter.

SERIES B EXERCISES

E 12-1B (LO1)

RECORDING TRANSACTIONS IN THE PROPER JOURNAL Identify the journal (sales, cash receipts, purchases, cash payments, or general) in which each of the following transactions should be recorded.

(a) Issued credit memo to customer for merchandise returned.
(b) Sold merchandise for cash.
(c) Purchased merchandise on account.
(d) Issued checks to employees in payment of wages.
(e) Purchased factory supplies on account.
(f) Sold merchandise on account.

E 12-2B (LO2)

✓ Sept. 1: Dr. Accounts Receivable/K. Smith, $1,890

JOURNALIZING SALES TRANSACTIONS Enter the following transactions in a sales journal. Use a 5% sales tax rate.

(continued)

Sept. 1 Sold merchandise on account to K. Smith, $1,800, plus sales tax. Sale No. 228.

3 Sold merchandise on account to J. Arnes, $3,100, plus sales tax. Sale No. 229.

5 Sold merchandise on account to M. Denison, $2,800, plus sales tax. Sale No. 230.

7 Sold merchandise on account to B. Marshall, $1,900, plus sales tax. Sale No. 231.

E 12-3B (LO3)

✓ Nov. 1: Cr. Accounts Receivable/Jean Haghighat, $750

JOURNALIZING CASH RECEIPTS Enter the following transactions in a cash receipts journal:

Nov. 1 Jean Haghighat made payment on account, $750.

12 Marc Antonoff made payment on account, $464.

15 Made cash sales, $3,763.

18 Will Mossein made payment on account, $241.

25 Made cash sales, $2,648.

E 12-4B (LO4)

✓ Jan. 3: Purchases Dr./Accounts Payable Cr., $6,000

JOURNALIZING PURCHASES TRANSACTIONS Enter the following transactions in a purchases journal like the one below.

Jan. 3 Purchased merchandise from Feng, $6,000. Invoice No. 416, dated January 1, terms 2/10, n/30.

12 Purchased merchandise from Miranda, $9,000. Invoice No. 624, dated January 10, terms n/30.

19 Purchased merchandise from J. B. Barba, $6,400. Invoice No. 190, dated January 18, terms 1/10, n/30.

26 Purchased merchandise from Ramirez, $3,700. Invoice No. 923, dated January 25, terms 1/15, n/30.

PURCHASES JOURNAL PAGE

DATE	INVOICE NO.	FROM WHOM PURCHASED	POST. REF.	PURCHASES DEBIT/ACCOUNTS PAYABLE CREDIT

E 12-5B (LO5)

✓ Apr. 19: Cash Cr., $4,950

JOURNALIZING CASH PAYMENTS Sandcastles Northwest uses a cash payments journal. Prepare a cash payments journal using the same format and account titles as illustrated in the chapter. Record the following payments for merchandise purchased:

Apr. 5 Issued Check No. 429 to Standard Industries for merchandise purchased April 3, $8,000, terms 2/10, n/30. Payment is made within the discount period.

19 Issued Check No. 430 to Finest Company for merchandise purchased April 10, $5,300, terms 1/10, n/30. A credit memo had previously been received from Finest Company for merchandise returned, $300. Payment is made within the discount period after deduction for the return dated April 12.

21 Issued Check No. 431 to Funny Follies for merchandise purchased March 21, $3,250, terms n/30.

29 Issued Check No. 432 to Classic Data for merchandise purchased April 20, $7,000, terms 2/10, n/30. Payment is made within the discount period.

SERIES B PROBLEMS

P 12-6B (LO2)
✓ Total Accounts Receivable Dr.: $13,072.50

SALES JOURNAL T. M. Maxwell owns a retail business and made the following sales during the month of July 20--. There is a 5% sales tax on all sales.

July 1	Sale No. 101 to Saga, Inc., $1,200, plus sales tax.
8	Sale No. 102 to Vinnie Ward, $2,100, plus sales tax.
15	Sale No. 103 to Dvorak Manufacturing, $4,300, plus sales tax.
21	Sale No. 104 to Vinnie Ward, $1,800, plus sales tax.
24	Sale No. 105 to Zapata Co., $1,600, plus sales tax. (Open a new account for this customer. Address is 789 N. Stafford Dr., Bloomington, IN 47401–6201.)
29	Sale No. 106 to Saga, Inc., $1,450, plus sales tax.

REQUIRED

1. Record the transactions in the sales journal. Total and verify the column totals and rule the columns.
2. Post the sales journal to the general ledger and accounts receivable ledger accounts. Use account numbers as shown in the chapter.

P 12-7B (LO3)
✓ Total Accounts Receivable Cr.: $3,481

CASH RECEIPTS JOURNAL Color Florists, a retail business, had the following cash receipts during January 20--. The sales tax is 5%.

Jan. 1	Received payment on account from Ray Boyd, $880.
3	Received payment on account from Clint Hassell, $271.
5	Made cash sales for the week, $2,800, plus tax. Bank credit card sales for the week, $1,200, plus tax. Bank credit card fee is 3%.
8	Received payment on account from Jan Sowada, $912.
11	Ray Boyd returned merchandise for a credit, $40, plus tax.
12	Made cash sales for the week, $3,100, plus tax. Bank credit card sales for the week, $1,900, plus tax. Bank credit card fee is 3%.
15	Received payment on account from Robert Zehnle, $1,100.
18	Robert Zehnle returned merchandise for a credit, $31, plus tax.
19	Made cash sales for the week, $2,230, plus tax.
25	Received payment on account from Dazai Manufacturing, $318.

Beginning general ledger account balances were as follows:

Cash	$2,890.75
Accounts Receivable	6,300.00

Beginning customer account balances were as follows:

R. Boyd	$1,400
Dazai Manufacturing	318
C. Hassell	815
J. Sowada	1,481
R. Zehnle	2,286

(continued)

REQUIRED

1. Record the transactions in the cash receipts journal. Total and verify the column totals and rule the columns. Use the general journal to record sales returns and allowances.
2. Post from the journals to the general ledger and accounts receivable ledger accounts. Use account numbers as shown in the chapter.

P 12-8B (LO2/3)

✓ Total Accounts Receivable Dr.: $7,853.80

SALES JOURNAL, CASH RECEIPTS JOURNAL, AND GENERAL JOURNAL Paul Jackson owns a retail business. The following sales, returns, and cash receipts are for April 20--. There is a 7% sales tax.

Apr. 1	Sold merchandise to O. L. Meyers, $2,100, plus sales tax. Sale No. 111.
3	Sold merchandise to Andrew Plaa, $1,000, plus sales tax. Sale No. 112.
6	O. L. Meyers returned merchandise from Sale No. 111 for a credit (Credit Memo No. 42), $50, plus sales tax.
7	Made cash sales for the week, $3,240, plus sales tax.
9	Received payment from O. L. Meyers for Sale No. 111, less Credit Memo No. 42.
12	Sold merchandise to Melissa Richfield, $980, plus sales tax. Sale No. 113.
14	Made cash sales for the week, $2,180, plus sales tax.
17	Melissa Richfield returned merchandise from Sale No. 113 for a credit (Credit Memo No. 43), $40, plus sales tax.
19	Sold merchandise to Kelsay Munkres, $1,020, plus sales tax. Sale No. 114.
21	Made cash sales for the week, $2,600, plus sales tax.
24	Sold merchandise to O. L. Meyers, $920, plus sales tax. Sale No. 115.
27	Sold merchandise to Andrew Plaa, $1,320, plus sales tax. Sale No. 116.
28	Made cash sales for the week, $2,800, plus sales tax.

Beginning general ledger account balances were as follows:

Cash	$2,864.54
Accounts Receivable	2,726.25

Beginning customer account balances were as follows:

O. L. Meyers	$2,186.00
K. Munkres	482.00
M. Richfield	58.25

REQUIRED

1. Record the transactions in the sales journal, cash receipts journal, and general journal. Total, verify, and rule the columns where appropriate at the end of the month.
2. Post from the journals to the general ledger and accounts receivable ledger accounts. Use account numbers as shown in the chapter.

P 12-9B (LO4)
✓ Total Purchases Dr.: $18,515

PURCHASES JOURNAL Ann Benton, owner of Benton's Galleria, made the following purchases of merchandise on account during the month of October:

Oct. 2	Purchase Invoice No. 321, $1,950, from Boggs Distributors.
7	Purchase Invoice No. 152, $2,915, from Wolfs Wholesaler.
10	Purchase Invoice No. 634, $3,565, from Komuro & Co.
16	Purchase Invoice No. 349, $2,845, from Fritz & McCord, Inc.
24	Purchase Invoice No. 587, $3,370, from Boggs Distributors.
26	Purchase Invoice No. 764, $2,240, from Sanderson Company.
31	Purchase Invoice No. 672, $1,630, from Wolfs Wholesaler.

REQUIRED

1. Record the transactions in the purchases journal. Total and rule the journal.
2. Post from the purchases journal to the general ledger and accounts payable ledger accounts. Use account numbers as shown in the chapter.

P 12-10B (LO4)
✓ Amelia & Vincente account balance: $7,810

PURCHASES JOURNAL, GENERAL LEDGER, AND ACCOUNTS PAYABLE LEDGER The purchases journal of Ryan's Rats Nest, a small retail business, is as follows:

PURCHASES JOURNAL — PAGE 1

	DATE		INVOICE NO.	FROM WHOM PURCHASED	POST. REF.	PURCHASES DEBIT/ACCOUNTS PAYABLE CREDIT	
	20--						
1	Jan.	3	121	Sandra's Sweets		4 4 9 0 00	1
2		5	641	Amelia & Vincente		5 9 2 0 00	2
3		9	215	Nobuko's Nature Store		2 6 8 0 00	3
4		15	227	Smith and Johnson Company		6 5 6 0 00	4
5		21	933	Hidemi, Inc.		1 3 0 0 00	5
6		30	650	Amelia & Vincente		1 8 9 0 00	6
7						22 8 4 0 00	7

REQUIRED

1. Post the total of the purchases journal to the appropriate general ledger accounts. Use account numbers as shown in the chapter.
2. Post the individual purchase amounts to the accounts payable ledger.

P 12-11B (LO5)
✓ Total Cash Cr.: $29,890

CASH PAYMENTS JOURNAL Kay Zembrowski operates a retail variety store. The books include a cash payments journal and an accounts payable ledger. All cash payments (except petty cash) are entered in the cash payments journal. Selected account balances on May 1 are as follows:

General Ledger

Cash	$40,000
Accounts Payable	20,000

(continued)

Accounts Payable Ledger	
Cortez Distributors	$4,200
Indra & Velga	6,800
Toy Corner	4,600
Troutman Outlet	4,400

The following transactions are related to cash payments for the month of May:

May 1 Issued Check No. 326 in payment of May rent (Rent Expense), $2,600.

4 Issued Check No. 327 to Cortez Distributors in payment of merchandise purchased on account, $4,200, less a 3% discount. Check was written for $4,074.

7 Issued Check No. 328 to Indra & Velga in partial payment of merchandise purchased on account, $6,200. A cash discount was not allowed.

11 Issued Check No. 329 to Toy Corner for merchandise purchased on account, $4,600, less a 1% discount. Check was written for $4,554.

15 Issued Check No. 330 to County Power and Light (Utilities Expense), $1,500.

19 Issued Check No. 331 to Builders Warehouse for a cash purchase of merchandise, $3,500.

25 Issued Check No. 332 to Troutman Outlet for merchandise purchased on account, $4,400, less a 2% discount. Check was written for $4,312.

30 Issued Check No. 333 to Rapid Transit Company for freight charges on merchandise purchased (Freight-In), $800.

31 Issued Check No. 334 to City Merchants for a cash purchase of merchandise, $2,350.

REQUIRED

1. Enter the transactions in a cash payments journal. Total, rule, and prove the cash payments journal.
2. Post from the cash payments journal to the general ledger and accounts payable ledger. Use general ledger account numbers as shown in the chapter.

P 12-12B (LO4/5)
✓ Total Cash Cr.: $10,760

KLOOSTER & ALLEN

PURCHASES JOURNAL, CASH PAYMENTS JOURNAL, AND GENERAL JOURNAL Debbie Mueller owns a small retail business called Debbie's Doll House. The cash account has a balance of $20,000 on July 1. The following transactions occurred during July:

July 1 Issued Check No. 314 for July rent, $1,400.

1 Purchased merchandise on account from Topper's Toys, Invoice No. 211, $2,500, terms 2/10, n/30.

3 Purchased merchandise on account from Jones & Company, Invoice No. 812, $2,800, terms 1/10, n/30.

5 Returned merchandise purchased from Topper's Toys receiving a credit memo on the amount owed, $400.

8 Purchased merchandise on account from Downtown Merchants, Invoice No. 159, $1,600, terms 2/10, n/30.

July 11 Issued Check No. 315 to Topper's Toys for merchandise purchased on account, less return of July 5 and less 2% discount.

13 Issued Check No. 316 to Jones & Company for merchandise purchased on account, less 1% discount.

15 Returned merchandise purchased from Downtown Merchants receiving a credit memo on the amount owed, $600.

18 Issued Check No. 317 to Downtown Merchants for merchandise purchased on account, less return of July 15 and less 2% discount.

25 Purchased merchandise on account from Columbia Products, Invoice No. 468, $3,200, terms n/30.

26 Purchased merchandise on account from Topper's Toys, Invoice No. 395, $1,430, terms 2/10, n/30.

29 Purchased merchandise on account from Jones & Company, Invoice No. 853, $2,970, terms 1/10, n/30.

31 Mueller withdrew cash for personal use, $2,500. Issued Check No. 318.

31 Issued Check No. 319 to Burnside Warehouse for a cash purchase of merchandise, $1,050.

REQUIRED

1. Record the transactions in the purchases journal, cash payments journal, and general journal. Total and rule the purchases and cash payments journals. Prove the cash payments journal.
2. Post from the journals to the general ledger and accounts payable ledger accounts. Use general ledger account numbers as shown in the chapter.

MANAGING YOUR WRITING

You have a part-time job as a bookkeeper at a local office supply store. The accounting records consist of a general journal and general ledger. The manager is concerned about efficiency and feels that too much time is spent recording transactions. In addition, there sometimes is difficulty determining the amount owed to specific suppliers. The manager knows you are an accounting student and asks for your suggestions to improve the accounting function.

Write a memo to the manager describing how to increase efficiency and accuracy by using different accounting records.

ETHICS CASE

Judy Baresford, the store manager of Comfort Futons, noticed that the amount of time the two bookkeepers were spending on accounts receivable, accounts payable, and cash receipts was increasing due to the store's increase in sales. A friend of Judy's who is also a store manager suggested that she might want to have some special journals designed that would reduce the amount of work involved in the day-to-day bookkeeping at her store. Judy approached Jon Fortner and Sue Stavio, the bookkeepers, and asked them

(continued)

to come up with a proposal for special journals. During lunch, Jon told Sue he thought designing special journals would be a lot of work and it was not in his job description. Sue told him not to worry because she would just copy pages of special journals from her accounting textbook and they could submit these journals as their own design. Jon liked the idea and they agreed to meet the next night, scan the journals into Word, and submit them to Judy the following morning.

1. Do you think Sue's suggestion is unethical? Why or why not?
2. In using the generic special journals from Sue's accounting textbook, what possible problems can you foresee?
3. If you were Judy, how would you respond to Sue and Jon's "plan"?

MASTERY PROBLEM

✓ Total Accounts Receivable Cr.: $7,235

KA KLOOSTER & ALLEN

During the month of October 20--, The Pink Petal flower shop engaged in the following transactions:

Oct. 1	Sold merchandise on account to Elizabeth Shoemaker, $1,000, plus tax of $50. Sale No. 222.
2	Issued Check No. 190 to Jill Hand in payment of October 1 balance of $500, less 2% discount.
2	Purchased merchandise on account from Flower Wholesalers, $4,000. Invoice No. 500, dated October 2, terms 2/10, n/30.
4	Purchased merchandise on account from Seidl Enterprises, $700. Invoice No. 527, dated October 4, terms 2/15, n/30.
5	Issued Check No. 191 in payment of telephone expense for the month of September, $150.
7	Sold merchandise for cash, $3,500, plus tax of $175.
9	Received payment from Leigh Summers in full settlement of account, $2,000.
11	Issued Check No. 192 to Flower Wholesalers in payment of October 1 balance of $1,500.
12	Sold merchandise on account to Leigh Summers, $2,000, plus tax of $100. Sale No. 223.
12	Received payment from Meg Johnson on account, $3,100.
13	Issued Check No. 193 to Seidl Enterprises in payment of October 4 purchase. Invoice No. 527, less 2% discount.
14	Meg Johnson returned merchandise for a credit, $300, plus sales tax of $15.
17	Returned merchandise to Vases Etc. for credit, $900.
24	Received payment from David's Decorating on account, $2,135.
27	Sold merchandise on account to David's Decorating, $3,000, plus tax of $150. Sale No. 224.
29	Issued Check No. 194 in payment of wages (Wages Expense) for the four-week period ending October 30, $900.

Selected account balances as of October 1 were as follows:

Account	Account No.	Debit	Credit
Cash	101	$18,225.00	
Accounts Receivable	122	9,619.00	
Accounts Payable	202		$5,120.00

The Pink Petal also had the following subsidiary ledger balances as of October 1:

Accounts Receivable:

Customer	Accounts Receivable Balance
David's Decorating 12 Jude Lane Hartford, CT 06117	$3,340.00
Elizabeth Shoemaker 52 Juniper Road Hartford, CT 06118	279.00
Meg Johnson 700 Hobbes Dr. Avon, CT 06108	4,000.00
Leigh Summers 5200 Hamilton Ave. Hartford, CT 06111	2,000.00

Accounts Payable:

Vendor	Accounts Payable Balance
Vases Etc. 34 Harry Ave. East Hartford, CT 05234	$3,120.00
Jill Hand 1009 Drake Rd. Farmington, CT 06082	500.00
Flower Wholesalers 43 Lucky Lane Bristol, CT 06007	1,500.00
Seidl Enterprises 888 Anders Street Newington, CT 06789	—

REQUIRED

1. Record the transactions in a sales journal (page 7), cash receipts journal (page 10), purchases journal (page 6), cash payments journal (page 11), and general journal (page 5). Total, verify, and rule the columns where appropriate at the end of the month.
2. Post from the journals to the general ledger, accounts receivable ledger, and accounts payable ledger accounts. Use account numbers as shown in the chapter.

CHALLENGE PROBLEM

This problem challenges you to apply your cumulative accounting knowledge to move a step beyond the material in the chapter.

✓ June 3: Cr. City Sales Tax Payable, $4.22

Screpcap Co. had the following transactions during the first week of June:

June 1	Purchased merchandise on account from Acme Supply, $2,700, plus freight charges of $160.
1	Issued Check No. 219 to Denver Wholesalers for merchandise purchased on account, $720, less 1% discount.
1	Sold merchandise on account to F. Colby, $246, plus 5% state sales tax plus 2% city sales tax.
2	Received cash on account from N. Dunlop, $315.
2	Made cash sale of $413 plus 5% state sales tax plus 2% city sales tax.
2	Purchased merchandise on account from Permon Co., $3,200, plus freight charges of $190.
3	Sold merchandise on account to F. Ayres, $211, plus 5% state sales tax plus 2% city sales tax.
3	Issued Check No. 220 to Ellis Co. for merchandise purchased on account, $847, less 1% discount.
3	Received cash on account from F. Graves, $463.
4	Issued Check No. 221 to Penguin Warehouse for merchandise purchased on account, $950, less 1% discount.
4	Sold merchandise on account to K. Stanga, $318, plus 5% state sales tax plus 2% city sales tax.
4	Purchased merchandise on account from Mason Milling, $1,630, plus freight charges of $90.
4	Received cash on account from O. Alston, $381.
5	Made cash sale of $319 plus 5% state sales tax plus 2% city sales tax.
5	Issued Check No. 222 to Acme Supply for merchandise purchased on account, $980, less 1% discount.

REQUIRED

1. Record the transactions in a general journal.
2. Assuming these are the types of transactions Screpcap Co. experiences on a regular basis, design the following special journals for Screpcap:
   (a) Sales journal
   (b) Cash receipts journal
   (c) Purchases journal
   (d) Cash payments journal

ANSWERS TO SELF-STUDY QUESTIONS AND EXERCISES

True/False Questions

1. T **2.** F (general journal is still needed) **3.** F (only credit sales) **4.** T **5.** T

Multiple Choice Questions

1. a **2.** a **3.** c **4.** c **5.** a

U REVU Exercises

1.

SALES JOURNAL PAGE 7

	DATE		SALE NO.	TO WHOM SOLD	POST. REF.	ACCOUNT RECEIVABLE DEBIT	SALES CREDIT	SALES TAX PAYABLE CREDIT	
1	June	1	214	Erin Lucas		882 00	840 00	42 00	1

2.

CASH RECEIPTS JOURNAL PAGE

	DATE			ACCOUNT CREDITED	POST. REF.	GENERAL CREDIT	ACCOUNTS RECEIVABLE CREDIT	SALES CREDIT	SALES TAX PAYABLE CREDIT	CASH DEBIT	
1	June	7		Erin Lucas			882 00			882 00	1
2		30						2150 00	107 50	2257 50	2
3		30		Rent Revenue		750 00				750 00	3
4											4

3.

PURCHASES JOURNAL PAGE

	DATE		INVOICE NO.	FROM WHOM PURCHASED	POST. REF.	PURCHASES DEBIT/ACCOUNTS PAYABLE CREDIT	
1	Apr.	6	131	Clever		1680 00	1
2							2

4.

CASH PAYMENTS JOURNAL PAGE

	DATE		CK NO.	ACCOUNT DEBITED	POST. REF.	GENERAL DEBIT	ACCOUNTS PAYABLE DEBIT	PURCHASES DEBIT	PURCHASES DISCOUNTS CREDIT	CASH CREDIT	
1	Aug.	2	193	Rent Expense		2200 00				2200 00	1
2		6	194	Mason Hardware			1700 00		34 00	1666 00	2
3		10	195					2730 00		2730 00	3
4											4

Chapter 13

MARK LENNHIAN/AP PHOTO

PHOTO: © CARY BENBOW

LEARNING OBJECTIVES

Careful study of this chapter should enable you to:

LO1 Explain the impact of merchandise inventory on the financial statements.

LO2 Describe the two principal systems of accounting for merchandise inventory—the periodic system and the perpetual system.

LO3 Compute the costs allocated to the ending inventory and cost of goods sold using different inventory methods.

LO4 Estimate the ending inventory and cost of goods sold by using the gross profit and retail inventory methods.

Accounting for Merchandise Inventory

With 11,000 employees serving 2 million customers weekly, Marsh operates 99 Marsh Supermarkets and five O'Malia's Food Markets in Indiana and Ohio. Headquartered in Indianapolis, Marsh also has 41 pharmacy locations, the largest pharmacy chain based in the state of Indiana. Known for its use of technology, Marsh has the distinction of being the first grocery store in the world to use electronic scanners to ring up purchases.

As you walk through a grocery store, have you ever wondered what the store paid for each item? It would be nice to know which items are "good buys" and which are "overpriced." What happens when management pays different amounts for identical products on the shelf? In this chapter, you will learn how merchandising firms determine which items were sold and which remain. That is, how they determine the cost of the goods sold and the cost of the goods remaining on the shelves at the end of the year.

In Chapters 10 and 11, you learned how to account for the purchase and sale of merchandise. One of the major reasons for keeping accounting records is to determine the net income (or net loss) of a business. A major component of net income is the gross profit. In Chapter 11, you learned how to compute gross profit. An abbreviated form of this calculation is shown below.

Calculation of Gross Profit		
Net sales		$110
Cost of goods sold		
Merchandise inventory, Jan. 1	$ 20	
Purchases	80	
Cost of goods available for sale	$100	
Less merchandise inventory, Dec. 31	30	
Cost of goods sold		70
Gross profit		$ 40

The terms goods and merchandise mean the same thing and are used interchangeably.

For a merchandising business, the cost of goods available for sale ($100) during the accounting period must be divided between cost of goods sold ($70) and ending merchandise inventory ($30). In Chapter 11, the costs assigned to these accounts were provided. In this chapter, you will learn how to determine the dollar amounts assigned to cost of goods sold and ending merchandise inventory. In Chapter 14, we will illustrate the end-of-period adjustments required to bring the cost of goods sold and merchandise inventory accounts up to date to reflect their proper balances.

THE IMPACT OF MERCHANDISE INVENTORY ON FINANCIAL STATEMENTS

LO1 Explain the impact of merchandise inventory on the financial statements.

A company's ending inventory must be reported accurately. An error in the reported inventory will cause errors on the income statement, statement of owner's equity, and balance sheet. In addition, since this year's ending inventory becomes next year's beginning inventory, financial statements for the following year will also contain errors.

Figure 13-1 illustrates the impact of an error in the *ending inventory*. The first pair of columns presents partial financial statements when the ending inventory is correct. For this illustration, sales, cost of goods sold, and operating expenses are assumed to be the same for 20-1 and 20-2. Thus, the same net income of $30 and beginning and ending merchandise inventories of $20 are reported for both years.

This year's ending inventory becomes next year's beginning inventory.

The second pair of columns in Figure 13-1 illustrates the effects of understating the ending inventory. Understating the ending inventory for 20-1 by $5 causes the cost of goods sold to be overstated by $5 and net income to be understated by $5. Since net income is reported on the statement of owner's equity, Erv Bultman's capital on December 31 is understated by $5. The understated capital also appears in the owner's equity section of the balance sheet. The understated ending inventory is reported in the current assets section of the balance sheet.

LEARNING KEY

If the ending inventory for 20-1 is understated, net income for 20-1 is understated and net income for 20-2 is overstated.

Even if the ending inventory for 20-2 is accurately reported, we still have a problem with the income statement. Since the ending inventory for 20-1 was understated, the beginning inventory for 20-2 is understated also ($15 instead of $20). This error causes cost of goods sold to be understated by $5 and net income to be overstated by $5.

FIGURE 13-1 Effect of Inventory Errors on Net Income

	ENDING INVENTORY FOR 20-1 IS CORRECT				ENDING INVENTORY FOR 20-1 IS UNDERSTATED				ENDING INVENTORY FOR 20-1 IS OVERSTATED			
	20-1		20-2		20-1		20-2		20-1		20-2	
Income Statement												
Sales		80		80		80		80		80		80
Cost of goods sold:												
Beginning merchandise inventory	20		**20**		20		**15**		20		**25**	
Add purchases (net)	40		40		40		40		40		40	
Cost of goods available for sale	60		60		60		55		60		65	
Less ending merchandise inventory	**(20)**		(20)		**(15)**		(20)		**(25)**		(20)	
Cost of goods sold		(40)		(40)		(45)		(35)		(35)		(45)
Gross profit		40		40		35		45		45		35
Operating expenses		(10)		(10)		(10)		(10)		(10)		(10)
Net income		30		30		25		35		35		25
Statement of Owner's Equity												
Erv Bultman, capital, January 1	100		130		100		125		100		135	
Net income	30		30		25		35		35		25	
Erv Bultman, capital, December 31		130		160		125		160		135		160
Balance Sheet (Partial)												
Current assets:												
Merchandise inventory		20		20		15		20		25		20
Owner's equity:												
Erv Bultman, capital		130		160		125		160		135		160

At this point, we can see that this inventory error "washes out" over the two-year period. The understated net income for 20-1 is offset by overstated net income in 20-2. Thus, Bultman's capital account as of December 31, 20-2, is reported accurately on the statement of owner's equity and balance sheet at $160. Assuming no future inventory errors, the financial statements for 20-3 and thereafter will be correct.

LEARNING KEY

If the ending inventory for 20-1 is overstated, net income for 20-1 is overstated and net income for 20-2 is understated.

The third pair of columns in Figure 13-1 illustrates the effects of overstating the ending inventory in 20-1. This causes net income to be overstated in 20-1 and understated in 20-2. As previously discussed, these errors "wash out" by the end of 20-2. Thus, Bultman's capital account is correct in the 20-2 financial statements.

It is very important to have an accurate count and valuation for the ending inventory. Since errors in the ending inventory have a direct effect on net income for the period, managers may be tempted to manipulate this amount to achieve a desired result: to either increase net income to make the company look good, or decrease net income to reduce taxes or smooth earnings. For this reason, observing and verifying the ending inventory is an important aspect of an external auditor's job.

U REVU

Complete U REVU-1 on **page 506** to test your basic understanding of LO1.

TYPES OF INVENTORY SYSTEMS: PERIODIC AND PERPETUAL

LO2 Describe the two principal systems of accounting for merchandise inventory—the periodic system and the perpetual system.

The two principal systems of accounting for merchandise inventory are the periodic and the perpetual systems. Entries made for inventory transactions under these systems are illustrated in Figure 13-2. Chapter 11 illustrated the periodic inventory system. As shown in Figure 13-2, under the **periodic inventory system**, no entries are made to the merchandise inventory or cost of goods sold account during the year. Thus, the balance in the merchandise inventory account is based on the physical count of inventory taken at the end of the last accounting period. The merchandise inventory and the cost of goods sold for the current period are not determined until the end of the current accounting period, when a physical inventory is taken. At that time, the following formula is applied to calculate cost of goods sold.

LEARNING KEY

Under the periodic inventory system, the ending inventory and cost of goods sold are determined at the end of the accounting period, when a physical inventory is taken.

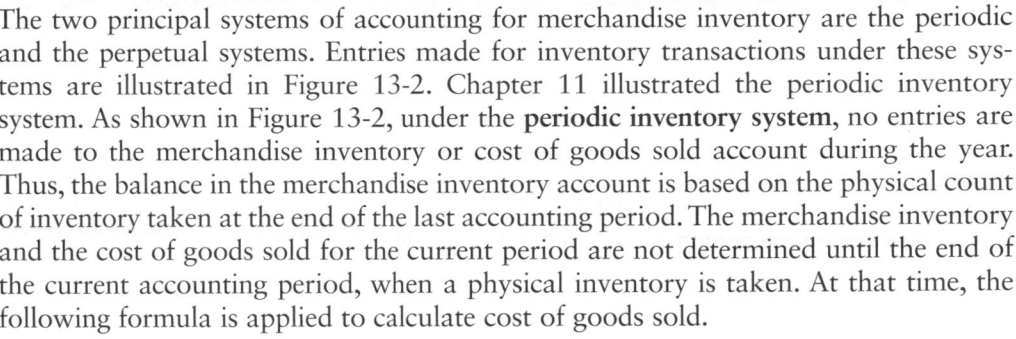

Beginning Inventory (based on last year's ending physical count)
+ Net Purchases (account balance at end of this year)
= Cost of Goods Available for Sale
− Ending Inventory (based on this year's ending physical count)
= Cost of Goods Sold (for this year)

Adjusting entries are needed at the end of the fiscal year to update the merchandise inventory account and cost of goods sold. These entries are illustrated in Chapter 14.

FIGURE 13-2 Entries for Periodic and Perpetual Inventory Systems

TRANSACTION	PERIODIC SYSTEM			PERPETUAL SYSTEM		
1. Purchased merchandise on account, $100.	Purchases	100		Merchandise Inventory	100	
	Accounts Payable		100	Accounts Payable		100
2. Paid freight charge, $30.	Freight-In	30		Merchandise Inventory	30	
	Cash		30	Cash		30
3. Sold merchandise on account, $80. The cost of the merchandise was $50.	Accounts Receivable	80		Accounts Receivable	80	
	Sales		80	Sales		80
				Cost of Goods Sold	50	
				Merchandise Inventory		50
4. Merchandise costing $10 was returned to the supplier.	Accounts Payable	10		Accounts Payable	10	
	Purchases Ret. & Allow.		10	Merchandise Inventory		10
5. Customers returned merchandise sold for $20. The cost of the merchandise was $15.	Sales Ret. and Allow.	20		Sales Ret. and Allow.	20	
	Accounts Receivable		20	Accounts Receivable		20
				Merchandise Inventory	15	
				Cost of Goods Sold		15
6. Paid for merchandise costing $100. The supplier granted a 2% discount for prompt payment.	Accounts Payable	100		Accounts Payable	100	
	Purchases Discounts		2	Merchandise Inventory		2
	Cash		98	Cash		98

As shown in Figure 13-2, under the **perpetual inventory system**, entries are made to the merchandise inventory and cost of goods sold accounts as transactions take place during the accounting period. The merchandise inventory account is debited for the cost of all goods purchased, including freight charges, and credited for the cost of all goods sold. In addition, this account is debited when customers return merchandise and is credited when suppliers grant returns, allowances, and discounts. Thus, the balance of the account represents the cost of goods on hand at all times. The cost of goods sold account is debited when merchandise is sold and credited when customers return merchandise. Thus, the balance of the account reflects the cost of goods sold at any point during the accounting period. No year-end adjusting entry is necessary as long as the physical inventory agrees with the amount reported in the merchandise inventory account. In Chapter 14, we will illustrate the proper adjustment if this is not true.

LEARNING KEY

Under the perpetual inventory system, cost of goods sold and the amount of merchandise inventory on hand are continually updated as merchandise is bought and sold.

FIGURE 13-4 Allocation of Goods Available for Sale to Cost of Goods Sold and Ending Inventory

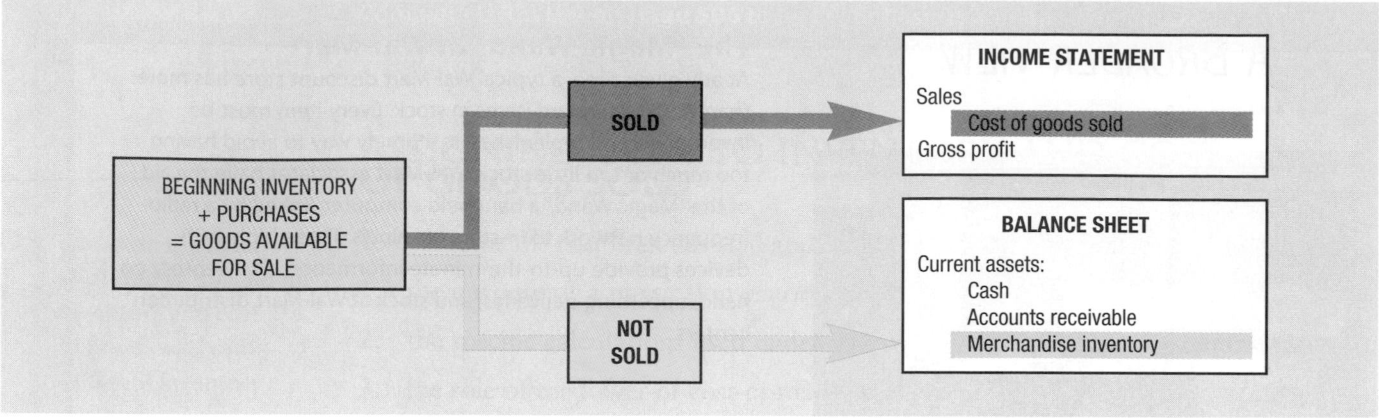

THE PERIODIC INVENTORY SYSTEM

Specific Identification Method

LEARNING KEY

The specific identification method requires that each inventory item have a distinguishing feature or marking to assure proper identification.

When each unit of inventory can be specifically identified, the **specific identification method** can be used. To use this method, inventory items must be physically different from each other, or they must have serial numbers. Examples include cars, motorcycles, furniture, appliances, and fine jewelry. When a unit is sold, its cost is determined from the supplier's invoice. Unless computerized, this method is practical only for businesses in which sales volume is relatively low and inventory unit value is relatively high. Otherwise, record keeping becomes expensive and time consuming.

To illustrate how specific identification costing works, assume the following data for an inventory of one specific model of children's bicycles:

Children's Bicycles (Model ZX007)

	Units	Unit Price	Total Cost
On hand at start of period	40	$62	$ 2,480
Purchased during period:			
1st purchase	60	65	3,900
2nd purchase	80	67	5,360
3rd purchase	70	68	4,760
Number of units available for sale	250		$16,500
On hand at end of period	50		
Number of units sold during period	200		

Of the 200 units sold during the period, the bicycle serial numbers show that 30 were from the beginning inventory, 50 were from the first purchase, 60 were from the second purchase, and 60 were from the last purchase. The cost of goods sold and the cost of inventory at the end of the period are determined as shown in Figure 13-5.

First-In, First-Out (FIFO) Method

LEARNING KEY

FIFO means **F**irst-**I**n, **F**irst-**O**ut.

Another widely used method of allocating merchandise cost is called the **first-in, first-out**, or **FIFO, method**. This costing method assumes that the first goods purchased were the first goods sold. Therefore, the latest goods purchased remain in inventory.

Whenever possible, a business will attempt to sell the older goods first. This is particularly true of businesses that sell perishable items or merchandise that may become obsolete. Grocery stores, fresh fruit stands, and computer software businesses are good examples. These businesses must rotate their stock forward. They pull the oldest bread,

FIGURE 13-5 Specific Identification Inventory Method

	COST OF GOODS SOLD			COST OF ENDING INVENTORY		
	Units	Unit Price	Total	Units	Unit Price	Total
Beginning inventory	30	$62	$ 1,860	10	$62	$ 620
1st purchase	50	65	3,250	10	65	650
2nd purchase	60	67	4,020	20	67	1,340
3rd purchase	60	68	4,080	10	68	680
Total	200		$13,210	50		$ 3,290
Alternative calculation if given goods available for sale and cost of goods sold or ending inventory.	Cost of goods available for sale Less cost of ending inventory Cost of goods sold		$16,500 (3,290) $13,210	Cost of goods available for sale Less cost of goods sold Cost of ending inventory		$16,500 (13,210) $ 3,290

milk, fruit, and vegetables to the front of the shelves and try to sell all copies of the current software before a new version arrives. FIFO costing is, therefore, widely used because it often follows the actual movement of goods. It assumes that the oldest units have been sold and the newest or freshest units are in the ending inventory.

Applying FIFO to the bicycle inventory data, the cost of goods sold and the cost of inventory at the end of the period are determined as shown in Figure 13-6.

FIGURE 13-6 FIFO Inventory Method

	COST OF GOODS SOLD			COST OF ENDING INVENTORY		
	Units	Unit Price	Total	Units	Unit Price	Total
Beginning inventory	40	$62	$ 2,480		$62	$ 0
1st purchase	60	65	3,900		65	0
2nd purchase	80	67	5,360		67	0
3rd purchase	20	68	1,360	50	68	3,400
Total	200		$ 13,100	50		$ 3,400
Alternative calculation if given goods available for sale and cost of goods sold or ending inventory.	Cost of goods available for sale Less cost of ending inventory Cost of goods sold		$ 16,500 (3,400) $ 13,100	Cost of goods available for sale Less cost of goods sold Cost of ending inventory		$ 16,500 (13,100) $ 3,400

Note that the 50 items on hand at the end of the period are considered to be those most recently purchased.

FIFO costing is widely used because businesses have used this method for a long time. Accountants are reluctant to change a long-followed method of accounting when such a change would affect the comparability of their income calculations over a period of years. **Consistency** based on comparability is an important accounting principle.

LEARNING KEY

The consistency principle of accounting suggests that a business should use the same accounting techniques from year to year.

Weighted-Average Method

Another method of allocating merchandise cost is called the **weighted-average method,** or **average cost method.** This costing method is based on the average cost of identical units.

Consider the bicycle inventory data again. The average cost of identical units is determined by dividing the total cost of units available for sale ($16,500) by the total number of units available for sale (250).

$$\frac{\$16{,}500 \text{ (cost of units available for sale)}}{250 \text{ (units available for sale)}} = \$66 \text{ weighted-average cost per unit}$$

The cost of goods sold and the cost of the end-of-period inventory are calculated as follows:

Cost of goods sold	200 units @ $66 =	$13,200
Cost of ending inventory	50 units @ $66 =	3,300
Total	250 units	$16,500

There is a logical appeal to the weighted-average method of allocating cost between goods sold and goods on hand. In this example, one-fifth (50) of the total units available (250) were unsold. The weighted-average method assigns one-fifth ($3,300) of the total cost ($16,500) to these goods.

LEARNING KEY

LIFO means **L**ast-**In**, **F**irst-**O**ut.

Last-In, First-Out (LIFO) Method

A fourth method of allocating merchandise cost is called the **last-in, first-out**, or **LIFO, method.** It assumes that the sales in the period were made from the most recently purchased goods. Therefore, the earliest goods purchased remain in inventory.

This physical flow is associated with businesses selling products that are not perishable or likely to become obsolete, and may be difficult to handle. Imagine a large barrel of nails at a lumberyard. Customers take nails from the top of the barrel. When the supply gets low, new nails are simply piled on top of the old ones. There is no need to rotate the nails from the bottom to the top of the barrel.

Applying LIFO to the bicycle inventory data, the cost of goods sold and the cost of inventory at the end of the period are determined as shown in Figure 13-7.

FIGURE 13-7 LIFO Inventory Method

	COST OF GOODS SOLD			COST OF ENDING INVENTORY		
	Units	Unit Price	Total	Units	Unit Price	Total
Beginning inventory	0	$62	$ 0	40	$62	$ 2,480
1st purchase	50	65	3,250	10	65	650
2nd purchase	80	67	5,360		67	0
3rd purchase	70	68	4,760	—	68	0
Total	200		$ 13,370	50		$ 3,130
Alternative calculation if given goods available for sale and cost of goods sold or ending inventory.	Cost of goods available for sale Less cost of ending inventory Cost of goods sold		$ 16,500 (3,130) $ 13,370	Cost of goods available for sale Less cost of goods sold Cost of ending inventory		$ 16,500 (13,370) $ 3,130

Note that the 50 units on hand at the end of the period are considered to be the 40 units in the beginning inventory plus 10 of the units from the first purchase.

The LIFO method has been justified on the grounds that the physical movement of goods in some businesses is actually last-in, first-out. This is rarely the case, but the method has become popular for other reasons. One persuasive argument for the use of the LIFO method is that it matches the most current cost of items purchased against

Although LIFO is acceptable under U.S. GAAP and many U.S. companies use this method for financial reporting and tax purposes, it is not permitted under International Financial Reporting Standards.

the current sales revenue. When the most current costs of purchases are subtracted from sales revenue, the impact of changing prices on the resulting gross profit figure is minimized. In the opinion of many accountants, this is proper and desirable.

Another reason for the popularity of the LIFO method is its effect on income taxes. When prices are rising, net income calculated under the LIFO method is less than net income calculated under either the FIFO or the weighted-average method. Since the net income amount under LIFO is less, the related income tax will be less. The reverse would be true if prices were falling. However, periods of falling prices over the past two centuries have been few and brief.

Opponents of the LIFO method contend that its use causes old, out-of-date inventory costs to be shown on the balance sheet. The theoretical and practical merits of FIFO versus LIFO are the subject of much professional debate.

Physical Flows and Cost Flows

LEARNING KEY

The inventory method used does not have to match the physical flow of goods.

Of the four inventory costing methods described, only the specific identification costing method will necessarily reflect cost flows that match physical flows of goods. Each of the other three methods—FIFO, weighted-average, and LIFO—is based on assumed cost flows. The assumed cost flows *are not required to reflect the actual physical movement of goods* within the company. Any one of the three assumed cost flow methods could be used under any set of physical flow conditions. For example, a fresh fruit stand with an actual FIFO flow of inventory may use LIFO for accounting purposes. Similarly, a supplier of building materials that sells nails, lumber, and sand off the top of the pile may use FIFO even though the physical flow of goods is LIFO.

Comparison of Methods

To compare the results of the four inventory methods, let's assume that the 200 bicycle units in our example were sold for $18,000. Figure 13-8 contrasts the ending inventory, cost of goods sold, and gross profit under each of the four methods.

FIGURE 13-8 Comparison of Inventory Methods

	SPECIFIC IDENTIFICATION		FIFO		WEIGHTED AVERAGE		LIFO	
Sales		$18,000		$18,000		$18,000		$18,000
Cost of goods sold:								
Beginning inventory	$ 2,480		$ 2,480		$ 2,480		$ 2,480	
Purchases	14,020		14,020		14,020		14,020	
Goods available for sale	$16,500		$16,500		$16,500		$16,500	
Less ending inventory	3,290		3,400		3,300		3,130	
Cost of goods sold		13,210		13,100		13,200		13,370
Gross profit		$ 4,790		$ 4,900		$ 4,800		$ 4,630

During periods of rising prices, we can observe the following: LIFO generally produces the highest cost of goods sold, lowest gross profit, and lowest ending inventory. Since the most recent units purchased are assumed to have been sold, the most recent costs are matched against revenues and this provides the best measure of gross profit and net income. After all, the units sold must be replaced at current prices. However, under LIFO, the first units purchased are assumed to remain in inventory (FISH: First-In, Still Here). This means that units purchased many years ago may remain in the ending inventory. These dollar amounts are likely to have little meaning when measuring the firm's performance or financial health.

LEARNING KEY

In periods of rising prices, LIFO produces the lowest net income and FIFO produces the highest net income.

FIFO generally produces the lowest cost of goods sold, highest gross profit, and highest ending inventory. Since the last units purchased are assumed to be in ending inventory, these most recent costs provide the best inventory measure on the balance sheet (LISH: Last-In, Still Here). However, under FIFO, the first units purchased are assumed to have been sold. This means that somewhat older prices are used to compute cost of goods sold and gross profit than under LIFO. Thus, these measures are somewhat less useful than those computed under LIFO.

The weighted-average inventory method produces measures between LIFO and FIFO. The specific identification method will produce measures based on the actual units sold.

The Internal Revenue Service requires the use of the same inventory method for tax and financial reporting purposes. Since LIFO generally produces the highest cost of goods sold, lowest gross profit, and lowest tax liability, many firms use the LIFO inventory method to minimize federal income taxes. The tax dollars saved are then available for other purposes.

As discussed earlier, keep the following in mind when selecting the inventory method to be used by a business:

1. The physical flow of the inventory does not need to match the flow assumed by the inventory method.
2. The consistency principle requires that the same accounting methods be followed from period to period. Although it is acceptable to make changes, it is not appropriate to switch back and forth from FIFO to LIFO based on the desire to maximize or minimize earnings for a given year.

THE PERPETUAL INVENTORY SYSTEM

Under the perpetual inventory system, a continuous record is maintained for the quantities and costs of goods on hand at all times. The general ledger account for Merchandise Inventory under such a system is somewhat like the account for Cash. It provides a chronological record of each addition (purchase) and subtraction (sale). The balance of the account at any time shows the cost of goods that should be on hand.

When perpetual inventory records are kept, the merchandise inventory account in the general ledger is usually a controlling account. A subsidiary ledger is maintained with an account for each type of merchandise. These accounts are often recorded on cards or in computer files. As shown in Figure 13-9, the subsidiary accounts are designed to handle additions and subtractions and determine the new balance after each change. Goods sold usually are assigned cost on either a FIFO, moving-average, or LIFO basis. Procedures for applying the FIFO method in a perpetual inventory system are similar to those illustrated for a periodic system. The first merchandise purchased is treated as the first merchandise sold. The illustration in Figure 13-9 is based on the FIFO method. The specific techniques used to apply the moving-average and LIFO methods in a perpetual system are more complicated. They are illustrated in the chapter appendix.

LEARNING KEY

A controlling account and subsidiary ledger are maintained for inventory in much the same way as for accounts receivable and accounts payable.

LOWER-OF-COST-OR-MARKET METHOD OF INVENTORY VALUATION

It is a well-established tradition in accounting that gains should not be recognized unless a sale has occurred. If the value of an asset increases while it is being held, no formal entry of the gain is made on the books. On the other hand, if an asset's value declines while it is being held, it is generally considered proper to recognize a loss. This is in keeping with the accounting practice of **conservatism,** which states that when in doubt, the lower asset value and net income measure should be used. Thus, we should never anticipate gains, but we should always anticipate and account for losses.

LEARNING KEY

The accounting practice of conservatism states that when in doubt, the lower asset value and net income measure should be used. Thus, when in doubt, we should not record gains, but we should record losses.

FIGURE 13-9 Perpetual Inventory Record: FIFO Method

DATE	PURCHASES			COST OF GOODS SOLD				INVENTORY ON HAND				
	Units	Cost/ Unit	Total	Units	Cost/ Unit	CGS	Cumulative CGS	Layer	Units	Cost/ Unit	Layer Cost	Total
Jan. 1 (BI)								(1)	40	$62	$2,480	$2,480
Feb. 15				30	$62	$ 1,860	$ 1,860	(1)	10	$62	$ 620	$ 620
Mar. 1								(1)	10	$62	$ 620	
	60	$65	$3,900					(2)	60	65	3,900	$4,520
Apr. 1				10	$62	$ 620		(2)	30	$65	$1,950	
				30	$65	1,950	$ 4,430					$1,950
May 15								(2)	30	$65	$1,950	
	80	$67	$5,360					(3)	80	67	5,360	$7,310
June 30				30	$65	$ 1,950		(3)	20	$67	$1,340	
				60	67	4,020	$10,400					$1,340
Aug. 28								(3)	20	$67	$1,340	
	70	$68	$4,760					(4)	70	68	4,760	$6,100
Oct. 30				20	$67	$ 1,340		(4)	50	$68	$3,400	
				20	68	1,360	$13,100					$3,400
Cost of Goods Sold during 20--							$13,100					
BI: Beginning Inventory												

As applied to inventory, conservatism means that if the value of inventory declines while it is being held, the loss should be recognized in the period of the decline. The purpose of the **lower-of-cost-or-market method** is to recognize such losses on the income statement and to report the lower inventory valuation on the balance sheet.

In applying the lower-of-cost-or-market method, "**cost**" means the dollar amount calculated using one of the four inventory costing methods. "**Market**" means the cost to replace the inventory. It is the price in the market in which goods are purchased by the business—not the price in the market in which they are normally sold by the business. The lower-of-cost-or-market method assumes that a decline in the purchase (replacement) price of inventory is accompanied by a decline in the selling price. In this sense, a decline in the purchase (replacement) price signals a decline in the value of the inventory.

To illustrate the lower-of-cost-or-market method, assume the following end-of-period inventory data for three items:

Item	Recorded Purchase Cost	End-of-Period Market Value	Lower-of-Cost-or-Market
1	$ 8,000	$ 7,000	$ 7,000
2	9,000	10,000	9,000
3	7,000	6,500	6,500
	$24,000	$23,500	$22,500

The illustration shows two ways to calculate the lower-of-cost-or-market. First, the lower-of-cost-or-market method can be applied to the total inventory. This involves comparing the $24,000 total cost with the $23,500 *total end-of-period market value*. Under the second approach, the method is applied to each item in inventory. This

Lower-of-cost-or-market may not be used with LIFO costing for tax purposes.

LEARNING KEY

Under lower-of-cost-or-market, market represents the cost to replace the inventory item, not the selling price.

involves comparing the $24,000 total cost with the $22,500 lower-of-cost-or-market value determined by comparing cost with market value for *each item*. Either approach is acceptable, but the one chosen should be applied consistently across periods.

The difference between the cost and market value is considered a loss due to holding inventory. Normally, it is charged to an account such as **Loss on Write-Down of Inventory**. For example, based on application of the method to the total inventory in the previous illustration, a $500 loss ($24,000 – $23,500) is recognized as follows:

14			Loss on Write-Down of Inventory		5 0 0 00		14
15			Merchandise Inventory			5 0 0 00	15
16			To recognize loss in value of inventory held				16

The loss due to write-down of inventory should be reported on the income statement as an expense. Although not a preferred treatment, some businesses include it in cost of goods sold if the amounts are small.

U REVU Complete U REVU-3 on **page 506** to test your basic understanding of LO3.

ESTIMATING ENDING INVENTORY AND COST OF GOODS SOLD

LO4 Estimate the ending inventory and cost of goods sold by using the gross profit and retail inventory methods.

Many businesses prepare monthly or quarterly financial statements. To do this, the business must estimate the inventory at the end of the month or quarter and the cost of goods sold for the period. This is not a problem for businesses using the perpetual inventory method. Although these amounts need to be verified by a physical inventory at the end of the year, the unverified amounts are generally reliable estimates and can be used for these "interim" statements.

Businesses using the periodic inventory method must use other methods to estimate the ending inventory and cost of goods sold. Two generally accepted methods are the gross profit method and the retail inventory method.

GROSS PROFIT METHOD OF ESTIMATING INVENTORY

Under the **gross profit method**, a business's normal gross profit (net sales – cost of goods sold) is used to estimate the cost of goods sold and ending inventory. To illustrate the gross profit method, assume the following data with respect to Groomer Company:

Inventory, start of period	$80,000
Net purchases, first month	$70,000
Net sales, first month	$110,000
Normal gross profit as a percentage of sales	40%

The estimated cost of goods sold for the month and the estimated merchandise inventory at the end of the month would be determined as shown in Figure 13-10.

This calculation is appropriate only if the firm's normal gross profit as a percentage of net sales has been relatively stable over time. This type of calculation also can be used to test the reasonableness of the amount of inventory that was computed on the basis of a physical count. A large difference between the two amounts might indicate a mistake in the count, a mistake in the costing of the items, or a marked change

FIGURE 13-10 Steps for the Gross Profit Method

STEP 1	Compute the cost of goods available for sale.	Cost of goods available for sale:		
		Inventory, start of period	$ 80,000	
		Net purchases, first month	70,000	
		Cost of goods available for sale:		$150,000
STEP 2	Estimate cost of goods sold by deducting the normal gross profit from net sales.	Estimated cost of goods sold:		
		Net sales	$110,000	
		Normal gross profit ($110,000 × 40%)	44,000	
		Estimated cost of goods sold		66,000
STEP 3	Estimate the ending inventory by deducting cost of goods sold from the cost of goods available for sale.	Estimated end-of-month inventory		$ 84,000

in the gross profit rate. The gross profit procedure also can be used to estimate the cost of an inventory that was destroyed by fire or other casualty.

RETAIL METHOD OF ESTIMATING INVENTORY

Many retail businesses, such as department and clothing stores, use a variation of the gross profit method to calculate cost of goods sold and ending inventory. The procedure used, called the **retail method** of inventory, requires keeping records of both the cost and selling (retail) prices of all goods purchased. This information can be used to estimate cost of goods sold and ending inventory, as shown in Figure 13-11.

FIGURE 13-11 Steps in the Retail Inventory Method

			COST	RETAIL
STEP 1	Compute the cost of goods available for sale at cost and retail.	Inventory, start of period	$ 60,000	$ 85,000
		Net purchases during period	126,000	163,000
		Goods available for sale	$186,000	$248,000
STEP 2	Compute the ending inventory at retail by subtracting sales at retail from goods available for sale at retail.	Less net sales for period		180,000
		Inventory, end of period, at retail		$ 68,000
STEP 3	Compute the cost-to-retail ratio by dividing the cost of goods available for sale by the retail value of the goods available for sale.	Ratio of cost-to-retail prices of goods available for sale ($186,000 ÷ $248,000)		75%
STEP 4	Estimate the cost of the ending inventory by multiplying the ending inventory at retail (step 2) by the cost-to-retail ratio.	Inventory, end of period, at estimated cost (75% of $68,000)	(51,000)	
STEP 5	Estimate cost of goods sold by a. multiplying sales at retail by the cost-to-retail ratio, or b. subtracting the estimated ending inventory from the cost of goods available for sale.	Estimated cost of goods sold (or, sales of $180,000 × 75% = $135,000)	$135,000	

U REVU Complete U REVU-4 on **page 506** to test your basic understanding of LO4.

LEARNING OBJECTIVES Key Points to Remember

LO1 Explain the impact of merchandise inventory on the financial statements.

The cost of goods available for sale during the accounting period must be divided between the cost of goods sold and the ending merchandise inventory. Cost of goods sold is reported on the income statement and used to determine the gross profit for the period. The ending merchandise inventory is reported as a current asset on the balance sheet. Figure 13-12 illustrates the allocation of cost of goods available for sale into cost of goods sold and ending inventory.

FIGURE 13-12 Allocation of Goods Available for Sale to Cost of Goods Sold and Ending Inventory

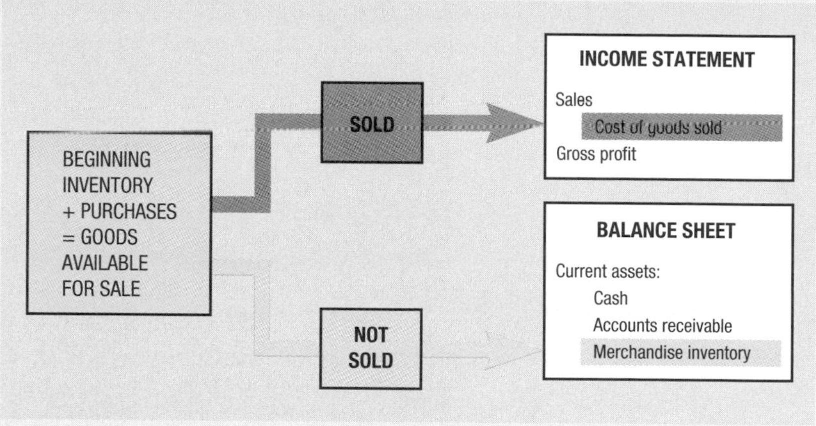

LO2 Describe the two principal systems of accounting for merchandise inventory—the periodic system and the perpetual system.

There are two systems of accounting for merchandise.

Periodic Inventory System

1. The purchases account is debited for the cost of all goods purchased.
2. The sales account is credited for the selling prices of all goods sold.
3. At the end of the accounting period, a physical inventory is taken, and the following formula is applied to calculate cost of goods sold:

   Beginning Inventory (last year's ending physical count)
   \+ Net Purchases (account balance at end of this year)
   = Cost of Goods Available for Sale
   − Ending Inventory (this year's ending physical count)
   = Cost of Goods Sold (for this year)

Perpetual Inventory System

1. The merchandise inventory account is debited for all purchases.
2. The cost of goods sold account is debited, and the merchandise inventory account is credited for all sales.
3. Thus, the merchandise inventory account provides a running balance of the goods on hand.

LO3 Compute the costs allocated to the ending inventory and cost of goods sold using different inventory methods.

One of the following four inventory methods is generally used to determine the costs assigned to the goods sold and ending inventory:

- Specific identification
- FIFO: first-in, first-out
- Weighted-average
- LIFO: last-in, first-out

(continued)

LEARNING OBJECTIVES Key Points to Remember

LO3 (concluded)	The actual physical flow of inventory does not have to match the method used. During periods of rising prices, LIFO produces the lowest net income, and FIFO produces the highest net income.
LO4 Estimate the ending inventory and cost of goods sold by using the gross profit and retail inventory methods.	Firms using the periodic inventory method often need to estimate their inventory. Two methods are used for this purpose. • **Gross Profit Method**—The firm's normal gross profit as a percentage of net sales is used to estimate cost of goods sold and ending inventory in three steps. 1. Compute the cost of goods available for sale. 2. Estimate cost of goods sold by deducting the normal gross profit (net sales × normal gross profit as percentage of net sales) from net sales. 3. Estimate the ending inventory by deducting cost of goods sold from the cost of goods available for sale. • **Retail Inventory Method**—The firm's ratio of cost-to-retail prices of goods available for sale is used to estimate ending inventory and cost of goods sold in five basic steps: 1. Compute the cost of goods available for sale at cost and retail. 2. Compute the ending inventory at retail by subtracting sales at retail from goods available for sale at retail. 3. Compute the cost-to-retail ratio by dividing the cost of goods available for sale by the retail value of the goods available for sale. 4. Estimate the cost of ending inventory by multiplying the ending inventory at retail (step 2) by the cost-to-retail ratio. 5. Estimate cost of goods sold by: a. multiplying sales at retail by the cost-to-retail ratio, or b. subtracting the estimated ending inventory from the cost of goods available for sale.

DEMONSTRATION PROBLEM

Fialka Company's beginning inventory and purchases during the fiscal year ended October 31, 20-2, were as follows:

		Units	Unit Price	Total Cost
November 1, 20-1	Beginning inventory	500	$25.00	$ 12,500
November 12, 20-1	1st purchase	600	26.25	15,750
December 28, 20-1	2nd purchase	400	27.50	11,000
March 29, 20-2	3rd purchase	1,000	28.00	28,000
May 31, 20-2	4th purchase	750	28.50	21,375
July 29, 20-2	5th purchase	350	29.00	10,150
August 30, 20-2	6th purchase	675	30.00	20,250
October 21, 20-2	7th purchase	225	31.00	6,975
		4,500		$126,000

There are 1,600 units of inventory on hand on October 31, 20-2.

(continued)

REQUIRED

1. Calculate the total amount to be assigned to cost of goods sold for the fiscal year and ending inventory on October 31, 20-2, under each of the following periodic inventory methods:
   (a) FIFO
   (b) LIFO
   (c) Weighted-average cost (round calculations to two decimal places)
2. Assume that the market price per unit (cost to replace) of Fialka's inventory on October 31, 20-2, was $29. Calculate the total amount to be assigned to the ending inventory on October 31, 20-2, under each of the following methods:
   (a) FIFO lower-of-cost-or-market
   (b) Weighted-average lower-of-cost-or-market
3. Assume that a fire destroyed Fialka's store and all inventory on October 31, just prior to taking a physical inventory. Thus, Fialka must estimate the ending inventory and cost of goods sold. During the fiscal year ended October 31, 20-2, net sales of $134,000 were made. The normal gross profit rate is 40%. Use the gross profit method to estimate the cost of goods sold for the fiscal year ended October 31, 20-2, and the inventory on October 31, 20-2.

Solution 1a.

FIFO INVENTORY METHOD

Date		Cost of Goods Sold			Cost of Ending Inventory		
20-1/-2		Units	Unit Price	Total	Units	Unit Price	Total
Nov. 1	Beginning inventory	500	$25.00	$ 12,500		$25.00	$ 0
Nov. 12	1st purchase	600	26.25	15,750		26.25	0
Dec. 28	2nd purchase	400	27.50	11,000		27.50	0
Mar. 29	3rd purchase	1,000	28.00	28,000		28.00	0
May 31	4th purchase	400	28.50	11,400	350	28.50	9,975
July 29	5th purchase		29.00	0	350	29.00	10,150
Aug. 30	6th purchase		30.00	0	675	30.00	20,250
Oct. 21	7th purchase		31.00	0	225	31.00	6,975
	Total	2.900		$ 78,650	1,600		$ 47,350
Alternative calculation if given goods available for sale and cost of goods sold or ending inventory.		Cost of goods available for sale		$126,000	Cost of goods available for sale		$126,000
		Less cost of ending inventory		(47,350)	Less cost of goods sold		(78,650)
		Cost of goods sold		$ 78,650	Cost of ending inventory		$ 47,350

1b.

Date		LIFO INVENTORY METHOD Cost of Goods Sold			Cost of Ending Inventory		
20-1/-2		Units	Unit Price	Total	Units	Unit Price	Total
Nov. 1	Beginning inventory		$25.00	$ 0	500	$25.00	$ 12,500
Nov. 12	1st purchase		26.25	0	600	26.25	15,750
Dec. 28	2nd purchase		27.50	0	400	27.50	11,000
Mar. 29	3rd purchase	900	28.00	25,200	100	28.00	2,800
May 31	4th purchase	750	28.50	21,375		28.50	0
July 29	5th purchase	350	29.00	10,150		29.00	0
Aug. 30	6th purchase	675	30.00	20,250		30.00	0
Oct. 21	7th purchase	225	31.00	6,975		31.00	0
	Total	2,900		$ 83,950	1,600		$ 42,050
Alternative calculation if given goods available for sale and cost of goods sold or ending inventory.		Cost of goods available for sale Less cost of ending inventory Cost of goods sold		$126,000 (42,050) $ 83,950	Cost of goods available for sale Less cost of goods sold Cost of ending inventory		$126,000 (83,950) $ 42,050

1c. Weighted-average method:
Average cost per unit: $126,000 ÷ 4,500 units = $28
Inventory, October 31, 20-2:
1,600 units @ $28 = $44,800
Cost of goods sold for 20-1/-2:
2,900 units @ $28 = $81,200

2a. FIFO lower-of-cost-or-market:

FIFO cost	$47,350
Market 1,600 units @ $29	46,400
Choose market	46,400

2b. Weighted-average lower-of-cost-or-market:

Weighted-average cost	$44,800
Market 1,600 units @ $29	46,400
Choose weighted-average cost	44,800

3. Estimated inventory on October 31, 20-2:

Inventory, November 1, 20-1	$ 12,500	
Net purchases, November 1, 20-1 through October 31, 20-2	113,500	
Cost of goods available for sale		$126,000
Estimated cost of goods sold:		
Net sales	$134,000	
Normal gross profit ($134,000 × 40%)	53,600	
Estimated cost of goods sold		80,400
Estimated inventory on October 31, 20-2		$ 45,600

KEY TERMS

average cost method (493) See weighted-average method.

conservatism (496) The accounting practice of conservatism states that we should never anticipate gains, but always anticipate and account for losses. As applied to inventory, conservatism means that if the value of inventory declines while it is being held, the loss should be recognized in the period of the decline.

consignee (491) The company holding the merchandise of another business to be sold.

consignment (491) Goods that are held by one business for sale but that are owned by another business.

consignor (491) The owner of the merchandise that is held by another business.

consistency (493) The principle that states that a business should use the same accounting methods from period to period. This improves the comparability of the financial statements over time.

cost (497) In applying the lower-of-cost-or-market method, cost means the dollar amount calculated using one of the four inventory costing methods.

first-in, first-out (FIFO) method (492) A method of allocating merchandise cost which assumes that the first goods purchased were the first goods sold and, therefore, that the latest goods purchased remain in inventory.

gross profit method (498) A method of estimating inventory in which a business's normal gross profit percentage is used to estimate the cost of goods sold and ending inventory.

in transit (491) Goods that are in the process of being shipped between the seller and the buyer.

inventory sheet (490) A form used for recording inventory items. It has columns for recording the description of each item, the quantity on hand, the cost per unit, and the extension.

last-in, first-out (LIFO) method (494) A method of allocating merchandise cost which assumes that the sales in the period were made from the most recently purchased goods. Therefore, the earliest goods purchased remain in inventory.

Loss on Write-Down of Inventory (498) This account is debited when the market value (replacement cost) of the inventory is below cost when applying the lower-of-cost-or-market method of inventory valuation. It is reported on the income statement as an expense.

lower-of-cost-or-market method (497) An inventory valuation method under which inventory is valued at the lower-of-cost-or-market value (replacement cost).

market (497) In applying the lower-of-cost-or-market method, market means the cost to replace the inventory. It is the prevailing price in the market in which goods are purchased—not the prevailing price in the market in which they are normally sold.

natural business year (490) A fiscal year that starts and ends at the time the stock of goods is normally at its lowest level.

periodic inventory system (489) Under this system, the ending inventory and cost of goods sold are determined at the end of the accounting period, when a physical inventory is taken.

perpetual inventory system (489) Under this system, the merchandise inventory and cost of goods sold accounts are updated when merchandise is bought and sold.

physical inventory (490) A physical count of the goods on hand.

retail method (499) A variation of the gross profit method that is used by many retail businesses, such as department and clothing stores, to estimate the cost of goods sold and ending inventory.

specific identification method (492) A method of allocating merchandise cost in which each unit of inventory is specifically identified.

weighted-average method (493) A method of allocating merchandise cost based on the average cost of identical units. The average cost of identical units is determined by dividing the total cost of units available for sale by the total number of units available for sale.

SELF-STUDY QUESTIONS AND EXERCISES

True/False Questions

1. LO1 An overstatement of ending inventory in the year 20-1 will cause net income to be overstated in the year 20-1.
2. LO1 An understatement of ending inventory in the year 20-1 will cause net income to be overstated in the year 20-2, assuming no other errors.
3. LO2 Under the perpetual system of accounting for inventory, the current merchandise inventory and the cost of goods sold are not determined until the end of the accounting period when a physical inventory is taken.
4. LO3 A fiscal year that starts and ends at the time the stock of goods is normally at its lowest level is known as a natural business year.
5. LO3 If goods are shipped FOB shipping point, the seller pays for the shipping costs.

Multiple Choice Questions

1. LO1 An understatement of ending inventory in the year 20-1 will cause the owner's equity account at the end of the year 20-2, assuming no other errors, to be

   (a) understated.
   (b) correctly stated.
   (c) overstated.
   (d) none of the above.

2. LO3 Goods held on consignment remain the property of the

   (a) consignee.
   (b) consignor.
   (c) buyer.
   (d) seller.

3. LO3 In times of rising prices, the inventory cost method that will yield the lowest net income is

   (a) FIFO.
   (b) weighted-average.
   (c) LIFO.
   (d) none of the above.

4. LO3 In times of rising prices, the inventory cost method that will yield the highest cost of goods sold is

   (a) LIFO.
   (b) weighted-average.
   (c) FIFO.
   (d) none of the above.

5. LO3 In the application of "lower-of-cost-or-market," market is the

   (a) lowest sales price.
   (b) highest sales price.
   (c) replacement cost.
   (d) average sales price.

U REVU **Exercises**

1. LO1 If the ending inventory is overstated by $10,000, indicate what, if anything, is incorrect about the following:

Cost of goods sold	__________
Gross profit	__________
Net income	__________
Ending owner's capital	__________

2. LO2 Using the following information, compute the ending balance of the merchandise inventory account under the perpetual inventory system.

a. Merchandise inventory, beginning balance	$ 20,000
b. Purchased merchandise on account	200,000
c. Sold merchandise on account	240,000
d. Cost of merchandise sold in (c)	120,000
e. Freight charges paid on inventory delivered to showroom	1,000
f. Refund provided to customers for merchandise returned	800
g. Cost of merchandise returned by customers	500

3. LO3 Use the following information to compute cost of goods sold under the FIFO and LIFO inventory methods. The firm sold 200 units.

	Units	Unit Price	Total
Beginning inventory	50	$ 5	$ 250
1st purchase	100	8	800
2nd purchase	150	10	1,500

4. LO4 Kulsrud Company would like to estimate the current inventory level. Using the gross profit method and the following information, estimate the current inventory level for Kulsrud Company.

Goods available for sale	$100,000
Net sales	150,000
Normal gross profit as a percent of sales	40%

The answers to the Self-Study Questions and Exercises are at the end of the chapter (pages 515–516).

APPLYING YOUR KNOWLEDGE

REVIEW QUESTIONS

LO1 1. What financial statements are affected by an error in the ending inventory?

LO2 2. What is the main difference between the periodic system of accounting for inventory and the perpetual system of accounting for inventory?

LO3 3. Is a physical inventory necessary under the periodic system? Why or why not?

LO3 4. Is a physical inventory necessary under the perpetual system? Why or why not?

LO3 5. In a period of rising prices, which inventory method will result in:

(a) the highest cost of goods sold?
(b) the lowest cost of goods sold?
(c) the highest ending inventory?

(d) the lowest ending inventory?
(e) the highest gross profit?
(f) the lowest gross profit?

LO3 6. What two factors are taken into account by the weighted-average method of merchandise cost allocation?

LO3 7. Which inventory method always follows the actual physical flow of merchandise?

LO3 8. When lower-of-cost-or-market is assigned to the items that comprise the ending merchandise inventory, what does "cost" mean? What does "market" mean?

LO4 9. List the three steps followed under the gross profit method of estimating inventory.

LO4 10. List the five steps followed under the retail method of estimating inventory.

SERIES A EXERCISES

E 13-1A (LO1)

INVENTORY ERRORS Assume that in year 1, the ending merchandise inventory is overstated by $50,000. If this is the only error in years 1 and 2, indicate which items will be understated, overstated, or correctly stated for years 1 and 2.

	Year 1	Year 2
Ending merchandise inventory	________	________
Beginning merchandise inventory	________	________
Cost of goods sold	________	________
Gross profit	________	________
Net income	________	________
Ending owner's capital	________	________

E 13-2A (LO2)

JOURNAL ENTRIES—PERIODIC INVENTORY Bill Diamond owns a business called Diamond Distributors. The following transactions took place during January of the current year. Journalize the transactions in a general journal using the periodic inventory method.

Jan. 5 Purchased merchandise on account from Prestigious Jewelers, $3,700.

8 Paid freight charge on merchandise purchased, $200.

12 Sold merchandise on account to Diamonds Unlimited, $4,900.

15 Received a credit memo from Prestigious Jewelers for merchandise returned, $600.

22 Issued a credit memo to Diamonds Unlimited for merchandise returned, $800.

E 13-3A (LO2)

JOURNAL ENTRIES—PERPETUAL INVENTORY Sandy Johnson owns a small variety store. The following transactions took place during March of the current year. Journalize the transactions in a general journal using the perpetual inventory method.

Mar. 3 Purchased merchandise on account from City Galleria, $2,700.

7 Paid freight charge on merchandise purchased, $175.

13 Sold merchandise on account to Amber Specialties, $3,000. The cost of the merchandise was $1,800.

18 Received a credit memo from City Galleria for merchandise returned, $500.

22 Issued a credit memo to Amber Specialties for merchandise returned, $400. The cost of the merchandise was $240.

E 13-4A (LO3)

✓ End. inv.: $45,500

ENDING INVENTORY COSTS Sandy Chen owns a small specialty store, named Chen's Chattel, whose year-end is June 30. Determine the total amount that should be included in Chen's Chattel's year-end inventory. A physical inventory taken on June 30 reveals the following:

Cost of merchandise on the showroom floor and in the warehouse	$37,800
Goods held on consignment (consignor is National Manufacturer)	6,400
Goods that Chen's Chattel, as the consignor, has for sale at the location of the Grand Avenue Vista	4,600
Sales invoices indicate that merchandise was shipped on June 29, terms FOB shipping point, delivered at buyer's receiving dock on July 3	3,800
Sales invoices indicate that merchandise was shipped on June 25, terms FOB destination, delivered at buyer's receiving dock on July 5	3,100

E 13-5A (LO3)

✓ 1. End. inv., FIFO: $300.00; Weighted-avg.: $242.50

LOWER-OF-COST-OR-MARKET Stalberg Company's beginning inventory and purchases during the fiscal year ended December 31, 20--, were as follows:

		Units	Unit Price	Total Cost
Jan. 1	Beginning inventory	10	$20	$200
Mar. 5	1st purchase	10	22	220
Sept. 9	2nd purchase	10	25	250
Dec. 8	3rd purchase	10	30	300
		40		$970

There are 10 units of inventory on hand on December 31.

1. Calculate the total amount to be assigned to the ending inventory under each of the following periodic inventory methods:
   (a) FIFO
   (b) Weighted-average (round calculations to two decimal places)
2. Assume that the market price per unit (cost to replace) of Stalberg's inventory on December 31, 20--, was $26. Calculate the total amount to be assigned to the ending inventory on December 31 under each of the following methods:
   (a) FIFO lower-of-cost-or-market
   (b) Weighted-average lower-of-cost-or-market
3. What journal entry would be made under lower-of-cost-or-market for parts 2(a) and (b) above?

SERIES A PROBLEMS

P 13-6A (LO3)

✓ Cost of goods sold, FIFO: $77,100; LIFO: $81,150; Weighted-avg.: $79,050; Specific I.D.: $78,450

SPECIFIC IDENTIFICATION, FIFO, LIFO, AND WEIGHTED-AVERAGE Hamilton Company's beginning inventory and purchases during the fiscal year ended September 30, 20-2, were as follows:

		Units	Unit Price	Total Cost
October 1, 20-1	Beginning inventory	300	$20.00	$ 6,000
October 18	1st purchase	500	21.50	10,750
November 25	2nd purchase	400	22.00	8,800
January 12, 20-2	3rd purchase	800	23.00	18,400
March 17	4th purchase	900	23.50	21,150
June 2	5th purchase	600	24.00	14,400
August 21	6th purchase	500	25.00	12,500
September 27	7th purchase	400	25.75	10,300
		4,400		$102,300

Use the following information for the specific identification method.

There are 1,000 units of inventory on hand on September 30, 20-2. Of these 1,000 units:

100 are from October 18, 20-1	1st purchase
300 are from January 12, 20-2	3rd purchase
100 are from March 17	4th purchase
200 are from June 2	5th purchase
100 are from August 21	6th purchase
200 are from September 27	7th purchase

REQUIRED

Calculate the total amount to be assigned to cost of goods sold for the fiscal year ended September 30, 20-2, and ending inventory on September 30, 20-2, under each of the following periodic inventory methods:

1. FIFO
2. LIFO
3. Weighted-average (round calculations to two decimal places)
4. Specific identification

P 13-7A (LO3)

✓ 1. Ending inv., FIFO: $13,825; LIFO: $8,000; Weighted-avg.: $10,500

COST ALLOCATION AND LOWER-OF-COST-OR-MARKET Douglas Company's beginning inventory and purchases during the fiscal year ended December 31, 20--, were as follows:

		Units	Unit Price	Total Cost
January 1, 20--	Beginning inventory	1,100	$ 8.00	$ 8,800
March 5	1st purchase	900	9.00	8,100
April 16	2nd purchase	400	9.50	3,800
June 3	3rd purchase	700	10.25	7,175
August 18	4th purchase	600	11.00	6,600
September 13	5th purchase	800	12.00	9,600
November 14	6th purchase	400	14.00	5,600
December 3	7th purchase	500	14.05	7,025
		5,400		$56,700

There are 1,000 units of inventory on hand on December 31.

REQUIRED

1. Calculate the total amount to be assigned to the ending inventory and cost of goods sold on December 31 under each of the following methods:

   (a) FIFO
   (b) LIFO
   (c) Weighted-average (round calculations to two decimal places)

2. Assume that the market price per unit (cost to replace) of Douglas's inventory on December 31 was $13. Calculate the total amount to be assigned to the ending inventory on December 31 under each of the following methods:

   (a) FIFO lower-of-cost-or-market
   (b) Weighted-average lower-of-cost-or-market

P 13-8A (LO4)
✓ Est. ending inv.: $80,800

GROSS PROFIT METHOD A fire completely destroyed all the inventory of Glisan Lumber Yard on August 5, 20--. Fortunately, the accounting records were not destroyed in the fire. The following information is provided by Glisan Lumber Yard for the time period January 1 through August 5:

Beginning inventory, **January 1, 20--**	**$100,000**
Net purchases, January 1 through August 5	420,000
Net sales, January 1 through August 5	732,000
Normal gross profit as a percentage of sales	40%

REQUIRED

Estimate the amount of merchandise inventory destroyed in the fire on August 5 using the gross profit method.

P 13-9A (LO4)
✓ Est. ending inv.: $39,000

RETAIL INVENTORY METHOD The following information is provided by Raynette's Pharmacy for the last quarter of its fiscal year ending on March 31, 20--:

	Cost	Retail
Inventory, start of period, January 1, 20--	$ 32,000	$ 52,000
Net purchases during the period	176,000	268,000
Net sales for the period		260,000

REQUIRED

1. Estimate the ending inventory as of March 31 using the retail inventory method.
2. Estimate the cost of goods sold for the time period January 1 through March 31 using the retail inventory method.

SERIES B EXERCISES

E 13-1B (LO1)

INVENTORY ERRORS Assume that in year 1, the ending merchandise inventory is understated by $40,000. If this is the only error in years 1 and 2, indicate which items will be understated, overstated, or correctly stated for years 1 and 2.

	Year 1	Year 2
Ending merchandise inventory	______	______
Beginning merchandise inventory	______	______
Cost of goods sold	______	______
Gross profit	______	______
Net income	______	______
Ending owner's capital	______	______

E 13-2B (LO2)

JOURNAL ENTRIES—PERIODIC INVENTORY Amy Douglas owns a business called Douglas Distributors. The following transactions took place during January of the current year. Journalize the transactions in a general journal using the periodic inventory method.

Jan. 5	Purchased merchandise on account from Elite Warehouse, $4,100.
8	Paid freight charge on merchandise purchased, $300.
12	Sold merchandise on account to Memories Unlimited, $5,200.
15	Received a credit memo from Elite Warehouse for merchandise returned, $700.
22	Issued a credit memo to Memories Unlimited for merchandise returned, $400.

E 13-3B (LO2)

JOURNAL ENTRIES—PERPETUAL INVENTORY Doreen Woods owns a small variety store. The following transactions took place during March of the current year. Journalize the transactions in a general journal using the perpetual inventory method.

Mar. 3 Purchased merchandise on account from Corner Galleria, $3,500.

7 Paid freight charge on merchandise purchased, $200.

13 Sold merchandise on account to Sonya Specialties, $4,250. The cost of the merchandise was $2,550.

18 Received a credit memo from Corner Galleria for merchandise returned, $900.

22 Issued a credit memo to Sonya Specialties for merchandise returned, $500. The cost of the merchandise was $300.

E 13-4B (LO3)

✓ Ending inv.: $53,700

ENDING INVENTORY COSTS Danny Steele owns a small specialty store, named Steele's Storeroom, whose year-end is June 30. Determine the total amount that should be included in Steele's Storeroom's year-end inventory. A physical inventory taken on June 30 reveals the following:

Cost of merchandise on the showroom floor and in the warehouse	$42,600
Goods held on consignment (consignor is Quality Manufacturer)	7,600
Goods that Steele's Storeroom, as the consignor, has for sale at the location of Midtown Galleria	8,300
Sales invoices indicate that merchandise was shipped on June 28, terms FOB shipping point, delivered at buyer's receiving dock on July 6	4,350
Sales invoices indicate that merchandise was shipped on June 26, terms FOB destination, delivered at buyer's receiving dock on July 1	2,800

E 13-5B (LO3)

✓ 1. Ending inv., FIFO: $800; Weighted-avg.: $697.20

LOWER-OF-COST-OR-MARKET Bouie Company's beginning inventory and purchases during the fiscal year ended December 31, 20--, were as follows:

		Units	Unit Price	Total Cost
Jan. 1	Beginning inventory	20	$30	$ 600
Mar. 5	1st purchase	22	34	748
Sept. 9	2nd purchase	24	35	840
Dec. 8	3rd purchase	22	40	880
		88		$3,068

There are 20 units of inventory on hand on December 31.

1. Calculate the total amount to be assigned to the ending inventory under each of the following periodic inventory methods:
   (a) FIFO
   (b) Weighted-average (round calculations to two decimal places)
2. Assume that the market price per unit (cost to replace) of Bouie's inventory on December 31, 20--, was $39. Calculate the total amount to be assigned to the ending inventory on December 31 under each of the following methods:
   (a) FIFO lower-of-cost-or-market
   (b) Weighted-average lower-of-cost-or-market
3. What journal entry would be made under lower-of-cost-or-market for parts 2(a) and (b) above?

SERIES B PROBLEMS

P 13-6B (LO3)

✓ Ending inv., FIFO: $19,075; LIFO: $14,350; Weighted-avg.: $16,290; Specific I.D.: $17,000

SPECIFIC IDENTIFICATION, FIFO, LIFO, AND WEIGHTED-AVERAGE Boyce Company's beginning inventory and purchases during the fiscal year ended September 30, 20-2, were as follows:

		Units	Unit Price	Total Cost
October 1, 20-1	Beginning inventory	400	$15.00	$ 6,000
October 18	1st purchase	300	16.50	4,950
November 25	2nd purchase	600	17.00	10,200
January 12, 20-2	3rd purchase	700	17.25	12,075
March 17	4th purchase	800	18.00	14,400
June 2	5th purchase	400	19.00	7,600
August 21	6th purchase	300	21.00	6,300
September 27	7th purchase	500	21.75	10,875
		4,000		$72,400

Use the following information for the specific identification method.

There are 900 units of inventory on hand on September 30, 20-2. Of these 900 units:

50 are from October 18, 20-1	1st purchase
300 are from January 12, 20-2	3rd purchase
100 are from March 17	4th purchase
200 are from June 2	5th purchase
50 are from August 21	6th purchase
200 are from September 27	7th purchase

REQUIRED

Calculate the total amount to be assigned to the cost of goods sold for the fiscal year ended September 30, 20-2, and ending inventory on September 30, 20-2, under each of the following periodic inventory methods:

1. FIFO
2. LIFO
3. Weighted-average (round calculations to two decimal places)
4. Specific identification

P 13-7B (LO3)

✓ 1. Cost of goods sold, FIFO: $55,950; LIFO: $64,300; Weighted avg.: $60,475

COST ALLOCATION AND LOWER-OF-COST-OR-MARKET Hall Company's beginning inventory and purchases during the fiscal year ended December 31, 20--, were as follows:

		Units	Unit Price	Total Cost
January 1	Beginning inventory	800	$11.00	$ 8,800
March 5	1st purchase	600	12.00	7,200
April 16	2nd purchase	500	12.50	6,250
June 3	3rd purchase	700	14.00	9,800
August 18	4th purchase	800	15.00	12,000
September 13	5th purchase	900	17.00	15,300
November 14	6th purchase	400	18.00	7,200
December 3	7th purchase	500	20.30	10,150
		5,200		$76,700

There are 1,100 units of inventory on hand on December 31.

REQUIRED

1. Calculate the total amount to be assigned to the ending inventory and cost of goods sold on December 31 under each of the following methods:
   (a) FIFO
   (b) LIFO
   (c) Weighted-average (round calculations to two decimal places)
2. Assume that the market price per unit (cost to replace) of Hall's inventory on December 31 was $16. Calculate the total amount to be assigned to the ending inventory on December 31 under each of the following methods:
   (a) FIFO lower-of-cost-or-market
   (b) Weighted-average lower-of-cost-or-market

P 13-8B (LO4)
✓ Est. inv.: $82,500

GROSS PROFIT METHOD A flood completely destroyed all the inventory of Bayside Waterworks Company on July 1, 20--. Fortunately, the accounting records were not destroyed in the flood. The following information is provided by Bayside Waterworks for the time period January 1 through July 1, 20--.

Beginning inventory, January 1, 20--	$ 60,000
Net purchases, January 1 through July 1	380,000
Net sales, January 1 through July 1	650,000
Normal gross profit as a percentage of sales	45%

REQUIRED

Estimate the amount of merchandise inventory destroyed in the flood on July 1 using the gross profit method.

P 13-9B (LO4)
✓ Est. cost of goods sold: $193,750

RETAIL INVENTORY METHOD The following information is provided by Beverly's Basket Corner for the last quarter of its fiscal year ending on March 31, 20--:

	Cost	Retail
Inventory, start of period, January 1, 20--	$ 50,000	$ 80,000
Net purchases during the period	220,000	352,000
Net sales for the period		310,000

REQUIRED

1. Estimate the ending inventory as of March 31 using the retail inventory method.
2. Estimate the cost of goods sold for the time period January 1 through March 31 using the retail inventory method.

MANAGING YOUR WRITING

Most major grocery chains have optical scanning devices at the checkout stands and they certainly reduce the time required to check out. What benefits do they provide to the business? Next time you go to the grocery store, take a few minutes to chat with the manager. Ask the manager to describe the benefits of the scanning devices over the old machines that required the clerk to key in each purchase. Pay particular attention to the linkage between the scanning devices and the inventory systems. Be sure to ask whether the grocery store is on a periodic or perpetual system.

After your visit, write a memo to your instructor describing the benefits of the scanning devices and how they are linked with the inventory system.

ETHICS CASE

Electronics, Inc., is a high-volume, wholesale merchandising company. Most of its inventory turns over four or five times a year. The company has had 50 units of a particular brand of computers on hand for over a year. These computers have not sold and probably will not sell unless they are discounted 60 to 70%. The accountant is carrying them on the books at cost and intends to recognize the loss when they are sold. This way, she can avoid a significant write-down in inventory on the current year's financial statements.

1. Is the accountant correct in her treatment of the inventory? Why or why not?
2. If the computers cost $1,000 each and their market value is 40% of their cost, journalize the entry necessary for the write-down.
3. In a short paragraph, explain what is meant by conservatism and how it ties in with the lower-of-cost-or-market method of accounting for inventory.
4. In groups of three or four, make a list of reasons why inventories of electronic equipment might have to be written down.

MASTERY PROBLEM

✓ 1. Cost of goods sold, FIFO: $64,250; LIFO: $75,000; Weighted-avg.: $69,600
✓ 2. Ending inv., FIFO LCM: $21,600; Weighted-avg. LCM: $17,400
✓ 3. Estimated inv.: $22,000

Tiller Company's beginning inventory and purchases during the fiscal year ended December 31, 20-2, were as follows:

		Units	Unit Price	Total Cost
January 1, 20-2	Beginning inventory	1,500	$10.00	$15,000
January 12	1st purchase	500	11.50	5,750
February 28	2nd purchase	600	14.50	8,700
June 29	3rd purchase	1,200	15.00	18,000
August 31	4th purchase	800	16.50	13,200
October 29	5th purchase	300	18.00	5,400
November 30	6th purchase	700	18.50	12,950
December 21	7th purchase	400	20.00	8,000
		6,000		$87,000

There are 1,200 units of inventory on hand on December 31, 20-2.

REQUIRED

1. Calculate the total amount to be assigned to the cost of goods sold for 20-2 and ending inventory on December 31 under each of the following periodic inventory methods:

   (a) FIFO
   (b) LIFO
   (c) Weighted-average (round calculations to two decimal places)

2. Assume that the market price per unit (cost to replace) of Tiller's inventory on December 31 was $18. Calculate the total amount to be assigned to the ending inventory on December 31 under each of the following methods:

   (a) FIFO lower-of-cost-or-market
   (b) Weighted-average lower-of-cost-or-market

3. In addition to taking a physical inventory on December 31, Tiller decides to estimate the ending inventory and cost of goods sold. During the fiscal year ended December 31, 20-2, net sales of $100,000 were made at a normal gross profit rate of 35%. Use the gross profit method to estimate the cost of goods sold for the fiscal year ended December 31 and the inventory on December 31.

CHALLENGE PROBLEM

This problem challenges you to apply your cumulative accounting knowledge to move a step beyond the material in the chapter.

✓ FIFO CGS 20-2: $4,250;
LIFO CGS 20-2: $4,200

Bhushan Company has been using LIFO for inventory purposes because it would prefer to keep gross profits low for tax purposes. In its second year of operation (20-2), the controller pointed out that this strategy did not appear to work and suggested that FIFO cost of goods sold would have been higher than LIFO cost of goods sold for 20-2. Is this possible?

20-1	Units	Cost/Unit
Purchase 1	100	$1.00
Purchase 2	200	2.00
Purchase 3	300	3.00
Ending inventory	200	

20-2	Units	Cost/Unit
Beginning inventory	200	
Purchase 4	150	$4.00
Purchase 5	250	5.00
Purchase 6	350	6.00
Ending inventory	50	

REQUIRED

Using the information provided, compute the cost of goods sold for 20-1 and 20-2 comparing the LIFO and FIFO methods.

ANSWERS TO SELF-STUDY QUESTIONS AND EXERCISES

True/False Questions

1. T
2. T
3. F (this is true for the periodic method)
4. T
5. F (the buyer pays)

Multiple Choice Questions

1. b 2. b 3. c 4. a 5. c

U REVU Exercises

1.

Cost of goods sold	Understated by $10,000
Gross profit	Overstated by $10,000
Net income	Overstated by $10,000
Ending owner's capital	Overstated by $10,000

2.

Beginning inventory	
Merchandise inventory, beginning balance	$ 20,000
Purchased merchandise on account	200,000
Cost of merchandise sold	(120,000)
Freight charges paid on inventory delivered to showroom	1,000
Cost of merchandise returned by customers	500
Ending inventory	$101,500

3.

FIFO cost of goods sold:	
50 units @ $ 5 =	$ 250
100 units @ $ 8 =	800
50 units @ $10 =	500
FIFO cost of goods sold	$1,550

LIFO cost of goods sold:	
150 units @ $10 =	$1,500
50 units @ $ 8 =	400
LIFO cost of goods sold	$1,900

4.

Estimated inventory using the gross profit method:		
Cost of goods available for sale		$ 100,000
Net sales	$150,000	
Normal gross profit ($150,000 × 40% = $60,000)	60,000	
Estimated cost of goods sold		90,000
Estimated inventory		$ 10,000

Chapter 13 Appendix

Perpetual Inventory Method: LIFO and Moving-Average Methods

LEARNING OBJECTIVES

Careful study of this appendix should enable you to:

LO1 Compute the costs allocated to the ending inventory and cost of goods sold using the perpetual LIFO inventory method.

LO2 Compute the costs allocated to the ending inventory and cost of goods sold using the perpetual moving-average inventory method.

In Chapter 13, you learned how to apply the LIFO and weighted-averge inventory methods under the periodic inventory system. Recall that all calculations under the periodic system are done at the end of the accounting period. Under the perpetual system, costs are computed every time merchandise is purchased and sold. These costs are used to maintain a running record of the cost of goods sold to date and the balance of inventory on hand.

PERPETUAL LIFO

LO1 Compute the costs allocated to the ending inventory and cost of goods sold using the perpetual LIFO inventory method.

When using the **perpetual LIFO inventory method,** every time inventory is purchased a new layer is formed. When inventory is sold, we assume that the most recently purchased layer is sold first. As those units are used up, units are taken from the next most recently purchased layer. To illustrate, let's assume that Phaler's Fishing Supplies has the following beginning inventory, purchases, and sales of one type of bobber during the month of June. Note that the beginning inventory also has layers based on the prices paid in earlier periods.

Date	Beginning Inventory and Purchases		Sales
	Units	Cost/Unit	Units
June 1 (BI)	20	$0.80	
	160	1.00	
	20	1.20	
June 4	300	1.50	
June 20			400
June 30	100	1.80	

BI: Beginning Inventory

As shown in Figure 13A-1, the beginning inventory of 200 units forms Phaler's first three layers of inventory. The purchase on June 4 forms a fourth layer (300 units @ $1.50 = $450). At this point, Phaler has a total of 500 units at a total cost of $650. On June 20, Phaler sells 400 units. Under perpetual LIFO, we assume that the 300 units purchased on June 4 are sold first, followed by 20 that cost $1.20 each and 80 units that cost $1.00 each from the beginning inventory. The cost of goods sold on June 20 is $554. The cost of the inventory on hand is $96. At this point, Phaler has 100 units remaining from the beginning inventory.

On June 30, Phaler purchases 100 units at $1.80 each. This forms a new fifth layer (100 @ $1.80 = $180). This layer is added to the two layers remaining from the beginning inventory for a total of 200 units at a total cost of $276 of inventory on hand on June 30. Note that the third ($1.20 layer) and fourth ($1.50 layer) layers of inventory are gone. They will never reappear. If Phaler makes additional sales before buying more inventory, they will come from the fifth layer at $1.80 each, followed by units from the second ($1.00) and then the first ($0.80) layers.

FIGURE 13A-1 Perpetual LIFO Inventory System

DATE	PURCHASES			COST OF GOODS SOLD				INVENTORY ON HAND				
	Units	Cost/ Unit	Total	Units	Cost/ Unit	CGS	Cumulative CGS	Layer	Units	Cost/ Unit	Layer Cost	Total
Jan. 1 (BI)								(1)	20	$0.80	$ 16.00	
								(2)	160	1.00	160.00	
								(3)	20	1.20	24.00	$200.00
June 4								(1)	20	$0.80	$ 16.00	
								(2)	160	1.00	160.00	
								(3)	20	1.20	24.00	
	300	$1.50	$450.00	→				(4)	300	1.50	450.00	$650.00
June. 20				300	$1.50	$450.00		(1)	20	$0.80	$ 16.00	
				20	1.20	24.00		(2)	80	1.00	80.00	$ 96.00
				80	1.00	80.00	$554.00					
June 30								(1)	20	$0.80	$ 16.00	
								(2)	80	1.00	80.00	
	100	$1.80	$180.00	→				(5)	100	1.80	180.00	$276.00
Cost of Goods Sold for June							$554.00					
BI: Beginning Inventory												

PERPETUAL MOVING-AVERAGE

LO2 Compute the costs allocated to the ending inventory and cost of goods sold using the perpetual moving-average inventory method.

When using the **perpetual moving-average inventory method**, every time inventory is purchased a new average cost per unit is calculated. When inventory is sold, the most recent average cost is used to measure cost of goods sold and the remaining inventory on hand. To illustrate, let's look again at the purchases and sales of Phaler's Fishing Supplies for the month of June.

Date	Beginning Inventory and Purchases		Sales
	Units	Cost/Unit	Units
June 1 (BI)	20	$0.80	
	160	1.00	
	20	1.20	
June 4	300	1.50	
June 20			400
June 30	100	1.80	

BI: Beginning Inventory

When using the moving average inventory method, it is best to do the calculations on a calculator or computer spreadsheet. Carry each calculation out to the number of decimal places allowed by the technology used. This will reduce rounding errors.

As shown in Figure 13A-2, a new average cost is calculated each time a purchase is made. The average cost of the June 1 beginning inventory is shown as $1.00 ($200 cost/200 units). To compute the average cost after buying more inventory on June 4, we take the cost of the inventory on hand ($200 + $450 = $650) and divide by the number of units on hand (200 + 300 = 500). Thus, the average cost of the inventory on hand on June 4 is $1.30 per unit. To compute the cost of the 400 units sold on June 20, multiply the 400 units by $1.30 to get the cost of goods sold of $520. The remaining cost of the inventory on hand is $130 ($650 – $520). The number of units on hand is reduced to 100 (500 – 400).

On June 30, 100 additional units are purchased. This increases the units on hand to 200 (100 + 100) and the cost of the inventory on hand to $310 ($130 + $180). Dividing the cost of the inventory on hand by the number of units on hand provides a new moving-average cost of $1.55 ($310 ÷ 200). If Phaler makes another sale before buying additional units, this average cost will be used to compute the cost of goods sold and determine the cost of the inventory remaining on hand. Note that selling inventory does not change the moving-average cost. This is because the units are being removed at the most recent average cost.

FIGURE 13A-2 Perpetual Moving-Average Inventory System

DATE	PURCHASES			COST OF GOODS SOLD				INVENTORY ON HAND AND AVG. COST/UNIT			
	Units	Cost/ Unit	Total	Units	Cost/ Unit	CGS	Cumulative CGS	Cost of Purchase or (Sale)	Cost of Inventory on Hand	Units on Hand	AVG. Cost/Unit
June 1 (BI)									$200.00	200.00	$1.0000
June 4	300.00	$1.50	$450.00					$ 450.00	650.00	500.00	1.3000
June 20				400.00	$1.30	$520.00	$520.00	(520.00)	130.00	100.00	1.3000
June 30	100.00	$1.80	$180.00					180.00	310.00	200.00	1.5500
Cost of Goods Sold during January							$520.00				

BI: Beginning Inventory

LEARNING OBJECTIVES Key Points to Remember

LO1 Compute the costs allocated to the ending inventory and cost of goods sold using the perpetual LIFO inventory method.	When using the perpetual LIFO inventory method, every time inventory is purchased, a new layer is formed. When inventory is sold, we assume the units were sold out of the most recent layer. As those units are used up, additional sales are taken from the next most recently purchased layer.
LO2 Compute the costs allocated to the ending inventory and cost of goods sold using the perpetual moving-average inventory method.	When using the perpetual moving-average inventory method, every time inventory is purchased, a new average cost per unit is calculated. When inventory is sold, the most recent average cost is used to measure cost of goods sold and the remaining inventory on hand.

KEY TERMS

perpetual LIFO inventory method (517) A method of allocating merchandise cost which assumes that every time inventory is purchased, a new layer is formed. When inventory is sold, units are sold out of the most recent layer. As those units are used up, additional sales are taken from the next most recently purchased layer.

perpetual moving-average inventory method (518) A method of allocating merchandise cost which assumes that every time inventory is purchased, a new average cost per unit is calculated. When inventory is sold, the most recent average cost is used to measure cost of goods sold and the remaining inventory on hand.

REVIEW QUESTION

LO1 1. Explain the primary difference between the periodic and perpetual inventory systems when calculating cost of goods sold and merchandise inventory.

SERIES A EXERCISE

E 13Apx-1A (LO1/2)

✓ CGS under perpetual LIFO: $3,345; CGS under perpetual moving-average: $3,250

PERPETUAL: LIFO AND MOVING-AVERAGE The beginning inventory, purchases, and sales for Myrl Sign Company for the month of April follow.

Date	Beginning Inventory and Purchases		Sales
	Units	Cost/Unit	Units
April 1 (BI)	100	$4.30	
	100	4.50	
	200	4.60	
April 20	400	5.50	
April 30			650

BI: Beginning Inventory

REQUIRED

Calculate the total amount to be assigned to cost of goods sold for April and the ending inventory on April 30, under each of the following methods:

1. Perpetual LIFO inventory method
2. Perpetual moving-average inventory method

SERIES A PROBLEM

P 13Apx-2A (LO1/2)

✓ CGS under perpetual LIFO: $1,900; CGS under perpetual moving-average: $1,856.64

PERPETUAL: LIFO AND MOVING-AVERAGE Kelley Company began business on January 1, 20-1. Purchases and sales during the month of January follow.

Date	Purchases		Sales
	Units	Cost/Unit	Units
Jan. 1	100	$1.00	
Jan. 4	400	1.10	
Jan. 5			300
Jan. 10	300	1.30	
Jan. 12			200
Jan. 15	200	1.35	
Jan. 18	500	1.60	
Jan. 22			800
Jan. 27			100
Jan. 31	300	1.80	

REQUIRED

Calculate the total amount to be assigned to cost of goods sold for January and the ending inventory on January 31, under each of the following methods:

1. Perpetual LIFO inventory method
2. Perpetual moving-average inventory method

SERIES B EXERCISE

E 13Apx-1B (LO1/2)

✓ CGS under perpetual LIFO: $5,435; CGS under perpetual moving-average: $5,395

PERPETUAL: LIFO AND MOVING-AVERAGE The beginning inventory, purchases, and sales for Harrington Equipment Company for the month of August follow.

Date	Beginning Inventory and Purchases		Sales
	Units	Cost/Unit	Units
Aug. 1 (BI)	100	$8.00	
	150	8.10	
	250	8.30	
Aug. 15	300	8.50	
Aug. 31			650

BI: Beginning Inventory

REQUIRED

Calculate the total amount to be assigned to cost of goods sold for August and the ending inventory on August 31, under each of the following methods:

1. Perpetual LIFO inventory method
2. Perpetual moving-average inventory method

SERIES B PROBLEM

P 13Apx-2B (LO1/2)

✓ CGS under perpetual LIFO: $3,720; CGS under perpetual moving-average: $3,665.25

PERPETUAL: LIFO AND MOVING-AVERAGE Vozniak Company began business on January 1, 20-1. Purchases and sales during the month of January follow.

Date	Purchases		Sales
	Units	Cost/Unit	Units
Jan. 1	100	$2.00	
Jan. 5	500	2.30	
Jan. 7			300
Jan. 12	300	2.40	
Jan. 15			300
Jan. 17	200	2.50	
Jan. 19	500	2.70	
Jan. 24			800
Jan. 28			100
Jan. 31	200	2.90	

REQUIRED

Calculate the total amount to be assigned to cost of goods sold for January and the ending inventory on January 31, under each of the following methods:

1. Perpetual LIFO inventory method
2. Perpetual moving-average inventory method

Chapter 14

COURTESY OF THE SCRANTON/WILKES-BARRE YANKEES/WWW.SWBYANKEES.COM

Adjustments and the Work Sheet for a Merchandising Business

The Scranton/Wilkes-Barre (Pa.) Yankees are the Class AAA affiliate of the New York Yankees. They play in the North Division of the International League with the Buffalo Bisons, Ottawa Lynx, Pawtucket Red Sox, Rochester Red Wings, and Syracuse Chiefs. The franchise was founded in 1989 when the Maine Guides moved to Pennsylvania. From 1989 to 2006, the team was the Class AAA International League affiliate of the Philadelphia Phillies known as the Red Barons.

The team is managed by Mandalay Sports Entertainment, which also operates several other Minor League teams. The Yankees play at PNC Field, which was built on Montage Mountain between Scranton and Wilkes-Barre and has a capacity of 10,310, including luxury suites with indoor and outdoor seating. It opened in 1989.

Often, we are expected to pay in advance for goods and services. This is true for season tickets for sporting events like the Scranton/Wilkes-Barre Yankees, magazine subscriptions, or tickets for popular operas or rock concerts. In return, we expect to receive the goods or services. In this chapter, you will learn proper accounting for cash receipts received in advance, which are known as unearned revenues.

LEARNING OBJECTIVES

Careful study of this chapter should enable you to:

LO1 Prepare an adjustment for merchandise inventory using the periodic inventory system.

LO2 Prepare an adjustment for unearned revenue.

LO3 Prepare a work sheet for a merchandising business.

LO4 Journalize adjusting entries for a merchandising business.

LO5 Prepare adjusting journal entries under the perpetual inventory system.

In Chapters 10 through 13, we learned how to account for the day-to-day transactions of a merchandising business. In this chapter, we focus on end-of-period adjustments and the preparation of the work sheet. Finally, in Chapter 15, we will complete the accounting cycle by preparing financial statements and closing entries.

A work sheet for a merchandising business is similar to the work sheet prepared for a service business (Chapter 5). It is used to prepare adjustments for supplies, prepaid insurance, wages earned but not paid, depreciation, and other necessary year-end adjustments. A merchandising business must also make an adjustment to properly report the amount of merchandise inventory held at the end of the accounting period. While revisiting the work sheet, we will also introduce a new adjustment for unearned revenue.

ADJUSTMENT FOR MERCHANDISE INVENTORY: PERIODIC INVENTORY SYSTEM

LO1 Prepare an adjustment for merchandise inventory using the periodic inventory system.

As discussed in Chapter 13, under the periodic inventory system when merchandise inventory is purchased, the purchases account is debited and Cash or Accounts Payable is credited. When inventory is sold, Cash or Accounts Receivable is debited and Sales is credited. Figure 14-1 provides a review of these entries.

FIGURE 14-1 Review of Entries for Purchase and Sale of Merchandise

TRANSACTION	ENTRY		
Purchase of merchandise	Purchases	xxx	
	Accounts Payable or Cash		xxx
Sale of merchandise	Accounts Receivable or Cash	xxx	
	Sales		xxx

Note that the merchandise inventory account is not debited or credited in either of these entries. Since sales and purchases have taken place during the year, the beginning balance of the merchandise inventory account no longer provides an accurate measure of the inventory held at the end of the year. Thus, an adjustment must be made. For other assets, like prepaid insurance, we would simply make an adjustment for the change in the asset account. *We do not follow this procedure for merchandise inventory.*

The adjustment for merchandise inventory is done in two steps.

Periodic Inventory Adjustments:
1. Take out the old.
2. Bring in the new.

1. Remove the beginning inventory from the merchandise inventory account by making the following entry:

Income Summary	old	
Merchandise Inventory		old

2. Enter the ending inventory in the merchandise inventory account by making the following entry:

Merchandise Inventory	new	
Income Summary		new

As discussed in Chapter 13, the quantity of inventory on hand at the end of the accounting period is determined by taking a physical count of the goods on hand. The cost of these goods is determined by using FIFO, LIFO, or another inventory method. Of course, this year's ending inventory becomes next year's beginning inventory.

To illustrate the adjustment for merchandise inventory, let's assume that Ponder's Bike Parts had a beginning merchandise inventory of $25,000. During the year, the entries shown in Figure 14-1 were made as merchandise was purchased and sold. At the end of the accounting period, a physical inventory of the merchandise determined that merchandise costing $30,000 was still on hand.

To appreciate the reason for the different adjustment process, recall the discussion in Chapter 13 of how the beginning and ending inventories are used when computing cost of goods sold. As shown in the bottom portion of Figure 14-2, the beginning inventory is added to purchases to compute cost of goods available for sale. The

FIGURE 14-2 Calculation of Cost of Goods Sold Using Information in the Income Statement Columns of the Work Sheet

Ponder's Bike Parts
Work Sheet (Partial)
For Year Ended December 31, 20 - -

	ACCOUNT TITLE	TRIAL BALANCE		ADJUSTMENTS		ADJUSTED TRIAL BALANCE		INCOME STATEMENT		BALANCE SHEET		
		DEBIT	CREDIT	DEBIT	CREDIT	DEBIT	CREDIT	DEBIT	CREDIT	DEBIT	CREDIT	
1								Beginning	Ending			1
2								Inventory	Inventory			2
3												3
4	Merchandise Inventory	25 000 00		STEP 2 30 000 00	25 000 00 STEP 1	30 000 00				30 000 00		4
5	Income Summary			STEP 1 25 000 00	30 000 00 STEP 2	25 000 00	30 000 00	25 000 00	30 000 00			5
6	Purchases	80 000 00				80 000 00		80 000 00				6
7	Purchases Returns/Allowances		1 000 00				1 000 00		1 000 00	Purchases Returns & Allow.		7
8	Purchases Discounts		500 00				500 00	Purchases	500 00	Purchases Discounts		8
9	Freight-In	700 00				700 00		700 00				9
10												10
11								Freight-In				11
12												12
13												13
14												14

Step 1: Remove beginning inventory	Income Summary	25,000	
	Merchandise Inventory		25,000
Step 2: Insert ending inventory	Merchandise Inventory	30,000	
	Income Summary		30,000

Cost of goods sold:				
Merchandise inventory, January 1			$ 25 000 00	
Purchases		$ 80 000 00		
Less: Purchases returns and allowances	$ 1 000 00			
Purchases discounts	500 00	1 500 00		
Net purchases		$ 78 500 00		
Add freight-in		700 00		
Cost of goods purchased			79 200 00	
Goods available for sale			$104 200 00	
Less merchandise inventory, December 31			30 000 00	
Cost of goods sold				$ 74 200 00

ending inventory is subtracted from cost of goods available for sale to compute cost of goods sold.

Many firms use the work sheet to prepare financial statements. Thus, all of the information needed to compute cost of goods sold should be readily available in the Income Statement columns of the work sheet. To provide this information, we need an adjustment technique that results in the beginning inventory being extended into the Income Statement *Debit* column so it can be *added* to purchases. Further, we need the ending inventory extended into the Income Statement *Credit* column so it will be *subtracted* when computing cost of goods sold. As shown in Figure 14-2, this can be accomplished in two steps by using the income summary account.

STEP 1 The beginning inventory ($25,000) is removed by crediting Merchandise Inventory. Income Summary is debited because this amount is used in the calculation of cost of goods sold and net income.

STEP 2 The ending inventory ($30,000) is entered by debiting Merchandise Inventory. Income Summary is credited because this amount is also used in the calculation of cost of goods sold and net income.

LEARNING KEY

Both the debit and credit amounts on the income summary line are extended to the Income Statement columns.

Note that the debit *and* credit adjustments made to Income Summary are extended into the Adjusted Trial Balance and Income Statement columns. *This is the only time individual figures, rather than the net amount, are extended on the work sheet.* It is done in this case because the individual amounts are needed for the calculation of cost of goods sold on the income statement (beginning inventory + purchases − ending inventory = cost of goods sold). Note, also, that all of the information needed to compute cost of goods sold is readily available in the Income Statement columns of the work sheet.

U REVU Complete U REVU-1 on **page 544** to test your basic understanding of LO1.

ADJUSTMENT FOR UNEARNED REVENUE

LO2 Prepare an adjustment for unearned revenue.

Some businesses require payment before delivering a product or performing a service. Examples include insurance companies, magazine publishers, apartment complexes, college food services, and professional sports and theater companies that sell season tickets. The cash received in advance is called **unearned revenue**. Since the cash has been received in advance, the company owes the customers the product or service, or must refund their money. Thus, unearned revenue is reported as a *liability* on the balance sheet.

LEARNING KEY

Remember, under the accrual basis of accounting, revenue is recorded when *earned* regardless of when cash is received.

To illustrate, let's assume that Brown County Playhouse sells season tickets for five plays produced throughout the year. Tickets sell for $10 for each play ($50 for a season ticket) and a maximum of 1,000 seats can be sold for each play. For simplicity, let's assume that all shows sell out during the first week that season tickets are available for sale. As shown below and in Figure 14-3, the sale of the tickets would be recorded as follows:

8		(1)	Cash	50,000.00		8
9			Unearned Ticket Revenue		50,000.00	9
10			Season ticket sales			10
11			($10 × 1,000 seats × 5 shows)			11

To prepare financial statements following production of the third show, an adjusting entry is needed to recognize that $30,000 ($10 × 1,000 seats × 3 shows) in ticket revenue has been earned. To do this, the following adjusting entry is made:

13			Adjusting Entries			13
14			Unearned Ticket Revenue		30 0 0 0 00		14
15			Ticket Revenue			30 0 0 0 00	15

The remaining balance of $20,000 in Unearned Ticket Revenue is reported as a current liability on the balance sheet.

FIGURE 14-3 Entries for Unearned Revenue

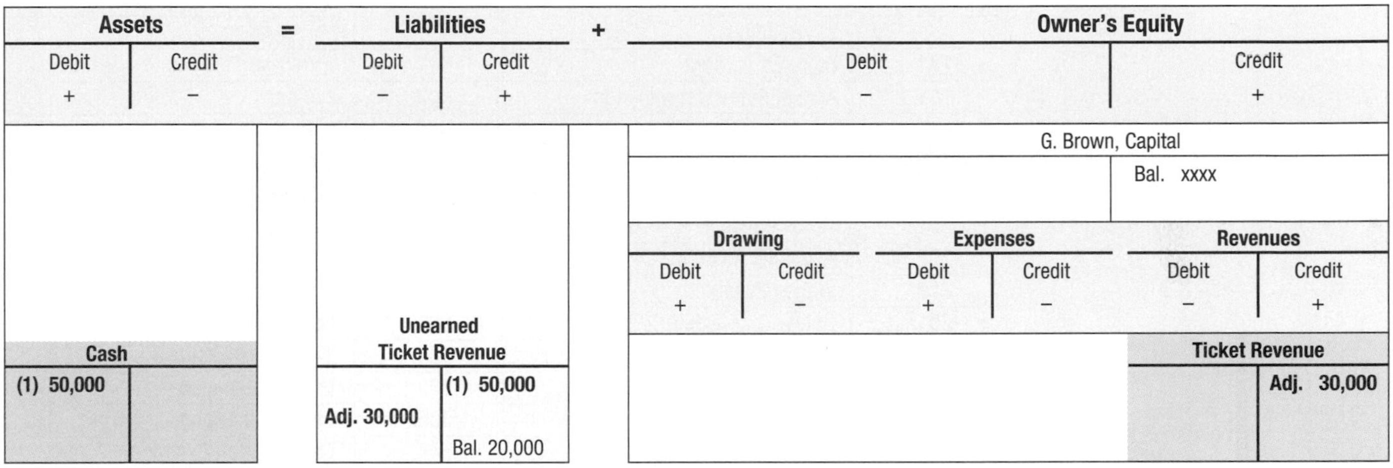

EXPANDED CHART OF ACCOUNTS

Let's take a look at where the new accounts for a merchandising business fit into a chart of accounts. Recall that the chart of accounts follows the form of the accounting equation (assets = liabilities + owner's equity + revenues − expenses). A chart of accounts for Northern Micro is provided in Figure 14-4. Note the classification of the new accounts introduced in Chapters 10 and 11 for a merchandising firm.

Merchandise Inventory is listed as a current asset. Since Northern Micro sells subscriptions to a computer magazine that it produces, Unearned Subscriptions Revenue is listed as a current liability, and Subscriptions Revenue is listed as a revenue. Sales Returns and Allowances and Sales Discounts are contra-revenue accounts. Recall, however, that Northern Micro does not offer sales discounts.

Purchases, Purchases Returns and Allowances, Purchases Discounts, and Freight-In are used to compute cost of goods sold. Thus, they are listed under this heading. Purchases Returns and Allowances and Purchases Discounts are often called contra-cost accounts or contra-purchases accounts.

Interest Expense is classified as "Other Expenses" instead of being listed under Operating Expenses. This is because it represents the expense of obtaining money to do business, rather than an expense directly associated with operating the business.

FIGURE 14-4 Chart of Accounts for Northern Micro

NORTHERN MICRO CHART OF ACCOUNTS			
Assets		**Revenue**	
Current Assets		401	Sales
101	Cash	401.1	Sales Returns and
122	Accounts Receivable		Allowances
131	Merchandise Inventory	**Other Revenue**	
141	Supplies	411	Interest Revenue
145	Prepaid Insurance	412	Rent Revenue
		413	Subscriptions Revenue
Property, Plant, and Equipment		**Expenses**	
161	Land	**Cost of Goods Sold**	
171	Building	501	Purchases
171.1	Accumulated Depreciation—	501.1	Purchases Returns and
	Building		Allowances
181	Store Equipment	501.2	Purchases Discounts
181.1	Accumulated Depreciation—	502	Freight-In
	Store Equipment	**Operating Expenses**	
Liabilities		511	Wages Expense
Current Liabilities		512	Advertising Expense
201	Notes Payable	513	Bank Credit Card
202	Accounts Payable		Expense
219	Wages Payable	521	Rent Expense
231	Sales Tax Payable	523	Supplies Expense
241	Unearned Subscriptions	525	Telephone Expense
	Revenue	533	Utilities Expense
Long-Term Liabilities		535	Insurance Expense
251	Mortgage Payable	540	Depreciation Expense—
			Building
Owner's Equity		541	Depreciation Expense—
311	Gary L. Fishel, Capital		Store Equipment
312	Gary L. Fishel, Drawing	549	Miscellaneous Expense
313	Income Summary		
		Other Expenses	
		551	Interest Expense

U REVU

Complete U REVU-2 on **page 544** to test your basic understanding of LO2.

PREPARING A WORK SHEET FOR A MERCHANDISING BUSINESS

LO3 Prepare a work sheet for a merchandising business.

The work sheet for a merchandising business is similar to the one shown in Chapter 5 for a service business. Recall the five steps taken to prepare a work sheet.

STEP 1 Prepare the trial balance.

STEP 2 Prepare the adjustments.

STEP 3 Prepare the adjusted trial balance.

STEP 4 Extend the adjusted trial balance amounts to the Income Statement and Balance Sheet columns.

STEP 5 Total the Income Statement and Balance Sheet columns to compute the net income or net loss.

The work sheet format and the five steps taken when preparing the work sheet are illustrated in Figure 14-5. Note that the new accounts introduced for a merchandising firm and the unearned revenue account are highlighted so that you can see their proper placement and extensions. (The abbreviation BI stands for beginning inventory; EI stands for ending inventory.) Pay particular attention to the extension of Income Summary. Both the debit and credit amounts for this account must be extended.

FIGURE 14-5 Overview of Work Sheet for a Merchandising Business

Name of Company
Work Sheet
For Year Ended December 31, 20 - -

	ACCOUNT TITLE	TRIAL BALANCE		ADJUSTMENTS		ADJUSTED TRIAL BALANCE		INCOME STATEMENT		BALANCE SHEET		
		DEBIT	CREDIT	DEBIT	CREDIT	DEBIT	CREDIT	DEBIT	CREDIT	DEBIT	CREDIT	
1		Step 1:		Step 2:		Step 3:		Step 4:				1
2		Prepare a		Prepare the		Prepare the		Extend Adjusted				2
3	(Insert Ledger Account Titles)	Trial Balance		Adjustments		Adjusted Trial Balance		Account Balances				3
4		Assets				Assets				Assets		4
5		Mdse. Inv. (BI)		EI	BI	Mdse. Inv. (EI)				Mdse. Inv. (EI)		5
6			Liabilities				Liabilities				Liabilities	6
7			Unearned				Unearned				Unearned	7
8			Revenues				Revenues				Revenues	8
9												9
10			Capital				Capital				Capital	10
11		Drawing				Drawing				Drawing		11
12												12
13	Income Summary			BI	EI	BI	EI	BI	EI			13
14												14
15			Revenues				Revenues		Revenues			15
16			Sales				Sales		Sales			16
17		Sales R&A				Sales R&A		Sales R&A				17
18		Sales Discounts				Sales Discounts		Sales Discounts				18
19												19
20		Expenses				Expenses		Expenses				20
21		Purchases				Purchases		Purchases				21
22			Purch. R&A				Purch. R&A		Purch. R&A			22
23			Purch. Discounts				Purch. Discounts		Purch. Discounts			23
24		Freight-In				Freight-In		Freight-In				24
25									Step 5:			25
26									Complete the work sheet			26
27									(1) Sum columns			27
28									(2) Compute net income (loss)			28
29												29
30								Net	Net	Net	Net	30
31								Income	Loss	Loss	Income	31
32												32

BI = Beginning Inventory
EI = Ending Inventory

A Broader View

ENDOPACK/ISTOCKPHOTO.COM

The Importance of Inventory

Note the important role of the ending inventory in the calculation of cost of goods sold in Figure 14-2. If the ending inventory is overstated for any reason, net income will also be overstated. Given this important relationship, auditors observe and verify the accuracy of the physical inventory. However, unethical managers, desperate to improve profits, have on occasion found ways to mislead auditors.

In one case, managers overstated inventory counts for items that the auditors had not physically verified. In another case, auditors found a barrel whose contents had been valued by management at thousands of dollars. It actually contained floor sweepings. Finally, there was a case where management called the auditor, the day after the inventory audit, to report that additional inventory had arrived and should be included in the inventory count. The auditor never verified that the inventory was real. It turned out to be a scam that helped the company double its reported profits for the year. These unfortunate events highlight the reason auditors must exercise great care when conducting an inventory audit.

ADJUSTMENTS FOR NORTHERN MICRO

Before preparing a work sheet for Northern Micro, let's review the preparation of adjustments in T account form. Figure 14-6 provides year-end adjustment information for Northern Micro. Figure 14-7 shows adjusting entries based on this information. The unadjusted balances for these accounts were taken from Northern Micro's trial balance.

PREPARING A WORK SHEET FOR NORTHERN MICRO

Let's prepare a work sheet for Northern Micro following the five steps illustrated in Figure 14-5.

STEP 1 In Figure 14-8, the Trial Balance columns are completed by copying the balances of all accounts from the general ledger (not shown).

STEP 2 In Figure 14-9, the adjustments are entered. These entries are exactly the same as those made in T account form in Figure 14-7.

STEP 3 In Figure 14-10, extensions are made to the Adjusted Trial Balance columns. Note that both the debit and credit amounts for Income Summary are extended.

STEP 4 In Figure 14-11, the Adjusted Trial Balance amounts are extended to the Income Statement and Balance Sheet columns.

STEP 5 In Figure 14-11, the work sheet is completed by totaling the Income Statement and Balance Sheet columns. The difference between the debits and credits for each pair of columns represents the net income or net loss.

FIGURE 14-6 Year-End Adjustment Data for Northern Micro

YEAR-END ADJUSTMENT DATA FOR NORTHERN MICRO	
(a, b)	A physical count showed that merchandise inventory costing $18,000 is on hand as of December 31.
(c)	Supplies remaining at the end of the year, $400.
(d)	Unexpired insurance on December 31, $600.
(e)	Depreciation expense on the building for the year, $4,000.
(f)	Depreciation expense on the store equipment for the year, $3,000.
(g)	Wages earned but not paid as of December 31, $450.
(h)	Northern Micro publishes a computer magazine. Subscribers pay in advance. Unearned subscriptions revenue as of December 31, $2,000.

FIGURE 14-7 Adjusting Entries for Northern Micro

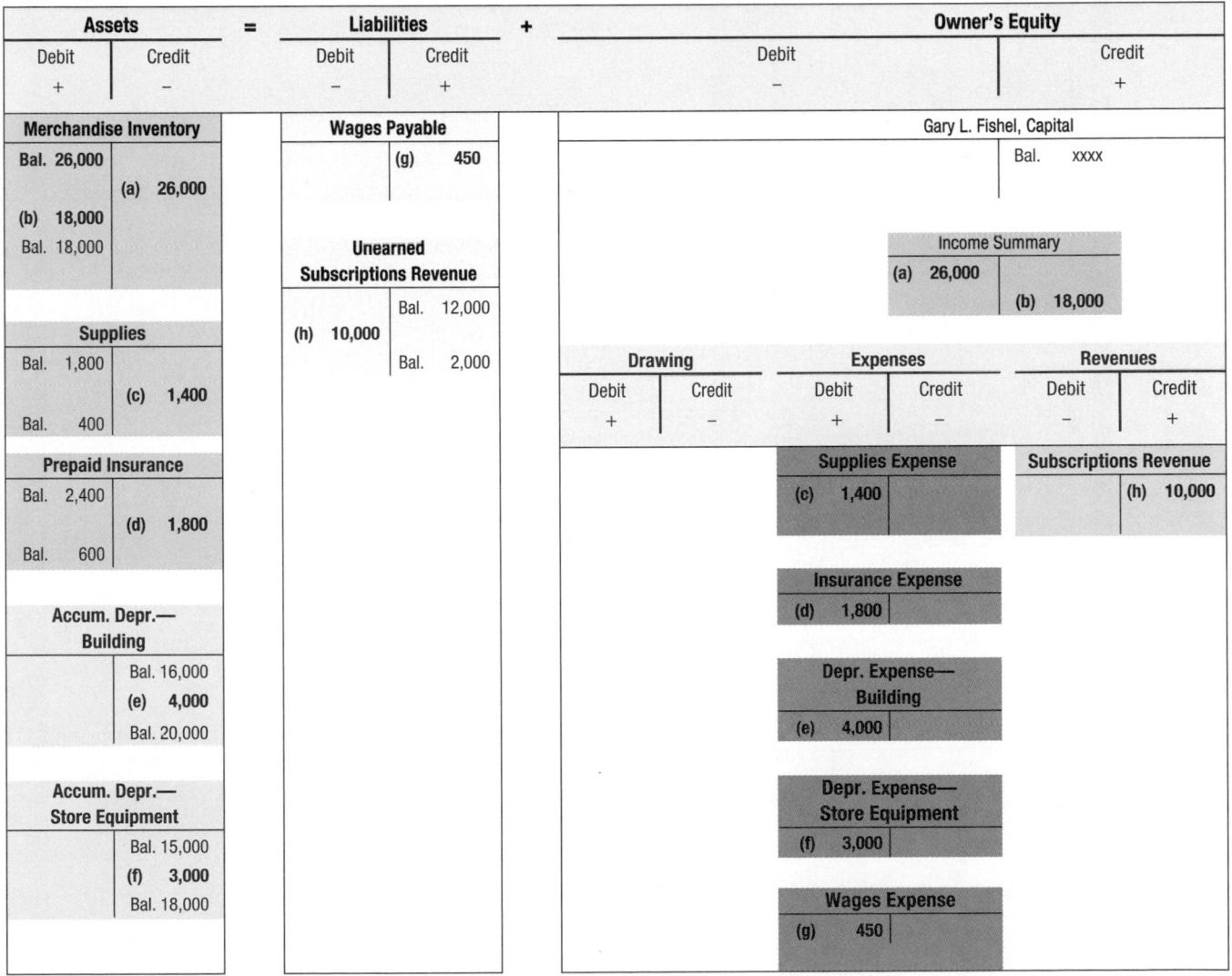

Assets = **Liabilities** + **Owner's Equity**

Assets Debit +	Assets Credit −	Liabilities Debit −	Liabilities Credit +	Owner's Equity Debit −	Owner's Equity Credit +

Assets

Merchandise Inventory	
Bal. 26,000	(a) 26,000
(b) 18,000	
Bal. 18,000	

Supplies	
Bal. 1,800	(c) 1,400
Bal. 400	

Prepaid Insurance	
Bal. 2,400	(d) 1,800
Bal. 600	

Accum. Depr.—Building	
	Bal. 16,000
	(e) 4,000
	Bal. 20,000

Accum. Depr.—Store Equipment	
	Bal. 15,000
	(f) 3,000
	Bal. 18,000

Liabilities

Wages Payable	
	(g) 450

Unearned Subscriptions Revenue	
	Bal. 12,000
(h) 10,000	
	Bal. 2,000

Owner's Equity

Gary L. Fishel, Capital	
	Bal. xxxx

Income Summary	
(a) 26,000	(b) 18,000

Drawing Debit +	Drawing Credit −	Expenses Debit +	Expenses Credit −	Revenues Debit −	Revenues Credit +

Supplies Expense	
(c) 1,400	

Insurance Expense	
(d) 1,800	

Depr. Expense—Building	
(e) 4,000	

Depr. Expense—Store Equipment	
(f) 3,000	

Wages Expense	
(g) 450	

Subscriptions Revenue	
	(h) 10,000

FIGURE 14-8 Step 1: Completion of the Trial Balance Columns

Northern Micro
Work Sheet
For Year Ended December 31, 20 - -

	ACCOUNT TITLE	TRIAL BALANCE		ADJUSTMENTS		ADJUSTED TRIAL BALANCE		INCOME STATEMENT		BALANCE SHEET		
		DEBIT	CREDIT	DEBIT	CREDIT	DEBIT	CREDIT	DEBIT	CREDIT	DEBIT	CREDIT	
1	Cash	20,000.00										1
2	Accounts Receivable	15,000.00										2
3	Merchandise Inventory	26,000.00										3
4	Supplies	1,800.00										4
5	Prepaid Insurance	2,400.00										5
6	Land	10,000.00										6
7	Building	90,000.00										7
8	Accum. Depr.—Building		16,000.00									8
9	Store Equipment	50,000.00										9
10	Accum. Depr.—Store Equipment		15,000.00									10
11	Notes Payable		5,000.00									11
12	Accounts Payable		10,000.00									12
13	Wages Payable											13
14	Sales Tax Payable		1,500.00									14
15	Unearned Subscriptions Revenue		12,000.00									15
16	Mortgage Payable		30,000.00									16
17	Gary L. Fishel, Capital		114,400.00									17
18	Gary L. Fishel, Drawing	20,000.00										18
19	Income Summary											19
20	Sales		214,000.00									20
21	Sales Returns and Allowances	1,200.00										21
22	Interest Revenue		900.00									22
23	Rent Revenue		8,000.00									23
24	Subscriptions Revenue											24
25	Purchases	105,000.00										25
26	Purchases Returns and Allowances		800.00									26
27	Purchases Discounts		1,000.00									27
28	Freight-In	300.00										28
29	Wages Expense	42,000.00										29
30	Advertising Expense	2,500.00										30
31	Bank Credit Card Expense	1,500.00										31
32	Rent Expense	20,000.00										32
33	Supplies Expense											33
34	Telephone Expense	3,500.00										34
35	Utilities Expense	12,000.00										35
36	Insurance Expense											36
37	Depr. Expense—Building											37
38	Depr. Expense—Store Equipment											38
39	Miscellaneous Expense	2,250.00										39
40	Interest Expense	3,150.00										40
41		428,600.00	428,600.00									41
42												42

STEP 1

FIGURE 14-9 Step 2: Preparation of the Adjustments

Northern Micro
Work Sheet
For Year Ended December 31, 20 - -

	ACCOUNT TITLE	TRIAL BALANCE		ADJUSTMENTS		ADJUSTED TRIAL BALANCE		INCOME STATEMENT		BALANCE SHEET		
		DEBIT	CREDIT	DEBIT	CREDIT	DEBIT	CREDIT	DEBIT	CREDIT	DEBIT	CREDIT	
1	Cash	20 000 00										1
2	Accounts Receivable	15 000 00										2
3	Merchandise Inventory	26 000 00		(b) 18 000 00	(a) 26 000 00							3
4	Supplies	1 800 00			(c) 1 400 00							4
5	Prepaid Insurance	2 400 00			(d) 1 800 00							5
6	Land	10 000 00										6
7	Building	90 000 00										7
8	Accum. Depr.—Building		16 000 00		(e) 4 000 00							8
9	Store Equipment	50 000 00										9
10	Accum. Depr.—Store Equipment		15 000 00		(f) 3 000 00							10
11	Notes Payable		5 000 00									11
12	Accounts Payable		10 000 00									12
13	Wages Payable				(g) 450 00							13
14	Sales Tax Payable		1 500 00									14
15	Unearned Subscriptions Revenue		12 000 00	(h) 10 000 00								15
16	Mortgage Payable		30 000 00									16
17	Gary L. Fishel, Capital		114 400 00									17
18	Gary L. Fishel, Drawing	20 000 00										18
19	Income Summary			(a) 26 000 00	(b) 18 000 00							19
20	Sales		214 000 00									20
21	Sales Returns and Allowances	1 200 00										21
22	Interest Revenue		900 00									22
23	Rent Revenue		8 000 00									23
24	Subscriptions Revenue				(h) 10 000 00							24
25	Purchases	105 000 00										25
26	Purchases Returns and Allowances		800 00									26
27	Purchases Discounts		1 000 00									27
28	Freight-In	300 00										28
29	Wages Expense	42 000 00		(g) 450 00								29
30	Advertising Expense	2 500 00										30
31	Bank Credit Card Expense	1 500 00										31
32	Rent Expense	20 000 00										32
33	Supplies Expense			(c) 1 400 00								33
34	Telephone Expense	3 500 00										34
35	Utilities Expense	12 000 00										35
36	Insurance Expense			(d) 1 800 00								36
37	Depr. Expense—Building			(e) 4 000 00								37
38	Depr. Expense—Store Equipment			(f) 3 000 00								38
39	Miscellaneous Expense	2 250 00										39
40	Interest Expense	3 150 00										40
41		428 600 00	428 600 00	64 650 00	64 650 00							41
42												42

Callouts: Line 3 adjustments: (b) debit — ENDING INVENTORY; (a) credit — BEGINNING INVENTORY. Line 19 adjustments: (a) debit — BEGINNING INVENTORY; (b) credit — ENDING INVENTORY.

STEP 1 (Trial Balance) STEP 2 (Adjustments)

FIGURE 14-10 Step 3: Extensions to the Adjusted Trial Balance Columns

Northern Micro
Work Sheet
For Year Ended December 31, 20 - -

	ACCOUNT TITLE	TRIAL BALANCE DEBIT	TRIAL BALANCE CREDIT	ADJUSTMENTS DEBIT	ADJUSTMENTS CREDIT	ADJUSTED TRIAL BALANCE DEBIT	ADJUSTED TRIAL BALANCE CREDIT	INCOME STATEMENT DEBIT	INCOME STATEMENT CREDIT	BALANCE SHEET DEBIT	BALANCE SHEET CREDIT	
1	Cash	20 000 00				20 000 00						1
2	Accounts Receivable	15 000 00				15 000 00						2
3	Merchandise Inventory	26 000 00		(b) 18 000 00	(a) 26 000 00	18 000 00						3
4	Supplies	1 800 00			(c) 1 400 00	400 00						4
5	Prepaid Insurance	2 400 00			(d) 1 800 00	600 00						5
6	Land	10 000 00				10 000 00						6
7	Building	90 000 00				90 000 00						7
8	Accum. Depr.—Building		16 000 00		(e) 4 000 00		20 000 00					8
9	Store Equipment	50 000 00				50 000 00						9
10	Accum. Depr.—Store Equipment		15 000 00		(f) 3 000 00		18 000 00					10
11	Notes Payable		5 000 00				5 000 00					11
12	Accounts Payable		10 000 00				10 000 00					12
13	Wages Payable				(g) 450 00		450 00					13
14	Sales Tax Payable		1 500 00				1 500 00					14
15	Unearned Subscriptions Revenue		12 000 00	(h) 10 000 00			2 000 00					15
16	Mortgage Payable		30 000 00				30 000 00					16
17	Gary L. Fishel, Capital		114 400 00				114 400 00					17
18	Gary L. Fishel, Drawing	20 000 00				20 000 00						18
19	Income Summary			(a) 26 000 00	(b) 18 000 00	26 000 00	18 000 00					19
20	Sales		214 000 00				214 000 00					20
21	Sales Returns and Allowances	1 200 00				1 200 00						21
22	Interest Revenue		900 00				900 00					22
23	Rent Revenue		8 000 00				8 000 00					23
24	Subscriptions Revenue				(h) 10 000 00		10 000 00					24
25	Purchases	105 000 00				105 000 00						25
26	Purchases Returns and Allowances		800 00				800 00					26
27	Purchases Discounts		1 000 00				1 000 00					27
28	Freight-In	300 00				300 00						28
29	Wages Expense	42 000 00		(g) 450 00		42 450 00						29
30	Advertising Expense	2 500 00				2 500 00						30
31	Bank Credit Card Expense	1 500 00				1 500 00						31
32	Rent Expense	20 000 00				20 000 00						32
33	Supplies Expense			(c) 1 400 00		1 400 00						33
34	Telephone Expense	3 500 00				3 500 00						34
35	Utilities Expense	12 000 00				12 000 00						35
36	Insurance Expense			(d) 1 800 00		1 800 00						36
37	Depr. Expense—Building			(e) 4 000 00		4 000 00						37
38	Depr. Expense—Store Equipment			(f) 3 000 00		3 000 00						38
39	Miscellaneous Expense	2 250 00				2 250 00						39
40	Interest Expense	3 150 00				3 150 00						40
41		428 600 00	428 600 00	64 650 00	64 650 00	454 050 00	454 050 00					41
42												42

Ending Inventory (line 3, adjusted trial balance debit)

Beginning Inventory (line 19, adjusted trial balance debit)

Both the debit and credit are extended (line 19)

Ending Inventory (line 19, adjusted trial balance credit)

STEP 1 (Trial Balance) | STEP 2 (Adjustments) | STEP 3 (Adjusted Trial Balance)

FIGURE 14-11 Step 4: Extensions to the Income Statement and Balance Sheet Columns Step 5: Completing the Work Sheet and Computing Net Income

Northern Micro
Work Sheet
For Year Ended December 31, 20 --

	ACCOUNT TITLE	TRIAL BALANCE		ADJUSTMENTS		ADJUSTED TRIAL BALANCE		INCOME STATEMENT		BALANCE SHEET		
		DEBIT	CREDIT	DEBIT	CREDIT	DEBIT	CREDIT	DEBIT	CREDIT	DEBIT	CREDIT	
1	Cash	20 000 00				20 000 00				20 000 00		1
2	Accounts Receivable	15 000 00				15 000 00				15 000 00		2
3	Merchandise Inventory	26 000 00		(b) 18 000 00	(a) 26 000 00	18 000 00				18 000 00		3
4	Supplies	1 800 00			(c) 1 400 00	400 00				400 00		4
5	Prepaid Insurance	2 400 00			(d) 1 800 00	600 00				600 00		5
6	Land	10 000 00				10 000 00				10 000 00		6
7	Building	90 000 00				90 000 00				90 000 00		7
8	Accum. Depr.—Building		16 000 00		(e) 4 000 00		20 000 00				20 000 00	8
9	Store Equipment	50 000 00				50 000 00				50 000 00		9
10	Accum. Depr.—Store Equipment		15 000 00		(f) 3 000 00		18 000 00				18 000 00	10
11	Notes Payable		5 000 00				5 000 00				5 000 00	11
12	Accounts Payable		10 000 00				10 000 00				10 000 00	12
13	Wages Payable				(g) 450 00		450 00				450 00	13
14	Sales Tax Payable		1 500 00				1 500 00				1 500 00	14
15	Unearned Subscriptions Revenue		12 000 00	(h) 10 000 00			2 000 00				2 000 00	15
16	Mortgage Payable		30 000 00				30 000 00				30 000 00	16
17	Gary L. Fishel, Capital		114 400 00				114 400 00				114 400 00	17
18	Gary L. Fishel, Drawing	20 000 00				20 000 00				20 000 00		18
19	Income Summary			(a) 26 000 00	(b) 18 000 00	26 000 00	18 000 00	26 000 00	18 000 00			19
20	Sales		214 000 00				214 000 00		214 000 00			20
21	Sales Returns and Allowances	1 200 00				1 200 00		1 200 00				21
22	Interest Revenue		900 00				900 00		900 00			22
23	Rent Revenue		8 000 00				8 000 00		8 000 00			23
24	Subscriptions Revenue				(h) 10 000 00		10 000 00		10 000 00			24
25	Purchases	105 000 00				105 000 00		105 000 00				25
26	Purchases Returns and Allowances		800 00				800 00		800 00			26
27	Purchases Discounts		1 000 00				1 000 00		1 000 00			27
28	Freight-In	300 00				300 00		300 00				28
29	Wages Expense	42 000 00		(g) 450 00		42 450 00		42 450 00				29
30	Advertising Expense	2 500 00				2 500 00		2 500 00				30
31	Bank Credit Card Expense	1 500 00				1 500 00		1 500 00				31
32	Rent Expense	20 000 00				20 000 00		20 000 00				32
33	Supplies Expense			(c) 1 400 00		1 400 00		1 400 00				33
34	Telephone Expense	3 500 00				3 500 00		3 500 00				34
35	Utilities Expense	12 000 00				12 000 00		12 000 00				35
36	Insurance Expense			(d) 1 800 00		1 800 00		1 800 00				36
37	Depr. Expense—Building			(e) 4 000 00		4 000 00		4 000 00				37
38	Depr. Expense—Store Equipment			(f) 3 000 00		3 000 00		3 000 00				38
39	Miscellaneous Expense	2 250 00				2 250 00		2 250 00				39
40	Interest Expense	3 150 00				3 150 00		3 150 00				40
41		428 600 00	428 600 00	64 650 00	64 650 00	454 050 00	454 050 00	230 050 00	252 700 00	224 000 00	201 350 00	41
42	Net Income							22 650 00			22 650 00	42
43								252 700 00	252 700 00	224 000 00	224 000 00	43
		STEP 1		STEP 2		STEP 3		STEPS 4 AND 5				

U REVU Complete U REVU-3 on **page 544** to test your basic understanding of LO3.

LO4 Journalize adjusting entries for a merchandising business.

ADJUSTING ENTRIES

Recall that making the adjustments on the work sheet has no effect on the actual accounts in the general ledger. Journal entries must be made to enter the adjustments into the accounting system. Figure 14-12 shows the adjusting entries for Northern Micro.

LEARNING KEY

Recall that the work sheet is just a planning tool. The adjusting entries must be entered in the general journal.

FIGURE 14-12 Adjusting Entries for Northern Micro

GENERAL JOURNAL — PAGE 3

	DATE		DESCRIPTION	POST. REF.	DEBIT	CREDIT	
1			Adjusting Entries				1
2	20-- Dec.	31	Income Summary		26 000 00		2
3			Merchandise Inventory			26 000 00	3
4							4
5		31	Merchandise Inventory		18 000 00		5
6			Income Summary			18 000 00	6
7							7
8		31	Supplies Expense		1 400 00		8
9			Supplies			1 400 00	9
10							10
11		31	Insurance Expense		1 800 00		11
12			Prepaid Insurance			1 800 00	12
13							13
14		31	Depr. Expense—Building		4 000 00		14
15			Accumulated Depr.—Building			4 000 00	15
16							16
17		31	Depr. Expense—Store Equipment		3 000 00		17
18			Accumulated Depr.—Store Equipment			3 000 00	18
19							19
20		31	Wages Expense		450 00		20
21			Wages Payable			450 00	21
22							22
23		31	Unearned Subscriptions Revenue		10 000 00		23
24			Subscriptions Revenue			10 000 00	24
25							25

U REVU Complete U REVU-4 on **page 544** to test your basic understanding of LO4.

LO5 Prepare adjusting journal entries under the perpetual inventory system.

ADJUSTING ENTRIES UNDER THE PERPETUAL INVENTORY SYSTEM

Under the perpetual inventory system, the merchandise inventory and cost of goods sold accounts are continually updated throughout the year to reflect purchases and sales of inventory. When inventory is purchased, the merchandise inventory account is debited and Cash or Accounts Payable is credited. When inventory is sold, two entries are made.

1. Cash or Accounts Receivable is debited and Sales is credited.
2. Cost of Goods Sold is debited and Merchandise Inventory is credited.

A comparison of the entries under the periodic and perpetual inventory systems is provided in Figure 14-13.

LEARNING KEY

Under the perpetual inventory system, cost of goods sold and the amount of merchandise inventory on hand are continually updated as merchandise is bought and sold.

FIGURE 14-13 Entries for Periodic and Perpetual Inventory Systems

TRANSACTION	PERIODIC SYSTEM			PERPETUAL SYSTEM		
Purchased merchandise on account, $800.	Purchases	800		Merchandise Inventory	800	
	Accounts Payable		800	Accounts Payable		800
Sold merchandise on account, $400. The cost of the merchandise sold was $300.	Accounts Receivable	400		Accounts Receivable	400	
	Sales		400	Sales		400
				Cost of Goods Sold	300	
				Merchandise Inventory		300

As discussed in Chapter 13, the perpetual inventory system does not eliminate the need for taking physical inventories. The perpetual records must be compared with the physical inventory to discover and correct any errors or losses of merchandise from theft, breakage, or spoilage. If a difference is found between the physical count and the amount in the perpetual inventory records, the records must be corrected by an adjusting entry. Some firms use Cost of Goods Sold to make this adjustment. A preferable approach is to use an account called **Inventory Short and Over**. For example, if the book balance is $3,840 and the physical count shows $3,710 worth of merchandise, the $130 shortage would be entered as follows:

Adjusting Entry

4		Inventory Short and Over		1 3 0 00		4
5		Merchandise Inventory			1 3 0 00	5
6		To adjust inventory per physical count				6

LEARNING KEY

A physical inventory is still important under the perpetual inventory system. It is used to verify the accuracy of the inventory records.

Similarly, if the book balance is $3,840 and the physical count shows $3,900 worth of merchandise, this $60 overage would be entered as follows:

Adjusting Entry

4		Merchandise Inventory		6 0 00		4
5		Inventory Short and Over			6 0 00	5
6		To adjust inventory per physical count				6

If Inventory Short and Over has a debit balance, the account is listed with other expenses on the income statement. If it has a credit balance, the account is listed with other revenues on the income statement.

Using a separate account, Inventory Short and Over, makes it easier for management to track inventory problems associated with errors, theft, breakage, and spoilage.

Further, it removes these items from the calculation of cost of goods sold and provides a better measure of the gross profit on sales.

A business that sells a wide selection of low-cost goods may not find it practical to keep a perpetual inventory. In contrast, a business that sells a few high-cost items (cars, fine jewelry, stereo equipment) can maintain such a record without incurring excessive processing costs. The increasing use of computers and optical scanning devices at the point of sale has enabled more businesses to switch from the periodic to the perpetual inventory system.

U REVU Complete U REVU-5 on **page 544** to test your basic understanding of LO5.

SELF-STUDY

LEARNING OBJECTIVES Key Points to Remember

LO1 Prepare an adjustment for merchandise inventory using the periodic inventory system.

Extra care is required for the end-of-period adjustment for merchandise inventory and the related extensions on the work sheet. The two-step adjustment process used on the work sheet is shown below. This technique is used so that all of the information required to compute cost of goods sold on the income statement is provided in the Income Statement columns of the work sheet.

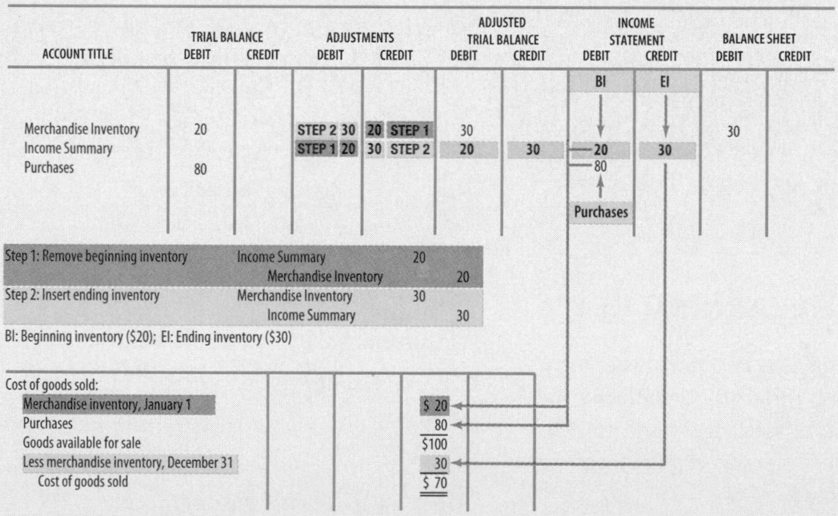
ACCOUNT TITLE
TRIAL BALANCE DEBIT CREDIT
ADJUSTMENTS DEBIT CREDIT
ADJUSTED TRIAL BALANCE DEBIT CREDIT
INCOME STATEMENT DEBIT CREDIT
BALANCE SHEET DEBIT CREDIT
BI
EI
Merchandise Inventory 20 STEP 2 30 20 STEP 1 30 30
Income Summary STEP 1 20 30 STEP 2 20 30 20 30
Purchases 80 80
Purchases
Step 1: Remove beginning inventory Income Summary 20 Merchandise Inventory 20
Step 2: Insert ending inventory Merchandise Inventory 30 Income Summary 30
BI: Beginning inventory ($20); EI: Ending inventory ($30)
Cost of goods sold:
Merchandise inventory, January 1 $ 20
Purchases 80
Goods available for sale $100
Less merchandise inventory, December 31 30
Cost of goods sold $ 70

LO2 Prepare an adjustment for unearned revenue.

Some firms receive cash before providing a service or selling a product. The cash received in advance is considered a liability, unearned revenue, until earned. The adjusting entry to recognize that unearned revenue has become earned is as follows:

Unearned Revenue	xxx	
Revenue		xxx

LEARNING OBJECTIVES Key Points to Remember

LEARNING OBJECTIVES	Key Points to Remember
LO3 Prepare a work sheet for a merchandising business.	Steps to follow when preparing a work sheet are as follows: 1. Prepare the trial balance. 2. Prepare the adjustments. 3. Prepare the adjusted trial balance. 4. Extend the adjusted trial balance amounts to the Income Statement and Balance Sheet columns. 5. Total the Income Statement and Balance Sheet columns to compute the net income or net loss.
LO4 Journalize adjusting entries for a merchandising business.	The work sheet is a useful tool when preparing end-of-period adjustments and financial statements. Remember: The work sheet is NOT a formal part of the accounting system. Adjustments made on the work sheet must be entered in a journal and posted to the ledger.

LO5 Prepare adjusting journal entries under the perpetual inventory system.	Under the perpetual inventory system, the cost of goods sold and merchandise inventory accounts are updated whenever merchandise is purchased or sold. Thus, the firm knows how much inventory should be on hand at any given point in time. However, the balance of the merchandise inventory account must be verified with an actual physical count of the inventory before issuing financial statements. If there is a difference, an adjusting entry is made. If the balance in the inventory account is greater than the physical count, the following entry is made:
	Inventory Short and Over xxx
	    Merchandise Inventory xxx
	If the balance in the inventory account is less than the physical count, the following entry is made:
	Merchandise Inventory xxx
	    Inventory Short and Over xxx

DEMONSTRATION PROBLEM

Aaron Patton owns and operates Patton's Bait Shop and Boat Rental. A year-end trial balance is shown on the next page.

Year-end adjustment data for Patton's Bait Shop and Boat Rental are as follows:

(a and b) A physical count shows that merchandise inventory costing $15,000 is on hand as of December 31, 20--.

(c) Supplies remaining at the end of the year, $200.

(d) Unexpired insurance on December 31, $300.

(e) Depreciation expense on the building for 20--, $2,000.

(f) Depreciation expense on the store equipment for 20--, $1,500.

(g) Wages earned but not paid as of December 31, $225.

(h) Unearned boat rental revenue as of December 31, $1,000.

(continued)

REQUIRED

1. Prepare a year-end work sheet.
2. Journalize the adjusting entries.
3. Compute cost of goods sold using the work sheet prepared for part (1).

Patton's Bait Shop and Boat Rental
Trial Balance
December 31, 20 - -

ACCOUNT TITLE	DEBIT BALANCE	CREDIT BALANCE
Cash	10,000.00	
Accounts Receivable	7,500.00	
Merchandise Inventory	19,000.00	
Supplies	900.00	
Prepaid Insurance	1,200.00	
Land	5,000.00	
Building	45,000.00	
Accumulated Depreciation—Building		8,000.00
Store Equipment	25,000.00	
Accumulated Depreciation—Store Equipment		7,500.00
Notes Payable		2,500.00
Accounts Payable		5,000.00
Wages Payable		
Unearned Boat Rental Revenue		11,000.00
Aaron Patton, Capital		77,900.00
Aaron Patton, Drawing	10,000.00	
Income Summary		
Sales		100,250.00
Sales Returns and Allowances	600.00	
Boat Rental Revenue		
Purchases	52,500.00	
Purchases Returns and Allowances		400.00
Purchases Discounts		500.00
Freight-In	150.00	
Wages Expense	21,000.00	
Advertising Expense	3,750.00	
Supplies Expense		
Telephone Expense	1,750.00	
Utilities Expense	6,000.00	
Insurance Expense		
Depreciation Expense—Building		
Depreciation Expense—Store Equipment		
Miscellaneous Expense	3,625.00	
Interest Expense	75.00	
	213,050.00	213,050.00

Solution 1.

Patton's Bait Shop and Boat Rental
Work Sheet
For Year Ended December 31, 20 --

	Account Title	Trial Balance Debit	Trial Balance Credit	Adjustments Debit	Adjustments Credit	Adjusted Trial Balance Debit	Adjusted Trial Balance Credit	Income Statement Debit	Income Statement Credit	Balance Sheet Debit	Balance Sheet Credit	
1	Cash	10,000.00				10,000.00				10,000.00		1
2	Accounts Receivable	7,500.00				7,500.00				7,500.00		2
3	Merchandise Inventory	19,000.00		(b) 15,000.00	(a) 19,000.00	15,000.00				15,000.00		3
4	Supplies	900.00			(c) 700.00	200.00				200.00		4
5	Prepaid Insurance	1,200.00			(d) 900.00	300.00				300.00		5
6	Land	5,000.00				5,000.00				5,000.00		6
7	Building	45,000.00				45,000.00				45,000.00		7
8	Accum. Depr.—Building		8,000.00		(e) 2,000.00		10,000.00				10,000.00	8
9	Store Equipment	25,000.00				25,000.00				25,000.00		9
10	Accum. Depr.—Store Equipment		7,500.00		(f) 1,500.00		9,000.00				9,000.00	10
11	Notes Payable		2,500.00				2,500.00				2,500.00	11
12	Accounts Payable		5,000.00				5,000.00				5,000.00	12
13	Wages Payable				(g) 225.00		225.00				225.00	13
14	Unearned Boat Rental Revenue		11,000.00	(h) 10,000.00			1,000.00				1,000.00	14
15	Aaron Patton, Capital		77,900.00				77,900.00				77,900.00	15
16	Aaron Patton, Drawing	10,000.00				10,000.00				10,000.00		16
17	Income Summary			(a) 19,000.00	(b) 15,000.00	19,000.00	15,000.00	19,000.00	15,000.00			17
18	Sales		100,250.00				100,250.00		100,250.00			18
19	Sales Returns and Allowances	600.00				600.00		600.00				19
20	Boat Rental Revenue				(h) 10,000.00		10,000.00		10,000.00			20
21	Purchases	52,500.00				52,500.00		52,500.00				21
22	Purchases Returns and Allowances		400.00				400.00		400.00			22
23	Purchases Discounts		500.00				500.00		500.00			23
24	Freight-In	150.00				150.00		150.00				24
25	Wages Expense	21,000.00		(g) 225.00		21,225.00		21,225.00				25
26	Advertising Expense	3,750.00				3,750.00		3,750.00				26
27	Supplies Expense			(c) 700.00		700.00		700.00				27
28	Telephone Expense	1,750.00				1,750.00		1,750.00				28
29	Utilities Expense	6,000.00				6,000.00		6,000.00				29
30	Insurance Expense			(d) 900.00		900.00		900.00				30
31	Depr. Expense—Building			(e) 2,000.00		2,000.00		2,000.00				31
32	Depr. Expense—Store Equipment			(f) 1,500.00		1,500.00		1,500.00				32
33	Miscellaneous Expense	3,625.00				3,625.00		3,625.00				33
34	Interest Expense	75.00				75.00		75.00				34
35		213,050.00	213,050.00	49,325.00	49,325.00	231,775.00	231,775.00	113,775.00	126,150.00	118,000.00	105,625.00	35
36	Net Income							12,375.00			12,375.00	36
37								126,150.00	126,150.00	118,000.00	118,000.00	37

(continued)

2.

GENERAL JOURNAL					PAGE 3
DATE		DESCRIPTION	POST REF.	DEBIT	CREDIT
		Adjusting Entries			
20-- Dec.	31	Income Summary		19,000.00	
		Merchandise Inventory			19,000.00
	31	Merchandise Inventory		15,000.00	
		Income Summary			15,000.00
	31	Supplies Expense		700.00	
		Supplies			700.00
	31	Insurance Expense		900.00	
		Prepaid Insurance			900.00
	31	Depreciation Expense—Building		2,000.00	
		Accumulated Depreciation—Building			2,000.00
	31	Depreciation Expense—Store Equipment		1,500.00	
		Accumulated Depreciation—Store Equipment			1,500.00
	31	Wages Expense		225.00	
		Wages Payable			225.00
	31	Unearned Boat Rental Revenue		10,000.00	
		Boat Rental Revenue			10,000.00

3.

Cost of goods sold:				
Merchandise inventory, January 1			$19,000.00	
Purchases		$52,500.00		
Less: Purchases returns and allowances	$ 400.00			
Purchases discounts	500.00	900.00		
Net purchases		$51,600.00		
Add freight-in		150.00		
Cost of goods purchased			51,750.00	
Goods available for sale			$70,750.00	
Less merchandise inventory, December 31			15,000.00	
Cost of goods sold				$55,750.00

KEY TERMS

Inventory Short and Over (537) An account used to adjust the perpetual inventory records when a difference exists between the physical count and the amount in the perpetual inventory records.

unearned revenue (526) Cash received in advance of delivering a product or performing a service.

SELF-STUDY QUESTIONS AND EXERCISES

True/False Questions

1. LO1 Under the periodic inventory system, the beginning inventory is removed from the merchandise inventory account with a credit to Merchandise Inventory and a debit to Income Summary.
2. LO1 Under the periodic inventory system, the ending inventory is entered by debiting Merchandise Inventory and crediting Income Summary.
3. LO2 The cash received in advance before delivering a product or performing a service is called unearned revenue.
4. LO2 Unearned revenue is adjusted into an expense account at the end of the accounting period.
5. LO2 Sales Returns and Allowances is classified as a contra-cost account on the income statement.

Multiple Choice Questions

1. LO2 Purchases Returns and Allowances and Purchases Discounts are classified as ________ on the income statement.
   (a) expense accounts
   (b) contra-cost accounts
   (c) revenue accounts
   (d) contra-revenue accounts
2. LO3 The first step in preparing a work sheet is to
   (a) prepare the trial balance.
   (b) prepare the income statement.
   (c) prepare the adjustments.
   (d) prepare the balance sheet.
3. LO3 The last step in preparing a work sheet is to
   (a) prepare the adjusted trial balance.
   (b) total the Income Statement and Balance Sheet columns to compute net income or net loss.
   (c) prepare the adjustments.
   (d) extend the Adjusted Trial Balance columns.
4. LO3 Unearned Revenue is extended into the ________ on the work sheet.
   (a) Adjustments columns
   (b) Balance Sheet columns
   (c) Income Statement columns
   (d) Trial Balance columns

5. LO3 The most useful tool in preparing end-of-period adjustments and financial statements is the
   (a) general ledger.
   (b) work sheet.
   (c) general journal.
   (d) physical inventory.

U REVU Exercises

1. LO1 Prepare the cost of goods sold section for Joseph's Gift Shop. The following amounts are known:

Beginning merchandise inventory	$ 20,000
Ending merchandise inventory	15,000
Purchases	171,000

2. LO2 The Venice Theatre sold and collected cash of $45,000 for season tickets. Upon collection of cash, Unearned Ticket Revenue was credited. At the end of the accounting period, $15,000 had been earned. Make the appropriate adjusting entry.

3. LO3 Information relating to inventory for Janie Par Gifts is provided below.

Beginning merchandise inventory	$120,000
Ending merchandise inventory	90,000
Purchases	250,000

   1. Set up a work sheet similar to the one provided below.
   2. Enter the appropriate information from above into the Trial Balance columns.
   3. Prepare appropriate adjusting entries and extensions across the work sheet.

	ACCOUNT TITLE	TRIAL BALANCE DEBIT	TRIAL BALANCE CREDIT	ADJUSTMENTS DEBIT	ADJUSTMENTS CREDIT	ADJUSTED TRIAL BALANCE DEBIT	ADJUSTED TRIAL BALANCE CREDIT	INCOME STATEMENT DEBIT	INCOME STATEMENT CREDIT	BALANCE SHEET DEBIT	BALANCE SHEET CREDIT	
1	Merchandise Inventory											1
2	Income Summary											2
3	Purchases											3

4. LO4 Using the partial work sheet provided below, prepare the adjusting entries for merchandise inventory.

	ACCOUNT TITLE	TRIAL BALANCE DEBIT	TRIAL BALANCE CREDIT	ADJUSTMENTS DEBIT	ADJUSTMENTS CREDIT	
1	Merchandise Inventory	50 0 0 0 00		(b) 60 0 0 0 00	(a) 50 0 0 0 00	1
2	Income Summary			(a) 50 0 0 0 00	(b) 60 0 0 0 00	2
3	Purchases	80 0 0 0 00				3

5. LO5 The following information is provided by Koffi Products:

Ending balance of merchandise inventory account	$50,000
Physical count of ending merchandise inventory	48,000

   Prepare the appropriate adjusting entry under the perpetual inventory system.

The answers to the Self-Study Questions and Exercises are at the end of the chapter (page 562).

APPLYING YOUR KNOWLEDGE

REVIEW QUESTIONS

LO1 1. A firm is preparing to make adjusting entries at the end of the accounting period. The balance of the merchandise inventory account is $200,000. If the firm is using the periodic inventory system, what does this balance represent?

LO1 2. What work sheet amounts are used to compute cost of goods sold?

LO1 3. Why are both the debit and credit amounts in the Adjustments columns on the Income Summary line of the work sheet extended to the Adjusted Trial Balance columns?

LO2 4. What is an unearned revenue?

LO2 5. Give three examples of unearned revenue.

LO3 6. List the five steps taken to prepare a work sheet.

LO3 7. What does the difference between the totals of the Income Statement columns represent? What does the difference between the Balance Sheet column totals represent?

LO5 8. A firm is preparing to make adjusting entries at the end of the accounting period. The balance of the merchandise inventory account is $100,000. If the firm is using the perpetual inventory system, what does this balance represent?

SERIES A EXERCISES

E 14-1A (LO1)

ADJUSTMENT FOR MERCHANDISE INVENTORY USING T ACCOUNTS: PERIODIC INVENTORY SYSTEM Sam Baker owns a business called Sam's Sporting Goods. His beginning inventory as of January 1, 20--, was $47,000, and his ending inventory as of December 31, 20--, was $53,000. Set up T accounts for Merchandise Inventory and Income Summary and perform the year-end adjustment for Merchandise Inventory.

E 14-2A (LO1)
✓ Cost of goods sold: $65,200

CALCULATION OF COST OF GOODS SOLD: PERIODIC INVENTORY SYSTEM Prepare the cost of goods sold section for Adams Gift Shop. The following amounts are known:

Beginning merchandise inventory	$26,000
Ending merchandise inventory	23,000
Purchases	71,000
Purchases returns and allowances	3,500
Purchases discounts	5,500
Freight-in	200

E 14-3A (LO2)

ADJUSTMENT FOR UNEARNED REVENUES USING T ACCOUNTS Set up T accounts for Cash, Unearned Ticket Revenue, and Ticket Revenue. Post the following two transactions to the appropriate accounts, indicating each transaction by letter:

(a) Sold 1,500 season tickets at $30 each, receiving cash of $45,000.
(b) An end-of-period adjustment is needed to recognize that $35,000 in ticket revenue has been earned.

REQUIRED

1. Complete the Adjustments columns, identifying each adjustment with its corresponding letter.
2. Complete the work sheet.
3. Enter the adjustments in a general journal.

Seaside Kite Shop
Trial Balance
December 31, 20 --

ACCOUNT TITLE	DEBIT BALANCE	CREDIT BALANCE
Cash	20,000.00	
Accounts Receivable	14,000.00	
Merchandise Inventory	25,000.00	
Supplies	8,000.00	
Prepaid Insurance	5,400.00	
Land	30,000.00	
Building	50,000.00	
Accumulated Depreciation—Building		20,000.00
Store Equipment	35,000.00	
Accumulated Depreciation—Store Equipment		14,000.00
Accounts Payable		9,600.00
Wages Payable		
Sales Tax Payable		5,900.00
Unearned Rent Revenue		8,900.00
Mortgage Payable		45,000.00
J. Kennington, Capital		65,410.00
J. Kennington, Drawing	26,000.00	
Income Summary		
Sales		118,000.00
Sales Returns and Allowances	1,700.00	
Rent Revenue		
Purchases	27,000.00	
Purchases Returns and Allowances		1,400.00
Purchases Discounts		1,800.00
Freight-In	2,100.00	
Wages Expense	32,000.00	
Advertising Expense	3,600.00	
Supplies Expense		
Telephone Expense	1,350.00	
Utilities Expense	8,000.00	
Insurance Expense		
Depreciation Expense—Building		
Depreciation Expense—Store Equipment		
Miscellaneous Expense	860.00	
	290,010.00	290,010.00

P 14-10A (LO1/2/3/4) **COMPLETION OF A WORK SHEET SHOWING A NET LOSS** The trial balance for Cascade Bicycle Shop, a business owned by David Lamond, is shown below. Year-end adjustment information is as follows:

✓ Adj. col. total: $72,650; Net loss: $45,760

KA KLOOSTER & ALLEN

(a and b) Merchandise inventory costing $22,000 is on hand as of December 31, 20--. (The periodic inventory system is used.)
(c) Supplies remaining at the end of the year, $2,400.
(d) Unexpired insurance on December 31, $1,750.
(e) Depreciation expense on the building for 20--, $4,000.
(f) Depreciation expense on the store equipment for 20--, $3,600.
(g) Unearned storage revenue as of December 31, $1,950.
(h) Wages earned but not paid as of December 31, $750.

Cascade Bicycle Shop
Trial Balance
December 31, 20 --

ACCOUNT TITLE	DEBIT BALANCE	CREDIT BALANCE
Cash	23 0 0 0 00	
Accounts Receivable	15 0 0 0 00	
Merchandise Inventory	31 0 0 0 00	
Supplies	7 2 0 0 00	
Prepaid Insurance	4 6 0 0 00	
Land	28 0 0 0 00	
Building	53 0 0 0 00	
Accumulated Depreciation—Building		17 0 0 0 00
Store Equipment	27 0 0 0 00	
Accumulated Depreciation—Store Equipment		9 0 0 0 00
Accounts Payable		3 8 0 0 00
Wages Payable		
Sales Tax Payable		3 0 5 0 00
Unearned Storage Revenue		5 6 0 0 00
Mortgage Payable		42 0 0 0 00
D. Lamond, Capital		165 7 6 0 00
D. Lamond, Drawing	33 0 0 0 00	
Income Summary		
Sales		51 0 0 0 00
Sales Returns and Allowances	2 4 0 0 00	
Storage Revenue		
Purchases	21 0 0 0 00	
Purchases Returns and Allowances		1 3 0 0 00
Purchases Discounts		1 9 0 0 00
Freight-In	1 8 0 0 00	
Wages Expense	35 0 0 0 00	
Advertising Expense	5 7 0 0 00	
Supplies Expense		
Telephone Expense	2 2 0 0 00	
Utilities Expense	9 6 0 0 00	
Insurance Expense		
Depreciation Expense—Building		
Depreciation Expense—Store Equipment		
Miscellaneous Expense	9 1 0 00	
	300 4 1 0 00	300 4 1 0 00

(continued)

REQUIRED

1. Complete the Adjustments columns, identifying each adjustment with its corresponding letter.
2. Complete the work sheet.
3. Enter the adjustments in the general journal.

P 14-11A (LO1/2/4)

✓ Adj. col. total: $88,155

WORKING BACKWARD FROM ADJUSTED TRIAL BALANCE TO DETERMINE ADJUSTING ENTRIES The partial work sheet shown below is taken from the books of Stark Street Computers, a business owned by Logan Cowart, for the year ended December 31, 20--.

Stark Street Computers
Work Sheet (Partial)
For Year Ended December 31, 20 --

	ACCOUNT TITLE	TRIAL BALANCE		ADJUSTMENTS		ADJUSTED TRIAL BALANCE		
		DEBIT	CREDIT	DEBIT	CREDIT	DEBIT	CREDIT	
1	Cash	18,000.00				18,000.00		1
2	Accounts Receivable	11,000.00				11,000.00		2
3	Merchandise Inventory	25,000.00				35,000.00		3
4	Supplies	8,000.00				2,820.00		4
5	Prepaid Insurance	5,400.00				1,225.00		5
6	Land	27,000.00				27,000.00		6
7	Building	48,000.00				48,000.00		7
8	Accum. Depr.—Building		20,000.00				27,000.00	8
9	Store Equipment	33,000.00				33,000.00		9
10	Accum. Depr.—Store Equipment		8,700.00				12,800.00	10
11	Accounts Payable		6,400.00				6,400.00	11
12	Wages Payable						1,300.00	12
13	Sales Tax Payable		5,700.00				5,700.00	13
14	Unearned Repair Revenue		8,200.00				1,800.00	14
15	Mortgage Payable		44,000.00				44,000.00	15
16	L. Cowart, Capital		80,025.00				80,025.00	16
17	L. Cowart, Drawing	35,000.00				35,000.00		17
18	Income Summary					25,000.00	35,000.00	18
19	Sales		122,000.00				122,000.00	19
20	Sales Returns and Allowances	2,250.00				2,250.00		20
21	Repair Revenue						6,400.00	21
22	Purchases	29,750.00				29,750.00		22
23	Purchases Returns and Allowances		1,850.00				1,850.00	23
24	Purchases Discounts		1,425.00				1,425.00	24
25	Freight-In	3,200.00				3,200.00		25
26	Wages Expense	37,000.00				38,300.00		26
27	Advertising Expense	4,125.00				4,125.00		27
28	Supplies Expense					5,180.00		28
29	Telephone Expense	1,650.00				1,650.00		29
30	Utilities Expense	9,150.00				9,150.00		30
31	Insurance Expense					4,175.00		31
32	Depr. Expense—Building					7,000.00		32
33	Depr. Expense—Store Equipment					4,100.00		33
34	Miscellaneous Expense	775.00				775.00		34
35		298,300.00	298,300.00			345,700.00	345,700.00	35

REQUIRED

1. Determine the adjusting entries by analyzing the difference between the adjusted trial balance and the trial balance.
2. Journalize the adjusting entries in a general journal.

P 14-12A **(LO1/2/3/4)**
✓ Adj. col. total: $92,335; Cost of goods sold: $33,145

WORKING BACKWARD FROM THE INCOME STATEMENT AND BALANCE SHEET COLUMNS OF THE WORK SHEET TO DETERMINE ADJUSTED TRIAL BALANCE AND ADJUSTING ENTRIES The partially completed work sheet from the books of Lewis Music Store, a business owned by Hugo Lewis, for the year ended December 31, 20--, is shown on page 552.

REQUIRED

1. Analyze the work sheet and determine the adjusted trial balance and the adjusting entries by working backward from the Income Statement and Balance Sheet columns.
2. Journalize the adjusting entries in a general journal.
3. Prepare the cost of goods sold section of the income statement for Lewis Music Store.

SERIES B EXERCISES

E 14-1B **(LO1)**

ADJUSTMENT FOR MERCHANDISE INVENTORY USING T ACCOUNTS: PERIODIC INVENTORY SYSTEM Sandra Owens owns a business called Sandra's Sporting Goods. Her beginning inventory as of January 1, 20--, was $33,000, and her ending inventory as of December 31, 20--, was $36,000. Set up T accounts for Merchandise Inventory and Income Summary and perform the year-end adjustment for Merchandise Inventory.

E 14-2B **(LO1)**
✓ Cost of goods sold: $58,100

CALCULATION OF COST OF GOODS SOLD: PERIODIC INVENTORY SYSTEM Prepare the cost of goods sold section for Havens Gift Shop. The following amounts are known:

Beginning merchandise inventory	$29,000
Ending merchandise inventory	27,000
Purchases	62,000
Purchases returns and allowances	2,800
Purchases discounts	3,400
Freight-in	300

E 14-3B **(LO2)**

ADJUSTMENT FOR UNEARNED REVENUES USING T ACCOUNTS Set up T accounts for Cash, Unearned Ticket Revenue, and Ticket Revenue. Post the following two transactions to the appropriate accounts, indicating each transaction by letter:

(a) Sold 1,200 season tickets at $20 each, receiving cash of $24,000.
(b) An end-of-period adjustment is needed to recognize that $19,000 in ticket revenue has been earned.

PROBLEM 14-12A

Lewis Music Store
Work Sheet
For Year Ended December 31, 20 --

	Account Title	Trial Balance Debit	Trial Balance Credit	Adjustments Debit	Adjustments Credit	Adjusted Trial Balance Debit	Adjusted Trial Balance Credit	Income Statement Debit	Income Statement Credit	Balance Sheet Debit	Balance Sheet Credit	
1	Cash	27,000.00								27,000.00		1
2	Accounts Receivable	13,300.00								13,300.00		2
3	Merchandise Inventory	34,000.00								38,000.00		3
4	Supplies	5,300.00								1,500.00		4
5	Prepaid Insurance	6,100.00								1,785.00		5
6	Land	31,000.00								31,000.00		6
7	Building	52,000.00								52,000.00		7
8	Accum. Depr.—Building		17,000.00								21,145.00	8
9	Store Equipment	39,000.00								39,000.00		9
10	Accum. Depr.—Store Equipment		11,900.00								14,875.00	10
11	Accounts Payable		6,250.00								6,250.00	11
12	Wages Payable										875.00	12
13	Sales Tax Payable		6,200.00								6,200.00	13
14	Unearned Rent Revenue		7,400.00								3,175.00	14
15	Mortgage Payable		46,000.00								46,000.00	15
16	H. Lewis, Capital		111,620.00								111,620.00	16
17	H. Lewis, Drawing	37,000.00								37,000.00		17
18	Income Summary							34,000.00	38,000.00			18
19	Sales		136,000.00						136,000.00			19
20	Sales Returns and Allowances	3,500.00						3,500.00				20
21	Rent Revenue								4,225.00			21
22	Purchases	39,000.00						39,000.00				22
23	Purchases Returns and Allowances		2,530.00						2,530.00			23
24	Purchases Discounts		1,975.00						1,975.00			24
25	Freight-In	2,650.00						2,650.00				25
26	Wages Expense	42,000.00						42,875.00				26
27	Advertising Expense	4,175.00						4,175.00				27
28	Supplies Expense							3,800.00				28
29	Telephone Expense	1,980.00						1,980.00				29
30	Utilities Expense	7,945.00						7,945.00				30
31	Insurance Expense							4,315.00				31
32	Depr. Expense—Building							4,145.00				32
33	Depr. Expense—Store Equipment							2,975.00				33
34	Miscellaneous Expense	925.00						925.00				34
35		346,875.00	346,875.00					152,285.00	182,730.00	240,585.00	210,140.00	35
36	Net Income							30,445.00			30,445.00	36
37								182,730.00	182,730.00	240,585.00	240,585.00	37

E 14-4B (LO3)

✓ Cost of goods sold: $73,400

WORK SHEET EXTENSIONS FOR MERCHANDISE INVENTORY ADJUSTMENTS: PERIODIC INVENTORY SYSTEM The following partial work sheet is taken from Nicole's Gift Shop for the year ended December 31, 20--. The ending merchandise inventory is $37,000.

1. Complete the Adjustments columns for the merchandise inventory.
2. Extend the merchandise inventory to the Adjusted Trial Balance and Balance Sheet columns.
3. Extend the remaining accounts to the Adjusted Trial Balance and Income Statement columns.
4. Prepare a cost of goods sold section from the partial work sheet.

Nicole's Gift Shop
Work Sheet (Partial)
For Year Ended December 31, 20 --

	ACCOUNT TITLE	TRIAL BALANCE		ADJUSTMENTS		
		DEBIT	CREDIT	DEBIT	CREDIT	
1	Merchandise Inventory	30,000 00				1
12	Income Summary					12
13	Purchases	85,000 00				13
14	Purchases Returns and Allowances		2,200 00			14
15	Purchases Discounts		2,500 00			15
16	Freight-In	100 00				16
17						17
18						18

E 14-5B (LO3)

✓ Beg. inv.: $49,000

DETERMINING THE BEGINNING AND ENDING INVENTORY FROM A PARTIAL WORK SHEET: PERIODIC INVENTORY SYSTEM From the following partial work sheet, indicate the dollar amount of beginning and ending merchandise inventory.

	ACCOUNT TITLE	ADJUSTMENTS		ADJUSTED TRIAL BALANCE		INCOME STATEMENT		BALANCE SHEET		
		DEBIT	CREDIT	DEBIT	CREDIT	DEBIT	CREDIT	DEBIT	CREDIT	
1	Merchandise Inventory	(b) 45,000 00	(a) 49,000 00	45,000 00				45,000 00		1
2	Income Summary	(a) 49,000 00	(b) 45,000 00	49,000 00	45,000 00	49,000 00	45,000 00			2

E 14-6B (LO4)

✓ (b)
Mdse. Inv. 30,000
Inc. Sum. 30,000

JOURNALIZE ADJUSTING ENTRIES FOR A MERCHANDISING BUSINESS The following partial work sheet is taken from the books of Carmen's Collies, a local pet kennel, for the year ended December 31, 20--. Journalize the adjustments in a general journal.

(continued)

Carmen's Collies
Work Sheet (Partial)
For Year Ended December 31, 20 - -

	ACCOUNT TITLE	TRIAL BALANCE DEBIT	TRIAL BALANCE CREDIT	ADJUSTMENTS DEBIT	ADJUSTMENTS CREDIT	
1	Merchandise Inventory	35,000.00		(b) 30,000.00	(a) 35,000.00	1
2	Supplies	4,500.00			(d) 3,100.00	2
3	Building	50,000.00				3
4	Accum. Depr.—Building		23,000.00		(e) 6,000.00	4
5	Wages Payable				(f) 1,300.00	5
6	Unearned Grooming Revenue		7,000.00	(c) 5,500.00		6
7	Income Summary			(a) 35,000.00	(b) 30,000.00	7
8	Grooming Revenue		24,000.00		(c) 5,500.00	8
9	Wages Expense	41,000.00		(f) 1,300.00		9
10	Supplies Expense			(d) 3,100.00		10
11	Depr. Expense—Building			(e) 6,000.00		11
12				80,900.00	80,900.00	12
13						13

E 14-7B (LO5)

JOURNAL ENTRIES UNDER THE PERPETUAL INVENTORY SYSTEM Sunita Computer Supplies entered into the following transactions. Prepare journal entries under the perpetual inventory system.

May 1 Purchased merchandise on account from Anju Enterprises, $200,000.

8 Purchased merchandise for cash, $100,000.

15 Sold merchandise on account to Salil's Pharmacy for $8,000. The merchandise cost $5,000.

E 14-8B (LO5)

JOURNALIZE ADJUSTING ENTRY FOR A MERCHANDISING BUSINESS: PERPETUAL INVENTORY SYSTEM On December 31, Anup Enterprises completed a physical count of its inventory. Although the merchandise inventory account shows a balance of $200,000, the physical count comes to $210,000. Prepare the appropriate adjusting entry under the perpetual inventory system.

SERIES B PROBLEMS

P 14-9B (LO1/2/3/4)

✓ Adj. col. total: $76,500;
Net income: $13,950

COMPLETION OF A WORK SHEET SHOWING A NET INCOME A trial balance for the Basket Corner, a business owned by Linda Palermo, is shown on page 567. Year-end adjustment information is provided below.

(a and b) Merchandise inventory costing $24,000 is on hand as of December 31, 20--. (The periodic inventory system is used.)
(c) Supplies remaining at the end of the year, $2,100.
(d) Unexpired insurance on December 31, $2,600.
(e) Depreciation expense on the building for 20--, $5,300.
(f) Depreciation expense on the store equipment for 20--, $3,800.
(g) Unearned decorating revenue as of December 31, $1,650.
(h) Wages earned but not paid as of December 31, $750.

REQUIRED

1. Complete the Adjustments columns, identifying each adjustment with its corresponding letter.

2. Complete the work sheet.
3. Enter the adjustments in a general journal.

Basket Corner
Trial Balance
December 31, 20 --

ACCOUNT TITLE	DEBIT BALANCE	CREDIT BALANCE
Cash	25 0 0 0 00	
Accounts Receivable	8 1 0 0 00	
Merchandise Inventory	32 0 0 0 00	
Supplies	7 1 0 0 00	
Prepaid Insurance	3 6 0 0 00	
Land	40 0 0 0 00	
Building	45 0 0 0 00	
Accumulated Depreciation—Building		16 0 0 0 00
Store Equipment	27 0 0 0 00	
Accumulated Depreciation—Store Equipment		5 5 0 0 00
Accounts Payable		3 6 0 0 00
Wages Payable		
Sales Tax Payable		6 2 0 0 00
Unearned Decorating Revenue		6 3 0 0 00
Mortgage Payable		36 0 0 0 00
L. Palermo, Capital		112 0 5 0 00
L. Palermo, Drawing	31 0 0 0 00	
Income Summary		
Sales		125 0 0 0 00
Sales Returns and Allowances	2 6 0 0 00	
Decorating Revenue		
Purchases	38 0 0 0 00	
Purchases Returns and Allowances		2 2 0 0 00
Purchases Discounts		1 7 0 0 00
Freight-In	1 9 0 0 00	
Wages Expense	38 0 0 0 00	
Advertising Expense	4 2 0 0 00	
Supplies Expense		
Telephone Expense	1 8 7 0 00	
Utilities Expense	8 4 0 0 00	
Insurance Expense		
Depreciation Expense—Building		
Depreciation Expense—Store Equipment		
Miscellaneous Expense	7 8 0 00	
	314 5 5 0 00	314 5 5 0 00

P 14-10B (LO1/2/3/4) ✓ Adj. col. total: $86,730; Net loss: $53,630

COMPLETION OF A WORK SHEET SHOWING A NET LOSS The trial balance for Oregon Bike Company, a business owned by Craig Moody, is shown on page 556. Year-end adjustment information is provided below.

(a and b) Merchandise inventory costing $26,000 is on hand as of December 31, 20--. (The periodic inventory system is used.)

(c) Supplies remaining at the end of the year, $2,500.

(d) Unexpired insurance on December 31, $1,820.

(continued)

(e) Depreciation expense on the building for 20--, $6,400.
(f) Depreciation expense on the store equipment for 20--, $2,800.
(g) Unearned rent revenue as of December 31, $2,350.
(h) Wages earned but not paid as of December 31, $1,100.

Oregon Bike Company
Trial Balance
December 31, 20 - -

ACCOUNT TITLE	DEBIT BALANCE	CREDIT BALANCE
Cash	27,000.00	
Accounts Receivable	12,000.00	
Merchandise Inventory	39,000.00	
Supplies	6,200.00	
Prepaid Insurance	5,800.00	
Land	32,000.00	
Building	58,000.00	
Accumulated Depreciation—Building		27,000.00
Store Equipment	31,000.00	
Accumulated Depreciation—Store Equipment		14,000.00
Accounts Payable		4,900.00
Wages Payable		
Sales Tax Payable		2,900.00
Unearned Rent Revenue		6,100.00
Mortgage Payable		49,000.00
C. Moody, Capital		169,500.00
C. Moody, Drawing	36,000.00	
Income Summary		
Sales		58,000.00
Sales Returns and Allowances	3,300.00	
Rent Revenue		
Purchases	19,000.00	
Purchases Returns and Allowances		900.00
Purchases Discounts		1,450.00
Freight-In	800.00	
Wages Expense	47,000.00	
Advertising Expense	6,200.00	
Supplies Expense		
Telephone Expense	1,860.00	
Utilities Expense	8,100.00	
Insurance Expense		
Depreciation Expense—Building		
Depreciation Expense—Store Equipment		
Miscellaneous Expense	490.00	
	333,750.00	333,750.00

REQUIRED

1. Complete the Adjustments columns, identifying each adjustment with its corresponding letter.
2. Complete the work sheet.
3. Enter the adjustments in a general journal.

P 14-11B (LO1/2/4)
✓ Adj. col. total: $88,805

WORKING BACKWARD FROM ADJUSTED TRIAL BALANCE TO DETERMINE ADJUSTING ENTRIES The partial work sheet shown below is taken from the books of Burnside Auto Parts, a business owned by Barbara Davis, for the year ended December 31, 20--.

Burnside Auto Parts
Work Sheet (Partial)
For Year Ended December 31, 20 - -

	ACCOUNT TITLE	TRIAL BALANCE		ADJUSTMENTS		ADJUSTED TRIAL BALANCE		
		DEBIT	CREDIT	DEBIT	CREDIT	DEBIT	CREDIT	
1	Cash	21,000.00				21,000.00		1
2	Accounts Receivable	8,300.00				8,300.00		2
3	Merchandise Inventory	32,000.00				36,000.00		3
4	Supplies	6,150.00				1,865.00		4
5	Prepaid Insurance	5,925.00				1,835.00		5
6	Land	41,750.00				41,750.00		6
7	Building	43,000.00				43,000.00		7
8	Accum. Depr.—Building		24,000.00				27,500.00	8
9	Store Equipment	25,400.00				25,400.00		9
10	Accum. Depr.—Store Equipment		12,400.00				14,750.00	10
11	Accounts Payable		8,100.00				8,100.00	11
12	Wages Payable						980.00	12
13	Sales Tax Payable		5,200.00				5,200.00	13
14	Unearned Rent-A-Junk Revenue		7,950.00				2,350.00	14
15	Mortgage Payable		26,000.00				26,000.00	15
16	B. Davis, Capital		109,130.00				109,130.00	16
17	B. Davis, Drawing	40,000.00				40,000.00		17
18	Income Summary					32,000.00	36,000.00	18
19	Sales		123,500.00				123,500.00	19
20	Sales Returns and Allowances	2,860.00				2,860.00		20
21	Rent-A-Junk Revenue						5,600.00	21
22	Purchases	32,525.00				32,525.00		22
23	Purchases Returns and Allowances		2,150.00				2,150.00	23
24	Purchases Discounts		2,400.00				2,400.00	24
25	Freight-In	3,175.00				3,175.00		25
26	Wages Expense	44,175.00				45,155.00		26
27	Advertising Expense	3,275.00				3,275.00		27
28	Supplies Expense					4,285.00		28
29	Telephone Expense	2,200.00				2,200.00		29
30	Utilities Expense	8,250.00				8,250.00		30
31	Insurance Expense					4,090.00		31
32	Depr. Expense—Building					3,500.00		32
33	Depr. Expense—Store Equipment					2,350.00		33
34	Miscellaneous Expense	845.00				845.00		34
35		320,830.00	320,830.00			363,660.00	363,660.00	35

REQUIRED

1. Determine the adjusting entries by analyzing the difference between the adjusted trial balance and the trial balance.
2. Journalize the adjusting entries in a general journal.

P 14-12B (LO1/2/3/4)

✓ Adj. col. total: $99,545;
Cost of goods sold: $31,975

WORKING BACKWARD FROM THE INCOME STATEMENT AND BALANCE SHEET COLUMNS OF THE WORK SHEET TO DETERMINE ADJUSTED TRIAL BALANCE AND ADJUSTING ENTRIES The partial work sheet shown on page 559 is taken from the books of Diamond Music Store, a business owned by Ned Diamond, for the year ended December 31, 20--.

REQUIRED

1. Analyze the work sheet and determine the adjusted trial balance and the adjusting entries by working backward from the Income Statement and Balance Sheet columns.
2. Journalize the adjusting entries in a general journal.
3. Prepare the cost of goods sold section of the income statement for Diamond Music Store.

MANAGING YOUR WRITING

A friend of yours recently opened Abracadabra, a sportswear shop specializing in monogrammed athletic gear. Most merchandise is special ordered for customers. However, a small inventory is on hand. Your friend does not understand why a physical inventory is necessary before preparing the financial statements. She knows how much she paid for all merchandise purchased. Why not simply use this amount for cost of goods sold? After all, it has been paid for. Write a brief memo explaining the purpose of the physical inventory and why she should not use the cost of purchases as cost of goods sold.

PROBLEM 14-12B

Diamond Music Store
Work Sheet
For Year Ended December 31, 20- -

	ACCOUNT TITLE	TRIAL BALANCE DEBIT	TRIAL BALANCE CREDIT	ADJUSTMENTS DEBIT	ADJUSTMENTS CREDIT	ADJUSTED TRIAL BALANCE DEBIT	ADJUSTED TRIAL BALANCE CREDIT	INCOME STATEMENT DEBIT	INCOME STATEMENT CREDIT	BALANCE SHEET DEBIT	BALANCE SHEET CREDIT	
1	Cash	31000 00								31000 00		1
2	Accounts Receivable	11980 00								11980 00		2
3	Merchandise Inventory	33600 00								39100 00		3
4	Supplie	7140 00								1965 00		4
5	Prepaid Insurance	5985 00								1235 00		5
6	Land	36200 00								36200 00		6
7	Building	51850 00								51850 00		7
8	Accum. Depr.—Building		13590 00								18875 00	8
9	Store Equipment	32675 00								32675 00		9
10	Accum. Depr.—Store Equipment		10290 00								14755 00	10
11	Accounts Payable		5895 00								5895 00	11
12	Wages Payable										1250 00	12
13	Sales Tax Payable		6375 00								6375 00	13
14	Unearned Rent Revenue		8850 00								2930 00	14
15	Mortgage Payable		42400 00								42400 00	15
16	N. Diamond, Capital		116350 00								116350 00	16
17	N. Diamond, Drawing	39500 00								39500 00		17
18	Income Summary							33600 00	39100 00			18
19	Sales		148000 00						148000 00			19
20	Sales Returns and Allowances	2800 00						2800 00				20
21	Rent Revenue								5920 00			21
22	Purchases	40700 00						40700 00				22
23	Purchases Returns and Allowances		2775 00						2775 00			23
24	Purchases Discounts		2325 00						2325 00			24
25	Freight-l	1875 00						1875 00				25
26	Wages Expense	47000 00						48250 00				26
27	Advertising Expense	4695 00						4695 00				27
28	Supplies Expense							5175 00				28
29	Telephone Expense	2250 00						2250 00				29
30	Utilities Expense	6825 00						6825 00				30
31	Insurance Expense							4750 00				31
32	Depr. Expense—Building							5285 00				32
33	Depr. Expense—Store Equipment							4465 00				33
34	Miscellaneous Expense	775 00						775 00				34
35		356850 00	356850 00					161445 00	198120 00	245505 00	208830 00	35
36	Net Income							36675 00			36675 00	36
37								198120 00	198120 00	245505 00	245505 00	37

ETHICS CASE

Jason Tierro, an inventory clerk at Lexmar Company, is responsible for taking a physical count of the goods on hand at the end of the year. He has been performing this duty for several years. This year, Jason was very busy due to a shortage of personnel at the company, so he decided to just estimate the amount of ending inventory instead of doing an accurate count. He reasoned that he could come very close to the true amount because of his past experience working with inventory. Besides, he was sure that the sophisticated computer program that Lexmar had just invested in kept an accurate record of inventory on hand.

1. What is your opinion of Jason's reasoning?
2. If Jason underestimates the dollar amount of ending inventory, what effect will it have on net income for the current accounting period?
3. Write a short paragraph explaining why a physical inventory should be taken at least once a year.
4. In groups of three or four, make a list of possible reasons that the actual ending inventory might not agree with the ending inventory according to a computer system.

MASTERY PROBLEM

✓ Adj. T.B. col. total: $695,325; Net income: $37,125

John Neff owns and operates Waikiki Surf Shop. A year-end trial balance is provided on page 561. Year-end adjustment data for the Waikiki Surf Shop are shown below.

(a and b) A physical count shows merchandise inventory costing $45,000 on hand as of December 31, 20--. Neff uses the periodic inventory system.
(c) Supplies remaining at the end of the year, $600.
(d) Unexpired insurance on December 31, $900.
(e) Depreciation expense on the building for 20--, $6,000.
(f) Depreciation expense on the store equipment for 20--, $4,500.
(g) Wages earned but not paid as of December 31, $675.
(h) Unearned boat rental revenue as of December 31, $3,000.

REQUIRED

1. Prepare a year-end work sheet.
2. Journalize the adjusting entries.

Waikiki Surf Shop
Trial Balance
December 31, 20 --

ACCOUNT TITLE	DEBIT BALANCE	CREDIT BALANCE
Cash	30,000 00	
Accounts Receivable	22,500 00	
Merchandise Inventory	57,000 00	
Supplies	2,700 00	
Prepaid Insurance	3,600 00	
Land	15,000 00	
Building	135,000 00	
Accumulated Depreciation—Building		24,000 00
Store Equipment	75,000 00	
Accumulated Depreciation—Store Equipment		22,500 00
Notes Payable		7,500 00
Accounts Payable		15,000 00
Wages Payable		
Unearned Boat Rental Revenue		33,000 00
J. Neff, Capital		233,700 00
J. Neff, Drawing	30,000 00	
Income Summary		
Sales		300,750 00
Sales Returns and Allowances	1,800 00	
Boat Rental Revenue		
Purchases	157,500 00	
Purchases Returns and Allowances		1,200 00
Purchases Discounts		1,500 00
Freight-In	450 00	
Wages Expense	63,000 00	
Advertising Expense	11,250 00	
Supplies Expense		
Telephone Expense	5,250 00	
Utilities Expense	18,000 00	
Insurance Expense		
Depreciation Expense—Building		
Depreciation Expense—Store Equipment		
Miscellaneous Expense	10,875 00	
Interest Expense	225 00	
	639,150 00	639,150 00

CHALLENGE PROBLEM

This problem challenges you to apply your cumulative accounting knowledge to move a step beyond the material in the chapter.

✓ **Net purchases in 20-1: $410,000**

Block Food's, a retail grocery store, has agreed to purchase all of its merchandise from Square Wholesalers. In return, Block receives a special discount on purchases. Over recent months, Square noticed that purchases by Block had been falling off. At first, Square simply thought that business might be down for Block and was hopeful that their purchases would pick up. When business with Block did not return to a normal level, Square requested financial statements from Block. Square's records indicate that Block purchased $300,000 worth of merchandise during 20-1, the most recent year.

(continued)

Selected information taken from Block's financial statements is as follows:

	12/31/-1	12/31/-0
Balance Sheet		
Inventory	$30,000	$20,000
Income Statement		
Cost of goods sold	$400,000	

REQUIRED

Compute net purchases made by Block during 20-1. Does it appear that Block violated the agreement?

ANSWERS TO SELF-STUDY QUESTIONS AND EXERCISES

True/False Questions

1. T 2. T 3. T 4. F (revenue is recognized) 5. F (contra-revenue account)

Multiple Choice Questions

1. b 2. a 3. b 4. b 5. b

U REVU Exercises

1.

Beginning merchandise inventory	$ 20,000
Purchases	171,000
Goods available for sale	$191,000
Less ending inventory	15,000
Cost of goods sold	$176,000

2.

Unearned Ticket Revenue	15,000	
Ticket Revenue		15,000

3.

	ACCOUNT TITLE	TRIAL BALANCE DEBIT	TRIAL BALANCE CREDIT	ADJUSTMENTS DEBIT	ADJUSTMENTS CREDIT	ADJUSTED TRIAL BALANCE DEBIT	ADJUSTED TRIAL BALANCE CREDIT	INCOME STATEMENT DEBIT	INCOME STATEMENT CREDIT	BALANCE SHEET DEBIT	BALANCE SHEET CREDIT	
1	Merchandise Inventory	120 000 00		(b) 90 000 00	(a)120 000 00					90 000 00		1
2	Income Summary			(a)120 000 00	(b) 90 000 00			120 000 00	90 000 00			2
3	Purchases	250 000 00				250 000 00		250 000 00				3

4.

10		Income Summary	50 000 00		10
11		Merchandise Inventory		50 000 00	11
12		Merchandise Inventory	60 000 00		12
13		Income Summary		60 000 00	13

5.

8		Inventory Short and Over	2 000 00		8
9		Merchandise Inventory		2 000 00	9
10					10

Chapter 14 Appendix

Expense Method of Accounting for Prepaid Expenses

LEARNING OBJECTIVES

Careful study of this appendix should enable you to:

LO1 Use the expense method of accounting for prepaid expenses.

LO2 Make the appropriate adjusting entries when the expense method is used for prepaid expenses.

THE EXPENSE METHOD

LO1 Use the expense method of accounting for prepaid expenses.

Under the **expense method** of accounting for prepaid expenses, supplies and other prepaid items are entered as expenses when purchased. Under this method, we must adjust the accounts at the end of each accounting period to record the unused portions as assets. To illustrate, let's assume that the following entry was made when office supplies were purchased:

4			Office Supplies Expense		4 2 5 00		4
5			Cash			4 2 5 00	5
6			Purchased office supplies				6

In the next section, we will illustrate the proper adjusting entry when using the expense method.

ADJUSTING ENTRIES UNDER THE EXPENSE METHOD

LO2 Make the appropriate adjusting entries when the expense method is used for prepaid expenses.

Office Supplies Expense was debited for a total of $425 during the period. An inventory taken at the end of the period shows that supplies on hand amounted to $150. The following adjusting entry is made for supplies on hand:

8			Office Supplies		1 5 0 00		8
9			Office Supplies Expense			1 5 0 00	9
10							10

As shown in the T accounts below, after this entry is posted, the office supplies expense account has a debit balance of $275. This amount is reported on the income statement as an operating expense. The office supplies account has a debit balance of $150. It is reported on the balance sheet as a current asset.

Office Supplies

Adj.	150		

Office Supplies Expense

	425	Adj.	150
Bal.	275		

Let's consider another example of the use of the expense method. The following entry was made for the payment of $6,000 for a three-year insurance policy:

				Debit	Credit	
11		Insurance Expense		6 0 0 0 00		11
12		Cash			6 0 0 0 00	12
13		Paid insurance premium				13

At the end of the first year, one-third of the premium has expired and two-thirds remains. Thus, $2,000 for insurance expense should be reported on the income statement and $4,000 in prepaid insurance should be reported on the balance sheet. The following adjusting entry is made:

				Debit	Credit	
15		Prepaid Insurance		4 0 0 0 00		15
16		Insurance Expense			4 0 0 0 00	16
17						17

As shown in the T accounts below, after this entry is posted, the prepaid insurance account has a debit balance of $4,000. The insurance expense account has a debit balance of $2,000.

Prepaid Insurance

	Debit		Credit
Adj.	4,000		

Insurance Expense

	Debit		Credit
	6,000	Adj.	4,000
Bal.	2,000		

The asset and expense methods of accounting for prepaid expenses give the same final result. In the **asset method**, the prepaid item is first debited to an asset account. At the end of each period, the amount consumed is debited to an expense account. In the expense method, the original amount is debited to an expense account. At the end of each accounting period, the portion not consumed is debited to an asset account.

LEARNING OBJECTIVES Key Points to Remember

LO1 Use the expense method of accounting for prepaid expenses.	Under the expense method, an expense account is debited when prepaid items are acquired.
LO2 Make the appropriate adjusting entries when the expense method is used for prepaid expenses.	At the end of the accounting period, an asset must be recognized for the amount of the prepaid item remaining. The expense account must be credited so that the ending balance represents the amount of the item consumed.

KEY TERMS

asset method (564) Under this method, the acquisition of a prepaid item is debited to an asset account.

expense method (563) Under this method, the acquisition of a prepaid item is debited to an expense account.

SERIES A EXERCISE

E 14Apx-1A (LO1/2)

EXPENSE METHOD OF ACCOUNTING FOR PREPAID EXPENSES Davidson's Food Mart paid $1,200 in advance to the local newspaper for advertisements that will appear monthly. The following entry was made:

4		Advertising Expense		1 2 0 0 00		4
5		Cash			1 2 0 0 00	5
6		Paid prepaid advertising				6

At the end of the year, December 31, 20--, Davidson received notification that advertisements costing $800 had been run. Prepare the adjusting entry.

SERIES B EXERCISE

E 14Apx-1B (LO1/2)

EXPENSE METHOD OF ACCOUNTING FOR PREPAID EXPENSES Ryan's Fish House purchased supplies costing $3,000 for cash. This amount was debited to the supplies expense account. At the end of the year, December 31, 20--, an inventory showed that supplies costing $500 remained. Prepare the adjusting entry.

Chapter 15

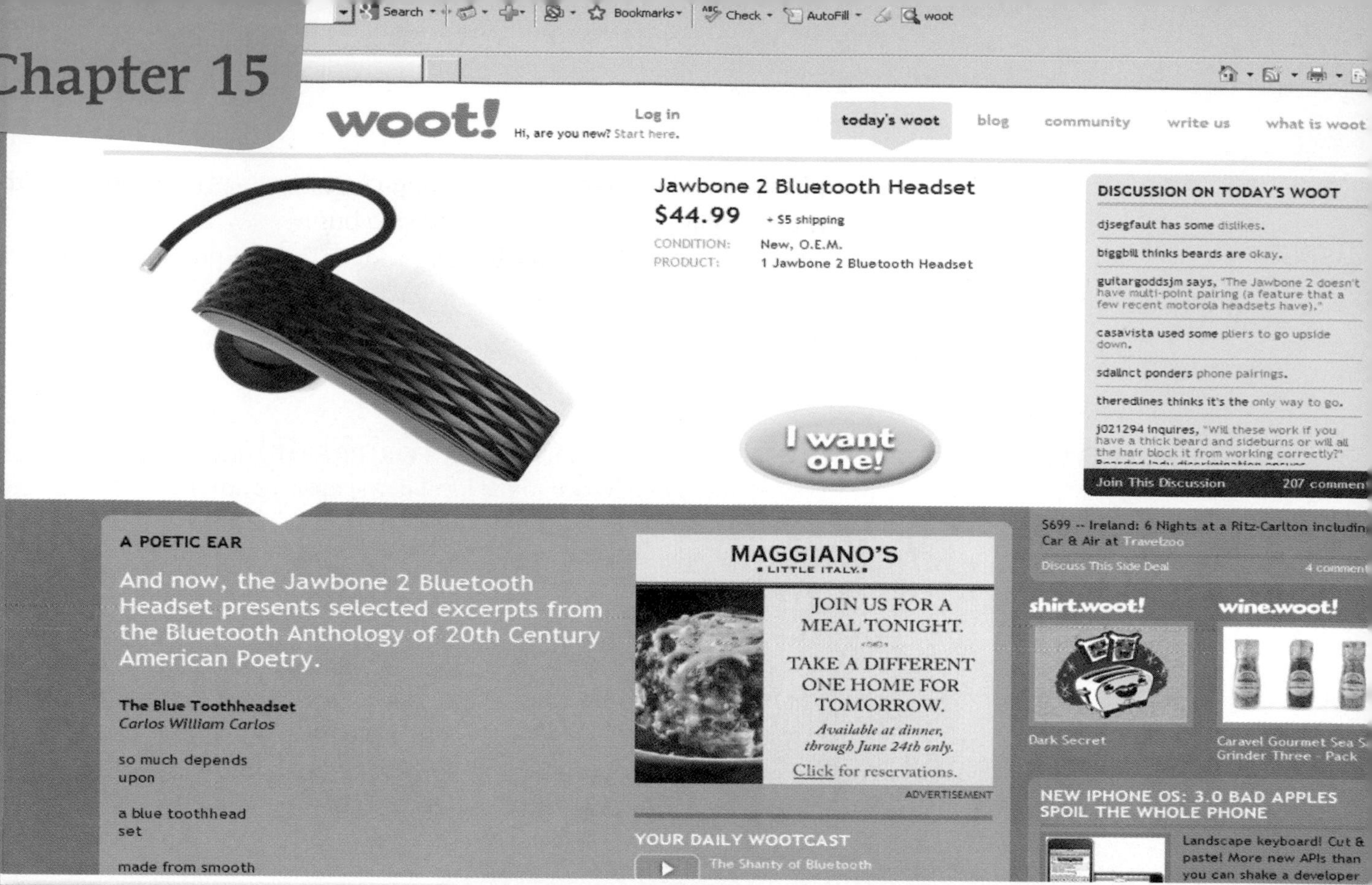

COURTESY OF WOOT.COM

LEARNING OBJECTIVES

Careful study of this chapter should enable you to:

LO1 Prepare a single-step and multiple-step income statement for a merchandising business.

LO2 Prepare a statement of owner's equity.

LO3 Prepare a classified balance sheet.

LO4 Compute standard financial ratios.

LO5 Prepare closing entries for a merchandising business.

LO6 Prepare reversing entries.

Financial Statements and Year-End Accounting for a Merchandising Business

"Woot" was originally a truncated expression commonly used by players of Dungeons and Dragons for "Wow, loot!" "Woot, Inc.," is an online store, founded in 2003, that focuses on "selling cool stuff cheap." The company is known for its honest item descriptions and limited customer service. For example, the Web site explains that the company doesn't take calls because its 100 employees are busy finding new products and shipping orders. Further, don't try to return something until all other options have been exhausted. If you want cheap prices, don't expect great service. This candor is refreshing, but we suspect they will help you out if you need it. The company claims profitability is anticipated by 2043. "By then we should be retired; someone smarter might take over and jack up the prices." Clever, but with revenues increasing from $2.3 million to $117.4 million over a recent three-year period, we suspect the company is doing just fine. Probably the most unique characteristic of this merchandiser is that it sells only one product each day. It is available from 12:00 A.M. until sold out, or 11:59 P.M., when a different product is posted. Missed a cool product? Too bad. You can't buy yesterday's item.

Though clearly unique, this business must perform year-end accounting in the same manner as other retailers. In this chapter, you will learn how Woot and other merchandising firms prepare financial statements, compute financial ratios to evaluate performance, and prepare closing and reversing entries. No matter how unique, businesses must follow similar accounting procedures so that profitability and financial health can be compared across years and with other companies.

The first six chapters of this text illustrated the accounting cycle for a service business. In this chapter, we complete the accounting cycle for a merchandising business.

In Chapter 14, we prepared the year-end work sheet and adjusting entries for Northern Micro. In this chapter, we will prepare financial statements, look briefly at financial statement analysis, and demonstrate closing and reversing entries.

THE INCOME STATEMENT

LO1 Prepare a single-step and multiple-step income statement for a merchandising business.

As you know, a primary purpose of the work sheet is to serve as an aid in preparing the financial statements. Figure 15-1 shows the completed work sheet for Northern Micro. We will use it to prepare financial statements.

The purpose of an income statement is to summarize the results of operations during an accounting period. The income statement shows the sources of revenue, types of expenses, and the amount of the net income or net loss for the period. Two forms of the income statement commonly used are the single step and the multiple step. The **single-step income statement** lists all revenue items and their total first, followed by all expense items and their total. The difference, which is either net income or net loss, is then calculated. A single-step income statement for Northern Micro is illustrated in Figure 15-2.

The use of the work sheet to prepare a **multiple-step income statement** is illustrated in Figure 15-3. This type of income statement is commonly used for merchandising businesses. The term "multiple-step" is used because the final net income is calculated on a step-by-step basis. Gross sales is shown first, less sales returns and allowances and sales discounts. This difference is called **net sales.** (Many published income statements begin with the amount of net sales.) Cost of goods sold is subtracted next to arrive at **gross profit** (sometimes called **gross margin**).

Operating expenses are then listed and subtracted from the gross profit to compute **income from operations** (sometimes called **operating income**). Operating expenses are directly associated with providing the primary goods and services of the business. Some companies divide operating expenses into the following subcategories.

Selling expenses. These expenses are directly associated with selling activities. Examples include:

- Sales Salaries Expense
- Sales Commissions Expense
- Advertising Expense
- Bank Credit Card Expense
- Delivery Expense
- Depreciation Expense—Store Equipment and Fixtures

FIGURE 15-1 Northern Micro Work Sheet

Northern Micro
Work Sheet
For Year Ended December 31, 20 - -

	Account Title	Trial Balance Debit	Trial Balance Credit	Adjustments Debit	Adjustments Credit	Adjusted Trial Balance Debit	Adjusted Trial Balance Credit	Income Statement Debit	Income Statement Credit	Balance Sheet Debit	Balance Sheet Credit	
1	Cash	20,000.00				20,000.00				20,000.00		1
2	Accounts Receivable	15,000.00				15,000.00				15,000.00		2
3	Merchandise Inventory	26,000.00		(b) 18,000.00	(a) 26,000.00	18,000.00				18,000.00		3
4	Supplies	1,800.00			(c) 1,400.00	400.00				400.00		4
5	Prepaid Insurance	2,400.00			(d) 1,800.00	600.00				600.00		5
6	Land	10,000.00				10,000.00				10,000.00		6
7	Building	90,000.00				90,000.00				90,000.00		7
8	Accum. Depr.—Building		16,000.00		(e) 4,000.00		20,000.00				20,000.00	8
9	Store Equipment	50,000.00				50,000.00				50,000.00		9
10	Accum. Depr.—Store Equipment		15,000.00		(f) 3,000.00		18,000.00				18,000.00	10
11	Notes Payable		5,000.00				5,000.00				5,000.00	11
12	Accounts Payable		10,000.00				10,000.00				10,000.00	12
13	Wages Payable				(g) 450.00		450.00				450.00	13
14	Sales Tax Payable		1,500.00				1,500.00				1,500.00	14
15	Unearned Subscriptions Revenue		12,000.00	(h) 10,000.00			2,000.00				2,000.00	15
16	Mortgage Payable		30,000.00				30,000.00				30,000.00	16
17	Gary L. Fishel, Capital		114,400.00				114,400.00				114,400.00	17
18	Gary L. Fishel, Drawing	20,000.00				20,000.00				20,000.00		18
19	Income Summary			(a) 26,000.00	(b) 18,000.00	26,000.00	18,000.00	26,000.00	18,000.00			19
20	Sales		214,000.00				214,000.00		214,000.00			20
21	Sales Returns and Allowances	1,200.00				1,200.00		1,200.00				21
22	Interest Revenue		900.00				900.00		900.00			22
23	Rent Revenue		8,000.00				8,000.00		8,000.00			23
24	Subscriptions Revenue				(h) 10,000.00		10,000.00		10,000.00			24
25	Purchases	105,000.00				105,000.00		105,000.00				25
26	Purchases Returns and Allowances		800.00				800.00		800.00			26
27	Purchases Discounts		1,000.00				1,000.00		1,000.00			27
28	Freight-In	300.00				300.00		300.00				28
29	Wages Expense	42,000.00		(g) 450.00		42,450.00		42,450.00				29
30	Advertising Expense	2,500.00				2,500.00		2,500.00				30
31	Bank Credit Card Expense	1,500.00				1,500.00		1,500.00				31
32	Rent Expense	20,000.00				20,000.00		20,000.00				32
33	Supplies Expense			(c) 1,400.00		1,400.00		1,400.00				33
34	Telephone Expense	3,500.00				3,500.00		3,500.00				34
35	Utilities Expense	12,000.00				12,000.00		12,000.00				35
36	Insurance Expense			(d) 1,800.00		1,800.00		1,800.00				36
37	Depr. Expense—Building			(e) 4,000.00		4,000.00		4,000.00				37
38	Depr. Expense—Store Equipment			(f) 3,000.00		3,000.00		3,000.00				38
39	Miscellaneous Expense	2,250.00				2,250.00		2,250.00				39
40	Interest Expense	3,150.00				3,150.00		3,150.00				40
41		428,600.00	428,600.00	64,650.00	64,650.00	454,050.00	454,050.00	230,050.00	252,700.00	224,000.00	201,350.00	41
42	Net Income							22,650.00			22,650.00	42
43								252,700.00	252,700.00	224,000.00	224,000.00	43

FIGURE 15-2 Single-Step Income Statement

Northern Micro Income Statement For Year Ended December 31, 20 - -		
Revenues:		
Net sales	$212 8 0 0 00	
Interest revenue	9 0 0 00	
Rent revenue	8 0 0 0 00	
Subscriptions revenue	10 0 0 0 00	
Total revenues		$231 7 0 0 00
Expenses:		
Cost of goods sold	$111 5 0 0 00	
Wages expense	42 4 5 0 00	
Advertising expense	2 5 0 0 00	
Bank credit card expense	1 5 0 0 00	
Rent expense	20 0 0 0 00	
Supplies expense	1 4 0 0 00	
Telephone expense	3 5 0 0 00	
Utilities expense	12 0 0 0 00	
Insurance expense	1 8 0 0 00	
Depreciation expense—building	4 0 0 0 00	
Depreciation expense—store equipment	3 0 0 0 00	
Miscellaneous expense	2 2 5 0 00	
Interest expense	3 1 5 0 00	
Total expenses		209 0 5 0 00
Net income		$ 22 6 5 0 00

LEARNING KEY

Although the formats for the single-step and multiple-step income statements are different, the reported net income is the same.

By showing other revenues and other expenses separately, it is possible to show income from operations. This makes it easier for the reader to see how the business is doing in its main activity.

General expenses. These expenses are associated with administrative, office, or general operating activities. Examples include:

- Rent Expense
- Office Salaries Expense
- Office Supplies Expense
- Telephone Expense
- Utilities Expense
- Insurance Expense
- Depreciation Expense—Office Equipment

Finally, other revenues are added and other expenses are subtracted to arrive at net income (or net loss). Note that the operating expenses are arranged according to the order given in the chart of accounts. They could also be listed by descending amount, with Miscellaneous Expense last.

FIGURE 15-6 Using a Work Sheet to Prepare a Report Form Classified Balance Sheet

Northern Micro
Work Sheet (Partial)
For Year Ended December 31, 20 --

	ACCOUNT TITLE	BALANCE SHEET DEBIT	BALANCE SHEET CREDIT
1	Cash	20,000 00	
2	Accounts Receivable	15,000 00	
3	Merchandise Inventory	18,000 00	
4	Supplies	400 00	
5	Prepaid Insurance	600 00	
6	Land	10,000 00	
7	Building	90,000 00	
8	Accum. Depr.—Building		20,000 00
9	Store Equipment	50,000 00	
10	Accum. Depr.—Store Equipment		18,000 00
11	Notes Payable		5,000 00
12	Accounts Payable		10,000 00
13	Wages Payable		450 00
14	Sales Tax Payable		1,500 00
15	Unearned Subscriptions Revenue		2,000 00
16	Mortgage Payable		30,000 00
17	Gary L. Fishel, Capital		114,400 00
18	Gary L. Fishel, Drawing	20,000 00	
19	Income Summary		
20	Sales		
21	Sales Returns and Allowances		
22	Interest Revenue		
23	Rent Revenue		
24	Subscriptions Revenue		
25	Purchases		
26	Purchases Returns and Allowances		
27	Purchases Discounts		
28	Freight-In		
29	Wages Expense		
30	Advertising Expense		
31	Bank Credit Card Expense		
32	Rent Expense		
33	Supplies Expense		
34	Telephone Expense		
35	Utilities Expense		
36	Insurance Expense		
37	Depr. Expense—Building		
38	Depr. Expense—Store Equipment		
39	Miscellaneous Expense		
40	Interest Expense		
41		224,000 00	201,350 00
42	Net Income		22,650 00
43		224,000 00	224,000 00

Northern Micro
Balance Sheet
December 31, 20 --

Assets			
Current assets:			
Cash		$20,000 00	
Accounts receivable		15,000 00	
Merchandise inventory		18,000 00	
Supplies		400 00	
Prepaid insurance		600 00	
Total current assets			$ 54,000 00
Property, plant, and equipment:			
Land		$10,000 00	
Building	$90,000 00		
Less accum. depr.—building	20,000 00	70,000 00	
Store equipment	$50,000 00		
Less accum. depr.—store equip.	18,000 00	32,000 00	
Total property, plant, and equipment			112,000 00
Total assets			$166,000 00
Liabilities			
Current liabilities:			
Notes payable	$ 5,000 00		
Accounts payable	10,000 00		
Wages payable	450 00		
Sales tax payable	1,500 00		
Unearned subscriptions revenue	2,000 00		
Mortgage payable (current portion)	500 00		
Total current liabilities		$19,450 00	
Long-term liabilities:			
Mortgage payable	$30,000 00		
Less current portion	500 00	29,500 00	
Total liabilities			$ 48,950 00
Owner's Equity			
Gary L. Fishel, capital			117,050 00*
Total liabilities and owner's equity			$166,000 00

*From statement of owner's equity.

Current assets are listed on the balance sheet from the most liquid to least liquid. **Liquidity** refers to the speed with which the company can convert the asset to cash. Cash is the most liquid asset and is always listed first. Notes Receivable, Accounts Receivable, and Merchandise Inventory often follow it on the balance sheet.

PROPERTY, PLANT, AND EQUIPMENT

Assets that are expected to be used for more than one year in the operation of a business are called **property, plant, and equipment.** Examples include land, buildings, office equipment, store equipment, and delivery equipment. Of these assets, only land is permanent; however, all of these assets have useful lives that are comparatively long. Typically, assets with longer useful lives are listed first.

The balance sheet of Northern Micro shows Land, Building, and Store Equipment. Land is not depreciated. Accumulated depreciation amounts are shown as deductions from the costs of the building and store equipment. The difference represents the **undepreciated cost**, or **book value**, of the assets. This amount less any salvage value will be written off as depreciation expense in future periods.

CURRENT LIABILITIES

The current portion of long-term debt, the amount due within one year, is reported as a current liability. The remainder is reported under long-term liabilities.

Current liabilities include those obligations that are due within one year or the normal operating cycle of the business, whichever is longer, and will require the use of current assets. As of December 31, the current liabilities of Northern Micro consist of Notes Payable, Accounts Payable, Wages Payable, Sales Tax Payable, Unearned Subscriptions Revenue, and the portion of Mortgage Payable that is due within the next year.

LONG-TERM LIABILITIES

Long-term liabilities include those obligations that will extend beyond one year or the normal operating cycle, whichever is longer. A common long-term liability is a mortgage payable.

A **mortgage** is a written agreement specifying that if the borrower does not repay a debt, the lender has the right to take over specific property to satisfy the debt. When the debt is paid, the mortgage becomes void. **Mortgage Payable** is an account that is used to reflect an obligation that is secured by a mortgage on certain property.

OWNER'S EQUITY

The permanent owner's equity accounts reported on the balance sheet are determined by the type of organization. The accounts for a sole proprietorship, a partnership, and a corporation differ. Northern Micro is a sole proprietorship and reports one owner's equity account, Gary L. Fishel, Capital. The balance of this account is taken from the statement of owner's equity. Partnerships are illustrated in Chapter 19 and corporations are discussed in Chapters 20 and 21.

U REVU Complete U REVU-3 on **page 592** to test your basic understanding of LO3.

FINANCIAL STATEMENT ANALYSIS

LO4 Compute standard financial ratios.

Both management and creditors are interested in using the financial statements to evaluate the financial condition and profitability of the firm. This can be done by making a few simple calculations.

BALANCE SHEET ANALYSIS

Recall the following:

1. Current assets include cash, items that will be converted to cash, and items that will be consumed within one year.
2. Current liabilities are obligations that will require the use of current assets.

Thus, the difference between current assets and current liabilities represents the amount of capital the business has available for current operations. This is called **working capital**.

Working Capital = Current Assets − Current Liabilities

The balance sheet in Figure 15-6 shows that Northern Micro has current assets of $54,000 and current liabilities of $19,450. Thus, the working capital at year end is $34,550 ($54,000 – $19,450). This amount should be more than adequate to satisfy current operating requirements.

Two measures of the firm's ability to pay its current liabilities are the **current ratio** and **quick ratio**. The formulas for calculating these ratios are as follows:

LEARNING KEY

Ratio analysis is most informative when the ratios are compared with past performance and with those of similar businesses.

				Northern Micro		
Current Ratio	=	Current Assets / Current Liabilities	=	$54,000 / $19,450	=	2.8 to 1
Quick Ratio	=	Quick Assets / Current Liabilities	=	$35,000 / $19,450	=	1.8 to 1

Northern Micro's current ratio of 2.8 to 1 is quite high, which indicates a favorable financial position. The traditional "rule of thumb" has been that a current ratio should be about 2 to 1, but many businesses operate successfully on a current ratio of 1.5 to 1. Although a rule of thumb is helpful, it is better to compare an individual company to industry averages, which are available in most public libraries or on the Internet.

Information on industry averages is available in various publications from Dun & Bradstreet, Standard & Poor's, and Moody's.

Quick assets include cash and all other current assets that can be converted into cash quickly, such as accounts receivable and temporary investments. Temporary investments are discussed in more advanced textbooks. The balance sheet in Figure 15-6 shows total quick assets of $35,000 ($20,000 in cash + $15,000 in accounts receivable). This produces a quick ratio of 1.8 to 1. Quick assets appear to be more than adequate to meet current obligations. The traditional rule of thumb has been that a quick ratio should be about 1 to 1, but many businesses operate successfully on a quick ratio of 0.6 to 1.

INTERSTATEMENT ANALYSIS

Interstatement analysis provides a comparison of the relationships between selected income statement and balance sheet amounts. A good example of interstatement analysis is the ratio of net income to owner's equity in the business. This ratio is known as **return on owner's equity**.

				Northern Micro
Return on Owner's Equity	=	Net Income / Average Owner's Equity	=	$22,650 / (($104,400 + $117,050) ÷ 2)
			=	$22,650 / $110,725
			=	20.5%

The statement of owner's equity in Figure 15-5 shows that the owner's equity of Northern Micro was $104,400 on January 1 and $117,050 on December 31. The net income for the year of $22,650 is 20.5% of the average owner's equity. A comparison of this ratio with the return on owner's equity in prior years should be of interest to the owner. It may also be of interest to compare the return on owner's equity of Northern Micro with the same ratio for other businesses of comparable nature and size.

A second ratio involving both income statement and balance sheet accounts is a measure of the time required to collect cash from credit customers. This financial measure is often computed in two ways. The **accounts receivable turnover** is the number of times the accounts receivable "turned over," or were collected, during the accounting period. Of course, a higher number indicates that cash is collected more quickly. This ratio is calculated as follows:

$$\text{Accounts Receivable Turnover} = \frac{\text{Net Credit Sales for the Period}}{\text{Average Accounts Receivable}}$$

Net credit sales is generally not reported in the financial statements. Use net sales, instead. As long as the proportion of cash and credit sales is reasonably stable over time, this ratio will provide a reasonable measure of the business's ability to collect receivables in a timely manner from year to year.

The accounts receivable turnover for Northern Micro for the year ended December 31 is computed as follows:

Net credit sales for the year (determined from the accounting records)	$110,000
Accounts receivable balance, January 1, 20-- (taken from last year's balance sheet)	10,000
Accounts receivable balance, December 31, 20--	15,000

Northern Micro

$$\text{Average Accounts Receivable} = \frac{\text{Beginning Balance} + \text{Ending Balance}}{2} = \frac{\$10,000 + \$15,000}{2} = \$12,500$$

$$\text{Accounts Receivable Turnover} = \frac{\text{Net Credit Sales for the Period}}{\text{Average Accounts Receivable}} = \frac{\$110,000}{\$12,500} = 8.8$$

The **average collection period** is calculated by dividing the number of days in the year (365) by the rate of turnover to determine the number of days credit customers take to pay for their purchases. Northern Micro's customers are taking about 42 days.

$$365 \text{ days} \div 8.8 = 41.5 \text{ days}$$

Comparing the average collection period with a business's credit terms offers an indication of whether customers are paying within the terms. If Northern Micro allows credit terms of n/45, an average collection period of 41.5 days would suggest that customers are paying on a timely basis.

A third ratio involving both income statement and balance sheet accounts is the rate of **inventory turnover**. This is the number of times the merchandise inventory turned over, or was sold, during the accounting period. This ratio is calculated as follows:

$$\text{Inventory Turnover} = \frac{\text{Cost of Goods Sold for the Period}}{\text{Average Inventory}}$$

If inventory is taken only at the end of each accounting period, the average inventory for the period can be calculated by adding the beginning and ending inventories and dividing their sum by two. Northern Micro's turnover for the year ended December 31 is computed as follows:

Cost of goods sold for the period	$111,500
Beginning inventory	26,000
Ending inventory	18,000

Northern Micro

$$\text{Average Inventory} = \frac{\text{Beginning Inventory} + \text{Ending Inventory}}{2} = \frac{\$26,000 + \$18,000}{2} = \$22,000$$

$$\text{Inventory Turnover} = \frac{\text{Cost of Goods Sold for the Period}}{\text{Average Inventory}} = \frac{\$111,500}{\$22,000} = 5.1$$

The **average days to sell inventory** can be computed by dividing the number of days in the year (365) by the inventory turnover. For Northern Micro, it takes about two months.

365 days ÷ 5.1 = 71.6 days

The higher the rate of inventory turnover, the smaller the profit required on each dollar of sales to produce a satisfactory gross profit. This is because the increase in the number of units sold offsets the smaller amount of gross profit earned per unit. For example, grocery stores have a very small gross profit on each item sold, but make up for this with a rapid inventory turnover. Other types of businesses, jewelers for example, need a high gross profit on each item because their inventory turnover is quite slow. Evaluations of Northern Micro's rate of inventory turnover would require comparison with prior years, other companies, or its industry.

U REVU

Complete U REVU-4 on **pages 592–593** to test your basic understanding of LO4.

CLOSING ENTRIES

LO5 Prepare closing entries for a merchandising business.

Closing entries for a service business were illustrated in Chapter 6. The process is essentially the same for a merchandising business. All revenues and expenses reported on the income statement must be closed to Income Summary. Then, the income summary and drawing accounts are closed to the owner's capital account. Keep in mind, however, that a few new accounts were needed for a merchandising business. These include Sales Returns and Allowances, Sales Discounts, Purchases Returns and Allowances, and Purchases Discounts. Since these are temporary accounts reported on the income statement, they also must be closed. The easiest way to complete the closing process is by using the work sheet to prepare the closing entries in four basic steps, as illustrated in Figures 15-7 and 15-8.

FIGURE 15-7 The Closing Process

THE CLOSING PROCESS FOR A MERCHANDISING BUSINESS

STEP 1 All income statement accounts with credit balances are debited, with an offsetting credit to Income Summary.

STEP 2 All income statement accounts with debit balances are credited, with an offsetting debit to Income Summary.

STEP 3 The resulting balance in Income Summary, which is the net income or loss for the period, is transferred to the owner's capital account.

ACCOUNT: Income Summary ACCOUNT NO. 331

DATE		ITEM	POST. REF.	DEBIT	CREDIT	BALANCE DEBIT	BALANCE CREDIT	Adjustments to:
20-- Dec.	31	Adjusting	J5	26,000.00		26,000.00		Remove Beg. Inventory
	31	Adjusting	J5		18,000.00	8,000.00		Enter End. Inventory
	31	Closing	J6		234,700.00		226,700.00	Closing step 1
	31	Closing	J6	204,050.00			22,650.00	Closing step 2
	31	Closing	J6	22,650.00		—	—	Closing step 3

STEP 4 The balance in the owner's drawing account is transferred to the owner's capital account.

FIGURE 15-8 Closing Entries for a Merchandising Business

Northern Micro
Work Sheet (Partial)
For Year Ended December 31, 20 - -

	ACCOUNT TITLE	INCOME STATEMENT DEBIT	INCOME STATEMENT CREDIT	BALANCE SHEET DEBIT	BALANCE SHEET CREDIT	
17	Gary L. Fishel, Capital				114,400.00	17
18	Gary L. Fishel, Drawing			20,000.00		18
19	Income Summary	26,000.00	18,000.00			19
20	Sales		214,000.00			20
21	Sales Returns and Allowances	1,200.00				21
22	Interest Revenue		900.00			22
23	Rent Revenue		8,000.00			23
24	Subscriptions Revenue		10,000.00			24
25	Purchases	105,000.00				25
26	Purchases Returns and Allow.		800.00			26
27	Purchases Discounts		1,000.00			27
28	Freight-In	300.00				28
29	Wages Expense	42,450.00				29
30	Advertising Expense	2,500.00				30
31	Bank Credit Card Expense	1,500.00				31
32	Rent Expense	20,000.00				32
33	Supplies Expense	1,400.00				33
34	Telephone Expense	3,500.00				34
35	Utilities Expense	12,000.00				35
36	Insurance Expense	1,800.00				36
37	Depr. Expense—Building	4,000.00				37
38	Depr. Expense—Store Equip.	3,000.00				38
39	Miscellaneous Expense	2,250.00				39
40	Interest Expense	3,150.00				40
41		230,050.00	252,700.00	224,000.00	201,350.00	41
42	Net Income	22,650.00			22,650.00	42
43		252,700.00	252,700.00	224,000.00	224,000.00	43
44						44

GENERAL JOURNAL PAGE 6

	DATE		DESCRIPTION	POST. REF.	DEBIT	CREDIT	
1	20--		Closing Entries				1
2	Dec.	31	Sales		214,000.00		2
3			Interest Revenue		900.00		3
4			Rent Revenue		8,000.00		4
5			Subscriptions Revenue		10,000.00		5
6			Purchases Returns and Allowances		800.00		6
7			Purchases Discounts		1,000.00		7
8			Income Summary			234,700.00	8
9							9
10		31	Income Summary		204,050.00		10
11			Sales Returns and Allowances			1,200.00	11
12			Purchases			105,000.00	12
13			Freight-In			300.00	13
14			Wages Expense			42,450.00	14
15			Advertising Expense			2,500.00	15
16			Bank Credit Card Expense			1,500.00	16
17			Rent Expense			20,000.00	17
18			Supplies Expense			1,400.00	18
19			Telephone Expense			3,500.00	19
20			Utilities Expense			12,000.00	20
21			Insurance Expense			1,800.00	21
22			Depreciation Exp.—Building			4,000.00	22
23			Depreciation Exp.—Store Equip.			3,000.00	23
24			Miscellaneous Expense			2,250.00	24
25			Interest Expense			3,150.00	25
26							26
27		31	Income Summary		22,650.00		27
28			Gary L. Fishel, Capital			22,650.00	28
29							29
30		31	Gary L. Fishel, Capital		20,000.00		30
31			Gary L. Fishel, Drawing			20,000.00	31
32							32

POST-CLOSING TRIAL BALANCE

A trial balance of the general ledger accounts taken after the temporary owner's equity accounts have been closed is called a **post-closing trial balance.** The purpose of the post-closing trial balance is to prove that the general ledger is in balance at the beginning of a new accounting period, before any transactions for the new accounting period are entered. It should also confirm that all temporary accounts have zero balances. Figure 15-9 shows a post-closing trial balance for Northern Micro.

> The post-closing trial balance must be prepared by taking the balances from the general ledger accounts. It should not be prepared from the balances on the work sheet. Using the general ledger accounts makes sure that all adjusting and closing entries were entered and posted correctly.

FIGURE 15-9 Post-Closing Trial Balance

Northern Micro
Post-Closing Trial Balance
December 31, 20 - -

ACCOUNT TITLE	ACCOUNT NO.	DEBIT BALANCE	CREDIT BALANCE
Cash	101	20,000 00	
Accounts Receivable	122	15,000 00	
Merchandise Inventory	131	18,000 00	
Supplies	141	400 00	
Prepaid Insurance	145	600 00	
Land	161	10,000 00	
Building	171	90,000 00	
Accumulated Depreciation—Building	171.1		20,000 00
Store Equipment	181	50,000 00	
Accumulated Depreciation—Store Equipment	181.1		18,000 00
Notes Payable	201		5,000 00
Accounts Payable	202		10,000 00
Wages Payable	219		450 00
Sales Tax Payable	231		1,500 00
Unearned Subscriptions Revenue	241		2,000 00
Mortgage Payable	251		30,000 00
Gary L. Fishel, Capital	311		117,050 00
		204,000 00	204,000 00

A BROADER VIEW

LESTER LEFKOWITZ/GETTY IMAGES

Who Cares About Tracking Financial Ratios?

Tracking a business's average collection period for receivables can help investors avoid making poor investments. Take the case of Kendall Square, a supercomputer maker. In an effort to increase sales and profits, Kendall Square recognized large amounts of revenues that had not actually been earned. Since no cash was received for these sales, accounts receivable increased dramatically (by 57%). Similarly, the average collection period increased to 157 days. Large increases in the average collection period should warn potential investors that something might be wrong. What happened at Kendall Square? Over $10 million of sales on account was never collected. This was equal to almost half of the revenues reported for the year. When eventually discovered, Kendall Square's stock price fell from $24.25 to $2.28 a share.

U REVU Complete U REVU-5 on **page 594** to test your basic understanding of LO5.

REVERSING ENTRIES

LO6 Prepare reversing entries.

Numerous adjusting entries are needed at the end of the accounting period to bring the account balances up to date for presentation in the financial statements. Although not required, some of these adjusting entries should be reversed at the beginning of the next accounting period. This is done to simplify the recording of transactions in the new accounting period. As its name implies, a **reversing entry** is the reverse or opposite of the adjusting entry.

ADJUSTING ENTRY

4	Dec.	31	Wages Expense		450 00		4
5			Wages Payable			450 00	5

REVERSING ENTRY (OPPOSITE)

7	Jan.	1	Wages Payable		450 00		7
8			Wages Expense			450 00	8

To see the advantage of using reversing entries, let's consider the effect of reversing Northern Micro's adjusting entry for wages earned, but not paid, at the end of the year. Figure 15-10 shows that accrued wages on December 31 were $450. These wages are for work performed by the employees on the last three days of the accounting period ($150 × 3 = $450). The employees will be paid on Friday, January 2, the normal payday.

Note that the adjusting and closing entries are the same, regardless of whether a reversing entry is made. However, the reversing entry on January 1 has an impact on the entry made when the employees are paid. **Without** a reversing entry, the payment on January 2, 20-2, must be split between reduction of the wages payable account for wages earned in 20-1 and Wages Expense for wages earned in 20-2. **With** a reversing entry, the bookkeeper simply debits Wages Expense and credits Cash, as is done on every other payday. Thus, the likelihood of error is reduced. Reversing entries are particularly important in large businesses where the individual recording the entry for wages may not even know what adjusting entries were made.

Not all adjusting entries should be reversed. To determine which adjusting entries to reverse, follow this rule: *Except for the first year of operations, reverse all adjusting entries that increase an asset or liability account from a zero balance.*

LEARNING KEY

Reverse all adjusting entries that increase an asset or liability account from a zero balance.

Except for the first year of operation, merchandise inventory, and contra-assets like accumulated depreciation, will have existing balances. Thus, they should never be reversed. The adjusting entries for Northern Micro are shown in Figure 15-11. Note that only the adjustment for accrued wages is reversed in Figure 15-12.

FIGURE 15-10 Adjusting, Closing, and Reversing Entries for Wages

	20-1 12/29/-1 Monday	20-1 12/30/-1 Tuesday	20-1 12/31/-1 Wednesday	20-2 1/1/-2 Thursday	20-2 1/2/-2 Friday
Wages Earned	150	150	150	150	150
Wages Paid	0	0	0	0	750
Total Earned			450		300
Total Paid			0		750
Accrued Wages on 12/31/-1			450		

Date	Without Reversing Entry			With Reversing Entry		
12/31/-1 Adj. Entry	Wages Expense	450		Wages Expense	450	
	Wages Payable		450	Wages Payable		450
12/31/-1 Closing Entry	Income Summary	42,450		Income Summary	42,450	
	Wages Expense		42,450	Wages Expense		42,450
1/1/-2 Rev. Entry	No Entry			Wages Payable	450	
				Wages Expense		450
1/2/-2 Payment of Payroll	Wages Expense	300		Wages Expense	750	
	Wages Payable	450		Cash		750
	Cash		750			

Without Reversing Entry

Description	Wages Expense (Debit)	Wages Expense (Credit)	Description
Bal.	42,000		
12/31/-1 Adj.	450		
		42,450	12/31/-1 Close
1/2/-2 Payroll	300		

Wages Payable			
		450	12/31/-1 Adj.
1/2/-2 Payroll	450		

Cash			
		750	1/2/-2 Payroll

With Reversing Entry

Description	Wages Expense (Debit)	Wages Expense (Credit)	Description
Bal.	42,000		
12/31/-1 Adj.	450		
		42,450	12/31/-1 Close
		450	1/1/-2 Reversing
1/2/-2 Payroll	750		
Bal.	300		

Wages Payable			
		450	12/31/-1 Adj.
1/1/-2 Reverse	450		

Cash			
		750	1/2/-2 Payroll

FIGURE 15-11 Which Adjusting Entries to Reverse?

GENERAL JOURNAL PAGE 5

	DATE		DESCRIPTION	POST. REF.	DEBIT	CREDIT		SHOULD THE ADJUSTMENT BE REVERSED?
1			Adjusting Entries				1	
2	20-- Dec.	31	Income Summary		26,000.00		2	Never reverse adjustments for merchandise inventory.
3			Merchandise Inventory			26,000.00	3	
4							4	
5		31	Merchandise Inventory		18,000.00		5	Never reverse adjustments for merchandise inventory.
6			Income Summary			18,000.00	6	
7							7	
8		31	Supplies Expense		1,400.00		8	No. No asset or liability with a zero balance has been increased.
9			Supplies			1,400.00	9	
10							10	
11		31	Insurance Expense		1,800.00		11	No. No asset or liability with a zero balance has been increased.
12			Prepaid Insurance			1,800.00	12	
13							13	
14		31	Depr. Expense—Building		4,000.00		14	Never reverse adjustments for depreciation.
15			Accum. Depr.—Building			4,000.00	15	
16							16	
17		31	Depr. Expense—Store Equipment		3,000.00		17	Never reverse adjustments for depreciation.
18			Accum. Depr.—Store Equipment			3,000.00	18	
19							19	
20		31	Wages Expense		450.00		20	Yes. A liability account with a zero balance has been increased.
21			Wages Payable			450.00	21	
22							22	
23		31	Unearned Subscriptions Revenue		10,000.00		23	No. No asset or liability with a zero balance has been increased.
24			Subscriptions Revenue			10,000.00	24	
25							25	

FIGURE 15-12 Reversing Entry for Northern Micro

GENERAL JOURNAL PAGE 7

	DATE		DESCRIPTION	POST. REF.	DEBIT	CREDIT	
1			Reversing Entries				1
2	20-- Jan.	1	Wages Payable		450.00		2
3			Wages Expense			450.00	3
4							4
5							5

U REVU

Complete U REVU-6 on **page 594** to test your basic understanding of LO6.

LEARNING OBJECTIVES Key Points to Remember

LO1 Prepare a single-step and multiple-step income statement for a merchandising business.

The general formats, for a single-step and multiple-step income statement are shown below.

Single-Step
Income Statement
For Year Ended December 31, 20--

Revenues:		
List all revenues	$xxx	
Total revenues		$xxx
Expenses:		
Cost of goods sold	$xxx	
List all other expenses	xxx	
Total expenses		xxx
Net income		$xxx

Multiple-Step
Income Statement
For Year Ended December 31, 20--

Revenue from sales:		
Sales	$xxx	
Less sales returns and allowances	xxx	
Net sales		$xxx
Cost of goods sold		xxx
Gross profit		$xxx
Operating expenses:		
List all operating expenses	$xxx	
Total operating expenses		xxx
Income from operations		$xxx
Other revenue:		
List all other revenue	$xxx	
Total other revenue		xxx
Other expenses:		
List all other expenses	$xxx	
Total other expenses		xxx
Net income		$xxx

LO2 Prepare a statement of owner's equity.

A statement of owner's equity has the following format:

Business Name
Statement of Owner's Equity
For Year Ended December 31, 20--

Capital, January 1, 20--		$xxx
Add additional investments		xxx
Total investment		$xxx
Net income for the year	$xxx	
Less withdrawals	xxx	
Increase in capital		xxx
Capital, December 31, 20--		$xxx

LEARNING OBJECTIVES Key Points to Remember

LO3 Prepare a classified balance sheet.

A classified balance sheet has the following major headings:

Business Name
Balance Sheet
December 31, 20--

Assets			
Current assets:			
List all current assets		$xxx	
Total current assets			$xxx
Property, plant, and equipment:			
List all property, plant, and equipment	$xxx		
Less accumulated depreciation (if appropriate)	xxx	$xxx	
Total property, plant, and equipment			xxx
Total assets			$xxx
Liabilities			
Current liabilities:			
List all current liabilities	$xxx		
Total current liabilities		$xxx	
Long-term liabilities:			
List all long-term liabilities	$xxx		
Total long-term liabilities		xxx	
Total liabilities			$xxx
Owner's Equity			
Owner's capital			xxx
Total liabilities and owner's equity			$xxx

LO4 Compute standard financial ratios.

The following measures of financial condition may be computed from financial statement information:

Working Capital = Current Assets − Current Liabilities

Current Ratio = Current Assets ÷ Current Liabilities

Quick Ratio = Quick Assets ÷ Current Liabilities

Return on Owner's Equity = Net Income ÷ Average Owner's Equity

$$\text{Accounts Receivable Turnover} = \frac{\text{Net Credit Sales for the Period}}{\text{Average Accounts Receivable}}$$

$$\text{Average Collection Period} = \frac{365}{\text{Accounts Receivable Turnover}}$$

$$\text{Inventory Turnover} = \frac{\text{Cost of Goods Sold for the Period}}{\text{Average Inventory}}$$

$$\text{Average Days to Sell Inventory} = \frac{365}{\text{Inventory Turnover}}$$

LEARNING OBJECTIVES Key Points to Remember

LO5 Prepare closing entries for a merchandising business.	The four steps in the closing process for a merchandising business are as follows: STEP 1 All income statement accounts with credit balances are debited, with an offsetting credit to Income Summary. STEP 2 All income statement accounts with debit balances are credited, with an offsetting debit to Income Summary. STEP 3 The resulting balance in Income Summary, which is the net income or loss for the period, is transferred to the owner's capital account. STEP 4 The balance in the owner's drawing account is transferred to the owner's capital account.
LO6 Prepare reversing entries.	Use the following rule to determine which adjusting entries to reverse: Except for the first year of operations, reverse all adjusting entries that increase an asset or liability account from a zero balance.

DEMONSTRATION PROBLEM

Tom McKinney owns and operates McK's Home Electronics. He has a store where he sells and repairs televisions and stereo equipment. A completed work sheet for 20-1 is provided on page 585. McKinney made a $20,000 additional investment during 20-1. The current portion of Mortgage Payable is $1,000. Net credit sales for 20-1 were $200,000, and the balance of Accounts Receivable on January 1 was $26,000.

REQUIRED

1. Prepare a multiple-step income statement.
2. Prepare a statement of owner's equity.
3. Prepare a balance sheet.
4. Compute the following measures of performance and financial condition for 20-1:
   (a) current ratio
   (b) quick ratio
   (c) working capital
   (d) return on owner's equity
   (e) accounts receivable turnover and the average number of days required to collect receivables
   (f) inventory turnover and the average number of days required to sell inventory
5. Prepare adjusting entries and indicate which should be reversed and why.
6. Prepare closing entries.
7. Prepare reversing entries for the adjustments where appropriate.

McK's Home Electronics
Work Sheet
For Year Ended December 31, 20-1

	ACCOUNT TITLE	TRIAL BALANCE DEBIT	TRIAL BALANCE CREDIT	ADJUSTMENTS DEBIT	ADJUSTMENTS CREDIT	ADJUSTED TRIAL BALANCE DEBIT	ADJUSTED TRIAL BALANCE CREDIT	INCOME STATEMENT DEBIT	INCOME STATEMENT CREDIT	BALANCE SHEET DEBIT	BALANCE SHEET CREDIT	
1	Cash	10 000 00				10 000 00				10 000 00		1
2	Accounts Receivable	22 500 00				22 500 00				22 500 00		2
3	Merchandise Inventory	39 000 00		(b) 45 000 00	(a) 39 000 00	45 000 00				45 000 00		3
4	Supplies	2 700 00			(c) 2 100 00	600 00				600 00		4
5	Prepaid Insurance	3 600 00			(d) 2 700 00	900 00				900 00		5
6	Land	15 000 00				15 000 00				15 000 00		6
7	Building	135 000 00				135 000 00				135 000 00		7
8	Accum. Depr.—Building		24 000 00		(e) 6 000 00		30 000 00				30 000 00	8
9	Store Equipment	75 000 00				75 000 00				75 000 00		9
10	Accum. Depr.—Store Equipment		22 500 00		(f) 4 500 00		27 000 00				27 000 00	10
11	Notes Payable		7 500 00				7 500 00				7 500 00	11
12	Accounts Payable		15 000 00				15 000 00				15 000 00	12
13	Wages Payable				(g) 675 00		675 00				675 00	13
14	Sales Tax Payable		2 250 00				2 250 00				2 250 00	14
15	Unearned Repair Fees		18 000 00	(h) 15 000 00			3 000 00				3 000 00	15
16	Mortgage Payable		45 000 00				45 000 00				45 000 00	16
17	Tom McKinney, Capital		151 600 00				151 600 00				151 600 00	17
18	Tom McKinney, Drawing	30 000 00				30 000 00				30 000 00		18
19	Income Summary			(a) 39 000 00	(b) 45 000 00	39 000 00	45 000 00	39 000 00	45 000 00			19
20	Sales		300 750 00				300 750 00		300 750 00			20
21	Sales Returns and Allowances	1 000 00				1 000 00		1 000 00				21
22	Sales Discounts	800 00				800 00		800 00				22
23	Repair Fees				(h) 15 000 00		15 000 00		15 000 00			23
24	Interest Revenue		1 350 00				1 350 00		1 350 00			24
25	Purchases	157 500 00				157 500 00		157 500 00				25
26	Purchases Returns and Allowances		1 200 00				1 200 00		1 200 00			26
27	Purchases Discounts		1 500 00				1 500 00		1 500 00			27
28	Freight-In	450 00				450 00		450 00				28
29	Wages Expense	63 000 00		(g) 675 00		63 675 00		63 675 00				29
30	Advertising Expense	3 750 00				3 750 00		3 750 00				30
31	Supplies Expense			(c) 2 100 00		2 100 00		2 100 00				31
33	Telephone Expense	5 250 00				5 250 00		5 250 00				32
33	Utilities Expense	18 000 00				18 000 00		18 000 00				33
34	Insurance Expense			(d) 2 700 00		2 700 00		2 700 00				34
35	Depr. Expense—Building			(e) 6 000 00		6 000 00		6 000 00				35
36	Depr. Expense—Store Equipment			(f) 4 500 00		4 500 00		4 500 00				36
37	Miscellaneous Expense	3 375 00				3 375 00		3 375 00				37
38	Interest Expense	4 725 00				4 725 00		4 725 00				38
39		590 650 00	590 650 00	114 975 00	114 975 00	646 825 00	646 825 00	312 825 00	364 800 00	334 000 00	282 025 00	39
40	Net Income							51 975 00			51 975 00	40
41								364 800 00	364 800 00	334 000 00	334 000 00	41

(continued)

Solution 1.

McK's Home Electronics
Income Statement
For Year Ended December 31, 20-1

Revenue from sales:				
Sales			$300,750.00	
Less: Sales returns and allowances		$ 1,000.00		
Sales discounts		800.00	1,800.00	
Net sales				$298,950.00
Cost of goods sold:				
Merchandise inventory, January 1, 20-1			$ 39,000.00	
Purchases		$157,500.00		
Less: Purchases returns and allowances	$1,200.00			
Purchases discounts	1,500.00	2,700.00		
Net purchases		$154,800.00		
Add freight-in		450.00		
Cost of goods purchased			155,250.00	
Goods available for sale			$194,250.00	
Less merchandise inventory, December 31, 20-1			45,000.00	
Cost of goods sold				149,250.00
Gross profit				$149,700.00
Operating expenses:				
Wages expense			$ 63,675.00	
Advertising expense			3,750.00	
Supplies expense			2,100.00	
Telephone expense			5,250.00	
Utilities expense			18,000.00	
Insurance expense			2,700.00	
Depreciation expense—building			6,000.00	
Depreciation expense—store equipment			4,500.00	
Miscellaneous expense			3,375.00	
Total operating expenses				109,350.00
Income from operations				$ 40,350.00
Other revenues:				
Repair fees			$ 15,000.00	
Interest revenue			1,350.00	
Total other revenues				16,350.00
Other expenses:				
Interest expense				4,725.00
Net income				$ 51,975.00

2.

McK's Home Electronics
Statement of Owner's Equity
For Year Ended December 31, 20-1

Tom McKinney, capital, January 1, 20-1		$131,600.00
Add additional investments		20,000.00
Total investment		$151,600.00
Net income for the year	$51,975.00	
Less withdrawals	30,000.00	
Increase in capital		21,975.00
Tom McKinney, capital, December 31, 20-1		$173,575.00

3.

McK's Home Electronics Balance Sheet December 31, 20 -1			
Assets			
Current assets:			
Cash		$ 10,000.00	
Accounts receivable		22,500.00	
Merchandise inventory		45,000.00	
Supplies		600.00	
Prepaid insurance		900.00	
Total current assets			$ 79,000.00
Property, plant, and equipment:			
Land		$ 15,000.00	
Building	$135,000.00		
Less accumulated depreciation	30,000.00	105,000.00	
Store equipment	$ 75,000.00		
Less accumulated depreciation	27,000.00	48,000.00	
Total property, plant, and equipment			168,000.00
Total assets			$247,000.00
Liabilities			
Current liabilities:			
Notes payable	$ 7,500.00		
Accounts payable	15,000.00		
Wages payable	675.00		
Sales tax payable	2,250.00		
Unearned repair fees	3,000.00		
Mortgage payable (current portion)	1,000.00		
Total current liabilities		$ 29,425.00	
Long-term liabilities:			
Mortgage payable	$ 45,000.00		
Less current portion	1,000.00	44,000.00	
Total liabilities			$ 73,425.00
Owner's Equity			
Tom McKinney, capital			173,575.00
Total liabilities and owner's equity			$247,000.00

4. (a) Current Ratio = Current Assets ÷ Current Liabilities
= $79,000 ÷ $29,425 = 2.68 to 1

(b) Quick Ratio = Quick Assets ÷ Current Liabilities
= $32,500 ÷ $29,425 = 1.10 to 1

(c) Working Capital = Current Assets – Current Liabilities
= $79,000 – $29,425 = $49,575

(d) Return on Owner's Equity = Net Income ÷ Average Owner's Equity

$$= \frac{\$51,975}{(\$131,600 + \$173,575) \div 2}$$

= $51,975 ÷ $152,587.50

= 34.1%

(continued)

(e) Accounts Receivable Turnover $= \dfrac{\text{Net Credit Sales for the Period}}{\text{Average Accounts Receivable}}$

$= \dfrac{\$200{,}000}{(\$26{,}000 + \$22{,}500) \div 2}$

$= \$200{,}000 \div 24{,}250$

$= 8.25$

Average number of days to collect an account receivable:
$365 \div 8.25 = 44.24$ days

(f) Inventory Turnover $= \dfrac{\text{Cost of Goods Sold for the Period}}{\text{Average Inventory}}$

$= \dfrac{\$149{,}250}{(\$39{,}000 + \$45{,}000) \div 2}$

$= \$149{,}250 \div 42{,}000$

$= 3.6$

Average number of days to sell inventory:
$365 \div 3.6 = 101.39$ days

5.

GENERAL JOURNAL PAGE 3

	DATE		DESCRIPTION	POST. REF.	DEBIT	CREDIT		SHOULD THE ADJUSTMENT BE REVERSED?
1			Adjusting Entries				1	
2	20-1 Dec.	31	Income Summary		39 000 00		2	Never reverse adjustments for merchandise inventory.
3			Merchandise Inventory			39 000 00	3	
4							4	
5		31	Merchandise Inventory		45 000 00		5	Never reverse adjustments for merchandise inventory.
6			Income Summary			45 000 00	6	
7							7	
8		31	Supplies Expense		2 100 00		8	No. No asset or liability with a zero balance has been increased.
9			Supplies			2 100 00	9	
10							10	
11		31	Insurance Expense		2 700 00		11	No. No asset or liability with a zero balance has been increased.
12			Prepaid Insurance			2 700 00	12	
13							13	
14		31	Depr. Expense—Building		6 000 00		14	Never reverse adjustments for depreciation.
15			Accum. Depr.—Building			6 000 00	15	
16							16	
17		31	Depr. Expense—Store Equipment		4 500 00		17	Never reverse adjustments for depreciation.
18			Accum. Depr.—Store Equipment			4 500 00	18	
19							19	
20		31	Wages Expense		675 00		20	Yes. A liability account with a zero balance has been increased.
21			Wages Payable			675 00	21	
22							22	
23		31	Unearned Repair Fees		15 000 00		23	No. No asset or liability with a zero balance has been increased.
24			Repair Fees			15 000 00	24	
25							25	

6.

	GENERAL JOURNAL					PAGE 4
	DATE		DESCRIPTION	POST. REF.	DEBIT	CREDIT	
1			Closing Entries				1
2	20-1 Dec.	31	Repair Fees		15,000.00		2
3			Sales		300,750.00		3
4			Interest Revenue		1,350.00		4
5			Purchases Returns and Allowances		1,200.00		5
6			Purchases Discounts		1,500.00		6
7			Income Summary			319,800.00	7
8							8
9		31	Income Summary		273,825.00		9
10			Sales Returns and Allowances			1,000.00	10
11			Sales Discounts			800.00	11
12			Purchases			157,500.00	12
13			Freight-In			450.00	13
14			Wages Expense			63,675.00	14
15			Advertising Expense			3,750.00	15
16			Supplies Expense			2,100.00	16
17			Telephone Expense			5,250.00	17
18			Utilities Expense			18,000.00	18
19			Insurance Expense			2,700.00	19
20			Depr. Expense—Building			6,000.00	20
21			Depr. Expense—Store Equipment			4,500.00	21
22			Miscellaneous Expense			3,375.00	22
23			Interest Expense			4,725.00	23
24							24
25		31	Income Summary		51,975.00		25
26			Tom McKinney, Capital			51,975.00	26
27							27
28		31	Tom McKinney, Capital		30,000.00		28
29			Tom McKinney, Drawing			30,000.00	29
30							30

7.

	GENERAL JOURNAL					PAGE 5
	DATE		DESCRIPTION	POST. REF.	DEBIT	CREDIT	
1			Reversing Entries				1
2	20-2 Jan.	1	Wages Payable		675.00		2
3			Wages Expense			675.00	3
4							4

KEY TERMS

accounts receivable turnover (574) The number of times the accounts receivable turned over, or were collected, during the accounting period. When 365 is divided by the turnover, this measure can be expressed in terms of the average number of days required to collect receivables.

average collection period (575) The number of days in the year (365) divided by the accounts receivable turnover. Provides an indication of the number of days credit customers take to pay for their purchases.

average days to sell inventory (576) The number of days in the year (365) divided by the inventory turnover. Provides an indication of the average number of days required to sell inventory.

book value (573) See undepreciated cost.

current assets (571) Cash and all other assets expected to be converted into cash or consumed within one year or the normal operating cycle of the business, whichever is longer.

current liabilities (573) Those obligations that are due within one year or the normal operating cycle of the business, whichever is longer, and will require the use of current assets.

current ratio (574) Current assets divided by current liabilities.

general expenses (569) Those expenses associated with administrative, office, or general operating activities.

gross margin (567) See gross profit.

gross profit (567) Net sales minus cost of goods sold.

income from operations (567) Gross profit minus operating expenses on a multiple-step income statement.

interstatement analysis (574) Compares the relationship between certain amounts in the income statement and balance sheet.

inventory turnover (575) The number of times the merchandise inventory turned over, or was sold, during the accounting period. When 365 is divided by the turnover, this measure can be expressed in terms of the average number of days required to sell inventory.

liquidity (572) Refers to the speed with which an asset can be converted to cash.

long-term liabilities (573) Those obligations that will extend beyond one year or the normal operating cycle, whichever is longer.

mortgage (573) A written agreement specifying that if the borrower does not repay a debt, the lender has the right to take over specific property to satisfy the debt.

Mortgage Payable (573) An account that is used to reflect an obligation that is secured by a mortgage on certain property.

multiple-step income statement (567) This statement shows a step-by-step calculation of net sales, cost of goods sold, gross profit, operating expenses, income from operations, other revenues and expenses, and net income.

net sales (567) Gross sales less sales returns and allowances and less sales discounts.

operating cycle (571) The length of time generally required for a business to buy inventory, sell it, and collect the cash.

operating income (567) See income from operations.

post-closing trial balance (578) A trial balance taken after the temporary owner's equity accounts have been closed.

property, plant, and equipment (572) Assets that are expected to be used for more than one year in the operation of a business.

quick assets (574) Cash and all other current assets that can be converted into cash quickly, such as accounts receivable and temporary investments.

quick ratio (574) Quick assets divided by current liabilities.

return on owner's equity (574) Net income divided by average owner's equity.

reversing entry (579) The opposite of the adjusting entry. It is made on the first day of the next accounting period and simplifies recording transactions in the new period.

selling expenses (567) Those expenses directly associated with selling activities.

single-step income statement (567) This statement lists all revenue items and their total first, followed by all expense items and their total.

undepreciated cost (573) Cost of plant and equipment less the accumulated depreciation amounts. Also called book value.

working capital (573) The difference between current assets and current liabilities, which represents the amount of capital the business has available for current operations.

SELF-STUDY QUESTIONS AND EXERCISES

True/False Questions

1. LO1 A multiple-step form of income statement calculates gross profit, before subtracting operating expenses.
2. LO3 Current assets include cash, items expected to convert into cash, and items that will be consumed during a year or the normal operating cycle, whichever is shorter.
3. LO3 Current assets are listed on the balance sheet in order of liquidity.
4. LO4 Working capital is the difference between current assets and current liabilities.
5. LO4 Accounts receivable turnover is the number of times merchandise inventory turned over or was sold during the accounting period.

Multiple Choice Questions

1. LO3 Which of these assets is *not* a current asset?

   (a) Cash
   (b) Accounts Receivable
   (c) Office Equipment
   (d) Merchandise Inventory

2. LO3 Which of these would be listed *first* on a balance sheet?

   (a) Accounts Receivable
   (b) Delivery Equipment
   (c) Accounts Payable
   (d) Prepaid Insurance

3. LO4 Which of these is considered a *quick asset*?

   (a) Merchandise Inventory
   (b) Accounts Receivable
   (c) Office Equipment
   (d) Prepaid Insurance

4. LO4 To calculate the accounts receivable turnover ratio, ______ is divided by average accounts receivable.
   (a) Net sales
   (b) Cost of goods sold
   (c) Total sales
   (d) Net credit sales

5. LO4 Inventory turnover is calculated by dividing cost of goods sold by
   (a) average accounts receivable.
   (b) average owner's equity.
   (c) average inventory.
   (d) accounts receivable turnover.

U REVU Exercises

Use the following work sheet for Yoder's Cool Stuff for U REVU Exercises 1, 2, and 3.

Yoder's Cool Stuff
Work Sheet
For Year Ended December 31, 20 --

	ACCOUNT TITLE	TRIAL BALANCE		ADJUSTMENTS		ADJUSTED TRIAL BALANCE		INCOME STATEMENT		BALANCE SHEET		
		DEBIT	CREDIT	DEBIT	CREDIT	DEBIT	CREDIT	DEBIT	CREDIT	DEBIT	CREDIT	
1	Cash	370.00				370.00				370.00		1
2	Accounts Receivable	650.00				650.00				650.00		2
3	Merchandise Inventory	2,000.00		(b) 4,000.00	(a) 2,000.00	4,000.00				4,000.00		3
4	Supplies	80.00			(c) 60.00	20.00				20.00		4
5	Prepaid Insurance	200.00			(d) 25.00	175.00				175.00		5
6	Delivery Equipment	8,000.00				8,000.00				8,000.00		6
7	Accum. Depr.—Delivery Equipment		2,000.00		(f) 1,000.00		3,000.00				3,000.00	7
8	Accounts Payable		1,800.00				1,800.00				1,800.00	8
9	Wages Payable				(e) 50.00		50.00				50.00	9
10	Pete Yoder, Capital		4,400.00				4,400.00				4,400.00	10
11	Pete Yoder, Drawing	150.00				150.00				150.00		11
12	Income Summary			(a) 2,000.00	(b) 4,000.00	2,000.00	4,000.00	2,000.00	4,000.00			12
13	Sales		12,650.00				12,650.00		12,650.00			13
14	Sales Returns and Allowances	500.00				500.00		500.00				14
15	Purchases	8,000.00				8,000.00		8,000.00				15
16	Wages Expense	650.00		(e) 50.00		700.00		700.00				16
17	Rent Expense	200.00				200.00		200.00				17
18	Supplies Expense			(c) 60.00		60.00		60.00				18
19	Telephone Expense	50.00				50.00		50.00				19
20	Insurance Expense			(d) 25.00		25.00		25.00				20
21	Depr. Expense—Delivery Equip			(f) 1,000.00		1,000.00		1,000.00				21
22		20,850.00	20,850.00	7,135.00	7,135.00	25,900.00	25,900.00	12,535.00	16,650.00	13,365.00	9,250.00	22
23								4,115.00			4,115.00	23
24								16,650.00	16,650.00	13,365.00	13,365.00	24
25												25

1. LO1 Prepare a multiple-step income statement for Yoder's Cool Stuff.

2. LO2 Prepare a statement of owner's equity for Yoder's Cool Stuff. Assume the beginning balance of Yoder's capital account was $3,400.

3. LO3 Prepare a balance sheet for Yoder's Cool Stuff.

4. LO4 Using the financial statements for Herman's Parts provided on page 593, compute the following ratios:
   (a) Working capital
   (b) Current ratio
   (c) Return on owner's equity
   (d) Inventory turnover

Herman's Parts
Income Statement
For Year Ended December 31, 20 - -

Revenue from sales:				
Sales	$28 000	00		
Less sales returns and allowances	500	00		
Net sales			$27 500	00
Cost of goods sold:				
Merchandise inventory, January 1, 20- -	$ 4 000	00		
Purchases	18 000	00		
Goods available for sale	$22 000	00		
Less merchandise inventory, December 31, 20--	6 000	00		
Cost of goods sold			16 000	00
Gross profit			$11 500	00
Operating expenses:				
Wages expense	$ 7 800	00		
Rent Expense	300	00		
Supplies expense	100	00		
Telephone expense	80	00		
Insurance expense	50	00		
Depr. expense—delivery equip.	1 000	00		
Total operating expenses			9 330	00
Net income			$ 2 170	00

Herman's Parts
Statement of Owner's Equity
For Year Ended December 31, 20 - -

Herman Gillespie, capital, January 1, 20--			$ 5 000	00
Add additional investment			1 000	00
Total investment			$ 6 000	00
Net income for the year	$ 2 170	00		
Less withdrawals for the year	1 000	00		
Increase in capital			1 170	00
Herman Gillespie, capital, December 31, 20--			$ 7 170	00

Herman's Parts
Balance Sheet
December 31, 20 - -

Assets				
Current assets:				
Cash	$ 500	00		
Accounts receivable	1 920	00		
Merchandise inventory	6 000	00		
Supplies	200	00		
Prepaid insurance	400	00		
Total current assets			$ 9 020	00
Property, plant, and equipment:				
Delivery equipment	$6 000	00		
Less accumulated depreciation	3 000	00	3 000	00
Total assets			$12 020	00
Liabilities				
Current liabilities:				
Accounts payable	$3 800	00		
Wages payable	1 050	00		
Total current liabilities			$ 4 850	00
Owner's Equity				
Herman Gillespie, capital			7 170	00
Total liabilities and owner's equity			$12 020	00

5. LO5 Using the work sheet provided on page 592 for Yoder's Cool Stuff, prepare the closing entries.
6. LO6 Pinto Company made the following adjusting entries at the end of the year. It is Pinto's fifth year in operation. Prepare the appropriate reversing entry(ies).

Depreciation Expense—Delivery Equipment	500.00	
Accumulated Depreciation—Delivery Equipment		500.00
Interest Expense	1,000.00	
Interest Payable		1,000.00

The answers to the Self-Study Questions and Exercises are at the end of the chapter (pages 611–613).

APPLYING YOUR KNOWLEDGE

REVIEW QUESTIONS

LO1 1. Describe the nature of the two forms of an income statement.

LO4 2. Name and describe the calculation of two measures that provide an indication of a business's ability to pay current obligations.

LO4 3. Describe how to calculate the following ratios:

(a) return on owner's equity
(b) accounts receivable turnover
(c) inventory turnover

LO5 4. Where is the information obtained that is needed in journalizing the closing entries?

LO5 5. Explain the function of each of the four closing entries made by Northern Micro.

LO5 6. What is the purpose of a post-closing trial balance?

LO6 7. What is the primary purpose of reversing entries?

LO6 8. What is the customary date for reversing entries?

LO6 9. What adjusting entries should be reversed?

SERIES A EXERCISES

E 15-1A (LO1)
✓ Net sales: $133,700

REVENUE SECTION, MULTIPLE-STEP INCOME STATEMENT Based on the information that follows, prepare the revenue section of a multiple-step income statement.

Sales	$140,000
Sales Returns and Allowances	3,500
Sales Discounts	2,800

E 15-2A (LO1)

✓ Cost of goods sold: $102,560

COST OF GOODS SOLD SECTION, MULTIPLE-STEP INCOME STATEMENT Based on the information that follows, prepare the cost of goods sold section of a multiple-step income statement.

Merchandise Inventory, January 1, 20--	$ 34,000
Purchases	102,000
Purchases Returns and Allowances	4,200
Purchases Discounts	2,040
Freight-In	800
Merchandise Inventory, December 31, 20--	28,000

E 15-3A (LO1)

✓ Cost of goods sold: $87,860; Net income: $15,634

MULTIPLE-STEP INCOME STATEMENT Use the following information to prepare a multiple-step income statement, including the revenue section and the cost of goods sold section, for Rau Office Supplies for the year ended December 31, 20--.

Sales	$148,300
Sales Returns and Allowances	1,380
Sales Discounts	2,166
Interest Revenue	240
Merchandise Inventory, January 1, 20--	26,500
Purchases	98,000
Purchases Returns and Allowances	2,180
Purchases Discounts	1,960
Freight-In	750
Merchandise Inventory, December 31, 20--	33,250
Wages Expense	23,800
Supplies Expense	900
Telephone Expense	1,100
Utilities Expense	7,000
Insurance Expense	1,000
Depreciation Expense—Equipment	3,100
Miscellaneous Expense	720
Interest Expense	3,880

E 15-4A (LO4)

✓ Current ratio: 4.64 to 1; Return on owner's equity: 28.9%; Inventory turnover: 3.13

FINANCIAL RATIOS Based on the financial statements for Jackson Enterprises (income statement, statement of owner's equity, and balance sheet) shown on the next pages, prepare the following financial ratios. All sales are credit sales. The Accounts Receivable balance on January 1, 20--, was $21,600.

1. Working capital
2. Current ratio
3. Quick ratio
4. Return on owner's equity
5. Accounts receivable turnover and average number of days required to collect receivables
6. Inventory turnover and average number of days required to sell inventory

(continued)

Jackson Enterprises
Income Statement
For Year Ended December 31, 20 - -

Revenue from sales:				
Sales			$184,200.00	
Less sales returns and allowances			2,100.00	
Net sales				$182,100.00
Cost of goods sold:				
Merchandise inventory, January 1, 20--			$ 31,300.00	
Purchases		$92,800.00		
Less: Purchases returns and allowances	$1,800.00			
Purchases discounts	1,856.00	3,656.00		
Net purchases		$89,144.00		
Add freight-in		933.00		
Cost of goods purchased			90,077.00	
Goods available for sale			$121,377.00	
Less merchandise inventory, December 31, 20--			28,177.00	
Cost of goods sold				93,200.00
Gross profit				$ 88,900.00
Operating expenses:				
Wages expense			$ 38,000.00	
Advertising expense			1,180.00	
Supplies expense			380.00	
Telephone expense			2,210.00	
Utilities expense			11,000.00	
Insurance expense			900.00	
Depreciation expense—building			4,000.00	
Depreciation expense—equipment			3,800.00	
Miscellaneous expense			530.00	
Total operating expenses				62,000.00
Income from operations				$ 26,900.00
Other revenues:				
Interest revenue			$ 1,800.00	
Other expenses:				
Interest expense			900.00	900.00
Net income				$ 27,800.00

Jackson Enterprises
Statement of Owner's Equity
For Year Ended December 31, 20 --

J. B. Gray, capital, January 1, 20--		$ 88,000.00
Net income for the year	$27,800.00	
Less withdrawals for the year	11,600.00	
Increase in capital		16,200.00
J. B. Gray, capital, December 31, 20--		$104,200.00

Jackson Enterprises Balance Sheet December 31, 20 --			
Assets			
Current assets:			
Cash		$20,800.00	
Accounts receivable		18,900.00	
Merchandise inventory		28,177.00	
Supplies		1,323.00	
Prepaid insurance		900.00	
Total current assets			$ 70,100.00
Property, plant, and equipment:			
Building	$90,000.00		
Less accumulated depreciation—building	28,000.00	$62,000.00	
Equipment	$33,000.00		
Less accumulated depreciation—equipment	7,500.00	25,500.00	
Total property, plant, and equipment			87,500.00
Total assets			$157,600.00
Liabilities			
Current liabilities:			
Accounts payable	$12,600.00		
Wages payable	500.00		
Sales tax payable	1,200.00		
Mortgage payable (current portion)	800.00		
Total current liabilities		$15,100.00	
Long-term liabilities:			
Mortgage payable	$39,100.00		
Less current portion	800.00	38,300.00	
Total liabilities			$ 53,400.00
Owner's Equity			
J. B. Gray, capital			104,200.00
Total liabilities and owner's equity			$157,600.00

E 15-5A (LO5)

CLOSING ENTRIES From the work sheet on page 598, prepare the following:

1. Closing entries for Gimbel's Gifts and Gadgets in a general journal.
2. A post-closing trial balance.

E 15-6A (LO6)

REVERSING ENTRIES From the work sheet used in Exercise 15-5A, identify the adjusting entry(ies) that should be reversed and prepare the reversing entry(ies).

E 15-7A (LO5/6)

ADJUSTING, CLOSING, AND REVERSING ENTRIES Prepare entries for (a), (b), and (c) listed below using two methods. First, prepare the entries without making a reversing entry. Second, prepare the entries with the use of a reversing entry. Use T-accounts to assist your analysis.

(a) Wages paid during 20-1 are $20,800.
(b) Wages earned but not paid (accrued) as of December 31, 20-1, are $300.
(c) On January 3, 20-2, payroll of $800 is paid, which includes the $300 of wages earned but not paid in December.

EXERCISE 15-5A

Gimbel's Gifts and Gadgets
Work Sheet
For Year Ended December 31, 20-1

	ACCOUNT TITLE	TRIAL BALANCE		ADJUSTMENTS		ADJUSTED TRIAL BALANCE		INCOME STATEMENT		BALANCE SHEET		
		DEBIT	CREDIT	DEBIT	CREDIT	DEBIT	CREDIT	DEBIT	CREDIT	DEBIT	CREDIT	
1	Cash	8,214.00				8,214.00				8,214.00		1
2	Accounts Receivable	6,720.00				6,720.00				6,720.00		2
3	Merchandise Inventory	14,210.00		(b) 16,800.00	(a) 14,210.00	16,800.00				16,800.00		3
4	Supplies	680.00			(c) 380.00	300.00				300.00		4
5	Prepaid Insurance	800.00			(d) 200.00	600.00				600.00		5
6	Building	80,000.00				80,000.00				80,000.00		6
7	Accum. Depr.—Building		13,600.00		(e) 4,000.00		17,600.00				17,600.00	7
8	Accounts Payable		5,280.00				5,280.00				5,280.00	8
9	Wages Payable				(f) 280.00		280.00				280.00	9
10	Sales Tax Payable		326.00				326.00				326.00	10
11	J. M. Gimbel, Capital		87,883.00				87,883.00				87,883.00	11
12	J. M. Gimbel, Drawing	8,000.00				8,000.00				8,000.00		12
13	Income Summary			(a) 14,210.00	(b) 16,800.00	14,210.00	16,800.00	14,210.00	16,800.00			13
14	Sales		86,000.00				86,000.00		86,000.00			14
15	Sales Returns and Allowances	1,840.00				1,840.00		1,840.00				15
16	Purchases	54,200.00				54,200.00		54,200.00				16
17	Purchases Returns and Allowances		2,813.00				2,813.00		2,813.00			17
18	Purchases Discounts		1,084.00				1,084.00		1,084.00			18
19	Freight-In	800.00				800.00		800.00				19
20	Wages Expense	16,800.00		(f) 280.00		17,080.00		17,080.00				20
21	Advertising Expense	784.00				784.00		784.00				21
22	Supplies Expense			(c) 380.00		380.00		380.00				22
23	Telephone Expense	2,100.00				2,100.00		2,100.00				23
24	Utilities Expense	1,310.00				1,310.00		1,310.00				24
25	Insurance Expense			(d) 200.00		200.00		200.00				25
26	Depr. Expense—Building			(e) 4,000.00		4,000.00		4,000.00				26
27	Miscellaneous Expense	386.00				386.00		386.00				27
28	Interest Expense	142.00				142.00		142.00				28
29		196,986.00	196,986.00	35,870.00	35,870.00	218,066.00	218,066.00	97,432.00	106,697.00	120,634.00	111,369.00	29
30	Net Income							9,265.00			9,265.00	30
31								106,697.00	106,697.00	120,634.00	120,634.00	31

SERIES A PROBLEMS

P 15-8A (LO1/2/3)

✓ Cost of goods sold: $37,740; Total assets: $39,850

INCOME STATEMENT, STATEMENT OF OWNER'S EQUITY, AND BALANCE SHEET Paulson's Pet Store completed the work sheet on page 600 for the year ended December 31, 20--. Owner's equity as of January 1, 20--, was $21,900. The current portion of Mortgage Payable is $500.

REQUIRED

1. Prepare a multiple-step income statement.
2. Prepare a statement of owner's equity.
3. Prepare a balance sheet.

P 15-9A (LO4)

✓ Working capital: $29,200; Quick ratio: 2.78 to 1; Accts. receivable turnover: 22.86

FINANCIAL RATIOS Use the work sheet and financial statements prepared in Problem 15-8A. All sales are credit sales. The Accounts Receivable balance on January 1, 20--, was $3,800.

REQUIRED

Prepare the following financial ratios:

(a) Working capital
(b) Current ratio
(c) Quick ratio
(d) Return on owner's equity
(e) Accounts receivable turnover and average number of days required to collect receivables
(f) Inventory turnover and average number of days required to sell inventory

P 15-10A (LO5/6)

✓ Net income: $10,610; Post-closing trial bal. col. totals: $79,650

WORK SHEET, ADJUSTING, CLOSING, AND REVERSING ENTRIES Ellis Fabric Store shows the trial balance on page 601 as of December 31, 20-1.

At the end of the year, the following adjustments need to be made:

(a and b) Merchandise inventory as of December 31, $28,900.
(c) Unused supplies on hand, $1,350.
(d) Insurance expired, $300.
(e) Depreciation expense for the year, $500.
(f) Wages earned but not paid (Wages Payable), $480.
(g) Unearned revenue on December 31, 20-1, $1,000.

(continued)

PROBLEM 15-8A

Paulson's Pet Store
Work Sheet
For Year Ended December 31, 20 - -

	ACCOUNT TITLE	TRIAL BALANCE		ADJUSTMENTS		ADJUSTED TRIAL BALANCE		INCOME STATEMENT		BALANCE SHEET		
		DEBIT	CREDIT	DEBIT	CREDIT	DEBIT	CREDIT	DEBIT	CREDIT	DEBIT	CREDIT	
1	Cash	15,860.00				15,860.00				15,860.00		1
2	Accounts Receivable	2,340.00				2,340.00				2,340.00		2
3	Merchandise Inventory	15,000.00		(b) 16,500.00	(a) 15,000.00	16,500.00				16,500.00		3
4	Supplies	800.00			(c) 200.00	600.00				600.00		4
5	Prepaid Insurance	600.00			(d) 150.00	450.00				450.00		5
6	Equipment	5,000.00				5,000.00				5,000.00		6
7	Accum. Depr.—Equipment		450.00		(e) 450.00		900.00				900.00	7
8	Accounts Payable		4,890.00				4,890.00				4,890.00	8
9	Wages Payable				(f) 300.00		300.00				300.00	9
10	Sales Tax Payable		860.00				860.00				860.00	10
11	Mortgage Payable		4,000.00				4,000.00				4,000.00	11
12	B. Paulson, Capital		23,900.00				23,900.00				23,900.00	12
13	B. Paulson, Drawing	1,200.00				1,200.00				1,200.00		13
14	Income Summary			(a) 15,000.00	(b) 16,500.00	15,000.00	16,500.00	15,000.00	16,500.00			14
15	Sales		71,510.00				71,510.00		71,510.00			15
16	Sales Returns and Allowances	1,340.00				1,340.00		1,340.00				16
17	Purchases	40,660.00				40,660.00		40,660.00				17
18	Purchases Returns and Allowances		1,020.00				1,020.00		1,020.00			18
19	Purchases Discounts		800.00				800.00		800.00			19
20	Freight-In	400.00				400.00		400.00				20
21	Wages Expense	22,300.00		(f) 300.00		22,600.00		22,600.00				21
22	Advertising Expense	300.00				300.00		300.00				22
23	Supplies Expense			(c) 200.00		200.00		200.00				23
24	Telephone Expense	684.00				684.00		684.00				24
25	Utilities Expense	716.00				716.00		716.00				25
26	Insurance Expense			(d) 150.00		150.00		150.00				26
27	Depr. Expense—Equipment			(e) 450.00		450.00		450.00				27
28	Miscellaneous Expense	150.00				150.00		150.00				28
29	Interest Expense	80.00				80.00		80.00				29
30		107,430.00	107,430.00	32,600.00	32,600.00	124,680.00	124,680.00	82,730.00	89,830.00	41,950.00	34,850.00	30
31	Net Income							7,100.00			7,100.00	31
32								89,830.00	89,830.00	41,950.00	41,950.00	32

Ellis Fabric Store
Trial Balance
For Year Ended December 31, 20-1

ACCOUNT TITLE	DEBIT BALANCE	CREDIT BALANCE
Cash	28,000.00	
Accounts Receivable	14,200.00	
Merchandise Inventory	33,000.00	
Supplies	1,600.00	
Prepaid Insurance	900.00	
Equipment	6,600.00	
Accumulated Depreciation—Equipment		1,000.00
Accounts Payable		15,620.00
Wages Payable		
Sales Tax Payable		850.00
Unearned Revenue		5,000.00
W. P. Ellis, Capital		71,200.00
W. P. Ellis, Drawing	21,610.00	
Income Summary		
Sales		74,500.00
Sales Returns and Allowances	1,850.00	
Interest Revenue		1,200.00
Purchases	41,500.00	
Purchases Returns and Allowances		1,800.00
Purchases Discounts		830.00
Freight-In	660.00	
Wages Expense	14,880.00	
Advertising Expense	810.00	
Supplies Expense		
Telephone Expense	1,210.00	
Utilities Expense	3,240.00	
Insurance Expense		
Depreciation Expense—Equipment		
Miscellaneous Expense	920.00	
Interest Expense	1,020.00	
	172,000.00	172,000.00

REQUIRED

1. Prepare a work sheet.
2. Prepare adjusting entries.
3. Prepare closing entries.
4. Prepare a post-closing trial balance.
5. Prepare reversing entry(ies).

SERIES B EXERCISES

E 15-1B (LO1)

✓ Net sales: $82,196

REVENUE SECTION, MULTIPLE-STEP INCOME STATEMENT Based on the information that follows, prepare the revenue section of a multiple-step income statement.

Sales	$86,200
Sales Returns and Allowances	2,280
Sales Discounts	1,724

E 15-2B (LO1)

✓ Cost of goods sold: $59,442

COST OF GOODS SOLD SECTION, MULTIPLE-STEP INCOME STATEMENT Based on the information that follows, prepare the cost of goods sold section of a multiple-step income statement.

Merchandise Inventory, January 1, 20--	$13,800
Purchases	71,300
Purchases Returns and Allowances	3,188
Purchases Discounts	1,460
Freight-In	390
Merchandise Inventory, December 31, 20--	21,400

E 15-3B (LO1)

✓ Cost of goods sold: $109,714; Net income: $12,040

MULTIPLE-STEP INCOME STATEMENT Use the following information to prepare a multiple-step income statement, including the revenue section and the cost of goods sold section, for Aeito's Plumbing Supplies for the year ended December 31, 20--.

Sales	$166,000
Sales Returns and Allowances	1,620
Sales Discounts	3,320
Interest Revenue	3,184
Merchandise Inventory, January 1, 20--	33,200
Purchases	111,300
Purchases Returns and Allowances	3,600
Purchases Discounts	2,226
Freight-In	640
Merchandise Inventory, December 31, 20--	29,600
Wages Expense	22,000
Supplies Expense	650
Telephone Expense	1,100
Utilities Expense	9,000
Insurance Expense	1,000
Depreciation Expense—Building	4,600
Depreciation Expense—Equipment	2,800
Miscellaneous Expense	214
Interest Expense	1,126

E 15-4B (LO4)

✓ Current ratio: 3.68 to 1; Return on owner's equity: 42.6%; Inventory turnover: 3.42

FINANCIAL RATIOS Based on the financial statements, shown on pages 603–604, for McDonald Carpeting Co. (income statement, statement of owner's equity, and balance sheet), prepare the following financial ratios. All sales are credit sales. The balance of Accounts Receivable on January 1, 20--, was $6,800.

1. Working capital
2. Current ratio
3. Quick ratio
4. Return on owner's equity
5. Accounts receivable turnover and the average number of days required to collect receivables
6. Inventory turnover and the average number of days required to sell inventory

McDonald Carpeting Co.
Income Statement
For Year Ended December 31, 20 --

Revenue from sales:				
Sales			$122,800.00	
Less sales returns and allowances			1,100.00	
Net sales				$121,700.00
Cost of goods sold:				
Merchandise inventory, January 1, 20--			$ 19,300.00	
Purchases		$62,800.00		
Less: Purchases returns and allowances	$2,800.00			
Purchases discounts	1,944.00	4,744.00		
Net purchases		$58,056.00		
Add freight-in		944.00		
Cost of goods purchased			59,000.00	
Goods available for sale			$ 78,300.00	
Less merchandise inventory, December 31, 20- -			16,700.00	
Cost of goods sold				61,600.00
Gross profit				$ 60,100.00
Operating expenses:				
Wages expense			$ 18,000.00	
Advertising expense			980.00	
Supplies expense			320.00	
Telephone expense			1,200.00	
Utilities expense			8,000.00	
Insurance expense			800.00	
Depreciation expense—building			3,500.00	
Depreciation expense—equipment			2,500.00	
Miscellaneous expense			200.00	
Total operating expenses				35,500.00
Income from operations				$ 24,600.00
Other revenues:				
Interest revenue			$ 2,800.00	
Other expenses:				
Interest expense			2,100.00	700.00
Net income				$ 25,300.00

McDonald Carpeting Co.
Statement of Owner's Equity
For Year Ended December 31, 20 - -

C. S. McDonald, capital, January 1, 20- -		$52,000.00
Net income for the year	$25,300.00	
Less withdrawals for the year	10,400.00	
Increase in capital		14,900.00
C. S. McDonald, capital, December 31, 20- -		$66,900.00

(continued)

McDonald Carpeting Co. Balance Sheet December 31, 20 - -			
Assets			
Current assets:			
Cash		$10,400.00	
Accounts receivable		8,900.00	
Merchandise inventory		16,700.00	
Supplies		1,200.00	
Prepaid insurance		700.00	
Total current assets			$37,900.00
Property, plant, and equipment:			
Building	$60,000.00		
Less accumulated depreciation—building	18,000.00	$42,000.00	
Equipment	$22,000.00		
Less accumulated depreciation—equipment	6,200.00	15,800.00	
Total property, plant, and equipment			57,800.00
Total assets			$95,700.00
Liabilities			
Current liabilities:			
Accounts payable	$ 8,400.00		
Wages payable	300.00		
Sales tax payable	1,000.00		
Mortgage payable (current portion)	600.00		
Total current liabilities		$10,300.00	
Long-term liabilities:			
Mortgage payable	$19,100.00		
Less current portion	600.00	18,500.00	
Total liabilities			$28,800.00
Owner's Equity			
C. S. McDonald, capital			66,900.00
Total liabilities and owner's equity			$95,700.00

E 15-5B (LO5)

CLOSING ENTRIES From the work sheet on page 605 prepare the following:

1. Closing entries for Balloons and Baubbles in a general journal.
2. A post-closing trial balance.

E 15-6B (LO6)

REVERSING ENTRIES From the work sheet in Exercise 15-5B, identify the adjusting entry(ies) that should be reversed and prepare the reversing entry(ies).

E 15-7B (LO5/6)

ADJUSTING, CLOSING, AND REVERSING ENTRIES Prepare entries for (a), (b), and (c) listed below using two methods. First, prepare the entries without making a reversing entry. Second, prepare the entries with the use of a reversing entry. Use T-accounts to assist your analysis.

(a) Wages paid during 20-1 are $20,080.
(b) Wages earned but not paid (accrued) as of December 31, 20-1, are $280.
(c) On January 3, 20-2, payroll of $840 is paid, which includes the $280 of wages earned but not paid in December.

EXERCISE 15-5B

Balloons and Baubles
Work Sheet
For Year Ended December 31, 20-1

	ACCOUNT TITLE	TRIAL BALANCE		ADJUSTMENTS		ADJUSTED TRIAL BALANCE		INCOME STATEMENT		BALANCE SHEET		
		DEBIT	CREDIT	DEBIT	CREDIT	DEBIT	CREDIT	DEBIT	CREDIT	DEBIT	CREDIT	
1	Cash	2,800.00				2,800.00				2,800.00		1
2	Accounts Receivable	4,200.00				4,200.00				4,200.00		2
3	Merchandise Inventory	8,600.00		(b) 7,500.00	(a) 8,600.00	7,500.00				7,500.00		3
4	Supplies	780.00			(c) 280.00	500.00				500.00		4
5	Prepaid Insurance	620.00			(d) 120.00	500.00				500.00		5
6	Equipment	3,000.00				3,000.00				3,000.00		6
7	Accum. Depr.—Equipment		600.00		(e) 300.00		900.00				900.00	7
8	Accounts Payable		1,800.00				1,800.00				1,800.00	8
9	Wages Payable				(f) 200.00		200.00				200.00	9
10	Sales Tax Payable		80.00				80.00				80.00	10
11	L. Marlow, Capital		12,200.00				12,200.00				12,200.00	11
12	L. Marlow, Drawing	2,000.00				2,000.00				2,000.00		12
13	Income Summary			(a) 8,600.00	(b) 7,500.00	8,600.00	7,500.00	8,600.00	7,500.00			13
14	Sales		31,000.00				31,000.00		31,000.00			14
15	Sales Returns and Allowances	800.00				800.00		800.00				15
16	Purchases	22,000.00				22,000.00		22,000.00				16
17	Purchases Returns and Allowances		1,800.00				1,800.00		1,800.00			17
18	Purchases Discounts		407.00				407.00		407.00			18
19	Freight-In	200.00				200.00		200.00				19
20	Wages Expense	1,200.00		(f) 200.00		1,400.00		1,400.00				20
21	Advertising Expense	300.00				300.00		300.00				21
22	Supplies Expense			(c) 280.00		280.00		280.00				22
23	Telephone Expense	700.00				700.00		700.00				23
24	Utilities Expense	480.00				480.00		480.00				24
25	Insurance Expense			(d) 120.00		120.00		120.00				25
26	Depr. Expense—Equipment			(e) 300.00		300.00		300.00				26
27	Miscellaneous Expense	110.00				110.00		110.00				27
28	Interest Expense	97.00				97.00		97.00				28
29		47,887.00	47,887.00	17,000.00	17,000.00	55,887.00	55,887.00	35,387.00	40,707.00	20,500.00	15,180.00	29
30	Net Income							5,320.00			5,320.00	30
31								40,707.00	40,707.00	20,500.00	20,500.00	31

SERIES B PROBLEMS

P 15-8B (LO1/2/3)

✓ Cost of goods sold: $75,350; Total assets: $117,750

INCOME STATEMENT, STATEMENT OF OWNER'S EQUITY, AND BALANCE SHEET Backlund Farm Supply completed the work sheet on page 607 for the year ended December 31, 20--. Owner's equity as of January 1, 20--, was $50,000. The current portion of Mortgage Payable is $1,000.

REQUIRED

1. Prepare a multiple-step income statement.
2. Prepare a statement of owner's equity.
3. Prepare a balance sheet.

P 15-9B (LO4)

✓ Working capital: $43,230; Quick ratio: 0.84 to 1; Accts. receivable turnover: 4.35

FINANCIAL RATIOS Use the work sheet and financial statements prepared in Problem 15-8B. All sales are credit sales. The Accounts Receivable balance on January 1 was $38,200.

REQUIRED

Prepare the following financial ratios:

(a) Working capital
(b) Current ratio
(c) Quick ratio
(d) Return on owner's equity
(e) Accounts receivable turnover and the average number of days required to collect receivables
(f) Inventory turnover and the average number of days required to sell inventory

P 15-10B (LO5/6)

✓ Net income: $4,590; Post-closing trial bal. columns: $53,500

WORK SHEET, ADJUSTING, CLOSING, AND REVERSING ENTRIES The trial balance for Darby Kite Store as of December 31, 20-1, is shown on page 608.

At the end of the year, the following adjustments need to be made:

(a and b) Merchandise inventory as of December 31, $23,600.
(c) Unused supplies on hand, $1,050.
(d) Insurance expired, $250.
(e) Depreciation expense for the year, $400.
(f) Wages earned but not paid (Wages Payable), $360.
(g) Unearned revenue on December 31, 20-1, $500.

REQUIRED

1. Prepare a work sheet.
2. Prepare adjusting entries.

(continued)

PROBLEM 15-8B

Backlund Farm Supply
Work Sheet
For Year Ended December 31, 20--

	Account Title	Trial Balance Debit	Trial Balance Credit	Adjustments Debit	Adjustments Credit	Adjusted Trial Balance Debit	Adjusted Trial Balance Credit	Income Statement Debit	Income Statement Credit	Balance Sheet Debit	Balance Sheet Credit	
1	Cash	10,180.00				10,180.00				10,180.00		1
2	Accounts Receivable	26,420.00				26,420.00				26,420.00		2
3	Merchandise Inventory	42,160.00		(b) 44,300.00	(a) 42,160.00	44,300.00				44,300.00		3
4	Supplies	4,360.00			(c) 860.00	3,500.00				3,500.00		4
5	Prepaid Insurance	3,000.00			(d) 750.00	2,250.00				2,250.00		5
6	Equipment	38,000.00				38,000.00				38,000.00		6
7	Accum. Depr.—Equipment		6,000.00		(e) 900.00		6,900.00				6,900.00	7
8	Accounts Payable		41,200.00				41,200.00				41,200.00	8
9	Wages Payable				(f) 420.00		420.00				420.00	9
10	Sales Tax Payable		800.00				800.00				800.00	10
11	Mortgage Payable		8,000.00				8,000.00				8,000.00	11
12	J. Backlund, Capital		57,000.00				57,000.00				57,000.00	12
13	J. Backlund, Drawing	6,800.00				6,800.00				6,800.00		13
14	Income Summary			(a) 42,160.00	(b) 44,300.00	42,160.00	44,300.00	42,160.00	44,300.00			14
15	Sales		141,800.00				141,800.00		141,800.00			15
16	Sales Returns and Allowances	1,310.00				1,310.00		1,310.00				16
17	Purchases	81,300.00				81,300.00		81,300.00				17
18	Purchases Returns and Allowances		2,900.00				2,900.00		2,900.00			18
19	Purchases Discounts		1,510.00				1,510.00		1,510.00			19
20	Freight-In	600.00				600.00		600.00				20
21	Wages Expense	41,300.00		(f) 420.00		41,720.00		41,720.00				21
22	Advertising Expense	400.00				400.00		400.00				22
23	Supplies Expense			(c) 860.00		860.00		860.00				23
24	Telephone Expense	800.00				800.00		800.00				24
25	Utilities Expense	1,300.00				1,300.00		1,300.00				25
26	Insurance Expense			(d) 750.00		750.00		750.00				26
27	Depr. Expense—Equipment			(e) 900.00		900.00		900.00				27
28	Miscellaneous Expense	200.00				200.00		200.00				28
29	Interest Expense	1,080.00				1,080.00		1,080.00				29
30		259,210.00	259,210.00	89,390.00	89,390.00	304,830.00	304,830.00	173,380.00	190,510.00	131,450.00	114,320.00	30
31	Net Income							17,130.00			17,130.00	31
32								190,510.00	190,510.00	131,450.00	131,450.00	32

Darby Kite Store
Trial Balance
For Year Ended December 31, 20-1

ACCOUNT TITLE	DEBIT BALANCE	CREDIT BALANCE
Cash	11,700.00	
Accounts Receivable	11,200.00	
Merchandise Inventory	25,000.00	
Supplies	1,200.00	
Prepaid Insurance	800.00	
Equipment	5,400.00	
Accumulated Depreciation—Equipment		800.00
Accounts Payable		7,100.00
Wages Payable		
Sales Tax Payable		250.00
Unearned Revenue		3,000.00
M. D. Akins, Capital		50,000.00
M. D. Akins, Drawing	10,500.00	
Income Summary		
Sales		55,490.00
Sales Returns and Allowances	1,450.00	
Purchases	34,500.00	
Purchases Returns and Allowances		1,100.00
Purchases Discounts		630.00
Freight-In	360.00	
Wages Expense	10,880.00	
Advertising Expense	740.00	
Supplies Expense		
Telephone Expense	1,100.00	
Utilities Expense	2,300.00	
Insurance Expense		
Depreciation Expense—Equipment		
Miscellaneous Expense	320.00	
Interest Expense	920.00	
	118,370.00	118,370.00

3. Prepare closing entries.
4. Prepare a post-closing trial balance.
5. Prepare reversing entry(ies).

MANAGING YOUR WRITING

A friend of yours has the opportunity to invest in a small business. She has come to you for advice on how she might determine whether this would be a good investment. In particular, she is concerned about how long it takes to sell the merchandise and collect receivables. Draft a memo suggesting various ratios that should be computed to evaluate the business's profitability, ability to pay its current obligations, and time required to sell inventory and collect receivables.

ETHICS CASE

Brian Marlow recently was hired to prepare Louise Michener Consulting's year-end financial statements. Brian just earned his CPA certificate, and Louise Michener was one of his first clients. Louise employs a bookkeeper, Martha Halling, who does the daily journal entries and prepares a year-to-date trial balance at the end of each month. Martha gives the December 31 trial balance to a CPA to make the adjustments and generate the financial statements. As Brian was looking through Louise Michener's books, he noticed two things. First, in each of the last three years, a different CPA had prepared the financial statements. Second, the amount shown on the December 31 trial balance for miscellaneous expense was quite high this year compared to prior years. Brian called Martha to find out if she knew why miscellaneous expense had such a high balance. Martha's response was "I just do what Louise tells me to do. If she wants to charge personal expenses to the company, it's none of my business."

1. What should Brian do?
2. How might Brian's decision affect Martha? Has Martha done anything unethical?
3. Write a short letter from Brian to Louise explaining why personal items should not be charged to a business.
4. In small groups, discuss the ethical responsibilities of an accountant relating to a client's books.

MASTERY PROBLEM

✓ Net income: $21,350;
Total assets: $99,000;
Current ratio: 2.65 to 1;
Return on owner's equity: 28.1%

KLOOSTER & ALLEN

Dominique Fouque owns and operates Dominique's Doll House. She has a small shop in which she sells new and antique dolls. She is particularly well known for her collection of antique Ken and Barbie dolls. A completed work sheet for 20-3 is shown on the next page. Fouque made no additional investments during the year and the long-term note payable is due in 20-9. No portion of the long-term note is due within the next year. Net credit sales for 20-3 were $35,300, and receivables on January 1 were $2,500.

REQUIRED

1. Prepare a multiple-step income statement.
2. Prepare a statement of owner's equity.
3. Prepare a balance sheet.
4. Compute the following measures of performance and financial condition for 20-3:
   (a) Current ratio
   (b) Quick ratio
   (c) Working capital
   (d) Return on owner's equity
   (e) Accounts receivable turnover and average number of days required to collect receivables
   (f) Inventory turnover and the average number of days required to sell inventory
5. Prepare adjusting entries and indicate which should be reversed and why.
6. Prepare closing entries.
7. Prepare reversing entries for the adjustments where appropriate.

(continued)

MASTERY PROBLEM

Dominique's Doll House
Work Sheet
For Year Ended December 31, 20 -3

	ACCOUNT TITLE	TRIAL BALANCE		ADJUSTMENTS		ADJUSTED TRIAL BALANCE		INCOME STATEMENT		BALANCE SHEET		
		DEBIT	CREDIT	DEBIT	CREDIT	DEBIT	CREDIT	DEBIT	CREDIT	DEBIT	CREDIT	
1	Cash	5,200.00				5,200.00				5,200.00		1
2	Accounts Receivable	3,200.00				3,200.00				3,200.00		2
3	Merchandise Inventory	22,300.00		(b) 24,600.00	(a) 22,300.00	24,600.00				24,600.00		3
4	Office Supplies	800.00			(c) 600.00	200.00				200.00		4
5	Prepaid Insurance	1,200.00			(d) 400.00	800.00				800.00		5
6	Store Equipment	85,000.00				85,000.00				85,000.00		6
7	Accum. Depr.—Store Equipment		15,000.00		(e) 5,000.00		20,000.00				20,000.00	7
8	Notes Payable		6,000.00				6,000.00				6,000.00	8
9	Accounts Payable		5,500.00				5,500.00				5,500.00	9
10	Wages Payable				(g) 200.00		200.00				200.00	10
11	Sales Tax Payable		850.00				850.00				850.00	11
12	Unearned Rent Revenue		1,000.00	(f) 700.00			300.00				300.00	12
13	Long-Term Note Payable		10,000.00				10,000.00				10,000.00	13
14	Dominique Fouque, Capital		75,800.00				75,800.00				75,800.00	14
15	Dominique Fouque, Drawing	21,000.00				21,000.00				21,000.00		15
16	Income Summary			(a) 22,300.00	(b) 24,600.00	22,300.00	24,600.00	22,300.00	24,600.00			16
17	Sales		130,500.00				130,500.00		130,500.00			17
18	Sales Returns and Allowances	900.00				900.00		900.00				18
19	Rent Revenue		25,000.00		(f) 700.00		25,700.00		25,700.00			19
20	Purchases	72,000.00				72,000.00		72,000.00				20
21	Purchases Discounts		750.00				750.00		750.00			21
22	Freight-In	1,200.00				1,200.00		1,200.00				22
23	Wages Expense	42,000.00		(g) 200.00		42,200.00		42,200.00				23
24	Rent Expense	6,000.00				6,000.00		6,000.00				24
25	Office Supplies Expense			(c) 600.00		600.00		600.00				25
26	Telephone Expense	1,500.00				1,500.00		1,500.00				26
27	Utilities Expense	7,600.00				7,600.00		7,600.00				27
28	Insurance Expense			(d) 400.00		400.00		400.00				28
29	Depr. Expense—Store Equipment			(e) 5,000.00		5,000.00		5,000.00				29
30	Interest Expense	500.00				500.00		500.00				30
31		270,400.00	270,400.00	53,800.00	53,800.00	300,200.00	300,200.00	160,200.00	181,550.00	140,000.00	118,650.00	31
32	Net Income							21,350.00			21,350.00	32
33								181,550.00	181,550.00	140,000.00	140,000.00	33

CHALLENGE PROBLEM

This problem challenges you to apply your cumulative accounting knowledge to move a step beyond the material in the chapter.

✓ **Average days to convert inventory to cash: 45.0 days**

John Byers owns and operates Byers Building Supplies. The following information was taken from his financial statements:

Balance Sheet	**12/31/-2**	**12/31/-1**
Accounts Receivable	$700	$500
Inventory	300	100
Income Statement		
Net Credit Sales	$7,200	
Cost of Goods Sold	5,000	

All sales are made on account.

REQUIRED

Based on the above information, on average, approximately how many days pass from the time Byers purchases inventory until he receives cash from customers?

ANSWERS TO SELF-STUDY QUESTIONS AND EXERCISES

True/False Questions

1. T
2. F (whichever is longer)
3. T
4. T
5. F (number of times accounts receivable turned over)

Multiple Choice Questions

1. c
2. a
3. b
4. d
5. c

U REVU Exercises

1.

Yoder's Cool Stuff
Income Statement
For Year Ended December 31, 20 - -

Revenue from sales:		
Sales	$12,650.00	
Less sales returns and allowances	500.00	
Net sales		$12,150.00
Cost of goods sold:		
Merchandise inventory, January 1, 20- -	$ 2,000.00	
Purchases	8,000.00	
Goods available for sale	$10,000.00	
Less merchandise inventory, December 31, 20--	4,000.00	
Cost of goods sold		6,000.00
Gross profit		$ 6,150.00
Operating expenses:		
Wages expense	$ 700.00	
Rent expense	200.00	
Supplies expense	60.00	
Telephone expense	50.00	
Insurance expense	25.00	
Depr. expense—delivery equip.	1,000.00	
Total operating expenses		2,035.00
Net income		$ 4,115.00

2.

Yoder's Cool Stuff
Statement of Owner's Equity
For Year Ended December 31, 20 - -

Pete Yoder, capital, January 1, 20--		$3,400.00
Add additional investment		1,000.00
Total investment		$4,400.00
Net income for the year	$ 4,115.00	
Less withdrawls for the year	150.00	
increase in capital		3,965.00
Pete Yoder, capital, December 31, 20--		$8,365.00

3.

Yoder's Cool Stuff
Balance Sheet
December 31, 20 - -

Assets		
Current assets:		
Cash	$ 370.00	
Accounts receivable	650.00	
Merchandise inventory	4,000.00	
Supplies	20.00	
Prepaid insurance	175.00	
Total current assets		$ 5,215.00
Property, plant, and equipment:		
Delivery equipment	$8,000.00	
Less accumulated depreciation	3,000.00	5,000.00
Total assets		$10,215.00
Liabilities		
Current liabilities:		
Accounts payable	$1,800.00	
Wages payable	50.00	
Total current liabilities		$ 1,850.00
Owner's Equity		
Pete Yoder, capital		8,365.00
Total liabilities and owner's equity		$10,215.00

4. a. Working capital:

Current assets	$9,020
– Current liabilities	4,850
	$4,170

b. Current ratio:

$$\frac{\text{Current Assets}}{\text{Current Liabilities}} = \frac{\$9,020}{\$4,850} = 1.86 \text{ to } 1$$

c. Return on owner's equity:

$$\frac{\text{Net Income}}{\text{Average Owner's Equity}} = \frac{\$2,170}{(\$5,000 + \$7,170)/2} = \frac{\$2,170}{\$6,085} = 35.7\%$$

d. Inventory turnover:

$$\frac{\text{Cost of Goods Sold}}{\text{Average Inventory}} = \frac{\$16,000}{(\$4,000 + \$6,000)/2} = \frac{\$16,000}{\$5,000} = 3.2$$

5.

DATE	DESCRIPTION	POST. REF.	DEBIT	CREDIT
	Closing Entries			
	Sales		12,650.00	
	Income Summary			12,650.00
	Income Summary		10,535.00	
	Sales Returns and Allowances			500.00
	Purchases			8,000.00
	Wages Expense			700.00
	Rent Expense			200.00
	Supplies Expense			60.00
	Telephone Expense			50.00
	Insurance Expense			25.00
	Depr. Expense—Delivery Equip.			1,000.00
	Income Summary		4,115.00	
	Pete Yoder, Capital			4,115.00
	Pete Yoder, Capital		150.00	
	Pete Yoder, Drawing			150.00

6.

Interest Payable	1,000.00	
Interest Expense		1,000.00

Do not reverse the adjustment for depreciation expense. The adjusting entry does not increase an asset or liability from a zero balance and does not make the subsequent entry easier.

COMPREHENSIVE PROBLEM 2: ACCOUNTING CYCLE WITH SUBSIDIARY LEDGERS, PART 1

During the second half of December 20-1, TJ's Specialty Shop engaged in the following transactions:

Dec. 16	Received payment from Lucy Greene on account, $1,960.
16	Sold merchandise on account to Kim Fields, $160, plus sales tax of $8. Sale No. 640.
17	Returned merchandise to Evans Essentials for credit, $150.
18	Issued Check No. 813 to Evans Essentials in payment of December 1 balance of $1,250, less the credit received on December 17.
19	Sold merchandise on account to Lucy Greene, $620, plus tax of $31. Sale No. 641.
22	Received payment from John Dempsey on account, $1,560.
23	Issued Check No. 814 for the purchase of supplies, $120. (Debit Supplies)
24	Purchased merchandise on account from West Wholesalers, $1,200. Invoice No. 465, dated December 24, terms n/30.
26	Purchased merchandise on account from Nathen Co., $800. Invoice No. 817, dated December 26, terms 2/10, n/30.
27	Issued Check No. 815 in payment of utilities expense for the month of December, $630.
27	Sold merchandise on account to John Dempsey, $2,020, plus tax of $101. Sale No. 642.
29	Received payment from Martha Boyle on account, $2,473.
29	Issued Check No. 816 in payment of wages (Wages Expense) for the two-week period ending December 28, $1,100.
30	Issued Check No. 817 to Meyers Trophy Shop for a cash purchase of merchandise, $200.

As of December 16, TJ's account balances were as follows:

Account	Account No.	Debit	Credit
Cash	101	$ 9,705	
Accounts Receivable	122	10,256	
Merchandise Inventory	131	21,800	
Supplies	141	1,035	
Prepaid Insurance	145	1,380	
Land	161	8,700	
Building	171	52,000	
Accum. Depr.—Building	171.1		$ 9,200
Store Equipment	181	28,750	
Accum. Depr.—Store Equipment	181.1		9,300
Accounts Payable	202		3,600
Wages Payable	219		
Sales Tax Payable	231		1,378
Mortgage Payable	251		12,525
Tom Jones, Capital	311		90,000
Tom Jones, Drawing	312	8,500	
Income Summary	313		
Sales	401		124,900

Sales Returns and Allowances	401.1	$ 1,430	
Purchases	501	64,400	
Purchases Returns and Allowances	501.1		$ 460
Purchases Discounts	501.2		698
Freight-In	502	175	
Wages Expense	511	26,100	
Advertising Expense	512	4,700	
Supplies Expense	524		
Telephone Expense	525	2,180	
Utilities Expense	533	6,900	
Insurance Expense	535		
Depr. Expense—Building	540		
Depr. Expense—Store Equipment	541		
Miscellaneous Expense	549	2,700	
Interest Expense	551	1,350	
		$252,061	$252,061

TJ's also had the following subsidiary ledger balances as of December 16:

Accounts Receivable Ledger

Customer	Balance
Martha Boyle 12 Jude Lane Hartford, CT 06117	$3,796
Anne Clark 52 Juniper Road Hartford, CT 06118	2,100
John Dempsey 700 Hobbes Dr. Avon, CT 06108	1,560
Kim Fields 5200 Hamilton Ave. Hartford, CT 06117	—
Lucy Greene 236 Bally Lane Simsbury, CT 06123	2,800

Accounts Payable Ledger

Vendor	Balance
Evans Essentials 34 Harry Ave. East Hartford, CT 05234	$3,600
Nathen Co. 1009 Drake Rd. Farmington, CT 06082	—
Owen Enterprises 43 Lucky Lane Bristol, CT 06007	—
West Wholesalers 888 Anders Street Newington, CT 06789	—

At the end of the year, the following adjustments (a)–(g) need to be made:

(a, b) Merchandise inventory as of December 31, $19,700.

(c) Unused supplies on hand, $525.

(d) Unexpired insurance on December 31, $1,000.

(e) Depreciation expense on the building for the year, $800.

(f) Depreciation expense on the store equipment for the year, $450.

(g) Wages earned but not paid as of December 31, $330.

Requirements and working papers for this problem are provided in two versions: General Journal based and Special Journals based. Complete the version as directed by your instructor.

(continued)

REQUIRED—GENERAL JOURNAL

For those not using working papers:

1. If you are not using the working papers, open a general ledger, an accounts receivable ledger, and an accounts payable ledger as of December 16. Enter the December 16 balance of each of the accounts, with a check mark in the Posting Reference column.

For working paper users and nonusers:

2. Enter transactions for the second half of December in the general journal. Post immediately to the accounts receivable and accounts payable ledgers.
3. Post from the journal to the general ledger.

REQUIRED—SPECIAL JOURNALS

For those not using working papers:

1. If you are not using the working papers:
   a. Open a general ledger, an accounts receivable ledger, and an accounts payable ledger as of December 16. Enter the following December 16 balances in the general ledger accounts and place a check mark in the Posting Reference column.

Cash	$ 11,500
Accounts Receivable	7,823
Accounts Payable	6,850
Sales Tax Payable	933
Sales	116,000
Purchases	60,500
Purchases Discounts	575

   b. Enter the December 16 balances in the rest of the general ledger accounts, as indicated in the trial balance, and place a check mark in the Posting Reference column.
   c. Enter the December 16 balances in the accounts receivable and accounts payable ledgers, as indicated in the subsidiary ledger account listings, and place a check mark in the Posting Reference column.
   d. Insert Dec. 1–15, Cumulative Amount, and the following amounts in the special journal columns.

   Sales Journal: Accounts Receivable Dr., 4,263; Sales Cr., 4,060; Sales Tax Payable Cr., 203.

   Cash Receipts Journal: Accounts Receivable Cr., 1,830; Sales Cr., 4,840; Sales Tax Pay. Cr., 242; Cash Dr., 6,912.

   Purchases Journal: Purchases Dr./Accts. Pay. Cr., 3,900.

   Cash Payments Journal: General Dr., 1,680; Accounts Payable Dr., 7,150; Purchases Discounts Cr., 123; Cash Cr., 8,707.

For working paper users and nonusers:

2. Enter transactions for the second half of December in the proper journals. If you are using the working papers, the cumulative amount of entries in the special journals for December 1–15 has been entered in these journals for you. Post immediately to the accounts receivable and accounts payable ledgers.
3. Post from the journals to the general ledger. Post the journals in the following order: general, sales, purchases, cash receipts, and cash payments.

REQUIRED—GENERAL JOURNAL (*continued*)

4. Prepare schedules of accounts receivable and accounts payable.
5. Prepare a year-end work sheet, an income statement, a statement of owner's equity, and a balance sheet. The mortgage payable includes $600 that is due within one year.
6. Journalize and post adjusting entries.
7. Journalize and post closing entries. (*Hint*: Close all expense and revenue account balances listed in the Income Statement columns of the work sheet. Then, close Income Summary and Tom Jones, Drawing to Tom Jones, Capital.)
8. Prepare a post-closing trial balance.
9. Journalize and post reversing entries for the adjustments where appropriate, as of January 1, 20-2.

REQUIRED—SPECIAL JOURNALS (*continued*)

4. Prepare schedules of accounts receivable and accounts payable.
5. Prepare a year-end work sheet, an income statement, a statement of owner's equity, and a balance sheet. The mortgage payable includes $600 that is due within one year.
6. Journalize and post adjusting entries.
7. Journalize and post closing entries. (*Hint*: Close all expense and revenue account balances listed in the Income Statement columns of the work sheet. Then, close Income Summary and Tom Jones, Drawing to Tom Jones, Capital.)
8. Prepare a post-closing trial balance.
9. Journalize and post reversing entries for the adjustments where appropriate, as of January 1, 20-2.

COMPREHENSIVE PROBLEM 2: ACCOUNTING CYCLE WITH SUBSIDIARY LEDGERS, PART 2

During the month of January 20-2, TJ's Specialty Shop engaged in the following transactions:

Jan.	1	Sold merchandise on account to Anne Clark, $3,000, plus tax of $150. Sale No. 643.
	2	Issued Check No. 818 to Nathen Co. in payment of January 1 balance of $800, less 2% discount.
	3	Purchased merchandise on account from West Wholesalers, $1,500. Invoice No. 678, dated January 3, terms 2/15, n/30.
	4	Purchased merchandise on account from Owen Enterprises, $2,000. Invoice No. 767, dated January 4, terms 2/10, n/30.
	4	Issued Check No. 819 in payment of telephone expense for the month of January, $180.
	8	Sold merchandise for cash, $3,600, plus tax of $180.
	9	Received payment from Lucy Greene in full settlement of account, $1,491.
	10	Issued Check No. 820 to West Wholesalers in payment of January 1 balance of $1,200.
	12	Sold merchandise on account to Martha Boyle, $1,000, plus tax of $50. Sale No. 644.
	12	Received payment from Anne Clark on account, $2,100.
	12	Issued Check No. 821 in payment of wages (Wages Expense) for the two-week period ending January 11, $1,100.
	13	Issued Check No. 822 to Owen Enterprises in payment of January 4 purchase. Invoice No. 767, less 2% discount.
	13	Martha Boyle returned merchandise for a credit, $800, plus sales tax of $40.
	17	Returned merchandise to Evans Essentials for credit, $300.
	22	Received payment from John Dempsey on account, $2,121.

(*continued*)

Jan. 26 Issued Check No. 823 in payment of wages (Wages Expense) for the two-week period ending January 25, $1,100.

27 Issued Check No. 824 in payment of utilities expense for the month of January, $630.

27 Sold merchandise on account to John Dempsey, $2,000, plus tax of $100. Sale No. 645.

Late in January, TJ's agreed to sell the business to a competitor. To agree on a selling price, financial statements are needed as of January 31 and for the month of January 20-2. To prepare these financial statements, TJ's must perform the same procedures it normally does at year-end.

At the end of January, the following adjustments (a)–(g) need to be made:

(a, b) Merchandise inventory as of January 31, $19,000.
(c) Unused supplies on hand, $115.
(d) Unexpired insurance on January 31, $968.
(e) Depreciation expense on the building for the month, $67.
(f) Depreciation expense on the store equipment for the month, $38.
(g) Wages earned but not paid as of January 31, $330.

REQUIRED—GENERAL JOURNAL

For those not using working papers:

1. If you are not using the working papers, open a general ledger, an accounts receivable ledger, and an accounts payable ledger as of January 1. Enter the January 1 balance of each of the accounts, with a check mark in the Posting Reference column. The beginning balances for Part 2 are the same as the balances from your solution to Part 1 of Comprehensive Problem 2.

For working paper users and nonusers:

2. Enter transactions for the month of January in the general journal. Post immediately to the accounts receivable and accounts payable ledgers.
3. Post from the journal to the general ledger.
4. Prepare schedules of accounts receivable and accounts payable.
5. Prepare a month-end work sheet, income statement, statement of owner's equity, and balance sheet. The mortgage payable includes $600 that is due within one year.
6. Journalize and post adjusting entries.
7. Journalize and post closing entries. (*Hint*: Close all expense and revenue account balances listed in the Income Statement columns of the work sheet. Then close Income Summary and Tom Jones, Drawing to Tom Jones, Capital.)
8. Prepare a post-closing trial balance.

REQUIRED—SPECIAL JOURNALS

For those not using working papers:

1. If you are not using the working papers, open a general ledger, an accounts receivable ledger, and an accounts payable ledger as of January 1. Enter the January 1 balance of each of the accounts, with a check mark in the Posting Reference column. The beginning balances for Part 2 are the same as the balances from your solution to Part 1 of Comprehensive Problem 2.

For working paper users and nonusers:

2. Enter transactions for the month of January in the proper journals. Post immediately to the accounts receivable and accounts payable ledgers.
3. Post from the journals to the general ledger. Post the journals in the following order: general, sales, purchases, cash receipts, and cash payments.
4. Prepare schedules of accounts receivable and accounts payable.
5. Prepare a month-end work sheet, income statement, statement of owner's equity, and balance sheet. The mortgage payable includes $600 that is due within one year.
6. Journalize and post adjusting entries.
7. Journalize and post closing entries. (*Hint*: Close all expense and revenue account balances listed in the Income Statement columns of the work sheet. Then close Income Summary and Tom Jones, Drawing to Tom Jones, Capital.)
8. Prepare a post-closing trial balance.

Specialized Accounting Procedures for Merchandising Businesses and Partnerships

PART 4

JOCHEN TACK/DAS FOTOARCHIV/BLACK STAR/ALAMY

Add Some Color to Your Learning!

Throughout the text, you will be introduced to many important terms and types of accounts. To help you learn the different terms and types of accounts, we have coded many of them using the following color key in Part 4:

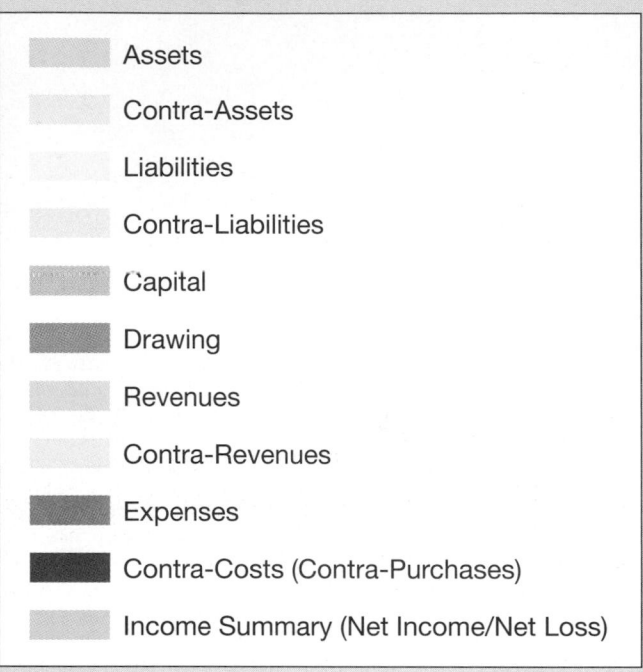

- Assets
- Contra-Assets
- Liabilities
- Contra-Liabilities
- Capital
- Drawing
- Revenues
- Contra-Revenues
- Expenses
- Contra-Costs (Contra-Purchases)
- Income Summary (Net Income/Net Loss)

Chapter 16

COMSTOCK/JUPITER IMAGES

Accounting for Accounts Receivable

Consumers are so accustomed to buying on account today that it is difficult for most businesses to function without making credit sales. Of course, this means businesses must manage their accounts receivable. To whom should credit sales be made? How much credit should be allowed? How much time should customers be allowed to pay their accounts? What should be done if a customer fails to make timely payments? What strategies can be used to encourage payment? Remember: Sales on account can be a good thing, but to succeed, the business must collect the cash. As you can see, the management of credit sales and accounts receivable can be challenging and complex.

You might recall from Chapter 9 that businesses can hire outside companies to manage payroll because of its complexity. Well, the same kind of outside service is available for managing accounts receivable. Receivables Performance Management (RPM) is a successful young company that offers such services. RPM was founded in 2002, and its revenues in a recent four-year period grew by more than 400%, from $3.9 million to $16.3 million. From its headquarters in Lynnwood, Washington, the company specializes in receivables management and collection services. It analyzes and manages the entire receivables process, not just the collection stage and handling delinquent accounts. Its clients include large utilities, telecommunication companies, banks, and many small businesses. In this chapter, you will learn how to account for accounts receivable, including accounting for accounts that cannot be collected.

LEARNING OBJECTIVES

Careful study of this chapter should enable you to:

LO1 **Apply the allowance method of accounting for uncollectible accounts.**

LO2 **Apply the percentage of sales and percentage of receivables methods of estimating uncollectible accounts.**

LO3 **Apply the direct write-off method of accounting for uncollectible accounts.**

Businesses generally are willing to sell goods and services on account. A major reason for doing so is to increase sales. Most of us simply tend to buy more if we can "charge it" rather than pay cash. In fact, one way a business can increase sales is to have easy credit policies and sell on account to virtually anyone. Unfortunately, some businesses and individuals who "charge it" then are unwilling or unable to "pay for it." Thus, a cost to a business of selling goods and services on account is that some of the accounts receivable will be uncollectible or bad debts. The more willing a business is to make sales on account, the more uncollectible accounts it is likely to have.

There are two methods of accounting for uncollectible accounts: (1) the allowance method and (2) the direct write-off method. The purpose of this chapter is to learn how to use these methods.

ALLOWANCE METHOD

LO1 Apply the allowance method of accounting for uncollectible accounts.

Bad debt expense is a loss from failure to collect an account receivable. The **allowance method** is a technique that attempts to recognize bad debt expense in the same period that the related credit sales are made. This method is consistent with the **matching principle,** which states that expenses should be matched with the revenues they helped to produce.

Under the accrual basis of accounting, the allowance method is generally required for financial reporting purposes. To use the allowance method, three steps are followed:

STEP 1 At the end of each accounting period, the amount of uncollectible accounts is estimated.

LEARNING KEY

Under the allowance method, bad debt expense is recorded as a *year-end adjustment.*

STEP 2 An adjusting entry is made to recognize the bad debt expense and reduce reported receivables for the amount of estimated uncollectible accounts. For example, if the estimated amount at December 31 is $900, the entry is as shown below and in Figure 16-1.

4	Dec.	31	Bad Debt Expense		900 00		4
5			Allowance for Bad Debts			900 00	5
6							6

FIGURE 16-1 Adjusting Entry for Bad Debt Expense

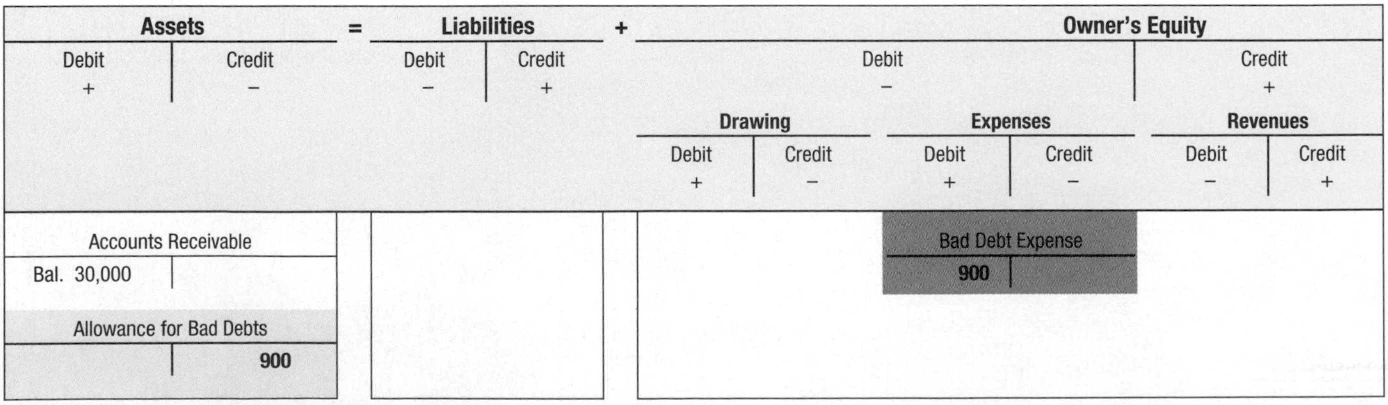

LEARNING KEY

In accounting for bad debts, Accounts Receivable is credited only when we can identify which customers are not going to pay.

Note that the credit is not to Accounts Receivable. This is because at this time we do not know which specific customers will fail to pay. Instead, a contra-asset account, Allowance for Bad Debts (also known as Allowance for Uncollectible Accounts or Allowance for Doubtful Accounts), is credited. The balance of this account is deducted from Accounts Receivable on the balance sheet. The remaining amount is known as the **net receivables** or **net realizable value** of accounts receivable because it is the amount the business expects to collect. Accounts receivable of $30,000 with an allowance of $900 would appear as follows:

Current assets:			
Accounts receivable	$30,000		
Less allowance for bad debts	900	$29,100	← Net receivables (Net realizable value)

STEP 3 In a subsequent period, when a specific uncollectible account is identified, an entry is made to write off the account and reduce the balance in Allowance for Bad Debts. For example, if the uncollectible account is $250, the entry is as follows:

8		Allowance for Bad Debts		250.00		8
9		Accounts Receivable/Customer Name			250.00	9
10		Wrote off uncollectible account				10

U REVU

Complete U REVU-1 on **page 638** to test your basic understanding of LO1.

ESTIMATING AND WRITING OFF UNCOLLECTIBLES

LO2 Apply the percentage of sales and percentage of receivables methods of estimating uncollectible accounts.

To use the allowance method, we need a way to estimate the amount of uncollectibles. Two basic methods are used: the percentage of sales method and the percentage of receivables method. A company chooses one method or the other and uses it consistently over time.

PERCENTAGE OF SALES METHOD

Some businesses apply the percentage of sales method based on sales rather than credit sales.

The **percentage of sales method** is based on the idea that some portion of the credit sales will not lead to collections. This way of viewing uncollectible accounts is illustrated in Figure 16-2 for total credit sales of $10,000. In this case, 1% ($100) of the credit sales for the year are estimated to be uncollectible. In other words, the company estimates that amount of cash will not be collected.

To apply this method, we focus on the relationship between the amount of credit sales during the year and the amount of uncollectible accounts. Assume that during 20-1 and 20-2, Chris Co. had total credit sales of $200,000 and that $2,000 of those credit sales had become uncollectible. Based on this experience, Chris could estimate its uncollectible accounts at 1% of credit sales.

$$\frac{\text{Uncollectible Accounts}}{\text{Credit Sales}} = \frac{\$2,000}{\$200,000} = 1\%$$

FIGURE 16-2 Percentage of Sales Method

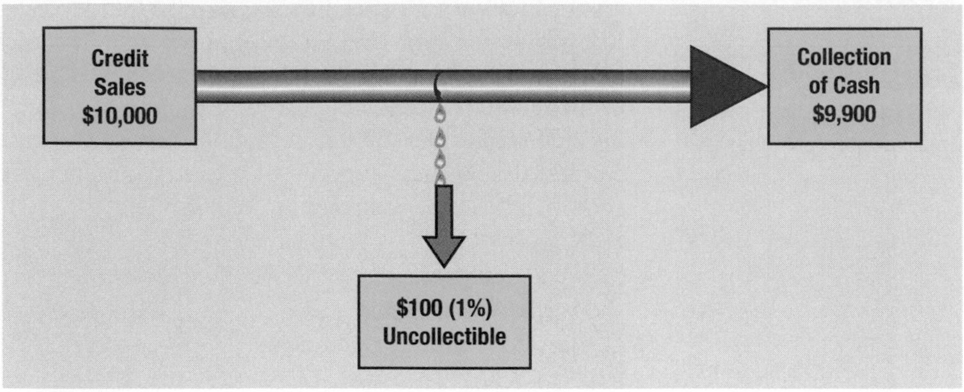

If during 20-3 Chris had credit sales of $120,000, the estimate of uncollectible accounts would be made as follows:

Credit sales	$ 120,000
Estimated % uncollectible	× 1%
Estimated uncollectible accounts	$ 1,200

Thus, the following adjusting entry would be made on December 31, 20-3:

4	Dec.	31	Bad Debt Expense		1,200.00		4
5			Allowance for Bad Debts			1,200.00	5
6							6

In T account form at the end of 20-3, Allowance for Bad Debts would appear as follows:

Allowance for Bad Debts

Debit		Credit	
		20-3	
		12/31	1,200

Assume that during the following year, 20-4, uncollectible accounts totaling $1,100 were written off as follows:

8			Allowance for Bad Debts		1,100.00		8
9			Accounts Receivable/Customer Names			1,100.00	9
10			Wrote off uncollectible accounts				10

After posting this entry, Allowance for Bad Debts would have a credit balance of $100.

Allowance for Bad Debts

Debit		Credit		
		20-3		
		12/31		1,200
20-4	1,100			
		20-4	Bal.	100

Accounts written off during 20-4

Assume that during 20-4, Chris had credit sales of $130,000. Based on experience, Chris would still estimate its uncollectible accounts at 1% of credit sales. This would yield estimated uncollectible accounts of $1,300 (1% × $130,000), and the following adjusting entry would be made on December 31, 20-4:

4	Dec.	31	Bad Debt Expense	1 3 0 0 00		4
5			Allowance for Bad Debts		1 3 0 0 00	5
6						6

This would increase the Allowance for Bad Debts balance to $1,400.

Allowance for Bad Debts

		20-3		
		12/31		1,200
20-4	1,100			
		20-4	Bal.	100
		12/31	Adj.	1,300
		12/31	Bal.	1,400

This demonstrates an important feature of the percentage of sales method. Allowance for Bad Debts may have a debit or credit balance prior to adjustment. This is a normal result of underestimating or overestimating uncollectible accounts. Under the percentage of sales method, any balance in Allowance for Bad Debts prior to adjustment is generally *ignored* in making the current period's adjusting entry.

LEARNING KEY

Percentage of sales method: When making the adjusting entry, ignore the balance in Allowance for Bad Debts prior to adjustment.

This is because the percentage of sales method focuses on the *current year's* credit sales. Any previous balance in the allowance account relates to credit sales and uncollectible accounts from *prior years*. In the above illustration, the balance was a credit of $100. This balance could have been a credit of $300 or a debit of $200, and it would not have mattered. The adjusting entry for uncollectible accounts would have been the same—$1,300.

There is one exception to ignoring the balance in Allowance for Bad Debts in making the adjustment. When a large debit or credit balance accumulates in the allowance account, the percentage of credit sales used to estimate uncollectible accounts should be increased or decreased. This provides a better estimate based on recent experience.

PERCENTAGE OF RECEIVABLES METHOD

The **percentage of receivables method** is based on the idea that some portion of the existing accounts receivable will not be collected. This way of viewing uncollectible accounts is illustrated in Figure 16-3 for accounts receivable of $2,000. In this case, 4% ($80) of the accounts receivable at the end of the year are estimated to be uncollectible. In other words, the company estimates that amount of cash will not be collected.

If a business is new and has no prior credit experience, industry averages or percentages for similar companies may be used for making estimates in initial years of operation.

To apply this method, we focus on the relationship between the amount of accounts receivable at the end of the year and the amount of uncollectible accounts. The simplest form of this method involves computing uncollectible accounts as a percentage of the Accounts Receivable balance. Assume that Craft Co. had an average Accounts Receivable balance at the end of the past two years of $110,000, and average uncollectible accounts of $4,400. Craft would estimate its percentage of uncollectible accounts as follows:

$$\frac{\text{Average Uncollectible Accounts}}{\text{Average Accounts Receivable}} = \frac{\$4,400}{\$110,000} = 4\%$$

FIGURE 16-3 Percentage of Receivables Method

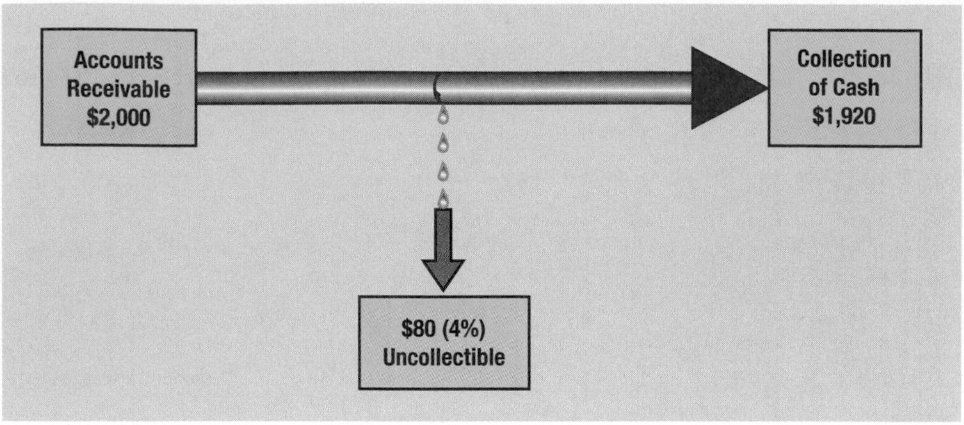

If the Accounts Receivable balance at the end of the current year was $120,000, the estimate of uncollectible accounts would be made as follows:

Accounts receivable	$120,000
Estimated % uncollectible	× 4%
Estimated uncollectible accounts	$ 4,800

Assuming Allowance for Bad Debts has a zero balance prior to adjustment, the following adjusting entry would be made at year-end:

					Debit	Credit	
4	Dec.	31	Bad Debt Expense		4,800.00		4
5			Allowance for Bad Debts			4,800.00	5
6							6

Although the above approach is simple, the estimate of uncollectible accounts is not very precise. This is because with this approach each dollar of receivables is treated as having the same chance of being uncollectible. In fact, we know that the older an amount is, the greater the chance it will be uncollectible.

Therefore, the percentage of receivables method usually is applied in a way that yields a better estimate of uncollectible accounts. Instead of using the total accounts receivable in making the estimate, each customer's account is analyzed to determine how long the amounts have been outstanding. Different percentages are then applied to amounts that have been outstanding for different lengths of time. Because of the emphasis on the length of time the accounts have been outstanding, this process is called **aging the receivables**.

An aging schedule similar to the one in Figure 16-4 is often used to analyze the receivables and estimate the uncollectible amount. As indicated in Figure 16-4, the following steps are used in preparing the aging schedule:

STEP 1 Categorize each account receivable according to the length of time the amounts have been outstanding.

STEP 2 Multiply the amount of receivables in each category by an estimate of the percent that will be uncollectible. This percentage is based on past experience and increases as the number of days past due increases.

STEP 3 Total the estimates for each category to determine the amount that is not expected to be collected.

FIGURE 16-4 Aging Schedule

		AGING SCHEDULE OF ACCOUNTS RECEIVABLE — December 31, 20-1									
					NUMBER OF DAYS PAST DUE						
		CUSTOMER	TOTAL	NOT YET DUE	1–30	31–60	61–90	91–180	181–365	OVER 365	
(1)	4	W. Billiard	$ 3,000.00	$ 2,500.00	$ 500.00						4
	5	K. Campbell	950.00			$ 650.00		$ 300.00			5
	6	J. Farley	4,325.00	3,800.00			$ 525.00				6
	7	L. Gilbert	1,900.00	1,500.00		400.00					7
	8	E. Rome	3,950.00	3,170.00					$ 780.00		8
	20	B. Zimmerman	200.00					200.00			20
(2)	21	Total	$100,500.00	$65,000.00	$18,000.00	$8,250.00	$6,310.00	$1,810.00	$ 780.00	$ 350.00	21
	22	Estimated percent									22
	23	uncollectible		× 2 %	× 5 %	× 10 %	× 20 %	× 30 %	× 50 %	× 80 %	23
(3)	24	Total est. uncollectible									24
	25	accounts	$ 5,500.00	$ 1,300.00	$ 900.00	$ 825.00	$1,262.00	$ 543.00	$ 390.00	$ 280.00	25
	26										26
	27		($ 5,500.00	= 1,300.00	+ 900.00	+ 825.00	+ 1,262.00	+ 543.00	+ 390.00	+ 280.00)	27
	28										28

Based on the aging schedule in Figure 16-4, uncollectible accounts would be estimated as $5,500 as indicated in the Total column. In other words, it is estimated that $5,500 of the $100,500 of accounts receivable at December 31, 20-1, will not be collected. Thus, assuming Allowance for Bad Debts has a zero balance prior to adjustment, the following adjusting entry would be made at December 31, 20-1:

4	Dec.	31	Bad Debt Expense	5,500.00		4
5			Allowance for Bad Debts		5,500.00	5
6						6

In T account form, Allowance for Bad Debts would appear as follows:

Allowance for Bad Debts

Debit	Credit
	20-1 12/31 Adj. 5,500

Assume that during the following year, 20-2, uncollectible accounts totaling $5,200 were written off as follows:

8			Allowance for Bad Debts	5,200.00		8
9			Accounts Receivable/Customer Names		5,200.00	9
10			Wrote off uncollectible accounts			10

Allowance for Bad Debts now would have a credit balance of $300.

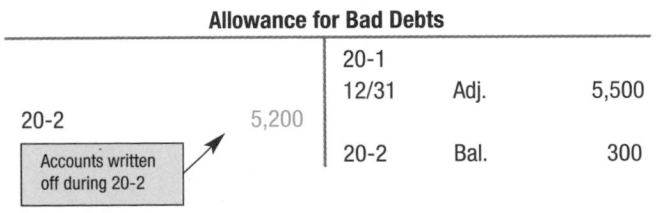

Allowance for Bad Debts

Debit	Credit
	20-1 12/31 Adj. 5,500
20-2 5,200	
Accounts written off during 20-2	20-2 Bal. 300

Assume that at the end of 20-2 another aging schedule like the one in Figure 16-4 is prepared, and that the estimated uncollectible amount is $5,700. To bring the credit balance in the allowance account to $5,700, an adjustment of $5,400 is needed.

Estimated uncollectible amount	$5,700
Current credit balance in account	– 300
Adjustment needed	$5,400

Thus, the following adjusting entry would be made on December 31, 20-2:

4	Dec.	31	Bad Debt Expense		5 4 0 0 00		4
5			Allowance for Bad Debts			5 4 0 0 00	5
6							6

This would increase the Allowance for Bad Debts balance to $5,700.

Allowance for Bad Debts

			20-1		
			12/31	Adj.	5,500
20-2		5,200			
			20-2	Bal.	300
			12/31	Adj.	5,400
			12/31	Bal.	5,700

Adjustment to increase the balance to $5,700

This demonstrates an important feature of the percentage of receivables method. Allowance for Bad Debts may have a debit or credit balance prior to adjustment. Under the percentage of receivables method, this balance must be considered in making the current period's adjusting entry.

This is because the percentage of receivables method focuses on the Accounts Receivable balance at the end of the year. That balance contains receivables from the current year and any remaining from prior years. The total Accounts Receivable balance consisting of current and prior year receivables is analyzed to determine the proper allowance account balance. The adjusting entry is then made to achieve that balance in the allowance account. In the above illustration, the balance prior to adjustment was a credit of $300. Therefore, the adjustment to bring the balance to $5,700 was $5,400 ($5,700 – $300). If the balance prior to adjustment had been a debit of $100, the necessary adjusting entry would have been $5,800.

LEARNING KEY

Percentage of receivables method: Unlike the percentage of sales method, when making the adjusting entry, consider the balance in Allowance for Bad Debts prior to adjustment.

Estimated uncollectible amount	$5,700
Current debit balance in account	+ 100
Adjustment needed	$5,800

Notice that the resulting credit balance in Allowance for Bad Debts after adjustment would once again be $5,700.

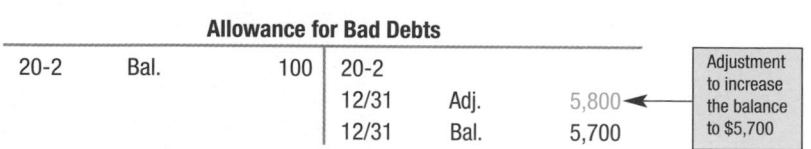

Allowance for Bad Debts

20-2	Bal.	100	20-2		
			12/31	Adj.	5,800
			12/31	Bal.	5,700

Adjustment to increase the balance to $5,700

to collect $95,000 after writing off his account. Management knew that there would be some uncollectible accounts. Now they know that McDonald is one of them.

RECOVERY OF ACCOUNTS PREVIOUSLY WRITTEN OFF—ALLOWANCE METHOD

Occasionally, an account that was written off is collected. For example, assume that a check for $500 was received on February 1 from Bill McDonald, whose account was written off on January 15. This requires two entries, as follows:

1. Reinstate the account.
2. Record the collection.

To reinstate an account, simply reverse the entry made to write off the account, as follows:

5	Feb.	1	Accounts Receivable/B. McDonald		500 00		5
6			Allowance for Bad Debts			500 00	6
7			Reinstated account receivable				7

To record the collection, the following entry is made:

9	Feb.	1	Cash		500 00		9
10			Accounts Receivable/B. McDonald			500 00	10
11			Collection on account				11

Instead of making these entries, it might be simpler to debit Cash and credit Allowance for Bad Debts. However, this shortcut should not be taken. Without the reinstatement, the subsidiary ledger will report only that McDonald's account was written off as uncollectible. With the reinstatement, the subsidiary ledger will reflect the fact that McDonald has paid his account. This information will be important to McDonald and the business should he desire credit in the future.

U REVU

Complete U REVU-2 on **page 638** to test your basic understanding of LO2.

DIRECT WRITE-OFF METHOD

LO3 Apply the direct write-off method of accounting for uncollectible accounts.

Under the **direct write-off method**, the bad debt expense is not recognized until it has been determined that an account is uncollectible. For example, assume that on August 15, John Lafollette's account for $500 is judged to be uncollectible. The following entry would be made:

5	Aug.	15	Bad Debt Expense		500 00		5
6			Accounts Receivable/J. Lafollette			500 00	6
7			Wrote off uncollectible account				7

ADVANTAGE AND DISADVANTAGES OF DIRECT METHOD

The direct write-off method has one advantage. It is very simple to apply. However, there are three disadvantages of using this method. First, efforts to collect the account often extend over many months. Thus, the revenue from the sale might be recognized in one period and the bad debt expense recognized in another. This violates the matching principle.

Second, the amount of bad debt expense recognized in a given period can be manipulated by management. This occurs because there is no general rule for deciding when an account becomes uncollectible. Thus, management can use its subjective judgment in deciding when to recognize bad debt expense.

Third, the amount of accounts receivable reported on the balance sheet does not represent the amount of cash actually expected to be collected. Thus, the assets are overstated by the amount of uncollectible accounts included in accounts receivable. For these reasons, the direct write-off method is generally not acceptable for financial reporting purposes. It is acceptable only if the amount of uncollectible accounts cannot be reasonably estimated and if the estimated amount is very small. This method is required, however, for income tax purposes.

To deduct bad debt expense for income tax purposes, the taxpayer must have attempted unsuccessfully to collect the account.

RECOVERY OF ACCOUNTS PREVIOUSLY WRITTEN OFF—DIRECT WRITE-OFF METHOD

Occasionally, an account that was written off is collected. The proper entries for the recovery depend on the period in which the cash is collected.

Write-Off and Recovery in Same Accounting Period

Assume the write-off and recovery are made in the same accounting period. In this case, first reinstate the account by reversing the entry for the write-off. Then, record the collection in the usual manner as shown below.

To write off account:

5	Aug.	15	Bad Debt Expense		5 0 0 00		5
6			Accounts Receivable/J. Lafollette			5 0 0 00	6
7			Wrote off uncollectible account				7

To reinstate account:

35	Dec.	20	Accounts Receivable/J. Lafollette		5 0 0 00		35
36			Bad Debt Expense			5 0 0 00	36
37			Reinstated account receivable				37

To record collection:

39	Dec.	20	Cash		5 0 0 00		39
40			Accounts Receivable/J. Lafollette			5 0 0 00	40
41			Collection on account				41

Profiles in Accounting

Ingry Valdes, Junior Accountant

After graduating from The College of Westchester with an associate degree in accounting, Ingry Valdes worked full time for a CPA firm as a bookkeeper, where she gained valuable experience. Her next job was as a junior accountant in a small nonprofit company. Ingry's responsibilities included preparation of bank reconciliations, write-up of accounts receivable and payables through QuickBooks, and preliminary tax preparation. According to Ingry, she was exposed to all aspects of accounting. These work experiences motivated Ingry's return to school for her baccalaureate degree and eventually her master's degree in accounting. Ingry's career goal is to become a licensed certified public accountant (CPA).

Write-Off and Recovery in Different Accounting Periods

What if the write-off is made in one period and the recovery in the following accounting period? In this case, first reinstate the account by debiting Accounts Receivable and crediting Uncollectible Accounts Recovered. This revenue account is credited instead of Bad Debt Expense because a credit to the expense account would understate bad debt expense for the current year. Uncollectible Accounts Recovered is reported on the income statement as other revenue. The entries for the write-off and recovery are shown below.

To write off account:

5	Aug.	15	Bad Debt Expense		500 00		5
6			Accounts Receivable/J. Lafollette			500 00	6
7			Wrote off uncollectible account				7

To reinstate account:

35	Jan.	20	Accounts Receivable/J. Lafollette		500 00		35
36			Uncollectible Accounts Recovered			500 00	36
37			Reinstated account receivable				37

To record collection:

39	Jan.	20	Cash		500 00		39
40			Accounts Receivable/J. Lafollette			500 00	40
41			Collection on account				41

U REVU

Complete U REVU-3 on **page 638** to test your basic understanding of LO3.

LEARNING OBJECTIVES Key Points to Remember

LO1 Apply the allowance method of accounting for uncollectible accounts.

To use the allowance method, apply three steps.

STEP 1 At the end of the period, estimate the uncollectible amount.

STEP 2 Make the following adjusting entry:

4		Bad Debt Expense		x x x xx		4
5		Allowance for Bad Debts			x x x xx	5

STEP 3 When an uncollectible account is identified, make the following entry:

8		Allowance for Bad Debts		x x x xx		8
9		Accounts Receivable/Customer Name			x x x xx	9
10		Wrote off uncollectible account				10

LO2 Apply the percentage of sales and percentage of receivables methods of estimating uncollectible accounts.

The *percentage of sales method* is based on the relationship between the amount of credit sales and the amount of uncollectible accounts. Any balance in Allowance for Bad Debts prior to adjustment is ignored in making the current period's adjusting entry.

The *percentage of receivables method* is based on the relationship between the amount of accounts receivable and the amount of uncollectible accounts. The estimate of uncollectibles is usually based on an aging of receivables. Any balance in Allowance for Bad Debts prior to adjustment is considered in making the current period's adjusting entry.

Under the allowance method, the actual write-off of an uncollectible account does not affect either the income statement or the balance sheet.

When an account is collected that has been written off, the account is reinstated and then the collection is recorded.

LO3 Apply the direct write-off method of accounting for uncollectible accounts.

Under the direct write-off method, bad debt expense is not recognized until an account is written off as uncollectible.

The entries for collection of an account previously written off depend on when the collection occurs. If the collection is in the same period as the write-off, the credit is to Bad Debt Expense. If the collection is in the following period, the credit is to Uncollectible Accounts Recovered.

DEMONSTRATION PROBLEM

Budke and Budke, a landscaping service, uses the allowance method to record the following transactions related to accounts receivable. Adjusting and closing entries completed during the current year ended December 31, 20--, are also described below.

Mar. 6 Received 50% of the $12,000 balance owed by Columbia Gardens, a bankrupt business, and wrote off the remainder as uncollectible.

June 12 Reinstated the account of Ramon Burgos, which had been written off in the previous year, and received $2,250 cash in full settlement.

Sept. 19 Wrote off the $13,800 balance owed by Kelly Richeson, who has no assets.

Nov. 9 Reinstated the account of Jackie Kwas, which had been written off in the preceding year, and received $2,175 cash in full settlement.

Dec. 27 Wrote off the following accounts as uncollectible, in compound entry form: Blair & Smith, $10,480; Landscapes Unlimited, $8,570; Beekman Brothers, $22,500; B. J. McKay, $9,300.

31 Based on an aging analysis of $1,460,000 of accounts receivable, it was estimated that $73,500 will be uncollectible. Made the adjusting entry.

31 Made the entry to close the appropriate account to Income Summary.

Selected accounts and beginning balances on January 1, 20--, are as follows:

122.1	Allowance for Bad Debts	$95,000 credit
313	Income Summary	—
532	Bad Debt Expense	—

REQUIRED

1. Open the three selected accounts.
2. Enter the transactions and the adjusting and closing entries in general journal form (page 12 for the first 2 entries; page 13 for all others). After each entry, post to the three accounts named.
3. Determine the net realizable value as of December 31, 20--.

Solution 1. and 2.

GENERAL LEDGER

ACCOUNT: Allowance for Bad Debts ACCOUNT NO. 122.1

DATE		ITEM	POST. REF.	DEBIT	CREDIT	BALANCE DEBIT	BALANCE CREDIT
20-- Jan.	1	Balance	✓				95 0 0 0 00
Mar.	6		J12	6 0 0 0 00			89 0 0 0 00
June	12		J13		2 2 5 0 00		91 2 5 0 00
Sept.	19		J13	13 8 0 0 00			77 4 5 0 00
Nov.	9		J13		2 1 7 5 00		79 6 2 5 00
Dec.	27		J13	50 8 5 0 00			28 7 7 5 00
	31	Adjusting	J13		44 7 2 5 00		73 5 0 0 00

ACCOUNT: Income Summary ACCOUNT NO. 313

DATE		ITEM	POST. REF.	DEBIT	CREDIT	BALANCE DEBIT	BALANCE CREDIT
20-- Dec.	31	Closing	J13	44 7 2 5 00		44 7 2 5 00	

ACCOUNT: Bad Debt Expense ACCOUNT NO. 532

DATE		ITEM	POST. REF.	DEBIT	CREDIT	BALANCE DEBIT	BALANCE CREDIT
20-- Dec.	31	Adjusting	J13	44 7 2 5 00		44 7 2 5 00	
	31	Closing	J13		44 7 2 5 00		

(continued)

GENERAL JOURNAL PAGE 12

DATE		DESCRIPTION	POST. REF.	DEBIT	CREDIT
20--					
Mar.	6	Cash		6,000.00	
		Accounts Receivable/Columbia Gardens			6,000.00
		Collection on account			
	6	Allowance for Bad Debts	122.1	6,000.00	
		Accounts Receivable/Columbia Gardens			6,000.00
		Wrote off uncollectible account			

GENERAL JOURNAL PAGE 13

DATE		DESCRIPTION	POST. REF.	DEBIT	CREDIT
20--					
June	12	Accounts Receivable/R. Burgos		2,250.00	
		Allowance for Bad Debts	122.1		2,250.00
		Reinstated account receivable			
	12	Cash		2,250.00	
		Accounts Receivable/R. Burgos			2,250.00
		Collection on account			
Sept.	19	Allowance for Bad Debts	122.1	13,800.00	
		Accounts Receivable/K. Richeson			13,800.00
		Wrote off uncollectible account			
Nov.	9	Accounts Receivable/J. Kwas		2,175.00	
		Allowance for Bad Debts	122.1		2,175.00
		Reinstated account receivable			
	9	Cash		2,175.00	
		Accounts Receivable/J. Kwas			2,175.00
		Collection on account			
Dec.	27	Allowance for Bad Debts	122.1	50,850.00	
		Accounts Receivable/Blair & Smith			10,480.00
		Accounts Receivable/Landscapes Unlimited			8,570.00
		Accounts Receivable/Beekman Brothers			22,500.00
		Accounts Receivable/B. J. McKay			9,300.00
		Wrote off uncollectible accounts			
		Adjusting Entry			
	31	Bad Debt Expense	532	44,725.00	
		Allowance for Bad Debts	122.1		44,725.00
		Closing Entry			
	31	Income Summary	313	44,725.00	
		Bad Debt Expense	532		44,725.00

3\.

Accounts receivable, December 31, 20--	$1,460,000
Less allowance for bad debts	73,500
Net realizable value	$1,386,500

KEY TERMS

aging the receivables (626) The process of estimating the uncollectible amount by analyzing account balances according to the length of time the accounts have been outstanding.

allowance method (622) A technique that attempts to recognize bad debt expense in the same period that the related credit sales are made.

bad debt expense (622) A loss from failure to collect an account receivable.

direct write-off method (631) A method in which the bad debt expense is not recognized until it has been determined that an account is uncollectible.

matching principle (622) A concept that requires expenses to be matched with the revenues they helped to produce.

net realizable value (623) The amount a business expects to collect from its accounts receivable; calculated as Accounts Receivable less Allowance for Bad Debts. Also called net receivables.

net receivables (623) See net realizable value.

percentage of receivables method (625) A method in which the current year's uncollectible accounts are estimated based on the relationship between the amount of accounts receivable and the amount of uncollectible accounts in prior years.

percentage of sales method (623) A method in which the current year's uncollectible accounts are estimated based on the relationship between the amount of credit sales and the amount of uncollectible accounts in prior years.

SELF-STUDY QUESTIONS AND EXERCISES

True/False Questions

1. LO1 There are two methods of accounting for uncollectible accounts: the allowance method and the direct write-off method.
2. LO1 The matching principle states that debits should be matched with credits.
3. LO2 Using the percentage of sales method, the balance in Allowance for Bad Debts must be taken into consideration before making the adjusting entry.
4. LO2 When an account is written off under the allowance method, there should be a debit to Bad Debt Expense.
5. LO3 Each time an account is written off under the direct write-off method, Bad Debt Expense is debited.

Multiple Choice Questions

1. LO1 The dollar difference between Accounts Receivable and Allowance for Bad Debts is called

   (a) book value.
   (b) interest value.
   (c) carrying value.
   (d) net realizable value.

2. LO2 A business has an ending balance in Accounts Receivable of $35,000; credit sales for the year of $300,000; and a credit balance in Allowance for Bad Debts of $800. If the percentage of sales method is used and the percentage is estimated at 1% of credit sales, what is the amount to be entered for the adjusting entry?

   (a) $3,000
   (b) $3,800
   (c) $2,200
   (d) $1,150

3. LO2 A business has an ending balance in Accounts Receivable of $35,000; credit sales for the year of $300,000; and a credit balance in Allowance for Bad Debts of $800. If the percentage of sales method is used and the percentage is estimated at 1% of credit sales, what is the ending balance in Allowance for Bad Debts *after* the adjusting entry?

   (a) $3,000
   (b) $3,800
   (c) $2,200
   (d) $1,150

4. LO2 A business has an ending balance in Accounts Receivable of $40,000; credit sales for the year of $500,000; and a debit balance in Allowance for Bad Debts of $300. If an aging analysis indicates that $4,800 should be the balance in Allowance for Bad Debts, the amount to be entered for the adjusting entry is

   (a) $4,800.
   (b) $4,500.
   (c) $5,000.
   (d) $5,100.

5. LO2 Under the allowance method, when an account is determined to be worthless, the journal entry to write off the account will include a

   (a) debit to Allowance for Bad Debts.
   (b) debit to Bad Debt Expense.
   (c) credit to Allowance for Bad Debts.
   (d) debit to Accounts Receivable.

U REVU **Exercises**

1. LO1 Beamon Department Store has an Accounts Receivable balance of $32,500 and an Allowance for Bad Debts balance of $1,100. Determine the net realizable value of Beamon's accounts receivable.

2. LO2 (a) Toni's Tech Shop has total credit sales for the year of $170,000 and estimates that 3% of its credit sales will be uncollectible. Allowance for Bad Debts has a credit balance of $275.

   Prepare the adjusting entry at year-end for the estimated uncollectible accounts.

   (b) Based on an aging of its accounts receivable, Kyle's Cyclery estimates that $3,200 of its year-end accounts receivable will be uncollectible. Allowance for Bad Debts has a debit balance of $280 at year-end.

   Prepare the adjusting entry at year-end for the estimated uncollectible accounts.

3. LO3 Fiona's Pharmacy uses the direct write-off method of accounting for bad debt expense. Prepare the journal entry on July 25 to write off $1,320 owed by P. Wahdia.

The answers to the Self-Study Questions and Exercises are at the end of the chapter (pages 648–649).

APPLYING YOUR KNOWLEDGE

REVIEW QUESTIONS

LO1 1. What method of accounting for uncollectible accounts is generally required for financial reporting purposes?

LO1 2. Describe the steps to follow when using the allowance method to account for uncollectible accounts.

LO1 3. Explain how to compute net realizable value.

LO2 4. Describe the process followed when estimating uncollectible accounts under the percentage of sales method.

LO2 5. Describe the process followed when estimating uncollectible accounts under the percentage (aging) of receivables method.

LO2 6. How does the balance in Allowance for Bad Debts before adjustment affect the amount of the year-end adjustment under the percentage of sales method? Under the percentage of receivables method?

LO2 7. Under the allowance method, what impact does the write-off of a customer's account have on the financial statements?

LO2 8. Under the allowance method, what journal entries are made if an account is collected that was previously written off?

LO3 9. Describe the accounting procedures when using the direct write-off method to account for uncollectible accounts.

LO3 10. What are three disadvantages of using the direct write-off method?

SERIES A EXERCISES

E 16-1A (LO1)
✓ 1. Net realizable value: $42,000

CALCULATION OF NET REALIZABLE VALUE J. B. Bucks owns a department store that has a $45,000 balance in Accounts Receivable and a $3,000 credit balance in Allowance for Bad Debts.

1. Determine the net realizable value of the accounts receivable.
2. Assume that an account receivable in the amount of $400 was written off using the allowance method. Determine the net realizable value of the accounts receivable after the write-off.

E 16-2A (LO2)
✓ 1. Dr. Bad Dept Exp.: $5,400

UNCOLLECTIBLE ACCOUNTS—PERCENTAGE OF SALES Ryan's Express has total credit sales for the year of $180,000 and estimates that 3% of its credit sales will be uncollectible. Record the end-of-period adjusting entry on December 31, in general journal form, for the estimated uncollectible accounts. Assume the following independent conditions existed prior to the adjustment:

1. Allowance for Bad Debts has a credit balance of $925.
2. Allowance for Bad Debts has a debit balance of $385.

E 16-3A (LO2)
✓ 2. Dr. Bad Debt Exp.: $4,525

UNCOLLECTIBLE ACCOUNTS—PERCENTAGE OF RECEIVABLES Tammie's Toyota Sales and Service estimates the amount of uncollectible accounts using the percentage of receivables method. After aging the accounts, it is estimated that $4,250 will not be collected. Record the end-of-period adjusting entry on December 31, in general journal form, for the estimated uncollectible accounts. Assume the following independent conditions existed prior to the adjustment:

1. Allowance for Bad Debts has a credit balance of $690.
2. Allowance for Bad Debts has a debit balance of $275.

E 16-4A (LO2)
✓ Sept. 27, Cr. Allow. for Bad Debts: $5,350

COLLECTION OF ACCOUNTS WRITTEN OFF—ALLOWANCE METHOD Julia Alvarez, owner of Alvarez Rentals, uses the allowance method in accounting for uncollectible accounts. Record the following transactions in general journal form:

July 7	Wrote off $5,350 owed by Randy Dalzell, who has no assets.
Aug. 12	Wrote off $2,870 owed by Jason Flint, who declared bankruptcy.
Sept. 27	Reinstated the account of Randy Dalzell, which had been written off on July 7, and received $5,350 cash in full settlement.

E 16-5A (LO2)
✓ 1(b). Dr. Bad Debt Exp.: $28,570

UNCOLLECTIBLE ACCOUNTS—PERCENTAGE OF SALES AND PERCENTAGE OF RECEIVABLES At the end of the current year, the accounts receivable account of

(*continued*)

Glenn's Nursery Supplies has a debit balance of $390,000. Credit sales are $2,800,000. Record the end-of-period adjusting entry on December 31, in general journal form, for the estimated uncollectible accounts. Assume the following independent conditions existed prior to the adjustment:

1. Allowance for Bad Debts has a credit balance of $1,760.
   (a) The percentage of sales method is used and bad debt expense is estimated to be 1% of credit sales.
   (b) The percentage of receivables method is used and an analysis of the accounts produces an estimate of $30,330 in uncollectible accounts.
2. Allowance for Bad Debts has a debit balance of $1,900.
   (a) The percentage of sales method is used and bad debt expense is estimated to be ¾ of 1% of credit sales.
   (b) The percentage of receivables method is used and an analysis of the accounts produces an estimate of $29,890 in uncollectible accounts.

E 16-6A (LO3)
✓ July 20, Dr. Bad Debt Exp.: $2,325

DIRECT WRITE-OFF METHOD Maria Rivera, owner of Rivera Pharmacy, uses the direct write-off method in accounting for uncollectible accounts. Record the following transactions in general journal form:

July 20 Wrote off $2,325 owed by Joe Balouka, who has no assets.

Oct. 15 Wrote off $1,675 owed by Alice Rose, who declared bankruptcy.

E 16-7A (LO3)
✓ Sept. 2, Cr. Bad Debt Exp.: $1,745

COLLECTION OF ACCOUNT WRITTEN OFF—DIRECT WRITE-OFF METHOD Como's Music Store uses the direct write-off method in accounting for uncollectible accounts. Record the following transactions in general journal form:

20-1

May 8 Wrote off $1,745 owed by Vickie Lawrence, who has no assets.

July 15 Wrote off $1,300 owed by Dan Utter, who declared bankruptcy.

Sept. 2 Reinstated the account of Vickie Lawrence, which had been written off on May 8, and received $1,745 cash in full settlement.

20-2

May 15 Reinstated the account of Dan Utter, which had been written off in the previous year, and received $1,300 cash in full settlement.

SERIES A PROBLEMS

P 16-8A (LO1/2)
✓ 3. $921,300

UNCOLLECTIBLE ACCOUNTS—ALLOWANCE METHOD Emery Nurseries used the allowance method to record the following transactions, adjusting entries, and closing entries during the year ended December 31, 20--:

Feb. 9 Received 60% of the $5,000 balance owed by Patty's Petunias, a bankrupt business, and wrote off the remainder as uncollectible.

May 28 Reinstated the account of Danielle Bell, which had been written off in the preceding year, and received $2,400 cash in full settlement.

Aug. 16 Wrote off the $8,200 balance owed by Rich Bouie as uncollectible.

Oct. 5 Reinstated the account of Bonnie McCelland, which had been written off in the preceding year, and received $3,600 cash in full settlement.

Dec. 28 Wrote off the following accounts as uncollectible, in compound entry form: Bloudeck & Rhodes, $14,450; Creative Landscapers, $16,100; Ramona Randol, $12,750.

31 Based on an aging analysis of the $980,000 of accounts receivable, it was estimated that $58,700 will be uncollectible. Made the adjusting entry.

31 Made the entry to close the appropriate account to Income Summary.

Selected accounts and beginning balances on January 1, 20--, are as follows:

122.1	Allowance for Bad Debts	$52,000 credit
313	Income Summary	—
532	Bad Debt Expense	—

REQUIRED

1. Open the three selected accounts.
2. Enter the transactions and the adjusting and closing entries in a general journal (page 6). After each entry, post to the three accounts named.
3. Determine the net realizable value as of December 31.

P 16-9A (LO2)

✓ 1(b). Dr. Bad Debt Exp.: $6,620

UNCOLLECTIBLE ACCOUNTS—PERCENTAGE OF SALES AND PERCENTAGE OF RECEIVABLES At the completion of the current fiscal year ending December 31, the balance of Accounts Receivable for Yang's Gift Shop was $30,000. Credit sales for the year were $355,200.

REQUIRED

Make the necessary adjusting entry in general journal form under each of the following assumptions. Show calculations for the amount of each adjustment and the resulting net realizable value.

1. Allowance for Bad Debts has a credit balance of $330.
   (a) The percentage of sales method is used and uncollectible accounts are estimated to be 2.0% of credit sales.
   (b) The percentage of receivables method is used and an analysis of the accounts produces an estimate of $6,950 in uncollectible accounts.
2. Allowance for Bad Debts has a debit balance of $400.
   (a) The percentage of sales method is used and uncollectible accounts are estimated to be 1.5% of credit sales.
   (b) The percentage of receivables method is used and an analysis of the accounts produces an estimate of $5,685 in uncollectible accounts.

P 16-10 A (LO2)

✓ 2. Dr. Bad Debt Exp.: $2,790

AGING ACCOUNTS RECEIVABLE An analysis of the accounts receivable of Johnson Company as of December 31, 20--, reveals the following:

Age Interval	Balance	Estimated Percent Uncollectible
Not yet due	$65,000	2%
1–30 days past due	4,500	5
31–60 days past due	3,550	10
61–90 days past due	1,650	25
91–180 days past due	1,200	35
181–365 days past due	650	55
Over 365 days past due	400	85
Total	$76,950	

(continued)

REQUIRED

1. Prepare an aging schedule as of December 31, 20--, by adding the following column to the three columns shown above: Estimated Amount Uncollectible.
2. Assuming that Allowance for Bad Debts had a credit balance of $620 before adjustment, record the end-of-period adjusting entry in general journal form to enter the estimate for uncollectible accounts.

P 16-11A (LO3)

✓ 20-2, Jan. 17, Cr. Uncoll. Accounts Recovered: $6,300

DIRECT WRITE-OFF METHOD Williams & Hendricks Distributors uses the direct write-off method in accounting for uncollectible accounts.

20-1	
Feb. 18	Sold merchandise on account to Merry Merchants, $17,500.
Mar. 22	Sold merchandise on account to Utter Unicorns, $14,300.
June 3	Received $10,000 from Merry Merchants and wrote off the remainder owed on the sale of February 18 as uncollectible.
Sept. 9	Received $8,000 from Utter Unicorns and wrote off the remainder owed on the sale of March 22 as uncollectible.
Nov. 13	Reinstated the account of Merry Merchants, which had been written off on June 3, and received $7,500 cash in full settlement.
20-2	
Jan. 17	Reinstated the account of Utter Unicorns, which had been written off on September 9 of the previous year, and received $6,300 cash in full settlement.

REQUIRED

Record these transactions in general journal form.

SERIES B EXERCISES

E 16-1B (LO1)

✓ 1. Net realizable value: $60,025

CALCULATION OF NET REALIZABLE VALUE Mary Martin owns a department store that has a $65,200 balance in Accounts Receivable and a $5,175 credit balance in Allowance for Bad Debts.

1. Determine the net realizable value of the accounts receivable.
2. Assume that an account receivable in the amount of $900 was written off using the allowance method. Determine the net realizable value of the accounts receivable after the write-off.

E 16-2B (LO2)

✓ 1. Dr. Bad Debt Exp.: $7,600

UNCOLLECTIBLE ACCOUNTS—PERCENTAGE OF SALES Nicole's Neckties has total credit sales for the year of $380,000 and estimates that 2% of its credit sales will be uncollectible. Record the end-of-period adjusting entry on December 31, in general journal form, for the estimated uncollectible accounts. Assume the following independent conditions existed prior to the adjustment:

1. Allowance for Bad Debts has a credit balance of $430.
2. Allowance for Bad Debts has a debit balance of $295.

E 16-3B (LO2)
✓ 2. Dr. Bad Debt Exp.: $4,495

UNCOLLECTIBLE ACCOUNTS—PERCENTAGE OF RECEIVABLES Charlie's Chevy Sales and Service estimates the amount of uncollectible accounts using the percentage of receivables method. After aging the accounts, it is estimated that $3,935 will not be collected. Record the end-of-period adjusting entry on December 31, in general journal form, for the estimated uncollectible accounts. Assume the following independent conditions existed prior to the adjustment:

1. Allowance for Bad Debts has a credit balance of $245.
2. Allowance for Bad Debts has a debit balance of $560.

E 16-4B (LO2)
✓ Sept. 23, Cr. Allow. for Bad Debts: $6,040

COLLECTION OF ACCOUNT WRITTEN OFF—ALLOWANCE METHOD Raynette Ramos, owner of Ramos Rentals, uses the allowance method in accounting for uncollectible accounts. Record the following transactions in general journal form:

July 9	Wrote off $6,040 owed by Sue Sanchez, who has no assets.
Aug. 15	Wrote off $4,790 owed by Lonnie Jones, who declared bankruptcy.
Sept. 23	Reinstated the account of Sue Sanchez, which had been written off on July 9, and received $6,040 cash in full settlement.

E 16-5B (LO2)
✓ 1(b). Dr. Bad Debt Exp.: $22,640

UNCOLLECTIBLE ACCOUNTS—PERCENTAGE OF SALES AND PERCENTAGE OF RECEIVABLES At the end of the current year, the accounts receivable account of Parker's Nursery Supplies has a debit balance of $350,000. Credit sales are $2,300,000. Record the end-of-period adjusting entry on December 31, in general journal form, for the estimated uncollectible accounts. Assume the following independent conditions existed prior to the adjustment:

1. Allowance for Bad Debts has a credit balance of $1,920.
   (a) The percentage of sales method is used and bad debt expense is estimated to be 1% of credit sales.
   (b) The percentage of receivables method is used and an analysis of the accounts produces an estimate of $24,560 in uncollectible accounts.
2. Allowance for Bad Debts has a debit balance of $1,280.
   (a) The percentage of sales method is used and bad debt expense is estimated to be ¾ of 1% of credit sales.
   (b) The percentage of receivables method is used and an analysis of the accounts produces an estimate of $22,440 in uncollectible accounts.

E 16-6B (LO3)
✓ July 19, Dr. Bad Debt Exp.: $1,935

DIRECT WRITE-OFF METHOD Brent Mussellman, owner of Brent's Barbells, uses the direct write-off method in accounting for uncollectible accounts. Record the following transactions in general journal form:

July 19	Wrote off $1,935 owed by Arnold Swartz, who has no assets.
Oct. 12	Wrote off $2,125 owed by Janice Strong, who declared bankruptcy.

E 16-7B (LO3)
✓ Sept. 20, Cr. Bad Debt Exp.: $2,360

COLLECTION OF ACCOUNT WRITTEN OFF—DIRECT WRITE-OFF METHOD Madonna's Music Store uses the direct write-off method in accounting for uncollectible accounts. Record the following transactions in general journal form:

20-1	
May 5	Wrote off $2,360 owed by Neal Dammond, who has no assets.
July 18	Wrote off $1,255 owed by Maxine Mouse, who declared bankruptcy.

(continued)

Sept. 20 Reinstated the account of Neal Dammond, which had been written off on May 5, and received $2,360 cash in full settlement.

20-2

May 11 Reinstated the account of Maxine Mouse, which had been written off in the previous year, and received $1,255 cash in full settlement.

SERIES B PROBLEMS

P 16-8B (LO1/2)

✓ 3. $1,107,850

KLOOSTER & ALLEN

UNCOLLECTIBLE ACCOUNTS—ALLOWANCE METHOD Lewis Warehouse used the allowance method to record the following transactions, adjusting entries, and closing entries during the year ended December 31, 20--:

Feb. 7 Received 70% of the $8,000 balance owed by Luxury Sofas, a bankrupt business, and wrote off the remainder as uncollectible.

May 26 Reinstated the account of Sandy Johnson, which had been written off in the preceding year, and received $3,725 cash in full settlement.

Aug. 15 Wrote off the $9,350 balance owed by Izumi Goto as uncollectible.

Oct. 6 Reinstated the account of Doreen Woods, which had been written off in the preceding year, and received $4,320 cash in full settlement.

Dec. 29 Wrote off the following accounts as uncollectible, in compound entry form: Schmidt & Yeager, $13,945; Economy Homes, $15,830; Davis Industries, $11,865.

31 Based on an aging analysis of the $1,175,000 of accounts receivable, it was estimated that $67,150 will be uncollectible. Made the adjusting entry.

31 Made the entry to close the appropriate account to Income Summary.

Selected accounts and beginning balances on January 1, 20--, are as follows:

122.1	Allowance for Bad Debts	$49,850 credit
313	Income Summary	—
532	Bad Debt Expense	—

REQUIRED

1. Open the three selected accounts.
2. Enter the transactions and the adjusting and closing entries in a general journal (page 6). After each entry, post to the three accounts named.
3. Determine the net realizable value as of December 31, 20--.

P 16-9B (LO2)

✓ 1(b). Dr. Bad Debt Exp.: $27,650

UNCOLLECTIBLE ACCOUNTS—PERCENTAGE OF SALES AND PERCENTAGE OF RECEIVABLES At the completion of the current fiscal year ending December 31, the balance of Accounts Receivable for Anderson's Greeting Cards was $180,000. Credit sales for the year were $1,950,000.

REQUIRED

Make the necessary adjusting entry in general journal form under each of the following assumptions. Show calculations for the amount of each adjustment and the resulting net realizable value.

1. Allowance for Bad Debts has a credit balance of $2,600.
   (a) The percentage of sales method is used and bad debt expense is estimated to be 1.5% of credit sales.
   (b) The percentage of receivables method is used and an analysis of the accounts produces an estimate of $30,250 in uncollectible accounts.
2. Allowance for Bad Debts has a debit balance of $1,900.
   (a) The percentage of sales method is used and bad debt expense is estimated to be 1.0% of credit sales.
   (b) The percentage of receivables method is used and an analysis of the accounts produces an estimate of $20,500 in uncollectible accounts.

P 16-10B (LO2)
✓ 2. Dr. Bad Debt Exp.: $9,792

AGING ACCOUNTS RECEIVABLE An analysis of the accounts receivable of Matsushita Company as of December 31, 20--, reveals the following:

Age Interval	Balance	Estimated Percent Uncollectible
Not yet due	$250,000	1.5%
1–30 days past due	17,000	4
31–60 days past due	12,800	9
61–90 days past due	8,200	20
91–180 days past due	4,600	30
181–365 days past due	4,200	45
Over 365 days past due	1,400	75
Total	$298,200	

REQUIRED

1. Prepare an aging schedule as of December 31, 20--, by adding the following column to the three columns shown above: Estimated Amount Uncollectible.
2. Assuming that Allowance for Bad Debts had a credit balance of $1,750 before adjustment, record the end-of-period adjusting entry in general journal form to enter the estimate for uncollectible accounts.

P 16-11B (LO3)
✓ 20-2, Jan. 11, Cr. Uncoll. Accounts Recovered: $5,800

KLOOSTER & ALLEN

DIRECT WRITE-OFF METHOD Lee and Chen Distributors uses the direct write-off method in accounting for uncollectible accounts.

20-1	
Feb. 16	Sold merchandise on account to Biggs and Daughters, $16,000.
Mar. 23	Sold merchandise on account to Lloyd Place, $12,800.
June 8	Received $12,000 from Biggs and Daughters and wrote off the remainder owed on the sale of February 16 as uncollectible.
Sept. 27	Received $7,000 from Lloyd Place and wrote off the remainder owed on the sale of March 23 as uncollectible.
Nov. 18	Reinstated the account of Biggs and Daughters, which had been written off on June 8, and received $4,000 cash in full settlement.
20-2	
Jan. 11	Reinstated the account of Lloyd Place, which had been written off on September 27 of the previous year, and received $5,800 cash in full settlement.

REQUIRED
Record these transactions in general journal form.

MANAGING YOUR WRITING

The heads of the marketing and finance areas at your business are arguing about tight versus easy credit policies. One feels the policy should be tightened, and the other feels it should be eased. The division manager is concerned about which approach to use and asks for your advice. Prepare a memo to the division manager stating arguments for and against tight and easy credit policies. The manager will use this information to decide on which policy to establish.

ETHICS CASE

Preston Enterprises uses the direct write-off method of accounting for uncollectible accounts. On October 12, a very large account was written off. The amount was subsequently recovered on December 15. Ray Preston, the owner of the company, instructed the accountant to not make a journal entry for the recovery and to hold the check in his desk until after the first of the year "for tax purposes."

1. If you were the accountant, what would you think of Preston's request?
2. If the December 15 entry is not made, how will it affect Preston's current year financial statements?
3. Assume the amount of the charge-off and the subsequent recovery was $10,000. Prepare the proper journal entries for October 12 and December 15.
4. In groups of two or three, discuss the possible consequences for the accountant holding the check in his desk drawer for a couple of weeks.

MASTERY PROBLEM

✓ 5. Net realizable value: $59,000

Sam and Robert are identical twins. They opened identical businesses and experienced identical transactions. However, they decided to estimate uncollectible accounts in different ways. Sam elected to use the percentage of sales method, and Robert elected to use the percentage of receivables method. Listed below are the beginning balances of Cash, Accounts Receivable, and Allowance for Bad Debts [items (a)–(c)], and summary transactions that occurred during the year [items (d)–(g)] for both businesses. Remember, both businesses experienced the same events: credit sales, collections of receivables, and write-offs. The only difference between the businesses is the method of estimating uncollectible accounts.

	Sam	Robert
(a) Balance of Cash, January 1, 20--	$300,000	$300,000
(b) Balance of Accounts Receivable, January 1	50,000	50,000
(c) Balance of Allowance for Bad Debts, January 1	5,000	5,000
(d) Sales on account during 20--	550,000	550,000
(e) Collections on account during 20--	530,000	530,000
(f) Uncollectible accounts written off during 20--	4,500	4,500
(g) Collections made on accounts written off during 20--	500	500

REQUIRED

1. Enter items (a) through (c) in two sets of general ledger accounts: one for Sam and one for Robert.

For Sam:

2. Prepare entries in a general journal (page 4) for summary transactions (d) through (g) for Sam.

3. Post the entries to a general ledger for Sam, using the following accounts and numbers.

Cash	101
Accounts Receivable	122
Allowance for Bad Debts	122.1
Sales	401
Bad Debt Expense	532

4. Sam estimates that 1% of all sales on account will be uncollectible. Calculate the estimated bad debt expense and make the appropriate adjusting entry in a general journal. Post the entry to the general ledger accounts on December 31, 20--.

5. Compute the net realizable value of Sam's accounts receivable on December 31, 20--.

For Robert:

6. Prepare entries in a general journal (page 4) for summary transactions (d) through (g) for Robert.

7. Post the entries to a general ledger for Robert, using the same accounts and numbers as were used for Sam.

8. Robert bases the estimate of uncollectible accounts on an aging schedule of accounts receivable. Using the following information, compute the estimated uncollectible amounts and make the appropriate adjusting entry in a general journal. Post the entry to the general ledger accounts on December 31, 20--.

Customers	**Invoice Dates and Amounts for Unpaid Invoices**					
Beets, D.	10/7	$2,300	11/15	$1,200	12/18	$8,500
Cook, L.	6/1	1,200	8/15	2,500		
Hylton, D.	9/23	4,300	10/22	2,500	12/23	2,800
Martin, D.	10/15	5,400	11/12	3,200	12/15	1,500
Stokes, D.	9/9	200	12/15	9,500		
Taylor, T.	11/20	400	12/10	1,400		
Thomas, O.	12/2	5,500				
Tower, R.	12/15	2,300				
Williams, G.	11/18	2,800	12/8	8,000		

All sales are billed n/30. The following aging chart is used to estimate the uncollectibles using the percentage of receivables method:

Age Interval	**Estimated Percent Uncollectible**
Not yet due	2%
1–30 days	5
31–60 days	10
61–90 days	25
91–120 days	50
Over 120 days	80

9. Compute the net realizable value of Robert's accounts receivable on December 31, 20--.

CHALLENGE PROBLEM

This problem challenges you to apply your cumulative accounting knowledge to move a step beyond the material in the chapter.

✓ 2. Dr. Bad Debt Exp.: $25,000

1. Martel Co. has $320,000 in Accounts Receivable on December 31, 20-1, the end of its first year of operations. The business is new, so it has no prior experience with uncollectible accounts. In Martel's overall industry, the percentage of uncollectible accounts receivable is about 3%. For companies similar to Martel in size and operations, the percentage is about 5%. Martel decides to use the overall industry experience as the basis for its estimate of uncollectible accounts.

   REQUIRED

   Prepare the adjusting entry on December 31, 20-1 for Martel Co.'s bad debt expense.

2. At the end of 20-2, Martel Co. had $380,000 in Accounts Receivable and a debit balance of $6,000 in Allowance for Bad Debts. Because it has been operating for only two years, Martel once again wants to base its estimate of uncollectible accounts on the industry average or the experience of similar companies. The industry and similar company percentages for the year were the same as in 20-1.

   REQUIRED

   Based on Martel Co.'s experience in 20-2, select the most appropriate basis (industry or similar company) for estimating its uncollectible accounts for 20-2. Prepare the adjusting entry on December 31, 20-2 for Martel Co.'s bad debt expense.

3. At the end of 20-3, Martel Co. had $410,000 in Accounts Receivable and a credit balance of $300 in Allowance for Bad Debts. Martel has now been in business for three years and wants to base its estimate of uncollectible accounts on its own experience.

   REQUIRED

   Assume that Martel Co.'s adjusting entry for bad debt expense on December 31, 20-2, was a debit to Bad Debt Expense and a credit to Allowance for Bad Debts of $25,000.

   (a) Estimate Martel's uncollectible accounts percentage based on its actual bad debt experience during the past two years.
   (b) Prepare the adjusting entry on December 31, 20-3, for Martel Co.'s bad debt expense.

ANSWERS TO SELF-STUDY QUESTIONS AND EXERCISES

True/False Questions

1. T
2. F (expenses matched with revenues)
3. F (balance in Allowance for Bad Debts is ignored)
4. F (debit to Allowance for Bad Debts)
5. T

Multiple Choice Questions

1. d
2. a
3. b
4. d (note the debit balance in the allowance account)
5. a

U REVU Exercises

1.

Accounts receivable	$32,500
Less allowance for bad debts	1,100
Net realizable value	$31,400

2.

				Debit	Credit	
1		(a) Bad Debt Expense		5 1 0 0 00*		1
2		Allowance for Bad Debts			5 1 0 0 00	2
3		*($170,000 total sales × 3% = $5,100				3
4		bad debt expense needed)				4
5						5
6		(b) Bad Debt Expense		3 4 8 0 00*		6
7		Allowance for Bad Debts			3 4 8 0 00	7
8		*($3,200 desired credit balance + $280				8
9		debit balance = $3,480 adjustment needed)				9

3.

				Debit	Credit	
1		Bad Debt Expense		1 3 2 0 00		1
2		Accounts Receivable/P.Wahdia			1 3 2 0 00	2
3		Wrote off uncollectible account				3

Chapter 17

COURTESY OF COLLEGE BOXES; WWW.COLLEGEBOXES.COM

LEARNING OBJECTIVES

Careful study of this chapter should enable you to:

LO1 **Describe a promissory note.**

LO2 **Calculate interest on and determine the due date of promissory notes.**

LO3 **Account for notes receivable transactions and accrued interest.**

LO4 **Account for notes payable transactions and accrued interest.**

Accounting for Notes and Interest

In the late 1990s, two Duke and Washington University students noticed many of their colleagues struggling with the same questions. How do we transport our stuff to and from the university? And where do we store our stuff in the summer? In response, each of them started a small business that provided transport and storage services for students at their schools. After graduation, they merged their efforts to form Collegeboxes, Inc.

Collegeboxes now serves over 50 schools nationally and has annual revenue of more than $2 million. The company provides packing materials, picks up packed goods, and either ships them to the intended destination or stores them in secure facilities until the end of summer or whenever needed. Students can store furniture, refrigerators, computers, bicycles, books, etc. In addition, the students can select the exact move out and move in dates. The convenience for the students and parents is very appealing.

For a business like Collegeboxes, there no doubt are times of the year when activity and revenues are substantial, and other times when hardly anything is happening. During the periods when cash inflow is slow, the company might need a short-term loan to meet its bills. A common way meeting this need is by signing a promissory note at a bank. In this chapter, you will learn about these notes, how to calculate interest on the amount borrowed, and how to account for both notes receivable and notes payable.

In Chapter 16, we learned how to account for accounts receivable. Recall that an account receivable is an unwritten promise by a customer to pay for goods or services. In this chapter, we will learn how to account for a more formal, written type of receivable called a promissory note.

After completing our study of notes receivable, we will learn to account for notes payable. You will see that a note payable is very similar to a note receivable. Both are promissory notes. We simply look at the note from two different points of view. A note receivable is someone's promise to pay you. A note payable is your promise to pay someone else.

THE PROMISSORY NOTE

LO1 Describe a promissory note.

A **promissory note** (usually called a note) is a written promise to pay a specific sum at a definite future date. The note must be signed by the person or business agreeing to make the payment, known as the **maker** of the note. The note must be payable to a specific person or business, known as the **payee**.

Notes are often used when credit is extended for 60 days or more, or when large amounts of money are involved. Figure 17-1 shows one form of promissory note. Sara Morney, the maker of the note, promises to pay a specific amount of money ($2,500) at a definite future time (September 7). Central Bank, the payee of the note, is to receive the specified amount of money. Notice that to Morney it is a note payable while to Central Bank it is a note receivable.

FIGURE 17-1 Promissory Note

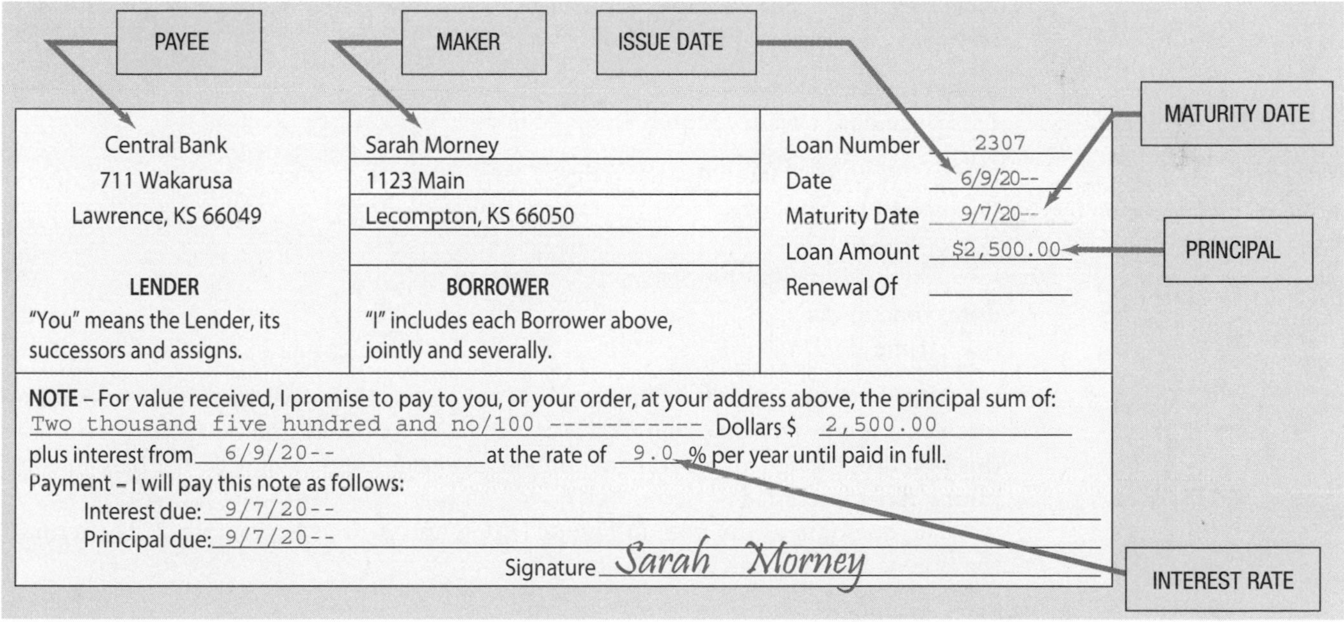

Central Bank
711 Wakarusa
Lawrence, KS 66049

LENDER
"You" means the Lender, its successors and assigns.

Sarah Morney
1123 Main
Lecompton, KS 66050

BORROWER
"I" includes each Borrower above, jointly and severally.

Loan Number 2307
Date 6/9/20--
Maturity Date 9/7/20--
Loan Amount $2,500.00
Renewal Of

NOTE – For value received, I promise to pay to you, or your order, at your address above, the principal sum of:
Two thousand five hundred and no/100 ----------- Dollars $ 2,500.00
plus interest from 6/9/20-- at the rate of 9.0 % per year until paid in full.
Payment – I will pay this note as follows:
Interest due: 9/7/20--
Principal due: 9/7/20--
Signature *Sarah Morney*

Notes may be interest bearing or non-interest bearing. An **interest-bearing note** is one with an explicit interest rate stated on the face of the note. The note in Figure 17-1 is a 9% interest-bearing note. A **non-interest-bearing note** is one on which no rate of interest is specified, although the note does include an interest component. Notes signed when borrowing from a bank often are of this type. This type of transaction is illustrated later in the chapter.

CALCULATING INTEREST AND DETERMINING DUE DATE

LO2 Calculate interest on and determine the due date of promissory notes.

To calculate interest on notes, three factors are used:

1. Principal of the note
2. Rate of interest
3. Term of the note

The **principal of the note** is the face amount of the note that the maker promises to pay at maturity. The principal is the base on which the interest is calculated. The principal of the note in Figure 17-1 is $2,500.

The **rate of interest** usually is expressed as a percentage, such as 8% or 10%. Ordinarily, an annual rate is used, but in some cases a monthly rate is quoted, such as 1½% a month. A rate of 1½% a month is equivalent to a rate of 18% a year payable monthly (1½% × 12 = 18%). The rate of interest on the note in Figure 17-1 is 9% per year.

The **term of the note** is the months or days from the issue date to the maturity date. The term of the note is used to calculate **time**, which is the term of the note stated as a fraction of a year. When the term of the note is specified in months, time is calculated on the basis of months. For example, a three-month note issued on June 1 is payable on September 1, and time is calculated as follows:

Time
3 mos./12 mos. = 3/12 = ¼ year

When the term of a note is specified in days or when the due date is specified in a note, time is computed using the exact number of days from the issue date of the note to the maturity date. In making this computation, the maturity date is counted but the issue date is not. For example, for a $1,000, 9% note dated March 1, with a due date of June 1, time is computed as follows:

LEARNING KEY

To compute the time of a note, count the maturity date; do *not* count the issue date.

Days in March	31	
Less issue date of note, March 1	1	
Days remaining in March		30
Add: Days in April		30
Days in May		31
Maturity date, June 1		1
Total time in days		92
Time = 92/360		

Notice the use of 360 in the denominator in the above calculation. In computing interest, it is common to use 360 days as a year. Many banks and business firms follow this practice, though all federal government agencies use 365 days as the base in computing daily interest.

The due date of the note in Figure 17-1 is specified as September 7. The term of the note is 90 days, calculated as follows:

Days in June	30	
Less issue date of note, June 9	9	
Days remaining in June		21
Add: Days in July		31
Days in August		31
Maturity date, September 7		7
Total time in days		90

CALCULATING INTEREST

The principal, interest rate, and time of the note are used in the following formula to calculate interest:

Interest = Principal × Rate × Time

For the $1,000, 9% note described on page 652, interest is calculated as follows:

I	=	P	×	R	×	T
	=	$1,000	×	0.09	×	92/360
	=	$23				

LEARNING KEY

I = P × R × T
I = amount of *interest*
P = amount of *principal*
R = *rate* of interest (annual)
T = *time*

For a $2,000, 8% note due in three months, interest is calculated as follows:

I	=	P	×	R	×	T
	=	$2,000	×	0.08	×	3/12
	=	$40				

For the note in Figure 17-1, interest is calculated as follows:

I	=	P	×	R	×	T
	=	$2,500	×	0.09	×	90/360
	=	$56.25				

The principal of the note plus interest equals the **maturity value** of the note. For example, the maturity value of the $1,000 note above is $1,023. Similarly, the maturity value of the $2,000 note is $2,040. Figure 17-2 uses a time line to illustrate the gradual accumulation of interest on the $1,000 note to its $1,023 maturity value.

FIGURE 17-2 Accumulation of Interest Time Line

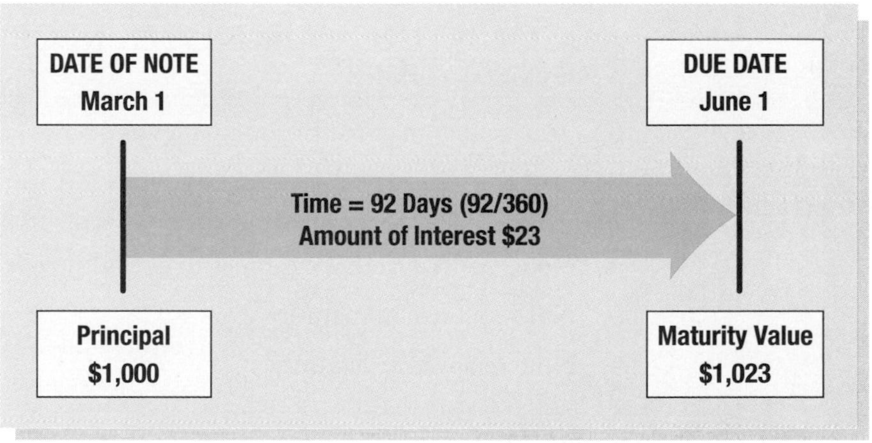

Most of the examples in this chapter are for notes of 90 days or less. Notes can be for much longer periods of time—two to five years is common with auto loans.

DETERMINING THE DUE DATE

As previously explained, the period of time between the issue date and the maturity date of a note may be stated in either months or days. If the term of the note is stated in months, the due date is determined by counting the number of months from the date the note was issued. The note is due on the date in the month of maturity that corresponds with the date the note was issued. For example, a three-month note dated August 10 would be due November 10. If there is no date in the month of maturity corresponding to the issue date, the due date is the last day of the month. For example, a three-month note dated January 31 would be due April 30.

If the term of the note is stated in days, the due date is the specified number of days after the issue date. To determine the due date, apply these three steps.

STEP 1 Subtract the issue date from the number of days in the month of issuance.

STEP 2 Add to the result of step 1 the number of days in as many months as possible without exceeding the time of the note.

STEP 3 Subtract the result of step 2 from the time of the note. The result is the date of the month the note is due.

To calculate the due date of the note in Figure 17-1, a 90-day note dated June 9, apply the three steps as follows:

STEP 1	Days in June		30
	Less issue date of note: June		9
	Result of step 1		**21**
STEP 2	Result of step 1		21
	Plus days in July		31
	Plus days in August		31
	Result of step 2		**83**
STEP 3	Time of note		90 days
	Less result of step 2		83
	Due date:	September	7

U REVU Complete U REVU-1 on **page 672** to test your basic understanding of LO2.

ACCOUNTING FOR NOTES RECEIVABLE TRANSACTIONS

LO3 Account for notes receivable transactions and accrued interest.

Businesses other than banks and savings and loans generally encounter seven types of transactions involving notes receivable.

1. Note received from a customer in exchange for assets sold
2. Note received from a customer to extend time for payment of an account
3. Note collected at maturity
4. Note renewed at maturity
5. Note discounted before maturity
6. Note dishonored
7. Collection of dishonored note

NOTE RECEIVED FROM A CUSTOMER IN EXCHANGE FOR ASSETS SOLD

When a business makes a large sale, it may accept a note for the amount of the sale. A business may be willing to accept the note for two reasons. First, the note is a formal, written promise to pay. This note can be converted to cash at a bank if necessary. Second, the note is likely to bear interest.

Assume that on June 1 Linesch Hardware Co. sells an industrial mower to Williams Manufacturing for $8,500. Williams gives Linesch a 180-day, 9% note for $8,500 in exchange for the mower. This transaction is entered by Linesch as follows:

1	June	1	Notes Receivable	8,500.00		1
2			Sales		8,500.00	2
3			Received note for merchandise sale			3

NOTE RECEIVED FROM A CUSTOMER TO EXTEND TIME FOR PAYMENT

When a customer's account is due, the customer may issue a note for all or part of the amount. Assume that Michael Putter owes Linesch Hardware Co. $2,000 on account. To settle the account, Putter gives Linesch a 90-day, 10% note dated June 8. This transaction is entered by Linesch as follows:

15	June	8	Notes Receivable	2,000.00		15
16			Accounts Receivable/M. Putter		2,000.00	16
17			Received note to settle account			17

If instead Putter gives a check for $250 and a note for $1,750 to settle the account, Linesch makes the following entry:

15	June	8	Cash	250.00		15
16			Notes Receivable	1,750.00		16
17			Accounts Receivable/M. Putter		2,000.00	17
18			Received cash and note to settle account			18

NOTE COLLECTED AT MATURITY

When a note receivable matures, it may be collected by one of the following:

1. The payee (in Figure 17-1, Central Bank)
2. The bank named in the note
3. A bank where it was left for collection

Assume that on September 6, Putter pays Linesch the $2,000 principal plus $50 interest on the note described above. Linesch makes the following entry:

31	Sept.	6	Cash	2,050.00		31
32			Notes Receivable		2,000.00	32
33			Interest Revenue		50.00	33
34			Received payment of note with interest			34

When a bank makes the collection, it notifies the payee that the net amount has been added to the payee's account. The bank uses a **credit advice** like the one in Figure 17-3 for this purpose.

Assume that Linesch left Putter's 90-day, 10% note for $2,000 at Planet Bank for collection. On September 6, the bank notifies Linesch that the note plus $50 interest

FIGURE 17-3 Credit Advice

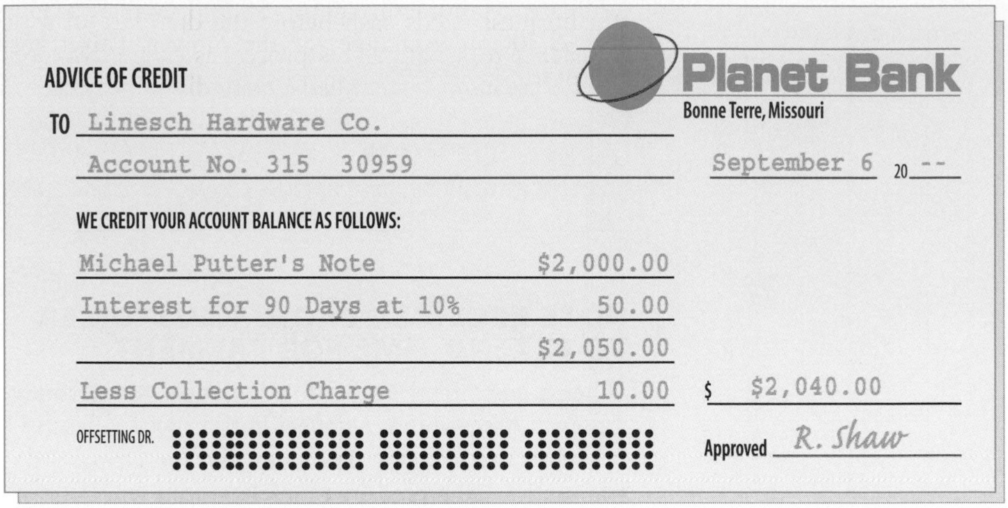
ADVICE OF CREDIT

Planet Bank
Bonne Terre, Missouri

TO Linesch Hardware Co.

Account No. 315 30959 September 6 20--

WE CREDIT YOUR ACCOUNT BALANCE AS FOLLOWS:

Michael Putter's Note	$2,000.00
Interest for 90 Days at 10%	50.00
	$2,050.00
Less Collection Charge	10.00

$ $2,040.00

OFFSETTING DR.

Approved R. Shaw

have been collected. The bank fee for collecting the note was $10. Linesch enters this transaction as follows:

37	Sept.	6	Cash		2,040.00		37
38			Collection Expense		10.00		38
39			Notes Receivable			2,000.00	39
40			Interest Revenue			50.00	40
41			Received payment of note with interest				41
42			less collection fee				42

NOTE RENEWED AT MATURITY

If the maker of a note is unable to pay the amount due at maturity, the payee may allow the maker to renew all or part of the note. Assume that at maturity of the $2,000 note, Putter pays only the $50 interest and gives a new 60-day, 10% note. Linesch enters this transaction as follows:

31	Sept.	6	Cash		50.00		31
32			Notes Receivable (new note)		2,000.00		32
33			Notes Receivable (old note)			2,000.00	33
34			Interest Revenue			50.00	34
35			Received new note plus interest on old note				35

If Putter pays $50 interest plus $500 on the principal and gives a new 90-day, 11% note for $1,500, Linesch makes the following entry:

31	Sept.	6	Cash		550.00		31
32			Notes Receivable (new note)		1,500.00		32
33			Notes Receivable (old note)			2,000.00	33
34			Interest Revenue			50.00	34
35			Received new note plus partial payment				35
36			and interest on old note				36

One of the reasons a business might prefer a promissory note from a customer is that the business can obtain cash by discounting the note at the bank.

NOTE DISCOUNTED BEFORE MATURITY

If a business needs cash before the due date of a note, it can endorse the note and transfer it to a bank. This process is called **discounting a note receivable.** The bank charges an interest fee called a **bank discount** for the **discount period,** the time between the date of discounting and the due date of the note. The difference between the maturity value of the note and the bank discount is called the **proceeds.** This is the amount of cash received by the business discounting the note.

Maturity Value − Discount = Proceeds

Assume that the $2,000, 10%, 90-day note receivable from Putter dated June 8 is discounted by Linesch at the bank on July 8 at a rate of 12%. To calculate the discount and proceeds, apply the following four steps:

STEP 1 Compute the maturity value of the note.

Face	+	Interest	=	Maturity Value
$2,000	+	$50	=	$2,050

STEP 2 Compute the number of days in the discount period—from the discount date to the due date.

Discount date	July 8	
Days in July		31
Less discount date	July	8
Remaining days in July		23
Plus days in August		31
Plus due date	September	6
Days in discount period		60

STEP 3 Compute the discount amount.

Maturity Value*	×	Discount Rate	×	Discount Period	=	Discount Amount
$2,050	×	12%	×	60/360	=	$41

*Note that in calculating the discount amount, the *maturity value* of the note is used, not the principal.

LEARNING KEY

To calculate the discount amount, use the maturity value of the note.

STEP 4 Compute the proceeds.

Maturity Value	−	Discount Amount	=	Proceeds
$2,050	−	$41	=	$2,009

Figure 17-4 shows a time line illustration of this transaction.

FIGURE 17-4 Discounted Note Receivable Time Line

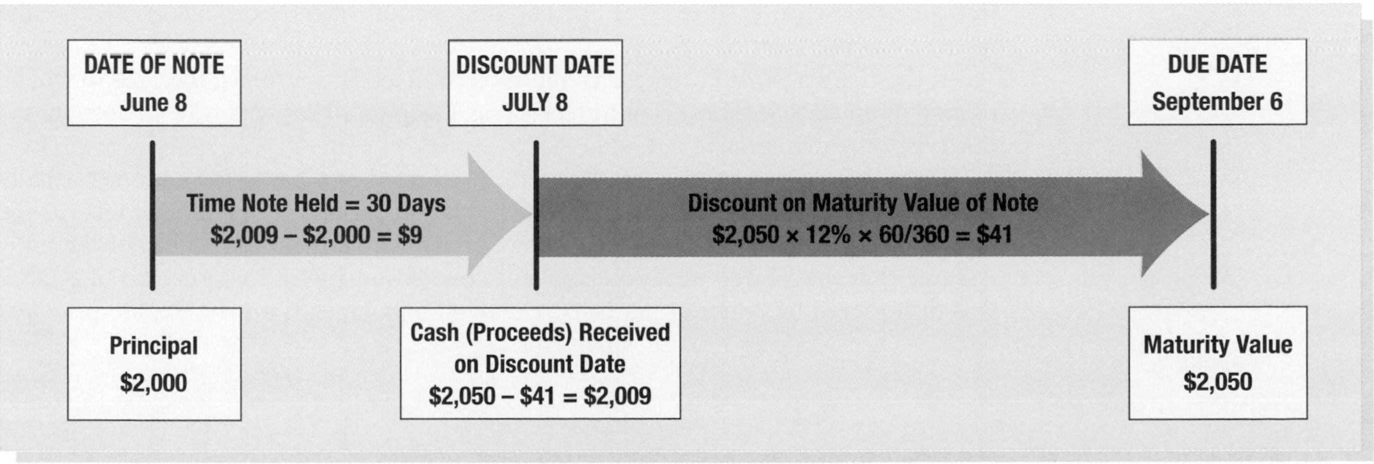

The excess of the $2,009 proceeds over the $2,000 face value of the note represents interest revenue of $9. Linesch enters this transaction as follows:

26	July	8	Cash	2009 00		26
27			Notes Receivable		2000 00	27
28			Interest Revenue		9 00	28
29			Discounted note receivable			29

If the proceeds from discounting a note are less than the face value of the note, the difference represents interest expense. For example, if the proceeds from discounting Putter's $2,000 note were only $1,992, Linesch would make the following entry:

26	July	8	Cash	1992 00		26
27			Interest Expense	8 00		27
28			Notes Receivable		2000 00	28
29			Discounted note receivable			29

When a note receivable is discounted, the business that endorses the note becomes potentially liable to the bank. If the maker of the note does not pay it at maturity, the business that discounted the note must pay the maturity value and any bank fees to the bank. This kind of potential liability that may become a real liability, depending on future events, is called a **contingent liability**. A contingent liability does not affect the accounting records. It is disclosed in the notes to the financial statements.

NOTE DISHONORED

If the maker of a note does not pay or renew it at maturity, the note is said to be **dishonored.** The maker of the note is still liable to the payee for the principal amount plus interest. But a dishonored note loses its legal status as a note receivable. Therefore, the payee transfers the amount due from Notes Receivable to Accounts Receivable. For example, if the $2,000, 10%, 90-day note from Putter is dishonored, Linesch makes the following entry:

16	Sept.	6	Accounts Receivable/M. Putter	2050 00		16
17			Notes Receivable		2000 00	17
18			Interest Revenue		50 00	18
19			Note receivable dishonored			19

Notice that the $50 difference between the maturity value and principal of the note is credited to Interest Revenue. This is done even though the amount has not been collected. Recall that under accrual accounting, revenue is recognized when earned, regardless of when cash is received. The time period of the note has passed, so the interest has been earned.

If the claim against Putter turns out to be completely worthless, the $2,050 will be treated as an uncollectible account receivable. Chapter 16 showed how to account for this type of transaction.

If the dishonored note is one that was discounted at a bank, the endorser usually must pay the bank the principal, interest, and any bank fees. The endorser records the total amount paid to the bank as an account receivable from the maker of the note. Assume that the $2,000 note receivable discounted on July 8 for proceeds of $2,009 was dishonored by Putter at maturity. The bank bills Linesch for the $2,000 principal of the note, $50 interest, and a $10 bank fee, a total of $2,060. Linesch pays the bank and makes the following journal entry:

23	Sept.	6	Accounts Receivable/M. Putter	2 0 6 0 00	
24			Cash		2 0 6 0 00
25			Paid bank for dishonored note		

Note that the $10 bank fee is included in the amount receivable from Putter. This is because the fee was incurred as a result of Putter's dishonoring of the note, and this is not Linesch's expense.

COLLECTION OF DISHONORED NOTE

What if a note that has been dishonored eventually is collected? When that occurs, the payee records collection of the account receivable. In addition, interest usually is charged for the period from the due date of the original note to the final collection date. Interest is based on the maturity value of the note plus the bank fee, if any, incurred when the note was dishonored. Let's look again at Putter's $2,000 note that Linesch discounted at the bank on July 8. When this note was dishonored on September 6, the $2,000 principal of the note, $50 interest, and $10 bank fee were transferred to Accounts Receivable. Assume that on October 16, Putter pays the original maturity value of the note plus the bank fee ($2,060) and interest for the period from September 6 to October 16. Interest would be computed as follows:

Original Maturity Value Plus Bank Fee	×	Rate	×	Time		
$2,060	×	10%	×	40*/360	=	$22.89

*Days in September	30
Less original maturity date of note	6
Days remaining in September	24
Plus due date in October	16
Total days	40

A BROADER VIEW

IAN DAGNALL/ALAMY

These Notes Were No Longer *Receivable*

The former chief financial officer (CFO) of Intermountain Mortgage Company, Inc. (IMC), in Billings, Montana, pleaded guilty to defrauding the company's mortgage loan lender. IMC's main line of business was originating, brokering, and servicing first and second mortgage loans. To fund these loans, the company obtained a line of credit from First Citizen's Bank of Billings and then sold the loans in a secondary market. This is a common practice with mortgage notes receivable.

Like all lenders, First Citizen's Bank relied on IMC's financial reports in order to continue to fund the line of credit. When IMC started to have financial difficulties that could cause it to lose the line of credit, the CFO began including fraudulent "notes receivable" on its financial reports. The reports claimed that IMC had sold these notes but had not yet received payment. In fact, these were no longer actual notes receivable because IMC had already been paid. After two years, 26 fraudulent notes receivable were listed in the financial reports provided to First Citizen's Bank. The fraud was uncovered during an investigation by the FBI. The former CFO was sentenced to a short time in prison, six months of house arrest, and five years of supervision.

Linesch would make the following journal entry:

16	Oct.	16	Cash		2,082.89		16
17			Accounts Receivable			2,060.00	17
18			Interest Revenue			22.89	18
19			Collected dishonored note with interest				19

NOTES RECEIVABLE REGISTER

When a business receives many notes, it may keep a **notes receivable register.** This is a detailed auxiliary record of notes receivable. Figure 17-5 shows an abbreviated version of a notes receivable register. A more complete register might also include the number of each note and where the note is payable. The information contained in the register is obtained directly from the notes.

FIGURE 17-5 Notes Receivable Register

NOTES RECEIVABLE REGISTER PAGE 1

DATE RECEIVED		MAKER	TIME	DUE DATE		AMOUNT	INTEREST RATE	INTEREST AMOUNT	DISCOUNTED BANK	DISCOUNTED DATE	DATE COLLECTED		REMARKS
20-- Apr.	4	L. Peters	60 days	June	3	400.00	8%	5.33			June	3	
	21	J. Slaw	60 days	June	20	600.00	9%	9.00			June	20	Renewal for $500
May	2	S. Alpart	30 days	June	1	700.00	9%	5.25			June	1	Sent for collection 5/30
	19	L. Shein	90 days	Aug.	17	800.00	9%	18.00					
June	20	J. Slaw	60 days	Aug.	19	500.00	9%	7.50					Renewal of 4/21 note

ACCRUED INTEREST RECEIVABLE

Under accrual accounting, revenue is recognized when it is earned. For notes receivable, interest literally is earned day by day. It would be impractical, however, to record the interest revenue each day. Instead, for notes that are received and due within a single accounting period, no entry is made for interest revenue until the note is due.

For notes that are received in one period and due in the following period, however, accrued interest must be recorded at the end of the period. **Accrued interest on notes receivable** is interest revenue that has been earned but not yet received. The amount of accrued interest can be computed from the notes themselves or from the notes receivable register. The notes receivable register in Figure 17-5 can be used as an example. At June 30, the end of this company's fiscal year, two notes are outstanding. Accrued interest on these notes is calculated as follows:

Principal	Issue Date	Rate of Interest	Days from Issue Date to June 30	Accrued Interest June 30
$800.00	May 19	9%	42	$8.40
500.00	June 20	9%	10	1.25
Total accrued interest on notes receivable				$9.65

The following adjusting entry is made on June 30 for the accrued interest:

16	June	30	Accrued Interest Receivable		9.65		16
17			Interest Revenue			9.65	17
18			Interest accrued on notes receivable				18

Accrued interest receivable is reported as a current asset on the balance sheet. Interest revenue is reported as other revenue on the income statement.

U REVU Complete U REVU-2 on **page 672** to test your basic understanding of LO3.

ACCOUNTING FOR NOTES PAYABLE TRANSACTIONS

LO4 Account for notes payable transactions and accrued interest.

Businesses generally encounter five types of transactions involving notes payable.

1. Note issued to a supplier in exchange for assets purchased
2. Note issued to a supplier to extend time for payment of an account
3. Note issued as security for cash loan
4. Note paid at maturity
5. Note renewed at maturity

NOTE ISSUED TO A SUPPLIER IN EXCHANGE FOR ASSETS PURCHASED

When a business makes a large purchase, it may give a note for the amount of the purchase. Assume that on June 1 Linesch Hardware Co. purchases a truckload of trees and shrubs from Evergreen Enterprises for $4,000. Linesch gives Evergreen a 90-day, 9% note for $4,000 in exchange for the trees and shrubs. This transaction is entered by Linesch as follows:

5	June	1	Purchases		4000 00		5
6			Notes Payable			4000 00	6
7			Issued note for inventory purchase				7

NOTE ISSUED TO A SUPPLIER TO EXTEND TIME FOR PAYMENT

When a firm's account with a supplier is due, the supplier may be willing to accept a note for all or part of the amount due. Assume that Linesch Hardware Co. owes Bella & Co. $700 on June 11. If Linesch issues Bella a 90-day, 10% note for $700, Linesch makes the following entry:

26	June	11	Accounts Payable/Bella & Co.		700 00		26
27			Notes Payable			700 00	27
28			Issued note to settle account				28

If instead, Linesch gives Bella a check for $200 and a 90-day, 10% note for $500, the entry by Linesch is as follows:

26	June	11	Accounts Payable/Bella & Co.		700 00		26
27			Cash			200 00	27
28			Notes Payable			500 00	28
29			Made partial payment and issued note				29
30			to settle account				30

NOTE ISSUED AS SECURITY FOR CASH LOAN

Businesses sometimes have brief periods during which receipts from customers are not adequate to finance operations. During such periods, businesses commonly borrow money from banks on short-term notes.

Interest-Bearing Notes

Assume that on June 16, Linesch borrows $6,000 from Planet Bank on a 60-day, 10½% note. This transaction is entered as follows:

38	June	16	Cash		6,000.00		38
39			Notes Payable			6,000.00	39
40			Issued note for bank loan				40

Non-Interest-Bearing Notes

When making a loan, banks often deduct interest in advance, using a procedure known as **discounting**. The nature of this transaction and the procedures for handling it are very similar to those for discounting notes receivable (see pages 657–658). To illustrate, suppose that Linesch borrowed $6,000 on a 60-day, non-interest-bearing note that the bank discounted at 10½%. No interest rate is stated on the face of a non-interest-bearing note, but clearly there is an interest component. In this case, it is the 10½% discount rate. The bank calculates the **bank discount** at 10½% and deducts this amount from the $6,000 face of the note. The amount of the discount and the proceeds to Linesch are calculated using three steps.

LEARNING KEY

As with discounting notes receivable, to calculate the discount amount, use the maturity value of the note.

STEP 1 Compute the maturity value of the note.

Face	+	Interest	=	**Maturity Value**
$6,000	+	0	=	$6,000

STEP 2 Compute the discount amount.

Maturity Value*	×	Discount Rate	×	Discount Period	=	**Discount Amount**
$6,000	×	10½%	×	60/360	=	$105

*Note that in calculating the discount amount, the *maturity value* of the note is used.

STEP 3 Compute the proceeds.

Maturity Value	–	Discount Amount	=	**Proceeds**
$6,000	–	$105	=	$5,895

Figure 17-6 shows a time line illustration of this transaction.

Linesch records receipt of the $5,895 proceeds ($6,000 – $105) from the loan as shown below and in Figure 17-7.

14	June	16	Cash		5,895.00		14
15			Discount on Notes Payable		105.00		15
16			Notes Payable			6,000.00	16
17			Issued note for bank loan				17

FIGURE 17-6 Discounted Note Payable Time Line

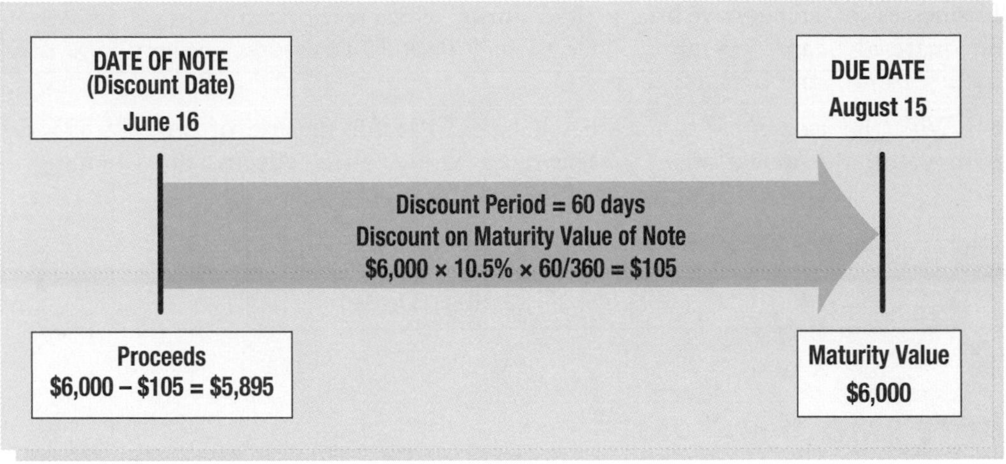

FIGURE 17-7 Journal Entry for Discounted Note Payable

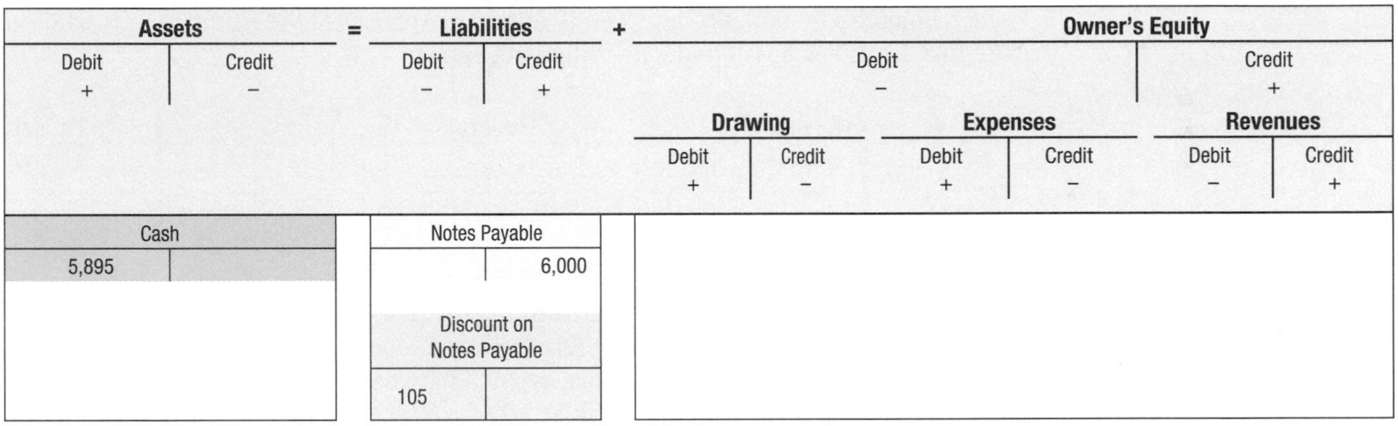
Assets
=
Liabilities
+
Owner's Equity
Debit +
Credit –
Debit –
Credit +
Debit –
Credit +
Drawing
Debit +
Credit –
Expenses
Debit +
Credit –
Revenues
Debit –
Credit +
Cash
5,895
Notes Payable
6,000
Discount on Notes Payable
105

The $105 debit to Discount on Notes Payable is an offset to the $6,000 note payable. Linesch's liability at this time is only $5,895, which is the net amount or **proceeds** received from the bank. Discount on Notes Payable is a **contra-liability account**. As shown in Figure 17-8, it is reported as a deduction from Notes Payable on the balance sheet.

FIGURE 17-8 Notes Payable and Related Discount on the Balance Sheet

Current liabilities:		
Notes payable	$6,000.00	
Less discount on notes payable	105.00	$5,895.00

Stated versus Effective Interest Rate

The stated rate of interest was 10½% on both the interest-bearing and discounted notes. Notice, however, that the real interest rates on the two notes are not the same. With the interest-bearing note, Linesch obtained $6,000 for 60 days at a cost of $105—exactly 10½%.

$$
\begin{aligned}
\$105 \div \$6{,}000 &= 1.75\% \text{ for 60 days} \\
&\quad \underline{\times 6} \quad (360 \div 60) \\
&= 10.5\% \text{ for 360 days}
\end{aligned}
$$

With the discounted note, Linesch paid $105 for the use of only $5,895 for 60 days—a rate of nearly 10.7%. This rate is known as the **effective rate** of interest.

$$
\begin{aligned}
\$105 \div \$5{,}895 &= 1.781\% \text{ for 60 days} \\
&\quad \underline{\times 6} \quad (360 \div 60) \\
&= 10.686\% \text{ for 360 days}
\end{aligned}
$$

NOTE PAID AT MATURITY

The proper entry to make when a note is paid at maturity depends on whether the note is interest bearing or non-interest bearing. For an interest-bearing note, the same entry is made for payment to a supplier or to a bank. For example, let's reconsider Linesch's $6,000, 60-day, 10½% note due August 15. When the note is paid on August 15, Linesch will make the following entry:

21	Aug.	15	Notes Payable		6 0 0 0 00		21
22			Interest Expense		1 0 5 00		22
23			Cash			6 1 0 5 00	23
24			Paid note with interest at maturity				24

For a non-interest-bearing note from a bank, the entry to record the payment of the note is different. This is because Discount on Notes Payable was debited when the money was borrowed. For example, recall Linesch's $6,000, 60-day, non-interest-bearing note discounted by the bank at 10½%. When the money was borrowed, the following entry was made:

14	June	16	Cash		5 8 9 5 00		14
15			Discount on Notes Payable		1 0 5 00		15
16			Notes Payable			6 0 0 0 00	16
17			Issued note for bank loan				17

The $105 discount gradually becomes interest expense. This expense is recognized when the $6,000 principal amount of the note is repaid on August 15, the due date. Linesch will enter the payment of the note at maturity as follows:

22	Aug.	15	Notes Payable		6 0 0 0 00		22
23			Interest Expense		1 0 5 00		23
24			Cash			6 0 0 0 00	24
25			Discount on Notes Payable			1 0 5 00	25
26			Paid note at maturity				26

NOTE RENEWED AT MATURITY

The payee of a note may allow the maker to renew all or a part of the note at maturity. For example, let's reconsider the $6,000 interest-bearing note that Linesch issued to Planet Bank on June 16. Assume that on August 15 Linesch pays $105 interest and $1,000 on the principal of this note and gives a new 60-day, 10½% note for $5,000. Linesch enters this transaction as follows:

27	Aug.	15	Notes Payable (old note)		6 000 00		27
28			Interest Expense		105 00		28
29			Cash			1 105 00	29
30			Notes Payable (new note)			5 000 00	30
31			Paid interest and part of principal on				31
32			old note and issued new note				32

NOTES PAYABLE REGISTER

When a business issues many notes, it may keep a **notes payable register**. This is a detailed auxiliary record of notes payable. An abbreviated version of a notes payable register is shown in Figure 17-9. A more complete register might also include the number of each note and where the note is payable. The information contained in the register is obtained directly from the notes.

FIGURE 17-9 Notes Payable Register

NOTES PAYABLE REGISTER PAGE 1

DATE ISSUED		PAYEE	TIME	DUE DATE		AMOUNT	INTEREST		DATE PAID		REMARKS
							RATE	AMOUNT			
20-- Apr.	14	L. Knoop	60 days	June	13	2 000 00	9%	30 00	June	13	Settled 2/14 invoice
May	13	Apex Bank	90 days	Aug.	11	8 000 00	10%	200 00			
June	2	S. Bront	30 days	July	2	1 500 00	11%	13 75			Settled 4/2 invoice

ACCRUED INTEREST PAYABLE

As with notes receivable, it also is necessary to record accrued interest on notes payable at the end of the period. For notes payable issued in one period and due in the following period, accrued interest payable must be recorded. **Accrued interest on notes payable** is interest expense that has been incurred but not paid. The amount of accrued interest can be computed from the notes themselves or from the notes payable register.

The proper entry for accrued interest on notes payable depends on whether the note is interest bearing or non-interest bearing. Assume that a $900, 60-day, 10% note was issued on May 31. On June 30, this company's fiscal year-end, an adjusting entry for accrued interest of $7.50 ($900 × 10% × 30/360) is recorded as follows:

19	June	30	Interest Expense		7 50		19
20			Accrued Interest Payable			7 50	20
21			Interest accrued on note payable				21

Assume instead that the $900, 60-day note was non-interest bearing and discounted at the bank at 10%. When the money was borrowed, the following entry was made:

23	May	31	Cash		885.00		23
24			Discount on Notes Payable*		15.00		24
25			Notes Payable			900.00	25
26			Issued note for bank loan				26
27							27

*$900 × 10% × 60/360 = $15

On June 30, part of the discount must be transferred from Discount on Notes Payable to Interest Expense. The note was issued on May 31, so 30 days of the 60-day life of the note have passed. Thus, half of the balance in Discount on Notes Payable should be recognized as interest expense. The following adjusting entry is made on June 30:

29	June	30	Interest Expense		7.50		29
30			Discount on Notes Payable			7.50	30
31			Interest accrued on note payable				31

Note that the credit is to Discount on Notes Payable rather than Accrued Interest Payable. This is because the bank already deducted the interest at the time the money was borrowed. Thus, there is no additional interest payable to recognize. There is an increase in a liability, but that liability is notes payable instead of accrued interest payable. As shown below, the credit to Discount on Notes Payable increases the carrying value of the notes payable.

LEARNING KEY

The adjusting entry for accrued interest on a note payable depends on whether the note is interest bearing or a non-interest-bearing note from a bank.

Balance Sheet:	May 31	June 30
Notes payable	$900.00	$900.00
Less discount on notes payable	(15.00)	(7.50)
	$885.00	$892.50

Interest expense is reported as other expense on the income statement. Accrued interest payable is reported as a current liability on the balance sheet. As previously illustrated in Figure 17-8 (page 663), discount on notes payable is reported as a contra-liability to notes payable on the balance sheet.

U REVU Complete U REVU-3 on **page 672** to test your basic understanding of LO4.

SELF-STUDY

LEARNING OBJECTIVES Key Points to Remember

LO1 Describe a promissory note.	A promissory note is a written promise to pay a specific sum at a future date. Notes are used when credit is extended for periods of 60 days or more, or when large amounts of money are involved. To the maker of a note, the note is a note payable. To the payee of a note, the note is a note receivable.

LEARNING OBJECTIVES Key Points to Remember

LO2 Calculate interest on and determine the due date of promissory notes.	The following formula is used to calculate interest on notes receivable and payable: I = P × R × T Interest = Principal × Rate × Time To determine the due date of a note with a term stated in months, count the number of months from the issue date of the note. To determine the due date of a note with a term stated in days, follow these steps. STEP 1 Subtract the issue date from the number of days in the month of issuance. STEP 2 Add to the result of step 1 the number of days in as many months as possible without exceeding the time of the note. STEP 3 Subtract the result of step 2 from the time of the note.
LO3 Account for notes receivable transactions and accrued interest.	Businesses generally encounter seven types of transactions involving notes receivable. 1. Note received from a customer in exchange for assets sold 2. Note received from a customer to extend time for payment of an account 3. Note collected at maturity 4. Note renewed at maturity 5. Note discounted before maturity 6. Note dishonored 7. Collection of dishonored note When a note receivable is discounted at a bank, four steps are applied to calculate the discount and proceeds as follows: STEP 1 Compute the maturity value of the note. STEP 2 Compute the number of days in the discount period. STEP 3 Compute the discount amount. STEP 4 Compute the proceeds. If a note receivable that was discounted at a bank is dishonored, the endorser of the note is liable to the bank for the maturity value of the note and any bank fees. Notes that are received in one period and due in the following period require an adjustment for accrued interest at the end of the period.
LO4 Account for notes payable transactions and accrued interest.	Businesses generally encounter five types of transactions involving notes payable. 1. Note issued to a supplier in exchange for assets purchased 2. Note issued to a supplier to extend time for payment of an account

(continued)

LEARNING OBJECTIVES Key Points to Remember

LO4 (concluded)

3. Note issued as security for cash loan
4. Note paid at maturity
5. Note renewed at maturity

When money is borrowed at a bank on a non-interest-bearing note that is discounted by the bank, three steps are used to calculate the discount and proceeds.

STEP 1 Compute the maturity value of the note.

STEP 2 Compute the discount amount.

STEP 3 Compute the proceeds.

Notes payable that are issued in one period and due in the following period require an adjustment for accrued interest at the end of the period. The proper entry depends on whether or not the note is interest bearing.

DEMONSTRATION PROBLEM

Barbar Brothers, partners in a wholesale hardware business, completed the following transactions involving notes and interest during the first half of 20--:

Jan.	11	Received a $900, 60-day, 10% note from Paul Heinsius in payment for sale of merchandise.
	18	Borrowed $10,000 from Landmark Bank issuing a 90-day, 11% note.
Feb.	6	Received an $875, 30-day, 9% note from Ana Fuentes in payment of an account receivable.
	21	Issued a $650, 60-day, 11% note to Swanson & Johnson, a supplier, in payment of an account payable.
Mar.	1	Received a $1,000, 90-day, 10% note from Steve Roberts, a customer, in payment of an account receivable.
	9	Received a check for $881.56 from Ana Fuentes in payment of note due March 8, including interest.
	12	Paul Heinsius dishonored his $900 note due March 12.
	31	Discounted the $1,000 note from Steve Roberts at Manchester Bank at a discount rate of 12%.
Apr.	11	Paul Heinsius paid the original maturity value of his note due March 12, plus interest at 10% on the maturity value for the 30 days from March 12 to April 11.
	18	Paid Landmark Bank for $10,000 note due today, including interest. (See January 18 transaction.)
	22	Paid Swanson & Johnson $61.92 on the note due today (interest of $11.92 plus $50 toward the principal), and issued a new $600, 60-day, 11% note.
May	31	Steve Roberts dishonored his $1,000 note due at the Manchester Bank yesterday. Paid Manchester Bank $1,000, plus interest, plus a $10 bank fee, for the dishonored note.

June 20 Issued a $750, 90-day, 9% note to Greene Acres, a supplier, for purchase of merchandise.

REQUIRED

Record each transaction in a general journal.

GENERAL JOURNAL PAGE 5

DATE		DESCRIPTION	POST. REF.	DEBIT	CREDIT
20-- Jan.	11	Notes Receivable		900 00	
		Sales			900 00
		Received note for merchandise sale			
	18	Cash		10000 00	
		Notes Payable			10000 00
		Isssued note for bank loan			
Feb.	6	Notes Receivable		875 00	
		Accounts Receivable/A. Fuentes			875 00
		Received note to settle account			
	21	Accounts Payable/Swanson & Johnson		650 00	
		Notes Payable			650 00
		Issued note to settle account			
Mar.	1	Notes Receivable		1000 00	
		Accounts Receivable/S. Roberts			1000 00
		Received note to settle account			
	9	Cash		881 56	
		Notes Receivable			875 00
		Interest Revenue			6 56
		Received payment of note with interest			
	12	Accounts Receivable/P. Heinsius		915 00	
		Notes Receivable			900 00
		Interest Revenue			15 00
		Note receivable dishonored			
	31	Cash		1004 50	
		Notes Receivable			1000 00
		Interest Revenue			4 50
		Discounted note receivable			
		Principal $1,000.00			
		Interest to maturity 25.00			
		Maturity value $1,025.00			
		Less discount			
		($1,025 × 12% × 60/360) 20.50			
		Cash proceeds $1,004.50			
Apr.	11	Cash		922 63	
		Accounts Receivable/P. Heinsius			915 00
		Interest Revenue			7 63
		Collected dishonored note with interest			

(continued)

Solution

GENERAL JOURNAL PAGE 6

	DATE		DESCRIPTION	POST REF.	DEBIT	CREDIT	
1	20-- Apr.	18	Notes Payable		10,000 00		1
2			Interest Expense		275 00		2
3			Cash			10,275 00	3
4			Paid note with interest at maturity				4
5							5
6		22	Notes Payable (old note)		650 00		6
7			Interest Expense		11 92		7
8			Cash			61 92	8
9			Notes Payable (new note)			600 00	9
10			Paid interest and part of principal on old note				10
11			and issued new note				11
12							12
13	May	31	Accounts Receivable/S. Roberts		1,035 00		13
14			Cash			1,035 00	14
15			Paid bank for dishonored note				15
16							16
17			Principal $1,000.00				17
18			Interest 25.00				18
19			Bank fee 10.00				19
20			$1,035.00				20
21							21
22	June	20	Purchases		750 00		22
23			Notes Payable			750 00	23
24			Issued note for inventory purchase				24
25							25

KEY TERMS

accrued interest on notes payable (665) Interest expense that has been incurred but not paid.

accrued interest on notes receivable (660) Interest revenue that has been earned but not yet received.

bank discount (note payable) (657) The amount that the bank deducts from the face of a note.

bank discount (note receivable) (657) An interest fee that the bank charges for the time between the date of discounting and the due date of the note.

contingent liability (658) A potential liability that may become a real liability depending on future events. In the case of a note discounted at a bank, the business that discounted the note must pay the maturity value and any bank fees if the maker of the note does not pay it at maturity.

contra-liability account (663) An account with a debit balance that is deducted from the related liability account.

credit advice (655) A notification to the payee that the bank has collected interest on a note and added the amount to the payee's account.

discount period (657) The time between the date of discounting and the due date of the note.

discounting (note payable) (662) The procedure, which banks often use, of deducting interest in advance when making a loan.

discounting a note receivable (657) Transferring a note receivable to a bank for cash.

dishonored (658) A note which the maker does not pay or renew at maturity.

effective rate (664) The interest amount paid divided by the proceeds received on a discounted note.

interest-bearing note (651) A note with an explicit interest rate stated on the face of the note.

maker (651) The person or business agreeing to make the payment on a note.

maturity value (653) The principal of the note plus interest equals the maturity value of the note.

non-interest-bearing note (651) A note on which no rate of interest is specified, although the note does include an interest component.

notes payable register (665) A detailed auxiliary record of notes payable.

notes receivable register (660) A detailed auxiliary record of notes receivable.

payee (651) The specific person or business to whom a note is payable.

principal of the note (652) The face amount of the note that the maker promises to pay at maturity. The principal is the base on which the interest is calculated.

proceeds (note payable) (663) The net amount received from the bank.

proceeds (note receivable) (657) The difference between the maturity value of the note and the bank discount. This is the amount of cash received by the business discounting the note.

promissory note (651) A written promise to pay a specific sum at a definite future date.

rate of interest (652) The rate at which interest is charged, usually expressed as an annual percentage, but in some cases a monthly rate is quoted.

term of the note (652) The months or days from the date of issue to the date of maturity.

time (652) The term of the note stated as a fraction of a year.

SELF-STUDY QUESTIONS AND EXERCISES

True/False Questions

1. LO2 The maturity value of a note includes both principal and interest.
2. LO3 When a note is renewed at maturity, the old note is cancelled and a new note is issued.
3. LO3 The difference between the maturity value of a note and the net proceeds is called discounting.
4. LO3 When a note is dishonored, the interest is not credited to Interest Revenue because it is not earned.
5. LO3 When a dishonored note is collected, interest is collected for the time between date of maturity and date of collection.

Multiple Choice Questions

1. LO2 Principal plus interest equals ________ of a note.

   (a) discount
   (b) net proceeds
   (c) interest rate
   (d) maturity value

2. LO3 Which account is debited for interest earned but not yet received?
   (a) Interest Revenue
   (b) Accrued Interest Receivable
   (c) Accrued Interest Payable
   (d) Interest Expense
3. LO3 The discount amount is calculated by multiplying the maturity value times the _______ times the discount period.
   (a) discount rate
   (b) interest rate
   (c) term of note
   (d) net proceeds
4. LO4 When a note payable is paid at maturity, what account is debited for the amount of the interest?
   (a) Interest Revenue
   (b) Notes Payable
   (c) Interest Expense
   (d) Discount on Notes Payable
5. LO4 Accrued interest payable is reported as a _______ on the balance sheet.
   (a) current asset
   (b) long-term asset
   (c) current liability
   (d) long-term liability

U REVU **Exercises**

1. LO2 On September 5, Y. Haun borrowed $4,000 from the bank, giving a 90-day, interest-bearing 10% note.
   (a) Calculate the interest on this note.
   (b) Determine the due date for this note.
2. LO3 Prepare general journal entries for the following transactions:
   (a) Received $250 plus a 60-day, 9% note for $1,000 in payment for an account receivable balance of $1,250.
   (b) Received $90 interest plus $500 principal on an old $3,000 note; the old note is renewed for 60 days at 12%.
   (c) Discounted at a rate of 12% a 120-day, 10% note issued 30 days ago for $6,000.
3. LO4 Prepare general journal entries for the following transactions:
   (a) Issued a $2,500, 30-day, 9% note in payment of an account payable.
   (b) Borrowed $3,000 cash from the bank, giving a 60-day, non-interest-bearing note discounted at 12% by the bank.
   (c) Paid the note in transaction (b) in full at maturity.

The answers to the Self-Study Questions and Exercises are at the end of the chapter (pages 683–684).

APPLYING YOUR KNOWLEDGE

REVIEW QUESTIONS

LO1 1. How does a note receivable differ from an account receivable?

LO2 2. What is the formula for calculating interest on notes?

LO2 3. In the formula for calculating interest, how is time computed?

LO2 4. What number of days is considered as a year by most banks and businesses in computing interest?

LO3 5. What seven types of transactions involving notes receivable do businesses generally encounter?

LO3 6. If a note receivable is discounted at a bank, on what amount and for what time period does the bank compute the discount?

LO3 7. If a note receivable that was discounted at a bank is dishonored by its maker, what is the responsibility of the person or business discounting the note?

LO3/4 8. On which notes receivable and notes payable is it necessary to record accrued interest at the end of the period?

LO4 9. What five types of transactions involving notes payable do businesses generally encounter?

LO4 10. When a business borrows money from a bank on a non-interest-bearing note, how are the bank discount and proceeds calculated?

LO4 11. What kind of account is Discount on Notes Payable, and how is it reported on the balance sheet?

LO4 12. What is the appropriate entry for accrued interest on notes payable for an interest-bearing note? For a non-interest-bearing note from a bank?

LO3/4 13. How are accrued interest receivable and accrued interest payable reported on the balance sheet?

SERIES A EXERCISES

E 17-1A (LO2)
✓ May 4 note: 74 days

KLOOSTER & ALLEN

TERM OF A NOTE Calculate total time in days for the following notes. (Assume there are 28 days in February.)

Date of Note	Due Date	Time in Days
May 4	July 17	________
August 17	October 1	________
July 5	September 5	________
December 11	February 5	________
March 24	May 16	________
January 6	March 18	________

E 17-2A (LO2)
✓ $5,000 note: $25

KLOOSTER & ALLEN

CALCULATING INTEREST Using 360 days as the denominator, calculate interest for the following notes using the formula I = P × R × T.

Principal	Rate	Time	Interest
$5,000	6.00%	30 days	________
1,000	7.50	60	________
4,500	8.00	120	________
950	6.80	95	________
1,250	7.25	102	________
2,900	7.00	90	________

E 17-3A (LO2)
✓ Aug. 12 note – Nov. 10

KLOOSTER & ALLEN

DETERMINING DUE DATE Determine the due date for the following notes. (Assume there are 28 days in February.)

Date of Note	Term of Note	Due Date
August 12	90 days	________
September 1	60	________
January 3	120	________

(*continued*)

Date of Note	Term of Note	Due Date
March 18	88	________
June 11	200	________
May 17	38	________

E 17-4 A (LO3)

✓ Feb. 15, Cr. Interest Rev.: $150

JOURNAL ENTRIES (NOTE RECEIVED, RENEWED, AND COLLECTED) Prepare general journal entries for the following transactions:

Jan. 16 Received a 30-day, 9% note in payment for merchandise sale of $20,000.

Feb. 15 Received $150 (interest) on the old (January 16) note; the old note is renewed for 30 days at 11%.

Mar. 17 Received principal and interest on the new (February 15) note.

19 Received a 60-day, 9% note in payment for accounts receivable balance of $8,000.

May 18 Received $120 (interest) plus $1,000 principal on the old (March 19) note; the old note is renewed for 60 days (from May 18) at 9%.

July 17 Received principal and interest on the new (May 18) note.

E 17-5A (LO3)

✓ June 2, Cr. Interest Rev.: $7.50

JOURNAL ENTRIES (NOTE RECEIVED, DISCOUNTED, DISHONORED, AND COLLECTED) Prepare general journal entries for the following transactions:

Apr. 6 Received a 120-day, 11% note in payment for accounts receivable balance of $3,000.

26 Discounted the note at a rate of 12%.

May 3 Received a 30-day, 10% note in payment for accounts receivable balance of $900.

June 2 The $900, 30-day, 10% note is dishonored.

5 The dishonored note is paid, plus interest at 10% on the maturity value.

E 17-6A (LO3)

✓ Cr. Interest Rev.: $58.50

JOURNAL ENTRIES (ACCRUED INTEREST RECEIVABLE) At the end of the year, the following interest is earned, but not yet received. Record the adjusting entry in a general journal.

Interest on $4,000, 90-day, 12% note (for 15 days)	$20.00
Interest on $7,000, 60-day, 11% note (for 18 days)	38.50
	$58.50

E 17-7A (LO4)

✓ July 1, Dr. Interest Exp.: $41.67

JOURNAL ENTRIES (NOTE ISSUED, RENEWED, AND PAID) Prepare general journal entries for the following transactions:

May 1 Purchased $5,000 worth of equipment from a supplier on account.

June 1 Issued a $5,000, 30-day, 10% note in payment of the account payable.

July 1 Paid $500 cash plus interest to the supplier, extending the note for 30 days from July 1.

31 Paid the note in full.

Aug. 10 Issued a $3,500, 60-day, 9% note to a supplier for purchase of merchandise.

E 17-8A (LO4)

✓ Discount: $100

JOURNAL ENTRIES (NOTE ISSUED FOR BANK LOAN) Prepare general journal entries for the following transactions:

July 15 Borrowed $5,000 cash from the bank, giving a 60-day non-interest-bearing note. The note is discounted 12% by the bank.

Sept. 13 Paid the $5,000 note, recognizing the discount as interest expense.

E 17-9A (LO4)

✓ Dr. Interest Exp.: $22.50

JOURNAL ENTRIES (ACCRUED INTEREST PAYABLE) At the end of the year, the following interest is payable, but not yet paid. Record the adjusting entry in the general journal.

Interest on $5,000, 60-day, 9% note (for 12 days)	$15.00
Interest on $2,500, 30-day, 12% note (for 9 days)	7.50
	$22.50

SERIES A PROBLEMS

P 17-10A (LO2/3)

✓ Feb. 13, Cr. Interest Rev.: $13.64

NOTES RECEIVABLE ENTRIES J. K. Pratt Co. had the following transactions:

20-1	
July 20	Received a $750, 30-day, 10% note from J. Akita in payment for sale of merchandise.
Aug. 19	J. Akita paid note issued July 20 plus interest.
25	Sold merchandise on account to L. Beene, $1,100.
Sept. 5	L. Beene paid $100 and gave a $1,000, 30-day, 12% note to extend time for payment.
Oct. 5	L. Beene paid note issued September 5, plus interest.
10	Sold merchandise to R. Harris for $750: $50 plus a $700, 30-day, 11% note.
Nov. 9	R. Harris paid $200 plus interest on note issued October 10 and extended the note ($500) for 30 days.
Dec. 9	R. Harris paid note extended on November 9, plus interest.
10	Sold merchandise on account to B. Kraus, $1,500.
15	B. Kraus paid $150 on merchandise purchased on account, and gave a $1,350, 30-day, 12% note to extend time for payment.
20-2	
Jan. 14	B. Kraus's note of December 15 is dishonored.
Feb. 13	Collected B. Kraus's dishonored note, plus interest at 12% on the maturity value.

REQUIRED

Record the transactions in a general journal.

P 17-11A (LO2/3)

✓ May 5, Cr. Interest Rev.: $4.25

NOTES RECEIVABLE DISCOUNTING Movado Suppliers had the following transactions:

Mar. 1	Sold merchandise on account to R. Sticca, $5,000.
20	R. Sticca gave a $5,000, 90-day, 12% note to extend time for payment.
30	R. Sticca's note is discounted at Commerce Bank at a discount rate of 15%.
Apr. 20	Received a $3,000, 60-day, 10% note from K. Jones in payment for sale of merchandise.
May 5	K. Jones's note is discounted at Commerce Bank at a discount rate of 12%.
June 19	K. Jones's note is dishonored. The bank bills Movado for the maturity value of the note plus a $40 bank fee.

(continued)

July 31 K. Jones's dishonored note is collected; Jones pays Movado the maturity value of the note, the $40 bank fee, and interest at 10% on the maturity value plus the bank fee.

Aug. 1 Sold merchandise on account to R. Brown, $5,600.

12 R. Brown paid $400 and gave a $5,200, 30-day, 12% note to extend time for payment.

Sept. 11 R. Brown paid $400, plus interest, and gave a new $4,800, 60-day, 14% note to extend time for payment.

26 R. Brown's note is discounted at Commerce Bank at a discount rate of 16%.

Nov. 10 R. Brown's note is dishonored. The bank bills Movado for the maturity value of the note plus a $40 bank fee.

Dec. 15 R. Brown's dishonored note is collected. Brown pays Movado the maturity value of the note, the $40 bank fee, and interest at 14% on the maturity value plus the bank fee.

REQUIRED

Record the transactions in a general journal.

P 17-12A (LO3)
✓ Accrued interest: $151.03

ACCRUED INTEREST RECEIVABLE The following is a list of outstanding notes receivable as of December 31, 20--:

Maker	Date of Note	Principal	Interest	Term	No. of Days
K. Savelin	12/15/--	$1,000	10%	60 days	16
R. Hillier	12/3/--	5,000	12	90	28
B. Miranda	11/30/--	2,800	8	90	31
R. Hansen	11/18/--	7,500	9	120	43

REQUIRED

1. Compute the accrued interest at the end of the year.
2. Prepare the adjusting entry in the general journal.

P 17-13A (LO4)
✓ June 4, Dr. Interest Exp.: $33.33

NOTES PAYABLE ENTRIES Milo Radio Shop had the following notes payable transactions:

Apr. 1 Borrowed $5,000 from Builder's Bank, signing a 90-day, 8% note.

5 Gave a $2,000, 60-day, 10% note to Breaker Parts Co. for purchase of merchandise.

10 Paid $500 cash and gave a $1,500, 30-day, 12% note to M. K. Reynolds in payment of an account payable.

May 10 Paid $500 cash, plus interest, and issued a new $1,000, 30-day, 14% note to M. K. Reynolds.

20 Borrowed $3,500 for 60 days from Builder's Bank on a non-interest-bearing note. The discount rate is 12%.

June 4 Paid $500 cash, plus interest, to Breaker Parts Co. (see April 5) and gave a new $1,500, 30-day, 12% note to extend time for payment.

9 Paid the principal and interest due on the $1,000 note to M. K. Reynolds. (See May 10.)

30 Paid the principal and interest due on the $5,000 note to Builder's Bank. (See April 1.)

July 4 Paid the principal and interest due on the $1,500 note to Breaker Parts Co. (See June 4.)

19 Paid the $3,500 non-interest-bearing note to Builder's Bank. (See May 20.)

REQUIRED

Record the transactions in a general journal.

P 17-14A (LO4)
✓ Accrued interest: $75.37

ACCRUED INTEREST PAYABLE The following is a list of outstanding notes payable as of December 31, 20--:

Maker	Date of Note	Principal	Interest	Term	No. of Days
B. Jones	12/1/--	$1,000	11%	90 days	30
M. Aguilar	11/25/--	2,500	9	80	36
T. Plant	12/14/--	3,800	12	120	17
W. Brand	11/19/--	1,900	10	180	42

REQUIRED

1. Compute the accrued interest at the end of the year.
2. Prepare the adjusting entry in the general journal.

SERIES B EXERCISES

E 17-1B (LO2)
✓ Aug. 17 note: 54 days

TERM OF A NOTE Calculate total time in days for the following notes. (Assume there are 28 days in February.)

Date of Note	Due Date	Time in Days
August 17	October 10	________
January 12	March 10	________
July 15	September 13	________
December 3	February 1	________
April 11	July 6	________
October 6	December 18	________

E 17-2B (LO2)
✓ $4,000 note: $46.67

CALCULATING INTEREST Using 360 days as the denominator, calculate interest for the following notes using the formula I = P × R × T.

Principal	Rate	Time	Interest
$4,000	7.00%	60 days	________
3,000	9.50	30	________
7,500	8.00	150	________
850	7.90	99	________
2,250	7.55	122	________
1,900	8.80	82	________

E 17-3B (LO2)
✓ July 11 note: Aug. 25

DETERMINING DUE DATE Determine the due date for the following notes. (Assume there are 28 days in February.)

Date of Note	Term of Note	Due Date
July 11	45 days	________
December 23	90	________
April 18	120	________
October 3	77	________
January 1	180	________
August 13	65	________

E 17-4B (LO3)
✓ June 21, Cr. Interest Rev.: $165

JOURNAL ENTRIES (NOTE RECEIVED, RENEWED, AND COLLECTED) Prepare general journal entries for the following transactions:

May 22	Received a 30-day, 9% note in payment for merchandise sale of $22,000.
June 21	Received $165.00 cash (interest) on the old (May 22) note; the old note is renewed for 30 days at 10%.
July 21	Received principal and interest on the new (June 21) note.
28	Received a 45-day, 7% note in payment for accounts receivable balance of $11,600.
Sept. 11	Received $101.50 cash (interest) plus $1,600 principal on the old (July 28) note; the old note is renewed for 60 days (from September 11) at 9%.
Nov. 10	Received principal and interest on the new (September 11) note.

E 17-5B (LO3)
✓ Oct. 5, Cr. Interest Rev.: $11

JOURNAL ENTRIES (NOTE RECEIVED, DISCOUNTED, DISHONORED, AND COLLECTED) Prepare general journal entries for the following transactions:

Aug. 4	Received a 120-day, 12% note in payment for accounts receivable balance of $4,000.
14	Discounted the note at a rate of 14%.
Sept. 5	Received a 30-day, 11% note in payment for accounts receivable balance of $1,200.
Oct. 5	The $1,200, 30-day, 11% note is dishonored.
Nov. 4	The dishonored note is paid, plus interest at 11% on the maturity value.

E 17-6B (LO3)
✓ Cr. Interest Rev.: $80

JOURNAL ENTRIES (ACCRUED INTEREST RECEIVABLE) At the end of the year, the following interest is earned, but not yet received. Record the adjusting entry in a general journal.

Interest on $6,000, 60-day, 11% note (for 24 days)	$44.00
Interest on $9,000, 90-day, 12% note (for 12 days)	36.00
	$80.00

E 17-7B (LO4)
✓ Aug. 14, Dr. Interest Exp.: $60

JOURNAL ENTRIES (NOTE ISSUED, RENEWED, AND PAID) Prepare general journal entries for the following transactions:

June 15	Purchased $6,000 worth of equipment from a supplier on account.
July 15	Issued a $6,000, 30-day, 12% note in payment of the account payable.
Aug. 14	Paid $600 cash plus interest to the supplier, extending the note for 30 days from August 14.
Sept. 13	Paid the note in full.
27	Issued a $5,000, 60-day, 10% note to a supplier for purchase of merchandise.

E 17-8B (LO4)
✓ Discount: $140

JOURNAL ENTRIES (NOTE ISSUED FOR BANK LOAN) Prepare general journal entries for the following transactions:

Sept. 15	Borrowed $7,000 cash from the bank, giving a 60-day non-interest-bearing note. The note is discounted 12% by the bank.
Nov. 14	Paid the $7,000 note, recognizing the discount as interest expense.

E 17-9B (LO4)
✓ Dr. Interest Exp.: $40.75

JOURNAL ENTRIES (ACCRUED INTEREST PAYABLE) At the end of the year, the following interest is payable, but not yet paid. Record the adjusting entry in the general journal.

Interest on $8,000, 90-day, 8% note (for 18 days)	$32.00
Interest on $4,500, 60-day, 10% note (for 7 days)	8.75
	$40.75

SERIES B PROBLEMS

P 17-10B (LO2/3)
✓ Jan. 13, Cr. Interest Rev.: $25.59

NOTES RECEIVABLE ENTRIES M. L. DiMaurizio had the following notes receivable transactions:

20-3	
June 20	Received a $2,400, 30-day, 10% note from K. Lorenzo in payment for sale of merchandise.
July 20	K. Lorenzo paid the note plus interest.
25	Sold merchandise on account to R. Boone, $5,600.
Aug. 4	R. Boone paid $600 and gave a $5,000, 30-day, 12% note to extend time for payment.
Sept. 3	R. Boone paid the note plus interest.
10	Sold merchandise to T. Akins for $3,000: $400 plus a $2,600, 30-day, 11% note.
Oct. 10	T. Akins paid $600, plus interest, and extended the note ($2,000) for 30 days.
Nov. 9	T. Akins paid the note plus interest.
10	Sold merchandise on account to J. Brown, $5,000.
25	J. Brown paid $1,000 and gave a $4,000, 30-day, 12% note to extend time for payment.
Dec. 25	J. Brown's note is dishonored.
20-4	
Jan. 13	J. Brown's dishonored note is collected, plus interest at 12% on the maturity value.

REQUIRED

Record the transactions in a general journal.

P 17-11B (LO2/3)
✓ July 5, Cr. Interest Rev.: $3.40

NOTES RECEIVABLE DISCOUNTING Madison Graphics had the following notes rcccivablc transactions:

May 1	Sold merchandise on account to L. Carney, $5,600.
20	L. Carney gave a $5,600, 90-day, 12% note to extend time for payment.
30	L. Carney's note is discounted at Commercial Bank at a discount rate of 15%.
June 20	Received a $2,400, 60-day, 10% note from P. Arnst in payment for sale of merchandise.
July 5	P. Arnst's note is discounted at Commercial Bank at a discount rate of 12%.

(*continued*)

Aug. 19 P. Arnst's note is dishonored. The bank bills Madison Graphics for the maturity value of the note plus a $30 bank fee.

31 P. Arnst's dishonored note is collected; Arnst pays Madison the maturity value of the note, the $30 bank fee, and interest at 10% on the maturity value plus the bank fee.

Sept. 1 Sold merchandise on account to B. Faust, $6,400.

12 B. Faust paid $400 and gave a $6,000, 30-day, 12% note to extend time for payment.

Oct. 12 B. Faust paid $400, plus interest, and gave a new $5,600, 60-day, 14% note to extend time for payment.

26 B. Faust's note is discounted at Commercial Bank at a discount rate of 14%.

Dec. 11 B. Faust's note is dishonored. The bank bills Madison Graphics for the maturity value of the note plus a $30 bank fee.

Dec. 27 B. Faust's dishonored note is collected. Faust pays Madison Graphics the maturity value of the note, the $30 bank fee, and interest at 14% on the maturity value plus the bank fee.

REQUIRED

Record the transactions in a general journal.

P 17-12B (LO3)

✓ Accrued interest: $94.02

ACCRUED INTEREST RECEIVABLE The following is a list of outstanding notes receivable as of December 31, 20--:

Maker	Date of Note	Principal	Interest	Term	No. of Days
P. Harrison	12/17/--	$1,200	11.0%	60 days	14
T. Rieber	12/3/--	4,000	12.0	90	28
K. Burke	12/1/--	2,200	9.0	90	30
A. Pai	11/28/--	4,500	8.5	120	33

REQUIRED

1. Compute the accrued interest at the end of the year.
2. Prepare the adjusting entry in the general journal.

P 17-13B (LO4)

✓ June 4, Dr. Interest Exp.: $50

NOTES PAYABLE Mary's Travel Agency had the following notes payable transactions:

Apr. 1 Borrowed $4,000 from Finance Bank, signing a 90-day, 8% note.

5 Gave a $3,000, 60-day, 10% note to Krenshaw Airline for purchase of merchandise.

10 Paid $400 cash and issued a $1,600, 30-day, 12% note to Andrew Adams in payment of an account payable.

May 10 Paid $400, plus interest, and gave a new $1,200, 30-day, 14% note to Andrew Adams.

20 Borrowed $4,500 for 60 days from Finance Bank on a non-interest-bearing note. The discount rate is 14%.

June 4 Paid $500, plus interest, to Krenshaw Airline (see April 5) and gave a new $2,500, 30-day, 12% note to extend time for payment.

9 Paid the principal and interest due on the $1,200 note to Andrew Adams. (See May 10.)

30 Paid the principal and interest due on the $4,000 note to Finance Bank. (See April 1.)

July 4 Paid the principal and interest due on the $2,500 note to Krenshaw Airline. (See June 4.)

19 Paid the $4,500 non-interest-bearing note to Finance Bank. (See May 20.)

REQUIRED

Record the transactions in a general journal.

P 17-14B (LO4)

✓ Accrued interest: $83.54

ACCRUED INTEREST PAYABLE The following is a list of outstanding notes payable as of December 31, 20--:

Payee	Date of Note	Principal	Interest	Term	No. of Days
X. Rayal	12/1/--	$1,200	11%	90 days	30
G. Richards	11/28/--	2,300	8	80	33
A. Gray	12/16/--	3,400	12	120	15
O. Hankins	11/13/--	2,900	10	180	48

REQUIRED

1. Compute the accrued interest at the end of the year.
2. Prepare the adjusting entry in the general journal.

MANAGING YOUR WRITING

You are purchasing a new car and plan to finance it through your employee credit union. The credit union has offered you two different promissory note plans, as follows:

Option 1: Three years at 9%, with interest payable annually.
Option 2: One year at 8%, renewable each year for up to three more years, at the then-current interest rate. Interest is payable at the end of each year.

Prepare a written report summarizing the advantages and disadvantages of each of these options.

ETHICS CASE

Rochelle needed to borrow $3,000 for three months in order to pay for college expenses while waiting for her scholarship to arrive. After Rochelle filled out the loan application, the loan officer at the bank asked her if she would like to pay the interest up front or at the maturity of the note. He went on to explain that it didn't make a difference, but he preferred that she pay it up front because it would make his paperwork easier. He also told Rochelle that the interest rate and amount would be the same. Rochelle agreed, signed the three-month, 12%, discounted note and left with a check for $2,910.

1. Did the loan officer offer Rochelle an acceptable explanation of the interest rate? Justify your answer.
2. What is the effective rate of interest on Rochelle's loan? Round to the nearest tenth of a percent.
3. In a short paragraph, explain the difference between an "interest-bearing" note and a "discounted" note.
4. In groups of two or three, discuss some common situations where the average person might misunderstand interest rate quotations.

MASTERY PROBLEM

✓ Nov. 1, Cr. Interest Rev.: $5.89

KA KLOOSTER & ALLEN

Eddie Edwards and Phil Bell own and operate The Second Hand Equipment Shop. The following transactions involving notes and interest were completed during the last three months of 20--:

Oct. 1	Issued a $6,800, 60-day, 10% note to Mac Farm Equipment for purchase of merchandise.
15	Received a $2,000, 60-day, 12% note from R. Chambers in payment for sale of merchandise.
Nov. 1	Discounted the note received from R. Chambers on October 15 at Merchants National Bank. The discount rate is 14%.
1	Borrowed $5,000 from First National Bank on a three-month, non-interest-bearing note that was discounted at 10%.
20	Received a $4,000, 90-day, 9% note from L. Revsine in payment of an account receivable.
30	Issued a check to Mac Farm Equipment in payment of the note issued on October 1, including interest.
Dec. 10	Issued a $3,000, 90-day, 9% note to Remak Tractors to extend time for payment of an account payable.
16	Received notification from Merchants National Bank that R. Chambers has dishonored his note. A check is issued to cover the note plus a $20 bank fee that must be paid to the bank.

REQUIRED

1. Prepare general journal entries for the transactions.
2. Prepare necessary adjusting entries for the notes outstanding on December 31.

CHALLENGE PROBLEM

This problem challenges you to apply your cumulative accounting knowledge to move a step beyond the material in the chapter.

REQUIRED

Prepare general journal entries on the books of both Mirror Co. and the other party (either Rosman Co., Kaw County Bank, or Lawrence Bank) for each of the following transactions:

✓ July 1, Lawrence Bank, Dr. Interest Rec.: $13.50

June 1	Rosman Co. gave Mirror Co. a $3,000, 90-day, 10% note to extend the time for payment of its account.
20	Mirror Co. borrowed $2,000 for 60 days from Kaw County Bank on a non-interest-bearing note. The discount rate was 12%.
July 1	Mirror Co. discounted Rosman Co.'s note at Lawrence Bank at a discount rate of 12%.
Aug. 19	Mirror Co. paid the $2,000 non-interest-bearing note to Kaw County Bank.
30	Rosman Co.'s $3,000 note (see June 1 transaction) was collected by Lawrence Bank. (Treat Lawrence Bank as the other party.)

ANSWERS TO SELF-STUDY QUESTIONS AND EXERCISES

True/False Questions

1. T
2. T
3. F (Difference is called the discount.)
4. F (Interest is credited to Interest Revenue; time has passed and interest has been earned.)
5. T

Multiple Choice Questions

1. d 2. b 3. a 4. c 5. c

U REVU Exercises

1. (a) $4,000 × 10% × 90/360 = $100

   (b) Sept. 25
   Oct. 31
   Nov. 30
   86
   Dec. 4
   90 Due date = Dec. 4

2.

1		(a)	Cash	250 00	
2			Notes Receivable	1000 00	
3			Accounts Receivable		1250 00
4			Received cash and note to settle account		
5		(b)	Cash	590 00	
6			Notes Receivable (new note)	2500 00	
7			Notes Receivable (old note)		3000 00
8			Interest Revenue		90 00
9			Received new note plus partial payment and		
10			interest on old note		
11		(c)	Cash	6014 00*	
12			Notes Receivable		6000 00
13			Interest Revenue		14 00
14			Discounted note receivable		
15			*Maturity value = $6,000 + ($6,000 × 10% × 120/360) = $6,200		
16			Discount amount = $6,200 × 12% × 90/360 = $186		
17			Proceeds = $6,200 − $186 = $6,014		

3.

					Debit	Credit
1		(a)	Accounts Payable		2,500.00	
2			Notes Payable			2,500.00
3			Issued note to settle account			
4		(b)	Cash		2,940.00	
5			Discount on Notes Payable		60.00*	
6			Notes Payable			3,000.00
7			Issued note for bank loan			
8			* Discount = \$3,000 × 12% × 60/360 = \$60			
9		(c)	Notes Payable		3,000.00	
10			Interest Expense		60.00	
11			Cash			3,000.00
12			Discount on Notes Payable			60.00
13			Paid note at maturity			

Chapter 18

COURTESY OF IMI IRVING MATERIALS, INC.

Accounting for Long-Term Assets

IMI is a privately held, employee-owned corporation with company headquarters in Greenfield, Indiana. It has four regional operation centers located in Greenfield, Indiana; Evansville, Indiana; Louisville, Kentucky; and Nashville, Tennessee. Skunk Irving founded IMI in 1946 as a building materials supplier. The company has 2,400 employees servicing six states through the four regional operation centers. Over the years, IMI has not only delivered quality concrete and aggregates but has also become a leader in the development of new technologies. IMI led the way in the design of the front discharge mixer that is now a staple of the concrete industry. IMI has also developed a number of concrete batch mixes and specialty admixtures that have revolutionized the construction processes.

IMI must make substantial investments in heavy equipment, like the truck shown above. In this chapter, you will learn how to account for long-term assets, such as equipment, from the time they are acquired until they are retired.

LEARNING OBJECTIVES

Careful study of this chapter should enable you to:

LO1 Determine the cost of property, plant, and equipment.

LO2 Explain the nature and purpose of depreciation.

LO3 Compute depreciation using the straight-line, declining-balance, sum-of-the-years'-digits, and units-of-production methods.

LO4 Account for repairs, maintenance, additions, improvements, and replacements to plant and equipment.

LO5 Account for the disposition of property, plant, and equipment.

LO6 Explain the nature of, purpose of, and accounting for depletion.

LO7 Explain the nature of and accounting for intangible assets.

Assets that are expected to provide benefits for a number of accounting periods are called **long-term assets**. Long-term assets that are **tangible** (have physical substance) and that are used in the operations of the business are called **property, plant, and equipment; plant assets;** or **fixed assets**. Examples include land, buildings, furniture, and equipment. Assets whose physical substance consists of natural resources that are consumed in the operation of the business are often called **wasting assets**. Examples include mines (coal, salt, and gold), stands of timber, and oil and gas wells. Long-term assets that have no physical substance are called **intangible assets**. Common examples include patents, copyrights, and trademarks.

All long-term assets except land gradually wear out or are used up as time passes. As an asset's useful life expires, a portion of the asset's cost is recognized as an expense. This is often referred to as "writing off" the asset. A different term is used to describe this expense for the different types of long-term assets. For plant assets, the expense is called **depreciation;** for natural resources, it is called **depletion;** and for intangible assets, it is called **amortization**. In this chapter, proper accounting for property, plant, and equipment; natural resources; and intangible assets is described and illustrated.

ACQUISITION COST OF PROPERTY, PLANT, AND EQUIPMENT

LO1 Determine the cost of property, plant, and equipment.

The cost of a long-term asset includes all amounts spent to acquire the asset and prepare it for its intended use. Purchases of long-term assets are entered by debiting the proper asset account and crediting either the cash or the proper liability account.

LAND

All costs incurred to purchase land and prepare it for its intended use are debited to the land account. These costs include legal and real estate fees as well as the cost of removing old buildings and grading the land to prepare it for its intended use. Special tax assessments for streets, sewers, or parks also are debited to the land account, because these items are viewed as permanent.

LAND IMPROVEMENTS

Costs related to land that are not permanent in nature are normally debited to the land improvements account. Common examples include the costs of planting trees and shrubs, installing fences, and paving parking areas. Items debited to the land improvements account are depreciated over their expected useful lives.

BUILDINGS

The cost of buildings that are purchased includes the purchase price, realtor and legal fees, and related taxes on the purchase. If the purchase price includes land, the cost of the land and building must be determined and accounted for separately. If the building is constructed, costs include all normal construction costs for material and labor and architectural and engineering fees. In addition, insurance premiums and interest on loans *while the building is being constructed* are considered part of the cost of the asset.

EQUIPMENT

The cost of equipment includes the purchase price, transportation charges, insurance while in transit, installation costs, and any other costs that are incurred up to the point of placing the asset in service.

TREATMENT OF INTEREST WHEN ACQUIRING OR CONSTRUCTING ASSETS

The proper treatment of interest depends on whether the asset is being purchased or constructed. Often, businesses must borrow money to buy major long-term assets. The method used to finance the *acquisition* of an asset should not affect its cost. For example, interest on a mortgage to purchase a building should not be included in the cost of the asset. We always use the **cash equivalent price,** which is the amount of cash that could have been paid for the asset on the date of purchase.

Interest costs are treated differently for assets being constructed. Interest incurred *while an asset is being constructed* should be included as part of the cost of the asset. Since the asset is not operational during the construction period, it is not generating revenues against which the interest could be matched. Thus, the interest is included in the cost of the asset and recognized as part of depreciation expense when the asset is placed in operation and begins generating revenues.

U REVU

Complete U REVU-1 on **page 709** to test your basic understanding of LO1.

DEPRECIATION

LO2 Explain the nature and purpose of depreciation.

The purpose of depreciation is to match a plant asset's cost with the revenues it helps to produce. As discussed in earlier chapters, the following is a typical adjusting entry made at the end of each accounting period:

5	Dec.	31	Depr. Expense—Delivery Equipment	541	1 0 0 00		5
6			Accum. Depr.—Delivery Equipment	185.1		1 0 0 00	6
7							7

LEARNING KEY

Depreciation matches an asset's cost with the revenues it helps generate.

LEARNING KEY

Since land does not wear out, no depreciation is recognized.

Recall that Depreciation Expense is reported on the income statement and Accumulated Depreciation is reported on the balance sheet as a contra-asset. Accumulated Depreciation is deducted from the asset account to report the book value, or undepreciated cost, of the asset. For example, a machine with a cost of $3,000 and accumulated depreciation of $600 would be reported on the balance sheet as follows:

Property, Plant, and Equipment		
Equipment	$3,000	
Less accumulated depreciation	600	$2,400

Keep in mind that depreciation is a process of *cost allocation,* not a process of valuation. Many factors cause the market values of plant assets to change over time. The recognition of depreciation is not intended to make the assets reflect their market values on the balance sheet. The net amounts reported on the balance sheet (book values) are merely the portions of the original costs that have not yet been allocated to expense.

LEARNING KEY

Market Value	=	Amount Asset Can Be Sold For
Book Value	=	Cost – Accumulated Depreciation

The recognition of depreciation is not intended to represent market values on the balance sheet.

The two major types of depreciation are physical and functional. **Physical depreciation** is the loss of usefulness because of deterioration from age and wear. **Functional depreciation** is the loss of usefulness because of inadequacy or obsolescence. As a business grows, some of its plant assets may become inadequate to handle the increased workload. As new manufacturing methods are developed, assets may become obsolete because there are faster, more efficient, or more effective assets that may be used to perform this work.

U REVU

Complete U REVU-2 on **page 709** to test your basic understanding of LO2.

DEPRECIATION METHODS

LO3 Compute depreciation using the straight-line, declining-balance, sum-of-the-years'-digits, and units-of-production methods.

Before we discuss the methods of calculating depreciation, there are several terms to be defined.

Cost The sum of all amounts spent to acquire an asset and prepare it for its intended use.

Useful Life The amount of service expected to be obtained from an asset. It can be expressed in years, hours of operation, units of production, or miles driven. There is no way of knowing exactly how long an asset will last or exactly what its output will be. Therefore, estimates must be made based on past experience and information from trade associations and engineers.

Salvage Value The estimated **scrap**, or market, **value** for the asset on its expected disposal date. This amount can be difficult to predict. Often, a zero salvage value is used if the asset is expected to have little or no value at the end of its useful life.

Depreciable Cost (Base) The original cost less salvage (or scrap) value.

Depreciable Cost = Original Cost − Salvage Value

Book Value The undepreciated cost of the asset.

Book Value = Cost − Accumulated Depreciation

There are several different ways of calculating the amount of depreciation for each period. The most commonly used methods for financial reporting purposes are the following:

1. Straight-line method
2. Declining-balance method
3. Sum-of-the-years'-digits method
4. Units-of-production method

STRAIGHT-LINE METHOD

Under the **straight-line method**, the depreciable cost of an asset is allocated equally over the years of the asset's useful life according to the following formula:

Straight-Line Method

$$\text{Annual Depreciation} = \frac{(\text{Cost} - \text{Salvage Value})}{\text{Estimated Useful Life}}$$

To illustrate, assume that a new asset costs \$10,000, has an expected life of four years, and has a \$1,000 estimated salvage value. Using the straight-line method, the amount of depreciation allocated to each year would be \$2,250, computed as follows:

Original Cost	–	Salvage Value	=	Depreciable Cost
$10,000	–	$1,000	=	$9,000
Depreciation Cost / Estimated Useful Life	=	$9,000 / 4 years	=	$2,250 annual depreciation

LEARNING KEY

Under the straight-line method, the same amount of depreciation is recorded each period.

The annual *rate* of depreciation is 25% (100% ÷ 4 years) of the depreciable cost.

A month is usually the shortest period that is used in depreciation accounting. An asset purchased on or before the fifteenth of the month is considered to have been owned for the full month. An asset purchased after the fifteenth of the month is considered to have been acquired the first of the next month.

With the straight-line method, the book value of the asset decreases uniformly period by period. As shown in Figure 18-1, the book value over several periods is a downward-sloping, perfectly straight line. That is how the method got its name.

DECLINING-BALANCE METHOD

Many plant assets require repairs and replacement of parts to keep them in service. Such expenses usually increase as the assets get older. Some accountants believe that depreciation expense, therefore, should be higher in the early years to offset the higher repair and maintenance expenses of the later years. Others suggest that assets contribute more to the business when they are comparatively new. For these reasons, it may be desirable to calculate depreciation in a way that will give larger write-offs in the early years of the asset's life. Depreciation methods that provide for a higher depreciation charge in the first year of an asset's life and gradually decreasing charges in subsequent years are called **accelerated depreciation methods.**

One popular accelerated method is the **declining-balance method.** As shown in the following formula, under this method, the book value is multiplied by a fixed rate.

Declining-Balance Method

$$\text{Annual Depreciation} = \text{Depreciation Rate} \times \text{Book Value at Beginning of Year}$$

LEARNING KEY

"Double" means double the straight-line rate. "Declining balance" means that we should multiply the rate by the declining beginning book value balance.

This method results in successively smaller depreciation charges as the book value declines year by year. The most common rate used is double the straight-line rate. For this reason, this technique is sometimes referred to as the **double-declining-balance method.**

FIGURE 18-1 Comparison of Depreciation Methods

Straight-Line Method

Year	Depr. Exp.	Accum. Depr.	Book Value
			10,000
1	2,250	2,250	7,750
2	2,250	4,500	5,500
3	2,250	6,750	3,250
4	2,250	9,000	1,000

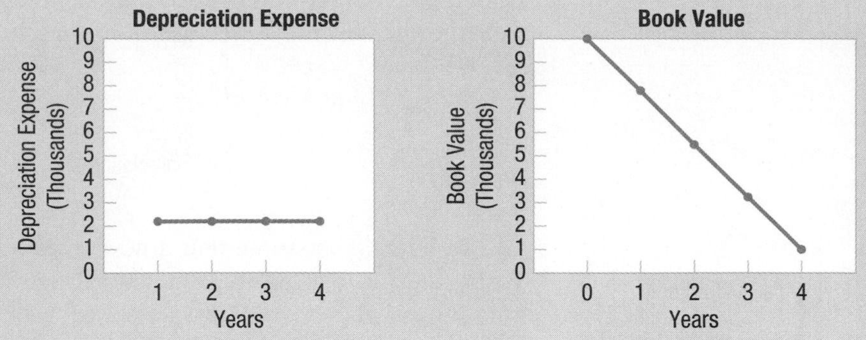

Double-Declining-Balance Method

Year	Depr. Exp.	Accum. Depr.	Book Value
			10,000
1	5,000	5,000	5,000
2	2,500	7,500	2,500
3	1,250	8,750	1,250
4	250	9,000	1,000

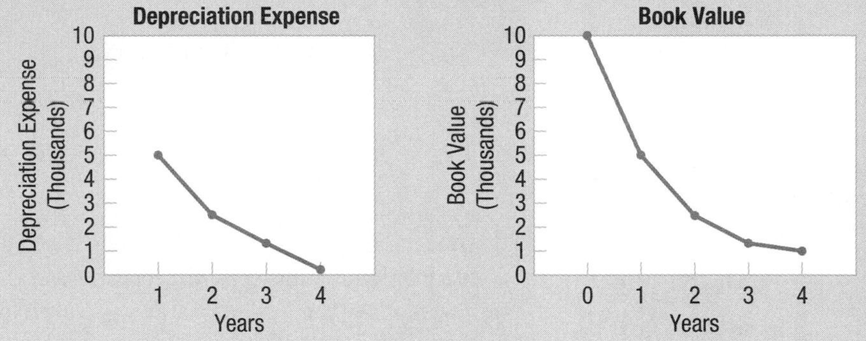

Sum-of the Years'-Digits Method

Year	Depr. Exp.	Accum. Depr.	Book Value
			10,000
1	3,600	3,600	6,400
2	2,700	6,300	3,700
3	1,800	8,100	1,900
4	900	9,000	1,000

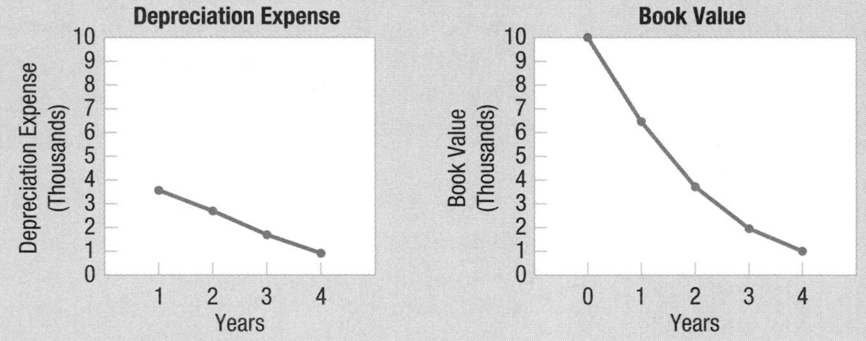

Units-of-Production Method

Year	Depr. Exp.	Accum. Depr.	Book Value
			10,000
1	2,400	2,400	7,600
2	4,000	6,400	3,600
3	2,000	8,400	1,600
4	600	9,000	1,000

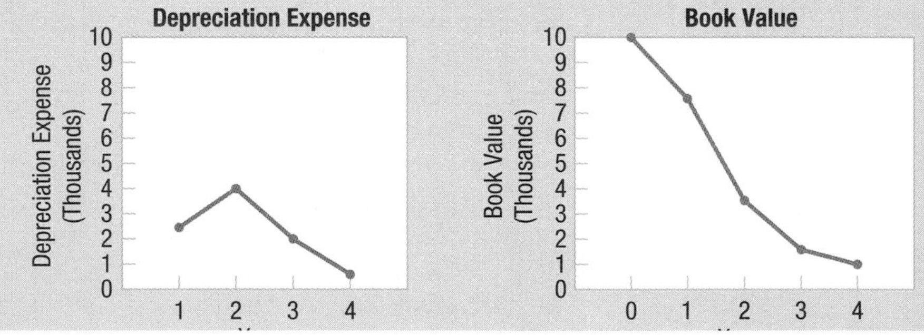

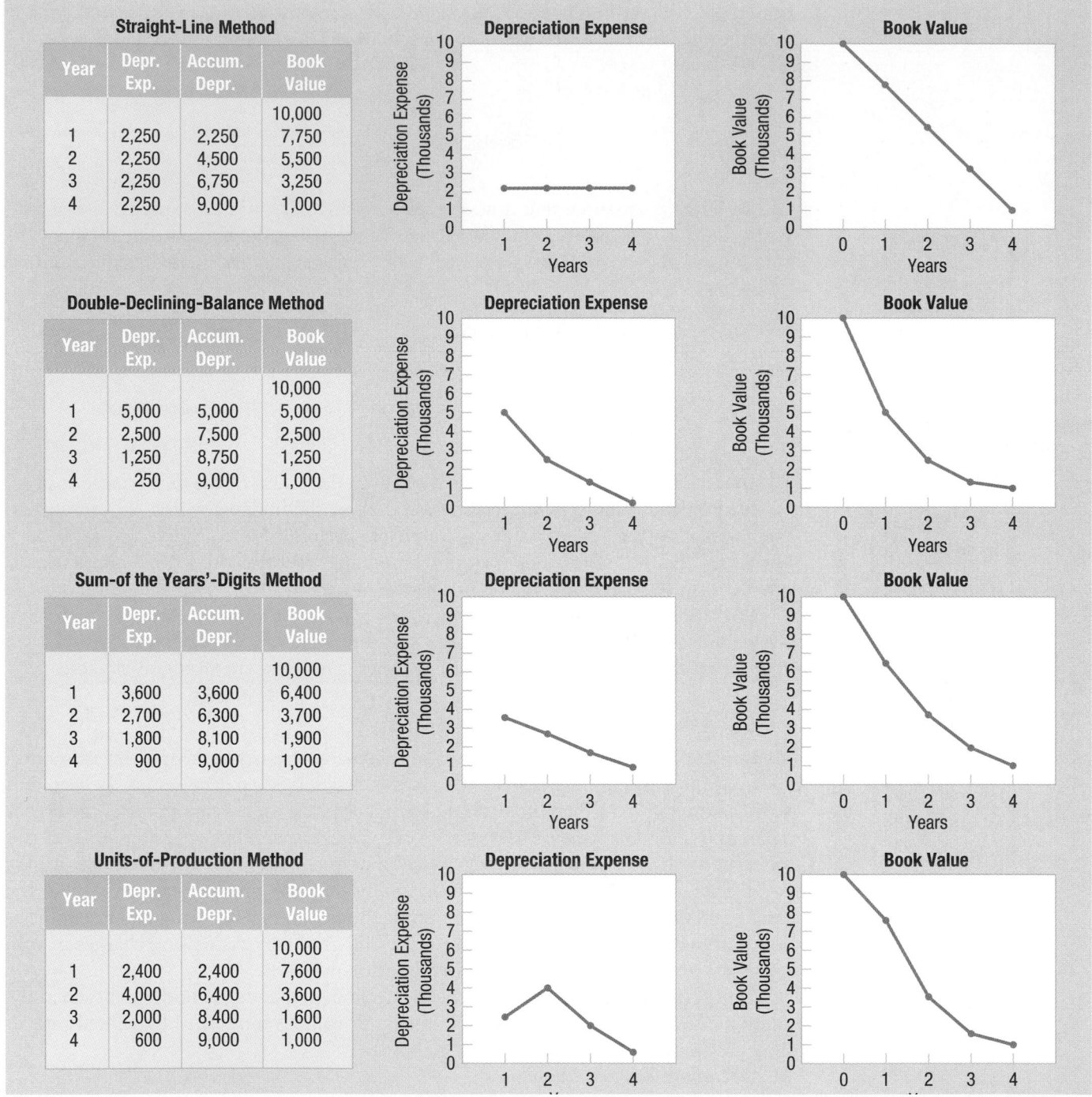

To illustrate, let's use the same asset as for the straight-line method. The asset cost $10,000, has an expected life of four years, and has a $1,000 estimated salvage value. Using the double-declining-balance method, the depreciation rate to be applied to the book value of the asset each year is 50%, computed as follows:

Straight-Line Rate = 25% (100% ÷ 4 years)

Double-Declining-Balance Rate = 50% (2 × 25%)

The annual depreciation and the book value at the end of each year are as follows:

Year	Book Value Beginning of Year	Rate	Annual Depreciation	Accumulated Depreciation End of Year	Book Value End of Year
1	$10,000	50%	$5,000	$5,000	$5,000
2	5,000	50	2,500	7,500	2,500
3	2,500	50	1,250	8,750	1,250
4	1,250	—	250*	9,000	1,000

*$250 = $1,250 (book value at beginning of year) – $1,000 (salvage value)

LEARNING KEY

Do not subtract the salvage value from the original cost before multiplying by the declining-balance rate.

The salvage value is not considered in determining the annual depreciation. However, the asset's book value should not be allowed to fall below its estimated salvage value. Thus, the amount of depreciation actually recorded in the final year (year 4) is limited to $250 ($1,250 – $1,000). As shown in Figure 18-1, with the declining-balance method, the book value declines rapidly in the early years and more slowly in the later years of an asset's life.

Declining-Balance Method for Partial Periods

If the asset was acquired at some time other than the beginning of the year, a change would be necessary in the computation of depreciation for the year. For example, if the asset was acquired on April 1, the depreciation for year 1 would be calculated as follows:

Year 1: $10,000 × 50% = $5,000 × 9/12 = $3,750

Depreciation for years 2 through 4 would then be calculated by applying the 50% depreciation rate to the book value of the asset at the beginning of each year, as follows:

Year	Book Value Beginning of Year	Rate	Annual Depreciation	Accumulated Depreciation End of Year	Book Value End of Year
2	$6,250*	50%	$3,125	$6,875	$3,125
3	3,125	50	1,563	8,438	1,562
4	1,562	—	562**	9,000	1,000

*$6,250 = $10,000 (cost) – $3,750 (depreciation for year 1)

**$562 = $1,562 (book value at beginning of year) – $1,000 (salvage value)

LEARNING KEY

An asset should not be depreciated below its estimated salvage value.

Depreciation in year 4 is limited to $562 because the asset should not be depreciated below its estimated salvage value. If the asset continued to be used in year 5, no depreciation would be recorded.

SUM-OF-THE-YEARS'-DIGITS METHOD

As shown in the following formula, under the **sum-of-the-years'-digits method**, the depreciation each year is determined by multiplying the depreciable cost by a schedule of fractions.

Sum-of-the-Years'-Digits Method

$$\text{Annual Depreciation} = (\text{Cost} - \text{Salvage Value}) \times \frac{\text{Remaining Useful Life}}{\text{Sum-of-the-Years'-Digits}}$$

The numerator in any year is the number of years of remaining life for the asset, measured from the beginning of the year. The denominator for all fractions is determined by listing the digits that represent the years of the estimated life of the asset and adding these digits. For example, suppose that the estimated life of an asset is four years. The sum of the digits (4 + 3 + 2 + 1) equals 10 (the denominator). The following formula can also be used to determine the denominator.

Calculating the Sum-of-the-Years'-Digits

$$S = N \times \frac{(N + 1)}{2}$$

S = sum of the digits
N = number of years of estimated life

If the life of the asset is four years:

$$S = 4 \times \frac{(4 + 1)}{2} = 4 \times (2.5) = 10$$

The denominator equals 10. Therefore, the fractions used for an asset with a four-year life would be 4/10, 3/10, 2/10, and 1/10. Applying these fractions to the asset in our illustration, the results are as follows:

Year	Depreciable Cost	Rate	Annual Depreciation	Accumulated Depreciation End of Year	Book Value End of Year
1	$9,000	4/10	$3,600	$3,600	$6,400
2	9,000	3/10	2,700	6,300	3,700
3	9,000	2/10	1,800	8,100	1,900
4	9,000	1/10	900	9,000	1,000

As shown in Figure 18-1, the pattern of decline in the book value using the sum-of-the-years'-digits method is accelerated. However, the write-off is not as rapid as it is with the double-declining-balance method.

Sum-of-the-Years'-Digits Method for Partial Periods

If the asset is acquired at some time other than the beginning of the year, a modification is necessary in the calculation. For example, if the asset is acquired on April 1, the depreciation for years 1 through 3 is calculated as follows:

Year 1:	$9,000	×	4/10	=	$3,600	×	9/12	=	$2,700
Year 2:	$9,000	×	4/10	=	$3,600	×	3/12	=	$ 900
	9,000	×	3/10	=	2,700	×	9/12	=	2,025
									$2,925
Year 3:	$9,000	×	3/10	=	$2,700	×	3/12	=	$ 675
	9,000	×	2/10	=	1,800	×	9/12	=	1,350
									$2,025

Depreciation for years 4 and 5 is calculated in a similar manner.

UNITS-OF-PRODUCTION METHOD

Under the **units-of-production method**, depreciation is based on the extent to which the asset was used during the year. As shown below, annual depreciation is computed in two steps. First, a depreciation charge per unit produced or consumed is computed. Second, this unit rate is multiplied by the number of units produced or consumed during the year.

Units-of-Production Method

$$\text{Step 1: Depreciation per Unit} = \frac{(\text{Cost} - \text{Salvage Value})}{\text{Estimated Useful Life in Units}}$$

$$\text{Step 2: Annual Depreciation} = \text{Depreciation per Unit} \times \begin{array}{l}\text{Number of Units Produced or}\\ \text{Consumed this Year}\end{array}$$

This method can be used for certain types of machinery, equipment, and vehicles. It is most appropriate for assets that receive varying amounts of use over time. For example, assume that a company purchases a car at a cost of $10,000 and expects that it can be sold for $1,000 after 90,000 miles of service. The calculation of depreciation for the first year when the car was driven 24,000 miles follows:

$$\text{Depreciable Cost} = \$10{,}000 \text{ Original Cost} - \$1{,}000 \text{ Salvage Value} = \$9{,}000$$

$$\text{Depreciation per Mile} = \frac{\$9{,}000 \text{ Depreciable Cost}}{90{,}000 \text{ Total Miles}} = \$0.10$$

$$\text{First-Year Depreciation} = 24{,}000 \text{ miles} \times \$0.10/\text{mile} = \$2{,}400$$

As shown in Figure 18-1, the depreciation expense and book value for each year do not follow a particular pattern. They are a function of the miles driven each year (24,000; 40,000; 20,000; and 6,000 in this illustration).

DEPRECIATION FOR FEDERAL INCOME TAX PURPOSES

A business is allowed to deduct depreciation expenses in calculating taxable income. Allowable depreciation methods for tax purposes vary depending on when the asset was acquired. For plant assets acquired before 1981, any of the four methods described in the previous sections is permitted. For plant assets acquired between 1981 and 1986, either the straight-line method or the **Accelerated Cost Recovery System (ACRS)** must be used. ACRS classifies all business plant assets into four different useful life categories. Most business assets fall into one of three categories: three-year, five-year, or 18-year property.

For plant assets acquired after 1986, either the straight-line method or the **Modified Accelerated Cost Recovery System (MACRS)** must be used. MACRS identifies eight categories of useful life for plant assets. Most business assets other than real estate fall into one of two categories: five year or seven-year property. ACRS and MACRS define depreciation rates for various categories. For example, the rates for five-year property are shown on page 694. In using these rates, salvage value is ignored. Note that depreciation under MACRS for a five-year asset must be spread over six years. This is because, regardless of when the asset is purchased, the MACRS depreciation rates assume one-half year's depreciation in year 1 and one-half year's depreciation in year 6. Note that MACRS offers an accelerated "write-off" of the asset and that both methods permit depreciating 100% of the cost of the asset.

LEARNING KEY

Under ACRS and MACRS, salvage value is ignored when computing the asset's depreciable cost.

Depreciation Rates for Five-Year Assets
ACRS and MACRS Depreciation

Year	ACRS	MACRS
1	15%	20.0%
2	22	32.0
3	21	19.2
4	21	11.5
5	21	11.5
6		5.8
	100%	100.0%

U REVU Complete U REVU-3 on **page 710** to test your basic understanding of LO3.

REPAIRS, MAINTENANCE, ADDITIONS, IMPROVEMENTS, AND REPLACEMENTS TO PLANT AND EQUIPMENT

LO4 Account for repairs, maintenance, additions, improvements, and replacements to plant and equipment.

LEARNING KEY

Repairs Expense is debited for normal repair and maintenance costs that do not extend the life of the asset or improve its usefulness.

Plant and equipment require normal repairs and maintenance for proper operating efficiency and quality. Replacement of minor parts, lubrication, and cleaning are typical examples of normal repairs and maintenance. These expenditures are debited to Repairs Expense, as follows:

5		Repairs Expense		x x x xx		5
6		Cash (or Supplies Inventory)			x x x xx	6
7		Made repairs				7

Additions or **improvements** to plant and equipment are accounted for in the same way. As the word implies, an addition indicates the company has added a new asset. For example, the addition of a wing to a building or the installation of partitions, shelving, sprinkler systems, or air conditioning systems would be additions. When making an improvement, sometimes called a **betterment**, the company substitutes a better component of a major asset for the one currently used. For example, a concrete floor might be substituted for a wooden one. Both additions and improvements enhance the quality and efficiency of the building or equipment. These expenditures are debited to the building or equipment account and credited to either the cash or a liability account, as follows:

9		Building or Equipment		x x x xx		9
10		Cash (or Liability)			x x x xx	10
11		Made addition (or improvement)				11

Since these improvements will benefit future periods, depreciation will be recognized in future periods.

Sometimes, component parts of assets are replaced with similar components. For example, a business may replace the engine in a truck with a similar engine, or replace a wooden floor with a new wooden floor. These **replacements** extend the lives of the truck or building beyond the original estimate, but do not improve their usefulness or efficiency. This expenditure is debited to Accumulated Depreciation and credited to either the cash or a liability account, as follows:

14		Accum. Depr.—Building or Equipment	x x x xx		14
15		Cash (or Liability)		x x x xx	15
16		Made replacement			16

Accumulated Depreciation is debited because the depreciation taken on the original engine or floor has been recaptured by replacing it with a new one. The debit to Accumulated Depreciation increases the book value of the asset. Since the new engine or floor will benefit future periods, additional depreciation will be taken in future periods.

Notice that the book value of the asset is increased regardless of whether we debit the asset account or the accumulated depreciation account. This increase in book value leads to an increase in the amount of depreciation recognized in future periods. To illustrate, assume that a business owns the following two computers that were purchased on January 1, 20-1:

	Computer A	Computer B
Cost	$6,500	$6,500
Salvage value	500	500
Depreciable base	$6,000	$6,000
Estimated life	3 years	3 years
Depreciation method	Straight-line	Straight-line
Depreciation expense		
20-1	$2,000	$2,000

At the beginning of 20-2, a disk drive is replaced on Computer A and a new tape drive backup unit is added to Computer B. Let's assume that the disk drive and tape backup units cost $400 each. The entries for the replacement of the disk drive to Computer A, which extends its life by an additional two years beyond the original estimate but does not increase its usefulness, and the addition of a new tape backup unit to Computer B are shown in T account form, as follows:

Computer A

	Debit		Credit
	6,500		

Computer B

	Debit		Credit
	6,500		
Jan. 1, 20-2	400		
Bal.	6,900		

Accum. Depr.—Computer A

	Debit		Credit
		Dec. 31, 20-1	2,000
Jan. 1, 20-2	400		
		Bal.	1,600

Accum. Depr.—Computer B

	Debit		Credit
		Dec. 31, 20-1	2,000

Note that after recording the expenditures on January 1, 20-2, Computers A and B both have book values of $4,900, as follows:

	Computer A	Computer B
Asset account balance	$ 6,500	$ 6,900
Accumulated depreciation	(1,600)	(2,000)
Book value	$ 4,900	$ 4,900

Compute depreciation expense for 20-2 as follows:

1. Compute the new depreciable base by deducting the salvage value from the book value of the computers after recording the expenditures.
2. Divide the new depreciable base by the remaining useful life, four years for Computer A and two years for Computer B.

	Computer A	Computer B
Book value	$4,900	$4,900
Salvage value	(500)	(500)
New depreciable base	$4,400	$4,400
Remaining useful life	4 years	2 years
Depreciation expense	$1,100	$2,200

Thus, depreciation expense is $1,100 for Computer A in 20-2 through 20-5 and $2,200 for Computer B in 20-2 and 20-3.

LEARNING KEY

Expenditures on plant and equipment are accounted for in the following ways:

- If the expenditures simply maintain the asset's operating condition, debit the Repairs Expense account.
- If the expenditures increase the asset's usefulness or efficiency, debit the asset account.
- If the expenditures extend the asset's useful life beyond the original estimate, but do not increase its usefulness or efficiency, debit the accumulated depreciation account.

U REVU

Complete U REVU-4 on **page 710** to test your basic understanding of LO4

LO5 Account for the disposition of property, plant, and equipment.

DISPOSAL OF PLANT ASSETS

A plant asset can be disposed of in several ways.

1. It may be discarded or retired.
2. It may be sold.
3. It may be exchanged or traded in for another asset.

Regardless of the method of disposal, any gain or loss that occurred on the disposal must be determined. This is done by comparing the market and book values of the asset on the date of disposal. *To determine the book value on the date of disposal, an adjusting entry must be made to record depreciation from the end of the previous period to the disposal date.* Gains and losses are determined, as follows:

Determining Gains and Losses on Disposal of Assets

Gain = Market Value Greater than Book Value

Loss = Market Value Less than Book Value

Gains are similar to revenue and increase net income. Losses are similar to expenses and reduce net income. They are reported on the income statement under Other Revenues and Other Expenses.

DISCARDING OR RETIRING PLANT ASSETS

A plant asset may be discarded or retired at any time. If its book value on the disposal date is zero, no gain or loss will be realized. If it is greater than zero, the book value of the discarded asset will represent a loss.

To illustrate, assume that a printer with a cost of $800 and accumulated depreciation of $800 is discarded. Because the printer is fully depreciated, its book value is zero and no gain or loss results from this transaction. The removal of the asset and related accumulated depreciation is recorded as follows:

5			Accum. Depr.—Office Equipment		800 00		5
6			Office Equipment			800 00	6
7			Discarded printer				7

However, if at the time the printer is discarded, the accumulated depreciation is $720, the book value is $80 and a loss results. In this case, the discard of the asset and recognition of the loss are recorded as follows:

9			Accum. Depr.—Office Equipment		720 00		9
10			Loss on Discarded Office Equipment		80 00		10
11			Office Equipment			800 00	11
12			Discarded printer				12

SELLING PLANT ASSETS

Now let's assume that this same printer is sold for $80 at the time its book value is $80. This transaction is entered as follows:

5			Cash		80 00		5
6			Accum. Depr.—Office Equipment		720 00		6
7			Office Equipment			800 00	7
8			Sold printer				8

No gain or loss results from this transaction because the printer's selling price, or market value, is equal to its book value.

If the printer is sold for $120 at the time its book value is $80, there is a gain of $40. In this case, the journal entry is as follows:

LEARNING KEY

Gains and losses are always computed by comparing the market and book values of the asset being sold or exchanged.

		Description		Debit	Credit	
5		Cash		120 00		5
6		Accum. Depr.—Office Equipment		720 00		6
7		Office Equipment			800 00	7
8		Gain on Sale of Printer			40 00	8
9		Sold printer				9

If, instead, the printer is sold for $50, there is a loss of $30. This transaction is recorded as follows:

		Description		Debit	Credit	
5		Cash		50 00		5
6		Accum. Depr.—Office Equipment		720 00		6
7		Loss on Sale of Printer		30 00		7
8		Office Equipment			800 00	8
9		Sold printer				9

EXCHANGE OR TRADE-IN OF PLANT ASSETS

When one plant asset is exchanged for another, a gain or loss is recognized if the exchange is considered to have "commercial substance." The gain or loss is computed by comparing the difference between the market and book values of the asset given up. Some fairly complex transactions may lack commercial substance. In our discussions, however, we will assume that all exchanges have commercial substance.

Occasionally, generally accepted accounting principles are modified. Accounting for exchanges of plant assets is a good example. Our discussion here is based on a new pronouncement issued by the Financial Accounting Standards Board.

If one asset is traded in on the purchase of another asset, a **trade-in allowance** may be granted. This trade-in allowance may be greater than, less than, or equal to the book value of the asset traded. If you have ever traded in a car for a newer model, you know that the trade-in allowance frequently is not equal to the fair market value. Therefore, the fair market value of the asset traded in must be determined to calculate the gain or loss on the exchange. For simplicity, however, we will assume in our illustrations that the trade-in allowance is equal to the market value of the old asset being traded.

To illustrate accounting for the exchange of plant assets, let's assume that an old delivery truck is traded for a new one. Relevant information for this transaction is as follows:

Old Delivery Truck		New Delivery Truck	
Cost	$8,000	Market value (new truck)	$30,000
Accumulated depreciation	6,900	Trade-in allowance (old truck)	1,000
Book value	$1,100	Cash required	$29,000

Gain or Loss on Exchange

$ 1,100	Book value
(1,000)	Market value (trade-in allowance)
$ 100	Loss

If the new truck has a fair market value of $30,000 and the **trade-in value** of the old truck is $1,000, then $29,000 is due in cash ($30,000 – $1,000). As discussed earlier, the gain or loss on the exchange is determined by comparing the market value of the old asset ($1,000) with its book value ($1,100). In this case, there is a $100 loss. The transaction is entered as follows:

5		Delivery Equipment (new truck)	30 000 00		5
6		Accum. Depr.—Delivery Equipment	6 900 00		6
7		Loss on Exchange of Delivery Equipment	100 00		7
8		Delivery Equipment (old truck)		8 000 00	8
9		Cash		29 000 00	9
10		Purchased a new truck			10

This entry has the following effects on the accounting records:

1. The original cost ($8,000) and accumulated depreciation ($6,900) for the old truck are removed from the books.
2. Cash is credited to show the amount paid ($29,000).
3. The new delivery equipment is entered on the books at its market value ($30,000).
4. The loss on the exchange is recognized ($100).

Now let's assume the same event, except that the market value and trade-in allowance for the old truck is $1,500. As shown below, this means that only $28,500 in cash is required and there is a $400 gain on the exchange ($1,500 – $1,100 = $400).

Old Delivery Truck	
Cost	$8,000
Accumulated depreciation	6,900
Book value	$1,100

New Delivery Truck	
Market value (new truck)	$30,000
Trade-in allowance (old truck)	1,500
Cash required	$28,500

Gain or Loss on Exchange	
$ 1,500	Market value (trade-in allowance)
(1,100)	Book value
$ 400	Gain

The proper entry is as follows:

5		Delivery Equipment (new truck)	30 000 00		5
6		Accum. Depr.—Delivery Equipment	6 900 00		6
7		Delivery Equipment (old truck)		8 000 00	7
8		Cash		28 500 00	8
9		Gain on Exchange of Delivery Equipment		400 00	9
10		Purchased a new truck			10

For tax purposes, gains and losses are not recognized on the exchange of similar assets ("like-kind" exchanges).

This entry has the following effects on the accounting records:

1. The original cost ($8,000) and accumulated depreciation ($6,900) for the old truck are removed from the books.
2. Cash is credited to show the amount paid ($28,500).
3. The new delivery equipment is entered on the books at its market value ($30,000).
4. The gain on the exchange is recognized ($400).

A BROADER VIEW

MARC ROMANELLI/THE IMAGE BANK/GETTY IMAGES

Value? Which Value?

Determining the market value of an asset is not always easy. For example, if you have ever traded your car for a newer one, you probably learned that the trade-in allowance is often different from what the dealer would "pay" for the car and different from what you might sell it for by advertising in the newspaper. To test this concept, try it. Next time you are shopping for a car, ask the dealer two questions. First, ask the dealer what trade-in allowance he or she would offer on your car. Then, ask what he or she would accept for the new car if you paid cash. The difference between the "cash price" and the cash that you must pay with a trade-in offers a measure of what the dealer is paying you for your old car. (See illustration below.) This amount probably is not the same as the trade-in allowance offered by the dealer and may not be the same as the amount you could sell the car for by advertising in the newspaper. Of course, you need this information to make a good decision on whether to trade your car or sell it yourself.

Sticker price of new car	$20,000	
Trade-in allowance	5,000	Cash price for new
Cash that must be paid	$15,000	car $18,000

The value of your old car to the dealer is $3,000. Compare this with what you might sell it for by advertising in the newspaper.

The accounting described above is also applied when a business exchanges one type of plant asset for another. For example, a pizza business may exchange a delivery truck for a pizza oven from another pizza business. Gains and losses are recognized on this type of exchange in the same manner as described above.

PROPERTY, PLANT, AND EQUIPMENT RECORDS

If a business has many depreciable assets, a summary general ledger account will be kept for each major class of assets. For example, separate accounts might be kept for buildings, equipment, and furniture. Each summary account has a related accumulated depreciation account. Subsidiary records in the form of cards or computer files support these summary accounts. A typical property, plant, and equipment record is shown in Figure 18-2.

FIGURE 18-2 Property, Plant, and Equipment Record

PROPERTY, PLANT, AND EQUIPMENT RECORD

Description	Computer	Account	Office Equipment
Age when acquired	New	Estimated salvage value	$500
Estimated life	5 years	Rate of annual depreciation based on cost less salvage value	20%

COST			DEPRECIATION RECORD			
Date Purchased	Description	Amount	Year	Rate	Amount	Total To Date
20-2 Jan. 9	ABC DE/3 MODEL50	5,000 00	20-2	20%	900 00	900 00
	Serial No. 8403637		20-3	20%	900 00	1,800 00
	American Micro		20-4	20%	450 00	2,250 00
	Less estimated salvage value	500 00	20			
	Depreciable cost	4,500 00	20			
			20			
			20			
			20			
			20			
			20			
			20			
			20			
			20			
			20			
			20			

SOLD, EXCHANGED, OR DISCARDED				
Date	Explanation	Amount Realized	Book Value on Disposal Date	Gain (Loss)
20-4 July 1	Sold	3,000 00	2,750 00	250 00

FULLY DEPRECIATED PLANT ASSETS

A plant asset is fully depreciated when the book value is equal to the salvage value. When an asset is fully depreciated, no further depreciation should be entered. Since the rate of depreciation is based on its *estimated* useful life, an asset may still be used after it is fully depreciated. In this case, the cost of the asset and the accumulated depreciation are left in the accounts. When the asset eventually is disposed of, the cost and accumulated depreciation should be removed from the accounts, as illustrated in previous sections.

U REVU Complete U REVU-5 on **page 710** to test your basic understanding of LO5

NATURAL RESOURCES

LO6 Explain the nature of, purpose of, and accounting for depletion.

The consumption or exhaustion of *natural resources* is called *depletion*. The purpose of depletion is to allocate the cost of these assets to the periods in which they are consumed. Computing *cost depletion* is similar to computing depreciation using the units-of-production method. The cost of the property, less the estimated salvage or residual value, is divided by the estimated number of units that the property contains. The result is the depletion expense per unit. This amount times the number of units removed and sold during the period is the depletion expense for the period.

To illustrate, assume a coal mine is acquired at a cost of $1,000,000. No salvage value is expected. The estimated recoverable amount of coal in the mine is 1,000,000 tons. During the current year, 180,000 tons of coal are mined and sold. The computation of the amount of depletion expense is as follows:

$$\frac{\$1{,}000{,}000}{1{,}000{,}000 \text{ tons}} = \$1 \text{ per ton}$$

$$180{,}000 \text{ tons} \times \$1 \text{ per ton} = \$180{,}000 \text{ depletion expense}$$

An adjusting entry is made at the end of the accounting period to recognize the depletion expense. For the coal mine, this entry is as follows:

11			Depletion Expense—Coal Mine	180 0 0 0 00		11
12			Accum. Depletion—Coal Mine		180 0 0 0 00	12
13						13

The difference between the cost of the mine and the amount of the accumulated depletion is the undepleted cost of the property.

Cost of coal mine	$1,000,000
Less accumulated depletion	180,000
Undepleted cost of mine	$ 820,000

Depletion Expense is reported as an operating expense on the income statement. Accumulated Depletion is reported on the balance sheet as a deduction from the related asset account, with the difference identified as undepleted cost of the asset. As was explained for depreciation, this undepleted cost of the wasting asset simply represents the cost not yet charged to operations. It is not intended to reflect the market value of the asset.

U REVU

Complete U REVU-6 on **page 710** to test your basic understanding of LO6

INTANGIBLE ASSETS

LO7 Explain the nature of and accounting for intangible assets.

In an accounting sense, the term "intangible" has come to have a very restricted meaning. Intangible assets refers to a limited group of valuable legal or economic rights that a firm may acquire. All items classified as intangibles are considered to be long-term assets. Major examples of intangibles include patents, copyrights, and trademarks.

PATENTS

A **patent** is a grant by the federal government to an inventor giving the exclusive right to produce, use, and sell an invention for a period of 20 years. A firm may purchase a patent from a prior patent owner or may develop its own and acquire an original patent from the government. If purchased, the amount paid represents the cost of the patent.

If a company carries on regular research and development activities to develop its own patents, the costs of such activities are treated as current expenses. If the government grants a patent on an invention the company develops, the cost of this patent includes only the fees paid to the government and to patent attorneys for their services. This amount is debited to an asset account and amortized over the patent's useful life.

Since the life of a patent is specifically limited, any cost assigned to it is allocated over no more than the number of years that the patent right will exist. The greatest number of years would be 20 if the firm developed and applied for the patent. If the expected useful or economic life of a patent is less than its legal life, the cost should be allocated over the shorter period.

With the straight-line method, the amortization each year is determined by dividing the cost of the patent by its expected life. Let's assume that a patent with 13 years to run is purchased at a cost of $12,000, and that the buyer expects the useful life of the patent to be only 10 years. In that event, $1,200 ($12,000 ÷ 10 years) would be amortized as expense for each of the 10 years. The adjusting entry for the amortization at the end of each year is as follows:

7		Patent Amortization		1 2 0 0 00		7
8		Patents			1 2 0 0 00	8

Patent amortization is usually treated as an operating expense. Since patents are assets, their unamortized cost is reported on the balance sheet as an intangible long-term asset.

COPYRIGHTS

A **copyright** is similar in many respects to a patent. It consists of a federal grant of the exclusive right to the reproduction and sale of a literary, artistic, or musical composition. A copyright is granted for life plus 70 years after the death of the holder. The cost of obtaining the initial copyright on a composition is nominal. It is treated as an ordinary expense. However, if an existing copyright is purchased, the cost may be large enough and the expected future value sufficient to warrant charging the cost to an asset account entitled Copyrights.

It is a rare case in which a copyright would have an economic life as long as its legal life. In most cases, the cost of a copyright is written off in a very few years. The write-off can be on a straight-line basis or in the proportion of the actual sales of the copyrighted item during the period to the total expected sales of the item. The amount of the write-off for each period is debited to Copyright Amortization (or Copyright Expense) and credited to Copyrights. Copyright amortization is treated as an operating expense. Any unamortized portion of the cost of copyrights is reported on the balance sheet as an intangible long-term asset.

TRADEMARKS

The practice of using a **trademark** or registered trade name to identify a firm's merchandise is widespread. Such designations can be legally protected by registering them with the United States Patent Office. As long as the trademark or trade name is continuously used, the trademark is legally enforceable.

Research and development costs incurred to develop a trademark are expensed as incurred. However, costs incurred to register a trademark are debited to an asset account and amortized over the trademark's useful life. These costs include attorney and registration fees.

If a trademark is acquired by purchase, its cost is debited to an asset account entitled Trademarks. The future value of a trademark or a trade name is highly uncertain. Conservatism suggests that any cost incurred in purchasing a trademark should be written off within a few years.

The amount written off each period is debited to Trademark Amortization and credited to Trademarks. The amount written off is reported as an operating expense. Any unamortized portion of the cost of trademarks or trade names is reported on the balance sheet as an intangible long-term asset.

U REVU

Complete U REVU-7 on **page 710** to test your basic understanding of LO7

LEARNING OBJECTIVES Key Points to Remember

LO1 Determine the cost of property, plant, and equipment.	The cost to acquire an asset includes the purchase price and all costs incurred to prepare the asset for its intended use.
LO2 Explain the nature and purpose of depreciation.	The purpose of depreciation is to match a plant asset's cost with the revenues it helps to produce.
LO3 Compute depreciation using the straight-line, declining-balance, sum-of-the-years'-digits, and units-of-production methods.	Depreciation methods for financial reporting purposes are as follows: *Straight-Line Method* $\text{Annual Depreciation} = \dfrac{(\text{Cost} - \text{Salvage Value})}{\text{Estimated Useful Life}}$ *Declining-Balance Method* $\text{Annual Depreciation} = \text{Depreciation Rate} \times \text{Book Value at Beginning of Year}$ *Sum-of-the-Years'-Digits Method* $\text{Annual Depreciation} = (\text{Cost} - \text{Salvage Value}) \times \dfrac{\text{Remaining Useful Life}}{\text{Sum-of-the-Years'-Digits}}$ *Units-of-Production Method* $\text{Depreciation per Unit} = \dfrac{(\text{Cost} - \text{Salvage Value})}{\text{Estimated Useful Life in Units}}$ $\text{Annual Depreciation} = \text{Depreciation per Unit} \times \text{Number of Units Produced or Consumed this Year}$

LO4 Account for repairs, maintenance, additions, improvements, and replacements to plant and equipment.	The entry for additions and improvements that increase the usefulness of equipment would be as follows:
	Building or Equipment xxx
	    Cash or Liability account xxx
	The entry for replacements that extend the life of the asset, but do not improve usefulness or efficiency, would be as follows:
	Accumulated Depreciation—Building or Equipment xxx
	    Cash or Liability account xxx
	To compute straight-line depreciation expense for the year following an addition, an improvement, or a replacement, use the following steps:
	1. Compute the new depreciable base by deducting the salvage value from the book value of the asset following the expenditures.
	2. Divide the new depreciable base by the remaining useful life.

LEARNING OBJECTIVES	Key Points to Remember
LO5 Account for the disposition of property, plant, and equipment.	Disposal of Plant Assets When an asset is discarded: 1. Remove cost and accumulated depreciation from accounting records. 2. If book value is greater than zero, recognize loss. When an asset is sold: 1. Remove cost and accumulated depreciation from accounting records. 2. Debit Cash for amount received. 3. Recognize gain or loss (market value – book value of asset sold). When an asset is traded in for another similar asset: 1. Debit new asset for its market value. 2. Remove cost and accumulated depreciation for asset traded in from accounting records. 3. Credit Cash for amount paid. 4. Record gain or loss on exchange (market value – book value of asset traded in).
LO6 Explain the nature of, purpose of, and accounting for depletion.	The consumption or exhaustion of natural resources is called *depletion*. The purpose of accounting for depletion is to allocate the cost of these assets to the periods in which they are consumed.
LO7 Explain the nature of and accounting for intangible assets.	The term *intangible assets* is used to refer to a limited group of valuable legal or economic rights (patent, copyright, and trademark) that a firm may acquire. Since the life of an intangible asset is limited, any cost assigned to it is allocated over no more than the number of years that the asset will exist.

DEMONSTRATION PROBLEM

Stillman Company purchased a new machine at the start of its current year at a cost of $37,500. The machine is expected to serve for five years and to have a salvage value of $3,000. Ronald L. Stillman, the chief executive officer, has asked for information as to the effects of alternative depreciation methods.

REQUIRED

1. Calculate the annual depreciation expense for each of the five years of expected life of the machine, the accumulated depreciation at the end of each year, and the book value at the end of each year using the following methods:

(continued)

(a) Straight-line
(b) Double-declining-balance
(c) Sum-of-the-years'-digits

2. Assume that in years 2 and 4 of the five-year life of this machine, revenues are $45,000 and costs and expenses other than depreciation are $25,000. Calculate the net income for years 2 and 4 using the same three depreciation methods used in part (1).

3. Assume that Stillman chose the double-declining-balance method of depreciation for this machine. Then, in the first week of year 5, the machine was exchanged (traded in) for similar equipment costing $45,000. The market value and trade-in allowance on the old machine was $4,000 and cash was paid for the balance. Prepare the necessary journal entry to record this exchange.

Solution 1.

	Year	Annual Depreciation Expense	Accumulated Depreciation End of Year	Book Value End of Year
a.	1	$ 6,900	$ 6,900	$30,600
	2	6,900	13,800	23,700
	3	6,900	20,700	16,800
	4	6,900	27,600	9,900
	5	6,900	34,500	3,000
b.	1	$15,000	$15,000	$22,500
	2	9,000	24,000	13,500
	3	5,400	29,400	8,100
	4	3,240	32,640	4,860
	5	1,860*	34,500	3,000
c.	1	$11,500	$11,500	$26,000
	2	9,200	20,700	16,800
	3	6,900	27,600	9,900
	4	4,600	32,200	5,300
	5	2,300	34,500	3,000

*The machine is not depreciated below its estimated salvage value of $3,000.

2.

Year 2	(a) Straight-Line Method	(b) Double-Declining-Balance Method	(c) Sum-of-the-Years'-Digits Method
Revenue	$45,000	$45,000	$45,000
Costs and expenses other than depreciation	25,000	25,000	25,000
Depreciation	6,900	9,000	9,200
Net income	$13,100	$11,000	$10,800

Year 4	(a) Straight-Line Method	(b) Double-Declining-Balance Method	(c) Sum-of-the-Years'-Digits Method
Revenue	$45,000	$45,000	$45,000
Costs and expenses other than depreciation	25,000	25,000	25,000
Depreciation	6,900	3,240	4,600
Net income	$13,100	$16,760	$15,400

3.

5			Equipment (new machine)	45 000 00		5
6			Accum. Depr.—Equipment	32 640 00		6
7			Loss on Exchange of Equipment	8 60 00		7
8			Equipment (old machine)		37 500 00	8
9			Cash		41 000 00	9
10			Purchased a new machine			10

Old Equipment		New Equipment	
Cost of old equipment	$37,500	Market value (new)	$45,000
Accumulated depreciation	32,640	Trade-in allowance (old)	4,000
Book value	$ 4,860	Cash required	$41,000
Book value	$ 4,860		
Trade-in (market value)	(4,000)		
Loss	$ 860		

KEY TERMS

Accelerated Cost Recovery System (ACRS) (693) A method of depreciation used for federal income tax purposes for plant assets acquired between 1981 and 1986.

accelerated depreciation methods (689) Depreciation methods that provide for a higher depreciation charge in the first year of an asset's life and gradually decreasing charges in subsequent years.

addition (694) The company has added a new asset. Examples include the addition of a wing to a building and the installation of shelving, sprinklers, and air conditioning.

amortization (686) The portion of an intangible asset's cost that is recognized as expense.

betterments (694) See improvements.

book value (688) The undepreciated cost of the asset (cost – accumulated depreciation).

cash equivalent price (687) The amount of cash that could have been paid for the asset on the date of purchase.

copyright (703) A grant by the federal government of the exclusive right to the reproduction and sale of a literary, artistic, or musical composition.

cost (688) The sum of all amounts spent to acquire an asset and prepare it for its intended use.

declining-balance method (689) An accelerated depreciation method in which the book value is multiplied by a fixed rate. A common rate is double the straight-line rate (the double-declining-balance method).

depletion (686) The consumption or exhaustion of natural resources.

depreciable cost (base) (688) The original cost less salvage (or scrap) value.

depreciation (686) The portion of a plant asset's cost that is recognized as expense.

double-declining-balance method (689) An accelerated depreciation method in which the book value is multiplied by double the straight-line rate.

fixed assets (686) See property, plant, and equipment.

functional depreciation (688) The loss of usefulness because of inadequacy or obsolescence.

improvements (694) The company substitutes a better component of a plant asset for the existing one, such as a marble floor for a wooden floor. Also known as betterments.

intangible assets (686) Long-term assets that have no physical substance (patents, copyrights, and trademarks).

long-term assets (686) Assets that are expected to provide benefits for a number of accounting periods.

Modified Accelerated Cost Recovery System (MACRS) (693) A method of depreciation used for federal income tax purposes for plant assets acquired after 1986.

patent (702) A grant by the federal government to an inventor giving the exclusive right to produce, use, and sell an invention for a period of 20 years.

physical depreciation (688) The loss of usefulness because of deterioration from age and wear.

plant assets (686) See property, plant, and equipment.

property, plant, and equipment (686) Long-term tangible assets that are used in the operations of the business. Also called plant assets or fixed assets.

replacements (695) A component of a plant asset is replaced with a similar component. That is, a wooden floor is replaced with a new wooden floor. These replacements extend the lives of the assets beyond the original estimates, but do not improve their usefulness or efficiency.

salvage value (687) The estimated market value of an asset on its expected disposal date.

scrap value (688) See salvage value.

straight-line method (689) A depreciation method in which the depreciable cost of an asset is allocated equally over the years of the asset's useful life.

sum-of-the-years'-digits method (691) A depreciation method in which the annual depreciation is determined by multiplying the depreciable cost by a schedule of fractions.

tangible assets (686) Long-term assets that have physical substance.

trade-in allowance (698) An allowance granted when one asset is traded in on the purchase of another similar asset.

trade-in value (699) See trade-in allowance.

trademark (703) A registered trade name or symbol that identifies a firm's merchandise.

units-of-production method (693) A depreciation method in which depreciation is based on the extent to which the asset was used during the year.

useful life (688) The amount of service expected to be obtained from an asset.

wasting assets (686) Assets whose physical substance consists of natural resources that are consumed in the operation of the business.

SELF-STUDY QUESTIONS AND EXERCISES

True/False Questions

1. LO1 All long-term assets wear out gradually or are gradually used up entirely.
2. LO1 Intangible assets are depreciated; plant assets are amortized.
3. LO2 Depreciation is a process of asset valuation; that is, book value is the same as true asset value.
4. LO3 The straight-line method of depreciation allocates the cost of an asset more rapidly than the sum-of-the-years'-digits method.
5. LO3 The units-of-production method of depreciation allocates the cost of an asset equally over each year of the useful life.

Multiple Choice Questions

1. LO3 Using the sum-of-the-years'-digits method, the denominator for a five-year useful life would be

   (a) 5. (c) 12.
   (b) 7. (d) 15.

2. LO5 A machine that cost $100 and had accumulated depreciation of $80 was sold for $20.

   (a) There was a $20 gain. (c) There was no gain or loss.
   (b) There was a $20 loss. (d) There was a $60 loss.

3. LO5 A computer was sold on April 1, 20-2, for $575. Its cost was $3,000, and accumulated depreciation as of December 31, 20-1, was $2,100 ($700 a year).

   (a) There was a gain of $150. (c) There was a gain of $325.
   (b) There was a loss of $150. (d) There was a loss of $325.

4. LO6 Cost depletion of natural resources is most like which of these depreciation methods?

   (a) straight-line (c) declining-balance
   (b) units-of-production (d) sum-of-the-years'-digits

5. LO7 Which of these is granted for life plus 70 years after the death of the holder?

   (a) patent (c) copyright
   (b) mineral rights (d) trademark

U REVU Exercises

1. LO1 The following costs were incurred to purchase a machine:

Purchase price	$50,000
Transportation costs	800
Insurance during transportation	100
Interest on loan during first month of asset's use	250

   Determine the acquisition cost.

2. LO2 The following information is provided for a building:

Cost	$500,000
Depreciation expense per year	25,000
Accumulated depreciation	100,000
Current market value	600,000

   How would information about the above building be reported on the balance sheet?

3. LO3 A machine costing $350,000 has a salvage value of $5,000 and an estimated life of three years. Prepare depreciation schedules reporting the depreciation expense, accumulated depreciation, and book value of the machine for each year under the double-declining-balance and sum-of-the-years'-digits methods. For the double-declining-balance method, round the depreciation rate to two decimal places.

4. LO4 Grandorf Company replaced the engine in a truck for $8,000 and expects the new engine will extend the life of the truck two years beyond the original estimated life. Related information is provided below.

Cost of truck	$65,000
Salvage value	5,000
Original estimated life	6 years

The truck was purchased on January 1, 20-1. The engine was replaced on January 1, 20-6. Using straight-line depreciation, compute depreciation expense for 20-6.

5. LO5 Prepare journal entries for the following transactions:

   a. A machine with a cost of $10,000 and accumulated depreciation of $8,000 was sold for $2,500.
   b. A machine with a cost of $10,000 and accumulated depreciation of $8,000 was traded for a new machine with a market value of $12,000. Cash of $9,500 was also paid.

6. LO6 Popilarz Mining acquired a coal mine at a cost of $4,000,000 with the expectation that 1,250,000 tons of coal would be mined over its lifetime. The estimated salvage value of the land is $250,000, and 100,000 tons of coal are mined in the first year. Compute the depletion expense for the first year.

7. LO7 Todd Company purchased a patent with a remaining life of 10 years for $100,000 cash. Prepare the journal entry for the acquisition and the first year's amortization. Assume straight-line amortization.

The answers to the Self-Study Questions and Exercises are at the end of the chapter (pages 721–723).

APPLYING YOUR KNOWLEDGE

REVIEW QUESTIONS

LO1 1. What costs should be included when measuring the total cost to acquire a long-term asset?

LO1 2. How should the cost of such activities as planting trees and shrubs be entered?

LO2 3. What are the two major types of depreciation?

LO3 4. What is meant by the "depreciable cost" of a plant asset?

LO3 5. What are the four most commonly used methods of calculating depreciation for financial reporting purposes? How do they differ in their application?

LO3 6. Which depreciation method provides the fastest write-off of an asset?

LO3 7. Explain how the depreciation method selected affects the balance sheet and income statement.

LO3 8. For assets acquired after 1986, what depreciation methods are allowed for federal income tax purposes?

LO4 9. How should additions or improvements representing an increase in the usefulness of plant assets be entered?

LO4 10. Explain what is meant by the "replacement" of a component of a plant asset.

LO5 11. What are the three major ways of disposing of a plant asset?

LO5 12. For what time interval should depreciation expense be entered on the date of an asset's disposal?

LO5 13. When a plant asset is sold, what must be known about the asset in order to determine the proper amount of gain or loss on the sale?

LO5 14. What details about a particular asset are provided by a property, plant, and equipment record?

LO6 15. What is the purpose of depletion?

LO3/6 16. Which depreciation method is similar to the method used to compute depletion expense?

LO7 17. Over what period of time should the cost of a patent be allocated if its economic life is expected to be less than its legal life?

LO7 18. How should the unamortized portion of the cost of a copyright be reported on the balance sheet?

LO7 19. How does conservatism suggest that the cost of a trademark or trade name be accounted for subsequent to acquisition?

SERIES A EXERCISES

E 18-1A **(LO1)**

COST OF PROPERTY, PLANT, AND EQUIPMENT Consider the following list of expenditures and indicate whether each would be debited to Land, Building, or Equipment as part of the cost to purchase these assets. Place a check mark in the appropriate column.

	Yes	No
Debit Land?		
Real estate fees	______	______
Cost to remove old buildings	______	______
Cost to pave parking areas	______	______
Tax assessment for streets	______	______
Debit Building?		
Cost of land on which the building is located	______	______
Legal fees related to purchase	______	______
Taxes related to purchase	______	______
Realtor fees	______	______
Interest on construction loan while building was under construction	______	______
Debit Equipment?		
Transportation charges	______	______
Insurance while in transit	______	______
Installation costs	______	______
Interest on loan to buy equipment	______	______

E 18-2A (LO3)
✓ Year 1: SL, $3,000; DDB, $6,750; SYD, $5,333.33

STRAIGHT-LINE, DECLINING-BALANCE, AND SUM-OF-THE-YEARS'-DIGITS METHODS A light truck is purchased on January 1 at a cost of $27,000. It is expected to serve for eight years and have a salvage value of $3,000. Calculate the depreciation expense for the first and third years of the truck's life using the following methods:

1. Straight-line
2. Double-declining-balance (round to two decimal places)
3. Sum-of-the-years'-digits (round to two decimal places)

E 18-3A (LO3)
✓ Depr. for year 1: $5,000

UNITS-OF-PRODUCTION METHOD The truck purchased in Exercise 18-2A is expected to be used for 96,000 miles over its eight-year useful life. Using the units-of-production method, calculate the depreciation expense for the first and third years of use if the truck is driven 20,000 miles in year 1 and 18,000 miles in year 3.

E 18-4A (LO4)

JOURNAL ENTRIES: REPAIRS, MAINTENANCE, ADDITIONS, IMPROVEMENTS, AND REPLACEMENTS Prepare the entries for the following transactions for Stepanski's Food Mart using a general journal:

1. Replaced the checkout computer in Checkout Stand A for $2,000 cash. The computer is part of the Checkout Stand. The replacement is expected to extend the life of the checkout stand.
2. Added a laser scanner to Checkout Stand B for $3,000 cash to decrease checkout time.
3. Cleaned scanner window on Checkout Stand A for $20 cash (normal maintenance).

E 18-5A (LO5)
✓ 1(a): Loss, $500; 1(b): No gain/loss; 1(c): Gain, $50; 2(a): Loss, $2,000; 2(b): Gain, $3,000

JOURNAL ENTRIES: DISPOSITION OF PLANT ASSETS Prepare the entries for the following transactions using a general journal:

1. Discarding an asset.
   - (a) On January 4, shelving units, which had a cost of $6,400 and had accumulated depreciation of $5,900, were discarded.
   - (b) On June 15, a hand cart, which had a cost of $1,500 and had accumulated depreciation of $1,350, was sold for $150.
   - (c) On October 1, a copy machine, which had a cost of $7,200 and had accumulated depreciation of $6,800, was sold for $450.
2. Exchange or trade-in of assets.
   - (a) On December 31, a drill press, which had a cost of $60,000 and had accumulated depreciation of $48,000, was traded in for a new drill press with a fair market value of $75,000. The old drill press and $65,000 in cash were given for the new drill press.
   - (b) On December 31, the old drill press in (a) and $60,000 in cash were given for the new drill press.

E 18-6A (LO6)
✓ 1. Depletion Exp.: $25,000; 2. Depletion Exp.: $500,000;

DEPLETION Prepare the following entries using a general journal:

1. A coal mine was acquired at a cost of $1,500,000 and estimated to contain 6,000,000 tons of ore. During the year, 100,000 tons were mined and sold. Prepare the journal entry for the year's depletion expense.
2. A silver mine was acquired at a cost of $3,000,000 and estimated to contain 750,000 tons of ore. During the year, 125,000 tons were mined and sold. Prepare the journal entry for the year's depletion expense.

SERIES A PROBLEMS

P 18-7A (LO3)
✓ Depr. exp. for year 8: (a) $7,000.00; (b) $1,968.89; (c) $1,555.56

STRAIGHT-LINE, DECLINING-BALANCE, AND SUM-OF-THE-YEARS'-DIGITS METHODS A machine is purchased January 1 at a cost of $59,000. It is expected to serve for eight years and have a salvage value of $3,000.

REQUIRED

Prepare a schedule showing depreciation for each year and the book value at the end of each year using the following methods:

(a) Straight-line
(b) Double-declining-balance (round to two decimal places)
(c) Sum-of-the-years'-digits (round to two decimal places)

P 18-8A (LO3)
✓ Depr. year 1: $4,300

UNITS-OF-PRODUCTION METHOD A machine is purchased January 1 at a cost of $59,000. It is expected to produce 130,000 units and have a salvage value of $3,000 at the end of its useful life.

Units produced are as follows:

Year 1	10,000
Year 2	8,000
Year 3	12,000
Year 4	16,000
Year 5	11,000

REQUIRED

Prepare a schedule showing depreciation for each year and the undepreciated cost at the end of each year using the units-of-production method (round calculations to two decimal places).

P 18-9A (LO3)
✓ 1. Depr. exp.: $8,075

CALCULATING AND JOURNALIZING DEPRECIATION Equipment records for Johnson Machine Co. for the year follow. Johnson Machine uses the straight-line method of depreciation. In the case of assets acquired by the fifteenth day of the month, depreciation should be computed for the entire month. In the case of assets acquired after the fifteenth day of the month, no depreciation should be considered for the month in which the asset was acquired.

Asset	Purchase Price	Useful Life	Salvage Value	Date Purchased
Truck #1	$20,000	8 years	$4,000	January 1
Truck #2	24,000	8	4,000	April 10
Tractor #1	18,000	5	3,000	May 1
Tractor #2	14,000	6	2,000	June 18
Forklift	40,000	10	4,000	September 1

REQUIRED

1. Calculate the depreciation expense for Johnson Machine as of December 31, 20--.
2. Prepare the entry for depreciation expense using a general journal.

P 18-10A (LO4)
✓1: Depr. exp. is $8,000 for each; 2: Sim. A—Dr. Accum. Depr., $3,000; 3: Sim. A—$5,900.00 per year

IMPACT OF IMPROVEMENTS AND REPLACEMENTS ON THE CALCULATION OF DEPRECIATION On January 1, 20-1, two flight simulators were purchased by a space camp for $68,000 each with a salvage value of $4,000 each and estimated useful lives of eight years. On January 1, 20-2, the hydraulic system for Simulator A was

(continued)

replaced for $3,000 cash and an updated computer for more advanced students was installed in Simulator B for $10,000 cash. The hydraulic system is expected to extend the life of Simulator A three years beyond the original estimate.

REQUIRED

1. Using the straight-line method, prepare general journal entries for depreciation on December 31, 20-1, for Simulators A and B.
2. Enter the transactions for January 20-2 in a general journal.
3. Assuming no other additions, improvements, or replacements, calculate the depreciation expense for each simulator for 20-2 through 20-8.

P 18-11A (LO5)
✓ Jan. 8, Loss: $200; Feb. 1, Gain, $200

DISPOSITION OF ASSETS: JOURNALIZING Mitchell Parts Co. had the following plant asset transactions during the year:

1. Assets discarded or sold:

Jan. 1 Motor #12, which had a cost of $2,800 and accumulated depreciation of $2,800, was discarded.

8 Motor #8, which had a cost of $4,400 and accumulated depreciation of $4,000, was sold for $200.

14 Motor #16, which had a cost of $5,600 and accumulated depreciation of $5,400, was sold for $450.

2. Assets exchanged or traded in:

Feb. 1 Motor #6, which had a cost of $6,000 and accumulated depreciation of $4,800, was traded in for a new motor (#22) with a fair market value of $7,000. The old motor and $5,600 in cash were given for the new motor.

9 Motor #9, which had a cost of $5,500 and accumulated depreciation of $5,000, was traded in for a new motor (#23) with a fair market value of $6,500. The old motor and $6,200 in cash were given for the new motor.

REQUIRED
Prepare general journal entries for the transactions.

P 18-12A (LO6)
✓ 1. Depletion exp. for year 1: $100,000

DEPLETION: CALCULATING AND JOURNALIZING Mineral Works Co. acquired a salt mine at a cost of $1,700,000. The estimated number of units available for production from the mine is 3,400,000 tons.

(a) During the first year, 200,000 tons are mined and sold.
(b) During the second year, 600,000 tons are mined and sold.

REQUIRED

1. Calculate the amount of depletion expense for both years.
2. Prepare general journal entries for depletion expense.

P 18-13A (LO7)
✓ 1. Patent amortization: $1,000

INTANGIBLE LONG-TERM ASSETS Track Town Co. had the following transactions involving intangible assets:

Jan. 1 Purchased a patent for leather soles for $10,000 and estimated its useful life to be 10 years.

Apr. 1 Purchased a copyright for a design for $15,000 with a life left on the copyright of 25 years. The estimated remaining (economic) life of the copyright is five years.

July 1 Purchased a trademark at a cost of $50,000. The estimated economic life of the trademark is 25 years. However, conservatism suggests it should be written off in five years.

REQUIRED

1. Using the straight-line method, calculate the amortization of the patent, copyright, and trademark.
2. Prepare general journal entries to record the end-of-year amortizations.

SERIES B EXERCISES

E 18-1B (LO1)
✓ Cost of asset: (a) $61,400; (b) $41,900; (c) $108,400

COST OF PROPERTY, PLANT, AND EQUIPMENT Lam Company purchased the following long-term assets. Determine the purchase cost of each asset.

(a) Ten computers:	
Purchase price	$60,000
Transportation costs	500
Insurance during transportation	100
Installation	800
Interest on loan to purchase computers	3,000
(b) Three acres of land:	
Purchase price	$30,000
Grading of land in preparation to build	10,000
Planting of trees around border	5,000
Fence on southern border	3,000
Tax assessment for sewer	1,000
Legal fees related to purchase	900
(c) Five-thousand-square-foot building:	
Purchase price	$102,000
Real estate fees	5,000
Land on which building is located	10,000
Legal fees related to purchase	600
Taxes related to purchase	800
Interest on mortgage to buy building	300

E 18-2B (LO3)
✓ Year 1: SL: $3,600; DDB: $7,600; SYD: $6,000

STRAIGHT-LINE, DECLINING-BALANCE, AND SUM-OF-THE-YEARS'-DIGITS METHODS A light truck is purchased on January 1 at a cost of $19,000. It is expected to serve for five years and have a salvage value of $1,000. Calculate the depreciation expense for the first and third years of the truck's life using the following methods:

1. Straight-line
2. Double-declining-balance
3. Sum-of-the-years'-digits

E 18-3B (LO3)
✓ Depr. for year 1: $3,240

UNITS-OF-PRODUCTION METHOD The truck purchased in Exercise 18-2B is expected to be used for 100,000 miles over its five-year useful life. Using the units-of-production method, calculate the depreciation expense for the first and third years of use if the truck is driven 18,000 miles in year 1 and 22,000 miles in year 3.

E 18-4B (LO4)

JOURNAL ENTRIES: REPAIRS, MAINTENANCE, ADDITIONS, IMPROVEMENTS, AND REPLACEMENTS Enter the following transactions for Larry's Lawn Service in a general journal:

1. Added a second mower deck to Tractor A for $550 cash to decrease mowing time.
2. Replaced the engine in Mower D for $200 cash. The replacement is expected to extend the life of the mower.
3. Lubricated engine of Tractor A for $25 cash (normal maintenance).

E 18-5B (LO5)

✓ 1(a): Loss, $300; 1(b): No gain/loss; 1(c): Gain, $100; 2(a): Gain, $2,500; 2(b): Loss, $2,500;

JOURNAL ENTRIES: DISPOSITION OF PLANT ASSETS Prepare the entries for the following transactions using a general journal:

1. Discarding an asset.
   (a) On January 4, shelving units, which had a cost of $7,200 and accumulated depreciation of $6,900, were discarded.
   (b) On June 15, a hand cart, which had a cost of $2,500 and accumulated depreciation of $2,250, was sold for $250.
   (c) On October 1, a copy machine, which had a cost of $5,200 and accumulated depreciation of $4,800, was sold for $500.
2. Exchange or trade-in of assets.
   (a) On December 31, a drill press, which had a cost of $50,000 and accumulated depreciation of $37,500, was traded in for a new drill press with a fair market value of $55,000. The old drill press and $40,000 in cash were given for the new drill press.
   (b) On December 31, the old drill press in (a) and $45,000 in cash were given for the new drill press.

E 18-6B (LO6)

✓ 1. Depletion Exp.: $77,000; 2. Depletion Exp.: $300,000

DEPLETION Prepare the following entries using a general journal:

1. A coal mine was acquired at a cost of $1,750,000 and estimated to contain 2,500,000 tons of ore. During the year, 110,000 tons were mined and sold. Prepare the journal entry for the year's depletion expense.
2. A silver mine was acquired at a cost of $2,000,000 and estimated to contain 500,000 tons of ore. During the year, 75,000 tons were mined and sold. Prepare the journal entry for the year's depletion expense.

SERIES B PROBLEMS

P 18-7B (LO3)

✓ Depr. exp. for year 1: (a) $9,000; (b) $19,250; (c) $16,000

STRAIGHT-LINE, DECLINING-BALANCE, AND SUM-OF-THE-YEARS'-DIGITS METHODS A machine is purchased January 1 at a cost of $77,000. It is expected to serve for eight years and have a salvage value of $5,000.

REQUIRED

Prepare a schedule showing depreciation for each year and the book value at the end of each year using the following methods:

(a) Straight-line
(b) Double-declining-balance (round to two decimal places)
(c) Sum-of-the-years'-digits (round to two decimal places)

P 18-8B (LO3)
✓ Depr. for year 1: $9,000

UNITS-OF-PRODUCTION METHOD A machine is purchased January 1 at a cost of $58,000. It is expected to produce 110,000 units and have a salvage value of $3,000 at the end of its useful life.

Units produced are as follows:

Year 1	18,000
Year 2	16,000
Year 3	20,000
Year 4	16,000
Year 5	12,000

REQUIRED

Prepare a schedule showing depreciation for each year and the undepreciated cost at the end of each year using the units-of-production method.

P 18-9B (LO3)
✓ Depr. exp.: $10,250

KA KLOOSTER & ALLEN

CALCULATING AND JOURNALIZING DEPRECIATION Equipment records for Byerly Construction Co. for the year follow. Byerly Construction uses the straight-line method of depreciation. In the case of assets acquired by the fifteenth day of the month, depreciation should be computed for the entire month. In the case of assets acquired after the fifteenth day of the month, no depreciation should be considered for the month in which the asset was acquired.

Asset	Purchase Price	Useful Life	Salvage Value	Date Purchased
Truck #1	$22,000	7 years	$1,000	January 17
Truck #2	24,000	5	4,000	March 23
Molding #1	18,000	5	3,000	May 14
Molding #2	24,000	6	6,000	July 1
Forklift	35,000	8	3,000	September 19

REQUIRED

1. Calculate the depreciation expense for Byerly Construction as of December 31, 20--.
2. Prepare the entry for depreciation expense using a general journal.

P 18-10B (LO4)
✓ 1: Depr. exp. is $600 each;
2: J–H A—Dr. Asset for $800;
3: J–H A—$866.67 per year

IMPACT OF IMPROVEMENTS AND REPLACEMENTS ON THE CALCULATION OF DEPRECIATION On January 1, 20-1, Dan's Demolition purchased two jackhammers for $2,500 each with a salvage value of $100 each and estimated useful lives of four years. On January 1, 20-2, a stronger blade to improve performance was installed in Jackhammer A for $800 cash and the compressor was replaced in Jackhammer B for $200 cash. The compressor is expected to extend the life of Jackhammer B one year beyond the original estimate.

REQUIRED

1. Using the straight-line method, prepare general journal entries for depreciation on December 31, 20-1, for Jackhammers A and B.
2. Enter the transactions for January 20-2 in a general journal.
3. Assuming no other additions, improvements, or replacements, calculate the depreciation expense for each jackhammer for 20-2 through 20-4.

P 18-11B (LO5)
✓ Jan. 8, Loss: $200; Feb. 1, Gain: $300

DISPOSITION OF ASSETS: JOURNALIZING Mayer Delivery Co. had the following plant asset transactions during the year:

1. Assets discarded or sold:

Jan. 1 Van #11, which had a cost of $8,800 and accumulated depreciation of $8,800, was discarded.

8 Van #7, which had a cost of $9,400 and accumulated depreciation of $9,000, was sold for $200.

14 Van #13, which had a cost of $7,600 and accumulated depreciation of $7,400, was sold for $250.

2. Assets exchanged or traded in:

Feb. 1 Van #8, which had a cost of $11,000 and accumulated depreciation of $8,800, was traded in for a new van (#20) with a fair market value of $13,000. The old van and $10,500 in cash were given for the new van.

9 Van #3, which had a cost of $7,500 and accumulated depreciation of $7,000, was traded in for a new van (#21) with a fair market value of $9,500. The old van and $9,200 in cash were given for the new van.

REQUIRED

Prepare general journal entries for the transactions.

P 18-12B (LO6)
✓ 1. Depletion exp. for year 1: $160,000

DEPLETION: CALCULATING AND JOURNALIZING Mining Works Co. acquired a copper mine at a cost of $1,200,000. The estimated number of units available for production from the mine is 3,000,000 tons.

(a) During the first year, 400,000 tons are mined and sold.
(b) During the second year, 700,000 tons are mined and sold.

REQUIRED

1. Calculate the amount of depletion expense for both years.
2. Prepare general journal entries for depletion expense.

P 18-13B (LO7)
✓ 1. Patent amortization: $1,000

INTANGIBLE LONG-TERM ASSETS B. J. Bakery had the following transactions involving intangible assets:

Jan. 1 Purchased a patent for a new pastry for $10,000 and estimated its useful life to be 10 years.

Apr. 1 Purchased a copyright for a cookie cutter design for $5,000 with a life left on the copyright of 15 years. Estimated that the future remaining (economic) life of the copyright is five years.

July 1 Purchased a trademark at a cost of $40,000. The estimated economic life on the trademark is 20 years. However, conservatism suggests it should be written off in five years.

REQUIRED

1. Using the straight-line method, calculate the amortization of the patent, copyright, and trademark.
2. Prepare journal entries to record the end-of-year amortizations using a general journal.

MANAGING YOUR WRITING

A friend owns and operates her own business and is concerned about completing her tax return. She owns several assets and uses straight-line depreciation for business purposes. She intended to use straight-line depreciation for tax purposes also, but recently heard about another method called MACRS. She has asked for your advice on which method to use on her tax return. Write a brief memo recommending a depreciation method and explaining why you believe it should be used.

ETHICS CASE

Creative Solutions purchased a patent from Russell Lazarus, an inventor. At the time of the purchase, the patent had two years remaining. The president of Creative Solutions decided to have the accountant amortize the cost of the patent, $200,000, over 10 years rather than two years. His reasoning was that the $200,000 has already been spent and stockholders might ask a lot of questions about a $100,000 expense showing up on the income statement but probably wouldn't pay much attention to a $20,000 expense.

1. What is Creative Solutions' ethical responsibility to the company's stockholders?
2. According to GAAP, how should the amortization of patents be treated?
3. Write a short paragraph explaining similarities and differences between plant assets and intangible assets.
4. In groups of two or three, determine an appropriate method of depreciation, depletion, or amortization of the following assets for financial reporting purposes: (a) a car used as a taxi, (b) a parcel of land that will be resold in a few years, (c) a computer that has a very short life and loses most of its value in the first year or two, (d) an ore mine, (e) research and development costs incurred to develop a trademark.

MASTERY PROBLEM

✓ 1(c). Loss on exchange: $4,750; 2(c). Gain: $3,500

On April 1, 20-3, Kwik Kopy Printing purchased a copy machine for $50,000. The estimated life of the machine is five years, and it has an estimated salvage value of $5,000. The machine was used until July 1, 20-6.

REQUIRED

1. Assume that Kwik Kopy uses straight-line depreciation and prepare the following entries:
   (a) Adjusting entries for depreciation on December 31 of 20-3 through 20-5.
   (b) Adjusting entry for depreciation on June 30, 20-6, just prior to trading in the asset.
   (c) On July 1, 20-6, the copy machine was traded in for a new copy machine. The market value of the new machine is $38,000. Kwik Kopy must trade in the old copy machine and pay $22,000 for the new machine.
2. Assume that Kwik Kopy uses sum-of-the-years'-digits depreciation and prepare the following entries:
   (a) Adjusting entries for depreciation on December 31, 20-3 through 20-5.

(continued)

(b) Adjusting entry for depreciation on June 30, 20-6, just prior to trading in the asset.

(c) On July 1, 20-6, the copy machine was traded in for a new copy machine. The market value of the new machine is $38,000. Kwik Kopy must trade in the old copy machine and pay $22,000 for the new machine.

CHALLENGE PROBLEM

This problem challenges you to apply your cumulative accounting knowledge to move a step beyond the material in the chapter.

✓ 4. Cumulative tax savings over eight years: $841.20

Don Burnette is starting a new home planning business. For years, people have asked Don to draw up the blueprints for their homes and he has done so in his spare time. Don has decided to go into business full time and believes that he will need to add one new draftsman each year for the next five years as his business grows. Don believes that the best way to design homes is by using home designing software on a computer. Thus, he plans to buy himself a new computer and a computer for each new associate who joins the company.

Don has heard that using MACRS for tax purposes will save him taxes and has asked you to develop a schedule illustrating the depreciation expense that would be recognized using straight-line depreciation for his income statement and MACRS depreciation for his tax return over the next eight years under the following assumptions:

1. Don will start his business on July 1, 20-1, and will purchase a new computer on that date.
2. Don will hire four new associates, one on July 1 of each year for the next four years, 20-2 through 20-5. He will also buy each associate a computer.
3. The computers cost $4,000, have useful lives of five years, and have no salvage value. Don will take a half-year's depreciation in the first and last year of each computer's life when computing straight-line depreciation. He will use the MACRS rates, which also assume a half-year convention in the first and last years of the asset's life.
4. As each computer completes its five-year life, Don will buy a new one to replace it.
5. Don's tax rate is 30%.

REQUIRED

1. Prepare a depreciation schedule showing the straight-line depreciation expense for years 20-1 through 20-8.
2. Prepare a depreciation schedule showing the MACRS depreciation for years 20-1 through 20-8. The MACRS rates are shown below.

Depreciation Rates for Five-Year Assets
MACRS Depreciation

Year	MACRS
1	20.0%
2	32.0
3	19.2
4	11.5
5	11.5
6	5.8
	100.0%

3. Compute the difference between straight-line depreciation and MACRS depreciation for each year, 20-1 through 20-8.
4. The differences in part (3) represent the differences in Don's taxable income each year. By using MACRS, how much does Don save in taxes each year, and in total?
5. Under what conditions would Don lose the accumulated tax savings?

ANSWERS TO SELF-STUDY QUESTIONS AND EXERCISES

True/False Questions

1. F (land is not used up)
2. F (reverse is true)
3. F (depreciation is a method of cost allocation)
4. F (the opposite is true)
5. F (the units-of-production method is based on the usage or output of the asset)

Multiple Choice Questions

1. d
2. c
3. b
4. b
5. c

U REVU Exercises

1.

Purchase price	$50,000
Transportation costs	800
Insurance during transportation	100
Total	$50,900

2.

Property, Plant, and Equipment		
Building	$500,000	
Less accumulated depreciation	100,000	$400,000

3.

Double-Declining-Balance Method

Year	Beginning Book Value	Rate	Annual Depreciation	Accumulated Depreciation End of year	Book Value End of Year
1	$350,000	0.67	$234,500	$234,500	$115,500
2	115,500	0.67	77,385	311,885	38,115
3	38,115	0.67	25,537	337,422	12,578

Sum-of the Years'-Digits Method

Year	Depreciable Base	Rate	Annual Depreciation	Accumulated Depreciation End of year	Book Value End of Year
1	$345,000	3/6	$172,500	$172,500	$177,500
2	345,000	2/6	115,000	287,500	62,500
3	345,000	1/6	57,500	345,000	5,000

4.

Cost	$65,000
Salvage value	5,000
Depreciable base	$60,000

Depreciation during years 20-1 through 20-5:

$60,000/6-year life = $10,000 per year × 5 = $50,000 (See also T accounts below)

Truck

Debit	Credit
65,000	

Accum. Depr.—Truck

Date	Debit	Credit	Date
		10,000	12/31/20-1
		10,000	12/31/20-2
		10,000	12/31/20-3
		10,000	12/31/20-4
		10,000	12/31/20-5
1/1/20-6	8,000		
		42,000	Bal.

New Depreciable Base 1/1/20-6:

Cost	$65,000
Accumulated depreciation	42,000 (See T account)
Book value	$23,000
Less salvage value	5,000
New depreciable base	$18,000

$$\frac{\text{New Depreciable Base}}{\text{Remaining Expected Life}} = \text{Depreciation Expense per Year}$$

$$\frac{\$18{,}000}{3} = \$6{,}000 \quad \text{Per year for remaining three years}$$

The depreciation expense for 20-6 is $6,000.

5. a

		Account	Debit	Credit	
1		Cash	2,500 00		1
2		Accumulated Depreciation—Machine	8,000 00		2
3		Machine		10,000 00	3
4		Gain on Sale of Machine		500 00	4
5		Sold machine			5

b.

6		Machine (new)		12,000.00				6
7		Accumulated Depreciation—Machine		8,000.00				7
8		Machine (old)				10,000.00		8
9		Cash				9,500.00		9
10		Gain on Exchange of Machine				500.00		10
11		Purchased new machine						11

6.

Cost of mine	\$4,000,000
Salvage value	250,000
Depletable cost	\$3,750,000

$$\frac{\text{Depletable cost}}{\text{Estimated recoverable amount}} \quad \frac{\$3{,}750{,}000}{1{,}250{,}000 \text{ tons}} = \$3.00 \text{ depletion per ton}$$

Depletion for first year = 100,000 tons × \$3.00 per ton = \$300,000 depletion

7.

1		Patents		100,000.00				1
2		Cash				100,000.00		2
3		Purchased a patent						3
4								4
5		Adjusting Entry						5
6		Patents Amortization		10,000.00				6
7		Patents				10,000.00		7

Chapter 19

Alwin C Ernst
1881–1948

Arthur Young
1863–1948

JUSTIN KASE ZNINEZ/ALAMY/COURTESY OF ERNST AND YOUNG

LEARNING OBJECTIVES

Careful study of this chapter should enable you to:

LO1 Describe the various types of partnerships, their characteristics, the partnership agreement, and the advantages and disadvantages of a partnership.

LO2 Prepare entries for the initial investments in a partnership.

LO3 Explain how partners are compensated and account for the allocation of net income.

LO4 Prepare financial statements reporting the allocation of net income and partnership equity.

LO5 Describe the actions that result in the dissolution of a partnership and account for the dissolution.

LO6 Describe how a partnership is liquidated and prepare associated entries and a statement of partnership liquidation.

Accounting for Partnerships

Born in Cleveland, Ohio, Alwin C. Ernst worked as a bookkeeper after leaving school. In 1903, he and his brother, Theodore, started Ernst & Ernst, a small public accounting firm.

Born in Glasgow, Scotland, Arthur Young graduated in law but became interested in investments and banking. In 1890, he moved to the United States to pursue his career in accounting. In 1906, he and his brother, Stanley, formed an accounting firm, Arthur Young & Company.

Although A. C. Ernst and Arthur Young were contemporaries and died within days of each other, they never met. In 1989, their names were joined when the accounting partnerships they started combined to create Ernst & Young, one of the "Big Four" accounting firms.

Many service businesses, like accounting and law firms, use the partnership form of business. In this chapter, you will learn to account for the formation, operation, dissolution, and liquidation of partnerships.

When two or more individuals engage in an enterprise as co-owners, the organization is known as a **partnership**. This form of organization is common to practically all types of enterprises. However, it is more popular among personal service enterprises than among merchandising businesses. For example, the partnership form of organization is quite common in the legal and public accounting professions. In this chapter, the important features of and accounting procedures for partnerships will be discussed and illustrated.

TYPES OF PARTNERSHIPS AND HOW THEY ARE FORMED

LO1 Describe the various types of partnerships, their characteristics, the partnership agreement, and the advantages and disadvantages of a partnership.

The Uniform Partnership Act states that "a partnership is an association of two or more persons who carry on, as co-owners, a business for profit." Partnerships are formed for many reasons. Primarily, however, they are formed on the belief that individuals with complementary resources and abilities can operate more profitably together than as individuals.

In the United States, there are three primary forms of a partnership: general, limited, and limited liability partnerships. Although state laws vary, the basic characteristics of these forms of partnerships are provided below.

General Partnership (or simply a partnership)

- All partners are **general partners** who actively participate in the operation and management of the partnership.
- General partners are subject to unlimited personal liability for any legal actions and debts of the firm.

Limited Partnership (LP)

- A limited partnership must have at least one general partner with the rights and responsibilities of partners in a general partnership.
- A limited partnership also has **limited partners**. Limited partners do not participate in the management of the business. They provide capital and are paid a return on their investment, and their liability is limited to the amount of their investment.

Limited Liability Partnership (LLP)

- All partners may actively participate in the operation and management of the firm.
- In general, LLP partners are personally liable for their own actions and the actions of those they supervise. They are not, however, personally liable for inappropriate actions by others in the firm. The LLP is a popular form of ownership for accounting and law firms.

CHARACTERISTICS OF PARTNERSHIPS

The characteristics of a partnership are different from those of the sole proprietorships we have accounted for in previous chapters. Some of the more important of these characteristics are listed as follows:

Co-Ownership of Assets

All assets held by a partnership are co-owned by all partners. If one partner contributes an asset to the business, the asset is jointly owned by all partners.

Mutual Agency

Any partner can bind the other partners to a contract if he or she is acting within the general scope of the business. Thus, if one partner signs a contract to purchase merchandise for the business, other partners are bound by that contract. On the other hand, if one partner contracts to buy a personal automobile, this is not part of normal business operations, and other partners would not be bound by it.

Limited Life

A partnership has a limited life. It may be dissolved as the result of any change in the ownership. These include death, bankruptcy, incapacity, withdrawal of a partner, addition of a new partner, or expiration of the time specified in the partnership agreement.

Unlimited Liability

In a general partnership, each partner is personally liable for all debts incurred by the partnership. If the partnership cannot pay a bill, creditors will expect payment from the personal assets of the partners. As discussed earlier, the liability can be limited for some or all of the partners by adopting other forms of a partnership.

Federal Income Taxes

Partnerships are not subject to federal income taxes. However, partnerships file federal income tax returns for informational purposes and notify partners of the amount of partnership income that must be reported on their individual federal (and state if appropriate) income tax returns. Note that partners are taxed on their share of net income, not the amount withdrawn.

LEARNING KEY

There must be a clear understanding of the key elements of the partnership: expectations for each partner, payments to partners, sharing of profits and losses, and dissolution of the partnership. The best way to do so is to put everything in writing.

THE PARTNERSHIP AGREEMENT

A written agreement containing the various provisions for operating a partnership is known as a **partnership agreement**. There is no standard form of partnership agreement, but the following provisions are essential:

1. Date of agreement
2. Names of the partners
3. Kind of business to be conducted
4. Length of time the partnership is to run
5. Name and location of the business
6. Investment of each partner
7. Basis on which profits or losses are to be shared by the partners
8. Limitation of partners' rights and activities
9. Salary allowances to partners
10. Division of assets upon dissolution of the partnership
11. Signatures of the partners

Figure 19-1 is an example of a partnership agreement.

FIGURE 19-1 Partnership Agreement

PARTNERSHIP AGREEMENT

THIS CONTRACT, made and entered into on the first day of January 20--, by and between Sam Mitchell of Indianapolis, Indiana, and Lisa Jenkins of the same city and state.

WITNESSETH: That the said parties have this day formed a partnership for the purpose of engaging in and conducting a wholesale and retail business in the city of Indianapolis under the following stipulations which are a part of this contract:

FIRST: The said partnership is to continue for a term of twenty-five years from January 1, 20--.

SECOND: The business is to be conducted under the firm name of Mitchell & Jenkins, at 2200 East Washington Street, Indianapolis, Indiana.

THIRD: The investments are as follows: Sam Mitchell, cash, $350,000; Lisa Jenkins, cash, $200,000. These invested assets are partnership property.

FOURTH: Each partner is to devote his/her entire time and attention to the business and to engage in no other business enterprise without the written consent of the other partner.

FIFTH: During the operation of the partnership, neither partner is to become surety or bonding agent for anyone without the written consent of the other partner.

SIXTH: Sam Mitchell is to receive a salary allowance of $36,000 a year, payable $1,500 in cash on the fifteenth day and last business day of each month. Lisa Jenkins is to receive a salary allowance of $48,000 a year, payable $2,000 in cash on the fifteenth day and last business day of each month. At the end of each annual fiscal period, the net income or the net loss shown by the income statement after the salaries of the two partners have been allowed is to be shared as follows: Sam Mitchell, 60 percent; Lisa Jenkins, 40 percent.

SEVENTH: Neither partner is to withdraw assets in excess of his/her salary, any part of the assets invested, or assets in anticipation of net income to be earned, without the written consent of the other partner.

EIGHTH: In the case of the death or the legal disability of either partner, the other partner is to continue the operations of the business until the close of the annual fiscal period on the following December 31. At that time, the continuing partner is to be given an option to buy the interest of the deceased or incapacitated partner at not more than 10 percent above the value of the deceased or incapacitated partner's proprietary interest as shown by the balance of his/her capital account after the books are closed on December 31. It is agreed that this purchase price is to be paid one-half in cash and the balance in four equal installments payable quarterly.

NINTH: At the conclusion of this contract, unless it is mutually agreed to continue the operation of the business under a new contract, the assets of the partnership, after the liabilities are paid, are to be divided in proportion to the net credit of each partner's capital account on that date.

IN WITNESS WHEREOF, the parties aforesaid have hereunto set their hands and affixed their seals on the day and year above written.

Sam Mitchell (Seal)
Sam Mitchell

Lisa Jenkins (Seal)
Lisa Jenkins

A BROADER VIEW

VARIO IMAGES GMBH & CO. KG/ALAMY

Partnerships: How Large Can They Go?

When we think of partnerships, we often picture small businesses with a few partners. This is often the case. However, some partnerships are quite large. Take PricewaterhouseCoopers, an international accounting firm, as an example. This partnership has over 8,500 partners guiding the efforts of over 155,000 personnel in 700 offices located in 153 countries. Worldwide revenues exceed $28 billion. This is not what you might call a "mom and pop" operation.

ADVANTAGES AND DISADVANTAGES

In comparison with the sole proprietorship, the partnership form of business offers certain advantages.

1. The ability and experience of the partners are combined in one enterprise.
2. More capital may be raised because the resources of the partners are combined.
3. Credit may be improved because each general partner is personally liable for partnership debts.

There also are some disadvantages of the partnership form of organization.

1. Unlimited liability is a major disadvantage of the general partnership form of ownership. This means that a partner could lose not only the amount invested, but also personal assets. Although this is also true for a sole proprietorship, it is not true for the corporate form of ownership, which will be introduced in Chapters 20 and 21. As discussed earlier, this disadvantage may be avoided for most partners by forming limited partnerships or limited liability partnerships.
2. Mutual agency can lead to serious problems if all partners do not act responsibly and consult each other before signing contracts. Yes, unwitting partners could be liable for swamp land purchased by another partner.
3. The interest of a partner in the partnership cannot be transferred without the consent of the other partners.
4. Termination of the partnership agreement, bankruptcy of the firm, death of one of the partners, or any change in partner membership dissolves the partnership.

ACCOUNTING FOR INITIAL INVESTMENTS

LO2 Prepare entries for the initial investments in a partnership.

Accounting for the various forms of a partnership is similar to accounting for a sole proprietorship. The main difference is that separate capital and drawing accounts are maintained for each partner. Care should be used when preparing the opening entry and entering any transactions that affect the respective interests of the partners.

CASH INVESTMENTS

A partnership may be formed by the investment of cash by the partners. In opening the books for a partnership, a separate journal entry is made for each partner's investment. The opening entries for Mitchell & Jenkins based on the partnership agreement shown in Figure 19-1 are as follows:

Description	Debit	Credit
Cash	350,000.00	
Sam Mitchell, Capital		350,000.00
S. Mitchell invested $350,000 in cash		
Cash	200,000.00	
Lisa Jenkins, Capital		200,000.00
L. Jenkins invested $200,000 in cash		

INVESTMENT OF CASH AND OTHER ASSETS

When forming a partnership, market values are used to measure the investment of each partner. This is reasonable. Investing $1,000 in cash is equivalent to investing an asset that could be sold for $1,000.

A partnership may also be formed by the investment of cash and other assets by the partners. Certain liabilities also may be assumed by the partnership. Each partner's capital account should be credited for the difference between the market value of the assets invested and liabilities assumed.

Instead of investing $200,000 in cash, assume that Jenkins invested:

1. inventory valued at $47,500 on which $10,500 was owed,
2. office equipment valued at $40,000,
3. delivery equipment valued at $92,000, on which $19,000 was owed on a note, and
4. $50,000 in cash.

The following opening entry would be made:

Description		Debit		Credit
Cash	4	50,000.00		
Inventory	1	47,500.00		
Office Equipment	2	40,000.00		
Delivery Equipment	3	92,000.00		
Notes Payable			3	19,000.00
Accounts Payable			1	10,500.00
Lisa Jenkins, Capital				200,000.00
L. Jenkins' investment in partnership				

PARTNERSHIPS FORMED FROM EXISTING BUSINESSES

Two or more sole proprietors may combine their businesses to form a partnership. Their respective balance sheets serve as the basis for the opening entries for the investments of such partners. For example, assume that on April 1, Donna Morning and Larry Knight form a partnership under the firm name of Morning & Knight Sports. The balance sheets shown in Figure 19-2 are made a part of the partnership agreement. They agree to invest their assets and that the partnership will assume the liabilities shown in their respective balance sheets. Each partner's investment is measured by the difference between the assets invested and the liabilities assumed. The profits and losses are to be shared on a 50-50 basis. In case of dissolution, the assets are to be distributed between the partners in the ratio of their capital interests at the time of dissolution.

LEARNING KEY

The difference between the assets invested and the liabilities assumed is each partner's investment.

When two sole proprietors decide to combine their businesses, assets should be recorded at their fair market values as of the date of formation of the partnership. For Morning and Knight, any accounts receivable known to be uncollectible as of March 31, 20--, should be written off. None were considered uncollectible in this case. The balance in Accounts Receivable is debited, and the amount of the Allowance for Bad Debts is credited in the books of the partnership. In this way, the accounts receivable are entered at their approximate fair market value.

FIGURE 19-2 Balance Sheets for Morning Sports and Knight Athletics Prior to the Formation of the Partnership

Morning Sports
Balance Sheet
March 31, 20--

Assets			Liabilities		
Cash		$ 6,344.00	Notes payable	$4,600.00	
Accounts receivable	$5,524.00		Accounts payable	9,082.00	
Less allowance for bad debts	430.00	5,094.00	Total liabilities		$13,682.00
Merchandise inventory		24,574.00			
Store equipment	$3,840.00		Owner's Equity		
Less accumulated depreciation	1,000.00	2,840.00	Donna Morning, capital		25,170.00
Total assets		$38,852.00	Total liabilities and owner's equity		$38,852.00

Knight Athletics
Balance Sheet
March 31, 20--

Assets			Liabilities		
Cash		$ 3,544.00	Notes payable	$ 6,000.00	
Accounts receivable	$5,280.00		Accounts payable	13,238.00	
Less allowance for bad debts	720.00	4,560.00	Total liabilities		$19,238.00
Merchandise inventory		29,692.00			
Supplies		286.00			
Office equipment	$4,320.00				
Less accumulated depreciation	1,100.00	3,220.00			
Store equipment	$4,800.00		Owner's Equity		
Less accumulated depreciation	1,200.00	3,600.00	Larry Knight, capital		25,664.00
Total assets		$44,902.00	Total liabilities and owner's equity		$44,902.00

LEARNING KEY

Assets should be recorded at their fair market values as of the date a partnership is formed.

Both Morning and Knight had been using the first-in, first-out (FIFO) method of inventory costing. Recall that under FIFO, the most recently purchased inventory is considered to be on hand. Thus, the values shown for merchandise inventories on their respective balance sheets are close to their fair market values as of March 31, 20--. If Morning or Knight had been using some other inventory costing method, the merchandise inventory amounts might have required restatement to reflect fair market value.

The fair market value of Morning's store equipment as of March 31, 20--, is $3,600. This amount should be entered on the books of the new partnership rather than the book value of $2,840 shown on Morning's balance sheet in Figure 19-2. In like manner, the fair market values of Knight's office equipment and store equipment as of March 31, 20--, are $3,850 and $4,200, respectively. These amounts should be entered on the books of the new partnership, rather than the respective book values of $3,220 and $3,600 shown on Knight's balance sheet. Once again, the difference between assets invested and liabilities assumed is credited to each partner's capital account. The opening entries for Morning & Knight Sports are as follows:

GENERAL JOURNAL PAGE 1

	DATE		DESCRIPTION	POST. REF.	DEBIT	CREDIT	
	20--						
1	Apr.	1	Cash		6,344.00		1
2			Accounts Receivable		5,524.00		2
3			Merchandise Inventory		24,574.00		3
4			Store Equipment		3,600.00		4
5			Allowance for Bad Debts			430.00	5
6			Notes Payable			4,600.00	6
7			Accounts Payable			9,082.00	7
8			Donna Morning, Capital			25,930.00	8
9			D. Morning's investment in partnership				9
10							10
11		1	Cash		3,544.00		11
12			Accounts Receivable		5,280.00		12
13			Merchandise Inventory		29,692.00		13
14			Supplies		286.00		14
15			Office Equipment		3,850.00		15
16			Store Equipment		4,200.00		16
17			Allowance for Bad Debts			720.00	17
18			Notes Payable			6,000.00	18
19			Accounts Payable			13,238.00	19
20			Larry Knight, Capital			26,894.00	20
21			L. Knight's investment in partnership				21

U REVU Complete U REVU-1 on **page 753** to test your basic understanding of LO2

PARTNER COMPENSATION AND THE ALLOCATION OF NET INCOME

LO3 Explain how partners are compensated and account for the allocation of net income.

In the absence of any agreement between the partners, profits and losses must be shared equally regardless of the partners' investments. Generally, however, the basis on which reported profits and losses are shared is a matter of agreement between the partners. If both partners invest similar amounts of assets in the business and devote the same amount of time to the operation of the business, they may elect to allocate profits and losses equally. However, if the contributions to the success of the business are not similar, they may agree to allocate profits and losses based on each partner's contribution. For example, one partner may contribute most of the assets but render no services, while the other partner may contribute less in assets but devote full time to operating the business. In this case, the partners may agree to allocate the net income or loss based on salary and interest allowances. One partner would have a higher salary allowance to reflect the greater number of hours devoted to running the business. The other partner would have a higher interest allowance to reflect the larger financial investment in the partnership.

LEARNING KEY

The partnership agreement should define the basis on which profits and losses are shared between the partners. The most common basis is the contribution of each partner to the success of the business.

Partner compensation is reported on the income statement but is not used to compute net income. Salary and interest are not listed on the income statement as expenses. Instead, these allowances indicate how net income is allocated to each partner's capital account. The **salary allowance** is generally based on the services provided by each partner to the operations of the business. The **interest allowance** is based on the balance of each partner's capital account.

Withdrawals in a partnership are essentially the same as discussed earlier for a sole proprietorship. In a partnership, however, the agreement often sets limits on the amount a partner may withdraw. For example, the Mitchell & Jenkins partnership agreement limits withdrawals to the amount of the salary allowance. To make an additional withdrawal, the written consent of the other partner is required. These agreements vary across partnerships. Since partners must pay federal income taxes on their share of net income, many partnership agreements permit the withdrawal of a partner's entire share of net income.

Withdrawals are not necessarily equal to the salary allowance.

PROFITS AND LOSSES SHARED EQUALLY

If the Mitchell & Jenkins partnership agreement shown in Figure 19-1 did not specify how the partners would be compensated, the profits and losses would be shared equally. If net income for the year was $190,800, the allocation would be reported on the income statement as shown in Figure 19-3.

FIGURE 19-3 Allocation of Profit and Loss (Equal Division)

Mitchell & Jenkins
Income Statement (Partial)
For Year Ended December 31, 20 --

	S. MITCHELL	L. JENKINS	TOTAL
Net income			$190 800 00
Allocation of net income	$95 400 00	$95 400 00	$190 800 00

Let's assume Mitchell and Jenkins withdrew $36,000 and $48,000, respectively, during the year. Mitchell withdrew $36,000 cash. Jenkins withdrew $40,000 in cash and $8,000 in inventory, as is often done by partners. The entries to record the withdrawals are the same as they would be for a sole proprietorship.

For Mitchell, we would make the following entry:

1			S. Mitchell, Drawing		36 0 0 0 00		1
2			Cash			$36 0 0 0 00	2
3							3

We need to be a little more careful with the withdrawal by Jenkins because the entry depends on the inventory method used as shown below.

	Periodic inventory method			Perpetual inventory method			
1	L. Jenkins, Drawing	48 0 0 0 00		L. Jenkins, Drawing	48 0 0 0 00		1
2	Cash		40 0 0 0 00	Cash		40 0 0 0 00	2
3	Purchases		8 0 0 0 00	Merchandise Inventory		8 0 0 0 00	3
4							4

Maintaining a record of each partner's share of net income and the amount of drawing each year requires a minor change in the way closing entries are made. Recall that four closing entries are made for sole proprietorships at the end of the accounting period. For a partnership, separate capital and drawing accounts are maintained for each partner. Thus, entries three and four must be changed as shown in Figure 19-4.

FIGURE 19-4 Closing Entries

CLOSING ENTRIES—SOLE PROPRIETOR	CLOSING ENTRIES—PARTNERSHIP
1. Close all revenues to Income Summary.	1. Close all revenues to Income Summary.
2. Close all expenses to Income Summary.	2. Close all expenses to Income Summary.
3. Close Income Summary to the owner's capital account.	3. Close Income Summary *by allocating each partner's share of net income or loss to the individual capital accounts.*
4. Close Drawing to the owner's capital account.	4. Close *each partner's drawing account to the individual capital accounts.*

Based on the income allocation shown in Figure 19-3, the third closing entry is as follows:

5			Income Summary		190 8 0 0 00		5
6			S. Mitchell, Capital			95 4 0 0 00	6
7			L. Jenkins, Capital			95 4 0 0 00	7

If Mitchell and Jenkins withdrew \$36,000 and \$48,000, the fourth closing entry would actually require two entries as shown below:

9			S. Mitchell, Capital		36 0 0 0 00		9
10			S. Mitchell, Drawing			36 0 0 0 00	10
11							11
12			L. Jenkins, Capital		48 0 0 0 00		12
13			L. Jenkins, Drawing			48 0 0 0 00	13

The four closing entries for a partnership are summarized in T account form in Figure 19-5.

FIGURE 19-5 Closing Process for a Partnership

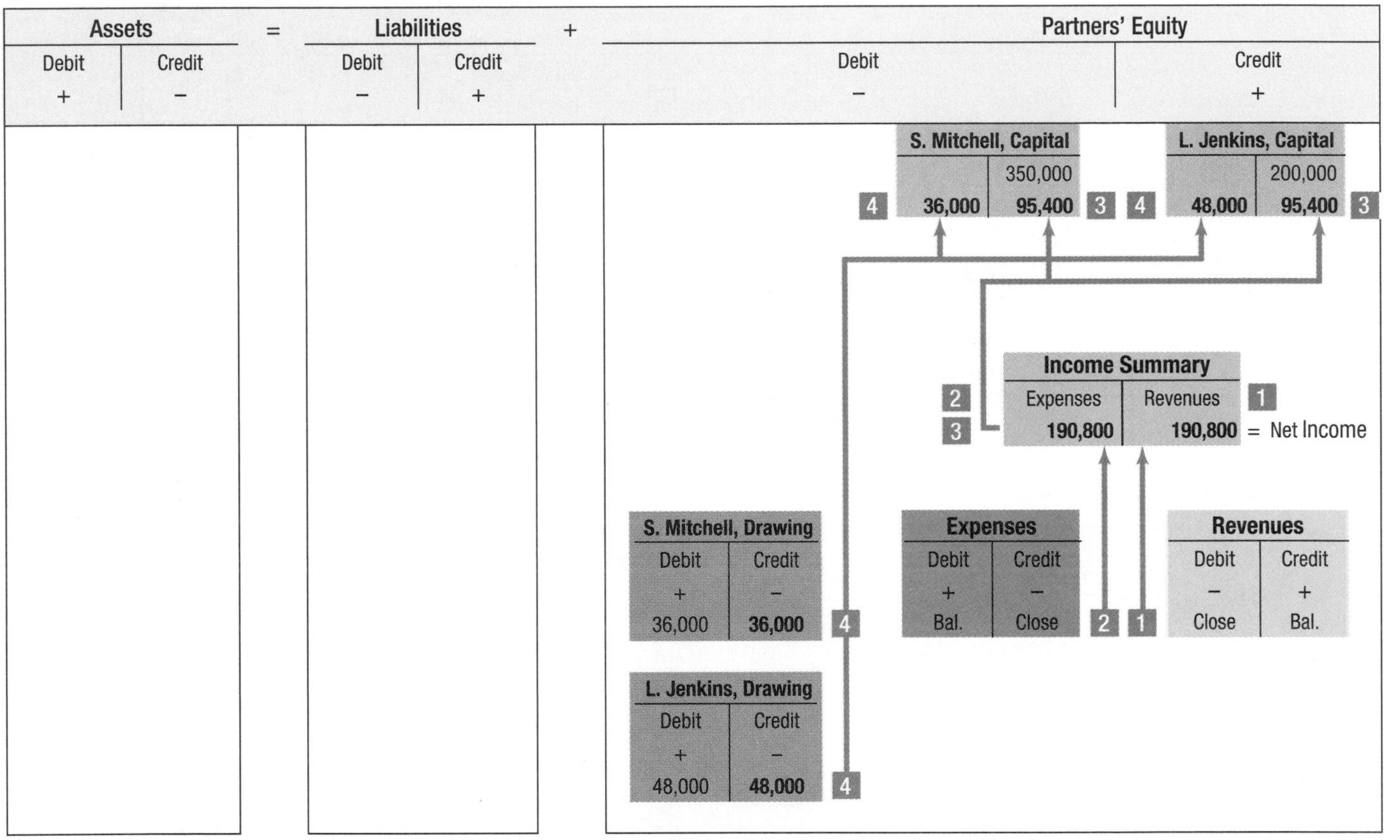

ALLOCATION OF PROFITS AND LOSSES WITH SALARY ALLOWANCES

Net Income Exceeds Salary Allowances

The partnership agreement in Figure 19-1 specifies that after providing for salary allowances of \$36,000 for Mitchell and \$48,000 for Jenkins, the remaining net income or loss is divided on a 60-40 basis. Recall that payments made to partners for salaries or other reasons are debited to the partners' drawing accounts. They are not considered an expense and are not included in the calculation of net income. Under these conditions, the allocation of net income would be reported on the income statement as shown in Figure 19-6.

FIGURE 19-6 Allocation of Profit and Loss when Net Income Exceeds Salary Allowances

If net income is greater than the salary allowances, the remaining income is allocated according to the ratio specified in the partnership agreement.

Net income		$190,800
Less salary allowances		(84,000)
Remaining income		$106,800
60% of $106,800	=	$64,080
40% of $106,800	=	$42,720

Mitchell & Jenkins
Income Statement (Partial)
For Year Ended December 31, 20 - -

	S. MITCHELL	L. JENKINS	TOTAL
Net income			$190,800.00
Allocation of net income:			
Salary allowances	$ 36,000.00	$48,000.00	$ 84,000.00
Remaining income	64,080.00	42,720.00	106,800.00
Allocation of net income	$100,080.00	$90,720.00	$190,800.00

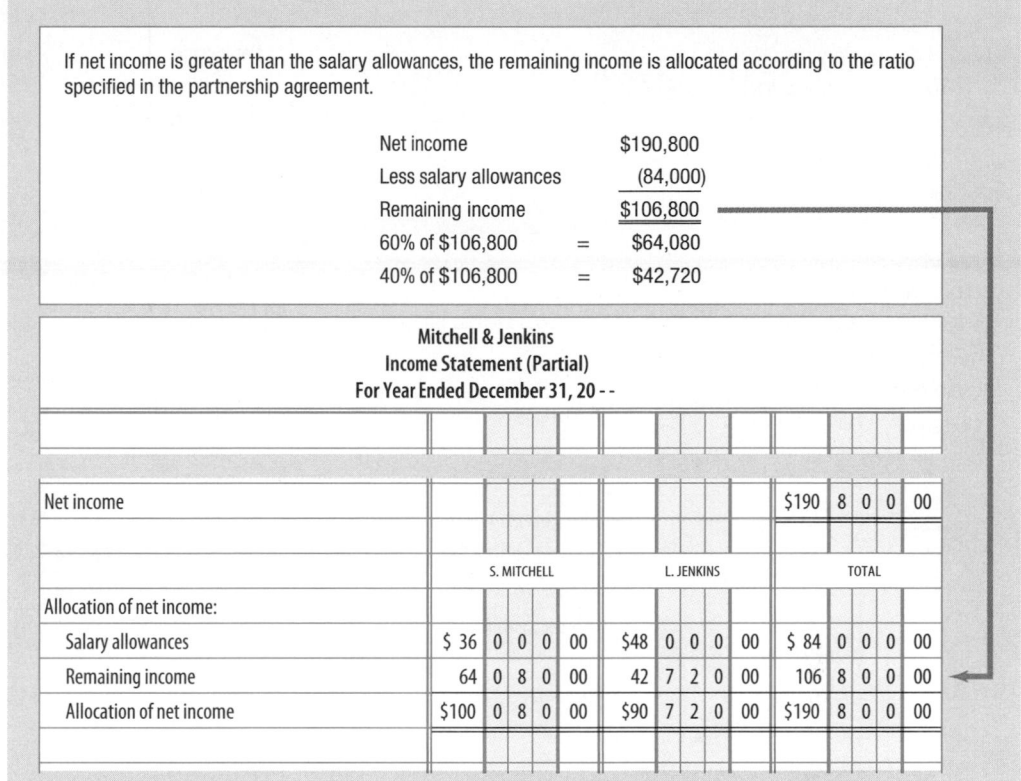

Based on the net income allocation shown above, the closing entry is as follows:

5	Dec.	31	Income Summary		190,800.00		5
6			S. Mitchell, Capital			100,080.00	6
7			L. Jenkins, Capital			90,720.00	7

Assuming that Mitchell and Jenkins withdrew their salaries as described in the partnership agreement, the balances in the drawing accounts at year-end would be $36,000 and $48,000, respectively. The drawing accounts would be closed to the partners' capital accounts at year-end in the same manner as illustrated earlier.

9	Dec.	31	S. Mitchell, Capital		36,000.00		9
10			S. Mitchell, Drawing			36,000.00	10
11							11
12			L. Jenkins, Capital		48,000.00		12
13			L. Jenkins, Drawing			48,000.00	13

Net Income Is Less than Salary Allowances

If the salary allowances are greater than net income, the earnings shortfall or deficiency is allocated to the partners according to the ratio specified in the partnership agreement. If net income for Mitchell and Jenkins is $44,000, the allocation is made as shown in Figure 19-7.

Think of the excess of salary allowances over net income as an economic loss to the partnership. Although net income of $44,000 is reported, the partnership did not generate enough revenues to cover expenses and the partners' salary allowances. This loss ($40,000) is allocated per the profit/loss sharing ratio to determine the proper allocation of the reported net income.

FIGURE 19-7 Allocation of Profit and Loss when Net Income is Less than Salary Allowances

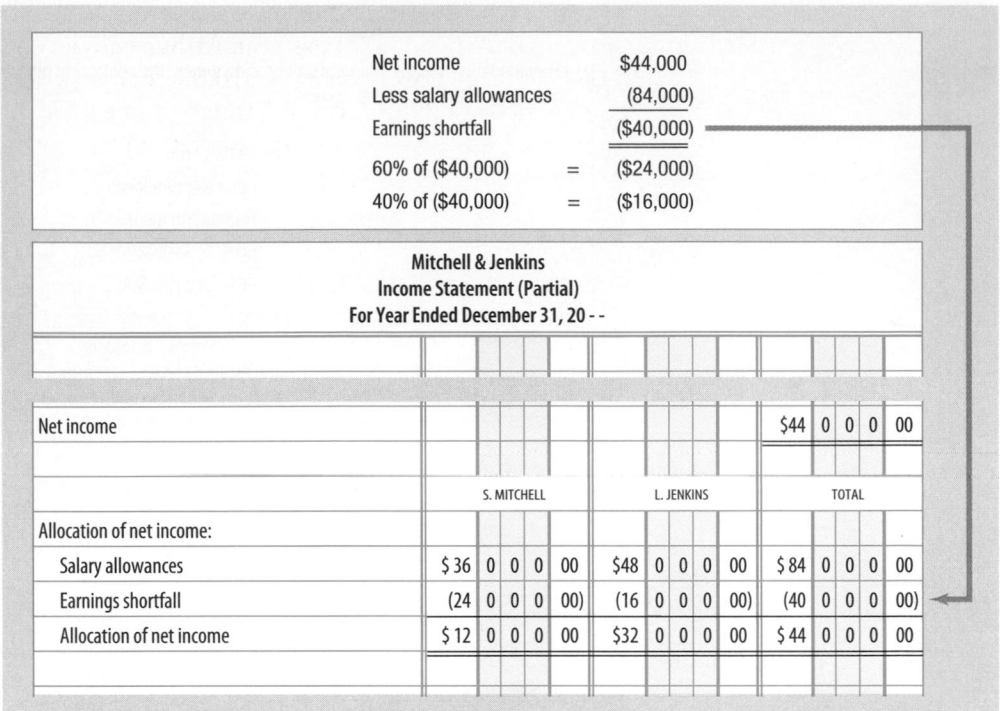

Net income		$44,000
Less salary allowances		(84,000)
Earnings shortfall		($40,000)
60% of ($40,000)	=	($24,000)
40% of ($40,000)	=	($16,000)

Mitchell & Jenkins
Income Statement (Partial)
For Year Ended December 31, 20 - -

	S. MITCHELL	L. JENKINS	TOTAL
Net income			$44,000.00
Allocation of net income:			
Salary allowances	$36,000.00	$48,000.00	$84,000.00
Earnings shortfall	(24,000.00)	(16,000.00)	(40,000.00)
Allocation of net income	$12,000.00	$32,000.00	$44,000.00

Given the lower profits of the partnership, let's assume in this case that Mitchell and Jenkins withdrew only $30,000 and $40,000 respectively, during this period. Based on the net income allocation in Figure 19-7, the closing entries are as follows:

5	Dec.	31	Income Summary	44,000.00		5
6			S. Mitchell, Capital		12,000.00	6
7			L. Jenkins, Capital		32,000.00	7
8						8
9			S. Mitchell, Capital	30,000.00		9
10			S. Mitchell, Drawing		30,000.00	10
11						11
12			L. Jenkins, Capital	40,000.00		12
13			L. Jenkins, Drawing		40,000.00	13

Note that the debits to the capital accounts ($30,000 + $40,000 = $70,000) exceed the credits ($12,000 + $32,000 = $44,000). Thus, the partners' capital accounts are decreasing. This is consistent with the concept of an earnings shortfall deficiency.

ALLOCATION OF PROFITS AND LOSSES WITH SALARY AND INTEREST ALLOWANCES

Net Income Exceeds Allowances

Partners may agree that the best method of allocating profits and losses is to base salaries on the services rendered by each partner and to provide interest on capital investments. The remainder is then shared equally, or according to a predefined ratio.

Assume that B. K. Kelly and S. B. Arthur form a partnership on January 1 of the current year. Kelly will devote full time to operating the business, invest $50,000, and draw a salary of $35,000 per year. Arthur will devote about 10 hours per week, invest $150,000, and draw a salary of $10,000 per year. The partners will be allowed interest of 10% on capital balances on January 1 of each year and the balance of earnings will be divided equally. Net income of $80,000 in the first year of operation would be allocated as reported in Figure 19-8.

Remember: These allocations are simply a method of assigning net income/loss to the partners' capital accounts. There are no cash flows here. Withdrawals by the partners are generally defined in the partnership agreement and are debited to the partners' drawing accounts.

FIGURE 19-8 Allocation of Profit and Loss when Net Income Exceeds Salary and Interest Allowances

Interest allowances:	Kelly:	$50,000 × 10% =	$ 5,000
	Arthur:	$150,000 × 10% =	$15,000

Net income	$80,000
Less salary and interest allowances	(65,000)
Remaining income	$15,000

$15,000 ÷ 2 = $7,500 allocated to each partner

Kelly and Arthur
Income Statement (Partial)
For Year Ended December 31, 20 - -

	B. K. KELLY	S. B. ARTHUR	TOTAL
Net income			$80,000.00
Allocation of net income:			
Salary allowances	$35,000.00	$10,000.00	$45,000.00
Interest allowances	5,000.00	15,000.00	20,000.00
Remaining income	7,500.00	7,500.00	15,000.00
Allocation of net income	$47,500.00	$32,500.00	$80,000.00

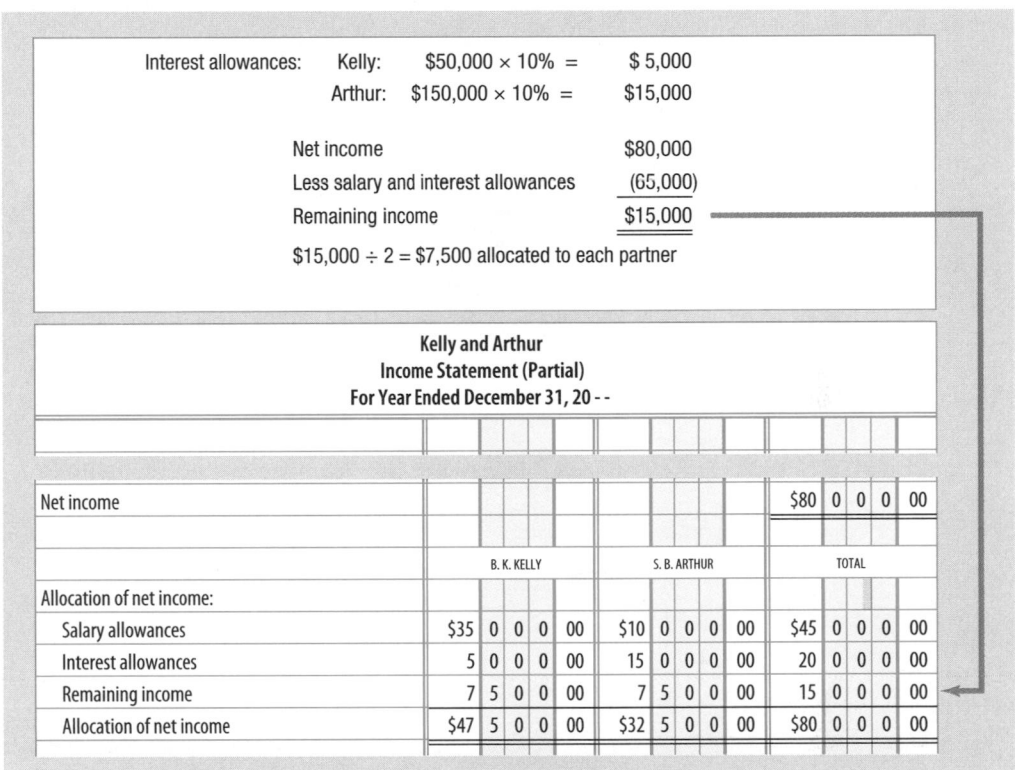

Based on the net income allocation shown in Figure 19-8, the closing entry is as follows:

5	Dec.	31	Income Summary		80,000.00		5
6			B. K. Kelly, Capital			47,500.00	6
7			S. B. Arthur, Capital			32,500.00	7

Net Income Is Less than Total Allowances

If Kelly and Arthur incurred a net loss of $20,000 in year 1, the allocation would be made as shown in Figure 19-9.

FIGURE 19-9 Allocation of Net Loss with Salary and Interest Allowances

Note that subtracting the allowances from a net loss makes the earnings shortfall larger.

Net Loss	$(20,000)
Less salary and interest allowances	(65,000)
Earnings shortfall	$(85,000)

($85,000) ÷ 2 = ($42,500) allocated to each partner

Kelly and Arthur
Income Statement (Partial)
For Year Ended December 31, 20 - -

	B. K. KELLY	S. B. ARTHUR	TOTAL
Net loss			$(20,000.00)
Allocation of net loss:			
Salary allowances	$35,000.00	$10,000.00	$45,000.00
Interest allowances	5,000.00	15,000.00	20,000.00
Earnings shortfall	(42,500.00)	(42,500.00)	(85,000.00)
Allocation of net loss	$(2,500.00)	$(17,500.00)	$(20,000.00)

The following closing entry would be made to allocate the loss of $20,000:

5	Dec. 31	B. K. Kelly, Capital		2,500.00		5
6		S. B. Arthur, Capital		17,500.00		6
7		Income Summary			20,000.00	7

U REVU Complete U REVU-2 on **page 753** to test your basic understanding of LO3

STATEMENTS FOR PARTNERSHIPS

LO4 Prepare financial statements reporting the allocation of net income and partnership equity.

The allocation of net income and its impact on the partners' capital balances should be disclosed in the financial statements. All three financial statements are affected: the income statement, statement of owners' (partners') equity, and balance sheet. As illustrated in the preceding section, the allocation is often reported in the lower portion of the income statement. In addition, the statement of partners' equity reflects the equity of each partner and summarizes the allocation of net income for the year.

Recall that the capital balances for Kelly and Arthur on January 1, 20--, were $50,000 and $150,000, respectively. Let's assume that Arthur invested an additional $10,000, net income was $80,000 and allocated as reported in Figure 19-8, and the partners withdrew only the salary portion of their compensation ($35,000 and $10,000, respectively) during the first year of operation. As shown in Figure 19-10, the statement of partners' equity reports this information and the income allocations reported on the income statement.

Interest allowances for year 2 would be computed as follows:
Kelly: $62,500 × 10% = $6,250
Arthur: $182,500 × 10% = $18,250
The additional investment is reported in the same manner as for a sole proprietorship.

FIGURE 19-10 Statement of Partners' Equity

Kelly and Arthur
Statement of Partners' Equity
For Year Ended December 31, 20 --

	B. K. KELLY	S. B. ARTHUR	TOTAL
Capital, January 1, 20 --	$50 000 00	$150 000 00	$200 000 00
Additional investments during the year		10 000 00	10 000 00
	$50 000 00	$160 000 00	$210 000 00
Net income for the year (see Figure 19-8)	47 500 00	32 500 00	80 000 00
	$97 500 00	$192 500 00	$290 000 00
Withdrawals	35 000 00	10 000 00	45 000 00
Capital, December 31, 20 --	$62 500 00	$182 500 00	$245 000 00

Finally, the partners' equity section of the balance sheet reports the equity of each partner. This is illustrated as follows:

Kelly and Arthur
Balance Sheet (Partial)
December 31, 20 - -

Partners' Equity		
B. K. Kelly, capital	$ 62 500 00	
S. B. Arthur, capital	182 500 00	
Total partners' equity		$245 000 00

U REVU Complete U REVU-3 on **page 753** to test your basic understanding of LO4

LO5 Describe the actions that result in the dissolution of a partnership and account for the dissolution.

DISSOLUTION OF A PARTNERSHIP

One of the primary characteristics of the partnership form of organization is its limited life. Any change in the members of the partnership results in **dissolution**. Dissolution of a partnership may occur because of the addition of a new partner, the death or withdrawal of one of the partners, or bankruptcy.

LEARNING KEY

The partnership is dissolved if there is any change in the members of the partnership.

Dissolution of the partnership does not necessarily imply that business operations will halt. It simply means that the partnership is dissolved. The business may continue with a new group of partners, or a different form of ownership. Any time the original partnership agreement is altered, a new partnership agreement must be prepared to replace the original agreement.

ADMITTING A NEW PARTNER

A new partner may be admitted by agreement among the existing partners. When this happens, the old partnership is dissolved and a new one is created. A new partner may buy into the business in three ways: (1) by purchasing an interest directly from existing partners, (2) by making a cash investment in the business, or (3) by contributing assets from an existing business.

Assume that Morning and Knight admit Sunny Noon as a new partner as of July 1, 20--, when Morning and Knight have capital interests of $30,000 and $20,000, respectively. Noon pays $12,000 to Morning for one-third of her interest and $12,000 to Knight for one-half of his interest. These cash payments go to the partners directly, not to the business. Thus, the following entry is made by the partnership:

	Date		Description	Debit	Credit	
	20--					
1	July	1	Donna Morning, Capital	10 0 0 0 00 *		1
2			Larry Knight, Capital	10 0 0 0 00 **		2
3			Sunny Noon, Capital		20 0 0 0 00	3
4			S. Noon admitted to partnership			4
5			*$30,000 × 1/3 = $10,000			5
6			**$20,000 × 1/2 = $10,000			6

The extra $2,000 ($12,000 – $10,000) paid to both Morning and Knight represents profit to them, but it has no effect on the *partnership's* financial statements.

Now, assume instead that Noon invested $25,000 cash in the new partnership. In this case, the following entry would be made to admit Noon:

	Date		Description	Debit	Credit	
	20--					
1	July	1	Cash	25 0 0 0 00		1
2			Sunny Noon, Capital		25 0 0 0 00	2
3			S. Noon admitted to partnership			3
4						4

Finally, let's assume that Noon had been operating her own business, which was then taken over by the new partnership. In this case, the balance sheet for Sunny Noon's Golf, shown in Figure 19-11, would serve as a basis for preparing the opening entry. The assets listed in the balance sheet are taken over, the liabilities are assumed, and Noon's capital account is credited for the difference.

FIGURE 19-11 Balance Sheet for Sunny Noon's Golf

Sunny Noon's Golf
Balance Sheet
June 30, 20 --

Assets			Liabilities		
Cash		$ 5 0 0 0 00	Notes payable	$9 0 4 8 00	
Accounts receivable	$14 2 9 0 00		Accounts payable	7 5 5 0 00	
Less allowance for bad debts	1 0 7 8 00	13 2 1 2 00	Total liabilities		$16 5 9 8 00
Merchandise inventory		27 2 9 0 00	Owner's Equity		
			Sunny Noon, capital		28 9 0 4 00
Total assets		$45 5 0 2 00	Total liabilities and owner's equity		$45 5 0 2 00

Noon has no knowledge of any uncollectible accounts receivable as of June 30, 20--, and has been using the FIFO method of inventory costing. Thus, the amounts reported on the balance sheet are reasonable approximations of market values. The entry to admit Noon as a partner, therefore, is as follows:

	Date		Description	Debit	Credit	
	20- -					
1	July	1	Cash	5,000.00		1
2			Accounts Receivable	14,290.00		2
3			Merchandise Inventory	27,290.00		3
4			Allowance for Bad Debts		1,078.00	4
5			Notes Payable		9,048.00	5
6			Accounts Payable		7,550.00	6
7			Sunny Noon, Capital		28,904.00	7
8			S. Noon admitted to partnership			8
9						9

WITHDRAWAL OF PARTNER

By agreement, a partner may retire and be permitted to withdraw assets equal to, less than, or greater than the amount of his or her interest in the partnership. The book value of a partner's interest is shown by the credit balance of the partner's capital account. The balance is computed after all profits or losses have been allocated in accordance with the partnership agreement and the books closed. If a retiring partner withdraws cash or other assets equal to the credit balance of his or her capital account, the transaction will have no effect on the capital of the remaining partners.

To illustrate, assume that several years after the formation of Morning, Noon, and Knight Sports, Sunny Noon decided to retire. The partners agreed to the withdrawal of cash equal to the amount of Noon's equity in the assets of the partnership. After bringing all accounts up to date, assume that the partners' capital accounts had credit balances as follows:

Donna Morning	$55,000
Sunny Noon	40,000
Larry Knight	45,000

If Noon withdraws $40,000 in cash, the entry on the books of the partnership is as follows:

	Date		Description	Debit	Credit	
12			Sunny Noon, Capital	40,000.00		12
13			Cash		40,000.00	13
14			S. Noon retired, withdrawing			14
15			$40,000 in equity settlement			15

Note that this transaction decreases cash and decreases the total capital of the partnership, but it does not affect the equity of the remaining partners. Morning still has an equity of $55,000 and Knight an equity of $45,000 in the partnership assets.

If a retiring partner agrees to withdraw less than the amount in his or her capital account, the transaction will increase the capital accounts of the remaining partners. For example, if Noon withdraws only $30,000 in settlement of the interest, the entry in the books of the partnership is as follows:

	Date		Description	Debit	Credit	
12			Sunny Noon, Capital	40,000.00		12
13			Cash		30,000.00	13
14			Donna Morning, Capital		5,500.00	14
15			Larry Knight, Capital		4,500.00	15
16			S. Noon retired, withdrawing			16
17			$30,000 in equity settlement			17

The difference between Noon's equity in the assets of the partnership and the amount of cash withdrawn is $10,000 ($40,000 – $30,000). This difference is divided between the remaining partners on the basis stated in the partnership agreement. In this case, it is divided according to the ratio of their capital interests after allocating net income and closing their drawing accounts. On this basis, Morning's capital account is credited for $5,500 and Knight's is credited for $4,500. The calculations are as follows:

Remaining Equity in Partnership

Morning	$ 55,000
Knight	45,000
Total	$100,000

Allocation to Morning: ($55,000 ÷ $100,000) × $10,000 = $5,500
Allocation to Knight: ($45,000 ÷ $100,000) × $10,000 = $4,500

If a retiring partner withdraws more than the amount in his or her capital account, the transaction will decrease the capital accounts of the remaining partners. Thus, if Morning and Knight allow Noon to withdraw $45,000 in settlement of Noon's interest, the entry in the books of the partnership is as follows:

12		Sunny Noon, Capital		40 000 00		12
13		Donna Morning, Capital		2 750 00		13
14		Larry Knight, Capital		2 250 00		14
15		Cash			45 000 00	15
16		S. Noon retired, withdrawing				16
17		$45,000 in equity settlement				17

The excess of the amount of cash withdrawn over Noon's equity in the partnership ($5,000) is divided between the remaining partners on the basis stated in the partnership agreement. Thus, Donna Morning, Capital is debited for $2,750 (55/100 of $5,000), while Larry Knight, Capital is debited for $2,250 (45/100 of $5,000).

When a partner retires from the business, the partner's interest may be purchased directly by one or more of the remaining partners or by an outside party. If the retiring partner's interest is sold to one of the remaining partners, the retiring partner's equity is merely transferred to the other partner. For example, assume that Noon's equity is sold to Morning. The entry for the transaction on the books of the partnership is as follows:

12		Sunny Noon, Capital		40 000 00		12
13		Donna Morning, Capital			40 000 00	13
14		D. Morning purchased S. Noon's				14
15		interest in partnership				15

The amount paid to Noon by Morning is a personal transaction and has no effect on the above entry. Any gain or loss resulting from the transaction is a personal gain or loss of the withdrawing partner and not of the business. Thus, whatever amount is involved, the credit in Noon's account is transferred to Morning's account.

DEATH OF A PARTNER

The death of a partner dissolves the partnership. On the date of death, the accounts are closed and the net income for the year to date is allocated to the partners' capital accounts. Most agreements call for an audit and revaluation of the assets at this time. The balance of the deceased partner's capital account is then transferred to a liability account with the deceased's estate. The surviving partners may continue the business or liquidate. If the business continues, the procedures for settling with the estate are the same as those described earlier for the withdrawal of a partner. Liquidation procedures are described in the following section.

U REVU

Complete U REVU-4 on **page 753** to test your basic understanding of LO5

LO6 Describe how a partnership is liquidated and prepare associated entries and a statement of partnership liquidation.

LEARNING KEY

When a partnership is liquidated, the assets are sold, liabilities are paid, and the remaining cash or other assets are distributed to the partners.

LIQUIDATION OF A PARTNERSHIP

Liquidation of a partnership generally means that the assets are sold, liabilities are paid, and the remaining cash or other assets are distributed to the partners. When normal operations are discontinued, adjusting and closing entries are made. Thus, only the assets, liabilities, and partners' equity accounts remain open. As the assets are sold, the cash realized is applied first to the claims of creditors. Once all liabilities are paid, the remaining cash and other assets are distributed to the partners according to their ownership interests as indicated by their capital accounts.

To illustrate, assume that after several years of operations, the partnership of Morning, Noon, and Knight Sports is to be liquidated. After making closing entries on May 31, 20--, the following accounts remain open. For simplicity, "Other Assets" and "Liabilities" are used as account titles. In actual practice, several asset, contra-asset, and liability accounts would be involved.

	Account Balance	
Account Title	Debit	Credit
Cash	$ 10,000	
Inventory	120,000	
Other Assets	220,000	
Liabilities		$ 80,000
Donna Morning, Capital		95,000
Larry Knight, Capital		120,000
Sunny Noon, Capital		55,000

Using these account balances, accounting for the liquidation of the partnership is illustrated in Figure 19-12. For convenience, let's assume that all assets are sold in one transaction on June 1, 20--, and all liabilities are paid at once on June 15, 20--. On June 18, cash settlements are made with the partners who share equally in all profits and losses.

GAIN ON SALE OF ASSETS

Assume that the noncash assets are sold for $370,000. Since these assets have a book value of $340,000, a gain of $30,000 on the sale is recognized. The gain is allocated to the partners' capital accounts according to the profit-and-loss sharing ratio. In this case, the gain is shared equally. Next, the liabilities are paid and the remaining cash distributed to the partners according to their capital account balances. A statement of partnership liquidation summarizing these transactions is provided in Figure 19-12.

FIGURE 19-12 Statement of Partnership Liquidation

Morning, Noon, and Knight Sports
Statement of Partnership Liquidation
For Period June 1–18, 20 --

	CASH	INVENTORY	OTHER ASSETS	LIABILITIES	CAPITAL		
					D. MORNING	L. KNIGHT	S. NOON
Balance before sale of assets	$ 10 000 00	$120 000 00	$220 000 00	$ 80 000 00	$ 95 000 00	$120 000 00	$ 55 000 00
Sale of noncash assets and							
allocation of gain	370 000 00	(120 000 00)	(220 000 00)		10 000 00	10 000 00	10 000 00
Balance after sale	$380 000 00	0	0	$ 80 000 00	$105 000 00	$130 000 00	$ 65 000 00
Payment of liabilities	(80 000 00)			(80 000 00)			
Balance after payment of liabilities	$300 000 00	0	0	0	$105 000 00	$130 000 00	$ 65 000 00
Distribution of cash to partners	(300 000 00)				(105 000 00)	(130 000 00)	(65 000 00)
Final balance	0	0	0	0	0	0	0

The entries for these transactions are as follows:

	20--						
1	June	1	Cash		370 000 00		1
2			Inventory			120 000 00	2
3			Other Assets			220 000 00	3
4			Gain on Sale of Assets			30 000 00	4
5			Sale of assets				5
6							6
7		1	Gain on Sale of Assets		30 000 00		7
8			Donna Morning, Capital			10 000 00	8
9			Larry Knight, Capital			10 000 00	9
10			Sunny Noon, Capital			10 000 00	10
11			Allocation of gain				11
12							12
13		15	Liabilities		80 000 00		13
14			Cash			80 000 00	14
15			Payment of liabilities				15
16							16
17		18	Donna Morning, Capital		105 000 00		17
18			Larry Knight, Capital		130 000 00		18
19			Sunny Noon, Capital		65 000 00		19
20			Cash			300 000 00	20
21			Distribution of cash to partners				21

LOSS ON SALE OF ASSETS

Using the same information for Morning, Noon, and Knight as given on page 743, assume that the noncash assets are sold for $295,000, resulting in a loss of $45,000. A statement of partnership liquidation reflecting the equal allocation of the loss on the sale of assets, payment of the liabilities, and distribution of the cash to the partners is illustrated in Figure 19-13.

FIGURE 19-13 Statement of Partnership Liquidation

Morning, Noon, and Knight Sports
Statement of Partnership Liquidation
For Period June 1–18, 20 - -

	CASH	INVENTORY	OTHER ASSETS	LIABILITIES	CAPITAL D. MORNING	CAPITAL L. KNIGHT	CAPITAL S. NOON
Balance before sale of assets	$ 10,000.00	$120,000.00	$220,000.00	$ 80,000.00	$ 95,000.00	$120,000.00	$ 55,000.00
Sale of noncash assets and							
allocation of loss	295,000.00	(120,000.00)	(220,000.00)		(15,000.00)	(15,000.00)	(15,000.00)
Balance after sale	$305,000.00	0	0	$ 80,000.00	$ 80,000.00	$105,000.00	$ 40,000.00
Payment of liabilities	(80,000.00)			(80,000.00)			
Balance after payment of liabilities	$225,000.00	0	0	0	$ 80,000.00	$105,000.00	$ 40,000.00
Distribution of cash to partners	(225,000.00)				(80,000.00)	(105,000.00)	(40,000.00)
Final balance	0	0	0	0	0	0	0

The entries for these transactions are as follows:

	Date		Description	Post. Ref.	Debit	Credit	
	20- -						
1	June	1	Cash		295,000.00		1
2			Loss on Sale of Assets		45,000.00		2
3			Inventory			120,000.00	3
4			Other Assets			220,000.00	4
5			Sale of assets				5
6							6
7		1	Donna Morning, Capital		15,000.00		7
8			Larry Knight, Capital		15,000.00		8
9			Sunny Noon, Capital		15,000.00		9
10			Loss on Sale of Assets			45,000.00	10
11			Allocation of loss				11
12							12
13		15	Liabilities		80,000.00		13
14			Cash			80,000.00	14
15			Payment of liabilities				15
16							16
17		18	Donna Morning, Capital		80,000.00		17
18			Larry Knight, Capital		105,000.00		18
19			Sunny Noon, Capital		40,000.00		19
20			Cash			225,000.00	20
21			Distribution of cash to partners				21

U REVU Complete U REVU-5 on **page 753** to test your basic understanding of LO6

LEARNING OBJECTIVES	Key Points to Remember

LO1 Describe the various types of partnerships, their characteristics, the partnership agreement, and the advantages and disadvantages of a partnership.

The partnership form of business includes the following three types:

General Partnership (or simply a partnership)
- All partners actively participate in the operation and management of the partnership.
- All partners are "general" partners and are subject to unlimited personal liability for any legal actions and debts of the firm.

Limited Partnership (LP)
- A limited partnership must have at least one general partner with the rights and responsibilities of partners in a general partnership.
- A limited partnership also has "limited" partners. Limited partners do not participate in the management of the business. They provide capital and are paid a return on their investment, and their liability is limited to the amount of their investment.

Limited Liability Partnership (LLP)
- All partners may actively participate in the operation and management of the firm.
- In general, LLP partners are personally liable for their own actions and the actions of those they supervise. They are not, however, personally liable for inappropriate actions by others in the firm. The LLP is a popular form of ownership for accounting and law firms.

Characteristics of a partnership include:

Co-ownership of assets
Mutual agency
Limited life
Unlimited liability
No federal income taxes

A partnership agreement includes the following:

1. Date of agreement
2. Names of the partners
3. Kind of business to be conducted
4. Length of time the partnership is to run
5. Name and location of the business
6. Investment of each partner
7. Basis on which profits or losses are to be shared by the partners
8. Limitation of partners' rights and activities
9. Salary allowances to partners
10. Division of assets upon dissolution of the partnership
11. Signatures of the partners

Advantages:

Combined experience of partners
Increased ability to raise capital
Improved credit standing

(continued)

LEARNING OBJECTIVES Key Points to Remember

LO1 (concluded)

Disadvantages:

- Unlimited liability of general partners
- Mutual agency
- Difficulty transferring the interests of partners to others
- Various events can cause the partnership to be dissolved

LO2 Prepare entries for the initial investments in a partnership.

The proper accounting for the formation of a partnership depends on the type of investment made by each partner. Cash investments are recorded by recognizing the cash and an equal amount of partnership capital as follows:

Cash	50,000.00	
Katherine Meisenheimer, Capital		50,000.00
K. Meisenheimer invested		
$50,000 in cash		

If a partner invests cash and other assets, the assets are entered at their market values. The partner's capital account is credited for the sum of the cash and the market value of assets contributed as follows:

Cash	10,000.00	
Inventory (market value)	20,000.00	
Office Equipment (market value)	8,000.00	
Delivery Equipment (market value)	15,000.00	
Sara Bates, Capital		53,000.00
S. Bates' investment in		
partnership		

If existing sole proprietorships are combined, the balance sheets of the proprietorships are used to prepare the entry for the formation of the partnership. Each partner's investment is measured by the difference between the market value of the assets invested and the liabilities assumed by the partnership as shown below. Before transferring receivables to the partnership, any known uncollectible accounts must be written off by the proprietorship.

Cash	5,000.00	
Accounts Receivable	20,000.00	
Merchandise Inventory (market value)	50,000.00	
Store Equipment (market value)	30,000.00	
Allowance for Bad Debts		2,000.00
Notes Payable		10,000.00
Accounts Payable		12,000.00
Alex Von Rosenberger, Capital		82,800.00
A. Von Rosenberger's investment		
in partnership		

LEARNING OBJECTIVES — Key Points to Remember

LO3 Explain how partners are compensated and account for the allocation of net income.

Partner compensation may be based on salary and interest allowances as well as an allocation of remaining profits as stated in the partnership agreement.

LO4 Prepare financial statements reporting the allocation of net income and partnership equity.

Partnership financial statements report the allocation of net income and partnership equity as shown in the statements below.

Kelly and Arthur
Income Statement (Partial)
For Year Ended December 31, 20 --

	B. K. KELLY	S. B. ARTHUR	TOTAL
Net income			$80 000 00
Allocation of net income:			
Salary allowances	$35 000 00	$10 000 00	$45 000 00
Interest allowances	5 000 00	15 000 00	20 000 00
Remaining income	7 500 00	7 500 00	15 000 00
	$47 500 00	$32 500 00	$80 000 00

Kelly and Arthur
Statement of Partners' Equity
For Year Ended December 31, 20 --

	B. K. KELLY	S. B. ARTHUR	TOTAL
Capital, January 1, 20 --	$50 000 00	$150 000 00	$200 000 00
Additonal investments during the year		10 000 00	10 000 00
	$50 000 00	$160 000 00	$210 000 00
Net income for the year	47 500 00	32 500 00	80 000 00
	$97 500 00	$192 500 00	$290 000 00
Withdrawals (salaries during the year)	35 000 00	10 000 00	45 000 00
Capital, December 31, 20 --	$62 500 00	$182 500 00	$245 000 00

Kelly and Arthur
Balance Sheet (Partial)
December 31, 20 --

Partners' Equity		
B. K. Kelly, capital	$ 62 500 00	
S. B. Arthur, capital	182 500 00	
Total partners' equity		$245 000 00

LO5 Describe the actions that result in the dissolution of a partnership and account for the dissolution.

Any change in the members of the partnership results in its dissolution. Accounting for the dissolution varies depending on whether a new partner is admitted or a partner withdraws, and whether an additional investment is made in the partnership or payments are made directly to existing partners.

LEARNING OBJECTIVES Key Points to Remember

LO6 Describe how a partnership is liquidated and prepare associated entries and a statement of partnership liquidation.	The steps in the liquidation process are as follows: 1. Assets are sold. 2. Gains or losses are allocated to the partners. 3. Liabilities are paid. 4. Remaining cash and other assets are distributed to the partners according to their capital accounts.

DEMONSTRATION PROBLEM

Mascha Schuurmans, Jolijn Brouwer, and Mirjam van Tuil are partners in Holland Law. They share profits and losses in a 50-30-20 ratio. The partnership agreement calls for annual salaries of $40,000, $35,000, and $30,000, respectively, and interest of 12% on their January 1 capital balances.* Any remaining net income (or net loss) is to be divided in accordance with the ratios used for sharing profits and losses.

The partners' capital balances as of January 1, 20-1, were Schuurmans, $120,000; Brouwer, $75,000; and van Tuil, $50,000. No additional investments were made during the year. The net income of the partnership for the year 20-1 was $160,000. Partners' withdrawals for the year were Schuurmans, $50,000; Brouwer, $40,000; and van Tuil, $35,000.

On March 4, 20-2, the partners decide to liquidate their law firm. On that date, the firm has a cash balance of $46,000, noncash assets of $274,000, and liabilities of $40,000. No additional investments or withdrawals were made in 20-2. Between March 5 and March 31, the noncash assets are sold for $290,000, the gain is divided according to the profit and loss sharing ratio, and the liabilities are paid. The remaining cash is then distributed to the partners.

*Salaries and interest are not recognized as expenses in the determination of net income.

REQUIRED

1. Prepare the lower portion of the income statement of Holland Law for the year ended December 31, 20-1, showing the division of the partnership net income for the year.
2. Prepare the general journal entry to close Income Summary to the partners' capital accounts as of December 31, 20-1.
3. Prepare a statement of partners' equity for Holland Law for the year ended December 31, 20-1.
4. Prepare a statement of partnership liquidation for Holland Law for the period March 5 through March 31, 20-2.
5. Prepare the general journal entries as of March 31, 20-2, for:
   (a) The sale of the noncash assets of the partnership
   (b) The division of any loss or gain on the sale of assets
   (c) The payment of partnership liabilities
   (d) The distribution of remaining cash to the partners

(continued)

Solution 1.

Holland Law
Income Statement (Partial)
For Year Ended December 31, 20 -1

	M. SCHUURMANS	J. BROUWER	M. VAN TUIL	TOTAL
Net income				$160,000.00
Allocation of net income:				
Salary allowances	$40,000.00	$35,000.00	$30,000.00	$105,000.00
Interest allowances	14,400.00	9,000.00	6,000.00	29,400.00
Remaining income	12,800.00	7,680.00	5,120.00	25,600.00
	$67,200.00	$51,680.00	$41,120.00	$160,000.00

2.

4						4
5	Dec.	31	Income Summary	160,000.00		5
6			Mascha Schuurmans, Capital		67,200.00	6
7			Jolijn Brouwer, Capital		51,680.00	7
8			Mirjam van Tuil, Capital		41,120.00	8
9						9

3.

Holland Law
Statement of Partners' Equity
For Year Ended December 31, 20 -1

	M. SCHUURMANS	J. BROUWER	M. VAN TUIL	TOTAL
Capital, January 1, 20 -1	$120,000.00	$ 75,000.00	$50,000.00	$245,000.00
Net income for the year	67,200.00	51,680.00	41,120.00	160,000.00
	$187,200.00	$126,680.00	$91,120.00	$405,000.00
Withdrawals	50,000.00	40,000.00	35,000.00	125,000.00
Capital, December 31, 20 -1	$137,200.00	$ 86,680.00	$56,120.00	$280,000.00

4.

Holland Law
Statement of Partnership Liquidation
For Period March 5–31, 20 -2

	CASH	NONCASH ASSETS	LIABILITIES	CAPITAL M. SCHUURMANS	CAPITAL J. BROUWER	CAPITAL M. VAN TUIL
Balance before sale of assets	$ 46,000.00	$274,000.00	$ 40,000.00	$137,200.00	$ 86,680.00	$ 56,120.00
Sale of noncash assets and allocation of gain	290,000.00	(274,000.00)		8,000.00	4,800.00	3,200.00
Balance after sale	$336,000.00	0	$ 40,000.00	$145,200.00	$ 91,480.00	$ 59,320.00
Payment of liabilities	(40,000.00)		(40,000.00)			
Balance after payment of liabilities	$296,000.00	0	0	$145,200.00	$ 91,480.00	$ 59,320.00
Distribution of cash to partners	(296,000.00)			(145,200.00)	(91,480.00)	(59,320.00)
Final balance	0	0	0	0	0	0

5.

		GENERAL JOURNAL					PAGE 1	
		DATE		DESCRIPTION	POST. REF.	DEBIT	CREDIT	
		20-2						
a.	1	Mar.	31	Cash		290,000 00		1
	2			Noncash Assets			274,000 00	2
	3			Gain on Sale of Assets			16,000 00	3
	4			Sale of assets				4
	5							5
b.	6		31	Gain on Sale of Assets		16,000 00		6
	7			Mascha Schuurmans, Capital			8,000 00	7
	8			Jolijn Brouwer, Capital			4,800 00	8
	9			Mirjam van Tuil, Capital			3,200 00	9
	10			Allocation of gain				10
	11							11
c.	12		31	Liabilities		40,000 00		12
	13			Cash			40,000 00	13
	14			Payment of liabilities				14
	15							15
d.	16		31	Mascha Schuurmans, Capital		145,200 00		16
	17			Jolijn Brouwer, Capital		91,480 00		17
	18			Mirjam van Tuil, Capital		59,320 00		18
	19			Cash			296,000 00	19
	20			Distribution of cash to partners				20

KEY TERMS

dissolution (739) Dissolving of the partnership resulting from any change in the members of the partnership.

general partner (725) A partner that participates in the management of the business and is personally responsible for any legal actions and debts of the firm.

general partnership (725) A partnership made up of general partners who actively participate in the management of the business and are personally liable for all debts of the partnership.

interest allowance (732) An allocation of partnership net income based on the balance of each partner's capital account.

limited liability partnership (LLP) (725) A partnership in which all partners may actively participate in the management of the firm, but whose personal liability is limited to their own actions and the actions of those they supervise.

limited partner (725) A partner who does not participate in the management of the business and whose liability is limited to the amount invested.

limited partnership (LP) (725) A partnership with at least one general partner and limited partners.

liquidation (743) The process of selling the assets, paying the liabilities, and distributing the remaining cash or other assets to the partners.

mutual agency (726) One partner can bind other partners to a contract if he or she is acting within the general scope of the business.

partnership (725) The form of organization in which two or more individuals engage in an enterprise as co-owners.

partnership agreement (726) A written agreement containing the various provisions for operating a partnership.

salary allowance (732) An allocation of partnership net income based on the services provided by each partner to the operations of the business.

unlimited liability (726) The concept that a general partner's personal assets may be claimed by a creditor to satisfy partnership debts.

SELF-STUDY QUESTIONS AND EXERCISES

True/False Questions

1. LO1 When two or more individuals engage in an enterprise as co-owners, the organization is known as a proprietorship.
2. LO1 Mutual agency is a characteristic of a partnership in which any partner can bind the other partners to a contract if he/she is acting within the general scope of the business.
3. LO1 Limited life is a characteristic of a partnership in which each partner is personally liable for all debts incurred by the partners.
4. LO1 One advantage of a partnership is that the interest of a partner cannot be transferred without the consent of the other partners.
5. LO2 When two or more sole proprietors form a partnership, their respective balance sheets serve as the basis for the opening entries for the investments of such partners.

Multiple Choice Questions

1. LO1 The basis on which profits and losses are to be shared among partners is
   (a) a matter of agreement among the partners.
   (b) the same as their withdrawal ratio.
   (c) the same as their investment ratio.
   (d) always equal among all partners.
2. LO1 In the absence of any agreement among partners, profits and losses must be shared
   (a) equally among all partners.
   (b) on the basis of their withdrawals.
   (c) on the basis of their investment ratio.
   (d) in accordance with the Uniform Partnership Act.
3. LO3 If the partnership agreement specifies how profits are to be shared but does not specify how losses are to be shared, the losses must be shared
   (a) equally among all partners.
   (b) on the basis of their withdrawals.
   (c) on the basis of their investment ratio.
   (d) none of the above.
4. LO5 After closing the temporary owner's equity accounts into Income Summary and after allocating the net income and closing the partners' drawing accounts, assume the partners' capital accounts had credit balances as follows: Abbott, $20,000; Barnes, $30,000; Costello, $45,000.

   If Abbott retired and withdrew $25,000 in settlement of her equity, the debit to her capital account would be in the amount of
   (a) $25,000.
   (b) $55,000.
   (c) $20,000.
   (d) $45,000.

5. LO5 After closing the temporary owner's equity accounts into Income Summary and after allocating the net income and closing the partners' drawing accounts, assume the partners' capital accounts had credit balances as follows: Abbott, $20,000; Barnes, $30,000; Costello, $45,000. The difference between the withdrawing partner's equity and amount of cash withdrawn is divided according to the ratio of the remaining partners' capital interests.

   If Costello retired and withdrew $40,000 in settlement of his equity, the amount entered in Abbott's capital account would be a

   (a) $2,000 credit.
   (b) $2,000 debit.
   (c) $3,000 credit.
   (d) $3,000 debit.

U REVU Exercises

1. LO2 On January 1, 20-1, Paul Dimmitt and Mike Stiglitz decided to form The Bogey Men, a partnership to offer golf instruction and equipment to beginning golfers. They promise to have you shooting bogey golf by next Thursday. Prepare the journal entry for the investment of $100,000 by each partner.

2. LO3 Dimmitt and Stiglitz are to receive salary allowances of $40,000 and $50,000, respectively. The remaining income is to be divided on a 60-40 basis. Net income for the year ended December 31, 20-1, was $200,000. Determine the amount of net income allocated to each partner.

3. LO4 Using the information in UREVU-2, prepare the lower portion of the income statement showing the allocation of net income between Dimmitt and Stiglitz.

4. LO5 On January 1, 20-5, the capital balances of Dimmitt and Stiglitz are $200,000 and $250,000, respectively. On that date, James Mantz paid Stiglitz $60,000 for one-fifth of Stiglitz's capital interest in The Bogey Men. In addition, Jack Sacks contributed $50,000 to the business for a $50,000 capital interest. Prepare journal entries for the transactions admitting Mantz and Sacks to the partnership.

5. LO6 On December 31, 20-8, the partners decided to liquidate The Bogey Men. The balance sheet reported the following information:

	Account Balance	
Account Title	**Debit**	**Credit**
Cash	$500,000	
Inventory	400,000	
Paul Dimmitt, Capital		$400,000
James Mantz, Capital		300,000
Jack Sacks, Capital		100,000
Mike Stiglitz, Capital		100,000

   From January 1 through 18, 20-9, partners sold off the inventory for $600,000 and then distributed the cash in proportion to their capital balances. At this time, the partners' shares in profits and losses are as follows:

Dimmitt	30%
Mantz	30%
Sacks	20%
Stiglitz	20%

   Prepare the journal entries to record the sale of inventory for $600,000 and the allocation of the gain or loss.

The answers to the Self-Study Questions and Exercises are at the end of the chapter (pages 764–765).

APPLYING YOUR KNOWLEDGE

REVIEW QUESTIONS

LO1 1. Identify 11 essential provisions of a partnership agreement.

LO1 2. Identify three advantages of a partnership as compared with a sole proprietorship.

LO1 3. Identify four disadvantages of a partnership form of business organization.

LO2 4. When two sole proprietors decide to combine their businesses, at what values should the noncash assets be taken over by the partnership?

LO3 5. In the absence of any agreement between the partners, how must profits and losses be shared? If the partnership agreement specifies how profits are to be shared, but there is no agreement as to how losses are to be shared, what must be true with respect to losses?

LO3 6. What factors generally are considered in determining the allocation of profits and losses?

LO5 7. Identify three ways in which a partnership may be dissolved.

LO5 8. When a new partner who has been the sole owner of a business is admitted to a partnership by having the partnership take over the old business, what usually serves as the basis for preparing the opening entry?

LO6 9. Describe the four accounting entries for the liquidation of a partnership.

SERIES A EXERCISES

E 19-1A (LO2)

PARTNERSHIP OPENING ENTRIES Lisa Morris and Joyce Laski agreed on September 1 to go into business as partners. According to the agreement, Morris is to contribute $45,000 cash and Laski is to contribute $65,000 cash. Provide a separate journal entry for the investment of each partner.

E 19-2A (LO3)

✓ 4. Rhea: $42,000

ENTRIES FOR ALLOCATION OF NET INCOME Karen Rhea and Wayne Sellevaeg decided to form a partnership on July 1, 20-1. Rhea invested $100,000 and Sellevaeg invested $50,000. For the fiscal year ended June 30, 20-2, a net income of $90,000 was earned. Determine the amount of net income that Rhea and Sellevaeg would receive under each of the following independent assumptions:

1. There is no agreement concerning the distribution of net income.
2. Each partner is to receive 10% interest on their original investment. The remaining net income is to be divided equally.
3. Rhea and Sellevaeg are to receive a salary allowance of $30,000 and $40,000, respectively. The remaining net income is to be divided equally.
4. Each partner is to receive 10% interest on their original investment. Rhea and Sellevaeg are to receive a salary allowance of $30,000 and $40,000, respectively. The remaining net income is to be divided as follows: Rhea, 40% and Sellevaeg, 60%.

E 19-3A (LO4)

✓ 1. Allocation of net income: Cooper, $40,000;
2. Capital: Cooper, $110,000

PARTIAL FINANCIAL STATEMENTS Karen Cooper and Alex Orme formed a partnership on May 1, 20-1. Cooper contributed $80,000 and Orme contributed $50,000. During the year, Cooper contributed an additional $20,000. The partnership agreement states that Cooper is to receive $30,000 and Orme is to receive $60,000 as a salary allowance. Any remaining net income is to be divided as follows: Cooper, 20% and Orme, 80%. The partnership earned net income of $140,000 for the fiscal year ending April 30, 20-2. During the first year of operation, Cooper and Orme withdrew $30,000 and $50,000, respectively.

1. Prepare the lower portion of the income statement showing the allocation of net income between Cooper and Orme for the fiscal year ended April 30, 20-2.
2. Prepare a statement of partners' equity showing each individual partner's equity for the fiscal year ended April 30, 20-2.

E 19-4A (LO5)
✓ 2. Ending capital bal.: Bowman, $80,000; Emery, $45,000

ADMITTING NEW PARTNERS Jeff Bowman and Kristi Emery, who have ending capital balances of $100,000 and $60,000, respectively, agree to admit two new partners to their business on August 18, 20--. Dan Bridges will buy one-fifth of Bowman's capital interest for $30,000 and one-fourth of Emery's capital interest for $20,000. Payments will be made directly to the partners. Anna Terrell will invest $50,000 in the business, for which she will receive a $50,000 capital interest.

1. Prepare general journal entries showing the transactions admitting Bridges and Terrell to the partnership.
2. Calculate the ending capital balances of all four partners after the transactions.

E 19-5A (LO6)
✓ Gain: $50,000

ENTRIES: PARTNERSHIP LIQUIDATION On liquidation of the partnership of J. Hui and K. Cline, as of November 1, 20--, inventory with a book value of $180,000 is sold for $230,000. Given that Hui and Cline share profits and losses equally, prepare the entries for the sale and the allocation of gain.

SERIES A PROBLEMS

P 19-6A (LO2)
✓ Cr. to Woodworth, Capital: $29,010

PARTNERSHIP OPENING ENTRIES On July 1, 20--, Susan Woodworth and Barbara Holly combined their two businesses to form a partnership under the firm name of Woodworth and Holly. The balance sheets of the two sole proprietorships are shown below and on the next page.

The balance sheets reflect fair market values except for the following:

(a) The fair market value of Woodworth's store equipment is $7,500.
(b) The fair market values of Holly's office equipment and store equipment are $6,100 and $6,800, respectively.

REQUIRED

Prepare the opening entry for the formation of the Woodworth and Holly partnership as of July 1, 20--, using fair market values. The difference between assets invested and liabilities assumed should be credited to each partner's capital account. Neither partner has knowledge of any uncollectible accounts receivable.

Woodworth's Antiques
Balance Sheet
June 30, 20 --

Assets			Liabilities		
Cash		$7,100.00	Notes payable	$2,500.00	
Accounts receivable	$4,500.00		Accounts payable	8,400.00	
Less allowance for bad debts	620.00	3,880.00	Total liabilities		$10,900.00
Merchandise inventory		21,430.00			
Store equipment	$8,200.00		**Owner's Equity**		
Less accumulated depreciation	1,300.00	6,900.00	Susan Woodworth, capital		28,410.00
Total assets		$39,310.00	Total liabilities and owner's equity		$39,310.00

(continued)

Holly's Unfinished Furniture Balance Sheet June 30, 20--					
Assets			Liabilities		
Cash		$ 4,520.00	Notes payable	$8,000.00	
Accounts receivable	$3,275.00		Accounts payable	6,300.00	
Less allowance for bad debts	475.00	2,800.00	Total liabilities		$14,300.00
Merchandise inventory		28,190.00			
Supplies		960.00			
Office equipment	$7,400.00				
Less accumulated depreciation	1,800.00	5,600.00			
Store equipment	$7,700.00		Owner's Equity		
Less accumulated depreciation	1,500.00	6,200.00	Barbara Holly, capital		33,970.00
Total assets		$48,270.00	Total liabilities and owner's equity		$48,270.00

P 19-7A (LO4)

✓ 1. Allocation of net income: Hiller, $79,700; 2. Capital: Hiller, $69,100

KA KLOOSTER & ALLEN

PREPARING PARTIAL FINANCIAL STATEMENTS AND CLOSING ENTRIES The partnership of Hiller and Roundtree, CPAs, showed revenues of $195,000 and expenses of $52,000 on their year-end work sheet. Their capital balances as of January 1, 20--, were $52,000 for B. Hiller and $48,000 for O. Roundtree. No additional investments were made during the year. As stated in their partnership agreement, after withdrawing salary allowances of $60,000 for Hiller and $40,000 for Roundtree, the partners each withdrew 5% interest on their January 1 capital balances. No additional withdrawals were made. Any remaining net income is to be divided on a 45-55 basis.

REQUIRED

1. Prepare the lower portion of the income statement of the partnership for the year ended December 31, 20--, showing the division of the partnership net income for the year.
2. Prepare a statement of partners' equity for the year ended December 31, 20--, and the partners' equity section of the balance sheet on that date.
3. Prepare closing entries for the partnership as of December 31, 20--. (For simplicity, use the account titles "Revenues" for all revenues and "Expenses" for all expenses.)

P 19-8A (LO5)

✓ 1. Cr. to Mike Kelly, Capital: $5,000; 2. Dr. to Mike Kelly, Capital: $7,500

ENTRIES FOR DISSOLUTION OF PARTNERSHIP The Kelly and Kelly Wrecking Company, a partnership, operates a general demolition business. Ownership of the company is divided among the partners, Mike Kelly, Kim Kelly, Larry Dennis, and Jim Wheeles. Profits and losses are shared equally. The books are kept on a calendar-year basis.

On September 15, after the business had been in operation for several years, Dennis died. Mrs. Dennis wished to sell her husband's interest in the partnership for $25,000. After the books were closed, the partners' capital accounts had credit balances as follows:

Mike Kelly	$50,000
Kim Kelly	25,000
Larry Dennis	35,000
Jim Wheeles	25,000

REQUIRED

1. Prepare the general journal entry required to enter the check issued to Mrs. Dennis in payment of her deceased husband's interest in the partnership. According to the partnership agreement, the difference between the amount paid to Mrs. Dennis and the book value of Larry Dennis's capital account is allocated to the remaining partners based on their ending capital account balances.
2. Assume instead that Mrs. Dennis is paid $50,000 for the book value of Larry Dennis's capital account. Prepare the necessary journal entry.
3. Assume instead that Jim Wheeles (with the consent of the remaining partners) purchased Dennis's interest for $40,000 and gave Mrs. Dennis a personal check for that amount. Prepare the general journal entry for the partnership only.

P 19-9A (LO6)

✓ 1. Cash distributed to partners: Baldwin, $55,000

STATEMENT OF PARTNERSHIP LIQUIDATION WITH GAIN After several years of operations, the partnership of Baldwin, Cowan, and Stewart is to be liquidated. After making closing entries on June 30, 20--, the following accounts remain open:

	Account Balance	
Account Title	**Debit**	**Credit**
Cash	$ 5,000	
Inventory	55,000	
Other Assets	180,000	
Liabilities		$40,000
R. J. Baldwin, Capital		50,000
N. R. Cowan, Capital		90,000
K. M. Stewart, Capital		60,000

The noncash assets are sold for $250,000. Profits and losses are shared equally.

REQUIRED

1. Prepare a statement of partnership liquidation for the period July 1–20, 20--, showing the following:
   (a) The sale of noncash assets on July 1
   (b) The allocation of any gain or loss to the partners on July 1
   (c) The payment of the liabilities on July 15
   (d) The distribution of cash to the partners on July 20
2. Journalize these four transactions in a general journal.

P 19-10A (LO6)

✓ 1. Distribution of cash to partners: Nelson, $30,000

STATEMENT OF PARTNERSHIP LIQUIDATION WITH LOSS After several years of operations, the partnership of Nelson, Pope, and Williams is to be liquidated. After making closing entries on March 31, 20--, the following accounts remain open:

	Account Balance	
Account Title	**Debit**	**Credit**
Cash	$ 15,000	
Inventory	40,000	
Other Assets	220,000	
Liabilities		$ 75,000
C. W. Nelson, Capital		40,000
J. R. Pope, Capital		60,000
M. L. Williams, Capital		100,000

(continued)

The noncash assets are sold for $230,000. Profits and losses are shared equally.

REQUIRED

1. Prepare a statement of partnership liquidation for the period April 1–15, 20--, showing the following:
   (a) The sale of the noncash assets on April 1
   (b) The allocation of any gain or loss to the partners on April 1
   (c) The payment of the liabilities on April 12
   (d) The distribution of cash to the partners on April 15
2. Journalize these four transactions in a general journal.

SERIES B EXERCISES

E 19-1B (LO2)

PARTNERSHIP OPENING ENTRIES Sharon Usher and Leann Gomez agreed on September 1 to go into business as partners. According to the agreement, Usher is to contribute $30,000 cash and Gomez is to contribute $50,000 cash. Provide a separate journal entry for the investment of each partner.

E 19-2B (LO3)
✓ 4. Clark: $35,500

ENTRIES FOR ALLOCATION OF NET INCOME John Clark and David Haase decided to form a partnership on July 1, 20-6. Clark invested $60,000 and Haase invested $40,000. For the fiscal year ended June 30, 20-7, a net income of $80,000 was earned. Determine the amount of net income that Clark and Haase would receive under each of the following independent assumptions:

1. There is no agreement concerning the distribution of net income.
2. Each partner is to receive 10% interest on their original investment. The remaining net income is to be divided equally.
3. Clark and Haase are to receive a salary allowance of $25,000 and $30,000, respectively. The remaining net income is to be divided equally.
4. Each partner is to receive 10% interest on their original investment. Clark and Haase are to receive a salary allowance of $25,000 and $30,000, respectively. The remaining net income is to be divided as follows: Clark, 30% and Haase, 70%.

E 19-3B (LO4)
✓ 1. Allocation of net income: Nolan, $33,000;
2. Capital: Nolan, $78,000

PARTIAL FINANCIAL STATEMENTS Randy Nolan and Jill Brenton formed a partnership on May 1, 20-1. Nolan contributed $50,000 and Brenton contributed $25,000. During the year, Nolan contributed an additional $10,000. The partnership agreement states that Nolan is to receive $15,000 and Brenton is to receive $50,000 as a salary allowance. Any remaining net income is to be divided as follows: Nolan, 40% and Brenton, 60%. The partnership earned net income of $110,000 for the fiscal year ending April 30, 20-2. During the first year of operation, Nolan and Brenton withdrew $15,000 and $40,000, respectively.

1. Prepare the lower portion of the income statement showing the allocation of net income between Nolan and Brenton for the fiscal year ended April 30, 20-2.
2. Prepare a statement of partners' equity, showing each individual partner's equity for the fiscal year ended April 30, 20-2.

E 19-4B (LO5)
✓ 2. Capital bal.: Rhodes, $60,000; Blair, $32,000

ADMITTING NEW PARTNERS Maria Rhodes and Craig Blair, who have ending capital balances of $90,000 and $40,000, respectively, agree to admit two new partners to their business on September 1, 20--. Lori Kinder will buy one-third of Rhodes's capital interest for $40,000 and one-fifth of Blair's capital interest for $12,000.

Payments will be made directly to the partners. Todd Gilbert will invest $30,000 in the business for which he will receive a $30,000 capital interest.

1. Prepare general journal entries showing the transactions admitting Kinder and Gilbert to the partnership.
2. Calculate the ending capital balances of all four partners after the transactions.

E 19-5B (LO6)
✓ Loss: $16,000

ENTRIES: PARTNERSHIP LIQUIDATION On liquidation of the partnership of L. Straw and M. Maury, as of February 9, 20--, assets with a book value of $156,000 are sold for $140,000. Given that the profit-and-loss ratio is 60% for Straw and 40% for Maury, prepare the entries for the sale and the allocation of loss.

SERIES B PROBLEMS

P 19-6B (LO2)
✓ Cr. to Bush, Capital: $32,960

KA KLOOSTER & ALLEN

PARTNERSHIP OPENING ENTRIES On July 1, 20--, Lisa Bush and Wally Dodge combined their two businesses to form a partnership under the firm name of Bush and Dodge. The balance sheets of the two sole proprietorships are shown below.

Bush's Grooming & Pet Supplies
Balance Sheet
June 30, 20--

Assets			Liabilities		
Cash		$4,600.00	Notes payable	$3,600.00	
Accounts receivable	$4,200.00		Accounts payable	7,690.00	
Less allowance for bad debts	480.00	3,720.00	Total liabilities		$11,290.00
Merchandise inventory		28,580.00			
Store equipment	$9,260.00		Owner's Equity		
Less accumulated depreciation	2,400.00	6,860.00	Lisa Bush, capital		32,470.00
Total assets		$43,760.00	Total liabilities and owner's equity		$43,760.00

Wally's Pet World
Balance Sheet
June 30, 20--

Assets			Liabilities		
Cash		$3,350.00	Notes payable	$6,000.00	
Accounts receivable	$4,150.00		Accounts payable	5,500.00	
Less allowance for bad debts	250.00	3,900.00	Total liabilities		$11,500.00
Merchandise inventory		27,240.00			
Supplies		845.00			
Office equipment	$8,830.00				
Less accumulated depreciation	3,400.00	5,430.00			
Store equipment	$9,175.00		Owner's Equity		
Less accumulated depreciation	4,250.00	4,925.00	Wally Dodge, capital		34,190.00
Total assets		$45,690.00	Total liabilities and owner's equity		$45,690.00

The balance sheets reflect fair market values except for the following:

(a) The fair market value of Bush's store equipment is $7,350.
(b) The fair market values of Dodge's office equipment and store equipment are $5,875 and $6,100, respectively.

(continued)

REQUIRED

Prepare the opening entry for the formation of the Bush and Dodge partnership as of July 1, 20--, using fair market values. The difference between assets invested and liabilities assumed should be credited to each partner's capital account. Neither partner has knowledge of any uncollectible accounts receivable.

P 19-7B (LO4)

✓ 1. Allocation of net income: Rummel, $52,140; 2. Capital: Rummel, $46,040

KLOOSTER & ALLEN

PREPARING PARTIAL FINANCIAL STATEMENTS AND CLOSING ENTRIES The partnership of Rummel and Kang, Stonecutters, showed revenues of $133,000 and expenses of $41,000 on the year-end work sheet. The capital balances as of January 1, 20--, were $41,000 for C. Rummel and $25,000 for V. Kang. No additional investments were made during the year. As stated in their partnership agreement, after withdrawing salary allowances of $43,000 for Rummel and $34,000 for Kang, the partners each withdrew 10% interest on their January 1 capital balances. No additional withdrawals were made. Any remaining net income is to be divided on a 60-40 basis.

REQUIRED

1. Prepare the lower portion of the income statement of the partnership for the year ended December 31, 20--, showing the division of the partnership net income for the year.
2. Prepare a statement of partners' equity for the year ended December 31, 20--, and the partners' equity section of the balance sheet on that date.
3. Prepare closing entries for the partnership as of December 31, 20--. (For simplicity, use the account titles "Revenues" for all revenues and "Expenses" for all expenses.)

P 19-8B (LO5)

✓ 1. Cr. to Cummings, Capital: $4,500; 2. Dr. to Cummings, Capital: $9,000

ENTRIES FOR DISSOLUTION OF PARTNERSHIP Cummings and Stickel Construction Company, a partnership, is operating a general contracting business. Ownership of the company is divided among the partners, Katie Cummings, Julie Stickel, Roy Hewson, and Patricia Weber. Profits and losses are shared equally. The books are kept on the calendar-year basis.

On August 10, after the business had been in operation for several years, Patricia Weber died. Mr. Weber wished to sell his wife's interest for $30,000. After the books were closed, the partners' capital accounts had credit balances as follows:

Katie Cummings	$90,000
Julie Stickel	60,000
Roy Hewson	50,000
Patricia Weber	40,000

REQUIRED

1. Prepare the general journal entry required to enter the check issued to Mr. Weber in payment of his deceased wife's interest in the partnership. According to the partnership agreement, the difference between the amount paid to Mr. Weber and the book value of Patricia Weber's capital account is allocated to the remaining partners based on their ending capital account balances.
2. Assume instead that Mr. Weber is paid $60,000 for the book value of Patricia Weber's capital account. Prepare the necessary journal entry.
3. Assume instead that Julie Stickel (with the consent of the remaining partners) purchased Weber's interest for $70,000 and gave Mr. Weber a personal check for that amount. Prepare the general journal entry for the partnership only.

P 19-9B (LO6)

✓ 1. Cash distributed to partners: Leonard, $67,000

STATEMENT OF PARTNERSHIP LIQUIDATION WITH GAIN After several years of operations, the partnership of Leonard, Mitchell, and Swanson is to be liquidated. After making closing entries on June 30, 20--, the following accounts remain open:

	Account Balance	
Account Title	Debit	Credit
Cash	$ 4,000	
Inventory	40,000	
Other Assets	150,000	
Liabilities		$44,000
B. J. Leonard, Capital		60,000
W. T. Mitchell, Capital		15,000
J. C. Swanson, Capital		75,000

The noncash assets are sold for $211,000. Profits and losses are shared equally.

REQUIRED

1. Prepare a statement of partnership liquidation for the period July 1–20, 20--, showing the following:
   (a) The sale of noncash assets on July 1
   (b) The allocation of any gain or loss to the partners on July 1
   (c) The payment of the liabilities on July 15
   (d) The distribution of cash to the partners on July 20
2. Journalize these four transactions in a general journal.

P 19-10B (LO6)

✓ 1. Cash distributed to partners: Delco, $15,000

STATEMENT OF PARTNERSHIP LIQUIDATION WITH LOSS After several years of operations, the partnership of Delco, Smith, and Walker is to be liquidated. After making closing entries on March 31, 20--, the following accounts remain open.

	Account Balance	
Account Title	Debit	Credit
Cash	$ 7,000	
Inventory	25,000	
Other Assets	185,000	
Liabilities		$17,000
D. W. Delco, Capital		30,000
C. S. Smith, Capital		90,000
T. R. Walker, Capital		80,000

The noncash assets are sold for $165,000. Profits and losses are shared equally.

REQUIRED

1. Prepare a statement of partnership liquidation for the period April 1–15, 20--, showing the following:
   (a) The sale of noncash assets on April 1
   (b) The allocation of any gain or loss to the partners on April 1
   (c) The payment of the liabilities on April 12
   (d) The distribution of cash to the partners on April 15
2. Journalize these four transactions in a general journal.

MANAGING YOUR WRITING

A friend, Joan Mellencamp, has mentioned that she is thinking about forming a partnership with a small group of colleagues. She is interested in learning about the advantages and disadvantages of the partnership form of ownership. In addition, she has asked for your advice on the kinds of issues that should be agreed upon in advance of the formation of the partnership. Write a memo to your friend explaining the advantages and disadvantages of a partnership and offer your advice on the issues that should be settled in advance.

ETHICS CASE

Kathy Lentz, Rob Snyder, and Tom Rohm were all general partners in a consulting business. Each partner owned one-third of the business. The partnership agreement stated that all three partners must approve vouchers for payments in amounts exceeding $5,000. While Tom was on vacation, Kathy and Rob decided to purchase a new computer system costing $6,800. A voucher was prepared and Rob signed both his and Tom's name. Kathy signed her name and gave the voucher to the accounts payable clerk who wrote the check for $6,800.

1. Why would a partnership agreement specify that all purchases over a certain amount be approved by all partners? Are there any circumstances that would warrant deviation from this policy?
2. What are the disadvantages of the partnership form of business ownership?
3. Write a short memo from Tom Rohm to Kathy Lentz and Rob Snyder expressing disapproval of the situation.
4. In groups of three or four, discuss some of the possible outcomes of this situation.

MASTERY PROBLEM

✓ 4. Distribution of cash to partners: I. Fleming, $71,500

Jim Bond, a plumber, has been working for Fleming's Plumbing Supplies for several years. Based on his hard work and the fact that he recently married Ivan Fleming's daughter, Jim has been invited to enter into a partnership with Fleming. The new partnership will be called Fleming and Bond's Plumbing Supplies. The terms of the partnership are as follows:

(a) Fleming will invest the assets of Fleming's Plumbing Supplies, and the partnership will assume all liabilities. The market values of the office and store equipment are estimated to be $18,000 and $8,000, respectively. All other values reported on the balance sheet are reasonable approximations of market values. Fleming has no knowledge of any uncollectible accounts receivable.
(b) Bond will invest $50,000 cash.
(c) Fleming will draw a salary allowance of $50,000 per year, and Bond will receive $30,000.
(d) Each partner will receive 10% interest on the January 1 balance of his capital account.
(e) Profits or losses remaining after allocating salaries and interest will be distributed as follows: Fleming, 60% and Bond, 40%.

Fleming's Plumbing Supplies
Balance Sheet
December 31, 20-1

Assets			Liabilities		
Cash		$ 13,544.00	Notes payable	$36,000.00	
Accounts receivable	$15,280.00		Accounts payable	18,082.00	
Less allowance for bad debts	1,720.00	13,560.00	Total liabilities		$ 54,082.00
Merchandise inventory		89,692.00			
Supplies		1,286.00			
Office equipment	$14,320.00				
Less accumulated depreciation	1,100.00	13,220.00			
Store equipment	$ 8,800.00		Owner's Equity		
Less accumulated depreciation	2,200.00	6,600.00	Ivan Fleming, capital		83,820.00
Total assets		$137,902.00	Total liabilities and owner's equity		$137,902.00

REQUIRED

1. Prepare the entries on January 1, 20-2, for the formation of the partnership.
2. Net income for the partnership for 20-2 was $150,000. Prepare the lower portion of the income statement reporting the allocation of the profits to each partner.
3. In December 20-4, Fleming's daughter, Penny, graduated from business college and asked to join the business as a partner. She has $30,000 to invest and it is agreed that Penny will be given a capital interest of $30,000. Profits and losses will be shared as follows: I. Fleming, 50%; J. Bond, 30%; P. Fleming, 20%. Prepare the entry for Penny's investment on January 1, 20-5.
4. After several years of operations, it is decided to liquidate the partnership. After making closing entries on July 31, 20-9, the following accounts remain open:

Cash	$ 20,000	
Inventory	150,000	
Office Equipment	30,000	
Accum. Depreciation—Office Equipment		$18,000
Store Equipment	22,000	
Accum. Depreciation—Store Equipment		15,000
Notes Payable		20,000
Ivan Fleming, Capital		80,000
Jim Bond, Capital		50,000
Penny Fleming, Capital		39,000

(a) On August 1, 20-9, the inventory is sold for $130,000.
(b) On August 3, the office equipment is sold for $10,000.
(c) On August 5, the store equipment is sold for $12,000.
(d) On August 10, the notes payable are paid.
(e) On August 15, the remaining cash is distributed to the partners according to the balances in their capital accounts.

Prepare a statement of partnership liquidation and related journal entries for the period August 1–15, 20-9.

CHALLENGE PROBLEM

This problem challenges you to apply your cumulative accounting knowledge to move a step beyond the material in the chapter.

✓ Allocation of net income: Dewi, $122,500

The partnership agreement for the law firm of Dewi, Cheetem, and Howe states that net income should be allocated in the following manner:

1. Salaries are to be paid as follows:
   - Dewi, $50,000 per year
   - Cheetem, $40,000 per year
   - Howe, $20,000 per year
2. Each partner is to be paid a bonus of 25% of all revenues he or she generated. During 20-1, each partner generated the following revenues:
   - Dewi, $250,000
   - Cheetem, $150,000
   - Howe, $100,000
3. Each partner receives 10% interest on the beginning balance of his or her capital account. Beginning balances of the capital accounts are as follows:
   - Dewi, $200,000
   - Cheetem, $100,000
   - Howe, $50,000

Net income for the year ended December 31, 20-1, was $240,000.

REQUIRED

Prepare the lower portion of the income statement showing the allocation of net income to Dewi, Cheetem, and Howe.

ANSWERS TO SELF-STUDY QUESTIONS AND EXERCISES

True/False Questions

1. F (partnership)
2. T
3. F (limited life is a characteristic of a partnership because the partnership is dissolved with any change in the partners)
4. F (this is a disadvantage)
5. T

Multiple Choice Questions

1. a 2. a 3. d 4. c 5. a

U REVU Exercises

1.

1		Cash		100,000.00		1
2		Paul Dimmitt, Capital			100,000.00	2
3		Investment in partnership				3
4		Cash		100,000.00		4
5		Mike Stiglitz, Capital			100,000.00	5
6		Investment in partnership				6

2.

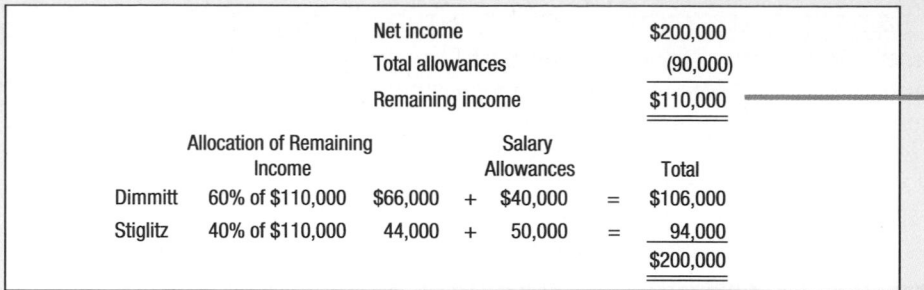

		Net income					$200,000
		Total allowances					(90,000)
		Remaining income					$110,000
	Allocation of Remaining Income			Salary Allowances			Total
Dimmitt	60% of $110,000	$66,000	+	$40,000	=		$106,000
Stiglitz	40% of $110,000	44,000	+	50,000	=		94,000
							$200,000

3.

The Bogey Men
Income Statement (Partial)
For Year Ended December 31, 20 - -

	P. Dimmitt	M. Stiglitz	TOTAL
Net income			$200,000.00
Allocation of net income:			
Salary allowances	$ 40,000.00	$50,000.00	$ 90,000.00
Remaining income	66,000.00	44,000.00	110,000.00
Allocation of net income	$106,000.00	$94,000.00	$200,000.00

4.

		Debit	Credit
	Mike Stiglitz, Capital	50,000.00	
	James Mantz, Capital		50,000.00
	Mantz admitted to partnership		
	Cash	50,000.00	
	Jack Sacks, Capital		50,000.00
	Sacks' investment in partnership		

5.

		Debit	Credit
	Cash	600,000.00	
	Inventory		400,000.00
	Gain on Sale of inventory		200,000.00
	Sale of inventory		
	Gain on Sale of Inventory	200,000.00	
	Paul Dimmitt, Capital		60,000.00
	James Mantz, Capital		60,000.00
	Jack Sacks, Capital		40,000.00
	Mike Stiglitz, Capital		40,000.00
	Allocation of gain		

COMPREHENSIVE PROBLEM 3: SPECIALIZED ACCOUNTING PROCEDURES

Siblings Jordan and Morgan Hartley are partners in a trendy toy store called ToyMania! Jordan, as senior partner, receives an annual salary allowance of $20,000 and 60 percent of all income/losses after salary and interest allowances are paid. Junior partner Morgan receives an annual salary allowance of $15,000 and 40 percent of all income/losses after salary and interest allowances are paid. The partners receive a 10 percent interest allowance at the end of the accounting period based on their respective January 1 capital account balances. Capital balances as of January 1 are $60,000 for Jordan Hartley and $40,000 for Morgan Hartley.

ToyMania! uses the allowance method for uncollectible accounts. Credit terms are 2/10, n/30. Longer payment terms are available by accepting interest-bearing notes receivable. Terms will vary depending on individual circumstances and will be provided in the related transactions. Notes under $1,000 are collected by ToyMania! while notes greater than $1,000 are collected by either Dean Bank or Marshall Bank. Interest is based on a 360-day year. Estimated uncollectibles are based on 3 percent of accounts receivable. Accounts are written off, as they are deemed uncollectible; however, efforts to collect all receivables continue for a two-year period.

ToyMania! occasionally writes notes to finance larger purchases and to extend time on accounts payable. Terms will be specified in the related transactions. Again, interest is based on a 360-day year.

Plant assets are depreciated using one of the various GAAP methods for depreciation. Fully depreciated assets that are useful remain in service until a sale, trade, or disposal is necessary. ToyMania! holds a patent on a toy which is amortized during year-end adjustments. The $25,000 patent's economic life is 10 years although the legal life is 20 years.

A periodic inventory system is maintained valuing inventory using the First-In, First-Out (FIFO) method. The lower-of-cost-or-market rule is applied by recognizing a loss on write-down of inventory when necessary. Beginning merchandise inventory on January 1 was $91,250.

Transactions for 20-1 are provided below.

Jan. 5 Reinstated the account of Christine Roby, which had been written off in the preceding year, and received $500 cash in full settlement.

14 Issued a $3,000, 3-month, 6% note to Zekir Computer Systems to purchase a new computer system (*Computer System*). The system, with an expected life of four years and no salvage value, will be depreciated using the double-declining-balance method.

Feb. 15 Received a $2,500, 6-month, 7% note from Carol Reynolds for sale of merchandise.

Mar. 11 Morgan Hartley invested an additional $5,000 into the business.

Apr. 1 Disposed of a cash register (*Store Equipment*) originally costing $675 with a $75 salvage value. Depreciation is computed on a monthly basis with adjusting entries made at the end of each year. Depreciation after eight years of use was $480 as of December 31. The cash register had an estimated life of 10 years.

12 Borrowed $5,000 from Dean Bank, signing a 75-day, 10% note.

14 Paid $500, plus interest, to Zekir Computer Systems (see January 14) and gave a new $2,500, 30-day, 8% note to extend time for payment.

May 1 Wrote off the $1,200 balance owed by Brenda Husband as uncollectible.

14 Paid the principal and interest due on the $2,500 note to Zekir Computer Systems. (See April 14.)

25 Paid $75 cash to Snowden's Service Station for an oil change, tire rotation, and coolant flushing on the company van.

June 1 Received a $1,700, 120-day, 8% note from Heidi Kruczkiewicz to settle an account receivable.

20 Reinstated the account of Brenda Husband, which had been written off last month, and received $1,200 cash in full settlement. (See May 1.)

22 Paid $30,000 cash to Klippi Construction for an addition (*Addition*) to the store so that more merchandise could be displayed. The addition has an estimated salvage value of $2,000 and an estimated life of 20 years. Depreciation is to be calculated using the straight-line method.

26 Paid the principal and interest due on the $5,000 note to Dean Bank. (See April 12.)

30 Upon opening the store, it was apparent that someone had entered the store illegally. Jordan and Morgan need to determine whether anything had been stolen. A physical inventory was taken and it was determined that approximately $67,500 in inventory was on hand, but they need to know how much inventory should have been on hand. Estimate the cost using the retail method based on the following information. Figures at cost: beginning inventory, $91,250; and net purchases, $70,000. Figures at retail: beginning inventory, $120,000; net purchases $95,000; and net sales, $125,000. Compare your estimate with the balance of $67,500. Does it appear that any inventory was stolen? *Space is provided for your calculations following the journal pages for the problem in your working papers.*

July 1 Heidi Kruczkiewicz's note (see June 1) is discounted at Marshall Bank at a discount rate of 12%.

8 Sold $4,250 in merchandise to Kim Sackett, terms 2/10, n/30.

10 Purchased merchandise on account for $15,000 from Dionis Distributing. Credit terms are 3/20, n/30.

18 Received payment in full from Kim Sackett, less discount, for merchandise sold on July 8.

30 Paid Dionis Distributing for merchandise purchased on account on July 10.

Aug. 1 Paid $500 to Snowden's Service Station to replace the exhaust system on the company van.

15 Received notification from Dean Bank that the principal and interest were collected on the note from Carol Reynolds. (See February 15.) The bank fee for collecting the note was $10.

22 Wrote off the $750 balance owed by Shelley Kozub as uncollectible.

Sept. 1 Traded the company car (*Automobile*) for a more stylish one at Plume Motors. The old car originally cost $13,000 and is depreciated up-to-date in the amount of $9,000. A trade-in allowance of $5,500 was given. The new car had a market value of $18,000 and the balance was paid in cash. The new car should last at least 100,000 miles and will be depreciated at $0.375 per mile.

9 Received a $2,000, 60-day, 7.5% note from Tammy Jones in payment of an account receivable.

15 Purchased $3,500 worth of toys from Dennis Designs, terms n/30.

Sept. 29 Received notification from Marshall Bank that Heidi Kruczkiewicz's note was dishonored. (See June 1 and July 1.) A check is issued to cover the maturity value plus a $50 bank fee that must be paid to the bank.

Oct. 15 Issued a $3,500, 90-day, 8% note to Dennis Designs to extend time for payment on an account payable.

20 Borrowed $10,000 for 180 days from Ohler-Cupplo Savings Association on a non-interest-bearing note. The discount rate is 7.5%.

Oct. 31 Sold $125 of merchandise for cash to Melinda Miller.

Nov. 1 Received a $500, 30-day, 5% note from Laura Nottingham in payment of an account receivable.

8 Received notification from Marshall Bank that Tammy Jones dishonored her note. (See September 9.) No fee was charged.

30 Heidi Kruczkiewicz's dishonored note is collected; Kruczkiewicz pays ToyMania! the maturity value of the note, the $50 bank fee, and interest at 9% on the maturity value plus bank fee. (See September 29.)

Dec. 1 Laura Nottingham paid the interest due on her note (see November 1), and gave a new note ($500) for 45 days at 8%.

14 Paid $2,000 to landscape and improve a grassy area on the lot. There will be no salvage value after 5 years and the landscaping will be depreciated using the sum-of-the-years'-digits method.

31 Sold building fixtures for $100. The original cost of the fixtures was $500 with an estimated 5-year life and no salvage value. Depreciation up-to-date is $300.

REQUIRED

1. Journalize the above transactions as needed.
2. Prepare selected adjusting entries using the following information.
   (a) Accrued interest receivable. (See December 1.)
   (b) Accrued interest payable. *Separate entries should be made for discounted and non-discounted notes.* (See October 15 and October 20.)
   (c) Depreciation for the year on the computer system put into service on January 14.
   (d) Depreciation for the year on the new car. 7,000 miles were traveled this period.
   (e) Depreciation for the year on the addition completed June 22.
   (f) Depreciation for the year on the landscaping recorded December 14.
   (g) Annual amortization on the patent.
   (h) Estimated uncollectibles are based on accounts receivable of $48,940. Current Allowance for Bad Debts balance is $375 credit.
   (i, j) Ending inventory valued at cost on December 31 is $102,000.
   (k) Ending inventory valued at market prices on December 31 is $100,500.
3. Prepare the following financial statements:
   (a) Partial Income Statement showing the allocation of net income. ToyMania! had a net income of $84,000 for the year. Each partner made withdrawals equal to his/her salary and interest allowances as stated in the partnership agreement.
   (b) Statement of Partners' Equity. No additional withdrawals were made after salary and interest allowances were allocated.
4. Prepare selected closing entries, referring to the financial statements as needed.
   (a) Close Income Summary to the capital accounts.
   (b) Close drawing accounts to the capital accounts.
5. Prepare reversing entries when appropriate.
6. Journalize the following transactions that occurred in the subsequent year.

Jan. 13 Paid the principal and interest due on the $3,500 note to Dennis Designs. (See October 15.)

15 Laura Nottingham paid her note plus interest. (See December 1.)

Apr. 18 Paid the principal on the $10,000 non-interest-bearing note to Ohler-Cupplo Savings Association. (See October 20.)

Accounting for Corporations and Manufacturing Businesses

PART 5

CREATAS/PHOTOLIBRARY

Add Some Color to Your Learning!

Throughout the text, you will be introduced to many important terms and types of accounts. To help you learn the different terms and types of accounts, we have coded many of them using the following color key in Part 5:

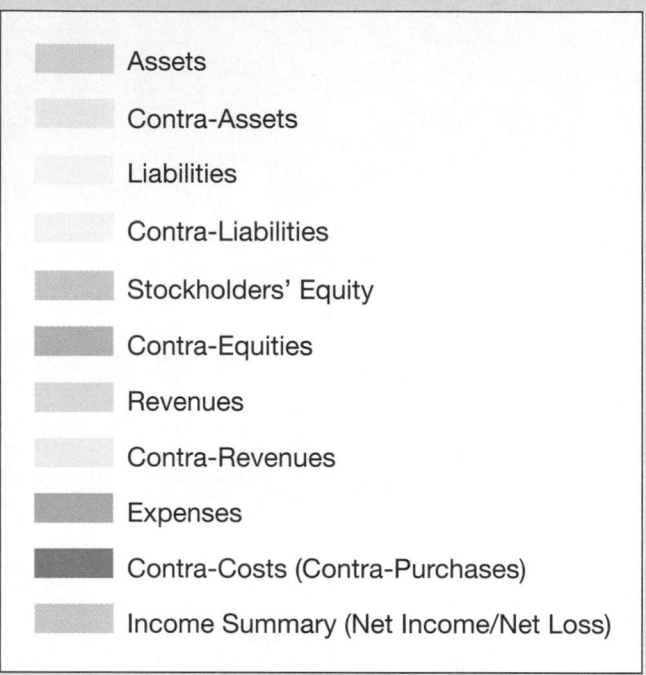

- Assets
- Contra-Assets
- Liabilities
- Contra-Liabilities
- Stockholders' Equity
- Contra-Equities
- Revenues
- Contra-Revenues
- Expenses
- Contra-Costs (Contra-Purchases)
- Income Summary (Net Income/Net Loss)

Chapter 20

Corporations: Organization and Capital Stock

If you have watched a James Bond movie, have you ever dreamed of zooming down the road in an exotic car like a Ferrari or Lamborghini? Based on the growth experience of Gotham Dream Cars, that's not an unusual dream. Gotham Dream Cars rents out extremely high-end cars, like Ferraris, Lamborghinis, Bentleys, Porsches, and Aston Martins, for as little as one day or as much as a month. The company also runs a Dream Car Tour in which participants drive six different exotic sports cars in one day over 120 miles of the area's best roads.

Gotham Dream Cars is headquartered in New York, where it was founded in 2003, and it has operations in both New York and Fort Lauderdale. Sales grew from $262,000 in 2004 to $2.9 million in 2007, and the numbers have continued to grow. The basis for Gotham Dream Cars' rental business is a fleet of 22 cars worth more than $4 million. A question that naturally comes to mind is how can you generate the money to begin and operate a business of this kind? One possibility is by incorporating. As you will learn in this chapter, one of the advantages of the corporate form of organization is that it makes it easier to raise capital. You will also learn about other advantages and some disadvantages of a corporation, types of ownership in a corporation, dividends, and how to account for some key transactions.

LEARNING OBJECTIVES

Careful study of this chapter should enable you to:

LO1 Describe the characteristics, formation, and organization of a corporation.

LO2 Describe stockholders' equity and the types of capital stock, and compute dividends on preferred and common stock.

LO3 Account for capital stock transactions.

LO4 Prepare the stockholders' equity section of a corporation balance sheet.

For most of this text, we have studied accounting for sole proprietorships. In Chapter 19, we focused on the partnership form of business. In this chapter, we turn our attention to the third type of business organization—the corporation.

It is important to learn about corporations because they play a major role in the economy. More businesses are organized as sole proprietorships and partnerships than as corporations in the United States. But corporations sell more goods and services in total than do sole proprietorships and partnerships combined.

THE CORPORATION

LO1 Describe the characteristics, formation, and organization of a corporation.

A corporation is a legal entity that exists separate and distinct from its owners. This is the key difference between corporations, sole proprietorships, and partnerships. The assets of sole proprietorships and partnerships legally belong to the owners. The liabilities of such businesses are legal liabilities of the owners. In contrast, a corporation's assets and liabilities are those of the business, not the owners. A corporation can own property, enter into contracts, and incur debt in its own name. It can sue and be sued.

ADVANTAGES AND DISADVANTAGES

In comparison with sole proprietorships and partnerships, the corporate form of organization offers five advantages:

1. *Limited liability of owners*. The owners of a corporation generally have no personal liability for the debts of the corporation. Their financial responsibility is limited to the amount they have invested. The limited liability feature is a major reason for the popularity of the corporate form of organization.
2. *Transferable ownership units*. The owners' equity in a corporation is called **capital stock**. The capital stock is divided into **shares** representing ownership rights in the corporation. These shares can be transferred from one person to another without the consent of the other owners and without disturbing the corporation's normal activities.
3. *Ease of raising capital*. The limited liability and transferable ownership characteristics make the corporation an attractive investment for many people. Therefore, a corporation generally can obtain capital by selling additional shares of stock.
4. *No mutual agency*. **Mutual agency** means that each owner has the power to act as an agent and engage in contracts for a business. In a corporation, individual owners do *not* have such power, unless the other owners have granted it to them.
5. *Unlimited life*. A corporation's life is specified in its charter. The charter either states the life as perpetual or provides for renewal if a limit is indicated. Changes of ownership through transfer of shares or death of owners have no effect on the life of a corporation.

Two disadvantages of the corporate form of organization are:

1. *Taxation of earnings*. A major disadvantage is that corporations must pay income taxes. In contrast, sole proprietorships and partnerships do not pay

income taxes. The earnings of sole proprietorships and partnerships are taxed only as the personal income of the owners.

In addition to the corporate income tax, the corporation's owners pay personal income tax on dividends they receive. **Dividends** are distributions of corporate income to the owners. Taxing corporate income both to the company that earns it and to the owners who receive it is called **double taxation.**

2. *Government regulation.* The corporation's activities may be regulated by federal, state, and local laws. These laws may restrict the corporation's ownership of real property, the purchase of its own stock, and the retention of its earnings. If a corporation does business in several states, each state may impose its own financial and tax reporting requirements.

FORMING A CORPORATION

In the United States, the power to create corporations rests largely with the states. To form a corporation, the **incorporators** file an application with the state in which the company is to be incorporated. After the application is approved, a legal document called a **charter**, or **articles of incorporation**, is prepared. The contents of the charter may vary, but it typically includes the following:

1. Name of the corporation
2. Location of the principal office
3. Purpose of the business
4. Description of the capital stock
5. Names and addresses of the incorporators

After the state approves the charter, the incorporators meet to elect a temporary board of directors and to prepare the corporation **bylaws**. The charter and bylaws provide the general guidelines for conducting the business.

Next, the corporation issues capital stock. Those who buy the stock become owners and are known as **stockholders**. Each stockholder receives a form called a **stock certificate** that shows the name of the stockholder and the number of shares owned.

ORGANIZATION OF A CORPORATION

The stockholders elect a **board of directors**. The board of directors determines corporate policies and selects the corporate officers. The officers generally manage the corporation and are responsible to the board. The officers usually consist of the president, one or more vice presidents, a secretary, and a treasurer. Figure 20-1 illustrates a common corporate organization, from the owners/stockholders through the employees.

FIGURE 20-1 Corporate Organization

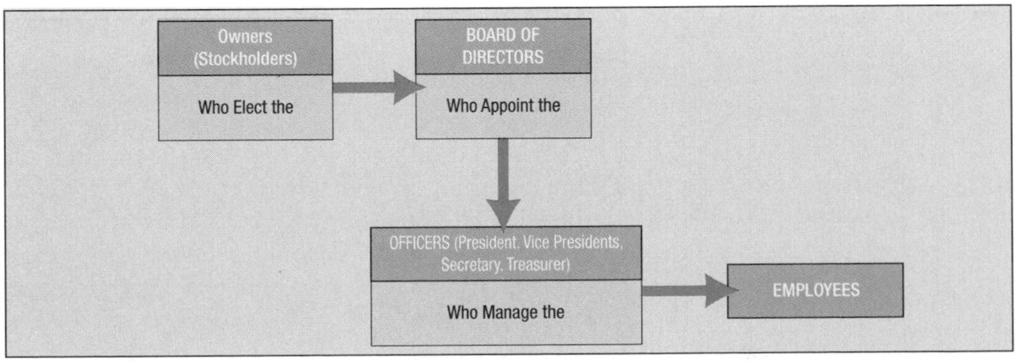

ORGANIZATION COSTS

The costs of organizing a corporation, such as incorporation fees, attorneys' fees, and promotion expenses, are called **organization costs**. Organization costs may be viewed as benefiting the entire life of a corporation, but accepted practice is to record them as expenses as they are incurred.

Assume that Neo Company was billed $8,000 for incorporation and attorney's fees. The journal entry for this transaction is as follows:

4		Organization Expenses		8,000.00		4
5		Accounts Payable			8,000.00	5
6		Corporate organization costs				6
7						7

Organization expenses are reported under Other Expenses on the income statement.

U REVU

Complete U REVU-1 on **page 793** to test your basic understanding of LO1.

STOCKHOLDERS' EQUITY AND TYPES OF CAPITAL STOCK

LO2 Describe stockholders' equity and the types of capital stock, and compute dividends on preferred and common stock.

A corporation's asset, liability, revenue, and expense accounts are generally the same as those for a sole proprietorship or partnership. The owners' equity accounts, however, are quite different, as shown in T account form in Figure 20-2.

In sole proprietorships and partnerships, the owners' capital accounts are affected by three types of events, identified by number in Figure 20-2.

1. Initial and subsequent investments in the business
2. Net income or losses during the life of the business
3. Withdrawals by the owners

The only difference between the sole proprietorship and partnership accounts is that the partnership has multiple capital and drawing accounts. The drawing accounts represent the amount withdrawn from the business during a given accounting period. Recall that each partner's drawing account is closed to his or her capital account. This closing process is shown as item 4 in the T accounts.

In a corporation, owners' equity is called **stockholders' equity**. More importantly, a distinction is made between capital invested by the owners and earnings retained in the business. The amount paid by the stockholders for their shares of stock is called **paid-in capital** and is generally recorded in two new types of accounts: Capital Stock and Additional Paid-In Capital. Both accounts are reported as part of stockholders' equity. These accounts will be explained in the following sections.

A corporation's net income (loss) is credited (debited) to another new account, Retained Earnings. Dividends are equivalent to withdrawals in a sole proprietorship or partnership. Dividends are debited to the dividends account in the same way that withdrawals are debited to Drawing in the sole proprietorship or partnership. Similarly, the dividends account is closed to Retained Earnings in the same way that Drawing is closed to the capital accounts in a sole proprietorship or partnership. Thus, **retained earnings**

FIGURE 20-2 Owners' Equity Accounts

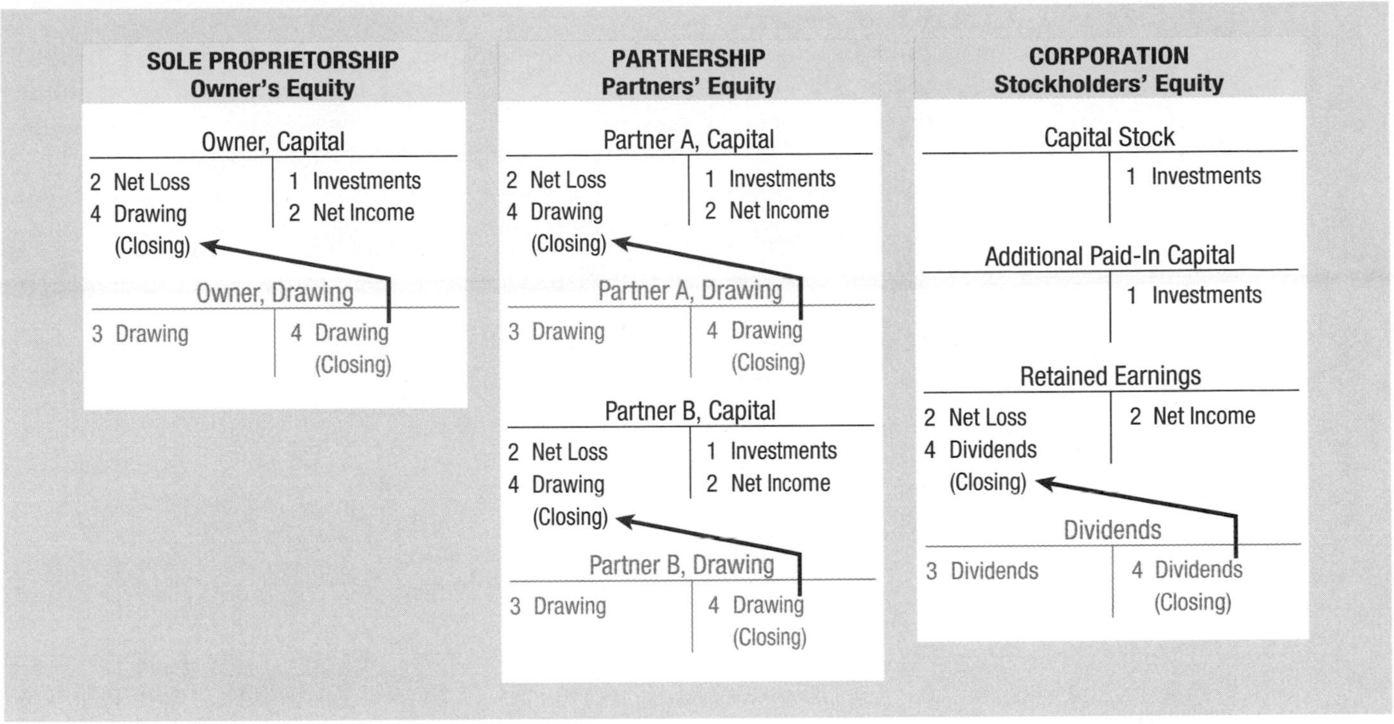

represents the accumulated earnings of the corporation that have not been paid out to stockholders as dividends.

We will look at a complete illustration of the stockholders' equity section of the corporate balance sheet near the end of the chapter. But to help you picture the paid-in capital and retained earnings accounts described here, Figure 20-3 illustrates the general format of the stockholders' equity section.

FIGURE 20-3 Stockholders' Equity Section Format

Paid-in capital:		
Capital stock	$xxx	
Additional paid-in capital:		
Paid-in capital in excess of par	xxx	
Total paid-in capital		$xxx
Retained earnings		xxx
Total stockholders' equity		$xxx

CAPITAL STOCK

Ownership rights in a corporation are represented by shares of capital stock issued by the corporation to the owners. As shown in Figure 20-4, the total number of shares the corporate charter authorizes a corporation to issue is called (1) **authorized stock.** Capital stock that has been sold and issued is called (2) **issued stock**. A corporation may buy back some of its own stock. This stock is known as (3) **treasury stock**. The issued stock less treasury stock equals (4) **outstanding stock,** which is the number of shares in the hands of stockholders.

FIGURE 20-4 Capital Stock

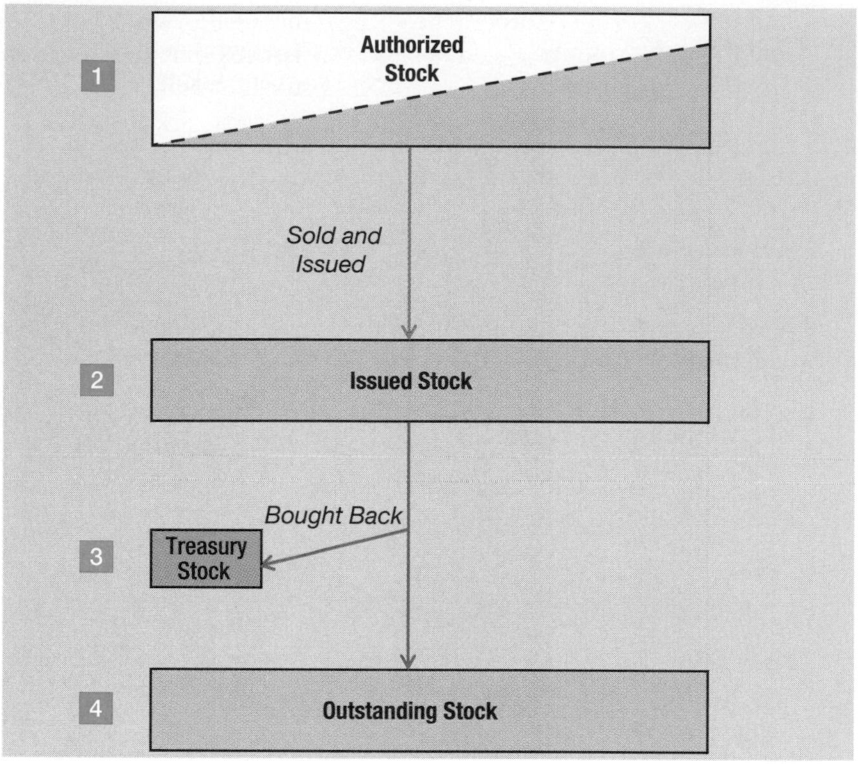

A corporation must maintain detailed records of who owns all shares of its stock.

Shares of stock commonly have a dollar amount per share printed on the stock certificate. This dollar amount is known as the **par value** of the stock. Par value is strictly a legal matter and has no direct relationship to the market value per share. **Market value** is the amount for which the stock can be sold on the open market. The par value has accounting importance, however, because it must be recorded in the capital stock account when stock is issued. If the stock is issued for more than its par value, the excess is credited to the paid-in capital in excess of par account.

Stock that has no dollar amount printed on it is called **no-par stock.** No-par stock sometimes is assigned a value per share by the board of directors. This amount is known as the **stated value** of the stock. From an accounting standpoint, par value and stated value stock are virtually the same.

COMMON STOCK

If a corporation issues only one class or type of stock, each share gives its owner the right to:

1. Vote at stockholders' meetings
2. Share in earnings distributions
3. Purchase additional shares in proportion to the owner's present holding, if more shares are issued by the corporation (This is called a **preemptive right.**)
4. Share in the assets if the corporation liquidates

Such stock is called **common stock.**

PREFERRED STOCK

Corporations sometimes issue two classes of stock—common stock and preferred stock. **Preferred stock** is stock that gives its owner certain preferences or rights superior to those of common stock. Usually, these preferences pertain to dividends or to distribution of assets at liquidation. To obtain these preferences, owners of preferred stock usually do not have one or more of the four rights stated previously. For example, preferred stock owners typically have no voting rights.

The owners of preferred stock usually have the right to dividends of a certain amount before owners of common stock can receive any dividends. The dividend preference is usually stated as a dollar amount per share or as a percentage of par value. For example, preferred stock might be described as "$50 par, $4 preferred stock," or "$50 par, 8% preferred stock."

To illustrate, assume that Pref Company has 2,000 shares of $50 par, $4 preferred stock, and 2,000 shares of $10 par common stock outstanding. The amount available for dividends for the year is $14,000. This $14,000 would be allocated between the preferred and common shares as follows:

1.	Total amount available for dividends	$14,000
2.	Dividend to preferred stock (2,000 shares × $4)	8,000
3.	Amount available for common stock	$ 6,000
	Dividends per share:	
	Preferred stock	$4
	Common stock ($6,000 ÷ 2,000 shares)	$3

Cumulative and Noncumulative Preferred Stock

Preferred stock on which any unpaid dividends accumulate from year to year is called **cumulative preferred stock**. The accumulated amounts and the current year preferred dividends must be paid to the preferred stockholders before the common stockholders can receive any dividends.

Assume that the Pref Company described in the previous illustration had no dividends available in year 1 of operation and $22,000 in year 2. Neither the preferred stock nor the common stock owners would receive any dividends in year 1. The dividends in year 2 for the cumulative and noncumulative preferred stock situations would be as follows:

	Year 2			
	Cumulative		Noncumulative	
Total amount available for dividends		$22,000		$22,000
Cumulative preferred dividend from prior year (2,000 shares × $4)	$8,000		$ 0	
Preferred dividend—current year (2,000 shares × $4)	8,000	16,000	8,000	8,000
Amount available for common stock		$ 6,000		$14,000
Dividends per share:				
Preferred		$8		$4
Common ($6,000 ÷ 2,000 shares)		$3		
($14,000 ÷ 2,000 shares)				$7

The cumulative feature of preferred stock is an important preference. Most preferred stock issued today is cumulative.

Preferred stock on which dividend claims do not accumulate from year to year is called **noncumulative preferred stock.** If in one year dividends are not declared, there is no carryover of dividends to the following years.

Participating and Nonparticipating Preferred Stock

Participating preferred stock gives its owners the right to share with common stock owners in dividends in excess of a stated dividend rate. If preferred dividends are limited to the stated dividend rate, the stock is called **nonparticipating.** It is unusual to find the participation feature in preferred stock today.

Convertible Preferred Stock

Convertible preferred stock gives its owner the right to convert that stock to common stock of the corporation. The number of shares of common stock that will be issued for each share of preferred stock is indicated on the preferred stock certificate. The purpose of the convertible feature is to make the preferred stock more attractive to potential investors. Common stock is riskier but normally has a better chance of increasing in market value.

U REVU

Complete U REVU-2 on **page 793** to test your basic understanding of LO2.

A BROADER VIEW

LUCAS SCHIFRES/LANDOV

Did You Say Company or Country?

This chapter introduces the corporate form of business. Corporations tend to be the largest business enterprises. In fact, the size of some corporations can be difficult to imagine. One way to appreciate the magnitude of some of the largest corporations is to compare them with countries.

In economic terms, the gross domestic product of a country is comparable to the sales of a corporation. Based on these yardsticks, consider the following:

1. Based on sales, Wal-Mart Stores is the largest corporation in the world. Its sales are larger than the gross domestic product of Greece or Denmark.
2. Royal Dutch Shell ranks third. Its sales are larger than the gross domestic product of Argentina or Venezuela.
3. Toyota Motor, which ranks 5th, has sales larger than the gross domestic product of Israel.

These comparisons give real meaning to the expression "big business."

CAPITAL STOCK TRANSACTIONS

LO3 Account for capital stock transactions.

Corporations issue capital stock in exchange for cash and noncash assets. Issuance for cash is the most common transaction.

ISSUING PAR VALUE STOCK AT PAR

If capital stock is issued at par for cash, Cash is debited and Common Stock or Preferred Stock is credited for the amount received. Assume that Linc Corp. issues 10,000 shares of $5 par common stock at par for $50,000 cash. The journal entry for this transaction is as follows:

5		Cash		50,000.00		5
6		Common Stock			50,000.00	6
7		Issued common stock at par				7

ISSUING PAR VALUE STOCK AT A PREMIUM

> **LEARNING KEY**
>
> Record the sale of par value stock at a price above par by debiting Cash and by crediting Capital Stock and Paid-In Capital in Excess of Par.

If stock is issued at a price above par, the amount received above par is known as a **premium.** Enter this transaction as follows:

1. Debit Cash for the amount received.
2. Credit Common Stock or Preferred Stock for the par amount.
3. Credit Paid-In Capital in Excess of Par for the amount above par.

Assume that Linc Corp. issues 10,000 shares of $5 par common stock for $60,000 cash. The journal entry for this transaction is as follows:

1. Amount received → Cash
2. Par amount → Common Stock*
3. Amount above par → Paid-In Capital in Excess of Par—Common Stock**

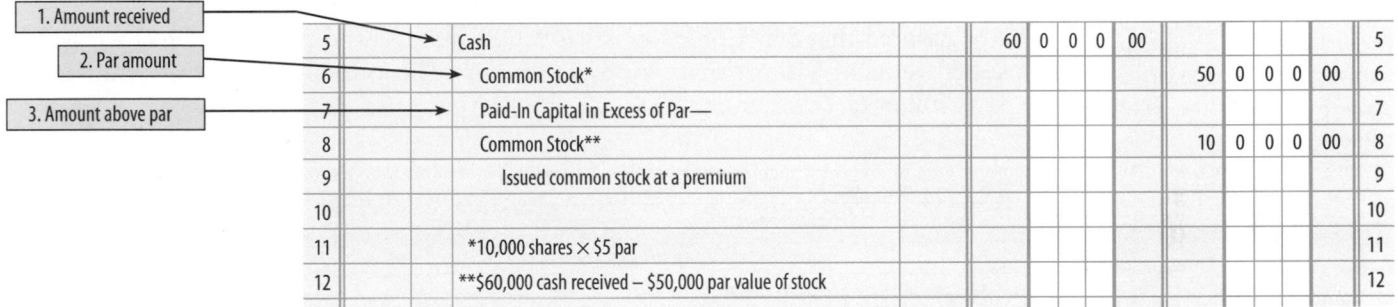

5		Cash		60,000.00		5
6		Common Stock*			50,000.00	6
7		Paid-In Capital in Excess of Par—				7
8		Common Stock**			10,000.00	8
9		Issued common stock at a premium				9
10						10
11		*10,000 shares × $5 par				11
12		**$60,000 cash received – $50,000 par value of stock				12

As shown in Figure 20-3 on page 775, Paid-In Capital in Excess of Par is reported as an addition to paid-in capital on the balance sheet.

ISSUING PAR VALUE STOCK AT A DISCOUNT

> **LEARNING KEY**
>
> Record the sale of par value stock at a price below par by debiting Cash and Discount on Capital Stock, and by crediting Capital Stock.

If par value stock is issued at a price below par, the difference between the par amount and the amount received is called a **discount.** Enter this transaction as follows:

1. Debit Cash for the amount received.
2. Debit Discount on Common Stock or Discount on Preferred Stock for the amount below par.
3. Credit Common Stock or Preferred Stock for the par amount.

Assume that Linc Corp. issues 2,000 shares of $50 par, 8% preferred stock for $96,000 cash. The journal entry for this transaction is as follows:

1. Amount received → Cash
2. Amount below par → Discount on Preferred Stock*
3. Par amount → Preferred Stock**

Cash	96 0 0 0 00	
Discount on Preferred Stock*	4 0 0 0 00	
Preferred Stock**		100 0 0 0 00
Issued preferred stock at a discount		
*$100,000 par value – $96,000 cash received		
**2,000 shares × $50 par		

Discount on Preferred Stock is reported as a deduction from paid-in capital on the balance sheet.

Stock is seldom issued at a discount for three reasons.

1. Firms generally set very low par values.
2. The purchaser is liable to the corporation's creditors for the difference between the par value and the amount paid.
3. This practice is illegal in many states.

ISSUING STOCK WITH A STATED VALUE

LEARNING KEY

Record the sale of no-par stock with a stated value in virtually the same manner as the sale of par value stock.

If no-par stock has a stated value, this value is treated virtually the same as par value in the accounts. Only a slight change in account titles is needed.

Assume that Stat Company issues 5,000 shares of no-par common stock with a stated value of $10 per share for $70,000 cash. The journal entry for this transaction is as follows:

Regardless of the amount for which par value or stated value stock is issued, the credit to Capital Stock is always for the par or stated value.

Cash	70 0 0 0 00	
Common Stock*		50 0 0 0 00
Paid-In Capital in Excess of Stated Value—		
Common Stock**		20 0 0 0 00
Issued common stock at a premium		
*5,000 shares × $10 stated value		
**$70,000 cash received – $50,000 stated		
value of stock		

Like Paid-In Capital in Excess of Par, Paid-In Capital in Excess of Stated Value is reported as an addition to paid-in capital on the balance sheet.

ISSUING NO-PAR STOCK

LEARNING KEY

Record the sale of no-par stock by debiting Cash and crediting Capital Stock.

Accounting for the issuance of no-par stock is generally simpler than for stock with a par or stated value. If no-par stock is issued, Cash is debited and Common Stock or Preferred Stock is credited for the amount received. No premium or discount is entered, regardless of the amount received.

Assume that Noll Company issues 5,000 shares of no-par common stock for $70,000 cash. The journal entry for this transaction is as follows:

5		Cash		70,000.00		5
6		Common Stock			70,000.00	6
7		Issued common stock				7

Similarly, if Noll issues 5,000 shares of no-par common stock for $40,000 cash, the journal entry is as follows:

5		Cash		40,000.00		5
6		Common Stock			40,000.00	6
7		Issued common stock				7

ISSUING STOCK FOR NONCASH ASSETS

Each transaction illustrated thus far has involved issuance of stock for cash. Corporations also sometimes issue stock for noncash assets. The accounting for this transaction can be more complicated because the value of the noncash assets received may need to be determined.

If stock is issued for noncash assets, follow this guideline.

> The assets received are recorded at the fair market value of the assets or of the stock, whichever can be more clearly determined.

Once the value of the noncash assets or the stock is determined, the journal entry for the stock issuance is very similar to those involving cash. Assume that Linc Corp. issues 5,000 shares of $5 par common stock for a truck. Linc's stock is not actively traded, so its market value is difficult to determine, but the truck has a known fair market value of $30,000. Thus, the fair market value of the truck is used to record this transaction. The journal entry is as follows:

11		Truck		30,000.00		11
12		Common Stock*			25,000.00	12
13		Paid-In Capital in Excess of Par—				13
14		Common Stock**			5,000.00	14
15		Issued common stock at a premium				15
16						16
17		*5,000 shares × $5 par				17
18		**$30,000 fair market value of truck				18
19		received – $25,000 par value of stock				19

Assume instead that Linc Corp. issues 10,000 shares of $5 par common stock for a building with several different appraisal values. Linc's stock is actively traded and has a fair market value of $7 per share. In this case, the fair market value of the stock, $70,000 (10,000 shares × $7), is used to record this transaction. The journal entry is as follows:

15		Building		70,000.00		15
16		Common Stock*			50,000.00	16
17		Paid-In Capital in Excess of Par—				17
18		Common Stock**			20,000.00	18
19		Issued common stock at a premium				19
20						20
21		*10,000 shares × $5 par				21
22		**$70,000 fair market value of stock				22
23		– $50,000 par value of stock				23

CAPITAL STOCK SUBSCRIPTIONS

Corporations sometimes accept subscriptions for capital stock. A **capital stock subscription** is an agreement in which a buyer (**subscriber**) contracts to buy shares of stock from a corporation at a specific price. The subscriber generally agrees to pay the amount in full on a specified date or in installments. The corporation does not issue the stock until the subscriber makes the full payment.

Accounting for stock subscriptions requires the use of some new accounts. Assume that Linc Corp. received subscriptions for 10,000 shares of its $5 par common stock for $60,000. The journal entry for this transaction is as follows:

	Common Stock Subscriptions Receivable		60 0 0 0 00	
	Common Stock Subscribed*			50 0 0 0 00
	Paid-In Capital in Excess of Par—			
	Common Stock**			10 0 0 0 00
	Received subscriptions for common stock			
	*10,000 shares × $5 par			
	**$60,000 subscription amount –			
	$50,000 par value of stock			

Some sources say Common Stock Subscriptions Receivable is an asset; others say it is contra-owners' equity. The SEC generally requires the contra-owners' equity treatment.

Common Stock Subscriptions Receivable looks like an asset, but current practice generally calls for treating it as a contra-equity account. It is reported as a deduction from the total of paid-in capital and retained earnings on the balance sheet. Common Stock Subscribed and Paid-In Capital in Excess of Par are reported as additions to paid-in capital on the balance sheet.

As the subscriber makes payments on the stock, the Common Stock Subscriptions Receivable balance is decreased. If the subscriber to Linc Corp.'s shares makes a payment of $40,000, the following journal entry is made:

	Cash		40 0 0 0 00	
	Common Stock Subscriptions Receivable			40 0 0 0 00
	Received subscription payment			

When the stock subscription has been fully paid, the corporation issues the stock. At this point, Common Stock Subscribed is debited and Common Stock is credited for the par amount of $50,000. The $10,000 premium on the stock issuance was already credited to Paid-In Capital in Excess of Par—Common Stock at the time the subscription was recorded. Assume the subscriber to Linc Corp.'s shares makes the final payment of $20,000 and Linc issues the 10,000 shares. The following journal entries are made:

	Cash		20 0 0 0 00	
	Common Stock Subscriptions Receivable			20 0 0 0 00
	Received subscription payment			
	Common Stock Subscribed		50 0 0 0 00	
	Common Stock			50 0 0 0 00
	Issued common stock			

The (a) subscription, (b) payments, and (c) issuance of the stock are shown in T account form in Figure 20-5.

FIGURE 20-5 Stock Subscription, Payments, and Issuance.

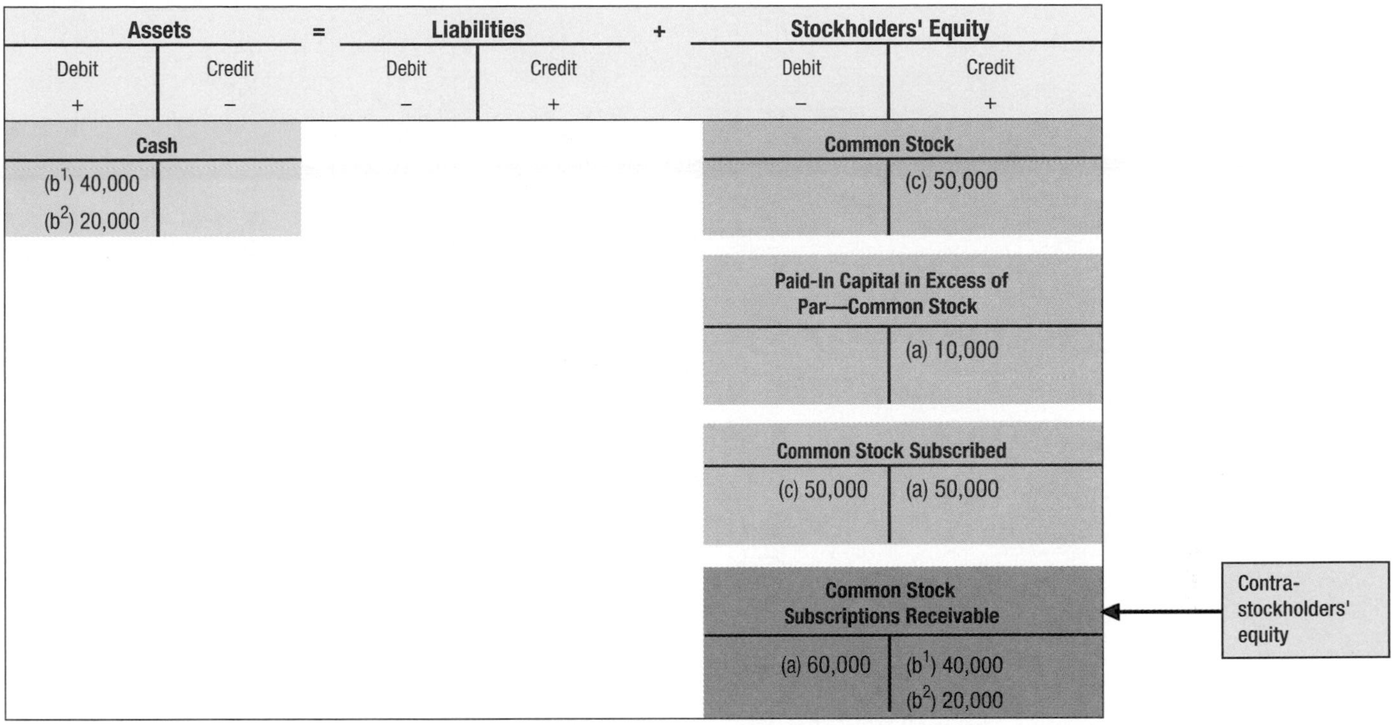

Subscriptions at par or below par, for no-par stock, and for stated value stock are accounted for in a similar manner. The only new accounts that require special care are the same in each instance: Common (or Preferred) Stock Subscriptions Receivable and Common (or Preferred) Stock Subscribed.

TREASURY STOCK

When a company buys back some of its own shares of stock, these shares are called treasury stock. When a corporation purchases its own stock, Treasury Stock is debited for the cost of the stock, regardless of any par or stated value. Assume Linc Corp. purchases 3,000 shares of its $5 par common stock for $6 per share, a total of $18,000. The journal entry for this transaction is as follows:

5			Common Treasury Stock		18 0 0 0 00		5
6			Cash			18 0 0 0 00	6
7			Purchased treasury stock				7

If treasury stock is subsequently sold, the transaction is handled as follows:

1. Cash is debited for the amount received.
2. Treasury Stock is credited for its cost.
3. Any difference between the amount received and the cost is debited or credited to Paid-In Capital from Sale of Treasury Stock.

Assume that Linc Corp. sells 2,000 of the 3,000 treasury shares for $7 per share, a total of $14,000. The journal entry is as follows:

15			Cash		14,000 00		15
16			Common Treasury Stock*			12,000 00	16
17			Paid-In Capital from Sale of Treasury Stock**			2,000 00	17
18			Sold treasury stock				18
19							19
20			*2,000 shares × $6 cost per share				20
21			**$14,000 cash received – $12,000 cost				21
22			of treasury shares				22

Assume that Linc Corp. subsequently sells the remaining 1,000 treasury shares for $5.50 per share, a total of $5,500. The journal entry for this transaction is as follows:

8			Cash		5,500 00		8
9			Paid-In Capital from Sale of Treasury Stock**		500 00		9
10			Common Treasury Stock*			6,000 00	10
11			Sold treasury stock				11
12							12
13			*1,000 shares × $6 cost per share				13
14			**$6,000 cost of treasury shares				14
15			– $5,500 cash received				15

LEARNING KEY

Treasury stock is *not* an asset. It is a contra-stockholders' equity account.

If treasury stock is sold for less than its cost and Paid-In Capital from Sale of Treasury Stock has a zero balance, the difference is debited to Retained Earnings.

Note that no gain or loss is recognized on treasury stock transactions. A corporation cannot realize a gain or incur a loss by dealing in its own shares.

Be careful in presenting treasury stock on the balance sheet. Treasury stock is *not* an asset. It is a contra-stockholders' equity account and is reported as a deduction from the total of paid-in capital and retained earnings. Paid-In Capital from Sale of Treasury Stock is reported as an addition to paid-in capital on the balance sheet.

SUMMARY OF CAPITAL STOCK TRANSACTION ACCOUNTS

In recording capital stock transactions, we have been introduced to many new accounts. Figure 20-6 summarizes these new accounts by type, purpose, and balance sheet presentation. Figure 20-7 shows each of these transactions in the accounting equation. Refer to these figures as you work the exercises and problems for this chapter.

FIGURE 20-6 Summary of Capital Stock Transaction Accounts

ACCOUNT	TYPE	PURPOSE	BALANCE SHEET PRESENTATION
Common Stock and Preferred Stock	Stockholders' Equity	If stock has par or stated value: Credited for par or stated value of stock issued If stock has no par or stated value: Credited for amount received for stock issued	Part of paid-in capital
Paid-In Capital in Excess of Par—Common and Preferred Stock Paid-In Capital in Excess of Stated Value—Common and Preferred Stock	Stockholders' Equity	Credited for amount by which issue price exceeds par or stated value of stock (Used only for stock with par or stated value)	Addition to paid-in capital
Discount on Common Stock and Preferred Stock	Contra-Stockholders' Equity	Debited for amount by which par or stated value exceeds issue price of stock	Deduction from paid-in capital
Common and Preferred Stock Subscibed	Stockholders' Equity	If stock has par or stated value: Credited for par or stated value of stock subscribed If stock has no par or stated value: Credited for amount of stock subscription	Addition to paid-in capital
Common and Preferred Stock Subscriptions Receivable	Contra-Stockholders' Equity	Debited for subscription price of stock	Deduction from total of paid-in capital and retained earnings
Paid-In Capital from Sale of Treasury Stock	Stockholders' Equity	Credited for excess of selling price over cost of treasury stock or Debited for excess of cost over selling price of treasury stock (if a credit balance)	Addition to paid-in capital
Treasury Stock—Common and Preferred	Contra-Stockholders' Equity	Debited for cost of stock purchased	Deduction from total of paid-in capital and retained earnings

FIGURE 20-7 Capital Stock Accounts in the Accounting Equation

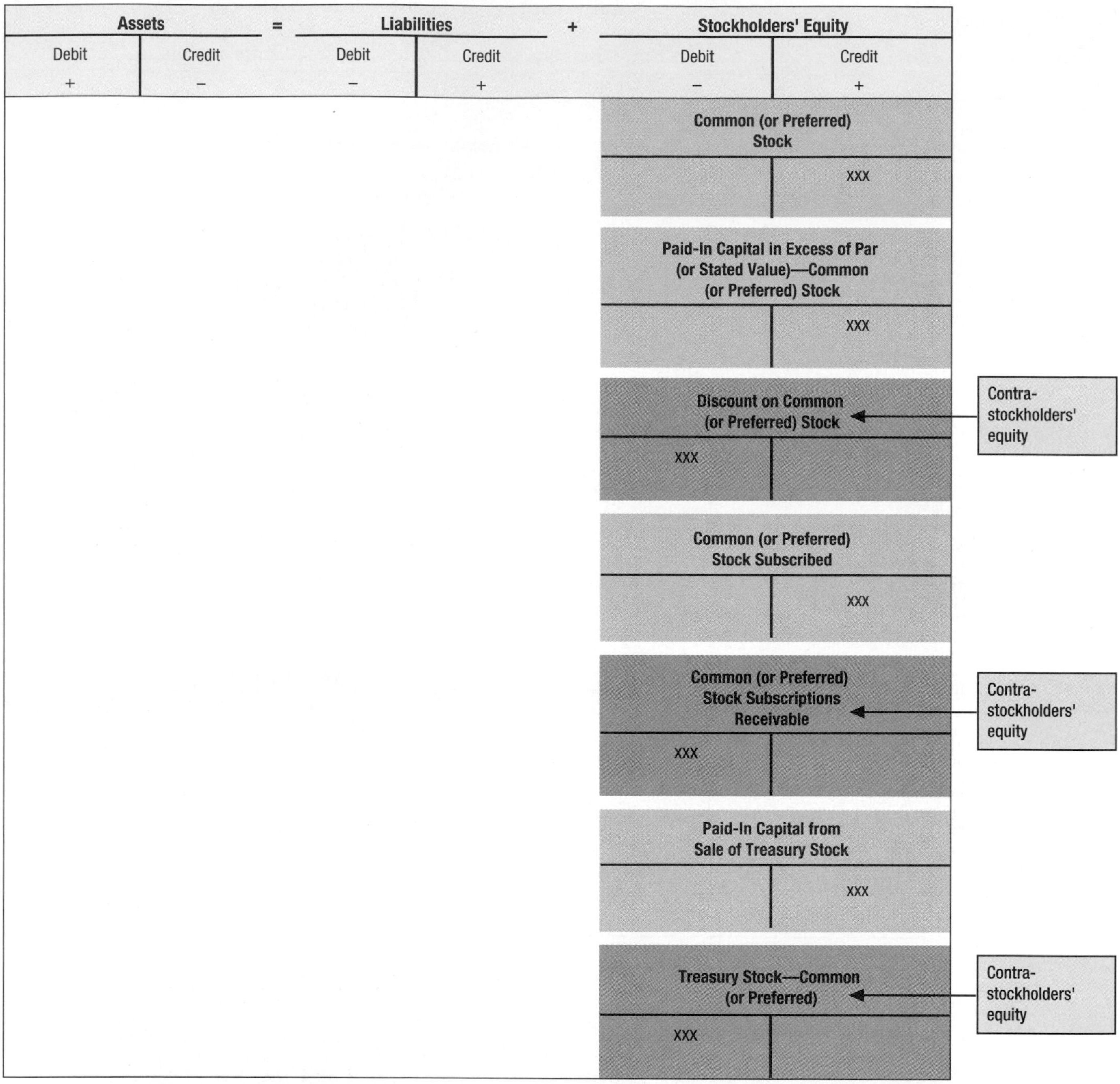

U REVU Complete U REVU-3 on **page 794** to test your basic understanding of LO3.

STOCKHOLDERS' EQUITY SECTION

LO4 Prepare the stockholders' equity section of a corporation balance sheet.

Now that we have seen the various accounts used in capital stock transactions, let's bring them together in a stockholders' equity section of the balance sheet. We will use Roland Company for this purpose.

After closing its books on December 31, Roland Company's stockholders' equity accounts have balances as shown at the top of page 787.

Figure 20-8 shows the stockholders' equity section prepared from these accounts. The line items are numbered to correspond with Roland Company's stockholders' equity accounts in the list shown below.

Account	Balance	Additional Information
(1) Preferred Stock Subscriptions Receivable	$ 20,000	
(2) Common Stock Subscriptions Receivable	30,000	
(3) Preferred Stock Subscribed	60,000	7%, $10 par, 6,000 shares
(4) Common Stock Subscribed	40,000	no-par, 4,000 shares
(5) Preferred Stock	140,000	7%, $10 par, 20,000 shares authorized, 14,000 shares issued
(6) Common Stock	163,000	no-par, 40,000 shares authorized, 16,300 shares issued
(7) Paid-In Capital in Excess of Par— Preferred Stock	56,000	
(8) Paid-In Capital from Sale of Treasury Stock	600	
(9) Common Treasury Stock	22,000 (Dr.)	no par, 2,000 shares, at cost
(10) Retained Earnings	60,000	

FIGURE 20-8 Stockholders' Equity Section

	Stockholders' Equity		
	Paid-in capital:		
(5)	Preferred stock, 7%, $10 par		
	(20,000 shares authorized; 14,000 shares issued)	$140 0 0 0 00	
(3)	Preferred stock subscribed (6,000 shares)	60 0 0 0 00	$200 0 0 0 00
(6)	Common stock, no par		
	(40,000 shares authorized; 16,300 shares issued)	$163 0 0 0 00	
(4)	Common stock subscribed (4,000 shares)	40 0 0 0 00	203 0 0 0 00
	Additional paid-in capital:		
(7)	Paid-in capital in excess of par—preferred stock	$ 56 0 0 0 00	
(8)	Paid-in capital from sale of treasury stock	6 0 0 00	56 6 0 0 00
	Total paid-in capital		$459 6 0 0 00
(10)	Retained earnings		60 0 0 0 00
			$519 6 0 0 00
(1)	Less: Preferred stock subscriptions receivable	$ 20 0 0 0 00	
(2)	Common stock subscriptions receivable	30 0 0 0 00	
(9)	Common treasury stock (2,000 shares at cost)	22 0 0 0 00	72 0 0 0 00
	Total stockholders' equity		$447 6 0 0 00

Note the following characteristics of this stockholders' equity presentation:

1. Stockholders' equity is separated by source:
   Paid-in capital—amounts contributed by owners
   Retained earnings—accumulated, undistributed earnings
2. Paid-in capital is separated by source:
   Preferred stock
   Common stock
   Stock subscriptions
   Paid-in capital in excess of par
   Paid-in capital from sale of treasury stock
3. Stock characteristics are indicated:
   Dividend rate for preferred stock—7%
   Par or no-par value

4. Numbers of shares authorized, subscribed, issued, and held as treasury stock are indicated.
5. Preferred stock is listed first. (This is because of its preferred claim to dividends and assets.)
6. Retained earnings is listed after all paid-in capital.
7. Preferred stock subscriptions receivable, common stock subscriptions receivable, and treasury stock are subtracted from the total of paid-in capital and retained earnings.

U REVU Complete U REVU-4 on **page 794** to test your basic understanding of LO4.

SELF-STUDY

LEARNING OBJECTIVES	Key Points to Remember
LO1 Describe the characteristics, formation, and organization of a corporation.	A corporation exists independently of its owners. Its assets and liabilities are those of the business. A corporation is formed according to the laws of the state in which it incorporates. It normally has a board of directors and four officers. Organization costs are expensed in the period they are incurred.
LO2 Describe stockholders' equity and the types of capital stock, and compute dividends on preferred and common stock.	A key characteristic of owners' equity in a corporation is the distinction between paid-in capital and retained earnings. Paid-in capital is the amount paid in by stockholders. Retained earnings is the accumulated earnings not paid out as dividends. Owners of capital stock generally have the right to: 1. Vote at stockholders' meetings 2. Share in earnings distributions 3. Purchase additional shares if more shares are issued by the corporation 4. Share in the assets if the corporation liquidates Owners of preferred stock generally give up the right to vote in order to have a preferential right to dividends and assets. Features such as cumulative and participating that may apply to preferred stock must be considered when calculating preferred stock and common stock dividends.
LO3 Account for capital stock transactions.	The accounting for par value and stated value stock is virtually the same. In each case, the difference between the par or stated value and the amount received at issuance is recorded as a premium or discount. • There is no premium or discount to account for when no-par stock is issued. • If stock is issued for noncash assets, the assets received are recorded at the fair market value of the assets or of the stock, whichever can be more clearly determined. • If capital stock subscriptions are received, the corporation does not issue the stock until the subscription is paid in full. • No gains or losses are recognized on treasury stock transactions.

LEARNING OBJECTIVES Key Points to Remember

LO4 Prepare the stockholders' equity section of a corporation balance sheet.	The stockholders' equity section of the corporate balance sheet has the following characteristics: 1. Stockholders' equity is separated into paid-in capital and retained earnings. 2. Paid-in capital is separated into preferred stock, common stock, stock subscriptions, paid-in capital in excess of par, and paid-in capital from sale of treasury stock. 3. The dividend rates for preferred stock and par or no-par value are indicated. 4. Numbers of shares authorized, subscribed, issued, and held as treasury stock are indicated. 5. Preferred stock is listed first. 6. Retained earnings is listed after all paid-in capital. 7. Preferred stock subscriptions receivable, common stock subscriptions receivable, and treasury stock are subtracted from the total of paid-in capital and retained earnings.

DEMONSTRATION PROBLEM

KLOOSTER & ALLEN

Stockholders' equity accounts and other related accounts of the JKL Manufacturing Corporation as of October 1, 20-1, the beginning of its fiscal year, follow.

Preferred Stock Subscriptions Receivable	$ 80,000
Preferred Stock, 8%, $10 par (200,000 shares authorized, 50,000 shares issued)	500,000
Preferred Stock Subscribed (10,000 shares)	100,000
Paid-In Capital in Excess of Par—Preferred Stock	50,000
Common Stock, $10 par (1,000,000 shares authorized, 200,000 shares issued)	2,000,000
Paid-In Capital in Excess of Par—Common Stock	500,000
Retained Earnings	2,250,000

During the fiscal year ended September 30, 20-2, JKL Manufacturing completed the following transactions affecting stockholders' equity:

(a) Received the balance due on preferred stock subscriptions and issued the necessary certificates.

(b) Purchased 10,000 shares of common treasury stock for $120,000.

(c) Received subscriptions for 8,000 shares of 8% preferred stock at $12 each, collecting one-fourth of the subscription price.

(d) Sold 6,000 shares of common treasury stock for $78,000.

(e) Issued 80,000 shares of common stock at $15, receiving cash.

(f) Sold 2,000 shares of common treasury stock for $22,000.

(g) Issued 100,000 shares of common stock with a market value of $15 per share in exchange for land for business expansion.

(continued)

REQUIRED

1. Prepare general journal entries for the transactions, identifying each transaction by the appropriate letter.
2. Prepare the stockholders' equity section of the balance sheet as of September 30, 20-2. The beginning retained earnings balance must be increased by the net income for the year, $720,000. The preferred stock was paid dividends at 8% on $600,000 par value of stock, and the common stock was paid dividends of $0.80 per share on 378,000 outstanding shares.

Solution 1.

GENERAL JOURNAL PAGE 1

DATE	DESCRIPTION	POST. REF.	DEBIT	CREDIT
(a)	Cash		80,000.00	
	Preferred Stock Subscriptions Receivable			80,000.00
	Received subscription payments			
	Preferred Stock Subscribed		100,000.00	
	Preferred Stock			100,000.00
	Issued preferred stock			
(b)	Common Treasury Stock		120,000.00	
	Cash			120,000.00
	Purchased treasury stock			
(c)	Cash		24,000.00	
	Preferred Stock Subscriptions Receivable		72,000.00	
	Preferred Stock Subscribed			80,000.00
	Paid-In Capital in Excess of Par—			
	Preferred Stock			16,000.00
	Received subscriptions for preferred stock			
(d)	Cash		78,000.00	
	Common Treasury Stock			72,000.00
	Paid-In Capital from Sale of Treasury Stock			6,000.00
	Sold treasury stock			
(e)	Cash		1,200,000.00	
	Common Stock			800,000.00
	Paid-In Capital in Excess of Par—			
	Common Stock			400,000.00
	Issued common stock at a premium			
(f)	Cash		22,000.00	
	Paid-In Capital from Sale of Treasury Stock		2,000.00	
	Common Treasury Stock			24,000.00
	Sold treasury stock			
(g)	Land		1,500,000.00	
	Common Stock			1,000,000.00
	Paid-In Capital in Excess of Par—			
	Common Stock			500,000.00
	Issued common stock at a premium			

2.

Stockholders' Equity										
Paid-in capital:										
Preferred stock, 8%, $10 par (200,000 shares authorized; 60,000 shares issued)	$ 600	0	0	0	00					
Preferred stock subscribed (8,000 shares)	80	0	0	0	00	$ 680	0	0	0	00
Common stock, $10 par (1,000,000 shares authorized; 380,000 shares issued)						3,800	0	0	0	00
Additional paid-in capital:										
Paid-in capital in excess of par—preferred stock	$ 66	0	0	0	00					
Paid-in capital in excess of par—common stock	1,400	0	0	0	00					
Paid-in capital from sale of treasury stock	4	0	0	0	00	1,470	0	0	0	00
Total paid-in capital						$5,950	0	0	0	00
Retained earnings*						2,619	6	0	0	00
						$8,569	6	0	0	00
Less: Preferred stock subscriptions receivable	$ 72	0	0	0	00					
Common treasury stock (2,000 shares at cost)	24	0	0	0	00	96	0	0	0	00
Total stockholders' equity						$8,473	6	0	0	00
* $2,250,000 + $720,000 – $48,000 – $302,400 = $2,619,600										

KEY TERMS

articles of incorporation (773) See charter.

authorized stock (775) The total number of shares the corporate charter authorizes a corporation to issue.

board of directors (773) A group elected by the stockholders to determine corporate policies and to select corporate officers.

bylaws (773) Together with the charter, the bylaws provide the general guidelines for conducting the business.

capital stock (772) Represents ownership rights in a corporation. Generally broken down into common and preferred stock.

capital stock subscription (782) An agreement in which a buyer contracts to buy shares of a corporation at a specific price.

charter (773) A legal document that includes the name of the corporation, the location of the principal office, the purpose of the business, the description of the capital stock, and the names and addresses of the incorporators.

common stock (776) Stock that gives its owner the right to vote at stockholders' meetings, share in earnings distributions, purchase additional shares if more shares are issued by the corporation, and share in the assets if the corporation liquidates.

convertible preferred stock (778) A type of preferred stock that gives its owners the right to convert the stock to common stock of the corporation.

cumulative preferred stock (777) Preferred stock on which unpaid dividends accumulate from year to year.

discount (779) The difference between the par amount and the amount received when the par value stock is issued at a price below par.

dividends (773) The distributions of corporate income to the owners.

double taxation (773) The process of taxing corporate income both to the company that earns it and to the owners who receive it.

incorporators (773) Those who form a corporation by filing an application with the state in which the company is to be incorporated.

issued stock (775) Capital stock that has been sold and issued.

market value (776) The amount for which the stock can be sold on the open market.

mutual agency (772) The power of each owner to act as an agent and engage in contracts for a business.

noncumulative preferred stock (778) Preferred stock on which dividend claims do not accumulate from year to year.

nonparticipating (778) Preferred stock on which the dividends are limited to the stated dividend rate.

no-par stock (776) Stock that has no dollar amount printed on it.

organization costs (774) The costs of organizing a corporation, such as incorporation fees, attorneys' fees, and promotion expenses.

outstanding stock (775) The number of shares in the hands of stockholders.

paid-in capital (774) The amount paid by stockholders for their shares of stock.

par value (776) The dollar amount printed on the share of stock.

participating (778) Preferred stock that has a right to share with common stock in dividends in excess of a stated dividend rate.

preemptive right (776) The right to purchase additional shares in proportion to the owner's present holding, if more shares are issued by the corporation.

preferred stock (777) Stock that has certain preferences or rights superior to common stock.

premium (779) The difference between the par value and the price of a stock when the stock is issued at a price above par.

retained earnings (774) The accumulated earnings of the corporation that have not been paid out to stockholders as dividends.

shares (772) Capital stock is divided into shares that represent ownership rights in the corporation.

stated value (776) Value per share assigned to no-par stock by the board of directors.

stock certificate (773) A form received by each stockholder that shows the name of the stockholder and the number of shares owned.

stockholders (773) Owners of the corporation.

stockholders' equity (774) Owners' equity within a corporation.

subscriber (782) A buyer who contracts to purchase shares of stock from a corporation at a specific price.

treasury stock (775) Shares of stock that have been bought back by the issuing company.

SELF-STUDY QUESTIONS AND EXERCISES

True/False Questions

1. LO1 Corporations do more dollar volume of business than sole proprietorships and partnerships combined.
2. LO1 Owners of corporations have no personal liability for debts of the corporation.
3. LO1 Dividends are not taxable because these earnings have already been taxed to the corporation.
4. LO1 Organization costs are recorded as an intangible asset and are generally amortized over a period of five years.
5. LO2 Convertible preferred stock is a type of preferred stock that gives its owners the right to convert the stock to common stock of the corporation.

Multiple Choice Questions

1. LO3 When par value stock is issued at a price above par, the amount above par is called a

   (a) discount.
   (b) market value.
   (c) stated value.
   (d) premium.

2. LO3 When par value stock is issued at a price below par, the amount below par is called a

   (a) discount.
   (b) market value.
   (c) stated value.
   (d) premium.

3. LO3 Shares of stock reacquired by the issuing company are called

   (a) par value stock.
   (b) no-par value stock.
   (c) treasury stock.
   (d) stock subscription.

4. LO3 Stock subscriptions receivable are listed as ________ on the balance sheet.

   (a) current liabilities
   (b) current assets
   (c) long-term assets
   (d) contra-stockholders' equity

5. LO3 Treasury stock is listed as a(n) _______ on the balance sheet.

   (a) current liability
   (b) current asset
   (c) deduction from stockholders' equity
   (d) addition to stockholders' equity

U REVU Exercises

1. LO1 AB Company incurred the following costs in organizing the corporation:

Attorneys' fees	$6,200
State incorporation fees	900

   Prepare the general journal entry to record payment of these costs on March 1.

2. LO2 Genous Company has 20,000 shares of common stock and 2,000 shares of cumulative, $20 par, $1 dividend, preferred stock outstanding. No dividends were declared in year 1 of operation. In year 2, $9,000 is available for dividends. Compute the dividends per share for common stock and preferred stock in year 2.

3. LO3 Prepare general journal entries for the following transactions of GOTE Company:
   (a) Received subscriptions for 10,000 shares of $2 par common stock for $80,000.
   (b) Received payment of $30,000 on the stock subscription in transaction (a).
   (c) Received the balance in full for the stock subscription in transaction (a) and issued the stock.
   (d) Purchased 1,000 shares of its own $2 par common stock for $7.50 a share.
   (e) Sold 500 shares of the stock on transaction (d) for $8.50 a share.
4. LO4 Prepare the stockholders' equity section of the balance sheet based on the following account balances:

Common stock, $2 par, 60,000 shares	$120,000
Preferred stock, $10 par, 5%, 4,000 shares	40,000
Common stock subscribed, $2 par, 3,000 shares	6,000
Retained earnings	17,000

The answers to the Self-Study Questions and Exercises are at the end of the chapter (pages 804–805).

APPLYING YOUR KNOWLEDGE

REVIEW QUESTIONS

LO1 1. Briefly describe five advantages of the corporate form of business organization. Describe two disadvantages.

LO1 2. What information usually is included in the charter?

LO1 3. Who elects the permanent board of directors?

LO1 4. Describe how to account for organization costs.

LO2 5. How do owners' equity accounts in a corporation differ from those in a sole proprietorship or partnership?

LO2 6. If a corporation issues only one class of stock, what four rights does each stockholder have?

LO3/4 7. How is paid-in capital in excess of par usually reported on the balance sheet? How is discount on capital stock usually reported?

LO3 8. If stock is issued for noncash assets, at what amount should the assets be recorded?

LO3/4 9. How is common stock subscriptions receivable usually reported on the balance sheet?

LO3/4 10. How is treasury stock usually shown on the balance sheet?

LO3/4 11. How is paid-in capital from sale of treasury stock usually shown on the balance sheet?

SERIES A EXERCISES

E 20-1A (LO1)
✓ Dr. Organization Expenses: $10,900

ORGANIZATION COSTS B&B Electric decided to incorporate and has incurred the following costs of organizing:

Incorporation fees	$ 400
Attorneys' fees	4,800
Promotion expenses	5,700

Prepare the entry to record payment of these organization costs for cash on January 31.

E 20-2A (LO2)
✓ Situation 2. Div. per share, common: $0.20

DIVIDEND ALLOCATIONS
Situation 1 Akimoto Company has the following stock outstanding:

Common Stock	Preferred Stock
50,000 shares	5,000 shares
$1 par value	$40 par, $2 dividend

The amount available for dividends this year is $40,000. Prepare the dividend allocation between the preferred and common shares.

Situation 2 Benitez Company has the following stock outstanding:

Common Stock	Preferred Stock
70,000 shares	Cumulative: 1,500 shares
$1 par value	$50 par, $2 dividend
	Noncumulative: 4,000 shares
	$50 par, $2 dividend

No dividends were declared in year 1 of operation. In year 2, there is $28,000 available for dividends. Prepare the dividend allocation between the preferred and common shares.

E 20-3A (LO3)
✓ (b) Cr. Paid-In Capital in Excess of Par—Common Stock: $5,000

STOCK ISSUANCE (PAR, NO-PAR, AND STATED VALUE) The following stock transactions occurred during January 20-- for Bremer Corporation:

(a) Issued 5,000 shares of $10 par common stock for $50,000 cash.
(b) Issued 4,000 shares of $10 par common stock for $45,000 cash.
(c) Issued 4,000 shares of $10 par common stock for $37,500 cash.
(d) Issued 5,000 shares of no-par common stock for $60,000 cash.
(e) Issued 3,000 shares of no-par common stock for $40,000 cash.
(f) Issued 5,000 shares of no-par common stock with a stated value of $8 per share for $40,000 cash.
(g) Issued 2,000 shares of no-par common stock with a stated value of $8 per share for $15,000 cash.
(h) Issued 3,000 shares of no-par common stock with a stated value of $8 per share for $26,000 cash.

Prepare general journal entries to record the stock transactions, identifying each transaction by letter.

E 20-4A (LO3)
✓ (b) Cr. Paid-In Capital in Excess of Par—Common Stock: $7,500

STOCK ISSUANCE (NONCASH ASSETS, SUBSCRIPTION, AND TREASURY STOCK) Smith & Cline had the following stock transactions during the year:

(a) Issued 5,000 shares of common stock with a $5 par value in exchange for real estate (land) with a fair market value of $27,500.
(b) Issued 7,500 shares of common stock with a $5 par value and $6 fair market value in exchange for a building with an uncertain fair market value.
(c) Received subscriptions for 10,000 shares of $6 par common stock for $65,000.
(d) Received subscriptions for 5,000 shares of $6 par common stock for $28,000.
(e) Received a payment of $30,000 on the stock subscription in transaction (c).
(f) Received the balance in full for the stock subscription in transaction (c) and issued the stock.
(g) Received the balance in full for the stock subscription in transaction (d) and issued the stock.
(h) Purchased 1,000 shares of its own $6 par common stock for $7 a share ($7,000).
(i) Sold 500 shares of the treasury stock in transaction (h) for $7.50 a share.
(j) Sold 500 shares of the treasury stock in transaction (h) for $6.75 a share.

Prepare general journal entries to record the transactions, identifying each by letter.

E 20-5A (LO4)
✓ Total paid-in capital: $110,000

STOCKHOLDERS' EQUITY SECTION After closing its books on December 31, Pro Parts' stockholders' equity accounts had the following balances:

Common stock subscriptions receivable	$ 4,000
Common stock, $5 par, 10,000 shares	50,000
Preferred stock, $10 par, 5%, 5,000 shares	50,000
Common stock subscribed, $5 par, 2,000 shares	10,000
Retained earnings	25,000

Prepare the stockholders' equity section of the balance sheet.

SERIES A PROBLEMS

P 20-6A (LO3)
✓ (e) Dr. Discount on Preferred Stock: $1,000

PAR AND NO-PAR, COMMON AND PREFERRED STOCK Hernandez Company had the following stock transactions during the year:

(a) Issued 25,000 shares of $1 par common stock for $25,000 cash.
(b) Issued 20,000 shares of $1 par common stock for $22,000 cash.
(c) Issued 22,000 shares of $1 par common stock for $21,000 cash.
(d) Issued 2,000 shares of $50 par, 8% preferred stock for $100,000 cash.
(e) Issued 1,000 shares of $50 par, 8% preferred stock for $49,000 cash.
(f) Issued 1,000 shares of $50 par, 8% preferred stock for $51,500 cash.
(g) Issued 2,500 shares of no-par common stock for $11,875 cash.
(h) Issued 1,500 shares of no-par, $7 preferred stock for $72,000 cash.

REQUIRED

Prepare general journal entries to record the transactions, identifying each transaction by letter.

P 20-7A (LO3)
✓ (f) Dr. Building: $90,000

STATED VALUE, COMMON AND PREFERRED STOCK, AND NONCASH ASSETS Kris Kraft Stores had the following stock transactions during the year:

(a) Issued 4,000 shares of no-par common stock with a stated value of $10 per share for $40,000 cash.

(b) Issued 6,000 shares of no-par common stock with a stated value of $8 per share for $50,000 cash.
(c) Issued 5,000 shares of no-par, 6% preferred stock with a stated value of $15 per share for $75,000 cash.
(d) Issued 3,000 shares of no-par, 6% preferred stock with a stated value of $20 per share for $58,000 cash.
(e) Issued 10,000 shares of $5 par common stock for land with a fair market value of $50,000.
(f) Issued 10,000 shares of $8 par common stock with a $9 fair market value for a building with an uncertain fair market value.
(g) Issued 8,000 shares of $50 par, 8% preferred stock for land with a fair market value of $405,000.

REQUIRED

Prepare general journal entries to record the transactions, identifying each transaction by letter.

P 20-8A (LO3)
✓ (c) Cr. Paid-In Capital in Excess of Par—Common Stock: $5,000

KA KLOOSTER & ALLEN

STOCK SUBSCRIPTIONS Juneau & Associates had the following stock transactions during the year:

(a) Issued 100,000 shares of $1 par common stock for $105,000 cash.
(b) Issued 12,000 shares of $10 par, 8% preferred stock for $128,000 cash.
(c) Received subscriptions for 10,000 shares of $10 par common stock for $105,000.
(d) Received subscriptions for 5,000 shares of $15 par, 8% preferred stock for $80,000.
(e) Received a payment of $55,000 on the common stock subscription.
(f) Received a payment of $40,000 on the preferred stock subscription.
(g) Issued 40,000 shares of $1 par common stock in exchange for a truck with a fair market value of $48,000.
(h) Received the balance in full for the common stock subscription and issued the stock.
(i) Issued 2,500 shares of no-par common stock with a stated value of $8 per share for $21,500 cash.
(j) Received the balance in full for the preferred stock subscription and issued the stock.

REQUIRED

Prepare general journal entries to record the transactions, identifying each transaction by letter.

P 20-9A (LO1/3)
✓ Sept. 18. Dr. Common Stock Subscribed: $100,000

KA KLOOSTER & ALLEN

STOCK SUBSCRIPTIONS AND TREASURY STOCK Brown & Brown formed a corporation and had the following stock transactions during the year:

June 30 Incurred the following costs of incorporation:

Incorporation fees	$ 800
Attorneys' fees	5,000
Promotion fees	7,000

July 15 Issued 5,000 shares of $10 par common stock for $52,000 cash.

21 Issued 4,000 shares of $20 par, 8% preferred stock for $79,500 cash.

(continued)

Aug. 1	Received subscriptions for 10,000 shares of $10 par common stock for $103,500.
15	Issued 10,000 shares of $10 par common stock in exchange for a building and fixtures with a fair market value of $110,000.
31	Received a payment of $53,500 for the common stock subscription.
Sept. 3	Purchased 1,000 shares of its own $10 par common stock for $11 a share.
12	Issued 3,500 shares of no-par common stock with a stated value of $8 per share for $30,000.
18	Received the balance in full for the common stock subscription and issued the stock.
30	Sold 500 shares of its treasury stock for $11.50 a share.
Oct. 15	Issued 5,000 shares of $20 par, 8% preferred stock in exchange for land with a fair market value of $108,000.
31	Sold 500 shares of its treasury stock for $10.75 a share.

REQUIRED

Prepare journal entries to record the transactions.

P 20-10A (LO4)
✓ Total paid-in capital: $491,000

STOCKHOLDERS' EQUITY SECTION After closing its books on December 31, 20—, Jackson Corporation's stockholders' equity accounts had the following balances:

Account	Balance	Additional Information
Preferred Stock Subscriptions Receivable	$ 15,000	
Common Stock Subscriptions Receivable	10,000	
Preferred Stock Subscribed	50,000	$4 dividend, $5 par, 10,000 shares
Common Stock Subscribed	30,000	$10 par, 3,000 shares
Preferred Stock	150,000	$4 dividend, $5 par, 30,000 shares
Common Stock	250,000	$10 par, 25,000 shares
Paid-In Capital in Excess of Par—Preferred Stock	10,000	
Paid-In Capital from Sale of Treasury Stock	1,000	
Common Treasury Stock	10,000	
Retained Earnings	75,000	

REQUIRED

Prepare the stockholders' equity section of the balance sheet for Jackson for the year ended December 31, 20--.

SERIES B EXERCISES

E 20-1B (LO1)
✓ Dr. Organization Expenses: $12,000

ORGANIZATION COSTS T&R TrackTown has decided to incorporate and has incurred the following costs of organizing:

Incorporation fees	$ 500
Attorneys' fees	6,800
Promotion fees	4,700

Prepare the entry to record payment of these organization costs for cash on January 20.

E 20-2B (LO2)
✓ Situation 2. Div. per share, common: $0.75

DIVIDEND ALLOCATIONS

Situation 1 Espino Company has the following stock outstanding:

Common Stock	Preferred Stock
100,000 shares	9,000 shares
$0.50 par value	$20 par, $2 dividend

The amount available for dividends this year is $50,000. Prepare the dividend allocation between the preferred and common shares.

Situation 2 Chiola Corporation has the following stock outstanding:

Common Stock	Preferred Stock
40,000 shares	Cumulative: 4,000 shares
$1 par value	$40 par, $2 dividend
	Noncumulative: 5,000 shares
	$40 par, $2 dividend

No dividends were declared in year 1 of operation. In year 2, there is $56,000 available for dividends. Prepare the dividend allocation between the preferred and common shares.

E 20-3B (LO3)
✓ (b) Dr. Discount on Common Stock: $5,000

STOCK ISSUANCE (PAR, NO-PAR, AND STATED VALUE) The following stock transactions occurred during January 20-- for Drexel Corporation:

(a) Issued 4,000 shares of $10 par common stock for $40,000 cash.
(b) Issued 5,000 shares of $10 par common stock for $45,000 cash.
(c) Issued 5,000 shares of $10 par common stock for $53,500 cash.
(d) Issued 6,000 shares of no-par common stock for $60,000 cash.
(e) Issued 4,000 shares of no-par common stock for $40,000 cash.
(f) Issued 6,000 shares of no-par common stock with a stated value of $8 per share for $48,000 cash.
(g) Issued 3,000 shares of no-par common stock with a stated value of $8 per share for $25,000 cash.
(h) Issued 4,000 shares of no-par common stock with a stated value of $8 per share for $30,500 cash.

Prepare general journal entries to record the stock transactions, identifying each transaction by letter.

E 20-4B (LO3)
✓ (b) Cr. Paid-In Capital in Excess of Par—Common Stock: $5,500

STOCK ISSUANCE (NONCASH ASSETS, SUBSCRIPTION, AND TREASURY STOCK) Brant & Evans had the following stock transactions during the year:

(a) Issued 6,000 shares of common stock with a $5 par value in exchange for real estate (land) with a fair market value of $33,500.
(b) Issued 5,500 shares of common stock with a $6 par value and $7 fair market value in exchange for a building with an uncertain fair market value.
(c) Received subscriptions for 11,000 shares of $5 par common stock for $58,000.
(d) Received subscriptions for 8,000 shares of $5 par common stock for $38,000.
(e) Received a payment of $29,000 on the stock subscription in transaction (c).
(f) Received the balance in full for the stock subscription in transaction (c) and issued the stock.
(g) Received the balance in full for the stock subscription in transaction (d) and issued the stock.
(h) Purchased 2,000 shares of its own $5 par common stock for $6 a share ($12,000).

(continued)

(i) Sold 1,000 shares of the treasury stock in transaction (h) for $6.50 a share.
(j) Sold 1,000 shares of the treasury stock in transaction (h) for $5.75 a share.

Prepare general journal entries to record the transactions, identifying each transaction by letter.

E 20-5B (LO4)
✓ Total paid-in capital: $220,000

STOCKHOLDERS' EQUITY SECTION After closing its books on December 31, Mel Brothers' stockholders' equity accounts have the following balances:

Common stock subscriptions receivable	$ 6,000
Common stock, $6 par, 15,000 shares	90,000
Preferred stock, $10 par, 8%, 10,000 shares	100,000
Common stock subscribed, $6 par, 5,000 shares	30,000
Retained earnings	50,000

Prepare the stockholders' equity section of the balance sheet.

SERIES B PROBLEMS

P 20-6B (LO3)
✓ (e) Dr. Discount on Preferred Stock: $3,000

PAR AND NO-PAR, COMMON AND PREFERRED STOCK Valdez Company had the following stock transactions during the year:

(a) Issued 24,000 shares of $1 par common stock for $26,000 cash.
(b) Issued 20,000 shares of $1 par common stock for $19,000 cash.
(c) Issued 18,000 shares of $1 par common stock for $18,000 cash.
(d) Issued 3,000 shares of $10 par, 7% preferred stock for $30,000 cash.
(e) Issued 4,000 shares of $15 par, 7% preferred stock for $57,000 cash.
(f) Issued 4,500 shares of $10 par, 7% preferred stock for $46,500 cash.
(g) Issued 1,800 shares of no-par common stock for $10,475 cash.
(h) Issued 1,100 shares of no-par, $7 preferred stock for $32,000 cash.

REQUIRED

Prepare general journal entries to record the transactions, identifying each transaction by letter.

P 20-7B (LO3)
✓ (f) Dr. Building: $99,000

STATED VALUE, COMMON AND PREFERRED STOCK, AND NONCASH ASSETS Dan's Hobby Stores had the following stock transactions during the year:

(a) Issued 5,000 shares of no-par common stock with a stated value of $10 per share for $50,000 cash.
(b) Issued 6,000 shares of no-par common stock with a stated value of $7 per share for $43,000 cash.
(c) Issued 5,000 shares of no-par, 6% preferred stock with a stated value of $18 per share for $88,600 cash.
(d) Issued 3,500 shares of no-par, 6% preferred stock with a stated value of $22 per share for $77,000 cash.
(e) Issued 10,000 shares of $9 par common stock for land with a fair market value of $90,000.
(f) Issued 11,000 shares of $8 par common stock with a $9 fair market value for a building with an uncertain fair market value.
(g) Issued 8,000 shares of $30 par, 6% preferred stock for land with a fair market value of $243,000.

REQUIRED

Prepare general journal entries to record the transactions, identifying each transaction by letter.

P 20-8B (LO3)

✓ (c) Dr. Discount on Common Stock: $2,000

KA KLOOSTER & ALLEN

STOCK SUBSCRIPTIONS Athletics West had the following stock transactions during the year:

(a) Issued 140,000 shares of $1 par common stock for $145,000 cash.
(b) Issued 9,000 shares of $18 par, 7% preferred stock for $162,800 cash.
(c) Received subscriptions for 10,000 shares of $12 par common stock for $118,000.
(d) Received subscriptions for 5,000 shares of $18 par, 7% preferred stock for $92,000.
(e) Received a payment of $59,000 on the common stock subscription.
(f) Received a payment of $46,000 on the preferred stock subscription.
(g) Issued 60,000 shares of $1 par common stock in exchange for a truck with a fair market value of $66,000.
(h) Received the balance in full for the common stock subscription and issued the stock.
(i) Issued 3,500 shares of no-par common stock with a stated value of $6 per share for $21,500 cash.
(j) Received the balance in full for the preferred stock subscription and issued the stock.

REQUIRED

Prepare general journal entries to record the transactions, identifying each transaction by letter.

P 20-9B (LO1/3)

✓ Sept. 18. Dr. Common Stock Subscribed: $100,000

KA KLOOSTER & ALLEN

STOCK SUBSCRIPTIONS AND TREASURY STOCK Rogers & Hart formed a corporation and had the following stock transactions during the year:

June 30 Incurred the following costs of incorporation:

Incorporation fees	$ 900
Attorneys' fees	6,000
Promotion fees	8,000

July 15 Issued 8,000 shares of $10 par common stock for $82,000 cash.
21 Issued 5,000 shares of $25 par, 8% preferred stock for $124,500 cash.
Aug. 1 Received subscriptions for 10,000 shares of $10 par common stock for $101,500.
15 Issued 10,000 shares of $10 par common stock in exchange for a building and fixtures with a fair market value of $104,800.
31 Received a payment of $51,500 for the common stock subscription.
Sept. 3 Purchased 1,000 shares of its own $10 par common stock for $11 a share.
12 Issued 2,800 shares of no-par common stock with a stated value of $8 per share for $21,400.
18 Received the balance in full for the common stock subscription and issued the stock.
30 Sold 500 shares of its treasury stock for $11.50 a share.
Oct. 15 Issued 4,000 shares of $25 par, 8% preferred stock in exchange for land with a fair market value of $105,000.
31 Sold 500 shares of its treasury stock for $10.75 a share.

(continued)

REQUIRED

Prepare journal entries to record the transactions.

P 20-10B (LO4)
✓ Total paid-in capital: $533,150

STOCKHOLDERS' EQUITY SECTION After closing its books on December 31, 20--, Merrill Corporation's stockholders' equity accounts have the following balances:

Account	Balance	Additional Information
Preferred Stock Subscriptions Receivable	$ 12,000	
Common Stock Subscriptions Receivable	30,000	
Preferred Stock Subscribed	40,000	$4 dividend, $5 par, 8,000 shares
Common Stock Subscribed	80,000	$10 par, 8,000 shares
Preferred Stock	120,000	$4 dividend, $5 par, 24,000 shares
Common Stock	280,000	$10 par, 28,000 shares
Paid-In Capital in Excess of Par—Preferred Stock	12,000	
Paid-In Capital from Sale of Treasury Stock	1,150	
Common Treasury Stock	24,000	
Retained Earnings	88,000	

REQUIRED

Prepare the stockholders' equity section of the balance sheet for Merrill Corporation for the year ended December 31, 20--.

MANAGING YOUR WRITING

Your boss started a construction company as a partnership with several other contractors 20 years ago. Twelve years later, the partners incorporated to gain access to additional capital by issuing common stock. Forty percent of the shares were sold to the general public, and 60% were acquired by the partners. In this way, the partners kept voting control of the business.

Now the company has an opportunity for a major expansion. To obtain additional capital to fund the expansion, the company is considering another stock offering. But the original partners do not want to lose voting control of the business. Your boss knows you are taking college business courses and asks whether there is a way the company can sell additional stock without the partners losing control of the business. Prepare a report for him describing the kinds of capital stock the company could issue that would accomplish his purpose.

ETHICS CASE

Tyler Corporation started its operations in March. During the first year of operation, a significant amount of money was spent on attorneys' fees and promotional expenses connected with organizing the corporation. The amount of revenue Tyler Corporation earned for the year was much higher than expected. Because of this, the accountant decided to charge the attorneys' fees and promotional expenses to advertising expense in the current year.

1. If the accountant simply was not aware of the proper treatment of these expenditures, were any ethical principles violated? Why or why not?
2. How would you have treated these expenditures?
3. Write a short memo from the accountant to the board of directors of Tyler Corporation explaining how costs of organizing a corporation are treated for accounting purposes.
4. In groups of two or three, discuss the difference between making unethical decisions and making careless decisions.

MASTERY PROBLEM

✓ 3. Total paid-in capital: $1,792,000

KA KLOOSTER & ALLEN

Stockholders' equity accounts and other related accounts of Gonzales Company as of January 1, 20--, the beginning of its fiscal year, are shown below.

Preferred stock subscriptions receivable	$ 50,000
Preferred stock, $10 par, 9% (200,000 shares authorized; 20,000 shares issued)	200,000
Preferred stock subscribed (10,000 shares)	100,000
Paid-in capital in excess of par—preferred stock	40,000
Common stock, $10 par (100,000 shares authorized; 60,000 shares issued)	600,000
Paid-in capital in excess of par—common stock	250,000
Retained earnings	750,000

During 20--, Gonzales Company completed the following transactions affecting stockholders' equity:

(a) Received $20,000 for the balance due on subscriptions for preferred stock with a par value of $40,000 and issued the stock.
(b) Purchased 10,000 shares of common treasury stock for $18 per share.
(c) Received subscriptions for 10,000 shares of common stock at $19 per share, collecting down payments of $45,000.
(d) Issued 15,000 shares of common stock in exchange for land with a fair market value of $290,000.
(e) Sold 5,000 shares of common treasury stock for $100,000.
(f) Issued 10,000 shares of preferred stock at $11.50 per share, receiving cash.
(g) Sold 3,000 shares of common treasury stock for $17 per share.

REQUIRED

1. Prepare general journal entries for the transactions, identifying each transaction by letter.
2. Post the journal entries to appropriate T accounts. The cash account has a beginning balance of $300,000.
3. Prepare the stockholders' equity section of the balance sheet as of December 31, 20--. Net income for the year was $825,000 and dividends of $400,000 were paid.

CHALLENGE PROBLEM

This problem challenges you to apply your cumulative accounting knowledge to move a step beyond the material in the chapter.

✓ (e) Dr. Retained Earnings: $1,000

Prepare general journal entries for the following transactions, identifying each transaction by letter:

(a) Gnu Company issued 5,000 shares of $1 par common stock to the Prendergas law firm as partial payment of fees incurred to incorporate the business. Gnu was short of cash, so Prendergas agreed to accept $10,000 cash and the shares of common stock in full settlement of its bill for $55,000.

(b) Gnu issued 50,000 shares of $1 par common stock in exchange for a parcel of land for building a shopping plaza. (The list price for the land was $400,000; a similar parcel in the same area sold last week for $380,000. During the past month, the price at which Gnu's common stock has traded on the open market has ranged from $5 to $12 per share. Two trades occurred yesterday at $7 and $10 per share.)

(c) Gnu purchased 10,000 shares of $1 par value common treasury stock for $70,000. (This is the only treasury stock that Gnu holds.)

(d) Gnu sold 4,000 shares of common treasury stock for $32,000.

(e) Gnu sold 5,000 shares of common treasury stock for $30,000.

ANSWERS TO SELF-STUDY QUESTIONS AND EXERCISES

True/False Questions

1. T
2. T
3. F (Dividends are taxable to the recipients.)
4. F (They are expensed when incurred.)
5. T

Multiple Choice Questions

1. d 2. a 3. c 4. d 5. c

U REVU Exercises

1.

Mar.	1	Organization Expenses	7 1 0 0 00	
		Cash		7 1 0 0 00
		Corporate organization costs		

2.

Total available for dividends		$9,000
Cumulative preferred dividend for year 1 (2,000 shares × $1)	$2,000	
Preferred dividend for year 2 (2,000 shares × $1)	2,000	4,000
Available for common stock		$5,000

Dividends per share:

Preferred	$2.00
Common ($5,000/20,000 shares)	$0.25

3.

(a)	Common Stock Subscriptions Receivable		80 000 00	
	Common Stock Subscribed			20 000 00
	Paid-In Capital in Excess of Par—Common Stock			60 000 00
	Received subscriptions for common stock			

(b)	Cash		30 000 00	
	Common Stock Subscriptions Receivable			30 000 00
	Received subscription payment			

(c)	Cash		50 000 00	
	Common Stock Subscriptions Receivable			50 000 00
	Received subscription payment			
	Common Stock Subscribed		20 000 00	
	Common Stock			20 000 00

(d)	Common Treasury Stock		7 500 00	
	Cash			7 500 00
	Purchased treasury stock			

(e)	Cash		4 250 00	
	Common Treasury Stock			3 750 00
	Paid-In Capital from Sale of Treasury Stock			500 00
	Sold treasury stock			

4.

Paid-in capital:		
Preferred stock, $10 par, 5%, 4,000 shares		$ 40,000
Common stock, $2 par, 60,000 shares	$120,000	
Common stock subscribed (3,000 shares)	6,000	126,000
Total paid-in capital		$166,000
Retained earnings		17,000
Total stockholders' equity		$183,000

Chapter 21

COURTESY OF WWW.BAMKO.NET

LEARNING OBJECTIVES

Careful study of this chapter should enable you to:

LO1 Account for corporate income taxes.

LO2 Explain the use of the retained earnings account.

LO3 Account for dividends and stock splits.

LO4 Account for appropriations of retained earnings.

LO5 Prepare a retained earnings statement.

Corporations: Taxes, Earnings, Distributions, and the Retained Earnings Statement

Chapter 20 opened with the story of Gotham Dream Cars. One way for the company to generate the capital it needed to begin and operate a business with those ultra-expensive cars was by incorporating. In this chapter, our study of corporations continues. We set the stage by looking at a very different kind of company—Bamko, Inc. Bamko designs, manufactures, and distributes a vast array of promotional products. These include items like shirts, hats, pants, watches, jackets, mugs, accessories, and many others. Bamko has thousands of customizable stock items or it can create from scratch virtually anything a client needs.

Bamko started in a small apartment in 1999 and has experienced phenomenal growth to rank in the top 1% of companies in the specialty advertising industry. It has doubled in size every year it has been in business, and in a recent four-year period its revenues grew more than 1600%, from $1.3 million to $22.5 million. The key question for a company like Bamko is not how to find the capital to start the business but how to fund this pace of growth. In this chapter, you will learn how the corporate form of organization can help. You will learn about cash dividends, stock dividends, and strategies for retaining earnings to help grow the business.

In Chapter 20, we learned that stockholders' equity is separated into paid-in capital (amounts contributed by owners) and retained earnings (amounts of accumulated earnings not paid out to stockholders). The emphasis in Chapter 20 was on accounting for paid-in capital, primarily the issuance of capital stock. In this chapter, we focus on retained earnings.

CORPORATE INCOME TAXES

LO1 Account for corporate income taxes.

In accounting for sole proprietorships and partnerships, we did not need to deal with income taxes. Sole proprietorships and partnerships, as businesses, do not pay taxes. But, as noted in Chapter 20, a disadvantage of corporations is that they must pay income taxes. To comply with the law and to determine net income, it is essential that the corporation correctly account for and pay corporate income taxes.

Most corporations must estimate their annual income taxes and make quarterly payments. To illustrate, assume Boot Corp. estimates that its income taxes for 20-1 will be $160,000. Based on this estimate, Boot will have to pay $40,000 ($160,000 ÷ 4) on April 15, June 15, September 15, and December 15. The journal entry for each payment is as follows:

5			Income Tax Expense		40,000 00		5
6			Cash			40,000 00	6
7			Made quarterly estimated tax payment				7

Corporations are subject to specific corporate tax rates different from those for individuals. Currently, there are eight tax brackets ranging from 15% to 39%.

The actual amount of income taxes typically differs from the estimated amount. Thus, at year-end, an adjusting entry is necessary to recognize the correct amount of income taxes for the year. Assume that as part of the year-end adjusting and closing process at Boot Corp., actual income taxes for the year are calculated as $163,000. The following adjusting journal entry would be made at December 31, 20-1:

5	Dec.	31	Income Tax Expense		3,000 00*		5
6			Income Tax Payable			3,000 00	6
7							7
8			*$163,000 actual – $160,000 estimated = $3,000				8

Income Tax Expense is closed to Income Summary at the end of the year in the same manner as other expense accounts. The following closing entry would be made at December 31, 20-1:

	Dec.	31	Income Summary		163,000 00		
			Income Tax Expense			163,000 00	

On March 15, 20-2, Boot Corp. would file its income tax return for the year ended December 31, 20-1, and pay the $3,000 income taxes due. The following entry would be made:

15	Mar.	15	Income Tax Payable	3,000.00		15
16			Cash		3,000.00	16
17			Made final 20-1 tax payment			17

Income taxes normally are reported as a separate expense item on the income statement, and are subtracted from income before income taxes. Assuming that Boot Corp. had income of $500,000 before considering income taxes, the bottom portion of Boot's income statement would appear as shown in Figure 21-1:

FIGURE 21-1 Bottom Portion of the Income Statement

Income before income taxes	$500,000.00
Income tax expense	163,000.00
Net income	$337,000.00

U REVU Complete U REVU-1 on **page 823** to test your basic understanding of LO1.

THE RETAINED EARNINGS ACCOUNT

LO2 Explain the use of the retained earnings account.

Two major sources of capital for every type of business are:

1. Capital that results from investments by the owners
2. Capital that results from earnings retained in the business

In a corporation, capital resulting from the retention of earnings is entered in the retained earnings account. A corporation usually distributes only a portion of its earnings to stockholders. The balance is retained as additional capital to help finance the growth of the business. This would be very important to Bamko, the company described in the chapter opener.

Generally, there are very few debits and credits to the retained earnings account. Typically, the only credit to the account is for the net income of a period. The only debits are for a net loss, closing the dividends account, and appropriations (special restrictions) of retained earnings. In this section, we will learn how to close the net income or net loss and the dividends for a period to the retained earnings account.

THE ADJUSTING AND CLOSING PROCESS

The adjusting and closing process at the end of the period is virtually the same for corporations as for sole proprietorships and partnerships. The accounts are adjusted and all revenue and expense accounts are closed to Income Summary. A credit balance in Income Summary represents net income; a debit balance signifies a net loss. Beyond this point, however, the closing procedures for corporations differ from those for sole proprietorships and partnerships. The balance of the income summary account of a corporation is transferred to the retained earnings account. For example, if the corporation has net income of $337,000 for the period, the following closing entry is made:

LEARNING KEY

In a corporation, close Income Summary to Retained Earnings.

18		Income Summary		337 0 0 0 00		18
19		Retained Earnings			337 0 0 0 00	19

If the corporation has a net loss of $52,000 for the period, the closing entry is as follows:

18		Retained Earnings		52 0 0 0 00		18
19		Income Summary			52 0 0 0 00	19

As noted in Chapter 20, the dividends account also is closed to Retained Earnings. If the corporation declares $30,000 in dividends, the closing entry is as shown below and in Figure 21-2.

18		Retained Earnings		30 0 0 0 00		18
19		Dividends			30 0 0 0 00	19

FIGURE 21-2 Closing the Dividends Account to Retained Earnings

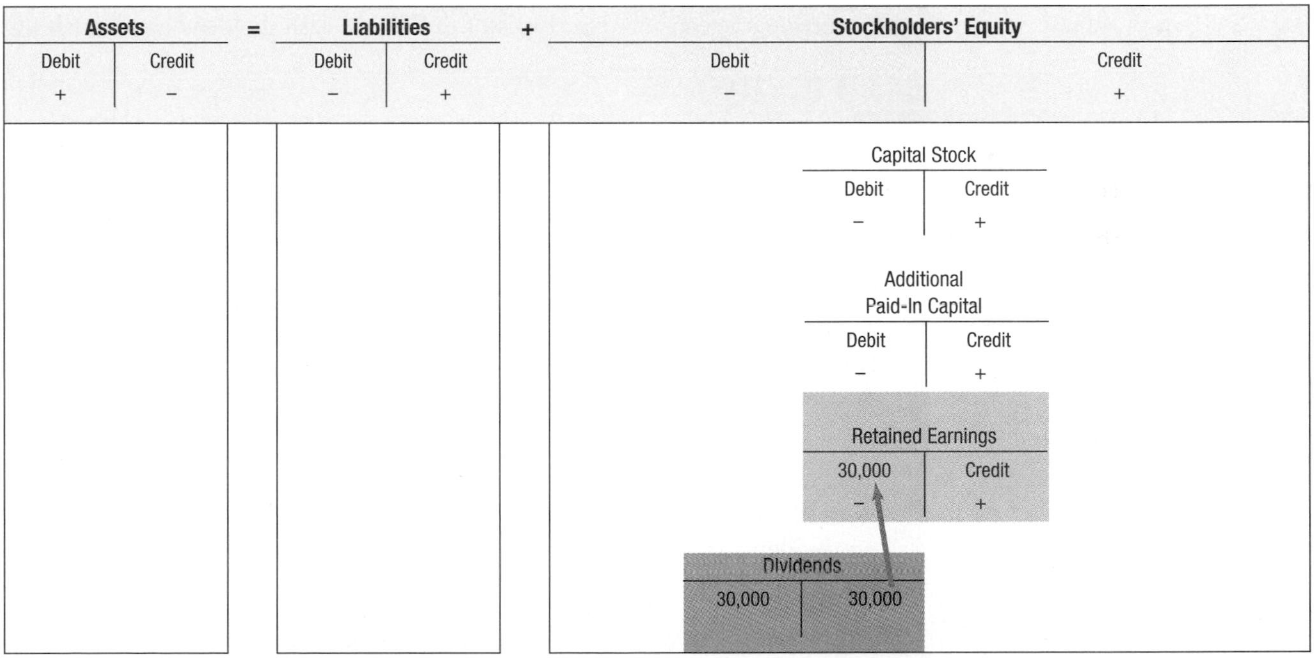

U REVU Complete U REVU-2 on **page 823** to test your basic understanding of LO2.

A BROADER VIEW

ALEKSEJ VASIC/ISTOCKPHOTO.COM

When Corporate Earnings Get Too Important

Earnings are important in virtually any business, but corporate managers sometimes become so focused on earnings growth that they "create" earnings that do not exist. This apparently is what happened at Kurzweil Applied Intelligence, Inc., a computerized speech recognition company based in Waltham, Massachusetts. Under pressure to produce consistently improving results, key executives at the company engaged in a scheme to regularly record fraudulent sales.

According to generally accepted accounting principles, a sale should be counted when goods are shipped from the company to the customer. Kurzweil took a different approach. Millions of dollars of sales were recorded based on shipments of goods to local warehouses for storage until "real" sales could occur. Most of these "real" sales never happened. The fraud was uncovered when Kurzweil's auditor investigated bills from the warehouses for storage of goods supposedly sold nine months previously.

ACCOUNTING FOR DIVIDENDS AND STOCK SPLITS

LO3 Account for dividends and stock splits.

A distribution of earnings by a corporation to its stockholders is known as a **dividend**. In this section, we consider two types of dividends: cash dividends and stock dividends.

CASH DIVIDENDS

A dividend payable in cash is known as a **cash dividend**. For a corporation to issue a cash dividend, three conditions are necessary.

1. Unrestricted retained earnings. In general, corporations can legally declare cash dividends only if the retained earnings balance is sufficient to cover the dividends.
2. Adequate cash balance. The retained earnings balance indicates whether a corporation can legally declare a dividend. But a corporation can pay a cash dividend only if an adequate amount of cash is available. Remember: Retained earnings is not the same as cash.
3. Declaration of dividend. Only the board of directors can declare a dividend. Regardless of the amount of cash or other assets accumulated by a corporation, no dividend can be paid unless the board of directors declares one.

Three dates are involved in the declaration and payment of dividends.

1. **Date of declaration**—the date on which the board of directors decides (declares) that a dividend is to be paid. This is the most important dividend date—when the corporation commits to paying the dividend.
2. **Date of record**—the date on which the names of stockholders entitled to receive the dividend are determined.
3. **Date of payment**—the date on which the dividend is actually paid by the corporation.

For example, assume that on February 1 the board of directors declares a dividend of $2 a share on common stock, payable on February 20 to stockholders of record on February 10. In this case, the date of declaration, date of record, and date of payment are as shown in Figure 21-3. To be eligible to receive the dividend, a stockholder's ownership of stock must be entered in the records of the corporation not later than February 10.

FIGURE 21-3 Dividend Dates

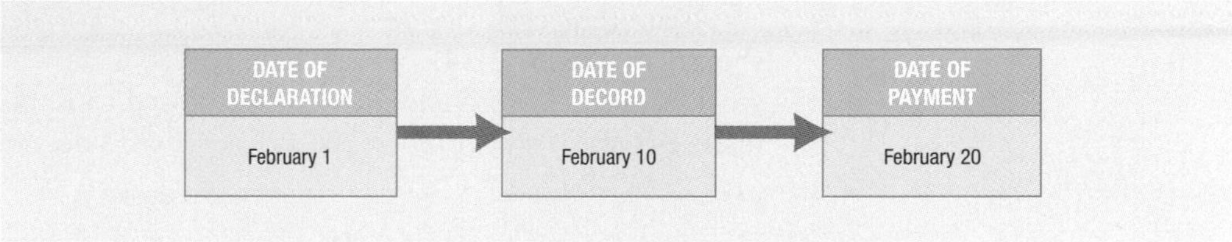

Dividends on different classes of capital stock should be accounted for separately. To illustrate, assume that on February 1 the board of directors declares the $2 per share dividend described above on 10,000 shares of common stock and a dividend of $4 per share on 4,000 shares of preferred stock. Both dividends are payable on February 20 to stockholders of record on February 10. These dividends are accounted for as follows:

Feb. 1 Date of Declaration:

4	Feb.	1	Cash Dividends		16 0 0 0 00		4
5			Preferred Dividends Payable			16 0 0 0 00	5
6			Declared preferred stock cash dividend				6
7							7
8		1	Cash Dividends		20 0 0 0 00		8
9			Common Dividends Payable			20 0 0 0 00	9
10			Declared common stock cash dividend				10

Feb. 10 Date of Record:

No journal entry is made. The date of record has no effect on the corporation accounts. This date simply determines which stockholders receive the dividends.

Feb. 20 Date of Payment:

18	Feb.	20	Preferred Dividends Payable		16 0 0 0 00		18
19			Cash			16 0 0 0 00	19
20			Paid preferred stock cash dividend				20
21							21
22		20	Common Dividends Payable		20 0 0 0 00		22
23			Cash			20 0 0 0 00	23
24			Paid common stock cash dividend				24

If a balance sheet is prepared between the date of declaration and date of payment, dividends payable accounts are reported as current liabilities.

As explained in Chapter 20, the dividends account is closed to Retained Earnings. If the two cash dividends described above were the only dividends declared for the year, the following closing entry would be made at December 31:

6	Dec.	31	Retained Earnings		36 0 0 0 00		6
7			Cash Dividends			36 0 0 0 00	7

Note that cash dividends reduce the stockholders' equity in the corporation, as shown in Figure 21-4. A cash dividend is a distribution of corporate assets to the stockholders. After Cash Dividends is closed to Retained Earnings, the retained earnings portion of stockholders' equity is reduced accordingly.

FIGURE 21-4 Effect of Cash Dividend

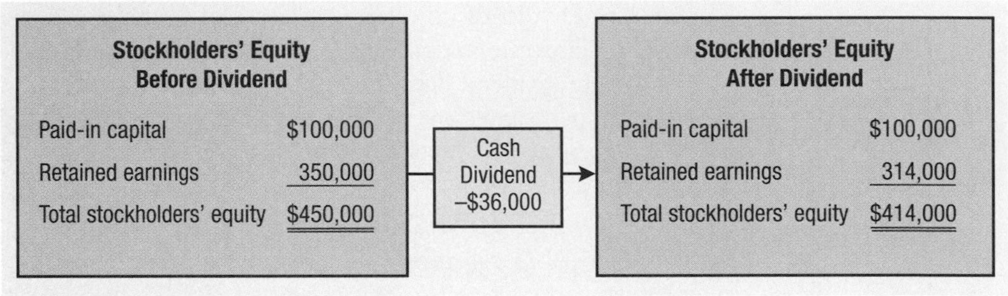

Stockholders' Equity
Before Dividend
Paid-in capital $100,000
Retained earnings 350,000
Total stockholders' equity $450,000
Cash
Dividend
–$36,000
Stockholders' Equity
After Dividend
Paid-in capital $100,000
Retained earnings 314,000
Total stockholders' equity $414,000

STOCK DIVIDENDS

A **stock dividend** is a proportionate distribution of shares of a corporation's own stock to its stockholders. Corporations may distribute this type of dividend for several reasons.

1. The company may be short of cash.
2. The company may want to increase the marketability of its shares by lowering the price per share. A greater number of shares outstanding decreases the price per share and makes wider ownership possible.
3. The corporation may want to transfer a portion of retained earnings to a paid-in capital category to indicate that it is unavailable for dividends.

Stock dividends usually involve issuing additional common shares to current common stockholders. Stock dividends typically are stated as a percentage of common stock outstanding. For example, a 10% stock dividend means that a stockholder receives one additional share for each 10 shares owned. Thus, the owner of 100 shares of common stock receives an additional 10 shares (10% × 100 shares = 10 shares).

Note that this 10% stock dividend does not give the stockholder any increased ownership in the corporation. As shown in Figure 21-5, *all* stockholders receive the 10% dividend, so everyone still owns the same portion of the corporation. Each stockholder owns 10% more shares, but each individual share is worth less.

When a stock dividend is declared, the proper journal entry depends on the dividend percentage. If the stock dividend is for less than 20%–25% of the outstanding shares, Stock Dividends is debited for the *market value* of the stock to be distributed.

LEARNING KEY

To record a stock dividend of less than 20%–25%, debit Stock Dividends for the *market value* of the shares distributed.

FIGURE 21-5 Effect of Stock Dividend

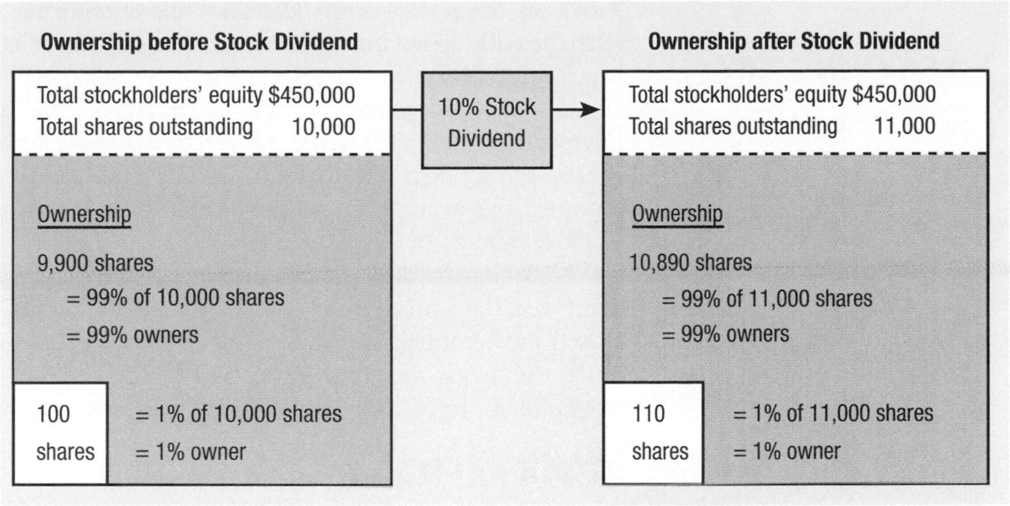

If the stock has neither par nor stated value, Stock Dividends Distributable is credited for the market value of the shares. If the stock has a par or stated value, Stock Dividends Distributable is credited for the par or stated value of the shares. The excess of the market value over par or stated value is credited to Paid-In Capital in Excess of Par (or Stated) Value—Common Stock.

To illustrate, assume that Diven Corp. has 4,000 shares of $5 par common stock outstanding. Diven declares a 10% stock dividend on March 5, payable on March 27 to stockholders of record on March 14. The market value of Diven's common stock on the date of declaration is $12 per share. This means that Diven will issue a total of 400 shares of common stock (4,000 shares × 10% = 400 shares) with a market value of $4,800 (400 shares × $12 = $4,800).

We account for this stock dividend as follows:

Mar. 5 Date of Declaration:

22	Mar.	5	Stock Dividends		4 8 0 0 00		22
23			Stock Dividends Distributable*			2 0 0 0 00	23
24			Paid-In Capital in Excess of Par—				24
25			Common Stock**			2 8 0 0 00	25
26			Declared stock dividend				26
27			*400 shares × $5 par				27
28			**$4,800 market value – $2,000 par value				28

Mar. 14 Date of Record:

No journal entry. As with cash dividends, the date of record has no effect on the corporation accounts.

Mar. 27 Date of Distribution:

14	Mar.	27	Stock Dividends Distributable		2 0 0 0 00		14
15			Common Stock			2 0 0 0 00	15
16			Distributed stock dividend				16

If a balance sheet is prepared between the date of declaration and the date of distribution, Stock Dividends Distributable is reported as an addition to common stock in the stockholders' equity section of the balance sheet. Stock Dividends Distributable is not a liability since no assets or services are owed.

LEARNING KEY

To record a stock dividend of more than 20%–25%, debit Stock Dividends for the par or stated value of the shares distributed.

If a stock dividend is more than 20%–25% of the outstanding shares, Stock Dividends is debited for the *par or stated value* rather than the market value of the shares to be distributed. Stock Dividends Distributable is credited for the same amount. The accounting on the date of distribution is the same as that illustrated for stock dividends of less than 20%–25%.

For stock with no par or stated value, Stock Dividends usually is debited for the average amount of paid-in capital per share of outstanding stock.

Note that stock dividends do not affect the assets, liabilities, or total stockholders' equity of the corporation. As with cash dividends, the stock dividends account is closed to Retained Earnings. However, there is no distribution of corporate assets. Stock dividends merely transfer part of the balance of the retained earnings account to one or more paid-in capital accounts.

STOCK SPLITS

A **stock split** is an exchange of one share of an old issue of stock for multiple shares of a new issue with a reduced par or stated value. The usual purpose of a stock split is to improve the marketability of the shares by reducing the market price per share. Having a greater number of shares outstanding also makes it possible to have a wider ownership of the stock.

Accounting for a stock split differs from accounting for a stock dividend. A stock split requires no formal journal entry and may be recognized simply by a memorandum notation in the general journal and in the appropriate capital stock accounts. Thus, stock splits do not affect the assets, liabilities, or any component of stockholders' equity of a corporation.

To illustrate, assume that Splice Corp. has 10,000 shares of $10 par common stock outstanding. Splice declares a two-for-one stock split. This means that Splice will issue a total of 20,000 shares of $5 par common stock in exchange for the 10,000 shares of $10 par common stock currently outstanding. Each stockholder will receive two shares of the new $5 par stock in exchange for one share of the old $10 par stock. The memorandum entry in the journal is as follows:

LEARNING KEY

No formal journal entry is made for a stock split.

22			Declared two-for-one stock split. Issued			22
23			20,000 shares of $5 par common stock in exchange for			23
24			10,000 shares of $10 par common stock.			24

SUMMARY OF DIVIDEND AND STOCK SPLIT TRANSACTIONS

We have seen that cash dividends, stock dividends, and stock splits affect stockholders' equity differently. Figure 21-6 briefly describes and summarizes the effects of these three transactions on the assets, paid-in capital, and retained earnings of the corporation. Refer to this figure as you work the exercises and problems for this chapter.

FIGURE 21-6 Summary of Dividend and Split Transactions

TRANSACTION	DESCRIPTION	JOURNAL ENTRIES			ASSETS	PAID-IN CAPITAL	RETAINED EARNINGS
Cash Dividend	Distribution of cash to stockholders	At declaration:			Decrease by amount of dividend distributed	No effect	Decrease by amount of cash dividend*
		Cash Dividends	xxx				
		Dividends Payable		xxx			
		At payment:					
		Dividends Payable	xxx				
		Cash		xxx			
Stock Dividend Less than 20%–25%	Distribution of corporation's stock to stockholders	At declaration:			No effect	Increase by market value of stock distributed	Decrease by market value of stock dividend*
		Stock Dividends	xxx				
		Stock Div. Distributable		xxx			
		Paid-In Capital in Excess of Par		xxx			
		At distribution:					
		Stock Div. Distributable	xxx				
		Common Stock		xxx			
More than 20%–25%	Distribution of corporation's stock to stockholders	At declaration:			No effect	Increase by par value of stock distributed	Decrease by par value of stock dividend*
		Stock Dividends	xxx				
		Stock Div. Distributable		xxx			
		At distribution:					
		Stock Div. Distributable	xxx				
		Common Stock		xxx			
Stock Split	Exchange of old stock for multiple shares of new stock	Memo notation			No effect	No effect	No effect

*Recall that Cash Dividends and Stock Dividends are closed to Retained Earnings at the end of the period.

U REVU Complete U REVU-3 on **page 823** to test your basic understanding of LO3.

APPROPRIATIONS OF RETAINED EARNINGS

LO4 Account for appropriations of retained earnings.

Thus far, we have examined how net income, net loss, cash dividends, and stock dividends affect retained earnings. One other event that affects retained earnings is an appropriation. A **retained earnings appropriation** is a restriction of retained earnings by the board of directors for a specific purpose. Recall that corporations may pay dividends only if the retained earnings balance is sufficient to do so. A retained earnings appropriation is used primarily to limit the availability of retained earnings for paying dividends.

To illustrate, assume that Chem Corp. has decided to build a new waste treatment plant. Chem Corp. has a retained earnings balance of $900,000. To financc a portion of the plant (and to inform people of its concern for the environment), the board of directors decides to appropriate $600,000 of retained earnings over a three-year period. At the end of each year for three years, the following journal entry would be made:

1		Retained Earnings*		200 0 0 0 00		1
2		Retained Earnings Appropriated				2
3		for Treatment Plant			200 0 0 0 00	3
4		Appropriated retained earnings for				4
5		treatment plant				5
6		*$600,000 ÷ 3 = $200,000				6

LEARNING KEY

The appropriation of retained earnings does not affect either total retained earnings or the cash and other assets of the corporation.

Notice two important things about the appropriation of retained earnings. First, total retained earnings is unaffected. Retained earnings is simply separated into two categories: appropriated and unappropriated. Retained earnings would appear in the Chem Corp. balance sheet at the end of year 1 as shown in Figure 21-7. The total retained earnings is $900,000, the same as it would be without the appropriation. Second, cash and other assets of the corporation are unaffected. Retained earnings is just a form of ownership interest in the assets of the corporation. All that a retained earnings appropriation does is restrict the corporation's ability to pay out its assets as dividends. In that sense, the *use* of corporate assets is restricted.

FIGURE 21-7 Retained Earnings Section of the Balance Sheet

Retained earnings:		
Appropriated for treatment plant	$200 000 00	
Unappropriated	700 000 00	
Total retained earnings		$900 000 00

After the retained earnings appropriation has served its purpose, the appropriated amount can be returned to retained earnings. To illustrate, let's return to the Chem Corp. example. At the end of three years, Retained Earnings Appropriated for Treatment Plant would have a balance of $600,000. Assume that the treatment plant is completed and that in year 4 the board of directors decides that the appropriation is no longer needed. The following journal entry would be made:

11			Retained Earnings Appropriated			11
12			for Treatment Plant	600 000 00		12
13			Retained Earnings		600 000 00	13
14			Returned appropriation to			14
15			retained earnings			15

The practice of appropriating retained earnings is unusual today. Stockholders generally do not regard the retained earnings balance as the total amount likely to be distributed as dividends. Thus, it generally is unnecessary to make appropriations to advise balance sheet readers that retained earnings is not all available for dividends. Restrictions on dividends can be described just as well in a footnote to the financial statements.

U REVU Complete U REVU-4 on **page 823** to test your basic understanding of LO4.

RETAINED EARNINGS STATEMENT

LO5 Prepare a retained earnings statement.

A **retained earnings statement** explains the change in the amount of retained earnings during the year. All of the information necessary to prepare the retained earnings statement is contained in the dividends accounts and the unappropriated and appropriated retained earnings accounts in the general ledger. If there are no appropriated retained earnings, the statement begins with the beginning of the year retained earnings balance. Net income for the year is added (or net loss is subtracted). Any cash and stock dividends are then subtracted to yield the end of the year retained earnings balance. This balance is the same amount that appears in the stockholders' equity section of the year-end balance sheet. Figure 21-8 shows the format for a retained earnings statement with no appropriated retained earnings.

FIGURE 21-8 Retained Earnings Statement without Appropriated Retained Earnings

Sample Corporation
Retained Earnings Statement
For Year Ended December 31, 20 - -

Retained earnings, January 1						$1,100	0	0	0	00
Add net income for the year						280	0	0	0	00
						$1,380	0	0	0	00
Less: Cash dividends	$30	0	0	0	00					
Stock dividends	20	0	0	0	00	50	0	0	0	00
Retained earnings, December 31						$1,330	0	0	0	00

If there are both appropriated and unappropriated retained earnings, each is shown separately in the retained earnings statement. To illustrate the preparation of this type of retained earnings statement, let's look again at Chem Corp. Assume that it is the end of the second year after beginning appropriations for the treatment plant. The appropriated and unappropriated retained earnings accounts from Chem's general ledger are shown in Figure 21-9.

FIGURE 21-9 Appropriated and Unappropriated Retained Earnings Accounts

Retained Earnings Appropriated for Treatment Plant

		Jan. 1	Bal.	200,000	
		Dec. 31		**200,000**	← Current year appropriation for treatment plant
			Bal.	400,000	

Retained Earnings—Unappropriated

Cash dividend →	Mar. 15	30,000	Jan. 1	Bal.	700,000	
Stock dividend →	June 15	20,000	Dec. 31		280,000	← Net income for the year
Current year appropriation for treatment plant →	**Dec. 31**	**200,000**				
				Bal.	730,000	

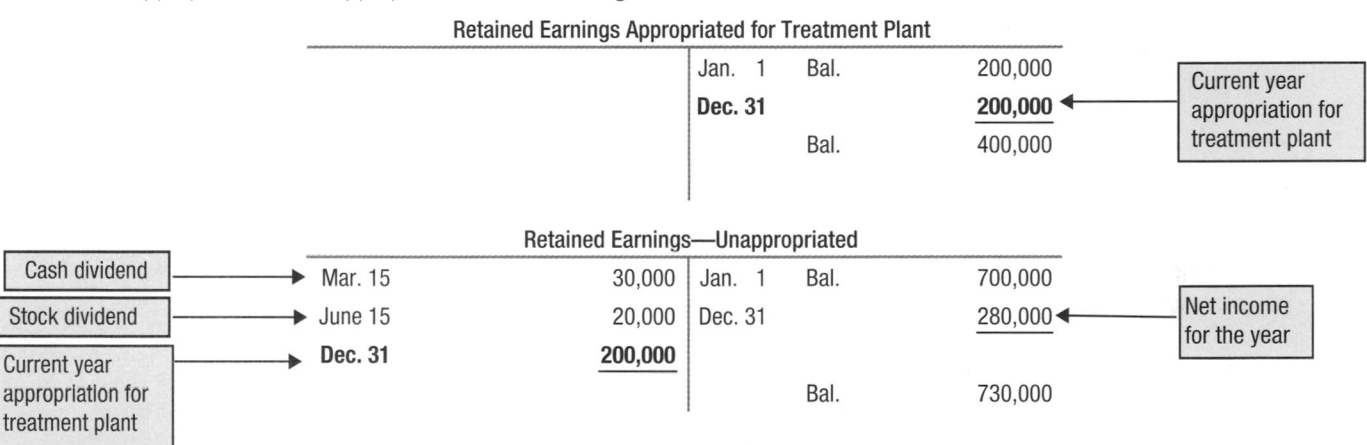

Figure 21-10 on page 818 shows a retained earnings statement prepared from these accounts.

Note the following characteristics of this retained earnings statement:

1. Appropriated retained earnings is presented first, followed by unappropriated retained earnings.
2. Changes in appropriated and unappropriated retained earnings are shown separately.
3. Current year appropriations of retained earnings are shown twice: as an increase in appropriated retained earnings and as a decrease in unappropriated retained earnings.
4. The ending unappropriated retained earnings balance is computed by adding net income for the year to the beginning-of-the-year balance, and then subtracting any dividends and current year appropriations.
5. Appropriated, unappropriated, and total retained earnings are shown separately.

FIGURE 21-10 Retained Earnings Statement with Appropriated and Unappropriated Retained Earnings

Chem Corporation
Retained Earnings Statement
For Year Ended December 31, 20-2

Appropriated:			
Appropriated for treatment plant, January 1		$200,000.00	
Current year appropriation (see below)		200,000.00	
Retained earnings appropriated, December 31			$ 400,000.00
Unappropriated:			
Balance, January 1	$700,000.00		
Add net income for the year	280,000.00	$980,000.00	
Less: Cash dividends	$ 30,000.00		
Stock dividends	20,000.00		
Transfer to appropriated for treatment plant	200,000.00	250,000.00	
Retained earnings unappropriated, December 31			730,000.00
Total retained earnings, December 31			$1,130,000.00

Current year appropriation (shown twice)

Appropriated shown first

Current year appropriation (shown twice)

U REVU

Complete U REVU-5 on **page 823** to test your basic understanding of LO5.

SELF-STUDY

LEARNING OBJECTIVES Key Points to Remember

LO1 Account for corporate income taxes.	Corporations must pay income taxes. Most corporations must estimate their annual income taxes and make quarterly payments.
LO2 Explain the use of the retained earnings account.	Earnings retained in a corporation are recorded by closing the income summary account to the retained earnings account at the end of the period.
LO3 Account for dividends and stock splits.	Three important dates in the declaration and payment of dividends are as follows: 1. Date of declaration 2. Date of record 3. Date of payment Journal entries are necessary on the date of declaration and date of payment.

(*continued*)

LEARNING OBJECTIVES	Key Points to Remember
LO3 (concluded)	For stock dividends of less than 20%–25%, Stock Dividends is debited for the market value of the shares to be distributed. For stock dividends of more than 20%–25%, Stock Dividends is debited for the par or stated value of the shares. A stock split requires no formal journal entry. A memorandum notation in the general journal and capital stock accounts is all that is necessary.
LO4 Account for appropriations of retained earnings.	A retained earnings appropriation has no effect on total retained earnings or on the assets of the corporation. An appropriation simply restricts the corporation's ability to pay out its assets as dividends.
LO5 Prepare a retained earnings statement.	A retained earnings statement explains the change in the amount of retained earnings during the year. If there are both appropriated and unappropriated retained earnings, each is shown separately on the retained earnings statement.

DEMONSTRATION PROBLEM

KLOOSTER & ALLEN

On January 1, 20-1, Grant Company's retained earnings account had the following balances:

Appropriated for warehouse	$ 25,000
Unappropriated retained earnings	650,000
	$675,000

During the year ended December 31, 20-1, Grant completed the following selected transactions:

Apr. 15	Estimated that its 20-1 income tax will be $40,000. Based on this estimate, it will make four quarterly payments of $10,000 each on April 15, June 15, September 15, and December 15.
20	Declared semiannual dividend of $0.30 per share on common stock to shareholders of record on May 5, payable May 15. Currently, 50,000 shares of $3 par stock are outstanding.
May 15	Paid the cash dividend.
June 15	Made estimated tax payment of $10,000.
Sept. 15	Made estimated tax payment of $10,000.
Oct. 20	Declared a semiannual dividend of $0.30 per share on common stock to shareholders of record on November 5, payable on November 15.
Nov. 4	Last year, Grant's board of directors appropriated $50,000 for a warehouse over a two-year period. Made this year's appropriation for $25,000.
15	Paid the cash dividend.
16	Declared a 10% stock dividend to shareholders of record on December 2, distributable on December 10. Market value of the common stock was estimated at $7 per share.

(continued)

Dec. 10 Issued certificates for common stock dividend.

15 Made estimated tax payment of $10,000.

On December 31, the following adjusting and closing entries were made:

31 Grant's actual 20-1 income tax is $44,000. This amount will be paid by March 15, 20-2. Made adjustment for the additional amount owed.

31 Net income for 20-1 was $98,000. Closed the income summary account.

31 Closed the cash dividends and stock dividends accounts.

REQUIRED

1. Prepare journal entries for the above transactions and for the adjusting and closing process.
2. Post all entries affecting the appropriated and unappropriated retained earnings accounts to T accounts.
3. Prepare a retained earnings statement for the year ended December 31, 20-1.

Solution 1.

GENERAL JOURNAL — PAGE 1

	DATE		DESCRIPTION	POST. REF.	DEBIT	CREDIT	
1	20-1 Apr.	15	Income Tax Expense		10,000.00		1
2			Cash			10,000.00	2
3			Made quarterly estimated tax payment				3
4							4
5		20	Cash Dividends		15,000.00		5
6			Common Dividends Payable			15,000.00	6
7			Declared common stock cash dividend				7
8							8
9	May	15	Common Dividends Payable		15,000.00		9
10			Cash			15,000.00	10
11			Paid common stock cash dividend				11
12							12
13	June	15	Income Tax Expense		10,000.00		13
14			Cash			10,000.00	14
15			Made quarterly estimated tax payment				15
16							16
17	Sept.	15	Income Tax Expense		10,000.00		17
18			Cash			10,000.00	18
19			Made quarterly estimated tax payment				19
20							20
21	Oct.	20	Cash Dividends		15,000.00		21
22			Common Dividends Payable			15,000.00	22
23			Declared common stock cash dividend				23
24							24
25	Nov.	4	Retained Earnings		25,000.00		25
26			Retained Earnings Appropriated for Warehouse			25,000.00	26
27			Appropriated retained earnings for warehouse				27
28							28
29		15	Common Dividends Payable		15,000.00		29
30			Cash			15,000.00	30
31			Paid common stock cash dividend				31

GENERAL JOURNAL					PAGE 2
DATE		DESCRIPTION	POST. REF.	DEBIT	CREDIT
20-1 Nov.	16	Stock Dividends		35,000.00	
		Stock Dividends Distributable ($3 × 5,000)			15,000.00
		Paid-In Capital in Excess of Par—			
		Common Stock ($4 × 5,000)			20,000.00
		Declared stock dividend			
Dec.	10	Stock Dividends Distributable		15,000.00	
		Common Stock			15,000.00
		Distributed stock dividend			
	15	Income Tax Expense		10,000.00	
		Cash			10,000.00
		Made quarterly estimated tax payment			
		Adjusting			
	31	Income Tax Expense		4,000.00	
		Income Tax Payable			4,000.00
		Closing			
	31	Income Summary		98,000.00	
		Retained Earnings			98,000.00
	31	Retained Earnings		30,000.00	
		Cash Dividends			30,000.00
	31	Retained Earnings		35,000.00	
		Stock Dividends			35,000.00

2.

Retained Earnings—Appropriated

Debit		Credit	
		Bal.	25,000
		Nov. 4	25,000
		Bal.	50,000

Retained Earnings—Unappropriated

Debit		Credit	
Nov. 4	25,000	Bal.	650,000
Dec. 31	30,000	Dec. 31	98,000
31	35,000		*748,000*
	90,000	Bal.	658,000

3.

Grant Company
Retained Earnings Statement
For Year Ended December 31, 20 -1

Appropriated:			
Appropriated for warehouse, January 1		$ 25,000.00	
Current year appropriation (see below)		25,000.00	
Retained earnings appropriated, December 31			$ 50,000.00
Unappropriated:			
Balance, January 1	$650,000.00		
Add net income for the year	98,000.00	$748,000.00	
Less: Cash dividends	$ 30,000.00		
Stock dividends	35,000.00		
Transfer to appropriated for warehouse	25,000.00	90,000.00	
Retained earnings unappropriated, December 31			658,000.00
Total retained earnings, December 31			$708,000.00

KEY TERMS

cash dividend (810) A dividend payable in cash.

date of declaration (810) The date on which the board of directors declares that a dividend is to be paid.

date of payment (810) The date on which the dividend is actually paid by the corporation.

date of record (810) The date on which the names of stockholders entitled to receive the dividend are determined.

dividend (810) A distribution of earnings by a corporation to its stockholders.

retained earnings appropriation (815) A restriction of retained earnings by the board of directors for a specific purpose.

retained earnings statement (816) A statement that explains the change in the amount of retained earnings during the year.

stock dividend (812) A proportionate distribution of shares of a corporation's own stock to its stockholders.

stock split (814) An exchange of one share of an old issue of stock for multiple shares of a new issue with a reduced par or stated value.

SELF-STUDY QUESTIONS AND EXERCISES

True/False Questions

1. LO1 Income taxes are a unique expense of the corporate form of business.
2. LO2 The adjusting and closing process at the end of the period is virtually the same for corporations as for sole proprietorships and partnerships.
3. LO3 A distribution of earnings by a corporation to its stockholders is known as a dividend.
4. LO3 A dividend payable in cash is known as a stock dividend.
5. LO3 When accounting for the declaration and payment of dividends, the date of record requires a journal entry.

Multiple Choice Questions

1. LO3 A proportionate distribution of shares of a corporation's own stock to its stockholders is called a(n)

   (a) stock dividend.
   (b) cash dividend.
   (c) stock split.
   (d) appropriation.

2. LO3 When a stock dividend is declared, the journal entry will include a credit to

   (a) Retained Earnings.
   (b) Stock Dividends Distributable.
   (c) Stock Dividends Payable.
   (d) Stock Dividends Declared.

3. LO3 Stock Dividends Distributable is classified on the balance sheet as a(n)

   (a) asset.
   (b) liability.
   (c) expense.
   (d) stockholders' equity.

4. LO3 The payment of a cash dividend will include a

   (a) debit to Dividends Declared.
   (b) credit to Dividends Payable.
   (c) credit to Cash.
   (d) debit to Retained Earnings.

5. LO4 When retained earnings is appropriated, total retained earnings
   (a) remains the same.
   (b) increases.
   (c) decreases.
   (d) increases or decreases, depending on the amount.

U REVU **Exercises**

1. LO1 Ozit Company made four quarterly income tax payments of $25,000 each during the year. On December 31, Ozit's actual income tax totals $103,000. Prepare the journal entry on December 31 to record the additional income tax owed.
2. LO2 DWP Company had net income of $183,000 and paid cash dividends totaling $16,000 throughout the year. Prepare the journal entries at December 31 to close Income Summary and Cash Dividends to Retained Earnings.
3. LO3 Teway Company declared and paid dividends in the current year as follows:
   (a) On May 31, declared cash dividend of $12,000 on common stock.
   (b) On June 20, paid the cash dividend declared in transaction (a).
   (c) On November 30, declared a 10% stock dividend on 50,000 shares of $2 par common stock with a market value of $7 per share.
   (d) On December 18, distributed the stock dividend declared in transaction (c).

   Prepare the journal entries for these transactions.
4. LO4 On September 30, Polmax Power Company's board of directors appropriated $300,000 of retained earnings for emission reduction plant modifications. Prepare the journal entry for this appropriation.
5. LO5 On January 1, 20--, MC Company had a retained earnings balance of $720,500. During the year, it paid cash dividends of $24,000 and stock dividends of $47,000, and had net income of $88,000. Prepare the retained earnings statement for MC Company for the year ended December 31, 20--.

The answers to the Self-Study Questions and Exercises are at the end of the chapter (pages 832–833).

APPLYING YOUR KNOWLEDGE

REVIEW QUESTIONS

LO1 1. What expense do corporations incur that sole proprietorships and partnerships do not?

LO2 2. What are the two major sources of capital for every type of business?

LO2 3. For what reason do corporations retain earnings in the business?

LO2 4. How do the procedures for closing Income Summary of a corporation differ from those of a sole proprietorship or partnership?

LO3 5. What are the three dates involved in the declaration and payment of dividends? What is the meaning of each date?

LO3 6. What is the effect of a cash dividend on the corporation accounts?

LO3 7. Give three reasons why a corporation may distribute a stock dividend.

LO3 8. Where should stock dividends distributable be reported on the balance sheet? Why?

LO3 9. What effect does a stock dividend have on the accounts of the corporation? A stock split?

LO4 10. What is the primary reason for appropriating retained earnings?

LO5 11. How are appropriated and unappropriated retained earnings shown on the retained earnings statement?

SERIES A EXERCISES

E 21-1A (LO1)
✓ Dec. 31. Dr. Income Tax Expense, $6,000

CORPORATE INCOME TAX Stanton Company estimates that its 20-1 income tax will be $80,000. Based on this estimate, it will make four quarterly payments of $20,000 each on April 15, June 15, September 15, and December 15.

1. Prepare the journal entry for April 15.
2. Assume that all four quarterly payments have been entered in the general journal. On December 31, Stanton's actual income tax amounts to $86,000. This amount will be paid by March 15, 20-2. Prepare the journal entry to record the additional income tax owed.

E 21-2A (LO2/3)
✓ 2. Cr. Stock Dividends, $18,000

CLOSING INCOME SUMMARY AND DIVIDENDS TO RETAINED EARNINGS Davidson Company had a net income of $120,000 and paid cash dividends of $24,000 for 20--. Wilson and Picket Company had a net loss of $30,000 and distributed a 10% stock dividend with a market value of $18,000.

1. Prepare the journal entries for Davidson as of December 31, 20--, to close Income Summary and Cash Dividends into Retained Earnings.
2. Prepare the journal entries for Wilson and Picket as of December 31, 20--, to close Income Summary and Stock Dividends into Retained Earnings.

E 21-3A (LO3)
✓ July 10. Dr. Cash Dividends, $40,000

COMMON AND PREFERRED CASH DIVIDENDS Wakui Company currently has 100,000 shares of $1 par common stock outstanding and 1,000 shares of $100 par preferred stock outstanding. On July 10, the board of directors declared a semiannual dividend of $0.40 per share on common stock to shareholders of record on August 1, payable on August 5.

On July 15, the board of directors declared a semiannual dividend of $10 per share on preferred stock to shareholders of record on August 5, payable on August 10.

Prepare journal entries for the declaration and payment of the common and preferred stock cash dividends.

E 21-4A (LO3)
✓ 1. Mar. 15. Dr. Stock Dividends, $60,000

STOCK DIVIDENDS Cruz Company currently has 100,000 shares of $1 par common stock outstanding. On March 15, a 10% stock dividend was declared to shareholders of record on April 2, distributable on April 14. Market value of the common stock was estimated at $6 per share.

1. Prepare journal entries for the declaration and distribution of the 10% common stock dividend.
2. Assume Cruz Company declared a stock dividend of 30% rather than 10%. Prepare journal entries for the declaration and distribution of the 30% common stock dividend.

E 21-5A (LO3)
✓ Memo entry only

STOCK SPLIT Goldstein Company has 100,000 shares of $10 par common stock outstanding. On July 1, the board of directors declared a two-for-one stock split.

Prepare a memorandum entry in the general journal indicating the new par value and the total number of outstanding shares of common stock.

E 21-6A (LO4)
✓ Oct. 2. Dr. Retained Earnings, $80,000

RETAINED EARNINGS APPROPRIATION On October 2, 20-1, the board of directors of Foxworth Company appropriated $80,000 of retained earnings for the purpose of buying a new sailboat (used for entertaining clients). On July 15, 20-2, the sailboat was purchased and the board of directors decided that the appropriation was no longer needed.

Prepare journal entries for the appropriation on October 2, 20-1, and the subsequent return on July 15, 20-2.

E 21-7A (LO5)
✓ Retained Earnings, Dec. 31: $75,000

RETAINED EARNINGS STATEMENT McGregor Company had the following balances and results for the current calendar year:

Retained earnings, January 1	$60,000
Cash dividends declared	5,000
Net income for the year	20,000

Prepare a retained earnings statement for the year ended December 31, 20--.

SERIES A PROBLEMS

P 21-8A (LO1/3)
✓ 1st Dec. 31 entry. Dr. Income Tax Expense, $5,000

CASH DIVIDENDS AND INCOME TAXES During the year ended December 31, 20-2, Bebeto Company completed the following selected transactions:

Apr. 15	Estimated that its 20-2 income tax will be $30,000. Based on this estimate, it will make four quarterly payments of $7,500 each on April 15, June 15, September 15, and December 15. Made the first payment.
25	Declared a semiannual dividend of $0.45 per share on common stock to shareholders of record on May 10, payable May 20. Currently, 80,000 shares of $1 par common stock are outstanding.
May 20	Paid the cash dividends.
June 15	Made estimated tax payment of $7,500.
Sept. 15	Made estimated tax payment of $7,500.
Oct. 25	Declared semiannual dividend of $0.45 per share on common stock to shareholders of record on November 10, payable on November 20.
Nov. 20	Paid the cash dividends.
Dec. 15	Made estimated tax payment of $7,500.
31	Bebeto's actual 20-2 income tax is $35,000. This amount will be paid by March 15, 20-3. Made adjustment for the additional amount owed.
31	Net income for 20-2 was $100,000. Closed the income summary account.
31	Closed the cash dividends account.

REQUIRED

Prepare journal entries for the transactions.

P 21-9A (LO3)
✓ Nov. 22. Dr. Stock Dividends, $40,000

CASH DIVIDENDS, STOCK DIVIDEND, AND STOCK SPLIT During the year ended December 31, 20--, Kuang-fu Company completed the following transactions:

Apr. 15	Declared a semiannual dividend of $0.80 per share on preferred stock and $0.50 per share on common stock to shareholders of record on May 5, payable on May 10. Currently, 4,000 shares of $100 par preferred stock and 50,000 shares of $1 par common stock are outstanding.
May 10	Paid the cash dividends.

(continued)

Oct. 15	Declared semiannual dividend of $0.80 per share on preferred stock and $0.50 per share on common stock to shareholders of record on November 5, payable on November 20.
Nov. 20	Paid the cash dividends.
22	Declared a 10% stock dividend to shareholders of record on December 8, distributable on December 16. Market value of the common stock was estimated at $8 per share.
Dec. 16	Issued certificates for common stock dividend.
20	Board of directors declared a two-for-one common stock split.

REQUIRED

Prepare journal entries for the transactions.

P 21-10A (LO3/4)

✓ Nov. 12. Dr. Cash Dividends, $19,500

CASH DIVIDEND AND APPROPRIATION OF RETAINED EARNINGS On January 1, 20--, MacMillan Company's retained earnings accounts had the following balances:

Appropriated for computer	$ 25,000
Appropriated for warehouse	80,000
Unappropriated retained earnings	600,000
	$705,000

During the year ended December 31, 20--, MacMillan completed the following selected transactions:

Mar. 16	Last year, MacMillan's board of directors appropriated $75,000 over a three-year period for a mainframe computer. Made this year's appropriation for $25,000.
Nov. 5	Purchased a new warehouse for $80,000, paying cash for the total amount.
5	The board of directors returned the amount of retained earnings set aside for the warehouse to unappropriated retained earnings.
12	Declared a cash dividend of $0.65 per share on common stock to shareholders of record on December 8, payable on December 19. Currently, 30,000 shares of common stock are outstanding.
Dec. 19	Paid the cash dividends.

REQUIRED

Prepare journal entries for the transactions.

P 21-11A (LO3/4/5)

✓ 3. Retained Earnings, Dec. 31: $1,094,000

RETAINED EARNINGS ACCOUNTS AND STATEMENT On January 1, 20--, Glover Company's retained earnings accounts had the following balances:

Appropriated for land acquisition	$ 60,000
Unappropriated retained earnings	900,000
	$960,000

During the year ended December 31, 20--, Glover completed the following selected transactions:

Mar. 20	Declared a semiannual dividend of $0.80 per share on preferred stock and $0.25 per share on common stock to shareholders of record on April 10, payable on April 15. Currently, 10,000 shares of $50 par preferred stock and 100,000 shares of $5 par common stock are outstanding.
Apr. 15	Paid the cash dividends.

June 16 Last year, Glover's board of directors appropriated $180,000 over a three-year period for the purchase of land for a future building site. Made this year's appropriation for $60,000.

Oct. 10 Declared semiannual dividend of $0.80 per share on preferred stock and $0.25 per share on common stock to shareholders of record on November 5, payable on November 10.

Nov. 10 Paid the cash dividends.

17 Declared a 5% stock dividend to shareholders of record on December 8, distributable on December 15. Market value of the common stock was estimated at $18 per share.

Dec. 15 Issued certificates for common stock dividend.

31 Net income for 20-- was $290,000. Closed the income summary account.

31 Closed the cash dividends and stock dividends accounts.

REQUIRED

1. Prepare journal entries for the transactions.
2. Post all entries affecting the appropriated and unappropriated retained earnings accounts to T accounts.
3. Prepare a retained earnings statement for the year ended December 31, 20--.

SERIES B EXERCISES

E 21-1B (LO1)
✓ Dec. 31. Dr. Income Tax Expense, $12,000

CORPORATE INCOME TAX Regis Company estimates that its 20-1 income tax will be $100,000. Based on this estimate, it will make four quarterly payments of $25,000 each on April 15, June 15, September 15, and December 15.

1. Prepare the journal entry for April 15.
2. Assume that all four quarterly payments have been entered in the general journal. On December 31, Regis's actual income tax amounts to $112,000. This amount will be paid by March 15, 20-2. Prepare the journal entry to record the additional income tax owed.

E 21-2B (LO2/3)
✓ 2. Cr. Stock Dividends, $15,000

CLOSING INCOME SUMMARY AND DIVIDENDS TO RETAINED EARNINGS Kennington Company had a net income of $90,000 and paid cash dividends of $18,000 for 20--. Mueller and Hanson Company had a net loss of $20,000 and distributed a 10% stock dividend with a market value of $15,000.

1. Prepare the journal entries for Kennington as of December 31, 20--, to close Income Summary and Cash Dividends into Retained Earnings.
2. Prepare the journal entries for Mueller and Hanson as of December 31, 20--, to close Income Summary and Stock Dividends into Retained Earnings.

E 21-3B (LO3)
✓ July 10. Dr. Cash Dividends, $30,000

COMMON AND PREFERRED CASH DIVIDENDS Ramirez Company currently has 100,000 shares of $1 par common stock outstanding and 5,000 shares of $50 par preferred stock outstanding. On July 10, the board of directors declared a semiannual dividend of $0.30 per share on common stock to shareholders of record on August 1, payable on August 5.

On July 15, the board of directors declared a semiannual dividend of $5 per share on preferred stock to shareholders of record on August 5, payable on August 10.

Prepare journal entries for the declaration and payment of the common and preferred stock cash dividends.

E 21-4B (LO3)
✓ 1. Mar. 15. Dr. Stock Dividends, $130,000

STOCK DIVIDENDS Martinez Company currently has 200,000 shares of $1 par common stock outstanding. On March 15, a 5% stock dividend was declared to shareholders of record on April 2, distributable on April 14. Market value of the common stock was estimated at $13 per share.

1. Prepare journal entries for the declaration and distribution of the 5% common stock dividend.
2. Assume Martinez Company declared a stock dividend of 30% rather than 5%. Prepare journal entries for the declaration and distribution of the 30% common stock dividend.

E 21-5B (LO3)
✓ Memo entry only

STOCK SPLIT Rogerson Company has 40,000 shares of $2 par common stock outstanding. On July 1, the board of directors declared a two-for-one stock split.

Prepare a memorandum entry in the general journal indicating the new par value and the total number of outstanding shares of common stock.

E 21-6B (LO4)
✓ Oct. 2. Dr. Retained Earnings, $400,000

RETAINED EARNINGS APPROPRIATION On October 2, 20-1, the board of directors of Carr Company appropriated $400,000 of retained earnings for the purpose of buying a new yacht (used for entertaining clients). On July 15, 20-2, the yacht was purchased and the board of directors decided that the appropriation was no longer needed.

Prepare journal entries for the appropriation on October 2, 20-1, and the subsequent return on July 15, 20-2.

E 21-7B (LO5)
✓ Retained Earnings, Dec. 31: $105,000

RETAINED EARNINGS STATEMENT Womack Company had the following balances and results for the current calendar year:

Retained earnings, January 1	$80,000
Cash dividends declared	15,000
Net income for the year	40,000

Prepare a retained earnings statement for the year ended December 31, 20--.

SERIES B PROBLEMS

P 21-8B (LO1/3)
✓ 1st Dec. 31 entry. Dr. Income Tax Expense, $14,000

CASH DIVIDENDS AND INCOME TAXES During the year ended December 31, 20-2, Tatu Company completed the following selected transactions:

Apr. 15	Estimated that its 20-2 income tax will be $160,000. Based on this estimate, it will make four quarterly payments of $40,000 each on April 15, June 15, September 15, and December 15. Made the first payment.
25	Declared a semiannual dividend of $0.50 per share on common stock to shareholders of record on May 10, payable May 20. Currently, 90,000 shares of $1 par common stock are outstanding.
May 20	Paid the cash dividends.
June 15	Made estimated tax payment of $40,000.
Sept. 15	Made estimated tax payment of $40,000.
Oct. 25	Declared semiannual dividend of $0.50 per share on common stock to shareholders of record on November 10, payable on November 20.
Nov. 20	Paid the cash dividends.

Dec. 15 Made estimated tax payment of $40,000.

31 Tatu's actual 20-2 income tax amounts to $174,000. This amount will be paid by March 15, 20-3. Made adjustment for the additional amount owed.

31 Net income for 20-2 was $196,000. Closed the income summary account.

31 Closed the cash dividends account.

REQUIRED

Prepare journal entries for the transactions.

P 21-9B (LO3)
✓ Nov. 22. Dr. Stock Dividends, $105,000

CASH DIVIDENDS, STOCK DIVIDEND, AND STOCK SPLIT During the year ended December 31, 20--, Baggio Company completed the following transactions:

Apr. 15 Declared a semiannual dividend of $0.65 per share on preferred stock and $0.45 per share on common stock to shareholders of record on May 5, payable on May 10. Currently, 6,000 shares of $50 par preferred stock and 70,000 shares of $1 par common stock are outstanding.

May 10 Paid the cash dividends.

Oct. 15 Declared semiannual dividend of $0.65 per share on preferred stock and $0.45 per share on common stock to shareholders of record on November 5, payable on November 20.

Nov. 20 Paid the cash dividends.

22 Declared a 10% stock dividend to shareholders of record on December 8, distributable on December 16. Market value of the common stock was estimated at $15 per share.

Dec. 16 Issued certificates for common stock dividend.

20 Board of directors declared a two-for-one common stock split.

REQUIRED

Prepare journal entries for the transactions.

P 21-10B (LO3/4)
✓ Nov. 12. Dr. Cash Dividends, $36,000

CASH DIVIDEND AND APPROPRIATION OF RETAINED EARNINGS On January 1, 20--, Krausert Company's retained earnings accounts had the following balances:

Appropriated for computer	$ 50,000
Appropriated for warehouse	70,000
Unappropriated retained earnings	800,000
	$920,000

During the year ended December 31, 20--, Krausert completed the following selected transactions:

Mar. 16 Last year, Krausert's board of directors appropriated $100,000 over a two-year period for a mainframe computer. Made this year's appropriation for $50,000.

Nov. 5 Purchased a warehouse for $70,000, paying cash for the total amount.

5 The board of directors returned the amount of retained earnings set aside for the warehouse to unappropriated retained earnings.

12 Declared a cash dividend of $0.90 per share on common stock to shareholders of record on December 8, payable on December 19. Currently, 40,000 shares of common stock are outstanding.

Dec. 19 Paid the cash dividends.

(continued)

REQUIRED

Prepare journal entries for the transactions.

P 21-11B (LO3/4/5)

✓ 3. Retained Earnings, Dec. 31: $989,000

RETAINED EARNINGS ACCOUNTS AND STATEMENT On January 1, 20--, Nguyen Company's retained earnings accounts had the following balances:

Appropriated for land acquisition	$ 75,000
Unappropriated retained earnings	825,000
	$900,000

During the year ended December 31, 20--, Nguyen completed the following selected transactions:

Mar.	20	Declared a semiannual dividend of $0.75 per share on preferred stock and $0.20 per share on common stock to shareholders of record on April 10, payable on April 15. Currently, 12,000 shares of $50 par preferred stock and 90,000 shares of $2 par common stock are outstanding.
Apr.	15	Paid the cash dividends.
June	16	Last year, Nguyen's board of directors appropriated $150,000 over a two-year period for the purchase of land for a future building site. Made this year's appropriation for $75,000.
Oct.	10	Declared semiannual dividend of $0.75 per share on preferred stock and $0.20 per share on common stock to shareholders of record on November 5, payable on November 10.
Nov.	10	Paid the cash dividends.
	17	Declared a 10% stock dividend to shareholders of record on December 8, distributable on December 15. Market value of the common stock was estimated at $13 per share.
Dec.	15	Issued certificates for common stock dividend.
	31	Net income for 20-- was $260,000. Closed the income summary account.
	31	Closed the cash dividends and stock dividends accounts.

REQUIRED

1. Prepare journal entries for the transactions.
2. Post all entries affecting the appropriated and unappropriated retained earnings accounts to T accounts.
3. Prepare a retained earnings statement for the year ended December 31, 20--.

MANAGING YOUR WRITING

The investments committee of your church has come to you for advice. One of the stocks held by the church has paid cash dividends for years. This year, the company issued a 10% stock dividend, so that the church received additional shares rather than cash. The committee is concerned about whether this stock dividend is really worth anything. One committee member argues the stock dividend is as good as cash; another argues that the dividend is worthless.

Write a brief report to the committee explaining the difference between a cash dividend and a stock dividend. Evaluate the value of the stock dividend compared with the cash dividend the church has received in prior years.

ETHICS CASE

Richard Petri is the chief financial officer at Computer Electronics, Inc. In this capacity, he attends all monthly board of directors meetings. A special meeting of the board of directors was called to discuss substantially increasing the amount of cash dividends paid to stockholders this year. The board voted unanimously to increase the dividend. Later that night, Richard called his uncle and hinted around that Computer Electronics, Inc., was going to make its stockholders very happy. His uncle didn't own any stock in Computer Electronics but went out and purchased 500 shares the next day.

1. Did Richard do anything unethical? Would your answer be different if Richard specifically stated that the dividends on Computer Electronics, Inc., were being increased substantially?
2. What should Richard's boss do if he finds out what Richard said to his uncle?
3. Write a short paragraph explaining the difference between cash dividends and stock dividends.
4. In groups of two or three, discuss possible reasons why a corporation might want to pay a very low or high dividend in any given year.

MASTERY PROBLEM

✓ 3. Retained Earnings, Dec. 31: $958,000

On January 1, 20--, Dover Company's retained earnings accounts had the following balances:

Appropriated for printing press	$ 50,000
Unappropriated retained earnings	800,000
	$850,000

During the year ended December 31, 20--, Dover completed the following selected transactions:

Mar. 15	Declared a semiannual dividend of $0.30 per share on preferred stock and $0.40 per share on common stock to shareholders of record on April 5, payable on April 10. Currently, 5,000 shares of $10 par preferred stock and 30,000 shares of $2 par common stock are outstanding.
Apr. 10	Paid the cash dividend.
July 2	Last year, Dover's board of directors appropriated $100,000 over a two-year period for a printing press. Made this year's appropriation for $50,000.
Sept. 15	Declared semiannual dividend of $0.30 per share on preferred stock and $0.40 per share on common stock to shareholders of record on October 5, payable on October 10.
Oct. 10	Paid the cash dividend.
Nov. 10	Board of directors declared a two-for-one common stock split.
Dec. 31	Net income for 20-- was $135,000. Closed the income summary account.
31	Closed the cash dividends account.

(continued)

REQUIRED

1. Prepare journal entries for the transactions.
2. Post all entries affecting the appropriated and unappropriated retained earnings accounts to T accounts.
3. Prepare a retained earnings statement for the year ended December 31, 20--.

CHALLENGE PROBLEM

This problem challenges you to apply your cumulative accounting knowledge to move a step beyond the material in the chapter.

✓ 1. (d) Dr. Cash Dividends, $57,200

LeeJin Corp. started a two-year period with 200,000 shares of $2 par common stock outstanding. During the two years, LeeJin had the following capital stock transactions:

(a) Declared a 10% common stock dividend. The market value of the common stock was estimated at $8 per share.
(b) Declared a cash dividend of $0.20 per share on common stock.
(c) Declared a 30% common stock dividend. The market value of the common stock was estimated at $9 per share.
(d) Declared a cash dividend of $0.20 per share on common stock.
(e) Declared a two-for-one stock split.
(f) Declared a cash dividend of $0.16 per share on common stock.

REQUIRED

1. Prepare general journal entries for each of the transactions. Identify each transaction by the appropriate letter. (Assume that any cash or share distributions have been completed and are a matter of record before the next transaction occurs.)
2. Compute the following:

(a) Number of shares of common stock outstanding after all the transactions have been completed.
(b) The par value per share of LeeJin's common stock after all the transactions have been completed.

ANSWERS TO SELF-STUDY QUESTIONS AND EXERCISES

True/False Questions

1. T 2. T 3. T 4. F (It is known as a cash dividend.)
5. F (Dates of declaration and payment require journal entries.)

Multiple Choice Questions

1. a 2. b 3. d 4. c 5. a

U REVU Exercises

1.

Dec.	31	Income Tax Expense		3,000.00	
		Income Tax Payable			3,000.00

2.

Dec.	31	Income Summary		183,000.00	
		Retained Earnings			183,000.00
		Retained Earnings		16,000.00	
		Cash Dividends			16,000.00

3.

(a)	May	31	Cash Dividends		12,000.00	
			Cash Dividends Payable			12,000.00
			Declared common stock cash dividend			
(b)	June	20	Cash Dividends Payable		12,000.00	
			Cash			12,000.00
			Paid common stock cash dividend			
(c)	Nov.	30	Stock Dividends		35,000.00	
			Stock Dividends Distributable*			10,000.00
			Paid-In Capital in Excess of Par—			
			Common Stock**			25,000.00
			Declared stock dividend			
			*50,000 shares × 10% × $2 par			
			*5,000 shares × $7 = $35,000 market value			
			−$10,000 par value			
(d)	Dec.	18	Stock Dividends Distributable		10,000.00	
			Common Stock			10,000.00
			Distributed stock dividend			

4.

Sep.	30	Retained Earnings		300,000.00	
		Retained Earnings Appropriated for			300,000.00
		Plant Modification			
		Appropriated retained earnings for			
		plant modification			

5.

MC Company
Retained Earnings Statement
For Year Ended December 31, 20- -

Retained earnings, January 1		$720,500.00
Add net income of the year		88,000.00
		$808,500.00
Less: Cash dividends	$24,000.00	
Stock dividends	47,000.00	71,000.00
Retained earnings, December 31		$737,500.00

Chapter 22

STEVE RUARK/AP PHOTO

LEARNING OBJECTIVES

Careful study of this chapter should enable you to:

LO1 Describe the types of bonds and how their sales price is determined.

LO2 Account for bonds issued at face value.

LO3 Account for bonds issued at a premium.

LO4 Account for bonds issued at a discount.

LO5 Account for bond redemption and bond sinking funds.

Corporations: Bonds

One of the greatest challenges facing the U.S. health care system is how to deliver quality health care at a reasonable cost. In addition to increasingly sophisticated and expensive medical treatments and technology, there is a shortage of doctors and other medical professionals. One way to address this problem is to enable doctors to be in more than one place at the same time. This might sound a little silly and "space-age," but this is what Intouch Health Company has done. Intouch Health develops, manufactures, and markets the Remote Presence Robotic System. This is a wireless, mobile robot with a two-way video and audio computer system. It allows physicians to monitor and interact with patients remotely. More than 200 robots are currently in use. They are most commonly used by doctors who are performing rounds on post-operation surgery patients, or who are on call but live some distance from emergency rooms. Founded in 2002 and located in Santa Barbara, California, Intouch Health has more than 50 patents or patents pending for its technology and products.

As we saw for Gotham Dream Cars and Bamko, Inc., in Chapters 20 and 21, it would require a large amount of capital to produce these robots and conduct research and development in this field. In Chapters 20 and 21, we learned how corporations can issue common stock and subsequently use accumulated earnings to provide capital. In Chapter 22, we will learn about a third major way to access a large amount of capital—corporate bonds.

In Chapters 20 and 21, we learned how to account for two major sources of funds for a corporation—capital stock and retained earnings. In this chapter, we turn our attention to a third major source of funds—bonds.

Bonds are similar to the promissory notes payable we saw in Chapter 17. Both are formal, written promises to pay an amount of money at a specified date. The main differences are that bonds are usually for larger sums of money and for longer time periods.

TYPES OF BONDS AND DETERMINATION OF SALES PRICE

LO1 Describe the types of bonds and how their sales price is determined.

A **bond** is a written promise to pay a specific sum of money at a specific future date. Bonds and stock often are mentioned in the same breath, but they are quite different. A bond is a debt of the corporation—a promise to pay certain amounts of money. If these payments are not made, the creditors can force the company into bankruptcy. Stock represents corporate ownership or equity; there is no promise to pay any definite amount of money. Bondholders are creditors of a corporation; stockholders are owners.

Bonds usually are issued in denominations of $1,000 each. For example, if a corporation issues $300,000 of bonds, this usually means it issues 300 individual bonds, each worth $1,000. This enables the issuing corporation to obtain large amounts of money by selling the bonds to many investors.

CLASSIFICATION OF BONDS

To appeal to different types of investors, bonds come with many different features. Based on some of these features, bonds can be classified as to (1) security, (2) timing of payment of principal, and (3) identification of ownership.

Security

All bonds are either secured or unsecured. A **secured bond** is one that is backed by specific corporate assets. A common type of secured bond is a **mortgage bond**—a bond secured by a mortgage on corporate property such as real estate or equipment.

An **unsecured bond** is backed solely by the general credit of the corporation, rather than by any specific assets. These bonds are called **debenture bonds**.

Timing of Payment of Principal

The **principal** of a bond is the amount to be paid to the bondholder at maturity. Based on the provisions made for payment of the principal, four types of bonds can be identified.

1. **Term bonds**—bonds that all have the same maturity date.
2. **Serial bonds**—bonds issued in a series so that a specified amount of the bonds matures each year.
3. **Convertible bonds**—bonds that give the holder the option of exchanging the bonds for capital stock of the corporation.
4. **Callable bonds**—bonds that give the issuing corporation the option of calling the bonds for redemption before the maturity date.

Identification of Ownership

There are two types of bonds according to identification of ownership.

1. **Registered bonds**—bonds whose ownership is recorded (registered) in the corporate records. The corporation maintains a record of the name and address of each owner. Any change of ownership must be registered with the corporation.
2. **Coupon bonds (bearer bonds)**—bonds whose ownership generally is not recorded by the corporation. Change of ownership is accomplished simply by delivering the bond. A coupon bond has interest coupons attached, one for each interest period during the life of the bond. As each coupon comes due, the holder of the bond removes the coupon and presents it to a bank for payment. Today, corporations rarely issue coupon bonds, but old ones are still in circulation.

DETERMINING SALES PRICE

At first glance, you would expect a \$1,000 bond to sell for \$1,000, its **face value**. But, for various reasons, bonds often do not sell at their face value. Two of the more important factors in determining the price at which bonds will sell are:

1. the rate of interest (**stated** or **coupon rate**) on the bonds, and
2. the current **market rate** of interest on similar investments.

The stated or coupon rate is the interest rate specified on the face of the bond. The market rate can be defined from two points of view. For the bond buyer, this is the rate that can be earned on similar investments. For the bond issuer, this is the rate that other companies in similar financial condition have to pay to borrow money.

To illustrate, assume that Watkin Corp. wants to sell \$400,000 of 10%, 10-year bonds. If the current market rate on similar investments is 10%, the bonds will sell at their face value of \$400,000. But if the current market rate is 11%, Watkin's bonds will sell at a **discount**, or at a price less than their face value of \$400,000. This is because the lower interest rate (10% vs. 11%) on Watkin's bonds makes them less valuable. In simple terms, investors will not pay full price for Watkin's bonds with a 10% interest rate if they can get a similar investment with an 11% interest rate.

LEARNING KEY

To determine whether a bond will sell at a price equal to, greater than, or less than face value, compare the stated and market interest rates.

What if the current market rate is 9%? In this case, Watkin's bonds will sell at a **premium**, or at a price in excess of their face value of \$400,000. This is because the higher interest rate (10% vs. 9%) on the bonds makes them more valuable.

Figure 22-1 summarizes the conditions in which bonds will sell at face value, premium, and discount.

Bond prices usually are stated using numbers such as 95, 99, or 102. These numbers are percentages of the face values of bond issues. Thus, a \$100,000 bond issue sold at 95 has a market price of \$95,000 (\$100,000 × 0.95). A similar issue sold at 102 has a market price of \$102,000. Numbers below 100 indicate discount issues. Numbers above 100 indicate premium issues.

FIGURE 22-1 Interest Rates and Bond Selling Prices

INTEREST RATES			SELLING PRICE	
Stated rate	=	Market rate	=	Face value
Stated rate	>	Market rate	>	Face value (Premium)
Stated rate	<	Market rate	<	Face value (Discount)

A Broader View

IMAGE COPYRIGHT HELEN & VLAD FILATOV, 2009/USED UNDER LICENSE FROM SHUTTERSTOCK.COM

Debt Can Be Dangerous

Lodgian is one of the largest independent owners of full-service hotels in the United States. It owns multiple Holiday Inn, Marriott, Hilton, and other properties. The independent auditors' report on this apparently strong company's 2008 financial statements included the following passage: "... the Company has been unable to refinance approximately $128 million of its debt on a long-term basis which raises substantial doubt about its ability to continue as a going concern." In other words, the independent auditors doubted that Lodgian would be able to survive as a business, because the company might not be able to meet its debt obligations.

This is a good example of the risk dimension of debt. By issuing stock, a company gives up ownership interest in the business. But when bonds and other types of debt are issued, a company runs the risk of going bankrupt if it cannot make the payments on its debts. Careful analysis and planning are needed in deciding how to finance a business.

U REVU Complete U REVU-1 on **page 853** to test your basic understanding of LO1.

ACCOUNTING FOR BONDS ISSUED AT FACE VALUE

LO2 Account for bonds issued at face value.

To illustrate the accounting for bonds, we will use bonds issued by Watkin Corp. Assume the following facts regarding these bonds:

Date of issue and sale:	April 1, 20-1
Principal amount:	$400,000
Denomination of each bond:	$1,000
Life of bonds:	10 years
Stated rate:	10%, payable semiannually each April 1 and October 1

ISSUANCE

Assume that on April 1, 20-1, the stated rate of 10% on Watkin's bonds is the same as the current market rate. In this case, the bonds will sell at their face value. The journal entry for the sale and issuance of Watkin's bonds at face value on April 1, 20-1, is as follows:

					Debit	Credit	
5	Apr.	1	Cash		400 0 0 0 00		5
6			Bonds Payable			400 0 0 0 00	6
7			Issued bonds at face value				7

Bonds payable is reported as a long-term liability on the corporation balance sheet.

INTEREST EXPENSE

The journal entry for the first semiannual interest payment of \$20,000 (10% × \$400,000 × ½ year) on October 1, 20-1, is as follows:

18	Oct.	1	Bond Interest Expense	20 0 0 0 00		18
19			Cash		20 0 0 0 00	19
20			Paid semiannual interest on bonds			20

On December 31, an adjusting entry is needed for interest accrued on the bonds since the last interest payment date, October 1, 20-1. Three months' interest has accrued (October 1–December 31), which amounts to \$10,000 (10% × \$400,000 × ¼ year). The adjusting entry therefore is as follows:

25	Dec.	31	Bond Interest Expense	10 0 0 0 00		25
26			Bond Interest Payable		10 0 0 0 00	26

After the October 1 and December 31 entries are posted, Bond Interest Expense and Bond Interest Payable appear in T account form as follows:

Bond Interest Expense

20-1		
Oct. 1	20,000	
Dec. 31	10,000	
	30,000	

Bond Interest Payable

	20-1	
	Dec. 31	10,000

The balance in the bond interest expense account is the total interest expense incurred from April 1 to December 31. Bond Interest Expense is reported as other expense on the income statement. The balance in the bond interest payable account is the accrued liability on December 31. Bond Interest Payable is reported as a current liability on the balance sheet.

The December 31, 20-1, adjusting entry normally is reversed as of January 1, 20-2, as follows:

8	Jan.	1	Bond Interest Payable	10 0 0 0 00		8
9			Bond Interest Expense		10 0 0 0 00	9

The next semiannual interest payment on April 1, 20-2, is made exactly like the entry on October 1, 20-1. After posting the reversing entry and the April 1 interest payment entry, Bond Interest Expense and Bond Interest Payable appear in T account form as follows:

Bond Interest Expense

20-1				
Oct. 1	20,000			
Dec. 31	10,000	Dec. 31	Close	30,000
20-2		20-2		
Apr. 1	20,000	Jan. 1	Rev.	10,000

Bond Interest Payable

			20-1	
			Dec. 31	10,000
20-2				
Jan. 1	Rev.	10,000		

U REVU

Complete U REVU-2 on **page 853** to test your basic understanding of LO2.

ACCOUNTING FOR BONDS ISSUED AT A PREMIUM

LO3 Account for bonds issued at a premium.

Recall that if the stated interest rate on bonds is greater than the current market rate, the bonds will sell at a premium. When bonds are issued at a premium, both bonds payable on the balance sheet and interest expense on the income statement are affected.

ISSUANCE

Assume that on April 1, 20-1, the stated rate of 10% on Watkin's bonds is greater than the current market rate, so that the bonds sell for 106. This means that the bonds sell for $424,000 ($400,000 × 106%), a premium of $24,000. The journal entry for the sale and issuance of Watkin's bonds at a premium on April 1, 20-1, is as follows:

5	Apr.	1	Cash		424 000 00		5
6			Bonds Payable			400 000 00	6
7			Premium on Bonds Payable			24 000 00	7
8			Issued bonds at a premium				8

Premium on Bonds Payable is an adjunct-liability account. It is added to bonds payable on the corporate balance sheet. On Watkin's balance sheet immediately after issuing the $400,000 of bonds for $424,000, the bonds payable and premium would appear as follows:

Long-term liabilities:		
Bonds payable	$400 000 00	
Premium on bonds payable	24 000 00	$424 000 00

The sum of bonds payable and premium on bonds payable is called the **carrying value** of the bonds.

INTEREST EXPENSE AND PREMIUM AMORTIZATION

When bonds are issued at a premium, the amount of interest actually paid is not the true interest expense. This is because the premium received when the bonds are issued effectively reduces the cost of borrowing. For example, Watkin received $424,000 for its bonds but will have to pay back only $400,000, the face value of the bonds. This $24,000 reduction ($424,000 – $400,000) in the cost of borrowing is spread over the life of the bond issue by adjusting interest expense on a regular basis.

In a sense, Premium on Bonds Payable is a "gain." Watkin received $424,000 in exchange for a promise to pay only $400,000, a "gain" of $24,000. This gain is spread as an "interest expense reduction" over the life of the bonds. As the premium is waiting to be spread, it is stored as a credit balance in an adjunct-liability account.

Figure 22-2 shows the "gain" from selling the $400,000 of bonds at a premium and how this gain is spread as an interest reduction over the life of the bonds.

The process of adjusting the bond interest expense account for any premium or discount is called **amortization** of the premium or discount. Two commonly used methods of amortizing premium (or discount) over the life of a bond are (1) effective interest and (2) straight-line. The effective interest method is recommended, but the straight-line method is much simpler to apply and generally provides acceptable results. We will use the straight-line method. The effective interest method is covered in the appendix.

FIGURE 22-2 Bonds Issued at a Premium

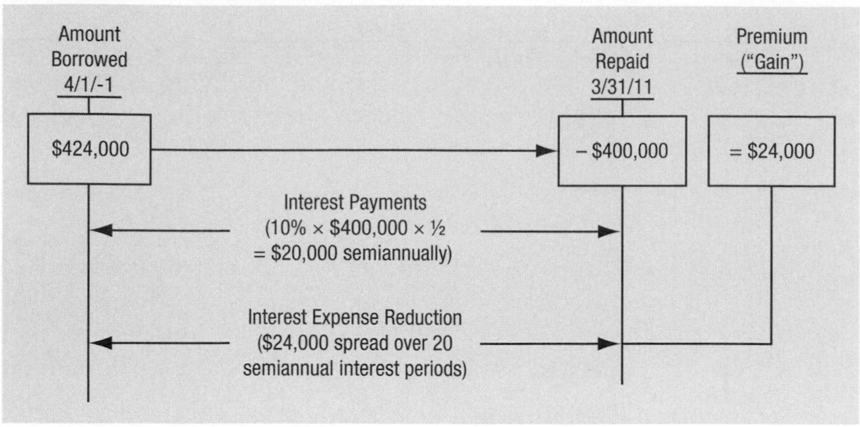

Using the straight-line method, $1,200 of the premium on Watkin's bonds is amortized each semiannual interest period, calculated as follows:

$$\frac{\text{Premium}}{\text{Life of Bonds}} \times \text{½ Year} = \frac{\$24,000}{10 \text{ Years}} \times \text{½ Year} = \$1,200$$

The entry for the first semiannual interest payment and amortization of bond premium on October 1, 20-1, is as follows:

18	Oct.	1	Bond Interest Expense	18,800.00		18
19			Premium on Bonds Payable	1,200.00		19
20			Cash		20,000.00	20
21			Paid semiannual interest and			21
22			amortized premium on bonds			22

LEARNING KEY

Premium amortization reduces the interest expense and carrying value of the bonds but has no effect on the amount of cash paid.

Note that the premium amortization does not affect the amount of cash paid. The amortization simply reduces the bond interest expense for the period and the carrying value of the bonds.

On December 31, an adjusting entry is needed both for accrued interest and for premium amortization for the period from October 1 through December 31. Three months' interest of $10,000 (10% × $400,000 × ¼ year) has accrued. Three months' premium of $600 ($24,000 ÷ 10 × ¼ year) should be amortized. The adjusting entry is as follows:

25	Dec.	31	Bond Interest Expense	9,400.00		25
26			Premium on Bonds Payable	600.00		26
27			Bond Interest Payable		10,000.00	27

After the April 1, October 1, and December 31 entries are posted, Cash, Bond Interest Expense, Bonds Payable, Premium on Bonds Payable, and Bond Interest Payable appear in the accounting equation as shown in Figure 22-3.

The December 31, 20-1, adjusting entry normally is reversed as of January 1, 20-2. The next semiannual interest and premium amortization entry on April 1, 20-2, is made exactly like the entry on October 1, 20-1. Columns 2, 3, and 4 in Figure 22-4 summarize the semiannual interest and premium amortization entries for the life of the bonds.

FIGURE 22-3 Bonds Payable and Related Accounts after Interest Accrual and Premium Amortization

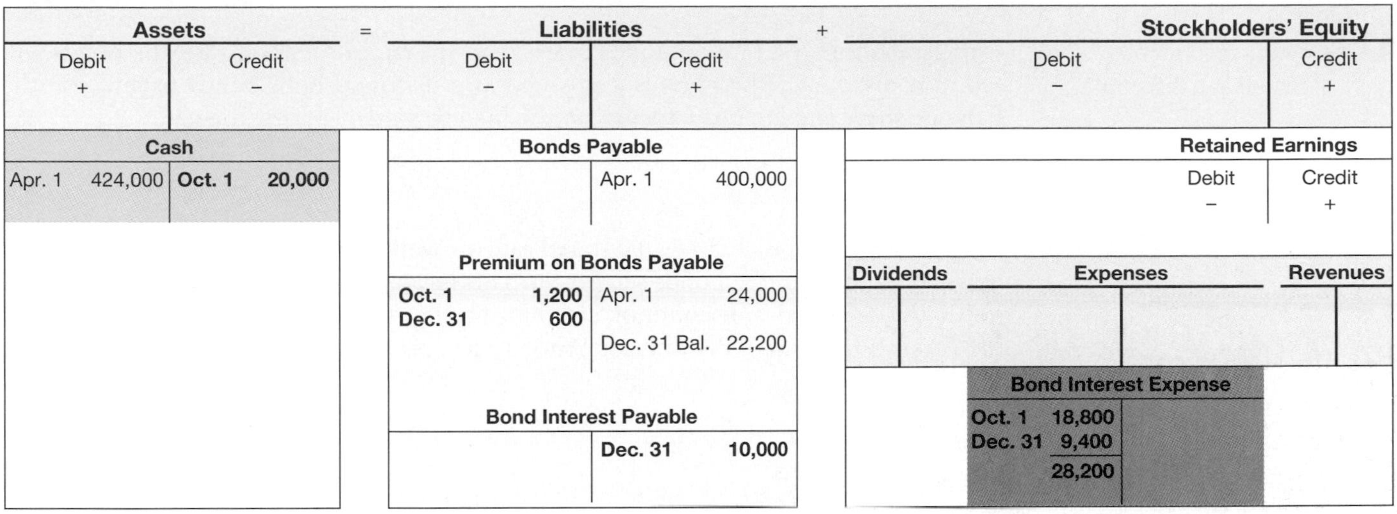

Assets = Liabilities + Stockholders' Equity
Debit + | Credit −
Debit − | Credit +
Debit − | Credit +
Cash
Apr. 1 424,000 | Oct. 1 20,000
Bonds Payable
Apr. 1 400,000
Premium on Bonds Payable
Oct. 1 1,200 | Apr. 1 24,000
Dec. 31 600
Dec. 31 Bal. 22,200
Bond Interest Payable
Dec. 31 10,000
Retained Earnings
Debit − | Credit +
Dividends
Expenses
Revenues
Bond Interest Expense
Oct. 1 18,800
Dec. 31 9,400
28,200

Consistent with the matching concept, note that the premium is spread over the period benefited—the 10-year life of the bonds.

Note that the effect of the premium amortization is to reduce both the interest expense for the period and the balance in the premium on bonds payable account. In fact, the premium on bonds payable account balance is gradually reduced to zero over the life of the bonds, as shown in column 6 of Figure 22-4. Recall that Premium on Bonds Payable is an adjunct-liability account. It is added to bonds payable on the balance sheet. The amount that Watkin will have to pay at maturity is $400,000. By amortizing the premium on bonds payable over the life of the bonds, the carrying value of the bonds decreases to $400,000 at maturity, as shown in column 7 of Figure 22-4.

FIGURE 22-4 Premium Amortization Schedule

BOND PREMIUM AMORTIZATION SCHEDULE
STRAIGHT-LINE METHOD

(1) Date	(2) Interest Expense Debit	(3) Premium on Bonds Payable Debit	(4) Cash Credit	(5) Bonds Payable Balance	(6) Premium on Bonds Payable Balance	(7) Carrying Value of Bonds [(5) + (6)]
4/1/-1				$400,000	$24,000	$424,000
10/1/-1	$18,800	$1,200	$20,000	400,000	22,800	422,800
4/1/-2*	18,800	1,200	20,000	400,000	21,600	421,600
10/1/-2	18,800	1,200	20,000	400,000	20,400	420,400
–	–	–	–	–	–	–
–	–	–	–	–	–	–
–	–	–	–	–	–	–
4/1/10	18,800	1,200	20,000	400,000	2,400	402,400
10/1/10	18,800	1,200	20,000	400,000	1,200	401,200
3/31/11	18,800	1,200	20,000	400,000	0	400,000

*The entry for the first interest payment each year assumes that the adjusting entry at December 31 of the preceding year was reversed.

U REVU Complete U REVU-3 on page 854 to test your basic understanding of LO3.

ACCOUNTING FOR BONDS ISSUED AT A DISCOUNT

LO4 Account for bonds issued at a discount.

If the stated interest rate on bonds is less than the current market rate, the bonds will sell at a discount. When bonds are issued at a discount, both bonds payable on the balance sheet and interest expense on the income statement are affected.

ISSUANCE

Assume that on April 1, 20-1, the stated rate on Watkin's bonds is less than the current market rate, so that the bonds sell for 96. This means that the bonds sell for $384,000 ($400,000 × 96%), a discount of $16,000. The journal entry for the sale and issuance of Watkin's bonds at a discount on April 1, 20-1, is as follows:

5	Apr.	1	Cash		384 0 0 0 00		5
6			Discount on Bonds Payable		16 0 0 0 00		6
7			Bonds Payable			400 0 0 0 00	7
8			Issued bonds at a discount				8

Discount on Bonds Payable is a contra-liability account. It is deducted from bonds payable on the corporate balance sheet. On Watkin's balance sheet immediately after issuing the $400,000 of bonds for $384,000, the bonds payable and discount would appear as follows:

Long-term liabilities:		
Bonds payable	$400 0 0 0 00	
Discount on bonds payable	16 0 0 0 00	$384 0 0 0 00

Bonds payable less the discount on bonds payable is called the carrying value of the bonds.

INTEREST EXPENSE AND DISCOUNT AMORTIZATION

When bonds are sold at a discount, we have a situation similar to what we saw in the case of bonds sold at a premium. The interest actually paid is not the true interest expense. This is because the discount given when the bonds are issued effectively increases the cost of borrowing. For example, Watkin received only $384,000 for its bonds but will have to pay back $400,000, the face value of the bonds. This $16,000 increase ($400,000 – $384,000) in the cost of borrowing is amortized over the life of the bond issue by adjusting interest expense on a regular basis.

In a sense, Discount on Bonds Payable is a "loss." Watkin received only $384,000 in exchange for a promise to pay $400,000, a "loss" of $16,000. This loss is spread as an "interest expense increase" over the life of the bonds. As the discount is waiting to be spread, it is stored as a debit balance in a contra-liability account.

Figure 22-5 shows the "loss" from selling the $400,000 of bonds at a discount and how this loss is spread as an interest increase over the life of the bonds.

Using the straight-line method, $800 of the discount on Watkin's bonds is amortized each semiannual interest period, calculated as follows:

$$\frac{\text{Discount}}{\text{Life of Bonds}} \times \tfrac{1}{2}\text{ Year} = \frac{\$16{,}000}{10\text{ Years}} \times \tfrac{1}{2}\text{ Year} = \$800$$

FIGURE 22-5 Bonds Issued at a Discount

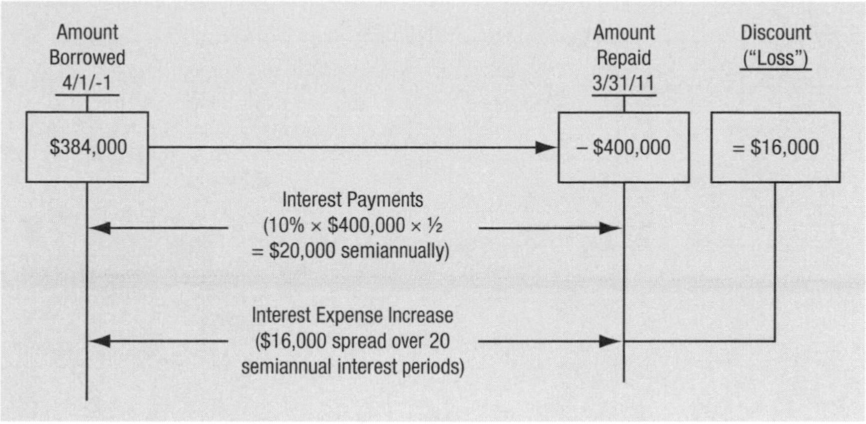

The entry for the first semiannual interest payment and amortization of bond discount on October 1, 20-1, is as follows:

18	Oct.	1	Bond Interest Expense		20,800.00		18
19			Discount on Bonds Payable			800.00	19
20			Cash			20,000.00	20
21			Paid semiannual interest and				21
22			amortized discount on bonds				22

LEARNING KEY

Discount amortization increases the interest expense and carrying value of the bonds but has no effect on the amount of cash paid.

Note that the discount amortization does not affect the amount of cash paid. The amortization simply increases the bond interest expense for the period and the carrying value of the bonds.

On December 31, an adjusting entry is needed both for accrued interest and for discount amortization for the period from October 1 through December 31. Three months' interest of $10,000 (10% × $400,000 × ¼ year) has accrued. Three months' discount of $400 ($16,000 ÷ 10 × ¼ year) should be amortized. The adjusting entry is as follows:

25	Dec.	31	Bond Interest Expense		10,400.00		25
26			Bond Interest Payable			10,000.00	26
27			Discount on Bonds Payable			400.00	27

After the October 1 and December 31 entries are posted, Cash, Bond Interest Expense, Bonds Payable, Discount on Bonds Payable, and Bond Interest Payable appear in the accounting equation as shown in Figure 22-6.

Consistent with the matching concept, note that the discount is spread over the period benefited—the 10-year life of the bonds.

The December 31 adjusting entry normally is reversed as of January 1, 20-2. The next semiannual interest and discount amortization entry on April 1, 20-2, is made exactly like the entry on October 1, 20-1. Columns 2, 3, and 4 in Figure 22-7 summarize the semiannual interest and discount amortization entries for the life of the bonds.

Note that the effect of the discount amortization is to increase the interest expense for the period and to decrease the balance in the discount on bonds payable account. In fact, the discount on bonds payable account balance is gradually reduced to zero over the life of the bonds, as shown in column 6 of Figure 22-7. Recall that Discount on Bonds Payable is a contra-liability account. It is subtracted from bonds payable on the balance sheet. The amount that Watkin will have to pay at maturity is $400,000. By amortizing the discount on bonds payable over the life of the bonds, the carrying value of the bonds increases to $400,000 at maturity, as shown in column 7 of Figure 22-7.

FIGURE 22-6 Bonds Payable and Related Accounts after Interest Accrual and Discount Amortization

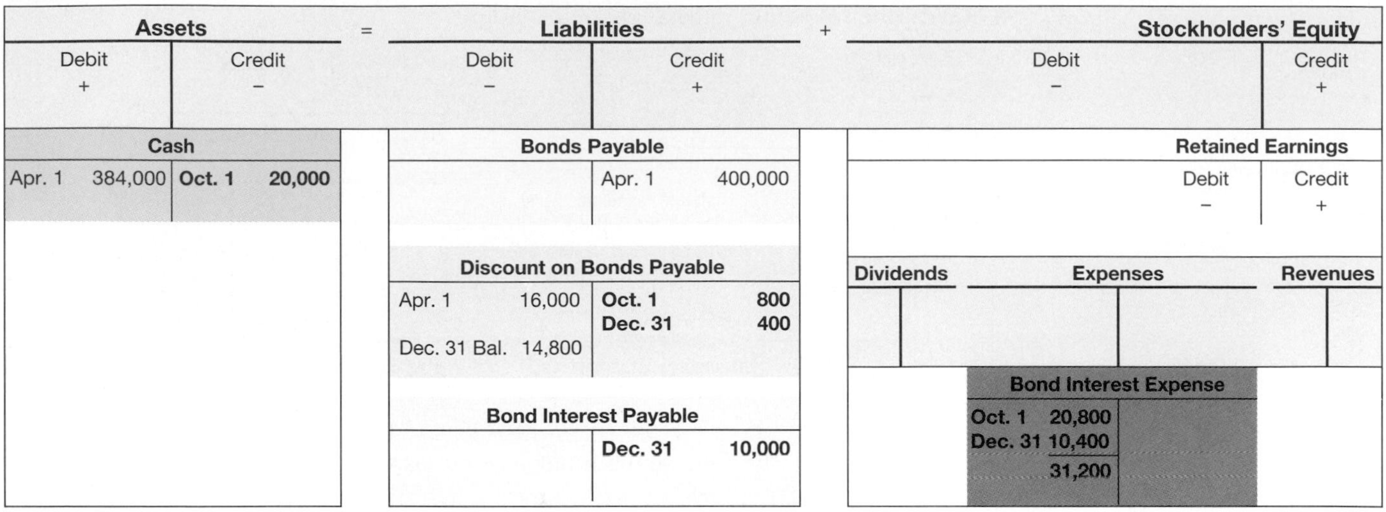

Assets = Liabilities + Stockholders' Equity
Debit + Credit −
Debit − Credit +
Debit − Credit +
Cash
Apr. 1 384,000 Oct. 1 20,000
Bonds Payable
Apr. 1 400,000
Retained Earnings
Debit − Credit +
Discount on Bonds Payable
Apr. 1 16,000 Oct. 1 800
Dec. 31 400
Dec. 31 Bal. 14,800
Dividends
Expenses
Revenues
Bond Interest Payable
Dec. 31 10,000
Bond Interest Expense
Oct. 1 20,800
Dec. 31 10,400
31,200

FIGURE 22-7 Discount Amortization Schedule

BOND DISCOUNT AMORTIZATION SCHEDULE
STRAIGHT-LINE METHOD

(1) Date	(2) Interest Expense Debit	(3) Discount on Bonds Payable Credit	(4) Cash Credit	(5) Bonds Payable Balance	(6) Discount on Bonds Payable Balance	(7) Carrying Value of Bonds [(5) − (6)]
4/1/-1				$400,000	$16,000	$384,000
10/1/-1	$20,800	$800	$20,000	400,000	15,200	384,800
4/1/-2*	20,800	800	20,000	400,000	14,400	385,600
10/1/-2	20,800	800	20,000	400,000	13,600	386,400
–	–	–	–	–	–	–
–	–	–	–	–	–	–
–	–	–	–	–	–	–
4/1/10	20,800	800	20,000	400,000	1,600	398,400
10/1/10	20,800	800	20,000	400,000	800	399,200
3/31/11	20,800	800	20,000	400,000	0	400,000

*The entry for the first interest payment each year assumes that the adjusting entry at December 31 of the preceding year was reversed.

U REVU Complete U REVU-4 on **page 854** to test your basic understanding of LO4.

ACCOUNTING FOR BOND REDEMPTION AND SINKING FUNDS

LO5 Account for bond redemption and bond sinking funds.

Proper accounting for bond redemption depends on whether the redemption is at maturity or before that date. Each of these conditions is explained in the following sections.

REDEMPTION AT MATURITY

Usually, bonds issued by a corporation are redeemed at face value at their maturity. By that date, the entire amount of any premium or discount should have been amortized. To enter the redemption, Bonds Payable is debited and Cash is credited for the face value of the bonds. For example, if the $400,000 of Watkin bonds are redeemed at maturity, the following journal entry is made:

22		Bonds Payable		400,000.00		22
23		Cash			400,000.00	23
24		Redeemed bonds at face value				24

REDEMPTION BEFORE MATURITY

Corporations may redeem part or all of a bond issue before maturity. If the bonds are callable, a corporation may call in the bonds before they mature. The call price is defined in the original bond agreement. If the bonds are not callable, a corporation can purchase its bonds in the open market at the market price. When bonds are redeemed before maturity, any accrued interest must be paid and the premium or discount amortization must be brought up to date. Entries for doing so are the same as those illustrated in previous sections of the chapter.

Redemption at a Loss

LEARNING KEY

To determine the amount of gain or loss on redemption of bonds, compare the redemption price with the carrying value of the bonds.

Usually, there is a gain or loss involved when bonds are redeemed before maturity. The gain or loss is the difference between the amount paid to redeem the bonds and the carrying value of the bonds. When bonds are issued at face value, the carrying value equals the face value throughout the life of the bonds. When bonds are issued at a premium or discount, the carrying value changes over the life of the bonds, as the premium or discount is amortized.

To illustrate, consider the Watkin Corp. $400,000, 10% bonds that were sold at face value. If $40,000 of the bonds are redeemed at 103, there is a loss of $1,200 on redemption of the bonds, calculated as follows:

Cash paid ($40,000 × 103%)	$41,200
Less carrying value (= face value) of bonds	40,000
Loss on redemption	$ 1,200

The journal entry for this transaction is as follows:

31		Bonds Payable		40,000.00		31
32		Loss on Bonds Redeemed		1,200.00		32
33		Cash			41,200.00	33
34		Redeemed bonds at a loss				34

Loss on Bonds Redeemed generally is reported as other expense near the bottom of the income statement.

Now consider the Watkin Corp. bonds that were sold at a premium (106) for $424,000. Assume that eight years after the issuance, Watkin redeems $40,000 of this issue at 103. The carrying value of these bonds is calculated as follows:

Issue price ($40,000 × 106%)	$42,400	
Face value	40,000	
Premium received at issuance		$ 2,400
Premium amortized per year ($2,400 ÷ 10 yrs.)	$ 240	
Number of years since issuance	× 8	
Total premium amortized in 8 years		1,920
Unamortized premium		$ 480
Face value		40,000
Carrying value		$40,480

Thus, after the interest payment and premium amortization have been entered on April 1, 20-9, the carrying value of the $40,000 of bonds is $40,480. There is a loss of $720 on redemption of the bonds, calculated as follows:

Cash paid ($40,000 × 103%)	$41,200
Less carrying value	40,480
Loss on redemption	$ 720

The journal entry for this transaction is as follows:

				Debit	Credit	
5	Apr.	1	Bonds Payable	40,000.00		5
6			Premium on Bonds Payable	480.00		6
7			Loss on Bonds Redeemed	720.00		7
8			Cash		41,200.00	8
9			Redeemed bonds at a loss			9

Redemption at a Gain

To illustrate the redemption of bonds at a gain, let's look again at two examples. Assume that $40,000 of Watkin's bonds that were issued at face value are redeemed at 98. In this case, Watkin has a gain of $800 on redemption of the bonds, calculated as follows:

Carrying value (= face value) of bonds	$40,000
Less cash paid ($40,000 × 98%)	39,200
Gain on bonds redeemed	$ 800

The journal entry for this transaction is as follows:

				Debit	Credit	
31			Bonds Payable	40,000.00		31
32			Gain on Bonds Redeemed		800.00	32
33			Cash		39,200.00	33
34			Redeemed bonds at a gain			34

Gain on Bonds Redeemed generally is reported as other income on the income statement.

Now consider the Watkin Corp. bonds that were sold at a discount (96) for $384,000. Assume that six years after issuance, Watkin redeems $40,000 of this issue at 98. The carrying value of these bonds is calculated as follows:

Face value	$40,000	
Issue price ($40,000 × 96%)	38,400	
Discount at issuance		$ 1,600
Discount amortized per year ($1,600 ÷ 10 yrs.)	$ 160	
Number of years since issuance	× 6	
Total discount amortized in 6 years		960
Unamortized discount		$ 640
Face value		$40,000
Less unamortized discount		640
Carrying value		$39,360

Thus, after the interest payment and discount amortization have been entered on April 1, 20-7, the carrying value of the $40,000 of bonds is $39,360. There is a gain of $160 on redemption of the bonds, calculated as follows:

Carrying value of bonds	$39,360
Less cash paid ($40,000 × 98%)	39,200
Gain on redemption	$ 160

The journal entry for this transaction is as follows:

5	Apr.	1	Bonds Payable		40,000.00		5
6			Discount on Bonds Payable			640.00	6
7			Gain on Bonds Redeemed			160.00	7
8			Cash			39,200.00	8
9			Redeemed bonds at a gain				9

BOND SINKING FUNDS

The formal written agreement for issuing bonds is called the **bond indenture.** Bond indentures for term bonds frequently require the accumulation and investment of money over a period of years. This is to provide the amount needed to redeem the bonds at maturity. Such accumulations are known as **bond sinking funds**. The sinking fund usually is administered by a trustee. The corporation makes periodic cash deposits with the trustee. The trustee is responsible for investing the cash and accumulating amounts necessary to redeem the bonds at maturity.

To illustrate, assume that the bond indenture for the Watkin bonds required Watkin to make deposits of $30,000 to a trustee each year. The entry for each deposit is as follows:

12			Bond Sinking Fund		30,000.00		12
13			Cash			30,000.00	13
14			Made sinking fund deposit				14

The bond sinking fund is a long-term asset and is reported under Investments on the corporation balance sheet.

The trustee invests the cash and adds any earnings on these investments to the sinking fund. Assume that Watkin's trustee reports sinking fund earnings of $2,800 for the year. The following entry is made:

26			Bond Sinking Fund		2,800.00		26
27			Sinking Fund Earnings			2,800.00	27
28			Annual sinking fund earnings				28

Sinking fund earnings are reported as other revenue on the corporation income statement.

When the bonds mature, the trustee sells all of the sinking fund investments. The corporation then deposits additional cash with the trustee so that the sum of the periodic deposits, the sinking fund earnings, and the additional cash is sufficient to redeem the bonds. When the Watkin bonds are redeemed at maturity by the trustee, the following entry is made:

5			Bonds Payable		400,000.00		5
6			Bond Sinking Fund			400,000.00	6
7			Redeemed bonds at face value				7

If any cash is left in the sinking fund after all of the bonds are redeemed, the cash is returned to the corporation. Assume that the sinking fund has a balance of $960 after all the bonds are redeemed. The following entry is made:

18			Cash		960.00		18
19			Bond Sinking Fund			960.00	19
20			Received sinking fund balance				20

U REVU Complete U REVU-5 on **page 854** to test your basic understanding of LO5.

SELF-STUDY

LEARNING OBJECTIVES Key Points to Remember

LO1 Describe the types of bonds and how their sales price is determined.

Bonds can be classified as to (1) security, (2) timing of payment of principal, and (3) identification of ownership. If the bond and market interest rates are equal, bonds will sell at face value. If the bond interest rate is greater than the market rate, bonds will sell at a premium. If the bond interest rate is less than the market rate, bonds will sell at a discount.

LO2 Account for bonds issued at face value.

LO3 Account for bonds issued at a premium.

LO4 Account for bonds issued at a discount.

The journal entries for bond issuance, interest payments, premium or discount amortization, and redemption can be summarized as follows:

	BONDS ISSUED AT		
	FACE	**PREMIUM**	**DISCOUNT**
Issuance	Cash Bonds Payable	Cash Bonds Payable Premium on Bonds Payable	Cash Discount on Bonds Payable Bonds Payable
Interest Payment and Amortization	Interest Expense Cash	Interest Expense Premium on Bonds Payable Cash	Interest Expense Discount on Bonds Payable Cash
Redemption at: Carrying Value	Bonds Payable Cash	Bonds Payable Premium on Bonds Payable Cash	Bonds Payable Discount on Bonds Payable Cash
< Carrying Value	Bonds Payable Gain on Redemption Cash	Bonds Payable Premium on Bonds Payable Gain on Redemption Cash	Bonds Payable Discount on Bonds Payable Gain on Redemption Cash
> Carrying Value	Bonds Payable Loss on Redemption Cash	Bonds Payable Premium on Bonds Payable Loss on Redemption Cash	Bonds Payable Loss on Redemption Discount on Bonds Payable Cash

LEARNING OBJECTIVES Key Points to Remember

LO5 Account for bond redemption and bond sinking funds.	The gain or loss on redemption of bonds is the difference between the amount paid to redeem the bonds and the carrying value of the bonds. Gains and losses on bonds redeemed are reported as other income or expense on the income statement. Bond sinking funds are used to accumulate the money needed for bond redemption. The sum of the amounts deposited in the sinking fund, sinking fund earnings, and any additional cash deposited in the sinking fund by the company when the bonds mature is used to redeem the bonds.

DEMONSTRATION PROBLEM

Brooks Inc.'s fiscal year ends December 31. Selected transactions for the period 20-1 through 20-8 involving bonds payable issued by Brooks are as follows:

20-1	
Nov. 30	Issued $800,000 of 10-year, 9%, callable bonds dated November 30, 20-1, for $776,000. Interest is payable semiannually on November 30 and May 31. The bond indenture provides that Brooks is to pay to the trustee bank $30,000 by June 15 of each year (except the tenth year) as a sinking fund for the retirement of the bonds on call or at maturity.
Dec. 31	Made the adjusting entry for interest payable and amortized one month's discount on the bonds (straight-line method).
20-2	
Jan. 2	Reversed the adjusting entry for interest payable and bond discount amortization.
May 31	Paid the semiannual interest on the bonds and amortized six months' discount.
June 15	Paid the sinking fund trustee $30,000.
Nov. 30	Paid the semiannual interest on the bonds and amortized six months' discount.
Dec. 31	Made the adjusting entry for interest payable and amortized one month's discount on the bonds.
31	Sinking fund earnings for the year were $1,100.
20-8	
June 15	Paid the sinking fund trustee $30,000.
Nov. 30	Paid the semiannual interest on the bonds and amortized six months' discount.
30	Redeemed the bonds, which were called at 102.

The balance in the bond discount account is $7,200 after the payment of interest and amortization of discount have been entered. The cash balance in the sinking fund is $320,000. The sinking fund trustee is paid the additional cash needed to redeem the bonds. (*Hint:* First make the entry for payment to the sinking fund, then make the entry for redemption of the bonds.)

REQUIRED

1. Enter the transactions in general journal form.
2. Calculate the carrying value of the bonds as of December 31, 20-2.

(continued)

Solution 1.

GENERAL JOURNAL PAGE 1

	DATE		DESCRIPTION	POST. REF.	DEBIT	CREDIT	
1	20-1 Nov.	30	Cash		776 0 0 0 00		1
2			Discount on Bonds Payable		24 0 0 0 00		2
3			Bonds Payable			800 0 0 0 00	3
4			Issued bonds at a discount				4
5							5
6			Adjusting Entry				6
7	Dec.	31	Bond Interest Expense		6 2 0 0 00		7
8			Bond Interest Payable			6 0 0 0 00	8
9			Discount on Bonds Payable*			2 0 0 00	9
10							10
11			Reversing Entry				11
12	20-2 Jan.	2	Bond Interest Payable		6 0 0 0 00		12
13			Discount on Bonds Payable		2 0 0 00		13
14			Bond Interest Expense			6 2 0 0 00	14
15							15
16	May	31	Bond Interest Expense		37 2 0 0 00		16
17			Discount on Bonds Payable			1 2 0 0 00	17
18			Cash			36 0 0 0 00	18
19			Paid semiannual interest and				19
20			amortized discount on bonds				20
21							21
22	June	15	Bond Sinking Fund		30 0 0 0 00		22
23			Cash			30 0 0 0 00	23
24			Made sinking fund deposit				24
25							25
26	Nov.	30	Bond Interest Expense		37 2 0 0 00		26
27			Discount on Bonds Payable			1 2 0 0 00	27
28			Cash			36 0 0 0 00	28
29			Paid semiannual interest and				29
30			amortized discount on bonds				30
31							31
32							32

*Amortization rate = $24,000 original discount ÷ 10 years = $2,400/year ÷ 12 months = $200/month

GENERAL JOURNAL PAGE 2

	DATE		DESCRIPTION	POST. REF.	DEBIT	CREDIT	
1			Adjusting Entry				1
2	20-2 Dec.	31	Bond Interest Expense		6,200.00		2
3			Bond Interest Payable			6,000.00	3
4			Discount on Bonds Payable			200.00	4
5							5
6		31	Bond Sinking Fund		1,100.00		6
7			Sinking Fund Earnings			1,100.00	7
8			Annual sinking fund earnings				8
9							9
10	20-8 June	15	Bond Sinking Fund		30,000.00		10
11			Cash			30,000.00	11
12			Made sinking fund deposit				12
13							13
14	Nov.	30	Bond Interest Expense		37,200.00		14
15			Discount on Bonds Payable			1,200.00	15
16			Cash			36,000.00	16
17			Paid semiannual interest and				17
18			amortized discount on bonds				18
19							19
20		30	Bond Sinking Fund		496,000.00		20
21			Cash			496,000.00	21
22			[($800,000 × 102%) – $320,000]				22
23			Made sinking fund deposit				23
24							24
25		30	Bonds Payable		800,000.00		25
26			Loss on Bonds Redeemed		23,200.00		26
27			Discount on Bonds Payable*			7,200.00	27
28			Bond Sinking Fund			816,000.00	28
29			Redeemed bonds at a loss				29

*Original discount on bonds payable	$24,000
Amortization for 7 years at $2,400/year	(16,800)
Unamortized discount on November 30, 20-8	$ 7,200

2.

Face value of bonds		$800,000
Original discount on bonds payable	$24,000	
Less:		
Discount amortized on December 31, 20-1	(200)	
Discount amortized during 20-2	(2,400)	
Balance of discount on bonds payable at December 31, 20-2		21,400
Carrying value of bonds, December 31, 20-2		$778,600

KEY TERMS

amortization (839) The process of adjusting the bond interest expense account for any premium or discount.

bearer bonds (836) See coupon bonds.

bond (835) A written promise to pay a specific sum of money at a specific future date.

bond indenture (847) The formal written agreement for issuing bonds.

bond sinking funds (847) The accumulation and investment of money over a period of years to provide the amount needed for the redemption of bonds.

callable bonds (835) Bonds that give the issuing corporation the option of calling the bonds for redemption before the maturity date.

carrying value (839) Bonds payable plus the premium or less the discount on bonds payable.

convertible bonds (835) Bonds that give the holder the option of exchanging the bonds for capital stock of the corporation.

coupon bonds (836) Bonds whose ownership generally is not recorded by the corporation. These bonds have interest coupons attached.

coupon rate (836) See stated rate.

debenture bonds (835) See unsecured bonds.

discount (836) The difference between the face value and the price of a bond when the current market interest rate is greater than the stated rate of that bond.

face value (836) The amount written on the face of the bond certificate.

market rate (836) The interest rate that can be earned on similar investments or the rate that other companies in similar financial condition have to pay to borrow money.

mortgage bonds (835) Bonds secured by a mortgage on corporate property such as real estate or equipment.

premium (836) The difference between the face value and the price of a bond when the current market interest rate is less than the stated rate of that bond.

principal (835) The amount to be paid to the bondholder at maturity.

registered bonds (836) Bonds whose ownership is recorded in the corporate records.

secured bonds (835) Bonds that are backed by specific corporate assets.

serial bonds (835) Bonds issued in a series so that a specified amount of the bonds matures each year.

stated rate (836) The rate of interest specified on the face of the bond.

term bonds (835) Bonds that all have the same maturity date.

unsecured bonds (835) Bonds backed solely by the general credit of the corporation issuing the bonds.

SELF-STUDY QUESTIONS AND EXERCISES

True/False Questions

1. LO1 A secured bond is one that is backed by specific corporate assets.
2. LO1 If the stated rate of interest on a bond is 9% and the current market rate on similar investments is 10%, the bond will sell at a premium.
3. LO2 When bonds are issued at face value, the debit to Cash and credit to Bonds Payable are for the same amount.
4. LO3 Amortization of the premium on bonds payable increases the bond interest expense and the carrying value of the bonds.
5. LO5 To determine the amount of gain or loss on redemption of bonds, compare the redemption price with the carrying value of the bonds.

Multiple Choice Questions

1. LO1 Bonds that give the holder the option of exchanging the bonds for capital stock in the corporation are called
   (a) debenture bonds.
   (b) serial bonds.
   (c) convertible bonds.
   (d) callable bonds.
2. LO3 If bonds with a face value of $200,000 are sold at 102, Cash is debited for
   (a) $200,000.
   (b) $202,000.
   (c) $204,000.
   (d) $196,000.
3. LO3 Ten-year bonds with a face value of $300,000 are sold at a premium of $6,000. If the premium is amortized using the straight-line method, each semiannual interest payment and amortization of bond premium will include a
   (a) debit to Premium on Bonds Payable.
   (b) credit to Premium on Bonds Payable.
   (c) debit to Cash.
   (d) credit to Bond Interest Expense.
4. LO4 If bonds are issued at a discount, the amortization of the discount over the life of the bonds causes the
   (a) face value to decrease each period.
   (b) face value to increase each period.
   (c) carrying value of the bonds to decrease.
   (d) carrying value of the bonds to increase.
5. LO5 Bond sinking fund earnings are
   (a) subtracted from the bond sinking fund.
   (b) added to the bond sinking fund.
   (c) subtracted from the current year interest expense.
   (d) added to the current year interest expense.

U REVU Exercises

1. LO1 Jibble Company wants to sell $300,000 of 8%, 10-year bonds. If the current market rate on similar investments is 9%, at what price will these bonds sell?
   (a) More than $300,000
   (b) $300,000
   (c) Less than $300,000
2. LO2 B&B Associates issued $300,000 of 8%, 10-year bonds at face value on April 1, 20-1. Interest is payable on September 30 and March 31. Prepare journal entries for the following:
   (a) Interest payment on the bonds on September 30.
   (b) Year-end adjustment for interest on the bonds.

3. LO3 Yingh Company issued $500,000 of 9%, 10-year bonds at 102 on July 1, 20-1. Interest is payable on December 31 and June 30. Prepare journal entries for the following:
   (a) Issuance of the bonds.
   (b) Interest payment and premium amortization on the bonds on December 31.
4. LO4 Mellis Company issued $300,000 of 8%, 10-year bonds at 97 on May 1, 20-1. Interest is payable on October 31 and April 30. Prepare journal entries for the following:
   (a) Issuance of the bonds.
   (b) Interest payment and discount amortization on the bonds on October 31.
5. LO5 FPD Company sold $300,000 of 9%, 10-year bonds at 97 six years ago. Prepare journal entries for each of the following possible redemptions of portions of these bonds:
   (a) FPD redeems $30,000 of the issue at 99. The unamortized discount is $360.
   (b) FPD redeems $40,000 of the bonds at 98. The unamortized discount is $480.

The answers to the Self-Study Questions and Exercises are at the end of the chapter (page 865).

APPLYING YOUR KNOWLEDGE

REVIEW QUESTIONS

LO1 1. Explain the difference between corporate bonds and stock from the standpoint of the issuing corporation.

LO1 2. Will a bond sell at a discount or at a premium if the stated rate is greater than the market rate on the bond? If the stated rate is less than the market rate?

LO1 3. Explain the meaning of a bond price quotation of 95. Of 102.

LO2 4. What accounts are affected when bonds are issued at face value?

LO3/4 5. How is Premium on Bonds Payable shown on the balance sheet? How is Discount on Bonds Payable shown?

LO3/4 6. How is the amount of bond premium or discount to be amortized in a period determined using the straight-line method?

LO3/4 7. How is the periodic interest expense affected by the amortization of the premium on bonds payable?

LO3/4 8. How is the periodic interest expense affected by the amortization of the discount on bonds payable?

LO5 9. When bonds are redeemed before maturity, how is the gain or loss on redemption determined? Why does the calculation differ for bonds issued at face value, at a premium, and at a discount?

LO5 10. Who usually administers a bond sinking fund?

LO5 11. How should sinking fund earnings be reported on the corporation income statement?

LO5 12. How should the bond sinking fund be reported on the corporation balance sheet?

SERIES A EXERCISES

E 22-1A (LO2)
✓ Dec. 31. Dr. Bond Interest Expense, $10,000

BONDS ISSUED AT FACE VALUE R & R Collectibles issued the following bonds:

Date of issue and sale:	April 1, 20-1
Principal amount:	$500,000
Sale price of bonds:	100
Denomination of bonds:	$1,000
Life of bonds:	10 years
Stated rate:	8%, payable semiannually on September 30 and March 31

Prepare journal entries for:

(a) Issuance of the bonds.
(b) Interest payment on the bonds on September 30.
(c) Year-end adjustment on the bonds.

E 22-2A (LO3)
✓ Dec. 31. Dr. Bond Interest Expense, $12,250

BONDS ISSUED AT A PREMIUM Velez Entertainment Co. issued the following bonds at a premium:

Date of issue and sale:	April 1, 20-1
Principal amount:	$500,000
Sale price of bonds:	104
Denomination of bonds:	$1,000
Life of bonds:	20 years
Stated rate:	10%, payable semiannually on September 30 and March 31

Prepare journal entries for:

(a) Issuance of the bonds at a premium.
(b) Interest payment and premium amortization on the bonds on September 30.
(c) Year-end adjustment on the bonds.

E 22-3A (LO4)
✓ Dec. 31. Dr. Bond Interest Expense, $9,000

BONDS ISSUED AT A DISCOUNT Brenner's Home Club issued the following bonds at a discount:

Date of issue and sale:	April 1, 20-1
Principal amount:	$500,000
Sale price of bonds:	98
Denomination of bonds:	$1,000
Life of bonds:	10 years
Stated rate:	7%, payable semiannually on September 30 and March 31

Prepare journal entries for:

(a) Issuance of the bonds at a discount.
(b) Interest payment and discount amortization on the bonds on September 30.
(c) Year-end adjustment on the bonds.

E 22-4A (LO2/5)
✓ (b) Dr. Loss on Bonds Redeemed, $3,200

REDEMPTION OF BONDS ISSUED AT FACE VALUE Levesque Lumber Co. issued $800,000 in bonds at face value 10 years ago and has paid semiannual interest payments through the years.

(a) Assume the bonds are redeemed at face value.
(b) Assume that $80,000 of the bonds are redeemed at 104.
(c) Assume that $80,000 of the bonds are redeemed at 96.

Prepare journal entries to record (a), (b), and (c).

E 22-5A (LO3/5)

✓ (a) Cr. Gain on Bonds Redeemed, $1,800

REDEMPTION OF BONDS ISSUED AT A PREMIUM Brighton Unlimited sold bonds at a premium for $630,000 (premium of $30,000) eight years ago.

(a) The corporation redeems $60,000 of this issue at 98. The unamortized premium is $600.
(b) The corporation redeems $90,000 of this issue at 102. The unamortized premium is $900.

Prepare journal entries to record the redemption in (a) and (b).

E 22-6A (LO4/5)

✓ (b) Dr. Loss on Bonds Redeemed, $100

REDEMPTION OF BONDS ISSUED AT A DISCOUNT Martinez Manufacturing sold bonds at a discount for $240,000 (discount of $10,000) seven years ago.

(a) The corporation redeems $25,000 of this issue at 96. The unamortized discount is $375.
(b) The corporation redeems $20,000 of this issue at 99. The unamortized discount is $300.

Prepare journal entries to record the redemption in (a) and (b).

E 22-7A (LO5)

✓ (b) Cr. Sinking Fund Earnings, $3,200

BOND SINKING FUNDS M. J. Adams Corporation pays $40,000 into a bond sinking fund each year for the future redemption of bonds. At the end of the first year, earnings on the sinking fund are $3,200. When the bonds mature, there is a balance in the sinking fund of $301,800, of which $300,000 is used to redeem the bonds.

Prepare journal entries to record:

(a) The initial sinking fund deposit.
(b) The first year's earnings.
(c) The redemption of the bonds.
(d) The return of excess cash to the corporation.

SERIES A PROBLEMS

P 22-8A (LO2)

✓ Dec. 31 entry: Dr. Bond Interest Expense, $7,500

KA KLOOSTER & ALLEN

BONDS ISSUED AT FACE VALUE Ito Co. issued the following bonds:

Date of issue and sale:	April 1, 20-1
Principal amount:	$300,000
Sale price of bonds:	100
Denomination of bonds:	$5,000
Life of bonds:	5 years
Stated rate:	10%, payable semiannually on September 30 and March 31

REQUIRED

Prepare journal entries for:

(a) Issuance of the bonds.
(b) Interest payment on the bonds on September 30, 20-1.
(c) Year-end adjustment on the bonds for 20-1.
(d) Reversing entry for the beginning of 20-2.
(e) Interest payments on the bonds for 20-2 (March 31 and September 30).
(f) Redemption at maturity.

P 22-9A (LO3)

✓ 2. Carrying value, Aug. 31, Year 2: $820,400

BONDS ISSUED AT A PREMIUM Bunkichi Corporation issued the following bonds at a premium:

Date of issue and sale:	March 1, 20-1
Principal amount:	$800,000
Sale price of bonds:	103
Denomination of bonds:	$1,000
Life of bonds:	10 years
Stated rate:	8%, payable semiannually on August 31 and February 28

REQUIRED

1. Prepare journal entries for:
   (a) Issuance of the bonds at a premium.
   (b) Interest payment and premium amortization on the bonds on August 31, 20-1.
   (c) Year-end adjustment on the bonds for 20-1.
   (d) Reversing entry for the beginning of 20-2.
   (e) Interest payments and premium amortization on the bonds for 20-2 (February 28 and August 31).
2. Calculate the carrying value of the bonds on August 31, 20-2.

P 22-10A (LO4)

✓ 2. Carrying value, Sept. 30, Year 2: $486,125

BONDS ISSUED AT A DISCOUNT Emerald, Inc., issued the following bonds at a discount:

Date of issue and sale:	April 1, 20-1
Principal amount:	$500,000
Sale price of bonds:	97
Denomination of bonds:	$1,000
Life of bonds:	20 years
Stated rate:	8%, payable semiannually on September 30 and March 31

REQUIRED

1. Prepare journal entries for:
   (a) Issuance of the bonds at a discount.
   (b) Interest payment and discount amortization on the bonds on September 30, 20-1.
   (c) Year-end adjustment on the bonds for 20-1.
   (d) Reversing entry for the beginning of 20-2.
   (e) Interest payments and discount amortization on the bonds for 20-2 (March 31 and September 30).
2. Calculate the carrying value of the bonds on September 30, 20-2.

P 22-11A (LO3/5)

✓ Mar. 1, 20-6 entry: Dr. Loss on Bonds Redeemed, $2,250

BONDS ISSUED AT A PREMIUM, REDEEMED AT A LOSS Perez Company issued the following bonds at a premium:

Date of issue and sale:	March 1, 20-1
Principal amount:	$400,000
Sale price of bonds:	103
Denomination of bonds:	$1,000
Life of bonds:	10 years
Stated rate:	12%, payable semiannually on August 31 and February 28

(continued)

REQUIRED

Prepare journal entries for:

(a) Issuance of the bonds.
(b) Interest payment and premium amortization on the bonds on August 31, 20-1.
(c) Year-end adjustment on the bonds for 20-1.
(d) Reversing entry for the beginning of 20-2.
(e) Redemption of $50,000 of the bonds on March 1, 20-6, at 106.

P 22-12A (LO4/5)
✓ Apr. 1, 20-4 entry: Cr. Gain on Bonds Redeemed, $1,150

BONDS ISSUED AT A DISCOUNT, REDEEMED AT A GAIN Cline & Co. issued the following bonds at a discount:

Date of issue and sale:	April 1, 20-1
Principal amount:	$500,000
Sale price of bonds:	98
Denomination of bonds:	$1,000
Life of bonds:	20 years
Stated rate:	9%, payable semiannually on September 30 and March 31

REQUIRED

Prepare journal entries for:

(a) Issuance of the bonds.
(b) Interest payment and discount amortization on the bonds on September 30, 20-1.
(c) Year-end adjustment on the bonds for 20-1.
(d) Reversing entry for the beginning of 20-2.
(e) Redemption of $50,000 of the bonds on April 1, 20-4, at 96.

P 22-13A (LO2/5)
✓ 2nd Dec. 31 entry: Dr. Bond Interest Expense, $12,500

BONDS ISSUED AT FACE VALUE WITH SINKING FUND Martin Manufacturing issued the following bonds:

Date of issue and sale:	April 1, 20-1
Principal amount:	$500,000
Sale price of bonds:	100
Denomination of bonds:	$10,000
Life of bonds:	10 years
Stated rate:	10%, payable semiannually on September 30 and March 31
Annual sinking fund requirement:	$34,000, payable June 1

REQUIRED

Prepare journal entries for:

(a) Issuance of the bonds.
(b) Deposit to sinking fund on June 1.
(c) Interest payment on the bonds on September 30, 20-1.
(d) Earnings of $2,400 on the sinking fund in 20-1.
(e) Year-end adjustment on the bonds for 20-1.
(f) Reversing entry for the beginning of 20-2.
(g) Interest payments on the bonds for 20-2 (March 31 and September 30).
(h) Redemption at maturity from the sinking fund.
(i) Return of excess cash of $1,050 from the sinking fund to the corporation.

SERIES B EXERCISES

E 22-1B (LO2)
✓ Dec. 31. Dr. Bond Interest Expense, $9,000

BONDS ISSUED AT FACE VALUE L & L Underwriters issued the following bonds:

Date of issue and sale:	April 1, 20-1
Principal amount:	$400,000
Sale price of bonds:	100
Denomination of bonds:	$1,000
Life of bonds:	20 years
Stated rate:	9%, payable semiannually on September 30 and March 31

Prepare journal entries for:

(a) Issuance of the bonds.
(b) Interest payment on the bonds on September 30.
(c) Year-end adjustment on the bonds.

E 22-2B (LO3)
✓ Dec. 31. Dr. Bond Interest Expense, $9,750

BONDS ISSUED AT A PREMIUM Bryant and Nelson Company issued the following bonds at a premium:

Date of issue and sale:	May 1, 20-1
Principal amount:	$500,000
Sale price of bonds:	103
Denomination of bonds:	$1,000
Life of bonds:	10 years
Stated rate:	12%, payable semiannually on October 31 and April 30

Prepare journal entries for:

(a) Issuance of the bonds at a premium.
(b) Interest payment and premium amortization on the bonds on October 31.
(c) Year-end adjustment on the bonds.

E 22-3B (LO4)
✓ Dec. 31. Dr. Bond Interest Expense, $8,150

BONDS ISSUED AT A DISCOUNT Beilke's Supply Stores issued the following bonds at a discount:

Date of issue and sale:	April 1, 20-1
Principal amount:	$400,000
Sale price of bonds:	97
Denomination of bonds:	$1,000
Life of bonds:	20 years
Stated rate:	8%, payable semiannually on September 30 and March 31

Prepare journal entries for:

(a) Issuance of the bonds at a discount.
(b) Interest payment and discount amortization on the bonds on September 30.
(c) Year-end adjustment on the bonds.

E 22-4B (LO2/5)
✓ (b) Dr. Loss on Bonds Redeemed, $750

REDEMPTION OF BONDS ISSUED AT FACE VALUE Okano Medical Lab issued $300,000 in bonds at face value 10 years ago and has paid semiannual interest payments through the years.

(a) Assume the bonds are redeemed at face value.
(b) Assume that $25,000 of the bonds are redeemed at 103.
(c) Assume that $25,000 of the bonds are redeemed at 97.

Prepare the journal entries to record (a), (b), and (c).

E 22-5B (LO3/5)

✓ (a) Cr. Gain on Bonds Redeemed, $3,000

REDEMPTION OF BONDS ISSUED AT A PREMIUM Miller & Miller sold bonds at a premium for $525,000 (premium of $25,000) eight years ago.

(a) The corporation redeems $50,000 of this issue at 95. The unamortized premium is $500.
(b) The corporation redeems $75,000 of this issue at 103. The unamortized premium is $750.

Prepare journal entries to record the redemption in (a) and (b).

E 22-6B (LO4/5)

✓ (b) Dr. Loss on Bonds Redeemed, $600

REDEMPTION OF BONDS ISSUED AT A DISCOUNT Medina Optical Supply sold bonds at a discount for $420,000 (discount of $20,000) eight years ago.

(a) The corporation redeems $25,000 of this issue at 94. The unamortized discount is $250.
(b) The corporation redeems $30,000 of this issue at 101. The unamortized discount is $300.

Prepare journal entries to record the redemption in (a) and (b).

E 22-7B (LO5)

✓ (b) Cr. Sinking Fund Earnings, $4,750

BOND SINKING FUNDS Sheng Corporation pays $50,000 into a bond sinking fund each year for the future redemption of bonds. At the end of the first year, earnings on the sinking fund are $4,750. When the bonds mature, there is a balance in the sinking fund of $502,125, of which $500,000 is used to redeem the bonds.

Prepare journal entries to record:

(a) The initial sinking fund deposit.
(b) The first year's earnings.
(c) The redemption of the bonds.
(d) The return of excess cash to the corporation.

SERIES B PROBLEMS

P 22-8B (LO2)

✓ Dec. 31 entry: Dr. Bond Interest Expense, $5,625

BONDS ISSUED AT FACE VALUE Ramona Arroyo Co. issued the following bonds:

Date of issue and sale:	April 1, 20-1
Principal amount:	$250,000
Sale price of bonds:	100
Denomination of bonds:	$5,000
Life of bonds:	10 years
Stated rate:	9%, payable semiannually on September 30 and March 31

REQUIRED

Prepare journal entries for:

(a) Issuance of the bonds.
(b) Interest payment on the bonds on September 30, 20-1.
(c) Year-end adjustment on the bonds for 20-1.
(d) Reversing entry for the beginning of 20-2.
(e) Interest payments on the bonds for 20-2 (March 31 and September 30).
(f) Redemption at maturity.

P 22-9B (LO3)

✓ 2. Carrying value, Aug. 31, Year 2: $256,937.50

BONDS ISSUED AT A PREMIUM Wang Corporation issued the following bonds at a premium:

Date of issue and sale:	March 1, 20-1
Principal amount:	$250,000
Sale price of bonds:	103
Denomination of bonds:	$500
Life of bonds:	20 years
Stated rate:	12%, payable semiannually on August 31 and February 28

REQUIRED

1. Prepare journal entries for:
   (a) Issuance of the bonds at a premium.
   (b) Interest payment and premium amortization on the bonds on August 31, 20-1.
   (c) Year-end adjustment on the bonds for 20-1.
   (d) Reversing entry for the beginning of 20-2.
   (e) Interest payments and premium amortization on the bonds for 20-2 (February 28 and August 31).
2. Calculate the carrying value of the bonds on August 31, 20-2.

P 22-10B (LO4)

✓ 2. Carrying value, Sept. 30, Year 2: $579,600

BONDS ISSUED AT A DISCOUNT Brandon, Inc., issued the following bonds at a discount:

Date of issue and sale:	April 1, 20-1
Principal amount:	$600,000
Sale price of bonds:	96
Denomination of bonds:	$1,000
Life of bonds:	10 years
Stated rate:	7%, payable semiannually on September 30 and March 31

REQUIRED

1. Prepare journal entries for:
   (a) Issuance of the bonds at a discount.
   (b) Interest payment and discount amortization on the bonds on September 30, 20-1.
   (c) Year-end adjustment on the bonds for 20-1.
   (d) Reversing entry for the beginning of 20-2.
   (e) Interest payments and discount amortization on the bonds for 20-2 (March 31 and September 30).
2. Calculate the carrying value of the bonds on September 30, 20-2.

P 22-11B (LO3/5)

✓ Mar. 1, 20-6 entry: Dr. Loss on Bonds Redeemed, $1,875

BONDS ISSUED AT A PREMIUM, REDEEMED AT A LOSS Blackwell Company issued the following bonds at a premium:

Date of issue and sale:	March 1, 20-1
Principal amount:	$500,000
Sale price of bonds:	103
Denomination of bonds:	$1,000
Life of bonds:	20 years
Stated rate:	12%, payable semiannually on August 31 and February 28

(continued)

REQUIRED

Prepare journal entries for:

(a) Issuance of the bonds.
(b) Interest payment and premium amortization on the bonds on August 31, 20-1.
(c) Year-end adjustment on the bonds for 20-1.
(d) Reversing entry for the beginning of 20-2.
(e) Redemption of $50,000 of the bonds on March 1, 20-6, at 106.

P 22-12B (LO4/5)

✓ Apr. 1, 20-4 entry: Cr. Gain on Bonds Redeemed, $950

BONDS ISSUED AT A DISCOUNT, REDEEMED AT A GAIN Ellis & Co. issued the following bonds at a discount:

Date of issue and sale:	April 1, 20-1
Principal amount:	$400,000
Sale price of bonds:	97
Denomination of bonds:	$1,000
Life of bonds:	10 years
Stated rate:	8%, payable semiannually on September 30 and March 31

REQUIRED

Prepare journal entries for:

(a) Issuance of the bonds.
(b) Interest payment and discount amortization on the bonds on September 30, 20-1.
(c) Year-end adjustment on the bonds for 20-1.
(d) Reversing entry for the beginning of 20-2.
(e) Redemption of $50,000 of the bonds on April 1, 20-4, at 96.

P 22-13B (LO2/5)

✓ 2nd Dec. 31 entry: Dr. Bond Interest Expense, $12,000

BONDS ISSUED AT FACE VALUE WITH SINKING FUND Creswell Entertainment issued the following bonds:

Date of issue and sale:	April 1, 20-1
Principal amount:	$600,000
Sale price of bonds:	100
Denomination of bonds:	$10,000
Life of bonds:	20 years
Stated rate:	8%, payable semiannually on September 30 and March 31
Annual sinking fund requirement:	$40,000, payable on June 1

REQUIRED

Prepare journal entries for:

(a) Issuance of the bonds.
(b) Deposit to sinking fund on June 1.
(c) Interest payment on the bonds on September 30, 20-1.
(d) Earnings of $3,000 on the sinking fund in 20-1.
(e) Year-end adjustment on the bonds for 20-1.
(f) Reversing entry for the beginning of 20-2.
(g) Interest payments on the bonds for 20-2 (March 31 and September 30).
(h) Redemption at maturity from the sinking fund.
(i) Return of excess cash of $1,900 from the sinking fund to the corporation.

MANAGING YOUR WRITING

The business where you work is considering issuing bonds to finance a major expansion. Your boss has just come from a lengthy meeting regarding the bonds, including the interest rate the bonds should carry. This has irritated your boss, who feels that the interest rate to use is obvious—the lowest one possible. This would yield the lowest interest expense to borrow the money. It seems stupid to pay big fees to financial advisors and lawyers when the question is so simple.

Write a report to your boss explaining how the issue price of the bonds (the net amount borrowed) is affected by the stated interest rate on the bonds. Include an explanation of how interest costs consist of more than just periodic interest payments.

ETHICS CASE

Alva Reese is 65 years old and getting ready to retire. She called her investment broker to help her decide what to do with the $50,000 that she has in the stock market. Alva told him that she didn't want any risky investments but hoped for an investment that was relatively safe and offered steady income. She had heard that bonds were safer than stocks and asked the broker how he felt about bonds. Her broker said bonds were a good safe choice and the ones he had in mind would offer her a high yield. He recommended that she invest all $50,000 in corporate callable bonds. Alva asked him to explain what callable bonds were and he told her the explanation was too technical but they were a safe investment that would serve her needs.

1. What information should the investment broker have given Alva?
2. Are all bonds safe? Why or why not?
3. Write a short paragraph describing how to determine the sales (trading) price of a bond.
4. In groups of three or four, make a list of the factors that Alva and the investment broker should consider before deciding how to invest the $50,000.

MASTERY PROBLEM

✓ 2. Carrying value, Dec. 31, Year 2: $610,600

KA KLOOSTER & ALLEN

Jackson, Inc.'s fiscal year ends December 31. Selected transactions for the period 20-1 through 20-8 involving bonds payable issued by Jackson are as follows:

20-1	
Oct. 30	Issued $600,000 of 10-year, 10%, callable bonds dated October 31, 20-1, for $612,000. Interest is payable semiannually on October 31 and April 30. The bond indenture provides that Jackson is to pay to the trustee bank $20,000 by May 15 of each year (except the tenth year) as a sinking fund for the retirement of the bonds on call or at maturity.
Dec. 31	Made the adjusting entry for interest payable and amortized two months' premium on the bonds (straight-line method).

(continued)

20-2	
Jan. 2	Reversed the adjusting entry for interest payable and bond premium amortization.
Apr. 30	Paid the semiannual interest on the bonds and amortized six months' premium.
May 15	Paid the sinking fund trustee $20,000.
Oct. 31	Paid the semiannual interest on the bonds and amortized six months' premium.
Dec. 31	Made the adjusting entry for interest payable and amortized two months' premium on the bonds.
31	Sinking fund earnings for the year were $900.
20-8	
May 15	Paid the sinking fund trustee $20,000.
Oct. 31	Paid the semiannual interest on the bonds and amortized six months' premium.
31	Redeemed the bonds, which were called at 97.

The balance in the bond premium account is $3,600 after the payment of interest and amortization of premium have been entered. The cash balance in the sinking fund is $200,000, which is applied to the redemption. Paid the sinking fund trustee the additional cash needed to pay off the bonds. (*Hint:* First make the entry for payment to the sinking fund, then make the entry for redemption of the bonds.)

REQUIRED

1. Enter the preceding transactions in general journal form.
2. Calculate the carrying value of the bonds as of December 31, 20-2.

CHALLENGE PROBLEM

This problem challenges you to apply your cumulative accounting knowledge to move a step beyond the material in the chapter.

✓ 1. Net savings = $27,000

On April 1, 20-1, Rebound Co. issued $300,000 of 10%, 10-year bonds, callable at 105 after three years, at face value. On April 1, 20-4, after completing three years of interest payments on the bonds, Rebound is considering calling the bonds and issuing $300,000 of new 8%, 10-year bonds at face value. The current market interest rate is only 8%, so Rebound thinks it might save money by taking this action.

REQUIRED

1. Compute the net savings to Rebound over the life of the original bond issue if it calls the old bonds and issues the new bonds.
2. Assuming Rebound calls the original bond issue, prepare the journal entry for the bond redemption.

ANSWERS TO SELF-STUDY QUESTIONS AND EXERCISES

True/False Questions

1. T 2. F (discount) 3. T 4. F (decreases) 5. T

Multiple Choice Questions

1. c 2. c 3. a 4. d 5. b

U REVU Exercises

1. (c) Less than $300,000

2.

(a)	Sep.	30	Bond Interest Expense		12,000 00	
			Cash			12,000 00
			Paid semiannual interest on bonds			
(b)	Dec.	31	Bond Interest Expense		6,000 00	
			Bond Interest Payable			6,000 00

3.

(a)	July	1	Cash		510,000 00	
			Bonds Payable			500,000 00
			Premium on Bonds Payable			10,000 00
			Issued bonds at a premium			
(b)	Dec.	31	Bond Interest Expense		22,000 00	
			Premium on Bonds Payable		500 00	
			Cash			22,500 00
			Paid semiannual interest and amortized premium on bonds			

4.

(a)	May	1	Cash		291,000 00	
			Discount on Bonds Payable		9,000 00	
			Bonds Payable			300,000 00
			Issued bonds at a discount			
(b)	Oct.	31	Bond Interest Expense		12,450 00	
			Discount on Bonds Payable			450 00
			Cash			12,000 00
			Paid semiannual interest and amortized discount on bonds			

5.

(a)			Bonds Payable		30,000 00	
			Loss on Bonds Redeemed		60 00	
			Discount on Bonds Payable			360 00
			Cash			29,700 00
			Redeemed bonds at a loss			
(b)			Bonds Payable		40,000 00	
			Discount on Bonds Payable			480 00
			Gain on Bonds Redeemed			320 00
			Cash			39,200 00
			Redeemed bonds at a gain			

Chapter 22 Appendix

Effective Interest Method

LEARNING OBJECTIVES

Careful study of this appendix should enable you to:

LO1 **Amortize premium on bonds payable using the effective interest method.**

LO2 **Amortize discount on bonds payable using the effective interest method.**

In Chapter 22, you learned how to amortize premium and discount on bonds payable using the straight-line method. In this appendix, the effective interest method of amortization is explained and illustrated.

The key to applying the effective interest method is the effective interest rate at which the bonds are issued. The **effective interest rate** is the market rate of interest on the date the bonds are issued. This rate is used to determine both the interest expense and the premium or discount amortization for the period.

LEARNING KEY

Under the effective interest method, the effective interest expense for the period is calculated by multiplying the *beginning-of-period* carrying value of the bonds by the effective interest rate.

Under the **effective interest method**, the beginning-of-period carrying value of the bonds multiplied by the effective interest rate is the **effective interest expense.** The difference between the effective interest expense and the cash interest payment is the amount of premium or discount to be amortized for the period.

AMORTIZATION OF PREMIUM USING THE EFFECTIVE INTEREST METHOD

LO1 Amortize premium on bonds payable using the effective interest method.

To illustrate the effective interest method of amortizing bond premium, assume the following bond issue for Prime Co:

Date of issue and sale:	April 1, 20-1
Principal amount:	\$400,000
Denomination:	\$1,000
Life:	10 years
Stated rate:	9%
Market rate at issue:	8%

LEARNING KEY

Under the effective interest method, the amount of premium or discount to be amortized for a period is the difference between the effective interest expense and the cash interest payment.

Because the stated rate exceeds the market rate, these bonds will sell at a premium, for \$427,181. The effective interest expense for the first semiannual interest period is \$17,087, the carrying value of the bonds, \$427,181, times the semiannual effective interest rate of 4%. The amount of bond premium to be amortized for the period is \$913, the difference between the effective interest expense (\$17,087) and the cash interest payment (\$18,000). The bond premium amortization schedule for the Prime Co. bonds for the first three and the last three interest periods is shown in Figure 22A-1.

The amount in column 2 is the semiannual cash interest payment. Column 3 contains the semiannual effective interest expense. This amount is computed by multiplying the beginning-of-period carrying value of the bond, which appears in the previous row of column 6, by the semiannual effective interest rate (4%). The difference between columns 2 and 3 is shown in column 4, the semiannual premium amortization. The unamortized premium is shown in column 5. As with the straight-line method of amortization, over the life of the bond, the unamortized premium decreases to zero and the carrying value of the bond decreases to its face value.

FIGURE 22A-1 Bond Premium Amortization Schedule

BOND PREMIUM AMORTIZATION SCHEDULE EFFECTIVE INTEREST METHOD					
(1)	(2)	(3)	(4)	(5)	(6)
Date	Cash Payment	Interest Expense [(6) in previous row × 4%]	Premium Amortization [(2) − (3)]	Unamortized Premium	Carrying Value of Bonds
4/1/-1				$27,181	$427,181
10/1/-1	$18,000	$17,087	$ 913	26,268	426,268
4/1/-2	18,000	17,051	949	25,319	425,319
10/1/-2	18,000	17,013	987	24,332	424,332
–	–	–	–	–	–
–	–	–	–	–	–
–	–	–	–	–	–
4/1/10	18,000	16,222	1,778	3,773	403,773
10/1/10	18,000	16,151	1,849	1,924	401,924
3/31/11	18,000	16,076*	1,924	0	400,000

*A $1 adjustment was subtracted to correct for rounding error.

AMORTIZATION OF DISCOUNT USING THE EFFECTIVE INTEREST METHOD

LO2 Amortize discount on bonds payable using the effective interest method.

To illustrate the effective interest method of amortizing bond discount, assume the following bond issue for Disco Co.:

Date of issue and sale:	April 1, 20-1
Principal amount:	$400,000
Denomination:	$1,000
Life:	10 years
Stated rate:	9%
Market rate at issue:	10%

Because the stated rate is less than the market rate, these bonds will sell at a discount, for $375,076. The effective interest expense for the first semiannual interest period is $18,754, the carrying value of the bonds, $375,076, times the semiannual effective interest rate of 5%. The amount of bond discount to be amortized for the period is $754, the difference between the effective interest expense ($18,754) and the cash interest payment ($18,000). The bond discount amortization schedule for the Disco Co. bonds for the first three and the last three interest periods is shown in Figure 22A-2.

The amount in column 2 is the semiannual cash interest payment. Column 3 contains the semiannual effective interest expense. This amount is computed by multiplying the beginning-of-period carrying value of the bond, which appears in the previous row of column 6, by the semiannual effective interest rate (5%). The difference between columns 2 and 3 is shown in column 4, the semiannual discount amortization. The unamortized discount is shown in column 5. As with the straight-line method of amortization, over the life of the bond the unamortized discount decreases to zero, and the carrying value of the bond increases to its face value.

FIGURE 22A-2 Bond Discount Amortization Schedule

BOND DISCOUNT AMORTIZATION SCHEDULE EFFECTIVE INTEREST METHOD					
(1)	(2)	(3)	(4)	(5)	(6)
Date	Cash Payment	Interest Expense [(6) in previous row × 5%]	Discount Amortization [(3) − (2)]	Unamortized Discount	Carrying Value of Bonds
4/1/-1				$24,924	$375,076
10/1/-1	$18,000	$18,754	$ 754	24,170	375,830
4/1/-2	18,000	18,791	791	23,379	376,621
10/1/-2	18,000	18,831	831	22,548	377,452
–	–	–	–	–	–
–	–	–	–	–	–
–	–	–	–	–	–
4/1/10	18,000	19,728	1,728	3,717	396,283
10/1/10	18,000	19,814	1,814	1,903	398,097
3/31/11	18,000	19,903*	1,903	0	400,000

*A $2 adjustment was subtracted to correct for rounding error.

LEARNING OBJECTIVES Key Points to Remember

LO1 Amortize premium on bonds payable using the effective interest method.	Under the effective interest method, the amount of premium to amortize for a period is the cash interest payment minus the effective interest expense on the bonds for the period.
LO2 Amortize discount on bonds payable using the effective interest method.	Under the effective interest method, the amount of discount to amortize for a period is the effective interest expense on the bonds for the period minus the cash interest payment.

KEY TERMS

effective interest expense (866) The beginning-of-period carrying value of the bonds multipled by the effective interest rate.

effective interest method (866) A method of amortizing bond discount or premium that uses the effective interest rate on the bonds.

effective interest rate (866) The market rate of interest on the date the bonds are issued.

In all exercises and problems, round amounts to the nearest whole dollar.

SERIES A EXERCISE

E 22Apx-1A (LO1)
✓ Dr. Premium on Bonds Payable, $456

On May 1, Holiday Company issued $200,000, 9%, 10-year bonds for $213,591 when the market rate was 8%. Prepare the general journal entry for the first semiannual interest payment and bond premium amortization on November 1, using the effective interest method.

SERIES A PROBLEM

P 22Apx-2A (LO1)

✓ Dec. 31 entry: Dr. Premium on Bonds Payable, $1,156

BOND PREMIUM AMORTIZATION Fields Company sold an issue of $800,000, 10%, 10-year bonds for $852,032 on March 1. The interest is payable semiannually on September 1 and March 1. The market rate of interest at the time the bonds were issued was 9%. Journalize the following transactions (round all amounts to the nearest dollar).

Sept. 1 Paid the first semiannual interest payment and amortized the bond premium, using the effective interest method.

Dec. 31 Made the adjusting entry for bond interest accrued and amortization of the bond premium from September 1. (*Hint:* Use the effective interest rate for the four-month period from September 1–December 31.)

Jan. 2 Reversed the adjusting entry for bond interest accrued and bond premium amortization as of December 31.

Mar. 1 Paid the second semiannual interest payment and amortized the bond premium.

SERIES B EXERCISE

E 22Apx-1B (LO2)

✓ Cr. Discount on Bonds Payable, $565

On May 1, Saxophone Corp. issued $300,000, 9%, 10-year bonds for $281,307 when the market rate was 10%. Prepare the general journal entry for the first semiannual interest payment and bond discount amortization on November 1, using the effective interest method.

SERIES B PROBLEM

P 22Apx-2B (LO2)

✓ Dec. 31 entry: Cr. Discount on Bonds Payable, $495

BOND DISCOUNT AMORTIZATION Zee Company sold an issue of $500,000, 9%, 10-year bonds for $468,845 on April 1. The interest is payable semiannually on October 1 and April 1. The market rate of interest at the time the bonds were issued was 10%. Journalize the following transactions (round all amounts to the nearest dollar).

Oct. 1 Paid the first semiannual interest payment and amortized the bond discount, using the effective interest method.

Dec. 31 Made the adjusting entry for bond interest accrued and amortization of the bond discount from October 1. (*Hint:* Use the effective interest rate for the three-month period from October 1–December 31.)

Jan. 2 Reversed the adjusting entry for bond interest accrued and bond discount amortization as of December 31.

Apr. 1 Paid the second semiannual interest payment and amortized the bond discount.

Chapter 23

COMSTOCK IMAGES/JUPITER IMAGES

LEARNING OBJECTIVES

Careful study of this chapter should enable you to:

LO1 Explain the purpose of the statement of cash flows.

LO2 Define operating, investing, and financing activities and describe transactions for each type of activity.

LO3 Describe the information needed to prepare a statement of cash flows.

LO4 Describe the direct and indirect methods of reporting cash flows from operating activities.

LO5 Describe the effects of changes in current assets and current liabilities on cash from operating activities under the indirect method.

LO6 Prepare a statement of cash flows under the indirect method using T accounts and including adjustments for current assets and current liabilities related to operations.

LO7 Prepare a statement of cash flows under the indirect method, including adjustments when the company:
- a. defines cash as "cash and cash equivalents,"
- b. reports depreciation expense,
- c. reports gains or losses on transactions not related to operating activities,
- d. has noncash investing and financing activities, and
- e. provides supplemental disclosures of cash flows.

LO8 Interpret the statement of cash flows.

Statement of Cash Flows

Costume Craze is an online retailer offering over 10,000 costumes for children, adults, and even pets that was founded by Kathleen, Matthew, and Kate Maloney. Kate serves as CEO. The company was started primarily to test a search engine optimization software program developed by Matthew. At that time, the company was known as Matthew's Robes, and only monk robes were offered for sale. Business was so good that the focus turned instead to expanding the costume product line. Today, clients include *The Early Show* on CBS, NFL cheerleading squads, World Wrestling Entertainment, and *The Tonight Show*. Odd as it may sound, the company once sold nearly 150 chicken costumes to a grocery store chain.

Headquartered in Pleasant Grove, Utah, the company operates year round, even though some costume businesses may be open just for the Halloween season. Costume Craze relies on Christmas, birthdays, theater productions, and other special events to keep cash coming in during the remainder of the year. So far, business is growing quite well. During a recent three-year period, revenues tripled from $2.4 million to $7.2 million. As with all companies, but especially important for new start-ups, cash flows must be monitored carefully. In this chapter, you will learn that the statement of cash flows clarifies where cash came from and how it was used by classifying cash flows into three categories: operating, investing, and financing activities. This information is critical to the success of any business and to an understanding of the firm's financial health.

A business must have an adequate amount of cash to operate. Without sufficient cash, suppliers and employees cannot be paid, debt cannot be retired, and dividends cannot be paid to stockholders. Managers, creditors, stockholders, and others pay close attention to a company's cash position and the economic events and transactions leading to changes in that position. The statement of cash flows provides information about the events that affect the cash position of a company.

NATURE AND PURPOSE OF THE STATEMENT OF CASH FLOWS

LO1 Explain the purpose of the statement of cash flows.

The managers of a business must generate net income (profitability) and keep the enterprise solvent (liquidity). The income statement reports on the company's profitability by matching revenues and expenses on an accrual basis. Revenues are recognized when earned, regardless of when the cash is received. Expenses are recognized as incurred, regardless of when the cash is paid. Although the accrual basis of accounting is an excellent method for measuring profitability, it does not explain why a company's liquidity has improved or worsened. The income statement does not explain, for example, why a company reporting substantial profits can have difficulty paying its bills on time.

It would seem logical that a profitable company would have plenty of cash. Net income brings in cash, either immediately or as soon as receivables are collected. However, the cash inflow resulting from profitable operations may be used to acquire long-term assets, to pay off long-term debt, or to pay stockholders in the form of dividends. Thus, an increase or decrease in cash results from a combination of operating, investing, and financing activities by management. The income statement alone does not adequately reflect all of these activities.

Management and outside users of the financial statements want to know how cash was generated and used during the period. The purpose of the **statement of cash flows** is to provide this information.

OPERATING, INVESTING, AND FINANCING ACTIVITIES

LO2 Define operating, investing, and financing activities and describe transactions for each type of activity.

The statement of cash flows categorizes all cash flows into three major types of activities: operating, investing, and financing.

LEARNING KEY

Cash flows from operating activities are primarily related to the revenues and expenses reported on the income statement.

OPERATING ACTIVITIES

Operating activities are transactions and events associated with selling a product or providing a service and are related to the revenues and expenses reported on the income statement. Since interest revenue, interest expense, and dividend revenue are reported on the income statement, they are also considered cash flows from operating activities. Figure 23-1 shows cash inflows and outflows from operating activities.

Operating activities represent the company's primary source of cash over the life of the business. Ultimately, net cash inflows from operating activities must be used to purchase plant and equipment, repay loans, and pay dividends to stockholders.

The proper reporting of dividends and interest on the statement of cash flows can be confusing. Here's an easy way to keep it straight. If the item is reported on the income statement (interest expense, interest revenue, and dividend revenue), it is classified as an operating activity on the statement of cash flows. If not (dividends), it is classified as a financing activity.

FIGURE 23-1 Cash Flows from Operating Activities

OPERATING ACTIVITIES	
Cash Inflows	**Cash Outflows**
1. Cash receipts from the sale of goods or services.	1. Payments for the acquisition of inventory.
2. Interest received on loans made to outside entities.	2. Payments to employees and the government.
3. Dividends received on investments made in the stock of other corporations.	3. Payments for interest on loans.
	4. Payments to other suppliers and for other expenses.

INVESTING ACTIVITIES

Investing activities include the following types of transactions:

1. The purchase and sale of long-term assets.
2. Buying and selling debt and equity securities.
3. Lending money and collecting the principal on the related loans.

Figure 23-2 shows typical transactions for cash inflows and outflows from investing activities.

FIGURE 23-2 Cash Flows from Investing Activities

INVESTING ACTIVITIES	
Cash Inflows	**Cash Outflows**
1. Proceeds from collection of principal amount of loans made to borrowers.*	1. Loans made by the company to other parties.
2. Proceeds from the sale of property, plant, and equipment; intangibles; and other productive assets.	2. Payments to acquire property, plant, and equipment; intangibles; and other productive assets.
3. Proceeds from the sale of investments in debt and equity securities.	3. Payments to acquire investments in debt and equity securities.
4. Proceeds from discounting notes receivable.	

*Note that interest received on loans is not included with investing activities. It is included with cash inflows from operating activities.

LEARNING KEY

Financing activities deal with the exchange of cash between the company and its stockholders and creditors.

FINANCING ACTIVITIES

Financing activities are transactions dealing with the exchange of cash between the company and its owners (stockholders) and creditors. Cash inflows and outflows include the types of transactions listed in Figure 23-3.

FIGURE 23-3 Cash Flows from Financing Activities

FINANCING ACTIVITIES	
Cash Inflows	**Cash Outflows**
1. Proceeds from additional investments by the owners or the issuance of stock.	1. Payments of dividends to stockholders or withdrawals by the owners.
2. Proceeds from borrowing money through the signing of a mortgage, issuing a bond, or other long- or short-term loans.	2. Payments to purchase treasury stock.
	3. Repayment of the principal on loans.*

* Note that interest payments on loans are not reported under financing activities. They are reported as cash outflows under operating activities.

Note: Amounts owed to suppliers of goods and services are not considered financing activities. They are used in the calculation of cash from operating activities.

U REVU

Complete U REVU-1 on **page 908** to test your basic understanding of LO2.

INFORMATION NEEDED TO PREPARE A STATEMENT OF CASH FLOWS

LO3 Describe the information needed to prepare a statement of cash flows.

To prepare a statement of cash flows, the following statements are needed:

1. Balance sheets for the beginning and end of the period.
2. Income statement for the period.
3. Statement of retained earnings for the period.

Additional information on major cash transactions is useful. This information and an analysis of all noncash balance sheet accounts are used to identify transactions involving cash flows during the year.

LEARNING KEY

The three major sections of the statement of cash flows focus on:

operating activities
investing activities
financing activities

The statement of cash flows is divided into three sections:

1. cash flows from operating activities,
2. cash flows from investing activities, and
3. cash flows from financing activities.

The sum of the cash generated or used by each of the three activities should equal the difference between the beginning and ending balance of the cash account. For example, if $5,000 was generated from operations, $2,000 used for investing activities, and $3,000 provided by financing activities, the cash balance must have increased by $6,000 ($5,000 – $2,000 + $3,000) during the year. The accuracy of the statement can be verified by computing the change in the balance of the cash account.

LEARNING KEY

Change in cash balance:

Cash from operating activities
± Cash from investing activities
± Cash from financing activities
= Change in cash balance

STATEMENT OF CASH FLOWS: DIRECT VS. INDIRECT METHODS

LO4 Describe the direct and indirect methods of reporting cash flows from operating activities.

A sure sign of financial difficulty for a business is the continuing need to sell assets or issue long-term debt to pay operating expenses. Therefore, an important factor in evaluating a company's financial condition is the ability to generate positive cash flows from operating activities. Cash generated from operating activities may be computed and reported using one of two methods. Under the **direct method,** revenues and expenses reported on the income statement are adjusted to reflect the amount of cash received or paid for each item. These adjusted revenues and expenses are reported on the statement of cash flows.

Under the **indirect method**, net income is reported first on the statement of cash flows as the primary source of cash from operating activities. However, this amount must be adjusted for transactions that affect net income *and* cash flows from operating activities, but by different amounts.

Throughout this chapter, colors will be used to help you recognize the three types of business activities as follows:

Green—Operating Activities
Blue—Investing Activities
Orange—Financing Activities

To illustrate the difference in the two methods, let's consider a firm with the following events:

1. Sales during the year amounted to $100, but accounts receivable increased by $10.
2. Wages expense for the year amounted to $40, but wages payable increased by $5.

Summary entries for these two events are shown below and would be the same regardless of the method used for the statement of cash flows.

(1)	Cash	90	
	Accounts Receivable	10	
	Sales		100
(2)	Wages Expense	40	
	Wages Payable		5
	Cash		35

Net income would be computed as follows:

Sales	$100
Wages expense	40
Net income	$ 60

Cash from operating activities, reported under the direct and indirect methods, is shown below.

DIRECT METHOD			INDIRECT METHOD	
Cash from customers	$90		Net income	$60
Cash paid to employees	(35)		Increase in accounts receivable	(10)
			Increase in wages payable	5
Cash from operating activities	$55	=	Cash from operating activities	$55

Direct Method. The direct adjustment of each line item of the income statement to compute cash from operating activities provides the source for the name of this method.

Under the direct method, each line of the income statement is converted to cash paid or received: Sales ($100) to cash from customers ($90), and wages expense ($40) to cash paid to employees ($35). Summing these amounts yields cash from operating activities of $55.

Under the indirect method, net income is listed first. However, the increase in accounts receivable ($10) decreases cash from operating activities, and the increase in wages payable increases cash from operating activities ($5). Summing net income and these indirect adjustments yields the same result as under the direct method: cash from operating activities of $55.

Although the direct and indirect methods provide different formats for reporting cash flows from operating activities, the two methods report the same net amount of cash provided or used by operating activities. In addition, investing and financing activities are reported in the same manner under the direct and indirect methods. Thus, only the operating activities section is different. The vast majority of companies use the indirect method. Thus, the indirect method is illustrated in this chapter. The Financial Accounting Standards Board, however, has been encouraging firms to switch to the direct method. The direct method is illustrated in the appendix to this chapter.

U REVU

Complete U REVU-2 on **page 908** to test your basic understanding of LO4.

CASH FLOWS FROM OPERATING ACTIVITIES: INDIRECT METHOD

LO5 Describe the effects of changes in current assets and current liabilities on cash from operating activities under the indirect method.

As you know, net income is measured using the accrual basis of accounting. Since increases and decreases in net income do not always increase or decrease cash from operating activities, the following adjustments must be made to net income to report cash flows from operating activities:

1. Changes in current assets related to operating activities.
2. Changes in current liabilities related to operating activities.
3. Noncash expenses.
4. Gains and losses on transactions not related to operating activities.

Adjustments for changes in current assets and current liabilities are discussed in this section of the chapter. Adjustments for noncash expenses and gains and losses not related to operating activities are discussed later.

LEARNING KEY

Under the indirect method, net income is considered the primary source of cash from operating activities. However, it must be adjusted for the following types of transactions:

1. transactions that impact net income and cash from operating activities, but by different amounts (items 1, 2, and 3 above), and
2. transactions that affect net income, but are not related to cash from operating activities (item 4 above).

CHANGES IN CURRENT ASSETS RELATED TO OPERATING ACTIVITIES

Accounts receivable, prepaid expenses, and inventories are examples of current assets related to operating activities. Increases in these assets reduce cash generated from operating activities; decreases have the opposite effect. If accounts receivable increased, cash received from customers was less than the sales revenue reported on the income statement. This increase is deducted from net income when computing cash generated from operating activities.

For example, if sales were $100,000 and accounts receivable increased by $5,000, think of the following entry:

Cash	95,000	
Accounts Receivable	5,000	
Sales		100,000

Since the revenue used to calculate net income ($100,000) is $5,000 greater than the cash received ($95,000), $5,000 must be subtracted from net income to compute cash from operating activities.

Similar adjustments are made for prepaid expenses. If prepaid expenses increased, cash paid during the period exceeded the expense reported on the income statement. This increase is deducted from net income. On the other hand, decreases in these assets increase cash from operating activities and must be added to net income when computing cash flows from operating activities.

For example, if rent expense was $30,000 and prepaid rent decreased by $2,000, think of the following entry:

Rent Expense	30,000	
Prepaid Rent		2,000
Cash		28,000

Since the rent expense used to calculate net income ($30,000) is $2,000 more than the cash paid ($28,000), $2,000 must be added to net income to compute cash from operating activities.

CHANGES IN CURRENT LIABILITIES RELATED TO OPERATING ACTIVITIES

Accounts payable, income tax payable, and salaries payable are examples of current liabilities related to operating activities. Not all current liabilities are related to operating activities. The declaration of dividends, for example, is not an operating activity and has no effect on net income. Therefore, changes in dividends payable do not require an adjustment to net income.

Changes in current liabilities require an adjustment opposite that of current assets. By increasing the amount owed to others, the company increases cash from operating activities in the current period. Thus, increases in current liabilities are added to net income to compute cash from operating activities. Decreases in current liabilities are deducted from net income to compute cash from operating activities.

An increase in salaries payable indicates that the expense recognized on the income statement for salaries is greater than the cash paid to employees. Thus, the increase in salaries payable must be added to net income to compute cash from operating activities. On the other hand, decreases in this account and other current liabilities reduce cash from operating activities and must be deducted from net income.

For example, if salaries expense was $5,000 and salaries payable increased by $500, think of the following entry:

Salaries Expense	5,000	
Salaries Payable		500
Cash		4,500

Since the expense ($5,000) is $500 greater than the cash paid ($4,500), $500 must be added to net income to compute cash from operating activities.

A decrease in income tax payable indicates that the expense recognized on the income statement for income taxes is less than the cash paid. Thus, the decrease in income tax payable must be subtracted from net income to compute cash from operating activities.

For example, if income tax expense was $40,000 and income tax payable decreased by $2,000, think of the following entry:

Income Tax Expense	40,000	
Income Tax Payable	2,000	
Cash		42,000

Since the expense ($40,000) is $2,000 less than the cash paid ($42,000), $2,000 must be subtracted from net income to compute cash from operating activities.

U REVU Complete U REVU-3 on **page 908** to test your basic understanding of LO5.

PREPARATION OF A STATEMENT OF CASH FLOWS UNDER THE INDIRECT METHOD: SIMPLEX

LO6 Prepare a statement of cash flows under the indirect method using T accounts and including adjustments for current assets and current liabilities related to operations.

To prepare the statement of cash flows under the indirect method, the following steps are used for Simplex Company. These steps will be expanded later in the chapter as we consider more complex events.

STEP 1 Compute the change in cash.

STEP 2 Set up T accounts with the beginning and ending balances for all noncash balance sheet accounts.

STEP 3 Compute cash flows from operating activities by:

(a) Reporting net income as the primary source of cash from operating activities.
(b) Adjusting net income for changes in current assets and current liabilities related to operating activities.

STEP 4 Identify cash flows from investing activities.

STEP 5 Identify cash flows from financing activities.

STEP 6 Prepare a statement of cash flows and verify the accuracy of the statement.

Figure 23-4 shows the financial statements and additional information for Simplex. This illustration requires adjustments to net income for changes in current assets and current liabilities. Adjustments for noncash expenses and gains and losses on the sale of long-term assets will be illustrated later in the chapter. The statement of cash flows will be prepared using the six steps listed above.

FIGURE 23-4 Financial Statements and Additional Information for Simplex

Simplex Company
Income Statement
For Year Ended December 31, 20-2

Net sales		$900,000.00
Cost of goods sold		600,000.00
Gross profit		$300,000.00
Operating expenses		177,000.00
Income before taxes		$123,000.00
Income tax expense		43,000.00
Net income		$ 80,000.00

FIGURE 23-4 Financial Statements and Additional Information for Simplex (*continued*)

Simplex Company
Statement of Retained Earnings
For Year Ended December 31, 20-2

Retained earnings, January 1, 20-2		$ 50,000.00
Net income	$80,000.00	
Less dividends	20,000.00	
Net increase in retained earnings		60,000.00
Retained earnings, December 31, 20-2		$110,000.00

Simplex Company
Comparative Balance Sheet
December 31, 20-2 and 20-1

	20-2	20-1	INCREASE (DECREASE)
Assets			
Current assets:			
Cash	$ 90,000.00	$200,000.00	$(110,000.00)
Accounts receivable	160,000.00	190,000.00	(30,000.00)
Merchandise inventory	180,000.00	200,000.00	(20,000.00)
Total current assets	$430,000.00	$590,000.00	(160,000.00)
Property, plant, and equipment:			
Land	$ 40,000.00	$ 40,000.00	0.00
Building	140,000.00		140,000.00
Equipment	100,000.00		100,000.00
Total property, plant, and equipment	$280,000.00	$ 40,000.00	240,000.00
Total assets	$710,000.00	$630,000.00	80,000.00
Liabilities			
Current liabilities:			
Notes payable	$ 60,000.00	$ 50,000.00	10,000.00
Accounts payable	120,000.00	180,000.00	(60,000.00)
Total liabilities	$180,000.00	$230,000.00	(50,000.00)
Stockholders' Equity			
Common stock ($5 par, 100,000 shares authorized;			
Issued: 58,000 in 20-2, 50,000 in 20-1)	$290,000.00	$250,000.00	40,000.00
Paid-in capital in excess of par—common stock	130,000.00	100,000.00	30,000.00
Retained earnings	110,000.00	50,000.00	60,000.00
Total stockholders' equity	$530,000.00	$400,000.00	130,000.00
Total liabilities and stockholders' equity	$710,000.00	$630,000.00	80,000.00

Additional Information for 20-2:

1. Acquired a building and equipment for cash just before the year-end.
2. Issued 8,000 shares of common stock for $8.75 per share.
3. Declared and paid cash dividends of $20,000.

STEP 1 Compute the change in cash.
As shown on the balance sheet in Figure 23-4, cash decreased by $110,000. When completed, the net increase or decrease in cash reported on the statement of cash flows will be compared with this amount to verify the accuracy of the statement of cash flows.

FIGURE 23-5 T Accounts for Simplex

Operating, Investing, and Financing Activities Affecting Cash

Cash

Operating Activities:			
(1) Net income	80,000		
(2) Decrease in accounts receivable	30,000		
(3) Decrease in inventory	20,000		
		60,000	(4) Decrease in accounts payable
Net cash provided by operating activities	70,000		
Investing Activities:			
		140,000	(5) Cash paid for building
		100,000	(6) Cash paid for equipment
Total cash used by investing activities		240,000	
Financing Activities:			
(7) Issued common stock	70,000		
		20,000	(8) Paid dividends
(9) Issued note payable	10,000		
Net cash provided by financing activities	60,000		

T Accounts for Indirect Method Statement of Cash Flows
Simplex Company

Accounts Receivable

BB	190,000		
		30,000	(2)
EB	160,000		

Notes Payable

		50,000	BB
		10,000	(9)
		60,000	EB

Common Stock

		250,000	BB
		40,000	(7)
		290,000	EB

Merchandise Inventory

BB	200,000		
		20,000	(3)
EB	180,000		

Accounts Payable

		180,000	BB
(4)	60,000		
		120,000	EB

Paid-In Capital in Excess of Par—Common Stock

		100,000	BB
		30,000	(7)
		130,000	EB

Land

BB	40,000		
EB	40,000		

Retained Earnings

		50,000	BB
(8)	20,000	80,000	(1)
		110,000	EB

Building

BB	—	
(5)	140,000	
EB	140,000	

Equipment

BB	—	
(6)	100,000	
EB	100,000	

BB: Beginning Balance
EB: Ending Balance

STEP 2 **Set up T accounts with the beginning and ending balances for all noncash balance sheet accounts.**

The T accounts provided in Figure 23-5 must be reconciled as the cash flow effects are determined. That is, debits or credits are made to each account to explain why the account increased or decreased. The related debits or credits are made to the cash account. This Cash T account represents a simple version of the statement of cash flows and is divided into three sections: operating, investing, and financing activities. Debits to the operating section represent additions to net income and credits represent deductions from net income. Debits to the investing and financing sections represent inflows of cash. Credits to these sections represent outflows of cash. As shown in Figure 23-6, this account will be very helpful in preparing the statement.

FIGURE 23-6 Statement of Cash Flows for Simplex

Simplex Company Statement of Cash Flows (Indirect Method) For Year Ended December 31, 20-2		
Cash flows from operating activities:		
Net income	$ 80,000.00	
Adjustments for changes in current assets and		
liabilities related to operating activities:		
Decrease in accounts receivable	30,000.00	
Decrease in inventory	20,000.00	
Decrease in accounts payable	(60,000.00)	
Net cash provided by operating activities		$ 70,000.00
Cash flows from investing activities:		
Purchased building	$(140,000.00)	
Purchased equipment	(100,000.00)	
Total cash used by investing activities		(240,000.00)
Cash flows from financing activities:		
Issued common stock	$ 70,000.00	
Paid dividends	(20,000.00)	
Issued note payable	10,000.00	
Net cash provided by financing activities		60,000.00
Net increase (decrease) in cash		$(110,000.00)
Cash balance, January 1, 20-2		200,000.00
Cash balance, December 31, 20-2		$ 90,000.00

STEP 3(a) **Compute cash flows from operating activities by reporting net income as the primary source of cash from operating activities.**
As reported on the income statement, net income is $80,000. Net income is the primary source of cash from operating activities and should be debited to Cash. Since net income increases retained earnings, Retained Earnings should be credited for $80,000 (Entry 1).

STEP 3(b) **Compute cash flows from operating activities by adjusting net income for changes in current assets and current liabilities related to operating activities.**
Increases in current assets related to operating activities require the use of cash and reduce cash from operating activities. On the other hand, decreases in current assets provide resources without using cash, thus increasing cash from operating activities. The opposite is true for current liabilities.

Accounts Receivable

Accounts receivable decreased by $30,000. If the amount that customers owe to the firm decreased, the amount of cash received by the firm has increased. This would represent an increase in cash from operating activities. A simple method of recording this event is to credit Accounts Receivable and debit Cash from operating activities (Entry 2) as shown in Figure 23-5. The credit to Accounts Receivable reconciles the account, and the debit to Cash is added to net income as one of the adjustments when calculating cash from operating activities.

We can also consider summary entries to reflect the decrease in accounts receivable. Simplex reports $900,000 in sales on the income statement (Figure 23-4). The balance sheet reports that accounts receivable decreased by $30,000. Thus, as shown in Figure 23-7, cash must have increased by $930,000.

FIGURE 23-7 Cash Received from Customers

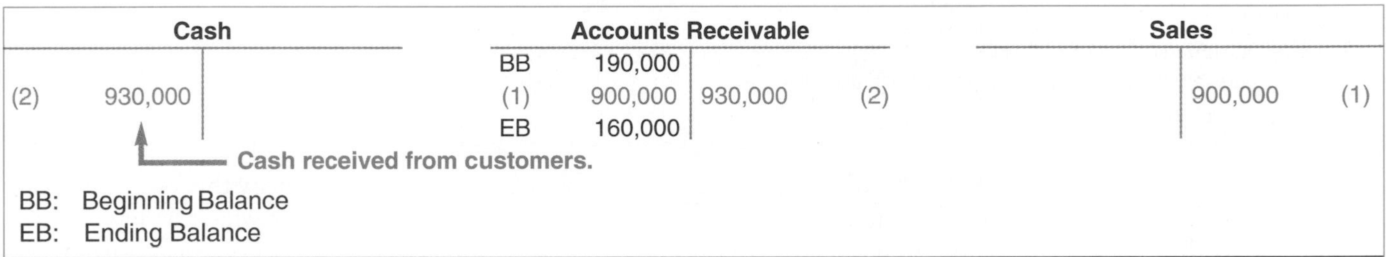

(1) Entry to record sales (assume all on account).	Accounts Receivable	900,000	
	Sales		900,000
(2) Credit required to reconcile Accounts Receivable. This represents the amount of cash collected from customers.	Cash	930,000	
	Accounts Receivable		930,000

Net income represents the primary source of cash from operating activities. To compute net income, Simplex recognized $900,000 in sales. Since Simplex actually received $930,000 in cash from its customers, $30,000 is added to net income when adjusting to compute cash from operating activities.

Merchandise Inventory and Accounts Payable

The balance sheet for Simplex (Figure 23-4) reports that merchandise inventory decreased by $20,000 and accounts payable decreased by $60,000. The reduction in inventory increases cash from operating activities. Instead of buying additional inventory to cover the amount sold, Simplex sold inventory that was in stock from last year. Thus, less cash was spent on inventory and cash from operating activities increased.

Simplex reduced the amount owed to suppliers, thus decreasing accounts payable. Making additional payments to suppliers to reduce accounts payable reduces cash from operating activities this year.

These relationships are most easily captured using the entries reported in Figure 23-5. The credit to Merchandise Inventory for $20,000 is offset by a debit to Cash under operating activities (Entry 3). The debit to Cash represents an addition to net income when computing cash from operating activities. The debit to Accounts Payable for $60,000 is offset by a credit to Cash under operating activities (Entry 4) and represents a deduction from net income when computing cash from operating activities.

Let's see why these relationships are true. As shown on the income statement in Figure 23-4, when computing net income, Simplex subtracted cost of goods sold of

FIGURE 23-8 Cash Paid to Suppliers for Merchandise

Cash		Merchandise Inventory		Accounts Payable		Cost of Goods Sold	
		BB 200,000			180,000 BB		
	640,000 (3)	(2) 580,000	600,000 (1)	(3) 640,000	580,000 (2)	(1) 600,000	
		EB 180,000			120,000 EB		

Purchases of merchandise.

Cash paid to suppliers for merchandise.

BB: Beginning Balance
EB: Ending Balance

(1) Entry to record cost of goods sold.	Cost of Goods Sold	600,000	
	Merchandise Inventory		600,000
(2) Debit required to reconcile the inventory account. This represents purchases for the period. Assume that all purchases were made on account.	Merchandise Inventory	580,000	
	Accounts Payable		580,000
(3) Debit required to reconcile Accounts Payable. This represents the amount of cash paid to suppliers for merchandise.	Accounts Payable	640,000	
	Cash		640,000

$600,000 from sales. Is this the amount of cash paid for inventory this year? Summary entries made for the acquisition and sale of inventory are provided in Figure 23-8. Thus, even though Simplex reported cost of goods sold of **$600,000**, cash of **$640,000** was actually paid for the merchandise inventory.

These facts fit nicely with the adjustments made to net income in Figure 23-5. By **adding** the decrease in inventory of $20,000 and **subtracting** the decrease of $60,000 in accounts payable, a net deduction of $40,000 was made to net income. This adjustment is consistent with the concept that Simplex subtracted $600,000 from sales to compute net income, but should subtract $640,000 to compute cash from operating activities, a net additional deduction of $40,000.

STEP 4 **Identify cash flows from investing activities.**

The balance sheet accounts related to investing activities are Land, Building, and Equipment. As reported under additional information on the balance sheet, a building and equipment were acquired for cash just before year-end. These acquisitions represent investing activities. As shown in Figure 23-4, the building account increased by $140,000. Thus, Building is debited for $140,000, and Cash is credited for $140,000 under investing activities (Entry 5). Similarly, equipment increased by $100,000. Thus, Equipment is debited for $100,000, and Cash is credited for $100,000 under investing activities (Entry 6). Both credits to the cash account represent outflows of cash from investing activities. There was no change in the land account. Thus, no reconciliation is required.

STEP 5 **Identify cash flows from financing activities.**

The balance sheet accounts related to financing activities are Notes Payable, Common Stock, Paid-In Capital in Excess of Par—Common Stock, and Retained Earnings. As reported in the additional information on the balance sheet in Figure 23-4, Simplex issued 8,000 shares of common stock for $8.75 per share, or a total of $70,000. This represents a financing activity and was recorded by making the following entry:

Cash	70,000	
Common Stock		40,000
Paid-In Capital in Excess of Par—Common Stock		30,000

To reconcile the accounts, credit Common Stock for $40,000 and Paid-In Capital in Excess of Par—Common Stock for $30,000, and debit Cash for

$70,000 under financing activities (Entry 7). This debit to Cash represents an inflow of cash from financing activities. By making these entries to the T accounts, Common Stock and Paid-In Capital in Excess of Par—Common Stock have been reconciled. For example, the beginning balance of Common Stock was $250,000. By crediting this account for $40,000, the balance is increased to $290,000, the ending balance.

The additional information also indicates that Simplex declared and paid cash dividends of $20,000. The entry for this event is as follows:

Dividends	20,000	
Cash		20,000

Since the dividends account is closed to Retained Earnings, the debit to the balance sheet accounts is actually made to Retained Earnings, and Cash is credited under financing activities (Entry 8).

Finally, the balance sheet reports an increase in notes payable of $10,000. Thus, Simplex borrowed $10,000. To reconcile the accounts, credit Notes Payable and debit Cash for $10,000 under financing activities (Entry 9). This represents an inflow of cash from financing activities.

STEP 6 **Prepare a statement of cash flows and verify the accuracy of the statement.** After analyzing all additional information and confirming that all noncash balance sheet accounts have been reconciled, the cash account in Figure 23-5 may be used to prepare the statement of cash flows shown in Figure 23-6. Instead of using debits and credits, the statement of cash flows employs additions and subtractions in each section.

Cash Flows from Operating Activities

The first section is cash flows from operating activities. Net income of $80,000 is reported first, followed by additions for the decreases in accounts receivable, $30,000, and inventory, $20,000. Finally, a deduction is made for the decrease in accounts payable ($60,000). By summing net income and the related adjustments, cash from operating activities of $70,000 is reported.

Cash Flows from Investing Activities

As shown in the cash account, investing activities included the purchase of a building and equipment for $140,000 and $100,000, respectively. Thus, the statement of cash flows reports these events and net cash used by investing activities of $240,000.

Cash Flows from Financing Activities

Finally, the cash account indicates three financing activities. Inflows of cash resulted from issuing common stock for $70,000 and a note payable for $10,000. These inflows are offset by an outflow from paying dividends of $20,000. Thus, the statement of cash flows reports these events and net cash provided by financing activities of $60,000.

Verifying the Accuracy of the Statement

By summing the cash flows from operating, investing, and financing activities ($70,000 – $240,000 + $60,000), the statement of cash flows reports a net decrease in cash of $110,000. Simplex's balance sheet reports that cash decreased by $110,000 ($200,000 – $90,000) during the year. The fact that these numbers agree provides some assurance that all cash flow activities have been included in the statement. This reconciliation is reported at the bottom of the statement of cash flows as shown in Figure 23-6.

U REVU

Complete U REVU-4 on **page 908** to test your basic understanding of LO6.

PREPARATION OF A STATEMENT OF CASH FLOWS UNDER THE INDIRECT METHOD: MULTIPLEX

LO7 Prepare a statement of cash flows under the indirect method, including adjustments when the company:
a. defines cash as "cash and cash equivalents."

This section of the chapter illustrates how to prepare a statement of cash flows for a more complex business. Steps similar to those followed to prepare the statement of cash flows for Simplex will be followed for Multiplex. In addition, a few steps will be expanded, and different techniques will be illustrated to provide a more complete understanding of the methods used to prepare the statement of cash flows. Additional concepts to be discussed for Multiplex include the following:

- Cash equivalents
- Noncash expenses
- Gains and losses on the sale of long-term assets
- Noncash investing and financing activities

CASH EQUIVALENTS

LEARNING KEY

A cash equivalent is a short-term, highly liquid investment that can be readily converted to a known amount of cash.

To earn a return on idle cash, many companies invest in short-term, highly liquid investments known as **cash equivalents**. To qualify as cash equivalents, the investments must be readily convertible to a *known* amount of cash, so that when cash is needed, the investments can be easily liquidated. Examples of cash equivalents include short-term investments in government notes and money market funds. These investments are considered the same as cash when preparing the statement of cash flows. Thus, the statement should explain the change in the amount of cash *and* cash equivalents held at the beginning and at the end of an accounting period.

U REVU

Complete U REVU-5 on **page 908** to test your basic understanding of LO7a.

NONCASH EXPENSES

LO7 Prepare a statement of cash flows under the indirect method, including adjustments when the company:
b. reports depreciation expense.
c. reports gains or losses on transactions not related to operating activities.

Depreciation expense and the amortization of intangible assets are examples of **noncash expenses**. These expenses reduce net income, but do not require an outflow of cash during the period. Thus, they are added to net income to compute cash flows from operating activities.

GAINS AND LOSSES ON TRANSACTIONS NOT RELATED TO OPERATING ACTIVITIES

Gains and losses on the sale of long-term assets are reported on the income statement and included in the calculation of net income. However, since these cash flows are not considered operating activities, the gains and losses should not be included in the calculation of cash from operating activities. Thus, net income must be adjusted on the statement of cash flows to compute cash from operating activities.

To illustrate, consider the financial statements for Stevie B's, shown in Figure 23-9. Let's assume no income tax and that all revenues and expenses for the period were for cash. Thus, the $300 of operating income reported on the income statement also represents cash from operating activities. During the accounting period, Stevie B's sold land that cost $200 for $250. Since this is not an operating activity, the gain of $50 is reported separately on the income statement.

FIGURE 23-9 Treatment of a Gain on the Statement of Cash Flows

Stevie B's
Income Statement
For Year Ended December 31, 20 -2

Sales (all cash)		$1,000.00
Wages expense (all cash)		700.00
Operating income		$ 300.00
Gain on sale of land		50.00
Net income		$ 350.00

Stevie B's
Balance Sheet
December 31, 20-2 and 20-1

Assets	20-2	20-1
Cash	$ 950.00	$ 400.00
Land	800.00	1,000.00
Total assets	$1,750.00	$1,400.00
Stockholders' Equity		
Common stock	$1,200.00	$1,200.00
Retained earnings	550.00	200.00
Total stockholders' equity	$1,750.00	$1,400.00
Additional information:		
Sold land that cost $200 for $250.		

Stevie B's
Statement of Cash Flows
For Year Ended December 31, 20-2

Cash flows from operating activities:		
Net income	$350.00	
Less gain on sale of land	(50.00)	
Net cash provided by operating activities		$300.00
Investing activities:		
Sold land		250.00
Net increase in cash		$550.00

On the statement of cash flows, this gain must be deducted from net income to compute cash from operating activities, $300. The entire amount of cash received from the sale of the land, $250, is reported as a cash inflow under investing activities.

U REVU

Complete U REVU-6 on **page 908** to test your basic understanding of LO7b and 7c.

LO7 Prepare a statement of cash flows under the indirect method, including adjustments when the company:
d. has noncash investing and financing activities.

NONCASH INVESTING AND FINANCING ACTIVITIES

Occasionally, firms will acquire assets by issuing debt. Acquiring assets is an investing activity and issuing debt is a financing activity, but no cash is involved in the transaction. Or, debt might be retired by issuing common stock. Similarly, retiring debt and issuing common stock are financing activities, but no cash is involved. As major events for the company, these transactions are of interest to users of the financial statements and should be included on the statement of cash flows. However, since no cash is involved, these transactions are *not* reported in the investing or financing sections of the statement. Instead, a separate section of the statement, **noncash investing and financing activities**, is used. For example, if a firm acquires a building by signing a mortgage for $500,000, the following entry would be made:

Building	500,000	
Mortgage Payable—Building		500,000

Since no cash is involved in this transaction, it is not reported in the investing or financing sections of the statement. Instead, it is reported in a separate section as follows:

Schedule of noncash investing and financing activities:	
Acquired a building by signing a mortgage	$500,000

LEARNING KEY

Noncash investing and financing activities involve no cash flows. Thus, they are not included in the investing and financing sections of the statement. However, these transactions represent a significant change in the company's financial position. Therefore, they are reported in a separate section of the statement of cash flows: Noncash investing and financing activities.

Figure 23-10 provides an income statement, statement of retained earnings, comparative balance sheet, and additional information about the cash flows for the period for Multiplex Corporation. We will use this information to prepare a statement of cash flows for Multiplex under the indirect method by following the steps listed on pages 888 to 897.

FIGURE 23-10 Financial Statements and Additional Information for Multiplex

Multiplex Corporation
Income Statement
For Year Ended December 31, 20-2

Net sales		$460,100.00
Cost of goods sold		270,100.00
Gross profit		$190,000.00
Operating expenses		120,750.00
Operating income		$ 69,250.00
Other revenues and gains:		
Interest revenue	$ 155.00	
Gain on sale of equipment	3,000.00	3,155.00
Other expenses:		
Interest expense		650.00
Income before taxes		$ 71,755.00
Income tax expense		24,000.00
Net income		$ 47,755.00

Multiplex Corporation
Statement of Retained Earnings
For Year Ended December 31, 20-2

Retained earnings, January 1, 20-2		$23,660.00
Net income	$47,755.00	
Less dividends	22,800.00	
Net increase in retained earnings		24,955.00
Retained earnings, December 31, 20-2		$48,615.00

FIGURE 23-10 Financial Statements and Additional Information for Multiplex *(continued)*

Multiplex Corporation
Comparative Balance Sheet
December 31, 20-2 and 20-1

	20-2		20-1		INCREASE (DECREASE)
Assets					
Current assets:					
Cash	$17,980.00		$20,000.00		$(2,020.00)
Government notes	1,800.00		3,200.00		(1,400.00)
Accrued interest receivable	100.00		300.00		(200.00)
Accounts receivable (net)	60,215.00		51,510.00		8,705.00
Merchandise inventory	64,570.00		67,500.00		(2,930.00)
Supplies and prepayments	4,000.00		2,750.00		1,250.00
Total current assets		$148,665.00		$145,260.00	3,405.00
Property, plant, and equipment:					
Store equipment	$48,000.00		$38,800.00		9,200.00
Less accumulated depreciation—store equipment	18,000.00	30,000.00	14,000.00	24,800.00	4,000.00
Delivery equipment	$47,000.00		$32,000.00		15,000.00
Less accumulated depreciation—delivery equipment	6,500.00	40,500.00	8,000.00	24,000.00	(1,500.00)
Office equipment	$38,000.00		$34,000.00		4,000.00
Less accumulated depreciation—office equipment	8,000.00	30,000.00	6,100.00	27,900.00	1,900.00
Total property, plant, and equipment		$100,500.00		$76,700.00	23,800.00
Total assets		$249,165.00		$221,960.00	27,205.00
Liabilities					
Current liabilities:					
Notes payable	$10,000.00		$11,800.00		(1,800.00)
Accounts payable	33,500.00		45,900.00		(12,400.00)
Income tax payable	3,000.00		2,000.00		1,000.00
Accrued and withheld payroll taxes	950.00		1,520.00		(570.00)
Accrued interest payable	100.00		80.00		20.00
Total current liabilities		$47,550.00		$61,300.00	(13,750.00)
Long-term liabilities:					
Note payable (3-year)		13,000.00			13,000.00
Total liabilities		$60,550.00		$61,300.00	(750.00)
Stockholders' Equity					
Common stock ($10 par, 100,000 shares authorized; Issued: 10,000 in 20-2 and 9,800 in 20-1)	$100,000.00		$98,000.00		2,000.00
Paid-in capital in excess of par—common stock	40,000.00		39,000.00		1,000.00
Retained earnings	48,615.00		23,660.00		24,955.00
Total stockholders' equity		188,615.00		160,660.00	27,955.00
Total liabilities and stockholders' equity		$249,165.00		$221,960.00	27,205.00

Additional information:

1. Depreciation expense for the year was $10,400 as follows:

Store equipment	$ 4,000
Delivery equipment	4,500
Office equipment	1,900
	$10,400

2. The following cash purchases were made:

Store equipment	$ 9,200
Delivery equipment	12,000
Office equipment	4,000
	$25,200

3. Delivery equipment was sold for $7,000.

Cost	$10,000
Accumulated depreciation	6,000
Book value	$ 4,000
Market value	7,000
Gain on sale of delivery equipment	$ 3,000

4. A $13,000, three-year note was issued to acquire delivery equipment with a market value of $13,000.
5. Declared and paid cash dividends of $22,800.
6. Issued 200 shares of common stock for $15 per share.

STEP 1 Compute the change in cash and cash equivalents.
Multiplex has cash equivalents (government notes) of $1,800 and $3,200 on December 31, 20-2 and 20-1, respectively. Thus, the statement of cash flows must explain why cash and government notes decreased by $3,420 during the year.

	20-2 Dec. 31	20-1 Dec. 31	Increase (Decrease)
Cash	$17,980	$20,000	$(2,020)
Government notes	1,800	3,200	(1,400)
Cash and cash equivalents	$19,780	$23,200	$(3,420)

STEP 2 Set up T accounts with the beginning and ending balances for all noncash (or cash equivalent) balance sheet accounts.
The purpose of the statement of cash flows is to report all transactions that resulted in cash receipts or payments. To provide a systematic method of searching for these transactions, all noncash (or cash equivalent) balance sheet accounts should be reconciled. The T accounts shown in Figure 23-11 (page 890) are helpful in completing this task. Figure 23-12 (page 891) shows the statement of cash flows for Multiplex. Instead of showing the cash effects in a Cash T account as we did for Simplex, the cash flow effects are entered directly on the statement of cash flows. Thus, the T accounts and statement of cash flows are provided on facing pages to make it easier to follow the "entries." In addition, we will illustrate the use of the T accounts and the Cash T account for selected adjustments throughout the chapter.

As with Simplex, the T accounts must be reconciled as the statement of cash flows is prepared. Each reconciling item has a debit and a credit. If a debit is made to a T account, an offsetting credit must be made either to another T account or on the statement of cash flows. Financial statements do not have debits and credits. However, we may use debits and credits to assist in the preparation of the statement as follows:

Debits—To enter cash receipts or additions to net income on the statement.
Credits—To enter cash payments or subtractions from net income on the statement.

Using this technique may help prevent errors when preparing the statement. Additions to net income and inflows of cash are shown on the statement of cash flows as positive numbers. Subtractions from net income and cash outflows are reported in parentheses ( ).

STEP 3(a) Compute cash flows from operating activities by reporting net income as the primary source of cash from operating activities.
Under the indirect method, net income is considered the primary source of cash. Therefore, it is listed first on the statement of cash flows, followed by any necessary additions or subtractions.

Since net income increases retained earnings, $47,755 is credited to the Retained Earnings T account (see item number 1). The credit to the T account (Figure 23-11) is offset by a debit (cash inflow or addition to net income) on the statement of cash flows (Figure 23-12).

The entry for net income **1** would appear as follows:

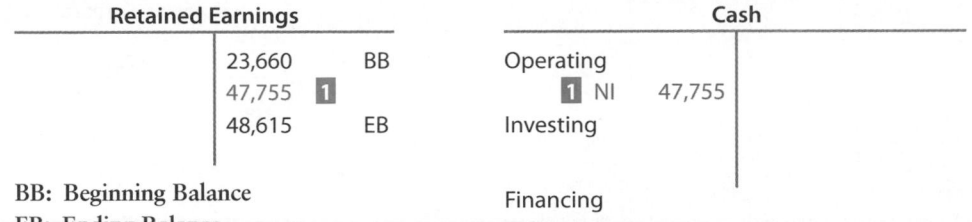

Retained Earnings

		23,660	BB
		47,755	**1**
		48,615	EB

Cash

Operating		
1 NI	47,755	
Investing		
Financing		

BB: Beginning Balance
EB: Ending Balance

Retained Earnings is not completely reconciled. We will watch for other transactions that impact retained earnings.

STEP 3(b) **Compute cash flows from operating activities by adjusting net income for changes in current assets and current liabilities related to operating activities.**

Multiplex has several current assets and current liabilities. Let's discuss changes in current assets first, followed by changes in current liabilities.

CHANGES IN CURRENT ASSETS RELATED TO OPERATING ACTIVITIES

Items **2** and **4** represent decreases in current assets related to operating activities. These decreases represent increases in cash from operating activities. They are reported as credits to each T account to reconcile each account and as additions to net income (debits) on the statement of cash flows.

The entry for the decrease in accrued interest receivable **2** would appear as follows:

Accrued Interest Receivable

BB	300		
		200	**2**
EB	100		

Cash

Operating		
NI	47,755	
2	200	
Investing		
Financing		

BB: Beginning Balance
EB: Ending Balance

Note that Accrued Interest Receivable has been reconciled and cash from operating activities has been increased by $200.

Items **3** and **5** represent increases in current assets related to operating activities. These increases represent reductions in cash from operating activities. They are reported as debits to the T accounts and as subtractions from net income (credits) on the statement of cash flows.

The entry for the increase in accounts receivable **3** would appear as follows:

Accounts Receivable (net)

BB	51,510	
3	8,705	
EB	60,215	

Cash

Operating			
NI	47,755		
		8,705	**3**
Investing			
Financing			

BB: Beginning Balance
EB: Ending Balance

FIGURE 23-11 T Accounts for Multiplex

T Accounts for Indirect Method Statement of Cash Flows
Multiplex Corporation

Accrued Interest Receivable

	Debit	Credit	
BB	300		
		200	2
EB	100		

Notes Payable

	Debit	Credit	
		11,800	BB
17	1,800		
		10,000	EB

Common Stock

	Debit	Credit	
		98,000	BB
		2,000	15
		100,000	EB

Accounts Receivable

	Debit	Credit	
BB	51,510		
3	8,705		
EB	60,215		

Accounts Payable

	Debit	Credit	
		45,900	BB
6	12,400		
		33,500	EB

Paid-In Capital in Excess of Par—Common Stock

	Debit	Credit	
		39,000	BB
		1,000	15
		40,000	EB

Merchandise Inventory

	Debit	Credit	
BB	67,500		
		2,930	4
EB	64,570		

Income Tax Payable

	Debit	Credit	
		2,000	BB
		1,000	7
		3,000	EB

Retained Earnings

	Debit	Credit	
		23,660	BB
16	22,800	47,755	1
		48,615	EB

Supplies and Prepayments

	Debit	Credit	
BB	2,750		
5	1,250		
a	4,000		

Accrued and Withheld Payroll Taxes

	Debit	Credit	
		1,520	BB
8	570		
		950	EB

Cash

	Debit	Credit	
BB	20,000		
		2,020	19
EB	17,980		

Government Notes

	Debit	Credit	
BB	3,200		
		1,400	19
EB	1,800		

Store Equipment

	Debit	Credit	
BB	38,800		
13	9,200		
EB	48,000		

Accrued Interest Payable

	Debit	Credit	
		80	BB
		20	9
		100	EB

Accumulated Depreciation—Store Equipment

	Debit	Credit	
		14,000	BB
		4,000	10
		18,000	EB

Long-Term Notes Payable

	Debit	Credit	
		—	BB
		13,000	18
		13,000	EB

Delivery Equipment

	Debit	Credit	
BB	32,000		
12	12,000	10,000	11
18	13,000		
EB	47,000		

Major entries of interest:

		Debit	Credit
Depreciation Expense	10	10,400	
Accum. Depr.—Store Equip.	10		4,000
Accum. Depr.—Delivery Equip.	10		4,500
Accum. Depr.—Office Equip.	10		1,900
Cash	11	7,000	
Accum. Depr.—Delivery Equipment	11	6,000	
Gain on Sale of Delivery Equip.	11		3,000
Delivery Equipment	11		10,000

Accumulated Depreciation—Delivery Equipment

	Debit	Credit	
		8,000	BB
11	6,000	4,500	10
		6,500	EB

Office Equipment

	Debit	Credit	
BB	34,000		
14	4,000		
EB	38,000		

Accumulated Depreciation—Office Equipment

	Debit	Credit	
		6,100	BB
		1,900	10
		8,000	EB

BB: Beginning Balance
EB: Ending Balance

FIGURE 23-12 Statement of Cash Flows for Multiplex (Indirect Method)

Multiplex Corporation
Statement of Cash Flows
For Year Ended December 31, 20-2

Cash flows from operating activities:			
Net income	$ 47,755.00	1*	
Adjustments for changes in current assets and liabilities related to operating activities:			
Decrease in accrued interest receivable	200.00	2	
Increase in accounts receivable	(8,705.00)	3	
Decrease in merchandise inventory	2,930.00	4	
Increase in supplies and prepayments	(1,250.00)	5	
Decrease in accounts payable	(12,400.00)	6	
Increase in income tax payable	1,000.00	7	
Decrease in accrued and withheld payroll taxes	(570.00)	8	
Increase in accrued interest payable	20.00	9	
Noncash expenses and other adjustments:			
Depreciation expense	10,400.00	10	
Gain on sale of delivery equipment	(3,000.00)	11	
Net cash provided by operating activities			$ 36,380.00
Cash flows from investing activities:			
Sold delivery equipment	$ 7,000.00	11	
Purchased delivery equipment	(12,000.00)	12	
Purchased store equipment	(9,200.00)	13	
Purchased office equipment	(4,000.00)	14	
Net cash used by investing activities			(18,200.00)
Cash flows from financing activities:			
Issued common stock	$ 3,000.00	15	
Paid cash dividends	(22,800.00)	16	
Retired notes payable	(1,800.00)	17	
Net cash used by financing activities			(21,600.00)
Net increase (decrease) in cash and cash equivalents		19	$ (3,420.00)
Cash and cash equivalents, January 1, 20-2			23,200.00
Cash and cash equivalents, December 31, 20-2			$ 19,780.00
Schedule of Noncash Investing and Financing Activities:			
Purchased delivery equipment by issuing a 3-year note		18	$ 13,000.00
Supplemental Disclosures of Cash Flow Information:			
Cash paid during the year for:			
Interest		20	$ 630.00
Income taxes		20	23,000.00

To compute cash paid for interest and taxes, prepare the following entries:

	Debit		Credit
Interest Expense (see income statement)	650.00		
Accrued Interest Payable (increase in Acc. Int. Pay.)			20.00
Cash (plug)		20	630.00
Income Tax Expense (see income statement)	24,000.00		
Income Tax Payable (increase in income tax payable)			1,000.00
Cash (plug)		20	23,000.00

*Note: Numbers show the relationship between the reconciling entries in the T Accounts and the items on the Statement of Cash Flows.

Note that Accounts Receivable has been reconciled and cash from operating activities has been decreased by $8,705.

CHANGES IN CURRENT LIABILITIES RELATED TO OPERATING ACTIVITIES

Items 6 and 8 represent decreases in current liabilities related to operating activities. These decreases reduce cash from operating activities. They are reported as debits to the T accounts and as subtractions from net income (credits) on the statement of cash flows.

The entry for the decrease in accounts payable 6 would appear as follows:

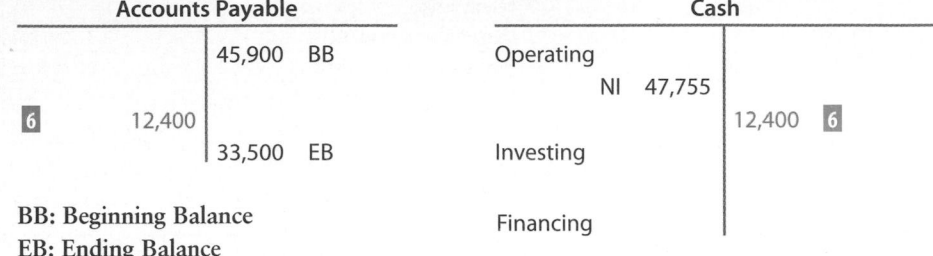

Accounts Payable

	45,900 BB
6 12,400	
	33,500 EB

BB: Beginning Balance
EB: Ending Balance

Cash

Operating	
NI 47,755	
	12,400 6
Investing	
Financing	

Note that Accounts Payable has been reconciled and cash from operating activities has been reduced by $12,400.

Items 7 and 9, the increases in Income Tax Payable and Accrued Interest Payable, indicate that Multiplex did not pay all of the tax and interest expense incurred during the period. Thus, these increases are reported as additions to net income (debits) in the calculation of cash flows from operating activities and as credits to the T accounts.

The entry for the increase in income tax payable 7 would appear as follows:

Income Tax Payable

	2,000 BB
	1,000 7
	3,000 EB

BB: Beginning Balance
EB: Ending Balance

Cash

Operating	
NI 47,755	
7 1,000	
Investing	
Financing	

Note that Income Tax Payable has been reconciled and cash from operating activities has been increased by $1,000.

STEP 3(c) **Compute cash flows from operating activities by adjusting net income for noncash expenses.**

Item 10 is for Depreciation Expense and represents noncash expenses. These expenses reduce net income on the income statement, but require no cash payments. Thus, they are added back to net income (debit) on the statement of cash flows. They are also entered as credits to the T accounts for Accumulated Depreciation—Store Equipment, Delivery Equipment, and Office Equipment.

The depreciation on the delivery equipment 10 would appear as follows:

Accumulated Depreciation—Delivery Equipment

Debit	Credit	
	8,000	BB
	4,500	10
	6,500	EB

BB: Beginning Balance
EB: Ending Balance

Cash

	Debit	Credit
Operating		
NI	47,755	
10	4,500	
Investing		
Financing		

Note that accumulated depreciation requires additional adjustments to be reconciled and cash from operating activities has been increased by $4,500. Also note that $10,400 is added back to net income in Figure 23-12. Above, we illustrated the adjustment for the depreciation on the delivery equipment. When preparing the statement of cash flows, we must adjust for the depreciation on all equipment: $4,000 on store equipment, $4,500 on delivery equipment, and $1,900 on office equipment for a total of $10,400 as shown below.

Depreciation Expense	10,400	
Accumulated Depreciation—Store Equipment		4,000
Accumulated Depreciation—Delivery Equipment		4,500
Accumulated Depreciation—Office Equipment		1,900

STEP 3(d) **Compute cash flows from operating activities by adjusting net income for gains and losses on transactions not related to operating activities.** The income statement reports a gain on the sale of equipment for $3,000. Further, the additional information indicates that the equipment was sold for $7,000. The cost of the equipment was $10,000, accumulated depreciation was $6,000, and the book value was $4,000. The entry for the sale of the equipment is shown below.

Cash	7,000	
Accum. Depr.—Delivery Equipment	6,000	
Delivery Equipment		10,000
Gain on Sale of Delivery Equipment		3,000

This transaction is related to investing activities, but increased net income by $3,000. Thus, the following adjustments are made to the statement of cash flows and T accounts. See entries marked 11.

1. Report the $7,000 cash inflow from investing activities. This represents a debit on the statement of cash flows under investing activities in Figure 23-12.
2. Debit Accumulated Depreciation—Delivery Equipment for $6,000. This helps reconcile the balance sheet account.
3. Credit Delivery Equipment for $10,000. This helps reconcile the balance sheet account.
4. Subtract the $3,000 gain from net income under cash from operating activities. Recall that a subtraction from net income is similar to a credit for analysis purposes. The $3,000 gain was included when computing net income of $47,755, but was not associated with operating activities; thus, subtract the $3,000 gain.

The entry for the sale of delivery equipment 11 would appear as follows:

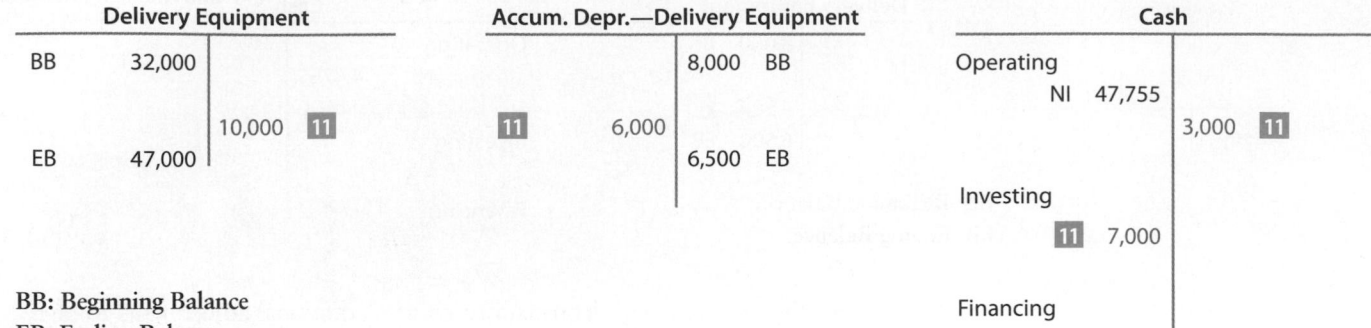

Delivery Equipment

	Debit	Credit	
BB	32,000		
		10,000	11
EB	47,000		

Accum. Depr.—Delivery Equipment

	Debit	Credit	
		8,000	BB
11	6,000		
		6,500	EB

Cash

	Debit	Credit	
Operating			
NI	47,755		
		3,000	11
Investing			
11	7,000		
Financing			

BB: Beginning Balance
EB: Ending Balance

Delivery Equipment is credited for $10,000 to remove the cost of the equipment sold. Accumulated Depreciation—Delivery Equipment is debited to remove the accumulated depreciation on the equipment sold. The inflow of cash of $7,000 from investing activities is debited to the cash account, and the $3,000 gain is credited to the operating section of the cash account to remove the gain that was included in net income.

STEP 4 Identify cash flows from investing activities.
Items 12, 13, and 14 are for purchases of equipment. These amounts are entered as debits to the T accounts to reconcile the equipment accounts and as outflows of cash (credits) under investing activities on the statement of cash flows.

The entry for the purchase of delivery equipment 12 would appear as follows:

Delivery Equipment

	Debit	Credit
BB	32,000	
12	12,000	
EB	47,000	

BB: Beginning Balance
EB: Ending Balance

Cash

	Debit	Credit	
Operating			
NI	47,755		
Investing			
		12,000	12
Financing			

Delivery Equipment is debited to show the acquisition, and Cash is credited to report the outflow of cash for investing activities.

STEP 5 Identify cash flows from financing activities.
Item 15 is for the issuance of common stock. The T accounts for Common Stock and Paid-In Capital in Excess of Par—Common Stock are credited ($2,000 and $1,000, respectively), and the $3,000 is shown as an inflow of cash (debit) from financing activities on the statement of cash flows.

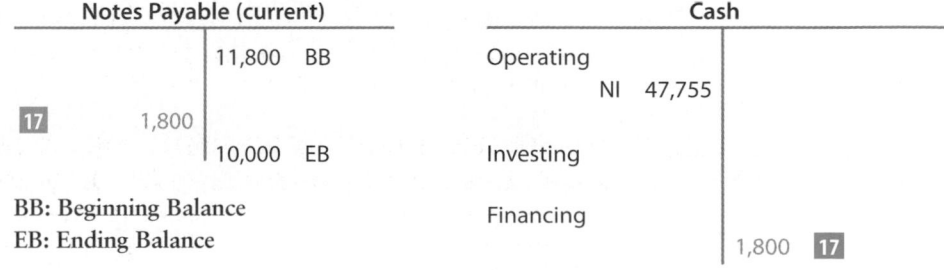

The entry for the issuance of common stock 15 would appear as follows:

Common Stock

		98,000	BB
		2,000	15
		100,000	EB

Paid-In Capital in Excess of Par—Common Stock

		39,000	BB
		1,000	15
		40,000	EB

Cash

Operating		
NI	47,755	
Investing		
Financing		
15	3,000	

BB: Beginning Balance
EB: Ending Balance

Note that Common Stock and Paid-In Capital in Excess of Par—Common Stock have been reconciled and an inflow of cash from financing activities has been recognized.

The statement of retained earnings in Figure 23-10 shows cash dividends of $22,800 were declared and paid during the year. Since dividends reduce retained earnings, $22,800 is debited to Retained Earnings. The outflow of cash (credit) is reported under financing activities as item 16.

The entry for the payment of dividends 16 would appear as follows:

Retained Earnings

		23,660	BB
16	22,800	47,755	(1)
		48,615	EB

Cash

Operating			
(1) NI	47,755		
Investing			
Financing			
		22,800	16

BB: Beginning Balance
EB: Ending Balance

Earlier, we credited Retained Earnings $47,755 (1) for net income. The above $22,800 debit to Retained Earnings for dividends 16 completes the reconciliation of the account. The dividends are credited to the cash account showing an outflow of cash from financing activities.

Item 17 represents the decrease of $1,800 in current notes payable. Therefore, Notes Payable is debited, and the $1,800 cash outflow (credit) is reported under financing activities on the statement of cash flows.

The entry for the reduction in notes payable 17 would appear as follows:

Notes Payable (current)

		11,800	BB
17	1,800		
		10,000	EB

Cash

Operating			
NI	47,755		
Investing			
Financing			
		1,800	17

BB: Beginning Balance
EB: Ending Balance

Noncash investing and financing activities are listed in a separate section of the statement.

STEP 6(a) **Prepare a statement of cash flows and disclose noncash investing and financing activities.**
A final review of all noncash balance sheet accounts reveals that Delivery Equipment and the long-term notes payable account have not yet been reconciled. This is consistent with the additional information (Figure 23-10) indicating that delivery equipment was acquired by issuing a three-year note for $13,000. Item 18 represents the issuance of the $13,000, three-year note for the acquisition of delivery equipment. Delivery Equipment is debited, and Long-Term Notes Payable is credited to reconcile these accounts. All debits and credits are made in the T accounts in Figure 23-11. Since there is no cash involved in this transaction, no entries are made in the investing or financing sections of the statement of cash flows. However, this event is noted in the schedule of noncash investing and financing activities on the statement of cash flows.

The entry for the purchase of delivery equipment by signing a three-year note 18 would appear as shown below. Note that when added to the previous adjustments (11 and 12), the accounts are reconciled.

Delivery Equipment

BB	32,000		
		10,000	(11)
(12)	12,000		
18	13,000		
EB	47,000		

Long-Term Notes Payable

		—	BB
		13,000	18
		13,000	EB

BB: Beginning Balance
EB: Ending Balance

STEP 6(b) **Prepare a statement of cash flows and verify the accuracy of the statement.**
After accounting for the changes in all noncash balance sheet accounts, the net increase or decrease in cash as reported on the statement of cash flows is computed. This is done by taking the sum of net cash flows provided by operating activities ($36,380), cash used by investing activities ($18,200), and cash used by financing activities ($21,600). To verify the accuracy of the statement, sum the decrease in Cash (item 19) and decrease in Government Notes (item 19) ($2,020 + $1,400) reported in Figures 23-10 and 23-11. This amount is the same as the $3,420 decrease in cash and cash equivalents (item 19) reported on the statement of cash flows, Figure 23-12.

This verification is reported at the bottom of the statement of cash flows. The $3,420 reduction in cash and cash equivalents is subtracted from the beginning balances of these accounts, $23,200, to compute the ending balance of cash and equivalents, $19,780.

U REVU Complete U REVU-7 on **page 908** to test your basic understanding of LO7d.

LO7 Prepare a statement of cash flows under the indirect method, including adjustments when the company:
e. provides supplemental disclosures of cash flows.

STEP 6(c) **Prepare a statement of cash flows and provide supplemental disclosures of cash flows.**

Companies using the indirect method are required to provide separate disclosure of the following information:

1. The change in accounts receivable.
2. The change in inventory.
3. The change in accounts payable.
4. Cash paid for interest.
5. Cash paid for income taxes.

These items are required so users of the financial statements can compute cash received from customers and cash paid to suppliers. The first three items have already been reported in the statement of cash flows.

CASH PAID FOR INTEREST

Additional disclosures include:
Cash paid for interest
Cash paid for income taxes

Multiplex reports $650 of interest expense on the income statement. As reported on the balance sheet, Accrued Interest Payable increased by $20. This means that Multiplex did not pay for all of the $650 of interest expense incurred this period. The $20 increase in the liability is deducted from Interest Expense to compute cash paid for interest ($630). This relationship is easily seen if we consider the summary entry made by Multiplex.

Interest Expense	650	
Interest Payable		20
Cash		630

CASH PAID FOR INCOME TAXES

Income tax expense of $24,000 is reported on the income statement. The balance sheet reports that Income Tax Payable increased by $1,000. Postponing the payment for taxes reduces the cash paid for income taxes by $1,000. Thus, $1,000 is deducted from Income Tax Expense to compute the income taxes paid in cash ($24,000 – $1,000 = $23,000). This relationship is easily seen if we consider the summary entry made by Multiplex.

Income Tax Expense	24,000	
Income Tax Payable		1,000
Cash		23,000

Cash paid for interest and income taxes must be reported as supplemental disclosures on the face of the statement of cash flows, or in the notes to the financial statements. The items marked 20 represent the disclosure of this information on the face of the statement of cash flows for Multiplex.

U REVU Complete U REVU-8 on **page 908** to test your basic understanding of LO7e.

INTERPRETING THE STATEMENT OF CASH FLOWS

LO8 Interpret the statement of cash flows.

The purpose of the statement of cash flows is to provide information on the sources and uses of cash. To do this, all cash-related activities are grouped into three categories: operating, investing, and financing. *An important indicator of the financial health of a business is the net cash used or provided by operating activities.* Both Simplex and Multiplex had positive cash flows from operations. This is important because these

LEARNING KEY

An important indicator of the financial health of a business is the net cash used or provided by operating activities.

funds are needed to purchase property, plant, and equipment to upgrade or expand operations. Expansion and renewal can be financed through borrowing or through the issuance of capital stock. However, loans must be repaid with interest, and dividends will be paid to stockholders in proportion to the amount invested. Ultimately, these funds must be generated from operations. A chronic inability to generate positive cash flows from operations is a sure sign of financial instability.

Information on investing and financing activities is also useful in evaluating the financial health of the company. For example, the statement of cash flows in Figure 23-12 shows that Multiplex generated $36,380 from operating activities. Net "spending" on investing and financing activities amounted to $39,800 ($18,200 + $21,600). Thus, cash and cash equivalents fell by $3,420. The major expenditures included a net outflow of $18,200 to purchase equipment and $22,800 paid for dividends. Approximately 63% ($22,800 ÷ $36,380) of the cash generated from operating activities went to the stockholders. If dividends begin to exceed the cash generated from operating activities, it could imply that the company is planning to go out of business.

Modest increases or decreases in cash balances are normal. Major fluctuations should be investigated and can generally be explained by current and expected future investment and financing activities.

A BROADER VIEW

Net Income versus Cash from Operating Activities: Eli Lilly Company

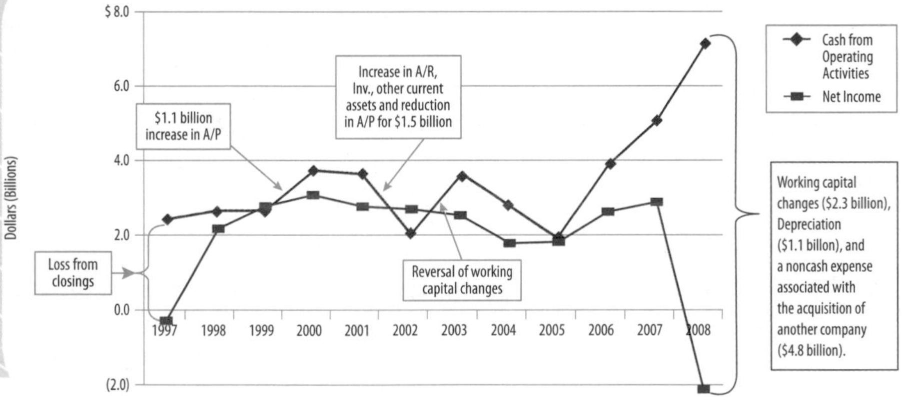

Since cash from operating activities (CFO) is related to revenues and expenses on the income statement, many financial statement users assume that CFO and net income (NI) are similar in value and move in the same direction. This relationship holds, except for a few considerations. For example, depreciation and amortization expenses reduce net income, but do not reduce cash. Thus, over the life of the firm, you should expect CFO to be greater than NI by the amount of depreciation and amortization expenses. However, for specific years, major differences between CFO and NI are easy to observe. As shown in the graph, Lilly reported a net loss of $385 million in 1997 while also reporting cash from operating activities of $2.4 billion. This occurred because Lilly reported a major expense associated with closing facilities that did not require the use of cash. In 2000, CFO increased substantially more than NI due to a $1.1 billion increase in accounts payable. By postponing payments to suppliers, Lilly effectively increased its CFO for 2000. In 2002, we see that cash from operating activities fell dramatically and dropped below NI. This was caused by major increases in receivables, inventories, other current assets, and a reduction in accounts payable for a combined reduction in CFO of $1.5 billion. Note that CFO bounced back up in 2003. This was partially caused by changes in current assets and current liabilities that increased CFO, a dramatic reversal of the previous year's reduction. In 2008, we see that CFO is $9.4 billion higher than the net loss. This unusually large difference is driven primarily by working capital changes ($2.3 billion), depreciation ($1.1 billion), and a noncash expense associated with the acquisition of another company ($4.8 billion).

LEARNING OBJECTIVES — Key Points to Remember

LO1 Explain the purpose of the statement of cash flows.

The purpose of the statement of cash flows is to report how cash was generated and used throughout the accounting period.

LO2 Define operating, investing, and financing activities and describe transactions for each type of activity.

The statement has three major sections that report on cash flows from operating, investing, and financing activities. Operating activities include transactions and events associated with selling a product or providing a service and are related to the revenues and expenses reported on the income statement. Investing activities are those transactions involving the purchase and sale of long-term assets, investments in debt and equity securities, and lending money and collecting the principal on the related loans. Financing activities are those transactions dealing with the exchange of cash between the company and its stockholders and creditors. The inflows and outflows associated with these types of activities are as follows:

OPERATING ACTIVITIES

Cash Inflows	Cash Outflows
1. Cash receipts from the sale of goods or services.	1. Payments for the acquisition of inventory.
2. Interest received on loans made to outside entities.	2. Payments to employees and the government.
3. Dividends received on investments made in the stock of other corporations.	3. Payments for interest on loans.
	4. Payments to other suppliers and for other expenses.

INVESTING ACTIVITIES

Cash Inflows	Cash Outflows
1. Proceeds from collection of principal amount of loans made to borrowers.*	1. Loans made by the company to other parties.
2. Proceeds from the sale of property, plant, and equipment; intangibles; and other productive assets.	2. Payments to acquire property, plant, and equipment; intangibles; and other productive assets.
3. Proceeds from the sale of investments in debt and equity securities.	3. Payments to acquire investments in debt and equity securities.
4. Proceeds from discounting notes receivable.	

*Note that interest received on loans is not included with investing activities. It is included with cash inflows from operating activities.

(continued)

LEARNING OBJECTIVES Key Points to Remember

LO2 (concluded)

FINANCING ACTIVITIES	
Cash Inflows	**Cash Outflows**
1. Proceeds from additional investments by the owners or the issuance of stock.	1. Payments of dividends to stockholders or withdrawals by the owners.
2. Proceeds from borrowing money through the signing of a mortgage, issuing a bond, or other long- or short-term loans.	2. Payments to purchase treasury stock.
	3. Repayment of the principal on loans.*

* Interest payments on loans are not reported under financing activities. They are reported as cash outflows under operating activities.

Note: Amounts owed to suppliers of goods and services are not considered financing activities. They are used in the calculation of cash from operating activities.

LO3 Describe the information needed to prepare a statement of cash flows.

To prepare a statement of cash flows, the following information is needed:

1. Balance sheets for the beginning and end of the period.
2. Income statement for the period.
3. Statement of retained earnings for the period.
4. Any additional information on major cash transactions.

LO4 Describe the direct and indirect methods of reporting cash flows from operating activities.

Under the direct method, cash from operating activities is determined by adjusting each revenue and expense on the income statement as shown below.

Income Statement	is converted to	**Cash from operating activities.**
Sales	is converted to	**Cash received from customers.**
Operating Expense	is converted to	**Cash paid for operating expenses.**

Under the indirect method, net income is considered the primary source of cash from operating activities. Thus, it is reported on the statement of cash flows under operating activities. However, net income must be adjusted for transactions that affect net income and cash flows from operating activities by different amounts.

LO5 Describe the effects of changes in current assets and current liabilities on cash from operating activities under the indirect method.

The effects of changes in current assets and liabilities on cash flows from operating activities are shown below.

Change in:		Impact on:
Current Asset	Current Liability	Cash from Operating Activities
Increase	Decrease	Decrease
Decrease	Increase	Increase

LEARNING OBJECTIVES Key Points to Remember

LO6 Prepare a statement of cash flows under the indirect method using T accounts and including adjustments for current assets and current liabilities related to operations.

Basic steps to prepare a statement of cash flows:

STEP 1 Compute the change in cash.

STEP 2 Set up T accounts with the beginning and ending balances for all noncash balance sheet accounts.

STEP 3 Compute cash flows from operating activities by:

(a) Reporting net income as the primary source of cash from operating activities.
(b) Adjusting net income for changes in current assets and current liabilities related to operating activities.

STEP 4 Identify cash flows from investing activities.

STEP 5 Identify cash flows from financing activities.

STEP 6 Prepare a statement of cash flows and verify the accuracy of the statement.

T accounts may be used to prepare the statement of cash flows. All noncash or cash equivalent balance sheet accounts should be set up in T accounts. As these accounts are reconciled, debits or credits are made to the cash account. Debits to Cash reflect additions to net income or inflows from investing or financing activities. Credits to Cash reflect deductions from net income or cash outflows from investing or financing activities. Using T accounts, the adjustment for an increase in accounts receivable would appear as follows:

Accounts Receivable (net)

	Debit	Credit
BB	51,510	
(3)	8,705	
EB	60,215	

BB: Beginning Balance
EB: Ending Balance

Cash

	Debit	Credit	
Operating			
NI	47,755		
		8,705	(3)
Investing			
Financing			

LO7 Prepare a statement of cash flows under the indirect method, including adjustments when the company:
(a) defines cash as "cash and cash equivalents,"
(b) reports depreciation expense,
(c) reports gains or losses on transactions not related to operating activities,

Cash equivalents are short-term, highly liquid investments that are readily convertible to a *known* amount of cash, so that when cash is needed, the investments can be easily liquidated.

Depreciation expense reduces net income, but does not reduce cash. Thus, under the indirect method, depreciation expense should be added to net income when computing cash from operating activities.

Gains and losses on the sale of equipment or retirement of debt impact net income, but are not related to operating activities. Thus, gains should be deducted and losses added to net income when computing cash from operating activities.

(continued)

LEARNING OBJECTIVES	Key Points to Remember
LO7 (concluded) **(d) has noncash investing and financing activities, and** **(e) provides supplemental disclosures of cash flows.**	Some major investing and financing transactions do not involve cash. Though not reported in the investing or financing sections of the statement of cash flows, these noncash investing and financing activities are disclosed in a separate schedule on the statement. The following supplemental disclosures are required under the indirect method: • The change in accounts receivable. • The change in inventory. • The change in accounts payable. • Cash paid for interest. • Cash paid for income taxes. **Complete steps to prepare a statement of cash flows.** STEP 1 Compute the change in cash and cash equivalents. STEP 2 Set up T accounts with the beginning and ending balances for all noncash (or cash equivalent) balance sheet accounts. STEP 3 Compute cash flows from operating activities by: (a) Reporting net income as the primary source of cash from operating activities. (b) Adjusting net income for changes in current assets and current liabilities related to operating activities. (c) Adjusting net income for noncash expenses. (d) Adjusting net income for gains and losses on transactions not related to operating activities. STEP 4 Identify cash flows from investing activities. STEP 5 Identify cash flows from financing activities. STEP 6 Prepare a statement of cash flows and: (a) Disclose noncash investing and financing activities. (b) Verify the accuracy of the statement. (c) Provide supplemental disclosures of cash flows.
LO8 Interpret the statement of cash flows.	An important indicator of the financial health of a company is the net cash used or provided by operating activities. These funds are needed to purchase property, plant, and equipment and pay dividends. Borrowing or issuing capital stock can be used to finance expansion, but these loans must be repaid with interest, and dividends must be paid to stockholders. These funds must ultimately be generated from operations.

DEMONSTRATION PROBLEM

Financial statements and additional information for Megaproducts, Inc., are provided below and on page 904.

Megaproducts, Inc.
Income Statement
For Year Ended December 31, 20-2

Net sales		$4,601,000.00
Cost of goods sold		2,701,000.00
Gross profit		$1,900,000.00
Operating expenses		1,242,504.00
Operating income		$ 657,496.00
Other revenues and expenses:		
Interest revenue	$ 1,550.00	
Interest expense	(6,440.00)	
Loss on sale of delivery equipment	(5,000.00)	(9,890.00)
Income before taxes		$ 647,606.00
Income tax expense		240,000.00
Net income		$ 407,606.00

Megaproducts, Inc.
Statement of Retained Earnings
For Year Ended December 31, 20-2

Retained earnings, January 1, 20-2		$236,622.00
Net income	$407,606.00	
Less dividends	128,000.00	
Net increase in retained earnings		279,606.00
Retained earnings, December 31, 20-2		$516,228.00

Additional information:

1. Delivery equipment was sold during the year for $10,000.

Cost	$ 50,000
Accumulated depreciation	(35,000)
Book value	$ 15,000
Market value	10,000
Loss	$ (5,000)

2. Depreciation expense for the year was $139,000 as follows:

Store equipment	$ 40,000
Delivery equipment	80,000
Office equipment	19,000
	$139,000

3. No other equipment was sold during the period. The following cash purchases were made:

Store equipment	$142,000
Delivery equipment	130,000
Office equipment	40,100
	$312,100

(continued)

4. Declared and paid cash dividends of $128,000.
5. Issued 2,000 shares of $10 par common stock for $15 per share.
6. Retired notes payable for $17,200 and acquired additional office equipment by issuing a note payable for $12,000.

Megaproducts, Inc.
Comparative Balance Sheet
December 31, 20-2 and 20-1

	20-2		20-1		INCREASE (DECREASE)
Assets					
Current assets:					
Cash	$ 171,786.00		$ 212,000.00		$ (40,214.00)
Government notes	26,000.00		20,000.00		6,000.00
Accrued interest receivable	300.00		700.00		(400.00)
Accounts receivable (net)	544,000.00		506,000.00		38,000.00
Merchandise inventory	645,678.00		675,120.00		(29,442.00)
Supplies and prepayments	40,150.00		27,356.00		12,794.00
Total current assets		$1,427,914.00		$1,441,176.00	(13,262.00)
Property, plant, and equipment:					
Store equipment	$ 530,000.00		$ 388,000.00		142,000.00
Less accumulated depreciation—store equipment	180,000.00	350,000.00	140,000.00	248,000.00	40,000.00
Delivery equipment	$ 400,000.00		$ 320,000.00		80,000.00
Less accumulated depreciation—delivery equipment	125,000.00	275,000.00	80,000.00	240,000.00	45,000.00
Office equipment	$ 392,000.00		$ 339,900.00		52,100.00
Less accumulated depreciation—office equipment	80,000.00	312,000.00	61,000.00	278,900.00	19,000.00
Total property, plant, and equipment		$ 937,000.00		$ 766,900.00	170,100.00
Total assets		$2,364,914.00		$2,208,076.00	156,838.00
Liabilities					
Current liabilities:					
Notes payable	$ 112,800.00		$ 118,000.00		(5,200.00)
Accounts payable	200,150.00		367,454.00		(167,304.00)
Income tax payable	125,000.00		100,000.00		25,000.00)
Accrued and withheld payroll taxes	9,896.00		15,200.00		(5,304.00)
Accrued interest payable	840.00		800.00		40.00
Total liabilities		$ 448,686.00		$ 601,454.00	(152,768.00)
Stockholders' Equity					
Common stock ($10 par, 1,000,000 shares authorized;					
Issued: 100,000 in 20-2 and 98,000 in 20-1)	$1,000,000.00		$ 980,000.00		20,000.00
Paid-in capital in excess of par—common stock	400,000.00		390,000.00		10,000.00
Retained earnings	516,228.00		236,622.00		279,606.00
Total stockholders' equity		1,916,228.00		1,606,622.00	309,606.00
Total liabilities and stockholders' equity		$2,364,914.00		$2,208,076.00	156,838.00

REQUIRED

1. Prepare a statement of cash flows explaining the change in cash and cash equivalents for the year ended December 31, 20-2.
2. Reconcile the cash and cash equivalents at the bottom of the statement of cash flows.

Solution

1. and 2.

T Accounts for Indirect Method Statement of Cash Flows
Megaproducts, Inc.

Accrued Interest Receivable

	Debit	Credit	
BB	700		
		400	2
EB	300		

Notes Payable

	Debit	Credit	
		118,000	BB
17	17,200	12,000	18
		112,800	EB

Common Stock

	Debit	Credit	
		980,000	BB
		20,000	16
		1,000,000	EB

Accounts Receivable

	Debit	Credit	
BB	506,000		
3	38,000		
EB	544,000		

Accounts Payable

	Debit	Credit	
		367,454	BB
6	167,304		
		200,150	EB

Paid-In Capital in Excess of Par—Common Stock

	Debit	Credit	
		390,000	BB
		10,000	16
		400,000	EB

Merchandise Inventory

	Debit	Credit	
BB	675,120		
		29,442	4
EB	645,678		

Income Tax Payable

	Debit	Credit	
		100,000	BB
		25,000	7
		125,000	EB

Retained Earnings

	Debit	Credit	
		236,622	BB
15	128,000	407,606	1
		516,228	EB

Supplies and Prepayments

	Debit	Credit	
BB	27,356		
5	12,794		
EB	40,150		

Accrued and Withheld Payroll Taxes

	Debit	Credit	
		15,200	BB
8	5,304		
		9,896	EB

Cash

	Debit	Credit	
BB	212,000		
		40,214	19
EB	171,786		

Store Equipment

	Debit	Credit	
BB	388,000		
12	142,000		
EB	530,000		

Accrued Interest Payable

	Debit	Credit	
		800	BB
		40	9
		840	EB

Government Notes

	Debit	Credit	
BB	20,000		
19	6,000		
EB	26,000		

Accumulated Depreciation—Store Equipment

	Debit	Credit	
		140,000	BB
		40,000	11
		180,000	EB

Delivery Equipment

	Debit	Credit	
BB	320,000		
13	130,000	50,000	10
EB	400,000		

Accumulated Depreciation—Delivery Equipment

	Debit	Credit	
		80,000	BB
10	35,000	80,000	11
		125,000	EB

Office Equipment

	Debit	Credit	
BB	339,900		
14	40,100		
18	12,000		
EB	392,000		

Accumulated Depreciation—Office Equipment

	Debit	Credit	
		61,000	BB
		19,000	11
		80,000	EB

Major entries of interest:

Cash	10	10,000	
Accum. Depr.—Delivery Equipment	10	35,000	
Loss on Sale of Del. Equip.	10	5,000	
Delivery Equipment	10		50,000
Depreciation Expense	11	139,000	
Accum. Depr.—Store Equip.	11		40,000
Accum. Depr.—Delivery Equip.	11		80,000
Accum. Depr.—Office Equip.	11		19,000

Note that Office Equipment and Notes Payable are affected by two transactions.

BB: Beginning Balance
EB: Ending Balance

(continued)

Megaproducts, Inc.
Statement of Cash Flows
For Year Ended December 31, 20-2

Cash flows from operating activities:				
Net income	$ 407,606.00	1		
Adjustments for changes in current assets and liabilities related to operating activities:				
Decrease in accrued interest receivable	400.00	2		
Increase in accounts receivable	(38,000.00)	3		
Decrease in merchandise inventory	29,442.00	4		
Increase in supplies and prepayments	(12,794.00)	5		
Decrease in accounts payable	(167,304.00)	6		
Increase in income tax payable	25,000.00	7		
Decrease in accrued and withheld payroll taxes	(5,304.00)	8		
Increase in accrued interest payable	40.00	9		
Noncash expenses and other adjustments:				
Loss on sale of delivery equipment	5,000.00	10		
Depreciation expense	139,000.00	11		
Net cash provided by operating activities				$ 383,086.00
Cash flows from investing activities:				
Sold delivery equipment	$ 10,000.00	10		
Purchase of store equipment	(142,000.00)	12		
Purchase of delivery equipment	(130,000.00)	13		
Purchase of office equipment	(40,100.00)	14		
Net cash used by investing activities				(302,100.00)
Cash flows from financing activities:				
Paid cash dividends	$(128,000.00)	15		
Issued common stock	30,000.00	16		
Retired notes payable	(17,200.00)	17		
Net cash used by financing activities				(115,200.00)
Net increase (decrease) in cash and cash equivalents			19	$ (34,214.00)
Cash and cash equivalents, January 1, 20-2				232,000.00
Cash and cash equivalents, December 31, 20-2				$ 197,786.00
Schedule of Noncash Investing and Financing Activities:				
Purchased office equipment by issuing a note payable			18	$ 12,000.00
Supplemental Disclosures of Cash Flow Information:				
Cash paid during the year for:				
Interest			20	$ 6,400.00
Income taxes			20	215,000.00

To compute cash paid for interest and taxes, prepare the following entries:

Interest Expense (see income statement)	6,440.00		
Accrued Interest Payable (increase in Acc. Int. Pay.)			40.00
Cash (plug)		20	6,400.00
Income Tax Expense (see income statement)	240,000.00		
Income Tax Payable (increase in income tax payable)			25,000.00
Cash (plug)		20	215,000.00

KEY TERMS

cash equivalents (884) Short-term, highly liquid investments that are considered the same as cash when preparing the statement of cash flows.

direct method (874) A method of preparing the statement of cash flows in which the revenues and expenses reported on the income statement are adjusted to reflect the amount of cash received or paid for each item.

financing activities (872) Transactions dealing with the exchange of cash between the company and its owners (stockholders) and creditors.

indirect method (874) A method of reporting cash from operating activities in which net income is adjusted for transactions that affect both net income and cash from operating activities, but in different ways.

investing activities (872) Transactions involving the purchase and sale of long-term assets, buying and selling debt and equity securities, and lending money and collecting the principal on the related loans.

noncash expenses (884) Expenses that reduce net income, but do not require an outflow of cash during the period.

noncash investing and financing activities (886) Investing and financing activities that involve no cash flows, but represent a significant change in the company's financial position.

operating activities (871) Transactions and events associated with selling a product or providing a service. They are related to the revenues and expenses reported on the income statement.

statement of cash flows (871) Statement of the cash flows associated with the operating, investing, and financing activities of the company.

SELF-STUDY QUESTIONS AND EXERCISES

True/False Questions

1. LO1 The purpose of the statement of cash flows is to provide information about total revenue and expenses.
2. LO2 Investing activities are those transactions dealing with the exchange of cash between the company and its stockholders and creditors.
3. LO5 An increase in accounts receivable is deducted from net income to compute cash from operating activities.
4. LO5 A decrease in inventory is added to net income to compute cash from operating activities.
5. LO8 (A BROADER VIEW) Generally, cash from operating activities should be greater than net income.

Multiple Choice Questions

1. LO2 The receipt of dividends on an investment is included on the statement of cash flows as a(n)

   (a) operating activity.
   (b) investing activity.
   (c) financing activity.
   (d) schedule of noncash investing and financing activities.

2. LO2 The purchase of new equipment is included on the statement of cash flows as a(n)

   (a) operating activity.
   (b) investing activity.
   (c) financing activity.
   (d) schedule of noncash investing and financing activities.

3. LO2 The payment of interest on a note payable is classified on the statement of cash flows as a(n)

   (a) operating activity.
   (b) investing activity.
   (c) financing activity.
   (d) schedule of noncash investing and financing activities.

4. LO2 The payment of a cash dividend to stockholders is classified on the statement of cash flows as a(n)

   (a) operating activity.
   (b) investing activity.
   (c) financing activity.
   (d) schedule of noncash investing and financing activities.

5. LO7 The acquisition of a building by signing a mortgage note payable is included on the statement of cash flows as a(n)

   (a) operating activity.
   (b) investing activity.
   (c) financing activity.
   (d) schedule of noncash investing and financing activities.

U REVU Exercises

1. LO2 Please classify the following activities as operating, investing, or financing.

   a. Received cash from the sale of goods.
   b. Paid cash to employees.
   c. Received interest on an investment.
   d. Paid cash for equipment.
   e. Paid principal on a loan.

2. LO4 The following events took place during the year.

   a. Sales during the year amounted to $500, and accounts receivable decreased by $30.
   b. Wage expense for the year amounted to $300 and wages payable decreased by $50.

   Compute cash from operating activities under the direct and indirect methods.

3. LO5 Indicate whether the following items increase or decrease cash from operating activities under the indirect method.

   a. Increase in accounts receivable.
   b. Increase in accounts payable.
   c. Increase in prepaid rent.
   d. Decrease in income taxes payable.

4. LO6 Describe how the following activities would be reported on a statement of cash flows prepared under the indirect method.

   a. Paid cash for equipment.
   b. Received cash from signing a long-term loan.
   c. Received cash for interest on an investment.
   d. Paid cash dividends to stockholders.

5. LO7(a) Kip Company has the following accounts on its balance sheet. Compute cash and cash equivalents.

Cash	$20,000
Government notes	5,000
Accounts receivable	30,000

6. LO7(b) and 7(c) Simon's Used Furniture earned net income of $50,000 during the year. All revenues and expenses were for cash except the following:

   a. Depreciation of $1,000.
   b. Gain on the sale of a delivery truck, $3,000.

   Compute cash from operating activities under the indirect method.

7. LO7(d) Brown Company signed a $500,000 mortgage to acquire an office building. How is this event reported on the statement of cash flows?

8. LO7(e) Brown Company also paid interest of $8,000 and income taxes of $40,000. How would this information be reported on the statement of cash flows?

Answers to the Self-Study Questions and Exercises are at the end of the chapter (pages 923–924).

REVIEW QUESTIONS

LO1 1. What is the primary purpose of the statement of cash flows?

LO1 2. Name the four principal financial statements comprising a full set of financial statements.

LO2 3. What are the three categories of cash flows shown on a statement of cash flows?

LO2 4. Name the types of cash flows associated with financing activities.

LO2 5. Name the types of cash flows associated with investing activities.

LO2 6. Name the types of cash flows associated with operating activities.

LO2 7. If a company pays cash dividends, where on the statement of cash flows should the payment be reported?

LO2 8. Where is cash received for interest reported on the statement of cash flows?

LO3 9. What information is needed to prepare a statement of cash flows?

LO4 10. Describe the direct method of reporting cash flows from operating activities.

LO4 11. Describe the indirect method of reporting cash flows from operating activities.

LO5 12. Under the indirect method of preparing a statement of cash flows, what adjustment is made to net income if accounts payable increased from last year?

LO5 13. Under the indirect method of preparing a statement of cash flows, what adjustment is made to net income if accounts receivable increased from last year?

LO6/7 14. List the six steps to be followed when preparing a statement of cash flows. Be sure to include all aspects of the statement's preparation.

LO7 15. Explain the procedure for verifying the accuracy of the statement of cash flows.

LO7 16. What are cash equivalents?

LO7 17. Under the indirect method of preparing a statement of cash flows, what adjustment is made for depreciation expense?

LO7 18. Under the indirect method of preparing a statement of cash flows, what adjustment is made for gains and losses on the sale of equipment.

LO7 19. Provide an example of a noncash investing and financing activity.

LO7 20. List the two supplemental disclosures required under the indirect method.

LO8 21. What is the most important value reported on the statement of cash flows when evaluating the financial health of a company?

SERIES A EXERCISES

E 23-1A (LO2)

IDENTIFICATION OF OPERATING, INVESTING, AND FINANCING ACTIVITIES The following activities took place during the current year. Indicate whether each activity is a cash inflow (+) or cash outflow (–), and whether it is an operating activity (O), an investing activity (I), or a financing activity (F).

(a) Proceeds from collection of principal amount of loans made to borrowers
(b) Cash receipts from the sale of goods
(c) Payments for interest on loans
(d) Payments of dividends to stockholders
(e) Payments to acquire investments in debt securities
(f) Dividends received on investments made in the stock of other corporations
(g) Repayment of the principal on loans
(h) Interest received on loans made to outside entities
(i) Salaries paid to employees
(j) Payments to acquire property, plant, and equipment and other productive assets
(k) Payments to purchase treasury stock
(l) Proceeds from the sale of common stock

E 23-2A (LO7)
✓ Increase in cash and cash equivalents: $17,000

CHANGE IN CASH AND CASH EQUIVALENTS Himes Company's balance sheets as of December 31, 20-2 and 20-1, showed the following with regard to cash and cash equivalents:

	20-2	20-1
Cash	$70,000	$50,000
Government notes	2,000	5,000

Compute the amount of change in cash and cash equivalents and indicate whether it represented an increase or a decrease.

E 23-3A (LO5)
✓ Net cash provided by operating activities: $26,000

ADJUSTING NET INCOME FOR CHANGES IN CURRENT ASSETS AND CURRENT LIABILITIES Lloyd Company reported net income of $25,000 for 20-2. The December 31 balances of the current assets and current liabilities are shown below.

	20-2	20-1
Accounts Receivable	$ 5,000	$ 3,000
Merchandise Inventory	25,000	30,000
Accounts Payable	20,000	18,000
Wages Payable	8,000	12,000

Compute cash provided by operating activities.

E 23-4A (LO7)
✓ Net cash provided by operating activities: $50,000

ADJUSTING NET INCOME FOR NONCASH EXPENSES After adjusting net income for changes in current assets and current liabilities, Penguin Tuxedo's cash from operating activities is $40,000. However, Penguin reports $10,000 in depreciation expense for the year. Compute cash from operating activities after considering the impact of depreciation.

E 23-5A (LO7)
✓ Net cash provided by operating activities: $400

GAINS AND LOSSES ON THE SALE OF LONG-TERM ASSETS The income statement for Hubbard's Professional Edge Tennis Camp follows. Assume that all revenues and expenses were for cash and that land was sold for $500. There were no other investing or financing activities during the year. The Cash balances at the beginning and end of the year were $100 and $1,000, respectively. Prepare a statement of cash flows under the indirect method.

Hubbard's Professional Edge Tennis Camp
Income Statement
For Year Ended December 31, 20-2

Sales (all cash)		$2,000.00
Wages expense (all cash)		1,600.00
Operating income		$ 400.00
Gain on sale of land		100.00
Net income		$ 500.00

E 23-6A (LO6)
✓ Net cash provided by financing activities: $60,000

CASH FLOWS FROM INVESTING AND FINANCING ACTIVITIES Rogerson Company's comparative balance sheet as of December 31, 20-2 and 20-1, showed the following with regard to investing and financing activities:

	20-2	20-1
Building	$130,000	$ 0
Equipment	90,000	0
Notes payable	30,000	20,000
Common stock at par	300,000	250,000
Paid-in capital in excess of par	80,000	50,000
Retained earnings	260,000	200,000

Net income for 20-2 was $90,000, and cash dividends of $30,000 were declared and paid. Rogerson did not sell any buildings or equipment and did not retire any debt. Determine the amount of cash received and paid for financing and investing activities and the cash flows as they would appear on Rogerson's statement of cash flows for the year ended December 31, 20-2.

E 23-7A (LO7)

NONCASH INVESTING AND FINANCING ACTIVITIES Norton's Sign Shop issued a $10,000, three-year note payable to acquire a new framing machine. Show how this transaction is reported on a statement of cash flows.

E 23-8A (LO7)
✓ Cash paid for interest: $1,500

CASH PAID FOR INTEREST Ball Company's income statement for 20-2 reported interest expense of $1,540. The comparative balance sheet as of December 31, 20-2 and 20-1, reported the following:

	20-2	20-1
Accrued interest payable	$260	$220

Compute the amount of cash paid for interest in 20-2.

SERIES A PROBLEMS

P 23-9A (LO7)
✓ Net cash provided by operating activities: $160,000

COMPUTE CASH PROVIDED BY OPERATING ACTIVITIES Mueller Company's condensed income statement for the year ended December 31, 20-2, was as follows:

Net sales	$900,000
Cost of goods sold	500,000
Gross profit	$400,000
Operating expenses	185,000
Income before taxes	$215,000
Income tax expense	75,000
Net income	$140,000

(continued)

Additional information obtained from Mueller's comparative balance sheets as of December 31, 20-2 and 20-1, was as follows:

	20-2	20-1
Cash and cash equivalents	$ 50,000	$ 10,000
Accounts receivable	80,000	90,000
Merchandise inventory	120,000	150,000
Accounts payable	60,000	80,000

REQUIRED

Prepare a partial statement of cash flows reporting cash provided by operating activities for the year ended December 31, 20-2.

P 23-10A (LO7)
✓ Net increase in cash and cash equivalents: $40,000

STATEMENT OF CASH FLOWS Refer to Problem 23-9A. The following additional information was obtained from Mueller's financial statements and auxiliary records for the year ended December 31, 20-2:

Acquired a new warehouse	$120,000
Bought new warehouse equipment	80,000
Issued a note to the bank	40,000
Issued additional common stock:	
Par value	50,000
Paid-in capital in excess of par	20,000
Declared and paid cash dividends	30,000

REQUIRED

Prepare a statement of cash flows for Mueller for the year ended December 31, 20-2.

P 23-11A (LO7)
✓ Net cash provided by operating activities: $206,070

COMPUTE CASH PROVIDED BY OPERATING ACTIVITIES Horn Company's condensed income statement for the year ended December 31, 20-2, was as follows:

Net sales		$1,220,000
Cost of goods sold		740,000
Gross profit		$ 480,000
Operating expenses		142,000
Operating income		$ 338,000
Other revenues and expenses:		
Interest revenue	$ 420	
Interest expense	(1,200)	(780)
Income before taxes		$ 337,220
Income tax expense		118,000
Net income		$ 219,220

Additional information obtained from Horn's comparative balance sheet and auxiliary records as of December 31, 20-2 and 20-1, was as follows:

	20-2	20-1
Accounts receivable	$135,000	$122,600
Merchandise inventory	145,300	158,900
Accounts payable	45,000	87,100
Income tax payable	2,000	1,000
Supplies and prepayments	11,300	6,800
Accrued and withheld payroll taxes	2,750	3,700
Accrued interest receivable	90	210
Accrued interest payable	240	160

Depreciation expense for 20-2, included in operating expenses on the income statement, was $32,000.

REQUIRED

Prepare a partial statement of cash flows reporting cash provided by operating activities for the year ended December 31, 20-2.

P 23-12A (LO7)
✓ Operating activities: $152,840
Investing activities: ($209,000)
Financing activities: $80,000

EXPANDED STATEMENT OF CASH FLOWS Financial statements for McDowell Company as well as additional information relevant to cash flows during the period are given below and on page 914.

McDowell Company
Income Statement
For Year Ended December 31, 20-2

Net sales		$1,890,000.00
Cost of goods sold		940,000.00
Gross profit		$ 950,000.00
Operating expenses		572,300.00
Operating income		$ 377,700.00
Other revenues and expenses:		
Interest revenue	$ 3,900.00	
Interest expense	(890.00)	
Loss on sale of store equipment	(15,000.00)	(11,990.00)
Income before taxes		$ 365,710.00
Income tax expense		133,000.00
Net income		$ 232,710.00

McDowell Company
Statement of Retained Earnings
For Year Ended December 31, 20-2

Retained earnings, January 1, 20-2		$360,000.00
Net income	$232,710.00	
Less dividends	60,000.00	
Net increase in retained earnings		172,710.00
Retained earnings, December 31, 20-2		$532,710.00

Additional information:

1. Store equipment was sold in 20-2 for $25,000. Additional information on the store equipment sold is provided below.

Cost	$ 70,000
Accumulated depreciation	(30,000)
Book value	$ 40,000
Market value	25,000
Loss on sale	$ 15,000

2. Depreciation expense for the year was $112,000.
3. The following purchases were made for cash:

Store equipment	$ 64,000
Delivery equipment	140,000
Office equipment	30,000
	$234,000

(continued)

McDowell Company
Comparative Balance Sheet
December 31, 20-2 and 20-1

	20-2		20-1		INCREASE (DECREASE)
Assets					
Current assets:					
Cash	$75,365.00		$40,325.00		$35,040.00
Government notes	6,800.00		18,000.00		(11,200.00)
Accrued interest receivable	720.00		610.00		110.00
Accounts receivable (net)	310,700.00		325,800.00		(15,100.00)
Merchandise inventory	685,400.00		540,200.00		145,200.00
Supplies and prepayments	27,000.00		39,000.00		(12,000.00)
Total current assets		$1,105,985.00		$963,935.00	142,050.00
Property, plant, and equipment:					
Store equipment	$470,000.00		$460,000.00		10,000.00
Less accumulated depreciation—store equipment	180,000.00	290,000.00	150,000.00	310,000.00	30,000.00
Delivery equipment	$530,000.00		$390,000.00		140,000.00
Less accumulated depreciation—delivery equipment	140,000.00	390,000.00	100,000.00	290,000.00	40,000.00
Office equipment	$430,000.00		$400,000.00		30,000.00
Less accumulated depreciation—office equipment	88,000.00	342,000.00	76,000.00	324,000.00	12,000.00
Total property, plant, and equipment		$1,022,000.00		$924,000.00	98,000.00
Total assets		$2,127,985.00		$1,887,935.00	240,050.00
Liabilities					
Current liabilities:					
Notes payable	$118,000.00		$102,000.00		16,000.00
Accounts payable	110,000.00		195,000.00		(85,000.00)
Income tax payable	20,000.00		25,000.00		(5,000.00)
Accrued and withheld payroll taxes	16,400.00		14,900.00		1,500.00
Accrued interest payable	875.00		1,035.00		(160.00)
Total current liabilities		$265,275.00		$337,935.00	(72,660.00)
Stockholders' Equity					
Common stock ($10 par, 300,000 shares authorized;					
Issued: 90,000 in 20-2 and 80,000 in 20-1)	$900,000.00		$800,000.00		100,000.00
Paid-in capital in excess of par—common stock	430,000.00		390,000.00		40,000.00
Retained earnings	532,710.00		360,000.00		172,710.00
Total stockholders' equity		1,862,710.00		1,550,000.00	312,710.00
Total liabilities and stockholders' equity		$2,127,985.00		$1,887,935.00	240,050.00

4. Declared and paid cash dividends of $60,000.
5. Issued 10,000 shares of $10 par common stock for $14 per share.
6. Acquired additional store equipment by issuing a note payable for $16,000.

REQUIRED

Prepare a statement of cash flows explaining the change in cash and cash equivalents for the year ended December 31, 20-2.

SERIES B EXERCISES

E 23-1B (LO2)

IDENTIFICATION OF OPERATING, INVESTING, AND FINANCING ACTIVITIES The following activities took place in Tomberlin Company during the most recent year. Indicate whether each activity is a cash inflow (+) or cash outflow (–), and whether it is an operating activity (O), investing activity (I), or financing activity (F).

(a) Payments to acquire productive assets
(b) Proceeds from the issuance of stock
(c) Interest received on loans made to outside entities
(d) Proceeds from the sale of productive assets
(e) Dividends received on investments made in the stock of other corporations
(f) Payments to other suppliers and for other expenses
(g) Payments of dividends to stockholders
(h) Payments to acquire investments in debt securities
(i) Payments for interest on loans
(j) Cash receipts from the sale of services
(k) Repayment of the principal on loans
(l) Payments for the acquisition of inventory

E 23-2B (LO7)
✓ Increase in cash and cash equivalents: $26,000

CHANGE IN CASH AND CASH EQUIVALENTS Pike Company's balance sheets as of December 31, 20-2 and 20-1, showed the following with regard to cash and cash equivalents:

	20-2	20-1
Cash	$90,000	$60,000
Government notes	4,000	8,000

Compute the amount of change in cash and cash equivalents and indicate whether it represented an increase or a decrease.

E 23-3B (LO6)
✓ Net cash provided by operating activities: $48,000

ADJUSTING NET INCOME FOR CHANGES IN CURRENT ASSETS AND CURRENT LIABILITIES Roberts Company reported net income of $50,000 for 20-2. The December 31 balances of the current assets and current liabilities are shown below.

	20-2	20-1
Accounts Receivable	$ 6,000	$10,000
Merchandise Inventory	60,000	50,000
Accounts Payable	36,000	40,000
Wages Payable	24,000	16,000

Compute cash provided by operating activities.

E 23-4B (LO7)
✓ Net cash provided by operating activities: $65,000

ADJUSTING NET INCOME FOR NONCASH EXPENSES After adjusting net income for changes in current assets and current liabilities, Cha Cha Dance Company's cash from operating activities is $60,000. However, Cha Cha reports $5,000 in patent amortization expense for the year. Compute cash from operating activities after considering the impact of amortization.

E 23-5B (LO7)
✓ Total cash provided by operating activities: $2,000

GAINS AND LOSSES ON THE SALE OF LONG-TERM ASSETS The income statement for Leadbetter's Golf Camp follows. Assume that all revenues and expenses were for cash and that land was sold for $600. There were no other investing or financing activities during the year. The Cash balances at the beginning and end of the year were $1,000 and $3,600, respectively. Prepare a statement of cash flows under the indirect method.

(continued)

Leadbetter's Golf Camp Income Statement For Year Ended December 31, 20-2		
Sales (all cash)		$5,000.00
Wages expense (all cash)		3,000.00
Operating income		$2,000.00
Loss on sale of land		200.00
Net income		$1,800.00

E 23-6B (LO6)
✓ Total cash used by investing activities: ($230,000)

CASH FLOWS FROM INVESTING AND FINANCING ACTIVITIES Hansen Company's comparative balance sheets as of December 31, 20-2 and 20-1, showed the following with regard to investing and financing activities:

	20-2	20-1
Building	$160,000	$ 0
Equipment	70,000	0
Notes payable	20,000	30,000
Common stock at par	260,000	200,000
Paid-in capital in excess of par	60,000	40,000
Retained earnings	220,000	160,000

Net income for 20-2 was $80,000, and cash dividends of $20,000 were declared and paid. Hansen did not sell any buildings or equipment and did not retire any debt. Determine the amount of cash received and paid for financing and investing activities and the cash flows as they would appear on Hansen's statement of cash flows for the year ended December 31, 20-2.

E 23-7B (LO7)

NONCASH INVESTING AND FINANCING ACTIVITIES Murry's consulting services issued a two-year, $5,000 note payable to acquire new office furniture. Show how this transaction is reported on the statement of cash flows.

E 23-8B (LO7)
✓ Cash paid for interest: $2,260

CASH PAID FOR INTEREST Mulligan Company's income statement for 20-2 reported interest expense of $2,190. The comparative balance sheet as of December 31, 20-2 and 20-1, reported the following:

	20-2	20-1
Accrued interest payable	$340	$410

Compute the amount of cash paid for interest in 20-2.

SERIES B PROBLEMS

P 23-9B (LO7)
✓ Net cash provided by operating activities: $155,000

COMPUTE CASH PROVIDED BY OPERATING ACTIVITIES Kennington Company's condensed income statement for the year ended December 31, 20-2, was as follows:

Net sales	$800,000
Cost of goods sold	475,000
Gross profit	$325,000
Operating expenses	148,000
Income before taxes	$177,000
Income tax expense	62,000
Net income	$115,000

Additional information obtained from Kennington's comparative balance sheet as of December 31, 20-2 and 20-1, was as follows:

	20-2	20-1
Cash and cash equivalents	$75,000	$ 20,000
Accounts receivable	50,000	75,000
Merchandise inventory	70,000	110,000
Accounts payable	25,000	50,000

REQUIRED

Prepare a partial statement of cash flows reporting cash provided by operating activities for the year ended December 31, 20-2.

P 23-10B (LO7)
✓ Net increase in cash and cash equivalents: $55,000

STATEMENT OF CASH FLOWS Refer to Problem 23-9B. The following additional information was obtained from Kennington's financial statements and auxiliary records for the year ended December 31, 20-2.

Acquired a new warehouse	$90,000
Bought new warehouse equipment	60,000
Issued a note to the bank	30,000
Issued additional common stock:	
Par value	30,000
Paid-in capital in excess of par	10,000
Declared and paid cash dividends	20,000

REQUIRED

Prepare a statement of cash flows for Kennington for the year ended December 31, 20-2.

P 23-11B (LO7)
✓ Net cash provided by operating activities: $179,395

COMPUTE CASH PROVIDED BY OPERATING ACTIVITIES Powell Company's condensed income statement for the year ended December 31, 20-2, was as follows:

Net sales		$1,160,000
Cost of goods sold		690,000
Gross profit		$ 470,000
Operating expenses		224,100
Operating income		$ 245,900
Other revenues and expenses:		
Interest revenue	$ 560	
Interest expense	(1,100)	(540)
Income before taxes		$ 245,360
Income tax expense		86,000
Net income		$ 159,360

Additional information obtained from Powell's comparative balance sheet and auxiliary records as of December 31, 20-2 and 20-1, was as follows:

	20-2	20-1
Accounts receivable	$122,700	$118,200
Merchandise inventory	116,800	139,300
Accounts payable	31,500	47,400
Income tax payable	10,000	15,000
Supplies and prepayments	10,900	5,200
Accrued and withheld payroll taxes	1,960	2,490
Accrued interest receivable	130	175
Accrued interest payable	230	110

(continued)

Depreciation expense for 20-2, included in operating expenses on the income statement, was $29,000.

REQUIRED

Prepare a partial statement of cash flows reporting cash provided by operating activities for the year ended December 31, 20-2.

P 23-12B (LO7)
✓ Operating activities: $99,300
Investing activities: ($237,000)
Financing activities: $180,000

EXPANDED STATEMENT OF CASH FLOWS Financial statements for McGinnis Company as well as additional information relevant to cash flows during the period are given below and on the next page.

McGinnis Company
Income Statement
For Year Ended December 31, 20-2

Net sales		$1,750,000.00
Cost of goods sold		890,000.00
Gross profit		$ 860,000.00
Operating expenses		590,600.00
Operating income		$ 269,400.00
Other revenues and expenses:		
Interest revenue	$ 2,700.00	
Interest expense	(750.00)	
Gain on sale of office equipment	15,000.00	16,950.00
Income before taxes		$ 286,350.00
Income tax expense		95,000.00
Net income		$ 191,350.00

McGinnis Company
Statement of Retained Earnings
For Year Ended December 31, 20-2

Retained earnings, January 1, 20-2		$320,000.00
Net income	$191,350.00	
Less dividends	40,000.00	
Net increase in retained earnings		151,350.00
Retained earnings, December 31, 20-2		$471,350.00

Additional information:

1. Office equipment was sold in 20-2 for $35,000. Additional information on the office equipment sold is provided below.

Cost	$100,000
Accumulated depreciation	(80,000)
Book value	$ 20,000
Market value	35,000
Gain on sale	$ 15,000

2. Depreciation expense for the year was $70,000.
3. The following purchases were made for cash:

Store equipment	$140,000
Delivery equipment	100,000
Office equipment	32,000
	$272,000

4. Declared and paid cash dividends of $40,000.
5. Issued 10,000 shares of $10 par common stock for $22 per share.
6. Acquired additional office equipment by issuing a note payable for $8,000.

McGinnis Company
Comparative Balance Sheet
December 31, 20-2 and 20-1

	20-2		20-1		INCREASE (DECREASE)
Assets					
Current assets:					
Cash	$103,420.00		$ 50,520.00		$ 52,900.00
Government notes	5,400.00		16,000.00		(10,600.00)
Accrued interest receivable	830.00		580.00		250.00
Accounts receivable (net)	300,600.00		309,200.00		(8,600.00)
Merchandise inventory	580,300.00		495,800.00		84,500.00
Supplies and prepayments	65,000.00		32,000.00		33,000.00
Total current assets		$1,055,550.00		$ 904,100.00	151,450.00
Property, plant, and equipment:					
Store equipment	$560,000.00		$420,000.00		140,000.00
Less accumulated depreciation—store equipment	120,000.00	440,000.00	90,000.00	330,000.00	30,000.00
Delivery equipment	$430,000.00		$330,000.00		100,000.00
Less accumulated depreciation—delivery equipment	150,000.00	280,000.00	120,000.00	210,000.00	30,000.00
Office equipment	$320,000.00		$380,000.00		(60,000.00)
Less accumulated depreciation—office equipment	30,500.00	289,500.00	100,500.00	279,500.00	(70,000.00)
Total property, plant, and equipment		$1,009,500.00		$ 819,500.00	190,000.00
Total assets		$2,065,050.00		$1,723,600.00	341,450.00
Liabilities					
Current liabilities:					
Notes payable	$117,000.00		$109,000.00		8,000.00
Accounts payable	135,000.00		185,000.00		(50,000.00)
Income tax payable	25,000.00		15,000.00		10,000.00
Accrued and withheld payroll taxes	15,800.00		13,400.00		2,400.00
Accrued interest payable	900.00		1,200.00		(300.00)
Total current liabilities		$ 293,700.00		$ 323,600.00	(29,900.00)
Stockholders' Equity					
Common stock ($10 par, 400,000 shares authorized;					
Issued: 80,000 in 20-2 and 70,000 in 20-1)	$800,000.00		$700,000.00		100,000.00
Paid-in capital in excess of par—common stock	500,000.00		380,000.00		120,000.00
Retained earnings	471,350.00		320,000.00		151,350.00
Total stockholders' equity		1,771,350.00		1,400,000.00	371,350.00
Total liabilities and stockholders' equity		$2,065,050.00		$1,723,600.00	341,450.00

REQUIRED

Prepare a statement of cash flows explaining the change in cash and cash equivalents for the year ended December 31, 20-2.

MANAGING YOUR WRITING

Direct Method

A friend of yours was looking at a schedule for the calculation of cash generated from operating activities prepared under the direct method and asked why depreciation expense is deducted from operating expenses. He is curious why depreciation is not considered an expense. Write a brief memo that explains why depreciation expense is deducted from operating expenses when preparing this schedule.

Indirect Method

A friend of yours was reading a statement of cash flows prepared under the indirect method and saw that depreciation expense was added when computing cash from operating activities. She is curious why depreciation is considered a source of cash. Write a brief memo that explains why depreciation expense is added to net income on the statement of cash flows and why it certainly is not a source of cash.

ETHICS CASE

Lyle McGee had been the chief accountant at L & B Corporation for well over 20 years. He routinely omitted noncash investing and financing activities from the statement of cash flows, even when they were significant events. When a junior accountant who had just been hired questioned this practice, Lyle told her that it doesn't make any difference how significant an item is "if it doesn't involve cash. Besides, we're a small company and our stockholders are only interested in the bottom line."

1. Is it possible that Lyle thinks he is treating the significant noncash investing and financing activities properly?
2. If you were the junior accountant, what would you do?
3. Suppose that Lyle wants the junior accountant to give him a refresher course on the statement of cash flows. Write a brief memo to Lyle explaining the purpose of the statement of cash flows. Include a description of both the direct and indirect methods. Also, explain the importance of including significant noncash investing and financing activities.
4. In groups of two or three, discuss which method of preparing the statement of cash flows is easier for you to understand, the direct or the indirect, and why.

MASTERY PROBLEM

Financial statements for Peachfield Corporation as well as additional information relevant to cash flows during the period follow.

Peachfield Corporation
Income Statement
For Year Ended December 31, 20-2

Net sales		$985,000.00
Cost of goods sold		515,000.00
Gross profit		$470,000.00
Operating expenses		299,400.00
Operating income		$170,600.00
Other revenues and expenses:		
Gain on sale of office equipment	$5,000.00	
Interest revenue	2,100.00	
Interest expense	(436.00)	6,664.00
Income before taxes		$177,264.00
Income tax expense		60,500.00
Net income		$116,764.00

Peachfield Corporation
Statement of Retained Earnings
For Year Ended December 31, 20-2

Retained earnings, January 1, 20-2		$141,973.00
Net income	$116,764.00	
Less dividends	20,000.00	
Net increase in retained earnings		96,764.00
Retained earnings, December 31, 20-2		$238,737.00

Additional information:

1. Office equipment was sold during the year for $75,000.

Cost	$ 80,000
Accumulated depreciation	(10,000)
Book value	$ 70,000
Market value	75,000
Gain	$ 5,000

2. Depreciation expense for the year was $62,400 as follows:

Store equipment	$24,000
Delivery equipment	27,000
Office equipment	11,400
	$62,400

3. No other equipment was sold during the year. The following purchases were made for cash.

Store equipment	$ 55,200
Delivery equipment	78,000
Office equipment	24,060
	$157,260

(continued)

4. Declared and paid cash dividends of $20,000.
5. Issued 11,200 shares of $10 par common stock for $118,000.
6. Issued a note payable for $10,700.
7. Additional store equipment was acquired by issuing a long-term note payable for $20,000.

Peachfield Corporation
Comparative Balance Sheet
December 31, 20-2 and 20-1

	2002		2001		INCREASE (DECREASE)
Assets					
Current assets:					
Cash	$102,072.00		$ 27,200.00		$ 74,872.00
Government notes	3,600.00		12,000.00		(8,400.00)
Accrued interest receivable	320.00		250.00		70.00
Accounts receivable (net)	152,945.00		140,905.00		12,040.00
Merchandise inventory	355,490.00		295,400.00		60,090.00
Supplies and prepayments	14,500.00		21,500.00		(7,000.00)
Total current assets		$ 628,927.00		$497,255.00	131,672.00
Property, plant, and equipment:					
Store equipment	$308,000.00		$232,800.00		75,200.00
Less accumulated depreciation—store equipment	108,000.00	200,000.00	84,000.00	148,800.00	24,000.00
Delivery equipment	$270,000.00		$192,000.00		78,000.00
Less accumulated depreciation—delivery equipment	75,000.00	195,000.00	48,000.00	144,000.00	27,000.00
Office equipment	$148,000.00		$203,940.00		(55,940.00)
Less accumulated depreciation—office equipment	38,000.00	110,000.00	36,600.00	167,340.00	1,400.00
Total property, plant, and equipment		$ 505,000.00		$460,140.00	44,860.00
Total assets		$1,133,927.00		$957,395.00	176,532.00
Liabilities					
Current liabilities:					
Notes payable	$ 65,480.00		$ 54,780.00		10,700.00
Accounts payable	53,500.00		125,473.00		(71,973.00)
Income tax payable	7,000.00		5,000.00		2,000.00
Accrued and withheld payroll taxes	8,760.00		7,644.00		1,116.00
Accrued interest payable	450.00		525.00		(75.00)
Total current liabilities		$ 135,190.00		$193,422.00	(58,232.00)
Long-term liabilities:					
Notes payable		20,000.00			20,000.00
Total liabilities		$ 155,190.00		$193,422.00	(38,232.00)
Stockholders' Equity					
Common stock ($10 par, 1,000,000 shares authorized;					
Issued: 50,000 in 20-2 and 38,800 in 20-1)	$500,000.00		$388,000.00		112,000.00
Paid-in capital in excess of par—common stock	240,000.00		234,000.00		6,000.00
Retained earnings	238,737.00		141,973.00		96,764.00
Total stockholders' equity		978,737.00		763,973.00	214,764.00
Total liabilities and stockholders' equity		$1,133,927.00		$957,395.00	176,532.00

REQUIRED

1. Prepare a statement of cash flows explaining the change in cash and cash equivalents.
2. Reconcile cash and cash equivalents at the bottom of the statement of cash flows.

CHALLENGE PROBLEM

This problem challenges you to apply your cumulative accounting knowledge to move a step beyond the material in the chapter.

✓ **Cash received from bond issuance: $797,423**

The long-term liabilities section of Guyton Enterprises follows. The bonds outstanding on January 1, 20-1, have an annual coupon rate of 4% and had been issued several years ago at a price to yield 5% per year. The discount is amortized using the effective interest method. On December 31, 20-1, $900,000, 5% bonds were issued at a price to yield 6%.

Long-Term Liabilities	December 31, 20-1	January 1, 20-1
Bonds payable	$1,900,000	$1,000,000
Discount on bonds payable	(202,461)	(104,651)
Total long-term liabilities	$1,697,539	$ 895,349

REQUIRED

Compute the cash received from issuing the bonds on December 31, 20-1. (*Hint*: If you have not covered the effective interest method, assume that bond interest expense for 20-1 was $44,767.)

ANSWERS TO SELF-STUDY QUESTIONS AND EXERCISES

True/False Questions

1. F (Cash flows)
2. F (Investing is buying and selling long-term assets, debt and equity securities, and lending money and collecting principal on the related loans.)
3. T
4. T
5. T

Multiple Choice Questions

1. a 2. b 3. a 4. c 5. d

U REVU Exercises

1. a. Operating
   b. Operating
   c. Operating
   d. Investing
   e. Financing

2. Direct method statement of cash flows:

Cash received from customers	$ 530
Cash paid to employees	(350)
Cash from operating activities	$ 180

Indirect method statement of cash flows:

Net income	$200
Decrease in accounts receivable	30
Decrease in wages payable	(50)
Cash from operating activities	$180

3. a. Decrease
   b. Increase
   c. Decrease
   d. Decrease

4. a. Outflow from investing activities
   b. Inflow from financing activities
   c. It is included in net income under operating activities. This one is difficult. Recall that the receipt of interest is defined as an operating activity. The interest revenue is included on the income statement and, thus, included in net income on the statement of cash flows. If the interest revenue is equal to the cash received, there is no need to make any additional adjustment to the statement.
   d. Cash outflow from financing activities.

5. Cash and cash equivalents:

Cash	$20,000
Government notes	5,000
Cash and cash equivalents	$25,000

6.

Net income	$50,000
Noncash expenses and other adjustments:	
Depreciation expense	1,000
Gain on sale of truck	(3,000)
Net cash provided by operating activities	$48,000

7. Noncash investing and financing activities:
   Signed mortgage to acquire office building $500,000

8. Interest and income tax expenses are included in net income under operating activities and adjusted for changes in interest and/or income taxes payable. Since the cash paid for these items is not readily recognizable, firms are required to report these amounts as supplemental disclosures as shown below.

   Supplemental disclosure of cash flow information:
   Cash paid during the year for:

Interest	$ 8,000
Income taxes	40,000

Chapter 23: Appendix

Statement of Cash Flows: The Direct Method

LEARNING OBJECTIVES

Careful study of this appendix should enable you to:

LO1 Describe the direct method of reporting cash flows from operating activities.

LO2 Prepare a schedule for the calculation of cash generated from operating activities under the direct method by adjusting revenues and expenses for changes in current assets and current liabilities associated with operations.

LO3 Prepare a schedule for the calculation of cash generated from operating activities under the direct method, including adjustments when the company reports:

a. changes in current assets and current liabilities associated with operations,

b. depreciation expense,

c. gains or losses on the sale of long-term assets,

d. receivables and payables associated with interest revenue, interest expense, and tax expense.

LO4 Prepare a statement of cash flows under the direct method.

This appendix illustrates the direct method of reporting cash flows from operating activities. As discussed earlier, the method of preparing the statement of cash flows only affects the presentation of cash flows from operating activities. The reporting of cash flows from investing and financing activities is identical under the direct and indirect methods.

THE DIRECT METHOD

LO1 Describe the direct method of reporting cash flows from operating activities.

Under the direct method, revenues and expenses reported on the income statement are adjusted to reflect the cash received or paid for each item. Since the investing and financing sections of the statement are identical under both methods, only the cash from operating activities section will be illustrated for Simplex.

CASH FROM OPERATING ACTIVITIES UNDER THE DIRECT METHOD: SIMPLEX

LO2 Prepare a schedule for the calculation of cash generated from operating activities under the direct method by adjusting revenues and expenses for changes in current assets and current liabilities associated with operations.

Simplex Company was used to illustrate the indirect method in the chapter. The same company is used here to provide the opportunity to compare the two methods. Figure 23A-1 provides the financial statements and additional information for Simplex.

To compute cash generated from operating activities, a schedule like the one shown in Figure 23A-2 is prepared. Revenues and expenses reported on the income statement are converted to cash received or paid for operating purposes. Column 1 reports the revenue or expense as reported on the income statement. Columns 2 and 3 are used to make additions or subtractions necessary to reflect the associated cash flows in column 4.

FIGURE 23A-1 Financial Statements and Additional Information for Simplex

Simplex Company
Income Statement
For Year Ended December 31, 20-2

Net sales		$900,000.00
Cost of goods sold		600,000.00
Gross profit		$300,000.00
Operating expenses		177,000.00
Income before taxes		$123,000.00
Income tax expense		43,000.00
Net income		$ 80,000.00

Simplex Company
Statement of Retained Earnings
For Year Ended December 31, 20-2

Retained earnings, January 1, 20-2		$ 50,000.00
Net income	$80,000.00	
Less dividends	20,000.00	
Net increase in retained earnings		60,000.00
Retained earnings, December 31, 20-2		$110,000.00

Simplex Company
Comparative Balance Sheet
December 31, 20-2 and 20-1

	20-2	20-1	INCREASE (DECREASE)
Assets			
Current assets:			
Cash	$ 90,000.00	$200,000.00	$(110,000.00)
Accounts receivable	160,000.00	190,000.00	(30,000.00)
Merchandise inventory	180,000.00	200,000.00	(20,000.00)
Total current assets	$430,000.00	$590,000.00	(160,000.00)
Property, plant, and equipment:			
Land	$ 40,000.00	$ 40,000.00	0.00
Building	140,000.00		140,000.00
Equipment	100,000.00		100,000.00
Total property, plant, and equipment	$280,000.00	$ 40,000.00	240,000.00
Total assets	$710,000.00	$630,000.00	80,000.00
Liabilities			
Current liabilities:			
Notes payable	$ 60,000.00	$ 50,000.00	10,000.00
Accounts payable	120,000.00	180,000.00	(60,000.00)
Total liabilities	$180,000.00	$230,000.00	(50,000.00)
Stockholders' Equity			
Common stock ($5 par, 100,000 shares authorized;			
Issued: 58,000 in 20-2, 50,000 in 20-1)	$290,000.00	$250,000.00	40,000.00
Paid-in capital in excess of par—common stock	130,000.00	100,000.00	30,000.00
Retained earnings	110,000.00	50,000.00	60,000.00
Total stockholders' equity	$530,000.00	$400,000.00	130,000.00
Total liabilities and stockholders' equity	$710,000.00	$630,000.00	80,000.00

Additional Information for 20-2:

1. Acquired a building and equipment for cash just before the year-end.
2. Issued 8,000 shares of common stock for $8.75 per share.
3. Declared and paid cash dividends of $20,000.

FIGURE 23A-2 Schedule for the Calculation of Cash Generated from Operating Activities for Simplex: Direct Method

Simplex Company
Schedule for the Calculation of Cash Generated from Operating Activities
For Year Ended December 31, 20-2

INCOME STATEMENT		ADDITIONS	DEDUCTIONS	CASH FLOWS	
Net sales	$900,000	1 $30,000		$930,000	Cash received from customers
Cost of goods sold	600,000	3 60,000	2 $(20,000)	640,000	Cash paid for merchandise
Gross profit	$300,000			$290,000	
Operating expenses	177,000			177,000	Cash paid for operating expenses
Income before taxes	$123,000			$113,000	
Income tax expense	43,000			43,000	Cash paid for income taxes
Net income	$ 80,000			$ 70,000	Cash generated from operating activities

1 The $30,000 reduction in receivables is added to sales to compute cash received from customers.

2 The $20,000 reduction in inventory is subtracted from cost of goods sold to compute the cost of merchandise purchased ($600,000 – $20,000 = $580,000).

3 Reducing the amount owed to suppliers (Accounts Payable) required the expenditure of additional cash. By adding the reduction in Accounts Payable to the cost of merchandise purchased, cash paid for merchandise is determined ($580,000 + $60,000 = $640,000).

CASH RECEIVED FROM CUSTOMERS

The income statement for Simplex reports $900,000 in sales during the year. Remember that revenues are recognized when earned, regardless of the amount of cash actually received. To prepare the statement of cash flows, these revenues must be converted to the amount of *cash received from customers during the year*.

If all sales were made for cash, it would not be necessary to adjust sales reported on the income statement. However, the balance sheet reports that accounts receivable decreased by $30,000 ($190,000 – $160,000) this year. The decrease in receivables increases the cash received from customers. This relationship is most easily understood by observing the summary entry in Figure 23A-3.

FIGURE 23A-3 Cash Received from Customers

Cash

	Debit	Credit
(2)	930,000	

← Cash received from customers.

Accounts Receivable

	Debit	Credit	
BB	190,000		
(1)	900,000	930,000	(2)
EB	160,000		

Sales

Debit	Credit	
	900,000	(1)

BB: Beginning Balance
EB: Ending Balance

		Debit	Credit
(1) Entry to record sales (assume all on account).	Accounts Receivable	900,000	
	Sales		900,000
(2) Credit required to reconcile Accounts Receivable. This represents the amount of cash collected from customers.	Cash	930,000	
	Accounts Receivable		930,000

Thus, on the schedule in Figure 23A-2, $30,000 is added to the $900,000 in sales reported on the income statement to show that $930,000 was received from customers during the past year.

CASH PAID FOR MERCHANDISE

Simplex reports cost of goods sold of $600,000 on the income statement. To determine cash generated from operating activities, cost of goods sold is adjusted to reflect *cash paid to suppliers for merchandise*. As under the indirect method, the impact of changes in merchandise inventory and accounts payable must be considered. This time, these changes will be used to adjust cost of goods sold.

Cost of goods sold, as reported on the income statement in Figure 23A-1, was \$600,000. However, the balance sheet reports that inventory *decreased* by \$20,000 (\$200,000 – \$180,000). The cost of merchandise purchased by Simplex, therefore, was \$580,000 (\$600,000 – \$20,000). Thus, \$20,000 is *deducted* from the cost of goods sold in column 3 of Figure 23A-2.

The balance sheet shows that Accounts Payable *decreased* by \$60,000 (\$180,000 – \$120,000). This indicates that in addition to paying for the purchases made this period, Simplex paid \$60,000 for merchandise purchased in prior periods. Thus, \$60,000 must be *added* to the cost of goods sold in column 2 of Figure 23A-2 to compute the cash paid for merchandise of \$640,000.

The impact of these two adjustments to cost of goods sold to compute cash paid to suppliers is summarized below.

Cost of Goods Sold	\$600,000
Less the reduction in merchandise inventory (\$200,000 – \$180,000)	(20,000)
Cost of merchandise purchased	\$580,000
Plus the reduction in accounts payable (\$180,000 – \$120,000)	60,000
Cash paid to suppliers	\$640,000

As discussed earlier for the indirect method, T accounts are also helpful in computing cash paid to suppliers as shown in Figure 23A-4.

FIGURE 23A-4 Cash Paid to Suppliers for Merchandise

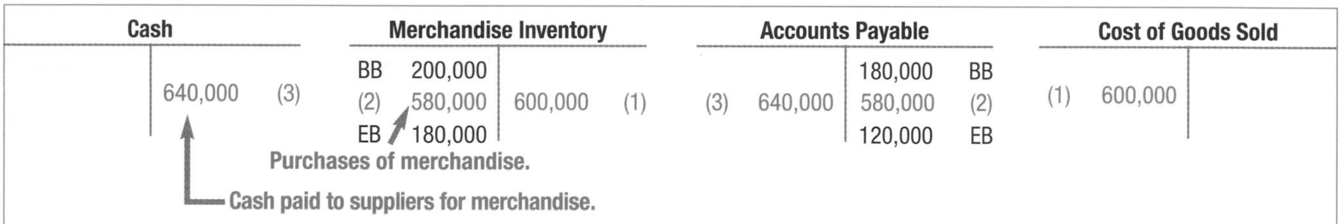

BB: Beginning Balance
EB: Ending Balance

(1) Entry to record cost of goods sold.	Cost of Goods Sold	600,000	
	Merchandise Inventory		600,000
(2) Debit required to reconcile the merchandise inventory account. This represents purchases for the period. Assume that all purchases were made on account.	Merchandise Inventory	580,000	
	Accounts Payable		580,000
(3) Debit required to balance Accounts Payable. This represents the amount of cash paid to suppliers for merchandise.	Accounts Payable	640,000	
	Cash		640,000

CASH PAID FOR OPERATING EXPENSES

Adjustments to operating expenses generally are necessary for items such as prepaid expenses, accrued liabilities, or depreciation on plant and equipment. Simplex does not have any of these items, so there is no need to adjust operating expenses. The entire \$177,000 of operating expenses is reported as a cash outflow. It is assumed that all of these expenses required cash outflows.

CASH PAID FOR INCOME TAXES

The balance sheet reports no receivables, payables, or other items related to income tax expense. Thus, tax expense reported on the income statement represents the amount of cash paid for taxes.

The schedule in Figure 23A-2 demonstrates that net income was $80,000, but only $70,000 in cash was generated from operating activities. All of the information in column 4 is reported on the statement of cash flows illustrated in Figure 23A-5. Though not discussed again in this appendix, note that cash flows from investing and financing activities are reported exactly as reported earlier under the indirect method.

FIGURE 23A-5 Statement of Cash Flows for Simplex—Direct Method.

Simplex Company Statement of Cash Flows For Year Ended December 31, 20-2		
Cash flows from operating activities:		
Cash received from customers		$ 930 000 00
Cash paid for merchandise	$(640 000 00)	
Cash paid for operating expenses	(177 000 00)	
Cash paid for income taxes	(43 000 00)	
Total cash disbursed for operating activities		(860 000 00)
Net cash provided by operating activities		$ 70 000 00
Cash flows from investing activities:		
Purchased building	$(140 000 00)	
Purchased equipment	(100 000 00)	
Total cash used by investing activities		(240 000 00)
Cash flows from financing activities:		
Issued note payable	$ 10 000 00	
Issued common stock	70 000 00	
Paid cash dividends	(20 000 00)	
Net cash provided by financing activities		60 000 00
Net increase (decrease) in cash		$(110 000 00)
Cash balance, January 1, 20-2		200 000 00
Cash balance, December 31, 20-2		$ 90 000 00

LO3 Prepare a schedule for the calculation of cash generated from operating activities under the direct method, including adjustments when the company reports:
a. changes in current assets and current liabilities associated with operations,
b. depreciation expense,
c. gains or losses on the sale of long-term assets,
d. receivables and payables associated with interest revenue, interest expense, and tax expense.

CASH FROM OPERATING ACTIVITIES UNDER THE DIRECT METHOD: MULTIPLEX

Simplex illustrated the basic adjustments needed for cash from operating activities under the direct method. Once again, Multiplex is used to illustrate additional concepts. The financial statements for Multiplex are provided in Figure 23A-6. The following additional concepts are addressed:

1. Adjustments to operating expenses for changes in current assets
2. Adjustments to operating expenses for changes in current liabilities
3. Adjustments to operating expenses for depreciation expense
4. Adjustments to interest revenue
5. Adjustments to interest expense
6. Adjustments to tax expense
7. Adjustments for gains or losses on the sale of long-term assets

FIGURE 23A-6 Financial Statements and Additional Information for Multiplex

Multiplex Corporation Income Statement For Year Ended December 31, 20-2		
Net sales		$460,100.00
Cost of goods sold		270,100.00
Gross profit		$190,000.00
Operating expenses		120,750.00
Operating income		$ 69,250.00
Other revenues and gains:		
Interest revenue	$ 155.00	
Gain on sale of equipment	3,000.00	3,155.00
Other expenses:		
Interest expense		650.00
Income before taxes		$ 71,755.00
Income tax expense		24,000.00
Net income		$ 47,755.00

Multiplex Corporation Statement of Retained Earnings For Year Ended December 31, 20-2		
Retained earnings, January 1, 20-2		$23,660.00
Net income	$47,755.00	
Less dividends	22,800.00	
Net increase in retained earnings		24,955.00
Retained earnings, December 31, 20-2		$48,615.00

Additional information:

1. Depreciation expense for the year was $10,400 as follows:

Store equipment	$ 4,000
Delivery equipment	4,500
Office equipment	1,900
	$10,400

2. The following cash purchases were made:

Store equipment	$ 9,200
Delivery equipment	12,000
Office equipment	4,000
	$25,200

3. Delivery equipment was sold for $7,000.

Cost	$10,000
Accumulated depreciation	6,000
Book value	$ 4,000
Market value	7,000
Gain on sale of delivery equipment	$ 3,000

4. A $13,000, three-year note was issued to acquire delivery equipment with a market value of $13,000.
5. Declared and paid cash dividends of $22,800.
6. Issued 200 shares of common stock for $15 per share

FIGURE 23A-6 Financial Statements and Additional Information for Multiplex (*continued*)

Multiplex Corporation
Comparative Balance Sheet
December 31, 20-2 and 20-1

	20-2		20-1		INCREASE (DECREASE)
Assets					
Current assets:					
Cash	$17,980.00		$20,000.00		$(2,020.00)
Government notes	1,800.00		3,200.00		(1,400.00)
Accrued interest receivable	100.00		300.00		(200.00)
Accounts receivable (net)	60,215.00		51,510.00		8,705.00
Merchandise inventory	64,570.00		67,500.00		(2,930.00)
Supplies and prepayments	4,000.00		2,750.00		1,250.00
Total current assets		$148,665.00		$145,260.00	3,405.00
Property, plant, and equipment:					
Store equipment	$48,000.00		$38,800.00		9,200.00
Less accumulated depreciation—store equipment	18,000.00	30,000.00	14,000.00	24,800.00	4,000.00
Delivery equipment	$47,000.00		$32,000.00		15,000.00
Less accumulated depreciation—delivery equipment	6,500.00	40,500.00	8,000.00	24,000.00	(1,500.00)
Office equipment	$38,000.00		$34,000.00		4,000.00
Less accumulated depreciation—office equipment	8,000.00	30,000.00	6,100.00	27,900.00	1,900.00
Total property, plant, and equipment		$100,500.00		$76,700.00	23,800.00
Total assets		$249,165.00		$221,960.00	27,205.00
Liabilities					
Current liabilities:					
Notes payable	$10,000.00		$11,800.00		(1,800.00)
Accounts payable	33,500.00		45,900.00		(12,400.00)
Income tax payable	3,000.00		2,000.00		1,000.00
Accrued and withheld payroll taxes	950.00		1,520.00		(570.00)
Accrued interest payable	100.00		80.00		20.00
Total current liabilities		$47,550.00		$61,300.00	(13,750.00)
Long-term liabilities:					
Notes payable (3-year)		13,000.00			13,000.00
Total liabilities		$60,550.00		$61,300.00	(750.00)
Stockholders' Equity					
Common stock ($10 par, 100,000 shares authorized; Issued: 10,000 in 20-2 and 9,800 in 20-1)	$100,000.00		$98,000.00		2,000.00
Paid-in capital in excess of par—common stock	40,000.00		39,000.00		1,000.00
Retained earnings	48,615.00		23,660.00		24,955.00
Total stockholders' equity		188,615.00		160,660.00	27,955.00
Total liabilities and stockholders' equity		$249,165.00		$221,960.00	27,205.00

CASH FLOWS FROM OPERATING ACTIVITIES: THE DIRECT METHOD

To compute cash flows from operating activities, prepare a schedule converting the accrual basis income statement to cash flows, as shown in Figure 23A-7. Following the same procedure used for Simplex, column 1 shows revenues and expenses as reported on the income statement. Columns 2 and 3 show additions and deductions to convert the accrual basis figures to the associated cash flows reported in column 4.

FIGURE 23A-7 Schedule for the Calculation of Cash Generated from Operating Activities (Direct Method)

Multiplex Corporation
Schedule for the Calculation of Cash Generated from Operating Activities
For Year Ended December 31, 20-2

INCOME STATEMENT		ADDITIONS	DEDUCTIONS	CASH FLOWS	
Net sales	$460,100		1 $ (8,705)	$451,395	Cash received from customers
Cost of goods sold	270,100	3 $12,400	2 (2,930)	279,570	Cash paid for merchandise
Gross profit	$190,000			$171,825	
Operating expenses	120,750	4 1,250	5 (10,400)		
		6 570		112,170	Cash paid for operating expenses
Operating income	$ 69,250			$ 59,655	
Interest revenue	155	7 200		355	Interest received
Gain on sale of equipment	3,000		8 (3,000)	0	Not related to operating activities
Interest expense	650		9 (20)	630	Interest paid
Income tax expense	24,000		10 (1,000)	23,000	Cash paid for income taxes
Net income	$ 47,755			$ 36,380	Cash generated from operating activities

1 The increase in accounts receivable reduced the amount of cash received from sales. Subtract this $8,705 increase from sales to compute cash received from customers.

2 The $2,930 decrease in inventory indicates that Multiplex purchased less inventory than it sold. Subtract this decrease from cost of goods sold to compute the cost of merchandise purchased for the year ($270,100 – $2,930 = $267,170).

3 The $12,400 decrease in accounts payable means that Multiplex paid cash to suppliers in excess of amounts purchased. Add the decrease in the amount owed to suppliers to the cost of merchandise purchased to compute cash paid for merchandise ($267,170 + $12,400 = $279,570).

4 The increase in supplies and prepayments indicates that Multiplex not only replenished these items for the amounts used during the period, but also increased the supplies on hand and prepayments. Thus, the cash paid for these items is greater than the expense recognized for the period. Add the increase of $1,250 to compute cash paid for operating expenses.

5 Depreciation is an operating expense but requires no cash outflow. Subtract the $10,400 ($4,000 + $4,500 + $1,900) in depreciation expense from operating expenses to compute cash paid for operating expenses.

6 By making payments to the government and reducing accrued and withheld payroll taxes, the amount of cash paid to the government this period was increased. Add the reduction of $570 to operating expenses to compute cash paid for operating expenses.

7 Add the reduction in accrued interest receivable of $200 to interest revenue to compute the amount of interest received in cash.

8 The gain on the sale of equipment is not related to operating activities. Selling equipment is an investing activity. Therefore, the gain is eliminated from the calculation of cash from operating activities.

9 Deduct the increase in accrued interest payable of $20 from interest expense to compute the amount of interest paid in cash.

10 Deduct the increase in income tax payable of $1,000 to compute income taxes paid in cash.

CASH RECEIVED FROM CUSTOMERS

The abbreviated income statement for Multiplex in Figure 23A-6 reports net sales of $460,100. The $8,705 increase in net receivables ($60,215 – $51,510) reported on the balance sheet means that cash was not received for all of the sales made during the year. Adjustment 1 in Figure 23A-7 deducts the increase in net receivables ($8,705) from net sales to compute cash received from customers of $451,395.

Of course, as demonstrated earlier, cash received from customers may also be computed using T accounts as shown in Figure 23A-8.

FIGURE 23A-8 Cash Received from Customers

Cash

	Debit	Credit
(2)	451,395	

↑ Cash received from customers.

Accounts Receivable

	Debit	Credit	
BB	51,510		
(1)	460,100	451,395	(2)
EB	60,215		

Sales

Debit	Credit	
	460,100	(1)

BB: Beginning Balance
EB: Ending Balance

	Account	Debit	Credit
(1) Entry to record sales (assume all on account).	Accounts Receivable	460,100	
	Sales		460,100
(2) Credit required to reconcile Accounts Receivable. This represents the amount of cash collected from customers.	Cash	451,395	
	Accounts Receivable		451,395

CASH PAID FOR MERCHANDISE

As discussed earlier, cost of goods sold must be adjusted for changes in merchandise inventory and accounts payable to compute cash paid for merchandise.

Merchandise Inventory

The balance sheet shows that inventory decreased by $2,930. This means that the cost of the goods **sold** exceeded the cost of the goods **purchased** during the year. Adjustment **2** in Figure 23A-7 deducts the decrease in inventory ($2,930) from the cost of goods sold to compute net purchases.

Accounts Payable

Multiplex reports a decrease in accounts payable of $12,400 on the balance sheet. This means that Multiplex paid for merchandise purchased this period *and* for merchandise purchased on account in prior periods. Adjustment **3** in Figure 23A-7 adds the $12,400 decrease in accounts payable to cost of goods sold. The combined adjustments for inventory and accounts payable result in $279,570 cash paid to suppliers for merchandise.

As illustrated earlier and in Figure 23A-9, T accounts are also helpful in determining cash paid to suppliers.

CASH PAID FOR OPERATING EXPENSES

The income statement shown in Figure 23A-6 reports $120,750 in operating expenses. The balance sheet and additional information provided in Figure 23A-6 are reviewed to identify necessary adjustments to compute cash paid for operating expenses.

Supplies and Prepayments

The balance sheet shows that supplies and prepayments increased by $1,250. The cash paid for these items was greater than the expense reported on the income statement. Adjustment **4** in Figure 23A-7 adds the increase of $1,250 to operating expenses to compute cash paid for operating expenses.

FIGURE 23A-9 Cash Paid to Suppliers for Merchandise

Cash				Merchandise Inventory				Accounts Payable				Cost of Goods Sold	
				BB	67,500					45,900	BB		
	279,570	(3)		(2)	267,170	270,100	(1)	(3)	279,570	267,170	(2)	(1)	270,100
				EB	64,570					33,500	EB		

Purchases of merchandise. Cash paid to suppliers for merchandise.

BB: Beginning Balance
EB: Ending Balance

(1) Entry to record cost of goods sold.	Cost of Goods Sold	270,100	
	Merchandise Inventory		270,100
(2) Debit required to reconcile the inventory account. This represents purchases for the period. Assume all purchases were made on account.	Merchandise Inventory	267,170	
	Accounts Payable		267,170
(3) Debit required to reconcile Accounts Payable. This represents the amount of cash paid to suppliers for merchandise.	Accounts Payable	279,570	
	Cash		279,570

Depreciation Expense

As reported under additional information in Figure 23A-6 (page 930), depreciation expense on all equipment amounted to $10,400. To recognize depreciation expense, Multiplex made the following adjusting entries at the end of the year:

4	Dec.	31	Depreciation Expense—Store Equipment		4,000	00			4
5			Accumulated Depreciation—Store Equipment				4,000	00	5
6									6
7		31	Depreciation Expense—Delivery Equipment		4,500	00			7
8			Accumulated Depreciation—Delivery Equipment				4,500	00	8
9									9
10		31	Depreciation Expense—Office Equipment		1,900	00			10
11			Accumulated Depreciation—Office Equipment				1,900	00	11

LEARNING KEY

Depreciation expense increases operating expenses, but requires no cash outflow. Therefore, deduct this amount from operating expenses to compute cash paid.

These entries increase operating expenses and reduce net income, but do not require an outflow of cash. Therefore, adjustment 5 in Figure 23A-7 deducts depreciation expense from the operating expenses to determine the cash paid for operating expenses.

Accrued and Withheld Payroll Taxes

The balance sheet in Figure 23A-6 shows that accrued and withheld payroll taxes decreased by $570. This decrease means that payments made to the government by Multiplex exceeded the payroll tax expense by $570. Thus, adjustment 6 in Figure 23A-7 adds the $570 decrease in the accrued and withheld payroll taxes account to operating expenses to compute cash paid for operating expenses.

As reported in column 4 of Figure 23A-7, after completing the adjustments related to operating expenses, cash paid for operating expenses is $112,170. Since supplies expense, prepaid expenses, depreciation expense, and payroll tax expense are all included in operating expenses, cash paid for operating expenses may also be computed by making the following summary entry:

Operating Expenses	120,750	
Supplies and Prepayments	1,250	
Accrued and Withheld Payroll Taxes	570	
Accumulated Depreciation—Store Equipment		4,000
Accumulated Depreciation—Delivery Equipment		4,500
Accumulated Depreciation—Office Equipment		1,900
Cash (**Cash paid for operating expenses**)	→	112,170

CASH RECEIVED FROM INTEREST

As reported on the balance sheet in Figure 23A-6, accrued interest receivable decreased by $200. This means that Multiplex received $200 in cash for interest earned in prior periods in addition to the cash received for interest earned this period. Adjustment 7 in Figure 23A-7 adds this amount to interest revenue ($155) to compute cash received from interest ($355). The need for this adjustment may also be seen in the following summary entry for interest revenue:

Cash	355	
Accrued Interest Receivable		200
Interest Revenue		155

GAIN ON SALE OF EQUIPMENT

As shown in Figure 23A-6, Multiplex reported a $3,000 gain on the sale of equipment on the income statement. Since this gain is not related to operating activities, adjustment 8 eliminates this gain when computing cash from operating activities.

CASH PAID FOR INTEREST

As reported on the balance sheet in Figure 23A-6, accrued interest payable increased by $20. This means that Multiplex did not pay all of the $650 of interest expense incurred this period. Adjustment 9 in Figure 23A-7 deducts the $20 increase in accrued interest payable from interest expense ($650) to compute cash paid for interest ($630). The need for this adjustment may also be seen in the following summary entry for interest expense:

Interest Expense	650	
Interest Payable		20
Cash		630

CASH PAID FOR INCOME TAXES

As shown in Figure 23A-6, income tax expense of $24,000 is reported on the income statement and an increase of $1,000 in income tax payable is reported on the balance sheet. Postponing the payment for taxes reduces cash paid for income taxes by $1,000. Thus, adjustment 10 in Figure 23A-7 deducts $1,000 from income tax expense ($24,000) to compute the income taxes paid in cash ($23,000). The need for this adjustment may also be seen in the following summary entry for income tax expense:

Income Tax Expense	24,000	
Income Tax Payable		1,000
Cash		23,000

PREPARING A STATEMENT OF CASH FLOWS: THE DIRECT METHOD

LO4 Prepare a statement of cash flows under the direct method.

As shown in Figure 23A-7, once the accrual basis revenues and expenses are adjusted, cash from operating activities is determined to be $36,380. This amount is shown at the bottom of column 4. All of the information from column 4 is presented on the statement of cash flows, shown in Figure 23A-10, under cash flows from operating activities.

FIGURE 23A-10 Statement of Cash Flows for Multiplex (Direct Method)

Muliplex Corporation Statement of Cash Flows (Direct Method) For Year Ended December 31, 20-2		
Cash flows from operating activities:		
Cash received from customers	$ 451,395.00	
Interest received	355.00	
Cash provided by operating activities		$ 451,750.00
Cash paid for merchandise	$(279,570.00)	
Cash paid for operating expenses	(112,170.00)	
Interest paid	(630.00)	
Income taxes paid	(23,000.00)	
Total cash disbursed for operating activities		(415,370.00)
Net cash provided by operating activities		$ 36,380.00
Cash flows from investing activities:		
Sold delivery equipment	$ 7,000.00	
Purchased delivery equipment	(12,000.00)	
Purchased store equipment	(9,200.00)	
Purchased office equipment	(4,000.00)	
Net cash used by investing activities		(18,200.00)
Cash flows from financing activities:		
Issued common stock	$ 3,000.00	
Paid cash dividends	(22,800.00	
Retired note payable	(1,800.00)	
Net cash used by financing activities		(21,600.00)
Net increase (decrease) in cash and cash equivalents		$ (3,420.00)
Cash and cash equivalents, January 1, 20-2		23,200.00
Cash and cash equivalents, December 31, 20-2		$ 19,780.00
Schedule of Noncash Investing and Financing Activities:		
Acquired delivery equipment by issuing a 3-year note		$ 13,000.00

The cash flows from investing and financing activities sections are identical to the sections presented in Chapter 23 under the indirect method. Under the direct method, there is no need for supplementary disclosures of cash paid for interest or taxes. These amounts are already reported in the statement.

LEARNING OBJECTIVES Key Points to Remember

LO1 Describe the direct method of reporting cash flows from operating activities.	Under the direct method, revenues and expenses reported on the income statement are adjusted to reflect the cash received or paid for each item.
LO2 Prepare a schedule for the calculation of cash generated from operating activities under the direct method by adjusting revenues and expenses for changes in current assets and current liabilities associated with operations.	A schedule for the calculation of cash generated from operating activities under the direct method is shown below. Current assets and current liabilities related to operating activities are used to adjust the revenues and expenses to cash receipts and cash payments. All of the adjustments below, except (5) and (9), illustrate adjustments for changes in current assets and current liabilities related to operating activities.

Sturm Corporation
Schedule for the Calculation of Cash Generated from Operating Activities
For Year Ended December 31, 20-2

INCOME STATEMENT		ADDITIONS		DEDUCTIONS		CASH FLOWS	
Net sales	$100			1	$ (5)	$95	Cash received from customers
Cost of goods sold	40	3	$8	2	(10)	38	Cash paid to suppliers
Gross profit	$ 60					$57	
Operating expenses	25	4	9	5	(6)		
		6	4			32	Cash paid for operating expenses
Operating income	$ 35					$25	
Interest revenue	5	7	1			6	Interest received
Interest expense	10			8	(7)	3	Interest paid
Gain on sale of store equipment	2			9	(2)	0	Gain not related to operating activities
Income tax expense	10	10	3			13	Cash paid for income taxes
Net income	$ 22					$15	Cash generated from operating activities

1. Accounts receivable increased by $5. Subtract this amount from net sales.
2. Inventory decreased by $10. Subtract this amount from cost of goods sold.
3. Accounts payable decreased by $8. Add this amount to cost of goods sold.
4. Supplies increased by $9. Add this amount to operating expenses.
5. Depreciation was $6. Subtract this amount from operating expenses.
6. Accrued payroll taxes decreased by $4. Add this amount to operating expenses.
7. Accrued interest receivable decreased by $1. Add this amount to interest revenue.
8. Accrued interest payable increased by $7. Subtract this amount from interest expense.
9. The gain on the sale of store equipment is reduced to zero. It is not related to operating activities.
10. Income taxes payable decreased by $3. Add this amount to income tax expense.

LEARNING OBJECTIVES — Key Points to Remember

LO3 Prepare a schedule for the calculation of cash generated from operating activities under the direct method, including adjustments when the company reports:

a. changes in current assets and current liabilities associated with operations,
b. depreciation expense,
c. gains or losses on the sale of long-term assets,
d. receivables and payables associated with interest revenue, interest expense, and tax expense.

Adjustments for receivables and payables associated with interest revenue, interest expense, and tax expense are treated the same as other current assets and current liabilities associated with operating activities. See adjustments 7, 8, and 10 on page 937.

Sturm reported $6 for depreciation expense. No cash is paid for depreciation. This amount is subtracted from operating expenses. See adjustment 5.

The gain on the sale of store equipment is related to an investing activity, not operating activities. Eliminate the gain of $2 as shown in adjustment 9.

LO4 Prepare a statement of cash flows under the direct method.

The investing and financing activities sections of the statement of cash flows are the same under the direct and indirect methods. Thus, only the operating activities section of the statement of cash flows under the direct method is shown below. The cash flows column from the illustration on page 937 is used to prepare this section.

Sturm Corporation
Statement of Cash Flows (Direct Method)
For Year Ended December 31, 20-2

Cash flows from operating activities:			
Cash received from customers		$95 00	
Interest received		6 00	
Cash provided by operating activities			$101 00
Cash paid to suppliers		$(38 00)	
Cash paid for operating expenses		(32 00)	
Cash paid for interest		(3 00)	
Cash paid for income taxes		(13 00)	
Total cash disbursed for operating activities			(86 00)
Net cash provided by operating activities			$15 00

REVIEW QUESTIONS

LO1 1. Describe the direct method of reporting cash flows from operating activities.

LO2 2. Under the direct method of preparing a statement of cash flows, what adjustment is made if accounts receivable increased from last year?

LO2 3. Under the direct method of preparing a statement of cash flows, what adjustments are made if merchandise inventory decreased and accounts payable increased from last year?

LO3 4. Under the direct method of preparing a statement of cash flows, what adjustment is made for depreciation expense?

LO3 5. Under the direct method of preparing a statement of cash flows, what adjustment is made for gains and losses on the sale of equipment?

SERIES A EXERCISES

E 23Apx-1A (LO2)
✓ Cash received from customers: $815,000

CASH RECEIVED FROM CUSTOMERS Potts Company's sales for 20-2 were $800,000. The Accounts Receivable balance as of December 31, 20-1, was $90,000. This same account had a balance of $75,000 as of December 31, 20-2. Compute the amount of cash received from customers in 20-2.

E 23Apx-2A (LO2)
✓ Cash paid for merchandise: $420,000

CASH PAID FOR MERCHANDISE Douglas Company's cost of goods sold for 20-2 was $400,000. Compute the amount of cash paid for merchandise in 20-2. The December 31, 20-2 and 20-1, balances of Merchandise Inventory and Accounts Payable were as follows:

	20-2	20-1
Merchandise Inventory	$60,000	$80,000
Accounts Payable	30,000	70,000

E 23Apx-3A (LO3)
✓ Cash paid for operating expenses: $332,200

CASH PAID FOR OPERATING EXPENSES The following information was obtained from Knox Company's income statement for 20-2, balance sheets as of December 31, 20-2 and 20-1, and auxiliary records:

Operating expenses for 20-2	$350,400
Depreciation expense for 20-2	22,000 (Included in operating expenses.)

	20-2	20-1
Supplies and prepayments	$9,600	$6,700
Accrued and withheld payroll taxes	2,900	3,800

Compute the amount of cash paid for operating expenses in 20-2.

E 23Apx-4A (LO3)
✓ Cash received for interest: $470

CASH RECEIVED FOR INTEREST Eary Company's income statement for 20-2 reported interest revenue of $430. The comparative balance sheet as of December 31, 20-2 and 20-1, reported the following:

	20-2	20-1
Accrued interest receivable	$150	$190

Compute the amount of cash received for interest in 20-2.

SERIES A PROBLEMS

P 23Apx-5A (LO2)
✓ Cash generated from operating activities: $160,000

SCHEDULE FOR CALCULATION OF CASH GENERATED FROM OPERATING ACTIVITIES Using the information provided in Problem 23-9A for Mueller Company, prepare the following:

1. A schedule for the calculation of cash generated from operating activities for Mueller Company for the year ended December 31, 20-2.
2. A partial statement of cash flows for Mueller Company reporting cash from operating activities under the direct method for the year ended December 31, 20-2.

P 23Apx-6A (LO3/4)
✓ Net cash provided by operating activities: $206,070

SCHEDULE FOR CALCULATION OF CASH GENERATED FROM OPERATING ACTIVITIES Using the information provided in Problem 23-11A for Horn Company, prepare the following:

1. A schedule for the calculation of cash generated from operating activities for Horn Company for the year ended December 31, 20-2.
2. A partial statement of cash flows for Horn Company reporting cash from operating activities under the direct method for the year ended December 31, 20-2.

P 23Apx-7A (LO3/4)
✓ Operating activities: $152,840
Investing activities: ($209,000)
Financing activities: $80,000

STATEMENT OF CASH FLOWS UNDER THE DIRECT METHOD Using the information provided in Problem 23-12A for McDowell Company, prepare the following:

1. A schedule for the calculation of cash generated from operating activities for McDowell Company for the year ended December 31, 20-2.
2. A statement of cash flows for McDowell Company prepared under the direct method for the year ended December 31, 20-2.

SERIES B EXERCISES

E 23Apx-1B (LO2)
✓ Cash received from customers: $735,000

CASH RECEIVED FROM CUSTOMERS Boyd Company's sales for 20-2 were $760,000. The Accounts Receivable balance as of December 31, 20-1, was $60,000. This same account had a balance of $85,000 as of December 31, 20-2. Compute the amount of cash received from customers in 20-2.

E 23Apx-2B (LO2)
✓ Cash paid for merchandise: $550,000

CASH PAID FOR MERCHANDISE Guild Company's cost of goods sold for 20-2 was $500,000. Compute the amount of cash paid for merchandise in 20-2. The December 31, 20-2 and 20-1, balances of Merchandise Inventory and Accounts Payable were as follows:

	20-2	20-1
Merchandise Inventory	$70,000	$50,000
Accounts Payable	60,000	90,000

E 23Apx-3B (LO3)
✓ Cash paid for operating expenses: $258,200

CASH PAID FOR OPERATING EXPENSES The following information was obtained from Busby Company's income statement for 20-2, balance sheets as of December 31, 20-2 and 20-1, and auxiliary records:

Operating expenses for 20-2	$290,500	
Depreciation expense for 20-2	30,000	(Included in operating expenses.)

	20-2	20-1
Supplies and prepayments	$7,100	$8,300
Accrued and withheld payroll taxes	3,800	2,700

Compute the amount of cash paid for operating expenses in 20-2.

E 23Apx-4B (LO3)
✓ Cash received for interest: $590

CASH RECEIVED FOR INTEREST Dowling Company's income statement for 20-2 reported interest revenue of $670. The comparative balance sheet as of December 31, 20-2 and 20-1, reported the following:

	20-2	20-1
Accrued interest receivable	$320	$240

Compute the amount of cash received for interest in 20-2.

SERIES B PROBLEMS

P 23Apx-5B (LO2)
✓ Cash generated from operating activities: $155,000

KA KLOOSTER & ALLEN

SCHEDULE FOR CALCULATION OF CASH GENERATED FROM OPERATING ACTIVITIES Using the information provided in Problem 23-9B for Kennington Company, prepare the following:

1. A schedule for the calculation of cash generated from operating activities for Kennington Company for the year ended December 31, 20-2.
2. A partial statement of cash flows for Kennington Company reporting cash from operating activities under the direct method for the year ended December 31, 20-2.

P 23Apx-6B (LO3/4)
✓ Net cash provided by operating activities: $179,395

SCHEDULE FOR CALCULATION OF CASH GENERATED FROM OPERATING ACTIVITIES Using the information provided in Problem 23-11B for Powell Company, prepare the following:

1. A schedule for the calculation of cash generated from operating activities for Powell Company for the year ended December 31, 20-2.
2. A partial statement of cash flows for Powell Company reporting cash from operating activities under the direct method for the year ended December 31, 20-2.

P 23Apx-7B (LO3/4)
✓ Operating activities: $99,300
Investing activities: ($237,000)
Financing activities: $180,000

STATEMENT OF CASH FLOWS UNDER THE DIRECT METHOD Using the information provided in Problem 23-12B for McGinnis Company, prepare the following:

1. A schedule for the calculation of cash generated from operating activities for McGinnis Company for the year ended December 31, 20-2.
2. A statement of cash flows for McGinnis Company prepared under the direct method for the year ended December 31, 20-2.

Chapter 24

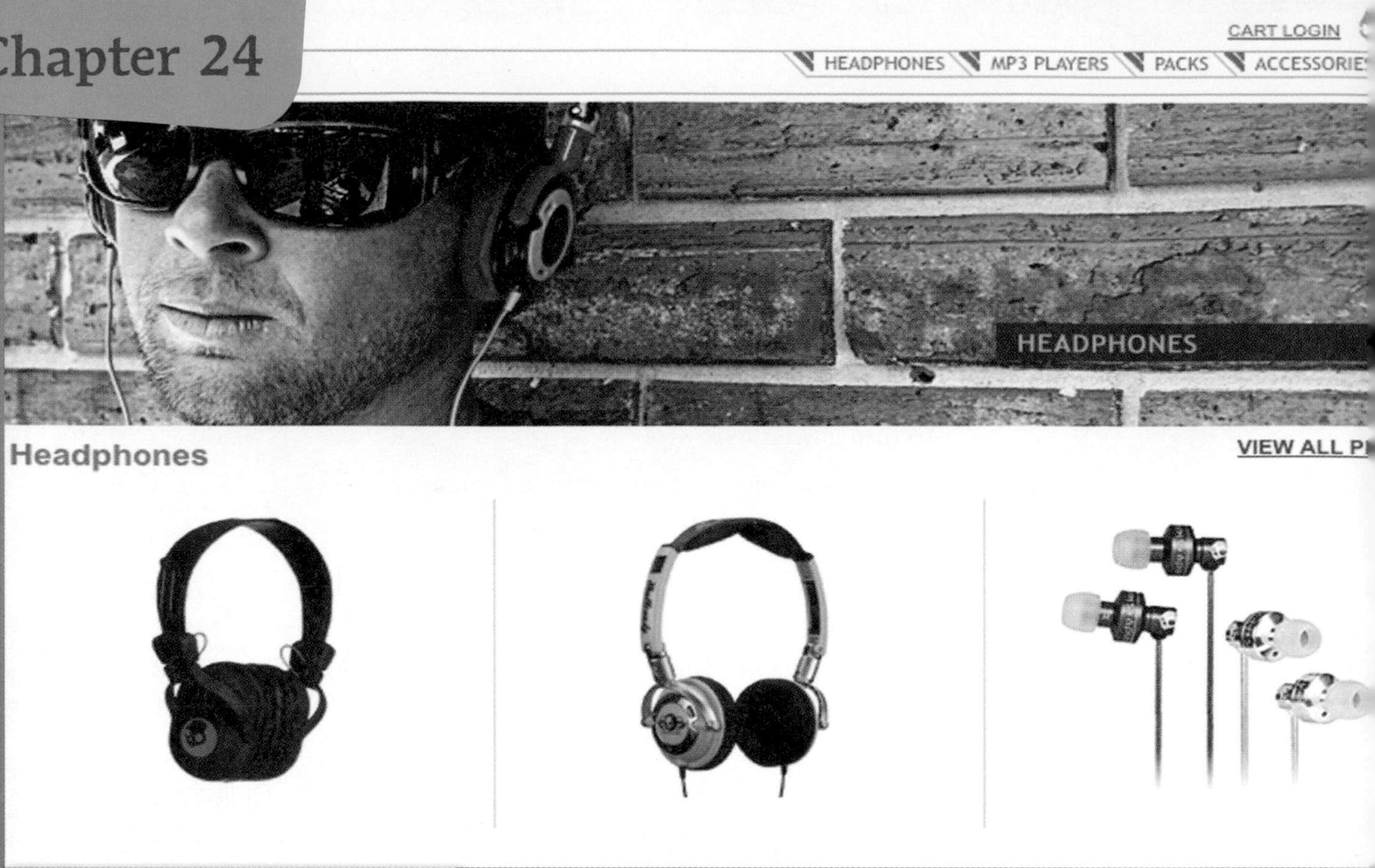

COURTESY OF WWW.SKULLCANDY.COM

LEARNING OBJECTIVES

Careful study of this chapter should enable you to:

LO1 **Perform horizontal and vertical analyses of the income statement and balance sheet.**

LO2 **Compute and explain liquidity measures.**

LO3 **Compute and explain activity measures.**

LO4 **Compute and explain profitability measures.**

LO5 **Compute and explain leverage measures.**

LO6 **Explain the components of ROA and ROE.**

LO7 **Compute and explain market measures.**

LO8 **Explain the limitations of financial statement analysis.**

Analysis of Financial Statements

Founded in 2003 by Rick Alden, Skullcandy manufactures audio products for cell phone and portable music devices. Building on Alden's background in snowboarding and skateboarding, Skullcandy designs and markets its products to these enthusiasts and those who listen to hip-hop and indie rock.

Over a recent three-year period, Skullcandy's revenues increased 4,077.4% to $35.7 million. Even so, it tries to maintain a small-company, edgy feel. For example, its entire office in Park City, Utah, is designed to look like a skateboard park with steel coping and concrete curbing.

Managers, employees, investors, and creditors need to continually evaluate the financial health of a company, especially when it is new and developing, like Skullcandy. In this chapter, you will learn how to perform horizontal and vertical analyses, compute standard financial ratios, and appreciate the limitations of these analyses.

This chapter demonstrates how to analyze financial statements to better understand the information obtained from them. Comparisons of financial statement variables over time and the calculation and interpretation of selected ratios will be presented.

COMPARATIVE ANALYSIS

LO1 Perform horizontal and vertical analyses of the income statement and balance sheet.

A business's financial statements supply information to management, current and potential owners and creditors, employees and their unions, government agencies, and sometimes the general public. Normally, interest centers on five aspects of the business.

1. **Liquidity measures**—the ability to pay current debts when they come due. Liquidity measures focus primarily on current assets and current liabilities.
2. **Activity measures**—the efficiency with which assets are used to generate profits.
3. **Profitability measures**—the ability to earn a satisfactory return on the investments in the business.
4. **Leverage**—the proportion of debt used to operate.
5. **Market measures**—the use of the market value of common stock as evidence of how the company is viewed by investors.

Financial statements can be much more informative if they are analyzed on a comparative basis. The following are four possible types of comparison:

1. with one or more previous periods
2. with data for the industry as a whole
3. with similar information for other businesses in the industry
4. with preset plans or goals (normally in the form of budgets)

We will use the financial statements of French Connection Importers (FCI) for the years ended December 31, 20-2 and 20-1, to illustrate the first type of analysis.

HORIZONTAL ANALYSIS

LEARNING KEY

In horizontal analysis, use the amount for the earlier year as the base when calculating the percentage change from year to year.

Comparing the amounts for the same item in the financial statements of two or more periods is called **horizontal analysis**. Figure 24-1 illustrates a horizontal analysis of the condensed comparative income statement of FCI for the two years under review, showing the amount and the percentage change in each item. In calculating the percentage change, the amount for the earlier year serves as the base. For example, to compute the percentage change in net sales, the increase or decrease in net sales for 20-2 is divided by net sales for 20-1.

Net sales in 20-2 were 17.9% greater than in 20-1. Cost of goods sold increased only 15.8%. Because of the smaller percentage increase in cost of goods sold, the percentage increase in the gross profit (23.9%) was greater than that for sales. Operating expenses increased only 12.7%, which was much less than the growth in sales. These events caused an increase of 36.6% in operating income. Although the percentage increase in other revenue was enormous (425.0%), the amount of this revenue was small. Because other expenses decreased 12.3%, income before income tax was 46.6% greater. The relative amount of income tax increased significantly (90.5%), and net income increased by 31.2%.

FIGURE 24-1 Comparative Income Statement—Horizontal Analysis

French Connection Importers
Comparative Income Statement
For Years Ended December 31, 20-2 and 20-1

	20-2	20-1	INCREASE (DECREASE)	PERCENT
Net sales	$835,950	$708,800	$127,150	17.9
Cost of goods sold	602,380	520,260	82,120	15.8
Gross profit	$233,570	$188,540	$ 45,030	23.9
Operating expenses	113,000	100,250	12,750	12.7
Operating income	$120,570	$ 88,290	$ 32,280	36.6
Other revenue	525	100	425	425.0
Other expenses	12,650	14,420	(1,770)	−12.3
Income before income taxes	$108,445	$ 73,970	$ 34,475	46.6
Income tax expense	36,600	19,210	17,390	90.5
Net income	$ 71,845	$ 54,760	$ 17,085	31.2

This horizontal analysis of the income statement indicates a major improvement in FCI's operating results. A 17.9% increase in net sales accompanied by apparently successful cost control resulted in a 31.2% increase in net income.

The condensed comparative balance sheet as of December 31, 20-2 and 20-1, presented in Figure 24-2, illustrates horizontal analysis. The most noteworthy changes in the balance sheet follow (numbers correspond to those in the margin of Figure 24-2).

1 *Increase (18.4%) in current assets and decrease (38.3%) in current liabilities.*

The increase in current assets is due primarily to the increases in cash (30.4%) and receivables (23.5%). These increases probably were needed to support the higher level of operating activity indicated by the 17.9% increase in net sales noted previously.

The decrease in current liabilities is caused by the reduction in notes payable and accounts payable. FCI apparently used some of the funds from its successful operations during 20-2 to pay off a large portion of its current liabilities.

2 *Increase in building (12.0%) and store equipment (11.1%).*

Increases in building and store equipment are important because they are signs of growth. It is common for long-term asset accounts to *decrease* simply because of depreciation and amortization. The decreases in delivery and office equipment and organization costs are examples of this tendency. *Increases* in the building and store equipment accounts mean that new long-term assets were acquired during 20-2.

3 *Increases in common stock (25.0%) and paid-in capital in excess of par (60.0%).*

Increases in common stock and paid-in capital in excess of par also indicate growth. Common stock with a par value of $15,000 was issued for $22,500 ($15,000 par + $7,500 paid-in capital in excess of par). Financing growth by issuing additional common stock is often desirable, particularly for a company carrying as much debt as FCI.

4 *Substantial increase (53.6%) in retained earnings.*

The large increase in retained earnings results from a highly profitable year (net income of $71,845) combined with a moderate dividend policy ($7,500). Retention of large amounts of earnings is another desirable way to finance corporate growth.

FIGURE 24-2 Comparative Balance Sheet—Horizontal Analysis

French Connection Importers
Comparative Balance Sheet
December 31, 20-2 and 20-1

	20-2	20-1	INCREASE (DECREASE)	PERCENT	
Assets					
Current assets:					
Cash	$ 25,695	$ 19,700	$ 5,995	30.4	
Government notes	5,000	1,000	4,000	400.0	
Accounts receivable (net)	61,750	50,000	11,750	23.5	
Merchandise inventory	55,500	54,250	1,250	2.3	
Supplies and prepayments	2,400	2,000	400	20.0	
Total current assets	$150,345	$126,950	$ 23,395	18.4	1
Property, plant, and equipment:					
Land	$ 40,000	$ 40,000	$ 0	0.0	
Building (net)	140,000	125,000	15,000	12.0	2
Store equipment (net)	100,000	90,000	10,000	11.1	2
Delivery and office equipment (net)	22,000	28,500	(6,500)	–22.8	
Organization costs	1,200	2,400	(1,200)	–50.0	
Total property, plant, and equipment	$303,200	$285,900	$ 17,300	6.1	
Total assets	$453,545	$412,850	$ 40,695	9.9	
Liabilities					
Current liabilities:					
Accrued and withheld payroll taxes	$ 2,500	$ 2,750	$ (250)	–9.1	
Notes payable	10,000	37,500	(27,500)	–73.3	
Accounts payable	40,000	59,000	(19,000)	–32.2	
Accrued interest payable	600	1,700	(1,100)	–64.7	
Income tax payable	13,600	13,400	200	1.5	
Dividends payable	7,500	6,000	1,500	25.0	
Total current liabilities	$ 74,200	$120,350	$(46,150)	–38.3	1
Long-term liabilities:					
Bonds payable	100,000	100,000	0	0.0	
Total liabilities	$174,200	$220,350	$(46,150)	–20.9	
Stockholders' Equity					
Common stock, $1 par	$ 75,000	$ 60,000	$ 15,000	25.0	3
Paid-in capital in excess of par	20,000	12,500	7,500	60.0	3
Retained earnings	184,345	120,000	64,345	53.6	4
Total stockholders' equity	$279,345	$192,500	$ 86,845	45.1	
Total liabilities and stockholders' equity	$453,545	$412,850	$ 40,695	9.9	

VERTICAL ANALYSIS

Reporting the amount of each item in a statement as a percentage of some designated total is called **vertical analysis.** Vertical analysis is most helpful when statements relating to two or more periods are compared.

Figure 24-3 shows FCI's condensed comparative income statement for the years ended December 31, 20-2 and 20-1. Each item is shown as a percentage of net sales for the year. This statement reveals that several factors contributed to FCI's increased profitability from 20-1 to 20-2. Both cost of goods sold and operating expenses decreased as a percentage of net sales. This allowed operating income to increase from 12.5% to 14.4% of net sales. Other expenses decreased from 2.0% to 1.5% of net sales, so that income before income taxes jumped from 10.4% to 13.0% of net sales. These positive factors were offset somewhat by the increase in taxes from 2.7% to 4.4% of net sales. However, net income as a percentage of net sales still increased from 7.7% to 8.6%.

LEARNING KEY

In vertical analysis of the income statement, each item is shown as a percentage of net sales for the year.

Vertical analysis of income statements automatically provides several important ratios. They include the following (numbers correspond to those in the margin of Figure 24-3):

1. **Cost of goods sold ratio**—ratio of cost of goods sold to net sales
2. **Gross profit ratio**—ratio of gross profit to net sales
3. **Operating expense ratio**—ratio of operating expenses to net sales
4. **Operating income ratio**—ratio of operating income to net sales
5. **Profit margin ratio** (also called **net income ratio**)—ratio of net income to net sales

FIGURE 24-3 Comparative Income Statement—Vertical Analysis

French Connection Importers
Comparative Income Statement
For Years Ended December 31, 20-2 and 20-1

	20-2	PERCENT*	20-1	PERCENT*	
Net sales	$835,950	100.0	$708,800	100.0	
Cost of goods sold	602,380	72.1	520,260	73.4	1
Gross profit	$233,570	27.9	$188,540	26.6	2
Operating expenses	113,000	13.5	100,250	14.1	3
Operating income	$120,570	14.4	$ 88,290	12.5	4
Other revenue	525	0.1	100	0.0	
Other expenses	12,650	1.5	14,420	2.0	
Income before income taxes	$108,445	13.0	$ 73,970	10.4	
Income tax expense	36,600	4.4	19,210	2.7	
Net income	$ 71,845	8.6	$ 54,760	7.7	5

*Percentages may not add due to rounding.

LEARNING KEY

In vertical analysis of the balance sheet, assets are shown as a percentage of total assets. Liabilities and stockholders' equity are shown as a percentage of total liabilities and stockholders' equity.

Vertical analysis is also performed on balance sheets. For assets, each item is shown as a percentage of the total assets. For liabilities and stockholders' equity, each item is shown as a percentage of the total equities (liabilities and stockholders' equity). Figure 24-4 shows a comparative balance sheet for FCI using vertical analysis. This statement reveals that current assets were a somewhat larger share (33.1% versus 30.7%) of total assets on December 31, 20-2, than on the same date in 20-1. In addition, current liabilities decreased dramatically (16.4% versus 29.2%) as a percentage of total equities. These two factors reflect a major improvement in FCI's current position. Retained earnings increased significantly in amount and as a percentage of total equities. Finally, the combination of favorable changes in current liabilities, common stock, paid-in capital in excess of par, and retained earnings resulted in total liabilities being a much smaller share (38.4% versus 53.4%) of total liabilities and stockholders' equity.

FIGURE 24-4 Comparative Balance Sheet—Vertical Analysis

French Connection Importers
Comparative Balance Sheet
December 31, 20-2 and 20-1

	20-2	PERCENT*	20-1	PERCENT*
Assets				
Current assets:				
Cash	$ 25,695	5.7	$ 19,700	4.8
Government notes	5,000	1.1	1,000	0.2
Accounts receivable (net)	61,750	13.6	50,000	12.1
Merchandise inventory	55,500	12.2	54,250	13.1
Supplies and prepayments	2,400	0.5	2,000	0.5
Total current assets	$ 150,345	33.1	$ 126,950	30.7
Property, plant, and equipment:				
Land	$ 40,000	8.8	$ 40,000	9.7
Building (net)	140,000	30.9	125,000	30.3
Store equipment (net)	100,000	22.0	90,000	21.8
Delivery and office equipment (net)	22,000	4.9	28,500	6.9
Organization costs	1,200	0.3	2,400	0.6
Total property, plant, and equipment	$ 303,200	66.9	$285,900	69.3
Total assets	$ 453,545	100.0	$412,850	100.0
Liabilities				
Current liabilities:				
Accrued and withheld payroll taxes	$ 2,500	0.6	$ 2,750	0.7
Notes payable	10,000	2.2	37,500	9.1
Accounts payable	40,000	8.8	59,000	14.3
Accrued interest payable	600	0.1	1,700	0.4
Income tax payable	13,600	3.0	13,400	3.2
Dividends payable	7,500	1.7	6,000	1.5
Total current liabilities	$ 74,200	16.4	$120,350	29.2
Long-term liabilities:				
Bonds payable	100,000	22.0	100,000	24.2
Total liabilities	$ 174,200	38.4	$220,350	53.4
Stockholders' Equity				
Common stock, $1 par	$ 75,000	16.5	$ 60,000	14.5
Paid-in capital in excess of par	20,000	4.4	12,500	3.0
Retained earnings	184,345	40.6	120,000	29.1
Total stockholders' equity	$ 279,345	61.6	$192,500	46.6
Total liabilities and stockholders' equity	$ 453,545	100.0	$412,850	100.0

*Percentages may not add due to rounding.

LIQUIDITY MEASURES

LO2 Compute and explain liquidity measures.

Liquidity measures indicate a company's ability to meet its current debts. These measures focus primarily on balance sheet amounts and on the company's ability to generate funds to liquidate current obligations.

WORKING CAPITAL

Working capital is the excess of a company's current assets over current liabilities. This measures whether current assets are sufficient to pay off current liabilities. The calculation of working capital for FCI at the end of each year is shown in Figure 24-5.

FIGURE 24-5 Calculation of Working Capital

		20-2	20-1
Working Capital	Current Assets	$150,345	$ 126,950
	– Current Liabilities	(74,200)	(120,350)
	= Working Capital	$ 76,145	$ 6,600

FCI's working capital position improved dramatically between 20-1 and 20-2. Current assets were barely sufficient to cover current liabilities on December 31, 20-1, whereas there is a substantial margin of working capital at the end of 20-2.

CURRENT RATIO

The **current ratio**, sometimes called **working capital ratio** because of its obvious linkage to working capital, is calculated by dividing current assets by current liabilities. The calculation of thc current ratio for FCI at the end of each year is shown in Figure 24-6.

FIGURE 24-6 Calculation of Current Ratio

			20-2	20-1
Current Ratio	Current Assets / Current Liabilities	=	$150,345 / $74,200	$126,950 / $120,350
			2.0 to 1	1.1 to 1

The current position of FCI improved greatly during the year ended December 31, 20-2. The general rule is that a current ratio of 2 to 1 or better is satisfactory, although this rule can be modified for certain types of businesses or the makeup of the current assets. If the current assets consist primarily of cash and short-term investments, a lower ratio may be fine. However, if current assets include high amounts of risky receivables and inventory that is not selling well, a higher ratio may be necessary to satisfy investors and creditors. FCI's current ratio was not acceptable in 20-1, but it improved to an acceptable level in 20-2.

QUICK OR ACID-TEST RATIO

Another frequently used measure of liquidity is the **quick** or **acid-test ratio.** This ratio is calculated by dividing "quick" assets—cash, temporary investments, and receivables—by current liabilities. The calculation of the quick ratio for FCI at the end of each year is shown in Figure 24-7.

FIGURE 24-7 Calculation of Quick Ratio

			20-2	20-1
Quick or Acid -Test Ratio	Quick Assets / Current Liabilities	=	$92,445 / $74,200	$ 70,700 / $120,350
			1.25 to 1	0.59 to 1
Quick Assets	Cash		$25,695	$19,700
	Government notes		5,000	1,000
	Accounts receivable (net)		61,750	50,000
			$92,445	$70,700

LEARNING KEY

Quick assets include cash, temporary investments, and receivables.

FCI's quick ratio improved during 20-2. As a general rule, the ratio should not be less than 1 to 1. FCI was far below that standard in 20-1, but the company's quick ratio at the end of 20-2 is acceptable.

If the liquidity measures are too low, it can be a sign that the company will be unable to pay its bills. This could require the company to raise cash through additional borrowing, selling assets, or issuing stock. Thus, investors and creditors generally prefer higher liquidity measures. It is possible, however, for the measures to be too high. Cash and most receivables are not "earning assets" (they do not produce goods or services to sell), and the return on most temporary investments is not large. Inventories are expensive to hold. They take up costly space, tie up money, and are subject to loss of value from various causes. Thus, management must try to maintain the optimal amount of each type of asset to maximize profits and pay bills on time.

U REVU

Complete U REVU-1 on **pages 970–971** to test your basic understanding of LO2.

ACTIVITY MEASURES

LO3 Compute and explain activity measures.

Activity measures focus primarily on the efficient use of assets. We discuss the speed with which receivables are collected and inventory is sold, as well as how efficiently assets are used to generate revenue.

ACCOUNTS RECEIVABLE TURNOVER

Since accounts receivable do not generally earn interest, and some receivables will never be collected, it is important to manage them carefully. The disadvantages of carrying receivables are accepted, however, because selling on account may generate greater sales and net income.

Accounts receivable turnover measures how promptly receivables are collected. It is calculated by dividing net sales on account by the average amount of net accounts receivable. It is preferable to calculate a monthly average of net receivables. However, if monthly figures are not available, averaging the beginning-of-year and end-of-year balances is acceptable if the receivables balance does not fluctuate widely. Only *accounts* receivable are considered. The calculations for FCI are shown in Figure 24-8.

FIGURE 24-8 Calculation of Accounts Receivable Turnover

			20-2	20-1
Accounts Receivable Turnover	Net Sales on Account / Average Accounts Receivable (Net)	=	$668,760 / $55,875 11.97	$567,040 / $45,000 12.60
Average Accounts Receivable	(Beginning Accounts Receivable + Ending Accounts Receivable) / 2	=	($50,000 + $61,750) / 2 $55,875	($40,000 + $50,000) / 2 $45,000
Average Collection Period	365 / Accounts Receivable Turnover	=	365 / 11.97 30.5 days	365 / 12.60 29.0 days

Note that beginning balances for 20-1 are not available on the current financial statements. These were taken from last year's financial statements.

Net sales *on account* is used in this ratio. However, this information is not generally available on the financial statements. Net sales may be used if net sales on account is not available. Using net sales will provide a useful measure across time periods as long as the proportion of cash and credit sales remains relatively stable.

Another way of examining accounts receivable turnover is to divide 365 days by the turnover figure to get the average collection period. This shows the number of days it takes a business to convert receivables into cash. Fluctuations in the average collection period over time should be investigated.

For FCI, Figure 24-8 shows that the average collection period is 30.5 days and 29.0 days, respectively, for the years ended December 31, 20-2 and 20-1. Although the accounts receivable turnover decreased slightly, both rates are quite good. The average number of days that receivables are on the books should not be greater than 1½ times the regular length of the credit period. FCI offered 30 days' credit to more customers in 20-2, which probably explains the slight decrease in turnover.

Faster collection of receivables is generally preferred. However, businesses are willing to wait for cash collections if extending credit increases sales. If the collection period increases substantially, however, it could be a sign that the firm's credit policy is too loose and too many customers may never pay. Or, worse yet, history has shown that some companies have attempted to pad revenues by booking bogus sales on account. Since these "sales" will never be collected, the collection period will increase substantially. Analysts have used this ratio to help identify unethical companies attempting to deceive investors and creditors.

MERCHANDISE INVENTORY TURNOVER

Every seller of goods would like to have maximum sales and a minimum inventory. **Merchandise inventory turnover** measures the relationship between sales and inventory. It is calculated by dividing cost of goods sold by average merchandise inventory. Again, calculating a monthly average of inventories is preferable. However, if monthly figures are not available, the average of the beginning-of-year and end-of-year inventories can be used. For FCI, the merchandise inventory turnover for each year is shown in Figure 24-9.

As with accounts receivable turnover, another way of examining merchandise inventory turnover is to divide 365 days by the turnover figure to get the average number of days required to sell the merchandise inventory. If all sales are made on

FIGURE 24-9 Calculation of Merchandise Inventory Turnover

			20-2	20-1
Merchandise Inventory Turnover	Cost of Goods Sold / Average Merchandise Inventory	=	$602,380 / $54,875 = 10.98	$520,260 / $52,500 = 9.91
Average Merchandise Inventory	(Beginning Merchandise Inventory + Ending Merchandise Inventory) / 2	=	($54,250 + $55,500) / 2 = $54,875	($50,750 + $54,250) / 2 = $52,500
Average Number of Days to Sell Inventory	365 / Merchandise Inventory Turnover	=	365 / 10.98 = 33.2 days	365 / 9.91 = 36.8 days

account, this is the average number of days it takes FCI to convert merchandise inventory into accounts receivable. This number of days plus the number of days to collect accounts receivable indicates the number of days to convert inventory into cash. Figure 24-9 shows that merchandise remained in stock an average of 33 days and 37 days, respectively, for the years ended December 31, 20-2 and 20-1.

The turnover increased slightly from 20-1 to 20-2. Both years show acceptable inventory turnover rates. FCI maintained a reasonable inventory turnover while significantly increasing its sales volume.

Many factors impact the merchandise inventory turnover. In general, faster turnover is preferred. However, the actions required to speed up turnover may be harmful to the company. For example, one way to speed up turnover would be to reduce prices, increase the number of sales, and, thus, increase cost of goods sold. Of course, this would reduce profit margins. Similarly, the firm could reduce inventory levels. While this is desirable, it could mean that merchandise is not available when customers want it. Thus, the firm would lose sales. It is also worth noting that inventory turnover levels vary considerably across industries. As you might suspect, inventory turnover at a fruit stand should be considerably faster than at a car dealership. Yet, both businesses could be equally profitable.

ASSET TURNOVER

The **asset turnover,** or **ratio of net sales to assets,** measures how efficiently a company used its assets to generate sales. The ratio is calculated by dividing net sales for the year by the average book value of the company's assets. The calculation for FCI is shown in Figure 24-10.

FIGURE 24-10 Calculation of Asset Turnover

			20-2	20-1
Asset Turnover	$\frac{\text{Net Sales}}{\text{Average Assets}}$	=	$\frac{\$835,950}{\$433,198}$	$\frac{\$708,800}{\$406,425}$
			1.9 to 1	1.7 to 1
Average Assets	$\frac{\text{Beginning Assets + Ending Assets}}{2}$	=	$\frac{\$412,850 + \$453,545}{2}$	$\frac{\$400,000 + \$412,850}{2}$
			$433,198	$406,425

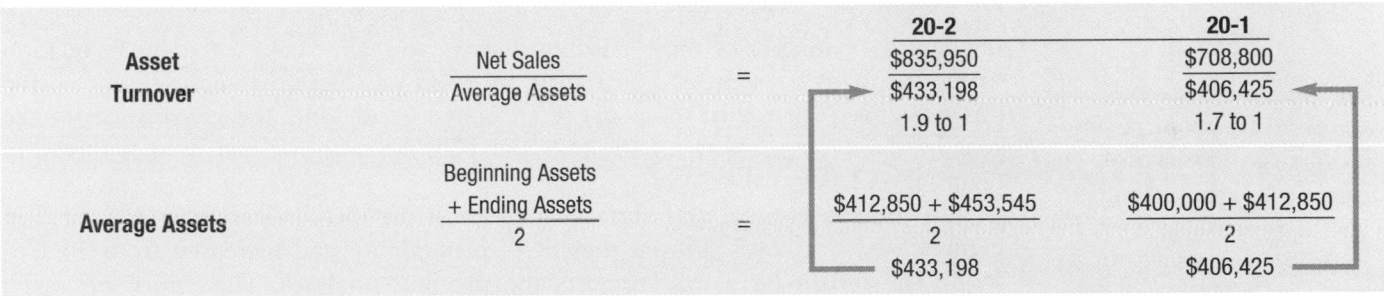

Asset turnover is heavily determined by the type of business. Those with little in the way of property, plant, and equipment, such as department stores, will have higher asset turnovers. Those in capital-intensive industries, like a company manufacturing large trucks, will have lower turnovers. Thus, it is important to compare turnover ratios with other companies in the same industry or with the historical performance of the company. FCI's asset turnover ratio increased modestly from 20-1 to 20-2.

U REVU Complete U REVU-2 on **pages 970–971** to test your basic understanding of LO3.

PROFITABILITY MEASURES

LO4 Compute and explain profitability measures.

Profitability measures indicate a company's ability to earn income by operating efficiently. These measures focus primarily on the profit margin and the relationship between key income statement and balance sheet amounts.

PROFIT MARGIN

As discussed earlier, the profit margin measures the amount of profit for each dollar of sales. We want to reinforce these calculations here because of the important role they play in ratios to be discussed later in the chapter. The ratio is calculated by dividing net income by net sales for the year. The calculation for FCI is shown in Figure 24-11.

FIGURE 24-11 Calculation of Profit Margin Ratio

			20-2	20-1
Profit Margin Ratio	Net Income / Net Sales	=	$71,845 / $835,950	$54,760 / $708,800
			8.6%	7.7%

Profit margins typically range from less than 1% to over 10%, depending on the industry. FCI earned 8.6% and 7.7% in 20-2 and 20-1, respectively. In other words, FCI earned 8.6 and 7.7 cents per dollar of sales, respectively, each year. This represents a strong and improving profit margin. This ratio should be compared over time and with other firms in the same industry.

RETURN ON ASSETS

Many analysts prefer to add interest expense (net of taxes) to the numerator of return on assets. This provides a measure of the efficient use of assets regardless of the method used to finance those assets.

Owners or managers of most businesses strive to realize large earnings in relation to the company's resources. The return on assets measures the success in achieving this objective. The **return on assets** is calculated by dividing the net income for the year by the average assets for the year. For FCI, the ratio for each year is shown in Figure 24-12.

Both the horizontal and vertical analyses of the income statement presented in Figures 24-1 and 24-3 showed that FCI's profitability had increased from 20-1 to 20-2. The return on assets supports the previous analyses. The return on assets increased from 13.5% in 20-1 to 16.6% in 20-2. This is a sign that management's performance improved during 20-2. To further evaluate management's performance, these results can be compared with those of similar companies or industry results.

FIGURE 24-12 Calculation of Return on Assets

			20-2	20-1
Return on Assets	Net Income / Average Assets	=	$71,845 / $433,198	$54,760 / $406,425
			16.6%	13.5%
Average Assets	(Beginning Assets + Ending Assets) / 2	=	($412,850 + $453,545) / 2	($400,000 + $412,850) / 2
			$433,198	$406,425

Within reasonable constraints, management strives to maximize sales and net income and minimize the assets required to operate. However, some industries require higher investments in plant and equipment to generate similar sales and profits. Thus, it is difficult to compare these measures across industries. It is best to evaluate these measures for the same firm over time, or with other firms in the same industry. Also, since book values are used to measure the assets, it is difficult to compare an older company (with older assets and lower book values) with a newer company (with newer assets and higher book values).

Stockholders' Equity includes Common Stock, Paid-in Capital in Excess of Par, and Retained Earnings. If FCI had preferred stock, the preferred dividends would be deducted from net income because these funds would not be available to common stockholders.

RETURN ON COMMON STOCKHOLDERS' EQUITY

Ultimately, the company must provide an adequate return to its common stockholders. Thus, **return on common stockholders' equity** is a very important performance measure. It is calculated by dividing net income available to common stockholders (net income less preferred dividends) for the year by the average common stockholders' equity during the year. For FCI, the calculation of the ratio for each year is shown in Figure 24-13.

FIGURE 24-13 Calculation of Return on Common Stockholders' Equity

			20-2	20-1
Return on Common Stockholders' Equity	Net Income Available to Common Stockholders / Average Common Stockholders' Equity	=	$71,845 / $235,923 30.5%	$54,760 / $183,750 29.8%
Average Common Stockholders' Equity	(Beginning Stockholders' Equity + Ending Stockholders' Equity) / 2	=	($192,500 + $279,345) / 2 $235,923	($175,000 + $192,500) / 2 $183,750

Net income increased from $54,760 in 20-1 to $71,845 in 20-2, leading to an increase in the return on common stockholders' equity from 29.8% to 30.5%. These rates of return are quite strong.

EARNINGS PER SHARE OF COMMON STOCK

LEARNING KEY

Earnings per share means *per share of common stock*. Thus, we must focus on earnings available to common stockholders.

One of the most important measures of profitability of the company is **earnings per share of common stock**. If only common stock is outstanding, earnings per share is calculated by dividing net income for the year by the average number of shares of common stock outstanding during the year. FCI had only common stock outstanding—60,000 shares throughout 20-1, and 60,000 shares at the beginning and 75,000 shares at the end of 20-2. The 15,000 additional shares were issued in the middle of the year, so the average number of shares outstanding during 20-2 was 67,500 [(60,000 + 75,000) ÷ 2]. Therefore, FCI's earnings per share for each year is calculated as shown in Figure 24-14.

If preferred shares are outstanding, the earnings per share of common stock is calculated after deducting preferred dividend requirements. For example, if a corporation has 40,000 shares of $10 par, 8% preferred stock, $32,000 must be subtracted from net income before dividing by the average number of common shares outstanding. If net income is $310,000, and the average shares of common stock outstanding is 80,000, the earnings per share of common stock is computed as follows:

Net income	$310,000
Less preferred dividend requirements (40,000 × $10 × 8%)	32,000
Earnings available to common stockholders	$278,000
Average number of shares of common stock outstanding	80,000
Earnings per share of common stock	$3.48

FIGURE 24-14 Calculation of Earnings per Share of Common Stock

			20-2	20-1
Earnings per Share of Common Stock	Net Income Available to Common Stockholders / Average Number of Common Shares Outstanding	=	$71,845 / 67,500 = $1.06	$54,760 / 60,000 = $0.91
Average Number of Common Shares Outstanding	(Beginning Shares Outstanding + Ending Shares Outstanding) / 2	=	(60,000 + 75,000) / 2 = 67,500	(60,000 + 60,000) / 2 = 60,000

Earnings per share is widely used as a measure of a company's performance. It is best tracked over time for the same company. Care must be taken to watch for major changes in the number of shares outstanding as these changes will have a significant impact on the measure.

U REVU Complete U REVU-3 on **pages 970–971** to test your basic understanding of LO4.

LEVERAGE MEASURES

LO5 Compute and explain leverage measures.

Leverage measures indicate the extent to which a company is being financed by debt and the ability of the company to meet its debt obligations. Two of these measures focus on balance sheet relationships, and another focuses on the income statement.

DEBT-TO-EQUITY RATIO

The **debt-to-equity ratio**, or **ratio of liabilities to stockholders' equity**, measures the extent of leverage, or proportion of borrowed capital, with which a business operates. This ratio is calculated by dividing total liabilities by total stockholders' equity. For FCI, the calculation of this ratio at the end of each year is shown in Figure 24-15.

FIGURE 24-15 Calculation of the Debt-to-Equity Ratio

			20-2	20-1
Debt-to-Equity Ratio	Total Liabilities / Total Stockholders' Equity	=	$174,200 / $279,345	$220,350 / $192,500
			0.62 to 1	1.14 to 1

This ratio was much lower on December 31, 20-2, than it was on December 31, 20-1. The reduction in the ratio appears to have been caused by three factors.

1. Stockholders' equity increased by issuance of common stock for $22,500.
2. Stockholders' equity increased by keeping a large portion of 20-2's earnings.
3. Both notes payable and accounts payable were significantly reduced during 20-2, so that total liabilities decreased.

On December 31, 20-1, the majority of the financing for FCI came from debt. Companies in low-risk industries with fairly stable earnings can operate with a high ratio of liabilities to stockholders' equity. Comparing FCI's ratio with the industry average would be helpful in evaluating the degree of leverage. If creditors view the debt-to-equity ratio as too high, it will be very difficult for the company to borrow additional funds.

ASSETS-TO-EQUITY RATIO

Another way to view financial leverage is by comparing total assets with total stockholders' equity. This **assets-to-equity ratio** is calculated by dividing total assets by total stockholders' equity. For FCI, the calculation of this ratio at the end of each year is shown in Figure 24-16.

FIGURE 24-16 Calculation of Assets-to-Equity Ratio

			20-2	20-1
Assets-to-Equity Ratio	Total Assets	=	$453,545	$412,850
	Total Stockholders' Equity		$279,345	$192,500
			1.6	2.1

We know that assets = liabilities + stockholders' equity. So, if there are no liabilities, assets will equal stockholders' equity, there is no leverage, and the ratio will equal 1:1. When this ratio exceeds 1:1, it means the firm is using debt to acquire assets. Some firms are very conservative and try to use as little debt as possible. Others are more aggressive and try to use other people's money to acquire assets and increase profits.

Of course, leverage is risky whether viewed as debt-to-equity or assets-to-equity. While leverage can increase profits in good times, it can also lead to reduced profits or losses in bad times. The key is whether the firm's return on the additional assets is greater than the interest on the debt used to acquire the assets. Thus, it is important to monitor the firm's ability to pay interest. This is discussed in our next measure of leverage, the times interest earned ratio.

TIMES INTEREST EARNED RATIO

When a business has long-term liabilities such as bonds payable or mortgage payable, creditors want to know the amount of earnings available to pay interest. The ratio of earnings before taxes and interest to the interest expense is called the **times interest earned ratio**.

FCI had bonds payable of $100,000 outstanding on December 31, 20-2 and 20-1. The interest rate on the bonds was 10.5%. Interest expense in each year was $10,500 ($100,000 × 10.5%). The calculation of the times interest earned ratio for each year is shown in Figure 24-17.

These times interest earned ratios would be very satisfactory to the bond holders of FCI and indicate that FCI is using leverage in a responsible manner. In many businesses, a ratio of 2 or 3 is considered adequate. Of course, if interest coverage is too low, it will be difficult to issue additional debt.

FIGURE 24-17 Calculation of Times Interest Earned Ratio

			20-2	20-1
Times Interest Earned	Income Before Taxes and Interest / Interest Expense	=	$118,945 / $10,500	$84,470 / $10,500
			11.3	8.0
Income Before Taxes and Interest	Net income		$ 71,845	$54,760
	Add: Income tax		36,600	19,210
	Bond interest		10,500	10,500
			$118,945	$84,470

U REVU Complete U REVU-4 on **pages 970–971** to test your basic understanding of LO5.

ANOTHER LOOK AT ROA AND ROE

LO6 Explain the components of ROA and ROE.

By employing three of the financial ratios that we have discussed, we are able to gain additional insight into how a company generates a return for its stockholders. First, we can break down the return on assets into two parts: profit margin and asset turnover as shown below in Figure 24-18 for FCI in 20-2.

FIGURE 24-18 Another Look at ROA

RETURN ON ASSETS			
	Net Income / Average Assets		
Profit Margin	×	**Asset Turnover**	
Net Income / Net Sales	×	Net Sales / Average Assets	
$71,845 / $835,950	×	$835,950 / $433,198	
		($412,850 + $453,545)/2	ROA
8.59%	×	1.93	= 16.6%

Recall that some analysts prefer to add interest (net of tax) to the numerator to provide a measure of ROA that ignores how the assets were financed. We can see that FCI uses a relatively modest profit margin and moderately fast asset turnover to produce its return on assets.

By adding a measure of leverage (assets-to-equity ratio), we can see how FCI uses leverage to enhance its return on assets to generate a better return on common stockholders' equity. Note that when the assets-to-equity ratio is used to help compute ROE, we use average assets and average common stockholders' equity. Ultimately, we are computing the return on stockholders' equity. Whenever we use income statement and balance sheet measures in a ratio, we must use the average for the balance sheet measure. Since net income was earned throughout the year, we must use the average amount of stockholders' equity that was available during the year. This calculation is shown in Figure 24-19 for FCI in 20-2.

FIGURE 24-19 Another Look at ROE

RETURN ON COMMON STOCKHOLDERS' EQUITY

$$\frac{\text{Net Income}}{\text{Average Common Stockholders' Equity}}$$

Profit Margin	×	Asset Turnover	×	Leverage Ratio		ROE
Net Income / Net Sales	×	Net Sales / Average Assets	×	Average Assets / Average Common Stockholders' Equity		
\$71,845 / \$835,950	×	\$835,950 / \$433,198	×	\$433,198 / \$235,923		
		(\$412,850 + \$453,545)/2		(\$192,500 + \$279,345)/2		
8.59%	×	1.93	×	1.84	=	30.5%
Or		16.6% (ROA)	×	1.84	=	30.5%

A BROADER VIEW

JOHN SOMMERS II/REUTERS/CORBIS

Different Ways to Generate Return on Assets

Return on assets may be broken down into two major ratios, profit margin and asset turnover. This view of ROA helps illustrate that there are different ways to be profitable. Some retail stores, like Staples, minimize investments in plant and equipment and focus on low prices. Thus, profit margins are lower, but asset turnover is higher. For every dollar in net sales, net income is rather small, perhaps only a nickel. However, these businesses are able to generate acceptable profits because they have many customers and must constantly restock the shelves. In contrast, companies like UPS must make large investments in trucks and airplanes to generate revenues. Therefore, they must have higher profit margins to compensate for lower asset turnover. As shown below, Staples and UPS have a similar return on assets, but very different profit margins and asset turnovers.

Return on Assets	=	Profit Margin	×	Asset Turnover
Net Income / Average Assets	=	Net Income / Net Sales	×	Net Sales / Average Assets

	Return on Assets	=	Profit Margin	×	Asset Turnover
Staples	\$834 / \$7,374	=	\$834 / \$16,079	×	\$16,079 / \$7,374
	11.3%		5.2%		2.18
UPS	\$3,870 / \$34,155	=	\$3,870 / \$42,581	×	\$42,581 / \$34,155
	11.3%		9.1%		1.25

Source: Annual Reports for each company. Dollars in millions.

Using this breakdown, we can see that FCI's use of leverage almost doubles (1.84) the return on assets when computing the return on common stockholders' equity. This appears to be a good use of leverage. Further, based on our earlier analysis of times-interest-earned, we know that FCI has no difficulty covering the interest payments.

U REVU Complete U REVU-5 on **pages 970–971** to test your basic understanding of LO6.

MARKET MEASURES

LO7 Compute and explain market measures.

Market measures use stock market prices to offer evidence of how the company is viewed by investors. Of course, we can compute these measures only if there is a ready market price for the stock. For these measures, we will assume FCI had market values of $9.00 and $7.00 per share of common stock in 20-2 and 20-1, respectively.

PRICE-EARNINGS RATIO (PE RATIO)

The **price-earnings ratio (PE ratio)** is often used by analysts and frequently cited on financial programs. It is computed by dividing the company's market price per share of common stock by the earnings per share of common stock. The calculations of the price earnings ratio for FCI are shown in Figure 24-20.

FIGURE 24-20 Calculation of Price-Earnings Ratio

			20-2	20-1
Price-Earnings Ratio	Market Price of Common Stock / Earnings per Share of Common Stock	=	$9.00 / $1.06	$7.00 / $0.91
			8.5	7.7

In general, a higher PE ratio suggests that investors have more confidence in a company's future earnings and growth than for a company with a low PE ratio. PE ratios vary considerably across industries, so it is important to compare ratios with companies in the same industry or with the company's own historical performance.

Some investors will use earnings per share or an estimate of future earnings to attempt to estimate the market value of the stock. If, for example, an investor believes the "correct" PE ratio for FCI is 12, an estimated market price of $12.72 ($1.06 EPS × 12) could be computed. This would suggest that FCI is "undervalued" by the market. Of course, these estimates are highly subjective.

BOOK VALUE PER SHARE OF COMMON STOCK

Book value per share of common stock is a measure of the ownership equity represented by each share. If a corporation has only common stock outstanding, book value per share is determined by dividing the total stockholders' equity as reported on the balance sheet by the number of shares outstanding at the end of the year. Book value per share means value per books, not the amount that stockholders would receive for their shares if sold or if the company liquidated.

FCI had 60,000 shares outstanding on December 31, 20-1, and 75,000 shares outstanding on December 31, 20-2. Therefore, the book value per share of common stock is calculated in Figure 24-21.

FIGURE 24-21 Calculation of Book Value per Share of Common Stock

			20-2	20-1
Book Value per Share of Common Stock	Common Stockholders' Equity / Number of Common Shares Outstanding	=	$279,345 / 75,000	$192,500 / 60,000
			$3.72	$3.21

When preferred shares are outstanding, the claims or equity of the preferred stock must be considered. These include liquidation values, dividends in arrears on cumulative preferred stock, and earnings available to participating preferred stock. For example, assume a corporation has 30,000 shares of $10 par, preferred stock with a liquidation value of $10.50 per share, and 60,000 shares of common stock outstanding. The total stockholders' equity in the company is $1,200,000. The book value per share of common stock is calculated as follows:

Total stockholders' equity	$1,200,000
Less liquidation claim of preferred stock ($10.50 × 30,000)	315,000
Balance applicable to common stock / Number of shares outstanding	$885,000 / 60,000
Book value per share of common stock	$14.75

As you probably noticed, market values are not used in these calculations. However, the market value of the common stock is often compared with its book value when attempting to determine whether the stock is valued properly. Since the market value of the company's assets generally exceeds their book values, the market value of the stock is generally well above its book value. Many investors watch for the market value of the stock to approach or fall below the book value and believe this is a good time to buy the stock. It's good to be cautious, however, since the price could be on its way to zero. Further analysis would be important.

U REVU

Complete U REVU-6 on **pages 970–971** to test your basic understanding of LO7.

LIMITATIONS OF FINANCIAL STATEMENT ANALYSIS

LO8 Explain the limitations of financial statement analysis.

Financial statement analysis can be a valuable tool in evaluating management performance. However, the methods of analysis need to be used cautiously and with an awareness of their limitations. The accounting system does not measure all aspects of operating a business. For example, the accounting numbers do not reflect the level of customer satisfaction with the company's products or the current employee morale. Further, the reported data are based on many estimates and approximations.

The period of time covered by the financial statements is another consideration. In this chapter, the analysis is based on only two years. A period of two consecutive years is not sufficient to establish a long-term trend. Many companies provide five- and ten-year summaries of operating results in published annual reports.

Profiles in Accounting

Jose Cortez, Financial Manager

As a financial manager, Jose has worked for both domestic and international companies, including Limited Brands and Neopost AG. He is currently the manager of store finance at Barnes & Noble, Inc., a Fortune 500 Company and the nation's largest bookseller, generating about $5 billion dollars annually. In his current role, he is responsible for the financial planning and analysis of approximately 800 super stores nationwide and leads a group of 5 financial analysts. His responsibilities have been designed to provide Barnes & Noble with a competitive advantage in reporting and strategizing for short-and long-terms goals.

Comparison of FCI's financial results with other companies and with its industry as a whole can be difficult because generally accepted accounting principles allow different methods of accounting for similar events. For example, the choice of different inventory and depreciation methods can significantly impact both the income statement and the balance sheet. At a minimum, the accounting methods used by the other companies must be identified, so that their possible effects on comparisons can be considered.

Finally, in using ratios, remember that the observed number is simply an expression of the relationship between two other numbers. Either the numerator or the denominator can cause a ratio to provide a distorted message. For example, a company with the same net income in two consecutive years could show a higher rate of return in the second year, simply because the total assets in the second year are lower due to depreciation.

SELF-STUDY

LEARNING OBJECTIVES	Key Points to Remember
LO1 Perform horizontal and vertical analyses of the income statement and balance sheet.	The financial statements can be much more informative and meaningful if they are analyzed on a comparative basis. The following are four possible types of comparisons: 1. with one or more previous periods 2. with data for the industry as a whole 3. with similar information for other businesses in the industry 4. with preset plans or goals (normally in the form of budgets) A comparison of the amounts for the same item in the financial statements of two or more periods is called *horizontal analysis.* Reporting the amount of each item in a statement as a percentage of some designated total is called *vertical analysis.*

LEARNING OBJECTIVES Key Points to Remember

LO2/3/4/5/7

Compute and explain liquidity, activity, profitability, leverage, and market measures of performance.

The following table summarizes the liquidity, activity, profitability, leverage, and market measures.

LIQUIDITY MEASURES	
Working Capital	Current Assets − Current Liabilities
Current Ratio	$\frac{\text{Current Assets}}{\text{Current Liabilities}}$
Quick (or Acid-Test) Ratio	$\frac{\text{Quick Assets}}{\text{Current Liabilities}}$

ACTIVITY MEASURES	
Accounts Receivable Turnover	$\frac{\text{Net Sales on Account}}{\text{Average Accounts Receivable (net)}}$
Also expressed in days	365 ÷ Accounts Receivable Turnover
Merchandise Inventory Turnover	$\frac{\text{Cost of Goods Sold}}{\text{Average Merchandise Inventory}}$
Also expressed in days	365 ÷ Merchandise Inventory Turnover
Asset Turnover	$\frac{\text{Net Sales}}{\text{Average Assets}}$

PROFITABILITY MEASURES	
Profit Margin Ratio	$\frac{\text{Net Income}}{\text{Net Sales}}$
Return on Assets	$\frac{\text{Net Income}}{\text{Average Assets}}$
Return on Common Stockholders' Equity	$\frac{\text{Net Income Available to Common Stockholders}}{\text{Average Common Stockholders' Equity}}$
Earnings per Share of Common Stock	$\frac{\text{Net Income Available to Common Stockholders}}{\text{Average Number of Common Shares Outstanding}}$

LEVERAGE MEASURES	
Debt-to-Equity Ratio	$\frac{\text{Total Liabilities}}{\text{Total Stockholders' Equity}}$
Assets-to-Equity Ratio	$\frac{\text{Total Assets}}{\text{Total Stockholders' Equity}}$
Times Interest Earned Ratio	$\frac{\text{Income Before Taxes and Interest}}{\text{Interest Expense}}$

MARKET MEASURES	
Price-Earnings Ratio	$\frac{\text{Market Price of Common Stock}}{\text{Earnings per Share of Common Stock}}$
Book Value per Share of Common Stock	$\frac{\text{Common Stockholders' Equity}}{\text{Number of Common Shares Outstanding at Year-End}}$

LEARNING OBJECTIVES — Key Points to Remember

LO6 Explain the components of ROA and ROE

The following table summarizes the components of return on assets (ROA) and return on equity (ROE).

COMPONENTS OF ROA AND ROE

Return on Assets	$\frac{\text{Net Income}}{\text{Average Assets}}$				
	Profit Margin	×	Asset Turnover		
	$\frac{\text{Net Income}}{\text{Net Sales}}$	×	$\frac{\text{Net Sales}}{\text{Average Assets}}$		
Return on Common Stockholders' Equity	$\frac{\text{Net Income}}{\text{Average Common Stockholders' Equity}}$				
	Profit Margin	×	Asset Turnover	×	Leverage Ratio
	$\frac{\text{Net Income}}{\text{Net Sales}}$	×	$\frac{\text{Net Sales}}{\text{Average Assets}}$	×	$\frac{\text{Average Assets}}{\text{Average Common Stockholders' Equity}}$

LO8 Explain the limitations of financial statement analysis.

Limitations of financial statement analysis include the following:

1. Factors not reported on the financial statements are also important in evaluating the financial health of a company.
2. Financial statement information is based on many estimates.
3. Statements from many years should be considered before drawing conclusions about long-term trends.
4. Comparisons across companies are difficult due to the possible use of different accounting techniques.
5. The cause of changes in key ratios must be investigated before drawing conclusions.

DEMONSTRATION PROBLEM

Garfinkle Inc.'s comparative financial statements for the years ending December 31, 20-2 and 20-1, are shown on pages 963 and 964. The market value of Garfinkle Inc.'s common stock at the end of 20-2 was $15 per share.

REQUIRED

1. Prepare a horizontal analysis of Garfinkle's comparative income statement for 20-2 and 20-1.
2. Prepare a vertical analysis of Garfinkle's comparative income statement for 20-2 and 20-1.
3. Prepare a horizontal analysis of Garfinkle's comparative balance sheet for 20-2 and 20-1.
4. Prepare a vertical analysis of Garfinkle's comparative balance sheet for 20-2 and 20-1.

5. Determine the following measures for 20-2 (round all calculations to two decimal places):
   (a) working capital
   (b) current ratio
   (c) quick ratio
   (d) accounts receivable turnover
   (e) average collection period for accounts receivable
   (f) merchandise inventory turnover
   (g) average number of days required to sell merchandise inventory
   (h) asset turnover
   (i) profit margin ratio
   (j) return on assets
   (k) return on common stockholders' equity
   (l) earnings per share of common stock
   (m) debt-to-equity ratio
   (n) assets-to-equity ratio
   (o) times interest earned ratio
   (p) ROA showing two components
   (q) ROE showing three components
   (r) price-earnings ratio
   (s) book value per share of common stock

Garfinkle Inc.
Comparative Income Statement
For Years Ended December 31, 20-2 and 20-1

	20-2	20-1
Sales (all on account)	$10,250,000	$6,515,200
Sales returns and allowances	250,000	115,200
Net sales	$10,000,000	$6,400,000
Cost of goods sold	6,800,000	4,160,000
Gross profit	$ 3,200,000	$2,240,000
Administrative expenses	$ 650,000	$ 448,000
Selling expenses	1,300,000	928,000
Total operating expenses	$ 1,950,000	$1,376,000
Operating income	$ 1,250,000	$ 864,000
Other expense (interest)	160,000	89,600
Income before income taxes	$ 1,090,000	$ 774,400
Income tax expense	390,000	234,400
Net income	$ 700,000	$ 540,000

(continued)

Garfinkle Inc.
Comparative Balance Sheet
December 31, 20-2 and 20-1

	20-2	20-1
Assets		
Current assets:		
Cash	$ 350,000	$ 250,000
Accounts receivable (net)	1,150,000	750,000
Inventories	1,440,000	960,000
Supplies and prepayments	60,000	40,000
Total current assets	$3,000,000	$2,000,000
Plant assets (net)	4,686,000	4,346,000
Total assets	$7,686,000	$6,346,000
Liabilities		
Current liabilities	$1,500,000	$1,300,000
Stockholders' Equity		
Common stock, $10 par	$4,500,000	$4,000,000
Retained earnings	1,686,000	1,046,000
Total stockholders' equity	$6,186,000	$5,046,000
Total liabilities and stockholders' equity	$7,686,000	$6,346,000

Solution

1. Horizontal analysis:

Garfinkle Inc.
Comparative Income Statement
For Years Ended December 31, 20-2 and 20-1

	20-2	20-1	INCREASE (DECREASE)	PERCENT
Sales (all on account)	$10,250,000	$6,515,200	$3,734,800	57.3
Sales returns and allowances	250,000	115,200	134,800	117.0
Net sales	$10,000,000	$6,400,000	$3,600,000	56.3
Cost of goods sold	6,800,000	4,160,000	2,640,000	63.5
Gross profit	$ 3,200,000	$2,240,000	$ 960,000	42.9
Administrative expenses	$ 650,000	$ 448,000	$ 202,000	45.1
Selling expenses	1,300,000	928,000	372,000	40.1
Total operating expenses	$ 1,950,000	$1,376,000	$ 574,000	41.7
Operating income	$ 1,250,000	$ 864,000	$ 386,000	44.7
Other expense (interest)	160,000	89,600	70,400	78.6
Income before income taxes	$ 1,090,000	$ 774,400	$ 315,600	40.8
Income tax expense	390,000	234,400	155,600	66.4
Net income	$ 700,000	$ 540,000	$ 160,000	29.6

2. Vertical analysis:

Garfinkle Inc.
Comparative Income Statement
For Years Ended December 31, 20-2 and 20-1

	20-2	PERCENT	20-1	PERCENT
Sales (all on account)	$10,250,000	102.5	$6,515,200	101.8
Sales returns and allowances	250,000	2.5	115,200	1.8
Net sales	$10,000,000	100.0	$6,400,000	100.0
Cost of goods sold	6,800,000	68.0	4,160,000	65.0
Gross profit	$ 3,200,000	32.0	$2,240,000	35.0
Administrative expenses	$ 650,000	6.5	$ 448,000	7.0
Selling expenses	1,300,000	13.0	928,000	14.5
Total operating expenses	$ 1,950,000	19.5	$1,376,000	21.5
Operating income	$ 1,250,000	12.5	$ 864,000	13.5
Other expense (interest)	160,000	1.6	89,600	1.4
Income before income taxes	$ 1,090,000	10.9	$ 774,400	12.1
Income tax expense	390,000	3.9	234,400	3.7
Net income	$ 700,000	7.0	$ 540,000	8.4

3. Horizontal analysis:

Garfinkle Inc.
Comparative Balance Sheet
December 31, 20-2 and 20-1

	20-2	20-1	INCREASE (DECREASE)	PERCENT
Assets				
Current assets:				
Cash	$ 350,000	$ 250,000	$ 100,000	40.0
Accounts receivable (net)	1,150,000	750,000	400,000	53.3
Inventories	1,440,000	960,000	480,000	50.0
Supplies and prepayments	60,000	40,000	20,000	50.0
Total current assets	$3,000,000	$2,000,000	$1,000,000	50.0
Plant assets (net)	4,686,000	4,346,000	340,000	7.8
Total assets	$7,686,000	$6,346,000	$1,340,000	21.1
Liabilities				
Current liabilities	$1,500,000	$1,300,000	$ 200,000	15.4
Stockholders' Equity				
Common stock, $10 par	$4,500,000	$4,000,000	$ 500,000	12.5
Retained earnings	1,686,000	1,046,000	640,000	61.2
Total stockholders' equity	$6,186,000	$5,046,000	$1,140,000	22.6
Total liabilities and stockholders' equity	$7,686,000	$6,346,000	$1,340,000	21.1

(continued)

4. Vertical analysis:

Garfinkle Inc.
Comparative Balance Sheet
December 31, 20-2 and 20-1

	20-2	PERCENT*	20-1	PERCENT*
Assets				
Current assets:				
Cash	$ 350,000	4.6	$250,000	3.9
Accounts receivable (net)	1,150,000	15.0	750,000	11.8
Inventories	1,440,000	18.7	960,000	15.1
Supplies and prepayments	60,000	0.8	40,000	0.6
Total current assets	$3,000,000	39.0	$2,000,000	31.5
Plant assets (net)	4,686,000	61.0	4,346,000	68.5
Total assets	$7,686,000	100.0	$6,346,000	100.0
Liabilities				
Current liabilities	$ 1,500,000	19.5	$1,300,000	20.5
Stockholders' Equity				
Common stock, $10 par	$4,500,000	58.5	$4,000,000	63.0
Retained earnings	1,686,000	21.9	1,046,000	16.5
Total stockholders' equity	$6,186,000	80.5	$5,046,000	79.5
Total liabilities and stockholders' equity	$7,686,000	100.0	$6,346,000	100.0

*Percentages may not add due to rounding.

5. (a) Working capital:

Current assets	$ 3,000,000
– Current liabilities	(1,500,000)
	$ 1,500,000

(b) Current ratio:

$$\frac{\text{Current assets}}{\text{Current liabilities}} = \frac{\$3,000,000}{\$1,500,000} = \underline{\underline{2.00 \text{ to } 1}}$$

(c) Quick ratio:

$$\frac{\text{Quick assets}}{\text{Current liabilities}} = \frac{\$1,500,000}{\$1,500,000} = \underline{\underline{1.00 \text{ to } 1}}$$

(d) Accounts receivable turnover:

$$\frac{\text{Net sales on account}}{\text{Average accounts receivable}} = \frac{\$10,000,000}{(\$750,000 + \$1,150,000) \div 2} = \underline{\underline{10.53}}$$

(e) Average collection period: $\frac{365}{10.53} = \underline{\underline{34.66 \text{ days}}}$

(f) Merchandise inventory turnover:

$$\frac{\text{Cost of goods sold}}{\text{Avg. merchandise inventory}} = \frac{\$6,800,000}{(\$960,000 + \$1,440,000) \div 2} = \underline{\underline{5.67}}$$

(g) Average number of days to sell inventory:

$(365 \div 5.67) = \underline{\underline{64.37 \text{ days}}}$

(h) Asset turnover:

$$\frac{\text{Net sales}}{\text{Average assets}} = \frac{\$10,000,000}{(\$6,346,000 + \$7,686,000) \div 2} = \underline{\underline{1.43 \text{ to } 1}}$$

(i) Profit margin ratio:

$$\frac{\text{Net income}}{\text{Net sales}} = \frac{\$700{,}000}{\$10{,}000{,}000} = \underline{\underline{7.0\%}}$$

(j) Return on assets:

$$\frac{\text{Net income}}{\text{Average assets}} = \frac{\$700{,}000}{(\$6{,}346{,}000 + \$7{,}686{,}000) \div 2} = \underline{\underline{9.98\%}}$$

(k) Return on stockholders' equity:

$$\frac{\text{Net income}}{\text{Avg. stockholders' equity}} = \frac{\$700{,}000}{(\$5{,}046{,}000 + \$6{,}186{,}000) \div 2} = \underline{\underline{12.46\%}}$$

(l) Earnings per share of common stock:

$$\frac{\text{Net income}}{\text{Avg. no. of common shares outstanding}} = \frac{\$700{,}000}{(400{,}000 \text{ shares} + 450{,}000 \text{ shares}) \div 2} = \underline{\underline{\$1.65}}$$

(m) Debt-to-equity ratio:

$$\frac{\text{Total liabilities}}{\text{Total stockholders' equity}} = \frac{\$1{,}500{,}000}{\$6{,}186{,}000} = \underline{\underline{0.24 \text{ to } 1}}$$

(n) Assets-to-equity ratio:

$$\frac{\text{Total assets}}{\text{Total stockholders' equity}} = \frac{\$7{,}686{,}000}{\$6{,}186{,}000} = \underline{\underline{1.24 \text{ to } 1}}$$

(o) Times interest earned ratio:

Net income	$ 700,000
Corporate income taxes	390,000
Interest expense	160,000
Income before taxes and interest	$1,250,000

$$\frac{\text{Income before taxes and interest}}{\text{Interest expense}} = \frac{\$1{,}250{,}000}{\$160{,}000} = \underline{\underline{7.81 \text{ times}}}$$

(p) ROA with 2 components: Profit margin ratio × Asset turnover

$$\frac{\text{Net income}}{\text{Average assets}} = \frac{\text{Net income}}{\text{Net sales}} \times \frac{\text{Net sales}}{\text{Average assets}}$$

$$\frac{\$700{,}000}{\$10{,}000{,}000} \times \frac{\$10{,}000{,}000}{\$7{,}016{,}000}$$

$$7.00\% \times 1.43\% = \underline{\underline{9.98\%}}$$

(q) ROE with 3 components:

		Profit margin ratio		Asset turnover		Leverage
$\frac{\text{Net income}}{\text{Average assets}}$	=	$\frac{\text{Net income}}{\text{Net sales}}$	×	$\frac{\text{Net sales}}{\text{Average assets}}$	×	$\frac{\text{Average assets}}{\text{Avg. stockholders' equity}}$
		$\frac{\$700{,}000}{\$10{,}000{,}000}$	×	$\frac{\$10{,}000{,}000}{\$7{,}016{,}000}$	×	$\frac{\$7{,}016{,}000}{\$5{,}616{,}000}$
		7.00%	×	1.43	×	1.25 = 12.46%

(r) Price-earnings ratio:

$$\frac{\text{Market price of stock}}{\text{Earnings per share}} \times \frac{\$15.00}{\$1.65} = 9.09$$

(s) Book value per share of common stock:

$$\frac{\text{Common stockholders' equity}}{\text{No. of common shares outstanding}} = \frac{\$6{,}186{,}000}{450{,}000 \text{ shares}} = \underline{\underline{\$13.75}}$$

KEY TERMS

accounts receivable turnover (949) The ratio of net sales on account to the average amount of net accounts receivable.

acid-test ratio (948) See quick ratio.

activity measures (943) Measure of the efficiency with which assets are used to generate a profit.

asset turnover ratio (951) A measure of how efficiently a company used its assets to generate sales. Also called ratio of net sales to assets.

assets-to-equity ratio (955) The ratio of total assets to total stockholders' equity.

book value per share of common stock (958) The ratio of common stockholders' equity to the number of common shares outstanding at the end of the year.

cost of goods sold ratio (946) The ratio of cost of goods sold to net sales.

current ratio (948) The ratio of current assets to current liabilities. Also called working capital ratio.

debt-to-equity ratio (954) The ratio of total liabilities to stockholders' equity. It is a measure of the extent of overall leverage or proportion of borrowed capital with which a business operates. Also called ratio of liabilities to stockholders' equity.

earnings per share of common stock (953) The ratio of net income available to common stockholders to the average number of shares of common stock outstanding during the year.

gross profit ratio (946) The ratio of gross profit to net sales.

horizontal analysis (943) A comparison of the amounts for the same item in the financial statements of two periods.

leverage (943) The proportion of debt to stockholders' equity.

leverage measures (954) Measures that indicate the extent to which a company is being financed by debt, and the ability of the company to meet its debt obligations.

liquidity measures (943) Measures that indicate a company's ability to meet its current debts as they come due.

market measures (943) The use of the market value of common stock as evidence of how the company is viewed by investors.

merchandise inventory turnover (950) The ratio of cost of goods sold to the average merchandise inventory.

net income ratio (946) See profit margin ratio.

operating expense ratio (946) The ratio of operating expenses to net sales.

operating income ratio (946) The ratio of operating income to net sales.

price-earnings ratio (PE ratio) (958) The price of the company's common stock divided by the earnings per share of common stock.

profit margin ratio (946) The ratio of net income to net sales.

profitability measures (943) Measures that indicate a company's ability to earn income by operating efficiently.

quick ratio (948) The ratio of quick assets to current liabilities. Also called the acid-test ratio.

ratio of liabilities to stockholders' equity (954) See debt-to-equity ratio.

ratio of net sales to assets (951) See asset turnover ratio.

return on common stockholders' equity (953) The ratio of net income available to common stockholders for the year to the average common stockholders' equity during the year.

return on assets (952) The ratio of net income for the year to the average assets for the year.

times interest earned ratio (955) The ratio of earnings before interest and taxes to interest expense.

vertical analysis (945) Reporting the amount of each item in a statement as a percentage of some designated total.

working capital (947) The excess of a company's current assets over current liabilities.

working capital ratio (948) See current ratio.

SELF-STUDY QUESTIONS AND EXERCISES

True/False Questions

1. LO1 A comparison of amounts for the same item in the financial statements of two or more periods is horizontal analysis.
2. LO1 It is common for long-term asset accounts to show a decrease in the net balance from year to year.
3. LO2 Working capital is calculated by dividing current assets by current liabilities.
4. LO3 In calculating accounts receivable turnover, only accounts receivable are considered; others, such as accrued interest receivable, are not included.
5. LO5 Leverage is the ability to pay debts when they come due.

Multiple Choice Questions

1. LO1 Financial statements are usually compared with
   (a) one or more previous periods.
   (b) data from the industry as a whole.
   (c) similar businesses in the industry.
   (d) all of the above.
2. LO2 Which of these is not a measure of liquidity?
   (a) working capital
   (b) current ratio
   (c) quick ratio
   (d) return on assets
3. LO2 Working capital is a measure of
   (a) liquidity.
   (b) profitability.
   (c) leverage.
4. LO4 The ability to earn a satisfactory return on investments is called
   (a) liquidity.
   (b) profitability.
   (c) leverage.
5. LO5 The times interest earned ratio is a measure of
   (a) liquidity.
   (b) profitability.
   (c) leverage.

U REVU Exercises

Financial statements for Esplanade Enterprises are provided below. Use these financial statements to complete the U REVU Exercises. (Round all calculations to two decimal places.)

Esplanade Enterprises
Income Statement
For Year Ended December 31, 20-2

	20-2
Net sales (on account)	$900,000
Cost of goods sold	600,000
Gross profit	$300,000
Operating expenses	167,000
Operating income	$133,000
Interest expense	10,000
Income before taxes	$123,000
Income tax expense	43,000
Net income	$ 80,000

Esplanade Enterprises
Balance Sheet
December 31, 20-2 and 20-1

	20-2	20-1
Assets		
Current assets:		
Cash	$ 90,000	$200,000
Accounts receivable	160,000	190,000
Merchandise inventory	180,000	200,000
Total current assets	$430,000	$590,000
Property, plant, and equipment:		
Land	$ 40,000	$ 40,000
Building	140,000	—
Equipment	100,000	—
Total property, plant, and equipment	$280,000	$ 40,000
Total assets	$710,000	$630,000
Liabilities		
Current liabilities:		
Notes payable	$ 20,000	$ 50,000
Accounts payable	40,000	60,000
Total current liabilities	$ 60,000	$110,000
Long-term liabilities:		
Bonds payable	120,000	120,000
Total liabilities	$180,000	$230,000
Stockholders' Equity		
Common stock ($5 par)	$290,000	$250,000
Paid-in capital in excess of par—common stock	130,000	100,000
Retained earnings	110,000	50,000
Total stockholders' equity	$530,000	$400,000
Total liabilities and stockholders' equity	$710,000	$630,000

1. LO2 Compute the following liquidity measures for Esplanade Enterprises for 20-2:
   a. Working capital
   b. Current ratio
   c. Quick ratio
2. LO3 Compute the following activity measures for Esplanade Enterprises for 20-2:
   a. Accounts receivable turnover and average collection period
   b. Merchandise inventory turnover and average number of days to sell inventory
   c. Asset turnover
3. LO4 Compute the following profitability measures for Esplanade Enterprises for 20-2:
   a. Profit margin ratio
   b. Return on assets (ROA)
   c. Return on common stockholders' equity (ROE)
   d. Earnings per share of common stock (EPS)
4. LO5 Compute the following leverage measures for Esplanade Enterprises for 20-2:
   a. Debt-to-equity ratio
   b. Assets-to-equity ratio
   c. Times interest earned ratio
5. LO6 Compute return on assets (ROA) using the two basic components and return on common stockholders' equity (ROE) using the three basic components for Esplanade Enterprises for 20-2:
6. LO7 Compute the following market measures for Esplanade Enterprises for 20-2:
   a. Price-earnings ratio (PE ratio) (The market value of Esplanade's common stock is $12.00 per share.)
   b. Book value per share of common stock

The answers to the Self-Study Questions and Exercises are at the end of the chapter (pages 981–983).

APPLYING YOUR KNOWLEDGE

REVIEW QUESTIONS

LO1 1. Financial statement analysis generally focuses on five main aspects of the business's financial health. What are they?

LO1 2. Describe four possible types of comparisons that may be made in financial statement analysis.

LO1 3. Why was the increase in FCI's operating income so much greater than the increase in its net sales?

LO1 4. What were the main causes of the decrease in FCI's current liabilities?

LO1 5. List five ratios that are automatically provided by the vertical analysis of income statements.

LO2 6. Identify three measures of liquidity calculated by FCI.

LO3 7. Identify three activity measures calculated by FCI.

LO4 8. Identify four measures of profitability calculated by FCI.

LO5 9. Identify three measures of the extent of leverage calculated by FCI.

LO6 10. Identify the two primary components of return on assets.

LO6 11. Identify the three primary components of return on common stockholders' equity.

LO7 12. Identify the two market measures calculated by FCI.

LO8 13. Briefly describe five limitations of financial statement analysis.

SERIES A EXERCISES

E 24-1A (LO2)

✓ (a) 2.17 to 1; (c) $1,716,800

ANALYSIS OF LIQUIDITY Based on the comparative income statement and balance sheet of Ace Kitchen Works, Inc., that follow, compute the following liquidity measures for 20-2 (round all calculations to two decimal places):

(a) Quick or acid-test ratio
(b) Current ratio
(c) Working capital

Ace Kitchen Works, Inc.
Comparative Income Statement
For Years Ended December 31, 20-2 and 20-1

	20-2	20-1
Net sales (on account)	$2,643,000	$2,176,400
Cost of goods sold	1,868,200	1,614,200
Gross profit	$ 774,800	$ 562,200
Operating expenses	244,600	221,800
Other expense (interest)	24,200	24,200
Income tax expense	161,900	101,200
Net income	$ 344,100	$ 215,000

Ace Kitchen Works, Inc.
Comparative Balance Sheet
December 31, 20-2 and 20-1

	20-2	20-1
Cash	$ 129,000	$ 106,800
Government notes	300,000	300,000
Accounts receivable (net)	892,400	787,400
Merchandise inventory	952,800	866,200
Supplies and prepayments	50,600	46,600
Land	108,200	108,200
Building (net)	330,000	390,600
Office equipment (net)	13,600	15,000
Total assets	$2,776,600	$2,620,800
Current liabilities (accounts payable)	$ 608,000	$ 507,200
Bonds payable	200,000	220,000
Total liabilities	$ 808,000	$ 727,200
Common stock ($10 par, 170,000 shares)	$1,700,000	$1,700,000
Retained earnings	268,600	193,600
Total stockholders' equity	$1,968,600	$1,893,600
Total liabilities and stockholders' equity	$2,776,600	$2,620,800

E 24-2A (LO3)

✓ (a) 3.15 or 115.87 days; (c) 0.98 to 1

ANALYSIS OF ACTIVITY MEASURES Based on the financial statement data in Exercise 24-1A, compute the following activity measures for 20-2 (round all calculations to two decimal places):

(a) Accounts receivable turnover
(b) Merchandise inventory turnover
(c) Asset turnover

E 24-3A (LO4)
✓ (b) 12.75%; (d) $2.02

ANALYSIS OF PROFITABILITY Based on the financial statement data in Exercise 24-1A, compute the following profitability measures for 20-2 (round all calculations to two decimal places):

(a) profit margin ratio
(b) Return on assets
(c) Return on common stockholders' equity
(d) Earnings per share of common stock

E 24-4A (LO5)
✓ (a) 0.41 to 1

ANALYSIS OF LEVERAGE Based on the financial statement data in Exercise 24-1A, compute the following leverage measures for 20-2 (round all calculations to two decimal places):

(a) Debt-to-equity ratio
(b) Times interest earned ratio (Bond interest is $24,200.)
(c) Assets-to-equity ratio

E24-5A (LO6)
✓ asset turnover 0.98

ANALYSIS OF ROA COMPONENTS Based on the financial statement data in Exercise 24-1A, compute ROA for 20-2 using its two basic components (round all calculations to two decimal places).

E24-6A (LO6)
✓ asset turnover 0.98

ANALYSIS OF ROE COMPONENTS Based on the financial statement data in Exercise 24-1A, compute ROE for 20-2 using its three basic components (round all calculations to two decimal places).

E24-7A (LO7)
✓ (a) 13.86

CALCULATION OF MARKET MEASURES Based on the financial statement data in Exercise 24-1A, compute the following market measures for 20-2 (round all calculations to two decimal places).

(a) Price-earnings ratio (The market price of Ace Kitchen Works' common stock was $28.00 on December 31, 20-2.)
(b) Book value per share of common stock

SERIES A PROBLEMS

P 24-8A (LO1)

✓	(Inc.)	%
NI	$32,139	52.8
Cash	$20,894	94.9
RE	$95,018	126.5

HORIZONTAL ANALYSIS OF COMPARATIVE FINANCIAL STATEMENTS Amounts from the comparative income statement and balance sheet of Miller Electronics Corporation for the last two years are as follows:

Miller Electronics Corporation
Comparative Income Statement
For Years Ended December 31, 20-2 and 20-1

	20-2	20-1
Net sales (on account)	$650,220	$420,600
Cost of goods sold	395,410	258,668
Gross profit	$254,810	$161,932
Administrative expenses	$ 63,518	$ 42,288
Selling expenses	65,992	43,936
Total operating expenses	$129,510	$ 86,224
Operating income	$125,300	$ 75,708
Interest expense	1,282	1,204
Income before income taxes	$124,018	$ 74,504
Income tax expense	31,005	13,630
Net income	$ 93,013	$ 60,874

(continued)

Miller Electronics Corporation
Comparative Balance Sheet
December 31, 20-2 and 20-1

	20-2	20-1
Assets		
Current assets:		
Cash	$ 42,900	$ 22,006
Receivables (net)	73,642	47,510
Merchandise inventory	92,060	50,396
Supplies and prepayments	3,788	1,158
Total current assets	$212,390	$121,070
Property, plant, and equipment:		
Office equipment (net)	$ 12,150	$ 8,490
Factory equipment (net)	105,360	71,190
Total property, plant, and equipment	$117,510	$ 79,680
Total assets	$329,900	$200,750
Liabilities		
Current liabilities:		
Notes payable	$ 10,000	$ 6,000
Accounts payable	43,524	30,242
Accrued and withheld payroll taxes	6,250	5,400
Total current liabilities	$ 59,774	$ 41,642
Stockholders' Equity		
Common stock ($10 par)	$100,000	$ 84,000
Retained earnings	170,126	75,108
Total stockholders' equity	$270,126	$159,108
Total liabilities and stockholders' equity	$329,900	$200,750

REQUIRED

Prepare a horizontal analysis. Add columns to show the amount of increase (decrease) and the percentage change. Round percentages to one decimal place.

P 24-9A (LO1)

✓

	20-2	20-1
CGS	60.8%	61.5%
Cash	13.0%	11.0%

KA KLOOSTER & ALLEN

VERTICAL ANALYSIS OF COMPARATIVE FINANCIAL STATEMENTS Refer to the financial statements in Problem 24-8A.

REQUIRED

Prepare a vertical analysis of the income statement and balance sheet. Show each item on the income statement as a percentage of the net sales for each year. On the balance sheet, show each asset item as a percentage of the total assets and each liability and equity item as a percentage of the total liabilities and stockholders' equity. Round percentages to one decimal place.

P 24-10A (LO2/3/4/5/7)

✓

	20-1
(a)	32.34%
(c)	$7.25
(e)	1.67 to 1
(g)	$79,428
(i)	5.21 or 70.06 days
(k)	2.23 to 1
(l)	62.88 times
(n)	1.26

RATIO ANALYSIS OF COMPARATIVE FINANCIAL STATEMENTS Refer to the financial statements in Problem 24-8A.

REQUIRED

Calculate the following ratios and amounts for 20-1 and 20-2 (round all calculations to two decimal places):

(a) Return on assets (Total assets on January 1, 20-1, were $175,750.)
(b) Return on common stockholders' equity (Total common stockholders' equity on January 1, 20-1, was $106,944.)

(c) Earnings per share of common stock (The average numbers of shares outstanding were 8,400 shares in 20-1 and 9,200 in 20-2.)
(d) Book value per share of common stock
(e) Quick ratio
(f) Current ratio
(g) Working capital
(h) Receivables turnover (Net receivables on January 1, 20-1, were $39,800.)
(i) Merchandise inventory turnover (Merchandise inventory on January 1, 20-1, was $48,970.)
(j) Debt-to-equity ratio
(k) Asset turnover (Assets on January 1, 20-1, were $175,750.)
(l) Times interest earned ratio
(m) Profit margin ratio
(n) Assets-to-equity ratio
(o) Price-earnings ratio (The market price of the common stock was $100.00 and $85.00 on December 31, 20-2 and 20-1, respectively.)

SERIES B EXERCISES

E 24-1B (LO2)
✓ (b) 3.87 to 1

ANALYSIS OF LIQUIDITY Based on the comparative income statement and balance sheet for Falcon Designers, Inc., given below and on the next page, compute the following liquidity measures for 20-2 (round all calculations to two decimal places):

(a) Quick or acid-test ratio
(b) Current ratio
(c) Working capital

E 24-2B (LO3)
✓ (b) 1.81 or 201.66 days

ANALYSIS OF ACTIVITY MEASURES Based on the financial statement data in Exercise 24-1B, compute the following activity measures for 20-2 (round all calculations to two decimal places):

(a) Accounts receivable turnover
(b) Merchandise inventory turnover
(c) Asset turnover

Falcon Designers, Inc.
Comparative Income Statement
For Years Ended December 31, 20-2 and 20-1

	20-2	20-1
Net sales (on account)	$1,850,800	$1,532,600
Cost of goods sold	1,150,400	1,010,500
Gross profit	$ 700,400	$ 522,100
Operating expenses	180,300	156,600
Other expenses (interest)	18,200	18,200
Income tax expense	160,600	107,600
Net income	$ 341,300	$ 239,700

(continued)

Falcon Designers, Inc.
Comparative Balance Sheet
December 31, 20-2 and 20-1

	20-2	20-1
Cash	$ 95,500	$ 79,700
Government notes	200,000	200,000
Accounts receivable (net)	639,300	570,600
Merchandise inventory	634,900	639,500
Supplies and prepayments	39,600	29,900
Land	81,900	78,400
Building (net)	227,500	289,300
Office equipment (net)	10,400	10,800
Total assets	$1,929,100	$1,898,200
Current liabilities (accounts payable)	$ 416,000	$ 394,500
Bonds payable	150,000	150,000
Total liabilities	$ 566,000	$ 544,500
Common stock ($10 par, 125,000 shares)	$1,250,000	$1,250,000
Retained earnings	113,100	103,700
Total stockholders' equity	$1,363,100	$1,353,700
Total liabilities and stockholders' equity	$1,929,100	$1,898,200

E 24-3B (LO4)
✓ (a) 18.44%;
(c) 25.13%

ANALYSIS OF PROFITABILITY Based on the financial statement data in Exercise 24-1B, compute the following profitability measures for 20-2 (round all calculations to two decimal places):

(a) Profit margin ratio
(b) Return on assets
(c) Return on common stockholders' equity
(d) Earnings per share of common stock

E 24-4B (LO5)
✓ (b) 28.58 times

ANALYSIS OF LEVERAGE Based on the financial statement data in Exercise 24-1B, compute the following leverage measures for 20-2 (round all calculations to two decimal places):

(a) Debt-to-equity ratio
(b) Times interest earned ratio (Bond interest is $18,200.)
(c) Assets-to-equity ratio

E24-5B (LO6)
✓ asset turnover 0.97

ANALYSIS OF ROA COMPONENTS Based on the financial statement data in Exercise 24-1B, compute ROA using its two basic components (round all calculations to two decimal places).

E24-6B (LO6)
✓ asset turnover 0.97

ANALYSIS OF ROE COMPONENTS Based on the financial statement data in Exercise 24-1B, compute ROE using its three basic components (round all calculations to two decimal places).

E24-7B (LO7)
✓ (a) 13.92

CALCULATION OF MARKET MEASURES Based on the financial statement data in Exercise 24-1B, compute the following market measures for 20-2 (round all calculations to two decimal places).

(a) Price-earnings ratio (The market price of Falcon Designers' common stock was $38.00 on December 31, 20-2.)
(b) Book value per share of common stock

SERIES B PROBLEMS

P 24-8B (LO1)

✓

	(Inc.)	%
NI	$17,497	23.9
Cash	$14,671	94.0
RE	$39,148	70.2

KA KLOOSTER & ALLEN

HORIZONTAL ANALYSIS OF COMPARATIVE FINANCIAL STATEMENTS Amounts from the comparative income statement and balance sheet of Johnson Stores, Inc., for the last two years are as follows:

Johnson Stores, Inc.
Comparative Income Statement
For Years Ended December 31, 20-2 and 20-1

	20-2	20-1
Net sales (on account)	$467,865	$305,145
Cost of goods sold	256,955	149,005
Gross profit	$210,910	$156,140
Administrative expenses	$ 43,876	$ 30,617
Selling expenses	44,994	31,293
Total operating expenses	$ 88,870	$ 61,910
Operating income	$122,040	$ 94,230
Interest expense	916	903
Income before income taxes	$121,124	$ 93,327
Income tax expense	30,280	19,980
Net income	$ 90,844	$ 73,347

Johnson Stores, Inc.
Comparative Balance Sheet
December 31, 20-2 and 20-1

	20-2	20-1
Assets		
Current assets:		
Cash	$ 30,275	$ 15,604
Receivables (net)	42,441	33,565
Merchandise inventory	49,460	34,636
Supplies and prepayments	7,119	6,403
Total current assets	$129,295	$ 90,208
Property, plant, and equipment:		
Office equipment (net)	$ 9,025	$ 6,062
Factory equipment (net)	72,090	52,930
Total property, plant, and equipment	$ 81,115	$ 58,992
Total assets	$210,410	$149,200
Liabilities		
Current liabilities:		
Notes payable	$ 4,000	$ 8,000
Accounts payable	30,233	14,821
Accrued and withheld payroll taxes	6,250	7,600
Total current liabilities	$ 40,483	$ 30,421
Stockholders' Equity		
Common stock ($10 par)	$ 75,000	$ 63,000
Retained earnings	94,927	55,779
Total stockholders' equity	$169,927	$118,779
Total liabilities and stockholders' equity	$210,410	$149,200

(continued)

REQUIRED

Prepare a horizontal analysis of the statements. Add columns to show the amount of increase (decrease) and the percentage change. Round percentages to one decimal place.

P 24-9B (LO1)

✓	20-2	20-1
CGS	54.9%	48.8%
Cash	14.4%	10.5%

VERTICAL ANALYSIS OF COMPARATIVE FINANCIAL STATEMENTS Refer to the financial statements in Problem 24-8B.

REQUIRED

Prepare a vertical analysis of the income statement and balance sheet. Show each item on the income statement as a percentage of the net sales for each year. On the balance sheet, show each asset item as a percentage of the total assets and each liability and equity item as a percentage of the total liabilities and stockholders' equity. Round percentages to one decimal place.

P 24-10B (LO2/3/4/5/7)

✓	20-1
(b)	73.06%
(d)	$18.85
(f)	2.97 to 1
(h)	9.76 or 37.40 days
(j)	0.26 to 1
(l)	104.35 times
(n)	1.26

RATIO ANALYSIS OF COMPARATIVE FINANCIAL STATEMENTS Refer to the financial statements in Problem 24-8B.

REQUIRED

Calculate the following ratios and amounts for 20-1 and 20-2 (round all calculations to two decimal places).

(a) Return on assets (Total assets on January 1, 20-1, were $111,325.)
(b) Return on common stockholders' equity (Total common stockholders' equity on January 1, 20-1, was $82,008.)
(c) Earnings per share of common stock (The average numbers of shares outstanding were 6,300 shares in 20-1 and 6,900 in 20-2.)
(d) Book value per share of common stock
(e) Quick ratio
(f) Current ratio
(g) Working capital
(h) Receivables turnover (Net receivables on January 1, 20-1, were $28,995.)
(i) Merchandise inventory turnover (Merchandise inventory on January 1, 20-1, was $32,425.)
(j) Debt-to-equity ratio
(k) Asset turnover (Assets on January 1, 20-1, were $111,325.)
(l) Times interest earned ratio
(m) Profit margin ratio
(n) Assets-to-equity ratio
(o) Price-earnings ratio (The market price of the common stock was $120.00 and $110.00 on December 31, 20-2 and 20-1, respectively.)

MANAGING YOUR WRITING

Many libraries have corporate annual reports and reports on the financial health of companies by financial analysts and rating agencies such as Standard and Poor's and Moody's. Go to the library and review financial information on two corporations in your favorite industry. Write a brief memo describing the information available and how it can be used to evaluate the financial health of a company.

ETHICS CASE

Jim Tennison, L & B Corporation's president, called the company's chief financial officer, Fred Harden, into his office late Friday afternoon. Jim had been reviewing the projected financial statements of L & B Corporation that would be issued as of year-end. Jim told Fred he was worried that the company's liquidity position had been declining over the past two years. Fred assured Jim that the company still had sufficient liquidity, and it had been steadily decreasing its debt. Jim said that there were three or four major stockholders who were very conservative and would raise lots of questions about the company's declining liquidity ratios. Jim and Fred then decided to take out a two-year loan secured by some land L & B Corporation owned, put the cash in the bank, and pay the loan off after January 1. Jim told Fred to account for the transaction as a long-term liability for financial reporting purposes. They agreed that this measure would solve the problem of liquidity at the annual stockholders' meeting because the company's ratios would be almost identical to last year. Jim was sure that most of the stockholders were only concerned with net income and ratios.

1. If you were a stockholder of L & B Corporation, how would you feel about Jim and Fred's idea? Have any ethical principles been violated?
2. If the transaction is booked as a debit to Cash and a credit to Long-Term Notes Payable, how will it affect the company's key current ratios and debt ratios?
3. Suppose Jim and Fred decide not to take out the loan. Write a brief note to the stockholders justifying a decrease in liquidity measures. Assure them that the company is still in the "safe range."
4. In groups of two or three, list as many reasons as possible, both positive and negative, for a decrease in net working capital.

MASTERY PROBLEM

✓ 3(a) $41,800
3(c) 0.58 to 1
4(b) 6.59 or 55.39 days
5(a) 7.60%
5(c) 14.96%
6(b) 45.76 times
7(a) 13.94

Comparative financial statements for Na Pali Coast Company for the years ending December 31, 20-1 and 20-2 are provided.

REQUIRED

1. Perform horizontal analysis of the comparative income statement and balance sheet. Round percentages to one decimal place.
2. Perform vertical analysis of the comparative income statement and balance sheet. Round percentages to one decimal place.
3. Compute the following liquidity measures for 20-2 (round all calculations to two decimal places):
   (a) Working capital
   (b) Current ratio
   (c) Quick or acid-test ratio
4. Compute the following activity measures for 20-2 (round all calculations to two decimal places):
   (a) Accounts receivable turnover and average number of days to collect receivables (Assume that sales on account for 20-2 were $120,000.)
   (b) Merchandise inventory turnover and average number of days to sell inventory
   (c) Asset turnover

(continued)

5. Compute the following profitability measures for 20-2 (round all calculations to two decimal places):
   (a) Profit margin ratio
   (b) Return on assets
   (c) Return on common stockholders' equity
   (d) Earnings per share of common stock
6. Compute the following leverage measures for 20-2 (round all calculations to two decimal places):
   (a) Debt-to-equity ratio
   (b) Times interest earned ratio (Assume interest expense for 20-2 was $1,200.)
7. Compute the following market measures for 20-2 (round all calculations to two decimal places):
   (a) Price-earnings ratio (The market price of Na Pali Coast Company's common stock was $23.00 on December 31, 20-2.)
   (b) Book value per share of common stock

Na Pali Coast Company
Comparative Income Statement
For Years Ended December 31, 20-2 and 20-1

	20-2	20-1
Net sales	$466,451	$291,613
Cost of goods sold	285,889	188,626
Gross profit	$180,562	$102,987
Operating expenses	125,650	78,200
Operating income	$ 54,912	$ 24,787
Other expenses	1,200	500
Income before income taxes	$ 53,712	$ 24,287
Income tax expense	18,250	7,285
Net income	$ 35,462	$ 17,002

Na Pali Coast Company
Comparative Balance Sheet
December 31, 20-2 and 20-1

	20-2	20-1
Assets		
Current assets:		
Cash	$ 8,600	$ 7,500
Government notes	3,000	2,000
Accounts receivable (net)	10,500	8,600
Merchandise inventory	53,600	33,200
Supplies and prepayments	4,500	3,200
Total current assets	$ 80,200	$ 54,500
Property, plant, and equipment:		
Land	$ 40,000	$ 40,000
Building (net)	200,000	150,000
Delivery equipment (net)	13,000	15,000
Office equipment (net)	5,400	6,000
Patents	5,000	6,000
Total property, plant, and equipment	$263,400	$217,000
Total assets	$343,600	$271,500

	20-2	20-1
Liabilities		
Current liabilities:		
Notes payable	$ 5,000	$ 3,000
Accounts payable	28,700	22,300
Accrued and withheld payroll taxes	4,200	5,600
Accrued interest payable	500	1,700
Total current liabilities	$ 38,400	$ 32,600
Long-term liabilities:		
Bonds payable	50,000	20,000
Total liabilities	$ 88,400	$ 52,600
Stockholders' Equity		
Common stock ($5 par)	$115,000	$100,000
Paid-in capital in excess of par	65,000	60,000
Retained earnings	75,200	58,900
Total stockholders' equity	$255,200	$218,900
Total liabilities and stockholders' equity	$343,600	$271,500

CHALLENGE PROBLEM

This problem challenges you to apply your cumulative accounting knowledge to move a step beyond the material in the chapter.

✓ **Days cash is outstanding for merchandise: 54.04 days**

Combining the information provided by various ratios can enhance your understanding of the financial condition of a business. Review the information provided for Na Pali Coast Company in the Mastery Problem. Using this information, respond to the following questions:

REQUIRED

1. Compute the average number of days required to sell inventory and collect cash from customers buying on account.
2. Note that Na Pali Coast Company also buys inventory on account. On average, how many days pass before Na Pali pays its creditors?
3. Using the information from your answers to parts (1) and (2), compute the number of days from the time Na Pali Coast pays for inventory until it receives cash from customers on account.

ANSWERS TO SELF-STUDY QUESTIONS AND EXERCISES

True/False Questions

1. T
2. T
3. F (WC = CA – CL)
4. T
5. F (Leverage is a measure of the extent to which debt is used to finance the business.)

Multiple Choice Questions

1. d 2. d 3. a 4. b 5. c

U REVU Exercises

1. a. Working capital = $430,000 – $60,000 = $370,000
   b. Current ratio = $430,000/$60,000 = 7.17 to 1
   c. Quick ratio = $250,000/$60,000 = 4.17 to 1

2. a. Accounts receivable turnover:

   $\frac{\text{Net sales on account}}{\text{Average accounts receivable}} = \frac{\$900,000}{\$175,000} = \underline{\underline{5.14}}$

   ($190,000 + $160,000)/2

   Average collection period 365/5.14 = 71.01 days

   b. Merchandise inventory turnover:

   $\frac{\text{Cost of goods sold}}{\text{Average merchandise inventory}} = \frac{\$600,000}{\$190,000} = \underline{\underline{3.16}}$

   ($200,000 + $180,000)/2

   Average number of days to sell inventory = 365/3.16 = 115.51

   c. Asset turnover:

   $\frac{\text{Net sales}}{\text{Average assets}} = \frac{\$900,000}{\$670,000} = \underline{\underline{1.34 \text{ to } 1}}$

   ($630,000 + $710,000)/2

3. a. Profit margin ratio:

   $\frac{\text{Net income}}{\text{Net sales}} = \frac{\$80,000}{\$900,000} = \underline{\underline{8.89\%}}$

   b. Return on assets (ROA):

   $\frac{\text{Net income}}{\text{Average assets}} = \frac{\$80,000}{\$670,000} = \underline{\underline{11.94\%}}$

   ($630,000 + $710,000)/2

   c. Return on common stockholders' equity (ROE):

   $\frac{\text{Net income}}{\text{Average common stockholders' equity}} = \frac{\$80,000}{\$465,000} = \underline{\underline{17.20\%}}$

   ($400,000 + $530,000)/2

   d. Earnings per share of common stock (EPS):

   $\frac{\text{Net income}}{\text{Average number of common shares outstanding}} = \frac{\$80,000}{54,000} = \underline{\underline{\$1.48}}$

   (50,000 + 58,000)/2

4. a. Debt-to-equity ratio:

   $\frac{\text{Total liabilities}}{\text{Total stockholders' equity}} = \frac{\$180,000}{\$530,000} = \underline{\underline{0.34 \text{ to } 1}}$

   b. Assets-to-equity ratio:

   $\frac{\text{Total assets}}{\text{Total stockholders' equity}} = \frac{\$710,000}{\$530,000} = \underline{\underline{1.34 \text{ to } 1}}$

   c. Times interest earned ratio:

   $\frac{\text{Income before taxes and interest}}{\text{Interest expense}} = \frac{\$133,000}{\$10,000} = \underline{\underline{13.30 \text{ times}}}$

Net income	$ 80,000
Income tax expense	43,000
Interest expense	10,000
Income before taxes and interest	$133,000

5. ROA with 2 components: **Profit margin ratio** × **Asset turnover**

$$\frac{\text{Net income}}{\text{Average assets}} = \frac{\text{Net income}}{\text{Net sales}} \times \frac{\text{Net sales}}{\text{Average assets}}$$

$$\frac{\$80{,}000}{\$900{,}000} \times \frac{\$900{,}000}{\$670{,}000}$$

($630,000 + $710,000)/2

$$8.89\% \times 1.34 = \underline{\underline{11.91\%^{*}}}$$

*Variance from 11.94% in 3b. due to rounding.

ROE with 3 components: **Profit margin ratio** × **Asset turnover** × **Leverage**

$$\frac{\text{Net income}}{\text{Average stockholders' equity}} = \frac{\text{Net income}}{\text{Net sales}} \times \frac{\text{Net sales}}{\text{Average assets}} \times \frac{\text{Average assets}}{\text{Avg. stockholders' equity}}$$

$$\frac{\$80{,}000}{\$900{,}000} \times \frac{\$900{,}000}{\$670{,}000} \times \frac{\$670{,}000}{\$465{,}000}$$

($630,000 + $710,000)/2 ($400,000 + $530,000)/2

$$8.89\% \times 1.34 \times 1.44 = \underline{\underline{17.15^{*}\%}}$$

*Variance from 17.20% in 3c. due to rounding.

6. a. Price-earnings ratio (PE ratio):

$$\frac{\text{Market price of common stock}}{\text{Earnings per share of common stock}} = \frac{\$12.00}{\$1.48} = \underline{\underline{8.11}}$$

b. Book value per share of common stock:

$$\frac{\text{Common stockholders' equity}}{\text{No. of common shares outstanding}} = \frac{\$530{,}000}{\$58{,}000} = \underline{\underline{\$9.14}}$$

Chapter 25

COURTESY OF VIZIO, INC.

LEARNING OBJECTIVES

Careful study of this chapter should enable you to:

LO1 **Explain the nature and purpose of departmental accounting.**

LO2 **Describe and compute departmental gross profit.**

LO3 **Describe and compute departmental operating income.**

LO4 **Describe and compute departmental direct operating margin.**

Departmental Accounting

As you marvel at the clarity and crispness of the picture on your HDTV or the power of the sounds blasting from your sound system, you probably don't think much about tracking the costs and profitability of these products. Okay, as budding accountants, maybe you do, but most folks would not. VIZIO is a highly successful and rapidly growing company (4,000%+ revenue increase in a recent four-year period) that certainly would need to do this tracking. VIZIO produces many models of LCD and HD TVs, plus multiple home theater systems, and a variety of accessories for such products. All of these are technology products, but LCD screens, home theater systems, and various accessories would involve different production components and processes. How would VIZIO know the profitability of these different products? One possibility is to organize the business into departments: e.g., LCD screens, home theater equipment and accessories. The activities of each department could then be separately accounted for and evaluated. In this chapter, we will learn how to account for departmental operations, including different measures of performance and how to interpret them.

Companies often engage in different types of profit-making activities. For example, a merchandiser might sell different products, such as lawn mowers and bicycles. A service business might provide different services, such as auditing and management consulting. Such businesses are often organized into separate segments called departments. In this chapter, we will examine how to account for a business organized into departments.

DEPARTMENTAL ACCOUNTING

LO1 Explain the nature and purpose of departmental accounting.

When a business sells several products or services, it can be difficult to obtain useful and accurate information about the business. An income statement prepared for the business as a whole might show that the business is reasonably profitable. This statement would not show that one portion of the business is highly successful while another portion is operating at a loss. Departmental accounting overcomes this problem by providing separate information about the revenues and expenses of each department.

Departmental reports are useful to management for three purposes: (1) planning, (2) control, and (3) performance evaluation.

1. Planning—Successful managers set goals and develop plans for achieving these goals. An important part of planning is identifying the strengths and weaknesses of the different parts of the firm. Departmental reports can be very helpful for this purpose.
2. Control—To properly control operations, managers must be able to identify revenues and expenses that are out of line. Departmental reports help management focus attention on problem areas or departments.
3. Performance evaluation—When a business is organized into departments, responsibility for each department can be assigned to a specific manager. Departmental reports can then be used to evaluate each manager's performance.

Departmental reports are usually not part of the basic financial statements. These reports are for internal management use only. This means the accounting rules for external reporting do not apply. Department reports can be prepared in whatever form management finds useful. Generally, only a departmental income statement is prepared. In the following sections, we will look at departmental income statements for Annie's Sporting Goods, which sells golf and tennis equipment. These income statements will be extended through three different levels: gross profit, operating income, and direct operating margin.

DEPARTMENTAL GROSS PROFIT

LO2 Describe and compute departmental gross profit.

Departmental gross profit is the difference between a department's net sales and cost of goods sold. Each element used to compute gross profit must be determined for each department. Recall that the following elements are used to compute gross profit:

Sales
Sales returns and allowances
Sales discounts
Inventory
Purchases

Purchases returns and allowances
Purchases discounts
Freight-in

Two ways of accumulating this information are:

1. Maintain separate general ledger accounts by department for each element (account) making up gross profit.
2. Maintain a single general ledger account for each element. The total in each account is assigned to the appropriate departments at the end of the accounting period.

DEPARTMENTAL INCOME STATEMENT SHOWING GROSS PROFIT

Figure 25-1 shows Annie's departmental income statement for the year 20--. The gross profit section is presented in condensed form. Gross profit is shown by department and in total.

FIGURE 25-1 Income Statement Showing Departmental Gross Profit

Annie's Sporting Goods
Income Statement
For Year Ended December 31, 20--

	GOLF	TENNIS	TOTAL
Net sales	$1,075,000.00	$640,300.00	$1,715,300.00
Cost of goods sold	545,280.00	420,900.00	966,180.00
Gross profit	$ 529,720.00	$219,400.00	$ 749,120.00
Operating expenses:			
Store clerks' wages expense			$ 80,250.00
Truck drivers' wages expense			83,900.00
Advertising expense			79,500.00
Store rent expense			22,800.00
Bad debt expense			17,900.00
Depreciation expense—delivery equipment			24,000.00
Other operating expenses			350,430.00
Total operating expenses			$ 658,780.00
Operating income			$ 90,340.00

This report shows that the golf department provides the majority of Annie's sales and gross profit. The report also reveals a large difference in the gross profit percentages of the two departments.

Golf department gross profit percentage: ($529,720 ÷ $1,075,000)	**49.3%**
Tennis department gross profit percentage: ($219,400 ÷ $640,300)	**34.3%**

These gross profit percentages provide a good example of how departmental reports can be useful for control and performance evaluation. Management should determine the causes of the difference between the departments' results and take appropriate action. Perhaps the normal retail markup on golf equipment is higher than that on tennis equipment. If so, management might want to emphasize selling golf equipment. If the normal retail markup on the two products is similar, the pricing policies for tennis equipment should be evaluated. The tennis department may be using an inadequate markup percentage. Another possibility is that the purchase prices for tennis equipment are too high. If so, the purchasing department should try to obtain better prices from vendors.

Once the causes of the difference are determined, the departmental information can be used for planning. Management can set quantitative goals for the departments for the following period. Performance comparisons then could be made both between the departments, as in Figure 25-1, and with established goals.

A higher gross profit or gross profit percentage does not necessarily mean that a department is more profitable overall. To evaluate overall profitability, departmental operating expenses must also be considered.

LEARNING KEY

An income statement showing departmental gross profit enables management to see whether each department is earning an adequate gross profit.

U REVU

Complete U REVU-1 on **page 1001** to test your basic understanding of LO2

DEPARTMENTAL OPERATING INCOME

LO3 Describe and compute departmental operating income.

Departmental operating income is the difference between a department's gross profit and its operating expenses. As with departmental gross profit, separate departmental accounts may be maintained for each operating expense. This approach is not common, however, because many operating expenses cannot be directly related to specific departments. Instead, a single general ledger account is maintained for each operating expense. The total of each expense is assigned or allocated to departments at the end of the period.

DIRECT AND INDIRECT OPERATING EXPENSES

Departmental operating expenses can be classified as direct and indirect. **Direct expenses** are incurred for the sole benefit of and are traceable directly to a specific department. **Indirect expenses** are incurred for the benefit of the business as a whole and cannot be traced directly to a specific department. Figure 25-2 provides examples of direct and indirect expenses for Annie's Sporting Goods.

FIGURE 25-2 Examples of Direct and Indirect Expenses

DIRECT EXPENSES	INDIRECT EXPENSES
Wages of golf department sales clerk	Cost of renting store space
Cost of advertising tennis equipment	Cost of advertising Annie's Sporting Goods store
Wages of driver who delivers golf equipment	Store manager's salary

To compute departmental operating income, direct expenses are *assigned* to departments based on the actual expenses incurred. If separate departmental accounts are used, the expenses are accumulated there. If separate departmental accounts are not used, the expenses are assigned to departments based on information contained in supporting records. For example, personnel records would show the departments in which employees work, and wages would be assigned accordingly.

Indirect expenses are *allocated* to departments on some reasonable basis, such as relative sales, cost of goods sold, or floor space, or the estimated time spent serving a given department. There are no rules like generally accepted accounting principles. The key is to use a "reasonable basis."

ASSIGNING AND ALLOCATING DEPARTMENTAL EXPENSES

To illustrate the computation of departmental operating income, we will assign and allocate the operating expenses of Annie's Sporting Goods. Annie's does not maintain separate general ledger departmental operating expense accounts.

Store Clerks' Wages Expense

Annie's employs five store clerks: two work solely in the golf department, one works in the tennis department, and two assist customers in both departments. Their wages are as follows:

EMPLOYEE NUMBER	DEPT.	WAGES	
1	Golf	$19,000	$36,000
2	Golf	17,000	
3	Tennis	15,250	
4	Both	13,000	$29,000
5	Both	16,000	
Total		$80,250	

Wages of $36,000 ($19,000 + $17,000) for the golf department clerks are assigned to golf. Wages of $15,250 for the tennis department clerk are assigned to tennis. Wages of $29,000 ($13,000 + $16,000) for the other two clerks are allocated between the departments based on the percentage of total net sales produced by each department.

$$\frac{\text{Golf Net Sales}}{\text{Total Net Sales}} = \frac{\$1{,}075{,}000}{\$1{,}715{,}300} = 62.67\%$$

$$\frac{\text{Tennis Net Sales}}{\text{Total Net Sales}} = \frac{\$640{,}300}{\$1{,}715{,}300} = 37.33\%$$

The total store clerks' wages expense is divided between the departments as follows:

	GOLF	TENNIS	TOTAL
Direct expense	$36,000	$15,250	$51,250
Indirect expense allocation:			
% × Total Expense			
62.67% × $29,000	18,174		18,174
37.33% × $29,000		10,826	10,826
	$54,174	$26,076	$80,250

Another reasonable basis for allocating the clerks' wages might be the percentage of total cost of goods sold. This is a good example of the judgment that must be made any time expenses need to be allocated.

Truck Drivers' Wages Expense

Annie's employs three delivery truck drivers, one of whom delivers only golf equipment. Their wages are as follows:

DRIVER NUMBER	PRODUCT DELIVERED	WAGES	
1	Golf	$29,000	
2	Both	26,500	$54,900
3	Both	28,400	
Total		$83,900	

Other reasonable bases for allocating the drivers' wages might be the cost of the equipment delivered or the number of units delivered.

Wages of the driver who delivers only golf equipment ($29,000) are assigned to that department. Wages of the other two drivers ($54,900) are allocated based on the relative dollar amount of golf and tennis equipment delivered by the drivers. Shipping and delivery records are used to estimate the percentages as approximately 70% golf and 30% tennis. The total drivers' wages expense is divided between the departments as follows:

			GOLF	TENNIS	TOTAL
Direct expense			$29,000		$29,000
Indirect expense allocation:					
%		Total Expense			
70%	×	$54,900	38,430		38,430
30%	×	$54,900		$16,470	16,470
			$67,430	$16,470	$83,900

Advertising Expense

Annie's total advertising expense is $79,500: $45,000 for newspaper advertising and $34,500 for radio. Newspaper advertising is classified as golf, tennis, or "mixed" based on the number of inches of copy space. The $45,000 of newspaper advertising is $17,000 for golf, $12,000 for tennis, and $16,000 mixed. All radio advertising is classified as mixed. The total mixed expense for advertising of $50,500 ($16,000 + $34,500) is allocated between departments based on the percentage of total net sales represented by each department. These percentages are 62.67% golf and 37.33% tennis, as calculated for store clerks' wages expense. The total advertising expense is divided between the departments as follows:

			GOLF	TENNIS	TOTAL
Direct expense			$17,000	$12,000	$29,000
Indirect expense allocation:					
%		Total Expense			
62.67%	×	$50,500	31,648		31,648
37.33%	×	$50,500		18,852	18,852
			$48,648	$30,852	$79,500

Store Rent Expense

Annie's rents 5,000 square feet of store space for $22,800 per year. This entire expense is an indirect expense, allocated on the basis of the relative number of square feet of floor space occupied by each department. The golf department occupies 3,200 square feet, or 64% of the floor space. The tennis department occupies the remaining 36% of floor space. The rent expense is divided between the departments as follows:

			GOLF	TENNIS	TOTAL
Indirect expense allocation:					
%		Total Expense			
64%	×	$22,800	$14,592		$14,592
36%	×	$22,800		$8,208	8,208
			$14,952	$8,208	$22,800

Bad Debt Expense

Annie's bad debt expense of $17,900 is treated as a direct expense. It is assigned to the departments based on experience with accounts written off. For the current year, $9,000 is assigned to golf and $8,900 to tennis.

Depreciation Expense—Delivery Equipment

Annie's has three delivery trucks, one of which is used to deliver only golf equipment. Total depreciation on the delivery equipment is $24,000 for the year, $9,000 of which relates to the golf delivery truck. The other $15,000 of depreciation is allocated on the basis of the relative dollar amount of golf and tennis equipment delivered with the other two trucks. These percentages are 70% golf and 30% tennis, as explained for the truck drivers' wages expense. The total depreciation expense on the delivery equipment is divided between the departments as follows:

			GOLF	TENNIS	TOTAL
Direct expense			$ 9,000		$ 9,000
Indirect expense allocation:					
%		Total Expense			
70%	×	$15,000	10,500		10,500
30%	×	$15,000		$ 4,500	4,500
			$19,500	$ 4,500	$24,000

Other Operating Expenses

Annie's other operating expenses totaled $350,430. This total includes a broad range of expenses, from managers' salaries to postage expense. These expenses are assigned and allocated using methods like those used for the various expenses previously described. A summary of the amounts assigned and allocated for other operating expenses is as follows:

	GOLF	TENNIS	TOTAL
Direct expense	$ 84,420	$ 31,980	$116,400
Indirect expense allocation	159,380	74,650	234,030
	$243,800	$106,630	$350,430

Departmental Operating Expense Summary

The assignment and allocation of departmental operating expenses can be summarized in a **departmental operating expense summary**. The summary in Figure 25-3 shows the following:

1. Classification of each operating expense as direct or indirect
2. Amount assigned or allocated to each department
3. Total operating expenses for each department

FIGURE 25-3 Departmental Operating Expense Summary

Annie's Sporting Goods
Departmental Operating Expense Summary
For Year Ended December 31, 20--

	TOTAL	GOLF			TENNIS		
		DIRECT	INDIRECT	TOTAL	DIRECT	INDIRECT	TOTAL
Store clerks' wages expense	$ 80,250.00	$ 36,000.00	$ 18,174.00	$ 54,174.00	$15,250.00	$ 10,826.00	$ 26,076.00
Truck drivers' wages expense	83,900.00	29,000.00	38,430.00	67,430.00		16,470.00	16,470.00
Advertising expense	79,500.00	17,000.00	31,648.00	48,648.00	12,000.00	18,852.00	30,852.00
Store rent expense	22,800.00		14,592.00	14,592.00		8,208.00	8,208.00
Bad debt expense	17,900.00	9,000.00		9,000.00	8,900.00		8,900.00
Depreciation expense—delivery equipment	24,000.00	9,000.00	10,500.00	19,500.00		4,500.00	4,500.00
Other operating expenses	350,430.00	84,420.00	159,380.00	243,800.00	31,980.00	74,650.00	106,630.00
Total	$658,780.00	$184,420.00	$272,724.00	$457,144.00	$68,130.00	$133,506.00	$201,636.00

DEPARTMENTAL INCOME STATEMENT SHOWING OPERATING INCOME

Figure 25-4 shows Annie's departmental income statement for the year 20--, with operating income by department and in total. Operating expense data on the statement were obtained from the departmental operating expense summary in Figure 25-3.

Compare this income statement with the one in Figure 25-1. Notice that the departmental gross profit, total operating expenses, and total operating income are the same in both statements. The difference is that Figure 25-4 shows operating expenses and operating income for each department.

Management can use this income statement to evaluate the overall performance of the two departments. For example, the income statement shows that the operating income and operating income percentage of the golf department are much higher than those of the tennis department.

LEARNING KEY

An income statement showing departmental operating income enables management to evaluate the overall performance of each department.

Golf department operating income percentage: ($72,576 ÷ $1,075,000)	**6.8%**
Tennis department operating income percentage: ($17,764 ÷ $640,300)	**2.8%**

FIGURE 25-4 Departmental Income Statement Showing Operating Income

Annie's Sporting Goods
Income Statement
For Year Ended December 31, 20 --

	GOLF	TENNIS	TOTAL
Net sales	$1,075,000.00	$640,300.00	$1,715,300.00
Cost of goods sold	545,280.00	420,900.00	966,180.00
Gross profit	$ 529,720.00	$219,400.00	$ 749,120.00
Operating expenses:			
Store clerks' wages expense	$ 54,174.00	$ 26,076.00	$ 80,250.00
Truck drivers' wages expense	67,430.00	16,470.00	83,900.00
Advertising expense	48,648.00	30,852.00	79,500.00
Store rent expense	14,592.00	8,208.00	22,800.00
Bad debt expense	9,000.00	8,900.00	17,900.00
Depreciation expense—delivery equipment	19,500.00	4,500.00	24,000.00
Other operating expenses	243,800.00	106,630.00	350,430.00
Total operating expenses	$ 457,144.00	$ 201,636.00	$ 658,780.00
Operating income	$ 72,576.00	$ 17,764.00	$ 90,340.00

Remember, however, that the golf department's gross profit and gross profit percentage are much higher than those of the tennis department. The golf department's operating income might be higher simply because the gross profit is higher. Further analysis shows that this is the case. As shown below, the operating expense percentage is lower for the tennis department than for the golf department.

		Golf	Tennis
Operating Expenses / Net Sales	=	$457,144 / $1,075,000	$201,636 / $640,300
Operating expense percentage		42.5%	31.5%

As noted in the discussion of the difference in gross profit percentages, departmental reports showing operating income can be used for control and performance evaluation. Management can determine the causes of the difference in operating income and take corrective action.

The departmental operating income data also can be used for planning. Quantitative operating income goals can be set for the following year, and departmental operating income can be evaluated against those goals.

However, management must be cautious in interpreting departmental operating income results. Most of Annie's operating expenses for both departments are indirect. They therefore are allocated between departments based on estimates. Indirect expenses, by definition, are incurred for the benefit of the business as a whole and cannot be traced directly to any department. Thus, the departments have no control over such expenses. Further, it might be possible to reduce some indirect expenses by eliminating a department, but most of these expenses would continue to be incurred. Many accountants argue that to properly evaluate departmental performance, an income measure should be used that considers only the direct expenses of each department.

U REVU Complete U REVU-2 on **page 1001** to test your basic understanding of LO3.

A BROADER VIEW

JEFF ZARUBA PHOTOGRAPHY

The Supply Chain—Reaching Beyond Your Department or Business

Businesses face increasing demands from their customers for higher quality, faster service, and lower costs. One way companies are responding to these demands is through supply-chain management. The supply chain includes all of the purchasing, production, storage, delivery, and sales functions across a set of businesses. Supply-chain management requires focusing on the entire supply chain across businesses instead of just on one's own department or business. By coordinating and participating with other companies, all partners in the chain can operate more efficiently. These arrangements can lead to some new challenges in measuring department performance.

DEPARTMENTAL DIRECT OPERATING MARGIN

LO4 Describe and compute departmental direct operating margin.

Departmental direct operating margin is the difference between a department's gross profit and its direct operating expenses. To compute departmental direct operating margin, the elements of gross profit and the direct operating expenses are needed for each department. For Annie's, this information was developed in the previous section. We can use it to prepare a departmental income statement showing departmental direct operating margin. The information in the departmental operating expense summary (Figure 25-3) and in the income statement (Figure 25-4) simply needs to be reorganized.

Annie's income statement for the year 20--, showing departmental direct operating margins, appears in Figure 25-5. To determine the departmental direct operating margins, the direct operating expenses listed in the departmental operating expense summary (Figure 25-3) are subtracted from the departmental gross profits.

Departmental Gross Profit − Direct Operating Expenses = Direct Operating Margin

Indirect expenses are then subtracted from the total direct operating margin to calculate total operating income. Note that the indirect expenses that are separated by department in the departmental operating expense summary (Figure 25-3) are combined in Figure 25-5. Indirect expenses are not allocated to specific departments in preparing this departmental income statement.

FIGURE 25-5 Departmental Income Statement Showing Direct Operating Margin

Annie's Sporting Goods
Income Statement
For Year Ended December 31, 20 - -

	GOLF	TENNIS	TOTAL
Net sales	$1,075,000.00	$640,300.00	$1,715,300.00
Cost of goods sold	545,280.00	420,900.00	966,180.00
Gross profit	$ 529,720.00	$219,400.00	$ 749,120.00
Direct operating expenses:			
Store clerks' wages expense	$ 36,000.00	$ 15,250.00	$ 51,250.00
Truck drivers' wages expense	29,000.00		29,000.00
Advertising expense	17,000.00	12,000.00	29,000.00
Bad debt expense	9,000.00	8,900.00	17,900.00
Depreciation expense—delivery equipment	9,000.00		9,000.00
Other operating expenses	84,420.00	31,980.00	116,400.00
Total direct operating expenses	$ 184,420.00	$ 68,130.00	$ 252,550.00
Departmental direct operating margin	$ 345,300.00	$151,270.00	$ 496,570.00
Indirect operating expenses:			
Store clerks' wages expense			$ 29,000.00
Truck drivers' wages expense			54,900.00
Advertising expense			50,500.00
Store rent expense			22,800.00
Depreciation expense—delivery equipment			15,000.00
Other operating expenses			234,030.00
Total indirect operating expenses			$ 406,230.00
Operating income			$ 90,340.00

The total operating expenses of $658,780 in Figure 25-4 are separated into direct and indirect operating expenses in Figure 25-5:

Total direct operating expenses	$252,550
Total indirect operating expenses	406,230
Total operating expenses	$658,780

Compare this income statement with the one in Figure 25-4. Notice that the departmental gross profit ($529,720 and $219,400), total operating expenses ($252,550 + $406,230 = $658,780), and total operating income ($90,340) are the same in each statement. The key difference between the statements is that only direct operating expenses ($252,550) are split between departments in Figure 25-5. This permits calculation of the direct operating margin for each department.

INTERPRETATION AND USE OF DIRECT OPERATING MARGIN

Management can use this form of income statement in several ways.

1. To evaluate departmental performance.
2. To determine the contribution a department makes to the overall operating income of the company.
3. To decide whether to discontinue a department.

Performance Evaluation

Recall that direct expenses are operating expenses that are traceable directly to a specific department. Departmental direct operating margin is calculated by subtracting only direct operating expenses from departmental gross profit. Thus, direct operating margin can be used to evaluate a department on the basis of only those expenses that it can control and for which it is directly responsible. The income statement in Figure 25-5 shows that the golf department's direct operating margin percentage is higher than that of the tennis department.

LEARNING KEY

Direct operating margin is a performance measure that focuses on the revenues and expenses that a department can control.

Golf department direct operating margin percentage: ($345,300 ÷ $1,075,000)	32.1%
Tennis department direct operating margin percentage: ($151,270 ÷ $640,300)	23.6%

Further analysis, however, shows that this is the case only because of the golf department's higher gross profit. In fact, the tennis department is controlling direct operating expenses more effectively than the golf department. The tennis department's direct operating expenses are only 10.6% ($68,130 ÷ $640,300) of net sales. The golf department's direct operating expenses are 17.2% ($184,420 ÷ $1,075,000) of net sales.

Note once again that this evaluation is based on comparisons between departments. If management sets quantitative goals for the departments, performance can also be evaluated relative to those goals.

Contribution to Overall Operating Income

Departmental direct operating margin also shows a department's contribution to the company's overall operating income. The conventional operating income in Figure 25-4 implies that the tennis department contributes only $17,764 to overall profits. In contrast, the departmental direct operating margin in Figure 25-5 shows that the tennis department contributes $151,270. This amount is available to cover the company's indirect operating expenses and operating income.

Decision to Discontinue

A third possible use of the departmental direct operating margin data is in deciding whether to discontinue a department. In making this decision, management must focus on the revenues and expenses that will be eliminated if a department is discontinued. This means focusing on departmental direct operating margin, not on operating income. Remember that the indirect expenses that are subtracted in calculating conventional operating income are expenses incurred for the business as a whole. Unless management can reduce these expenses by eliminating a department, such expenses will be incurred even if a department is discontinued.

To illustrate, assume that R & R Company is deciding whether to discontinue one of its three departments. Operating results for the current year for each department, for the business as a whole, and for departments A and B only are shown in Figure 25-6.

FIGURE 25-6 R & R Company

	DEPARTMENT A	DEPARTMENT B	DEPARTMENT C	TOTAL	DEPARTMENTS A & B ONLY
Net sales	$210 000 00	$185 000 00	$170 000 00	$565 000 00	$395 000 00
Cost of goods sold	115 000 00	110 000 00	96 000 00	321 000 00	225 000 00
Gross margin	$ 95 000 00	$ 75 000 00	$ 74 000 00	$244 000 00	$170 000 00
Direct operating expenses	55 000 00	45 000 00	54 000 00	154 000 00	100 000 00
Departmental direct operating margin	$ 40 000 00	$ 30 000 00	$ 20 000 00	$ 90 000 00	$ 70 000 00
Indirect operating expenses	27 000 00	22 000 00	25 000 00	74 000 00	74 000 00
Operating income (loss)	$ 13 000 00	$ 8 000 00	$ (5 000 00)	$ 16 000 00	$ (4 000 00)

Operating income results show that department C is operating at a $5,000 loss. However, eliminating department C would actually reduce rather than increase R & R's total operating income, as shown in the last column for departments A and B only. This reduction in operating income would occur because department C's direct operating margin is $20,000. This $20,000 is available to cover the indirect operating expenses and add to the operating income of the firm. If department C is eliminated, the remaining departments must absorb the indirect operating expenses of $25,000 allocated to department C. Thus, the schedule lists indirect operating expenses as $74,000 both in the Total column and in the Departments A and B Only column.

Note in Figure 25-6 that the difference between the total operating income of $16,000 and the operating loss of $4,000 for Departments A and B Only is $20,000. This $20,000 is department C's departmental direct operating margin. This amount would be lost if the department were eliminated. In general, if a department has a positive departmental direct operating margin, it should not be discontinued. The only exception would be when management has a plan to reduce indirect expenses by at least the amount of that department's direct operating margin.

It can be difficult to determine which expenses will change if a department is discontinued. Part of the plan to discontinue a department might be to expand in some other area. The effects of other changes on departmental expenses must be considered in making a decision to discontinue.

U REVU

Complete U REVU-3 on **page 1001** to test your basic understanding of LO4.

SELF-STUDY

LEARNING OBJECTIVES	Key Points to Remember
LO1 **Explain the nature and purpose of departmental accounting.**	Departmental reports provide information about the revenues and expenses of each department. These reports are useful to management for planning, control, and performance evaluation.
LO2 **Describe and compute departmental gross profit.**	Departmental gross profit is the difference between a department's net sales and cost of goods sold. A departmental income statement showing gross profit can help management identify problems with both the sales prices and purchase prices of its products.
LO3 **Describe and compute departmental operating income.**	Departmental operating income is the difference between a department's gross profit and its operating expenses. Departmental operating expenses are either direct or indirect. Direct expenses are incurred for the sole benefit of a specific department. Indirect expenses are incurred for the benefit of the business as a whole. Direct expenses are assigned to departments based on actual expenses incurred. Indirect expenses are allocated to departments on various reasonable bases. A departmental income statement showing departmental operating income permits evaluation of both the gross profit and operating expense performance of a department.

LEARNING OBJECTIVES Key Points to Remember

LO4 Describe and compute departmental direct operating margin.	Departmental direct operating margin is the difference between a department's gross profit and its direct operating expenses. A departmental income statement showing departmental direct operating margin focuses attention on revenues and expenses under the control of a department manager. Such a statement can be very useful for performance evaluation, evaluating contribution to overall operating income, and deciding whether to discontinue a department.

DEMONSTRATION PROBLEM

Kristen Owen and Stephen Kaplan are partners who own OK Cycling. They sell outdoor bicycles and exercise bicycles. They keep accounts and prepare reports on a departmental basis. Direct expenses are assigned and indirect expenses are allocated to departments by various means. Selected operating information for the year ended December 31, 20--, is as follows:

	Outdoor Bicycles	Exercise Bicycles
Net sales	$1,612,500	$1,150,600
Cost of goods sold	935,420	791,800
Direct operating expenses:		
Store clerks' wages expense	45,000	19,500
Truck drivers' wages expense	26,000	10,000
Advertising expense	16,000	20,000
Depreciation expense—delivery equipment	12,000	0
Bad debt expense	12,000	11,700
Other operating expenses	92,080	44,840
Indirect operating expenses:		
Store clerks' wages expense	26,400	14,850
Truck drivers' wages expense	62,800	22,250
Advertising expense	48,200	20,500
Depreciation expense—delivery equipment	13,800	5,700
Store rent expense	21,600	14,400
Other operating expenses	197,360	111,190

REQUIRED

1. Prepare an income statement showing departmental operating income.
2. Prepare another income statement showing departmental and total direct operating margins.
3. For the first statement, determine which department has the higher operating income percentage.
4. For the second statement, determine which department has the higher direct operating margin percentage.
5. Which of the two measures is more meaningful for decision-making purposes? Why?

(continued)

Solution

1.

OK Cycling
Income Statement
For Year Ended December 31, 20 --

	OUTDOOR BICYCLES	EXERCISE BICYCLES	TOTAL
Net sales	$1,612,500.00	$1,150,600.00	$2,763,100.00
Cost of goods sold	935,420.00	791,800.00	1,727,220.00
Gross profit	$ 677,080.00	$ 358,800.00	$1,035,880.00
Operating expenses:			
Store clerks' wages expense	$ 71,400.00	$ 34,350.00	$ 105,750.00
Truck drivers' wages expense	88,800.00	32,250.00	121,050.00
Advertising expense	64,200.00	40,500.00	104,700.00
Depreciation expense—delivery equipment	25,800.00	5,700.00	31,500.00
Store rent expense	21,600.00	14,400.00	36,000.00
Bad debt expense	12,000.00	11,700.00	23,700.00
Other operating expenses	289,440.00	156,030.00	445,470.00
Total operating expenses	$ 573,240.00	$ 294,930.00	$ 868,170.00
Operating income	$ 103,840.00	$ 63,870.00	$ 167,710.00

2.

OK Cycling
Income Statement
For Year Ended December 31, 20 --

	OUTDOOR BICYCLES	EXERCISE BICYCLES	TOTAL
Net sales	$1,612,500.00	$1,150,600.00	$2,763,100.00
Cost of goods sold	935,420.00	791,800.00	1,727,220.00
Gross profit	$ 677,080.00	$ 358,800.00	$1,035,880.00
Direct operating expenses:			
Store clerks' wages expense	$ 45,000.00	$ 19,500.00	$ 64,500.00
Truck drivers' wages expense	26,000.00	10,000.00	36,000.00
Advertising expense	16,000.00	20,000.00	36,000.00
Depreciation expense—delivery equipment	12,000.00	0.00	12,000.00
Bad debt expense	12,000.00	11,700.00	23,700.00
Other operating expenses	92,080.00	44,840.00	136,920.00
Total direct operating expenses	$ 203,080.00	$ 106,040.00	$ 309,120.00
Departmental direct operating margin	$ 474,000.00	$ 252,760.00	$ 726,760.00
Indirect operating expenses:			
Store clerks' wages expense			$ 41,250.00
Truck drivers' wages expense			85,050.00
Advertising expense			68,700.00
Depreciation expense—delivery equipment			19,500.00
Store rent expense			36,000.00
Other operating expenses			308,550.00
Total indirect operating expenses			$ 559,050.00
Operating income			$ 167,710.00

3. Operating income percentage:

For outdoor bicycles:

$$\frac{\text{Operating Income}}{\text{Net Sales}} = \frac{\$103{,}840}{\$1{,}612{,}500} = 6.4\%$$

For exercise bicycles:

$$\frac{\text{Operating Income}}{\text{Net Sales}} = \frac{\$63{,}870}{\$1{,}150{,}600} = 5.6\%$$

Outdoor bicycles has the higher operating income percentage.

4. Direct operating margin percentage:

For outdoor bicycles:

$$\frac{\text{Direct Operating Margin}}{\text{Net Sales}} = \frac{\$474{,}000}{\$1{,}612{,}500} = 29.4\%$$

For exercise bicycles:

$$\frac{\text{Direct Operating Margin}}{\text{Net Sales}} = \frac{\$252{,}760}{\$1{,}150{,}600} = 22.0\%$$

Outdoor bicycles has the higher direct operating margin percentage.

5. Most accountants believe that the departmental direct operating margin is more meaningful for decision-making purposes than departmental operating income. This is because the direct operating margin takes into account only the direct expenses of operating each department, while departmental operating income is affected by various allocations of indirect operating expenses.

OK Cycling's results demonstrate the importance of the direct operating margin. The answers to requirements 3 and 4 clearly show that the exercise bicycle department is less profitable than the outdoor bicycle department. Yet, the exercise bicycle department is still making a major contribution to the business. Its operating income is $63,870. More importantly, its direct operating margin is $252,760. Without the exercise bicycle department, OK Cycling would be operating at a loss of $85,050 ($167,710, the present total operating income, minus $252,760, the exercise bicycle department's direct operating margin).

KEY TERMS

departmental direct operating margin (993) The difference between a department's gross profit and its direct operating expenses.

departmental gross profit (985) The difference between a department's net sales and cost of goods sold.

departmental operating expense summary (991) A summary of the assignment and allocation of departmental operating expenses which shows the classification of each operating expense as direct or indirect, the amount assigned or allocated to each department, and total operating expenses for each department.

departmental operating income (987) The difference between a department's gross profit and its operating expenses.

direct expenses (987) Operating expenses that are incurred for the sole benefit of and are traceable directly to a specific department.

indirect expenses (987) Operating expenses that are incurred for the benefit of the business as a whole.

SELF-STUDY QUESTIONS AND EXERCISES

True/False Questions

1. LO2 Departmental gross profit is the difference between a department's net sales and operating expenses.
2. LO2 The gross profit percentage can be computed by dividing gross profit by net sales.
3. LO3 Departmental operating income is the difference between a department's gross profit and its operating expenses.
4. LO3 Direct expenses are operating expenses incurred for the benefit of the business as a whole and untraceable directly to a specific department.
5. LO4 Departmental direct operating margin is the difference between a department's gross profit and its direct operating expenses.

Multiple Choice Questions

1. LO2 The difference between a department's net sales and cost of goods sold is called
   (a) departmental gross profit.
   (b) departmental direct operating income.
   (c) departmental operating income.
   (d) net income.
2. LO3 Operating expenses incurred for the sole benefit of and traceable directly to a specific department are called
   (a) budgeted expenses.
   (b) normal expenses.
   (c) indirect expenses.
   (d) direct expenses.
3. LO3 A base used in the text to allocate store rent expense to specific departments is
   (a) net sales.
   (b) square footage.
   (c) number of employees.
   (d) number of customers.
4. LO3 The difference between a department's gross profit and its operating expenses is called
   (a) departmental gross profit.
   (b) departmental direct operating margin.
   (c) departmental operating income.
   (d) net income.
5. LO4 The difference between a department's gross profit and its direct operating expenses is called
   (a) departmental gross profit.
   (b) departmental direct operating margin.
   (c) departmental operating income.
   (d) net income.

U REVU **Exercises**

1. LO2 JW Enterprises is organized into three departments: Department A, Department B, and Department C. At the end of the current year, the sales and cost of goods sold of the three departments are as follows:

	Dept. A	Dept. B	Dept. C
Sales	$46,000	$53,000	$21,000
Cost of goods sold	32,500	33,100	11,090

Compute the gross profit for each department and for the business in total.

2. LO3 The sales, gross profit, and condensed total operating expenses of departments A and B for YH Company for the current year are as follows:

	Dept. A	Dept. B
Sales	$120,000	$180,000
Gross profit	42,000	84,000
Total operating expenses	13,200	31,800

Compute the operating income and operating income percentage for each department.

3. LO4 The sales, gross profit, and condensed direct operating expenses of departments A and B of Beedles Distributors for the current year are as follows:

	Dept. A	Dept. B
Sales	$300,000	$400,000
Gross profit	140,000	210,000
Direct operating expenses	65,000	90,000

Compute the direct operating margin and direct operating margin percentage for each department.

The answers to the Self-Study Questions are at the end of the chapter (page 1011).

APPLYING YOUR KNOWLEDGE

REVIEW QUESTIONS

LO1 1. For what purposes are departmental reports useful to management?

LO2 2. In what two ways can the information necessary to compute departmental gross profit be accumulated?

LO3 3. In what two ways can departmental operating expense data be accumulated?

LO3 4. What is the difference between direct and indirect operating expenses?

LO3 5. On what basis are direct expenses assigned to departments?

LO3 6. On what basis are indirect expenses allocated to departments?

LO3 7. What information is contained in a departmental operating expense summary?

LO3 8. Why must management be cautious in interpreting departmental operating income results?

LO4 9. Distinguish between departmental gross profit, departmental operating income, and departmental direct operating margin.

LO4 10. In what ways can an income statement showing departmental direct operating margin be used by management?

SERIES A EXERCISES

E 25-1A (LO2)

✓ Gross profit, running shoes dept.: $12,600

GROSS PROFIT SECTION OF DEPARTMENTAL INCOME STATEMENT Bill Walters and Alice Jennings are partners in a business called Walters and Jennings Sportswear that sells athletic footwear. They have organized the business on a departmental basis as follows: running shoes, walking shoes, and specialty shoes. At the end of the first year of operation, the sales and cost of goods sold for the three departments are as follows:

	Running Shoes	Walking Shoes	Specialty Shoes
Sales	$36,000	$42,000	$12,000
Cost of goods sold	23,400	23,520	7,680

Prepare the gross profit section of a departmental income statement for the year ended December 31, 20--. Show the gross profit for each department and for the business in total.

E 25-2A (LO3)

✓ Rent expense, dept. A: $5,216

ALLOCATING OPERATING EXPENSE—SQUARE FEET Wray Company rents 10,000 square feet of store space for $32,600 per year. The amount of square footage by department is as follows:

Department A:	1,600 sq. ft.
Department B:	2,200 sq. ft.
Department C:	3,800 sq. ft.
Department D:	2,400 sq. ft.

Allocate the annual rent expense among the four departments on the basis of relative square feet of floor space occupied.

E 25-3A (LO3)

✓ Advertising expense, deluxe: $7,200

ALLOCATING OPERATING EXPENSE—RELATIVE NET SALES Tina Domingo owns a car stereo store. She has divided her store into three departments. Net sales for the month of July are as follows:

Deluxe:	$36,000
Standard:	30,000
Economy:	54,000

Advertising expense for July was $24,000.

Allocate the advertising expense among the three departments on the basis of relative net sales.

E 25-4A (LO3)

✓ Truck expense, dept. 1: $5,760

ALLOCATING OPERATING EXPENSE—MILES DRIVEN Mercado Lopez owns a furniture store that offers free delivery of merchandise delivered within the local area. Mileage records for the three sales departments are as follows:

Department 1:	36,000 miles
Department 2:	48,000 miles
Department 3:	16,000 miles

The cost of using the truck for the last year, including depreciation, was $16,000.

Allocate the cost of the truck among the three departments on the basis of miles driven.

E 25-5A (LO3)
✓ Purchasing dept. expense, West Division: $6,600

ALLOCATING OPERATING EXPENSE—PURCHASE ORDERS The purchasing department of Brindley Company performs the purchasing function for the entire business. The numbers of purchase orders processed during the most recent month are as follows:

West Division:	33 purchase orders
East Division:	47 purchase orders
Central Division:	20 purchase orders

The monthly cost of operating the purchasing department, including personnel, was $20,000.

Allocate the cost of the purchasing department using the number of purchase orders processed as an allocation base.

E 25-6A (LO4)
✓ Direct operating margin, dept. A: $48,000

DEPARTMENTAL DIRECT OPERATING MARGIN AND DIRECT OPERATING MARGIN PERCENTAGE The sales, gross profit, and condensed direct and indirect operating expenses of departments A and B of Pan Fei International are as follows:

	Dept. A	Dept. B	Total
Sales	$200,000	$300,000	$500,000
Gross profit	70,000	140,000	210,000
Direct operating expenses	22,000	53,000	75,000
Indirect operating expenses			50,000

Compute the departmental direct operating margin and direct operating margin percentage for each department.

SERIES A PROBLEMS

P 25-7A (LO2/3)
✓ 2. Gross profit %, commercial sales: 40%

KA KLOOSTER & ALLEN

INCOME STATEMENT WITH DEPARTMENTAL GROSS PROFIT AND OPERATING INCOME Thomas and Hill Distributors has divided its business into two departments: commercial sales and industrial sales. The following information is provided for the year ended December 31, 20--:

Net sales, commercial sales department	$630,000
Net sales, industrial sales department	470,000
Cost of goods sold, commercial sales department	378,000
Cost of goods sold, industrial sales department	188,000
Warehouse wages expense	99,400
Truck drivers' wages expense	88,200
Advertising expense	66,000
Warehouse lease expense	30,000
Depreciation expense—delivery equipment	11,000
Other operating expenses	115,000

REQUIRED

1. Prepare an income statement showing departmental gross profit and total operating income.
2. Calculate departmental gross profit percentages.

P 25-8A (LO2/3)
✓ 2. Operating income %, breads: 21.5%

INCOME STATEMENT WITH DEPARTMENTAL OPERATING INCOME AND TOTAL OPERATING INCOME Carmella Campillo owns a business called Campillo's Bakery. She has divided her business into two departments: breads and pastries. The following information is provided for the fiscal year ended June 30, 20--:

	Breads	Pastries
Net sales	$182,000	$98,000
Cost of goods sold	72,800	58,800
Wages expense	30,000	20,000
Advertising expense	16,000	4,000
Other operating expenses	24,000	10,000

REQUIRED

1. Prepare an income statement showing departmental operating income and total operating income.
2. Calculate departmental operating expense and operating income percentages.

P 25-9A (LO2/3/4)
✓ 2. Direct operating margin %, commercial property: 15.4%

INCOME STATEMENT WITH DEPARTMENTAL DIRECT OPERATING MARGIN AND TOTAL OPERATING INCOME Durwood Thomas operates the business Thomas Security that sells security equipment for commercial property and residential homes. The following information is provided for the year ended December 31, 20--:

	Commercial Property	Residential Homes
Net sales	$465,000	$135,000
Cost of goods sold	279,250	54,000
Direct operating expenses:		
Advertising expense	35,000	20,000
Store clerks' wages expense	30,000	18,000
Truck drivers' wages expense	15,000	15,000
Bad debt expense	8,000	3,000
Depreciation expense—delivery equipment	6,000	4,000
Other operating expenses	20,000	10,000

Indirect operating expenses:	
Store clerks' wages expense	$10,000
Advertising expense	15,000
Store rent expense	20,000
Other operating expenses	10,000

REQUIRED

1. Prepare an income statement showing departmental direct operating margin and total operating income.
2. Calculate departmental direct operating margin percentages.

P 25-10A (LO4)
✓ 1. Operating income, depts. A & C only: $5,000

WHETHER TO DISCONTINUE A DEPARTMENT Williams and Lloyd Company is trying to decide whether to discontinue department B. Operating results for the year just ended for each of the company's three departments and for the entire operation are as follows:

	Dept. A	Dept. B	Dept. C	Total
Net sales	$380,000	$260,000	$290,000	$930,000
Cost of goods sold	210,000	140,000	160,000	510,000
Gross profit	$170,000	$120,000	$130,000	$420,000
Direct operating expenses	100,000	90,000	80,000	270,000
Departmental direct operating margin	$ 70,000	$ 30,000	$ 50,000	$150,000
Indirect operating expenses	40,000	35,000	40,000	115,000
Operating income (loss)	$ 30,000	$ (5,000)	$ 10,000	$ 35,000

REQUIRED

1. Prepare an additional column that combines departments A and C only.
2. Review all data and decide if department B should be discontinued. Defend your decision.

SERIES B EXERCISES

E 25-1B (LO2)
✓ Gross profit, letters dept.: $1,600

GROSS PROFIT SECTION OF DEPARTMENTAL INCOME STATEMENT Nicole Lawrence and Josh Doyle are partners in a business that sells cheerleading uniforms. They have organized the business, called L and D Uniforms, on a departmental basis as follows: letters, sweaters, and skirts. At the end of the first year of operation, the sales and cost of goods sold for the three departments are as follows:

	Letters	Sweaters	Skirts
Sales	$3,000	$12,000	$8,000
Cost of goods sold	1,400	5,900	4,750

Prepare the gross profit section of a departmental income statement for the year ended December 31, 20--. Show the gross profit for each department and for the business in total.

E 25-2B (LO3)
✓ Rent expense, dept. A: $9,600

ALLOCATING OPERATING EXPENSE—SQUARE FEET Johnson Company rents 5,000 square feet of store space for $40,000 per year. The amount of square footage by department is as follows:

Department A:	1,200 sq. ft.
Department B:	1,400 sq. ft.
Department C:	1,500 sq. ft.
Department D:	900 sq. ft.

Allocate the annual rent expense among the four departments on the basis of relative square feet of floor space occupied.

E 25-3B (LO3)
✓ Advertising expense, football: $2,000

ALLOCATING OPERATING EXPENSE—RELATIVE NET SALES Amelia Diaz owns a sporting goods store. She has divided her store into three departments. Net sales for the month of July are as follows:

Football:	$10,000
Basketball:	6,000
Baseball:	9,000

Advertising expense for July was $5,000.

Allocate the advertising expense among the three departments on the basis of relative net sales.

E 25-4B (LO3)
✓ Truck expense, dept. 1: $800

ALLOCATING OPERATING EXPENSE—MILES DRIVEN Herbert Quiong owns a furniture store that offers free delivery of merchandise delivered within the local area. Mileage records for the three sales departments are as follows:

Department 1:	4,000 miles
Department 2:	13,000 miles
Department 3:	8,000 miles

The cost of using the truck for the last year, including depreciation, was $5,000.

Allocate the cost of the truck among the three departments on the basis of miles driven.

E 25-5B (LO3)
✓ Purchasing dept. expense, West Division: $8,700

ALLOCATING OPERATING EXPENSE—PURCHASE ORDERS The purchasing department of Stokes Company performs the purchasing function for the entire business. The numbers of purchase orders processed during the most recent month are as follows:

West Division:	29 purchase orders
East Division:	37 purchase orders
Central Division:	34 purchase orders

The monthly cost of operating the purchasing department, including personnel, was $30,000.

Allocate the cost of the purchasing department using the number of purchase orders processed as an allocation base.

E 25-6B (LO4)
✓ Direct operating margin, dept. A: $75,000

DEPARTMENTAL DIRECT OPERATING MARGIN AND DIRECT OPERATING MARGIN PERCENTAGE The sales, gross profit, and condensed direct and indirect operating expenses of departments A and B of Robin Sun Enterprises are as follows:

	Dept. A	Dept. B	Total
Sales	$300,000	$400,000	$700,000
Gross profit	110,000	180,000	290,000
Direct operating expenses	35,000	72,000	107,000
Indirect operating expenses			78,000

Compute the departmental direct operating margin and direct operating margin percentage for each department.

SERIES B PROBLEMS

P 25-7B (LO2/3)

✓ 2. Gross profit %, retail sales: 44%

INCOME STATEMENT WITH DEPARTMENTAL GROSS PROFIT AND OPERATING INCOME Bacon and Hand Distributors has divided its business into two departments: retail sales and wholesale sales. The following information is provided for the year ended December 31, 20--:

Net sales, retail sales department	$570,000
Net sales, wholesale sales department	830,000
Cost of goods sold, retail sales department	319,200
Cost of goods sold, wholesale sales department	398,400
Warehouse wages expense	110,000
Truck drivers' wages expense	90,500
Advertising expense	70,000
Warehouse lease expense	40,000
Depreciation expense—delivery equipment	12,000
Other operating expenses	130,000

REQUIRED

1. Prepare an income statement showing departmental gross profit and total operating income.
2. Calculate departmental gross profit percentages.

P 25-8B (LO2/3)

✓ 2. Operating income %, domestic yarn: 10.5%

INCOME STATEMENT WITH DEPARTMENTAL OPERATING INCOME AND TOTAL OPERATING INCOME Sonya McDowell owns a business called The Knitting Chamber. She has divided her business into two departments: domestic yarn and international yarn. The following information is provided for the fiscal year ended June 30, 20--:

	Domestic Yarn	International Yarn
Net sales	$60,000	$40,000
Cost of goods sold	37,200	28,000
Wages expense	10,000	5,000
Advertising expense	2,500	1,500
Other operating expenses	4,000	1,000

REQUIRED

1. Prepare an income statement showing departmental operating income and total operating income.
2. Calculate departmental operating expense and operating income percentages.

P 25-9B (LO2/3/4)

✓ 2. Direct operating margin %, furniture: 7.2%

INCOME STATEMENT WITH DEPARTMENTAL DIRECT OPERATING MARGIN AND TOTAL OPERATING INCOME Tom Peterson owns the business Peterson's Furniture and Appliances. The following information is provided for the year ended December 31, 20--:

	Furniture Department	Appliances Department
Net sales	$390,000	$810,000
Cost of goods sold	234,000	405,000
Direct operating expenses:		
Advertising expense	30,000	60,000
Store clerks' wages expense	40,000	90,000

(continued)

	Furniture Department	Appliances Department
Truck drivers' wages expense	$35,000	$65,000
Bad debt expense	4,000	9,000
Depreciation expense—delivery equipment	4,000	8,000
Other operating expenses	15,000	50,000

Indirect operating expenses:	
Store clerks' wages expense	$20,000
Advertising expense	15,000
Store rent expense	50,000
Other operating expenses	25,000

REQUIRED

1. Prepare an income statement showing departmental direct operating margin and total operating income.
2. Calculate departmental direct operating margin percentages.

P 25-10B (LO4)
✓ 1. Operating income, depts. B & C only: $20,000

WHETHER TO DISCONTINUE A DEPARTMENT Mueller and Kenington Company is trying to decide whether to discontinue department A. Operating results for the year just ended for each of the company's three departments and for the entire operation are as follows:

	Dept. A	Dept. B	Dept. C	Total
Net sales	$680,000	$730,000	$690,000	$2,100,000
Cost of goods sold	400,000	380,000	360,000	1,140,000
Gross profit	$280,000	$350,000	$330,000	$ 960,000
Direct operating expenses	230,000	240,000	210,000	680,000
Departmental direct operating margin	$ 50,000	$110,000	$120,000	$ 280,000
Indirect operating expenses	70,000	70,000	70,000	210,000
Operating income (loss)	$ (20,000)	$ 40,000	$ 50,000	$ 70,000

REQUIRED

1. Prepare an additional column that combines departments B and C only.
2. Review all data and decide if department A should be discontinued. Defend your decision.

MANAGING YOUR WRITING

Two department heads are engaging in an argument. The head of department A argues that department A makes a greater contribution to profits, having produced a higher operating income for three years. The business probably would be better off if department B were discontinued. In fact, department income statements from the last three years show department A had higher operating income than department B. Department B had an operating loss in two of the three years.

Write a memo addressing the following two issues:

1. What are the proper accounting measures to use to determine which department is making a greater contribution to the profits of the business?
2. What are the proper accounting measures to use to decide whether to discontinue one of the departments?

ETHICS CASE

Melanie Sanders and Joyce O'Dell were department heads at Hobgood's Toy and Hobby Store. They had been friends for a long time. Mr. Hobgood, the owner of the store, let the department heads make all decisions relating to the store's operations. During the summer the hobby department usually had a higher gross profit, but during the holidays the toy department usually caught up. This year the toy department wasn't doing well at all, mainly because a new discount toy store had opened less than a mile away. In early December, Melanie, the toy department manager, asked Joyce if she would mind charging all the remaining year's advertising and shipping expenses to the hobby department. Melanie went on to explain that she was afraid Mr. Hobgood would get upset if he found out the toy department wasn't doing well during the last quarter. She said she had a plan for next year to earn more revenue but was vague on what it involved. Joyce knew the hobby department's year-to-date earnings were above average but she felt uncomfortable with what Melanie had asked her to do.

1. What is your reaction to Melanie's idea?
2. If Joyce decides to let Melanie charge all advertising and shipping expenses to the hobby department in December, what impact will it have on the financial statements?
3. Write a short paragraph stating both the short- and long-run implications of Melanie's idea.
4. In groups of three or four, make a list of some suggestions to help Hobgood's Toy and Hobby Store earn more revenue.

MASTERY PROBLEM

✓ 2b. Direct operating margin %, grocery: 11.0%

Bob's Acme Supermarket has been in operation for many years, offering high-quality groceries, produce, and meat at reasonable prices. Accounting records are maintained on a departmental basis with assignment of direct expenses and allocation of indirect expenses through the use of various procedures. Selected operating information for the year ended December 31, 20--, is as follows:

	Grocery	Meat	Produce	Total
Net sales	$2,104,890	$660,500	$345,800	$3,111,190
Cost of goods sold	1,683,912	462,350	207,480	2,353,742
Direct operating expenses:				
Store clerks' wages expense	125,000	58,000	38,500	221,500
Advertising expense	25,000	38,500	18,400	81,900
Depreciation expense—store equipment	10,800	15,000	12,000	37,800
Other operating expenses	28,200	28,540	35,600	92,340
Indirect operating expenses:				
Store clerks' wages expense	12,000	5,000	4,000	21,000
Advertising expense	7,000	2,000	1,000	10,000
Depreciation expense—store equipment	35,000	10,000	5,000	50,000
Store rent	60,000	20,000	20,000	100,000
Other operating expenses	25,500	4,500	18,450	48,450

(continued)

REQUIRED

1. (a) Prepare an income statement showing departmental operating income.
   (b) Compute the gross profit percentage and operating income percentage for each department (round to the nearest tenth of a percent).
2. (a) Prepare an income statement showing departmental and total direct operating margins.
   (b) Compute the departmental direct operating margin percentage for each department (round to the nearest tenth of a percent).
3. Should Bob be concerned about the profitability of the three departments? Should any of the departments be discontinued?

CHALLENGE PROBLEM

This problem challenges you to apply your cumulative accounting knowledge to move a step beyond the material in the chapter.

✓ **Total operating income, depts. A, B, & D: $60,250**

The results of the operating activities of Kobe Company for the current year are as follows:

	Dept. A	Dept. B	Dept. C	Total
Net sales	$590,000	$735,000	$450,000	$1,775,000
Cost of goods sold	365,000	545,750	267,000	1,177,750
Gross margin	$225,000	$189,250	$183,000	$ 597,250
Direct operating expenses	127,000	97,000	209,000	433,000
Direct operating margin	$ 98,000	$ 92,250	$ (26,000)	$ 164,250
Indirect operating expenses	61,000	52,000	20,000	133,000
Operating income (loss)	$ 37,000	$ 40,250	$ (46,000)	$ 31,250

Based on these results, Kobe is considering discontinuing department C and establishing a new department D. The estimated revenues and expenses of the new department are as follows:

	Dept. D
Net sales	$480,000
Cost of goods sold	270,000
Direct operating expenses	185,000

In addition, the proposed change will cause total indirect operating expenses to increase by $22,000.

REQUIRED

Determine whether Kobe should discontinue department C and establish department D.

ANSWERS TO SELF-STUDY QUESTIONS AND EXERCISES

True/False Questions

1. F (net sales – cost of goods sold) 2. T 3. T 4. F (traceable) 5. T

Multiple Choice

1. a 2. d 3. b 4. c 5. b

U REVU Exercises

1.

	Dept. A	Dept. B	Dept. C	Total
Sales	$46,000	$53,000	$21,000	$120,000
Cost of goods sold	32,500	33,100	11,090	76,690
Gross profit	$13,500	$19,900	$ 9,910	$ 43,310

2.

	Dept. A	Dept. B
Gross profit	$42,000	$84,000
Total operating expenses	13,200	31,800
Operating income	$28,800	$52,200

Operating income percentages:
Dept. A: $28,800/$120,000 = 24%
Dept. B: $52,200/$180,000 = 29%

3.

	Dept. A	Dept. B
Gross profit	$140,000	$210,000
Direct operating expenses	65,000	90,000
Direct operating margin	$ 75,000	$120,000

Direct operating margin percentages:
Dept. A: $75,000/$300,000 = 25%
Dept. B: $120,000/$400,000 = 30%

Chapter 26

COURTESY OF EVOLVE PROGRAMS

LEARNING OBJECTIVES

Careful study of this chapter should enable you to:

LO1 Describe the three manufacturing costs.

LO2 Describe the three inventories of a manufacturing business.

LO3 Describe and illustrate how manufacturing costs and inventories affect the financial statements of a manufacturing business.

LO4 Define and describe how to operate a job order cost accounting system.

LO5 Describe a process cost accounting system.

Manufacturing Accounting: The Job Order Cost System

As you have eaten at different restaurants or had service performed by auto or electronics technicians, have you noticed the variety of "uniforms" the staff wear? These shirts and jackets generally are more than clothing. They are part of the company's brand or image. A major contributor to this apparel and branding is Evolve, a company based in Denver, Colorado. Evolve designs and manufactures products by working directly with its customers to create customized apparel. Founded in 2002, Evolve already had revenue of over $10 million only six years later.

An interesting question for a company like Evolve is how to cost and price the special orders it receives from customers. A client might want 1,000; 5,000; or even 10,000 shirts or jackets with a special design, logo, etc. What does it cost to produce this order, and what should Evolve charge for it? In this chapter, you will learn about a job-order costing system that can help answer these questions. This system enables us to track production costs by (job) order and provides information to help determine what price to charge.

In the final two chapters of this book, we will study how to account for a manufacturing business. From an accounting standpoint, the key difference between a manufacturing and a merchandising business involves inventory. The manufacturer makes the items it sells; the merchandiser purchases inventory in final form for resale. This makes accounting for a manufacturer more complicated. Special cost accounting systems are needed to accumulate the costs of manufacturing the products. Multiple inventory accounts must be kept. Both the income statement and balance sheet are affected by these accounting changes.

MANUFACTURING COSTS

LO1 Describe the three manufacturing costs.

The costs incurred to manufacture a product can be classified into three primary elements of manufacturing cost:

1. Materials
2. Labor
3. Factory overhead

As illustrated in Figure 26-1, these costs come together in a conversion process that produces completed products, commonly called finished goods.

FIGURE 26-1 The Manufacturing Process

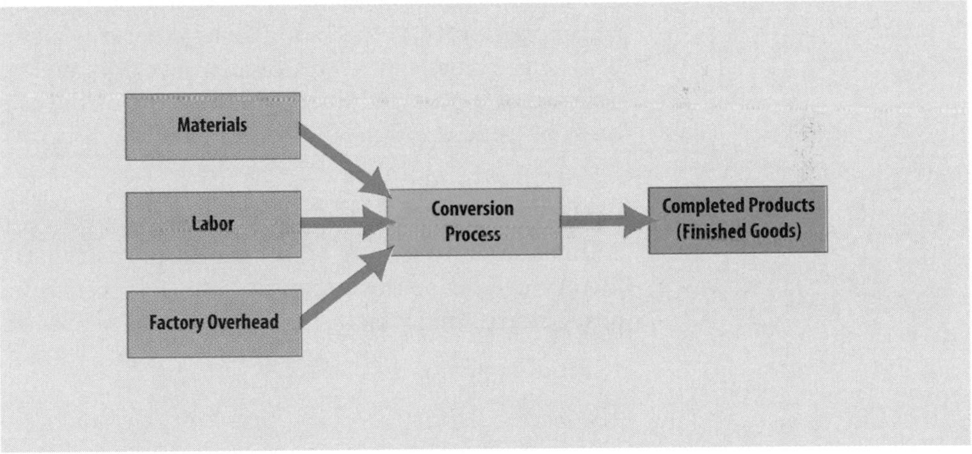

MATERIALS

Various materials are needed to manufacture a product. A manufacturer of automobiles requires items such as sheet metal, bar steel, plastic, fabric, and tires. A manufacturer of electric guitars requires wood, plastic, electrical wire, magnets, nuts, and screws. In many instances, the only distinction between materials and finished goods is their relationship to a particular manufacturer. The finished goods of one manufacturer may be the materials of another. For example, flour is finished goods to a miller but materials to a baker. Similarly, silver may be finished goods to a mining company but materials to a manufacturer of silverware. Materials used in manufacturing are classified as:

1. Direct materials
2. Indirect materials

Direct materials enter into and become a major part of the finished product. Thus, the leather and linings used in the manufacture of shoes are direct materials. Similarly, the sheet metal, bar steel, fabric, and many other materials used in the manufacture of an automobile are direct materials.

Indirect materials are used in the manufacturing process but do not become a major part of the finished product. Thus, oil and grease used in the operation of machinery are indirect materials. Such materials are often called **factory supplies**. Indirect materials also may include inexpensive items such as nails, screws, and washers. These items may become a part of the finished product, but their small cost is most easily accounted for as part of indirect materials.

LABOR

Wages and salaries paid to factory workers and supervisors are part of the cost of manufacturing a product. These wages and salaries are classified as:

1. Direct labor
2. Indirect labor

Direct labor includes the wages of employees who are directly involved in converting materials into finished goods. Such workers may do assembly work or operate factory machinery. These wages are charged directly to the cost of the products being manufactured.

Indirect labor includes the wages and salaries of employees who devote their time to supervision or to work of a general nature. Such workers may include superintendents, inspectors, timekeepers, receiving clerks, and janitors. The costs of these employees cannot be charged directly to the cost of the products being manufactured. They must be included in the indirect costs of the factory operation.

FACTORY OVERHEAD

All manufacturing costs other than direct materials and direct labor are classified as **factory overhead**. This group of costs is sometimes described as **manufacturing overhead, indirect manufacturing cost**, or **factory burden**. Factory overhead consists of:

1. Indirect materials
2. Indirect labor
3. Other factory overhead

Indirect materials and indirect labor have already been discussed. Other factory overhead includes a variety of items, such as:

- Depreciation of factory buildings and equipment
- Repairs to factory buildings and equipment
- Insurance on factory buildings and equipment
- Property taxes on factory buildings and equipment
- Heat, light, and power

INVENTORIES

LO2 Describe the three inventories of a manufacturing business.

In accounting for a merchandising business, we used only a single inventory account, Merchandise Inventory. Because a manufacturing business acquires materials in one form and converts them into a different form for final sale, we need three inventory accounts:

1. Materials Inventory
2. Work in Process Inventory
3. Finished Goods Inventory

Materials Inventory consists of the materials acquired to be used in production. This account includes both direct and indirect materials.

Work in Process Inventory consists of products on which work has been started but is not yet finished at the end of the accounting period. Materials, labor, and overhead costs of producing a product are accumulated in this account until the product is completed.

Finished Goods Inventory contains products that have been completed and are ready for sale. All materials, labor, and overhead costs of completed products are accumulated in this account until the products are sold.

FLOW OF MANUFACTURING COSTS

LEARNING KEY

Direct materials and direct labor go directly into Work in Process. Indirect materials and indirect labor go through Factory Overhead, and then into Work in Process.

The flow of the three manufacturing costs through the three inventory accounts is illustrated in Figure 26-2. The figure shows how direct materials and direct labor flow directly into Work in Process. Indirect materials and indirect labor become part of Factory Overhead, which flows into Work in Process. All manufacturing costs then flow from Work in Process into Finished Goods when the manufacturing process is completed.

FIGURE 26-2 Flow of Manufacturing Costs

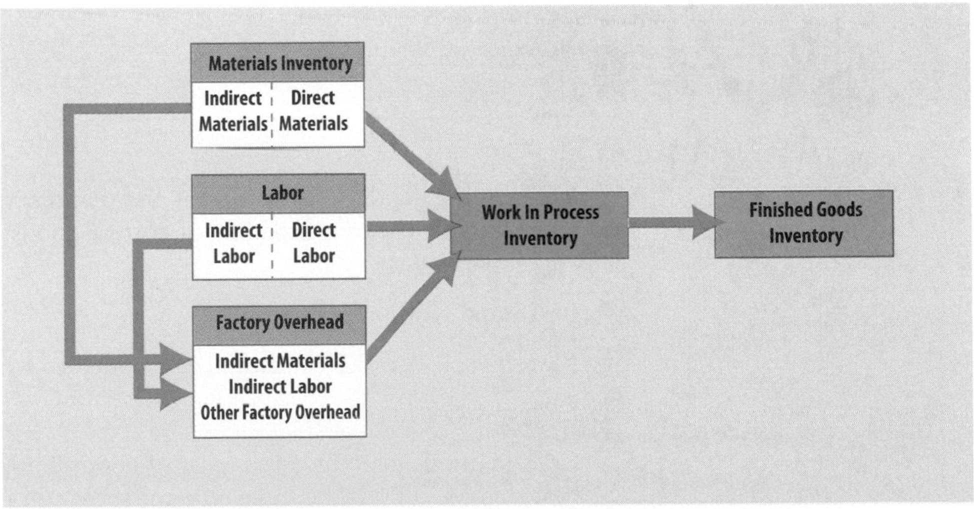

U REVU Complete U REVU-1 on **page 1034** to test your basic understanding of LO2.

FINANCIAL STATEMENT EFFECTS

LO3 Describe and illustrate how manufacturing costs and inventories affect the financial statements of a manufacturing business.

The financial statements of a manufacturing business are very similar to those of a merchandiser. The main differences are in the cost of goods sold section of the income statement and the inventories on the balance sheet.

INCOME STATEMENT

The key difference between the manufacturing and merchandising company income statements is highlighted in Figure 26-3. The purchases made by a merchandiser are the goods that eventually are sold. In contrast, the purchases made by a manufacturer are merely purchases of materials. The cost of manufacturing a product includes not only materials, but also labor and overhead. Thus, *cost of goods manufactured* on the manufacturer's income statement replaces *purchases* on the merchandiser's income statement.

FIGURE 26-3 Cost of Goods Sold Sections

Merchandising Company Partial Income Statement	
Cost of goods sold:	
Merchandise inventory, January 1, 20 --	$10 000 00
Purchases	42 000 00
Merchandise available for sale	$52 000 00
Merchandise inventory, December 31, 20 --	8 000 00
Cost of goods sold	$44 000 00

Manufacturing Company Partial Income Statement	
Cost of goods sold:	
Finished goods inventory, January 1, 20 --	$10 000 00
Cost of goods manufactured	42 000 00
Goods available for sale	$52 000 00
Finished goods inventory, December 31, 20 --	8 000 00
Cost of goods sold	$44 000 00

The cost of goods sold section of the manufacturer's income statement is commonly supplemented by a schedule of cost of goods manufactured (see Figure 26-4). This schedule shows:

1. Beginning work in process.
2. Materials, labor, and overhead costs added to work in process during the period.
3. Ending work in process.
4. Cost of goods manufactured (cost of goods completed during the period). Note that this $42,000 is the same amount shown in Figure 26-3.

FIGURE 26-4 Schedule of Cost of Goods Manufactured

1	Work in process, January 1, 20--			$ 6,000.00
	Direct materials:			
	Materials inventory, January 1, 20--	$ 3,000.00		
	Materials purchases	15,800.00		
	Materials available	$ 18,800.00		
	Materials inventory, December 31, 20--	2,500.00		
	Cost of materials used	$16,300.00		
	Less indirect materials included in overhead	800.00		
2	Cost of direct materials used		$15,500.00	
	Direct labor		16,500.00	
	Overhead		8,000.00	
	Total manufacturing costs			40,000.00
	Total work in process during the period			$46,000.00
3	Work in process, December 31, 20--			4,000.00
4	Cost of goods manufactured			$42,000.00

If no indirect materials from the materials inventory are charged to overhead, it is not necessary to subtract the indirect materials cost in computing the cost of direct materials used.

The *cost of direct materials used* of $15,500 is calculated in almost the same way the cost of goods sold is calculated in a merchandiser's income statement. Beginning inventory of materials plus purchases equals materials available. This amount less the ending inventory of materials equals cost of materials used. Some of these materials were indirect and charged to overhead. So the indirect materials cost is subtracted to compute the cost of direct materials used.

The cost of goods manufactured of $42,000 represents:

1 The amount *transferred out* of work in process during the period.

2 The amount *added* to finished goods during the period.

Work in Process			Finished Goods	
	42,000	1 ⟶ 2	42,000	

BALANCE SHEET

A manufacturer's balance sheet has three inventory accounts rather than the single merchandise inventory account used by a merchandiser. The current assets section of the manufacturer's balance sheet might appear as shown in Figure 26-5. The three inventories are listed in decreasing order of liquidity, with finished goods first and materials last.

FIGURE 26-5 Current Assets Section of Manufacturer's Balance Sheet

Current assets:		
Cash		$17,000.00
Accounts receivable (net)		12,000.00
Inventories:		
Finished goods	$8,000.00	
Work in process	4,000.00	
Materials	2,500.00	14,500.00
Supplies		2,300.00
Total current assets		$45,800.00

U REVU

Complete U REVU-2 on **page 1035** to test your basic understanding of LO3.

JOB ORDER COST ACCOUNTING

LO4 Define and describe how to operate a job order cost accounting system.

A **cost accounting system** is a system for accumulating detailed information about the cost of producing a product. Product cost information is needed for three purposes:

1. To assist in setting selling prices. A product's selling price must be sufficient to provide a gross profit and contribute to net income.
2. To assist in controlling production costs. If the actual costs of producing a product exceed the planned costs, management can take corrective action.
3. To assist in determining the net income or loss. When products are manufactured, the manufacturing costs must be accumulated to determine inventories, cost of goods sold, and net income or loss.

The two basic types of inventory cost accounting systems are:

1. Job order cost system.
2. Process cost system.

A **job order cost system** provides a separate record of the cost of producing each individual product or group of products. If products are made to customers' orders or in separately identifiable "lots" or "batches," a job order cost system is appropriate. A printing shop, consulting firm, or custom shirt and jacket maker like Evolve in the chapter opener would use such a system.

A BROADER VIEW

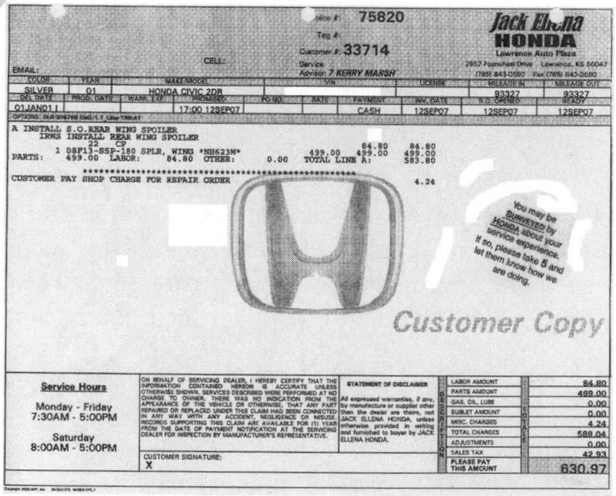

Job Cost Systems—So Common You Find Them by Accident

Throughout this book, we have seen the accounting side of many items we regularly encounter in our everyday lives: managing our checking account, deductions for taxes on our paychecks, purchases we make with our credit cards, and use of promissory notes to borrow money. In this chapter, we see yet another accounting item that is far more common than we probably realize—the job order cost system.

Presented on the left is Job Order 75820 used by Jack Ellena Honda to repair Becca Fenili's car. If you ever had your car repaired or serviced, even something as minor as an oil change, you probably were part of a job order. In fact, any repairs or servicing of any kind—on TVs, computers, lawn tractors, etc.—usually are based on a job order system. You can see accounting issues almost everywhere. It is indeed an important language to learn.

A **process cost system** accumulates manufacturing costs by process, such as cutting, painting, or finishing. Each unit of product passing through the process during a period of time is assigned a share of the costs. A business that manufactures cement, chemicals, or flour would use such a system.

PERPETUAL INVENTORIES

A cost accounting system uses perpetual inventories. To understand the journal entries and flow of information in a cost accounting system, we need to recall how a perpetual inventory system works.

Chapter 13 demonstrated how a perpetual inventory system works for a merchandising business. The merchandise inventory account is increased for each purchase and decreased for each sale.

A manufacturing business has three inventory accounts: Materials, Work in Process, and Finished Goods. Inventory costs flow through all three of these accounts. This makes a manufacturing business's perpetual inventory system more complex than that of a merchandising business. The following four inventory movements and journal entries are illustrated in Figure 26-6:

FIGURE 26-6 Flow of Costs Through Manufacturing Inventory Accounts

INVENTORY MOVEMENTS	JOURNAL ENTRIES
1 Materials are purchased.	Increase Materials
2 Materials are put into the manufacturing process.	Decrease Materials Increase Work in Process
3 Product is completed.	Decrease Work in Process Increase Finished Goods
4 Completed product is sold.	Decrease Finished Goods Increase Cost of Goods Sold

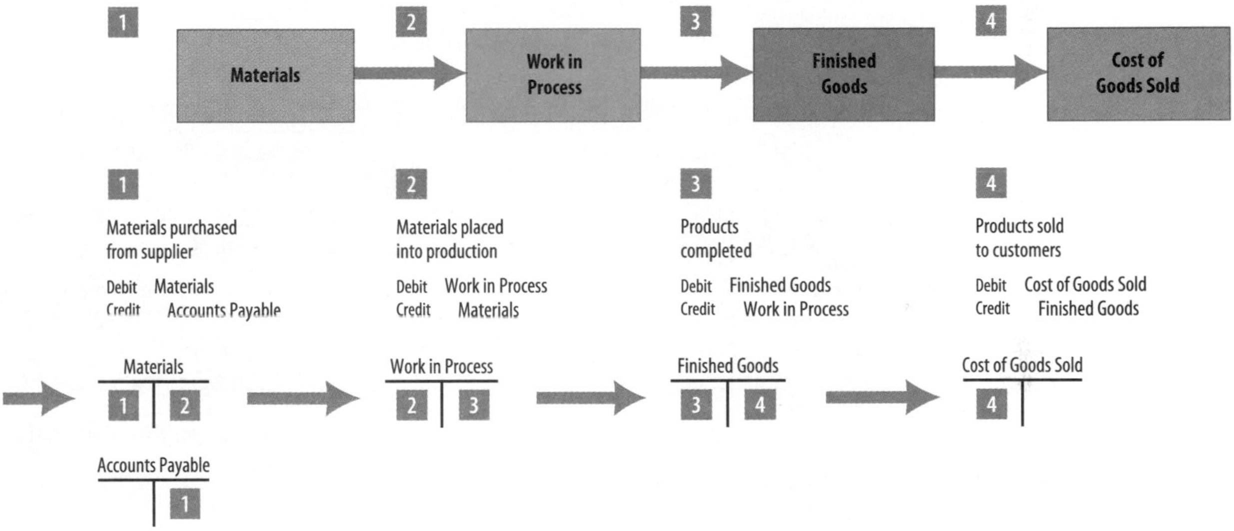

ACCOUNTING FOR MATERIALS

When materials are purchased, their cost is debited to Materials. If materials costing $1,300 are purchased on account, the following journal entry is made:

4			Materials		1,300.00		4
5			Accounts Payable			1,300.00	5
6			Purchased materials on account				6

The materials account in the general ledger is a control account. A separate account for each type of material is kept in a subsidiary ledger called a **materials ledger** or **stores ledger**. Each subsidiary account shows the quantity and cost of the material received and issued and the resulting balance.

Materials are issued from the storeroom to production based on a form called a **materials requisition.** This form is both an authorization to the storekeeper to issue materials and a source document showing the movement of materials. Figure 26-7 illustrates one form of materials requisition. If these are direct materials, the following journal entry is made:

The job number is placed after Work in Process.

8			Work in Process (Job No. 319)		2,100 00		8
9			Materials			2,100 00	9
10			Issued direct materials to production				10

Note that the debit to Work in Process also indicates the job to which the materials are charged. This job is in the job cost ledger, a subsidiary ledger for Work in Process. This ledger is explained later in the chapter.

FIGURE 26-7 Materials Requisition

MATERIALS REQUISITION

Requested by: Susan Korman   Req. No. 439
Date: January 19, 20--   Approved: C.D.
Charge to: Job No. 319 Materials

Item No.	Description	Quantity	Unit Cost	Total Cost
SP10	16" Plastic Truck Body	500	$4.20	$2,100.00

Received By: S.K.   Date Received: January 19, 20--

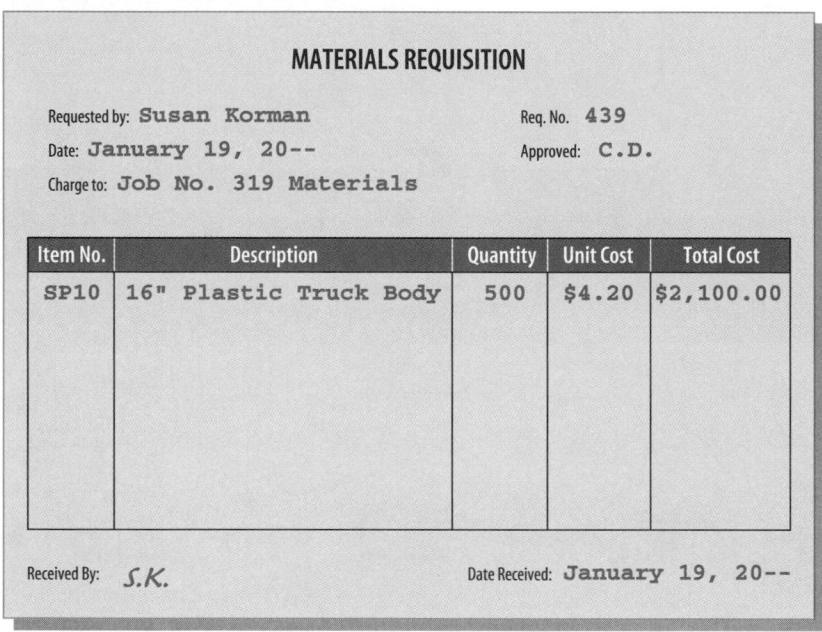

Figure 26-8 shows Job No. 319 with $2,100 of direct materials charged to it.

FIGURE 26-8 Job No. 319 with Direct Materials

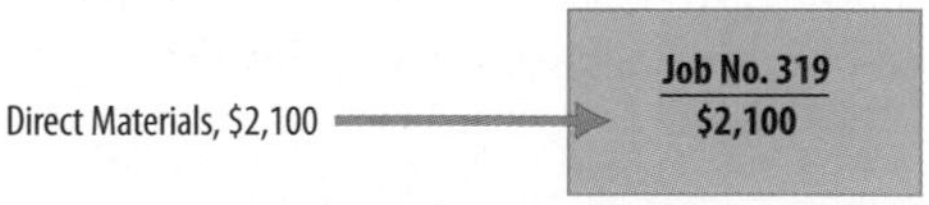

Materials requisitions also are used to issue indirect materials. Since indirect materials are part of overhead, the following journal entry is made to issue $250 of indirect materials to production:

13			Factory Overhead		250 00		13
14			Materials			250 00	14
15			Issued indirect materials to production				15

Notice that no job number is indicated for these overhead costs. This is because overhead costs relate to many different jobs. These and other overhead costs are accumulated and will be applied to specific jobs. This application process is illustrated later in the chapter.

ACCOUNTING FOR LABOR

Chapter 8 showed how to account for employee earnings and payroll deductions. A job order cost accounting system uses the same procedures, except more detail is involved. The earnings of workers whose services are direct labor are charged to the jobs on which they worked. The earnings of workers whose services are indirect labor are charged to the proper factory overhead accounts. This requires keeping a record of the time worked and labor cost incurred on each job. One way of doing so is to require the direct labor employees to complete a **daily time sheet** or **time ticket** like the one in Figure 26-9.

In businesses with computer-based timekeeping systems, a record of time and labor costs on each job can be generated automatically. Employees' barcode time cards (Chapter 8, Figure 8-2) are inserted into a computer at their workstations. The labor costs are then distributed by the computer system.

FIGURE 26-9 Daily Time Sheet

ToyJoy Manufacturing Co.

DAILY TIME SHEET

Name Charles Rhome Date 1/27/--

Job No.	Start	Stop	Hours		Equiv. Hours	Rate	Amount Earned
			Reg.	O.T.			
319	8:00	12:00	4		4	10.00	40.00
319	1:00	5:00	4		4	10.00	40.00
							80.00

Approved B.R.

Time sheets normally are summarized by days, weeks, or months to provide the direct labor cost for each job. This summary is used to make the journal entry for the direct labor costs incurred. Based solely on the time sheet in Figure 26-9, the entry is as follows:

4		Work in Process (Job No. 319)	80 00		4
5		Wages Payable		80 00	5
6		Incurred direct labor costs			6

The debit to Work in Process also indicates the job to which the direct labor is charged.

Figure 26-10 shows Job No. 319 with $2,100 of direct materials and $80 of direct labor charged to it.

FIGURE 26-10 Job No. 319 with Direct Materials and Direct Labor

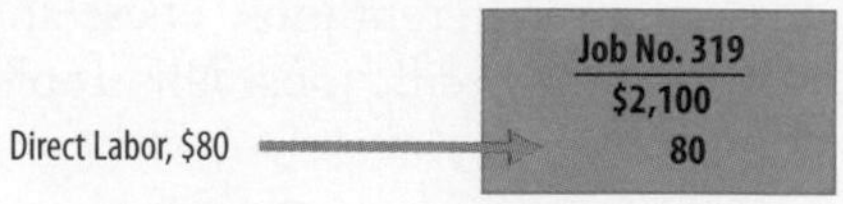

Employees who perform indirect labor also use time sheets. Since indirect labor is part of overhead, the following journal entry is made if indirect labor costs of $110 are incurred:

8			Factory Overhead	110 00		8
9			Wages Payable		110 00	9
10			Incurred indirect labor costs			10

As we saw with indirect materials, notice that no job number is indicated for these indirect labor overhead costs. They are accumulated and will be applied to specific jobs.

ACCOUNTING FOR FACTORY OVERHEAD

Factory overhead includes all manufacturing costs other than direct materials and direct labor. The previous two sections showed how to charge indirect materials and indirect labor to Factory Overhead. Similarly, other overhead costs such as depreciation of factory buildings, utilities, and repairs are charged to Factory Overhead. For example, the factory lighting bill of $870 is recorded as follows:

12			Factory Overhead	870 00		12
13			Accounts Payable		870 00	13
14			Incurred factory lighting costs			14

The factory overhead account generally is a control account in the general ledger. Details of the different types of factory overhead costs are accumulated in a **factory overhead ledger**. This subsidiary ledger contains separate accounts for indirect materials, indirect labor, utilities, repairs, and other costs.

By using a factory overhead control account and subsidiary ledger, we can readily accumulate actual factory overhead costs. The major problem in a job order cost accounting system, however, is assigning a reasonable amount of overhead costs to each job. The nature of many factory overhead costs complicates the problem. Most factory overhead costs, such as depreciation of factory buildings, do not vary with the volume of production. Further, some types of overhead, such as heating costs, vacation pay, and repairs, are incurred irregularly throughout the year. These costs do not apply solely to the products manufactured in the months in which the costs occurred.

Predetermined Overhead Rate

Because of the difficulties of relating actual overhead costs to specific jobs, overhead is applied to jobs based on a **predetermined overhead rate**. The basic idea is that we estimate the total overhead costs and total production activity for the year. The overhead is then spread among the jobs based on the amount of production activity on each job. Common measures of production activity are direct labor hours, direct labor costs, and machine hours.

LEARNING KEY

Actual overhead costs are accumulated in factory overhead accounts. Overhead costs are applied to jobs using a predetermined overhead rate.

To illustrate, assume that ToyJoy Manufacturing Co. estimates its factory overhead costs at \$366,000 and direct labor costs at \$610,000 for the coming year. ToyJoy's predetermined overhead application rate based on direct labor costs is 60%.

$$\frac{\text{Estimated Factory Overhead Costs}}{\text{Estimated Direct Labor Costs}} = \frac{\$366{,}000}{\$610{,}000} = 60\%$$

As each job is completed during the year, 60% of the direct labor cost incurred on the job is added as the job's share of factory overhead. Assume that Job No. 319 had total direct labor costs of \$5,040. Factory overhead applied to this job is \$3,024.

Direct labor cost	\$5,040
Application rate	×60%
Overhead cost applied	\$3,024

The entry to apply the overhead cost to Job No. 319 is as follows:

4			Work in Process (Job No. 319)		3,024.00		4
5			Factory Overhead			3,024.00	5
6			Applied overhead to work in process				6

The debit to Work in Process also indicates the job to which the overhead is charged.

Figure 26-11 shows Job No. 319 with \$2,100 of direct materials, \$5,040 (\$80 + \$4,960) of direct labor, and \$3,024 of overhead charged to it.

FIGURE 26-11 Job No. 319 with Direct Materials, Direct Labor, and Overhead

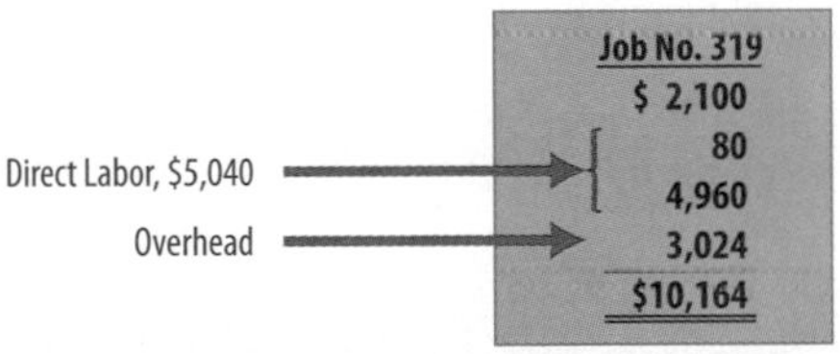

LEARNING KEY

Direct materials, direct labor, and applied factory overhead costs are accumulated on a job cost sheet.

ACCOUNTING FOR WORK IN PROCESS—THE JOB COST SHEET

In the three previous sections, we saw materials, labor, and overhead costs charged to a specific job (No. 319) that was part of work in process. The accumulation of the materials, labor, and overhead charges was illustrated in Figures 26-8, 26-10, and 26-11. In a job order cost accounting system, Work in Process is a control account with a subsidiary ledger (**job cost ledger**). This ledger is made up of job cost sheets. A **job cost sheet** is a document for recording the direct materials and direct labor costs incurred and factory overhead costs applied on a specific job. The job cost sheet for Job No. 319 is illustrated in Figure 26-12. As the direct materials and direct labor costs are incurred on a specific job, they are entered on a cost sheet. When the job is completed, factory overhead is applied at the predetermined rate. Note that the total cost (\$10,164) is the same as in Figure 26-11.

FIGURE 26-12 Job Cost Sheet

ToyJoy
Manufacturing Co.

JOB COST SHEET

Job No. 319 Date Started Jan. 14, 20--

Item RC Truck

For Fun Time Wholesalers Date Completed Feb. 12, 20--

Direct Materials		Direct Labor		Factory Overhead
Req. No.	Amount	Hours	Amount	
439	$2,100	410	$4,260	Direct Labor $5,040
		70	780	Overhead Rate 60%
				Overhead Applied $3,024

Summary	
Direct Materials	$ 2,100
Direct Labor	5,040
Overhead	3,024
Total Cost	$10,164
Units Completed	500

ACCOUNTING FOR COMPLETED JOBS

After a job has been completed, all of the costs accumulated on the job cost sheet are transferred to finished goods. For Job No. 319 (Figure 26-12), the entry is as follows:

The product number is placed after the inventory account title

9			Finished Goods (No. R4)		10 1 6 4 00		9
10			Work in Process (Job No. 319)			10 1 6 4 00	10
11			Transferred work in process to finished goods				11

The credit to Work in Process indicates the job that has been completed (Job No. 319). The debit to Finished Goods indicates the completed product number (R4). Finished Goods is a control account in the general ledger. A separate account for each product is kept in a subsidiary ledger called a **finished goods ledger**.

In T account form, product R4 would appear in the finished goods ledger as follows:

Product R4

Job #297	13,400	
Job #319	10,164	

Notice that the finished goods subsidiary ledger account shows the costs both by product and by job. Remember that in a job cost system, costs are accumulated by job.

At this point, the job has been completed and the costs have been transferred from Work in Process to Finished Goods. Since the costs are no longer in Work in Process, the job cost sheet is removed from the job cost ledger and filed for future reference.

ACCOUNTING FOR SALES

Each time a sale occurs, both the sale and the cost of the goods sold are recorded. Assume that the 500 RC trucks produced in Job No. 319 are sold to RC Time for $13,900 on account. The entry for this sale is as follows:

4			Accounts Receivable		13,900.00		4
5			Sales			13,900.00	5
6							6
7			Cost of Goods Sold		10,164.00		7
8			Finished Goods (No. R4)			10,164.00	8
9			Made sale on account				9

The credit to Finished Goods also indicates the completed product that was sold (No. R4).

FLOW OF JOB ORDER COST THROUGH THE ACCOUNTS

In the preceding sections, we have made journal entries for events ranging from the purchase of materials through the sale of a finished product. We also used three different subsidiary ledgers. It might be helpful at this point to review the complete flow of costs in a job order cost system. Figure 26-13 summarizes the journal entries in T account form and ties in the subsidiary ledgers with the related control accounts for the following nine events:

1 Materials purchased from suppliers.

2 Direct materials issued to production (work in process).

3 Indirect materials issued to production (overhead).

4 Direct labor costs incurred (work in process).

5 Indirect labor costs incurred (overhead).

6 Other factory overhead costs incurred (e.g., utilities, depreciation).

7 Overhead applied to completed jobs at predetermined rate.

8 Jobs completed.

9 Finished goods sold to customers.

FIGURE 26-13 Flow of Job Order Costs

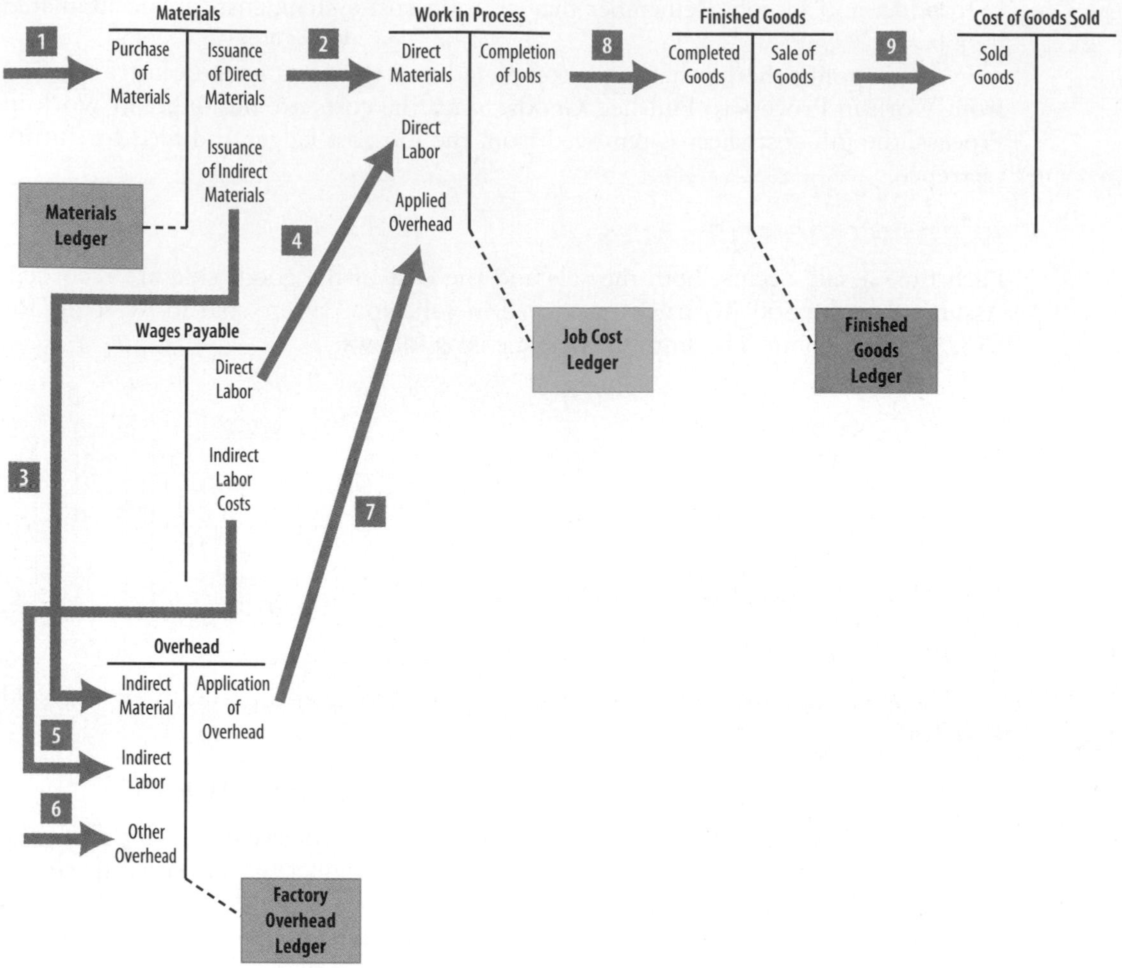

Note the linkage between each of the control accounts and its related subsidiary ledger. Each time an entry affects one of these control accounts, the related subsidiary ledger must be updated accordingly. All nine events require entries in both a control account and a subsidiary ledger.

UNDERAPPLIED AND OVERAPPLIED FACTORY OVERHEAD

We apply factory overhead to completed jobs based on a predetermined rate. This rate is based on *estimates* of the total factory overhead costs and total production activity for the year. It is unlikely that these estimates will be exactly correct. When either estimate is too high or too low, the amount of factory overhead cost actually incurred will differ from the amount applied. If the amount of applied overhead is greater than actual overhead cost incurred, the difference is called **overapplied overhead**. If the amount applied is less than actual overhead cost incurred, the difference is called **underapplied overhead**.

Figure 26-14 shows two versions of ToyJoy's factory overhead account after entries for actual and applied overhead have been made for the year. In Case 1, factory overhead is *under*applied by $900 ($185,000 – $184,100). Overhead costs of $900 were incurred that were not applied to goods produced. In Case 2, factory overhead is *over*applied by $1,000 ($185,000 – $186,000). Overhead costs of $1,000 more than were actually incurred were applied to goods produced.

FIGURE 26-14 Factory Overhead Account

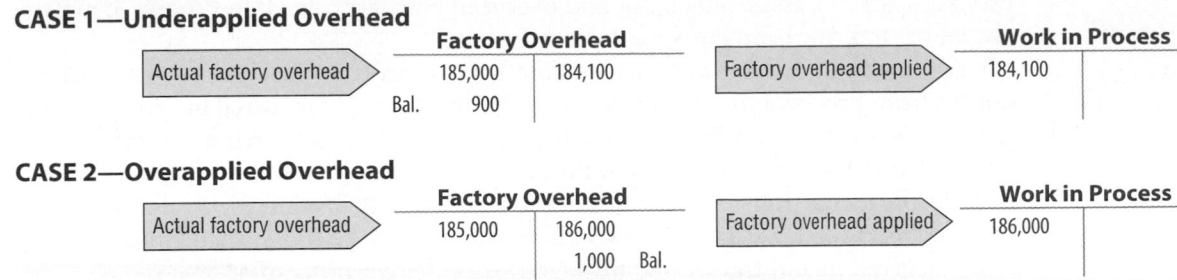

CASE 1—Underapplied Overhead

Actual factory overhead →

	Factory Overhead	
	185,000	184,100
Bal.	900	

Factory overhead applied →

Work in Process	
184,100	

CASE 2—Overapplied Overhead

Actual factory overhead →

Factory Overhead		
185,000	186,000	
	1,000	Bal.

Factory overhead applied →

Work in Process	
186,000	

If underapplied or overapplied overhead is a large amount, it should be spread among the work in process, finished goods, and cost of goods sold accounts, based on the relative size of these accounts.

What should we do with the underapplied or overapplied balance in the factory overhead account? Three accounts were affected by the overhead applications during the year: Work in Process, Finished Goods, and Cost of Goods Sold. First, overhead was applied to Work in Process. When the goods were completed, overhead was transferred to Finished Goods as part of the work in process. When the goods were sold, overhead was transferred to Cost of Goods Sold as part of the finished goods. We could spread the balance among these three accounts. This would require considerable cost and effort, and the accuracy achieved is generally viewed as not worth the trouble. Instead, unless the amount is large, the underapplied or overapplied overhead commonly is transferred to Cost of Goods Sold by an adjusting entry. The adjusting entries for each case shown in Figure 26-14 would be as follows:

CASE 1—Underapplied Overhead

4			Cost of Goods Sold		9 0 0 00		4
5			Factory Overhead			9 0 0 00	5

CASE 2—Overapplied Overhead

7			Factory Overhead		1 0 0 0 00		7
8			Cost of Goods Sold			1 0 0 0 00	8

U REVU Complete U REVU-3 on **page 1035** to test your basic understanding of LO4.

PROCESS COST ACCOUNTING

LO5 Describe a process cost accounting system.

The job order cost system described in the previous section accumulates costs by job. This system is useful for costing separately identifiable products or batches of product. In a process cost system, costs are accumulated by process or department. This system is useful for costing similar or identical products. Good examples include basic models of most automobiles, or wooden bookshelves.

LEARNING KEY

In a process cost system, costs attach to products as the products move from one process to another.

As products move through the manufacturing process in a process cost system, costs of processing "attach" to the products. These costs are then passed on to the next processing operation where additional costs attach to the product. This sequence continues through the final production of finished goods.

The production of unassembled wooden bookshelves in a process cost system is illustrated in Figure 26-15. Notice how different manufacturing costs are added at different processing stages. Materials, labor, and overhead costs are incurred in Process 1. In Process 2, only labor and overhead costs are added. In Process 3, materials, labor, and overhead costs are incurred again.

Also notice how the costs accumulate from process to process. The costs of the output from Process 1 are the materials, labor, and overhead incurred in Process 1. The costs of the output from Process 2 include both the costs transferred in from Process 1 and the additional costs incurred in Process 2. The costs of the output from Process 3 include the costs transferred in from Processes 1 and 2, plus the additional costs incurred in Process 3. Thus, the costs ultimately transferred to Finished Goods include costs incurred in and transferred through three different processing operations.

FIGURE 26-15 Process Cost System

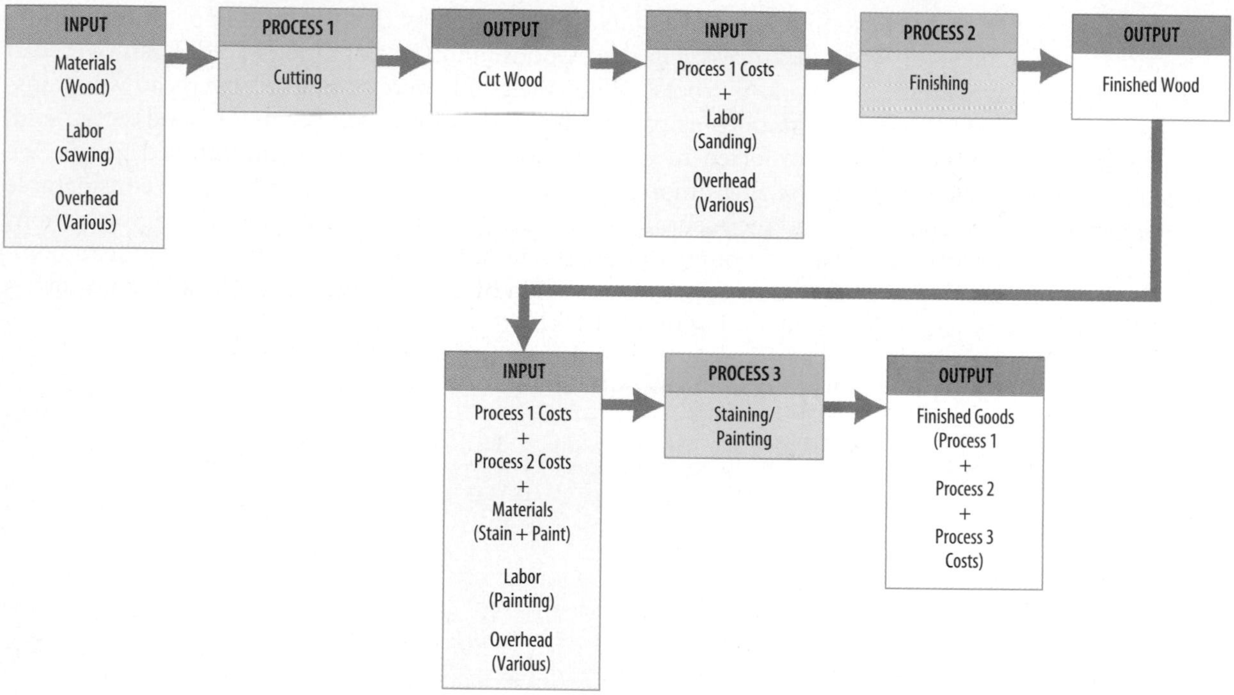

To function effectively, a process cost system must also have the following features:

- Work in process accounts. Each processing department has a separate work in process account.
- Overhead application rates. Each processing department has a separate predetermined overhead application rate.
- Costs per unit. Costs are calculated per unit to allocate costs to products moving through the processes.

  The number of units is computed for each process based on:

  1. units in process at the beginning of the period,
  2. units started and completed during the period, and
  3. units still in process at the end of the period.

The cost per unit must be computed separately for materials, labor, and overhead.

In general, process cost systems are more complicated than job order cost systems. Process cost systems are fully explained and illustrated in more advanced texts.

LEARNING OBJECTIVES	Key Points to Remember
LO1 **Describe the three manufacturing costs.**	The three primary elements of manufacturing cost are materials, labor, and factory overhead. These three costs come together in a conversion process to produce completed products, as shown in Figure 26-1.
LO2 **Describe the three inventories of a manufacturing business.**	Three inventories are needed in a manufacturing business: materials, work in process, and finished goods. Materials inventory consists of materials acquired to be used in production. Work in process inventory consists of products started but not yet finished. Finished goods inventory contains completed products.
LO3 **Describe and illustrate how manufacturing costs and inventories affect the financial statements of a manufacturing business.**	There are two main differences in the financial statements of a manufacturer and a merchandiser: (1) cost of goods sold on the income statement and (2) inventories on the balance sheet. Purchases on the merchandiser's income statement is replaced by cost of goods manufactured on the manufacturer's income statement. The manufacturer's balance sheet has three inventory accounts: Finished Goods, Work in Process, and Materials.
LO4 **Define and describe how to operate a job order cost accounting system.**	A job order cost system provides a separate record of the cost of each product or group of products that is produced. A cost accounting system with perpetual inventories is used to accumulate information about the cost of producing each product. Under this system, at least one of the three inventory accounts is affected every time (1) materials are purchased, (2) materials are placed in production, (3) products are completed, or (4) products are sold, as shown in Figure 26-6. Three important documents used in a job order cost system are the materials requisition, daily time sheet, and job cost sheet. Overhead is applied to jobs based on a predetermined overhead rate. Underapplied or overapplied overhead normally is transferred to Cost of Goods Sold. Four subsidiary ledgers are used in a job cost system: the materials ledger, factory overhead ledger, job cost ledger, and finished goods ledger. Figure 26-13 shows the use of these four ledgers.
LO5 **Describe a process cost accounting system.**	In a process cost system, costs are accumulated by process or department rather than by job.

KLOOSTER & ALLEN

DEMONSTRATION PROBLEM

Mantel Manufacturing Company uses a job order cost accounting system. The following is a summary of transactions completed during its first year of operations:

(a) Purchased materials on account, $435,000.

(b) (1) Issued *direct materials* to production.

Job No. 1	$ 55,000	Job No. 4	$119,000
Job No. 2	76,000	Job No. 5	65,000
Job No. 3	59,800	Job No. 6	18,000

(2) Issued *indirect materials* to production, $11,900.

(c) (1) Incurred factory labor costs.

Job No. 1	$34,000	Job No. 4	$76,000
Job No. 2	40,000	Job No. 5	38,000
Job No. 3	29,000	Job No. 6	12,000

(2) Incurred indirect labor costs, $10,000.

(d) Incurred other factory overhead costs, $96,000.

(e) Depreciation expense on factory equipment, $29,000.

(f) Applied factory overhead, 65% of direct labor cost incurred on jobs.

(g) Finished Job Nos. 1, 2, 4, and 5 as products A, B, D, and E, respectively.

(h) Shipped products A, B, and D and billed customers for $158,000, $210,000, and $362,000, respectively.

REQUIRED

1. Prepare general journal entries for the foregoing transactions. Make compound entries for (b), (c), and (f), but with separate debits for each job. (Use journal page numbers 7 and 8.)
2. Post the entries to the general ledger T accounts for Work in Process and Finished Goods, and determine the ending balances in these accounts.
3. Determine the balances in the job cost ledger to support the balance in the work in process account.
4. Determine the balances in the finished goods ledger to support the balance in the finished goods account.
5. Determine the amount of underapplied or overapplied overhead.

Solution 1.

GENERAL JOURNAL PAGE 7

		DATE	DESCRIPTION	POST. REF.	DEBIT	CREDIT	
(a)	1		Materials		435 0 0 0 00		1
	2		Accounts Payable			435 0 0 0 00	2
	3						3
(b)	4		Work in Process (Job No. 1)		55 0 0 0 00		4
	5		Work in Process (Job No. 2)		76 0 0 0 00		5
	6		Work in Process (Job No. 3)		59 8 0 0 00		6
	7		Work in Process (Job No. 4)		119 0 0 0 00		7
	8		Work in Process (Job No. 5)		65 0 0 0 00		8
	9		Work in Process (Job No. 6)		18 0 0 0 00		9
	10		Materials			392 8 0 0 00	10

		Date	Description	Post. Ref.	Debit	Credit	
	11						11
	12		Factory Overhead		11,900.00		12
	13		Materials			11,900.00	13
	14						14
(c)	15		Work in Process (Job No. 1)		34,000.00		15
	16		Work in Process (Job No. 2)		40,000.00		16
	17		Work in Process (Job No. 3)		29,000.00		17
	18		Work in Process (Job No. 4)		76,000.00		18
	19		Work in Process (Job No. 5)		38,000.00		19
	20		Work in Process (Job No. 6)		12,000.00		20
	21		Wages Payable			229,000.00	21
	22						22
	23		Factory Overhead		10,000.00		23
	24		Wages Payable			10,000.00	24
	25						25
(d)	26		Factory Overhead		96,000.00		26
	27		Accounts Payable			96,000.00	27
	28						28
(e)	29		Factory Overhead		29,000.00		29
	30		Accumulated Depreciation			29,000.00	30
	31						31
(f)	32		Work in Process (Job No. 1)		22,100.00		32
	33		Work in Process (Job No. 2)		26,000.00		33
	34		Work in Process (Job No. 3)		18,850.00		34
	35		Work in Process (Job No. 4)		49,400.00		35
	36		Work in Process (Job No. 5)		24,700.00		36
	37		Work in Process (Job No. 6)		7,800.00		37
	38		Factory Overhead			148,850.00	38
	39						39
(g)	40		Finished Goods (Product A)		111,100.00		40
	41		Work in Process (Job No. 1)			111,100.00	41
	42						42
	43		Finished Goods (Product B)		142,000.00		43
	44		Work in Process (Job No. 2)			142,000.00	44
	45						45
	46		Finished Goods (Product D)		244,400.00		46
	47		Work in Process (Job No. 4)			244,400.00	47
	48						48
	49		Finished Goods (Product E)		127,700.00		49
	50		Work in Process (Job No. 5)			127,700.00	50

GENERAL JOURNAL PAGE 8

		Date	Description	Post. Ref.	Debit	Credit	
(h)	1		Accounts Receivable		158,000.00		1
	2		Sales			158,000.00	2
	3						3
	4		Cost of Goods Sold		111,100.00		4
	5		Finished Goods (Product A)			111,100.00	5

(continued)

6				6
7	Accounts Receivable	210 0 0 0 00		7
8	Sales		210 0 0 0 00	8
9				9
10	Cost of Goods Sold	142 0 0 0 00		10
11	Finished Goods (Product B)		142 0 0 0 00	11
12				12
13	Accounts Receivable	362 0 0 0 00		13
14	Sales		362 0 0 0 00	14
15				15
16	Cost of Goods Sold	244 4 0 0 00		16
17	Finished Goods (Product D)		244 4 0 0 00	17
18				18

2.

Work in Process

Debit	Credit
55,000	111,100
76,000	142,000
59,800	244,400
119,000	127,700
65,000	*625,200*
18,000	
34,000	
40,000	
29,000	
76,000	
38,000	
12,000	
22,100	
26,000	
18,850	
49,400	
24,700	
7,800	
770,650	
Bal. 145,450	

Finished Goods

Debit	Credit
111,100	111,100
142,000	142,000
244,400	244,400
127,700	*497,500*
625,200	
Bal. 127,700	

3. In job cost ledger:

Job No. 3	$107,650
Job No. 6	37,800
	$145,450

4. Product E: $127,700

5.

Factory Overhead

Debit	Credit
11,900	148,850
10,000	
96,000	
29,000	
146,900	*148,850*
	1,950 (Overapplied overhead)

KEY TERMS

cost accounting system (1018) A system for accumulating detailed information regarding the cost of producing a product.

daily time sheet (1021) A record of the time worked and labor cost incurred on each job.

direct labor (1014) The wages of employees who are directly involved in converting materials into finished goods.

direct materials (1014) Those materials that enter into and become a major part of the finished product.

factory burden (1014) See factory overhead.

factory overhead (1014) All manufacturing costs other than direct materials and direct labor.

factory overhead ledger (1022) The subsidiary ledger in which details of the different types of factory overhead costs are accumulated.

factory supplies (1014) See indirect materials.

Finished Goods Inventory (1015) The account that contains the costs of products that have been completed and are ready for sale.

finished goods ledger (1024) The subsidiary ledger in which a separate account for each product is kept.

indirect labor (1014) The wages and salaries of employees who devote their time to supervision or to work of a general nature.

indirect manufacturing cost (1014) See factory overhead.

indirect materials (1014) Those materials used in the manufacturing process that do not become a major part of the finished product.

job cost ledger (1023) A subsidiary ledger for the work in process control account that is made up of job cost sheets.

job cost sheet (1023) A document for recording the direct materials, direct labor, and factory overhead costs incurred on a specific job.

job order cost system (1018) The system that provides a separate record of the cost of each individual product or group of products that is produced.

manufacturing overhead (1014) See factory overhead.

Materials Inventory (1015) The account that includes all the materials (both direct and indirect) acquired to be used in production.

materials ledger (1019) The subsidiary ledger that shows the quantity and cost of material received and issued, and the resulting balance for each type of material.

materials requisition (1020) A form used to issue materials from the storeroom to production.

overapplied overhead (1026) The amount by which applied overhead is greater than the actual overhead cost incurred.

predetermined overhead rate (1022) The rate used to apply overhead, based on production activity such as direct labor hours, direct labor costs, or machine hours; used because of the difficulties of relating specific overhead costs to specific jobs.

process cost system (1018) The system that accumulates manufacturing costs by process, such as cutting, painting, or finishing, and assigns each unit of product passing through the process a share of the costs.

stores ledger (1019) See materials ledger.

time ticket (1021) See daily time sheet.

underapplied overhead (1026) The amount by which applied overhead is less than the actual overhead cost incurred.

Work in Process Inventory (1015) The account in which materials, labor, and overhead costs of producing a product are accumulated until the product is completed.

SELF-STUDY QUESTIONS AND EXERCISES

True/False Questions

1. LO1 Both direct and indirect materials enter into and become major parts of the finished product.
2. LO1 Factory overhead is also known as manufacturing overhead, indirect manufacturing cost, or factory burden.
3. LO2 Work in Process Inventory consists of three items: materials, labor, and factory overhead.
4. LO2 Finished Goods Inventory consists of only those items finished and sold during the period.
5. LO5 A process cost system is useful for costing separately identifiable products or batches of product.

Multiple Choice Questions

1. LO1 Which of these would most likely be treated as an *indirect* material? (Assume you are manufacturing tables.)

   (a) wood (c) glue
   (b) lacquer (d) table legs

2. LO3 The cost of goods sold section of the income statement for a manufacturing company would contain which of the following?

   (a) purchases (c) direct labor
   (b) cost of goods manufactured (d) no inventory account

3. LO4 When total anticipated factory overhead is $500,000 and budgeted direct labor hours are 200,000, what is the predetermined factory overhead rate based on direct labor hours?

   (a) $2.50/hour (c) $10/hour
   (b) $5.00/hour (d) It cannot be determined.

4. LO4 When direct labor hours for Job 101 are 30 and the predetermined factory overhead rate is $5/direct labor hour, what is the applied factory overhead amount?

   (a) $250 (c) $150
   (b) $500 (d) It cannot be determined.

5. LO4 Underapplied or overapplied factory overhead is normally charged or credited to which account?

   (a) Materials (c) Finished Goods
   (b) Work in Process (d) Cost of Goods Sold

U REVU Exercises

1. LO2 Different manufacturing costs and inventory accounts are listed in the left column below. For each cost or account, indicate the other manufacturing cost or inventory account into which it flows. Item (a) is completed as an example.

   a. Indirect materials Factory Overhead
   b. Direct materials ____________
   c. Indirect labor ____________
   d. Direct labor ____________
   e. Factory overhead ____________
   f. Work in process inventory ____________

2. LO3 Prepare a schedule of cost of goods manufactured for the year ended December 31, 20--, based on the following information. (Assume that all materials inventory items are direct materials.)

Work in process, January 1	\$29,700
Materials inventory, January 1	15,400
Materials purchases	16,800
Materials inventory, December 31	18,200
Direct labor	13,300
Overhead	7,700
Work in process, December 31	14,700

3. LO4 Prepare general journal entries for the following transactions.

a. Purchased materials on account, \$26,400.
b. Issued direct materials to Job No. 6, \$21,000.
c. Issued indirect materials (factory overhead), \$3,700.
d. Incurred direct labor, Job No. 6, \$12,900.
e. Incurred indirect labor (factory overhead), \$5,000.
f. Incurred other indirect costs (factory overhead; credit Accounts Payable), \$2,300.
g. Applied factory overhead to Job No. 6, \$7,740.

The answers to the Self-Study Questions and Exercises are at the end of the chapter (pages 1045–1046).

APPLYING YOUR KNOWLEDGE

REVIEW QUESTIONS

LO1 1. Why is the accounting for a manufacturing business more complicated than that for a merchandising business?

LO1 2. What are the three primary elements of manufacturing cost?

LO1 3. What are the two major types of materials, and how do they differ?

LO1 4. Distinguish between direct and indirect labor.

LO1 5. Describe and give three examples of factory overhead.

LO2 6. What are the three inventories needed in a manufacturing business?

LO2 7. Describe the flow of materials, labor, and overhead into Work in Process.

LO3 8. What are the main differences between the financial statements of a manufacturing and a merchandising business?

LO4 9. For what three reasons is product cost information needed by a manufacturing business?

LO4 10. What two purposes are served by a materials requisition form?

LO4 11. What information is provided by the daily time sheet?

LO4 12. Explain how to calculate a predetermined overhead rate.

LO4 13. What costs are entered on the job cost sheet?

LO4 14. Describe underapplied and overapplied overhead. What is commonly done with the underapplied or overapplied balance in the factory overhead account?

LO5 15. Briefly describe the difference between a job order cost system and a process cost system.

SERIES A EXERCISES

E 26-1A (LO3)
✓ Cost of goods sold: $49,000

COST OF GOODS SOLD SECTION The following information is supplied for R&D Manufacturing Co. and WP West Co. (a merchandising company). Prepare the cost of goods sold sections for the income statements of both companies for the year ended 20--.

	R&D Manufacturing	WP West
Merchandise inventory, January 1		$57,000
Finished goods inventory, January 1	$57,000	
Merchandise purchases		36,000
Cost of goods manufactured	36,000	
Merchandise inventory, December 31		44,000
Finished goods inventory, December 31	44,000	

E 26-2A (LO3)
✓ Total manufacturing costs: $98,000

SCHEDULE OF COST OF GOODS MANUFACTURED The following information is supplied for Morales Mining and Manufacturing Company. Prepare a schedule of cost of goods manufactured for the year ended December 31, 20--. Assume that all materials inventory items are direct materials.

Work in process, January 1	$70,000
Materials inventory, January 1	28,000
Materials purchases	32,000
Materials inventory, December 31	24,000
Direct labor	44,000
Overhead	18,000
Work in process, December 31	56,000

E 26-3A (LO4)
✓ Jan. 20 entry: Dr. Factory Overhead (Indirect Mats.), $4,000

JOURNAL ENTRIES FOR MATERIAL, LABOR, AND OVERHEAD Jones Manufacturing Corporation had the following transactions for its job order costing operation. Prepare general journal entries to record these transactions.

Jan. 1	Purchased materials on account, $15,000.
15	Issued direct materials to Job No. 101, $10,000.
20	Issued indirect materials (factory overhead), $4,000.
31	Incurred direct labor, Job No. 101, $8,000.
31	Incurred indirect labor (factory overhead), $2,000.
31	Incurred other indirect costs (factory overhead; credit Accounts Payable), $1,500.

E 26-4A (LO4)
✓ Entry for underapplied factory overhead: Dr. Cost of Goods Sold, $200

JOURNAL ENTRIES FOR FACTORY OVERHEAD Huang Company manufactures toys. It keeps a factory overhead account where actual factory overhead costs are recorded as a debit, and factory overhead applied is recorded as a credit. At the end of the month, under- or overapplied factory overhead is calculated and transferred to the cost of goods sold account. For the month of January, Huang had the following overhead transactions. Make appropriate general journal entries to record factory overhead and factory overhead applied, and to close the under- or overapplied factory overhead to the cost of goods sold account.

Jan. 1	Paid rent, $1,000.
10	Paid electricity bill, $250.
15	Paid repair expense, $1,500.

Jan. 21	Vacation pay for machine operator, $500 (Wages Payable).
31	Depreciation expense for the month, $450.
31	Factory overhead applied was $3,500.

E 26-5A (LO4)
✓ (1) $10/direct labor hour

PREDETERMINED FACTORY OVERHEAD RATE Lovejoy Enterprises calculates a predetermined factory overhead rate so that factory overhead may be applied to production during the month. It calculates the overhead using three different methods and then decides which one to use. Total estimated factory overhead costs are $500,000. Total estimated direct labor hours are 50,000. Total estimated direct labor costs are $800,000. Total machine hours are estimated to be 100,000.

Calculate the predetermined overhead application rates based on (1) direct labor hours, (2) direct labor costs, and (3) machine hours.

E 26-6A (LO4)
✓ 1st Apr. 30 entry: Dr. Finished Goods, $17,500

JOURNAL ENTRIES FOR MATERIAL, LABOR, OVERHEAD, AND SALES Micro Enterprises had the following job order transactions during the month of April. Record the transactions in the general journal, including issuance of materials, labor, and factory overhead applied; completed jobs sent to finished goods inventory; closing of the under- or overapplied factory overhead to the cost of goods sold account; and sale of finished goods.

Apr. 1	Purchased materials on account, $35,000.
10	Issued direct materials to Job No. 33, $10,000.
11	Issued direct materials to Job No. 34, $8,000.
12	Issued direct materials to Job No. 35, $11,000.
25	Incurred direct labor: On Job No. 33, $6,000 On Job No. 34, $4,000 On Job No. 35, $5,000
25	Applied factory overhead: To Job No. 33, $1,500 To Job No. 34, $1,200 To Job No. 35, $1,600
30	Transferred Job Nos. 33–35 to the finished goods inventory account as products F, G, and H.
30	Sold products F, G, and H for $20,000, $16,000, and $22,000, respectively.
30	Actual factory overhead for Job Nos. 33–35, $4,220.

SERIES A PROBLEMS

P 26-7A (LO4)
✓ (d): Dr. Work in Process: (Job No. 300), $8,000

KA KLOOSTER & ALLEN

JOURNAL ENTRIES FOR MATERIAL, LABOR, AND OVERHEAD Eto Manufacturing had the following transactions during the month:

(a) Purchased raw materials on account, $70,000.
(b) Issued direct materials to Job No. 300, $25,000.
(c) Issued indirect materials to production, $10,000.
(d) Paid biweekly payroll and charged direct labor to Job No. 300, $8,000.
(e) Paid biweekly payroll and charged indirect labor to production, $3,000.

(continued)

(f) Issued direct materials to Job No. 301, $20,000.
(g) Issued indirect materials to production, $4,000.
(h) Paid miscellaneous factory overhead charges, $6,000.
(i) Paid biweekly payroll and charged direct labor to Job No. 301, $10,000.
(j) Paid biweekly payroll and charged indirect labor to production, $2,000.

REQUIRED

Prepare general journal entries for transactions (a) through (j).

P 26-8A (LO4)
✓ 1. (h) Product J: Dr. Finished Goods, $16,000

JOB ORDER COSTING TRANSACTIONS B & L Enterprises makes garage doors. During the month of February, the company had four job orders: 303, 304, 305, and 306. Overhead was applied at predetermined rates, while actual factory overhead was recorded as incurred. All four jobs were completed.

(a) Purchased raw materials on account, $40,000.
(b) Issued direct materials to production:

Job No. 303:	$8,000
Job No. 304:	9,000
Job No. 305:	7,000
Job No. 306:	8,500

(c) Issued indirect materials to production, $5,000.
(d) Incurred direct labor costs:

Job No. 303:	$5,000
Job No. 304:	4,000
Job No. 305:	4,800
Job No. 306:	5,200

(e) Charged indirect labor to production, $3,100.
(f) Paid electricity, heating oil, and repair bills for the factory and charged to production, $4,900.
(g) Applied factory overhead to each of the jobs using a predetermined factory overhead rate as follows:

Job No. 303:	$3,000
Job No. 304:	3,500
Job No. 305:	3,000
Job No. 306:	3,500

(h) Finished Job Nos. 303–306 and transferred to the finished goods inventory account as products J, K, L, and M.
(i) Sold products J, K, L, and M for $19,000, $18,500, $16,000, and $18,300, respectively.

REQUIRED

1. Prepare general journal entries to record transactions (a) through (i).
2. Post the entries to the work in process and finished goods T accounts only.

P 26-9A (LO4)
✓ 3: Balance in job cost ledger, $66,600

JOB ORDER COSTING WITH UNDER- AND OVERAPPLIED FACTORY OVERHEAD M. Evans & Sons manufactures parts for radios. For each job order, it maintains ledger sheets on which it records direct labor, direct materials, and factory overhead applied. The factory overhead control account contains postings of actual overhead costs. At the end of the month, the under- or overapplied factory overhead is charged to the cost of goods sold account.

Factory overhead is applied on the basis of direct labor hours. For Job Nos. 101, 102, 103, and 104, direct labor hours are 12,000, 10,000, 11,000, and 18,000, respectively. The overhead application rate is $1.20/direct labor hour.

(a) Purchased raw materials on account, $50,000.
(b) Issued direct materials:

Job No. 101:	$10,000
Job No. 102:	8,000
Job No. 103:	9,000
Job No. 104:	15,000

(c) Issued indirect materials to production, $8,000.

(d) Incurred direct labor costs:

Job No. 101:	$22,000
Job No. 102:	19,000
Job No. 103:	20,500
Job No. 104:	30,000

(e) Charged indirect labor to production, $15,000.
(f) Paid electricity bill, taxes, and repair fees for the factory and charged to production, $8,000.
(g) Depreciation expense on factory equipment, $30,000.
(h) Applied factory overhead to Job Nos. 101–104 using the predetermined factory overhead rate (see above).
(i) Finished Job Nos. 101–103 and transferred to the finished goods inventory account as products N, O, and P.
(j) Sold products N and O for $50,000 and $45,400, respectively.
(k) Transferred under- or overapplied factory overhead balance to the cost of goods sold account.

REQUIRED

1. Prepare general journal entries to record transactions (a) through (k).
2. Post the entries to the work in process and finished goods T accounts only and determine the ending balances in these accounts.
3. Compute the balance in the job cost ledger and make certain this balance agrees with that in the work in process control account.

SERIES B EXERCISES

E 26-1B (LO3)
✓ Cost of goods sold: $13,750

COST OF GOODS SOLD SECTION The following information is supplied for A&B Manufacturing Co. and JC Yoshino Co. (a merchandising company). Prepare the cost of goods sold sections for the income statements of both companies for the year ended 20--.

	A&B Manufacturing	JC Yoshino
Merchandise inventory, January 1		$15,750
Finished goods inventory, January 1	$15,750	
Merchandise purchases		11,000
Cost of goods manufactured	11,000	
Merchandise inventory, December 31		13,000
Finished goods inventory, December 31	13,000	

E 26-2B (LO3)
✓ Total manufacturing costs: $25,000

SCHEDULE OF COST OF GOODS MANUFACTURED The following information is supplied for Sanchez Welding and Manufacturing Company. Prepare a schedule of cost of goods manufactured for the year ended December 31, 20--. Assume that all materials inventory items are direct materials.

Work in process, January 1	$20,500
Materials inventory, January 1	11,000
Materials purchases	12,000
Materials inventory, December 31	13,000
Direct labor	9,500
Overhead	5,500
Work in process, December 31	10,500

E 26-3B (LO4)
✓ Jan. 20 entry: Dr. Factory Overhead (Indirect Mats.), $3,000

JOURNAL ENTRIES FOR MATERIAL, LABOR, AND OVERHEAD Rich Manufacturing Corporation had the following transactions for its job order costing operation. Prepare general journal entries to record these transactions.

Jan. 1 Purchased materials on account, $22,000.
15 Issued direct materials to Job No. 1, $18,000.
20 Issued indirect materials (factory overhead), $3,000.
31 Incurred direct labor, Job No. 1, $11,000.
31 Incurred indirect labor (factory overhead), $4,000.
31 Incurred other indirect costs (factory overhead; credit Accounts Payable), $1,500.

E 26-4B (LO4)
✓ Entry for underapplied factory overhead: Dr. Cost of Goods Sold, $500

JOURNAL ENTRIES FOR FACTORY OVERHEAD Bandy Company manufactures toys. It keeps a factory overhead account where actual factory overhead costs are recorded as a debit and factory overhead applied is recorded as a credit. At the end of the month, under- or overapplied factory overhead is calculated and transferred to the cost of goods sold account. For the month of January, Bandy had the following overhead transactions. Make appropriate general journal entries to record factory overhead and factory overhead applied, and to close the under- or overapplied factory overhead to the cost of goods sold account.

Jan. 1 Paid rent, $2,000.
10 Paid electricity bill, $500.
15 Paid repair expense, $3,000.
21 Vacation pay for machine operator, $500 (Wages Payable).
31 Depreciation expense for the month, $500.
31 Factory overhead applied was $6,000.

E 26-5B (LO4)
✓ (1) $20/direct labor hour

PREDETERMINED FACTORY OVERHEAD RATE Marston Enterprises calculates a predetermined factory overhead rate so that factory overhead may be applied to production during the month. It calculates the overhead using three different methods and then decides which one to use. Total estimated factory overhead costs are $600,000. Total estimated direct labor hours are 30,000. Total estimated direct labor costs are $1,200,000. Total machine hours are estimated to be 200,000.

Calculate the predetermined overhead application rates based on (1) direct labor hours, (2) direct labor costs, and (3) machine hours.

E 26-6B (LO4)

✓ 1st Apr. 30 entry: Dr. Finished Goods, $18,800

JOURNAL ENTRIES FOR MATERIAL, LABOR, OVERHEAD, AND SALES Alert Enterprises had the following job order transactions during the month of April. Record the transactions in the general journal, including issuance of materials, labor, and factory overhead applied; completed jobs sent to finished goods inventory; closing of the under- or overapplied factory overhead to the cost of goods sold account; and sale of finished goods.

Apr.	1	Purchased materials on account, $28,000.
	10	Issued direct materials to Job No. 26, $11,000.
	11	Issued direct materials to Job No. 27, $9,000.
	12	Issued direct materials to Job No. 28, $7,000.
	25	Incurred direct labor: On Job No. 26, $6,000 On Job No. 27, $4,000 On Job No. 28, $5,000
	25	Applied factory overhead: To Job No. 26, $1,800 To Job No. 27, $1,500 To Job No. 28, $1,400
	30	Transferred Job Nos. 26–28 to the finished goods inventory account as products Q, R, and T.
	30	Sold products Q, R, and T for $20,600, $16,000, and $14,900, respectively.
	30	Actual factory overhead for Job Nos. 26–28, $4,500.

SERIES B PROBLEMS

P 26-7B (LO4)

✓ (d): Dr. Work in Process (Job No. 200), $4,500

KA KLOOSTER & ALLEN

JOURNAL ENTRIES FOR MATERIAL, LABOR, AND OVERHEAD Shiar Manufacturing had the following transactions during the month:

(a) Purchased raw materials on account, $22,500.
(b) Issued direct materials to Job No. 200, $11,250.
(c) Issued indirect materials to production, $4,000.
(d) Paid biweekly payroll and charged direct labor to Job No. 200, $4,500.
(e) Paid biweekly payroll and charged indirect labor to production, $1,250.
(f) Issued direct materials to Job No. 201, $10,000.
(g) Issued indirect materials to production, $2,500.
(h) Paid miscellaneous factory overhead charges, $4,500.
(i) Paid biweekly payroll and charged direct labor to Job No. 201, $4,250.
(j) Paid biweekly payroll and charged indirect labor to production, $900.

REQUIRED

Prepare general journal entries for transactions (a) through (j).

P 26-8B (LO4)

✓ 1. (h) Product W: Dr. Finished Goods, $16,100

JOB ORDER COSTING TRANSACTIONS D & K Enterprises makes wicker baskets. During the month of August, the company had four job orders: 501, 502, 503, and 504. Overhead was applied at predetermined rates, while actual factory overhead was recorded as incurred. All four jobs were completed.

(continued)

(a) Purchased raw materials on account, $44,000.
(b) Issued direct materials to production:

Job No. 501:	$8,200
Job No. 502:	9,100
Job No. 503:	7,300
Job No. 504:	8,500

(c) Issued indirect materials to production, $5,000.
(d) Incurred direct labor costs:

Job No. 501:	$4,800
Job No. 502:	4,100
Job No. 503:	4,800
Job No. 504:	5,000

(e) Charged indirect labor to production, $3,300.
(f) Paid electricity, heating oil, and repair bills for the factory and charged to production, $5,200.
(g) Applied factory overhead to each of the jobs using a predetermined factory overhead rate as follows:

Job No. 501:	$3,100
Job No. 502:	3,300
Job No. 503:	3,300
Job No. 504:	3,800

(h) Finished Job Nos. 501–504 and transferred to the finished goods inventory account as products W, X, Y, and Z.
(i) Sold products W, X, Y, and Z for $17,500, $18,000, $16,900, and $19,000, respectively.

REQUIRED

1. Prepare general journal entries to record transactions (a) through (i).
2. Post the entries to the work in process and finished goods T accounts only.

P 26-9B (LO4)
✓ 3: Balance in job cost ledger, $47,700

JOB ORDER COSTING WITH UNDER- AND OVERAPPLIED FACTORY OVERHEAD J. Bowen & Co. manufactures screen doors. For each job order, it maintains ledger sheets on which it records direct labor, direct materials, and factory overhead applied. The factory overhead control account contains postings of actual overhead costs. At the end of the month, the under- or over-applied factory overhead is charged to the cost of goods sold account.

Factory overhead is applied on the basis of direct labor hours. For Job Nos. 201, 202, 203, and 204, direct labor hours are 10,000, 11,000, 11,000, and 12,000, respectively. The overhead application rate is $1.50/direct labor hour.

(a) Purchased raw materials on account, $45,000.
(b) Issued direct materials:

Job No. 201:	$10,000
Job No. 202:	11,000
Job No. 203:	9,500
Job No. 204:	12,200

(c) Issued indirect materials to production, $7,500.

(d) Incurred direct labor costs:

Job No. 201:	$18,000
Job No. 202:	19,000
Job No. 203:	20,500
Job No. 204:	17,500

(e) Charged indirect labor to production, $11,000.
(f) Paid electricity bill, taxes, and repair fees for the factory and charged to production, $7,000.
(g) Depreciation expense on factory equipment, $40,000.
(h) Applied factory overhead to Job Nos. 201–204 using the predetermined factory overhead rate (see above).
(i) Finished Job Nos. 201–203 and transferred to the finished goods inventory account as products C, D, and E.
(j) Sold products C and D for $47,000 and $49,000, respectively.
(k) Transferred under- or overapplied factory overhead balance to the cost of goods sold account.

REQUIRED

1. Prepare general journal entries to record transactions (a) through (k).
2. Post the entries to the work in process and finished goods T accounts only and determine the ending balances in these accounts.
3. Compute the balance in the job cost ledger and make certain this balance agrees with that in the work in process control account.

MANAGING YOUR WRITING

Joan owns a print shop and has a difficult time figuring out what to bid on jobs. She knows how to estimate the cost of materials and labor on different jobs but is confused about how to handle many other costs she knows she incurs to run the shop. These include utilities, cleaning staff, property taxes on the building, and other expenses. Many of these types of costs vary from month to month. In addition, she often does not know the amounts until some time after jobs are completed.

Write a memo to Joan explaining how she should apply her overhead costs in developing bids on her jobs.

ETHICS CASE

Ben Reese is a painter for a small manufacturing plant. Sometimes he works directly on the product and sometimes he performs routine maintenance on the plant's three buildings. He is paid $11.50 an hour and fills out a time sheet at the end of each week. His supervisor then fills in the specific jobs that will be charged with Ben's time. On Friday afternoon, Ben's supervisor, Ralph Brooks, said he needed Ben to do a job off the plant site. Ralph explained that he had just installed a wooden garage door on his house and needed it painted. He told Ben to leave a couple of hours early and "just sign out as though you had stayed until quitting time." Even though this request made Ben uncomfortable, he did what the boss said.

1. What would you have done if you were Ben? Justify your answer.
2. How do you suppose Ralph will account for Ben's hours away from the plant?

(continued)

3. Write a short paragraph explaining the difference between direct labor and indirect labor. Include how each is assigned to specific jobs.
4. In groups of two or three, come up with some suggestions on measures a company can take to prevent a situation like this from happening.

MASTERY PROBLEM

✓ 3: Balance in job cost ledger, $97,260

Forester Manufacturing Company uses a job order cost accounting system to keep track of finished jobs and jobs in process. All production is either to customer order or to specification. The following is a summary of transactions completed during the month of August:

(a) Purchased materials (direct and indirect) on account, $158,000.

(b) Requisitioned materials from storerooms, $149,000 (direct materials, $122,000; indirect materials, $27,000). Charged to jobs as follows:

Job No. 805:	$34,000
Job No. 806:	44,000
Job No. 807:	20,000
Job No. 808:	24,000

(c) Incurred factory labor cost for the month, $211,800 (direct labor, $150,000; indirect labor, $61,800). Charged to jobs as follows:

Job No. 805:	$25,500
Job No. 806:	39,800
Job No. 807:	51,400
Job No. 808:	33,300

(d) Incurred other factory overhead costs, $85,000 (depreciation expense, $10,000; miscellaneous factory expense on account, $75,000).

(e) Applied factory overhead, 120% of direct labor cost incurred on jobs. (Make a separate debit for each job.)

(f) Finished Job Nos. 805, 806, and 807 and placed them in stock as products X, Y, and Z, respectively.

(g) Sold products X, Y, and Z on account for $123,000, $150,000, and $168,000, respectively. Costs of products sold were $90,100, $122,000, and $140,000, respectively. (Products Y and Z included some items from the beginning inventory of finished goods and some from the current period's production.)

The beginning balances in the inventory accounts were as follows:

Work in Process	$0
Finished Goods	$76,000 (Product Y, $46,000; Product Z, $30,000).

REQUIRED

1. Prepare general journal entries for the foregoing transactions.
2. Post the entries to the general ledger T accounts for Work in Process and Finished Goods, and compute the ending balances in these accounts.
3. Determine the job cost ledger balance to support the balance in the work in process account.
4. Determine the amount of under- or overapplied factory overhead.

CHALLENGE PROBLEM

This problem challenges you to apply your cumulative accounting knowledge to move a step beyond the material in the chapter.

✓ 2: Net income = $75,750

For its most recent year of operations, Unovap Co. had sales of $950,000, cost of goods sold of $680,000, and operating expenses of $190,000. Its ending inventories were as follows:

Raw material	$30,000
Work in process	88,000
Finished goods	32,000

In addition, it has $5,000 of underapplied overhead which has not yet been transferred to any other accounts.

REQUIRED

1. Transfer the underapplied overhead to Cost of Goods Sold and calculate the net income for the year.
2. Spread the underapplied overhead among Work in Process, Finished Goods, and Cost of Goods Sold, and calculate the net income for the year.
3. (a) What is the difference in the net income based on the two different approaches to accounting for the underapplied overhead?

   (b) How would you recommend accounting for the underapplied overhead in this case?

ANSWERS TO SELF-STUDY QUESTIONS AND EXERCISES

True/False Questions

1. F (only direct materials)
2. T
3. T
4. F (items finished and not sold)
5. F (It is useful for costing similar or identical products.)

Multiple Choice Questions

1. c 2. b 3. a 4. c 5. d

U REVU Exercises

1.	a. Indirect materials	Factory Overhead
	b. Direct materials	Work in Process Inventory
	c. Indirect labor	Factory Overhead
	d. Direct labor	Work in Process Inventory
	e. Factory overhead	Work in Process Inventory
	f. Work in process inventory	Finished Goods Inventory

2.

Work in process, January 1, 20--			$29,700
Direct materials:			
Materials inventory, January 1, 20--	$15,400		
Materials purchases	16,800		
Materials available for use	$32,200		
Materials inventory, December 31, 20--	18,200		
Cost of direct materials used		$14,000	
Direct labor		13,300	
Overhead		7,700	
Total manufacturing costs			35,000
Total work in process during period			$64,700
Work in process, December 31, 20--			14,700
Cost of goods manufactured			$50,000

3.

a.	Materials Inventory	26,400	
	Accounts Payable		26,400
b.	Work in Process (Job No. 6)	21,000	
	Materials Inventory		21,000
c.	Factory Overhead (indirect materials)	3,700	
	Materials Inventory		3,700
d.	Work in Process (Job No. 6)	12,900	
	Wages Payable		12,900
e.	Factory Overhead (indirect labor)	5,000	
	Wages Payable		5,000
f.	Factory Overhead (miscellaneous)	2,300	
	Accounts Payable		2,300
g.	Work in Process (Job No. 6)	7,740	
	Factory Overhead		7,740

Chapter 27

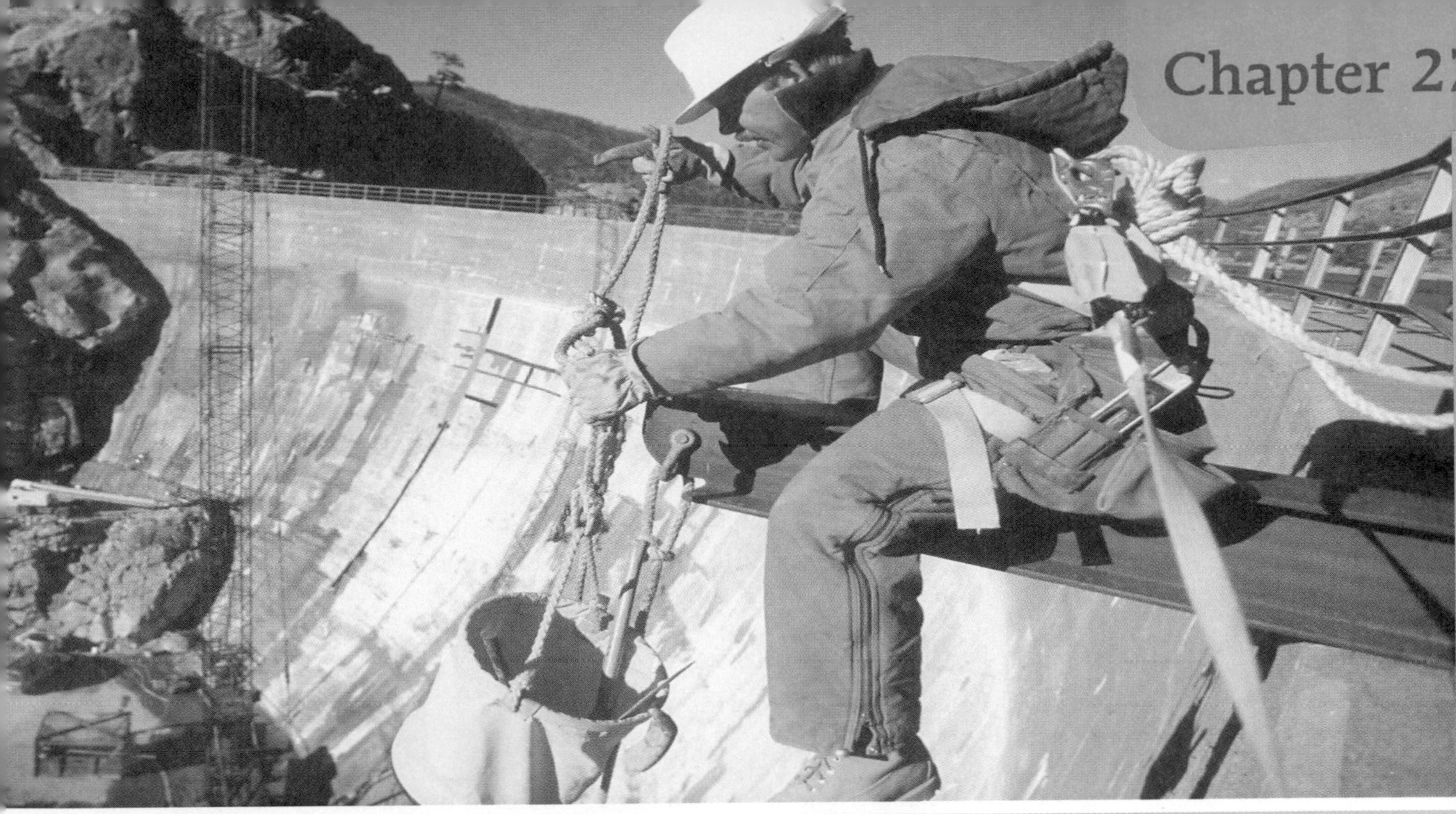
JOHN BURKE/PHOTOLIBRARY

Manufacturing Accounting: The Work Sheet and Financial Statements

Throughout this text, we have emphasized how accounting is relevant to many aspects of our lives. It therefore seems fitting that we conclude with an example of its relevance even in dealing with natural disasters. When hurricanes, tornadoes, or earthquakes strike, someone needs to pick up the pieces. The government often is viewed as this someone. But the government must engage private businesses to do much of the actual work. SRS is one of those businesses.

SRS was founded in 2001 and is located in Gallatin, Tennessee. The company provides construction management and disaster recovery services, often working with FEMA (Federal Emergency Management Agency) and the U.S. Army Corps of Engineers. Their work includes projects like building construction, demolition, road building, and installation of underground utilities. Many of these projects involve millions of dollars and extend over long periods of time. It is common for SRS to end its fiscal year with many projects in process. The accounting for these projects can be challenging. In this chapter, you will learn how to make year-end adjustments for construction projects that are in process and the importance of making these adjustments correctly.

LEARNING OBJECTIVES

Careful study of this chapter should enable you to:

LO1 **Prepare a 10-column work sheet for a manufacturing company.**

LO2 **Prepare work sheet adjusting entries to (1) apply factory overhead to ending work in process, (2) record additional actual factory overhead, (3) record under- or overapplied overhead, (4) record other expenses not involving overhead, and (5) provide for corporate income taxes.**

LO3 **Prepare financial statements for a manufacturing company.**

LO4 **Prepare adjusting, closing, and reversing journal entries for a manufacturing company.**

In Chapters 14 and 15, we learned how to use the work sheet to prepare financial statements for a merchandising company. In this chapter, we use a work sheet to prepare financial statements for a manufacturing company. Both the work sheet and financial statements of a manufacturer differ from those of a merchandiser.

THE WORK SHEET FOR A MANUFACTURING COMPANY

LO1 Prepare a 10-column work sheet for a manufacturing company.

The work sheet for a manufacturing company is similar to the one illustrated in Chapter 14 for a merchandising company. The same five steps are used to prepare both work sheets.

STEP 1 Prepare the trial balance.

STEP 2 Prepare the adjustments.

STEP 3 Prepare the adjusted trial balance.

STEP 4 Extend the adjusted trial balance amounts to the Income Statement and Balance Sheet columns.

STEP 5 Total the Income Statement and Balance Sheet columns to compute the net income or net loss.

Figure 27-1 shows the Trial Balance and Adjustments columns of ToyJoy Manufacturing Co.'s work sheet. The Trial Balance columns were completed by copying the balances of all accounts from the general ledger (not shown). The following accounts and related adjustments are different from the Chapter 14 illustration and are highlighted in the work sheet:

1. Finished Goods Inventory, Work in Process Inventory, and Materials Inventory
2. Cost of Goods Sold
3. Factory Overhead
4. Income Tax Expense and Income Tax Payable

INVENTORIES

Instead of a single merchandise inventory account, the manufacturer has three inventory accounts—Finished Goods, Work in Process, and Materials. The manufacturer purchases materials (Materials Inventory) and converts them (Work in Process Inventory) to completed products (Finished Goods Inventory) for sale to customers. These three inventories are shown as the first three boxes in Figure 27-2

COST OF GOODS SOLD

The cost of goods sold account is related to the inventory accounts. Cost of Goods Sold appears on the work sheet because ToyJoy uses a perpetual inventory system. With a perpetual inventory system, the movement of goods from materials to work in process to finished goods to cost of goods sold is recorded as the movement occurs. This movement of goods and the related journal entries were shown in Chapter 26 as Figure 26-6, which is reproduced on page 1050 as Figure 27-2. The use of a perpetual inventory system has two important effects on ToyJoy's work sheet compared with the one presented in Chapter 14 for a business using the periodic inventory method.

FIGURE 27-1 Partial Work Sheet

ToyJoy Manufacturing Co.
Work Sheet (Partial)
For Year Ended December 31, 20--

	ACCOUNT TITLE	TRIAL BALANCE DEBIT	TRIAL BALANCE CREDIT	ADJUSTMENTS DEBIT	ADJUSTMENTS CREDIT	
1	Cash	25,763 00				1
2	Government Notes	5,000 00				2
3	Accounts Receivable	66,485 00				3
4	Allowance for Bad Debts		460 00		(g) 1,405 00	4
5	Finished Goods Inventory	35,614 00				5
6	Work in Process Inventory [1]	9,990 00		(a) 2,700 00		6
7	Materials Inventory	9,275 00				7
8	Factory Supplies	5,542 00			(b) 5,020 00	8
9	Prepaid Insurance	8,060 00			(c) 6,520 00	9
10	Land	40,000 00				10
11	Factory Building	178,000 00				11
12	Accumulated Depreciation—Factory Building		30,000 00		(d) 7,500 00	12
13	Factory Equipment	155,000 00				13
14	Accumulated Depreciation—Factory Equipment		40,640 00		(d) 13,500 00	14
15	Office Equipment	21,300 00				15
16	Accumulated Depreciation—Office Equipment		4,925 00		(h) 2,000 00	16
17	Interest Payable				(f) 800 00	17
18	Accounts Payable		39,685 00			18
19	Income Tax Payable [4]				(i) 7,300 00	19
20	Bonds Payable		100,000 00			20
21	Capital Stock		75,000 00			21
22	Paid-In Capital in Excess of Par		20,000 00			22
23	Retained Earnings		132,690 00			23
24	Cash Dividends	15,000 00				24
25	Sales		835,948 00			25
26	Interest Revenue		430 00			26
27	Factory Overhead [3]	155,080 00	185,982 00	(b) 5,020 00	(a) 2,700 00	27
28				(c) 6,520 00		28
29				(d) 21,000 00		29
30				(e) 1,062 00		30
31	Cost of Goods Sold [2]	601,581 00			(e) 1,062 00	31
32	Wages Expense	91,316 00				32
33	Advertising Expense	5,264 00				33
34	Bad Debt Expense			(g) 1,405 00		34
35	Utilities Expense—Office	5,690 00				35
36	Depreciation Expense—Office Equipment			(h) 2,000 00		36
37	Interest Expense	8,800 00		(f) 800 00		37
38	Income Tax Expense [4]	23,000 00		(i) 7,300 00		38
39		1,465,760 00	1,465,760 00	47,807 00	47,807 00	39

1. The costs of goods sold are accumulated in Cost of Goods Sold as sales occur during the year. Thus, Cost of Goods Sold is not computed by means of an adjustment process at the end of the period as we did in Chapter 14.

FIGURE 27-2 Flow of Costs Through Manufacturing Inventory Accounts

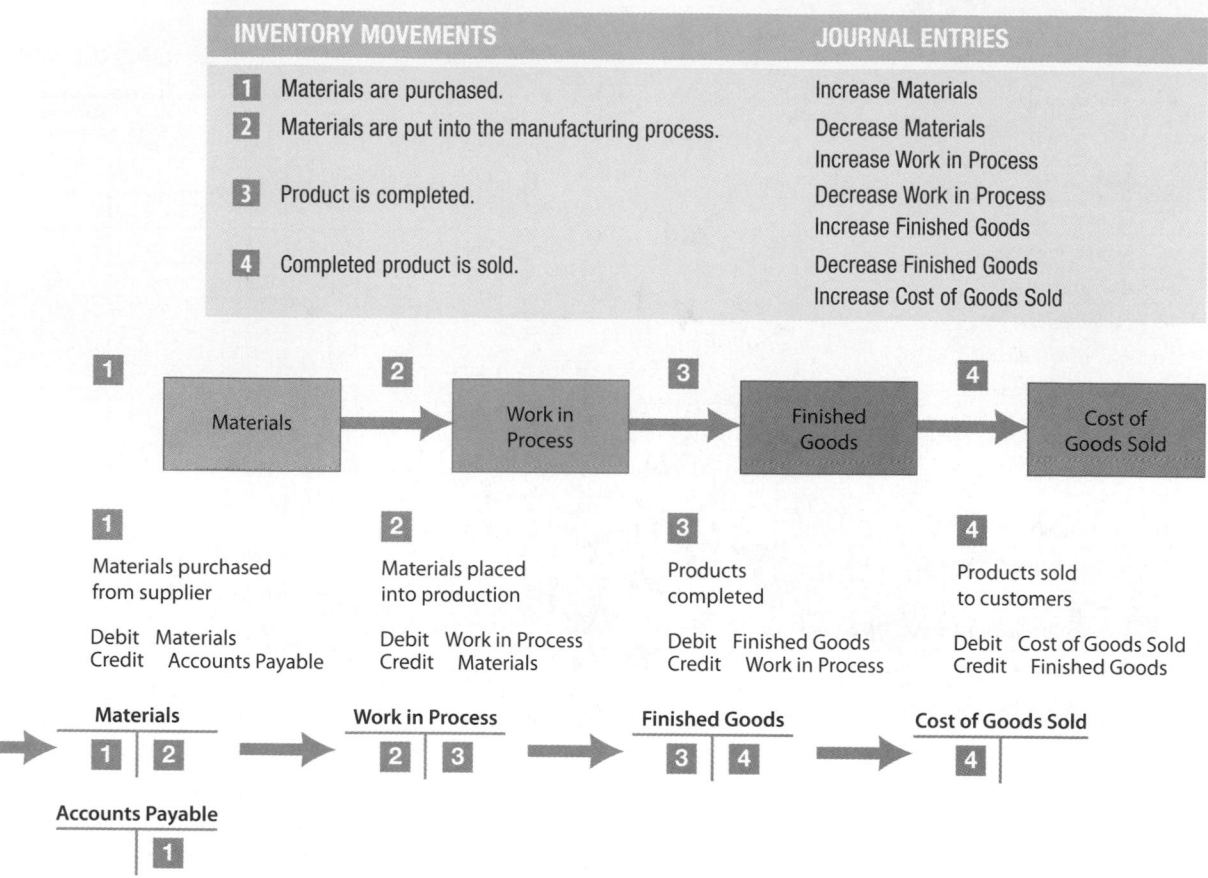

INVENTORY MOVEMENTS	JOURNAL ENTRIES
1 Materials are purchased.	Increase Materials
2 Materials are put into the manufacturing process.	Decrease Materials Increase Work in Process
3 Product is completed.	Decrease Work in Process Increase Finished Goods
4 Completed product is sold.	Decrease Finished Goods Increase Cost of Goods Sold

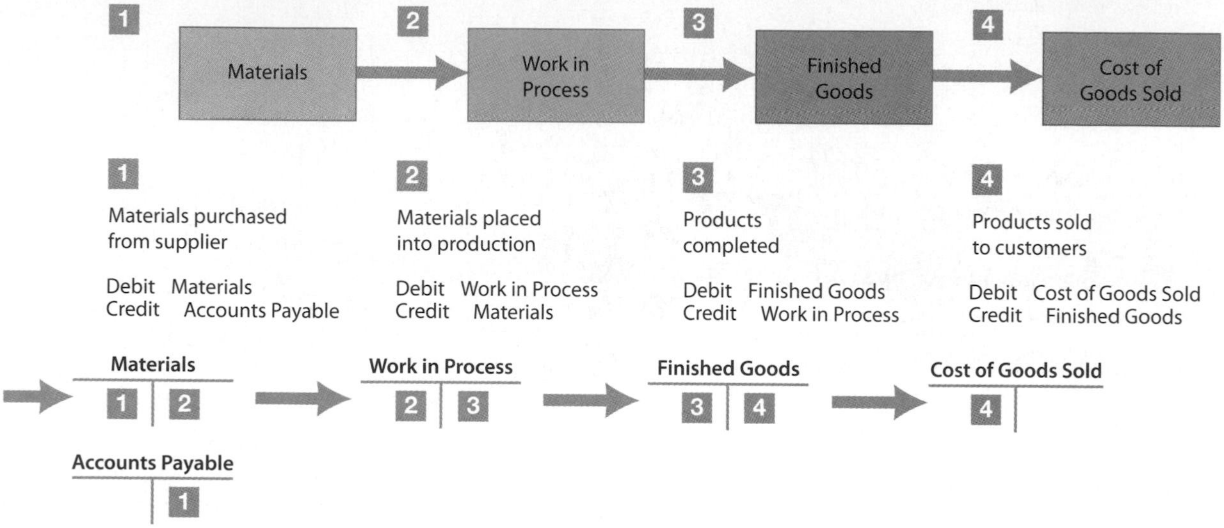

LEARNING KEY

Because ToyJoy uses a perpetual inventory system, Cost of Goods Sold contains the costs recorded as sales were made during the year. The inventory accounts reflect the ending balances.

2. The inventory accounts (Materials, Work in Process, and Finished Goods) reflect ending rather than beginning balances.

As explained in Chapters 13 and 14, a physical count of the inventory still is necessary to verify the accuracy of the perpetual inventory records. If a difference is found between the physical count and the amount in the perpetual inventory records, the records must be corrected by an adjusting entry. The physical counts of ToyJoy's inventories agreed with the amounts in the books, so no adjustments for this purpose were necessary.

FACTORY OVERHEAD

The factory overhead account appears solely because ToyJoy is a manufacturer. Factory overhead exists as part of the cost of manufacturing products. Both the debit ($155,080) and credit ($185,982) totals are shown for this account.

The debit represents the actual overhead costs incurred. The credit represents overhead applied to production. Both the debit and credit balances are shown for completeness of presentation, and because both amounts are useful in preparing financial statements.

INCOME TAX

Income Tax Expense and Income Tax Payable appear because ToyJoy is a corporation. As explained in Chapter 21, income taxes are an expense of doing business as a corporation.

ADJUSTING ENTRIES

LO2 Prepare work sheet adjusting entries to (1) apply factory overhead to ending work in process, (2) record additional actual factory overhead, (3) record under- or overapplied overhead, (4) record other expenses not involving overhead, and (5) provide for corporate income taxes.

The second pair of amount columns in Figure 27-1 contains the adjustments labeled (a) through (i). Data for adjusting the accounts are as follows:

(a)	Factory overhead to be applied to work in process ending inventory	$ 2,700
(b)	Factory supplies consumed	5,020
(c)	Insurance expired on factory building and equipment	6,520
(d)	Depreciation on:	
	factory building	7,500
	factory equipment	13,500
(e)	Overapplied factory overhead	1,062
(f)	Accrual of interest payable	800
(g)	Estimate of uncollectible accounts, based on an aging of accounts receivable	1,865
(h)	Depreciation on office equipment	2,000
(i)	Provision for corporate income taxes	7,300

The adjustments that are similar to those illustrated in Chapter 14 will be explained very briefly. Adjustments (a), (b), (c), (d), (e), and (i) are new and will be explained more fully.

APPLY FACTORY OVERHEAD TO ENDING WORK IN PROCESS

LEARNING KEY

Factory overhead must be applied to Work in Process at the end of the year.

Adjustment (a)

As jobs were completed during the year, factory overhead was applied to them at a rate of 60% of direct labor costs. At the end of the year, several jobs are still in process. To correctly state the work in process ending inventory, factory overhead must be applied to these jobs. It should be applied using the same basis as for finished goods. The job cost ledger (not shown here) shows total direct labor costs of $4,500 on jobs in process at December 31. An adjustment is needed to apply $2,700 (60% of the direct labor costs) to work in process. Debit Work in Process Inventory and credit Factory Overhead.

RECORD ADDITIONAL ACTUAL FACTORY OVERHEAD

Adjustment of individual jobs in work in process is unnecessary. This issue is addressed again later in the chapter.

Adjustment (b)

A physical count of factory supplies at the end of the year shows that $5,020 of factory supplies were used during the year. Since factory supplies expense is part of factory overhead, debit Factory Overhead and credit Factory Supplies for $5,020. The factory supplies expense account in the factory overhead ledger (not shown here) also is debited for this amount.

Adjustment (c)

A review of the insurance policy files shows that $6,520 of insurance on the factory building and equipment has expired. Since factory building and equipment insurance expense is part of factory overhead, debit Factory Overhead and credit Prepaid Insurance for $6,520. Also, debit the factory building and equipment insurance expense account in the factory overhead ledger.

Adjustment (d)

Depreciation expense for the year was $7,500 on the factory building and $13,500 on the factory equipment, a total of $21,000. Depreciation expense on the factory building and factory equipment is part of factory overhead. Therefore, debit Factory Overhead for $21,000, and credit Accumulated Depreciation—Factory Building for $7,500 and Accumulated Depreciation—Factory Equipment for $13,500. Also, debit the depreciation expense—factory building and equipment account in the factory overhead ledger for $21,000.

Notice that adjustments (b), (c), and (d) are *debited* to Factory Overhead. Recall from Chapter 26 that actual factory overhead expenses are debited to Factory Overhead.

RECORD UNDER- OR OVERAPPLIED OVERHEAD

Adjustment (e)

This adjustment is needed because overhead was overapplied during the year. Figure 27-3 shows the factory overhead account in T account form. The amounts shown are:

1 debit and credit "balances" from the December 31 trial balance

2 debits for adjustments (b), (c), and (d)

3 credit for adjustment (a)

4 total actual overhead and overhead applied

5 debit for adjustment (e), which makes the total debits and credits equal in the account

FIGURE 27-3 Factory Overhead T Account

Factory Overhead

1			155,080			185,982	1
		(b)	5,020		(a)	2,700	3
2		(c)	6,520				
		(d)	21,000				
4	(Actual overhead)		187,620	(Overhead applied)		188,682	4
5	Overapplied overhead	(e)	1,062				
	Totals		188,682			188,682	

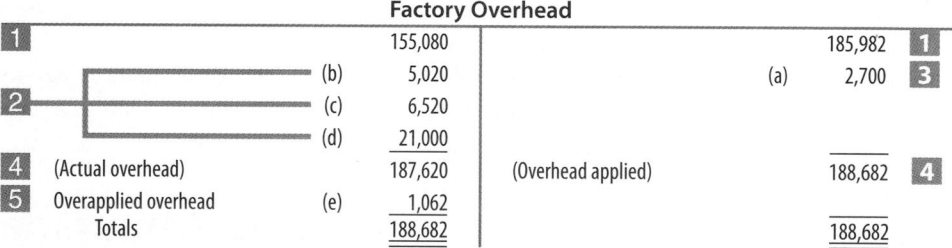

The two item 4 amounts in Figure 27-3 show that actual overhead for the year was $187,620, while overhead applied was $188,682. Thus, overhead was *overapplied* by $1,062. Debit Factory Overhead and credit Cost of Goods Sold for $1,062 to adjust for overapplied overhead.

RECORD OTHER EXPENSES NOT INVOLVING OVERHEAD

Adjustment (f)

Interest of $800 is accrued at the end of the year on the bonds payable. Debit Interest Expense and credit Interest Payable.

Adjustment (g)

The estimated amount of uncollectible accounts at the end of the year, based on an aging of accounts receivable, is $1,865. Allowance for Bad Debts had a credit balance of $460, so the necessary adjustment is $1,405 ($1,865 – $460). Debit Bad Debt Expense and credit Allowance for Bad Debts.

Adjustment (h)

Depreciation expense for the year on the office equipment was $2,000. Debit Depreciation Expense—Office Equipment and credit Accumulated Depreciation—Office Equipment.

PROVIDE FOR CORPORATE INCOME TAXES

Adjustment (i)

Corporate income tax for the year is $30,300. As shown in Figure 27-1, income tax expense of $23,000 had been recorded during the year. Therefore, an adjustment of $7,300 is needed ($30,300 – $23,000 = $7,300). Debit Income Tax Expense and credit Income Tax Payable.

COMPLETING THE WORK SHEET

LEARNING KEY

The factory overhead account balances are not extended to the Income Statement or Balance Sheet Columns.

Figure 27-4 on page 1054 shows ToyJoy's full 10-column work sheet. Note the handling of the factory overhead account. The total debits and total credits of $188,682 appear in the Adjusted Trial Balance columns. But neither of these amounts is extended to the Income Statement or Balance Sheet columns. Figure 27-5 shows why this procedure is followed. Factory overhead costs are (1) incurred, (2) applied to Work in Process, (3) transferred to Finished Goods with completed products, and (4) transferred to Cost of Goods Sold when goods are sold.

The factory overhead amounts are not extended because they have already been transferred to Work in Process, Finished Goods, and Cost of Goods Sold. These three account balances, which contain the factory overhead amounts, are extended to the appropriate Income Statement and Balance Sheet columns.

A BROADER VIEW

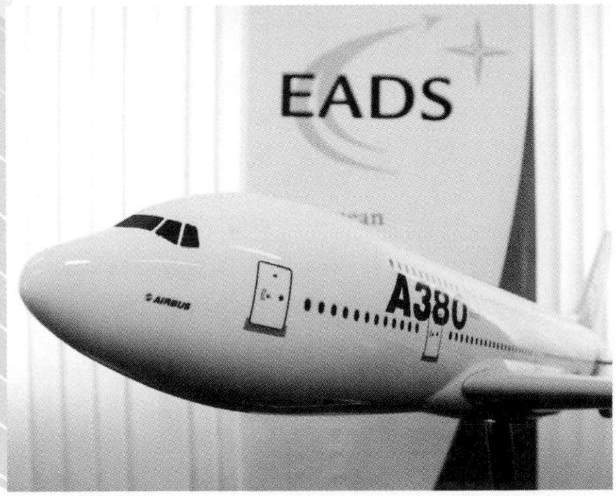

JAN PITMAN/AP PHOTO

Work in Process Inventory—This Stuff Really Matters

When you study the year-end accounting procedures for a manufacturing company, you might question whether all the adjustments really matter in the real world. One way to answer that question is to consider the financial statements of a real company.

EADS N.V. is the European parent company of Airbus, a leading aircraft manufacturer, and several other companies in related industries. In 2008, EADS reported net income of $2.25 billion (€1.6 billion). At the close of 2008, the ending inventory for EADS included $17.27 billion of work in process. Think about the accounting implications of these figures. The work in process inventory for EADS is almost eight times ($17.27 billion ÷ $2.25 billion = 7.68) the size of its net income. This means that a relatively small percentage error in work in process inventory could have a significant effect on the net income. Clearly, the year-end adjustments can be quite important for a company like EADS.

FIGURE 27-4 Work Sheet

ToyJoy Manufacturing Co.
Work Sheet
For Year Ended December 31, 20 --

	ACCOUNT TITLE	TRIAL BALANCE		ADJUSTMENTS		ADJUSTED TRIAL BALANCE		INCOME STATEMENT		BALANCE SHEET		
		DEBIT	CREDIT	DEBIT	CREDIT	DEBIT	CREDIT	DEBIT	CREDIT	DEBIT	CREDIT	
1	Cash	25 763 00				25 763 00				25 763 00		1
2	Government Notes	5 000 00				5 000 00				5 000 00		2
3	Accounts Receivable	66 485 00				66 485 00				66 485 00		3
4	Allowance for Bad Debts		460 00		(g) 1 405 00		1 865 00				1 865 00	4
5	Finished Goods Inventory	35 614 00				35 614 00				35 614 00		5
6	Work in Process Inventory	9 990 00		(a) 2 700 00		12 690 00				12 690 00		6
7	Materials Inventory	9 275 00				9 275 00				9 275 00		7
8	Factory Supplies	5 542 00			(b) 5 020 00	522 00				522 00		8
9	Prepaid Insurance	8 060 00			(c) 6 520 00	1 540 00				1 540 00		9
10	Land	40 000 00				40 000 00				40 000 00		10
11	Factory Building	178 000 00				178 000 00				178 000 00		11
12	Accum. Depr.—Factory Building		30 000 00		(d) 7 500 00		37 500 00				37 500 00	12
13	Factory Equipment	155 000 00				155 000 00				155 000 00		13
14	Accum. Depr.—Factory Equip.		40 640 00		(d) 13 500 00		54 140 00				54 140 00	14
15	Office Equipment	21 300 00				21 300 00				21 300 00		15
16	Accum. Depr.—Office Equipment		4 925 00		(h) 2 000 00		6 925 00				6 925 00	16
17	Interest Payable				(f) 800 00		800 00				800 00	17
18	Accounts Payable		39 685 00				39 685 00				39 685 00	18
19	Income Tax Payable				(i) 7 300 00		7 300 00				7 300 00	19
20	Bonds Payable		100 000 00				100 000 00				100 000 00	20
21	Capital Stock		75 000 00				75 000 00				75 000 00	21
22	Paid-In Capital in Excess of Par		20 000 00				20 000 00				20 000 00	22
23	Retained Earnings		132 690 00				132 690 00				132 690 00	23
24	Cash Dividends	15 000 00				15 000 00				15 000 00		24
25	Sales		835 948 00				835 948 00		835 948 00			25
26	Interest Revenue		430 00				430 00		430 00			26
27	Factory Overhead	155 080 00	185 982 00	(b) 5 020 00	(a) 2 700 00	188 682 00	188 682 00	Not extended				27
28				(c) 6 520 00								28
29				(d) 21 000 00								29
30				(e) 1 062 00								30
31	Cost of Goods Sold	601 581 00			(e) 1 062 00	600 519 00		600 519 00				31
32	Wages Expense	91 316 00				91 316 00		91 316 00				32
33	Advertising Expense	5 264 00				5 264 00		5 264 00				33
34	Bad Debt Expense			(g) 1 405 00		1 405 00		1 405 00				34
35	Utilities Expense—Office	5 690 00				5 690 00		5 690 00				35
36	Depr. Expense—Office Equip.			(h) 2 000 00		2 000 00		2 000 00				36
37	Interest Expense	8 800 00		(f) 800 00		9 600 00		9 600 00				37
38	Income Tax Expense	23 000 00		(i) 7 300 00		30 300 00		30 300 00				38
39		1,465 760 00	1,465 760 00	47 807 00	47 807 00	1,500 965 00	1,500 965 00	746 094 00	836 378 00	566 189 00	475 905 00	39
40	Net Income							90 284 00			90 284 00	40
41								836 378 00	836 378 00	566 189 00	566 189 00	41

FIGURE 27-5 Flow of Overhead Costs in a Manufacturing Accounting System

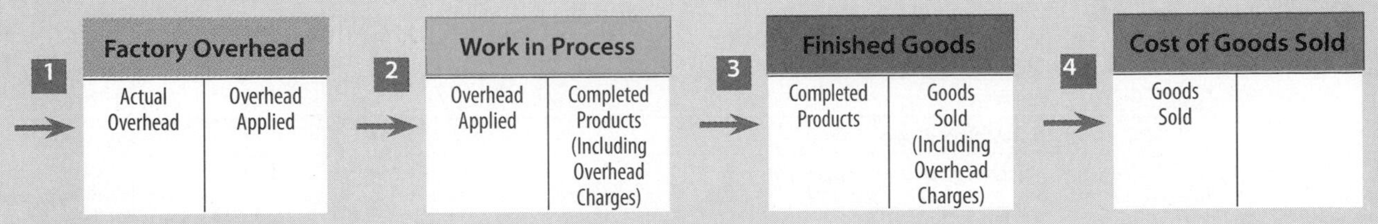

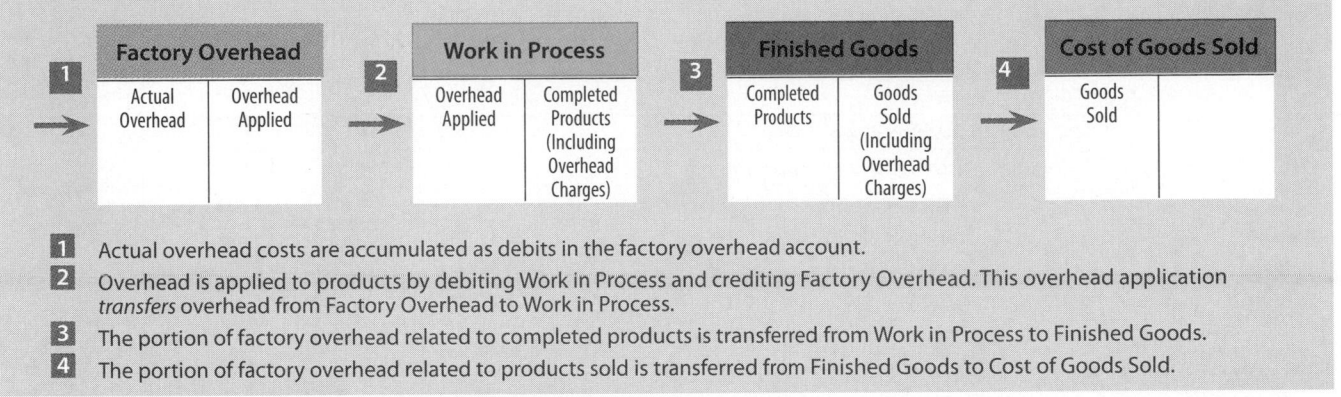

1. Actual overhead costs are accumulated as debits in the factory overhead account.
2. Overhead is applied to products by debiting Work in Process and crediting Factory Overhead. This overhead application *transfers* overhead from Factory Overhead to Work in Process.
3. The portion of factory overhead related to completed products is transferred from Work in Process to Finished Goods.
4. The portion of factory overhead related to products sold is transferred from Finished Goods to Cost of Goods Sold.

U REVU Complete U REVU-1 on **page 1070** to test your basic understanding of LO2.

FINANCIAL STATEMENTS

LO3 Prepare financial statements for a manufacturing company.

ToyJoy's financial statements include an income statement, retained earnings statement, balance sheet, and statement of cash flows. The statement of cash flows is essentially the same in format as the one illustrated in Chapter 23, so it is not presented here. We will focus on the statements prepared from the enhanced work sheet for a manufacturing business.

INCOME STATEMENT

ToyJoy's income statement is presented in Figure 27-6. All income statement data were obtained from the Income Statement columns of the work sheet, except for the cost of goods sold section. To prepare this section, the beginning finished goods inventory was taken from the finished goods account in the general ledger (not shown). The cost of goods manufactured was taken from the schedule of cost of goods manufactured (Figure 27-7, page 1057). The ending finished goods inventory is from the Balance Sheet columns of the work sheet.

ToyJoy uses a perpetual inventory system, so cost of goods sold is already known, as shown in the work sheet in Figure 27-4. The procedures described here are simply to show the calculation of cost of goods sold on the income statement.

A manufacturer's income statement is commonly supported by a schedule of cost of goods manufactured like the one in Figure 27-7. The ending materials and work in process inventories are from the Balance Sheet columns of the work sheet. Other data for this schedule, listed in the order in which they appear, were obtained from the following sources.

DATA	SOURCE OF DATA
Work in process inventory, January 1	Work in process account in general ledger
Materials inventory, January 1	Materials inventory account in general ledger
Purchases	Materials inventory account in general ledger
Indirect materials charged to production	Materials inventory account in general ledger
Direct labor	Work in process account in general ledger
Overhead	Factory overhead account in general ledger

FIGURE 27-6 Income Statement

ToyJoy Manufacturing Co. Income Statement For Year Ended December 31, 20 --		
Net sales		$835,948.00
Less cost of goods sold:		
Finished goods inventory, January 1	$ 24,569.00	
Cost of goods manufactured	611,564.00	← From Schedule
Cost of goods available for sale	$636,133.00	
Finished goods inventory, December 31	35,614.00	
Cost of goods sold		600,519.00
Gross profit		$235,429.00
Operating expenses:		
Wages expense	$ 91,316.00	
Advertising expense	5,264.00	
Bad debt expense	1,405.00	
Utilities expense—office	5,690.00	
Depreciation expense—office equipment	2,000.00	
Total operating expenses		105,675.00
Operating income		$129,754.00
Other revenue:		
Interest revenue		430.00
		$130,184.00
Other expense:		
Interest expense		9,600.00
Income before income taxes		$120,584.00
Income tax		30,300.00
Net income	To Retained Earnings Statement →	$ 90,284.00

RETAINED EARNINGS STATEMENT

The retained earnings statement appears in Figure 27-8. The retained earnings balance at January 1 and the cash dividends for the year are taken from the Balance Sheet columns of the worksheet. The net income for the year can be taken from the Income Statement columns of the worksheet or from the income statement. The only distinctive feature of the retained earnings statement arises from ToyJoy being organized as a corporation. As a corporation, ToyJoy pays dividends, in this case, $15,000.

BALANCE SHEET

ToyJoy's balance sheet is presented in Figure 27-9 on page 1058. Data for this statement were taken from the Balance Sheet columns of the work sheet, except for the retained earnings. This amount was taken from the retained earnings statement. Note that the retained earnings amount on the balance sheet ($207,974) also can be calculated from the work sheet. It is the sum of (1) the retained earnings balance shown on the work sheet ($132,690) plus (2) the net income for the year ($90,284) less (3) the cash dividends for the year ($15,000).

(1) Beginning balance	$132,690
(2) Net income	90,284
(3) Cash dividends	(15,000)
Ending balance	$207,974

FIGURE 27-7 Schedule of Cost of Goods Manufactured

ToyJoy Manufacturing Co. Schedule of Cost of Goods Manufactured For Year Ended December 31, 20 --			
Work in process, January 1			$ 11,940.00
Direct materials			
Materials inventory, January 1	$ 12,992.00		
Materials purchases	124,580.00		
Materials available	$137,572.00		
Materials inventory, December 31	9,275.00		
Cost of materials used		$128,297.00	
Less indirect materials included in overhead		3,200.00	
Cost of direct materials used		$125,097.00	
Direct labor		299,597.00	
Factory overhead		187,620.00	
Total manufacturing costs			612,314.00
Total work in process during the period			$624,254.00
Work in process, December 31			12,690.00
Cost of goods manufactured		To Income Statement	$611,564.00

Two main differences in this balance sheet compared with those for merchandising companies are:

1. Since this is a manufacturing company, there are three inventory accounts listed: Finished Goods, Work in Process, and Materials.
2. Since ToyJoy is a corporation, the stockholders' equity section contains information regarding capital stock, paid-in capital in excess of par, and retained earnings.

FIGURE 27-8 Retained Earnings Statement

ToyJoy Manufacturing Co. Retained Earnings Statement For Year Ended December 31, 20 --			
Retained earnings, January 1		$132,690.00	
Net income for the year (after provision for income taxes of $30,300)		90,284.00	From Income Statement
		$222,974.00	
Less cash dividends ($1.00 per share) — Corporate Dividends		15,000.00	
Retained earnings, December 31		$207,974.00	To Balance Sheet

FIGURE 27-9 Balance sheet

ToyJoy Manufacturing Co.
Balance Sheet
December 31, 20--

Assets			
Current assets:			
Cash		$ 25,763.00	
Government notes		5,000.00	
Accounts receivable	$ 66,485.00		
Less allowance for bad debts	1,865.00	64,620.00	
Inventories:			
Finished goods	$ 35,614.00		
Work in process	12,690.00		
Materials	9,275.00	57,579.00	
Factory supplies		522.00	
Prepaid insurance		1,540.00	
Total current assets			$155,024.00
Property, plant, and equipment:			
Land		$ 40,000.00	
Factory building	$178,000.00		
Less accumulated depreciation	37,500.00	140,500.00	
Factory equipment	$155,000.00		
Less accumulated depreciation	54,140.00	100,860.00	
Office equipment	$ 21,300.00		
Less accumulated depreciation	6,925.00	14,375.00	
Total property, plant, and equipment			295,735.00
Total assets			$450,759.00
Liabilities			
Current liabilities:			
Interest payable		$ 800.00	
Accounts payable		39,685.00	
Income tax payable		7,300.00	
Total current liabilities			$ 47,785.00
Long-term liabilities:			
Bonds payable			100,000.00
Total liabilities			$147,785.00
Stockholders' Equity			
Common stock ($5 par value, 50,000 shares authorized; 15,000 shares issued)		$ 75,000.00	
Paid-in capital in excess of par		20,000.00	
Retained earnings		207,974.00	
Total stockholders' equity			302,974.00
Total liabilities and stockholders' equity			$450,759.00

Three inventories

Corporate section

From Retained Earnings Statement

U REVU

Complete U REVU-2 on **page 1070** to test your basic understanding of LO3.

LO4 Prepare adjusting, closing, and reversing journal entries for a manufacturing company.

JOURNAL ENTRIES

Most of ToyJoy's adjusting, closing, and reversing entries are similar to those illustrated in Chapters 14 and 15 for a merchandising company. We will comment only on selected adjustments.

ADJUSTING ENTRIES

The entries appearing in the Adjustments columns of the work sheet are journalized as shown in Figure 27-10 below. For ease of identification, each entry includes the coding letter from the work sheet.

FIGURE 27-10 Adjusting Entries

GENERAL JOURNAL

DATE		DESCRIPTION	POST. REF.	DEBIT	CREDIT	
		Adjusting Entries				
20-- Dec.	31	Work in Process Inventory		2,700.00		Aggregate
(a)		Factory Overhead			2,700.00	
(b)	31	Factory Overhead (Factory Supplies Expense)		5,020.00		Identify subsidiary
		Factory Supplies			5,020.00	
(c)	31	Factory Overhead (Factory Building and Equipment,				Identify subsidiary
		Insurance Expense)		6,520.00		
		Prepaid Insurance			6,520.00	
(d)	31	Factory Overhead (Depreciation Expense—				Identify subsidiary
		Factory Building and Equipment)		21,000.00		
		Accumulated Depreciation—Factory Building			7,500.00	
		Accumulated Depreciation—Factory Equipment			13,500.00	
(e)	31	Factory Overhead		1,062.00		
		Cost of Goods Sold			1,062.00	
(f)	31	Interest Expense		800.00		
		Interest Payable			800.00	
(g)	31	Bad Debt Expense		1,405.00		
		Allowance for Bad Debts			1,405.00	
(h)	31	Depreciation Expense—Office Equipment		2,000.00		
		Accumulated Depreciation—Office Equipment			2,000.00	
(i)	31	Income Tax Expense		7,300.00		
		Income Tax Payable			7,300.00	

Notice two things about these adjusting entries.

1. In adjustment (a), the application of factory overhead to ending work in process, no entries are made to the individual jobs in the job cost ledger. Aggregate work in process must be adjusted so that it is reported correctly on the financial statements. The individual jobs require no adjustment because they are not reported on any financial statements. The aggregate adjustment will be reversed at the beginning of the following period.
2. In adjustments (b), (c), and (d), the factory overhead account and the related subsidiary accounts are identified. Both the general ledger and subsidiary ledger accounts are adjusted for these actual overhead amounts.

CLOSING ENTRIES

Six steps are used to close ToyJoy's temporary accounts.

STEP 1 Transfer the debit balance in the factory overhead account to Income Summary and close the subsidiary factory overhead accounts.

STEP 2 Transfer the credit balance in the factory overhead account to Income Summary.

STEP 3 Transfer the balances of the sales and interest revenue accounts to Income Summary.

STEP 4 Transfer the balances of the cost of goods sold and all expense accounts to Income Summary.

STEP 5 Transfer the balance of Income Summary to Retained Earnings.

STEP 6 Transfer the balance of Cash Dividends to Retained Earnings.

Figure 27-11 shows the journal entries corresponding to these six steps. Entries (3), (4), (5), and (6) are essentially the same as the ones we used for a merchandising company in chapter 15. Entries (1) and (2) require explanation.

The T account in Figure 27-3 on page 1052 shows that the factory overhead account has a zero balance after all adjustments are entered. This account must still be "closed" to close the factory overhead subsidiary ledger accounts. This is the purpose of entries (1) and (2) in Figure 27-11.

Entry (1) closes the total debit amount in the factory overhead account to Income Summary. At the same time, the related factory overhead subsidiary ledger accounts are closed. (The detail for each subsidiary ledger account is omitted here.) Entry (2) closes the total credit amount in factory overhead to Income Summary.

LEARNING KEY

Reverse the adjusting entry to apply overhead to Work in Process.

REVERSING ENTRIES

ToyJoy reverses two of the adjusting entries made on December 31. Entry (1) in Figure 27-12 is related to the accrued interest on bonds payable. The purpose of this type of reversing entry was explained in Chapter 15. Entry (2) is unique to a manufacturing company. This entry reverses the adjusting entry to apply factory overhead to Work in Process. This reversal facilitates applying factory overhead to completed jobs in the following year. Recall that factory overhead is applied at a predetermined rate when a job is completed. If this reversing entry were not made, it would be necessary to keep track of which jobs already had a partial overhead application from a prior year's adjustment.

FIGURE 27-11 Closing Entries

GENERAL JOURNAL

	DATE		DESCRIPTION	POST. REF.	DEBIT	CREDIT		
1			Closing Entries				1	
2	20-- Dec.	31	Income Summary		188,682 00		2	Step 1
3	(1)		Factory Overhead (Subsidiary ledger accounts)			188,682 00	3	
4							4	
5	(2)	31	Factory Overhead		188,682 00		5	Step 2
6			Income Summary			188,682 00	6	
7							7	
8	(3)	31	Sales		835,948 00		8	Step 3
9			Interest Revenue		430 00		9	
10			Income Summary			836,378 00	10	
11							11	
12	(4)	31	Income Summary		746,094 00		12	Step 4
13			Cost of Goods Sold			600,519 00	13	
14			Wages Expense			91,316 00	14	
15			Advertising Expense			5,264 00	15	
16			Bad Debt Expense			1,405 00	16	
17			Utilities Expense—Office			5,690 00	17	
18			Depreciation Expense—Office Equipment			2,000 00	18	
19			Interest Expense			9,600 00	19	
20			Income Tax Expense			30,300 00	20	
21							21	
22	(5)	31	Income Summary		90,284 00		22	Step 5
23			Retained Earnings			90,284 00	23	
24							24	
25	(6)	31	Retained Earnings		15,000 00		25	Step 6
26			Cash Dividends			15,000 00	26	

FIGURE 27-12 Reversing Entries

GENERAL JOURNAL PAGE

	DATE		DESCRIPTION	POST. REF.	DEBIT	CREDIT	
1			Reversing Entries				1
2	20-- Jan.	1	Interest Payable		800 00		2
3	(1)		Interest Expense			800 00	3
4							4
5	(2)	1	Factory Overhead		2,700 00		5
6			Work in Process Inventory			2,700 00	6
7							7

Note that the adjustment for corporate income tax is not reversed. The purpose of reversing entries is to simplify the recording of routine transactions. Corporate income taxes are a specialized rather than routine transaction, so this adjustment is not reversed.

U REVU

Complete U REVU-3 on **page 1070** to test your basic understanding of LO4.

LEARNING OBJECTIVES	Key Points to Remember
LO1 **Prepare a 10-column work sheet for a manufacturing company.**	Five steps are used to prepare a 10-column work sheet for a manufacturing company: 1. Prepare the trial balance. 2. Prepare the adjustments. 3. Prepare the adjusted trial balance. 4. Extend the adjusted trial balance amounts to the Income Statement and Balance Sheet columns. 5. Total the Income Statement and Balance Sheet columns to compute the net income or net loss. The new accounts and related adjustments on the work sheet are Finished Goods Inventory, Work in Process Inventory, Materials Inventory, Cost of Goods Sold, Factory Overhead, Income Tax Expense, and Corporate Income Tax Payable.
LO2 **Prepare work sheet adjusting entries to (1) apply factory overhead to ending work in process, (2) record additional actual factory overhead, (3) record under- or overapplied overhead, (4) record other expenses not involving overhead, and (5) provide for corporate income taxes.**	Overhead must be applied to work in process at year-end. Adjustments for additional amounts of actual overhead are debited to Factory Overhead on the work sheet. After all adjustments are made for actual and applied overhead, an adjustment must be made for under- or overapplied overhead. An adjustment also is necessary for corporate income taxes. The factory overhead account balances are extended to the Adjusted Trial Balance columns but not to the Income Statement or Balance Sheet columns on the work sheet.
LO3 **Prepare financial statements for a manufacturing company.**	The main differences between a manufacturer's income statement and that of a merchandiser are the cost of goods sold section and the supplementary schedule of cost of goods manufactured. The only distinctive feature of ToyJoy's retained earnings statement is the deduction for dividends, because ToyJoy is a corporation. Two main differences in ToyJoy's balance sheet are the three inventory accounts and the stockholders' equity section.
LO4 **Prepare adjusting, closing, and reversing journal entries for a manufacturing company.**	Each of the adjustments on the work sheet must be journalized. All revenue and expense accounts and both the debit and credit totals of Factory Overhead must be closed to Income Summary. Income Summary and Cash Dividends must be closed to Retained Earnings. Reverse the adjusting entry for Interest Expense and the adjustment to apply factory overhead to work in process.

DEMONSTRATION PROBLEM

KA KLOOSTER & ALLEN

Montgomery Manufacturing Co. manufactures and sells a limited line of products per customer order. Nothing is purchased for resale in its original form. The company rents offices and a factory building, and it owns neither real estate nor delivery equipment. It does have its own office and factory equipment. The company uses a perpetual inventory system and keeps its accounts on the calendar year basis. The trial balance of the general ledger as of December 31, 20--, is illustrated below. Data for the year-end adjustment of the accounts follow the trial balance.

Montgomery Manufacturing Co.
Trial Balance
December 31, 20 - -

ACCOUNT TITLE	DEBIT BALANCE	CREDIT BALANCE
Cash	56,115.00	
Accounts Receivable	90,928.00	
Allowance for Bad Debts		1,800.00
Finished Goods Inventory	63,180.00	
Work in Process Inventory	41,256.00	
Materials Inventory	46,845.00	
Office Supplies	2,916.00	
Factory Supplies	4,633.00	
Prepaid Insurance	5,589.00	
Factory Equipment	185,022.00	
Accumulated Depreciation—Factory Equipment		34,956.00
Office Equipment	19,530.00	
Accumulated Depreciation—Office Equipment		2,421.00
Notes Payable		27,000.00
Interest Payable		
Accounts Payable		38,590.00
Income Tax Payable		
Capital Stock		135,000.00
Retained Earnings		38,131.00
Cash Dividends	10,000.00	
Sales		842,157.00
Factory Overhead	44,212.00	60,585.00
Cost of Goods Sold	455,393.00	
Wages Expense	115,663.00	
Advertising Expense	24,680.00	
Office Rent Expense	13,180.00	
Office Supplies Expense		
Bad Debt Expense		
Insurance Expense—Office Equipment		
Depreciation Expense—Office Equipment		
Interest Expense	1,498.00	
Income Tax Expense		
	1,180,640.00	1,180,640.00

(continued)

Data for year-end adjustments are as follows:

(a) Interest payable		$ 168
(b) Office supplies expense		900
(c) Factory supplies expense		1,870
(d) Depreciation of office equipment		960
(e) Depreciation of factory equipment		22,560
(f) Insurance expense on:		
office equipment	$ 120	
factory equipment	1,590	1,710
(g) Provision for uncollectible accounts (based on percentage of sales)		1,000
(h) Provision for corporate income taxes		60,560
(i) Factory overhead to be applied to work in process		4,729

Physical counts of the inventories agreed with the amounts in the books.

Additional information needed to prepare the income statement and schedule of cost of goods manufactured is as follows:

Finished goods inventory, January 1	$219,692
Materials inventory, January 1	23,000
Purchases for the year	114,500
Direct labor	156,897
Work in process inventory, January 1	36,500
Indirect materials charged to production	4,500

REQUIRED

1. Prepare a 10-column work sheet for the year ended December 31, 20--. After the factory overhead account is adjusted, the total debits will differ from the total credits. Enter the under- or overapplied overhead on the work sheet by transferring it to Cost of Goods Sold. [Label this adjustment (j).]
2. Prepare an income statement with a supporting schedule of cost of goods manufactured.
3. Journalize the adjusting journal entries from the work sheet. [For parts (3), (4), and (5), use journal page numbers 15–17.]
4. Prepare closing entries.
5. Prepare reversing entries.

Solution 1.

Montgomery Manufacturing Co.
Work Sheet
For Year Ended December 31, 20 --

	ACCOUNT TITLE	TRIAL BALANCE DEBIT	TRIAL BALANCE CREDIT	ADJUSTMENTS DEBIT	ADJUSTMENTS CREDIT	ADJUSTED TRIAL BALANCE DEBIT	ADJUSTED TRIAL BALANCE CREDIT	INCOME STATEMENT DEBIT	INCOME STATEMENT CREDIT	BALANCE SHEET DEBIT	BALANCE SHEET CREDIT	
1	Cash	56,115.00				56,115.00				56,115.00		1
2	Accounts Receivable	90,928.00				90,928.00				90,928.00		2
3	Allowance for Bad Debts		1,800.00		(g) 1,000.00		2,800.00				2,800.00	3
4	Finished Goods Inventory	63,180.00				63,180.00				63,180.00		4
5	Work in Process Inventory	41,256.00		(i) 4,729.00		45,985.00				45,985.00		5
6	Materials Inventory	46,845.00				46,845.00				46,845.00		6
7	Office Supplies	2,916.00			(b) 900.00	2,016.00				2,016.00		7
8	Factory Supplies	4,633.00			(c) 1,870.00	2,763.00				2,763.00		8
9	Prepaid Insurance	5,589.00			(f) 1,710.00	3,879.00				3,879.00		9
10	Factory Equipment	185,022.00				185,022.00				185,022.00		10
11	Accum. Depr.—Factory Equip.		34,956.00		(e) 22,560.00		57,516.00				57,516.00	11
12	Office Equipment	19,530.00				19,530.00				19,530.00		12
13	Accum. Depr.—Office Equip.		2,421.00		(d) 960.00		3,381.00				3,381.00	13
14	Notes Payable		27,000.00				27,000.00				27,000.00	14
15	Interest Payable				(a) 168.00		168.00				168.00	15
16	Accounts Payable		38,590.00				38,590.00				38,590.00	16
17	Income Tax Payable				(h) 60,560.00		60,560.00				60,560.00	17
18	Capital Stock		135,000.00				135,000.00				135,000.00	18
19	Retained Earnings		38,131.00				38,131.00				38,131.00	19
20	Cash Dividends	10,000.00				10,000.00				10,000.00		20
21	Sales		842,157.00				842,157.00		842,157.00			21
22	Factory Overhead	44,212.00	60,585.00	(c) 1,870.00	(i) 4,729.00	70,232.00	70,232.00					22
23				(e) 22,560.00	(j) 4,918.00							23
24				(f) 1,590.00								24
25	Cost of Goods Sold	455,393.00		(j) 4,918.00		460,311.00		460,311.00				25
26	Wages Expense	115,663.00				115,663.00		115,663.00				26
27	Advertising Expense	24,680.00				24,680.00		24,680.00				27
28	Office Rent Expense	13,180.00				13,180.00		13,180.00				28
29	Office Supplies Expense			(b) 900.00		900.00		900.00				29
30	Bad Debt Expense			(g) 1,000.00		1,000.00		1,000.00				30
31	Insurance Exp.—Office Equip.			(f) 120.00		120.00		120.00				31
32	Depr. Expense—Office Equip.			(d) 960.00		960.00		960.00				32
33	Interest Expense	1,498.00		(a) 168.00		1,666.00		1,666.00				33
34	Income Tax Expense			(h) 60,560.00		60,560.00		60,560.00				34
35		1,180,640.00	1,180,640.00	99,375.00	99,375.00	1,275,535.00	1,275,535.00	679,040.00	842,157.00	526,263.00	363,146.00	35
36	Net Income							163,117.00			163,117.00	36
37								842,157.00	842,157.00	526,263.00	526,263.00	37

(continued)

2.

Montgomery Manufacturing Co.
Schedule of Cost of Goods Manufactured
For Year Ended December 31, 20 --

Work in process, January 1			$ 36,500.00
Direct materials			
Materials inventory, January 1	$ 23,000.00		
Materials purchases	114,500.00		
Materials available	$137,500.00		
Materials inventory, December 31	46,845.00		
Cost of materials used		$ 90,655.00	
Less indirect materials included in overhead		4,500.00	
Cost of direct materials used		$ 86,155.00	
Direct labor		156,897.00	
Factory overhead		70,232.00	
Total manufacturing costs			313,284.00
Total work in process during the period			$349,784.00
Work in process, December 31			45,985.00
Cost of goods manufactured			$303,799.00

Montgomery Manufacturing Co.
Income Statement
For Year Ended December 31, 20 --

Net sales		$842,157.00
Less cost of goods sold:		
Finished goods inventory, January 1	$219,692.00	
Cost of goods manufactured	303,799.00	
Cost of goods available for sale	$523,491.00	
Finished goods inventory, December 31	63,180.00	
Cost of goods sold		460,311.00
Gross profit		$381,846.00
Operating expenses:		
Wages expense	$115,663.00	
Advertising expense	24,680.00	
Office rent expense	13,180.00	
Office supplies expense	900.00	
Bad debt expense	1,000.00	
Insurance expense—office equipment	120.00	
Depreciation expense—office equipment	960.00	
Total operating expenses		156,503.00
Operating income		$225,343.00
Other expense:		
Interest expense		1,666.00
Income before income taxes		$223,677.00
Income tax		60,560.00
Net income		$163,117.00

3.

GENERAL JOURNAL PAGE 15

	DATE		DESCRIPTION	POST. REF.	DEBIT	CREDIT	
1			Adjusting Entries				1
2	20-- Dec.	31	Interest Expense		168 00		2
3	(a)		Interest Payable			168 00	3
4							4
5	(b)	31	Office Supplies Expense		900 00		5
6			Office Supplies			900 00	6
7							7
8	(c)	31	Factory Overhead		1 870 00		8
9			Factory Supplies			1 870 00	9
10							10
11	(d)	31	Depr. Expense—Office Equipment		960 00		11
12			Accum. Depr.—Office Equipment			960 00	12
13							13
14	(e)	31	Factory Overhead (Depr. Expense—Factory Equip.)		22 560 00		14
15			Accum. Depr.—Factory Equipment			22 560 00	15
16							16
17	(f)	31	Factory Overhead (Insurance Expense)		1 590 00		17
18			Insurance Expense—Office Equipment		120 00		18
19			Prepaid Insurance			1 710 00	19
20							20
21	(g)	31	Bad Debt Expense		1 000 00		21
22			Allowance for Bad Debts			1 000 00	22
23							23
24	(h)	31	Income Tax Expense		60 560 00		24
25			Income Tax Payable			60 560 00	25
26							26
27	(i)	31	Work in Process Inventory		4 729 00		27
28			Factory Overhead			4 729 00	28
29							29
30	(j)	31	Cost of Goods Sold		4 918 00		30
31			Factory Overhead			4 918 00	31

(continued)

4.

GENERAL JOURNAL PAGE 16

DATE		DESCRIPTION	POST. REF.	DEBIT	CREDIT
		Closing Entries			
20-- Dec.	31	Income Summary		70,232.00	
		Factory Overhead			70,232.00
	31	Factory Overhead		70,232.00	
		Income Summary			70,232.00
	31	Sales		842,157.00	
		Income Summary			842,157.00
	31	Income Summary		679,040.00	
		Cost of Goods Sold			460,311.00
		Wages Expense			115,663.00
		Advertising Expense			24,680.00
		Office Rent Expense			13,180.00
		Office Supplies Expense			900.00
		Bad Debt Expense			1,000.00
		Insurance Expense—Office Equipment			120.00
		Depr. Expense—Office Equipment			960.00
		Interest Expense			1,666.00
		Income Tax Expense			60,560.00
	31	Income Summary		163,117.00	
		Retained Earnings			163,117.00
	31	Retained Earnings		10,000.00	
		Cash Dividends			10,000.00

5.

GENERAL JOURNAL PAGE 17

DATE		DESCRIPTION	POST. REF.	DEBIT	CREDIT
		Reversing Entries			
20-- Jan.	1	Interest Payable		168.00	
		Interest Expense			168.00
	1	Factory Overhead		4,729.00	
		Work in Process Inventory			4,729.00

SELF-STUDY QUESTIONS AND EXERCISES

True/False Questions

1. LO1 ToyJoy Manufacturing Co. in Chapter 27 uses a periodic inventory system.
2. LO1 Under the perpetual inventory system, Cost of Goods Sold is debited each time the finished goods inventory is sold.
3. LO2 On the work sheet, the factory overhead account shows both debit and credit totals in the Trial Balance columns.
4. LO2 The credit total of Factory Overhead represents actual factory overhead costs.
5. LO2 The adjustment for factory overhead applied to work in process at the end of the accounting period includes a debit to the factory overhead account.

Multiple Choice Questions

1. LO2 The adjustment for the amount of factory supplies used during the year includes a
   (a) debit to Factory Supplies.
   (b) debit to Factory Overhead.
   (c) credit to Factory Overhead.
   (d) debit to Supplies Expense.
2. LO2 The adjustment for depreciation expense for the year on the factory building includes a
   (a) debit to Depreciation Expense.
   (b) credit to Factory Overhead.
   (c) credit to Accumulated Depreciation.
   (d) debit to Accumulated Depreciation.
3. LO2 At the end of the accounting period, a credit balance in the factory overhead account represents
   (a) overapplied factory overhead.
   (b) actual factory overhead.
   (c) underapplied factory overhead.
   (d) revenue earned.
4. LO4 During the closing process, the credit total in the factory overhead account is debited to
   (a) Work in Process Inventory.
   (b) Factory Overhead Expense.
   (c) Cost of Goods Sold.
   (d) Income Summary.
5. LO4 The adjusting entry to apply factory overhead to Work in Process is reversed at the beginning of the next accounting period and includes a
   (a) debit to Work in Process Inventory.
   (b) debit to Factory Overhead.
   (c) credit to Factory Overhead.
   (d) credit to Cost of Goods Sold.

U REVU Exercises

1. LO2 Prepare adjusting entries at December 31 for J P Company based on the following data.
   (a) Factory overhead is applied at a rate of 75% of direct labor costs. At the end of the year, the direct labor costs associated with the jobs in process totaled $8,000.
   (b) A physical count of factory supplies at the end of the year shows that $4,920 of factory supplies were used during the year.
   (c) Depreciation expense for the year on the factory building was $8,700 and on factory equipment was $11,600, a total of $20,300.
   (d) The factory overhead account has a debit balance of $186,500 and a credit balance of $183,900 [after recording adjustments (a) through (c)].

2. LO3 Prepare a schedule of cost of goods manufactured for Samo Company for the year ended September 30, 20-2, based on the following information.

Work in process, October 1, 20-1	$ 8,960
Materials inventory, October 1, 20-1	6,825
Materials purchases	96,530
Direct labor	196,420
Actual factory overhead	119,315
Work in process, September 30, 20-2	12,780
Materials inventory, September 30, 20-2	9,730
Indirect materials charged to production	5,040

3. LO4 Prepare closing journal entries for Adjent Company for the year ended December 31, based on the following data.

Factory overhead, debit and credit balances	$135,400
Sales	588,000
Cost of goods sold	395,400
Salaries expense	64,900
Office supplies expense	2,100
Depreciation expense—office equipment	4,000
Utilities expense—office	3,700
Bad debt expense	1,300
Income tax expense	23,000

The answers to the Self-Study Test Questions are at the end of the chapter (pages 1088–1089).

REVIEW QUESTIONS

LO1 1. What accounts and related adjustments are new in the work sheet of ToyJoy Manufacturing Co.?

LO1 2. How does the use of a perpetual inventory system affect the accounts on the work sheet?

LO2 3. Why must Work in Process Inventory be adjusted for factory overhead applied at year-end?

LO2 4. What is the relationship between the debit and credit balances in the factory overhead account when the overhead is said to be underapplied? Overapplied?

LO2 5. Why are the balances in the factory overhead account not extended to the Income Statement and Balance Sheet columns of the work sheet?

LO3 6. What are the distinctive features of ToyJoy's income statement? Its retained earnings statement? Its balance sheet?

LO4 7. When the adjustment is made to apply overhead to ending work in process, why are no entries made in the job cost ledger?

LO4 8. Describe the procedures for closing the factory overhead account.

LO4 9. Which adjusting entries are reversed by ToyJoy?

SERIES A EXERCISES

E 27-1A **(LO2)**
✓ Factory overhead overapplied: $4,400

ADJUSTING ENTRIES INCLUDING ADJUSTMENT FOR UNDERAPPLIED/ OVERAPPLIED FACTORY OVERHEAD Prepare the December 31 adjusting journal entries for Johnson Company. Data are as follows:

(a) Factory overhead is applied at a rate of 60% of direct labor costs. At the end of the year, the direct labor costs associated with the jobs still in process totaled $6,000.
(b) A physical count of factory supplies at the end of the year shows that $4,630 of factory supplies were used during the year.
(c) A review of the insurance policy files shows that $5,190 of insurance on the factory building and equipment has expired.
(d) Depreciation expense for the year on the factory building was $8,200 and on factory equipment was $12,400, a total of $20,600.
(e) The factory overhead account has a debit balance of $178,300 and a credit balance of $182,700 [after recording adjustments (a) through (d)].

Was factory overhead under- or overapplied for the year?

E 27-2A **(LO3)**
✓ Cost of goods manufactured: $287,500

SCHEDULE OF COST OF GOODS MANUFACTURED Prepare a schedule of cost of goods manufactured for Tomas Company for the year ended June 30, 20-2. Information to prepare the schedule is as follows:

(continued)

Work in process, July 1, 20-1	$ 6,400
Materials inventory, July 1, 20-1	4,875
Materials purchases	68,950
Direct labor	140,300
Actual factory overhead	85,225
Work in process, June 30, 20-2	7,700
Materials inventory, June 30, 20-2	6,950
Indirect materials charged to production	3,600

E 27-3A (LO4)

✓ Factory supplies adjustment, Dr. Factory Overhead (Factory Supplies Expense): $3,400

ADJUSTING JOURNAL ENTRIES Prepare the December 31 adjusting journal entries for Hanna Company. Data for the end of the year adjustments are as follows:

Factory overhead to be applied to work in process ending inventory	$8,200
Interest receivable	680
Provision for uncollectible accounts	4,100
Office supplies consumed	960
Factory supplies consumed	3,400
Insurance expired on factory building and equipment	2,500
Depreciation on factory building	7,300
Depreciation on factory equipment	3,700

E 27-4A (LO4)

✓ Final closing entry, Dr. Income Summary: $119,660

CLOSING JOURNAL ENTRIES Prepare closing journal entries for Medina Company for the year ended December 31. Data for the closing entries are as follows:

Factory overhead, debit and credit balance	$193,460
Sales for the year	840,300
Interest revenue	800
Cost of goods sold	560,400
Salaries expense	93,800
Office supplies expense	2,200
Depreciation expense—office equipment	5,800
Utilities expense—office	6,100
Bad debt expense	1,940
Advertising expense	8,700
Interest expense	9,600
Income tax expense	32,900

E 27-5A (LO4)

✓ Final reversing entry, Dr. Factory Overhead: $3,180

REVERSING JOURNAL ENTRIES Prepare reversing journal entries for Rogerson Company on January 1, 20-2. The following year-end adjustments were made:

20-1			
Dec. 31	Interest Receivable	140	
	Interest Revenue		140
31	Interest Expense	930	
	Interest Payable		930
31	Work in Process Inventory	3,180	
	Factory Overhead		3,180

SERIES A PROBLEMS

P 27-6A (LO1/2/3)

✓ Net income: $104,845

WORK SHEET, ADJUSTING ENTRIES, AND FINANCIAL STATEMENTS Herrera Company had the following trial balance columns on its work sheet:

Herrera Company
Trial Balance
December 31, 20 - -

ACCOUNT TITLE	DEBIT BALANCE	CREDIT BALANCE
Cash	30,300.00	
Government Notes	5,000.00	
Interest Receivable		
Accounts Receivable	34,000.00	
Allowance for Bad Debts		530.00
Finished Goods Inventory	24,000.00	
Work in Process Inventory	9,000.00	
Materials Inventory	8,500.00	
Office Supplies	3,100.00	
Factory Supplies	3,800.00	
Land	100,000.00	
Factory Building	120,000.00	
Accumulated Depreciation—Factory Building		10,000.00
Factory Equipment	40,000.00	
Accumulated Depreciation—Factory Equipment		5,000.00
Interest Payable		
Accounts Payable		13,800.00
Income Tax Payable		
Bonds Payable		80,000.00
Capital Stock		50,000.00
Paid-In Capital in Excess of Par		30,000.00
Retained Earnings		92,400.00
Cash Dividends	30,000.00	
Sales		405,100.00
Interest Revenue		300.00
Factory Overhead	78,630.00	89,300.00
Cost of Goods Sold	190,700.00	
Wages Expense	70,000.00	
Office Supplies Expense		
Bad Debt Expense		
Utilities Expense—Office	4,400.00	
Interest Expense	7,000.00	
Income Tax Expense	18,000.00	
	776,430.00	776,430.00

(continued)

Data for adjusting the accounts are as follows:

(a) Factory overhead to be applied to work in process ending inventory	$3,100
(b) Interest receivable	75
(c) Interest payable	600
(d) Estimate of uncollectible accounts, based on an aging of accounts receivable	2,930
(e) Office supplies consumed	2,900
(f) Factory supplies consumed	3,300
(g) Factory building depreciation	5,000
(h) Factory equipment depreciation	4,000
(i) Overapplied factory overhead	1,470
(j) Provision for corporate income taxes	6,100
(k) Physical counts of the inventories agreed with the amounts in the books.	

Additional information needed to prepare the financial statements is as follows:

Beginning inventories:	
Finished goods, January 1	$18,000
Work in process, January 1	7,300
Materials inventory, January 1	9,500
Materials purchases for the year	51,500
Direct labor	60,000
Actual factory overhead	90,930
Indirect materials charged to production	3,400

REQUIRED

1. Prepare a work sheet.
2. Prepare the following financial statements and schedule:
   (a) income statement
   (b) schedule of cost of goods manufactured
   (c) retained earnings statement
   (d) balance sheet

P 27-7A (LO1/3)

✓ 2. Retained Earnings, Dec. 31: $93,810

FINANCIAL STATEMENTS The Income Statement and Balance Sheet columns of Endo Company's work sheet are shown on the next page.

Additional information needed to prepare the financial statements is as follows:

Materials inventory, January 1	$ 3,760
Work in process inventory, January 1	5,315
Finished goods inventory, January 1	16,225
Materials purchases	135,340
Direct labor	75,000
Actual factory overhead	92,000
Indirect materials charged to production	5,300

REQUIRED

1. Prepare an income statement and a schedule of cost of goods manufactured for the year ended December 31, 20--.
2. Prepare a retained earnings statement for the year ended December 31, 20--.
3. Prepare a balance sheet as of December 31, 20--.

PROBLEM 27-7A

Endo Company
Work Sheet (Partial)
For Year Ended December 31, 20 --

	ACCOUNT TITLE	INCOME STATEMENT DEBIT	INCOME STATEMENT CREDIT	BALANCE SHEET DEBIT	BALANCE SHEET CREDIT	
1	Cash			13,350.00		1
2	Government Notes			3,500.00		2
3	Interest Receivable			65.00		3
4	Accounts Receivable			24,100.00		4
5	Allowance for Bad Debts				1,225.00	5
6	Finished Goods Inventory			18,800.00		6
7	Work in Process Inventory			6,740.00		7
8	Materials Inventory			4,300.00		8
9	Office Supplies			320.00		9
10	Factory Supplies			410.00		10
11	Prepaid Insurance			600.00		11
12	Land			25,000.00		12
13	Factory Building			80,000.00		13
14	Accum. Depr.—Factory Building				20,150.00	14
15	Factory Equipment			90,000.00		15
16	Accum. Depr.—Factory Equipment				27,000.00	16
17	Interest Payable				450.00	17
18	Accounts Payable				16,000.00	18
19	Income Tax Payable				3,550.00	19
20	Bonds Payable				50,000.00	20
21	Capital Stock				40,000.00	21
22	Paid-In Capital in Excess of Par				15,000.00	22
23	Retained Earnings				80,225.00	23
24	Cash Dividends			25,000.00		24
25	Sales		397,110.00			25
26	Interest Revenue		325.00			26
27	Factory Overhead					27
28						28
29	Cost of Goods Sold	292,500.00				29
30	Wages Expense	44,200.00				30
31	Office Supplies Expense	1,200.00				31
32	Bad Debt Expense	2,450.00				32
33	Utilities Expense—Office	1,500.00				33
34	Interest Expense	2,550.00				34
35	Income Tax Expense	14,450.00				35
36		358,850.00	397,435.00	292,185.00	253,600.00	36
37	Net Income	38,585.00			38,585.00	37
38		397,435.00	397,435.00	292,185.00	292,185.00	38
39						39
40						40

P 27-8A (LO1/2/4)

✓ 2. Final closing entry, Dr. Income Summary: $76,090

ADJUSTING, CLOSING, AND REVERSING ENTRIES A partial work sheet for Baldwin Company is shown on the next page.

Data for adjusting the accounts are as follows:

(a) Factory overhead to be applied to work in process ending inventory	$3,600
(b) Interest receivable	140
(c) Interest payable	1,200
(d) Estimate of uncollectible accounts, based on an aging of accounts receivable	2,370
(e) Office supplies consumed	3,700
(f) Factory supplies consumed	4,200
(g) Insurance on factory building and equipment expired	5,100
(h) Factory building depreciation	5,000
(i) Factory equipment depreciation	4,000
(j) Underapplied factory overhead	1,300
(k) Provision for corporate income taxes	5,900

REQUIRED

1. Prepare the December 31 adjusting journal entries for Baldwin Company.
2. Prepare the December 31 closing journal entries for Baldwin Company.
3. Prepare the reversing journal entries as of January 1, 20-2, for Baldwin Company.

SERIES B EXERCISES

E 27-1B (LO2)

✓ Factory overhead underapplied: $3,500

ADJUSTING ENTRIES INCLUDING ADJUSTMENT FOR UNDERAPPLIED/OVERAPPLIED FACTORY OVERHEAD Prepare the December 31 adjusting journal entries for Keiser Company. Data are as follows:

(a) Factory overhead is applied at a rate of 80% of direct labor costs. At the end of the year, the direct labor costs associated with the jobs still in process totaled $7,000.

(b) A physical count of factory supplies at the end of the year shows that $3,750 of factory supplies were used during the year.

(c) A review of the insurance policy files shows that $4,360 of insurance on the factory building and equipment has expired.

(d) Depreciation expense for the year on the factory building was $9,400 and on factory equipment was $11,600, a total of $21,000.

(e) The factory overhead account has a debit balance of $146,700 and a credit balance of $143,200 [after recording adjustments (a) through (d)].

Was factory overhead underapplied or overapplied for the year?

PROBLEM 27-8A

Baldwin Company
Work Sheet (Partial)
For Year Ended December 31, 20 -1

	ACCOUNT TITLE	TRIAL BALANCE		ADJUSTMENTS		ADJUSTED TRIAL BALANCE		INCOME STATEMENT		BALANCE SHEET		
		DEBIT	CREDIT	DEBIT	CREDIT	DEBIT	CREDIT	DEBIT	CREDIT	DEBIT	CREDIT	
1	Cash	41 200 00				41 200 00						1
2	Government Notes	6 000 00				6 000 00						2
3	Interest Receivable			(b) 140 00		140 00						3
4	Accounts Receivable	32 000 00				32 000 00						4
5	Allowance for Bad Debts		920 00		(d) 1 450 00		2 370 00					5
6	Finished Goods Inventory	21 000 00				21 000 00						6
7	Work in Process Inventory	10 200 00		(a) 3 600 00		13 800 00						7
8	Materials Inventory	9 100 00				9 100 00						8
9	Office Supplies	4 200 00			(e) 3 700 00	500 00						9
10	Factory Supplies	5 100 00			(f) 4 200 00	900 00						10
11	Prepaid Insurance	6 200 00			(g) 5 100 00	1 100 00						11
12	Land	80 000 00				80 000 00						12
13	Factory Building	120 000 00				120 000 00						13
14	Accum. Depr.—Factory Building		20 000 00		(h) 5 000 00		25 000 00					14
15	Factory Equipment	50 000 00				50 000 00						15
16	Accum. Depr.—Factory Equip.		8 000 00		(i) 4 000 00		12 000 00					16
17	Interest Payable				(c) 1 200 00		1 200 00					17
18	Accounts Payable		16 400 00				16 400 00					18
19	Income Tax Payable				(k) 5 900 00		5 900 00					19
20	Bonds Payable		90 000 00				90 000 00					20
21	Capital Stock		60 000 00				60 000 00					21
22	Paid-In Capital in Excess of Par		40 000 00				40 000 00					22
23	Retained Earnings		46 780 00				46 780 00					23
24	Sales		410 200 00				410 200 00					24
25	Interest Revenue		500 00		(b) 140 00		640 00					25
26	Factory Overhead	91 800 00	105 200 00	(f) 4 200 00	(a) 3 600 00	110 100 00	110 100 00					26
27				(g) 5 100 00	(j) 1 300 00							27
28				(h) 5 000 00								28
29				(i) 4 000 00								29
30	Cost of Goods Sold	203 500 00		(j) 1 300 00		204 800 00						30
31	Salaries Expense	80 000 00				80 000 00						31
32	Office Supplies Expense			(e) 3 700 00		3 700 00						32
33	Bad Debt Expense			(d) 1 450 00		1 450 00						33
34	Utilities Expense—Office	6 700 00				6 700 00						34
35	Interest Expense	8 000 00		(c) 1 200 00		9 200 00						35
36	Income Tax Expense	23 000 00		(k) 5 900 00		28 900 00						36
37		798 000 00	798 000 00	35 590 00	35 590 00	820 590 00	820 590 00					37
38												38

E 27-2B (LO3)

✓ Cost of goods manufactured: $685,956

SCHEDULE OF COST OF GOODS MANUFACTURED Prepare a schedule of cost of goods manufactured for Verdi Company for the year ended June 30, 20-2. Assume that all materials inventory items are direct materials. Information to prepare the schedule is as follows:

Work in process, July 1, 20-1	$ 20,760
Materials inventory, July 1, 20-1	12,348
Materials purchases	154,008
Direct labor	330,576
Actual factory overhead	201,384
Work in process, June 30, 20-2	17,940
Materials inventory, June 30, 20-2	15,180

E 27-3B (LO4)

✓ Factory Supplies adjustment, Dr. Factory Overhead (Factory Supplies Expense): $4,160

ADJUSTING JOURNAL ENTRIES FOR A MANUFACTURING BUSINESS Prepare the December 31 adjusting journal entries for Ortiz Company. Data for the end of the year adjustments are as follows:

Factory overhead to be applied to work in process ending inventory	$7,780
Interest receivable	435
Provision for uncollectible accounts	3,876
Office supplies consumed	750
Factory supplies consumed	4,160
Insurance expired on factory building and equipment	3,200
Depreciation on factory building	6,800
Depreciation on factory equipment	4,200

E 27-4B (LO4)

✓ Final closing entry, Dr. Income Summary: $44,655

CLOSING JOURNAL ENTRIES Prepare closing journal entries for Armour Company for the year ended December 31. Data for the closing entries are as follows:

Factory overhead, debit and credit balance	$186,250
Sales for the year	930,600
Interest revenue	920
Cost of goods sold	710,500
Salaries expense	98,100
Office supplies expense	3,500
Depreciation expense—office equipment	6,130
Utilities expense—office	7,460
Bad debt expense	2,275
Advertising expense	9,250
Interest expense	8,300
Income tax expense	41,350

E 27-5B (LO4)

✓ Final reversing entry, Dr. Factory Overhead: $4,250

REVERSING ENTRIES Prepare reversing journal entries for Hendrix Company on January 1, 20-2. The following year-end adjustments were made:

20-1			
Dec. 31	Interest Receivable	230	
	Interest Revenue		230
31	Interest Expense	875	
	Interest Payable		875
31	Work in Process Inventory	4,250	
	Factory Overhead		4,250

SERIES B PROBLEMS

P 27-6B (LO1/2/3)

✓ Net Income: $73, 790

WORK SHEET, ADJUSTING ENTRIES, AND FINANCIAL STATEMENTS Woods Company's trial balance columns from its work sheet are shown on the next page. Data for adjusting the accounts are as follows:

(a) Factory overhead to be applied to work in process ending inventory	$ 4,300
(b) Interest receivable	100
(c) Interest payable	700
(d) Estimate of uncollectible accounts, based on an aging of accounts receivable	4,110
(e) Office supplies consumed	3,200
(f) Factory supplies consumed	6,700
(g) Factory building depreciation	10,000
(h) Factory equipment depreciation	6,000
(i) Underapplied factory overhead	7,690
(j) Provision for corporate income taxes	8,100
(k) Physical counts of the inventories agreed with the amounts in the books.	

Additional information needed to prepare the financial statements is as follows:

Beginning inventories:	
Finished goods, January 1	$ 22,300
Work in process, January 1	12,400
Materials inventory, January 1	7,900
Materials purchases for the year	18,700
Direct labor	90,300
Actual factory overhead	104,290

Assume that all materials inventory items are direct materials

REQUIRED

1. Prepare a work sheet.
2. Prepare the following financial statements and schedule:
   (a) income statement
   (b) schedule of cost of goods manufactured
   (c) retained earnings statement
   (d) balance sheet

(continued)

PROBLEM 27-6B

Woods Company
Trial Balance
December 31, 20 - -

ACCOUNT TITLE	DEBIT BALANCE	CREDIT BALANCE
Cash	28 4 0 0 00	
Government Notes	6 0 0 0 00	
Interest Receivable		
Accounts Receivable	32 8 0 0 00	
Allowance for Bad Debts		6 1 0 00
Finished Goods Inventory	26 1 0 0 00	
Work in Process Inventory	10 2 0 0 00	
Materials Inventory	9 3 0 0 00	
Office Supplies	4 2 0 0 00	
Factory Supplies	8 6 0 0 00	
Land	80 0 0 0 00	
Factory Building	160 0 0 0 00	
Accumulated Depreciation—Factory Building		30 0 0 0 00
Factory Equipment	60 0 0 0 00	
Accumulated Depreciation—Factory Equipment		20 0 0 0 00
Interest Payable		
Accounts Payable		16 0 0 0 00
Income Tax Payable		
Bonds Payable		100 0 0 0 00
Capital Stock		60 0 0 0 00
Paid-In Capital in Excess of Par		20 0 0 0 00
Retained Earnings		111 4 0 0 00
Cash Dividends	40 0 0 0 00	
Sales		410 7 0 0 00
Interest Revenue		5 0 0 00
Factory Overhead	81 5 9 0 00	92 3 0 0 00
Cost of Goods Sold	198 3 0 0 00	
Wages Expense	78 7 0 0 00	
Office Supplies Expense		
Bad Debt Expense		
Utilities Expense—Office	4 9 0 0 00	
Interest Expense	9 0 0 0 00	
Income Tax Expense	23 4 2 0 00	
	861 5 1 0 00	861 5 1 0 00

P 27-7B (LO1/3)

✓ 2. Retained Earnings, Dec. 31: $99,270

FINANCIAL STATEMENTS The Income Statement and Balance Sheet columns of Wen Company's work sheet are shown on the next page.

Additional information needed to prepare the financial statements is as follows:

Materials inventory, January 1	$ 4,750
Work in process inventory, January 1	3,600
Finished goods inventory, January 1	14,560
Materials purchases	115,090
Direct labor	110,000
Actual factory overhead	96,850
Indirect materials charged to production	4,100

PROBLEM 27-7B

Wen Company
Work Sheet (Partial)
For Year Ended December 31, 20 --

	ACCOUNT TITLE	INCOME STATEMENT		BALANCE SHEET		
		DEBIT	CREDIT	DEBIT	CREDIT	
1	Cash			16,450.00		1
2	Government Notes			6,000.00		2
3	Interest Receivable			210.00		3
4	Accounts Receivable			19,700.00		4
5	Allowance for Bad Debts				1,600.00	5
6	Finished Goods Inventory			16,250.00		6
7	Work in Process Inventory			7,600.00		7
8	Materials Inventory			4,550.00		8
9	Office Supplies			465.00		9
10	Factory Supplies			375.00		10
11	Prepaid Insurance			700.00		11
12	Land			30,000.00		12
13	Factory Building			60,000.00		13
14	Accum. Depr.—Factory Building				15,230.00	14
15	Factory Equipment			85,000.00		15
16	Accum. Depr.—Factory Equipment				23,000.00	16
17	Interest Payable				600.00	17
18	Accounts Payable				14,450.00	18
19	Income Tax Payable				3,150.00	19
20	Bonds Payable				40,000.00	20
21	Capital Stock				30,000.00	21
22	Paid-In Capital in Excess of Par				20,000.00	22
23	Retained Earnings				83,020.00	23
24	Cash Dividends			12,500.00		24
25	Sales		410,150.00			25
26	Interest Revenue		650.00			26
27	Factory Overhead					27
28						28
29	Cost of Goods Sold	312,350.00				29
30	Wages Expense	43,100.00				30
31	Office Supplies Expense	2,250.00				31
32	Bad Debt Expense	1,750.00				32
33	Utilities Expense—Office	4,000.00				33
34	Interest Expense	3,100.00				34
35	Income Tax Expense	15,500.00				35
36		382,050.00	410,800.00	259,800.00	231,050.00	36
37	Net Income	28,750.00			28,750.00	37
38		410,800.00	410,800.00	259,800.00	259,800.00	38
39						39

(continued)

REQUIRED

1. Prepare an income statement and a schedule of cost of goods manufactured for the year ended December 31, 20--.
2. Prepare a retained earnings statement for the year ended December 31, 20--.
3. Prepare a balance sheet as of December 31, 20--.

P 27-8B (LO1/2/4)

✓ 2. Final closing entry, Dr. Income Summary: $65,510

KA KLOOSTER & ALLEN

ADJUSTING, CLOSING, AND REVERSING ENTRIES A partial work sheet for Milnor Company is shown on the next page.

Data for adjusting the accounts are as follows:

(a)	Factory overhead to be applied to work in process ending inventory	$4,400
(b)	Interest receivable	190
(c)	Interest payable	1,420
(d)	Estimate of uncollectible accounts, based on an aging of accounts receivable	4,450
(e)	Office supplies consumed	4,200
(f)	Factory supplies consumed	3,800
(g)	Insurance on factory building and equipment expired	6,800
(h)	Factory building depreciation	8,000
(i)	Factory equipment depreciation	5,000
(j)	Overapplied factory overhead	4,340
(k)	Provision for corporate income taxes	6,400

REQUIRED

1. Prepare the December 31 adjusting journal entries for Milnor Company.
2. Prepare the December 31 closing journal entries for Milnor Company.
3. Prepare the reversing journal entries as of January 1, 20-2, for Milnor Company.

PROBLEM 27-8B

Milnor Company
Work Sheet (Partial)
For Year Ended December 31, 20 -1

	ACCOUNT TITLE	TRIAL BALANCE DEBIT	TRIAL BALANCE CREDIT	ADJUSTMENTS DEBIT	ADJUSTMENTS CREDIT	ADJUSTED TRIAL BALANCE DEBIT	ADJUSTED TRIAL BALANCE CREDIT	INCOME STATEMENT DEBIT	INCOME STATEMENT CREDIT	BALANCE SHEET DEBIT	BALANCE SHEET CREDIT	
1	Cash	39,600.00				39,600.00						1
2	Government Notes	8,000.00				8,000.00						2
3	Interest Receivable			(b) 190.00		190.00						3
4	Accounts Receivable	40,000.00				40,000.00						4
5	Allowance for Bad Debts		1,250.00		(d) 3,200.00		4,450.00					5
6	Finished Goods Inventory	24,000.00				24,000.00						6
7	Work in Process Inventory	12,300.00		(a) 4,400.00		16,700.00						7
8	Materials Inventory	8,700.00				8,700.00						8
9	Office Supplies	5,500.00			(e) 4,200.00	1,300.00						9
10	Factory Supplies	4,950.00			(f) 3,800.00	1,150.00						10
11	Prepaid Insurance	7,450.00			(g) 6,800.00	650.00						11
12	Land	90,000.00				90,000.00						12
13	Factory Building	130,000.00				130,000.00						13
14	Accum. Depr.—Factory Building		40,000.00		(h) 8,000.00		48,000.00					14
15	Factory Equipment	70,000.00				70,000.00						15
16	Accum. Depr.—Factory Equip.		10,000.00		(i) 5,000.00		15,000.00					16
17	Interest Payable				(c) 1,420.00		1,420.00					17
18	Accounts Payable		17,200.00				17,200.00					18
19	Income Tax Payable				(k) 6,400.00		6,400.00					19
20	Bonds Payable		120,000.00				120,000.00					20
21	Capital Stock		50,000.00				50,000.00					21
22	Paid-In Capital in Excess of Par		30,000.00				30,000.00					22
23	Retained Earnings		72,310.00				72,310.00					23
24	Sales		395,200.00				395,200.00					24
25	Interest Revenue		800.00		(b) 190.00		990.00					25
26	Factory Overhead	84,560.00	108,100.00	(f) 3,800.00	(a) 4,400.00	112,500.00	112,500.00					26
27				(g) 6,800.00								27
28				(h) 8,000.00								28
29				(i) 5,000.00								29
30				(j) 4,340.00								30
31	Cost of Goods Sold	194,600.00			(j) 4,340.00	190,260.00						31
32	Wages Expense	90,000.00				90,000.00						32
33	Office Supplies Expense			(e) 4,200.00		4,200.00						33
34	Bad Debt Expense			(d) 3,200.00		3,200.00						34
35	Utilities Expense—Office	7,200.00				7,200.00						35
36	Interest Expense	9,000.00		(c) 1,420.00		10,420.00						36
37	Income Tax Expense	19,000.00		(k) 6,400.00		25,400.00						37
38		844,860.00	844,860.00	47,750.00	47,750.00	873,470.00	873,470.00					38
39												39

MANAGING YOUR WRITING

You and a fellow student are arguing about the "value" of Chapter 27. She says that the chapter is mostly review. The work sheet and financial statements were fully covered in Chapter 15. Chapter 27 is a similar story with some cosmetic differences. You have just begun an impressive defense of Chapter 27 when your professor overhears the argument and decides to give the entire class the following assignment.

Prepare a report describing (1) the ways in which the manufacturer's work sheet differs from the merchandiser's and (2) the differences between the merchandiser's financial statements in Chapter 15 and the manufacturer's financial statements in Chapter 27.

ETHICS CASE

Kevin Ryan is an accountant for Warick Corporation, a medium-size manufacturing firm. One of his responsibilities is to review the adjusting entries at the end of each accounting period. Mary Sellers is a new accountant at Warick Corporation. She is a recent graduate and this is her first accounting job. One of the duties Kevin assigned Mary was to prepare the adjusting entries. After reviewing Mary's work, Kevin came to the conclusion that Mary did not understand the adjusting process for a manufacturing company. During their review meeting, Kevin told Mary that he was concerned about her ability to do the job. Mary admitted not having a sound knowledge of the adjusting and closing process but asked Kevin to give her another month to catch on. Kevin said he would have to think about it over the weekend and he would get back to her on Monday. That weekend, Kevin was offered a much better paying job with a large manufacturing company in the same city. He immediately accepted the position. When he gave his boss notice that he would be leaving Warick, his boss asked him how Mary was doing. Kevin said he thought she'd do just fine.

1. Do you think Kevin should have told his boss about Mary's poor performance? Why or why not?
2. How will Kevin's decision to not say anything affect Mary?
3. Write a short incident report concerning Mary's poor job performance and subsequent conference with Kevin. Assume Kevin writes the report and it will be placed in Mary's personnel file.
4. In groups of two or three, discuss what alternatives Kevin had in this situation. Come to a group consensus on the best alternative.

MASTERY PROBLEM

✓ 2. Retained Earnings, Dec. 31: $284,124

Reese Manufacturing Company manufactures and sells a limited line of products made to customer order. The company uses a perpetual inventory system and keeps its accounts on a calendar year basis. A 10-column work sheet is presented on page 1086.

Additional information needed to prepare the income statement and schedule of cost of goods manufactured is as follows:

Finished goods inventory, January 1	$ 85,454
Materials inventory, January 1	11,633
Purchases for the year	96,437
Direct labor	107,740
Work in process inventory, January 1	22,600
Indirect materials charged to production	3,200

REQUIRED

1. Prepare an income statement and schedule of cost of goods manufactured for the year ended December 31, 20--.
2. Prepare a retained earnings statement for the year ended December 31, 20--.
3. Prepare a balance sheet as of December 31, 20--.
4. Prepare the adjusting, closing, and reversing entries.

(continued)

MASTERY PROBLEM

Reese Manufacturing Company
Work Sheet
For Year Ended December 31, 20 --

	ACCOUNT TITLE	TRIAL BALANCE		ADJUSTMENTS		ADJUSTED TRIAL BALANCE		INCOME STATEMENT		BALANCE SHEET		
		DEBIT	CREDIT	DEBIT	CREDIT	DEBIT	CREDIT	DEBIT	CREDIT	DEBIT	CREDIT	
1	Cash	49,423.00				49,423.00				49,423.00		1
2	Accounts Receivable	78,096.00				78,096.00				78,096.00		2
3	Allowance for Bad Debts		5,074.00		(g) 956.00		6,030.00				6,030.00	3
4	Finished Goods Inventory	42,675.00				42,675.00				42,675.00		4
5	Work in Process Inventory	39,675.00		(i) 1,567.00		41,242.00				41,242.00		5
6	Materials Inventory	22,353.00				22,353.00				22,353.00		6
7	Office Supplies	3,546.00			(b) 800.00	2,746.00				2,746.00		7
8	Factory Supplies	1,878.00			(c) 1,389.00	489.00				489.00		8
9	Prepaid Insurance	1,500.00			(f) 1,454.00	46.00				46.00		9
10	Factory Equipment	186,674.00				186,674.00				186,674.00		10
11	Accum. Depr.—Factory Equip.		23,501.00		(e) 12,553.00		36,054.00				36,054.00	11
12	Office Equipment	46,986.00				46,986.00				46,986.00		12
13	Accum. Depr.—Office Equip.		2,916.00		(d) 923.00		3,839.00				3,839.00	13
14	Notes Payable		12,470.00				12,470.00				12,470.00	14
15	Interest Payable				(a) 132.00		132.00				132.00	15
16	Accounts Payable		10,356.00				10,356.00				10,356.00	16
17	Income Tax Payable				(h) 45,725.00		45,725.00				45,725.00	17
18	Capital Stock		72,000.00				72,000.00				72,000.00	18
19	Retained Earnings		195,341.00				195,341.00				195,341.00	19
20	Cash Dividends	36,000.00				36,000.00				36,000.00		20
21	Sales		532,027.00				532,027.00		532,027.00			21
22	Factory Overhead	52,356.00	65,446.00	(c) 1,389.00	(i) 1,567.00	67,654.00	67,654.00					22
23				(e) 12,553.00	(j) 641.00							23
24				(f) 1,356.00								24
25	Cost of Goods Sold	281,407.00		(j) 641.00		282,048.00		282,048.00				25
26	Wages Expense	58,380.00				58,380.00		58,380.00				26
27	Advertising Expense	11,450.00				11,450.00		11,450.00				27
28	Office Rent Expense	5,443.00				5,443.00		5,443.00				28
29	Office Supplies Expense			(b) 800.00		800.00		800.00				29
30	Bad Debt Expense			(g) 956.00		956.00		956.00				30
31	Insurance Exp.—Office Equip.			(f) 98.00		98.00		98.00				31
32	Depr. Expense—Office Equip.			(d) 923.00		923.00		923.00				32
33	Interest Expense	1,289.00		(a) 132.00		1,421.00		1,421.00				33
34	Income Tax Expense			(h) 45,725.00		45,725.00		45,725.00				34
35		919,131.00	919,131.00	66,140.00	66,140.00	981,628.00	981,628.00	407,244.00	532,027.00	506,730.00	381,947.00	35
36	Net Income							124,783.00			124,783.00	36
37								532,027.00	532,027.00	506,730.00	506,730.00	37
38												38
39												39
40												40

CHALLENGE PROBLEM

This problem challenges you to apply your cumulative accounting knowledge to move a step beyond the material in the chapter.

✓ **2. Revised net income: $56,670**

Drafts of the condensed income statement and balance sheet of Allofe Co. for the current year are shown below. Shortly after preparing these draft financial statements, Allofe discovered that an error had been made in the year-end adjustment process. Overhead of $2,500 had not been applied to the ending work in process.

Allofe Co.
Condensed Income Statement
For Year Ended December 31, 20--

Net sales	$501,570
Cost of goods sold	360,312
Gross profit	$141,258
Operating expenses	87,088
Net income	$ 54,170

Allofe Co.
Condensed Balance Sheet
December 31, 20--

Assets	
Current assets	$ 93,014
Property, plant and equipment (net)	177,441
Total assets	$270,455
Liabilities	
Current liabilities	$ 28,671
Long-term liabilities	60,000
Total liabilities	$ 88,671
Stockholders' Equity	
Paid-in capital	$ 57,000
Retained earnings	124,784
Total stockholders' equity	$181,784
Total liabilities and stockholders' equity	$270,455

REQUIRED

1. Identify all adjusting and closing entries that would be affected by this error and prepare the missing portions of the entries.
2. Prepare a revised condensed income statement for Allofe.

(In solving this problem, assume that corporate income tax is not affected by the error.)

ANSWERS TO SELF-STUDY QUESTIONS AND EXERCISE

True/False Questions

1. F (perpetual)
2. T
3. T
4. F (debit total)
5. F (credit)

Multiple Choice Questions

1. b 2. c 3. a 4. d 5. b

U REVU Exercises

1.

(a) Work in Process Inventory	6,000	
Factory Overhead		6,000
(b) Factory Overhead (Factory Supplies Expense)	4,920	
Factory Supplies		4,920
(c) Factory Overhead (Depreciation Expense—Factory Building and Equipment)	20,300	
Accumulated Depreciation—Factory Building		8,700
Accumulated Depreciation—Factory Equipment		11,600
(d) Cost of Goods Sold	2,600	
Factory Overhead		2,600

2.

Work in process, October 1, 20-1			$ 8,960
Direct materials			
Materials inventory, October 1, 20-1	$ 6,825		
Materials purchases	96,530		
Materials available	$103,355		
Materials inventory, September 30, 20-2	9,730		
Cost of materials used		$ 93,625	
Less indirect materials charged to production		5,040	
Cost of direct materials used		$ 88,585	
Direct labor		196,420	
Overhead		119,315	
Total manufacturing costs			404,320
Total work in process during period			$ 413,280
Work in process, September 30, 20-2			12,780
Cost of goods manufactured			$ 400,500

3.

Dec. 31	Income Summary	135,400	
	Factory Overhead (Subsidiary ledger accounts)		135,400
31	Factory Overhead	135,400	
	Income Summary		135,400
31	Sales	588,000	
	Income Summary		588,000
31	Income Summary	494,400	
	Cost of Goods Sold		395,400
	Salaries Expense		64,900
	Office Supplies Expense		2,100
	Depreciation Expense—Office Equipment		4,000
	Utilities Expense—Office		3,700
	Bad Debt Expense		1,300
	Income Tax Expense		23,000
31	Income Summary	93,600	
	Retained Earnings		93,600

Module Accounting for a Professional Service Business: The Combination Journal

LEARNING OBJECTIVES

Careful study of this module should enable you to:

LO1 Explain the differences between the modified cash and accrual bases of accounting.

LO2 Describe special records for a professional service business using the modified cash basis.

LO3 Describe and use a combination journal to record transactions of a professional service business.

LO4 Post from the combination journal to the general ledger.

LO5 Prepare a work sheet, financial statements, and adjusting and closing entries for a professional service business.

Professional service businesses include law, dentistry, medicine, optometry, architecture, engineering, and accounting. As discussed in Chapter 5, many small professional service businesses do not need to prepare financial statements in strict compliance with generally accepted accounting principles (GAAP). This is because they don't need to raise large amounts of money from investors or creditors who expect GAAP financial statements. Thus, many of these businesses use the modified cash basis. This simplifies the accounting process and provides results similar to the accrual basis if receivables and payables are minimal. If at some point GAAP financial statements are needed, an accountant can convert the modified cash basis statements to the accrual basis which is required under GAAP.

Small professional service businesses may also use a combination journal as the book of original entry, instead of a general journal, or special journals (illustrated in Chapter 12). The purpose of this module is to illustrate accounting for a professional service business using the modified cash basis of accounting and a combination journal.

THE MODIFIED CASH AND ACCRUAL BASES OF ACCOUNTING

LO1 Explain the differences between the modified cash and accrual bases of accounting.

The modified cash and accrual bases of accounting are the same except for three types of events. The accounting differences for these three events are shown in Figure M-1. First, expenses for services received are not recorded until paid. Thus, accounts payable is not used under the modified cash basis for services received. Second, under the modified cash basis, accrued expenses are not recognized. Examples of accrued

FIGURE M-1 Modified Cash Basis vs. Accrual Basis of Accounting

DIFFERENCES BETWEEN MODIFIED CASH AND ACCRUAL BASES OF ACCOUNTING		
Event	**Accrual basis**	**Modified cash basis**
Expenses Bills for services received, but not yet paid.	Expense Accounts Payable	No entry. (Record when paid.)
Wages earned by employees, but not yet paid.	Wages Expense Wages Payable	No entry. (Record when paid.)
Revenues Services provided on account.	Accounts Receivable Professional Fees	No entry. (Record when cash is received.)

expenses include wages that were earned by the employees, but not yet paid, and interest expense that has been incurred, but not yet paid. Thus, no end-of-period adjusting entries are made for these types of events. This means that other records must be used to maintain information on amounts owed for wages, interest, and other expenses. Typically, these bills are filed chronologically by due date.

The modified cash basis is the same as the accrual basis, except receivables and payables are not recognized for revenues and operating expenses.

Finally, under the modified cash basis, revenues from services performed on account are not recorded until cash is received. Thus, no accounts receivable are entered in the accounting system. This means that other records must be used to maintain information on amounts owed by clients and patients. These records generally include an appointment record and a client or patient ledger record. These records are illustrated in Figures M-2 and M-3.

FIGURE M-2 Appointment Record

Date: 6/4/--

Time	Patient	Medical Service	Fees	Payments
8:00	Dennis Rogan	OV	40.00	40.00
15				
30	Rick Cosier	OV;EKG	120.00	
45				
9:00	George Hettenhouse	OV;MISC	50.00	
15				
30	Sam Frumer	OV;LAB	75.00	75.00
45				
10:00	Dan Dalton	OV	40.00	
15				
30	Wally Bell	OV;X	65.00	
45				
11:00	Mike Groomer	X	40.00	40.00
15				
30				
45				
12:00				
15				
30				
45				
1:00	Mike Tiller	OV;LAB	80.00	
15				
30	Peggy Hite	OV;PHYS	190.00	
45				
2:00				
15				
30				
45				
3:00	Vivian Winston	OV;MISC	40.00	
15				
30				
45				
4:00	Hank Davis	OV	40.00	40.00
15				
30				
45				
	Bill Sharp			150.00
	Phil Jones			80.00
	Diane Gallagher			200.00
			780.00	625.00

FIGURE M-3 Client or Patient Ledger Account

Patient Name Dennis Rogan
Address 1542 Hamilton Avenue Cincinnati OH 45240-5524
Phone Number 555-1683

Date	Service Rendered	Time	Debit	Credit	Balance
20--					
June 4	Office Visit	8:00	40.00		40.00
4				40.00	—

U REVU

Complete U REVU-1 on **page 1109** to test your basic understanding of LO1.

ACCOUNTING FOR A PROFESSIONAL SERVICE BUSINESS

LO2 Describe special records for a professional service business using the modified cash basis.

The appointment record, shown in Figure M-2, is used to schedule appointments and to maintain a record of the services rendered, fees charged, and payments received. It also serves as a source document for the patient ledger records, shown in Figure M-3, which show the amount owed by each client or patient for services performed. A copy of this record may also be used for billing purposes.

THE COMBINATION JOURNAL

LO3 Describe and use a combination journal to record transactions of a professional service business.

The two-column general journal illustrated in Chapter 4 can be used to enter every transaction of a business. However, in most businesses, there are many similar transactions that involve the same account or accounts. Cash receipts and payments are good examples. Suppose that in a typical month there are 30 transactions that result in an increase in cash and 40 transactions that cause a decrease in cash. In a two-column general journal, this would require entering the account Cash 70 times, using a journal line each time.

A considerable amount of time and space is saved if a journal contains **special columns** for cash debits and cash credits. At the end of the month, the special columns for cash debits and credits are totaled. The total of the Cash Debit column is posted as one amount to the debit side of the cash account and the total of the Cash Credit column is posted as one amount to the credit side of the cash account. Thus, instead of receiving 70 postings, Cash receives only two: one debit and one credit. This method requires much less time and reduces the risk of making posting errors.

LEARNING KEY

The totals of special journal columns are posted as one amount to the account. This saves time and reduces the possibility of posting errors.

If other accounts are used frequently, special columns can be added for these accounts. **General Debit** and **General Credit columns** are used for accounts not affected by many transactions. A journal with such special and general columns is called a **combination journal.**

Many small professional enterprises use a combination journal to record business transactions. To demonstrate the use of a combination journal, let's consider the medical practice of Dr. Ray Bonita. Bonita uses the modified cash basis of accounting. The chart of accounts for his medical practice is shown in Figure M-4. The transactions for the month of June, his first month in practice, are provided in Figure M-5.

FIGURE M-4 Chart of Accounts

RAY BONITA, M.D. CHART OF ACCOUNTS			
Assets		**Revenue**	
101	Cash	401	Medical Fees
141	Medical Supplies		
142	Office Supplies	**Expenses**	
145	Prepaid Insurance	511	Wages Expense
182	Office Furniture	521	Rent Expense
182.1	Accum. Depr.—Office Furn.	523	Office Supplies Expense
185	Medical Equipment	524	Medical Supplies Expense
185.1	Accum. Depr.—Med. Equip.	525	Telephone Expense
		526	Laboratory Expense
Liabilities		535	Insurance Expense
202	Accounts Payable	541	Depr. Exp.—Office Furn.
		542	Depr. Exp.—Med. Equip.
Owner's Equity			
311	Ray Bonita, Capital		
312	Ray Bonita, Drawing		
313	Income Summary		

FIGURE M-5 Summary of Transactions for Ray Bonita's Medical Practice

June 1	Ray Bonita invested cash to start a medical practice, $50,000.
2	Paid for a one-year liability insurance policy, $6,000. Coverage began on June 1.
3	Purchased medical equipment for cash, $22,000.
4	Paid bill for laboratory work, $300.
5	Purchased office furniture on credit from Bittle's Furniture, $9,000.
6	Received cash from patients and insurance companies for medical services rendered, $5,000.
7	Paid June office rent, $2,000.
8	Paid part-time wages, $3,000.
9	Purchased medical supplies for cash, $250.
15	Paid telephone bill, $150.
15	Received cash from patients and insurance companies for medical services rendered, $10,000.
16	Paid bill for laboratory work, $280.
17	Paid part-time wages, $3,000.
19	Purchased office supplies for cash, $150.
20	Received cash from patients and insurance companies for medical services rendered, $3,200.
22	Paid the first installment to Bittle's Furniture, $3,300.
23	Purchased medical supplies for cash, $200.
24	Paid bill for laboratory work, $400.
25	Purchased additional furniture from Bittle's Furniture, $4,000. A down payment of $500 was made, with the remaining payments expected over the next four months.
27	Paid part-time wages, $2,500.
30	Received cash from patients and insurance companies for medical services rendered, $7,000.
30	Bonita withdrew cash for personal use, $10,000.

A combination journal for Bonita's medical practice is illustrated in Figure M-6. Note that special columns were set up for Cash (Debit and Credit), Medical Fees (Credit), Wages Expense (Debit), Laboratory Expense (Debit), Medical Supplies

FIGURE M-6 Combination Journal: Modified Cash Basis

COMBINATION JOURNAL

PAGE 1

	DATE	CASH DEBIT	CASH CREDIT	DESCRIPTION	POST. REF.	GENERAL DEBIT	GENERAL CREDIT	MEDICAL FEES CREDIT	WAGES EXPENSE DEBIT	LABORATORY EXPENSE DEBIT	MEDICAL SUPPLIES DEBIT	OFFICE SUPPLIES DEBIT	
1	20-- June 1	50 000 00		Ray Bonita, Capital	311		50 000 00						1
2	2		6 000 00	Prepaid Insurance	145	6 000 00							2
3	3		22 000 00	Medical Equipment	185	22 000 00							3
4	4		300 00		—					300 00			4
5	5			Office Furniture	182	9 000 00							5
6				Accounts Payable—Bittle's Furn.	202		9 000 00						6
7	6	5 000 00			—			5 000 00					7
8	7		2 000 00	Rent Expense	521	2 000 00							8
9	8		3 000 00		—				3 000 00				9
10	9		250 00		—						250 00		10
11	15		150 00	Telephone Expense	525	150 00							11
12	15	10 000 00			—			10 000 00					12
13	16		280 00		—					280 00			13
14	17		3 000 00		—				3 000 00				14
15	19		150 00		—							150 00	15
16	20	3 200 00			—			3 200 00					16
17	22		3 300 00	Accounts Payable—Bittle's Furniture	202	3 300 00							17
18	23		200 00		—						200 00		18
19	24		400 00		—					400 00			19
20	25		500 00	Office Furniture	182	4 000 00							20
21				Accounts Payable—Bittle's Furn.	202		3 500 00						21
22	27		2 500 00		—				2 500 00				22
23	30	7 000 00			—			7 000 00					23
24	30		10 000 00	Ray Bonita, Drawing	312	10 000 00							24
25		75 200 00	54 030 00			56 450 00	62 500 00	25 200 00	8 500 00	980 00	450 00	150 00	25
26		(101)	(101)			(✓)	(✓)	(401)	(511)	(526)	(141)	(142)	26

Note: The account numbers in the Posting Reference column and at the bottom of the special columns are inserted as posting is completed. The same is true for the (✓) at the bottom of the General Debit and Credit columns.

Proving the Combination Journal:

Debit columns:		**Credit columns:**	
Cash	75,200	Cash	54,030
General	56,450	General	62,500
Wages Expense	8,500	Medical Fees	25,200
Laboratory Expense	980		141,730
Medical Supplies	450		
Office Supplies	150		
	141,730		

LEARNING KEY

Set up special columns for the most frequently used accounts.

(Debit), and Office Supplies (Debit). Special columns were set up for these accounts because they will be used frequently in this business. Other businesses might set up special columns for different accounts depending on the frequency of their use. Of course, General Debit and Credit columns for transactions affecting other accounts are also needed.

JOURNALIZING IN A COMBINATION JOURNAL

The following procedures were used to enter the transactions for Bonita for June:

General Columns

Enter transactions in the *general columns* in a manner similar to that used for the *general journal*. Look at the entry for June 5 in Figure M-6.

(a) Enter the name of the debited account (Office Furniture) first at the extreme left of the Description column.

(b) Enter the amount in the General Debit column.

(c) Enter the name of the account credited (Accounts Payable—Bittle's Furniture) on the next line, indented.

(d) Enter the amount in the General Credit column.

General and Special Accounts

Some transactions affect both a *general account and a special account*. Look at the entry for June 1 in Figure M-6.

(a) Enter the name of the general account in the Description column.

(b) Enter the amount in the General Debit or Credit column.

(c) Enter the amount of the debit or credit for the special account in the appropriate special column.

Enter all of this information on the same line.

Special Accounts

Many transactions affect only *special accounts*. Look at the entry for June 6 in Figure M-6.

(a) Enter the amounts in the appropriate special debit and credit columns.

(b) Do not enter anything in the Description column.

(c) Place a dash in the **Posting Reference column** to indicate that this amount is not posted individually. It will be posted as part of the total of the special column at the end of the month. (The posting process is described later in this chapter.)

Description Column

In general, the **Description column** is used for the following:

(a) To enter the account titles for the General Debit and General Credit columns.

(b) To identify specific creditors when assets are purchased on account (see entry for June 5).

Note: For firms using the accrual basis of accounting, this column also would be used to identify specific customers receiving services on account (accounts receivable) and specific businesses that provided services on account (accounts payable).

(c) To identify specific creditors when payments are made on account (see entry for June 22).

(d) To identify adjusting, closing, and reversing entries.

(e) To identify amounts forwarded. When more than one page is required during an accounting period, amounts from the previous page are brought forward. In this situation, "Amounts Forwarded" is entered in the Description column on the first line.

PROVING THE COMBINATION JOURNAL

At the end of the accounting period, all columns of the combination journal should be totaled and ruled. The sum of the debit columns should be compared with the sum of the credit columns to verify that they are equal. The proving of Bonita's combination journal for the month of June is shown at the bottom of Figure M-6 on page 1094.

U REVU Complete U REVU-2 on **page 1109** to test your basic understanding of LO3.

POSTING FROM THE COMBINATION JOURNAL

LO4 Post from the combination journal to the general ledger.

Accounts debited or credited in the general columns are posted individually throughout the month in the same manner followed for the general journal. A different procedure is used for special columns. Figure M-7 describes the procedures to follow in posting from the combination journal.

FIGURE M-7 Posting from a Combination Journal

GENERAL COLUMNS	Since a combination journal is being used, enter "CJ" and the page number in each general ledger account's Posting Reference column. Once the amount has been posted to the general ledger account, the account number is entered in the Posting Reference column of the combination journal. Accounts in the general column should be posted daily. The check marks at the bottom of the General Debit and Credit columns are entered at the end of the month and serve as a reminder that these totals should not be posted.
SPECIAL COLUMNS	1. Post the totals of the special columns to the appropriate general ledger accounts. 2. Once posted, enter the account number (in parentheses) beneath the column and "CJ" and the page number in each general ledger account's Posting Reference column.

LEARNING KEY

Amounts in the General column are posted individually. Only the totals of the special columns are posted.

Portions of the combination journal in Figure M-6 and general ledger accounts for Cash, Office Furniture, Accounts Payable, and Medical Fees are shown in Figure M-8 to illustrate the effects of this posting process. Note that the individual debits and credits in the General columns are posted individually throughout the month. Only the totals of the Special columns are posted at the end of the month.

To see the advantages of posting a combination journal compared with the general journal, simply compare the accounts in Figure M-8 with the same accounts in Chapter 4, Figure 4-12. Note the number of postings required for the general journal and combination journal.

FIGURE M-8 Posting the Combination Journal

COMBINATION JOURNAL (only selected transactions are shown) PAGE 1

	Date		Cash Debit	Cash Credit	Description	Post. Ref.	General Debit	General Credit	Medical Fees Credit	
5	20-- June	5			Office Furniture	182	9 000 00			5
6					Accts. Payable—Bittle's Furn.	202		9 000 00		6
7		6	5 000 00			—			5 000 00	7
12		15	10 000 00			—			10 000 00	12
16		20	3 200 00			—			3 200 00	16
17		22		3 300 00	Accts. Payable—Bittle's Furn.	202	3 300 00			17
20		25		500 00	Office Furniture	182	4 000 00			20
21					Accts. Payable—Bittle's Furn.	202		3 500 00		21
23		30	7 000 00			—			7 000 00	23
25			75 200 00	54 030 00			56 450 00	62 500 00	25 200 00	25
26			(101)	(101)			(✓)	(✓)	(401)	26

GENERAL LEDGER

ACCOUNT: Cash ACCOUNT NO. 101

Date		Item	Post. Ref.	Debit	Credit	Balance Debit	Balance Credit
20-- June	30		CJ1	75 200 00		75 200 00	
	30		CJ1		54 030 00	21 170 00	

ACCOUNT: Office Furniture ACCOUNT NO. 182

Date		Item	Post. Ref.	Debit	Credit	Balance Debit	Balance Credit
20-- June	5		CJ1	9 000 00		9 000 00	
	25		CJ1	4 000 00		13 000 00	

ACCOUNT: Accounts Payable ACCOUNT NO. 202

Date		Item	Post. Ref.	Debit	Credit	Balance Debit	Balance Credit
20-- June	5		CJ1		9 000 00		9 000 00
	22		CJ1	3 300 00			5 700 00
	25		CJ1		3 500 00		9 200 00

ACCOUNT: Medical Fees ACCOUNT NO. 401

Date		Item	Post. Ref.	Debit	Credit	Balance Debit	Balance Credit
20-- June	30		CJ1		25 200 00		25 200 00

Color Key:
Red— Posting totals of Special columns.
Blue— Posting individual debits and credits in General columns.

	Number of Postings		
	General Journal	Combination Journal	
Cash	13	2	(Special columns for cash)
Delivery Equip./ Office Furniture	3	2	(No special column)
Accounts Payable	3	3	(No special column)
Delivery/Medical Fees	3	1	(Special column for Medical Fees)

Clearly, using the combination journal can be quite efficient.

LEARNING KEY

Beginning cash balance
+ Cash debits to date
− Cash credits to date
Current cash balance

DETERMINING THE CASH BALANCE

The debits and credits to Cash are not posted until the end of the accounting period. Therefore, the cash balance must be computed when this information is needed. The cash balance may be computed at any time during the month by taking the beginning balance and adding total cash debits and subtracting total cash credits to date. Figure M-9 shows the calculation of Bonita's cash balance on June 15.

U REVU Complete U REVU-3 on **page 1109** to test your basic understanding of LO4.

PERFORMING END-OF-PERIOD WORK FOR A PROFESSIONAL SERVICE BUSINESS

LO5 Prepare a work sheet, financial statements, and adjusting and closing entries for a professional service business.

Once the combination journal has been posted to the general ledger, the end-of-period work sheet is prepared in the same way as described in Chapter 5. Recall that financial statements are prepared and end-of-period work is normally performed at the end of the fiscal year. For illustration purposes, we will perform these activities at the end of Bonita's first month of operations.

PREPARING THE WORK SHEET

Bonita's work sheet is illustrated in Figure M-10 on page 1100. Adjustments were made for the following items:

(a) Medical supplies remaining on June 30, $350.

(b) Office supplies remaining on June 30, $100.

(c) Prepaid insurance expired during June, $500.

(d) Depreciation on office furniture for June, $200.

(e) Depreciation on medical equipment for June, $300.

PREPARING FINANCIAL STATEMENTS

Since this is the first month of Dr. Bonita's medical practice, we know the beginning balance of owner's equity is zero. We also know the $50,000 balance in the capital account on the work sheet is the result of his investment during June. With this information, we can prepare the financial statements directly from the work sheet. In future periods, the balance of the capital account on the work sheet will reflect the beginning balance plus any additional investments. Thus, we will need to examine Bonita's capital account for investments made during the period and report those separately on the statement of owner's equity. Bonita's financial statements are illustrated in Figure M-11 on page 1101.

FIGURE M-9 Determining the Cash Balance

COMBINATION JOURNAL — PAGE 1

	DATE		CASH DEBIT	CASH CREDIT	DESCRIPTION	POST. REF.	GENERAL DEBIT	GENERAL CREDIT	MEDICAL FEES CREDIT	WAGES EXPENSE DEBIT	LABORATORY EXPENSE DEBIT	MEDICAL SUPPLIES DEBIT	OFFICE SUPPLIES DEBIT	
1	20-- June	1	50 0 0 0 00		Ray Bonita, Capital	311		50 0 0 0 00						1
2		2		6 0 0 0 00	Prepaid Insurance	145	6 0 0 0 00							2
3		3		22 0 0 0 00	Medical Equipment	185	22 0 0 0 00							3
4		4		3 0 0 00		—					3 0 0 00			4
5		5			Office Furniture	182	9 0 0 0 00							5
6					Accounts Payable—Bittle's Furn.	202		9 0 0 0 00						6
7		6	5 0 0 0 00			—			5 0 0 0 00					7
8		7		2 0 0 0 00	Rent Expense	521	2 0 0 0 00							8
9		8		3 0 0 0 00		—				3 0 0 0 00				9
10		9		2 5 0 00		—						2 5 0 00		10
11		15		1 5 0 00	Telephone Expense	525	1 5 0 00							11
12		15	10 0 0 0 00			—			10 0 0 0 00					12
13			65 0 0 0 00	33 7 0 0 00										13

Beginning balance	$ 0
Add cash debits	65,000
Total	$65,000
Less cash credits	33,700
Cash balance, June 15	$31,300

FIGURE M-10 Work Sheet for Ray Bonita, M.D.

Ray Bonita, M.D.
Work Sheet
For Month Ended June 30, 20 - -

	ACCOUNT TITLE	TRIAL BALANCE		ADJUSTMENTS		ADJUSTED TRIAL BALANCE		INCOME STATEMENT		BALANCE SHEET		
		DEBIT	CREDIT	DEBIT	CREDIT	DEBIT	CREDIT	DEBIT	CREDIT	DEBIT	CREDIT	
1	Cash	21,170.00				21,170.00				21,170.00		1
2	Medical Supplies	450.00			(a) 100.00	350.00				350.00		2
3	Office Supplies	150.00			(b) 50.00	100.00				100.00		3
4	Prepaid Insurance	6,000.00			(c) 500.00	5,500.00				5,500.00		4
5	Office Furniture	13,000.00				13,000.00				13,000.00		5
6	Accum. Depr.—Office Furniture				(d) 200.00		200.00				200.00	6
7	Medical Equipment	22,000.00				22,000.00				22,000.00		7
8	Accum. Depr.—Medical Equipment				(e) 300.00		300.00				300.00	8
9	Accounts Payable		9,200.00				9,200.00				9,200.00	9
10	Ray Bonita, Capital		50,000.00				50,000.00				50,000.00	10
11	Ray Bonita, Drawing	10,000.00				10,000.00				10,000.00		11
12	Medical Fees		25,200.00				25,200.00		25,200.00			12
13	Wages Expense	8,500.00				8,500.00		8,500.00				13
14	Rent Expense	2,000.00				2,000.00		2,000.00				14
15	Office Supplies Expense			(b) 50.00		50.00		50.00				15
16	Medical Supplies Expense			(a) 100.00		100.00		100.00				16
17	Telephone Expense	150.00				150.00		150.00				17
18	Laboratory Expense	980.00				980.00		980.00				18
19	Insurance Expense			(c) 500.00		500.00		500.00				19
20	Depr. Expense—Office Furniture			(d) 200.00		200.00		200.00				20
21	Depr. Expense—Medical Equipment			(e) 300.00		300.00		300.00				21
22		84,400.00	84,400.00	1,150.00	1,150.00	84,900.00	84,900.00	12,780.00	25,200.00	72,120.00	59,700.00	22
23	Net Income							12,420.00			12,420.00	23
24								25,200.00	25,200.00	72,120.00	72,120.00	24
25												25
26												26
27												27
28												28
29												29

FIGURE M-11 Financial Statements for Ray Bonita, M.D.

Ray Bonita, M.D.
Income Statement
For Month Ended June 30, 20 --

Revenue:		
Medical fees		$25,200.00
Expenses:		
Wages expense	$8,500.00	
Rent expense	2,000.00	
Office supplies expense	50.00	
Medical supplies expense	100.00	
Telephone expense	150.00	
Laboratory expense	980.00	
Insurance expense	500.00	
Depreciation expense—office furniture	200.00	
Depreciation expense—medical equipment	300.00	
Total expenses		12,780.00
Net income		$12,420.00

Ray Bonita, M.D.
Statement of Owner's Equity
For Month Ended June 30, 20 --

Ray Bonita, capital, June 1, 20 --		$
Investment during June		50,000.00
Total investment		$50,000.00
Net income for June	$12,420.00	
Less withdrawals for June	10,000.00	
Increase in capital		2,420.00
Ray Bonita, capital, June 30, 20 --		$52,420.00

Ray Bonita, M.D.
Balance Sheet
June 30, 20 --

Assets		
Current assets:		
Cash	$21,170.00	
Medical supplies	350.00	
Office supplies	100.00	
Prepaid insurance	5,500.00	
Total current assets		$27,120.00
Property, plant, and equipment:		
Office furniture	$13,000.00	
Less accumulated depreciation—office furniture	200.00	12,800.00
Medical equipment	$22,000.00	
Less accumulated depreciation—medical equipment	300.00	21,700.00
Total assets		$61,620.00
Liabilities		
Current liabilities:		
Accounts payable		$ 9,200.00
Owner's Equity		
Ray Bonita, capital		52,420.00
Total liabilities and owner's equity		$61,620.00

PREPARING ADJUSTING AND CLOSING ENTRIES

Adjusting and closing entries are made in the combination journal in the same manner demonstrated for the general journal in Chapter 6. We simply use the Description and General Debit and Credit columns. These posted entries are illustrated in Figures M-12 and M-13.

FIGURE M-12 Adjusting Entries

COMBINATION JOURNAL

	Date		Cash Debit	Cash Credit	Description	Post. Ref.	General Debit	General Credit	
1					Adjusting Entries				1
2	20-- June	30			Medical Supplies Expense	524	100 00		2
3					Medical Supplies	141		100 00	3
4		30			Office Supplies Expense	523	50 00		4
5					Office Supplies	142		50 00	5
6		30			Insurance Expense	535	500 00		6
7					Prepaid Insurance	145		500 00	7
8		30			Depr. Expense—Office Furniture	541	200 00		8
9					Accum. Depr.—Office Furn.	182.1		200 00	9
10		30			Depr. Expense—Medical Equip.	542	300 00		10
11					Accum. Depr.—Medical Equip.	185.1		300 00	11

FIGURE M-13 Closing Entries

COMBINATION JOURNAL

	Date		Cash Debit	Cash Credit	Description	Post. Ref.	General Debit	General Credit	
12									12
13					Closing Entries				13
14	20-- June	30			Medical Fees	401	25 200 00		14
15					Income Summary	313		25 200 00	15
16		30			Income Summary	313	12 780 00		16
17					Wages Expense	511		8 500 00	17
18					Rent Expense	521		2 000 00	18
19					Office Supplies Expense	523		50 00	19
20					Medical Supplies Expense	524		100 00	20
21					Telephone Expense	525		150 00	21
22					Laboratory Expense	526		980 00	22
23					Insurance Expense	535		500 00	23
24					Depr. Expense—Office Furn.	541		200 00	24
25					Depr. Expense—Med. Equip.	542		300 00	25
26		30			Income Summary	313	12 420 00		26
27					Ray Bonita, Capital	311		12 420 00	27
28		30			Ray Bonita, Capital	311	10 000 00		28
29					Ray Bonita, Drawing	312		10 000 00	29

U REVU Complete U REVU-4 on **page 1110** to test your basic understanding of LO5.

LEARNING OBJECTIVES — Key Points to Remember

LO1 Explain the differences between the modified cash and accrual bases of accounting.

As shown below, there are three basic differences between the modified cash and accrual bases of accounting.

DIFFERENCES BETWEEN MODIFIED CASH AND ACCRUAL BASES OF ACCOUNTING		
EVENT	**ACCRUAL BASIS**	**MODIFIED CASH BASIS**
Expenses		
Bills for services received, but not yet paid.	Expense Accounts Payable	No entry. (Record when paid.)
Wages earned by employees, but not yet paid.	Wages Expense Wages Payable	No entry. (Record when paid.)
Revenues		
Services provided on account.	Accounts Receivable Professional Fees	No entry. (Record when cash is received.)

LO2 Describe special records for a professional service business using the modified cash basis.

Special records are required for a professional service business using the modified cash basis. Since accounts receivable are not entered in the accounting system, other records must be maintained to keep track of amounts owed by clients and patients. These records generally include an appointment record and a client or patient ledger record.

LO3 Describe and use a combination journal to record transactions of a professional service business.

A combination journal is used by some businesses to improve the efficiency of recording and posting transactions. It includes general and special columns. The headings for a typical combination journal for a doctor's office are shown below.

COMBINATION JOURNAL PAGE 1

DATE	CASH		DESCRIPTION	POST. REF.	GENERAL		MEDICAL FEES CREDIT	WAGES EXPENSE DEBIT	LABORATORY EXPENSE DEBIT	MEDICAL SUPPLIES DEBIT	OFFICE SUPPLIES DEBIT
	DEBIT	CREDIT			DEBIT	CREDIT					

LO4 Post from the combination journal to the general ledger.

Rules for posting a combination journal are as follows:

1. Amounts entered in the general columns are posted individually to the general ledger on a daily basis.
2. The totals of the special columns are posted to the general ledger at the end of the month.

LO5 Prepare a work sheet, financial statements, and adjusting and closing entries for a professional service business.

The work sheet, financial statements, adjusting entries, and closing entries are prepared in the same manner as discussed in Chapters 5 and 6. Remember, however, that under the modified cash basis, adjustments are made only for prepaid items and depreciation of plant and equipment.

DEMONSTRATION PROBLEM

Maria Vietor is a financial planning consultant. She developed the following chart of accounts for her business:

Vietor Financial Planning
Chart of Accounts

Assets	**Revenues**
101 Cash	401 Professional Fees
142 Office Supplies	
	Expenses
Liabilities	511 Wages Expense
202 Accounts Payable	521 Rent Expense
	523 Office Supplies Expense
Owner's Equity	525 Telephone Expense
311 Maria Vietor, Capital	526 Automobile Expense
312 Maria Vietor, Drawing	533 Utilities Expense
313 Income Summary	534 Charitable Contributions Expense

Vietor completed the following transactions during the month of December of the current year:

Dec.	1	Vietor invested cash to start a consulting business, $20,000.
	3	Paid December office rent, $1,000.
	4	Received a check from Aaron Bisno, a client, for services, $2,500.
	6	Paid Union Electric for December heating and light, $75.
	7	Received a check from Will Carter, a client, for services, $2,000.
	12	Paid Smith's Super Service for gasoline and oil purchases, $60.
	14	Paid Comphelp for temporary secretarial services obtained through them during the past two weeks, $600.
	17	Purchased office supplies on account from Cleat Office Supply, $280.
	20	Paid Cress Telephone Co. for local and long-distance business calls during the past month, $100.
	21	Vietor withdrew cash for personal use, $1,100.
	24	Made donation to the National Multiple Sclerosis Society, $100.
	27	Received a check from Ellen Thaler, a client, for services, $2,000.
	28	Paid Comphelp for temporary secretarial services obtained through them during the past two weeks, $600.
	29	Made payment on account to Cleat Office Supply, $100.

REQUIRED

1. Enter the transactions in a combination journal. Establish special columns for Professional Fees, Wages Expense, and Automobile Expense. Vietor uses the modified cash basis of accounting. (Refer to the Chapter 4 Demonstration Problem to see how similar transactions were recorded in a general journal. Notice that the combination journal is much more efficient.)
2. Prove the combination journal.
3. Post these transactions to a general ledger.
4. Prepare a trial balance.

Solution 1. and 2.

COMBINATION JOURNAL

PAGE 1

	DATE		CASH DEBIT	CASH CREDIT	DESCRIPTION	POST. REF.	GENERAL DEBIT	GENERAL CREDIT	PROFESSIONAL FEES CREDIT	WAGES EXPENSE DEBIT	AUTOMOBILE EXPENSE DEBIT	
1	20– Dec.	1	20000 00		Maria Vietor, Capital	311		20000 00				1
2		3		1000 00	Rent Expense	521	1000 00					2
3		4	2500 00			—			2500 00			3
4		6		75 00	Utilities Expense	533	75 00					4
5		7	2000 00			—			2000 00			5
6		12		60 00		—					60 00	6
7		14		600 00		—				600 00		7
8		17			Office Supplies	142	280 00					8
9					Accounts Payable—Cleat Office Supply	202		280 00				9
10		20		100 00	Telephone Expense	525	100 00					10
11		21		1100 00	Maria Vietor, Drawing	312	1100 00					11
12		24		100 00	Charitable Contributions Expense	534	100 00					12
13		27	2000 00			—			2000 00			13
14		28		600 00		—				600 00		14
15		29		100 00	Accounts Payable—Cleat Office Supply	202	100 00					15
16			26500 00	3735 00			2755 00	20280 00	6500 00	1200 00	60 00	16
17			(101)	(101)			(✓)	(✓)	(401)	(511)	(526)	17
18												18

Proving the Combination Journal:

Debit columns:		**Credit columns:**	
Cash	26,500	Cash	3,735
General	2,755	General	20,280
Wages Expense	1,200	Professional Fees	6,500
Automobile Expense	60		30,515
	30,515		

(continued)

3.

GENERAL LEDGER

ACCOUNT: Cash — ACCOUNT NO. 101

DATE		ITEM	POST. REF.	DEBIT	CREDIT	BALANCE DEBIT	BALANCE CREDIT
20-- Dec.	31		CJ1	26,500.00		26,500.00	
	31		CJ1		3,735.00	22,765.00	

ACCOUNT: Office Supplies — ACCOUNT NO. 142

DATE		ITEM	POST. REF.	DEBIT	CREDIT	BALANCE DEBIT	BALANCE CREDIT
20-- Dec.	17		CJ1	280.00		280.00	

ACCOUNT: Accounts Payable — ACCOUNT NO. 202

DATE		ITEM	POST. REF.	DEBIT	CREDIT	BALANCE DEBIT	BALANCE CREDIT
20-- Dec.	17		CJ1		280.00		280.00
	29		CJ1	100.00			180.00

ACCOUNT: Maria Vietor, Capital — ACCOUNT NO. 311

DATE		ITEM	POST. REF.	DEBIT	CREDIT	BALANCE DEBIT	BALANCE CREDIT
20-- Dec.	1		CJ1		20,000.00		20,000.00

ACCOUNT: Maria Vietor, Drawing — ACCOUNT NO. 312

DATE		ITEM	POST. REF.	DEBIT	CREDIT	BALANCE DEBIT	BALANCE CREDIT
20-- Dec.	21		CJ1	1,100.00		1,100.00	

ACCOUNT: Income Summary — ACCOUNT NO. 313

DATE		ITEM	POST. REF.	DEBIT	CREDIT	BALANCE DEBIT	BALANCE CREDIT
20--							

ACCOUNT: Professional Fees — ACCOUNT NO. 401

DATE		ITEM	POST. REF.	DEBIT	CREDIT	BALANCE DEBIT	BALANCE CREDIT
20-- Dec.	31		CJ1		6,500.00		6,500.00

ACCOUNT: Wages Expense — ACCOUNT NO. 511

DATE		ITEM	POST. REF.	DEBIT	CREDIT	BALANCE DEBIT	BALANCE CREDIT
20-- Dec.	31		CJ1	1,200.00		1,200.00	

ACCOUNT: Rent Expense — ACCOUNT NO. 521

DATE		ITEM	POST. REF.	DEBIT	CREDIT	BALANCE DEBIT	BALANCE CREDIT
20-- Dec.	3		CJ1	1,000.00		1,000.00	

ACCOUNT: Office Supplies Expense — ACCOUNT NO. 523

DATE		ITEM	POST. REF.	DEBIT	CREDIT	BALANCE DEBIT	BALANCE CREDIT
20--							

ACCOUNT: Telephone Expense — ACCOUNT NO. 525

DATE		ITEM	POST. REF.	DEBIT	CREDIT	BALANCE DEBIT	BALANCE CREDIT
20-- Dec.	20		CJ1	100.00		100.00	

ACCOUNT: Automobile Expense — ACCOUNT NO. 526

DATE		ITEM	POST. REF.	DEBIT	CREDIT	BALANCE DEBIT	BALANCE CREDIT
20-- Dec.	31		CJ1	60.00		60.00	

ACCOUNT: Utilities Expense — ACCOUNT NO. 533

DATE		ITEM	POST. REF.	DEBIT	CREDIT	BALANCE DEBIT	BALANCE CREDIT
20-- Dec.	6		CJ1	75.00		75.00	

ACCOUNT: Charitable Contributions Expense — ACCOUNT NO. 534

DATE		ITEM	POST. REF.	DEBIT	CREDIT	BALANCE DEBIT	BALANCE CREDIT
20-- Dec.	24		CJ1	100.00		100.00	

4.

Vietor Financial Planning
Trial Balance
December 31, 20 - -

ACCOUNT TITLE	ACCOUNT NO.	DEBIT BALANCE	CREDIT BALANCE
Cash	101	22,765.00	
Office Supplies	142	280.00	
Accounts Payable	202		180.00
Maria Vietor, Capital	311		20,000.00
Maria Vietor, Drawing	312	1,100.00	
Professional Fees	401		6,500.00
Wages Expense	511	1,200.00	
Rent Expense	521	1,000.00	
Telephone Expense	525	100.00	
Automobile Expense	526	60.00	
Utilities Expense	533	75.00	
Charitable Contributions Expense	534	100.00	
		26,680.00	26,680.00

KEY TERMS

combination journal (1092) A journal with special and general columns.

Description column (1095) The column in the combination journal used to enter the account titles for the General Debit and General Credit columns; to identify specific creditors when assets are purchased, or payments made, on account; to identify amounts forwarded; and to identify adjusting, closing, and reversing entries.

General Credit column (1092) The column in the combination journal used to credit accounts that are used infrequently.

General Debit column (1092) The column in the combination journal used to debit accounts that are used infrequently.

Posting Reference column (1095) The column in the combination journal where the account number is entered after posting to accounts from the General Debit and Credit columns.

special columns (1092) Columns in combination journals for frequently used accounts.

SELF-STUDY QUESTIONS AND EXERCISES

True/False Questions

1. LO1 Under the accrual basis of accounting, revenues are recorded when earned.
2. LO1 The modified cash basis of accounting is used by most large businesses.
3. LO1 The modified cash basis uses the accrual basis when recording revenues and expenses.
4. LO1 Under the modified cash basis, interest expense is recorded when paid.
5. LO1 Many small professional service businesses use the modified cash basis.

Multiple Choice Questions

1. LO1 Using the modified cash basis, when a business provides services on account, ________ is debited.

   (a) no entry
   (b) Accounts Receivable
   (c) Cash
   (d) Owner's Equity

2. LO1 Using the modified cash basis, when wages are earned but not paid, ________ is debited.

   (a) Wages Expense
   (b) no entry
   (c) Wages Payable
   (d) Accrued Wages

3. LO3 Which of these would make the best "special column" in a combination journal?

   (a) Office Equipment
   (b) Prepaid Insurance
   (c) Revenue
   (d) Telephone Expense

4. LO3 Verifying that debit column totals equal credit column totals is the process of

(a) debiting.
(b) proving.
(c) closing.
(d) adjusting.

5. LO4 Posting from the combination journal is accomplished by placing " ________ "and the page number in the Posting Reference column of the general ledger account.

(a) G
(b) DJ
(c) J
(d) CJ

U REVU Exercises

1. LO1 Using the information provided below, compute net income using the accrual and modified cash bases.

a. Revenues earned for the year, $500,000.
b. Cash collected from patients and insurance companies during the year, $520,000.
c. Total expenses incurred during the year, $300,000.
d. Bills for services received this year (expenses), but not yet paid, $5,000.
e. Bills for services received last year, but paid this year, $3,000.
f. Wages earned by employees this year, but not yet paid, $10,000.
g. Wages earned by employees last year, but paid this year, $15,000.

2. LO3 Tom Durkin, M.D., uses the modified cash basis and the combination journal provided below to record entries for his medical practice.

Date	Cash		Description	General		Medical Fees Credit	Wages Expense Debit	Laboratory Expense Debit	Medical Supplies Debit	Office Supplies Debit
	Debit	Credit		Debit	Credit					

Indicate which columns would be used for the debits and credits for the following transactions.

a. Medical services provided for cash.
b. Wages incurred, but not paid.
c. Cash paid for laboratory expenses.
d. Purchased medical supplies on account.

3. LO4 Indicate the manner in which the information in the columns of the combination journal shown below is posted.

a. Insert an "a" at the bottom of the column if the individual transaction amounts are posted throughout the month.
b. Insert a "b" if the column total is posted at the end of the month.

Date	Cash		Description	General		Medical Fees Credit	Wages Expense Debit	Laboratory Expense Debit	Medical Supplies Debit	Office Supplies Debit
	Debit	Credit		Debit	Credit					

4. LO5 Using the information and combination journal provided below, prepare the June 30 adjusting entries for the following:

a. Medical supplies used, $4,000.
b. Depreciation on office furniture, $2,000.

Date	Cash		Description	General		Medical Fees Credit	Wages Expense Debit	Laboratory Expense Debit	Medical Supplies Debit
	Debit	Credit		Debit	Credit				

The answers to the Self-Study Questions and Exercises are at the end of the Module (pages 1121–1122).

APPLYING YOUR KNOWLEDGE

REVIEW QUESTIONS

LO1 1. Explain when revenues are recorded under the modified cash basis and accrual basis of accounting.

LO1 2. Explain when wages expense is recorded under the modified cash basis and accrual basis of accounting.

LO2 3. Explain the purpose of an appointment record.

LO2 4. Explain the purpose of a patient ledger account.

LO3 5. Explain the purpose of a special column in the combination journal.

LO3 6. Explain the purpose of the General columns in the combination journal.

LO3/4 7. How does the use of the combination journal save time and space in entering cash transactions?

LO3 8. Explain the purpose of the Description column in the combination journal.

LO3 9. What is the purpose of proving the totals in the combination journal?

LO4 10. When an entry is posted from the combination journal to a ledger account, what information is entered in the Posting Reference column of the combination journal? In the Posting Reference column of the ledger account?

SERIES A EXERCISES

E M-1A (LO1/3)

✓ General Debit total: $2,715; Cash Debit total: $11,100

JOURNAL ENTRIES Jean Akins opened a consulting business. Journalize the following transactions that occurred during the month of January of the current year using the modified cash basis and a combination journal. Set up special columns for Consulting Fees (credit) and Wages Expense (debit).

Jan. 1	Invested cash in the business, $10,000.
2	Paid office rent, $500.
3	Purchased office equipment on account from Business Machines, Inc., $1,500.
5	Received cash for services rendered, $750.
8	Paid telephone bill, $65.
10	Paid for a magazine subscription (miscellaneous expense), $15.
11	Purchased office supplies on account from Leo's Office Supplies, $300.
15	Paid for one-year liability insurance policy, $150.
18	Paid part-time help, $500.
21	Received cash for services rendered, $350.
25	Paid electricity bill, $85.
27	Withdrew cash for personal use, $100.
29	Paid part-time help, $500.

E M-2A **(LO1/3)**

✓ Total debits: $19,191

JOURNAL ENTRIES Bill Rackes opened a bicycle repair shop. Journalize the following transactions that occurred during the month of October of the current year. Use the modified cash basis and a combination journal with special columns for Repair Fees (credit) and Wages Expense (debit). Prove the combination journal.

Oct. 1	Invested cash in the business, $15,000.
2	Paid shop rental for the month, $300.
3	Purchased bicycle parts on account from Tracker's Bicycle Parts, $2,000.
5	Purchased office supplies on account from Downtown Office Supplies, $250.
8	Paid telephone bill, $38.
9	Received cash for services, $140.
11	Paid for a sports magazine subscription (miscellaneous expense), $15.
12	Made payment on account for parts previously purchased, $100.
14	Paid part-time help, $300.
15	Received cash for services, $350.
16	Paid electricity bill, $48.
19	Received cash for services, $250.
23	Withdrew cash for personal use, $50.
25	Made payment on account for office supplies previously purchased, $50.
29	Paid part-time help, $300.

SERIES A PROBLEMS

P M-3A (LO3/4/5)

✓ 2. Cash bal., 1/12: $10,310;
3. Total journal credits: $15,499;
5. Trial bal. total debits: $13,460

JOURNALIZING AND POSTING TRANSACTIONS AND PREPARING A TRIAL BALANCE Angela McWharton opened an on-call nursing services business. She rented a small office space and pays a part-time worker to answer the telephone. Her chart of accounts is shown below.

Angela McWharton Nursing Services
Chart of Accounts

Assets
101 Cash
142 Office Supplies
181 Office Equipment

Liabilities
202 Accounts Payable

Owner's Equity
311 Angela McWharton, Capital
312 Angela McWharton, Drawing
313 Income Summary

Revenues
401 Nursing Care Fees

Expenses
511 Wages Expense
512 Advertising Expense
521 Rent Expense
525 Telephone Expense
526 Transportation Expense
533 Electricity Expense
549 Miscellaneous Expense

McWharton's transactions for the first month of business are as follows:

Jan. 1	Invested cash in the business, $10,000.
1	Paid January rent, $500.
2	Purchased office supplies on account from Crestline Office Supplies, $300.
4	Purchased office equipment on account from Office Technology, Inc., $1,500.
6	Received cash for nursing services rendered, $580.
7	Paid telephone bill, $42.
8	Paid electricity bill, $38.
10	Received cash for nursing services rendered, $360.
12	Made payment on account for office supplies previously purchased, $50.
13	Reimbursed part-time worker for use of personal automobile (transportation expense), $150.
15	Paid part-time worker, $360.
17	Received cash for nursing services rendered, $420.
18	Withdrew cash for personal use, $100.
20	Paid for newspaper advertising, $26.
22	Paid for gas and oil, $35.
24	Paid subscription for journal on nursing care practices (miscellaneous expense), $28.
25	Received cash for nursing services rendered, $320.
27	Made payment on account for office equipment previously purchased, $150.
29	Paid part-time worker, $360.
30	Received cash for nursing services rendered, $180.

REQUIRED

1. Journalize the transactions for January using the modified cash basis and page 1 of a combination journal. Set up special columns for Nursing Care Fees (credit), Wages Expense (debit), and Transportation Expense (debit).
2. Determine the cash balance as of January 12 (using the combination journal).
3. Prove the combination journal.
4. Set up general ledger accounts from the chart of accounts and post the transactions from the combination journal.
5. Prepare a trial balance.

P M-4A (LO3/4/5)

✓ 2. Cash bal., 11/12: $5,949; 3. Total journal credits: $6,499; 5. Trial Bal. total debits: $18,155; Adjusted Trial Bal. total debits: $18,455; Net income: $1,842; 7. Capital, 11/30: $6,772; Total assets, 11/30: $13,947

KLOOSTER & ALLEN

JOURNALIZING AND POSTING TRANSACTIONS AND PREPARING FINANCIAL STATEMENTS Sue Reyton owns a suit tailoring shop. She opened her business in September with a cash investment of $5,430. She rents a small work space and has an assistant to receive job orders and process claim tickets. Her trial balance shows her account balances for the first two months of business (September and October). No adjustments were made in September or October.

Sue Reyton Tailors
Trial Balance
October 31, 20 - -

ACCOUNT TITLE	ACCOUNT NO.	DEBIT BALANCE	CREDIT BALANCE
Cash	101	5,711.00	
Tailoring Supplies	141	1,000.00	
Office Supplies	142	485.00	
Prepaid Insurance	145	100.00	
Tailoring Equipment	188	3,800.00	
Accumulated Depreciation—Tailoring Equipment	188.1		
Accounts Payable	202		4,125.00
Sue Reyton, Capital	311		5,430.00
Sue Reyton, Drawing	312	500.00	
Tailoring Fees	401		3,600.00
Wages Expense	511	800.00	
Advertising Expense	512	33.00	
Rent Expense	521	600.00	
Telephone Expense	525	60.00	
Electricity Expense	533	44.00	
Miscellaneous Expense	549	22.00	
		13,155.00	13,155.00

Reyton's transactions for November are as follows:

Nov. 1 Paid November rent, $300.

2 Purchased tailoring supplies on account from Sew Easy Supplies, $150.

3 Purchased a new button hole machine on account from Seam's Sewing Machines, $3,000.

5 Earned first week's revenue: $400 in cash.

8 Paid for newspaper advertising, $13.

9 Paid telephone bill, $28.

10 Paid electricity bill, $21.

(continued)

Nov. 12	Earned second week's revenue: $200 in cash, $300 on account.
15	Paid part-time worker, $400.
16	Made payment on account for tailoring supplies, $100.
17	Paid for magazine subscription (miscellaneous expense), $12.
19	Earned third week's revenue: $450 in cash.
21	Paid for prepaid insurance for the year, $500.
23	Received cash from customers (previously owed), $300.
24	Paid for newspaper advertising, $13.
26	Paid for special delivery fee (miscellaneous expense), $12.
29	Earned fourth week's revenue: $600 in cash.

Additional accounts needed are as follows:

313	Income Summary
523	Office Supplies Expense
524	Tailoring Supplies Expense
535	Insurance Expense
542	Depreciation Expense—Tailoring Equipment

November 30 adjustments are as follows:

(a) Tailoring supplies on hand, $450.
(b) Office supplies on hand, $285.
(c) Prepaid insurance expired over past three months, $150.
(d) Depreciation on tailoring equipment for the last three months, $300.

REQUIRED

1. Journalize the transactions for November using the modified cash basis and page 5 of a combination journal. Set up special columns for Tailoring Fees (credit), Wages Expense (debit), and Advertising Expense (debit).
2. Determine the cash balance as of November 12.
3. Prove the combination journal.
4. Set up general ledger accounts, including the additional accounts listed above, entering the balances as of November 1, 20--. Post the entries from the combination journal.
5. Prepare a work sheet for the three months ended November 30, 20--.
6. Record the adjusting entries on page 6 of the combination journal and post to the general ledger accounts.
7. Prepare an income statement and statement of owner's equity for the three months ended November 30, and a balance sheet as of November 30, 20--. (Assume that Reyton made an investment of $5,430 on September 1, 20--.)
8. Record closing entries on page 6 of the combination journal and post to the general ledger accounts.

SERIES B EXERCISES

E M-1B (LO1/3)

✓ General Debit total: $2,129; Cash Debit total: $9,400.

JOURNAL ENTRIES Bill Miller opened a bookkeeping service business. Journalize the following transactions that occurred during the month of March of the current year. Use the modified cash basis and a combination journal with special columns for Bookkeeping Fees (credit) and Wages Expense (debit).

Mar. 1	Invested cash in the business, $7,500.
3	Paid March office rent, $500.
5	Purchased office equipment on account from Desk Top Office Equipment, $800.
6	Received cash for services rendered, $400.
8	Paid telephone bill, $48.
10	Paid for a magazine subscription (miscellaneous expense), $25.
11	Purchased office supplies, $200.
14	Received cash for services rendered, $520.
16	Paid for a one-year insurance policy, $200.
18	Paid part-time worker, $400.
21	Received cash for services rendered, $380.
22	Made payment on account for office equipment previously purchased, $100.
24	Paid electricity bill, $56.
27	Withdrew cash for personal use, $200.
29	Paid part-time worker, $400.
30	Received cash for services rendered, $600.

E M-2B (LO1/3)

✓ Total debits: $14,349

JOURNAL ENTRIES Amy Anjelo opened a delivery service. Journalize the following transactions that occurred in January of the current year. Use the modified cash basis and a combination journal with special columns for Delivery Fees (credit) and Wages Expense (debit). Prove the combination journal.

Jan. 1	Invested cash in the business, $10,000.
2	Paid shop rental for the month, $400.
3	Purchased a delivery cart on account from Walt's Wheels, $1,000.
5	Purchased office supplies, $250.
6	Paid telephone bill, $51.
8	Received cash for delivery services, $428.
11	Paid electricity bill, $37.
12	Paid part-time employee, $480.
13	Paid for postage stamps (miscellaneous expense), $29.
15	Received cash for delivery services, $382.
18	Made payment on account for delivery cart previously purchased, $90.
21	Withdrew cash for personal use, $250.

(continued)

Jan. 24	Paid for a one-year liability insurance policy, $180.
26	Received cash for delivery services, $292.
29	Paid part-time employee, $480.

SERIES B PROBLEMS

P M-3B (LO3/4/5)

✓ 2. Cash bal., 7/14: $4,786; 3. Total journal credits: $9,472; 5. Trial bal. total debits: $8,190

JOURNALIZING AND POSTING TRANSACTIONS AND PREPARING A TRIAL BALANCE J. B. Hoyt opened a training center at the marina where he provides private water-skiing lessons. He rented a small building at the marina and has a part-time worker to assist him. His chart of accounts is shown below.

Water Walking by Hoyt
Chart of Accounts

Assets
101 Cash
142 Office Supplies
183 Skiing Equipment

Liabilities
202 Accounts Payable

Owner's Equity
311 J. B. Hoyt, Capital
312 J. B. Hoyt, Drawing
313 Income Summary

Revenues
401 Training Fees

Expenses
511 Wages Expense
521 Rent Expense
525 Telephone Expense
526 Transportation Expense
533 Electricity Expense
537 Repair Expense
549 Miscellaneous Expense

Transactions for the first month of business are as follows:

July 1	Invested cash in the business, $5,000.
2	Paid rent for the month, $250.
3	Purchased office supplies, $150.
4	Purchased skiing equipment on account from Water Fun, Inc., $2,000.
6	Paid telephone bill, $36.
7	Received cash for skiing lessons, $200.
10	Paid electricity bill, $28.
12	Paid part-time worker, $250.
14	Received cash for skiing lessons, $300.
16	Paid for gas and oil (transportation expense), $60.
17	Received cash for skiing lessons, $250.
20	Paid for repair to ski rope, $20.
21	Made payment on account for skiing equipment previously purchased, $100.
24	Received cash for skiing lessons, $310.
26	Paid for award certificates (miscellaneous expense), $18.
28	Paid part-time worker, $250.
30	Received cash for skiing lessons, $230.
31	Paid for repair to life jacket, $20.

REQUIRED

1. Journalize the transactions for July using the modified cash basis and page 1 of a combination journal. Set up special columns for Training Fees (credit), Wages Expense (debit), and Repair Expense (debit).
2. Determine the cash balance as of July 14, 20--.
3. Prove the combination journal.
4. Set up general ledger accounts from the chart of accounts and post the transactions from the combination journal.
5. Prepare a trial balance.

P M-4B (LO3/4/5)

✓ 2. Cash bal., 6/12: $4,832; 3. Total journal credits: $4,587; 5. Trial Bal. total debits: $13,023; Adjusted Trial Bal. total debits: $13,283; Net income: $2,928; 7. Capital, 6/30: $7,028; Total assets, 6/30: $9,008

KA KLOOSTER & ALLEN

JOURNALIZING AND POSTING TRANSACTIONS AND PREPARING FINANCIAL STATEMENTS Molly Claussen owns a lawn care business. She opened her business in April with a cash investment of $5,000. She rents a small shop area where she stores her equipment and has an assistant to receive orders and process accounts. Her trial balance shows her account balances for the first two months of business (April and May). No adjustments were made at the end of April or May.

Molly Claussen's Green Thumb
Trial Balance
May 31, 20 - -

ACCOUNT TITLE	ACCOUNT NO.	DEBIT BALANCE	CREDIT BALANCE
Cash	101	4 6 0 4 00	
Lawn Care Supplies	141	5 8 8 00	
Office Supplies	142	2 4 3 00	
Prepaid Insurance	145	1 5 0 00	
Lawn Care Equipment	189	2 4 0 8 00	
Accumulated Depreciation—Lawn Care Equipment	189.1		
Accounts Payable	202		1 0 8 0 00
Molly Claussen, Capital	311		5 0 0 0 00
Molly Claussen, Drawing	312	8 0 0 00	
Lawn Care Fees	401		4 0 3 3 00
Wages Expense	511	6 0 0 00	
Rent Expense	521	4 0 0 00	
Telephone Expense	525	8 8 00	
Electricity Expense	533	6 2 00	
Repair Expense	537	5 0 00	
Gas and Oil Expense	538	1 2 0 00	
		10 1 1 3 00	10 1 1 3 00

Transactions for June are as follows:

June 1 Paid shop rent, $200.
2 Purchased office supplies, $230.
3 Purchased new landscaping equipment on account from Earth Care, Inc., $1,000.
5 Paid telephone bill, $31.
6 Received cash for lawn care fees, $640.
8 Paid electricity bill, $31.
10 Paid part-time worker, $300.
11 Received cash for lawn care fees, $580.
12 Paid for a one-year insurance policy, $200.

(continued)

June 14	Made payment on account for landscaping equipment previously purchased, $100.
15	Paid for gas and oil, $40.
19	Paid for mower repairs, $25.
21	Received $310 cash for lawn care fees and earned $480 on account.
24	Withdrew cash for personal use, $100.
26	Paid for edging equipment repairs, $20.
28	Received cash from customers (previously owed), $480.
29	Paid part-time worker, $300.

Additional accounts needed are as follows:

313 Income Summary
523 Office Supplies Expense
524 Lawn Care Supplies Expense
535 Insurance Expense
542 Depreciation Expense—Lawn Care Equipment

June 30 adjustments are as follows:

(a) Office supplies on hand, $273.
(b) Lawn care supplies on hand, $300.
(c) Prepaid insurance expired over past three months, $100.
(d) Depreciation on lawn care equipment for past three months, $260.

REQUIRED

1. Journalize the transactions for June using the modified cash basis and page 5 of a combination journal. Set up special columns for Lawn Care Fees (credit), Repair Expense (debit), and Wages Expense (debit).
2. Determine the cash balance as of June 12.
3. Prove the combination journal.
4. Set up general ledger accounts including the additional accounts listed above, entering balances as of June 1, 20--. Post the entries from the combination journal.
5. Prepare a work sheet for the three months ended June 30, 20--.
6. Record the adjusting entries on page 6 of the combination journal and post to the general ledger accounts.
7. Prepare an income statement and statement of owner's equity for the three months ended June 30, and a balance sheet as of June 30, 20--. Assume that Claussen invested $5,000 on April 1, 20--.
8. Record the closing entries on page 6 of the combination journal and post to the general ledger accounts.

MANAGING YOUR WRITING

Your friend is planning to start her own business and has asked you for advice. In particular, she is concerned about which method of accounting she should use. She has heard about the modified cash and accrual methods of accounting. However, she does not really understand the differences. Write a memo that explains each method and the type of business for which each method is most appropriate.

ETHICS CASE

Nancy Bowles, the owner of Bowles Services, a sole proprietorship, rushed into the office late Monday morning carrying a deposit receipt from the bank. Upon handing the receipt to Sarah, the accountant, she instructed her to debit Cash and credit Professional Fees for the full $10,000. When Sarah examined the source document, she saw that the cash had come from the account of Richard Bowles, Nancy's father. Nancy explained to Sarah that she was applying for a bank loan and needed to "show that her company earned more year-to-date income than it actually had." Nancy used the rationale that the company would earn at least $10,000 in revenue during the next few months but the financial statements the bank required were as of the end of this month.

1. Does Nancy's explanation make sense? Is it ethical?
2. How should this transaction be entered in Bowles Services' books? Does it matter whether the modified cash basis or accrual basis of accounting is used?
3. Make a written list of all the consequences Nancy might face as a result of recording this transaction as a debit to Cash and a credit to Professional Fees.
4. Break up into groups of two and role play Nancy's and Sarah's point of view in this situation.

MASTERY PROBLEM

✓ 1. Total debits to General Dr. col. of CJ: $112,705; 2. Total debits of CJ: $305,305; 4. Total debits on trial bal.: $232,200

KA KLOOSTER & ALLEN

John McRoe opened a tennis resort in June 20--. Most guests register for one week, arriving on Sunday afternoon and returning home the following Saturday afternoon. Guests stay at an adjacent hotel. The tennis resort provides lunch and dinner. Dining and exercise facilities are provided in a building rented by McRoe. A dietitian, masseuse, physical therapist, and athletic trainers are on call to assure the proper combination of diet and exercise. The chart of accounts and transactions for the month of June are provided below. McRoe uses the modified cash basis of accounting.

McRoe Tennis Resort
Chart of Accounts

Assets
101 Cash
142 Office Supplies
144 Food Supplies
184 Tennis Facilities
184.1 Accum. Depr.—Tennis Facilities
186 Exercise Equipment
186.1 Accum. Depr.—Exercise Equip.

Liabilities
202 Accounts Payable

Owner's Equity
311 John McRoe, Capital
312 John McRoe, Drawing
313 Income Summary

Revenue
401 Registration Fees

Expenses
511 Wages Expense
521 Rent Expense
523 Office Supplies Expense
524 Food Supplies Expense
525 Telephone Expense
533 Utilities Expense
535 Insurance Expense
536 Postage Expense
541 Depr. Exp.—Tennis Facilities
542 Depr. Exp.—Exercise Equip.

(continued)

June 1	McRoe invested cash in the business, $90,000.
1	Paid for new exercise equipment, $9,000.
2	Deposited registration fees in the bank, $15,000.
2	Paid rent for month of June on building and land, $2,500.
2	Rogers Construction completed work on new tennis courts that cost $70,000. The estimated useful life of the facility is five years, at which time the courts will have to be resurfaced. Arrangements were made to pay the bill in July.
3	Purchased food supplies on account from Au Naturel Foods, $5,000.
5	Purchased office supplies on account from Gordon Office Supplies, $300.
7	Deposited registration fees in the bank, $16,200.
10	Purchased food supplies on account from Au Naturel Foods, $6,200.
10	Paid wages to staff, $500.
14	Deposited registration fees in the bank, $13,500.
16	Purchased food supplies on account from Au Naturel Foods, $4,000.
17	Paid wages to staff, $500.
18	Paid postage, $85.
21	Deposited registration fees in the bank, $15,200.
24	Purchased food supplies on account from Au Naturel Foods, $5,500.
24	Paid wages to staff, $500.
28	Deposited registration fees in the bank, $14,000.
30	Purchased food supplies on account from Au Naturel Foods, $6,000.
30	Paid wages to staff, $500.
30	Paid Au Naturel Foods on account, $28,700.
30	Paid utility bill, $500.
30	Paid telephone bill, $120.
30	McRoe withdrew cash for personal use, $1,500.

REQUIRED

1. Enter the transactions in a combination journal (page 1). Establish special columns for Registration Fees (credit), Wages Expense (debit), and Food Supplies (debit).
2. Prove the combination journal.
3. Post these transactions to a general ledger.
4. Prepare a trial balance as of June 30.

CHALLENGE PROBLEM

This problem challenges you to apply your cumulative accounting knowledge to move a step beyond the material in the module.

✓ NI modified cash basis: $7,000; NI accrual basis: $7,300

Gerald Resler recently opened a financial consulting business. Summary transactions for the month of June, his second month of operation, are provided below.

1. Cash collected from clients for consulting fees, $10,000. $1,500 of the $10,000 was for consulting fees earned in May, but received in June.
2. Consulting fees earned in June, but to be received in July, $2,000.
3. Supplies on hand at the beginning of June amounted to $500. All purchases of supplies are made on account. Supplies purchased during June, $1,000. At the end of June, $600 worth of supplies remained unused.
4. Paid cash on account to suppliers during June, $800. $200 of the $800 was for purchases of supplies made in May.
5. Wages paid to an assistant, $2,000. Of this $2,000, $300 had been earned in May. In addition, the assistant earned $500 in June, which will be paid next month.
6. Purchased a laptop. Paid $1,200 cash in June and will pay the balance of $1,200 in July. Gerald expects to use the laptop for two years at which time he expects that it will be obsolete and have a zero salvage value.

REQUIRED

Prepare income statements for the month of June using the modified cash and accrual bases.

ANSWERS TO SELF-STUDY QUESTIONS AND EXERCISES

True/False Questions

1. T
2. F (Large businesses use the accrual basis.)
3. F (See Figure M-1)
4. T
5. T

Multiple Choice Questions

1. a
2. b
3. c
4. b
5. d

U REVU Exercises

1.

	ACCRUAL BASIS	MODIFIED CASH BASIS	
Revenues earned	$500,000		
Cash received from patients and insurance companies			$520,000
Expenses incurred	300,000	$300,000	
Bills received, but not yet paid		(5,000)	
Bills from last year, but paid this year		3,000	
Wages earned this year, but not yet paid		(10,000)	
Wages earned last year, but paid this year		15,000	303,000
	$200,000		$217,000

2.

	Debit	Credit
a.	Cash Debit	Medical Fees Credit
b.	No Entry	No Entry
c.	Laboratory Expense Debit	Cash Credit
d.	Medical Supplies Debit	General Credit

3.

Date	Cash		Description	General		Medical Fees Credit	Wages Expense Debit	Laboratory Expense Debit	Medical Supplies Debit	Office Supplies Debit
	Debit	Credit		Debit	Credit					
	b	b		a	a	b	b	b	b	b

4.

Date	Cash		Description	General		Medical Fees Credit	Wages Expense Debit	Laboratory Expense Debit	Medical Supplies Debit
	Debit	Credit		Debit	Credit				
20--			Adjusting Entries						
June 30			Medical Supplies Expense	4,000					
			Medical Supplies		4,000				
30			Depr. Exp—Off. Furn.	2,000					
			Accum. Depr—Off. Furn.		2,000				

*Page references in bold indicate defined terms.

D

E

L

M

N

Q

R